THE BOOK

OF THE

PROPHET EZEKIEL.

THEOLOGICALLY AND HOMILETICALLY EXPOUNDED

BY

FR. WILHELM JULIUS SCHRÖDER, B.D.,

LATE PASTOR OF THE REFORMED CHURCH AT ELBERFELD, PRUSSIA.

TRANSLATED, ENLARGED, AND EDITED

BY

PATRICK FAIRBAIRN, D.D.,

LATE PRINCIPAL OF THE FREE CHURCH COLLEGE, GLASGOW,

AND

REV. WILLIAM FINDLAY, M.A.,

LARKHALL, SCOTLAND,

AIDED BY

REV. THOMAS CRERAR, M.A., AND REV. SINCLAIR MANSON, M.A.

Wipf & Stock

PUBLISHERS

Eugene, Oregon

Wipf and Stock Publishers
199 W 8th Ave, Suite 3
Eugene, OR 97401

The Book of the Prophet Ezekiel
an Exegetical and Doctrinal Commentary
By Schröder, Wilhelm Julius
ISBN 13: 978-1-55635-407-6
ISBN 10: 1-55635-407-x
Publication date 4/6/2007
Previously published by Charles Scribner, 1876

LIST OF CONTRIBUTORS

TO THE CRITICAL, DOCTRINAL, AND HOMILETICAL COMMENTARY ON THE BIBLE.

GENERAL EDITORS:

Rev. JOHANN PETER LANGE, D.D.,
Consistorial Counselor and Professor of Theology in the University of Bonn.

Rev. PHILIP SCHAFF, D.D., LL.D.,
Professor of Sacred Literature in the Union Theological Seminary, New York.

I. CONTRIBUTORS TO THE GERMAN EDITION.

Rev. C. A. AUBERLEN, Ph.D., D.D.,
Professor of Theology in the University of Basle, Switzerland.

Rev. KARL CHR. W. F. BAHR, D.D.,
Ministerial Counselor at Carlsruhe.

Rev. KARL BRAUNE, D.D.,
General Superintendent at Altenburg, Saxony.

Rev. PAULUS CASSEL, Ph.D.,
Professor in Berlin.

Rev. CHR. FR. DAVID ERDMANN, D.D.,
Gen. Superintendent of Silesia, and Prof. Honorarius of Theology in the University of Breslau.

Rev. F. R. FAY,
Pastor in Crefeld, Prussia.

Rev. G. F. C. FRONMULLER, Ph.D.,
Pastor at Kemnath, Würtemberg.

Rev. KARL GEROK, D.D.,
Prelate and Chief Chaplain of the Court, Stuttgart.

Rev. PAUL KLEINERT, Ph.D., B.D.,
Professor of Old Testament Exegesis in the University of Berlin.

Rev. CHRIST. FR. KLING, D.D.,
Dean of Marbach on the Neckar, Würtemberg.

Rev. GOTTHARD VICTOR LECHLER, D.D.,
Professor of Theology, and Superintendent at Leipzig.

Rev. CARL BERNHARD MOLL, D.D.,
General Superintendent in Königsberg.

Rev. C. W. EDWARD NAEGELSBACH, Ph.D.,
Dean at Bayreuth, Bavaria.

Rev. J. J. VAN OOSTERZEE, D.D.,
Professor of Theology in the University of Utrecht.

Rev. C. J. RIGGENBACH, D.D.,
Professor of Theology in the University of Basle.

Rev. OTTO SCHMOLLER, Ph.D., B.D.,
Urach, Würtemberg.

Rev. FR. JULIUS SCHROEDER, D.D.,
Pastor at Elberfeld, Prussia.

Rev. FR. W. SCHULTZ, D.D.,
Professor of Theology in Breslau.

Rev. OTTO ZOECKLER, D.D.,
Professor of Theology in the University at Greifswald.

II. CONTRIBUTORS TO THE ANGLO-AMERICAN EDITION.

Rev. CHARLES A. AIKEN, Ph.D., D.D.,
Professor of Christian Ethics and Apologetics at Princeton, N. J.

Rev. SAMUEL RALPH ASBURY, M.A.,
Philadelphia.

Rev. GEORGE R. BLISS, D.D.,
Professor in Crozer Theological Seminary, Upland, Pa.

Rev. CHAS. A. BRIGGS, D.D.,
Professor of Oriental Languages in the Union Theological Seminary, New York.

Rev. TALBOT W. CHAMBERS, D.D.,
Pastor of the Collegiate Reformed Dutch Church, New York.

Rev. THOMAS J. CONANT, D.D.,
Brooklyn, N. Y.

Rev. E. R. CRAVEN, D.D.,
Newark, N. J.

Rev. HOWARD CROSBY, D.D., LL.D.,
Chancellor of the University of New York.

LIST OF CONTRIBUTORS.

Rev. JOHN A. BROADUS, D.D.,
Professor of New Testament Exegesis at Louisville, Ky.

Rev. CHAS. ELLIOTT, D.D.,
Professor of Biblical Literature and Exegesis, Chicago, Ill.

Rev. L. J. EVANS, D.D.,
Professor of New Test. Exegesis in Lane Theol. Seminary, Cincinnati.

Rev. PATRICK FAIRBAIRN, D.D.,
Principal and Professor of Divinity in the Free Church College, Glasgow.

Rev. WILLIAM FINDLAY, M.A.,
Pastor of the Free Church, Larkhall, Scotland.

Rev. JOHN FORSYTH, D.D., LL.D.,
Chaplain and Prof. of Ethics and Law in U. S. Military Academy, West Point, N. Y.

Rev. FREDERIC GARDINER, D.D.,
Prof. of the Literature of the O. T. in Berkeley Divinity School, Middletown, Ct.

Rev. ABRAHAM GOSMAN, D.D.,
Lawrenceville, N. J.

Rev. W. HENRY GREEN, D.D., LL.D.,
Professor of Oriental Literature in the Theol. Seminary at Princeton, N. J.

Rev. JAMES B. HAMMOND, M.A.,
New York.

Rev. HORATIO B. HACKETT, D.D.,
Professor of Biblical Exegesis in the Theological Seminary, Rochester, N. Y.

Rev. CHESTER D. HARTRANFT, D.D.,
New Brunswick, N. J.

Rev. EDWIN HARWOOD, D.D.,
Rector of Trinity Church, New Haven, Conn.

Rev. W. H. HORNBLOWER, D.D.,
Professor of Sacred Rhetoric, etc., in the Theol. Seminary at Alleghany, Pa.

Rev. JOHN F. HURST, D.D.,
President of the Drew Theological Seminary, Madison, N. J.

Rev. A. C. KENDRICK, D.D., LL.D.,
Professor of Greek in the University of Rochester, N. Y.

TAYLER LEWIS, LL.D.,
Professor of Oriental Languages in Union College, Schenectady, N. Y.

Rev. JOHN LILLIE, D.D.,
Kingston, N. Y.

Rev. SAMUEL T. LOWRIE, D.D.,
Philadelphia, Pa.

Rev. J. FRED. McCURDY, M.A.,
Ass't Professor of the Hebrew Language in the Theol. Sem. at Princeton, N. J.

Rev. CHARLES M. MEAD, Ph.D.,
Professor of the Hebrew Language and Literature in the Theol. Sem., Andover, Mass.

Rev. GEO. E. DAY, D.D.,
Professor in Yale Divinity School, New Haven, Conn.

Rev. J. ISADOR MOMBERT, D.D.,
Philadelphia, Pa.

Rev. DUNLOP MOORE, D.D.,
New Brighton, Pa.

Miss EVELINA MOORE,
Newark, N. J.

JAMES G. MURPHY, LL.D.,
Professor in the General Assembly's and the Queen's College at Belfast.

Rev. HOWARD OSGOOD, D.D.,
Professor of the Interpretation of the Old Test. in the Theol. Sem., Rochester, N. Y.

Rev. JOSEPH PACKARD, D.D.
Professor of Biblical Literature in the Theological Seminary at Alexandria, Va.

Rev. DANIEL W. POOR, D.D.,
Professor of Church History in the Theological Seminary at San Francisco, Cal.

Rev. MATTHEW B. RIDDLE, D.D.,
Professor of New Testament Exegesis in the Theol. Seminary at Hartford, Conn.

Rev. CHAS. F. SCHAEFFER, D.D.,
Professor of Theology in the Evangelical Lutheran Seminary at Philadelphia.

Rev. WILLIAM G. T. SHEDD, D.D., LL.D.,
Professor of Systematic Theology in the Union Theological Seminary, New York.

Rev. CHAS. C. STARBUCK, M.A.,
Formerly Tutor in the Theological Seminary at Andover, Mass.

Rev. P. H. STEENSTRA,
Professor of Biblical Literature at Cambridge, Mass.

Rev. JAMES STRONG, D.D.,
Professor of Exegetical Theology in the Drew Theological Seminary, Madison, N. J.

Rev. W. G. SUMNER, M.A.,
Professor in Yale College, New Haven, Conn.

Rev. C. H. TOY, D.D.,
Professor of Hebrew and Old Testament Exegesis, Louisville, Ky.

Rev. E. A. WASHBURN, D.D., LL.D.,
Rector of Calvary Church, New York.

WILLIAM WELLS, M.A., LL.D.,
Professor of Modern Languages in Union College, New York.

Rev. C. P. WING, D.D.,
Carlisle, Pa.

Rev. E. D. YEOMANS, D.D.,
Orange, N. J.

PREFACE.

THE thirteenth volume of this work embraces the Commentaries on the Prophetical Books of Ezekiel and Daniel.

I. The Commentary on EZEKIEL was prepared (1873) by my friend, the Rev. F. W. J. SCHRÖDER, Pastor of the First Reformed Church at Elberfeld, a gentleman of thorough theological education, sound views, and great pulpit abilities. He intended to devote himself to an academic career, took the degree of B.D. (*Lic. Theol.*), in the University of Berlin, and began a Commentary on the Old Testament somewhat similar to that of LANGE, issuing a volume on Genesis, which was well received. But when the celebrated Dr. F. W. KRUMMACHER removed from Elberfeld to Berlin (in 1847), Mr. SCHRÖDER, on his recommendation, was selected his successor, and continued in this pastoral charge till his death, in February, 1876. He looked forward with great interest to the appearance of the English translation of his work, on which he spent much labor and care.

The English edition was intrusted to the Rev. Dr. FAIRBAIRN, of Glasgow, one of the fathers and founders of the Free Church of Scotland, and himself the author of a valuable Commentary on Ezekiel, as well as other well known theological works.[1] His lamented death delayed the work. But he had associated with him his pupil and friend, the Rev. WM. FINDLAY, M.A., of Larkhall, Scotland, who, in connection with two other Scotch ministers, the Rev. THOMAS CRERAR, M.A., of Cardross, and the Rev. SINCLAIR MANSON, M.A., Free Church College, Glasgow, completed the task. The translation has been executed as follows:

Rev. WM. FINDLAY, pp.	1–179.
Rev. THOS. CRERAR,	180-240.
Rev. Dr. FAIRBAIRN,	241–331, (close of chap. XXXIV).
Rev. S. MANSON,	331–492.

[1] Dr. PATRICK FAIRBAIRN was born in January, 1805, and died August 6, 1874. See the Biographical Sketch by Prof. DOUGLAS, D.D. (his successor), in the "Monthly Record" of the Free Church of Scotland, for Oct. 1, 1874, pp. 217-218, and the Memoir prefixed to FAIRBAIRN'S "Pastoral Epistles," Edinburgh, 1875.

Many of the additions, which are numerous, have been extracted from Dr. FAIRBAIRN'S Commentary and from his manuscript notes. His forte lay in the development of principles and comprehensive views rather than in critical notes and details. The chief additions are on the English literature of Ezekiel (p. 30), the vision of the Cherubim (pp. 52–54), the symbolical actions (pp. 77–78), the 390 days (p. 81), the abominations in the Temple (pp. 104–106), Noah, Daniel and Job (p. 151), the marriage union of Jehovah and Israel (pp. 161–162), the Jewish Sabbath (p. 197), the Prince of Tyre (pp. 262-263), the Assyrian cedar (p. 284), the image of the Shepherd (p. 318), the divine promises in Chaps. XXXIV–XXXVII (pp. 352–353), Gog and Magog (pp. 372–373), and especially on the vision of the Temple (pp. 439–444).

II. The Commentary on DANIEL is the work of Prof. ZÖCKLER (1870), whom the readers of LANGE already know as one of the largest and ablest contributors to the Old Testament part of this Commentary.

The English edition of DANIEL is the work of the Rev. Dr. STRONG, of Drew Theological Seminary, aided by the Rev. G. MILLER, B.D., of Walpach Centre, N. J., who prepared the first draft of the translation. DR. STRONG has inserted the Biblical Text with its emendations and Critical Notes, and has made all the additions to the Commentary. The most extensive of these are the synoptical view of Daniel's prophecies, in tabular form, given in the Introduction, originally prepared by Dr. STRONG for another work, and the excursus on the Seventy Weeks. Dr. STRONG has everywhere added the interpretations of later or unnoticed Commentaries, especially those of Dr. KEIL and MOSES STUART. He differs from the German author with respect to the genuineness of certain parts of Chap. XI (vers. 5–39), and hopes he has fully vindicated the complete integrity of the text, as well as cleared up those difficulties which the author has confessedly left unsolved. Dr. ZÖCKLER himself admits, in the Preface, that his doubts concerning Chap. XI. are purely subjective, (the supposed *analogia visionis propheticæ*,) and that the external testimonies are all in favor of the integrity of the text.

PHILIP SCHAFF.

NEW YORK, *Oct.*, 1876.

THE PROPHET EZEKIEL.

INTRODUCTION.

§ 1. NAME OF THE PROPHET, AND ITS MEANING.

In Hebrew, Jĕchedsĕqēl; according to the Greek translation, Jezeki-el; in Sirach in Grecized form, Jezeki-elos, as Josephus also writes the name; in Latin (Vulgate), Ezechi-el; Luther, Heseki-el.

יחזקאל is a compound either of יחזק אל (Ewald) or of יחזק אל (Gesenius). In the former case the meaning of the name, according to prevailing linguistic usage, would be the intransitive one: "*God* is *strong* (firm)" (Hengstenberg: "or he in relation to whom God becomes strong"); in the other case the name of the prophet would mean: "*God strengthens*," *i.e.* "whom God makes firm (hardens)" (Baumgarten: "whose character is a personal confirmation of the strengthening of God"). The verb חזק may be compared with ἰσχύω (ἰσχύς), "to *be* strong;" in its radical meaning it has a transitive character ("to straiten," "to press," "to make firm," "to fetter"). Hiller in the *Onomasticon sacrum* translates the name Ezekiel: *Deus prævalebit;* and a similar explanation is given by Witsius also (Treatise, *De Prophetis in capt. Babyl.*, *Miscell. s.* i. 19, 6), J. H. Michaelis, and others.

The names of the prophets have their providential element, so that they may produce the impression of emblems in word. What the character of the time is in the divine judgment and the special task of the prophet, his calling from God, and therefore also his comfort against men, appear to have found expression in the name.

"Like all the names of the canonical prophets, the name of Ezekiel also is not such a name as he had borne from his youth, but an official name which he had assumed at the beginning of his calling" (Hengstenberg).

When passages like chap. i. 3, iii. 14 in Ezekiel are quoted for the explanation of his name, we arrive at no further result than something like what may be said distinctively of the prophetic order in general,—this *compulsion* of the human spirit by the Spirit of God, as a result of superior divine power. The holy men of God were Φερόμενοι ὑπὸ πνεύματος ἁγίου, 2 Pet. i. 21; God carried them along with Him (Ezek. iii. 14), proved Himself first of all in themselves to be the strong God. But while "the hand of Jehovah was upon him," and "was strong upon him," there is besides a *distinctive*, *peculiar* element in Ezekiel, as contrasted *e.g.* with Jeremiah (comp. his first appearance, Jer. i. 4–7, xx. 7), or even as in the case of Jonah. The interpretation of the name assumes a *more individual* aspect only when passages like chap. iii. 8, 9 are also taken into consideration. *Hard against hard* (חזק) is accordingly the mission of our prophet, the *counter-hard* he is to be according to God's will. *God stands fast* to His purpose, alike as respects judgment and as respects salvation: *this is the stamp of the time according to God* in the name of Ezekiel, the *objective* programme of his mission for those to whom he is sent, and let the heathen also know it. And for the accomplishment of such a task *God strengthens* him (the *subjective* side), *i.e.* in conformity with his nature, which is, of course, of another type from that of his parallel Jeremiah (§§ 2, 4). Ezekiel has not the "tender heart" and "soft disposition," but is "an individuality already endowed by nature with admirable strength of mind" (Hävernick). Where the man is *iron*, the divine preparation consists in this, that God makes him *steel*, hardens him,—lends to his natural power and energy the consecration of a *sword of God* (Isaiah = God (is) salvation, God (is) gracious; Ezekiel = God (is) hard).

Appendix.—"We may suppose that pious parents in those very corrupt times wished to testify their faith and to recommend it to their children by bestowing on them names so significant: that God will support the pious with His might, and carry through the covenant of His grace with His strong hand" (Witsius).—"The name is borrowed from the invincible might of God and our Saviour, and our prophet was able to comfort and fortify himself against all temptations and difficulties in his office by the mere remembrance even of his name and its meaning" (J. H. Michaelis).—"This prophet strengthened and fortified the souls of the Israelites, and on this account he was so named through Divine Providence from his birth; *i.e.* he was to express the might and strength of God, which He would manifest in the future redemption. For the prophets' names were by no means given them at the will and pleasure of their parents, but they got such names from above, through Divine Providence, as corresponded with their sphere of activity and their deeds" (Abarbanel). "God, the Strong, imparts power, gives strength and continuance. Thus might, power, strength from the hand which alone is strong; with human impotence nothing is ever done" (W. Neumann).—"Many explain the name of the prophet in this way: 'he who is strengthened by the Lord;' others in this way: 'he who holds fast to God;' and the man who will discharge his office with success must be strengthened by the Lord, for mere natural strength is too powerless to bear such a burden and to withstand the violence of the enemy. Let a man therefore hold fast to God, in order that he may overcome through the power of the Most High; let him do so with prayer, in order that his work may have a blessed result" (J. F. Starck).

§ 2. HIS POSITION AMONG "THE FOUR GREATER PROPHETS."

As is well known, the acceptance of *four* so-called "greater prophets," including Daniel as such after Ezekiel, in Luther's translation of the Bible, rests on the precedent of the Vulgate, which in this had been anticipated by the Greek translation of the LXX. and also by Josephus, while the editions and MSS. of the Hebrew Bible reckon only *three* גדולים—Isaiah, Jeremiah, Ezekiel—and place Daniel among the כתובים.

If the designation of the "greater" prophets has a mere outward reference to the size of their books which have come down to us, a deeper instinct has *combined the three*, and then also added *the fourth*. We have here the *fourfold Old Testament gospel.*

The fact that in the Talmud, as in German and French codices (comp. W. Neumann on Jeremiah, pp. 10 sqq.), Jeremiah is the first, and Ezekiel and Isaiah follow him,—of which Kimchi gives this as the explanation: "As the books of Kings (being those which precede) close with the devastation, and the whole of Jeremiah is occupied with the devastation, and as Ezekiel on the other hand ends with comfort, and Isaiah is wholly comfort," the Talmudists had joined "devastation with devastation, and comfort with comfort,"—gives no help indeed to a deeper understanding of the connection, but we see, although this order of succession differs from the Rabbinical one of the Masoretic text, in the one case as in the other a prophetic *triad*, and that consisting of the *same* persons. The *one* arrangement is predominantly *according to contents*, the *other* is *chronological.*

The *Calwer Handbuch* thus expresses itself: "Ezekiel forms with Isaiah and Jeremiah a glorious *triad.* While Isaiah exhibits the servant of God marching along in exalted greatness, and Jeremiah exhibits him gently admonishing, silently suffering, Ezekiel is the one who, in the first place, breaking in pieces the hard hearts with the hammer of the law, represents the strict inexorable judge, but thereafter, pouring soothing balm into the open wounds, approves himself as the healing physician. Faith, love, hope, would be a suitable inscription over these three prophetic books also."

Whether, then, we make the ascent *from* Isaiah with the Rabbins, or *to* Isaiah with the Talmudists, in either arrangement Ezekiel has *Jeremiah* as a neighbour; and consequently for his position in the triad this juxtaposition, which is also otherwise confirmed (§ 3), is first of all to be noticed. What *Jeremiah's* policy of the kingdom of God is in its *melancholy* way, in presence of the temple and while still in the holy city, *that same* is the *choleric*[1] *Ezekiel, far from the sanctuary among those already carried away.* "*Humble yourselves therefore under the mighty hand of God, that He may exalt you in His time,*"—so runs the preaching of *both, this* is their *harmonious note;* thus an announcement of *judgment*, of the full measure of punishment; just as Calvin says, that "God has made Jeremiah and Ezekiel

[1] The Ezekiel of Michael Angelo on the roof of the Sistine Chapel is correctly described by H. Grimm in his *Life of Michael Angelo,* "with the upper part of the body eagerly bent forward, the right hand stretched out in the act of demonstration, holding in the left an unrolled parchment; it is as if one saw the thoughts chasing one another in his mind."

the instruments of arraigning the Jews as guilty, and of holding up before them the sentence of condemnation."[1]

But if Ezekiel is *parallel with Jeremiah*, he may also further, like him, be made to approach Isaiah. In a theological point of view, Christ is certainly *above all* and the beginning of the way of God with sinners, God's will and purpose from eternity. The "*salvation* of Jehovah," therefore, takes the *lead* among the prophets also, and *Isaiah* has his place *before Jeremiah*. Historically, on the other hand, Christ appears as the *end* of the law; where sin abounded, grace did much more abound; and out of the curse on Israel came the blessing to all nations. *This* is, *as far as the law is concerned*, the historical transition, and in fact that *from Ezekiel to Isaiah*. For, as is included in the meaning of the name Ezekiel, not merely does the judgment stand fast, but *the salvation likewise stands fast* through God.

"As Isaiah has the calling to bring the word of Jehovah to Israel at the time when the necessity of the judgment of the captivity to be suspended over them had publicly manifested itself, and as Jeremiah discharged the prophetic office when this great and fearful turn of affairs burst forth upon the city of Jerusalem and the house of David, so Ezekiel has the prophetic calling to introduce personally the stiff-necked house of Israel into their thousand years' school of trial—into the wilderness of the heathen" (Baumgarten). ("As Isaiah proclaims the wrath of God in words of thunder, and Jeremiah wails in deep plaintive tones, so Ezekiel spreads out a multitude of splendid pictures, like banners, under which the scattered people are again to gather and comfort themselves, above all the picture of the ideal temple. With Isaiah, power of intellect predominates; with Jeremiah, depth of feeling; with Ezekiel, fancy." Wolfg. Menzel.)

If, finally, we add to the position of our prophet in the triad with respect to Jeremiah and with respect to Isaiah his position *with respect to Daniel*, the fourth and additional greater prophet, then we have *again a parallelism*. The *parallel of Ezekiel with Jeremiah* has reference to their labours *inwardly among Israel*; the parallel of *Ezekiel with Daniel* has reference to their labours *outwardly upon the heathen*. What is the case with *Daniel* in an *extraordinary* way and *in subordination to* his official position in the *world-empire* of Nebuchadnezzar, that is *Ezekiel's ordinary calling and office*. "It is not merely the circumstances of the theocracy in itself that Ezekiel keeps in his eye," says Hävernick, "but also its relation to the heathen world, chap. xxv.–xxxii. It is meant that we should clearly perceive by means of his word, directed to the mightiest, wisest, and proudest nations of the earth, the relation of that heathenism, which was certainly and for ever sinking, to that theocracy, which was at present indeed in a vanquished condition, but yet was ripening for an everlasting victory over the world." Comp. the article *Prophetenthum des A. T.*, by Oehler. (Herzog, *Encycl.* xii. pp. 230 sqq.)—Richter: "Ezekiel encounters the heathen symbolism of Babylon, just as Daniel encounters the heathen magic of the Chaldeans."

§ 3. THE CIRCUMSTANCES OF HIS LIFE, INCLUDING WHAT IS TRADITIONAL.

Ezekiel was of *priestly extraction*, like Jeremiah and Zechariah also. (The name occurs again in 1 Chron. xxiv. 16 in a priestly-Levitical connection.) His father is called (chap. i. 3) "*Buzi* the priest,"[2] of whom Holy Scripture relates nothing else. Witsius connects the name בּוּזִי, "*i.e.* my insult," with the time, which was "full of disgrace and shame." Jewish curiosity has discovered *Jeremiah* concealed under that name, who, as is alleged, was called "a despised one," and was Ezekiel's father. It passes current generally with the Jews as a rule: that the fathers of the prophets also must have been prophets, if we find them mentioned by name in the Holy Scriptures.

His extraction, and that from "the more respectable priestly families," is evidenced, according to Hävernick, "also by that closer relation in which the prophet (chap. xi.) appears to have stood to the more distinguished members of the priesthood."—Ewald: "As these, the first of the exiles, were in general only richer or more respectable Israelites: he

[1] Umbreit draws a parallel between Ezekiel and Jeremiah in the following way:—"Both of priestly descent, but Jeremiah is only a prophet; Ezekiel does not even in a strange land put off the priestly costume, and roots himself firmly in strictly Levitical ordinance, although he gives it a new form in a free spirit. Jeremiah is more the prophet of the Reformed Church development; Ezekiel represents outwardly the system of priestly continuance of Catholicism."

[2] Unless by הַכֹּהֵן (Hengstenberg, Bunsen) Ezekiel *himself* is to be designated as the "priest among the prophets."

sprang besides from that branch of Levi to which, in preference to the ordinary Levites, the peculiar priestly dignity belonged, chap. i. 3, viz. the sons of Zadok, chap. xl. 46, xliii. 19, xliv. 10, 15, xlv. 3 sqq., xlviii. 11; comp. 1 Kings i. sqq."

Born in the kingdom of *Judah*, in the reign of King Josiah, he lived there till he was carried away into exile. His childhood and youth fall accordingly into the period of the following kings: Josiah (the Pious); Jehoahaz, whom Pharaoh Necho sent captive to Egypt after three short months; Jehoiakim, the ungodly vassal of Egypt; and Jehoiachin, who reigned only three months and ten days. The "*captivity of King Jehoiachin*" is with Ezekiel from the commencement (chap. i. 2) and throughout an event of such moment,—besides, he designates it expressly (chap. xl. 1) as "*our* captivity,"—that he was without doubt among those who were *at that time carried captive to Babylon by Nebuchadnezzar* (2 Kings xxiv. 14 sqq.).

He belonged, accordingly, not to the poor and mean people who remained behind in the land (דלת עם־הארץ). If we take 1 Cor. i. 26 sqq. as not merely a New Testament point of view, then the choice of Ezekiel as a prophet is certainly interesting. If we fall in with the view, that a certain externality and splendour is proper to the Old Testament everywhere, then the prophet who is to be reckoned with the more distinguished Jews shares this Old Testament peculiarity. Certainly the Chaldeans took not only what had importance as regards rank, influence, property, power, and skill, but, if not "above all," yet in addition, the more spiritual portion of the nation with them, for which Hengstenberg makes Jer. xxiv. pass as a proof. This happened about the year B.C. 599 (Winer, 598; Bunsen, 597).

Josephus, who certainly makes a mistake in the outset in asserting that Ezekiel was already carried away under Jehoiakim, designates him as παῖς ὤν at the time, which Baumgarten (Herzog, *Real-Encyclop.* iv. p. 297), following the lead of J. H. Michaelis, translates not as "a boy," but "in his youthful years." "As it is not till the fifth year after the captivity of Jeconiah that he is called to the prophetic office (chap. i. 2)," this notice has "an internal probability." On the other hand, Hävernick thinks there is "little probability" that Ezekiel "left his home very young." In favour of "a more advanced age, testimony is certainly borne by the matured, thorough-going priestly spirit which prevails in his prophecies; unquestionably he had already for a considerable time performed priestly services in the temple, for he betrays the most exact acquaintance with the ancient sanctuary in its separate parts (chap. viii., chap. xl.-xliii.); with which also the proportionally brief period of 27 years, being the period of his sojourn in exile (comp. chap. i. 1 with chap. xxix. 17), corresponds, in so far as it is not exactly probable that the prophet long survived this period." If Hengstenberg is right on chap. i. 1 (see the exposition),—at all events, this hypothesis of the older expositors also recommends itself in preference to others,—then Ezekiel *at the time of his exile* was *in the 25th year of his age*, and we would have to place *the birth of our prophet* in the last quarter of the 7th century B.C.

When he *entered on the prophetic office* in the year B.C. 593 at the Chebar, where the exiles had been planted as colonists, *Jeremiah* had already been acting as a prophet for more than 30 years. According to Bleek, "it cannot indeed be doubted that Ezekiel also had known him personally, had often heard him, and had also read sayings of his." But certainly we know nothing of it; only he shows evidently that he presupposes the older contemporary as his companion in spirit, quotes him, leans upon him, is conscious to himself, personally and officially, of having a common calling with Jeremiah.[1] *Later tradition* has constructed out of such relationship, in express form, the position of *an assistant of Jeremiah.*

In a case where already in the law (Num. viii. 24, comp. chap. iv. 3, 23, 30) an earlier age for service, for the time of the setting up of the tabernacle, was contemplated, and where David had appointed even the 20th year for entrance on the Levitical service (1 Chron. xxx.; 2 Chron. xxxi. 17; Ezra iii. 8), the emphasis which Hengstenberg has laid upon Ezekiel's 30th year for the same, as being "a man of priestly family," appears unsuitable. Before his entrance on the prophetic office in this year, there lie, of course, five years of the exile, in which Ezekiel, far from the sanctuary at Jerusalem, could no more execute the priestly calling to which he was born; but that he *performed priestly duty* before this time

[1] "And this was no natural coincidence, that they prophesied, the one at Jerusalem, the other in Chaldea, in such a way as from one mouth, like two singers, the one accompanying the other's voice. For we can wish no better harmony than that which exhibits itself in these two servants of God" (Calvin).

is likewise probable.[1] His coming forth as a prophet in his 30th year compensated in an extraordinary way for an incongruity in his life, viz. his compulsory retirement as priest before the time fixed by the law.

Theodoret concludes from chap. xxiv. that Ezekiel was a *Nazarite* (?). We see from this chapter that he was *married;* his wife died in the ninth year of his banishment. Passages like chap. iii. 24, viii. 1, show him to us *settled down* in every shape, in possession of a house of his own.

Everything else connected with his life, on the other hand, belongs to that manifold tradition which has become *legend*, just as "outside his own book there is no further mention of him in the canonical Scriptures of the Old Testament" (Bleek); the apocryphal Jesus Sirach alone mentions him with commendation (chap. xlix.). As to the writings of Ezekiel falsely so called, see Fabricius, *Codex pseudep. V. T.* i.

Thus there is a fabulous report of a meeting between him and Pythagoras, who, as is well known, is reported to have gone in quest of the temple wisdom of the Egyptians also; he is said to have been a disciple of Ezekiel, nay, to have been Ezekiel himself.—So miracles are attributed to him, such as leading the Jews dryshod across the river Chebar, drowning the Chaldeans therein, and the like.—So he is said to have been murdered by a fellow-exile, a Jewish prince or judge, whose idolatry he reproved—to have died as a martyr. See in the Romish Martyrology at the 10th April, Ezekiel's day in the calendar.—His corpse is said to have been conveyed into the same sepulchral cavern in which Shem's and Arphaxad's bones had been deposited. "In the middle ages there was shown, some days' journey from Bagdad, his tomb, to which the Jews made pilgrimages from Parthia and Media" (Winer); and down even to the present day it is said to be a place of pious veneration. Comp. Witsius, *Misc. s.* i. 19, 10–11.

Ezekiel prophesied from the seventh year before, up to at least the sixteenth year after the destruction of Jerusalem,—22–23 years. He would accordingly have been upwards of fifty years of age. *The whole of his active service as a prophet belongs to the exile.*

§ 4. THE HISTORICAL BACKGROUND AND THE LABOURS OF THE PROPHET.

1. *The general background as connected with the history of the world.* 2. *The more special Jewish* (Israelitish?) *one.* 3. *The labours of the prophet during the first seven years.* 4. *His labours after the destruction of Jerusalem.*

1. *Egypt*, at this period no longer mysteriously closed as of old, has opened itself to strangers under Psammetichus, who has attained to power by means of strangers; *old Egypt goes to meet its self-dissolution.* New Egypt, however, as characterized, for example, by the genial circumnavigation of the whole of Africa under his successor Pharaoh Necho, rather than conquests on the Syrian border and the capture of Jerusalem, is not able to maintain itself; with the defeat at Carchemish (Circesium) B.C. 606, or 605, or 604, the star of the Pharaohs is already near the horizon.

It is in part a period of *gigantic downfalls, Ezekiel's period in the history of the world.* The power of the *Assyrians*, to which the kingdom of Israel and the Syrians had fallen a prey, succumbed to the coalition of the *Chaldeans and Medes.* Nineveh, stretching three days' journey along the Tigris, is since then (606, 625?) that range of hills consisting of immense heaps of ruins opposite Mosul, which more recent excavations have made so interesting. *Nebuchadnezzar* the *Conqueror*, the *Destroyer*, remains the leader of fashion for this period in the East.

According to Silberschlag's *Chronology of the World* (pp. 81, 83), there emerges already about this period the Heraclide *Caranus*, the alleged founder of the Macedonian empire, just as the *birth* of *Cyrus* is to be noticed.

In *Athens*, *Draco*, at the command of the people, wrote (B.C. 622 or 624) his code. The people said it was written with blood. Draco must therefore be followed by a *Solon;* and his more humane legislation also still belongs to this period. It is the period of the so-called "*seven wise men of Greece*," also of the lyric poet *Alcæus*, and of the greatest poetess

[1] "How he spent his time up till this the greatest turning-point of his life, is not reported to us; but he lived certainly in the exercise of a predominantly priestly-judicial care for his people, studied the law, and read the writings of the prophets who lived before him" (Umbreit).

of whom Greece boasted, the Lesbian *Sappho*.—For *Rome* contemporary chronology notes *Tarquinius Priscus*, the fifth of those legendary "*seven kings*," who in succession strengthened and consolidated the city and the state.

2. *The more special historic background*, on which *the labours of our prophet* display themselves, consists of *the occurrences connected with the Jews, their circumstances and conditions from the time of the captivity of King Jehoiachin* (or *Jeconiah*).

At home in the fatherland there is residing at Jerusalem *the last king of the house of David*. The *Babylonian servitude* has already begun under *Jehoiakim*, when Daniel and his companions were taken along with him to Babylon (Hävernick, Hengstenberg). According to the usual view, it began with the captivity of Jehoiachin. Set up as he was by Nebuchadnezzar, Mattaniah, at the time 21 years of age, the uncle of the *captive Jehoiachin*, was in truth a servant of Nebuchadnezzar, although he was called king over the worthless remnant left behind after the draining away of the strength of Judah, and had, perhaps under the impression of "Jehovah's righteousness," been named Zedekiah by Nebuchadnezzar (2 Kings xxiv. 17 sqq.; 2 Chron. xxxvi. 10 sqq.; Jer. xxxvii. 1; Ezek. xvii. 13 sqq.). Over-confidence in his own power and tact among the people, as well as with the great ones, the court party,—obstinate defiance throughout as regards the isolated prophetic voice of Jeremiah,—so much the more willing an ear for the allurements of the lying prophets, —incentive on the part of his neighbours, the small kingdoms of Tyrus, Sidon, Edom, Ammon, Moab, turned the head of this king by Nebuchadnezzar's grace, alike as to the serious oaths which bound his conscience as respects his liege lord (2 Chron. xxxvi. 13), and as to the inevitable consequences which such an act of perjury and treachery must bring with it. If not yet in the fourth year of the reign of Zedekiah, when the king himself even made a journey as far as Babylon, and did obeisance there, in order to remove any suspicion and for the renewal of his homage, yet certainly his overweening, defiant pride did take shape when Hophra (Wahprahet, Apries) had succeeded Necho's son on the throne of Egypt. *Negotiations with Egypt* were entered upon; but even before the Egyptian weapons were at hand, *Zedekiah rose up in rebellion for himself* in the ninth year (588?), provoking Nebuchadnezzar's wrath to an open outbreak. Quicker than Egypt's promised help was the vengeance of the Chaldean, laying waste the defenceless land, before the walls of Jerusalem; and when Hophra, after the city had already for almost a year withstood the besiegers, at length draws near for its relief, he is driven back to Africa without striking a blow. Jerusalem, now surrounded anew, and without any prospect of help, and besides reduced within to the last extremity by famine, can no longer hold out. The enemy has made a breach in the walls. Zedekiah succeeds in making his escape on the following night from the lost city; but the Chaldeans pursuing him, arrest him in his flight, and bring him and those belonging to him before Nebuchadnezzar, who had taken up his headquarters at the northern boundary of Palestine. His children and adherents are slain before his eyes, and his own eyes the infuriated conqueror causes to be put out. Dragged in chains to Babylon, he ends his life there in prison (2 Chron. xxxvi.; Jer. xxxix.; 2 Kings xxv.). The walls of Jerusalem were thrown down by Nebuchadnezzar's command, the temple burnt, as well as the royal palace and all the other prominent buildings. After most thorough pillage, and after the hand of the executioner had inflicted yet additional judgment at Riblah (Jer. lii.), the remainder of the people, with their wives and children, down to the poor vine-dressers and peasants, were *carried into the Babylonian captivity* (B.C. 586 or 587 [588]). Over those who still remained in the land a Jewish governor, Gedaliah, was placed, at whose side stood Jeremiah. There gathered also around him those who had escaped captivity by flight. But Gedaliah was murdered, and before the vengeance of the Chaldeans, in spite of the remonstrance of Jeremiah, the last remnant of the people fled to Egypt, where they settled down. The prophet they compelled to go along with them.

Comp. *Abriss der Urgeschichte des Orients nach Lenormant, Manuel d'hist. anc. de l'Orient*, by M. Busch, i., Duncker, i. p. 829 sqq.

Jeremiah had during this period, while the destinies of the kingdom of Judah were being accomplished, to take his stand not only against *the kings and their great ones*, but scarcely less against *the people* also, who oscillated between the madness of heathenish lusts and a *hypocritical self-righteousness* from their being the people of God. A *degenerate priesthood* and *the false prophets* give to the night-picture its demoniac shading. "Made a defenced city, and an iron pillar, and brazen walls," *the prophet of mourning and of tears* stands alone with his God beside the basket full of "figs, which are not to be eaten," and which are to become a terror and a proverb to all the world, and a curse (Jer. xxiv.). In prison and scourged, in the pit full of mire, subjected to hunger and deadly peril, as well as when receiving the distinctions of the Chaldean, to whom he was under the necessity of promising the victory, and even upon the ruins of Jerusalem and with the last remnants of Judah, Jeremiah remains *the watchman of his native land* (Jer. xxxix. xl.). His occasional relations to the colonists in Babylon (Jer. xxix. li.), as well as the close of his life in Egypt (Jer. xlii.–xliv.), make no essential change in this character. It is only similarly elegiac, tragic, if one will, that as Josiah, the pious king under whom Jeremiah's prophetic mission began, must fall at Megiddo in conflict with the Egyptians, so it was just in Egypt that Jeremiah also disappeared.

To the *occurrences* just narrated *the labours of Ezekiel bear reference.* He *supplements and continues those of his parallel Jeremiah.*

His visions, discourses, and actings are the accompaniment of the inward and outward corruption of Judah; the final decision there forms the basis of the principal division in the writings of our prophet (§ 5).

The *circumstances* at the river Chebar were certainly not in general the same with these in the fatherland, which were ever fluctuating, and never properly decided till the destruction of Jerusalem;—they were settled, in so far clear, as they were the circumstances of exile, of Babylonian captivity; although this captivity, as is plain from many a circumstance, in God's providence has unmistakeable traces of forbearance, of preservation in it. Nebuchadnezzar's procedure, even with respect to those who remained behind at the very end in their native land, is based upon *a secret conviction of their being the people of promise*, which reminds one involuntarily of the *prophecies of Balaam*, who was of course from the Euphrates. However much he feels himself to be a conqueror, he appears to know also that it is given him *to execute a judgment of God;* he shows, as is quite explicable in this way, many a surprising consideration for those who are the objects of the judgment.

It would be of importance for the history of heathenism to find the connection between Melchizedek and Balaam and Nebuchadnezzar. The strong heathenisms lead us to suppose a strong original consciousness of God.

Thus the exiles were *no slaves* of the Chaldeans. Probably lands had been let out to them in consideration of a tribute. So far as we know, it did not amount to bond-service, as in Egypt formerly. So much the easier was it to establish *a kind of civil commonwealth* in the strange land. This people, moreover, are like the cactuses, both as respects the contrast of odd angular forms with splendid blossom, and because when torn away, even on the most barren soil, they also take root again immediately and continue their existence. Even in Egypt what an organic connection had remained unbroken! And so we perceive, in chap. viii. 1, "*the elders of Judah*" *assembled around Ezekiel.* The whole mode of procedure on such an occasion shows certainly that these Jews have no longer any temple, can no longer offer any sacrifices, looks *like the later synagogue worship in its first beginnings.* There would also be no want of *mockery and derision* on the part of the heathen (comp. Dan. v.). But yet the permission to hear the will and counsel of Jehovah from the mouth of His prophet exists. *Religious persecution found no place*, although the tolerance of the Chaldeans might come into stern collision with the exclusive confession of Jehovah (Dan. iii.). Such was *outwardly* the condition of the Jews during the exile in *civil* and in *religious* respects.

Before we frame for ourselves a picture of the *inner condition* of the exiles, and thus of the whole of our prophet's labours and of their peculiar character, there is a preliminary question: *Whether and in how far the labours of Ezekiel had respect also to the exiles of the former separate kingdom of Israel, who had been carried into captivity more than a century before?* (Comp. J. J. Hess, *Geschichte der Regenten von Juda nach d. Exilio*, i. p. 3 ff.)

The decision of this question depends, fortunately, not on the mere geographical determination of the "river, *Chebar*" (Ezek. 2. 3) and *Habor* (2 Kings xvii. 6, xviii. 11). While Umbreit, Hävernick, Winer, Gesenius, Ritter, Bleek, Bunsen identify the two, and understand the sufficiently well-known *Mesopotamian* Chabōras (Syriac, Chebar or Chabur; Arabic, Chabur; in Strabo, 'Αβόῤῥας), which rises to the north of Ras el Ain at the foot of the Masian Mountains, receives the Mygdonius and falls into the Euphrates at Circesium, by which means, even locally, Ezekiel would be placed at the same time among the exiles of the ten tribes;—Ewald, Delitzsch, Keil, Baumgarten, Bähr (Lange on 2 Kings, p. 183) distinguish "Chebar" and "Habor." The "river Chebar" is to them the river indicated in Upper Mesopotamia; "Habor," on the other hand, a tributary of the Tigris, in northern Assyria, which gives very much the impression of what is sought, although it is called *Khabur Chasaniæ* (J. Wickelhaus *in der deutsch. morgenl. Zeitschr.* v. p. 467 sqq.). If one cannot admit the identity of "Chebar" and "Habor," it agrees at all events much better with the text in 2 Kings xvii. 6, xviii. 11, especially if one compares 1 Chron. v. 26, to take וּבְחָבוֹר along with בַּחְלַח, and to interpret the one like the other, viz. in both cases *as a province*, understanding it of the mountainous region "Chaboras" (Ptol. vi. 1) between Media and Assyria—a view which Jewish tradition would support, as it banishes the ten tribes thither. But the *relation of the exiles of Israel to those of Judah* is not at all affected through a local separation of the two. This rested on quite a different basis from anything that could be denied as a result of geographical investigations, or that could be proved only by means of such. The breaking off of the separate kingdom of Israel was in its very origin almost entirely of a political nature. The God-fearing among the separate tribes had never lost the religio-national unity of the people of God out of their hearts. And so Ezekiel's representations also (chap. xvi. xxiii. etc.) embrace Judah and Israel together as regards the hope, just as in the corruption. With the downfall of the state, both the peculiar court religion—in other words, state religion—of the kingdom of Israel and the whole separation, which had been upheld only with much exertion, came to the ground. Finally, as the exile, which at a later period absorbed Judah also, compensated in outward respects for the wide separation from each other which had existed for a hundred years and upwards, so still more it brought *the separated ones inwardly to one another.* The same land, the same suffering! The latter had its influence on the better portion at least. For Judah, however, the fruit of the chastisement experienced could not possibly be the mere quickening of her own piety; prophetic prediction certainly (such as Jer. xxx. 3 sqq.) set before her the prospect of Israel also being reunited with her in the restoration! The pious ones of Judah must have awaked to the consciousness of a holy mission, of a task of love with respect to the sheep of the ten tribes which had been torn away from David's flock. The *furtherance, the realization of this consciousness, lay throughout within the sphere of Ezekiel's labours* (comp. Ezek. xxxvii. 16 sqq., xlvii. 13). Whatever of a hindering, resisting element it might possibly have encountered from the other side—say, in the priests, officials, prophets of the Israelitish state religion, or in general in heathenishly inclined individuals of the ten tribes—had already in course of time been removed out of the way, had certainly passed into heathenism. The *kernel of Israel* yielded themselves to the attempts at approach on the part of Judah, *attached themselves to her, ranged themselves under her.* In this way is explained the naming of Judah and Benjamin only in the edict of Cyrus (Ezra i.), although it was published in the whole of his kingdom, and therefore also where exiles from Israel had their abode; just as in fact the people collectively got the name of Judah. Though it might be the case that the preponderating majority of the Jews were united in doing so, and that at the commencement a proportionally small number of Israelites returned, because these latter, on account of their much longer exile, had more difficulty in getting themselves disentangled; yet Anna (Luke ii. 36) was "of the tribe of Asher," and Paul testifies (Acts xxvi. 7) of his own nation as τὸ δωδεκάφυλον, and the millions of Jews who were at the time of Christ and afterwards in the dispersion can hardly be traced back to Judah and Benjamin merely (comp. Herzog, *Real-Encyclopädie*, i. p. 651 sqq., and Hengstenberg's *History of the Kingdom of God*, ii. p. 285 sqq. [Clark's Trans.]).

3. For the position of our prophet *among the exiles of Judah*, the occurrence of the final decision with respect to Jerusalem, *the destruction of the city and the temple, and the downfall of the kingdom of Judah also*, is the event from the date of which the prophetic labours of Ezekiel, which had hitherto been related to those of his parallel Jeremiah as supplementary and confirmatory, gain the character of an independent *continuation* of the same. Comp. Ezek. iii. 12 sqq., xxiv. 26 sqq., xxxiii. 21 sqq. With the apparently for ever lost father-

land, the prophet of the fatherland also now steps into the background. All is now *exile*, and *Ezekiel* is *the prophet of the exile.* Hitherto Judah abroad and Judah at home had remained in the closest possible connection, and the co-operation of Ezekiel with Jeremiah had been the prophetic corrective of this relation. Comp. Ezek. iv. v. vi. vii., etc. The deportation of King Jehoiachin had at the same time laid hold in part of those members of the covenant people who, in an inward and spiritual point of view, come into consideration. On the whole, it was already significant for *those carried away captive with Jehoiachin*, that they had complied with the counsel of Jeremiah, and his preaching of unconditional submission to the Chaldean power. They are favourably contrasted in this respect alike with those who *remained behind until the captivity under Zedekiah* (Jer. xxix. 16 sqq.; Ezek. xiv. 22 sqq.), and especially with those who fled at last to Egypt, whose description is given in Jer. xliv.; comp. Ezek. xxxiii. 23 sqq. But a reaction did not fail when, after Jehoiachin's captivity, *Zedekiah maintained himself in the government for eleven additional years.* What a king! what a government! and yet!? Yea, it came to this, that Nebuchadnezzar was compelled to raise the siege of Jerusalem before the actually approaching Egyptian auxiliaries! Had not Jeremiah perhaps taken too gloomy a view of matters, spoken with exaggeration of a seventy years' bondage under Babylon? Comp. Ezek. xii. Those who remained behind were able, not without the semblance of hope, of a prospect of continuance, to boast of the enjoyment of the holy land, of the possession of the sanctuary at Jerusalem; they boasted of being (Ezek. xi. 15 sqq.), and appeared to be, the patriots, the faithful worshippers of Jehovah; while upon the captives who had given ear to Jeremiah, as upon himself, there might fall the suspicion of being cowards, fugitives,—of being, if not exactly ungodly traitors, at least persons who had been unconsciously misled. In such circumstances there were not wanting for pious hearts even certain hours of severe temptation, when they might be on the verge of despair. What inference, then, may thence be drawn with respect to the rest—the large, more or less fleshly-minded mass of those carried captive with Jehoiachin! They were the children of their fathers in disposition also (comp. Ezek. ii. 3 ff., iii. 7 ff.); the foolish imaginations of those still dwelling in Palestine were to them thoroughly congenial, they dreamt similar dreams, the delusive power of Egypt had currency with them also; and false prophets and soothsayers, who corresponded with the anti-Jeremian party at Jerusalem, found only too much acceptance in their midst (Jer. xxix. 8 sqq., 21 sqq.; Ezek. xiii.). Ezekiel's labours during *this* period, during the *first seven years* of his prophetic office, *among those carried captive with Jehoiachin*, which are delineated for us more specially in accordance with such circumstances and these *inner conditions* of the exiles so far as regards their *spiritual* historical background, accompanied, supported,—as we have said, completed and confirmed the labours of Jeremiah, who on his part, as Jer. xxix. shows, by his word extended his influence to the exiles also.

4. The fall of Jerusalem increased the community of the exile by means of the still more extensive deportation which was decreed for Judah in consequence of this occurrence (Ezek. xxxiii. 31 sqq.). What had hitherto upheld the pride and the frivolity of the majority of the nation, had now come to the ground; the stern reality had followed the hope of which they dreamed; the overweening trust in human help had received a deadly blow. That in the case of many great despondency took the place of great defiance; that with the hope, according to which they dreamed of the future, and according to which they gladly allowed the false prophets to prophesy of it, all hope of every kind disappeared, and that no trust in the Lord won a place for itself, was natural, was in accordance with human nature. Those *carried captive with Zedekiah* were on the whole desperate, determined men. They were also later of coming into the school of the exile, where this had already been able to exercise a wholesome influence upon their predecessors. Although need and misery in themselves are just as capable of making men worse as of making them better, yet we must take into consideration for the result, whether the one or the other, a rougher state of mind or one more prepared by divine grace. Those who brought along with them from home into the strange land the sympathy for heathenish ways, would the less resist apostasy and a complete passing over into heathenism, where they found themselves in the midst of the heathen world, the more easily they could in this way avoid mockery and contempt on the part of the heathen, and spend a happier, more pleasant life. The 137th Psalm disavows even in the remembrance every weakening of the Jewish patriotic feeling, of the home-sickness for Jerusalem; yet how many a one, especially in so tolerable a condition as existed outwardly during the exile, was fixed

down by that plot of ground which he purchased, and whose produce made him comfortable, perhaps much more so than he was before in Palestine! For an influential bearing on the world also (the original divine destination of the Jewish character for the world's salvation), through preparatory training for its commerce, for enriching business transactions throughout the whole world, the circumstances of the exile, especially after the destruction of Jerusalem, may have had their influence. Meanwhile there lay as a burden upon the pious portion of the exiles the whole pressure not merely of the misery of the strange land, far from the land of their fathers, which was in fact the pledge of all God's promises, so that for them the exile embodied the question, and made it a standing one: Where is now thy God? but, inasmuch as now that which had been announced from Moses onwards through the prophets had really occurred, there was in addition the much heavier burden on their conscience, that they beheld themselves under a judgment of God, under a punishment long enough held back—that they were suffering from no mere vicissitude of political misfortune. If, in weighing the misfortune of the children and the guilt of the fathers, the righteousness of Jehovah was to be held up, and the way of earnest conversion before self-righteous misconception as before frivolous mockery (comp. ch. xviii.), so, where in the present instance the feeling of guilt on the part of afflicted consciences broke down all courage, and a divine sadness wrestled with despair under the wrath of God, comfort and the promise of salvation above and beyond all misery had their authorized place. If, therefore, *up to the fall of Jerusalem*, in order to confirm Jeremiah, the work of our prophet had been chiefly *a preaching of repentance*, not of course without thought of salvation, of forbearance and deliverance (*e.g.* ch. vi. 8 sqq., ix. 4 sqq.), —*after the destruction of the city and the temple* the activity of Ezekiel manifests itself predominantly in the *announcement of salvation*, although on the ground of the preceding call to that conversion which alone saves, and along with the repetition of the same. Comp. ch. xxxiii. xxxiv.

§ 5. CONTENTS AND DIVISION OF THE BOOK.

1. The work of our prophet, the picture of his prophetic life,—and this is most truly his life-picture,—is furnished us first of all by the contents of his book, according to Umbreit's description, "as in a prophetic diary carried on by himself." "Where the work of the prophets was *par excellence* a spiritual one, consisting in the preaching of the word, there the communication and preservation of this word is itself the portraiture of their activity, in very deed their prophetic biography. The latter is the case with Ezekiel" (Hävernick).

The very first three chapters give us a glimpse *as into a programme.* Still more as regards the object of the *vision* in ch. i., with which the book opens, than as regards the divine commission in ch. ii. and iii., the prophet appears to us at the very beginning as he will be up to the end in the peculiarity of his prophetic work according to the divine appointment. This is *not merely* that he is to be a *prophet in the exile*, which is the only thing Calvin makes prominent, but rather that he has to represent *the glory of Jehovah in the exile. This is the key to his prophetic labours in their strictest individuality.* As regards the *divine commission* to the prophet in ch. ii. and iii., what stands opposed *on man's part* to the carrying out of the same, partly *outside* (ch. ii. 3 sqq.), partly *in* himself (ch. ii. 8 sqq.), just as what is said with respect to the equipment of Ezekiel on *God's* part (ch. iii. 4 sqq.), is immediately connected with what is very similar in the case of Jeremiah (see the exposition).

Ch. iv. and v., however, change the scene entirely to the (§ 4) foresaid *parallelism of Ezekiel and Jeremiah*, which we found significant as regards the first labours of our prophet: from a *fourfold* (ch. iv. 1–3, 4 sqq., 9 sqq., v. 1 sqq.) *symbolical representation* of the impending *fate of Jerusalem and its inhabitants*, the accompanying interpretation of the symbols leads to *two almost Jeremian discourses of rebuke* against Judah, ch. vi. and vii.

What was already made prominent in these discourses of rebuke as *guilt, the idolatrous apostasy from Jehovah*, is represented with the plastic art of heathen worship and a liturgical vividness—*by the vision of the abominations in the temple* (ch. viii.), in which from the first the "image of jealousy" and the glory of Jehovah (ch. i.) confront each other (ch. viii. 3, 4), and *this latter* (ch. ix. 3 sqq.) causes *the judgment* to be carried out inexorably *on the guilty*, especially *on the city* (ch. x.).

As the 11th chapter, in which the vision closes, once more, and through a striking case of death, brings into prominence *the leaders* of the people (the demagogues), so the *symbolical transaction* in ch. xii. singles out the lot of *the king* at Jerusalem, so that with the "bread" and "water" a termination is reached in the meantime of the misery which is to come upon the land and its inhabitants. The only thing remaining is, that the prophet should announce the execution of the punishment as being one that is *near*, ver. 21 sqq.

The circumstance that his repeated (vers. 21 sqq., 26 sqq.) *previous announcement of the nearness* of the judgment takes the shape in ch. xiii. of a *discourse against the false prophets and prophetesses*, cannot (according to ch. xii. 24) lie outside the context, and the explanation come to with the *idolatrous seekers after oracles* in ch. xiv. easily fits into it; the elders of the people who are guilty of such consultation are just sitting before the prophet, and the guilt, essentially similar to their own, of *faithless Jerusalem* (ver. 12 sqq.) justifies to their consciences the righteousness of the punishment in the one case as in the other, just as such justification will also take place through the remnant from Jerusalem (vers. 22, 23), who will come to be seen by them. But after *Jerusalem* has been depicted in ch. xv. as *a vine tree for the burning*, especially after she has been depicted in detail as *a lewd adulteress* in ch. xvi.,—idolatry in that case being adultery and lewdness,—and after the *riddle with respect to the royal house of David* in ch. xvii. is followed by the thorough *statement of the divine righteousness* in ch. xviii., and lastly by *the lamentation* in ch. xix. over the perishing kingdom of Israel, ch. xx. merely contains in addition a *survey* of the objective as well as subjective guidance of the people from of old, for the purpose in ch. xxi. of setting forth with the most living distinctness *the express announcement of the nearness* of the judgment (comp. ver. 12), and then *alike the punishment and* (with equal sharpness) *the guilt—Jerusalem's in particular, and Judah's ana Israel's in common*—are portrayed in ch. xxii. and xxiii.

In ch. xxiv. the predicted *nearness* of the judgment is *a fact* of such a kind, that the prophet must for himself write down the day, that the fact of the death of his wife furnishes the mournful illustration, and that the prophet does *not* now *any longer speak*, but *is silent* respecting Jerusalem.

But during this silence *respecting Israel* the prophetic word goes forth with loud voice *against those without*,[1] such as *Ammon* (comp. ch. xxi. 33 sqq.) and *Moab*, *Edom*, *the Philistines* (ch. xxv.), then *Tyrus* and *Sidon* (ch. xxvi.–xxviii.), and lastly *Egypt* (ch. xxix.–xxxii.). There is no passing, as in the case of Paul, from the synagogue to the heathen. Neither is it the joy with Zion's joy, but the joy in Zion's suffering, that forms the point of departure. They are therefore predictions of *judgment; the downfall of Jerusalem determines the colour and tone of these chapters*, which appear *like an appendix to what goes before.* The judgment begins at the house of God, yet it will not spare the rest of the world. And here the predominating element as regards the carrying out of the judgment and the foreign nations that are named is *the connection with Nebuchadnezzar*, just as on the other hand *the more intimate historical relation to Jerusalem down to the last days of Judah.* (As to the chronology, see § 6, and the introductory observations to ch. xxv.–xxxii.)

These predictions rightly form *the transition to the predominantly comforting labours of Ezekiel after the destruction of Jerusalem.* For the ever repeated closing statement as the judgments are announced, "and ye shall," or "thou shalt," or "they shall know that I am the Lord" (comp. ch. xxv. 5, 7, 11), necessarily contained for the exiles *the* consolation, that the malicious delight in Judah's misery (ch. xxv. 3, 6, xxvi. 2) is not to issue in contempt for Judah's God also (ch. xxv. 8, xxviii. 2, 6, 22, xxix. 3, 9), but that their Judge will rather seat Himself in judgment on their false heathen friends also, especially on Egypt (ch. xxix. 6, 7, 16). If Jehovah made Himself known *in such a way* to the heathen, then the judgments over them and their gods, with whom Israel had sinned, to whom they had looked up in trust or in despair, removed at the same time many a stone out of that path which the people had to tread for their salvation. But with their conversion to the only true God—that was the path—the former more *negative* consolation arising from those judgments on the heathen nations grew into a *very positive* one for the people of Jehovah. As already, in the previous announcements of Judah's punishment (comp. ch. vi. 9, xi. 16 sqq., xvi. 60 sqq., xvii. 22 sqq.,

[1] A similar juxtaposition of predictions *respecting the heathen* is found both in Jeremiah (ch. xlvi.–li., at the close) and in Isaiah (ch. xiii.–xxiii.). Comp. Delitzsch, *Comm. on Isaiah*, p. 294 sqq. [Clark's Trans.]. In Isaiah, as in Ezekiel, it is a provisional temporary silence; in Jeremiah, one that is final respecting Israel.

xx. 40 sqq.), *prospects of salvation* are opened up, so the closing note of the prediction of judgment on Sidon (ch. xxviii. 25 sqq.), on Egypt (ch. xxix. 21), is *express* consolation for the exiles. Now what comes in the shape of *consolation*, as being salvation for the people of God, cannot in the end be accomplished without *blessing* for the heathen world, in which and for which Israel is placed from the beginning as a *mediator* of salvation. The judgments on one and another and another of the heathen nations are consummated, of course, in the additional judgment on the heathen world-power antagonistic to the kingdom of God; yet the salvation of the Jews comes to be for the good of the human race. The recovery of the consciousness of her peculiar spiritual calling as a nation must be the highest, the *full consolation* for Israel, to whom alike her own judgment and that on the heathen shaped themselves into a process of purification for her divine world-task.

The *silence of Ezekiel* (ch. xxiv.) had been accordingly, as the predictions with respect to the other nations have informed us, not merely for judgment on Israel, but at the same time *a waiting for the promise of God with respect to His people*, and that *from among the heathen also*. Comp. ch. xlvii. 1 sqq., 22, 23.

As the prophet *is now entering again on his labours among the children of his people*, it is thus suitable that in ch. xxxiii. he *again* becomes *conscious* of his *prophetic mission* from God,[1] when this has to take effect in face of the fact now accomplished and in view of the present situation. The promise of ch. xxxiv. starts therefore from the shepherds of Israel, under whom the sheep have been scattered; in their stead *the Lord Jehovah will interest Himself in the flock*, and, when it is again gathered, will make His servant David the *one shepherd* amid blessings which have as their aim mankind generally. And as the bad shepherds furnish the occasion for the restoration of the *Head*, so we have for that of the *members Edom* as a nation (ch. xxxv.), in contrast with which ch. xxxvi. celebrates *the mountains of Israel* and *the sanctification of the name of Jehovah in His people* (ver. 23 sqq.), to which prospect so rich in promise a temporary conclusion is furnished in ch. xxxvii. by *the vision of the resurrection and quickening of the dead bones*, as well as by *the symbolical action with the one stick out of the two sticks* (ver. 15 sqq.), which is intended to signify *the reuniting of Israel with Judah under the One King David.*

The bearing toward *what is without*, the *world-position* of the people of God in *this* connection, as following upon their *inward* restoration (which has hitherto been the object of promise), is brought into view by ch. xxxviii. and xxxix. *against Gog of Magog.* In this symbolical and typical representation of the powers hostile to the kingdom of God, the glory of the Lord will be perfected alike in the consuming judgment toward Gog, and in glorifying mercy toward Israel.

The *close of the book* (ch. xl.–xlviii.) is devoted to the *prophetic portrayal of the divine glory in the glory of His kingdom;* the temple and its service (ch. xl.–xlvi.), the holy land and the holy city "Jehovah Shammah" (ch. xlvii. and xlviii.), furnish the types consecrated from of old for the purpose.

2. The statement of the *contents* which we have thus attempted, as it has at the same time shown the profound *inner connection*, the *carrying out of the all-dominating idea of the glory of Jehovah*, is still further confirmed by *the division of the book.*

The collection of visions, emblematical actions and facts, of discourses and predictions, of which it is composed, is divided, alike by the downfall of Jerusalem and by the silence of the prophet with respect to his own people, into the *two principal parts:* (1) Ch. i.–xxiv.: The Prophecy *of Judgment;* (2) Ch. xxxiii.–xlviii.: The Prophecy *of the Mercies* of God toward His people in the world.[2] A *third transition-section* is formed by ch. xxv.–xxxii.: *announcements of judgment on the seven heathen nations*, *i.e.* cities.

[1] Especially when the symbolical representation (ch. ii. 8–iii. 3) of this mission and of the divine charge to the prophet from the outset made the taste of sweetness follow after the lamentation and woe.

[2] By these two principal parts of the book is Josephus (*Antiq.* x. 5. 1) perhaps to be explained, who, in speaking of Jeremiah, says further: "But it is not he alone that predicted such things to the people beforehand, but the prophet Ezekiel also, who πρῶτος περὶ τούτων δύο βιβλία γράψας κατέλιπεν." By Hävernick and others the πρῶτος is referred to Jeremiah. Umbreit: "The first large half of his book contains the bitter element of his discourse, the second the sweet element, *i.e.* the promise of the coming times of redemption; the first begins with the departure of the glory of Jehovah from the old profaned temple, the second closes with the return of the same into the new cleansed sanctuary."

HITZIG: "The oracles of Ezekiel are put together in an arranged, organic book. Against the sum-total of forty-eight chapters no objection is to be brought: it cannot therefore be regarded as an accident, if at ch. xxiv., exactly with the half, the series of domestic predictions before the fall of Jerusalem comes to an end. This, which is forthwith (ch. xxv. 2 sqq.) presupposed as having taken place, forms the middle and crowning point of the book. The foreign oracles, words of threatening against seven neighbouring nations, from the commencement and for the most part date from the period after the downfall of Judah, and are occasioned by this very catastrophe; the whole collection was placed suitably at the beginning of the second part, which is in this way just the more sharply contrasted with the first." Hengstenberg (*Christology*, 2d edit.) likewise distinguishes two principal parts, but in this way: "Predictions before the destruction (ch. i.–xxxii.), and after the destruction (ch. xxxiii.–xlviii.); in the former the tendency being mainly to counteract the foolish illusions, to call to repentance as the only means of salvation; in the latter to combat despair by portraying that salvation before the eyes of the people, etc." Similarly also Hävernick: "Two great sections, of which the destruction of Jerusalem forms the turning-point (ch. i.–xxxii. and xxxiii.–xlviii.). In the former period Ezekiel discharges the prophetic office of *rebuke*, afterwards the office of comforting and of *promise*." On the other hand, Kliefoth looks upon "the collection of predictions against foreign nations as a separate part of the book," and makes this division: "The Introduction, ch. i. 1–iii. 21; the First Part, ch. iii. 22–xxiv. 27; the Second Part, ch. xxv. 1–xxxiii. 20; the Third Part, ch. xxxiii. 21–xlviii. 35." De Wette: "The *first* part is arranged with perfect accuracy according to the chronology; the foreign oracles in the *second* part, however, are grouped together in accordance with an arrangement by contents. This collection is, as it were, a supplement or episode, inasmuch as at ch. xxiv. 27 a resting-point is given, or because several of these predictions really belong to the period between ch. xxiv. 27 and xxxiii. 21, while the others are ranged with them because of the similarity of their contents. With the tidings of the destruction of Jerusalem at ch. xxxiii. 21 the prediction advances a step, and the whole of the *third* part belongs to this period after the destruction." Neteler distributes each of the three parts of the book into four sections, and each section into four pieces.

The twofold division of the book, as Hitzig makes it, is an example of arithmetical division: 2 into 48 gives 24 chapters to each. As to the details of *subdivision*, he looks upon each of the principal parts as forming three unequal sections: I. (1) ch. i.–vii.; (2) ch. viii.–xix.; (3) ch. xx.–xxiv. II. (1) ch. xxv.–xxxii.; (2) ch. xxxiii.–xxxix.; (3) xl.–xlviii. According to Hitzig, the thing aimed at was merely "to incorporate the mass of the oracles." (!) If this appears to be too little for an "arranged, organic book," Kliefoth's principle of division, according to the formula, "And the word of Jehovah came to me thus," gives the impression of something that is too artificial. Our position must be this: The chronological element cannot be the determining one everywhere, nor even for the most part, as regards the division in detail; for neither are the dates so generally given, nor do they even regulate a separate part, such as ch. xxv. sqq. More tenable as a division of our book in respect to details—more tenable even than one furnished by the matter-of-fact, *historico*-material element—is that afforded by the *inner* substance, a method by which we shall have to look *at the fundamental idea of the glory of Jehovah manifesting itself in judament and pitying grace.*

SUBDIVISION OF THE PRINCIPAL PARTS.

A. FIRST PRINCIPAL PART: CH. I.–XXIV.

The Prophecy of Judgment.

I. *The Divine Mission of Ezekiel:* ch. i.–iii. 11.

1. The Vision of the Glory of Jehovah, ch. i.
2. The Divine Commission to the Prophet, ch. ii. 1–iii. 11.

II. *The First Execution of the Divine Commission:* ch. iii. 12–vii. 27.

1. The Installation and Instructions, ch. iii. 12–27.
2. The Four Signs and their Interpretation, ch. iv. 1–v. 17.
3. The Two Discourses of Rebuke, ch. vi. and vii.

III. *The Subsequent Execution of Divine Commissions:* ch. viii.–xxiv.

1. The Vision, ch. viii.–xi.
   (1) Of the Abominations in the Temple, ch. viii.
   (2) Of the Judgment on the Guilty, ch. ix.
   (3) In particular of the Coals of Fire on the City, ch. x.
   (4) Of the Leaders of the People, ch. xi.

2. The Signs, ch. xii. 1–20.
   (1) The Sign of the Departure of the King, ch. xii. 1–16.
   (2) The Sign of Bread and Water, ch. xii. 17–20.

3. The Near Execution of the Punishment, ch. xii. 21–xxiv. 27.
   (1) The repeated Preliminary Announcement, ch. xii. 21–28.
   (2) The Discourse against the False Prophets and Prophetesses, ch. xiii.
   (3) The Testimony against the Idolatrous Seekers after Oracles, ch. xiv
   (4) The Parable of the Vine Tree for the Burning, ch. xv.
   (5) The Story of the Lewd Adulteress, ch. xvi.
   (6) The Riddle about the Royal House of David, ch. xvii.
   (7) The Laws of the Divine Punitive Righteousness, ch. xviii.
   (8) The Lamentation over the Kings of Israel, ch. xix.
   (9) The Survey of the Leading of the People from of old, ch. xx.
   (10) The Approaching Judgment, ch. xxi.
   (11) The Conviction of the Ripeness for Judgment:
      a. as well of Jerusalem in particular, ch. xxii.
      b. as of Judah and Israel collectively, ch. xxiii.
   (12) The Marking down of the Event that is taking place, the Discourse in Signs, and the Virtual Sign (the Silence of Ezekiel), ch. xxiv.

A—B. Ch. xxv.–xxxii.

The Transition from the Prophecy of Judgment to the Prophecy of Mercy by means of the Predictions against

I. 1. Ammon,
   2. Moab,
   3. Edom,
   4. The Philistines,
   } Ch. xxv.

II. 1. Tyrus, ch. xxvi. 1–xxviii. 19.
   2. Sidon, ch. xxviii. 20–26.

III. Egypt, ch. xxix.–xxxii.

B. Second Principal Part: Ch. xxxiii.–xlviii.

The Prophecy of the Mercies of God toward His People in the World.

I. *The Renewal of the Divine Mission of Ezekiel,* ch. xxxiii.

1. His office of Watchman in itself, ch. xxxiii. 1–20.
2. The same in view of the Event that has taken place (the re-opening of the mouth of Ezekiel), and in face of the state of affairs as well as of hearts, ch. xxxiii. 21–33.

II. *The Divine Promises.*

1. Against the Shepherds of Israel of the Shepherd Mercy of Jehovah toward His Flock, and of His Servant David, ch. xxxiv.
2. Against Edom with respect to the Mountains of Israel in consequence of the Self-sanctification of the Name of Jehovah, ch. xxxv. and xxxvi.
3. (1) In the Vision of the Resurrection and Requickening of the Dead Bones, ch. xxxvii. 1–14.

(2) By means of the Symbolical Action with the One Stick out of the Two Sticks, along with the Interpretation, ch. xxxvii. 15–28.

4. Against Gog of Magog for the Glorification of Jehovah in the World, ch. xxxviii. and xxxix.

5. In the Vision of Glory.

(1) Of the Temple and its Services, ch. xl.–xlvi.

(2) Of the Holy Land and of the Holy City, ch. xlvii. and xlviii.

§ 6. CHRONOLOGICAL SKETCH ACCORDING TO THE DATES IN THE BOOK.

Day.	Month.	Year of the Captivity of King Jehoiachin.	CHAPTERS.
5	4	5	Ch. i.–vii.
5	6	6	,, viii.–xix.
10	5	7	,, xx.–xxiii.
10	10	9	,, xxiv. xxv. ?
12	10	10	,, xxix. 1–16, xxx. 1, 19. ?
1	1	11	,, xxvi.–xxviii.
7	1	11	,, xxx. 20–26.
1	3	11	,, xxxi.
5	10	12	,, xxxiii. (ch. xxxiv.–xxxix. ?)
1	12	12	,, xxxii. 1–16.
15	12	12	,, xxxii. 17–32.
10	1	25	,, xl.–xlviii.
1	1	27	,, xxix. 17–21.

It is clear from this chronological sketch, so far as dates in the book make it possible, that several of the predictions of judgment on the heathen encroach on the second principal part of the book. As the prophecy of the divine mercy begins on the ground of the renewed call to conversion, and with repeated earnest accusation of Israel (ch. xxxiii. xxxiv. xxxvi.), so the promises of God for His people are accompanied by the tone of judgment on the hostile world-powers, their judgment and downfall—comp. ch. xxxv. xxxviii. xxxix.—as contrast, background, as well as necessary transition to the glorification of the Lord in His kingdom; and so there belong also to this class the predictions, ch. xxxii. 1–16, 17–32, ch. xxix. 17–21, xxx. 1–19, which thus occupy in the transition section (A—B) a preparatory place.

It is likewise clear from the above table, that many a question will have to be answered just by the detailed exposition of the passages referred to, and perhaps only in accordance with probability.

§ 7. THE CHARACTERISTICS OF EZEKIEL'S PROPHECY.

J. Görres says, in the second volume of his *History of the Myths of the Asiatic World* (p. 477), of our prophet: "Like a flame from heaven, Ezekiel blazes up darkly glowing, a great strong nature, his imagination a furnace of seething metal, genuinely oriental in his whole character." Giving prominence to more than the mere natural peculiarity of Ezekiel, Hengstenberg draws the picture in his *Christology:* "A spiritual Samson, who with strong arm grasped the pillars of the idol temple and dashed it to the ground; a powerful gigantic nature, which by that very circumstance was fitted effectively to combat the Babylonian spirit of the age, which was fond of powerful, gigantic, grotesque forms, standing alone, but equal to a hundred trained in the schools of the prophets."

We may begin the discussion of the characteristics, as Ezekiel's book of prophecies exhibits them, by pointing back to the interpretation of *his name* (§ 1). *His prophetic peculiarity and manner of representation is reflected* first of all *in general*, and that throughout, *in his name.* Comp. also § 2.[1]

Then, *in particular*, above other things, emphasis must be laid on *the priestly stamp* which the prophecy of Ezekiel bears. If Keil (*Bibl. Comm.* p. 9) appears to have his difficulties in this respect, he is certainly right as against the opposite views brought forward by him; but this *predominantly* "symbolical and allegorical dress," which is "carried out into the most minute details," as it belongs to Ezekiel above "all other prophets," could with difficulty in the case of a Jew be better obtained than in the Levitical service, than in the temple at Jerusalem, than by means of a priestly education and training,—in short, in a priestly-Levitical way. A Levite lived in the Mosaic worship, a priest lived in the midst of symbolism and allegory; he became accustomed to it (especially if he brought along with him a mind suited for it, and possessed the sanctified imagination of Ezekiel) from his surroundings, from his whole actings, as it were involuntarily as his prevailing mode of expression. Thus "lie the elements," as Keil, following Hävernick, remarks, for the vision at the very commencement (ch. i.), "in the enthronement of Jehovah above the cherubim on the lid of the ark of the covenant," consequently in what was of necessity the crowning-point of a priest's life and of priestly contemplation, according to Lev. xvi. As the glory of Jehovah is the ruling element in the whole book, its priestly keynote is thus sufficiently indicated; but the closing chapters, with the prophetic description of the new temple, etc., completely reveal the priest-prophet, and are only to be explained from a genuine priestly fancy.[2]

A further characteristic of the method of Ezekiel's prophecy is *a lofty ideality*, a high figurativeness leaving far behind it the usual forms of existence, *side by side on the other hand with a severe realism, encountering sensualism sensually.* Both elements in their contrasts, in their conflict with one another, give to the prophetic form of Ezekiel an *eminently original vivacity.*

His sojourn in exile may be looked upon as contributing to this in a twofold respect: in the first place, in so far as our prophet was thereby withdrawn from the proper scene of events; and in the second place, inasmuch as he was at the same time placed in the midst of the Babylonian world.

If Jeremiah is himself present on the scene of events, is every instant enduring his part in the vicissitude of actual occurrences, has to interfere in the circumstances lying immediately before him, and if therefore he led a more stirring outward life, his style corresponds therewith—that of more popular prophetic discourse; his whole activity takes its complexion from the particular actual occurrence. Ezekiel, on the other hand, far as he was from Judea, standing face to face with the imaginings of the exiles (whatever inner connection these forced with the fatherland), amid the most diverse rumours, dispositions, and feelings, was *pointed to the divine communication by means of revelation.* It is therefore only fitting if he

[1] "Above all others, the prophet is distinguished by an uncommon power and energy. Ezekiel is one of the most imposing organs of the Spirit of God in the Old Covenant, a really gigantic phenomenon. In opposition to the present, he steps forth with all sternness and iron consistency, an inflexible nature, encountering the abomination with an immoveable spirit of boldness, with words full of consuming fire. Unceasingly he holds up the one thing that was needful before the deaf ears and hard hearts of the people. The overpowering element of his eloquence rests on this union in it alike of imposing strength and indefatigable consistency."—(Hävernick, *Comment.* p. xiv.)

[2] Ewald asserts that in this last great section of his book Ezekiel "begins already to look on what the people regard as sacred and the priesthood of Israel with that timidity and externality which becomes ever more prevalent after his time," and sees therein "just a consequence of the one-sided literary conception of antiquity according to mere books and traditions, as well as of the depression of intellect increased by the longer duration of the exile and bondage of the people." The exposition will as decidedly reject the alleged "timidity and externality," as Hävernick rightly points to this, what "a high spirit" rather, "which, looking away from all the pains and sufferings of the present, lives in the future and the reconstruction of the kingdom of God with fresh enthusiasm, meets us just in the second part of Ezekiel." If, however, the *detailed character of the description* were to make the impression of "externality," then this is a peculiarity of the prophet in the very first chapter of his book, and characterizes his popular addresses no less than his visions. One may look upon this at the same time as the later literary style; but the manner of Ezekiel is once for all to take a penetrating view of his subject on all sides, as he himself wholly lives and moves therein, and to exhaust it as far as possible. The more tranquil outward (public) life of Ezekiel, as compared with Jeremiah, is therefore not yet the "learned" "literary leisure" which Ewald makes it out to be.

[3] In this as in many other respects, Ezekiel may be compared with Tertullian.

looks at things as from afar, thus *from the divine idea of Jehovah's self-accomplishing glory.* His activity thus *ideally* conditioned concerns itself with the certain fact chiefly *according to its essence*, in its *necessity* and character of fact *as such.* On the height, it is not so much the ever-recurring gust of wind, the whirling dust, the falling of the heavy raindrops, and anon the first flash of lightning, the rolling of the first thunder, that affects us; it is especially the existence of the thunder-cloud coming from afar that has the power to engross our attention. In the distance from where the event actually occurs as an isolated phenomenon, the prophetic life will be for the most part *internal*,—a *contemplative*, *ideal* one; instead of the separate occurrences, by means of which the fact is accomplished on its theatre, there will meet us here, according to individuality and surroundings, as well as (in the case of a prophet) ever under the special divine impulse (in vision), the separate *forms of representation*, by means of which the contemplative spirit seeks to put in shape for itself and others *the ruling idea of the whole.* Hence, to make of Ezekiel a recluse and pedant,—to fancy him, as Ewald does, "a mere literary man confined to his own house and the narrow limits of domestic life" (*The Prophets of the Old Covenant*, ii. p. 210),—will appear to a believer in an extraordinary divine revelation to be an idea which may be mentioned because of its singularity, not refuted. Only on the standpoint of rationalistic or naturalistic materialism, where one makes the prophets at his own hand (comp. another passage at p. 203), are such conceptions and representations at home. The high position of Ezekiel in God's fixed purpose—the more so that he has his abode far from the sinking fatherland, among his fellow-captives by the Chebar—explains, in connection with his *poetic gift* (acknowledged even by Ewald), sufficiently the lofty ideality of his prophetic mode of representation.[1]

As to what has been maintained on the other side with respect to the "influence of the Babylonian spirit and taste on the form of his prophecy," viz. in reference to his symbolism, we must agree with Keil in the view, that the admission "of Old Testament ideas and views," alike for the contents and for the form, *in general* is sufficient (comp. the work referred to, p. 6 sqq.); on the other hand, as respects *the filling up of the picture in detail*, the exposition may indeed specify *many an Assyro-Babylonian feature.*

Thus ch. xl. sqq., with their *architectural finish and picturesqueness of detail*, transport us in a lively way *into the midst of the immense architectural labours of Nebuchadnezzar*, by means of which, when returned home from his victories, he transformed his metropolis Babylon into the finest[2] city of the world, not merely adorning and enlarging it, but fortifying it quite as much, just as, in like manner, in order to preserve the original territory of the kingdom, the land of Shinar, and the capital, from the Medes, he caused the so-called Median wall to be carried across from the Euphrates to the Tigris. The late Professor Hengstenberg said to me long ago, in course of a conversation about the last chapters of Ezekiel, the prophet must certainly have had a "knowledge of building," just as, *e.g.*, Riggenbach's treatise also on the tabernacle betrays such knowledge. At all events, the probability is as great of there being a natural substratum for the detailed restoration of the divine visions at the close of his book in what the priest of Judah in Babylonian exile, by means of Nebuchadnezzar's[3] immense buildings in city and country, was able to appropriate from what he saw

[1] "The flame of the divine wrath, the mighty rushing of the Spirit of the Lord, the holy majesty o Jehovah, as the seer has beheld it, is wonderfully reproduced in his discourse" (Hävernick).

[2] For this we have the ocular testimony (thoroughly confirmed by lately discovered inscriptions) of Herodotus, who visited Babylon in course of the fifth century before our era. The city had the form of a rectangle (comp. Ezek. xlviii. 30 sqq.). Herodotus describes the wall 200 feet high with its 100 gates (comp. also Ezek. xl. xlii.), with posts and thresholds of massive bronze. The deep and swiftly flowing Euphrates (comp. Ezek. xlvii.) intersected Babylon, discharging itself into the Erythræan Sea. The outer wall served as a work of defence. In the midst of the one half of the city was the royal palace, with large, strongly fortified enclosure; in the midst of the other half of the city was the sanctuary of Bel with its brazen gates (comp. ch. xlviii. 21 sqq.). *Herodotus' description of Babylon reads like a parallel to Ezek.* xl.–xlviii. (The circumference of Babylon, as the great outer wall determined it, was, according to the measurements of Oppert, the topographer of the old Chaldean city, seven times that of modern Paris; the inner and more contracted wall embraced still a much larger area than London.) "In symbolical effect," says Lange on one occasion, "human culture becomes a picture of divine worship."

[3] Nebuchadnezzar as a builder outstripped all his predecessors (Fr. Lenormant, *Manuel*, ii. 17 sqq.). He rebuilt almost entirely the royal city of the old Cushite rulers, lying on the eastern bank of the Euphrates; a gigantic new palace rose there at his command, recognizable even at the present day in

and understood in this connection. Nay rather, *in contrast with the buildings of Nebuchadnezzar, the building of Jehovah* rises up in Ezekiel as *the architectural antithesis of the kingdom of God to the kingdoms* of this world, as these latter are symbolized and typified by the world-empire of Nebuchadnezzar. In this way, face to face with "the dominion of the world-powers," as Auberlen designates the stadium of the Babylonian captivity "in the history of the development of the kingdom of God," a significant memento was set up. Our view is, that the impression which the melting and expenditure of brass and of gold necessary for the gigantic buildings of Nebuchadnezzar, and the innumerable brick kilns, were fitted to make, is to be met with in comparisons such as Ezek. i. 4, 7, 13, 27, viii. 2, x. 2, xxii. 20, 22, etc.

But especially the *designedly sensual realism*[1] of the representation, of the singular mode of expression in chapters like ch. xvi. and xxiii., seems to have borrowed its colouring from the so notorious *gross sensuality of the Babylonian idolatry*, in which the most unbridled, most shameless naturalism prevailed. Thus Herodotus relates of the temple of Bel, that in the chapel in the uppermost tower "there is a bed quite prepared," and that "no one spends the night in it but a woman of the land whom the god appoints." Bilitta, or Mylitta, the great goddess of nature, who combined the contrasted qualities of the heavenly and the popular Venus, Tauth and Zarpanit, demanded usually of every woman of the land once in her life her prostitution to a stranger as an offering. So Nana or Zarpanit, worshipped at Kutha, bore the surname of Succoth-Benoth, which likewise points to such prostitutions in honour of the goddess. Comp. the apocryphal epistle of Jeremiah, vers. 42, 43.

the hill of rubbish Kasr, one of the largest. An artificial hill was the site of the celebrated "hanging gardens," which were intended to represent to his Median consort Amytis her beautiful fatherland; terraces rising step by step one above the other, an "Isola Bella" on land, according to Oppert the great rubbish-deposit of Amram. Of the "temple of the foundations of the earth," called also Bit Saggatu ("the temple which raises its head"), that very ancient terraced pyramid of the royal city, with the alleged tomb of the god Bel-Merodach and an esteemed oracle, Nebuchadnezzar says in an inscription: "Bit Saggatu is the great temple of heaven and earth, the dwelling of the lord of the gods, Merodach. I have restored his sanctuary, the seat of the supreme authority, overlaying it with pure gold." A second terraced pyramid was erected by him beside it as a temple for the goddess Zarpanit. On the side of the "secular city" (Hallat) on the west bank of the Euphrates, now Hillah, where the captives from the different countries and Jews also were settled, Nebuchadnezzar restored the tower of Babel, and built therein the great temple of Bel, called Bit-Zida, and "the temple of the seven heavenly spheres." An inscription discovered some years ago, and translated, calls it "the terrace-tower, the everlasting house, the temple of the seven lights of the earth (planets), to which the oldest mention of Borsippa (*i.e.* 'the tower of the languages') is attached, which the first king built, but was not able to finish; men had forsaken it since the days of the flood, expressing their words in confusion. The earthquake and the thunder had shaken the crude brick, and had split the burnt brick of the facing; the crude brick of the foundation-walls had sunk down into hillocks." Herodotus also gives a description of this building restored as a temple. General Rawlinson has pointed out that the seven storeys with the sanctuary of the god above were painted as with the colours of the seven heavenly bodies; the succession of colours represented at the same time the succession of the days of the week. The cuneiform inscriptions of Nebuchadnezzar enumerate other temples besides, which he restored or erected anew, and likewise in the other cities of Chaldea. Those of Kai also, on the Euphrates at Babylon, were finished by him; but just as he cared for "the city of his kingdom" (so he calls it in his inscriptions), so in like manner he cared for the remaining portions of his land: he restored the celebrated royal canal (Naharwalkor), and below Sippara he caused an immense lake to be dug for the purpose of irrigation. It is certainly to be conceded that such activity in building on the part of Nebuchadnezzar will somehow be reflected in the prophetic form of Ezekiel, whose labours were carried on in presence of it.

[1] "As the symbolism and application of similitudes, images, and proverbs is in general only a means to an end, that of illustrating the truths to be brought forward, and of strengthening by means of illustration the effect of the word and the discourse, so the like end is also served by the detail and circumstantiality of the representation, and even by the repetition of thoughts and expressions under new points of view. The people to whom Ezekiel had to preach repentance by the announcement of divine judgment and salvation were a rebellious race, of brazen face and hardened heart. If he wished to exercise towards these faithfully and conscientiously the office of watchman committed to him by the Lord, he must both rebuke the sins of the people with strong words and in drastic fashion, and portray the terrors of the judgment vividly before their eyes, and also set forth in a way that would strike the senses that salvation which was to spring up thereafter for the penitent."—KEIL. "Est atrox, vehemens, tragicus, totus in δεινώσει, in sensibus elatus, fervidus, acerbus, indignabundus. In eo genere, ad quod unice videtur a natura comparatus, nimirum vi, impetu, pondere, granditate, nemo ex omni scriptorum numero eum unquam æquavit."—LOWTH.

From the circumstance that our prophet was placed in the midst of the Babylonian world, yet another peculiarity characterizing him and his book is explained, viz. his *surprisingly accurate knowledge of foreign nations and their affairs* (comp. ch. xxvi. sqq., xxxviii., xxxix.). In this respect he makes the impression of a man who has travelled much and far. Naturally, Ewald finds in this a confirmation of his strange view of Ezekiel sitting over his books, of the "literary and learned man" at the expense of the genuine prophet.[1] It is true: "the position and circumstances of the nations and countries of the earth are described by him with a comprehensiveness and a historical vividness such as belongs to no other prophet." But for this there was no need in the kingdom of Babylon of any far-fetched "learning;" it was enough, with an actual interest and the necessary mental endowments,—which even the *mastery of his materials* possessed by Ezekiel sufficiently shows,—if there were simply open eyes and ears, for Babylon was one of the centres of eastern commerce (Ezek. xvii. 4, xvi. 29), as its geographical position, where Higher and Lower Asia meet, between two great rivers, which placed it in connection with the Persian Gulf and the Indian Ocean, amply justifies, and as may also be shown in other ways. At this market-place so situated, the caravans of the east and west came together, and the mariners of Africa, Arabia, and India met one another. Here they obtained by barter the products of Babylonian industry, which was employed, down even to the villages, *e.g.* in woollen and linen weaving, in the manufacture of garments and carpets. Babylonian weapons, furniture, jewellery, and other fancy goods were articles not less desired. On the other hand, there came to Babylon wines from Armenia, precious stones and large dogs from India, as also the finest woollen stuffs from Persia, perfumes, spices, gold, ivory, and ebony from Arabia and Ethiopia. In the city of Babylon the great world-roads converged (comp. Lenormant, p. 35 sqq.). In addition, a powerful navy; Babylonian ships sailed over the Persian Gulf. According to Strabo, there were factories and colonies of Babylonians in distant lands.

One sees that the Babylonian exile had a similar task to that of the sojourn of the people in Egypt in former days; it was only a *more advanced secular school* for the Jews.

If now we must specify *vision and symbolism* as being, *to a considerable extent*, the characteristic of Ezekiel's prophecy, there is thus expressed a departure from the previous fundamental form of prophecy, viz. inspired popular discourse (which is the peculiarity *e.g.* of Isaiah, and also of Jeremiah even), and an approach to Daniel's peculiarity. What steps more into the background with Isaiah, Jeremiah, and other prophets (Isa. vi.; Jer. xxiv.), begins to be more prominent in Ezekiel, although "the word of Jehovah" also comes to him repeatedly along with it.[2] The lower form of dream is not found in our prophet; but divine revelation comes to him in a waking state, in the higher form of vision (Ezek. i., viii. sqq., xl. sqq.); and just as in the dream plastic symbolism is the rule, so symbolic representation, figurative and allegorical discourse, parabolic speech, the enigmatic is the seer's mode of expression in word as in action (Ezek. i., xv., xvii., iii., iv., v., etc.). HESS: "One might call it pantomimic." The more that God is unveiled before the prophet, in so much the more veiled a way does he shape his reproduction of what he has seen for the profane multitude. (Comp. in this connection the phenomena in the case of one who has risen from the dead. Auberlen quotes also Matt. xiii. 10 sqq.[3]) Only when Ezekiel is to be at the same time an expositor, and he is so almost throughout (ch. i. 28, iv. 3, 13 sqq., xvii.),—it is in this way the transition is made in his case to the plain word, to the prophetic popular discourse,—do logical thought and conceptions again make their appearance. That *being* in the Spirit (Rev. i. 10, iv. 2), as distinguished from this *speaking* in the Spirit, is the *apocalyptic element* of Ezekiel. He testifies of

[1] And yet Ewald concedes, and in words copiously recognises (pp. 204–206), a public ministry of Ezekiel, and that with "clearest consciousness of his being a genuine prophet," and "more plainly expressed than in the case of any earlier prophet."

[2] "We find in the prophet partly a purely didactive mode of discourse tranquilly unfolding itself, similar to what is to be found in the older prophets, ch. xii.–xix. The style is then the usual one of prophetic rhetoric," etc. (Häv.).

[3] "That mode of representation, because it introduces us immediately to the inner world of the prophetic spirit, has a mysterious, ofttimes obscure and enigmatic character. The prophet loves this mode of speech so much the more, when it rouses attention and inquiry, and the more impressively a word of such a kind touches men's hearts. Jerome designates our book as: scripturarum oceanum et mysteriorum Dei labyrinthum" (Häv.). Perhaps, for the idea of *Theosophy* (comp. the article of Lange in *Herzog* xvi.), the Old Testament point of connection may be got from Ezekiel.

it from the beginning (ch. i. 1): that "the heavens were opened," and "he saw visions of God." (Comp. the profound remarks of Auberlen on the three forms of Old Testament revelation, Theophany, Prophecy, Apocalypse, in his *Daniel and Revelation*, p. 70 sqq.[1])

We shall also in the case of Ezekiel be able to speak of "*a look that is all-embracing*," according to Auberlen the one peculiarity of apocalypse, just as we shall meet in our prophet with the other peculiarity remarked by him, "*specialty of prediction*," that apocalypse "gives more of the detail of universal history and more eschatological detail than prophecy," not exactly in the way in which it occurs in Daniel, but yet in similar fashion. Hävernick says: "Rightly did Witsius call the *donum prophetiæ* of our prophet *incomparabile*. True indeed, he grasps the future more in its general features,—the most comprehensive possible form of the kingdom of God as a whole,—but along with that there are not wanting also remarkable glimpses into the detail of the future, predictions strictly so called, on which by means of their exact fulfilment the seal of truth and of divine enlightenment on the part of the prophet is impressed, ch. xxvi. sqq., xii. 12 sqq., xxiv.; comp. ch. xxxiii." (ch. xi. 10; comp. with Jer. lii. 10). Year, month, and day are given us; it is the prophet's conscious intention to remove every suspicion of a *vaticinii post eventum*.

But apart from these *definite predictions*, the general sensuousness, *the complete visibility of the prophetic form of Ezekiel* is the suitable counterpart of *the Chaldean world which so caught the eye*, and amid which Israel is in a state of dread; and still more was it, on the other hand, adapted for the comfortless despondency and almost despair of those banished thither, from whom everything visible, which had been to them a pledge of the divine favour,—land, and city, and temple, and the beautiful ordinances of divine worship,—seemed to have vanished for ever, *to comfort* them against the whole aspect of things visible with something visible from God, and *as it were palpably heavenly*. For this purpose there lies *a security from God* in the appearance of Ezekiel, *a sacramental character*, one might say, to which, equally with the most definite predictions, a number of *formulas recurring through the whole book* contribute, such as. "and they shall know that I am Jehovah," or, "they shall know that a prophet is in their midst," "and the word of Jehovah came unto me, saying," "the hand of Jehovah came upon me," or the like, "as I live, saith the Lord Jehovah," "I, Jehovah, have said it," etc. ("Thus saith Jehovah the Lord" occurs, according to Kliefoth's reckoning, 121 times.) To perceive in such formulas (as Ewald does) "as it were an encouraging of themselves on the part of the fainting prophetic order," or even the boastful, stupid weakness of old age, is to misunderstand the intentional emphasizing of the divine origin and contents, which Ezekiel claims for his announcements. Not less does our prophet over and over again emphasize the divine commission, the divine impulse, to speak this, to do this or that (ch. vi. 1, xiii. 2, 17, xvi. 2, xvii. 2, xxxv. 2, xxxvi. 1, xxxviii. 2, iii. 1 sqq., iv. 4 sqq., xii. 1 sqq., xxi. 24 sqq., etc.). This is the more suitable in confronting his doubting, unbelieving, and rebellious hearers, especially for the opening apocalypse, where, in the case of the visions and symbols, mere human imagination might very greatly deceive itself and impose upon others. But Ezekiel is from the first set by Jehovah to speak and to execute the words of Him who thus commissioned him, and of Him only; his whole book is the fulfilment, and nothing more, of the symbolic procedure in ch. ii. 8 sqq.

In connection with this we must also understand the *standing address* of God to the prophet "son of man," viz. of one who of himself would be quite incapable of such communications, flesh of flesh, man of man!

As regards the *close connection of Ezekiel with the Pentateuch*, Keil is perfectly right in asserting that he has this "in common with all the prophets." "Along with his immediate predecessor Jeremiah, he is distinguished in this respect from the earlier prophets by the fact that the *verbal references* in both become *more frequent* and appear *more prominent*, which is

[1] To this category belongs also the significant occurrence of the number seven: thus, seven times prophecy about Egypt (ch. xxix. sqq.); and so, seven nations against whom judgment is predicted (ch. xxv. sqq.), by means of an intentional separation of Tyre and Sidon. Kliefoth has shown that, even as respects the whole book, according to the formula, "and the word of Jehovah came unto me, saying," it consists of 7 × 7 words of God: "an arrangement according to the number seven," says he, "which we find in the book of Zechariah and in the Apocalypse, carried out in a different fashion; for what these prophets predict will be fulfilled and accomplished, like God's work of creation, in seven days." Comp. besides, on Apocalypse and Prophecy, Lange on Genesis, p. 36.

accounted for chiefly by the circumstance, that the apostasy from the law had become so great, in consequence of which the judgments already threatened in the Pentateuch were falling upon them," etc. Ewald says that Ezekiel "makes use of the Pentateuch as a matter of pure learning" and certainly without genuine "prophetic originality and independence;" but the complete proof to the contrary is already furnished by his mode of understanding—which is not only sensible, but a result of his being filled with the Holy Ghost—this very ceremonial law in an eschatological or Christological respect. In reference to the moral law, we may compare, as against Ewald, ch. xviii., for example, of which chapter Umbreit remarks that it "brings out in the most splendid manner the ethical character of our priestly prophet." "If one sees in the ceremonial law narrow and narrowing forms, crippling our mental freedom, then certainly the entering on the same, as Ezekiel does, itself appears as a narrow-mindedness. But the law has a higher significance for the prophet; and with how free a step intellectually—with all his attachment, fidelity, love to the same—he enters on the subject, is shown by the deeper apprehension of the ideas which are enstamped on the ordinances of the law and of the spiritual import of the legal forms, so that, as the very section ch. xl. sqq. shows, he stands in a relation of nowise slavish dependence on the law, but has clearly recognised its exact significance for the period of the Old and of the New Covenants, alike in their agreement and in their diversity" (HÄV.). How different is Ezekiel's way of dealing with the law from that of Ezra, also a priest, the scribe! Comp. besides Oehler (HERZOG'S *Real-Encycl.* xii. pp. 227, 229). "The position of Ezekiel among the exiles," remarks the latter, "is to be compared relatively with that of the prophets in the kingdom of the ten tribes;—among the captives of Israel, where the tendency to idolatry was deeply rooted (Ezek. xiv. 3 sqq.), and where also still later (Isa. lxv.) the apostasy spread mightily, to preserve a religious community, within which the Church of the future might be perpetuated. This object was also served by the maintenance in particular of the sabbath-festival, a salutary fence for the people thrown among the heathen, a protection against the ways of the heathen," etc.

As to the "*literary* style" of Ezekiel, Ewald's judgment is, that his mode of representation "seldom falls away, like that of Jeremiah, easily recovers itself, and as a rule is beautifully rounded off; his language has already, scattered here and there, many an Aramaic and otherwise foreign element, the influx of the exile, yet fortunately it leans most on the older models; the discourse is rich in rare comparisons, often charming, and at the same time striking, full of manifold turnings (which are often beautifully elaborated), and where it rises higher, of genuine dramatic liveliness; it has also a certain evenness and repose, in contrast with Jeremiah," etc. Comp. Häv. *Comm.* p. xxiii; Keil, *Comm.* p. 10; Zunz, *Gottesdienstl. Vortr. d. Juden*, p. 159, who adduce, besides, the expressions original to Ezekiel, not occurring elsewhere, which perhaps are formed by himself. Schiller (as Richter tells us) read Ezekiel with the greatest pleasure, because of his finished glorious pictures, and wished even yet to learn Hebrew, in order to be able to read him correctly. Herder calls our prophet "the Æschylus and Shakespeare of the Hebrews."

§ 8. COMPOSITION, COLLECTION, ARRANGEMENT, GENUINENESS OF THE BOOK.

The book which bears Ezekiel's name is *pervaded throughout by one and the same spirit alike of God and of man.* In all its separate parts there meets us, as respects contents and form, mode of representation and language, the same very peculiar stamp of this prophet. Ewald acknowledges: "Even the slightest attention shows, that everything in it really proceeds from his hand." DE WETTE: "That Ezekiel, who usually speaks of himself in the first person, has written down everything himself, is a matter of no doubt." GESENIUS: "The book belongs to that not very numerous class, which from beginning to end maintain a unity of tone, which is evinced by favourite expressions and peculiar phrases; and by this circumstance alone every suspicion of spuriousness as regards particular sections might be averted."

"Groundless doubts," De Wette calls them (*Introd.* 7th edit.). Those of some of the Rabbins (comp. H. Witsii, *Misc. s.* i. ch. xix. 9) "were merely dogmatic;" the learned Jew Zunz has lost himself on the same path towards the Persian epoch. KEIL, *Introd.* p. 362 [Clark's Trans.].

But although, as Keil concludes, "the genuineness of Ezekiel's prophecies is at present

(1868) acknowledged with one voice by all critics, just as also no doubt any longer exists on this point, that the writing down and editing of the same in the book handed down to us has been executed by the prophet himself:" "yet as to the manner in which the whole book originated, its collection and arrangement, a general understanding has by no means been arrived at" (HÄVERNICK).

The "want of arrangement," which Jahn remarked in his Introduction, because of the interruption of the chronological sequence by the prophecies against foreign nations (ch. xxix. 17 sqq.; xxvi. 1, xxix. 1, xxxv., xxxviii., xxxix.),[1] may in general be regarded as cleared up by §§ 5 and 6, as to the detail the exposition will have to step forward; to ascribe it to the "copy of the transcriber or collector," is, from perplexity, to adopt a view which explains nothing.

Eichhorn in his *Introduction* adopted the supposition of small separate book-rolls, upon one of which, for the sake of economy, often two prophecies of the most diverse periods were written, the collector having shrunk from the trouble of re-transcribing them, and contented himself with the putting together of the separate rolls (!!).

In support of the view which ascribes *the collection also to Ezekiel himself*, Hävernick in his *Comm.* urges the following: (1) the systematic arrangement, which throughout corresponds to the contents, and combines strictly chronological sequence with arrangement according to subject-matter (in the prophecies against foreign nations); (2) the closest internal connection in the whole and in the separate parts, where every separate section looks back to the preceding; (3) the occasional closing notices, which in the collection of the whole have been appended most suitably by the prophet himself.

Ewald makes our book "first to have originated gradually from several layers, the mass not to have been written till several years after the destruction of Jerusalem in the leisure of domestic life;" it is "quite possible that Ezekiel began to write down many a thing even before the destruction of Jerusalem" (ch. xvii. 19, xii. 13, xvii. 20). Comp. said work, p. 213 sqq.

In favour of the *written* composition *by Ezekiel*, ch. ii. 9, 10 is certainly not without significance.[2] And where our prophet had not the temple with the people flocking together for *oral* address before him, where he could approach his auditory, the exiles scattered throughout the Chaldean empire, only by means of *written* communication, there is no necessity whatever, in support of a *speedy* written composition of the separate discourses, prophecies, visions, to draw the inference from Jer. xxix. that there was also a more extensive written intercourse between the place of exile and the fatherland. Yet Bleek in his *Introd.* urges, as an argument for their being originally committed to writing, and that not long after the revelation, the sentences with respect to the Jews in Jerusalem before the destruction of the city and with respect to the foreign nations, whilst he finds a later re-touching not unlikely. If it was "the prophetic custom of this period especially" (HÄV.), comp. Dan. vii. 1, Jer. xxxvi., *to commit* prophecies *to writing immediately*, then must the view, that in the case of Ezekiel also *the written composition of the separate parts* preceded the collection and arrangement of the whole by the prophet,—a view which is specially favoured by the very uniform setting of the separate pieces, by the similarity of the inscriptions, where they are found, by the recurring insertion with the formula "and the word of Jehovah came unto me,"—appear so much the more natural. Prophecies like those which form the close of the book, must have been sketched in writing before being orally delivered, and may afterwards have been amplified. The dates of Ezekiel are by no means "kept in so general a form" as Ewald asserts; year, month, and day are given, rather like the deliberate consciousness of the moment, than at random according to a very much later recollection. The peculiar description

[1] DE WETTE: "Of course ch. xxxv. ought to stand beside ch. xxvi., but it has also a suitable place here (much the same as Isa. lxiii. 1–6); but ch. xxxviii. and xxxix. have more a home than a foreign reference, and with perfect right are attached to ch. xxxvii."

[2] "It was the more likely for the prophet from the first to commit to writing the contents of the prophetic revelation entrusted to him by Jehovah, inasmuch as the beginning of the discourses which he had to deliver to the people was represented to him in the form of a writing. The inward necessity of writing, however, was much more urgently present as regards that portion of the prophetic announcement which was to be realized after the threatenings should have fulfilled their purpose, than in the case of the threatenings themselves, with which the prophet had to begin."—BAUMGARTEN.

in detail of our prophet may also certainly be traced back with Hävernick to the strength and freshness of a present revelation and ecstasy, and may be used as an argument for written composition before the preparation of the whole. Comp. besides, Kliefoth, p. 81 sqq.

That "the Masoretic text" is "more faulty than in almost any other book of the Old Testament," is an exaggeration on the part of Ewald. Just as little was it "still in the hands of the LXX. in a far purer form" (HITZIG). But yet the comparison of the latter, as well as of the Peschito, is interesting for settling, or at least throwing light upon difficult cases. To the Alexandrian Philo the Greek translation of Ezekiel, with whom certainly he had the greatest sympathy, appears not to have been at all accessible. (FRANKEL, *Vorstudien zu der Sept.* p. 39.)

§ 9. THE CHRISTOLOGY OF EZEKIEL.

"The Old Testament Christology is a result of this circumstance, that the divine promise comes forth *from the judgment of God*" (LANGE); and the fall of Jerusalem may be looked upon as the element which determines the second group of the Messianic prophecies. Comp. Lange, *Pos. Dog.* p. 674. And so throughout the announcement of future salvation has as its *precursor the judicial activity of Jehovah.* There there is no rest, till the last extremity has been reached, and the last drops of Judah have been scattered among the heathen. This background of *judgment*, on which the Christological prophecy of Ezekiel displays itself, is therefore the universal Old Testament one of the prophets,[1] just as he occupies it specially in common with Jeremiah.

Thus Ezekiel (ch. xi. 13) cries with loud voice, that God is making a full end of the remnant of Israel, and receives *thereupon* the promise (ver. 16), that the Eternal Himself will be "as a sanctuary" to the exiles for the short time of their banishment. Out of *apparently complete extermination in judgment* there rises up what in a certain measure already forms a preparation for the close of the book.

Yet *the priestly* element can neither on this account, nor on the whole, be regarded as *the peculiarity* of Ezekiel's Christology. The utmost we can maintain is, that it is a *predominant* element in the manner of our prophet's conception and representation (comp. § 7) in this respect also. For the *priestly* conception is certainly to be found in Jeremiah too, for example, and just in ch. iii. 14–17, where Hävernick finds "Jeremiah's fundamental idea" of the Messianic salvation expressed. It can also with difficulty be shown, at least in the case of Ezekiel, that, as Lange asserts, "the kingly office of the Messiah steps into the background;" it may be admitted with respect to His prophetic office. For, in accordance with Exod. xix. 6, —"the gospel of the Old Testament" (to use the words of Ewald),—the *kingdom* remains the keynote, and the all-pervading view of the Messiah is that of the King, whether resting on 2 Sam. vii., or going back to Gen. xlix. Not only does Ezekiel share such an expectation with all the prophets, but immediately on his opening up the Messianic prospect, in ch. xvii. 22–24, we have the planting of the cedar "on the high mountain of Israel," *i.e.* the raising up of the Davidic kingdom, to whose protection the nations will submit themselves (comp. besides on ch. xx. 33, 37). The "coming One" of ch. xxi. 32, "whose right it is" ("perhaps with allusion to the already Messianically interpreted passage, Gen. xlix. 10," remarks Bleek), is at all events a king. And just to the same effect we shall have to interpret ch. xxix. 21, especially the causing "the horn to bud forth." But now even in ch. xxxiv.,—while, with Tholuck, we must admit that "the name of shepherd corresponds to that of ruler in its ethical idea,"—where Jehovah takes upon Himself the care of the flock scattered under the bad

[1] Tholuck (*Die Propheten und ihre Weissagungen*, pp. 37 sqq., 78) gathers up "all prophecies under the category of that holy order of retributive justice which bears sway in the history of mankind." (Zephaniah is in outline this prophetic theodicy of God in history.) "As law and retribution are inter changeable ideas, it was a matter of necessity that legal exhortations should become the prophecy of retribution in the future—for individuals and for whole nations, closing with the prospect of the last judgment, by means of which the idea of the theocracy is destined to reach its ultimate fulfilment." Hävernick (*Vorl. über die Theologie d. Alten Testaments*, p. 147): "Prophecy keeps in its eye the future of the people, while it, as it were, gives up the present. From the judgment upon the theocracy as chastisement comes forth the salvation. The judgment upon the nations is nothing but the glorification of the theocracy, as a victorious power over heathendom. Every announcement of judgment upon the world is therefore, in reality, Messianic, like that of the theocratic judgment."

shepherds (ver. 11 sqq.), this is to be done by means of His servant David, so that the servant of the Lord is neither the people, nor the true Israel, nor the prophetic order, nor even the Messiah-prophet, but, as ver. 24 expressly says, "the prince." Comp. in addition, ch. xxxvii. 22, 24, 25: "My servant David shall be prince over them," etc., "and David My servant shall be their prince for ever."

We may accordingly assert rather, that the *kingly office* is *prominent* in Ezekiel's picture of the Messiah, and that, along with the prophetic office, the Messianic priesthood as well remains in the background with our prophet. At ch. xxi. 31 [26, Eng. vers.] the priestly dignity, which Tholuck holds to be still a matter of controversy, appears at most in union with the kingly. Among the priests of the temple (ch. xl. sqq.) the high priest is not named, but a high-priestly mode of acting is made the duty of the priests. These are to become a high-priesthood, just as the whole temple becomes a holy of holies. That "the Lord" is "at the same time the high priest," is not to be inferred from this circumstance. Undoubtedly "the man" in ch. xliii. 6 is neither the one nor the other; and when it is there said by the glory of Jehovah, when it enters, with respect to the ark of the covenant, "the place of My throne," this comes rather from the lips of God as King, than from the lips of a high priest.

On the whole, the peculiarity of Ezekiel in his Christological relations may perhaps be said to attach *less to the personality*, which, as so circumstanced and clothed with such an office, by this or that other work, mediates the Messianic salvation, *than to this salvation itself.* As with Jeremiah already expressly the "Jehovah our Righteousness" of the Messiah (ch. xxiii. 6) passes over to the Messianic people (ch. xxxiii. 16), so Ezekiel's prophecy occupies itself peculiarly with the *Messianic salvation of the people.* That of course is, just as elsewhere also in the prophets, that Judah, and along with Judah Israel also, is to return from the exile. The deliverance from Babylon and that other very different redemption run into one another, just like the destruction of Jerusalem and the last judgment in the eschatological discourses of Jesus. Nor can it be looked upon as anything peculiar, that this outward return is conceived of Messianically as an internal one, as conversion to the Lord; for the case is the same with Jeremiah (ch. xxiv. 5 sqq., xxxi. 10 sqq., xxx. 18 sqq.). But although the subjective side is not forgotten, that the remnant shall remember and loathe themselves (Ezek. vi. 9, xviii. 31 even, xxxvi. 31 sqq.), yet the *objective* testimony *preponderates* even in ch. xi. 16: "I will be to them as a sanctuary." Of course this "Jehovah as a sanctuary" may be looked upon as Ezekiel's parallel to Jeremiah's "Jehovah our Righteousness," and compared with Jer. iii. 16, 17, Ezek. xx. 40 sqq. The fundamental idea of Israel is "a kingdom *of priests*," "a *holy* people," whose head is the King-priest, the Messiah, ch. xxxvii. 23, 28. If, however, Jeremiah, in describing the Messianic salvation, as it will be accomplished in the people, as they will be put in possession of it, speaks of the "heart," which God will give, to know Him, of the "new covenant," where God "puts His law in their inward part and writes it on their heart," of the "*one* heart and *one* way" (Jer. xxxii. 39 sqq.), Ezekiel on his part, and that just at ch. xi. 19, employs similar language, but the "new spirit," like "the spirit" occurring before in ch. i. 12, 20 sqq., is characteristic, is something additional (ch. xviii. 31); comp. besides, ch. xvi. 60 sqq. The Messianic salvation of the people (quite in harmony with the character of the book, according to ch. i.) is described as a *sanctifying* or *glorifying of God in*, as well as *upon* Israel (ch. xx. 41, xxviii. 25, xxxix. 27; comp. John xvi. 14). Based on this thought there arises the cleansing (ch. xxxvi. 22 sqq.; comp. ch. xxxvi. 32, 33, xxxvii. 23), which the Messianic period holds out in prospect (ver. 25), and the gift of a new heart and new spirit (ver. 26), which again (ver. 27) is made to include in it the fact, that God puts *His Spirit* in their breast. The *putting of the Divine Spirit* in the whole house of Israel forms the kernel of the very characteristic vision of ch. xxxvii. (comp. ver. 14), and is expressly spoken of in ch. xxxix. 29 as *the outpouring of the Spirit of Jehovah* upon the house of Israel. *That* and nothing else is *the peculiarity of the Christology of Ezekiel;* in other words: *the development of the Messiah*, the Spirit-anointed of God, *the Christ, into Christianity* in the *true Israel.* Hence, "the peculiar blessing of the temple" (ch. xl. sqq.) is "its water-spring," ch. xlvii. (LANGE), which is at the same time the key to the understanding of these closing chapters of our book (John vii. 38, 39). Its Christology moves already within the circle of the economy of the Holy Spirit; nay, even ch. i. of our prophet is to be understood in accordance with John xvi. 14. One might say: *ecclesiastically*, while Daniel prophesies of the Messiah in His kingdom above all *politically*, on the side of the world. Comp. besides, the following section.

§ 10. OF THE USE, THEOLOGICAL IMPORT, AND DIFFERENT WAYS OF UNDERSTANDING THE BOOK OF EZEKIEL.

Starke's *Bibelwerk*, v. p. 1703, says at § 14: "Godly readers find in this book profit and edification enough," to wit, in general: "in distress and trouble comfort and consolation," as well as "the most delightful instruction as to a God-pleasing walk." "Everywhere one perceives how earnestly God seeks to awaken men, and to deliver them from the power of darkness, sometimes by promises, sometimes by threatenings, but sometimes also, if words are going to prove of no avail, by means of public calamities." "But in particular the prophet serves—(1) to give us the knowledge of the divine mercy, righteousness, truth, and power; (2) to give us the knowledge of the hatefulness of sin, for whose sake whole kingdoms are laid waste; (3) he gives us rules as to what every one has to do in his office on the breaking out of God's judgments; (4) he warns us how we are to be on our guard, etc., against false security, apostasy, presumption, hypocrisy, and the like; (5) and how, in the midst of the greatest corruption and severest oppression of the Church, we ought not to lose heart altogether, but to believe assuredly, that, as God is able to punish and exterminate His enemies, so also He is able to improve, protect, and make His Church glorious."

Ewald shows how this *use* for all time connects itself with the *immediate aims* of Ezekiel in the publication of his book, when he remarks among other things: "For one thing, he had to show that Jerusalem must fall, because it was in itself, and had been for long, in a state of irremediable confusion and perversity, and therein at the same time for the living there lay the right lesson and warning for the future; but, secondly, he must also set forth the certainty of a better future, and of the indestructibility of the true Church, and bring out clearly the genuine hope as opposed to despair, as well as in opposition to hasty and vain expectations; in keeping alive the sacred fire during the long period of the exile this book certainly had no small influence," etc. Jesus Sirach expresses himself in these terms about our prophet, according to Fritzsche's translation (ch. xlix. 8, 9): "Ezekiel beheld the vision of glory, which the Lord caused him to see upon the chariot of the cherubim; for he made mention of the enemies in wrath, and did good to those who walked in right ways; but he comforted Jacob, and delivered them by assured hope."[1]

As regards the *import* of Ezekiel *theologically considered*, we shall the more readily abide by what the son of Sirach makes a starting-point, as *the glory of God* has already repeatedly been found by us to be of importance in getting at the contents of our book. In this way Ezekiel's theology is characteristically indicated. If, distinctively, God's "majesty" expresses His incomparable and immeasurable exaltation above heaven and earth, that unique, absolutely perfect independence of His being, in virtue of which He is God alone, in whom the greatness, power, beauty, continuance, and splendour of life are properly inherent, then Ezekiel makes known to us the *glory* of Jehovah as being the self-*representation* of the divine life-form *in order to manifestation*. As the "majesty" would be the sum of all supramundane divine attributes, so, according to him, the *glory* is the whole *manifestation* of God *in* mundane things. As the divine "majesty"—which by this means is shown to be moral—has as its counterpart the "holiness" of God, in accordance with which God is Himself pure, so the divine *glory* finds its counterpart in the *righteousness* of God, in virtue of which God, as Cleanser or Sanctifier, alike in *judgment* and in *mercy*, *restores* as well as *displays* His glory in the world. The *righteousness of God* is, next to the *glory of God*, and in connection therewith, *the peculiar theologoumenon of Ezekiel*. From this theological standpoint he delineates the downfall of Jerusalem, and likewise the downfall of the heathen nations referred to. Both have refused in free surrender to consecrate themselves to God, but have as much as ever they could in their own case treated God profanely, and made the world on its part unclean. The divine righteousness *in judgment*, as it is executed on both, adjusts this disorder, this contradiction as regards God's manifestation in the world, as regards His divine glory, through their being taken away by force, inasmuch as God consecrates to Himself the one as well as the other as a sacrifice, and in this way making atonement for the sin by means of the punishment, cleanses the world also, which is destined to be and to become full of His glory, and thus restores His glory in this respect. From the same theological standpoint *mercy* and salvation also are

[1] Gregory sets up Ezekiel as a teacher and pattern *for preachers*.

conceived of in Ezekiel, and in fact *under the presupposition* of a *substitution.* "For the righteousness of God," says Beck (*Lehrsätze*, p. 115 sqq.), "is hallowed not merely in punishing, but also in putting again to rights and creating anew, when He puts His law as light and spirit outwardly and inwardly in the life, and sets up with creative power in the world, as its everlasting salvation, the reign of law which had been interrupted by sin." The self-manifestation of His glory is on this side, in fact, also its *restoration* through righteousness, but still more its blissful and lovely *exhibition.* Although a substitutionary suffering of the Servant of God, as in Isa. liii., is not met with in Ezekiel, yet the cleansing of Ezek. xxxvi. 25 is conceived of as one *effected by priestly mediation;* and the fact that substitution is no strange thought to our prophet, that such a view is with him fundamental, and will therefore also be presupposed by him for the salvation of Israel through the mercy of God, is shown by the tetralogy of recurring passages, ch. xiv. 14, 16, 18, 20. As there is no one now among the people, either prophet, or priest, or king, able to step into the breach, a substitution is demanded, by means of which full atonement can be made, by means of which righteousness gains the victory, and the glory of Jehovah in grace and mercy comes to be manifested. (Comp. besides, Oehler's very suggestive article in Herzog, ix. p. 419.) Hence the word of the prophet ever again just demands *conversion to God*, with whom all things are possible, while the delusion of a substitutionary suffering of the children for the guilt of their fathers is dismissed in the most energetic and decided way in ch. xviii. For the righteousness which Ezekiel holds up as a righteousness for man is "*to do* what is lawful and right," "to deal *truly*" (ch. xviii. 5, 9), "*to be* righteous," and not to depart from righteousness, therefore also to *remain* righteous (vers. 24, 26): so that these children can neither know themselves to be guiltless, so as even to be capable of a substitution for their fathers, nor durst they allow themselves to be satisfied with a righteousness of pious pretence (in contrast with one that is personal and actual, and real and abiding); [1] but they are to make themselves a new heart and a new spirit (ver. 31). As in particular this closing demand of the 18th chapter, in which the whole discourse about righteousness culminates, lets it be seen that the way of Israel's thoughts hitherto has been a false one, inasmuch as the matter in hand is more a conversion, will involve the new birth, a new creation, so in this way there rises into view, at the same time, as the true way for every man, the way *to God*, and therein *the way of God*, that God who "has no pleasure in the death of him that dieth" (vers. 32, 33, ch. xxxiii.), as *the way of life.* Each for himself, so runs with Ezekiel the antithesis to all fancied substitution in the judgment of God, an antithesis which leads to death (ver. 4). But as God wills the life of him who "turns from his way," the true way of life must offer a better, even a true substitution.

Baumgarten, however, gives less prominence (Herzog's *Real-Encyl.* iv. p. 298 sqq.) to such an *ethico-theological* meaning of our book than to an *eschatological* one, when he asserts, "that according to Scripture Israel's state of captivity by no means ceases after the return of a few thousands to Jerusalem under Cyrus, but continues down to the present day, and will last until the general conversion of Israel." The interpretation attempted from this point of view of the vision in ch. i., of the "prophetic word during the exile," of the "labours of Ezekiel during Israel's captivity,"—one may apply to it Baumgarten's own words—"drags into the passage with one's own hand the very thing that is to be proved from it." Here, however, the opportunity presents itself, before we enter on the exposition of the book of Ezekiel, of discussing the *different modes of interpreting* it. Baumgarten finds in the passage quoted, that in Ezek. i.–iii. (comp. ch. xi. 22, 23) "it is shown most clearly that a new method of revelation on God's part is to begin, wherewith there is given in Israel, even without the instrumentality of the sanctuary and the priestly service, a possibility of further development and progress;" and then, in support of this view, he brings forward "as a new (?) beginning of inner development" the "prophetic position and labours of Ezekiel during the exile," in connection with which reference is made to Ezek. viii. 1, xi. 25, xiii. 24 (xiv. 1), xx. 1, xxiv. 19, xxxiii. 31, 32, just as the continuation is found "in the ordinance of the synagogue down to the present day." "What, above all, the meaning of the last third of the book amounts

[1] "The bad sort of mere outward righteousness and sham holiness (says Baumgarten), which was one day to bring blasphemy and bloody persecution on the holy and righteous King of Israel and Him who was demonstrated to be the Son of God, as well as on His Spirit-anointed messengers of peace. Hence, also, Ezekiel's prophetic labours in word and deed are directed far more against this deepest and most lasting corruption, than against all else."

to," Baumgarten gives as follows, ch. xxxvi. xxxvii. : "a resurrection of the dead and buried nation, and an everlasting spring for their frost-bound land, as soon as the spirit of prophecy shall prove mighty enough, in the power of its divine source, to breathe upon and wake up this field of the dead,—which the prophet even is able to do as yet only in type (ch. xxxvii. 3, 7),—when the spirit of the prophetic word shall have entirely filled the Gentile world, or (?) when the fulness of the Gentiles shall have come in, and by this means shall have the power and the task to wake up the dead people of God (Rom. xi. 25, 26)."—Ch. xl.–xlviii. : "For when Israel as a nation is converted to their God, how can they, how dare they exhibit their faith and obedience otherwise, than in the forms and ordinances which Jehovah has given to this nation? And is it not plain, that only after this conversion will the whole law in all its parts receive that fulfilment, which it has always hitherto demanded in vain? The Church of God is to find its goal in the condition here seen and described by the prophet of Israel (!). At that goal the Gentiles finally enter again into the community of Israel (!), and find in the law of Israel their national (!) statute-book, according to the will of God. We must accustom ourselves to recognise in these lofty and glorious descriptions not merely the final shape of Israel, but also the ultimate model for the converted and incorporated Gentiles (comp. ch. xlvii. 22?)." This is not the place to enter on a fuller treatment of this extreme development of a view of our prophet, in support of which the Epistle to the Galatians and that to the Hebrews do not appear to have been written, nor Acts xv. to have been meant; it must just be left to characterize itself. Tholuck (*Die Propheten und ihre Weissag.* p. 151 sqq.) says: "Although in scarcely any other department of Scripture has there been the same fluctuation with respect to the hermeneutical principles as in the exposition of the prophets, yet we may take the liberty of saying, that throughout all periods and sections of the Church the *typological* character of prophecy has been usually taken for granted. In reference alike to Old Testament prophecy in general, and to our prophet also in particular, we shall have to distinguish more exactly the following different modes of interpretation (comp. with Tholuck, the valuable article of Oehler on 'Prophecy,' Herzog's *Real-Encycl.* xvii. p. 644 sqq.):—1. The *allegorical* interpretation, which, with a one-sided development, must degenerate into arbitrariness, as the exegesis of the ancient Church shows us. 2. The *historical* interpretation of the Antiochean school, then of a Grotius, now of the rationalistico-naturalistic criticism. 3. The *symbolical* (*e.g.* HÄV., HENGST.) and the *mystical* interpretation (*e.g.* of the *Berleburg Bible*). 4. The *typical* interpretation, which is combined sometimes with the symbolical, sometimes with the allegorical, sometimes with the historical, just as in general all these interpretations are mixed in the different expositors. If one chooses to call the historical the *realistic* interpretation, the other interpretations may be contrasted with it as *idealistic;* and if they are not to escape a certain measure of censure by being designated as "spiritualistic," as is done by Oehler, then the opposite interpretation might not without reason admit of being designated as a materialistic one. Pietism in former days, just as it revived Jewish legality to the hurt of the ideality of free Christian life, bordered with its chiliasms on a view of the prophetic word, which Jerome ('down till Lyra and Luther, an authority in the exposition of the prophets.'—THOLUCK) had condemned as Judaizing": "Ut quæ Judæi et nostri, immo non nostri Judaizantes, carnaliter futura contendunt, nos spiritualiter jam transacta doceamus," sqq. "A comparatively small fraction," Tholuck calls them, "who, just as recently again most of the English and a number of South German, especially Wurtemberg theologians have done, held themselves bound by the letter to understand *literally* what is said of the return of Israel, of the taking possession of the lands of the heathen, of the new temple, and sacrificial worship."

As regards the general view lying at the foundation of the following exposition of the book of Ezekiel, it coincides with Oehler in this, that prophecy is directed *to the end*, as being at the same time *the goal of the history of Israel.* There belongs to it, therefore, *an eschatological* character *in general*, and inasmuch as the history of Israel is determined essentially and distinctively *by the law* (Rom. ii. 17 sqq.), and *Christ* is the *end* of the law, the *eschatological* character of Old Testament prophecy must be, especially in its position towards the law, nay, in the law, to a large degree the *Christological* one. For "all the prophets and the law (itself) prophesied until John the Baptist" (Matt. xi. 13); in Him, therefore, to whom John could point with his finger, this prophecy ceases; it has become fulfilment (2 Cor. i. 20; Matt. v. 18; Heb. i. 1; 1 John ii. 18; 1 Pet. iv. 7). The development of such fulfilment of prophecy as it is given in Christ, embraces, as may be understood, *the perfecting of the Church*, so that in *this* sense, and as regards *this* relation, there occur also *eschatological elements* in the *narrower* acceptation of the word in the Old Testament prophets, *apocalyptic* features in their picture of the Messiah. But as the development of Christ in the perfecting of the Church is *that which takes place through the Holy Ghost*; for which reason the eschatological tenets of the Christian faith stand rightly in the third article,—the end of the ways of God in this respect is not flesh, but (now that the Word has become flesh) the *glorified* corporeity, a *new* heaven and a *new* earth, wherein dwelleth righteousness (Rom. xiv. 17),—so also nothing can be taken into view, for the eschatology *strictly so called*, which would result in a national Israel and an establishing of its law, or even in a Jewish-Christian redeemed humanity, especially as in Christ neither Jew nor Greek availeth anything (Gal. iii. 28), and the law has come in between merely, and that because of sin, until the Seed of promise should come, unto whom it had to serve as a schoolmaster only (Rom. v. 20; Gal. iii. 19, 24). "Prophecy contents itself," says Tholuck in the work referred to, "with setting forth the full realization of the kingdom planted in Israel, and along with that the satisfying of the religio-moral need of redemption on the part of mankind, as the ultimate goal of the earlier history of mankind." Tholuck, therefore, looks upon "the realization of the pictures in Ezek. xl. sqq., in the spiritual sense, as having already taken place in the Christian Church," while Oehler again, especially because of Rom. xi. 26,[1] at the same time holds strongly, as an essential element of all prophecy, that of Ezekiel included, the actual "restoration of the covenant people, preserved as they are even in their rejection for the fulfilment of their destiny." Comp. besides, the reasons which, according to Tholuck (p. 197 sqq.), stand opposed to a "gross realistic" view of the last chapters of Ezekiel. Hävernick (*Vorles. über die Theologie des A. T.*) expresses himself thus (p. 165): "The closing predictions of Ezekiel have in earlier times been usually understood typically, and referred directly to the person of Christ, the apostles and Christian affairs in general, and in this way the typical system in principle degenerated into a wild allegory. This mode of interpretation has called forth the other extreme, according to which the prophets are permitted to determine nothing else beforehand but the state of things as it was really to take place (but did not take place) after the exile, prophecy being thus transformed into a new legislation. Hence the prophetico-symbolical interpretation is most correct, according to which those representations are to be understood in the sense which they had already for one living under the Old Testament theocracy, viz. as symbols, whose true and full significance is to be realized only in the new Church."

(On prophecy in general one may compare also the thoughtful and profound statement by Beck, *Christl. Lehrwissenschaft*, p. 354 sqq.)

[1] We may be permitted to take this opportunity of casting a glance on this oft-mentioned passage, without attempting (for time would fail us for such a purpose) to defend the following interpretation in view of the context in Rom. ix.–xi. First of all it is to be observed, that in Rom. xi. 25 the apostle speaks of a μυστήριον τοῦτο, placing the pronoun after the substantive, whereby τοῦτο is made to refer not to what follows, but to what has been already said: "the foresaid mystery." Let one compare Eph. v. 32 and 1 Cor. xi. 25 with ver. 26. Then, further, and this is the most important consideration, exegetical tradition must submit to be told, that ἀπὸ μέρους, if one translates it as hitherto: "in part," is not very appropriate in any of the passages where it occurs elsewhere (Rom. xv. 15, 24; 2 Cor. i. 14; ii. 5). Μέρος (μοῖρα) is the portion that is due (Rev. xxi. 8), and so ἀπὸ μέρους will mean: as is due, in due measure, or: of right. The LXX. give their support to this meaning, and it suits admirably in the New Testament passages in question. *The foresaid mystery* is that discussed in Rom. ix. sqq., which is spoken of to the Ephesians also, namely: *that Christ hath made in Himself of Jews and Gentiles*, these two, *one new man* (Eph. ii. 15), so that *all believers* from among *Jews* as well as *Gentiles* are *one in Christ* (Gal. iii. 28), *Israel after the Spirit*, the *Israel of God* (Gal. vi. 16). This mystery we ought to know well, in order that we may not in our self-sufficiency forget, *that hardening has happened to the nation of Israel according to desert*, of right, which judgment of hardening endures unto the end, *until the fulness of the Gentile nations be come in*, namely, *in Israel's place as a nation*, καὶ οὕτω (ver. 26), *i.e.* and *so* (but not: and then), *in this way all Israel* shall be *saved*. That is to say: when the silently and continually growing temple of God shall be built up to the last stone (Eph. ii. 21), in this way shall *all Israel*, i.e. *all that belong to it in truth* (Rom. ix. 6), in this way shall all the children of the promise attain to salvation, which would be the ἀπολύτρωσις τῆς περιποιήσεως, the full salvation (Eph. i. 14), the ἀποκάλυψις τῶν υἱῶν τοῦ θεοῦ (Rom. viii. 19). And with this agrees also the Pauline application of the quotation from Isa. lix. 20, viz. not: for Zion (לְצִיּוֹן), Sept. ἕνεκεν Σιών, but ἐκ Σιών; thus (οὕτω), when the salvation comes from the Jews to the Gentiles. Comp. Doctrinal Reflections on Deut. xxx. (Lange's Com.).

Extremely interesting is the view of Ezekiel, to which the unknown painter of the lately rediscovered noteworthy wall-paintings in the remarkable double church of the 12th century, at Schwarz-Rheindorf, opposite Bonn, has given expression. (Comp. SIMONS, *Die Doppelkirche zu Schwarz-Rheindorf;* KUGLER, *Handbuch der Kunstgeschichte*, ii. 3 Aufl. pp. 96, 180 sqq.; *Rheinlands Baudenkmale des Mittelalters*, 7 Heft.) Formerly a collegiate church, it left free for the canonesses, whose places were in the upper chapel, the look (through a round opening, with balustrade) at the high altar in the lower church area. From this lower church the wall-paintings taken from the book of Ezekiel rise up, closing with a representation from the Revelation of John, above the altar of the upper church. These lower wall-paintings after Ezekiel place together, *e.g.* the vision of Ezekiel in ch. i., and the transfiguration of Christ; the manifold abominations in the temple (Ezek. viii. sqq.), and the expulsion of the buyers and sellers by the Saviour; and opposite one another Ezekiel's visions of judgment, and the final self-judgment of Israel by the crucifixion of the Messiah. What Kugler (following Hohe) mistakenly interprets as the figure of "a saint," is the Apostle Paul, marked out as such by his long Roman garment and his youthful form (Acts vii. 58), as well as by the threefold halo (2 Cor. xii. 2, "up to the third heaven"), to whom, on the other side, corresponds Peter, as he who has the keys of the Church upon earth, the temple of Ezekiel. The whole, down to the minutest details, is a spirited exegesis of our prophet, in the style of the middle ages.

§ 11.

1. **Rabbinical.**—RASCHI, as he is usually called, R. Salomon ben Isaaki, incorrectly named "Jarchi," Latin by BREITHAUPT, *Commentarius Hebr. in proph. majores, etc.; Lat. vers. ed. J. Fr. Breithaupt*, 4, Gotha 1713.—DAVID KIMCHI ("Radak," according to Jewish abbreviation) in BUXTORF'S *Rabbinical Bible.*—ISAAC ABARBANEL, Amsterdam edition, 1641, fol.—SALOMON BEN MELECH (called "Michlal Jophi"), edition in fol., with ABENDANA'S additions, Amsterdam, 1685.—Of *more recent Jewish* expositions, L. PHILIPPSON, *Israelitische Bibel*, 2 Ausg., Leipzig 1858, ii. Theil, was used.

2. **Patristic.**—ORIGEN, *Homiliæ XIV. in Ezechielem*, ἐκλογαὶ εἰς τὸν ἰεζεκιήλ.—GREGORY NAZIANZEN, *Annotatio de quatuor apud Ezechielem animalibus.*—THEODORET, Ἑρμηνεία τῆς προφητείας τοῦ θείου ἰεζεκιήλ.—JEROME, *Explanationes in Ezech., lib. XIV.*—ORIGEN, *Homiliæ XXVIII in prophetas Jerem. et Ezech.*—GREGORY THE GREAT, *Homiliæ in Ezech. proph.*

3. **Later, embracing Romish, Reformed, Lutheran.**—RHABANUS MAURUS, Commentary in his *Opera*, Cologne edit. 1627, fol.—RUPERT VON DEUTZ, in his *Commentarius de operibus sanctæ trinitatis*, and on the Gospel of Matthew, *sub titulo: De gloria et honore filii hominis*, Cologne edit. of his works.—C. SANCTIUS, *In Ezech. et Dan.*, 1612, 1619.—MALDONATUS, *Comment. in præc. s. scr. libr. V. T.*, Paris 1643, fol.—CORNELIUS A LAPIDE, *Comment. in omnes, scr. s. libr.*, last edit., Venice 1730.—CALMET, *Comment. lit. sur tous les livres de l'ancien et du nouv. Test.*, Latin by MANSI, Würzburg 1792, Part X.—HIER. PRADUS, *Comment. in Ezech.*, and VILLALPANDUS, *In Ezech. expl. et app. urb.*, etc., Rome 1596–1604.—*Die Propheten Ezechiel und Daniel als Fortsetzung des* v. BRENTANO'*schen. A. T. von.* DERESER. Frankf. a M. 1810.

CALVIN, *Prælectiones in Ezech. proph. viginta capita priora*, Amsterdam edit.; see Collective Works, 1667, in the 4th volume.—LUDOV. LAVATER, *Homiliæ seu commentarii in libr. v. prophetiam Ezech.*, Zurich 1571 (Preface by Beza to Coligny).—OECOLAMPADIUS, *Comment. in Ezech.*, Basle 1543, fol.—CONR. PELLICANUS, *Comment in libr. V. et N. Test.*, Zurich 1532 sqq., 4th volume.—JOHN PISCATOR, *Analysis, scholia, et observationes in omnes V. et N. T. libr.*, Herborn 1605 sqq.—PISCATOR'S *Biblework*, 4, Herborn 1603, Part 4.—POLANUS, *Comment. in Ezech.*, Basle 1607.—TOSSANI'S *Bible*, Minden 1716, fol.—The *Critici Sacri*, tom. iv., pars 1, in which we have: SEBASTIAN MÜNSTER, FRANCISCUS VATABLUS, SEBASTIAN CASTALIO, ISIDORUS CLARIUS, JOH. DRUSIUS, HUGO GROTIUS, and *Ludovici Capelli excerpta ex Villalpando ad cap.* 40–42 *et* 46 *Ezechielis.*—POOLE, *Synopsis criticorum*, vol. iii.—COCCEIUS in his *Opera omnia*, vol. iii.—VENEMA, *Lectiones academ. ad Ezech. usque ad cap.* 21.—CLERICUS, *In prophetas*, etc., Amsterdam 1731, fol.—HENRY, *Exposition of the Old and New T.*—W. NEWCOME, *An Attempt towards an Improved Version, a Metrical Arrangement, and an Explanation on the Prophet Ezekiel*, Dublin 1788.—GREENHILL, *Exposition of the Prophecy of Ezekiel.*

LUTHER, *Auslegung etlicher Kapitel des Ezechiel und Daniel.*—VICTOR STRIGEL, *Ezechiel pr. ad Hebr.*, sqq., Leipsic 1597.—NIK. SELNECCER, *Auslegung Ezechiels latein. und deutsch.*—LUC. OSIANDER, *Biblia Lat.*, etc., Tübingen 1588, fol.—ABR. CALOVIUS, *Biblia illustr. q. etiam exhibent et censent annot. H. Grotii*, Frankf. 1672, fol.—JOACH. LANGE, *Prophetisches Licht una Recht*, Halle 1732.—J. H. MICHAELIS in his Hebrew Bible with Annotations.—*Die Tübinger Bibel*, ed. PFAFF, 1729, fol.—*Summarien* (so-called Wurtemberg), *oder gründliche Ausleg.* ff. 3 Aufl., fol., Leipzig 1721.—JOH. FR. STARCK, *Comment. in proph. Ezech.*, Frankfort 1731. —JOH. GEORG STARKE, *Synopsis*, etc., Part 5, Leipzig 1747.—JOH. DAVID MICHAELIS, *Ueb. des A. T. mit Anmerkungen für Ungelehrte.* The 10th part, which contains Ezekiel and Daniel, Göttingen 1781.—TELLER, *Das englische Bibelwerk.*—MOLDENHAUER, *Uebers. und Erkl. d. h. BB. d. A. T*, Quedlinburg 1744.—HEZEL, *Die Bibel mit Anm.*, Lemgo 1780.—J. CH. F. SCHULZE, *Scholia in V. T.* (G. L. Bauer), Nurnberg 1783–97.—DATHE, *Proph. majores*, ed. 2, Halle 1785.—VOLLBORTH, *Ezechiel übers. mit Anm.*, Göttingen 1787.—*Berleburger Bibel*, 3 Theil, 1730.

4. More recent.—J. G. EICHHORN, *Die hebr. Propheten*, 1 Band, Göttingen 1816.—DINTER, *Schullehrer-Bibel*, 4 Theil, Neustadt 1828.—ROSENMÜLLER, *Scholia in Ezech.*, ed. 2, 1826, 2 Parts, and the same *in comp. red.*, 1833.—MAURER, *Comm. gram. crit. in V. T.*, Part 2d, Leipsic 1836.—UMBREIT, *Prakt. Comm. über d. Proph. Ezech.*, Hamburg 1843.—HÄVERNICK, *Comm. über den Proph. Ezech.*, Erlangen 1843.—RICHTER, *Erkl. Hausbibel*, in the 4th vol. p. 523 sqq., Barmen 1837.—V. GERLACH (SCHMIEDER), *Bibelwerk*, 4 Bd. 1 Abth.—HEIM UND HOFFMANN, *Die 4 grossen Proph. aus den Schriften der Reformatoren*, Stuttgart 1839.—EWALD, *Die Propheten des A. B.* im 2 Theil, 2 Ausg., Göttingen 1868.—HITZIG, *Der Proph. Ezech. erkl.*, Leipzig 1847.—BUNSEN, *Die Bibel*, 2 Theil, p. 599 sqq., Leipzig 1860. —DIEDRICH, *Der Proph. Jerem. und Ezech. kurz erkl.*, Neu-Ruppin 1863.—KLIEFOTH, *Das Buch Ezechiels*, 2 Abtheilungen, 1864.—HENGSTENBERG, *Die Weissagungen des Proph. Ezech.*, 1 Thl. 1867, 2 Theil 1868.—C. FR. KEIL, *Bibl Komment. über den Propheten Ezech.*, Leipzig 1868.—B. NETELER, *Die Gliederung des Buches Ezechiels ff.*, Münster 1870.

For Specialties.—P. TISCHINGER, *Singularia Ezechielis*, Schwabach 1743.—BÖTTCHER, *Proben altt. Schrifterkl.*, Leipzig 1833, p. 218 sqq. über Kap. 40 sqq.—W. NEUMANN, *Die Wasser des Lebens, Ezech.* 47, Berlin 1849.—REINKE, Die mess. Weiss, Giessen 1859.—HENGSTENBERG, *History of the Kingdom of God*, etc. [Clark's Trans., Edinburgh 1871–72.]—HOFFMANN, *Das gelobte Land in den Zeiten des getheilten Reiches bis zur babylon. Gefangenschaft*, Basel 1871. (Written from a fresh point of view, an attractive lecture.)

APPENDIX.

[Only two distinct works on the Prophecies of Ezekiel have of late years been issued from the British press: one by Patrick Fairbairn, D.D., the editor of the present translation, in the Lange series, published by the Messrs. Clark of Edinburgh, first edition in 1851, third edition in 1863; and another by the late Dr. E. Henderson in 1855, Hamilton, Adams, & Co., London. The latter work consists only of 219 pages, of which considerably more than the half is occupied by the text.—P. F.]

THE PROPHET EZEKIEL.

A. FIRST PRINCIPAL PART.—Ch. i.–xxiv.

THE PROPHECY OF JUDGMENT.

I. THE DIVINE MISSION OF EZEKIEL.—Ch. i.–iii. 11.

1. The Vision of Glory (Ch. i.).

It has been customary, as at Isa. vi. and Jer. i., so also here, to read Ezekiel's *call* to be a prophet as if it were his ordination or consecration to office. But even in the case of Isa. vi., where the official activity of the prophet does not certainly first begin, but where we find ourselves already in the midst of his labours, one has been compelled for this reason to individualize and to define more exactly; and instead of making it a call *to the prophetic office in general*, has made it a call *to a special mission*. This necessity, which is occasioned there by the position of the 6th chapter, would not indeed be present here; for the history of *Ezekiel's* call would be found exactly in the right, or at least in an unexceptionable place, namely, at the commencement of his official activity. It would be just as in the case of Jeremiah (ch. i. 4 sqq.), only not in equally simple circumstances, so far as the vision is concerned. But as regards *Jeremiah's* case, the historical call at a definite period of his life is from the first the element that falls into the background; what above all is prominent, is *the divine consecration and appointment of Jeremiah as a prophet even before his appearance and birth in time.* It is a thoroughly *ideal* history the history of the call of the prophet *Jeremiah*, and *not to be compared with what Ezekiel relates to us in these chapters* (i.–iii.). If then we keep by that which lies before us, is it *anywhere a call to the prophetic office that is spoken of?* If we bring closely together the detailed vision of Ezek. i., and the more compressed, briefer one of Isa. vi. 1–4, then also Ezek. ii. 3 sqq. contains merely the *mission* of Ezekiel, which is represented as a *divine* one, just as Isa. vi. 8 sqq. contains that of Isaiah. It is this, and by no means to tell us how Ezekiel was called to be a prophet, that is the essential element in the opening chapters of our book. So much does the idea of the prophetic *mission from God* dominate the whole, that neither does the real incongruity of how a sinner among sinners is permitted to be the seer of the holy God (comp. Isa. vi. 5 sqq.), nor the seeming incongruity of how a man who is not eloquent, and too young, is sent as a prophet (comp. Jer. i. 6 sqq.), come to a solution, but *Ezekiel has simply to open his mouth and to eat what is given him by God* (ch. ii. 8 sqq.). The question, therefore, is not, how he becomes qualified for the office of a prophet,—thus Isaiah, if such a view is held in his case, in the relation alleged, but more correctly perhaps for his special commission, is qualified by the removal of sin (Isa. vi. 6 sqq.); or Jeremiah, by means of the touch of Jehovah's hand (Jer. i. 9);—the question rather turns on this point simply, *in what capacity Ezekiel will have to discharge his prophetic office, to execute his mission.* The distinction between the *call* in general and a *mission* in particular might admit of being expressed as that between something more subjective and what is more objective, in some such way as this: that, in the call, the prophet as subject stands in the foreground; in the mission, the objective matter of fact preponderates, in which and through which the prophet has to develope his activity, which is Ezekiel's case. For the more general call, of course in its individual character in the case of each, one might have to confine himself in the case of Ezekiel as well as of Isaiah to their names (§ 1), while Jeremiah's name seems rather to express his mission. *The divine legitimation of the mission of Ezekiel* is the primary meaning of ch. i.–iii. On the whole, it approximates too much the peculiar nature of the prophetic office to the priestly and the kingly, when we speak in this way of the consecration of a prophet. The mission of a prophet is at all events in actual fact equivalent to his consecration to the prophetic office.

CHAPTER I.

1 AND it came to pass in the thirtieth year, in the fourth *month*, on the fifth *day*
of the month, as I was in the midst of the captivity, by the river Chebar, that
2 the heavens were opened, and I saw visions of God. On the fifth of the month
—it was the fifth year [from the time] of the carrying away captive of king
3 Jehoiachin—The word of Jehovah came in reality unto Ezekiel the priest, the
son of Buzi, in the land of the Chaldeans by the river Chebar; and the hand of
4 Jehovah came upon him there. And I saw, and, behold, a stormy wind came
out of the north, a great cloud, and fire flashing into itself, and brightness round
about it [the cloud], and out of the midst of it [the fire] as the look of the brightness
5 of gold, out of the midst of the fire. And out of the midst thereof [of the fire]
appeared the likeness of four living creatures. And this was their appearance:
6 they had the likeness of a man. And every one had four faces, and every one
7 of them four wings. And their feet were straight feet; and the sole of their
feet was like the sole of a calf's foot; and sparkling like the look of bright brass.
8 And they had the hands of a man under their wings on their four sides; and
9 they four had their faces and their wings. Joined one to another were their
wings; they turned not when they went; they went every one straight forward.
10 As for the likeness of their faces, they four had the face of a man, and the face
of a lion on the right side: and they four had the face of an ox on the left side;
11 and they four had the face of an eagle. And their faces and their wings were
separated above; in every one two were joined, and two covering their bodies.
12 And they went every one straight forward: whither the spirit was to go, they
13 went; they turned not when they went. As for the likeness of the living
creatures, their appearance was like kindled, burning coals of fire, like the
appearance of torches: this [the fire] was going round between the living creatures;
14 and the fire had brightness, and out of the fire went forth lightning. And the
living creatures ran and returned as the appearance of a flash of lightning.
15 And I saw the living creatures, and, behold, one wheel was upon the earth
16 beside the living creatures, for its four faces. The appearance of the wheels
and their make was like unto the look of the precious stone of Tartessus: and
they four had one likeness; and their appearance and their make was as it were
17 a wheel in the midst of a wheel. When they went, they went upon their four
18 sides: they turned not when they went. As for their felloes, there was a high-
ness about them, and fearfulness was about them; and their felloes were full
19 of eyes round about them four. And when the living creatures went, the wheels
went beside them; and when the living creatures were lifted up from the
20 earth, the wheels were lifted up. Whithersoever the spirit was to go, they
[the living creatures] went, thither was also the spirit to go [in the wheels]; and the
wheels were lifted up beside them: for the spirit of the living creature was in
21 the wheels. When those went, they also went; and when those stood, these
also stood; and when those were lifted up from the earth, the wheels were lifted
22 up beside them: for the spirit of the living creature was in the wheels. And a
likeness was over the heads of the living creature [ver. 20]—an expanse, like unto
23 the look of the terrible crystal, stretched out over their heads above. And
under the expanse were their wings straight, the one toward the other: to every
24 one two which covered, to every one two which covered their bodies. And I
heard the noise of their wings, like the noise of many waters, as the voice of the
Almighty, *to wit*, in their going, the noise of tumult, as the noise of an host:
25 when they stood, they let down their wings. And there came a voice from
above the expanse which was over their head: when they stood, they let down

26 their wings. And above the expanse that was over their head was there as the
appearance of a sapphire stone, the likeness of a throne: and upon the likeness
27 of the throne the likeness as the appearance of a man above upon it. And I saw
as the look of the brightness of gold, as the appearance of fire, a house round
about it; from the appearance of his loins and upwards, and from the appearance
of his loins and downwards, I saw as it were the appearance of fire, and bright-
28 ness round about Him. As the appearance of the bow that will be in the cloud
on the day of heavy rain, so was the appearance of the brightness round about.
This was the appearance of the likeness of the glory of Jehovah. And I saw, and fell
upon my face, and heard the voice of one that spake.

Ver. 2. Sept.: . . . τη αἰχμαλωσιας Ιωακειμ—
Ver. 3. . . . ἐπ' ἐμε χειρ κυριου. (Syr., Arab., and some MSS.: עלי.)
Ver. 4. . . . πυρ εξεστραπτον . . ὡς ὁρασις ἠλεκτρου . . . κ. φεγγος ἐν αὐτω. *Vulg.:* ignis involvens . . .
Ver. 5. . . . ὡς ὁμοιωμα . . . ζωων—animalium.

Ver. 6. Other readings: מהם, מהן; להמה, להן, להנה.

Ver. 7. . . . κ. πτερωτοι οἱ ποδες αὐτων, κ. σπινθηρες ὡς ὁ ἐξεστραπτων χαλκος, κ. ἐλαφραι αἱ πτερυγες αὐτων—et scintillae quasi aspectus aeris candentis.

Ver. 9. ἐχομεναι ἑτερα της ἑτερας. K. τα προσωπα αὐτων οὐκ ἐπεστρεφοντο ἐν τω βαδιζειν αὐτα (anoth. read.: בלכתם).

Ver. 10. Anoth. read.: לארבעתן.
Ver. 11. K. αἱ πτερυγες αὐτων ἐκτεταμεναι ἀνωθεν—

Ver. 12. Anoth. read.: בלכתם.
Ver. 13. K. ἐν μεσω των ζωων ὁρασις ὡς ἀνθρακων . . . λαμπαδων συστρεφομενων ἀνα μεσον των ζωων . . . (anoth. read.: מראיהן).
Ver. 14. . . . ὡς εἰδος του βεζεκ.
Ver. 16. Other readings: ומראה; ומעשיהן, wanting in Sept.; ומראיהן.
Ver. 17. Anoth. read.: רבעיהם.
Ver. 18. . . . οὐδε οἱ νωτοι αὐτων . . . κ. ἰδον αὐτα, κ. οἱ νωτοι—

Ver. 20. Οὐ ἀν ἠν ἡ νεφελη ἐκει το πνευμα του πορευεσθαι (ילכו שמה' ללכת are wanting in some MSS. The Greek and Syriac translators and the Targ. (?) omit הרוח ללכת).
Ver. 22. Sept., Vulg., Syr., Chald., Arab. read החיות.
Ver. 23. . . . αἱ πτερυγες αὐτων ἐκτεταμεναι, πτερυσσομεναι ἑτερα τη ἑτερα, ἑκαστω δυο συνεζευγμεναι,—(ולאיש שת' מכ' להנה are wanting in some MSS., Vulg., Sept., and Arab.)
Ver. 24. . . . ὑδατος πολλου, ὡς φωνην ἰκανου . . . φωνη του λογου ὡς φωνη παρεμβολης.
Ver. 25. בעמדם תר' כנפיהן are wanting in some MSS., in Sept.?, Syr., and Arab.
Ver. 27. . . . ὡς ὁρασιν πυρος ἐσωθεν αὐτου κυκλω—

EXEGETICAL REMARKS.

Vers. **1–3** a *preface*, which contains *introductory matter in general—specially to the vision which immediately follows*, what is most necessary respecting the *time*, *person*, *place*, and *subject-matter* on hand. This latter, the subject-matter, is "visions of God" in the plural, which are separated by means of the expression: "and I saw, and, behold" (vers. 4, 15), properly into two visions only, vers. 4–14, and 15–28; but it will commend itself to treat vers. 22–28 as a separate conclusion completing both visions.

Vers. 1–3.—*Preface, Introductory.*

Ver. 1. "**And it came to pass.**"—The imperf. with ו consecut., as usual without Dagesh forte, indicating a *continuation*, an *advance*, connection with something going before, begins, as often elsewhere, so also here the book of Ezekiel. Since there is no real connection, as in the case of Exodus, Ezra, a connection *in thought* is to be assumed, as in the case of Ruth, Esther. The chronology, still more the inner relationship (comp. the Introduction, §§ 2, 3, 4), suggests a connection with Jeremiah. Hengstenberg, while he lays stress upon the similar commencements, by which Joshua is connected with the Pentateuch, the book of Judges with Joshua, the books of Samuel and also Ruth with the book of Judges, understands, besides a special connection of Ezekiel with Jeremiah (whose letter (Jer. xxix.), directed shortly before to the exiles, formed as it were the programme for the labours of our prophet), *in general* (as in the case of the book of Esther) *the incorporation* (*represented by such a commencement*) *in a chain of sacred books*, a connection with a preceding sacred literature. In a more definite way Athanasius brought into connection with this the passage in Josephus (*Antiq.* x.)—comp. Introd. § 5—and made out that *the one book of Ezekiel*, with which the present one is *here connected by means of* ו, had gone amissing through the negligence of the Jews. Pradus cites Augustine (on Ps. iv.) and Gregory the Great in support of a view according to which this ו is intended to connect *the outward word* of the prophet *with what he had heard inwardly*, with the inward vision (CORN. A LAPIDE: "What he had formerly seen in his spirit or heard from God he connects by means of 'and' with something else which he saw and heard thereafter, and which he now relates"). Very many expositors have been quite content with a pleonastic Hebrew idiom, and with changing the sense of the future into that of the preterite. (According to Keil, appealing to Ewald (*Ausf. Lehrb.* § 231, *b*), it is merely "something annexed to a circle of what is finished—a circle already mentioned, or assumed as known.")—**In the thirtieth year,** etc. Where the divine legitimation of Ezekiel for his labours about to be described, and at the same time for his literary labours—this book of his—is to be shown, and where accordingly the prophet speaks of himself in the first person, going on immediately to say: "as I," so that ואני in such close juxtaposition with בשלשים שנה looks like the usual phrase בן שלשים שנה, there it ought to appear as simple as it is natural to think, with Origen and Gregory, of the thirtieth year of Ezekiel's life. There was no necessity whatever for Hengstenberg (comp. Introd. § 3) to urge the significance "as respects the man of priestly family." The appointment of the thirtieth year in Num. iv., with a view to "the carrying of the sanctuary during the journey through the wilderness—a work requiring the full vigour of manhood," cannot in actual fact be applied to Ezekiel; and we must then in a figurative way compare his prophetic labours in exile, especially his preaching of the glory of the Lord, and the circumstance that through Ezekiel's exercise of the prophetic office the Lord became to the exiles as a sanctuary in the captivity (ch. xi. 16), with that carrying of the tabernacle during the time of the wilderness. For "theological exposition," of course, "the entrance on office of the Baptist and of Christ after completing their thirtieth year" may be kept in view. The indefiniteness of the statement of time, "in the thirtieth year," is not greater than the indefiniteness with respect to the person: "as I." As the latter indefiniteness is removed in ver. 3 by the mention of the name, etc., so (according to Kliefoth, and also Keil) the corresponding addition: *in the fourth month, on the fifth day*, by the repetition in ver. 2 of the fifth *of the month*, viz. the fifth day of the forementioned fourth month, is brought into connection with the objectivity of the "fifth year from the carrying away captive of king Jehoiachin," and in this way relieved of all want of clearness, while at the same time expressly separated from the date: "in the thirtieth year," just as this latter itself is so much the more evidently left to its simplest, natural acceptation of the thirtieth year *of the prophet's life*. If then ver. 2 afterwards supplies the period according to which Ezekiel adjusts his first, subjective date, the supposition of another so-called "publicly current era" is superfluous, apart from the fact, that no such era has hitherto been pointed out. Recourse has been had (1) to a *Jewish* era, and (2) to a *Babylonian* one. (1.) Thus Hitzig adheres to the opinion of many Jewish expositors, that the reference is to the thirtieth year *from a jubilee*[1] (comp. on ch. xl. 1), but combats what is yet so necessary, the more exact definition, *e.g.*, of Raschi, that in this way the reckoning is from the *eighteenth year of king Josiah*, important on account of the finding of the book of the law, etc. (2 Kings xxii. sqq.; 2 Chron. xxxiv. sqq.); while Hävernick declares this reckoning (already that of the Chaldee Paraphrast, Jerome, Grotius, and also Ideler) "the only tenable one," as also that which is "alone suited to the context:" "that with the last period of prosperity there stands contrasted the last period of misfortune (under Jehoiachin): the numbers are prophetically significant statements, pointing to the weighty circumstance of the prophet's making his appearance in a memorable, fatal time." We must therefore assume a "priestly" mode of reckoning. Calvin lays stress upon the Greek analogy of Olympiads, as well as the Roman one of reckoning according to consulates, and in favour of the jubilee under Josiah brings forward the peculiarly solemn passover-feast at that time. (2.) For accepting a *Babylonian* era one might urge the sojourn of Ezekiel in Babylon, especially his peculiar attention to chronology, which dates from this seat of astronomical science. In this case the fifth year of the captivity of Jehoiachin has been reckoned as the year B.C. 595, and the thirtieth year from that as the year B.C. 625, when Nabopolassar ascended the Chaldean throne; and either the eighteenth year of Josiah has been taken as contemporaneous therewith, or the era of Nabopolassar merely has been clung to (*e.g.* by Scaliger, Perizonius). But the reckoning does not agree; according to Bunsen, at least, the fifth year of the captivity of Jehoiachin would be the year B.C. 593. Perizonius wished therefore to be at liberty to read in Ezekiel the thirty-second instead of the thirtieth year. J. D. Michaelis helps himself by making the reckoning start not from Nabopolassar's ascending the throne, but from the conquest of Nineveh and Babylon by him. Comp. besides in Hitzig.—The **fourth month,** since the first (Nisan) coincides for the most part with our March, corresponds to our June, or, according to J. D. Michaelis, Hitzig, Bunsen, to July nearly. The (probably Babylonian) name of it would be Tammuz; but the prophet follows still the custom of antiquity, which, with only some exceptions, did not give names to the separate months, but merely numbered them.—

ואני בתוך־הגולה. As the *time* is indicated by "in the thirtieth year," so also next the place is indicated in a personal way: **as I was**, *etc.* That the clause might by itself mean, *cum essem in medio captivorum*, is beyond a doubt; but that the LXX. in this case translate more correctly than the Vulgate is not less undoubtedly clear from ch. iii. 11, 15. Hitzig's solution (favoured by Klief., Keil): "in the district (region) of their (the exiles') dwelling-places (settlements)," is superfluous; more accurate is his remark: "and besides he himself was a captive." Rightly Ewald: **in the midst of the captivity**. The historical dates in the prophetic books have a certain designedness, something symbolic about them,—are at all events not simply historical notices; they are intended to be understood in the light of the idea, exactly as that was to be realized in the case in hand, and hence characteristically as regards the prophet in question. *In the midst of the misery the prophet was to behold the glory of God for his people* (comp. Introd. § 5). Calvin on this occasion enters into a polemic against the notion of the Jews, as if the hand of God were shortened towards the holy land, etc. Ezekiel was, according to ch. iii. 11, 15, alone by the river, and did not go, till he had had the vision, among the multitudes of his countrymen who dwelt or happened to be nearest him.—**By the river Chebar**, comp. Introd. § 4 (Calvin attaches indeed no importance to it, but he mentions the

[1] The Jews reckon the jubilee year from the fourteenth year after the taking possession of the land of Canaan, and place the destruction of Jerusalem in the thirty-sixth year of the jubilee: so that the fifth year of Jehoiachin's captivity = the thirtieth of the jubilee.

opinion of those who regard the rivers as places consecrated for revelations, inasmuch as they give prominence to their symbolical character [“the lighter element of water,” while “the earth appears heavier”], or inasmuch as others think of the “cleansing” power of water and the like. A kind of spiritual reference to Ps. cxxxvii. 1 Calvin looks upon as forced.) Hengstenberg compares Dan. viii. 2, x. 4; Ezekiel is “removed to the Chebar, because there he is far from the bustle of men, and allured to great thoughts by the rushing of the water.”[1] And then it is alleged he was “there only in vision,” as is clear from ch. iii. 12, 14! As if, forsooth, the Spirit could not have carried him to and from the actual river! Then we must understand “in the midst of the captivity” likewise as being in vision. In Daniel it is expressly said at ch. viii. 2 to be in vision, and at ch. x. 4 as well as here it is to be conceived of as not being so. At Ezek. viii. 3, xi. 24, the definition as to its being in vision is expressly added. (Some have also formed to themselves a conception of the sojourn by the water after the analogy of the Romish Ghetto, as Martial says instead of Jew *transtiberinus*.)—The personal reference is kept up still in the description of the *subject* in hand, of what took place: **the heavens were opened, and I saw**—; so much is *the divine authorization of Ezekiel* the leading thought. The opening of the heavens refers, as respects the form, as regards the character of the vision, to this vision which follows. There is in this respect nothing more general intended by it (John i. 52), as Keil seems to hint. Comp., however, Matt. iii. 16; Mark i. 10; Luke iii. 21; Acts vii. 56, x. 10, 11; Rev. iv. 1, xix. 11. As regards what is essential in all ways and forms, Calvin will be right in maintaining, that “God opens His heavens, not that in reality they are cleft asunder, but inasmuch as, after the removal of all hindrances, He enables the eyes of believers to penetrate to His heavenly glory.” As Jerome has already said: fide credentis intellige, eo quod cœlestia sint illi reserata mysteria. (Grotius makes the heavens to be rent open by repeated flashes of lightning.) “He who says this, testifies that what he has seen he has not seen as something which has come out of the earth or existed first on the earth, but that it has descended from heaven, and consequently been visions of God” (COCCEIUS). If the opening of the heavens depicts the manner of the thing, *how* it happened, then the expression, **visions of God** (ch. xl. 2), specifies *the thing itself* under discussion, and that first of all in accordance with what follows, where the next thing is *vision*. The genitive relation cannot be rendered by: sublime visions, or the like (as Calvin already rejects as frigid the interpretation: visiones præstantissimas, quia divinum vocatur in scriptura quidquid excellit), but it might perhaps, in accordance also with linguistic usage elsewhere, pass as equivalent to: divine visions, *i.e.* in the manner of Isa. vi., 1 Kings xxii. 19, 2 Kings vi. 17, etc. (Hitzig: heavenly visions). Quia ex cœlo demonstratas, ideoque divinas et a Deo ostensas (COCCEIUS). As genitive of the subject (*auctoris*) it might be interpreted in accordance with Num. xxiv. 4, 16, either: visions which God (as well as they) sees; or: visions which God gives to see (which proceed from God); which would correspond with the aim of the following vision, that of legitimating Ezekiel's call as a divine one. “The divine visions stand opposed to the visions of one's own heart, the empty fancies of false prophets, Jer. xxiii. 25, 26” (HENGSTENBERG). “Otherwise it would have been incredible, that a prophet should have arisen out of Chaldea. Nazareth even (John i. 47) was still situated in the promised land. Thus the divine call needed to be confirmed as such in a special way” (CALV.). As genitive of the object the meaning would be, visions which have reference to God, have Him as their object; which suits the contents of the vision as expressed at ver. 28. Here: visions of God; in Jer. i. 1: words of Jeremiah.—וָאֶרְאֶה is the complete form without apocope, as after the ו consecut. not seldom in the first person and in the later books.

Ver. 2 is occupied with a reference to the dates. It was *the fifth year from the carrying away captive of king Jehoiachin*, and it is meant of the “objective common era” (HENGSTENBERG),[1] just as also in the sequel of this notice (ver. 3), which is better inserted immediately than later. Ezekiel—a thing which does not occur elsewhere in the book (ch. xxiv. 24!)—speaks of himself in the *third* person. Without verses 2, 3, with ver. 1 simply pushed forward to ver. 4, we would have the impression that a private document, a leaf of the prophet's journal, lay before us. The explicit statement of ver. 2 was the more necessary, where already in ver. 1 the fifth of the fourth month was to be explained with reference to this fixed period, the most important of course for the immediate hearers of the prophet, and therefore easily intelligible for them, and also retained by the prophet throughout, but for others not equally clear. That vers. 2, 3 “interrupt” (EWALD) the connection cannot be alleged; we shall find the opposite.—גּוֹלָה in ver. 1 is essentially the same as גָּלוּת in ver. 2, the distinction to be made being perhaps this, that the former refers more to the *condition*, the latter to the *action*.—As to the historical fact, see 2 Kings xxiv. 6 sqq., 2 Chron. xxxvi. 9 sqq.—יוֹיָכִין as here, in 2 Kings, 2 Chron. יְהוֹיָכִין, is called in Jer. xxii. 24, 28 כָּנְיָהוּ, in ch. xxiv. 1 of the same book יְכָנְיָהוּ, and in ch. xxvii. 20 יְכָנְיָה.—Kliefoth, on the basis of the detailed exposition in Hävernick, gives prominence as regards this period, on the one hand, to the unpleasant impression of the first circular letter (Jer. xxix.) to the exiles, and on the other hand, to the inflaming of their minds by the later prophetic announcement in Jer. li. 59 sqq. Comp. in the remainder of the Introd. § 5. “That it was already the fifth year, is held up as a reproach to the stiffneckedness of the Jews” (CALV.). The appearance of Ezekiel took place in the most hopeful period of the reign of Zedekiah, when false prophecy was making its voice heard at home and abroad. To all this *seeming and fancied glory*, opposed as it was to the divine word of the true prophets, Ezekiel's *vision of glory* formed *the divine antithesis*.

[1] Corn. a Lap. ingeniously compares the gentle murmuring of the waters to the effect of music upon Elisha (2 Kings iii. 15).

[1] Namely, the exile, for which reason he does not reckon according to the year of the reign of Zedekiah.

Ver. 3. הָיֹה הָיָה, inf. absol., *in solemnly rhetorical fashion emphasizing the divine attestation of the prophet:* really, expressly, quite certainly. The full unquestionable reality of the transaction is to be indicated.—Though ver. 1 spoke of the person, time, place, subject-matter, all the elements of the introduction, yet ver. 2 reverted to the time; and so ver. 3 speaks anew first of all of the subject-matter as דבר יי׳, which came to Ezekiel, by which expression this same subject-matter, linking itself on to ver. 1 (there, "visions of God;" here, "the word of Jehovah"), is now designated according to its *intrinsic*, its essential character as the product of the Spirit (1 Thess. ii. 13). It is at the same time the exact announcement of what follows, and the introduction thereto; for at ver. 28 there is a transition from the "I saw" to the "I heard the voice of one that spake," and this latter is shown from ch. ii. 4 to be "the Lord Jehovah."—As to the *name* of the prophet and that of *his father*, as well as the *priestly* rank of both, with which the personal description is completed, comp. Introd. §§ 1, 3. For the purpose in a quite objective way of making more prominent *his divine legitimation*, Ezekiel speaks of himself *as of a third person.* (Like the LXX., the Syriac and Arabic versions presuppose עלי, the reading of several Codd.) *Humility* also, in a case where he had been deemed worthy of such a revelation (comp. the similar mode of expression in 2 Cor. xii. 2 sqq.), recommended his speaking in the third person.—The renewed mention of the place is not a mere repetition of the words: **by the river Chebar**, but a more exact definition alike of this river, and especially of the phrase: "in the midst of the captivity," both being defined by בארץ כשדים,—in the sense, however, of **land of the Chaldeans**=land *of the enemy*, to which at the close of the verse שם again points back, emphatically, as Calvin remarks. This locality was only too significant a corrective of presumption on the one hand, as of despair on the other, or rather of fleshly narrow-mindedness in general.—If then, finally, the subject-matter is again brought into prominence, and that as respects its producing cause, viz. that **the hand of Jehovah came upon him,** this certainly is not said without reference to the statement: "and I fell upon my face," in ver. 28, and might indeed have preceded the words: **the word of Jehovah came in reality** (HITZIG); but the immediately following subject-matter (ver. 4) demanded this or some such transition at the close of the verse. Thus verses 2, 3 complete the section. The formula of transition used is one that occurs again (Introd. § 7), ch. iii. 22, xxxvii. 1, xl. 1. Comp. 2 Kings iii. 15. The expression **the hand of Jehovah** always means a *divine manifestation of power*, but in the sense of *action*, consequently with *will* and *intention*, by means of which self-will and refusal on the part of man are laid in the dust, and the man is *prepared for the divine purpose.* For whatever may be the natural basis subjectively (intellectually, morally, and spiritually), as well as objectively (as respects the nexus in the history of the time or of the individual), the prophetic word as God's word, as visions of God, is neither a product of one's own effort and exertion, reflection and investigation, nor a result of mere human instruction. It is not gifts, not study that makes the prophet, just as also we do not meet with inclination as a prophetic factor, but constraint must be put upon them,—the prophets needed to be *overpowered.* Thus something lies in the עליו יד יי׳. Comp. Jer. xx. 7. If this appears in a still stronger form where instead of וַתְּהִי, *e.g.* at ch. viii. 1, we have וַתִּפֹּל, ch. xi. 5 certainly explains יד יי׳ by רוּח יי׳; it is the power *of the Spirit.* "He has thus expressed the energy of the divine Spirit" (THEODORET). Hence the prophetic preparation in consequence of this is rightly given by Oehler in the first place as a divine knowledge (comp. Jer. xxiii. 18 with Amos iii. 7), to which there cannot be wanting as a second element the sanctifying as well as strengthening efficacy (Ps. l. 16 sqq.; Mic. iii. 8). J. Fr. Starck quotes: impulsus inopinatus, illuminatio extraordinaria, spiritus prophetiæ vehemens, afflatus Spiritus Sancti singularis. "Thus he saw what other men did not see, then he recollected all that he had seen and heard, and understood the meaning of the Lord and did His commandment." Cocc. (On old pictures of the prophets, as well as in the frescoes of the church at Schwarz-Rheindorf, a hand is painted, which is stretched from heaven.)

Vers. 4–28.—*Ezekiel's Vision of the Glory of Jehovah.*

Isaac Casaubon, in his once far-famed *Exercitationes*, xvi. *de reb. sacr. et eccl. adv. Baronium* (Geneva 1655), asserts: "in the whole of the Old Testament there is nothing more obscure than the beginning and the end of the book of Ezekiel." Under the same impression Calvin declares, that "he acknowledges that he does not understand this vision." Jerome had pronounced that "in its interpretation all the synagogues of the Jews are dumb, giving as their reason that it transcends man's capacity, *et de hac et de ædificatione templi, quod in ultimo hujus prophetæ scribitur, aliquid velle conari.*" The Jewish designation for the following vision is מֶרְכָּבָה, "chariot" or "team of four," in accordance with the four living creatures and the four wheels. HÄVERNICK: "It formed the basis and the point of support for the later mystic theology in its endless gnostic speculations about the divine essence and the higher spirit-world." As their natural theology is called among the Jews בְּרֵאשִׁית, so the mystic is called מֶרְכָּבָה. One is not to read before reaching his thirtieth year either the beginning of Genesis, or the Song of Songs, or the beginning and end of the book of Ezekiel; such is the admonition of Jewish tradition. Comp. ZUNZ, *Die gottesdienstl. Vortr. d. Juden*, p. 162 sqq. (the most important work of more recent times in this department).

Umbreit, while he denies him the poetic gift, ascribes to Ezekiel "in the rarest degree the ability which is characteristic of the painter, of making visible to the eye what he has seen." But even the celebrated picture of Raphael in the Pitti Gallery at Florence may pass as a criticism of this assertion. There there is more than one feature quite passed over: what is separate appears grouped together; what is united, on the other hand, appears divided. To the artistic conception of the greatest painter the vision of Ezekiel presented itself with difficulty. We shall be compelled to assert even more positively, that with all the "exactitude of delineation, and with the plastic art in the giving of details" (UMBREIT), an obscurity remains over the whole, even merely as respects the setting it before the eye, an *invisibility*, which is not certainly to be ascribed to "overcrowding," but which lies in the subject-matter, the object of the vision, which results from the thing itself. The representation of Ezekiel wrestles with its subject, as the amplification, the repetition and recurrence again to what has been said, shows. It must indeed be the case, according to Exod. xxxiii., that (vers. 22, 23) only the "back parts" of the glory of God are capable of being seen by man here upon earth. Comp. 1 John iii. 2. Certainly, if Ezekiel, because he had been carried out of the body, were to have seen the "face" of the glory of God, his after-remembrance in the body of what he had seen would not have been capable of being expressed. Comp. 2 Cor. xii. 4, 3. The "unapproachable light," in which God dwells (1 Tim. vi. 16), remains from the time of the Sinaitic keynote theophany onwards for the whole of the Old Testament. Exod. xix. 9, 16, 20, 21 (Deut. iv. 11, v. 19); Lev. xvi. 2; 1 Kings viii. 12; Ps. xcvii. 2 (xviii. 12).

We may quote the remark of Umbreit, that Ezekiel "repeats more frequently than any other prophet the statement: the word of Jehovah was thus made known to me, as if he had felt the word like a burden, and was unable to reproduce it as such in a very worthy manner; it is only to set down its symbol that he feels himself called in his inmost being." There is also to be found in Ezekiel as compared with the older prophets a greater complication in the symbolism, in which *the following vision* especially is expressed in its plastic art. Comp. Introd. § 7.

Inasmuch as it is *vision*, and consequently the divine element is represented *visibly* in *pictures*, these pictures have a divine import, are *symbols*, so that there belongs to them at the same time a concealing, relatively veiling character, especially as regards the people. The *word* of God must accordingly come in addition to the *vision* of God, in order to explain it for the prophet and the people. Comp. the distinction between ὀπτασίας and ἀποκαλύψεις κυρίου, 2 Cor. xii. 1.

But it is not so much a peaceful picture which presents itself to our prophet, as rather a *phenomenon of a very excited character inwardly as well as outwardly*; a circumstance which must not remain unnoticed in the interpretation. The *storm* brings *great clouds* therefore. A strong brisk *fire*, which spreads its brightness round about, forms the interior of the cloud brought by the storm. Such is the first, outermost part of the vision, its porch as it were, which the prophet first of all enters (ver. 4). On a nearer view there are formed out of the intensive fire of the cloud *as it were four "living creatures,"* which have at first sight the appearance of a man, and are therefore to be carried back in thought to this in general, whatever else in detail more exact description perceives in them. And so the fourfold group of the creatures is individualized in a *fourfoldness* of each of them: *man, lion, ox, eagle.* In spite of such fourfoldness, which is perhaps also clear from other circumstances (thus they have wings, and at the same time the foot-soles of a calf, and yet the hands of a man, comp. at ver. 7), prominence is given expressly to a mutuality of relation, *the unity of a whole*, vers. 9, 12, 15, 20, 21, 22 (vers. 5–14). Then, further, as the direction out of the north (ver. 4) has given the tendency of the vision in its immediate *historical* reference, so *the wheels* also bring the whole into connection *with the earth*. The more expressive connecting link will be the number four, the *symbolic* number (passing over from the living creatures to the wheels) of the cosmical relations, in which God reveals Himself. (BÄHR, *Symbolism of the Mosaic Cultus*, i. p. 341.) The *glory of Jehovah from heaven* manifests itself with this second part of the vision as a *glorifying of Jehovah upon earth*, inasmuch as "the spirit of the living creature" unites in the closest way wheels and creatures (vers. 15–21). Lastly, the holy of holies of the vision is opened with the *vault* as of heaven over the heads of the *chajah*. The living creatures, into union with which the wheels are taken up by means of the "spirit," are by means of the "voice," which comes from above the vault, and that while they are at rest, united to Him who is enthroned there, who looked like a man. From Him ultimately everything proceeds, just as to Him ultimately everything tends. As in the holy of holies of the tabernacle and of the temple, the vision culminates in *the enthroning of Jehovah in His glory*. Hence, too, it cannot be passed over without remark, that in this very excited phenomenon a *thrice-repeated advance* makes itself known. The first time the fire-cloud כְּעֵין הַחַשְׁמַל מִתּוֹךְ הָאֵשׁ (ver. 4). The second time the fire-picture of the *chajoth* כְּגַחֲלֵי־אֵשׁ בֹּעֲרוֹת כְּמַרְאֵה הַלַּפִּדִים (vers. 13, 7), with the height and dreadfulness and כְּעֵין תַּרְשִׁישׁ of the wheels (vers. 18, 16). The third time: the רָקִיעַ כְּעֵין הַקֶּרַח הַנּוֹרָא, and the throne כְּמַרְאֵה אֶבֶן סַפִּיר, and the fire-bright appearance of the Glorious One thereon, the description of which, however, at last terminates significantly in: "As the appearance of the bow," etc. *Fire, brightness, light*,—this remains the common feature all three times; it forms consequently *the fundamental characteristic of the vision* as respects its interpretation, in which, however, the meaning of the closing *rainbow* in the cloud must not be left out.

Let us now attempt to get at the meaning of the vision. Although the separate symbols must be left over to the exegesis, yet *the symbolism as a whole* must be understood beforehand, according to which the import of the vision, especially in comparison and connection with other similar visions of the Old Testament, will come to light. Ezekiel himself leaves us in no doubt as to the meaning of his vision, for he says expressly at the close: הוּא מַרְאֵה דְמוּת כְּבוֹד יי׳. It is therefore *Jehovah's glory* that presented itself to him, and presents itself to us in the vision. In so far as this can be distinguished more in its personal relation to Himself, and on the other side more in its active manifestation and execution of His will, as Jehovah's *glory* and as His *glorification*, the הוּא of ch. i. 28 may, by a glance at ch. x. 4, 19, be more precisely explained by Keil (following Hitzig), but for the interpretation of the vision in ch. i. it is not advisable. As to the idea כבוד for "glory," comp. on ch. i. 28. Although the כָּבוֹד of God stands for the *appearance*, hence for what is manifest (Introd. § 10), yet the *figurative representation* of the same must not be taken as a matter of course for the *essential idea.* Gesenius says incorrectly in his Pocket Dictionary: "The Hebrew conceives (?) of it as a clear shining fire, from which fire issues, and which is usually enveloped in smoke;" for the Hebrew *conceives* of it rather (comp. Ges. himself) as "weight, dignity, *gravitas.*" To the divine *essence* there belongs a corresponding sovereign *dignity* and sovereign *power*,—a glory (*Herrlichkeit* from "*hehr*"), as well as a dominion (*Herrschaft* from "*Herr*"). The two things conceived of as one idea, and not merely in antithesis to the world, but in the world as *the light and the life* of the world, is the כָּבוֹד of God—*the significance of God for the world.* The heavens declare the glory of God (Ps. xix. 1), and the whole earth is full of His glory (Isa. vi. 3). Without it there is nothing but "power and matter" (Büchner), and our view of the world is an atomistic one. Although the manifest *aim* of creation has been turned by reason of sin into the *goal*, yet Ps. xcvii. 6 says and prophesies: "The heavens declare His righteousness, and all nations see His glory;" and in Num. xiv. 21 Jehovah swears by His life, that the glory of Jehovah shall fill the whole earth. If with this far-reaching look at the world's goal, and on the broad foundation of the divine aim as regards the world ("Jehovah" is certainly everywhere "Elohim"), Ezekiel's vision of Jehovah's glory shapes itself *first of all* and *predominantly* as *the righteousness* of the Holy One, who will execute *the judgment upon Jerusalem*, and thus also upon that portion of Israel not yet in banishment by the Chebar, *such a thing* is easily understood as being *necessary for that historical period*, alike from the situation of affairs and as regards the persons. And this it is that is symbolized by the fire-*cloud* in particular, as well as in general by the fire-*style*, in which the whole is kept. Nevertheless there comes forth as *the kernel* of the fire-cloud the fire-picture of the four *chajoth*, whose meaning is as little reached when one goes back and gives them a Judaistic interpretation as the cherubim in the tabernacle or in the temple, as when one christianizes them by anticipation, as Kliefoth does, as the "universality of the economy of salvation founded by Christ when He appeared, in contrast with the particularism and territorialism of the previous economy of salvation." It might rather be nearer the mark to adopt a third view which would keep fast hold of the *glory* of God as the original *aim* of the creation of heaven and earth as well as the ultimate *goal* of the history of the world; in connection with which the idea of *life*, so frequent with Ezekiel, pervading as it does the whole book, must not be overlooked (ch. xviii. 23; xxxiii. 11; the whole of ch. xxxvii.; ch. xviii. 9, 13, 17, 19, 21, 24, 28, 32; ch. xxxiii. 12, 13, 15, 16; iii. 18, 21; xvi. 6; xx. 11, 13, 21, 25; xlvii. 9; xiii. 18, 19, 22; vii. 13; v. 11; xiv. 16, 18, 20; xvii. 16, 19; xviii. 3; xx. 3, 31, 33; xxxiii. 11, 27; xxxiv. 8; xxxv. 11: comp. xxvi. 20; xxxii. 23, 24, 25, 26, 27, 32). For as God's glory has its side for Him, according to which it is the self-representation of His *life* in a majesty invisible for man, so, on the other side, heaven and earth and the world of creatures mirror forth *the divine life* in a visible *glory of God*, inasmuch as through them God's peculiar nature and power come to be seen in a manifoldness and fulness of *life.* This is His "fame," His "honour," which become known from creation conformably to its original design, according to which the investigation of nature was meant to be, as Prof. Fichte says, "an uninterrupted worship, a rational and intelligent glorification of that uncreated wisdom which manifests itself in nature." And in like manner (according to Beck), "all the threads of life, which the divine faithfulness in revelation preserves within the circle of sinful mankind from the beginning onwards, and evermore strengthens and perfects in a part of the same, converge at the end in a central manifestation of life: ἡ ζωὴ ἐφανερώθη, 1 John i. 2. The revelation *of life* in actual fact breaks the death-power of sin, 2 Tim. i. 10; *life* is the substance of salvation" (*Lehrwissenschaft*, i. p. 448); and this *life*-development of salvation exercises, on the one hand, a preserving, renewing, and perfecting influence on the still remaining life-power of the world, and on the other hand, a relaxing, judging, and annihilating influence on the death-power of sin, works creatively, so that man and the earthly system come forth as a new creation in eternal and unchangeable life from the catastrophe of conflict and judgment. *As arising from such a connection of the life and glory of God, must the spiritual symbolism of the chajoth also be understood in Ezekiel.* The retrospective reference to the cherubim of the ark has certainly its truth, but not till ch. x. (comp. at ch. ix. 3 the explanation with respect to the cherubs in general), where Ezekiel also (ver. 20) expressly brings them forward; and even there (vers. 15, 17, 20) they are called, as here and at ch. iii. 13, "chajoth" or "chajah." Their *symbolic* character is necessarily clear even from the symbolic connection in which they appear. The prophet saw also merely a "likeness" of four living creatures, consequently what looked like four living creatures. To their symbolic character corresponds also their designation; the biblical ideas of life and death have a symbolic colouring. But, in particular, support is entirely wanting in Holy Scripture for conceiving of these "living creatures," as Keil would have us, as "beings who of all the creatures of heaven and earth possess and exhibit life in the fullest sense of the word, and who on this very account of all spiritual beings stand the nearest to the God of the spirits of all flesh, who lives from eternity to eternity, and surround His throne on every side." What would thus be affirmed of "creatures," is applicable properly to the Son alone (John i. 4); and how would such "representatives and bearers of the eternal blessed life" harmonize even with the uniquely prominent position of man made in the image of God in the Bible! In opposition to actual individual beings of such a kind, in opposition to "angelic beings of a higher order," there speaks too evidently their fourfold form, whose meaning, as already settled by the Rabbins, is this, that the vital power according to four types (of man above all and in general because of his life being in highest potency, because of his spirit and its eternal destiny),—comp. Bähr, *Symb.* i. p. 342 sqq.,—is to find an expression, is to be represented in a fulness of the highest possible significance. From the reproach of being "abstract ideas or ideal forms of the imagination," which would thus be "represented as living beings," the purely symbolic view is released by this circumstance, that certainly the four types are taken from real life, only the manner of their application and their juxtaposition being ideal. There can be no question of abstraction, where rather the individual element is specially realized by means of the idea of the whole, viz. life. Hengstenberg ["The Cherubim" at the close of his "Ezekiel," Clark's Trans.], who in Bähr's interpretation emphasizes not so much the "ideal creature" as "the living creation," limits it, however, to the earth, holding that it must be viewed altogether apart from the heavenly creature. Passages, however, such as Gen. ii. 7, ix. 16, which he cites, leave sufficient room for the idea of *the living creature in general*, since, according to Gen. ii. 7, there by no means belongs to the living creature "a double element, the earthly material and the quickening breath of God;" but these two constitute merely the earthly man, and he rather becomes "a living soul" from the fact that God "breathed into his nostrils the breath of life," just as Gen. ix. 16 also limits "every living creature" by means of the words "among all flesh that is upon the earth," the thing spoken of being life upon earth. Theodoret, however, may be right, that the angels likewise are living creatures, and that the relation of mortality is the distinction between their life and that of man. The contrast with death is not less justified than that "with what is lifeless," and the expression the "living" God scarcely allows the idea of the living creature to be confined to man and beasts. Neither does "the number four in itself" point exclusively to the earth; comp. Bähr in the work quoted, i. p. 156 sqq. Only the composition of the number four, consisting as it does of man, lion, ox, and eagle, has, according to the ingenious exposition of Hengstenberg, much of an earthly appearance. That ox and calf alternate in ch. i. 7 (Rev. iv. 7), does indeed make the representation of the (tame) cattle by means of the ox and that of the wild animals by means of the lion very probable. But the flying of the eagle would certainly be sufficiently represented by two wings, while the four wings expressly mentioned (ch. i. 6) point beyond this requisite, and in their parallel (ver. 8) with the hands of a man—which give prominence to the human element—allow us on their side to conjecture something *superterrestrial* beyond man and beast, as Keil has rightly remarked. When Hengstenberg makes use of the cherubs of the tabernacle and in Solomon's temple for his exposition, one does not easily understand how the furnishing of their human form with wings is to spring from this cause, that the class of birds "in the history of creation opens the series of living creatures, just as man closes it;" for in Gen. i. 20 the aquatic animals still take the precedence, and in fact the large ones (ver. 21), which play such a part in Holy Scripture. Just as little can "the bird" take "the last place," as being also that which is relatively "lower," which is contradicted, as has been said, by the four wings. There is to be noticed in ver. 11 (23) the parallel to Isa. vi. 2 (comp. ch. iii. 12). Perhaps, also, when speaking of "the noise of their wings" (ver. 24), the comparison כְּקוֹל מַחֲנֶה (after Gen. xxxii. 2, 3) is worthy of notice. The cherubs in Solomon's temple (and also on the stands of the basins,[1] 1 Kings vii. 29) represented not life upon earth, according to its two extremities, but the terrestrial and superterrestrial life of creation. Thus only do the "lions and oxen" before us gain their significance: wild animals and cattle, the strictly *animal* world as contrasted with the earthly and heavenly *spiritual* world in their combination in the winged human figure. Otherwise they would not be necessary representations, inasmuch as they were certainly already represented by means of the irrational bird. With the "palm trees" and "flowers" (1 Kings vi. 29; Ezek. xli. 18, 19, 25), the *significant* vegetable world, too, was added to the earthly creation; while, in the following vision, storm, clouds, fire, light (ver. 4) set before our eyes almost literally passages like Ps. civ.: "O LORD, my God, Thou art very great. Thou clothest Thyself with splendour and glory, wrapping Thyself round with light as a garment,—who maketh clouds His chariot, walketh upon the wings of the wind, making His messengers winds, His servants flaming fire." Ps. l.: "Our God shall come, etc. Fire devoureth before Him, and round about Him it is very tempestuous; He calleth the heavens from above, and the earth, to judge His people,—and the heavens declare His righteousness." Ps. xviii.: "He bowed the heavens and came down, and cloudy darkness was under His feet, and He rode upon the cherub, and did fly, and was poised upon the wings of the wind, made darkness His covering, etc. At the brightness that was before Him His clouds passed away, hail and coals of fire." Although it will have to be conceded to Hengstenberg, that the *earthly* reference of the life of creation *preponderates* in the vision of Ezekiel, quite similarly as on the other side the human type preponderates, *yet the whole* continues to have *an undeniably superterrestrial character*. The fire-cloud with the four living creatures appears to the prophet (comp. ver. 1) *out of the opened heavens*, and it is only the *wheels* (ver. 15 sqq.) that intentionally set down the heavenly phenomenon as being at the same time something earthly. It is meant to be *the human-earthly creation in the fulness of its vital power*, as appearing from the background of the heaven-stirred, and also *spirit*-like *elemental powers* (*air, fire*), and still more (comp. Rev. iv. 8, 9; v. 8, 14; xix. 4) as *offering itself continually after the manner of the heavenly messengers and servants in obedience and voluntary surrender* (ὡς ἐν οὐρανῷ καὶ ἐπὶ τῆς γῆς, Matt. vi. 10), *in unceasing activity of service to His honour, and thus continually glorifying Him* (ver. 19 sqq.). This we may suppose to be the most intrinsically heavenly element in the vision. It is certainly the case with *the spectacle at the revelation on Sinai*, which, moreover, unmistakably furnishes the key-note here, that the law was given in fire and cloud, but not less through the mediation of angels (Deut. xxxiii. 2; Heb. ii. 2; Acts vii.

[1] To which Vitringa (*Observ. s.* iv. 1) traces back the vision of Ezekiel.

53, 38; Gal. iii. 19). Hengstenberg speaks strikingly of ch. i. as "the great panorama of the universe;" and there, certainly, the reference indicated could not be wanting. If the "spirit" (ver. 12) determines the first vital operation of the chajoth, their motion, and if (vers. 20, 21) it is also the determining element for the motion of the wheels, then the (as one may express it) more spiritual motion of the whole, but especially of the chajoth, viz. "the noise of their wings" (ver. 24), is determined negatively, *i.e.* is brought to silence, to rest, by the voice from above (ver. 25); so that with this voice from the throne, and therefore with Him who is upon it (ver. 26 sqq.), each and all are united, and express themselves as well as move as He pleases (ver. 24), or rest according to His intimation. In this way the God of hosts, whom Hengstenberg only co-ordinates with Him who is enthroned upon the chajoth, is rather at the same time declared to be this latter, or the chajoth seem in such manner to be embraced in the idea of the heavenly hosts. To see in the wheels, then, "the powers of nature," is certainly not so natural as to abide by the view of Hitzig, who appeals in support of it to Dan. vii. 9. Keil also must after all admit the idea of a throne-*chariot*. A throne which is to move upon the earth can hardly be conceived of without wheels. It is not so much, however, "to show the possibility and the ease with which the throne moves to all the four quarters of the world," as rather to express *the motion in the most living* manner and expressly *for the earth*, specially *in the first place with a view to Jerusalem*, corresponding to the historical circumstances: it is for this reason that we have to do with wheels. The eyes in the wheels are parallel with the faces in the chajoth, and both are to be understood in connection with the "spirit" (רוּחַ), and perhaps also not without reference to "the noise of the wings" (2 Chron. xvi. 9). *The sovereignty of Him who rules in heaven*, whom all serve as to Him all live, *as it is ready from heaven to manifest itself livingly upon earth*, is represented at the close as being the sovereignty "*as of a man*," which, when we take into account *the rainbow* of ver. 28 (notwithstanding the preponderating judicial character of the whole), allows of the coming forth full of promise—*as the ultimate goal*, as the victory *of righteousness—of the kindness and love of God toward man* (Tit. iii. 4), *in grace and mercy toward Israel, and for the salvation of the world*, so that the vision would have its fulfilment *in Christ* (comp. John xii. 41 with Isa. vi.), Rev. iv.

After this interpretation of the symbolism of the vision as a whole, its *meaning for the prophetic mission of Ezekiel* (comp. the introductory remarks to ch. i.-iii.) must be clear thus far, that above all the prophet will have to announce *judgment*, not merely in the first place *upon Jerusalem*, but farther *upon the heathen also*. To this the *fire*-characteristic points, which remains with the vision from beginning to end, and behind which whatever promise of mercy is in it steps into the background for the time, so that the prophet *falls down* under the impression received (ver. 28). For a so-called "consecration as a prophet," this certainly would be too special in its tenor. For this one would be under the necessity of extracting, and that at the same time under a misapprehension "of the dependence of our theophany on that manifestation of God at Sinai," as Keil does, "in a more general way the symbols of that righteousness, holiness, and grace which God manifests in the upholding, governing, and perfecting of His kingdom." On the other hand, *by means of the fire-character of judgment*, which expressed its special tendency, this vision was *an introduction of Ezekiel forthwith into his sphere of labour*. Nothing else had the prophet at first to testify to the exiles, for their obstinacy with all its ungodly hopes was still founded on the apparent continuance of Jerusalem. The more *such high ecstasy*—a throwing inwards or spiritualizing, which has its sphere on the boundary of corporeal life (ver. 28), as Oehler brings out prominently—along with the *mission* of Ezekiel *attested his call as a prophet*, the less need was there of an official consecration for him; his mission under such a vision was so in the highest degree, or at least made a call, calling, consecration to the prophetic office be presupposed in a decided manner in his case, as the Talmudists, even in reference to הָיֹה הָיָה in ver. 3 (in the interest certainly of the prophecy, as they assert, being attached to the ark), show therefrom, that Ezekiel was already before a prophet in the holy land. The vision does not by any means consecrate him as a prophet; but it certainly does transfer him to those banished to Tel-Abib (ch. iii. 12 sqq.); it *thus realizes itself as a mission*. And pervading as it does the whole book, it likewise stamps and illustrates the prophetic activity of Ezekiel, ch. iii. 23, viii. 4, xliii. 2. The vision is, however, not merely as regards its fire-character, a programme for our prophet, but its much *more essential* contents informed him that he would have to represent *the glory of Jehovah*. Judgment in the first place, from the very beginning, however, not without mercy, but rather a glorification of the living God in His people to be accomplished in a glory of vital power, on the basis of creation, and thus from the outset with a view to the whole earth.[1] The meaning of the chajoth in the vision, whence their designation (purposely not called cherubim in ch. i.), and their so-varied form, and the accompaniment of spirit-moved wheels full of eyes are explained, cannot be settled by pointing to the Lord's dwelling among His people in the holy of holies of the temple, nor explained by the "œcumenical character of the new economy of salvation, for the setting up of which the Lord shall appear upon earth" (which is said to be represented in the fourfold figure of the cherubs and wheels); nor even can it be expressed characteristically enough with Keil in this way, that "the moving of the throne to all quarters of the world is made conspicuous, not merely in order to indicate the spread of the kingdom of God over the whole earth, but in order to reveal the Lord and King, whose power stretches over the whole world," etc. (p. 28). *The prophecy of glory is the characteristic of Ezekiel, whereby he stands distinguished from all prophets.* With its destination for *the exile*,—this too must be added in reference to the *meaning of the following vision for the prophetic mission of Ezekiel*,—harmonizes the making *God*

[1] At the same time, perhaps with the hint of a creation in the future, a creative renewal.

prominent, on the ground of the manifold fulness of life in His creation, *as Himself the Living One* in ruling, reigning, as well as all-filling uniqueness of life and glory. And so He must break forth in judgment on Jerusalem, where He is degraded to a lifeless, powerless, and therefore no longer believed in idol, side by side with other false gods. And as such He must manifest Himself to the heathen world, into whose power His people have been already, will be completely, given. The *living* God, and as such glorious, has, however, no pleasure in the death of the wicked, of him that dieth, as Ezekiel repeatedly testifies to the exiles; rather is the quickening of Israel to new life (ch. xxxvii.), the stream of life (ch. xlvii.), His significant promise. As *I live*, why will *ye die*, O house of Israel? may be pronounced in this connection to be the prophetic voice of Ezekiel in the exile.

If we compare *other similar visions* in the Old Testament, in order to throw more light on the characteristic of Ezekiel's, the Talmudists have identified that of Isaiah in ch. vi. with that of Ezekiel, the only difference being as if a townsman and a countryman were to behold a king. But apart from the circumstance (introductory remarks to ch. i.–iii.), that in the case of Isaiah it is after the self-legitimation in actual fact by means of the preceding discourses, which are designated as חָזוֹן (ch. i. 1), הַדָּבָר אֲשֶׁר חָזָה (ch. ii. 1), and which thus presuppose his consecration as a prophet, and not till ch. vi. that the divine confirmation and introduction of the judicial mission of the prophet is related, so characteristically winding up what goes before as well as introducing what follows, while in the case of Ezekiel the vision opens his book; the theme with Isaiah is the thrice-*Holy* One over against the *sin* which has become ripe for the judgment of hardening, whereas, on the other hand, Ezekiel sees the *glory* of Jehovah in the midst of the *misery* of the exile. For Him who visibly appears as above the world, there is something becoming in the "holy, holy, holy" (comp. on the other hand, Ezek. iii. 12), in holiness He manifests Himself in the heavens; and the circumstance that His glory fills the whole earth (ver. 3), shows how His intramundane manifestation (Introd. § 10), in accordance with His heavenly holiness, must take shape in righteousness upon the earth. In accordance therewith, in accordance with the character of holiness belonging to Isaiah's vision, it is also *seraphim* that hover around the throne, that call one to another the "holy," etc., and one of whom must hallow the prophet, who declares himself personally, and as a member of the community, unclean. How different what is said in Ezekiel as to the *chajoth!* And, accordingly, Ezekiel becomes like a *dead man*, whereas Isaiah became conscious to himself of being a *sinner*. As regards the visions of the Mosaic period, which are likewise appearances in glory, Exod. xxiv. 17 resembles the vision of Ezekiel in its pervading fire-character, and ver. 10 of the same chapter resembles the closing picture in Ezek. i. 26; but in Moses' vision (Exod. xxxiii., xxxiv.) the glory of Jehovah is spoken of as "all His goodness" (כל טובי. Comp. ch. xxxiii. 19 with xxxiii. 22, 23), with which corresponds also the revelation in word (ch. xxxiii. 19, xxxiv. 6, 7) in its main import. The preponderance of revelation *in word* and of the fulness of God's *love* is in this case the distinguishing element on the one hand from Ezekiel's vision, and on the other from that of Isaiah. Lastly, the vision of Daniel in ch. vii. is closely related to that of Isaiah by means of the *fulness of majesty* of the divine *holiness* in ver. 9, just as it in so far coincides with Ezekiel's, when at ver. 12 mention is made of "respite *of life* for a season and time," while to the Son of man in ver. 14 is given an "*everlasting dominion*." The four beasts out of the sea (ver. 3) present themselves, on the contrary, as the antithesis to the four chajoth. (Comp. in the New Testament, besides Rev. at the passage already quoted, Matt. xvii. 5; 2 Pet. i. 17.)

The *different interpretations* of the following vision, from the multitude of persons and views, and because many of the differences are in matters of subordinate importance, can be brought forward in passing survey merely. Vitringa (in the work already quoted, IV. ch. ii. 2) makes Abarbanel divide the interpretation of the *Jewish* teachers into three classes: (1.) The *traditional* interpretation of the *ancient* school, viz. *angels*, in which mention is made of the four classes of the heavenly hosts, as leaders of which Michael, Gabriel, Uriel, Raphael are named, and the wheels also, by comparison with Dan. vii. 10, are held to be *spiritual beings* of higher or lower rank than the chajoth. (2.) The *philosophizing* interpretation *e.g.* of Maimonides, who brought in the Aristotelian physics. (3.) The *historical* interpretation (Kimchi), viz. of the four *world-monarchies*, Babylon, Persia, Greece, and Rome, which are said to be meant by the wheels, while the chajoth are the *heavenly spirits of these kingdoms*. The *Christian* expositors held fast in general the idea of Divine *Providence*, as it manifests itself either in nature or in the kingdom of grace. The former is, for example, the opinion of Calvin even, of a Lapide, of Bochart: the chajoth are to them heavenly spirits, the wheels, the great movements in the world and the church in accordance with God's decrees. The interpretation of the kingdom of grace more specially is the almost universal one in the ancient Church, according to which the chajoth are the *four evangelists*. LUTHER: "The vision of Ezekiel is nothing else but a revelation of the kingdom of Christ here upon earth in all the four quarters of the whole world." So also Osiander, Cocceius. If not the evangelists, then the apostles or certain things predicated of Christ (ARND.: Incarnation, Sacrifice, Resurrection, Ascension) are dragged in. The wheels, according to some, are meant to symbolize the Church, and that in her apostles, prophets, evangelists, and pastors; while, according to others, the chajoth represent the living Church of the New Testament, and the wheels the holy angels. (Origen found the four human passions represented. Some also have wished to find the four ensigns of the camp of Israel therein. According to others, Nebuchadnezzar himself; the king as a man, flew like an eagle, imposed the yoke of an ox, and became cruel like the lion! and more of the like sort. Comp. Jerome.) The *æsthetico-theologizing* interpretation of Umbreit is as follows: "The life-creating Spirit brings the Almighty, but He is not in the storm, nor in the cloud,—it is only His chariot-throne,—

nor in the fire—that is only the power of the natural life;—but neither is He the light, not even the gleam (eye) of the metal in its look of greatest splendour is the eye of God. Even the four living creatures, the old well-known Mosaic pictures of the cherubim over the ark of the covenant, are not Himself, but the natural life of the creatures in its endlessly divided multiplicity and unity, as well as in its restlessly moving power, reaching in the likeness of man the phenomenon of highest beauty. The destination of the four living creatures is shown by the wheels, the elements, which the free, formative principle of the divine Spirit appropriates to itself in the creation of the creatures; we see into the soul of nature. The third part of the vision lifts us up to heaven: My thoughts are not your thoughts, etc. (Isa. lv. 8, 9). The firmament, even with its crystal splendour, does not give us the likeness of God. It is the fourth part of the prophetic vision that first lets us see the glory of the Eternal King; we sink down with the prophet before this spectacle, but man bears God's image, and the Word was made flesh, full of grace and truth, surrounded with the light of the rainbow of grace."

Vers. 4–14.—*The Fire-Cloud* (ver. 4) *and the Fire-Picture of the Four Living Creatures* (vers. 5–14).

The Fire-Cloud, ver. 4. That which is set in motion in what presents itself to the prophet in vision (**and I saw**), and must rouse his attention as well as ours (**and, behold**), is described in the outset by means of the moving cause, viz. רוח סערה, which, by reason of the repeatedly emphasized רוח in what follows, is by no means = סערה (Isa. xxix. 6). רוּחַ, in place of רֶוַח, is properly "a drawing together," in manifold applications, but always with the idea of *life* in the background, figuratively or in actual fact, which cannot be without significance for the already mentioned fundamental idea of the vision as a keynote,—a keynote which we have pointed out in Ezekiel generally. We might almost translate: *spirit* of storm. (UMBREIT: "The storm announces the approach of the life-producing Spirit, who moved creatively upon the waters, poured His breath into the creatures, and who ever renews the face of the earth" (Ps. civ. 30). But comp. Jer. xxiii. 19. Swiftly and violently, irresistibly devastating! MALDONATUS: "Such were the Chaldeans, and harsh besides, cruel, heartless, unfeeling people.") סערה, of the violent impulse, the dashing, roaring along; in Jon. i. 11 סער, of the raging violence of the sea when roused by the storm. (**And I saw,** viz. visions of God; **and, behold,** this was specially the vision which I saw.) מן־הצפון—the article, because of this quarter of the heavens being universally known and standing alone, and perhaps also because to his circle of hearers and readers under the existing historical circumstances the quarter could not be a matter of question, but was determined by these. At all events, although צָפוֹן from a verb "to hold back," "to conceal," "to hide" (צָפַן, Ezek. vii. 22), might be conjectured to be something *mysterious*, yet "the idea of the hill of the gods" is not rendered probable by anything here; and Hitzig is under the necessity of paving the way for it in our passage by saying: "As the course of the sun makes the south appear inclined downwards, the north, it is conjectured (!!), lies higher, rises up to heaven with its high mountain chains, Lebanon, Caucasus, etc." A "*sacred* quarter of the heavens in the north" (EWALD) is not to be seen in the Bible. Nor are we necessitated to think of the north, as the land of *gold* of many of the nations of antiquity, by the mere comparison כעין החשמל; and Zech. vi. 1 sqq. (HERDER, UMBREIT) belongs still less to this category, since in that passage there is just as much mention of south as of north, and the abode of God is in some quite different place; comp. ver. 5 with ver. 1. Rather is the fundamental idea of what is *concealed* justified by the *darkness* which appears to the senses, alike by reason of the beclouding of the northern heavens, in contrast with the south, which is richer in light and poorer in rain, and also in respect of distance, of remoteness. This natural view of the north is, as is well known, the common one with the poets; but the mediating idea of darkness is also here, where a "great cloud" stands next at least for the outer part of the symbol, without our being compelled on that account to think of the dark holy of holies with the ark of the covenant and the cherubim, and that in a similar way the theophany presents itself here to our prophet; but perhaps for the meaning, the inner sense, we may, with Kliefoth, compare ch. viii. 1 sqq., x. 19, xi. 23, xliii. 2, as showing that God comes from the north when He comes to judgment, and, on the other hand, that He comes from the east for salvation and grace; only we must not overlook as the ultimate reason for this the *historical situation* of Israel, as well as of the prophet and the vision, and consequently it is to be explained with BUNSEN: "an allusion to *the Chaldeans coming from the north against Jerusalem*, Jer. i. 14; comp. Ezek. xxvi. 7." And therefore the prophet does not need to have been transported in spirit to Jerusalem (HÄVERNICK), "into the temple, where one naturally expects the priest," for the prophets, as Hävernick even does not deny, assign to the north the Assyrians and Babylonians, that is, "the region pregnant with destiny" (HENGSTENBERG); from Syria usually the inroad of the Asiatic world-powers was made, because the east side of the holy land was protected by means of the great trackless Arabia Deserta. We shall also certainly have to take into account the relation of Ezekiel to Jeremiah (comp. Introd. § 4), and along with that the parallel of the seething pot, Jer. i. 13, iv. 6, vi. 1. ("Against the north was the coalition of Jer. xxvii., Ezek. xxv. sqq. directed, which gave occasion for Ezekiel making his appearance. The storm from the north drives all the sanguine hopes which were founded on this coalition like withered leaves before it."—HENGSTENBERG.) The moving cause manifests its working by means of the phenomenon of a **great cloud** (HITZIG: "a thunder cloud;" the *chariot* of God afterwards appearing more prominently), with its far-reaching and compact bulk covering the heavens; but not so much a cloud of a veiling character, as a cloud to serve as a visible sign of the impending *judgment*, Nah. i. 3; Joel ii. 2;

Ps. xcvii. 2, xviii. 10 sqq. GROTIUS: "The great host of the Chaldeans, Jer. iv. 13; comp. also Ezek. xxxviii. 9."—We are not, with a Lapide, to think of rain, hail, and still less of the arrows of the Chaldeans. The divine judicial character of the cloud is indicated by the well-known metaphor of *fire* (Deut. iv. 24, xxxii. 22), here אש מתלקחת—Exod. ix. 24 (the parallel with Egypt is not unimportant): *catching itself mutually* (Hithp.), *i.e.* not merely; formed into a ball, a lump of fire, but at the same time flashing through and through itself, the flashes seizing one another, and as it were kindling themselves on one another. (POLANUS: "The fire which consumed the city was in itself, its own sins." J. FR. STARCK thinks of the camp-fire, and even of the sacred fire which the Chaldeans carried before them!) This fire in the cloud, because *unceasingly*, "livingly,"[1] as Ewald expresses it, "moving hither and thither in it," is the abiding characteristic kernel of the cloud. Comp. ver. 13 sqq. Hence, also, **brightness round about it.** לוֹ refers to ענן, because אשׁ, although not without exception, is as a rule feminine. The cloud is the subject at present under discussion; and as its size determines the form, so the fire determines its substance, which, while it makes the cloud a fire-cloud, imparts to it also brightness round about. But with this "brightness round about it," the *light*, and consequently the well-founded hope of love, grace, mercy, comes to its rights over the alarm-producing fire, cloud, and storm. The illusions of the transgressors and of a dead faith must not be destroyed to the injury of the believers. It is not yet indeed the "cheerful" brightness, as in ver. 28, for it proceeds immediately from the fire, but this fire is an abiding, essential one; and the sun pierces through the stormy element of his immediate mode of manifestation, and in its deepest ground the light is God, who is love. Hitzig and Hengstenberg also refer לוֹ to the whole. Why? Storm and brightness do not tally; the fire has brightness of itself (ver. 13); thus, in fact, the cloud only remains. According to Hengstenberg, we have certainly to think of a brightness contrasted with the fire (!). The older expositors keep firmly and exclusively by the terrible majesty and glory of the presence of God. In quite an opposite direction, UMBREIT: "The light which pours forth the joy of existence on every side; for in the brightness of light life steps forth from its dark fire-ground into manifestation, and unfolds itself in its immeasurable fulness; God said at first: Let there be light." מתוכה, as מתוך־האשׁ afterwards shows, refers to אשׁ, which is thereby at the same time proved to be feminine. But מתוך־ is not a mere resumption of מתוכה, which, especially as the latter occurs again in ver. 5, would certainly be too pleonastic. The *contents* of the cloud, *by way of preparation for what follows*, present themselves to the seer in such a form that he uses the comparison as to the effect of the internal fire upon him—כעין החשמל. ("*To look like*—because the matter in hand is not realities, but only the imperfect *forms* of realities."—HENGSTENBERG.) הַחַשְׁמַל only here, חַשְׁמַל in ver. 27, החשמלה in viii. 2 with ה paragogic, a word which has been the subject of much comment, perhaps formed by Ezekiel himself (Introd. § 7). [According to Bochart (*Hieroz.* iii.), it is to be looked upon as a compound of חשׁ = Aramaic נחשׁ = נְחֹשֶׁת, "brass," and a Chaldaic word (questionable, however) מַלְלָא, "gold;" while, according to Gesenius, with more certainty (?) it is to be regarded as = נְחֹשֶׁת קָלָל in ver. 7 (HITZIG: this is the Hebrew translation of the word), and a compound of נָחשׁ with נ thrown off and the syllable מַל "smooth" = "shining;" and thus in the former case it would mean "gold-brass," in the latter, "shining brass." Hävernick and Maurer have recourse to the Syriac, in order to get in this way "a metallic product wrought in the fire, and therefore (?) emitting sparks," which does not at all suit the context here. E. Meier holds it to be a (perhaps dialectic) expansion of כֶּתֶם: חַשְׁמַל = חַתְמַל = כַּתְמַל, "pure, solid gold." Fürst, in the Concordance, explains it as from חָשַׁם, like כָּתַם, "brightness," with the termination *al* affixed: "bright metal;" Keil, according to the analogy of כַּרְמֶל and כֶּרֶם, as from חשם, "probably *to glow*, with ל affixed: glowing brass." That חָשַׁם "probably" means "to glow," is a statement that goes for nothing, and just as unproved is the derivation of the meaning "to be bright," from כָּתַם, although the interchange of שׁ and ת, and of ח and כ, would have nothing surprising in it, for the root כתם, which occurs as a verb only once in the Niphal in Jer. ii. 22, might there perhaps mean: to be engraved, much the same as: to be recorded, were not this meaning generalized, as Hupfeld (on Ps. xvi. 1) convincingly shows, from the more correct one: to be soiled, stained, which is also proved by the old translations, and which, besides, suits best the antithesis in Jer. ii., and if it did not need to support itself on the similarity of the fundamental idea of כתם and כתב (to write). Because כֶּתֶם is gold, to assume for כָּתַם, and thus for חָשַׁם, a meaning: to be bright, or: to be red-hot, is mere arbitrariness, inasmuch as, if the fundamental meaning: to conceal, to keep safe as a jewel or secret, is incapable of proof from the Arabic, a meaning synonymous to the Hebrew and Aramaic one (to be soiled), viz. to be dark-coloured, lies before us in Arabic, just as it alone corresponds to the usual designation of gold in all languages as the yellow, the dark metal, in contrast with the white silver. Besides, כתם properly signifies: to hold back, which is traced back to a fundamental idea like: to divide, to separate, so that כֶּתֶם, "gold," might perhaps mean what is separated, as being what is purified, pure, held back. For חשם Meier seeks to point as a kindred meaning to the fundamental idea: to be firm, strong (hence in Arabic: to be fat,

[1] "A shifting motion, a glowing life," but not "the picture of the co-operating powers of creative life, shining in the gold of the earth, burning in the colours, and boiling in the blood," as Umbreit raves.

thick, and hard), so that חשמל might originally have designated: what is hard, firm, hence: brass, solid metal in general; while it would then have been transferred more definitely to a peculiarly bright brass.] To an impression of *peculiar brightness* the context of our passage points with indisputable necessity; nor must this brightness be conceived of apart from the fire, since it proceeds **out of the midst of it,** and כעין ה־ has the more exact definition מתוך האש side by side with it. The question may, however, be asked, whether what is glaringly bright and destructive is to be indicated thereby, or not rather a *glory* of look that is *full of life*, which is favoured not merely by the immediately appearing kernel of fire and the picture of the "chajoth," but also by the ingenious remark of Keil, that in all the three passages חשמל has its reference to Him who is enthroned above. We shall thus be compelled to abide by the view hinted at above on the "brightness round about it," inasmuch as in the whole vision the "brightness" appears not indeed separated from the fire, but yet distinct from it, although not contrasted with it. [The Syriac translator has simply omitted the difficult word in question here, but at ver. 27 and ch. viii. 2 he has given a conjectural interpretation: "divine look." The Chaldee Paraphrase keeps it as it stands. The Sept. and Vulg. translate it by ἤλεκτρον, *electrum*, which must not be confounded with "amber" (*sucinum*). Neither can the name be given to this latter from ἤλεκτρον, nor (as Buttmann, *Mythologus* II., will have it) can the converse be the case, for the colour of amber is of too mild a brightness for it, the comparison of the same with the precious metals may rest on much else, and the meaning: amber, leads to a derivation from ἕλκειν, ἑλκηστρον, ἕλκτρον (the drawer, draw-stone), while ἤλεκτρον is derived from ἠλέκτωρ (the beaming sun, ἥλιος, Empedocles so named the element of fire), or at least a more fiery brightness than that of amber was the synonym. The brightness of amber does not certainly correspond sufficiently to the comparison in our verse, where a metal, not precious stones of any kind, is thought of; nor does the transparency of its brightness suffice here. Now the ἤλεκτρον, everywhere mentioned along with gold and silver, was, according to the testimonies of the ancients (see Pape, *Greek Lexicon*), a natural metallic mixture of three or four parts of gold and one part of silver, which was also artificially prepared. (According to Oken, the "electrum" of the Mountain of Serpents in Siberia is gold, with an alloy of 36 per cent. of silver.) Hitzig, Bleek (*Vorles. über die Apokalypse*), and others mention the peculiar χαλκολίβανον (Rev. i. 15, ii. 18), which is said to be compounded of the Greek χαλκός and the Hebrew לָבָן (= white-shining brass), but which might also mean "brass from Lebanon" (EBRARD, PESCHITO, ETHIOPIC VERS.). The Talmudists explain חשמל as from חש, "quickness," and מל, "rest" (or "speaking" and "silence"). It passed also for the name of an angel with the Rabbins, and in fact for that of Ezekiel's teacher. (See Leigh, *Crit. S.* p. 174.) It has even been read backwards: למשח, and **understood of the Messiah (Calov. *Bib. Ill.*),** who united the divine and human natures in Himself (Maldonatus, Pradus). J. F. Starck compares also the pillar of cloud and fire (Exod. iii. 2), specially for the exiles!]. Usage always employs עין only of things, never of persons. "*As the look* of chasmal" means, moreover, not merely: as the aspect thereof, as it looks, but this as well: as it, so to speak, looks, looks on us. In the most poetic way, Umbreit, at all events, understands כעין ה־: "the eye of metal, as the same concentrates itself when melting in a look of the greatest brightness (the so-called silver look!); perhaps it was a technical expression of the smelters, possibly compounded of נחש and מלא: fulness of brass, when the brass appears in the fulness of its brightness." J. D. Michaelis translates: "a great cloud, under which the lightnings flashed through one another, and gilded its edge by the reflection (an aurora round about it), but in the middle it looked like glowing metal in the midst of the fire."

The Fire-Picture of the Four Living Creatures (vers. 5–14).

Ver. 5. Not only what the prophet sees, but even his seeing itself is something progressive. It is by no means as if Ezekiel had first sketched the outlines, and were now depicting the interior also, for he has reproduced for us in ver. 4 alike inside and outside what was first seen, but his seeing itself grows more penetrating, and what looked upon him out of the midst of the fire (hence the repetition ומתוכה), like chasmal looking out of the fire, shapes itself in the progressive advance of the vision to דמות. Derived as it is from דמה, and cognate with the Sanscrit *sama* (*similis*), דמות is not so much: form, as: **likeness,** *similitude*, a substantival "like as," and is used of what is living, but also of what is without life (ver. 26).—With respect to the four חיות (not "beasts," as Luther makes them, following the Vulg.), see what is said in the introductory remarks to vers. 4–28. (According to Hofmann, Ezekiel was in this way "to become aware that what he saw was not a thing, but a life. The intention was to represent to the prophet what there is about the presence of Jehovah: the judgment on His unholy people announced itself therein. Creature life, into which the unbroken fulness of the being of God pours itself, in order therein to become a manifoldness of power, serves the eternal God for the purpose of making Himself present to His world.") Formerly: *the judgment of God rushing on*, now: how not merely the power of the Chaldeans, against which one hoped at Jerusalem to accomplish everything with human leagues (Introd. § 4, 2) and one's own prudence, but *the whole creation in the entire universe*, heaven and earth, *is ready to execute this judgment of the living God!* This threatening character the vision obtained from its connection with ver. 4, and from the circumstance that the *chajoth* came forth out of the fire (HENGSTENBERG). But in this way, at the same time, its symbolical character is manifest: life out of fire!—מַרְאֶה (ver. 1) is "vision," *what* is seen (חָזוֹן); מַרְאֶה: *how* it is seen, hence: "appearance." As to the plural form מראיהן here and in ver. 13, and with מַעֲשֵׂיהֶם in ver. 16, comp. Ewald, *Ausf. Lehrb.* § 256; Gesenius, *Gram.* § 91. 9.—What first struck the prophet as being prominent in the vision, was "the likeness of a *man*." (לְהֵנָּה with the full tone.) Likeness to man, where God has made man like God, is just the fulness of the times, Gal. iv. 4; Phil. ii. 7, 8. The angels also assume the ways of man; for man is a microcosm. "All forms of the creature reach in his person a phenomenon of the highest beauty" (UMBREIT). At all events, man stands among the living creatures of the earthly world in the first, as in the highest place. In this way, first of all, the impression *in general* is stated, as Ezekiel received it from the four *chajoth*. What special feature in them produced this impression in his case, will become clear in the further progress of his description. And just because it will be expressly stated, a limit is drawn against arbitrariness in the application of man's corporeal form as a rule.

Ver. 6. Just as, on the one hand, *man, i.e.* (*inwardly* considered)-what is *spiritual*, what has *spiritual* life, characterizes the vision, so, on the other hand, in a *more outward* respect it is significantly defined by its *fourfold* character. Not only are there "four *chajoth*" in all (ver. 5), but "four faces" (ver. 10) are found "in each, and four wings" (vers. 8, 9, 11, 23; comp. ch. x. 8) likewise "in each of them." If the number 3, as the designation of the true, highest, most perfect being, is the number of God, then must the number 4 represent the conditional, dependent being, which has proceeded from the true being, and be the number of the *world*, as the *sum* of all created things. Time and space, the two most general forms of the universe, bear the number 4 in themselves, etc. (According to Bähr, comp. *Symb.* i. p. 156 sqq.)—להם masculine form, which Hengstenberg here, as in what follows, explains from the masculine name cherubim standing in the background, which, however, here lies as yet too far off. The more probable supposition, as a Lapide has already shown, is the collective אָדָם masc., this being the impression in general of the *chajoth*. As happens so frequently in looking at the sense, the reference to the grammatical form is let go—פָּנִים and also the dual כְּנָפַיִם stand as plurals. Some have incorrectly translated פנים: form, guise, so that each had only *one*, and that a human face and head, but had besides a fourfold figure, or expression of countenance, or head-ornament. No less incorrectly, some have assigned to every face 4 wings, and thus to each of the 4 *chajoth* 16, which would give a sum total of 64 wings. The Chaldee paraphrast understands just as many faces, and 256 wings in all.

Ver. 7. Now that we have passed from the faces to the wings, in going downwards their *legs* (masc. suff.) come into consideration, not merely in the sense of the lower part only, the foot proper, which is distinguished as כַּף רֶ־. ורגליהם is either conceived of distributively (HITZIG): and each of their legs was רגל ישרה, without bending inwards of the knee, rising straight up (comp. ver. 23), or the dual is to be understood thus: as respects their 2 legs, it was (generically, without reference to the number, so KEIL) a leg standing erect. ישר is, what is firm, "does not need to bend, to turn" (EWALD), without joints (MAIMONIDES), without front and back, smooth and symmetrical (PHILIPPSON): with which also the calf's foot agrees. Thus there is nothing of likeness to man in this connection, except the upright carriage in general, which results therefrom, but is not made prominent here. On the contrary, for the **sole of the foot,** even in special contrast to what is human, the comparison is taken from the beast, from the *calf, i.e.* the foot proper stood firmly, symmetrically rounded off (עָגֹל), while the human foot is extended lengthwise. (Hitzig makes the circumstance that "they present in no direction a decided front," as also the "want of distinction" in the legs, parallel with the *chajoth* "facing towards the four quarters of heaven." Similarly Hävernick before him: "These feet fulfil the object of being able to move in all directions, without turning round (ver. 9); they symbolize the idea of freedom of motion." The *human* element of the vision, which in general is prominent, will be strengthened, next to the *upright carriage*, by the *legs* also being *two* in number, which is not indeed stated, but is certainly to be understood. This human element is represented, because of the bestial element as well as in spite of it, by the masc. suffix. As the the lion also—which, according to Bähr, is to come into consideration because of his strength, power, and fearful character—is not mentioned in the detail, the substitution of the calf for the bull (ver. 10) may possibly here set the latter also aside, so far as regards the power of generation, just as Hengstenberg takes into consideration "only the representation of cattle, to ward off all heterogeneous ideas." "Although each has a lion's face, yet none has a lion's feet or claws for tearing in pieces, nor those of the eagle, not even the foot of a man."—COCC.)—ונצצים masc. is meant, according to Hitzig, also to refer to the cherubim, yet Hengstenberg (because of Rev. i. 15) admits that "the reference, in point of fact, is specially to the feet," and as Gesenius maintains that רגל is masc., although "rarely," the explanation of Keil is at all events more probable: and *the legs sparkled*, etc. Hengstenberg's limitation to the "sole of the foot:" "they were (there, on the sole of the foot) sparkling," is not forced, although it would apply to the legs also. PHILIPPSON: shining like a brazen hoof. (Ewald takes נצצים as "feathers," as already the Sept., which omits what is said of the sole of the foot, but instead makes the feet "feathered.")—נחשת, **brass,** is also in Dan. x. 6 masc.; GESENIUS: χαλκός, copper. קָלָל, GESENIUS: shining; BOCHART: polished, burnished; HENGSTENBERG (with a reference to Rev. i. 15), "properly: light [in weight]; but because what is light [in colour] is represented as lighter [in weight] than what is dark, just as what is sharp is represented as lighter than what is blunt, equivalent to: glowing, light brass." Hitzig grants the possibility of a derivation of "light" [in colour] from "to be light" [in weight], but asserts that קלל is manifestly a substantive in the genitive, possibly from קלה (to burn), meaning the red-hot or smelting furnace, akin to עֲלִיל, a crucible. "The sending forth of sparks refers to the special mission in hand, which is one of wrath" (HENGSTENBERG). But the comparison with the effect of *light brass* attributes to them (HÄVERNICK), at the same time, something glorious, according to UMBREIT, "imperishable freshness." (?)—If the faces in general serve to express the quality in view, then, from the fact of there being four of them, this quality is expressly shown to have its sphere *in the world;* and the four wings in general portray the prompt, rapid dexterity towards the respective sides. (UMBREIT: "The living motion and the unceasing vibration of creaturely existence.") In addition, there is the firmness, the steadiness of the carriage, the sure and certain tread (*βοείῳ ποδί*). UMBREIT: "The forcibly-pressed sole of the ox." A mere symbol of fitness for service, viz. *as regards God,* although of "any kind of rendering of service (as messengers or ambassadors of God) for men" nothing is said (HÄV.). It is *the creation glorifying the living God in its ever ready power and fulness of life.*

Ver. 8. For וידו the Qeri reads וִידֵי. Hengstenberg, on the other hand, upholds (comp. ch. x. 8) the singular ידו, either: "his man's hand," or: "his hand, that of a man," because of the ideal comprehension of the quaternity in the unity of the cherub. Hitzig likewise conjectures the singular; the suffix, according to him, presupposes (ch. x. 3, iii. 21) the genitive אדם. Ewald accepts the Qeri: "and man's hands," as also Keil, who declares ו to be an old mistake of the transcriber for י. Häv., Maurer, and before them Kimchi, explain the concise form of the Kethibh by understanding an ellipse, punctuating וְיָדָו, and taking the suffix distributively, thus: and his (each one of the four's) hands were hands of a man (יְדֵי אָדָם). KEIL: "The wings sat accordingly on the shoulders, from which the hands proceeded." Hence four wings, and are there not also four *hands?* and this also because of the four sides? The designation as *man's* hands determines nothing as to their number. Comp. on ver. 9. UMBREIT: "By means of the man's hands the mention of the bestial appearance is meant to be weakened.". With the "hands" the description will ascend to the "faces;" for just as on occasion of the hands, the "wings," as we saw, were very suitably mentioned "on their four sides," so, because the "four sides" are formed by means of the four faces on each of the *chajoth,* mention may be made of the "faces" as well as of the "wings:" **and they four had their faces and their wings** (רבע, as is known, from ארבע, "four," signifies the fourth part, or here: one side of four (ver. 17). The emphasizing of the number *four* down to the minutest detail is to be noted). Häv. connects the last words with vers. 9 and 10: "and as regards their faces and their wings in the four, their wings were," etc. Similarly Ewald. It cannot be objected to this, that here the topic is no longer the faces; even in ver. 9 the contrary is the case, but still more so in ver. 10.

Ver. 9. But the wings which come into consideration here (comp. ver. 11) reach still higher than the faces; a more exact description, therefore, which (as in ver. 6) likewise proceeds from above downwards, will have to begin with these wings. There is a going down (ver. 7), and a going up (ver. 8), and a going down again (ver. 11), just as the eye is accustomed to do in such an act of looking. The joining is (with Kliefoth, Keil) to be conceived of in this way: that the right upper wing of the chajoth was joined to the left upper wing of its neighbour at the tip. HENGSTENBERG: "This pair of wings is stretched upwards, so that the one wing stands over against the other, and is in so far (!) joined to it." One does not see how this can still be called a joining. The connection of the joining of the wings with the going straight forward, which Hitzig holds to be impossible, is pointed out by Ewald in the words: "The wings of all so firmly interlaced with one another, that all moved straight forward with wonderful coherence." Comp. for the joining of the wings, vers. 11 and 23, also Exod. xxv. 20, 1 Kings vi. 27, for the expression חברות אשה אל־אחותה, Exod. xxvi. 3.—יִסַּבּוּ (Niph. of סבב) shows that it is meant to be a joining of all together, not a joining of the wings of each separate chajoth-form just for itself. That they needed not to turn בלכתן (fem. suff.), **when they went** (vers. 12, 17), is of course at once intelligible from the joining of their wings, but is expressed still more strongly (and for this reason the *face* of each is spoken of) by means of איש אל עבר פניו, *i.e.* in whatever direction they went they always followed their face. Similarly with על in Exod. xxv. 37.—The change in the gender of the suffixes in this way in one and the same line, makes one almost think that *the diversity of the life of creation* in *this* respect is to be characterized in the chajoth.

Ver. 10. Now comes the detailed description of the four faces. First, **the face of a man,** which, as being turned toward the prophet, had determined his impression of the vision as a whole (ver. 5). Maimonides understood it even of the other three also, and distinguished in these only an expression corresponding to the animals named. Just as the man's face *in front* is put without this definition, so similarly the eagle's face also is not defined more exactly as being the one *behind.* The definition לארבעתן at the close applies to the man's face also, and besides, this latter is immediately preceded by the general פניהם. Hengst. claims for it the east side, as being the principal side, for the lion on the right the south, for the ox on the left the north. The position of the eagle behind shows (as against Hengst.) a background pointing higher up. Comp. the introductory remarks to vers. 4–28. The right and left of the description may be fixed either with respect to the man's face, or to the quarter of the heavens (יָמִין, south side, just as שְׂמֹאול, north), or to the prophet. As to the *meaning of the faces,*—the part of the body which, as may be understood, is capable of expressing more than any other what is characteristic, and that in the way that is most spirited, most in accordance with the idea in view,—see the introductory remarks to vers. 4–28. BÄHR : The ox (bull), the symbol of the generative, creative power of God ; the lion, the symbol of the royal majesty of the Sovereign and Judge ; the eagle, the symbol of the divine omnipresence and omniscience ; man, the symbol of the absolute spirituality of God, of the divine wisdom. GROTIUS : Man denoting the goodness, the lion the wrath (punitive justice) of God, the eagle His swiftness to do good, the ox His slowness to wrath. BOCHART : The ox the emblem of constancy and firmness ; man, of humanity, gentleness, and φιλανθρωπία ; the lion, of generosity and strength ; the eagle, of vigour, and of the sublimity of a heavenly nature. DE WETTE : The strength, power, wisdom of God, and His nearness. UMBREIT : The reason, sovereignty, creative power, and omnipresence of God. (What becomes of the veto of the second commandment ! ?)

Ver. 11. The description, which might now have done with the "faces," nevertheless repeats them (remaining, as they certainly do, the *principal* subject),—at ver. 8 in moving upwards, now in coming down to the lower parts—along with the **wings: ופניהם וכנפיהם**, which Häv., Klief., Keil rightly refuse to translate : "and (these are) their faces; and their wings were" (HENGST.), since the clause belongs rather to what follows, as already Ewald has taken it, inasmuch as *the faces also* were **separated** (the root-meaning of פָּרַד,—"spread out," because of the reference to the nearer וכנפיהם) "from **above**" (מלמעלה, which likewise gives greater prominence to this reference), *i.e.* were not (à la Janus) on the same head, but *on four heads*, or rather necks. EWALD : "Both faces and wings not hanging down loosely, but stretched upwards." In this way an *act of worship* is depicted in the *heads*, just as a *soaring* is intended to be expressed by means of the *wings*.—With the reference to the wings, by means of which the description goes downwards, there is a return to what has already been said (ver. 9), but it is conceived of more definitely, and joined with new matter. **Every one** (not of the four chajoth, but of what is spoken of in ver. 10, viz. the four faces, inasmuch as the description gives what the prophet saw, who, standing before each of the four faces, always beheld two wings, alike on the right and on the left, joined to one another) had **two joined,** viz. wings : חוברות איש, either belonging to לאיש, or as Keil : איש, an abbreviation for the אשה אל־ found in ver. 9. The meaning is clear, according to ver. 9. Since, then, the joining is expressed only as regards the four pairs of wings (in all) above, which together represent a square, the pairs of wings lower down are to be conceived of *without* such connection, each with its neighbour, which would also have no object. With these pairs of wings the chajoth covered their bodies. גְּוִיָּה, properly belly, denotes the body in this respect. As this is covered, the conjecture readily suggests itself, that it is conceived of neither as feathered nor as covered with hair, hence not like an animal, but likewise after the similitude of a man. BUNSEN : "which served for covering the body, and are to be conceived of as before and behind." UMBREIT : "in order to show their holy fear and reverence." Comp. Isa. vi. 2, where, however, this [*ne videant*] seems to be expressed by the covering of their faces; while the covering of the feet there, corresponding to the covering of the bodies here [*ne videantur*], symbolizes the *profound distance of the creature.*

Ver. 12. The lower part being now quite reached, taking up what has been said in ver. 9, their *going*, their movement is described, but along with the mention of the *moving principle.* Ver. 4 (comp. there) רוח סערה, here הרוח, which in any case does not denote the wind. HITZ. : the instinct, which does not suit the human element of the chajoth ; but also not : the will or the like (UMBREIT : "most unrestricted freedom"), since it is exactly such a movement that is meant to be set aside throughout the whole context. **The spirit** is conceived of manifestly according to its *divine* reference and power of influencing, although not as the Holy Spirit or the Spirit of Christ. Comp. vers. 20, 21. (HENGST. : "The life-breath of God, who dwells in the creature, and leads it according to the laws which He prescribes for it, to the ends which He sets for it.—Num. xvi. 22.") All quarters of the world are facing them, whether they go backward or forward, to the right or to the left. The facility of movement given in this way is—by means of the fastening of the wings outwardly, by means of "the spirit" (absolutely), *i.e.* "the spirit of the living creature" (vers. 20, 21) inwardly—united to the whole.

Ver. 13. The completed description of the chajoth, going back to ver. 5, merely adds what corresponds to the מתוכה of ver. 5 : out of the midst of the fire, their appearance was first of all *in themselves :* **like kindled coals** (from נָחַל, to kindle) **of fire, burning.** Is it primarily as depicting the lightning of the kindled wrath of God (following Ps. xviii. 8)? or is it to be referred specially to the eyes of the chajoth? (GROT. : "after God's long patience, eager for vengeance.")—בערות cannot easily be referred with Bunsen to חיות. The accumulation of synonymous expressions is still more unmistakable than the gradation of the same remarked by Häv. ; it is rather like a movement from the beginning of the fire to its rising up like flames, and to its breaking forth in lightning (Gen. xv. 17). לַפִּיד (λαμπάδες, *lampas*, lamp) is that which sends up light in motion, that which sends forth flame quickly, flickeringly toward us; hence what already resembles lightning. אש may, in accordance with the fiery element of all these comparisons, and where the chajoth themselves come forth from the fire, be looked upon as that to which היא refers. So Keil, Ewald. It can neither refer to דמות, by reason of the meaning, nor to מראה (masc.), for a linguistic reason. Hengst. correctly remarks that the fire appears separated from the living creatures (ver. 4). It forms the power that gives the keynote, just as the spirit is the moving principle. And along with this the **brightness** is emphasized, as in ver. 4 also. Comp. there.—לאש and ומן־האש confirm the reference of היא given above. בָּרָק,

from to break through, to break forth: lightning, denoting the threatening effect outwards. (Hofm. compares Gen. iii. 24.)

Ver. 14. Next we have the appearance of the *movement* of the chajoth. רצוא ושוב, infin. absol. for the finite verb, here with the noun-subject (GESEN. *Heb. Gram.* p. 215, BAGSTER'S edit.). A mere indication of what they did, not a "short description" as well (Ew.). רצוא, from רצא = רוץ, according to Häv.: an Aramaistic form. Their שׁוּב, however, was no נָסַב, their return (*i.e.* going back) no turning. Comp. on vers. 9, 12.—בָּזָק only here, in sound like בָּרָק in ver. 11, akin in meaning also, but not identical with it, Häv., Hengst.: "spark-fire;" Klief., Keil: denoting the zigzag of lightning. It is perhaps meant to be an individualizing of the lightning.

Vers. 15–21.—*The Wonderful Wheels upon the Earth.*

Vers. 4–14, which contain *the first vision* which Ezekiel saw, hang directly suspended between heaven and earth; there is need of connection alike with what is above and with what is below. The fire-cloud, as regards the spirit of the storm which impels it, and out of its midst the fire-picture of the chajoth, as regards the principle which moves them, are certainly governed from a higher region, and are no less certainly destined for the earth. It is, in the first place, this latter destination which is furnished by vers. 15–21.

Ver. 15 introduces the *second* vision in a way similar to that in which ver. 4 introduces the first. But the fact that it is said: **and I saw the living creatures, and, behold, a wheel,** brings into immediate prominence the connection, which what follows will have to bring out in detail and to give the reason for. The wheel shows itself בארץ, which is not to be thought of, with Kliefoth, in the case of the chajoth also, for these, forming as they certainly do the kernel of the cloud, are to be conceived of rather as being above the earth. There is thus for the second vision, *in its look towards the earth* (and the historical scene of events), a repetition of the idea, which was symbolized at the close *by the movement of the chajoth.* The simplest, most natural symbolism of this idea, *i.e.* in reference to earthly affairs, is the *wheel*, appearing as it does as mere motion, which only waits for the moment (comp. ch. x. 13, 2). This is, as regards the idea,[1] the connection of the in no wise "disturbing" החיות with אופן; and in accordance with this linking together of the second and primarily earthly vision with the first, that connection is also localized by means of אצל ה־, not = "neighbourhood" (HITZIG), but: **beside.**—As *one* wheel is spoken of, so also the chajoth in the vision are conceived of together as a unity; hence the singular suffix פניו. So already the Syriac. Nor are sixteen wheels meant to be indicated, with reference to each of the four faces of each of the four chajoth, but four wheels (ver. 16, ch. x. 9), corresponding to the four *front* sides, the human faces of the chajoth. Each being always between two faces of the separate chajoth on the right and on the left, the four wheels formed an outer square round the four chajoth. First of all Ezekiel had to say, although in general merely, where, in what position as regards the chajoth he saw the wheels; the relative position of "wheel" and chajoth took the precedence, not "the nature of an individual wheel,"—which would be the case, according to Häv., Maurer, Klief., if פניו were to be referred to אופן: "according to its fourfold face," equivalent to: "with fourfold face,"—for then we should have here already the wheel within a wheel specially mentioned, which comes after in ver. 16. As to the meaning of the wheels, comp. the introductory remarks to vers. 4–28. How little in this connection the basin-stands of 1 Kings vii. come into consideration, Klief. on Häv. and Keil has pointed out exhaustively (i. p. 91). To refer to "heathen works of art of Babylon," as Häv. does, explains nothing, while the conception of a *throne-chariot* rolling along over the earth gives a vivid unity to what goes before and what follows. It is to misunderstand the characteristic of these visions, this predominance of the ideas over everything, when one brings as an objection to such a conception partly the רָקִיעַ of ver. 22, partly the chariot not being named. Hengst. indicates very correctly the "impression as a whole" as being that of "a kind of vehicle, in which the Lord took the place of the charioteer, the living creature the place of the chariot, the wheels lowermost, as usual in a chariot." Züllig, in his pamphlet *The Cherubim-Chariot* (Heidelb. 1832), fears that "these wheels, standing there detached, might perhaps also some day roll away by themselves, and leave the throne standing," and therefore adopts the supposition, referring to 1 Kings vii. (like Vitringa before him), of a connection with the wheels, in opposition to which Umbreit: "the prophet was in spirit for the spirit, but not for the eye."

Ver. 16. The general is followed by the special. —**Make,** not: the material of which, but: the way in which they were made, added to the **appearance,** because we are dealing here not with what is living—כעין, comp. on ver. 4.—תרשיש, "the chrysolite, which with the ancients undoubtedly had a yellow colour" (BÄHR, 10. 9). "Probably of clear fire" (HITZIG). Perhaps from *Tartessus*, a Phœnician possession in Spain (similarly אוֹפִיר, for gold of Ophir). But whether is it so named because from thence, or on account of its solidity? The probable root, תָּרַשׁ (not רָשַׁשׁ), means, according to the Arabic: to be hard, solid (comp. תְּרִזָה תָּרַז); the word formed by doubling the third radical, as so frequently, means a fortified place, fortress. Spain is, however, rich in precious stones. It is said to be the modern topaz (gold-topaz), which commonly has small four-sided columns, whose surfaces are again divided into two, and which also appears bluish and quite white; according to Hengst. the jasper, which, however, has mostly a beautiful red, and also a brown and green colour. The chrysolite is pistachio-green, beautifully transparent and shining. That **they four had one likeness,** *i.e*

[1] HÄV.: An intensification of the thought of the *power and fulness of life* by means of the wheels, where the form must give way entirely to the essence, to the idea.

that the wheel apparently alike was found with all the four chajoth, explains the plural of the wheels as being four, but also how the same could before be conceived of as one, when a general statement was made.—לְאַרְבַּעְתָּן may also be referred to דְּמוּת; KEIL: "All four had one sort of shape." Comp. ver. 8.—**Appearance and make** are repeated, as it is the latter especially that now comes to be spoken of: not for the purpose of expressing superfluously a second time the likeness of the wheels, as Ewald (and before him Sanctius): "the one and the other of the foresaid four," or as Umbreit: "coinciding as well in their relation," but as Bunsen and the most: "each one consisted of two wheels, which intersected each other at right angles;" "double wheels, the one set into the other" (HENGST.). Cruciform! Such a construction had the effect—(Ver. 17) That they could *go in all four directions* (GROTIUS: the dispersion of the Jews into all the four quarters of the world, Isa. xliii. 5, 6) *without turning*. Comp. vers. 8, 9, 12. The fem. suff. lets the reference to the chajoth peep through here also, so that the wheels, as already from the commencement in ver. 15, are conceived of throughout along with the chajoth, and as determined by them. Hence first בלכתם, and at the end בלכתן. It is certainly to be noticed that in the description of the chajoth the masc. gend. has its turn, and with the wheels the fem. gend. As in the former case the human element predominates, so in the latter the connection with the chajoth; and this the more necessarily, as the wheels are here described by themselves.

Ver. 18 concludes this description in parallel terms with the chajoth of the vision. וְגַבֵּיהֶן וְגֹבַהּ alliteratively: "height," in the sense of sublimity, first of all characterized the rings of the wheels. What the wings were in the chajoth, that the גֹּבַהּ was in the wheels; as in the former fire and the like, so in the latter **fearfulness**; lastly, to the faces of the chajoth corresponded the **eyes round about**, where we are to think of the nails glancing like eyes. (Instead of גביהן we have now גבתם. Ewald for the latter: spokes? 1 Kings vii. 33. J. D. Mich., according to another punctuation: "could see, for the felloes of the four wheels were quite full of eyes.") The face has its life plastically in the eye. HÄV.: "the most beautiful evidence of the power of life." With the fearfulness (KEIL) the being **full of eyes** has as little to do as it has with intelligence and wisdom (HÄV.), or with the circumstance that "on the power of nature everywhere the stamp of reason is impressed" (HENGST.). But perhaps we have in this way represented to us—visible, of course, it could not be made—the idea of the "spirit," how it moved the living creatures; as will also be immediately explained in detail.

Ver. 19. Mention was already made in ver. 17 of the movement of the wheels by themselves, although not without relation to the chajoth, comp. there; now their relation to the chajoth is spoken of in detail. UMBREIT: "The wheels stand beside the living creatures, but when the latter move, the former must of themselves follow the impulse."—Ver. 20: עַל, not "weaker," for אֶל (HÄV.); but the מֵעַל going before has an influence, as being the last mentioned and most significant direction, and it is therefore again adopted. The LXX. have, instead of עַל, read עָב, "cloud-darkness"!—הרוח is **the spirit** of ver. 12, as it is also expressly called; but the chajoth are gathered up in the unity of the singular חיה: רוח החיה. Ver. 21, comp. ver. 22, where certainly it cannot be taken otherwise. Hence neither: the living spirit (or wind), nor: breath of life, living soul, nor: spirit of life, principle of life, nor even: the spirit of the living creatures. The *repetition* of the description not only *depicts* to us the simultaneous movement, but lays *emphasis* on this simultaneousness, and quite peculiarly on the circumstance, that the simultaneous movement is based *on there being one spirit* (כי): whither the spirit of the chajoth went, just thither went the spirit in the wheels, which was identically the same. Bunsen encloses in brackets as a gloss the words: **thither was the spirit to go.** HENGST.: "if the spirit impelled to go thither, then the wheels were lifted up," etc. KLIEF.: "whither the wind stood to go, thither they went (having the wind for going, *i.e.*) under the wind, driven by the wind." (!)—At ver. 21, in connection with the repetition of the simultaneousness of the movement of chajoth and wheels, and as an important preparation for vers. 24, 25, the new element of *rest* is added; it was hitherto, of course, only motion.

Vers. 22–28.—*The Heavenly Enthroned One.*

After vers. 15–21 have connected the first vision with what is below, with the earth, the whole vision of glory is now (vers. 22–28) completed in this second vision by connecting it with what is above, and thus receives a heavenly conclusion. "Now comes the culminating point of the theophany" (HÄV.). Ver. 22: It was not heaven, it was only something *like* it; and this is strongly emphasized; hence ודמות (comp. on ver. 4) put first. But not as Hengst.: "the likeness of a vault," in a genitive relation; the latter is an explanatory apposition (KEIL).—רקיע, **an expanse**, without the article; J. D. MICH.: "a floor!" (from רקע, to push, to stamp, to beat flat, to extend, to stretch), from Gen. i. onwards a technical term for the firmament dividing what is above from what is below, but which, as the atmosphere of the earth, remains in the background. In this way *the transition to the heavenly enthroned One is indicated*. Comp. ch. x. 1.—החיה, comp. on ch. i. 15, 20. כעין, comp. on ch. i. 4.—הקרח הנורא: the article, because of קרח being universally known (from קרח, "to make smooth"), from its likeness to ice: **the crystal.** The *pellucid transparency* is the point of the comparison (Exod. xxiv. 10; Rev. iv. 6). The dazzling clearness and purity is the occasion of the epithet **fearful.** ("The crystal is designated as fearful, because it excites awe by its splendour, in which that of the Creator is reflected. Fearfulness had also already, ver. 18, been attributed to the wheels. There the comparison is with the chrysolite, here with the crystal." HENGST.) Keil also remarks that it was not the vault of heaven that was over the heads of the chajoth,—it neither stretched over them, nor did it even sink down over them, but that it was merely a covering like it, looking fearful as the crystal, that appeared; EWALD: "no ordinary chariot-frame" (comp. ver. 11). ("**Stretched out**, a standing expression for the relation of heaven to earth, Isa. xl. 22, xlii. 5, xliv. 24; Jer. x. 12. We have here a mere **over**, not that the heads supported it; they are not at all immediately under the vault, for the wings project above them [vers. 19, 23]." HENGST.)—Ver. 23. Now הרקיע, viz. the forementioned. **Under** it were the wings of the chajoth **straight** (comp. on ver. 7), raised aloft, standing erect. The legs down, the wings up, a firm, imposing attitude.—Since, according to vers. 9 and 11, one wing was joined to the other wing, the four chajoth may be taken together in pairs for the representation, but not that every two wings downwards (KLIEFOTH), analogous to the connection above, likewise covered each other as neighbours; but the representation is rather an intentional and impressive repetition, in order, as a preparation for what follows, to portray solemnly the covering of the bodies (comp. on ver. 11). According to Hengst. the representation is meant to express merely: *every separate* cherub, so that without it the sense might be, that only one ("one had two which covered him") had two wings covering his body. (?) More correctly Keil: להנה corresponds to לאיש, analogously to the לאחת להם of ver. 6. Ewald supplies after the first להנה (quoting Isa. vi. 2), פְּנֵיהֶם. In opposition to this, Hengst. rightly remarks: "The tips of the wings (of the pair of wings serving for flight) reach along to the vault. For support they are not adapted, and particularly for this reason, that the wings (ver. 24) make a loud noise, and are therefore in free motion; and further, because upon occasion they are let down. The wheels also do not support the chariot. The local proximity seems only to indicate the connection between the several provinces of creation, is meant to represent the creation as a united whole."

Ver. 24. Not less vividly than the covering of the under part is the movement in the upper part (hence קול־כנפים) depicted, and that as a loud, powerful one (comp. ver. 14). "Hitherto the prophet was describing only what he saw, now also what he heard" (J. H. MICHAELIS). The quickening influence of the "spirit" gets here as its expression the **noise** (voice), ch. x. 5. Do they show in this way a "longing to fulfil their mission, and that consequently the time of this fulfilment draws near" (HENGST.)? Calvin makes the command in this voice bring about the movement of the wheels corresponding to the living creatures. The comparison is a threefold one: (1) **as the noise** (voice) **of many waters**, ch. xliii. 2 (Rev. xiv. 2, xix. 6); Isa. xvii. 12, 13; (2) **as the voice of the Almighty**, which may mean the thunder, as also every other similar manifestation of God (Rev. xiv. 2, xix. 6; Ps. xxix. 3 sqq.); (3) **noise** (voice) **of tumult** (הֲמֻלָּה, of the sound which is produced with lips brought together and closed, "to hum;" a dull, confused noise, Jer. xi. 16), **as the noise** (voice) **of an host.** (Arbitrarily and strangely, J. D. Michaelis: "as the rushing of a waterfall, as a thunder of the Most High, their words, as the voice of a whole army;" and in connection therewith he remarks: "just such a representation, as when in Homer Mars cries [only in Hebrew it is no god, but merely a team of the thunder-chariot of God], and so cries as if 10,000 men cried at once. I do not look upon Ezekiel in other respects as a beautiful writer, but every one certainly must find the picture here beautiful, and still more so with the distinction between God, of whom it is somewhat unworthy, and the draught beast before His thunder-chariot.") The "voice" (the sounding קול), however, which Ezekiel hears in this way, accompanied the movement of the chajoth, with which also that joining of the wings in ver. 9 took place; for *when they rested* (ver. 21) *they let down their wings* (Piel).

Ver. 25. This remark with respect to the resting of the chajoth enables us to form a conjecture as to what determines their resting; for as regards their motion the already repeatedly mentioned "spirit" might suffice. The "noise of their wings" also, especially where it was represented as "like the voice of the Almighty," admonishes us to listen higher, as indeed the "expanse" (vers. 22, 23) even must direct our looks upward. "**And there came a voice,**" etc. (J. D. MICH.: "Above the floor which was over their heads it thundered.") In this way our conjecture is verified, what we had to expect as following up what goes before is realized. There is no statement here as to the quarter from which the loud sound came which was heard during the motion of the wings, as Keil maintains. It is a "*voice*" also which comes, but the circumstance that "*it came*" (ויהי) depicts something *making its appearance suddenly*, so that the vision up to the last brings before us an occurrence of an exceedingly stirring character (comp. introd. remarks to vers. 4–28).—**In their standing** (now equivalent to: when they stood, when their motion ceased at the voice) **they let down their wings** (which were of course raised when they walked or rose up from the earth, ver. 19 sqq.), which is repeated verbatim from ver. 24, not, however, "in order to round off this subject" (KEIL), but in order now at the same time to explain it to us as respects its cause. ("A voice issues from above the vault, which yet for a time puts a restraint on the impetuosity of the instruments of the divine wrath." HENGST.) Although in what follows we are to reach a goal hitherto aimed at, mention may well be made here even of grace charging the judgment *in general* to stand still.—The *letting down* of the upper wings corresponds to their covering themselves with the lower wings. As the latter represents in general reverential distance, and that of the creature when in motion, so the former represents in particular their most submissive silence, their deep reverential rest before the only living God, as soon as His voice is heard, Ps. lxxvi. 9, xlvi. 7, 11. (UMBR.: "Is this not, in short, an allusion to the death of the creature? It is the voice of Him who kills and makes alive.")

Ver. 26. וממעל, the strongest expression for

above; "the *highest* Object in the vision" (HENGST.) is meant to be expressed.—סַפִּיר, from סָפַר, to make smooth, *shining*, that which *gives forth light*. "It cannot be decided whether the ancients gave this name to a sky-blue, or dark blue, or violet stone" (BÄHR). HENGST.: "on account of the heaven-like colour, Exod. xxiv. 10, where the whiteness or bright lustre of the sapphire stands in connection with the purity of the heavens, and denotes the infinite eminence of God's dominion over the earth with its impotence, sin, unrighteousness." HITZIG: "The sapphire of the ancients is our *lapis lazuli*, as in Exod. xxiv. 10 an opaque stone, and on account of the light blue colour of the heavens, a blue one." (J. D. MICH.: "The throne had thus the colour of the pure heaven which is above the clouds; beneath it all that is gloomy, or fire and lightning, the throne itself bright and pure, heaven-like blue.") The sapphire is perfectly transparent; at all events, it is *on account of its bright lustre* that it is taken as a comparison. The beautiful blue colour is merely incidental. But it is more worthy of notice how Ezekiel, where the Most High is in question, as already at vers. 22, 24, so especially here, repeats and emphasizes in the strongest way the merely *analogical*, purely *emblematic* character of his representation; דמות, כְּ three times, and yet again כְּ. As in the case of the chajoth what first made its appearance was "the likeness of a man" (ver. 5), so here it is said, **the likeness as the appearance of a man** (Dan. vii. 13). Comp. on ver. 5. The human element is thus up to the end, just as on the other hand the fiery element is throughout, characteristic of the vision. (Comp. introd. remarks to vers. 4–28.)

Ver. 27. ואֵרא, as in ver. 15 and ver. 4; parallel to ואשמע, ver. 24.—כעין חשמל, comp. on ver. 4.—There is thus also a retrospective reference to the fire-cloud, viz. by means of what formed the climax of its impression. But farther, the "*chasmal-look*" effects the transition from the human element of Him who sits upon the throne to the other side of His appearance, in order, finally, however, in a manner corresponding to the first human impression, to bring about the conclusion at the culminating point of the whole. The intermediate term betwixt "as the appearance of a man" and **as the appearance of fire**, etc., is thus the *bright lustre* of the chasmal, as was brought out on ver. 4; and brightness also will, as we shall see, form the medium of transition at the close. בֵּית־לָהּ סָבִיב, belonging most naturally to כְּמַרְאֵה־אֵשׁ = **as the appearance of fire, of a house round about it**, *i.e.* of a fire which takes the shape of a house enclosing round; HITZIG: "which has an enclosure round;" HENGST.: "a house round about it, *i.e.* which is enclosed round, in order to indicate the extent of its burning." Perhaps also it is meant in this way to depict a fire that is hemmed in. To refer לּה to דמות כסא, in ver. 26, lies too far off, and gives no sense; and there is just as little in favour of translating בית־לה by: "within the same," for which certainly the expression is מִבֵּית לְ.

We have to go back in thought to the fire-cloud in ver. 4. (Ewald makes out of בית something white, clear, בַּיִץ [?].) In this way mention **is** made generally of the brightness of light and the form of fire, *i.e.* of two different things.—There follows the application to Him who sits upon the throne, alike in an upward and in a downward direction. ו is explicative. The **loins** come into consideration, because He sits. As, then, **from the appearance** of these, looking **downwards**, the prophet says: **I saw as the appearance of fire**, there must remain self-evidently (and ch. viii. 2 puts it beyond doubt) for the **upwards** the brightness of light, which is not expressly added for this reason, because it is understood of itself after the separation and application of the fire, because, farther, "as the look of chasmal" had been the first thing which was spoken of before mention of the "as the appearance of fire," and because the "brightness" is mentioned in a way thoroughly sufficient in ver. 28. לוֹ refers, without doubt, expressly to Him who sits upon the throne; comp. on the other hand, on ver. 4, from which the words are borrowed. The **brightness** must accordingly be understood as being above, round the upper part of the body. On the other hand J. D. Mich.: "Like glowing metal inwardly, encircled round and round with fire, so the upper part of the body; the lower part of the body like fire, which produced a reflection round itself, and the reflection looked like a rainbow."

Ver. 28. The **bow** is that **in the cloud**, hence, as is also indicated still more definitely, the *rainbow*, whose meaning is fixed from Gen. ix. 13 sqq. onwards. We might almost describe the substance of the whole vision physically as a thunderstorm, which melts away in a rainbow, in which case the significance of this latter natural phenomenon in Holy Scripture throughout might be the thought in view. Thus simple, after all, is the *tout ensemble*, with all its complication in detail. But perhaps the mention of the **cloud** refers back likewise to ver. 4, just as the manifold retrospective references to the commencement of the vision are characteristic of its rounded close. The fire-cloud is changed, by means of the sun-like brightness round about Him who sits upon the throne, into a bearer of the bow of peace and of the covenant, the token of *grace after and* (springing) *out of judgment*. In this way the gospel and Christ break through, as in a grammatico-historical way exegesis even may expound the letter (Rev. iv. 3, x. 1). "From the north the vision appears to Ezekiel, but in the rainbow it vanishes from him; for he is to prophesy of judgment and ruin first, but of grace and everlasting salvation afterwards" (KLIEFOTH). This harmony of the vision, as it appears in the *tout ensemble*, and in the detail, and entirely confirmed as it is by the remainder of the Book of Ezekiel, is obliterated, if the rainbow is to signify nothing but "royal dignity," or is to come into consideration as the "most beautiful picture," *i.e.* on account of the beauty of its colours, to which, however, according to Hitzig, there is no second reference. J. D. Mich. asserts that the reflection, like a rainbow, is drawn from the smelting-furnaces of the precious metal, that when silver is smelted, there shows itself, at the moment of the separation of the vitrified **dross**, lead, or the like, over the pure, glowing metal something resembling a rainbow (the silver-gleam, comp. Umbr. on ver. 4). But Häv. also passes by the main thing, when he limits the human form, celebrating as it does its heavenly manifestation in brightness generally, and such a brightness as this, to a divine condescension for the prophet merely.—Keil, Klief., Hengst., Hitzig, and others, because of ch. x. 4. 19, confine הוא to the appearance of Him who sits upon the throne, including the veil of light, but "excluding the throne and cherubim." Comp. introd. remarks to vers. 4–28, where already it is brought out, that the application which is made of our vision in ch. x. must not be permitted to influence the interpretation of the much more general contents of ch. i. This only may be said: The vision of glory in ver. 26 sqq. likewise points to His Deity itself, which still infinitely transcends all His glory in the creature and its impending glorification upon earth (pp. 39, 40). Hence also דמות כבוד. "Strictly speaking, the prophet conceives of the δόξα τοῦ κυρίου as in itself so sublime that it cannot be described; it is a reflection, which only suggests the reality" (Häv.). כבוד (see as to the meaning p. 40), linguistically from כָּבֵד (כָּבַד), to be "drawing together," "drawing down," "*heavy*." This fundamental idea is in itself one derived from the senses, and even where, by transference to human relations, it becomes a metaphysical one, something abstract, like *gravis, gravitas, pondus,* βαρύς (comp. 2 Cor. iv. 17, βάρος δόξης), and means intellectual weight, importance, significance, it rests on real *power*, as money-power (riches), or high position, etc., without כבוד on this account being=riches or royalty; rather does it continue to be the *weight* which one is able to put in the scale *on the ground of such power.* If *in consequence of this* a *nimbus* gathers round the possessor of the power, because power adorns itself as readily as it is wont to be adorned through recognition and service on the part of others, it is natural that, for the purpose of expressing the weight of him who is powerful, and in order to represent, to give visibility to this power, the idea of brightness, splendour, greatness, dignity, respect, renown may enter, without כבוד itself having this meaning *radically.* Thus it is used κατ᾽ ἐξοχὴν of God's showing forth of His power, of His manifestation and presence (the "Shechinah," according to Jewish terminology), where the thought of the principal sphere of His manifestation, viz. the bright heavens, also exerts its influence; but the כבוד יי is, according to the fundamental idea of the word: the *power* of life belonging to God, in light that is invisible for man, except in that reflected splendour which adorns the creatures, man pre-eminently, but also the whole creation of God in general: *God's sovereignty in glory, as it belongs to Him alone.*—ואראה, comp. on ver. 1. The close of the vision. At the same time we have set before us the impression which it produced in the prophet's case, its immediate, first result. HENGST.: "He falls down before the majesty of God in His wrath." HÄV.: "Although Jehovah did not suffer to be wanting tokens of His grace and love, yet he could not bear to look upon His glory." HITZIG: "He is thrown down in a state of unconsciousness." KEIL: "Having fallen to the ground before the terrible revelation of the glory of Jehovah under a feeling of his own impotence and sinfulness." (Luke v. 8.) ["In the first place: because of the extraordinary vision, and from astonishment thereat. Secondly: from fear and humility; for if the seraphim veil their face before God, how should not mortal man fall to the earth when he sees the glory of God? Thirdly: in adoration of God" (A LAPIDE).] It is an overpowering impression, hence the power of God shown in the כבוד יי (comp. on the other hand Isa. vi. 5), quite corresponding to the fundamental idea. Ch. iii. 23, xliii. 3; Dan. viii. 17, 18, x. 7 sqq.; comp. especially Matt. xvii. 6 (Acts ix. 7, 8); Rev. i. 17.—ואשמע, now something else than in ver. 24; but the "voice" was that of ver. 25. In this way a transition is made to what follows. "He says, however: **of one that spake,** and not of God, because, lying upon his face, he could not see and recognise the speaker. Acts ix. 4 sqq." (A LAPIDE). As is clear otherwise from the context, the falling down and hearing, like all that has preceded, are to be conceived of within the sphere of the vision.

ADDITIONAL NOTE ON CH. I. 4–28.

[To gather up now the leading features and symbolic purport of this wonderful vision, we can easily perceive that the groundwork of it was derived from the patterns of divine things in the most holy place in the temple; yet very considerably modified and changed, to adapt it to the present occasion. Here also there is the throne of the divine Majesty, but not wearing the humble and attractive form of the mercy-seat; more like Sinai, with its electric clouds, and pealing sounds, and bursting effusions of living flame. Here, too, are the composite forms about the throne—the cherubim with outstretched wings touching each other; but instead of the two cherubic figures of the temple, four, each with four hands, four wings, four faces, looking in so many directions, doubtless with respect to the four quarters of the earth toward which the divine power and glory was going to manifest itself. These four are here further represented as peculiarly *living creatures,* full of life and motion, and not only with wings for flight, but wheels also of gigantic size beside them, revolving with lightning speed, and all resplendent with the most intense brightness. The general correspondence between what Ezekiel thus saw in the visions of God and what was to be found in the temple, indicated that it was the same God who dwelt between the cherubim in the temple, and who now appeared to His servant on the banks of the Chebar; while the differences bespoke certain manifestations of the divine character to be now at hand, such as required to be less prominently displayed in His ordinary procedure.

1. That He appeared specially and peculiarly as the God of holiness; this, first of all, was intimated by the presence of the cherubim. For here, as in the temple, the employment of these composite forms pointed back to their original destination in the garden of Eden, to keep the way to the tree of life, from which man had been debarred on account of sin; ideal creatures, as the region of pure and blessed life they occupied, had now become to men an ideal territory. Yet still they were creatures, not of angelic, but of

human mould; they bore the predominant likeness of man, with the likenesses superadded of the three highest orders of the inferior creation (the lion, the ox, the eagle). "It is an ideal combination; no such composite creature as the cherub exists in the actual world, and we can think of no reason why the singular combination it presents of animal forms should have been set upon that of man as the trunk or centre of the whole, unless it were to exhibit the higher elements of humanity in some kind of organic connection with certain distinctive properties of the inferior creation. The nature of man is immensely the highest upon earth, and towers loftily above all the rest, by powers peculiar to itself. And yet we can easily conceive how this very nature of man might be greatly raised and ennobled, by having superadded to its own inherent qualities, those of which the other animal forms here mentioned stand as the appropriate types."—"These composite forms are here called חַיּוֹת, for which the Septuagint, and John in the Apocalypse, use the synonymous term ζῶα, *living ones*. The frequency with which this name is used of the cherubim is remarkable. In Ezekiel and the Apocalypse together it occurs nearly thirty times, and may consequently be regarded as peculiarly expressive of the symbolical meaning of the cherubim. It presents them to our view as exhibiting the property of life in its highest state of power and activity; as forms of creaturely existence, altogether instinct with life. And the idea thus conveyed by the name is further substantiated by one or two traits associated with them in Ezekiel and the Apocalypse. Such, especially, is the very singular multiplicity of eyes attached to them, appearing primarily in the mystic wheels that regulated their movements, and at a later stage (ch. x. 12), in the cherubic forms themselves. For the eye is the symbol of intelligent life, the living spirit's most peculiar organ and index; and to represent the cherubim as so strangely replenished with eyes, could only be intended to make them known as wholly inspirited. Hence, in ver. 20, 'the spirit of the living creatures' is said to have been in the wheels; where the eye was, there also was the intelligent, thinking, directive spirit of life. Another and quite similar trait is the quick and restless activity ascribed to them by Ezekiel, who represents them as 'running and returning' with lightning speed, and then by John, when he describes them as 'resting not day and night.' Incessant motion is one of the most obvious symptoms of a plenitude of life. We instinctively associate the property of life even with the inanimate things that exhibit motion—such as fountains and running streams, which are called living in contradistinction to stagnant pools, that seem comparatively dead. So that creatures which appeared to be all eyes, all motion, are, in plain terms, those in which the powers and properties of life are quite peculiarly displayed; but life, it must be remembered, most nearly and essentially connected with God—life as it is or shall be held by those who dwell in His immediate presence, and form, in a manner, the very enclosure and covering of His throne—pre-eminently, therefore, holy and spiritual life."[1]

[1] The *Typology of Scripture*, 3d edit. vol. i. pp. 229-248, where the whole subject of the cherubim is fully investigated.

2. But this idea of holy and spiritual life, as connected with the presence and glory of God, was greatly strengthened in the vision by the fervid appearance, as of metallic brightness and flashes of liquid flame, which shone from and around all the parts and figures of the vision. It denoted the intense and holy severity in God's working, which was either to accomplish in the objects of it the highest good, or to produce the greatest evil. Precisely similar in meaning, though somewhat differing in form, was the representation in Isaiah's vision (ch. vi.), where, instead of the usual name cherubim, that of seraphim is applied to the symbolical attendants of God—the *burning ones*, as the word properly signifies—burning forms of holy fire, the emblems of God's purifying and destroying righteousness. Hence their cry one to another was, "Holy, holy, holy, is the Lord God of hosts." And in token of the twofold working of this holiness, it was by the application of a burning coal to his lips that the prophet, as the representative of the elect portion of the people, was hallowed for God's service, while in the message that follows, the ungodly mass are declared to be *for burning* (as the word literally is in ver. 13). The same element that refined and purified the one for God's service, was to manifest itself in the destruction of the other. And it is this also that is symbolically taught here by the dazzling light, the glowing embers, and fiery coruscations, with which all was enveloped and emblazoned. It made known God's purpose to put forth the severer attributes of His character, and to purify His Church by "the spirit of judgment and by the spirit of burning."

3. Even these fiery appearances, however, in the cherubim and the other objects of the vision, did not sufficiently express what was here meant to be conveyed; and, therefore, to make out the idea more completely, wheels of vast proportions were added to the cherubim. The prophet would thus render palpable to our view the gigantic and terrible energy which was going to characterize the manifestations of the God of Israel. A spirit of awful and resistless might was now to appear in His dealings; not proceeding, however, by a blind impulse, but in all its movements guided by a clear-sighted and unerring sagacity. How striking a representation did such a spirit find for itself in the resolute agency and stern utterances of Ezekiel! In this respect he comes nearest of all the later prophets to Elijah.

4. Finally, above the cherubim of glory and their wonderful wheel-work was seen, first, the crystal firmament, and then, above the firmament, the throne of God, on which He Himself sat in human form—a form, as here displayed, beaming with the splendour of heavenly fire, but, at the same time, bearing the engaging aspect of a man, and surrounded with the attractive and pleasing halo of the rainbow. In this shone forth the mingled majesty and kindness of God—the overawing authority on the one hand, and the gracious sympathy and regard on the other, which were to distinguish His agency as now to be put forth for the reproof of sin among the covenant-people, and the establishment of truth and righteousness. The terror which the manifestation was fitted to inspire, was terror only to the guilty, while, for the penitent and believing, there was to be the brightest display of covenant love and faithfulness. Especially was this indicated by

the crowning appearance of the rainbow, which, from being the token of God's covenant with Noah, in respect to the future preservation of the earth, was like the hanging out from the throne of the Eternal of a flag of peace, giving assurance to all, that the purpose of Heaven was to preserve rather than to destroy, and to fulfil that which was promised in the covenant. Even if the divine work now to be carried forward in the spiritual world should require, as in the natural world of old, a deluge of wrath for its successful accomplishment, still the faithfulness and love of God would be sure to the children of promise, and would only shine forth the more brightly at last, in consequence of the tribulations which might be needed to prepare the way for the ultimate good.

Such, then, was the form and import of this remarkable vision. There was nothing about it accidental or capricious; all was wisely adjusted and arranged, so as to convey beforehand suitable impressions of that work of God to which Ezekiel was now called to devote himself. It was substantially an exhibition, by means of emblematical appearances and actions, of the same views of the divine character and government, which were to be unfolded in the successive communications made by Ezekiel to the covenant-people. By a significant representation, the Lord gathered into one magnificent vision the substance of what was to occupy the prophetic agency of His servant, as in later times was done by our Lord to the evangelist John, in the opening vision of the Apocalypse.—FAIRBAIRN'S *Ezekiel*, pp. 30-34.—W. F.]

DOCTRINAL.

1. Thus God provides a helper for His servant Jeremiah, in a sphere where the latter, for far more than thirty years, has called without ceasing, with small result. But it was no small relief, that Jeremiah at Jerusalem heard the Holy Spirit assenting to and coinciding with him from the exile. Thus the truth was confirmed by the mouth of two witnesses (after CALVIN). "Let every one, therefore, do what belongs to his office, and God will doubtless raise up others, if it is necessary, to help us. Thus he associated with Joseph, who took Christ from the cross, Nicodemus." (LUDW. LAVATER.)

2. "As Ezekiel here, at thirty years of age, sees the heavens opened by a river, so Jesus, according to Matt. iii. 16; comp. with Luke iii. 21" (HENGST.). "As a type of Christ, who at thirty years of age came for baptism. . . . The priests entered on their office at the same age; John the Baptist began at thirty years of age the preaching of repentance" (JEROME). Comp. however, Introd. § 3, and the exeg. remarks on ver. 1.

3. Herein is shown the inestimable goodness of God, in that He raised up the prophet for Himself as it were out of hell; for Babylon was like the deepest abyss, and from thence must the voice of the retribution, as well as of the grace of God, sound forth. Thus the light breaks forth from the blackest darkness, and, at the same time, to the shame of the Jews, who had despised the voice of so many prophets (after CALVIN). "God calls the land of Canaan His own land; in that land He had a house and people, to whom He had given it as an inheritance. And now, when He began to lead the people forth from it, He yet did not forsake them, but went as it were with them into the exile, and gave them, even in the midst of the heathen in an unclean land, prophets who, like Daniel and Ezekiel, saw the greatest things,—a thing which has no longer happened to the Jews scattered over the earth after the last destruction of the temple; for prophecy departed from them. But Christ's disciples preached the gospel: which they, however, despised, and, in this way, turned the Spirit of God out of the synagogue. Where God is, there is vision, *i.e.* revelation by means of His word: there He dwells, where His word is loved and believed; there is the sanctuary (ch. xi. 16), which the time approaching was to show, when He would march along in the wilderness (Ps. lxviii. 7), *i.e.* would have His kingdom among the heathen in the whole world" (COCC.).

4. "Although a thousand heavens were to open, what piercing look would reach as far as the glory of God? How small the sun appears, and yet it is so much greater than the earth! And then the rest of the stars! And so, when He opens the heavens, God must, at the same time, give His servants new eyes. The eyes of Stephen, therefore, were doubtless enlightened with unusual power, so that he could penetrate in vision beyond what mere man was able to do; and so also, at the baptism of Christ, John the Baptist was raised above the clouds" (CALVIN).

5. He says at ver. 3 that God's word came to him; and thus God alone is to be heard, and the prophets for no other reason than this, that they cause us to hear God's word. Every doctor of the Church must first be a scholar, every teacher first a hearer. God must retain His rights as the only Guide and Teacher. The prophets, where they demand audience of us, demand it only for God's word (after CALVIN). "The prophet is to be distinguished essentially from the later scribes and disciples of the Rabbins. In his case it is not said: it stands written, or: such and such a master speaks, but: thus hath Jehovah spoken, or: the word of Jehovah came unto me, and the like. The true prophets are 'taught' not of a human master, but of Jehovah (Isa. l. 4)" (OEHLER).

6. This order: visions of God *first* (ver. 1), and *then* Jehovah's word, has its significance for biblical prophecy. Comp. Ezek. xiii. 2 sqq., where the false prophets prophesy without having seen. The prophet is certainly one who gives expression to something which he has seen, just as Oehler correctly defines internal vision as being the psychical form of prophecy; hence also the designation "seer" (חֹזֶה poetic, more solemn than the more usual רֹאֶה), and the circumstance that Isaiah (ch. ii. 1) "sees" the "word"; comp. Amos i. 1; Hab. i. 1, ii. 1.

7. The section, vers. 1-3, is meant to contain "an exact description of the state of prophetic inspiration or ecstasy" (HÄV.) in its threefold operation with a single cause. The four particulars: "the heavens were opened," "I saw visions of God," "the word of Jehovah came unto Ezekiel," "the hand of Jehovah came upon him there," may, in the first place, indicate: the two first the plastic part of the vision in ch. i., the two latter the phonetic part of it, viz. what follows in ch. ii. and iii. Then, as regards the

state of Ezekiel, we may admit a gradation in them, if we admit that they are successive. The subjectivity of the man is recognized even as regards its locality; how much more as regards its mental, moral, spiritual individuality, and its determination by the history of the time and of the individual. What, however, predominates is the objective, the divine. The *ego* of the prophet neither throws itself out upon the external world around, nor in upon itself; it is, from its usual activity being at rest, in a certain measure, carried away from itself as well as from the whole world, but by this means collected in an unusually receptive way for a higher order of things, for God and divine influence. This is the essential element of the ἔκστασις (Acts x. 10, xi. 5, xxii. 17), a being in the spirit, a being carried away from the earth, and rapt up into heaven. The contrast is the γίνεσθαι ἐν ἑαυτῷ (Acts xii. 11), the ἐν νοΐ εἶναι (1 Cor. xiv. 14); comp. THOLUCK, *Die Propheten und ihre Weissagungen*, p. 53 sqq., HENGST., *Christology*, 2d edit. iii. [Clark's Trans.], OEHLER, *Herzog's Encycl.* xvii. p. 627 sqq., LANGE, *Philosop. Dogmatik*, p. 447.

8. With a correct feeling,—one might say, with Christian intelligence,—the section, Ezek. i., is the haphtorah of the first Jewish day of Pentecost, on which besides ch. iii. 12 is read (comp. J. F. SCHRÖDER, *Satzungen und Gebräuche des talm. rabb. Judenth.* pp. 224, 214 sqq.).

9. The *fire-cloud* was characteristic. At Exod. xiii. 21, 22 Jehovah introduces Himself to His people for their entire guidance to Canaan by means of a cloud, in which by night there was fire. This cloud formed, in the Red Sea, the wall of separation between Israel and Egypt, for judgment and ruin to the latter (Exod. xiv.). Over the tabernacle (Exod. xl. 34 sqq.) it signified the divine presence (כְּמַרְאֵה־אֵשׁ, Num. ix. 15); in it appears the glory of the Lord, and that in very important, solemn crises of the journey through the wilderness (comp. Exod. xvi. 10; Num. xiv. 10, xvi. 19, xvii. 7, and other passages). The fire of this cloud had already flashed upon Moses out of that thorn bush on occasion of his mission to Israel (Exod. iii.); it was thoroughly known to the people from Sinai onwards (Exod. xix.). Thus there could scarcely be anything more familiar to the pious consciousness of the people. But it was not the cloud which had again filled the house of the Eternal in the time of Solomon (1 Kings viii.), nor was it even the fire (2 Chron. vii.); *i.e.* it must have had a different meaning, when a fire-cloud came from the north, and when it appeared in the land of Babylon. The fire in it is also quite manifest; that which envelopes it, and at the same time stands over against the scorching heat of the sun in the wilderness, is absent from it. (Comp. on the other hand, Isa. iv. 5 sqq., lx. 1.)

10. Hengst. draws attention to Ezekiel's opposition "to the vicious realism which will know nothing of the distinction between the thought and its vesture." "Appearance," "likeness," "appearance of the likeness," and the like, are peculiar to Ezekiel, "for the purpose of guarding against that vicious realism, which professes, indeed, to represent the interests of the faith against a 'false spiritualism,' but which is, in truth, nothing else but weakness in the exposition of Scripture."

11. "Man, in his ideality, the centre of life, which conditions all the other forms. The highest form of animal life: the suffering and bleeding life-form, the sacrificial animal, the bullock; the ruling life-form, exhibiting itself in royal freedom, the lion; the life-form which soars above the earth, free from toil, engaged in vision, the eagle. Above these three culminating points of the animal world, man, the intellectual life-form, which reproduces all those preliminary grades in a higher unity, but is always the one along with the other, when he corresponds with his destination: the tragic sacrificial animal, the fighting, conquering lion, the contemplative eagle, basking in the light—all this is *one* spirit; and just in this unity he is man. Every animal-form with Ezekiel is an ethical symbol. Everything living belongs to the spirit, falls to it, and is offered up to it: this is signified by the bullock. Everything living enjoys, contends, and overcomes, because it represents the spirit: this is expressed by the lion. Everything living lulls itself in a state of dreamy intoxication in the sunlight of the spirit: this is represented by the eagle. But everything living culminates in man: the inspiration of suffering, the inspiration of action, and the inspiration of contemplation; man is the image of God as regards his destiny. But Christ is the perfect, the glorified man, the God-man. Now, as man expands his fulness in the world, so does the God-man in the gospel, the element of the world's glorification; and as the riches of man branch out in the world, so do those of Christ in the Gospels. It was a far-reaching thought, when Irenæus referred the peculiarity of the four Gospels to the four animal-forms of Ezekiel" (LANGE).

12. If, in accordance with the representation given in the introductory remarks to ch. i. 4–28, Ezekiel's vision of glory, with its universality preceding the particular historical application in ch. x., symbolizes the human and earthly life of creation,—in its peculiarity as well with respect to its general place in the cosmos,—in like fulness of power as of unity and all-sidedness of movement (ver. 19 sqq.),—as a life not only of heavenly origin, *i.e.* from the beginning divinely-established (ver. 4), but also completely dependent on heaven (ver. 22 sqq.), and after the manner of the heavenly spirits, hence angel-like, always ready for service,—for purposes of judgment, but also of mercy:—then there lies therein every possibility of a passing over from the sphere of the merely natural in creation to what belongs to the history of the world in the preparatory revelation of God's glory in the midst of Israel, as well as in its fulfilment and completion in Christ among mankind. On the basis of this truth, the various interpretations of the vision in ch. i. admit of being harmonized.

13. "All things were," according to Col. i. 16, "created by Him and for Him," *i.e.* Him "who is the image (likeness) of the invisible God, the first-born before all creation" (ver. 15). Now, the vision of Ezekiel culminates in a "likeness (image) as the appearance of a man" on a throne (ver. 26), and this occupant of a throne is none other than Jehovah, and so the "likeness as the appearance of a man" must be the "image of the invisible God," according to Col. i. As the life of creation, in accordance with its origin, appears at its highest point in man, whom God has

created in His own image, after His own likeness, and therefore there is the "likeness of a man" in the four living creatures (ver. 5): so much more in accordance with its goal, as regards the destiny of its life and the goal of its development, everything which exists in any stage of life up to the highest of the invisible world culminates in the Son of man, who is the essential image of God, so that whoever sees Him sees God; hence the "likeness as the appearance of a man" upon the throne. The culmination of the vision of Ezekiel is thus the culmination of the whole creation in the Son of man, who is the Son of God; and in this way there lies expressed in the sphere of creation the very same thing which will also come to be expressed for the recovery from the fall and from the misdevelopment in mankind, for the redemption, so that grace already lies before us in nature archetypally. This is the grand all-embracing universalism of ch. i. The consecration alike of Israel and of mankind to God is the Christian provision, viz. that which is accomplished in Christ; is the glorifying of Christ by the Holy Ghost (John xvi. 14), *i.e.* the revelation of the power and dignity, the significance (כבוד, ver. 28) which Christ has as the reflection of the Father's glory, and at the same time the revelation in power and splendour of His victory over sin and death.

14. The glory of God, as the effulgent almightiness of divine life, must certainly show itself "in the warding off and annihilation of death, of transitoriness and of corruption," for which Nitzsch points away to "the glorification of Christ and of Christians in the resurrection (John xvii. 22; Rom. vi. 4, viii. 11, 30; 1 Pet. iv. 14)."

15. According to the interpretation in John xii. 41 of Isa. vi., it may be said also in reference to Ezek. i., that "the name of Jesus" is "the secret of Jehovah's name become manifest" (DELITZSCH). The divine glory (1) is symbolized in the Old Covenant, and that partly in outwardly visible phenomena, *e.g.* the cloud-guide, the signs on Sinai, partly in such ornaments connected with divine worship as the cherubim above the ark of the covenant in the most holy place of the tabernacle and the temple; and (2) it is personified with full powers in the manifold angelophanies, from which the Angel of the Lord, of the Presence, of the Covenant, is separated in important respects; (3) just as in like manner in the Old Testament representation of wisdom there begins, especially in what the prophets see in vision, a hypostatizing of the glory of God, which is already, in a manner full of promise, hinting at the incarnation of the Word (λόγος), in whom the abstract principle of wisdom and the spiritually living element in the expression of revelation are combined in one. (Comp. Lange on John i.) "In Christ the Shechinah has appeared in full realization." "The *Logos*, when on the way to become man, is one with the δόξα of the Father." This means more exactly, according to Heb. i. 3: He reflects the rays of the divine δόξα: He is its refulgence and effulgence, in the same way as the sunlight is related to the sun.

16. We have given prominence at ver. 28 to the overpowering element in the effect of the vision upon Ezekiel, and also (7) emphasized the predominance of the divine factor in the state of our prophet. We shall have occasion to complete what has been said in ch. ii. But here even, as Hengst. has brought out fully (*Gesch. Bil.* p. 141), the distinction between a prophet like Ezekiel and a Balaam, a Saul and the like, is to be maintained. "Inspiration assumed a character so violent, casting soul and body to the ground, only where it found beforehand an imperfect state." The more it can be taken for granted that "the ordinary consciousness is penetrated by the Spirit," the more "does the Spirit in the case of His extraordinary manifestations come into His own." We would otherwise have to expect the falling down of Ezekiel at the beginning of the chapter (comp. Num. xxiv. 4). At the close of the vision it is not explained from the divine power of the Spirit qualifying the seer beforehand for seeing, but from what is seen in its own significance, its own importance, especially over against human sinfulness. It is an embodied *Kurie eleison.*

HOMILETIC HINTS.

Ver. 1. The important "and" in Holy Scripture: (1) the catena of prophets and men of God; (2) the coincidence of times and occurrences; (3) the nexus of the divine leadings of Israel and of mankind.—"Pious people do not live thoughtlessly, like the ungodly, but mark closely days, months, and years in which special grace was shown them by God" (J. G. STARKE).—"With enemies even the pious find an asylum; Joseph with the Egyptians, David with the Philistines, Ezekiel with the Chaldeans. Whoever has God for his friend, remains alive among the lions, keeps a whole skin in the fiery furnace, and will be quite safe among whatever enemies he may be" (J. F. STARCKE).—"As Ezekiel is in the midst of them, one might say that in general judgments the pious also are taken along with others, and have to endure the like sufferings, as if there were no difference between the one and the other (Mal. iii. 18); but God preserves them in the midst of the flames; where the ungodly perish, the pious are kept safe; where it goes ill with the former, it goes well with the latter; and even if the body should be laid hold of, yet not the soul, which is bound up in the bundle of the living" (STCK.).—For intercourse with God, lonely retired places are the most suitable; here *the river*, there the wilderness (Hos. ii. 14, 16), elsewhere the closet, Matt. vi. 6 (after STCK.).—"If *the heavens* are *opened* to us in baptism, be on thy guard, that they be not shut to thee because of thy sins! The pious man, when he dies, will find the heavens opened; the ungodly will find hell open" (STCK.).—"'Visions *of God*': for Satan also has visions, by means of which he bewitches unbelievers" (L. LAVATER).—"We are not, however, on this account to expect and demand from God divine visions, when we have Moses and the prophets (Luke xvi.). It is certainly not impossible for God to unveil to us the future, and to reveal His will by means of visions; but under the New Covenant He has not promised such things" (STCK.).—"The Lord stooped to him, and his spirit was caught up to see God" (SCHMIEDER).—"Those whom God calls to the office of teaching and preaching, He furnishes also with necessary gifts. Luke xxi. 15" (O.).

Ver. 2. "The lie has a bad memory; on the other hand, the truth remains true to itself" (STCK.).—*Jehoiachin's* list of sins stands recorded shortly in 2 Kings xxiv. 9. Moreover, he was not so much *taken* prisoner; it was rather that he gave himself up as a prisoner, ver. 12. Ver. 3: "Ezekiel does not bring forward his dreams or imaginations, but according to 2 Pet. i. 21, God's revelation" (L. Lav.).—To the servants of God the *word of God* is entrusted for those who are to hear them. How could they otherwise raise such a claim to be heard in all the situations of life!? Woe to the unfaithful stewards! Woe to the disobedient hearers!—What a veto against all pride, self-will, and obstinacy, ought the servants of the word to have in that very word, whose servants merely and not masters they are! (Ps. cxv. 1.)—"The son of *Buzi, i.e.* contempt, is *Ezekiel, i.e.* God's strength; in other words, the man whom the world contemns, that very one God strengthens" (A Lapide).—"Humility adorns every one, but most of all the teacher, John i. 27" (St.).—The guidance of a servant of God among men consists of two parts: (1) God's *word;* (2) God's *hand.*—The goodness of God shown in the leading of His servants: (1) He compensates them richly for what they were obliged to sacrifice (Ezekiel for his hereditary priesthood, by means of the prophetic office derived from the Spirit); (2) His power is mighty in their misery (Ezekiel's home in God while in a state of exile from his native land, his divine freedom while led captive by man); (3) He fills their solitude with the glorious knowledge of Himself; (4) the heavens are opened to them above the earth, so that they see God instead of men.

Ver. 4 sqq. The glory of the Lord (1) present in nature, (2) proclaimed in the word, (3) experienced in faith.—Ver. 4: Nebuchadnezzar and Jehovah do not exclude one another; the former is merely the servant, and the latter the Master. The king of Babylon must perform what he has been sent to by the King of heaven and earth (Deut. xxxii. 30).—"With the one word *Storm!* the prophet places himself in rugged opposition to the false prophets, who with *one* mouth proclaimed serene tranquillity (Matt. viii. 26)" (Hengst.).—The storm which makes a clearance among the imaginations of the flesh is God's judgments, alike upon individuals and upon whole nations.—"The ungodly are like the storm, but God's storm outstorms them" (Stck.). —"*Out of* the north, not towards the north. The judgment must begin at the house of God" (H.).—"If they have become like the Egyptians in their practices, they need not wonder if an Egyptian fate also befalls them. They have not, in fact, wished it otherwise" (H.).—"The *cloud* of sins draws toward it the cloud of punishments" (Stck.).—"Behold, the Judge standeth before the door!" Jas. v. 9.—"*Fire* consumed Sodom; fire consumed the tent with the rebels in Israel; everlasting fire is sure to the ungodly" (Stck.). —"From this flows of itself the exhortation to repentance, in order that the sun may appear after the cloud" (H.).—"The contrast of the false prophets and of the true is not that of salvation and judgment, but that of salvation without punishment and without repentance, and of salvation which after judgment falls to the lot of the penitent people,—of mere gospel, crying, Peace, peace, when there is no peace, and of the law and the gospel, each in its own time. A prophet who proclaimed only punishment would be no less a false prophet than one who holds out in prospect nothing but peace. Law and gospel, each in its entire fulness,—this is even to the present day the characteristic mark of the true servants of God" (H.).—"Quæ putatur pœna, medicina est" (Jerome).—"As fiery rays shoot forth from the thick clouds, so in the midst of His judgments God causes a ray of His mercy to be seen" (St.).—"The *brightness* gleams only out of the far distance. But Exod. xxxiv. 6 must stand before our eyes, if the suffering called forth by sin is to bring forth the healthful fruit of righteousness" (H.).

Ver. 5 sqq. "He who appears for judgment is the Almighty, whom everything living serves (just as everything can also be quickened into life for His purposes, the wheels!); who is there that can pluck out of His hand?" (after H.).—The four *living creatures,* four living pictures of suitable instruments for God: (1) from the fire, *i.e.* zeal for God, all their acting as well as speaking must proceed; (2) they have, *a.* to confront the whole world; *b.* nevertheless, they may rise with confidence above the whole world on wings of prayer and meditation; (3) at the same time, *a.* they stand firm, sure, and stedfast, while everything around them reels to and fro; *b.* and their walk shines in the darkness of this world in a worthy, pure, divine manner.—The number four in Ezekiel in its significance for the mission and the missionary call of the Church of God.

Ver. 5. "Preachers have the *likeness of a man,* inasmuch as they imitate Christ in work, grace, suffering, and glory. They stamp in this way the Crucified One in the hearts of their hearers, 1 Cor. i. 23, ii. 2" (Gregory).—Ver. 6: "Similarly a believing soul also wishes for itself *wings* in His service, and four, yea, a thousand tongues, wherewith to praise Him" (Berl. B.).—Ver. 7: "Like pillars, honest servants of God and true believers ought to stand *straight* and erect in the house of God, and not suffer themselves to be bent after the will of men, nor to be corrupted through their own lusts, so as to get crooked feet" (Berl. B.).—The world ought to be permitted to look at our *feet* also, and to praise our Father in heaven, Matt. v. 16.—"We are in the world, but we ought not to be of the world," John xvii. 16.—"It is the fire of the divine Spirit that is meant, or love in our conduct, as it shines or becomes manifest to men's consciences" (Cocc.).

Ver. 8. "*Hands and wings* are together, just as we should not fail in carrying out our pious thoughts also" (after Scriver).—"The hands covered with the wings ought to teach thee humility; as Jerome says: Conceal thy hands where God has helped thee, and say, The Lord has done it; His name be praised! but not thy industry, thy wisdom, thy labour, thy care, and the like" (Stck.).—"Wherever and to whatever God calls thee, have not merely thy hands ready, but also thy heart; let that say: Thy will, O God, I gladly do! and thy mouth also for praise, and thy ear also, to hear and to hearken" (Stck.). —"The hand *under the wing;* see the hidden manner of acting of the Most High" (L. Lav.).—"The power of work under the wing of contemplation, Martha under Mary" (Gregory).—Ver. 9: "*United* power is stronger. *With wings united* in prayer, and stretched out for unwearied labour, we may hope for good success in all things" (STCK.).—"Through harmony, even small things grow, while the greatest even fade away through discord. Where there is *one* heart and *one* soul, there is God Himself and His blessing, Ps. cxxxiii.; Acts iv. 32" (STCK.).—The work is common; let the labour be the same; else the one pulls down what the other builds up.—*Straight forward*, a glorious matter also with servants of God: (1) The man who turns is not fit for the kingdom of God (Luke ix. 62), since whatever can stop or unnecessarily hinder, even though it cannot cause us to deviate, is behind; (2) that to which God sends and has called us, lies wholly and always before us, and the way is narrow. Towards this let the eagle's wing, the lion's courage, the ox's strength, the man's spirit, strive with all their powers! (Phil. iii. 14.)—Ver. 11: "The wings portray the faith which lifts us up to Christ; and therewith we also cover all our own worthiness, wisdom, strength, righteousness; for he who is righteous by faith is so as being an unrighteous and condemned man" (COCC.).—"So also the Saviour sent forth the disciples two by two to preach the gospel in concord and humility" (B. B.).

Ver. 12 sqq. "The creature in itself cannot and ought not to be the object of love, of trust, and of fear" (H.).—As *the Spirit* impels those who serve God, so zeal for the honour of God has the sway over them, and the outcome is pure life and motion.—Ver. 13: Of Basil it is said that his speech was thunder, his life lightning.—Ver. 14: "The pious soul never has rest; it has always something to contend with. Believers strive vehemently after what is heavenly, and return to God, while they ascribe all the honour of their works to Him" (GREGORY).—"The Church is continually in motion in the world. She has no fixed place, like Israel in Canaan; and wherever she is, she will move forward. If she is resisted, so much the more powerfully she breaks through the opposition. Wherever she comes, she subdues men to herself; and if she is driven out, she returns with power" (COCC.).

Living creatures and wheels! A glimpse into the divine government upon earth. (1) There all is life,—even what is in itself without life becomes life,—while in the case of man everything tends to death and becomes death. (2) There we see incessant movement in work, directed towards every quarter of the world, and to God's goal as its aim, while the world passes away with its lust as well as with its works in judgment.

Ver. 15 sqq. "The word of God may be compared to the *wheel* (1) because of its circuit through the world; (2) because of its unity in all quarters of the world; (3) because of the Spirit who works along with the word; (4) because of the glorious perfections of the word" (STCK.).—Ver. 16: "In the gospel thou findest the brightness of eternal truth, the light of heavenly doctrines, in manifold play of colours" (STCK.).—"There is, however, but *one* word, *one* gospel, alike in the Old and in the New Testament: the same in paradise, the same on David's harp, the same in the prophets and the apostles, and in the work and word of Christ Himself, Acts xv. 11" (STCK.).—As wheel in wheel, so the New in the Old Testament ("Novum in V. latet, Vetus in N. patet." AUGUSTINE).

Ver. 18. Starck compares the height of the word of God (Rom. xi. 33), and the fearfulness of its earnestness against the ungodly; then, farther, let one perceive therein the eye of divine Providence, the gospel which is all eye and light, etc.—"These are *the eyes* which watch over the Church" (A LAPIDE).—On the other hand, the world pictures to itself its good fortune as blind, in fact, its love also, and even its righteousness.—"But look thou what thou doest, thou who wouldst gladly be hidden from God, for He has very many eyes in His invisible instruments, which thou seest not, while they see thee well" (B. B.).—Ver. 19: "This is no chariot which rolls along with its wheels on the earth merely, and these are no animals which crawl along the earth merely; their instinct is upwards, and thither they point our way" (B. B.).

Vers. 20, 21. "Pious teachers and preachers are governed and impelled by the Spirit of God. O happy Churches, which have such teachers! Acts xviii. 5" (ST.).—"The divine care also accompanies godly men everywhere, and follows them step by step in all their undertakings; it moves and governs them, and does not leave them for an instant. Therefore also they do not move except under the impulse of the Holy Spirit, to which they give heed. They are ordered and regulated in all things according to the will of God" (B. B.).—Ver. 21: "That the course of the gospel is sometimes arrested for a season, arises from the decree of God" (O.).

Ver. 22. "The heaven or the heavens, in contrast with the poor earth standing in the singular, in the Old Testament is throughout the most illustrious proof of God's greatness (Ps. xix.); and the God of heaven is frequently called, in order to denote His omnipotence, the God of hosts, of the powers of heaven" (H.).—"The heaven is everywhere above us, in order that we may seek what is above, since as yet we have not full possession" (STCK.).—"The *terrible crystal* reminds us that nothing unclean enters the new Jerusalem" (STCK.).—"The throne of grace is founded in the righteousness of Christ, Ps. lxxxix. 14, xcvii. 2, of which this crystal foundation may be an emblem" (B. B.).—Ver. 23: "Faith unites the Church militant to the Church triumphant, and to the throne of God" (COCC.).—"The natural man, full of self-love and self-complacency, has neither wings for flying nor for covering himself, and is on that very account, with all his imagined riches, miserable and poor, naked and bare" (B. B.).—Ver. 24: "Like *the noise of the wings* is the uproar which God's word occasions. So was it in the time of the apostles" (STCK.).—"By which some understand the prayer and the ardour of spirit in the Church militant,—movements, however, which in the world also awaken a noise and alarm" (B. B.).—Ver. 25: "The voice in heaven is the voice and authority of the King, of Christ, by which He holds the nations in allegiance, so that they dare not inopportunely disturb His Church, Song viii. 4" (COCC.).—Ver. 26: "He *sat* upon the throne; for the Lord and Judge of all is of tranquil mind,—is not, like men, disturbed by passions. Above all, He who moves all, Himself unmoved" (B. B.).—Ver. 27: "As in 2 Thess. i. 8, 9, Christ is revealed in fire against the despisers of the gospel, so the *fire* here is directed against the despisers of the law" (H.).—Ver. 28: "However severe God's judgments are, yet He does not forget His covenant."—"After the storm the sun shines, after the rain follows the rainbow, after the cross the rest, after the tears the joy. Such is the vicissitude in this world; constant felicity is reserved for the world to come" (STCK.).—Without judgment no grace.—"This was at the same time a foreshadowing of the glorious appearing of Christ in the flesh with His kingdom, 1 Tim. iii. 16" (B. B.).—The glorious throne-chariot of Jehovah: (1) its nature: cloud, living creatures, wheels, throne; (2) its meaning: in the kingdom of nature, for the kingdom of grace; (3) its object: judgment and salvation.—"How glorious is the fatherland of the children of God! Little have the prophets seen of it in vision; but we are to have it all face to face" (after RICHTER).—Just when Israel's glory was about to disappear under Babylon, then Jehovah reveals His glory in Babylon.—"Let us learn, if we wish to be apt hearers of the divine word, to put no trust in our own powers, but humbly submitting ourselves to God, to hang on His lips, and to look to Him" (L. LAV.).—"In the sinner there is no ability to stand before God and before His light and glory, unless he is enabled to do so by the Spirit of God" (COCC.).—So also the *glory* of Jesus Christ which appeared to Paul, when in fulness of love the question was put to him: Why persecutest thou me? threw him to the ground. Yes; it is grace that does it most of all.

2. THE DIVINE COMMISSION TO THE PROPHET (CH. II. 1–III. 11).

CH. II. 1. And He said unto me, Son of man, stand upon thy feet, and I will speak
2 with thee. And the spirit entered into me as He spake unto me, and set me
3 upon my feet, and I heard Him that spake unto me. And He said unto me, Son
of man, I send thee to the sons of Israel, to heathens, the rebels, who rebelled
against me. They and their fathers have been revolters from me down to this
4 very day. And the sons! stiff of face and hard of heart are they, I do send thee
unto them [ver. 3]; and thou sayest unto them, Thus saith the Lord Jehovah.
5 And they, whether they hear or whether they forbear,—for they are a house of
6 rebelliousness,—know then that a prophet was in their midst. And thou, son of
man, thou art not to be afraid of them, neither of their words art thou to be
afraid; for [although] prickles and thorns are with thee, and thou art dwelling
among scorpions, of their words thou art not to be afraid, and at their face thou
7 art not to be terrified, for they are a house of rebelliousness. And thou speakest
my words unto them, whether they hear or whether they forbear; for they are
8 rebelliousness. And thou, son of man, hear what I say unto thee: Thou must
not be rebelliousness, like the house of rebelliousness. Open thy mouth, and eat
9 what I give unto thee. And I saw, and behold, an hand sent [stretched] unto me;
10 and behold, in it a book-roll. And He spread it out before me; and it was
written within and without, and on it were written lamentations, and groaning,
and woe.

CH. III. 1. And He said unto me, Son of man, that which thou shalt find eat; eat
2 this roll, and go, speak unto the house of Israel. And I opened my mouth, and
3 He caused me to eat this roll. And He said unto me, Son of man, thy belly
shalt thou cause to eat, and thy bowels shalt thou fill with this roll which I give
4 thee. And I did eat; and it became in my mouth as honey for sweetness. And
He said unto me, Son of man, go, get thee unto the house of Israel, and thou
5 speakest in my words unto them. For not to a people obscure of lip and difficult
6 of tongue art thou sent,—to the house of Israel. Not to many nations obscure
of lip and difficult of tongue, whose words thou canst not hear [understandest not],—
7 although I have not sent thee to them, *they* would hearken unto thee. Yet the
house of Israel, they will not be willing to hearken unto thee, for they are not
willing to hearken unto me; for all the house of Israel, hard of forehead and stiff
8 of heart are they. Behold, I have made thy face hard against their face, and thy
9 forehead hard against their forehead. As an adamant harder than stone have I
made thy forehead: thou shalt not fear them, and thou shalt not be terrified at
10 their face, for they are a house of rebelliousness. And He said unto me, Son of
man, all my words that I shall speak unto thee, receive in thine heart and hear
11 in thine ears. And go, get thee to the captivity, to the children of thy people,
and thou speakest unto them, and sayest unto them, Thus saith the Lord
Jehovah, whether they hear or whether they forbear.

Ch. ii. Ver. 2. Sept.: . . . ἐπ' ἐμε πνευμα κ. ἀνελαβεν με κ. ἐξηγειρεν με κ. ἐστησι με—
Ver. 3. . . . τ. οἰκον τ. Ἰσρ. τους παραπικραινοντας με, οἰτινες—
Ver. 5. . . . ἠ πτωηθωσιν, διοτι—

Ch. ii. Ver. 6. . . . *μηδε ἐκστης ἀπο προσωπου αὐτων, διοτι παροιστρησουσιν κ. ἐπισυστησονται ἐπι σε κυκλῳ—*
Ver. 7. Anoth. read.: בית מרי (Sept., Syr., Arab., Chald.: עם).
Ver. 10. . . . *γεγραμμενα ἠν τα ὀπισθεν κ. τα ἐμπροσθεν—*

Ch. iii. Ver. 1. . . . *ἀνθρωπου, καταφαγε τ. κεφαλιδα . . . υἱοις 'Ισρ.* (Anoth. read.: בני, Vulg., Syr., Arab.)
Ver. 2. K. *διηνοιξεν.*
Ver. 3. . . . *το στομα σου φαγεται κ. ἡ κοιλια . . . της δεδομενης εἰς σε . . . μελι γλυκαζον.*
Ver. 5. . . . *βαθυχειλον κ. . . . σὺ ἐξαποστελλη προς τ. οἰκ.*
Ver. 6. . . . *ἀλλογλωσσους οὐδὲ στιβὰρους τη γλωσση ὀντας . . . κ. εἰ προς τοιουτους . . . οὑτοι ἀν εἰσηκουσαν σου.*
Ver. 7. . . . *φιλονεικοι εἰσιν κ.—*
Ver. 9. K. *ἐσται, διαπαντος κραταιοτερον πετρας . . . μηδε πτοηθης ἀπο—*
Ver. 10. . . . *οὑς λελαληκα μετα σου—*
Ver. 11. . . . *ἐαν ἀρα ἐνδωσιν.*

EXEGETICAL REMARKS.

In accordance with the character of the vision of ch. i. as discussed at p. 31, the *installation of Ezekiel to his sphere of labour* must now take place, the vision must be realised *as a mission* (first of all *in words*). But before *the mission* comes to be expressed *in words* (it is said, first of all, merely, ver. 1, **and I will speak with thee**), the prophet is restored, so to speak, physically, *i.e.* as regards mind and body, to the *status quo.*

Vers. 1, 2.—*The Divine Raising up of Ezekiel in order to the Divine Commission.*

Ver. 1. **And He spake.** The "voice of one that spake" (ch. i. 28, comp. ver. 25) must be that of Him who sits upon the throne (ver. 26).—בן־אדם, *man of men.* By this expression Ezekiel is immediately contrasted with Him who is speaking to him; for of Him it is said at ch. i. 26: "*the likeness as the appearance* of a man." Jehovah merely *appeared* "as a man," Ezekiel *is* a **son of man.** (Cocc. certainly = *mi frater*, Ps. xxii. 22; Heb. ii. 11, 12.) Hence the view that this form of address is meant to distinguish him from the *angels*—apart from such a conception of the chajoth in ch. i.—says too little. On the other hand, it would increase the distinction so as to produce a conflict with the raising up of the prophet which follows, if a *humbling* of him were meant to be signified by this expression (RASCHI),—in order that he may not after such visions exalt himself *as being only a man* (2 Cor. xii. 7). It is perhaps meant to be said at the commencement,—but even more for those who have to hear him than for Ezekiel himself; and on this account it becomes a stereotyped (HÄVER.: more than 80 times) form of address to the prophet,—that he would not to be able to give such revelations *from himself* (comp. Introd. § 7). But this man of men is called: one whom God strengthens (comp. Introd. § 1). His legitimation for the Church lies as much in the one as in the other; in other words, in both together (1 Cor. xv. 10). The expression **son of man** is meant to say to Israel: "Thus saith *the Lord Jehovah.*"—As regards the divine raising up of Ezekiel which is intended, his falling down comes, first of all, to be considered: **stand upon thy feet.** This human element, which has come to be expressed, is established by the form of address on the part of Jehovah; yet without the design of humbling the prophet (*e.g.* as the Jews say, because driven out of Jerusalem, like Adam out of Eden!), rather with compassionate condescension (*ob φιλανθρωπίαν*—POLANUS), a divine *ecce homo.* Then, farther, it corresponds with the stereotyping of this form of address to Ezekiel, and also with an exaltation of him, as respects his prophetic mission, when it is remembered in connection therewith that the vision of ch. i., with all its direct and special applicability to Israel of that time, had a general human character, and a horizon embracing the whole world: the likeness of a man predominated in the chajoth, the likeness as the appearance of a man was the description of Him who sat on the throne, the number four had the sway numerically over the whole. With this distinction from ch. ix., x., the mission of Ezekiel takes place, who at the same time is addressed as "son of man," as prophet not merely of Israel, but of mankind generally. [ROSENM.: *pro simplici* אָדָם *homo.* HÄVERN.: a standing humiliation, corresponding with the time of the exile, and the strong, powerful nature of Ezekiel, and at the same time, a lesson for his hearers to look quite away from man. HENGST.: the form of address admits what lies before the eyes in looking at the frivolous objections of the multitude. HITZIG: a self-reflection of the prophet as to the distance between God and him. KLIEF.: because God speaks with him as man to man, as a man talks with his friend. KEIL: the weakness and frailty of man, in contrast with God, which appears the more prominent in the case of Ezekiel, through the preponderance of vision, for the people as for him a sign of the power of God in weakness, who can raise Israel even up again, miserable as she is among the heathen. UMBR.: "The call of grace out of the mouth of Him who by the sight of His glory has cast man to the ground in the consciousness of his sin."]—Ezekiel is *to rise to his feet* (comp. Dan. viii. 18; Matt. xvii. 7; Acts xxvi. 16; Exod. xxxiii. 21), primarily, a corporeal lifting up of the prophet, in order, however, that God *may talk with him.* אֹתָךְ, the accusative particle אות for the prep. את (Ew., *Lehrb.* § 264; GES. § 101). Comp. ch. iii. 22, 24, 27.

Ver. 2. For the divine summons the divine preparation is not wanting, important for all coming time (ch. iii. 24; comp. Rev. i. 17). רוח, coming in this way, by means of God's word, is not "the consciousness, the thinking power" of the prophet, his "animal spirits" (HITZIG), comp. on ch. i. 28; for the **spirit** *comes* into him, does not so much return to him (how would he have been able, ch. i. 28, in a state of unconsciousness, to hear one speaking?); but also not the Holy Spirit for the purpose of inspiration, but: the spirit who was also in the chajoth and in the wheels, ch. i. (HENGSTENBERG); just as the context makes us think of that first. God gives him the spirit to set him on his feet, but also to catch His words; on account of the latter, this divine quickening is at the same time expressed as a coming of the "spirit" into him; it is a quickening of mind and body conjointly.

which brings about the transition from the revelation in vision (מראה) *to the revelation by word.* (HÄVERN.: the Spirit of God, partly as power that overmasters, seizes him, partly as that victorious, divine power—in himself—of genuine courage and noble alacrity in his calling?) An interesting parallel in 1 Kings x. 5.—מִדַּבֵּר (ch. xliii. 6)=מִתְדַּבֵּר partic. Hithp.; in ch. i. 28, מְדַבֵּר partic. Piel. RASCHI: "The Shechinah talked within itself in its glory." In that case, אֵלַי=*of* me. אֵת with the participle=Him who (EWALD, *Lehr.* p. 569 sqq.).

Ver. 3–iii. 11.—*The Divine Commission to the Prophet.*

Vers. 3–7. *What Opposition he has to encounter from his Hearers, as well as the Divine Consolation thereanent.*

Ver. 3. **And He spake unto me**—is continually repeated anew, characteristically, indicating the momentary character of the divine communications.—The mission is portrayed after the manner of the address. בני, for which the LXX. have read בֵּית. The **sons** (children) **of Israel** in general are brought down to the level of גוים (which expression is not used for the tribes and families, nor does it, as HITZIG, KLIEF., mean merely isolated portions of the people),—גּוֹי (from גָּוָה), that which is brought together, like ἔθνος, that which hangs together by means of ἔθος, custom, in distinction from λαός—(comp. Hos. i. 9) which is farther explained by: **the rebels,** and may be illustrated by comparison with Ps. ii. 1. The article emphasizes them as such in a decided way, and the clause: **which rebelled against me,** impressively repeats what is applicable to them. (HENGST.: They are described first according to what they ought to have been, sons of him who wrestled and prevailed in faith with God and man; then according to what they really are, a microcosm, as it were, of the whole heathen world, whose religion and morals were reflected in them; the plural goes even beyond Isa. i. 4. Polanus refers it to Judah and Israel.) How general the statements are is shown by what follows: **they and their fathers**—(Jer. iii. 25). The echo makes itself heard still in the speech of Stephen, Acts vii. 51-53.—עצם, a Pentateuchal word.

Ver. 4. But since it is **the sons** to whom the divine mission directs the prophet, they are put forward, as it were pointed out with the finger, but by no means as "children of God," as Hävern. will have it. **Stiff** is something thoroughly bad (Isa. xlviii. 4); it is otherwise with **hard** (Heb. xiii. 9), which may at all events be determined by circumstances (comp. ch. iii. 8, 9). Here the **face** determines the character of the **heart**, and of its hardness as one that is evil. This evil hardness of the heart explains the before-mentioned faithlessness "down to this very day." The stiffness of the face excludes alike the emotion of shame and the tears of repentance.—**Thee** (thus to those who are חִזְקִי־לֵב, one of the חִזְקִי־אֵל), to the hard-hearted one who is hard (firm) in God, comp. **Ezekiel's name, Introd. § 1** (ch. iii. 8, 9).—**Thus saith the Lord Jehovah.** And here we are by no means, with J. H. Michaelis, to add in thought: etc. Just this short statement, without any addition, is of indescribable majesty as opposed to the rebels; in connection with it, Virgil's *quos ego* may suggest itself to us. [Sept.: κύριος κύριος. Vulg.: *Dominus deus.* PHILIPPS.: the Lord, the Eternal. Other Jewish translators: God the Lord.] It is a short form of Exod. xx. 2.—Because אֲדֹנָי, according to which יְהוָה is usually punctuated, immediately precedes, יֱהוִה gets the points of אֱלֹהִים.—Ver. 5. **And they** strongly emphasizes those who have been mentioned. To supply out of ver. 7: and speak my words unto them, or the like (HENGST.), is not necessary, is even unsuitable, inasmuch as "thus saith the Lord Jehovah" precedes (comp. ch. iii. 11), and also confuses the meaning of the sentence, which finds its apodosis after the expressively resumed המה in וידאו: **they know then,** or: "they know, however," etc. Nevertheless, היה preserves the meaning of **was** (not: is), although, as both cases are supposed: "hearing" and "forbearing," *i.e.* neglecting to hear, המה וידעו' ought not to be so much as: they will then learn by experience, viz. by the fulfilment of the threatenings, which could certainly be applicable to the latter case only. Here the matter in hand is not yet so much hearing and being converted, or not, as is the case afterwards in ch. iii. 17 sqq., but only *the mere giving ear in general, or the refusing even that;* and thus, even whether the prophet finds hearers or not, his "thus saith the Lord Jehovah" is a fact; they know by means of this testimony, which sounded among them, although they may hear nothing farther, that a prophet has been among them. God has by this given sufficient testimony to Himself (John xv. 22). Thus the אם־ואם makes the very least supposition which can be made, and gives the reason for this lowest supposition, hearing as well as forbearing to hear, by means of the clause: **for a house, etc.,** and hence also יֶחְדָּלוּ with full accentuation.—For נביא, comp. Lange's *Comment. on Deuteronomy,* Doct. Reflect. on ch. xiii.

Ver. 6. But whatever opposition the prophet may have to encounter as regards those to whom he is sent, in reference to his own person (hence the subjective negation אל)—so runs now *the divine consolation*—he has nothing to fear (Jer. i. 8, 17; Matt. x. 26, 28), either from themselves or from their words, which with men usually look worse than themselves, and frequently also are worse, since one pulls down another by such means: slander behind backs creates prejudice, and renders abortive the labours of the preacher. **"Thou art not to be afraid"** impressively repeated, thus: no, not at all. סרבים, only here, is taken by some literally, as an adjective (GESEN.): rebellious; by some figuratively, as a substantive (MEIER): straggling briars, or something hard, that injures: prickles, possibly also something for beating: a whip, scourge. Keil: stinging nettles, thorns. סַלּוֹן, here like סִלּוֹן, ch. xxviii. 24. Elsewhere also a figurative and non-figurative expression are combined (Ps. xxvii. 1).—כִּי, according to Keil: **if, but** better: although. It gives the reason for the charge.—אוֹתָךְ is explained by what follows as being the **with** of association (ch. iii. 15; Deut. viii. 15; 1 Kings xii. 11, 14). A gradation: briars, thorns, scorpions! חתת Niphal: to be broken, to pass away, to despair (ch. iii. 9).—**Face**, because it is stiff (ver. 4).—**House** (ver. 5), here again with special reference to his "*dwelling*." Ver. 7: ch. iii. 4; ii. 5. מרי at the close, but with heightened meaning, as it were the incarnation of it. Ch. xliv. 6.

Ver. 8–iii. 11. *What Opposition he might have to encounter in himself, and the Divine Strengthening against it.*

Ver. 8. Hitherto it was the commission as such, viz. a divine one, now it is the same commission as respects what it will contain את אשר־. Inasmuch as Ezekiel belongs to *that* house, מרי (as hitherto always in pause-form) is attributed to him also. It has been understood as an adjective, or elliptically (supply אִישׁ, ver. 7: אַנְשֵׁי). Comp. Jonah; Exod. iv. 13; Jer. i. 6. The divine commission is symbolized by means of the following demand, with which every objection is cut off. (Illustrating, at the same time, the form of expression in John vi.) With appetite, hunger, we have here nothing to do.—Ver. 9: ואראה, comp. ch. i. 1: consequently in vision. בו, because יד is of the common gender; others make the suffix neuter, alleging that יד is always feminine.—מגלת־, written after the manner of the Pentateuch on the skin of an animal, Ps. xl. 7; Heb. x. 7 (Rev. x. 2). J. D. Michaelis makes the remark here: such a book rolled about a rounded piece of wood looks not unlike a baker's roll (!).—Ver. 10. God spreads out this roll before him, so that he can ascertain what follows, the contents of the divine commission, can become acquainted with his mission. It was a so-called opisthograph (LUCIAN: *Vit. Auct.* ix.), PLINY, *Ep.* 49. Written over inside, and *on the back* (comp. Rev. v. 1), not merely, as usual, the inside alone; **within and without**, indicating a writing *of great size*, whose fulness of contents is also clear at once to every one, by which writing we are to understand the book of our prophet, whose character, as will immediately appear, is to be specified as קינה (wailing, mourning, lamentation, xix. 1), הגה (from the low sound), and הי (according to GESEN., for נְהִי; Ew.: a sound of wailing=הוֹי). Comp. therewith, Exod. xxxi. 18; Zech. v. 1; Jer. xxxvi. 18; Dan. v. 25.

Ch. iii. 1. What he *finds before him* (ch. ii. 8, 9); he would certainly not seek it for himself. After the acceptance without objection (symbolized by the eating), the speaking to the house of Israel is to take place: ולך דבר, ἀσυνδέτως, without ו between them, *one* idea. Only what God imparts to him he is to preach, and that immediately: and therefore nothing of his own, and no delay in accordance with his own judgment (2 Tim. iv. 2). The objectivity and sovereignty of the divine word are strongly emphasized. Comp. Deut. xviii. 18; Jer. i. 9 (Matt. x. 20).—Ver. 2. A symbolical transaction, and also taking place in vision (Deut. viii. 3; Ps. cxix. 130, 131).—Ver. 3. An intensification of the thought to the highest degree, so that the prophet is not merely to be willing to accept (to "eat"), but what he has accepted is to be his food, on which he lives, and that which fills his inner man, which determines his activity outwardly. Comp. Ps. xl. 8; John iv. 31–34 (1 Tim. iv. 6; Luke vi. 45). Double accusative—ואכלה, with emphasis (GESEN. *Gramm.* § 126), neut.: as respects sweetness, as sweet as honey. A frequent comparison as applied to the fear of God, His word and the like (comp. Jer. xv. 16). The bitter element (Rev. x. 9, 10) is perhaps presupposed in what he saw written on the roll (ch. ii. 10; comp. Rom. ix. 2). In this way the bitter element would come first, and so much the greater an act of obedience would the prophet's eating appear. And so Klief. might legitimately emphasize the sweet after-taste, and also point to this, that Ezekiel, after and during all the misery which he has to announce, will have also something sweet in his mouth in saying it, or even in merely knowing it respecting Israel. Comp. Introd. § 5; comp. however, ver. 14 also.

Ver. 4. לך־בא; comp. the imperative in vers. 1, 11. A more expressive repetition of the command in the mission. Hence the sweet taste which the prophet experienced in ver. 3 symbolizes, *first of all, his alacrity;* thus the divine preparation, the strengthening experienced in respect of that which would possibly offer resistance in himself; so that there may be a retrospective reference to the main hindrance, namely, that which lay with Israel (ch. ii. 3–7).—Ver. 5. It seems like a relief that Ezekiel is not sent to עמקי־, which certainly stands for those speaking a language foreign to a Jew (comp. Isa. xxxiii. 19), as is also explained in so many words in ver. 6, and which, in parallelism here with heavy tongue, will mean not so much "deep" of sound, as rather, in accordance with the cognate idea of deep, viz. *obscure as regards the interpretation,*—is there a reference to the widely-opened lips of the stammering tongue? The plural, because of the collective עם. So already CALVIN.—אתה שלוח, standing in the middle, refers alike to the positive and to the negative part of the sentence; we may supply: *but.*—The **house of Israel** is the prophet's *own* house (ver. 11), in whose case, therefore, lip and tongue have not the stamp of *strangeness* for him.—Ver. 6. This more general thought in ver. 5 receives in ver. 6 a peculiar colouring, inasmuch as, on the one hand, the **many nations** are made prominent by the side of Israel,—Ezekiel's sphere of labour is *small and contracted* in comparison,—and inasmuch as, on the other hand, stress is laid upon the circumstance: "*whose words* (if they had to speak to thee) *thou* wouldst *not* understand"—thus the hindrance as regards their lip and tongue would lie with the prophet. But in the latter respect, it is rather that he has to speak ("and speakest in my words," vers. 4, 11), and not so much to hear. The subject in hand is the power of comprehension which the prophet is to meet with. Now, this is a contrast which lies in thought between the lines. But another connected therewith (just as it is hinted by the contrast drawn between Israel and the heathen, to whom Israel was compared above in ch. ii. 3) is expressed in so many words: אם לא אליהם, where ובית ישׂ־ in ver. 7 is to be understood as the principal clause, and המה־ as in parenthesis, so that the sense is: Ezekiel is sent not to those whom he ought to understand, and cannot understand, but to Israel, who ought to hear him, and will not hearken to him. Those to whom God does not send him would throw no hindrance in his way; although he might not be able to understand them, they would *hearken unto him*—שמע with אל, contrasted indeed with the inability to understand on his part, as well as, of course, on their part also; but only the former reference comes to be considered when the question is as to the right accomplishment of his task, that of speaking God's words; it does not indeed signify "assent" (HENGST.), but a *giving heed*, and therefore what presupposes *interest* at least, if not *desire*, and what might possibly lead to more, perhaps, as Kimchi remarks: they would seek after an interpreter of thy words. But although the prophet is sent not to such, but rather to Israel, yet (ver. 7) **the house of Israel** does not manifest even the interest which heathens would show, for they *will* not even pay any attention to Ezekiel, not to speak of becoming obedient to his words. The relief is thus only seeming. Comp. Matt. xxiii. 37. [Similar and different explanations: For the most part אם־לא is understood as a formula of swearing, or as an asseveration (verily), and the sentence hypothetically (if I sent thee); comp. on the other hand Hitzig, Keil. For אם־לא, Ew. reads אם־לא instead of לו, just as a Lap. does, instead of לוא! The old translations omit לא without hesitation, while the Masoretes, on the other hand, mark the verse because of its threefold לא. HITZIG, KEIL: אם־לא = "but," referring אליהם and המה to Israel, and ישמעו אליך = they are able, ought to understand thee. The latter expression, however, does not mean the same thing as "to hearken to any one." COCC.: If I had not sent thee to them (Israel), those others (the heathen) would hearken to thee. The words have also been understood interrogatively: if I had not sent thee to them, would not those others hearken to thee?] The meaning we have given harmonizes with the history of Naaman the Syrian, of the book of Jonah, of the woman of Canaan, of the heathen centurion (Matt. viii.). Comp. also Matt. xi. 21 sqq., xii. 41.—**Not unto thee,** because **not unto me**: what a *strengthening* of Ezekiel! That must have changed his wrath into the sorrow of love, ch. xx. 8; comp. Matt. x. 24, 25; John xv. 20.—כל־בית considered as a whole, so that the exceptions do not come into consideration. The wicked hardness of the heart (comp. on ch. ii. 4) is here attributed to the forehead, because it finds expression there; that the stiffness of the "heart" is here expressed, proves the correctness of the explanation given on ch. ii. 4 of the hardness as applied to the heart (Isa. xlviii. 4; Jer. iii. 3; Exod. xxxii. 9; Matt. xix. 8).

Ver. 8. The divine *strengthening* of Ezekiel, now quite clearly expressed, while his labours have become more difficult, and not, as it appeared, more easy, offers itself as the explanation of his name (comp. on ch. ii. 4). It is also not without design that the word used in reference to him is not "stiff," but **hard,** which we find repeatedly. A divine confronting. Comp. Jer. i. 18, xv. 20.—Ver. 9. The thought is still further intensified by means of the comparison. שָׁמִיר (from שָׁמַר, to hold fast; hence: to keep) means something hard; hence a thorn; here the hardest of precious stones. **Harder than stone,** a proverbial expression of the diamond. Bochart, comparing the σμύρις, emery, understands a substance for grinding and polishing. Comp. also P. Cassel on "Schemir." According to the Jewish Hagada and Turkish legend: a wonderful worm, whose blood is said to have cut through the stones without noise at the building of Solomon's temple. לא־, the admonition sounds like a prohibition and promise in one. Comp. ch. ii. 6, 5.—Ver. 10. The conclusion and return to the prophet himself, in view of the possible resisting element in him (ch. ii. 8 sqq.). An allusion at the same time to the symbolic transaction in ver. 1 sqq.—**All the words,** but those which God will first speak to him.—The **heart** first, because otherwise the **ears** are of little use (Acts xvi. 14).—Ver. 11 (ver. 15). Comp. ver. 4. The "house of Israel" there is the "golah" (**captivity**) here, as a community, a society, which lies nearer to the prophet, because of its being his own people. **Thy,** not: My (Exod. xxxii. 7), ch. xxxiii. 2, 12, 17. As often דִּבֵּר and אמר together, the words to be spoken following the latter (ch. ii. 4). At the same time, a setting forth clearly of the position that he has to speak. Comp. ch. ii. 5, 7, iii. 27.

DOCTRINAL.

1. "A deeper meaning lies in this awakening word. First, the creature falls down in silence before the infinitude of the Creator; this is humility, the basis and root of all religious conduct. But he whom the Creator has permitted to come but little short of being himself God, whom He has crowned with glory and honour (Ps. viii. 5), is not to remain lying in half-conscious, silent adoration; he is to rise to his feet, that he may hear the word of God. But certainly he cannot set himself upon his feet; the Spirit must raise him up as a spirit, if he is to understand what God says. Lo, this is the holy psychology of Holy Scripture, this is the freedom of the highest thinking about God, which comes through God and from God" (UMBREIT).

2. The overmastering divine factor in the prophets does not, however, suffer them to appear by any means unconscious. Ezekiel falling down upon the earth, becomes, even in the midst of the divine revelation, and under the impression of it, thoroughly conscious of what is earthly and human in his own self as contrasted with it [*i.e.* the revelation]. If this self of the prophet stands in a receptive attitude in that part of the revelation made to him which is pure vision, yet plastic fancy gives symbolic form to the expression, so as to be understood by men, in similitudes drawn from the earthly world, and memory is able to reproduce for us what has been seen. But still farther, where, as in ch. ii., what has been inwardly received and experienced is expressed in

words as idea and thought, Ezekiel must first rise to his feet, and become capable in spirit of understanding the divine commission. Besides, a vast elevation of the mere natural life is the unmistakable characteristic of our section; comp. ch. ii. 5, 6, iii. 8, 9.

3. John also, although he had lain on the Lord's breast, at sight of Him (Rev. i.) fell at His feet as one dead. And by this as a standard, that very great familiarity which proclaims itself in so many prayers of far lesser saints ought to learn to measure and to moderate itself. There is, however, in our prayers more fancy and sham feeling than real intercourse with the Lord.

4. "An image of the new birth. When God bids us rise from the death in which we are lying (Eph. ii. 1, 5, v. 14), He at the same time imparts to us His Spirit, who quickens us and raises us up. Similarly is it with our strengthening in all that is good. We are to do our duty; and He brings it about that we are able to do it, Phil. ii. 13" (Cocc.).

5. "God does not cast down His own in order to leave them lying on the ground; but He lifts them up immediately afterwards. In believers, in other words, the haughtiness of the flesh is in this way corrected. If, therefore, we often see the ungodly terrified at the voice of God, yet they are not, like believers, after the humiliation, told to be of good courage," etc. (Calv.)

6. "It was only when the Spirit was added that some effect was produced by the voice of God. God works, indeed, effectually by means of His word; but the effectiveness is not bound up with the sound, but proceeds from the secret impulse of the Spirit. The working of the Spirit is here connected with the word of God, yet in such a way, that we may see how the external word is of no consequence unless it is animated by the power of the Spirit. But when God speaks, He at the same time adds the effectual working of His Spirit" (Calv.).

7. "Signs without the word are in vain. What fruit would there have been if the prophet had merely seen the vision, but no word of God had followed it? And this may be applied to the sacraments also, if they were mere signs before our eyes; it is the word of God only that makes the sacraments in some measure living, just as is the case with the visions" (Calv.).

8. By means of the repeated וַיֹּאמֶר the divine revelation in word is identified with the revelation of glory in ch. i., which was to appear as the "Shechinah" in the Messiah, according to the Targums falling back upon the older tradition. One of the steps towards the *Logos* in John i.

9. "In Jehovah and His covenant-relation to Israel lies the necessity of His revelation; His testimony, the tidings from Him, *must* be heard in the midst of Israel. Thus Jehovah Himself wills not merely the conversion, but also the hardening of the people (Isa. vi. 9 sqq.), in so far as, first of all, He merely wills the preaching of Himself. Hence, if on the one hand the prophetic preaching must be traced back strictly to the will of God, is to be looked upon as an outcome and transcript of it, not less is this the case as regards its effects; the hearing and not hearing of the same is likewise God's will, since otherwise He would be under the necessity of withholding His word itself" (Häv.).

10. The symbolical procedure with the book-roll belongs manifestly to the vision, is of the nature of vision, however much, as narrated, it resembles an external occurrence. Bordering, according to Tholuck, on "the rhetorical domain of metaphor," the representation teaches, at all events, how cautiously the exposition of Ezekiel will have to proceed in this respect.

11. Umbreit remarks on ch. iii. 1 sqq.: "Here we have the right expression for enabling us to form a judgment and estimate of true inspiration. The divine does not remain as a strange element in the man; it becomes his own feeling thoroughly, penetrates him entirely, just as food becomes a part of his bodily frame." "And the written book of the seer," he says in conclusion, "bears quite the stamp of something thoroughly pervaded alike by the divine and human."

12. A parallel to the symbolical transaction in Ezekiel, of which Hävernick remarks that it "is the reality of an inner state, of the highest spiritual excitement, of the true and higher entering into the divine will," is presented by the second book of Esdras, xiv. 38 sqq. Comp. the difference of this "dead, apocryphal imitation," by means of which the thought of pure, divine inspiration is meant to be expressed.

13. The unintelligibility of the language of the heathen world for the prophet is to be taken in a purely formal sense; for as respects the material element, the substance, the manner of the thinking, and not of the mere speaking, there is nothing at all said. For the prophet this inner side of the heathen languages would, it is true, present equal difficulty, if not even more, than that outer one. But emphasis is laid on the willingness of the heathen in spite of both, their pricking up their ears in order to understand, which was wanting in Israel. And therefore, what hinders the understanding lies in the case of the heathen merely in the language; in the case of Israel, on the other hand, in this very circumstance. That the language of Israel was the holy language in which God had spoken from the beginning to them, must as regards the import also have lightened the labours of Ezekiel, and consequently have produced a relief in this respect, where, in the case of the heathen, the language brought with it an additional difficulty. It is sometimes easier to exert an influence upon men of the world than upon men who are familiar with the "language of Canaan" (Isa. xix. 18) from childhood up. Just because Israel at once understood what the topic was in Ezekiel's mouth ("he spake, of course, merely what Moses and the other prophets had spoken," Cocc.), their disgust and repugnance towards God's word as soon as possible turned aside out of his way. The alleviation through the disposition of heart on the part of the heathen became in this case the reverse through the disposition of heart on the part of Israel.

14. "The distinction which Greeks and Romans made between their language and that of the barbarians, reduces itself to that of culture. It is otherwise with the distinction between the language of Israel and that of the heathen nations. Israel's language is formed by means of God's word, while the languages of the heathen nations were formed from purely human developments" (Klief.).

15. There is thus in Ezekiel the same hopeful

(although, in reference to Israel, mournful) outlook into the heathen world, which in the Old Covenant already announces the days of the New. "It follows from the stress laid on the receptivity of the heathen, that salvation will yet at some future time be offered to them in an effectual way" (HÄV.).

HOMILETIC HINTS.

Ver. 1. The name *Son of man* belongs above all to Him who did not fall to the ground before the vision of the divine glory, but descended from the midst of the enjoyment of this glory to our earth.—Ezekiel and Christ, type and antitype.—Daniel also is so addressed (ch. viii. 17); and if Ezekiel saw God as a man, Daniel saw the Lord of an everlasting dominion as a son of man (ch. vii.). Thus they bore upon them the stamp of the future, of the fulness of the times.—"I know thy weakness, that thou art a man, and canst not bear the splendour of the divine majesty" (B. B.).—"Although preachers are compared to angels, yet they continue men, and ought to keep this always in mind" (STCK.).—"Even the most pious and most gifted teachers are subject to human infirmities, Gal. ii. 11" (ST.).—"Because teachers are men, hearers ought also to learn to bear patiently with their infirmities, 2 Cor. xii. 13" (ST.).—"We ought not to remain lying on the ground, either in sin, or from laziness of the flesh, or with slavish fear, when God calls us" (STCK.).—"So long as man still lies on the ground, God cannot use him for His service" (ST.).

Ver. 2. "Let visions be ever so great, yet they are not so useful as the word" (B. B.).—God's glory is not meant to kill, but rather to make alive.—"It is the Lord Himself, who fills His children with dismay, that also comforts them again, Hos. vi. 1" (O.).—"The world smiles, in order to rage; flatters, in order to deceive; allures, in order to kill; lifts up, in order to bring low" (CYPRIAN).—"A herald of God ought to stand high above the world, with his spirit in heaven" (A L.).—"The man whom God sends, He also qualifies for it, and furnishes with the necessary powers, giving him also His *Spirit*, as is ever still the experience of the servants of God" (STCK.).—The real prophetic anointing: "the spirit came into me."—To whomsoever God gives an office, He gives understanding also. The fact that so many void of understanding are in office, may easily arise from this circumstance, that they have their office from men. For it is the Spirit of God, and not the clerical band, that makes the prophet.—"If God's Spirit does not uphold, teach, guide, rule, strengthen, keep us, we are nothing" (STCK.).—There is a difference between our setting ourselves on our feet, and God's Spirit setting us on our feet. The feet indeed remain our own, but the way along which they run is, like the power by which they are able to do so, God's, and the steps are also sure steps.—"O that we were at all times disposed to hear Him who speaks to us!" (STCK.)—Vers. 1, 2. At the installation of a preacher in his office: (1) What the congregation ought to consider: that the preacher is only a man, but one whom God sets on his feet by His Spirit; (2) What the preacher ought to consider: all this, as well as in particular that God wishes to speak with him, and that he also ought to have been a hearer ere he comes before his hearers.

Ver. 3. "When God demands obedience from us, He does not always promise a happy issue of our labour; but we ought to allow ourselves to be satisfied with His command, even if our labour should appear ridiculous in the eyes of men: our labour is nevertheless well-pleasing before God" (CALVIN).—"Hence the true prophet does not go of his own accord, just as he does not force himself upon the people, and does not come to seek honour and good days with them" (STCK.).—"So God stretches out His hand to sinners" (ST.).—"Even at worldly courts ambassadors of princes are a token of friendship" (STCK.).—Every sinner is a rebel against God.—It is a noticeable feature of the Jews of the present day in general, that they make heathens of themselves, and also take part in revolution against Church and State.—The apple does not fall far from the tree.—There is also a hereditary sin of nations: *e.g.* French vanity, German cosmopolitanism (want of a fixed centre, *Zerfahrenheit*), English selfishness (egoism).

Ver. 4. "Through the habit of sinning the countenance becomes stiff, just as the heart becomes hard in sinning" (STCK.).—"And yet the countenance is the noblest, as the heart is the best part of man, Prov. xxiii. 26; Matt. xv. 19" (STCK.).—"Judas Iscariot, *e.g.*, had a stiff countenance: his question Matt. xxvi. 25, his kiss" (L.).—"Thus saith the Lord" is the watchword of God against all opposition of men, the right war-cry.—Ver. 5. "Ezekiel may, of course, have thought with himself as Moses did, Exod. iv. 1" (ST.).—Preachers ought not to look to, to reckon upon hearers, but to listen to the Lord alone.—To preach God's word compensates even in the case of empty churches.—A full church, therefore, is not always a testimony for the preacher, 2 Tim. iv. 3.—"It serves, at all events, as a testimony, although no other result is attained by the preaching" (L.).—Ver. 6. *Fear* is a word which does not belong to any vocation of a preacher; but as little also does man-pleasing, which is often merely a form of fear.—"The comparison with thorns has reference in general to their unfruitfulness, in particular to their tendency to wound, to injure, their being interlaced together, their seeming bloom, their ultimate burning. As regards the expression scorpions, we are to think of the poison, the secret sting, the cunning. And what a wilderness must the house of Israel be! Ezekiel does not go to strayed sheep, but dwells with scorpions" (STCK.).—"In none of the prophetic books is the rigorous spirit of Moses more perceptible than in the case of Ezekiel" (ROOS). Because God knows our fear, therefore He speaks so repeatedly against it.—Ver. 7. Rebelliousness may well grieve the servant of God, may even rouse him to anger, but ought never to degrade him to the level of a dumb dog.—Spiritual dignitaries are those who carry the word of God high above themselves, even when it meets with nothing but contradiction.—"And fathers of families also are to be like preachers" (L.).

Ver. 8. The enemies of a preacher are not what is worst for him; his friends are often worse than his worst enemies, and his worst enemy of all by far may be his own self. Therefore, know thyself.—"Preachers ought to be patterns, not imitators and followers of the flock" (ST.).—"What an influence the surroundings of a preacher have upon him! And Ezekiel belonged to the same people" (L.).—Many a strange thing happens to one when he is with God. On the other hand, the demand: "Open thy mouth, and eat," is what we should naturally expect; for what does not man eat, and how many useless books are devoured with the greatest eagerness!—"By the mere looking at food no one gets his hunger satisfied, but it must be taken and eaten: and so also the mere hearing and reading of the word of God does not save, but it must be appropriated, and afterwards lived upon" (St.).—Ver. 9. "The word of God is very tender and delicate,—a sweet and deep invitation" (B. B.).—"The hand which presents the Scripture, is the same which also presents to believers the crown, 2 Tim. iv. 7, 8" (Stck.).—Ver. 10. "Such unfolding takes place with prayer on the part of believers, Eph. i.; Ps. cxix. 18 (with burning heart, Luke xxiv. 32; just as in the future with praise and jubilant acclamation, Rev. v. 9), with searching (John v. 39; Matt. vii. 8), and not without manifold temptations" (Fessel).—"This book-roll may also be applied to the bad conscience of the sinner, as well as to the condition of a soul under assault from outward oppression, likewise to the book of the law, to the misery of the damned, as well as used in the sense of a reward-book for the ungodly," etc. (Stck.)—So man finds in his life first the *lamentations* over the vanity of all things, then there wakes up the *sighing* over himself, and the last is the *woe* of dying.

Ver. 8-ch. iii. 3. The wonderful food of Ezekiel in general (Matt. iv. 4) and in particular (John iv. 34).—It served him: for protection, for instruction, for strengthening, for quickening.

Ch. iii. 1. "Ezekiel is no prophet of his own heart. Instead of murmuring against the poor instrument who has received so weighty a commission, let them repent" (H.).—"Comede et pasce, saturare et eructa, accipe et sparge, confortare et labora" (Jer.).—"A teacher must have the word of God not merely on his lips and in his mouth, but in his heart, and converted into nourishment and strength" (St.).—"The maxim: 'Eat what is set before you' (Luke x. 8), applies also to the divine revelation. The position of a chooser, which, instead of the motto, 'what I find,' puts 'what I like,' belongs to what is evil" (H.).—"Without having eaten this roll, no one ought to go and preach" (B. B.).—As against resistance from *without* we are *comforted;* as against opposition from *within*, from ourselves, we are *strengthened*. In the first case there is *suffering*, in the second it may come to *sin*.—Ver. 2. "The word of God is the right food of souls" (St.).—Ver. 3. "By our *taste* our life is determined" (Plato).—"The *sweet* taste means Ezekiel's approbation of God's judgment and commands" (Calv.).—"It is infinitely sweet and lovely to be the organ and spokesman of the Most High" (H.).—"In the case of those who eagerly hear the word of God, it goes into their heart, and as it were into their bowels; it becomes a treasure within them, out of which they bring forth, in overflowing abundance, necessary and wholesome instruction for others" (B. B., St.).—"Even a difficult office ought to be undertaken and discharged with joy; for God can sweeten even what is bitter in it" (St.).—"Even the most painful divine truths have for the spiritually-minded man a gladdening and quickening side" (H.).—"It is in general the quiet secret of all who suffer in true faith, that in their inmost being wormwood turns to honey" (Umbr.).

Ver. 4 sqq. "It was not yet the time of the heathen; it was still Israel's time, to whom also the Lord Himself would come, whose forerunners the prophets were" (Cocc.).—Ver. 7. *Forehead* and *heart* in their psychological correspondence.—Where there is the fear of God in the heart, shame still sits upon the forehead.—Ver. 8. "For hard people hard ministers also are suitable, Prov. xx. 30" (W.). For the rough block a rough wedge.—"God gives His prophet merely a firm countenance and forehead, but not a hard heart. In order to encounter a hard heart, a firm forehead indeed is necessary, but never a hard heart. The heart is to be full of love, and from love the firm forehead even is to be gained" (A L.).—Vers. 8, 9. "He who has to contend with the popular spirit is lost, unless he has a firm hold of Omnipotence. He who has not God decidedly with him, must come to terms with the majority" (H.).—"Firm preachers of this stamp were Nathan against David, Elijah, John the Baptist, Stephen" (A L.). Comp. Matt. xvi. 18. Nevertheless, the diamond does not occur either in Exod. xxviii. 17 sqq. or in Rev. xxi. 19 sqq. Christ will rather be a magnet, John xii. 32.—"God imparts to such a strength which far surpasses the strength of the learned. For God never yields to man. Not that the spirit referred to is a stiff-necked spirit, but God gives them words so powerful and mighty, that no one can gainsay them, Luke xxi. 15" (B. B.).—"This is that 'holy to the Lord' which shone forth on the forehead of the high priest, just as it belongs to all the servants of God" (Stck.).—"Carnal men stumble thereat, all who wish to be flattered or spared; for what is to the one class a stone for building, is to the other a stone of offence" (B. B.).—Ver. 10. "Whoever is to *hear*, must have confidence in him who speaks, and longing to hear, in order that he may lend his ear to the word. The *heart*, above everything, must be present, else the man does not hear, Acts xvi. 14" (Cocc.).—Ver. 11. "The fact, that it is his own people to whom he had to go, at the same time laid Ezekiel under a solemn obligation" (Stck.).—"We must first hear, then we are to speak" (Cocc.).

II. THE FIRST EXECUTION OF THE DIVINE COMMISSION.—Ch. iii. 12–vii. 27.

1. The Installation and Instructions (Ch. iii. 12–27).

12 And the spirit lifted me up, and I heard behind me a sound of a great
13 tumultuous noise: Praised be the glory of Jehovah from His place. And
[I heard] the noise of the wings of the living creatures striking one upon another,
and the noise of the wheels beside them, and the sound of a great tumultuous

14 noise. And the spirit lifted me up, and took me, and I went bitterly, in the
15 heat of my spirit, and [but] the hand of Jehovah was strong upon me. And I
came to the captivity at Tel-abib, who dwelt by the river Chebar, and where
16 they were sitting, there I also sat stunned [starr] in their midst seven days. And
it came to pass at the end of seven days, that the word of Jehovah came unto
17 me, saying, Son of man, I have given thee as a watchman to the house of Israel;
18 and thou hearest a word at my mouth, and thou warnest them from me. If I
say unto the wicked, Thou shalt surely die; and thou warnest him not, and
speakest not to warn the wicked from his wicked way, to save his life,—he, the
wicked, shall die in [because of] his iniquity; but his blood will I require at thine
19 hand. But if thou dost warn the wicked, and he doth not turn from his
wickedness and from his wicked way, he shall die in [because of] his iniquity;
20 but thou hast delivered thy soul. And if the righteous doth turn from his
righteousness, and commit iniquity, and I give a stumbling-block before him,
he shall die, for thou didst not warn him; in his sin he shall die, and his
righteousness which he hath done shall not be remembered; but his blood will
21 I require at thine hand. But if thou dost warn him as a righteous man, not to
sin as being righteous, and he sinneth not, he shall surely live, because he is
22 warned; and thou hast delivered thy soul. And the hand of Jehovah came
upon me there, and He said unto me, Arise, go forth to the valley, and there will
23 I speak with thee. And I arose, and went forth to the valley: and, behold, the
glory of Jehovah standing there, as the glory which I saw by the river Chebar:
24 and I fell upon my face. And the spirit came into me, and set me upon my
feet, and He spake with me, and said unto me: Go, shut thyself within thine
25 house. And thou, son of man, behold, they give [lay] bands upon thee, and bind
26 thee in them, and thou shalt not go out among them. And thy tongue will I make
to cleave to the roof of thy mouth, and thou art dumb, and thou shalt not be to
27 them a man that reproveth; for they are a house of rebelliousness. But when I
speak with thee, I will open thy mouth, and thou sayest unto them, Thus saith
the Lord Jehovah: He that heareth, let him hear; and he that forbeareth, let
him forbear: for they are a house of rebelliousness.

Ver. 13. Sept.: K. *εἰδον φωνην*—
Ver. 14. K. *το πνευμα κυριου ἐξηρεν με*—
Ver. 15. . . . *εἰς τ. αἰχμαλωσιαν μετεωρος, κ. περιηλθον τ. κατοικουντας . . . τ. ὀντας ἐκει, κ. ἐκαθισα ἐκει*—(some MSS. and Syr. omit ואשר המה' שם).

Ver. 19. Another reading: הוא רשע בעונו. Sept. and Arab. have read הרשע for the omitted הרשעה which precedes.

Ver. 25. . . . *δησουσιν σε ἐν αὐτοις, κ. συ μη ἐξελθης ἐξ αὐτων.*

EXEGETICAL REMARKS.

Vers. 12–15. *After the Installation of Ezekiel in his Sphere of Labour by means of the Commission in Word, there follows now the Installation in actual Fact.*

Ver. 12. רוח cannot possibly be anything else here than it has always been hitherto. Both Keil and Klief. unnecessarily bring in "a wind," which, however, according to Keil, carried the prophet through the air not in body, but in spirit, ch. viii. 3, xi. 1, 24. But here, also, just as in ver. 14, there is no reference to being carried through the air. The *lifting up by the spirit* corresponds entirely to the raising up in ch. ii. 2. Only what was there raising up from the earth, in order to stand and hear, is here rather (and that also because of the higher situation of Tel-abib) lifting up from the place of hearing, in order to go and speak; and at the same time, Ezekiel hears immediately behind him קול רעש גדול, by which is signified to him *the marching forth* of the divine glory, with which movement of the same, *his installation in actual fact commences in highest fashion.* His mission, shadowed forth by the character of the vision of glory, begins in this way to be realized in actual fact. Thus, **and the spirit lifted me up** is connected with **and I heard,** etc., and what Ezekiel hears with his actual introduction to his sphere of labour. As the spirit qualified him (ch. ii. 2) to *hear* Him that spake to him, so the spirit moves, lifts him up to do what he is told (ver. 11). Comp. besides, 1 Kings xviii. 12, 46; Matt. iv. 1; Acts viii. 39. The lifting up quite harmonizes with this influence of the spirit, just as it entirely corresponds with the character of the vision (vers. 24, 25) in the midst of which it occurs. And because the prophet is moved to betake himself to his fellow-countrymen, he also hears what he hears **behind** him.—The *great tumultuous noise* (ver. 13, ch. xxxvii. 7; Isa. ix. 5; Jer. x. 22) takes an articulate form, first of all, as *praise of the glory of Jehovah,* whereby our view (given at p. 39) of something super-terrestrial, heavenly, in the chajoth is **only** confirmed. It is not said who gave utterance to this praise; and nothing in the context, at least, compels us to think of heavenly spirits. Thus there remain in fact for it only the chajoth; and for this we may compare not merely Rev. iv. 8 sqq., but even Isa. vi. 3.—**From His place**, no matter whether we refer it to Jehovah or His כבוד, denotes very suitably, what Keil denies, not indeed so much as: who now leaves His place (HENGST.), nor what is said in ch. ix. 3, still less the temple (HÄV.), which is not at all the subject in hand, but perhaps, that from the place where Jehovah's glory has manifested itself to the prophet, and just as it manifested itself, its praise must and will go forth, and that immediately, over Israel (first), and into the whole world, and among all mankind (Mic. i. 3). Hence, also, as respects Ezekiel's doings and labours, how remarkably in this way the praise of the divine glory introduces him to his sphere of action! ממקומו is certainly too far off from ואשמע, to which Keil wishes to refer it! Philippson refers ממקומו to "the creation embraced in the vision: Praised be, etc., from the place where it is borne along, where it tarries" (Isa. xiii. 13). —Ver. 13: comp. ch. i. 24, 9, 11, 23, 15, 20, 21. This was in a manner the musical accompaniment of the laudation expressed above in words. וקול dependent on ואשמע in ver. 12.—נשק, to arrange, to join together. Hiphil: to strike on one another.—It ends, as it began, in the **great tumultuous noise.** ("The life of the creatures is the boundless sphere of the praise of the Creator of heaven and earth [Ps. cxlviii.]. This is the fugue notes of the sublimest music, which makes the universe itself ring. Finely and beautifully for the melodious harmony, we have the happy expression, that the wings *kiss* one another: fearful as is the sound of the striking of wings, and of the wheel-work of creation, yet there is unison and love in it; at last comes the soft, gentle whisper, as in the case of Elijah!" —UMBREIT.)

Ver. 14 (ch. xi. 24) as at ver. 12; the ecstatic lifting up is designated as a being *laid hold of*, a being taken (לקח). Nothing in the context points to "taking away" (J. H. MICH.); on the contrary, he **went** (ואלך), as he had been commanded in vers. 1, 4, 11. *Now*, therefore, a *corporeal* movement of the prophet in space took place, but not by means of wind through the air (JER., KLIEF.). The vision, as to the matter of it, is at an end with (vers. 12, 13) the laudation and great tumultuous noise (comp. Gen. xvii. 22); Keil unnecessarily adopts the view that it ends only with ver. 21. Personally, as respects the person of Ezekiel, the vision ends when he is ecstatically lifted up and laid hold of by the spirit, and not by wind, inasmuch as the power of the spirit put an end to all lingering and loitering in him, and prepared him, so that he betook himself to the quarter that was necessary, as was also expressly indicated to him by the departure of the divine glory. And with this the following description necessarily corresponds. **Bitterly, in the heat of my spirit**—thus he describes what is in *his* spirit, when he goes now on his own feet, after the spirit lifted him up and laid hold of him, so that he could neither stand still, nor move off in any other direction. The subjectivity of the prophet comes into the foreground (so already Calvin has it). The taste that was so sweet before (ver. 3) is followed (as in Rev. x. 9, 10) by a bitter after-taste; the joyousness which Ezekiel felt during the vision, gives place, when the vision ends, to bitterness (Matt. xxvi. 41). This **bitterness** expresses the *special feeling* of the prophet, while **the heat** designates the *general* character of his *mental state.* בחמת רוחי, reflecting the fiery style of the vision he has had, shows Ezekiel's spirit *raised to glowing heat by the wrath of God*, by the unavoidable judgment on Israel which he has to announce. In so far there is as yet no difference which would have to be got rid of or repressed; the difference respects not so much the relation to God, as the relation *to Israel.* It is in this direction that the interpretation of מר is to be sought (have the LXX. read רם?), and that simply as an expression for the *pain* which the prophet specially feels when he goes to his people. That is the human element of bitterness in his divine wrath. Distress and sorrow undoubtedly say too little,—HITZIG: "because the days of cheerful, sportive innocence are now over for him" (!)—but neither is it the "bitterness of fiery wrath because of the hardening of Israel, because of his commission with no prospect of success" (KEIL); and just as little have we to think, with Hengsten., of "holy irritation." In Ezekiel's spirit there is the wrath of God (Jer. xv. 17); but love to his people feels it bitter,—feels bitter pain. Hence: **the hand of Jehovah was strong upon me** (חזקה, according to the ingenious remark of Hitzig, different from כבד in Ps. xxxii. 4), where we must not compare either ch. i. 3 or Isa. viii. 11, but equivalent **to:** God strengthened him, as the Jewish expositors render it, with an allusion to the name Ezekiel. ו may be the simple **and,** not "since" (EWALD), nor as Hengst., who derives the indignation and heat of spirit from the powerful divine influence in him.

Ver. 15. The bitterness of the pain, and the glow of the wrath, and the strengthening of the Almighty, obtain a corresponding plastic expression in the behaviour of the prophet, as soon as he finds himself in the midst of his fellow-exiles. —תל אביב, the dwelling-place of Ezekiel, probably "hill of corn-ears," so called from the elevated situation and richness in grain of this colonial settlement; for other combinations with Tel in Babylon, see GESEN. *Lex.*, ROSENM.; comp. besides, Introd. pp. 7, 8. Jerome gives a symbolical meaning to the name of the place. The LXX. appear to have thought of a form תָּלַל and סָבַב. (The Kethib ואשר has given rise to many far-fetched interpretations. Even a second river has been made of it. The Qeri reads וָאֵשֵׁב, that he has not only come hither, but also remained [!], not to speak of other explanations. It is simply to be read וַאֲשֶׁר, and to be connected with שָׁם: **and where.**) **Seven days**—not because the week is the unity that most readily suggests itself for a plurality of days (HITZ.), nor as a standard period for cleansing, consecration, preparation for holy service (KEIL), but, if this number shadows forth anything, **then,** according to its leading symbolical signification (BÄHR, *Symb.* i. pp. 187 sqq., 193 sqq.), the *covenant* relation of God to Israel, by which the wrath as well as the pain of the prophet might be excited. Comp. Job ii. 13; Gen. l. 10; 1 Sam. xxxi. 13 (Ps. cxxxvii. 1).—משמים partic. Hiph. HITZ.: sunk in fixed silence; KEIL: motionless and still. Comp. Ezra ix. 3, 4. (HENGST.: in a state of horror. But how is this conceivable during the whole seven days?)—Häv. finds in the text two classes of exiles: those who had recently settled near the Chaboras, and the old inhabitants of former times belonging to the kingdom of the ten tribes still dwelling there. Comp. Introd. pp. 7, 8.

Vers. 16-27. *To the Installation of Ezekiel in actual Fact there is appended an Admonition of a more general Character* (vers. 16-21); *and a special One having reference to his Sphere of Labour* (vers. 22-27).

Ver. 16. The *admonition* after the installation comes to Ezekiel in a *new revelation.* (In the usual Hebrew text we find between ימים and ויהי דבר־ the sign *Pisca:* פסקא באמצע פסוק, *i.e.* a pause in the middle of the verse.)—Ver. 17. There is first an admonition of a *more general* character, but less, as Hitz. supposes, with respect to the relation between the revelation and him, that he is to speak only when he receives a revelation, than *as to how he is to look upon himself in reference to his sphere of labour;* for the latter reference is that which predominates in what follows. צֹפֶה partic., not subst., from צפה, "to draw round," to draw over, to cover, to take care of, hence: "to keep one's eyes on anything,"—the *seer*, the *look-out*, who from his watch-tower, which, in the case of the prophet, is the divine standpoint, turns to account the revelations which are made to him for the weal and woe of the people entrusted to his care as a watchman. Comp. 1 Sam. xiv. 16; 2 Sam. xiii. 34, xviii. 24; Jer. vi. 17; Hab. ii. 1; Isa. lvi. 10; Ezek. xxxiii. 1 sqq.—With the judicial character which predominates in the mission of Ezekiel, the **word from My mouth** is not revelation in general, but announcement, hint, command, sentence in connection with the threatening judgment of God, with a view thereto, and determined thereby; and, therefore, זהר in Hiph. not: to enlighten in the sense of to teach (Heb. xiii. 17), but in the sense of to caution, to warn. ממני is explained in accordance with the preceding מפי. HÄV.: "partly in compliance with definite divine instructions received, partly with continual appeal and reference thereto."

Ver. 18. The רשע, like the צדיק in what follows, is not so much a rhetorical personification of the species (HENGST.), and that of the people on the one hand, of the little flock on the other, but a characteristic individualization, for this preliminary period of the New Covenant; already the individuals are separating themselves from Israel as a national whole according to their individual qualification, *i.e.* as they exhibit themselves in their procedure towards the divine judgment on Israel, and the public preaching takes the shape of the special care of souls; and in this way the national mission of the prophetic order, on the one hand, enters more deeply into its spiritual significance, and, on the other hand, brings into prominence its general human side.—**If I say unto the wicked,** in accordance with ver. 17: "thou hearest a word at my mouth," equivalent to: when thou hearest what I say unto the wicked, that I announce unto him inevitable *ruin* in the impending judgment (Luke x. 16; 1 Thess. iv. 8).—מוֹת תמות, the original threatening on the transgressor of the divine word (Gen. ii. 17) is nothing new, unheard of, is only applied here (Gen. xx. 7) to the individual. In order to make his duty quite clear to the prophet, to free it from every objection, whether springing from his own heart, or coming from his fellow-men, or from surrounding circumstances, to fix it for all cases, and thus to enforce it very strongly, the simple **and thou warnest him not** is expanded still farther into what follows, **and speakest not to warn,** etc., implying at the same time repetition and urgency. Although the nation as a whole is lost (ch. iii. 7), the return of the individual is nevertheless, nay, so much the more, to be sought (Acts xx. 31; 2 Tim. iv. 2). The substance of such warning: "of" and "from *his* way;" it is consequently not the judgment of God, this way of God with Israel, for this may issue in life, inasmuch as it awakens to return, to repentance, but it is his *own* way and will, the life of *self*-will on the part of the רשע, which, in accordance with God's righteousness, is changed into death, just as it *is* in its root a dying, because departure from God, from the divine way, pointed out in the law. There lies at the root of רשע (if not, as contrasted with צדק, the meaning of what is crooked, awry—HUPF. on Ps. i. 1—and thus deviation from the straight, right way, yet at least) apostasy from God (Ps. xviii. 22 [21]). He is one who, according to the divine law, the rule for Israel as a nation, appears unrighteous, here as everywhere the opposite of צדיק.—הָרְשָׁעָה, which the LXX. in ver. 19 also have passed over, refers to דרכו (like אֹרַח), construed as feminine, perhaps in order to emphasize the significance of the figurative expression.—לחיתו, the object of the warning, perhaps at the same time: *to bring him to life again* (Ps. xxx. 4 [3]; Hos. vi. 2; Eph. ii. 5).—עָוֹן, properly: what is not straight, perverted in consequence of deviating from the straight, right way, hence: *unrighteousness,* and also: *iniquity.* In his perversity the unrighteous man necessarily brings upon himself death as a consequence; there is an עון קץ, as it is expressed in ch. xxi. 30 [E. V. 25].—The close of the verse likewise contains an allusion to a passage in Genesis, Gen. ix. 5 (xlii. 22), only with this difference, that בקש stands instead of דרש, which latter Ges. explains as: to go after any one, thus of a more active reclamation; while בקש means more a looking after, a seeking with the eyes. It is the life, which is in the blood, of those in Israel which is entrusted to the prophet as a watchman. For this Jehovah, the Supreme Proprietor, demands a reckoning. The prophet who forgets his duty, which he owes to the unrighteous in God's stead, becomes a manslaughterer, a murderer of that man, **and is regarded** as such by God.

Ver. 19. **What the way of deliverance is for**

the unrighteous man, is shown, viz. *return*, alike inwardly (**wickedness**) and outwardly. The deliverance of soul, as regards the prophet (here נפש, formerly דם Gen. ix. 4), is preservation from the divine avenging of blood.—Ver. 20. Antithetic parallelism of this and the following verse with the two preceding. Hengst., holding fast by the people in his interpretation, denies the personal contrast in צדיק; they are, according to him, designated as wicked at present, as righteous with reference to their destiny and better past. The description of the **righteous man** does not certainly rise above a certain outward legality and isolated **righteousnesses.** Ver. 18: באמרי, here בשוב.—**His righteousness** is that attained by him as regards the law of Israel, the national-legal righteousness; hence, also, departure therefrom is quite conceivable as "committing wickedness (iniquity);" and, for the decision of the matter, the **stumbling-block** is **given** by God; *i.e.*, to such a righteous man (comp. however, Prov. iv. 11, 12, xv. 19) the exile, or the state of matters in Jerusalem, becomes a temptation from God, in so far as, for the purpose of deciding the condition of the man, such like outward circumstances are arranged by Him, but not: a stumbling-block "on which he may die" (Ew.); for הוא ימות begins the apodosis, just as in ver. 18 הוא רשע, **he shall die,**—so it is decided as to the apostate righteous man, who has become like the wicked (ch. xviii. 24), and therefore must appear still worse than he; just as the stumbling-block to be given by God brings him also in actual fact to utter ruin. The parallel, however, with ver. 18 necessarily implies neglect in warning on the part of the prophet; and as such omission is presupposed, so also the death of this "righteous" man, his ruin in the Chaldean divine judgment, must be expressly (כי) referred to the prophet, and, consequently, the possibility of another result be presupposed. How the case will be in reality with this man, who is worse than the רשע, is shown by the statement: **in his sin he shall die,** which points, not to a false step arising from mere weakness, ignorance, but to *wickedness become a habit.* The individualizing description of our verse (as already in ver. 19) gives additional proof of the fearful corruption of Israel as a whole, which was disclosed in what precedes (ch. ii. 3). **His righteousnesses** mean, according to Hengst., "the good works of pious ancestors, Ps. cxxxii. 1" (!). They are the legal deeds of the "righteous man," or collectively: what he has done in accordance with the law, works without reference to the state of the heart. [Rosenm. reads צִדְקָתוֹ as a collective singular with the plural of the verb תִזָּכַרְןָ.] Comp. besides, on ver. 18.—Ver. 21. ואתה כי as in ver. 19; but the issue of the case is exactly the opposite: there warning without return, here warning which attains its object. After the three dark pictures which precede, this is drawn in colours so much the brighter. *It is the righteous man as he ought to be:* and hence also the emphatic mode of expression. Comp. besides, 1 John iii. 8, 9, ii. 1, iii. 6.—כי as in vêr. 20. Comp. besides, on ver. 19.

In vers. 22–27 there follows a quite *special* instruction for Ezekiel as to his sphere of labour, **which** is introduced by a special demand in vêr. 22. Comp. ch. i. 3. It is at Tel-abib, also, that this divine revelation is made to the prophet. Hengst. consistently asserts that there is no actual change of place, that Ezekiel's betaking himself to the valley, like his presence at the Chebar, takes place in the inner region of the spirit (!).—The **valley,** as distinguished from the height on which Tel-abib was situate, is not exactly the plain extending to the river—not הַשָּׂדֶה, but הבקעה, a certain valley between the mountain-walls there. It is not so much the solitude (HENGST.) as the subsequent renewal of the earlier vision of glory which leads to the choice of this locality. (2 Cor. vi. 17; Ps. xlv. 10, 11; comp. Ezek. xxxvii. 1, 2.)

Ver. 23; comp. ch. i. 28. The vision begins with: **and, behold.** עמד indicated to him the standing background and protection for his labours, or the Judge before the door!—Ver. 24; comp. ch. ii. 2. Hitzig's conjecture seems a correct one, that this definite ordering of the prophet into the house is connected with the preceding summons to go forth; it appears at least so much the more visible,—which is certainly of importance, if the prophet was, in the first place, to preach to the eye merely of his countrymen. If his procedure in ver. 15 was a sermon, this *shutting of himself up within his house* is, primarily, nothing else,—an action, a condition of Ezekiel's, meant for a sermon; just as in his case, more readily than in that of any of the other prophets, the inward becomes outward, and the outward is inward. His isolation from the midst of his countrymen in the valley *for God* is now followed by his isolation *among them* within his own house; the former a momentary one, the latter of a more enduring character. This latter symbolical sermon is further defined as a *non in publicum prodire* (ver. 25), and more exactly as a silence on the part of the voice calling to repentance (ver. 26). Those who are so very eager after what is visible are accordingly directed, first of all, to look at what the prophet will do (ch. xii. 6, 11). That would necessarily excite attention, and curiosity would necessarily, with ever growing intensity, desire to have it explained, what Ezekiel's acting has in view, what it means. This is certainly the primary reason why the prophet is not only summoned away by God (ver. 22 sqq.) from the midst of his countrymen, but also receives the command to shut himself up in his house in their midst. The shutting himself up in his house is therefore, of course, symbolic, although, at the same time, it explains to us the way in which ch. iv and v. are to be understood, viz. as domestic occurrences. It has been regarded as a picture of the future of Ezekiel's own prophetic destiny (HÄV.), and also as a picture of Jerusalem under investment (EPHRAEM SYRUS, JER.), inasmuch as it was falsely assumed that there was a connection with what follows immediately, or at a later stage. (RASCHI: that thou mayest show them that they are unworthy of admonition. GROT.: in order to await the suitable time for speaking.) Moreover, this **house** of the prophet is the innocent cause of all the "leisure of domestic life," amid which, according to Ewald, Ezekiel was almost exclusively occupied in literary pursuits.

Ver. 25. The shutting himself up in his house is not intended to shut out his countrymen from him; for what he is to do there is for the house of Israel (ch. iv. 3 sqq.), is done before their eyes (ver. 12; comp. also ch. viii. 1); but he (ואתה) is to be for them one who is shut up, *i.e.* in the first place, *one who is not to go forth into their midst.*—For **son of man,** comp. on ch. ii. 1.—**Behold, they lay,** etc., can only be his countrymen, and that not as being members of his family, who take him for a madman (A Lapide),—a view which nothing in the context favours. But Hitzig's view (accepted by Keil) of invisible, heavenly powers, which bound Ezekiel ("as it were bands of enchantment"!), is quite opposed to the context. Ver. 25 by no means moves in the same line with ver. 26; but in ver. 26 the transition is made from men to God. Ch. iv. 8, according to Keil's own explanation, has no connection with this. Everything depends on whether we are to look upon the *binding* of the prophet as intended to prevent him leaving his house, which would, indeed, fall in with the shutting himself up in it commanded by God, but which would correspond little with the disposition of the prophet's countrymen, who do not certainly wish what God wishes, but much rather the contrary! (Hence, perhaps, Kimchi: Go into thine house, and thou shalt be shut up therein, just as if they had bound thee with bands.) We are not to assert with Keil that a fettering by means of these would be irreconcilable with ch. iv. and v., since a fettering of this description might take place afterwards, and Ezekiel, meanwhile, might again have become free; and just as little is it to be regarded as a decisive objection to this view, that no trace of such assault is to be discovered elsewhere; our passage itself might contain the missing trace. But ולא תצא בתוכם is rather (as also Hengst.) =*but thou* (ואתה) *wilt* (shalt) *not go forth to them.* Instead of hindering him from speaking, his countrymen will, on the contrary, in their curiosity, do everything, will even lay violent hands upon him, that he may come forth and speak to them; they will throw bands over him, will bind him with them, in order the more easily to bring him forth. All that they gain thereby, besides his not going forth himself to them in such a case, will be, that, notwithstanding their efforts, he will not speak to them, since—ver. 26—God will hinder it. The shutting himself up in his house is to become something more definite, viz. *the shutting of his mouth at the same time,* and that as an איש מוכיח, which is here equivalent in meaning to "a declaimer against vice," in an almost exclusively formal respect, since they are **a house of rebelliousness** (ch. iii. 5), and nothing material is to be accomplished among them as a whole. Comp. on ver. 18.

Ver. 27. ובדברי points back to באמרי in ver. 18. Thus the silence of Ezekiel is even here already a judgment of God upon Israel: for the opening of his mouth has for its object the communication of the divine revelation to his countrymen. Comp. besides, on ch. ii. 4, iii. 11, ii. 5, 7 (Rev. ii. 7, xxii. 11). The reference of vers. 25–27 is primarily to ch. iv., v.; in a less degree it is carried on to ch. vii.; but perhaps ch. xxiv. 27 and ch. xxxiii. 22 refer to vers. 26, 27. Comp. there. In general, vers. 26, 27 express the entire dependence of the prophet, alike in silence and in speaking, on God, and consequently his divine legitimation; in particular, the remaining dumb imposed upon him—but that as regards the other character of his prophetic labours from ch. xxxiv. onwards—may be applied to the period down to the destruction of Jerusalem, as characteristic of this period, and therefore significantly repeated at its close. Comp. besides, on ch. v. 5.

Additional Note on Ch. iii. 12–27.

[This section, which should have formed a separate chapter, records the entrance of Ezekiel on his high vocation, and contains the first message delivered to him respecting it. His former place of abode, it would seem, was not the most advantageously situated for prosecuting with success the work committed to him; and, in consequence, he removed to Tel-abib, which is nowhere else mentioned, but was, in all probability, the best peopled locality, or the chief town of the Jewish colony. When he came and saw the captives dwelling there, in a dejected and mournful condition, he sat down among them for seven days continuously—sitting being the common attitude of grief (Ezra ix. 3; Lam. i. 1–3), and seven days being the usual period for the manifestation of the heaviest sorrow (Job ii. 13). By thus spending, at the outset, so many days of desolation and sadness, he gave proof of his deep fellow-feeling with his exiled brethren in their depressed condition, and showed how entirely he entered into their state. Thus sorrowing in their sorrow, and breathing the tenderness of a sympathizing spirit toward them, he sought to win their confidence, and secure a favourable hearing for the words of mercy and of judgment which he was from time to time to press upon their notice.

The prophet, however, did not go alone to this mournful field of prophetic agency. He was borne thither under the conscious might of the Spirit of God, and was attended by the symbols of the divine presence and glory. When he rose to proceed on his course, the whole machinery of the heavenly vision began also to move; and amid the crashing or tumultuous noise which broke upon his spiritual ear, he heard the words, "Blessed be the glory of Jehovah from His (or its) place"—certainly a somewhat peculiar utterance, and one not found in any other part of Scripture; yet not materially different from another in frequent use, "Blessed be the name of the Lord." The glory of Jehovah here was that manifested glory which had appeared in vision to the prophet, and which was, in other words, a revelation of His glorious name. To pronounce it blessed from its place, was in effect to bless God Himself, as thus and there revealing His adorable perfections and divine will. And as the prophet was going to be the representative and herald of these in a sphere where there was much to damp his spirit, and withstand his faithful agency, it was fit that he should go with the solemn word pealing in his ears, from those ideal ministers of heaven, "Blessed be the glory of the Lord." As much as to say, Let this above all be magnified; whatever is experienced or done, let nothing interfere with that pure and majestic glory of Jehovah, which has now in emblem been exhibited.

In regard to the message communicated to the prophet after the seven days of sadness had expired, there is also something peculiar in it; for it is only Ezekiel among the prophets who is described as a watchman appointed by God, to give timely and faithful warning to the people. Habakkuk speaks of standing upon his watch-tower (ch. ii. 1), but this was only in respect to his eager and anxious outlook for the manifestations he was expecting of divine power and faithfulness. Ezekiel alone is represented as called to do for others the part of a watchman; and in doing it he was most strictly charged, on the one hand, to receive all his instructions from God as to the existence of whatever danger there might be in the condition of the people, and, on the other, to sound a loud and solemn alarm when he might perceive it actually besetting them. That such should have been the distinctive character given to his position and calling, manifestly bespoke the very perilous condition of those to whom he was sent. It indicated that he had something else to do than merely to sympathize with them in their afflicted state, and speak soothing words to their downcast and drooping spirits. It was to be his rather to open their eyes to the profounder evils that encompassed them, to break the spell of inveterate and cherished delusions, and raise the cry of danger where none was suspected. So that the very form of the commission given to him was like the deliverance of a strong and impressive testimony to the people of the latent corruptions and imminent perils with which they were beset.

If we look also to the substance of the communication, or to the particular instructions given to the prophet concerning the discharge of his office, we see at once the grand principle disclosed on which the destiny of Israel was to turn. The question, whether life or death, blessing or cursing, was to be their portion, hung upon another, whether they were to make righteousness or sin their choice? Their return to righteousness was the indispensable condition of their restoration to blessing. If, in despite of this, the wicked should persevere in his evil ways, or even the righteous man should turn aside and practise iniquity, a visitation of wrath must be looked for—the original sentence against sin, to which the language designedly points, that the purpose of God in this respect might be seen to be fixed and unalterable—the sentence, that he who transgresses "shall surely die," must take effect; for God is unchangeably the same, and what he appointed at first as the wages of sin must continue to be its wages still.

But while this part of the charge cut off all hope from a backsliding and impenitent people, the other part of it held out ample encouragement to such as remained stedfast in the covenant of God, or repented of their evil ways. The man who continued to love the paths of righteousness, and the man also who, after having forsaken, again returned to them, was to be assured of the blessings of life; these should as surely live as the others should die. For the prophet, as God's watchman, was to represent the mercy as well as the justice of God's administration; he was to have a wakeful eye upon the good, not less than the evil, that appeared among the people; and was to stretch out the hand of fellowship, and display the banner of divine love and protection, in behalf of all who might be inclined or moved to cleave to the service of Heaven. Thus were they to know from the outset that, for the people as a whole, and for each individual amongst them, this one path lay open for their return to peace and blessing.—FAIRBAIRN'S *Ezekiel*, pp. 40–43.—W. F.]

DOCTRINAL.

1. The revelation of the glory of God, because it is revelation, has always accordingly its special locality (מָקוֹם). If heaven, above all, is reckoned the place from which it beams forth (Deut. xxvi. 15; 2 Chron. xxx. 27; Isa. lxiii. 15; Hab. ii. 20; Zech. ii. 17; 1 Kings viii. 39), yet even of it 1 Kings viii. 27 is true; how much more of all places of revelation upon earth! Thus God Himself remains ὁ Θεὸς and ὁ πατὴρ τῆς δόξης (Acts vii. 2; Eph. i. 17), the independent Possessor and Dispenser of glory, and the self-revelation of God made in Christ is the full revelation of His glory (Luke ii. 14); for to Him the angels of God descend, just as from Him also and from no other spot on earth they again ascend (John i. 52). From God, wherever He manifests Himself, on Sinai, in the temple, His praise goes forth accordingly with its destination for the whole world.

2. The praise of God is the glory of God, which is reflected in the blessedness of the creature, especially of man. "It is a momentary celebration beforehand of the eternal perfection, which, momentary though it be, has already an element of eternity in itself," says Lange with respect to the prayer of the doxology.

3. The servants of God, however mightily, however completely they fulfil their task, so that Ezekiel can speak of the "heat (glow) of *his* spirit," yet always remain men, *i.e.* if חמה signifies the holy wrath of God as distinguished from חרה, the being angry as the effect of passion, yet we shall meet with pain in the prophet's natural love to his people; just as Jesus the Son of man has tears over Jerusalem (Luke xix. 41). Pain is more active than sorrow, which is more a passive state. We ought to be full of the wrath of God over sin, especially where it has already become punishment, the judgment of hardening; but our feeling towards the sinners can only be pain, because of our love to them as men, as in the case of Ezekiel, or sorrow, if we wish to distinguish the melancholy, sorrowful Jeremiah (comp. Jer. vi. 11) in this way from the choleric, energetic Ezekiel. The servant of God, who should not find the latter emotions in himself, according to character and the circle in which he is placed, would need to bethink himself, and to mourn over himself. Wrath without love is of the devil, but not of God; just as a love which cannot be angry may be mere nature, mere human weakness.

4. Even a silent preacher may be a loud and very impressive sermon. In certain circumstances silence may be even more expressive than speaking. "This is the wisdom of him who is truly called," says Umbreit, "that he is sometimes silent, sometimes speaks; but that when he speaks, he lets the divine word stream forth freely without fear and trembling as to whether it is understood; for the light is not to be put under a bushel; it has a right to shine, because it is light."

5. The prophetic office of watchman, in accordance with the similitude of one who is posted on a height, or a watch-tower, has a twofold applica

tion. Inasmuch as the watchman has, in the first place, to keep a look-out—but what meets the prophetic eye is presented to him in vision, or by means of a revelation in word—the office of watchman is identical with the general designation of the prophets as "seers" (Doct. Reflect. 6 on ch. i. 1–3). Thus it is the circumstance of their descrying or not descrying that makes them "watchmen," not the circumstance that they have always to speak or to be silent accordingly (Hitz.); for the former, at least as regards Ezekiel, is still dependent on divine instructions. In Ezekiel's case, the opening of his mouth by God forms the transition to the second and more definite application and interpretation of the similitude of a watchman, viz. that the watchman has to announce the approaching danger, and therefore to warn against it. As such he is certainly not "the mere watchman, *i.e.* (as Ew. expresses it) the sharp but quiet, calm observer of men, in order to warn each at the right time." The whole of the people as such, as well as in their governing heads, is what is entrusted to the watchman. But the application of the figure of the watchman, in the direction of warning, rests on the more general duty of prophecy, to be the controlling power of the national life according to the divine law in all respects. Only the warning of the prophetic watchman is of a more special kind, not as regards the law, but in view of the judgments of God,—an express turning to account of the future which he has seen for the immediate present in its existing state.

6. If we find with Ezekiel—of course, on the basis of the nation as a whole, of the theocratic nationality of Israel—individualization already taking place (comp. ch. xxxiii. 1 sqq.), such individualization, in view of the period in the kingdom of God, is a sign of this period, and more than the personification, so frequent elsewhere, of what accords with the law and what is contrary to it, in the ideal picture of the righteous man, just as in his opposite, the רָשָׁע. Israel as a whole, in contradiction to its idea, begins to resolve itself into the ὅσοι δὲ of John i. 12. Comp. on ch. ix. 4.

7. In times when the axe is laid at the root of a whole nation, the mission of those who were originally destined for the whole becomes of itself the work of saving individuals.

8. The emphasizing (in ch. xviii. still more explicit) of the statement as to the personal responsibility of the individual has reference to the theocratic delusion and superstition of the hypocrites, the secure, which the false prophets still flattered, according to which the individual, because a descendant of Abraham according to the flesh, might hold himself assured of belonging to a nationality where, and where alone, a sure salvation was to be found.

9. The illustration of the prophet's office by means of the sixth commandment, supported by Gen. ix., shows not merely how πνευματικός the νόμος is, but what an idea of life ought to be familiar to the ministers of the word. They are not, as it were, in accordance with the world's policy, "to live and let live."

10. The disputed question, as to whether the righteous can fall away, as the Lutheran theology along with that of the Jesuits asserts, and which the Reformed doctrine, on the other hand, denies, demands for its solution that we should make the distinction between law and grace. That the man who is righteous according to the law may apostatize unto death, is the very thing asserted in ch. iii. 20; comp. xviii. 24. Just in the same way, it is denied in ch. iii. 21 with respect to him who is justified by faith, and who remains righteous when admonished by the Spirit. Only this distinction must not be applied so as to become a distinction between the Old and New Testament, as is done by Hävernick. For the righteousness of God is *one and the same* in both (comp. Rom. iv.). The legal standpoint, although not in its national form, yet in its externality, runs through the period of the New Covenant, just as the evangelical standpoint is not strange to the period of the Old Covenant, although mediated—not obscured—under the law by means of the symbolism of sacrifice.

11. "As the sinner may turn from his way and be saved, so a righteous man may fall away from his righteousness and become a wicked man. The man who is really and truly righteous cannot do so in such a way as to be lost; but he may fall into heinous transgressions, and appear for the time stripped of his faith, like the sun under a cloud, like fire beneath the ashes (David, Peter). But there are also those who believe for a time (1 John ii. 19), who become quite manifest during temptation, and also after it is ended, when it is all over with them."—Lavater.

12. If we speak of a snare which God lays for man, this cannot be sin, what is evil, but the position in which God places man with a view to his own personal decision, as well as with a view to the decision regarding him; and, in fact, this cannot be misfortune merely, but also so-called good fortune, the former leading to despair, the latter conducing to hardening in false security. Of course a snare of God in a definite development of sin may also be already punishment, the beginning of divine judgment.

13. Around the warning as neglected or administered by the prophet, four cases group themselves, four types for all time: the wicked man in general, who goes to destruction without warning,—this being the relative and ever-increasing guilt of Christendom; the wicked man in particular, who, in spite of warning, chooses the way of death; the righteous man, who is so merely in form, whether a conscious hypocrite or not,—just as nominal Christians in the mass have fallen away from the Church in critical times of persecution,—he who without warning falls under the judgment, in connection with whose case the Church ought to remember her duty, as opposed to the Pietism of the future, the diplomatic or government Pietism, as well as the "soldierly-pious" element ("*militär-fromm*"); lastly, the upright and sincere righteous man, who also remains so, who lets himself be warned. Of the four, then, there is one against three. What a conclusion may be drawn from this numerical relation of individuals to the whole!

14. No mere declaimer against vice, still less one who is this in the disguise of a homiletic mask, or who labours thereat as being his profession, is in accordance with God's word. That man only ought to reprove his brethren who has a commission from God for it, and only when he has that commission. "God does not permit mortal men, according to their mere will and pleasure, to condemn or to absolve. And although

He sends forth His servants, yet He does not Himself renounce His authority, in virtue of which the supreme sovereignty remains with Him. He is the One Lawgiver, who is able to save and to destroy (Jas. iv. 12)" (CALV.). The so-called "in virtue of our office" is by no means sufficient for this, but our own conscience must legitimate our doing it.

HOMILETIC HINTS.

Ver. 12. "He had come unto me for the purpose of drawing me out of myself, and taking me into Himself" (B. B.).—"The Holy Spirit lifts us up from the earth towards heaven; and where He rules, the man hastens in willing obedience to God to perform his duties" (STCK.).—"Scripture is full of examples of how God has *lifted up* rulers of the people and His prophets by His Spirit to higher things. Moses thinks no longer of his sheep, but of the people whom he has to lead forth; David is drawn by the Spirit from the flock to something higher; the apostles openly confess Christ, and conspicuous among them Peter, whom a maid had formerly frightened; even with respect to Saul we read of the elevating influence of the Spirit" (L. L.).—"Lest he should execute his work with fleshly zeal, the *Spirit* is sent him as a Guide. Hence for a time he is transported out of himself, raised on high beyond the bounds of the lower and merely human mode of representation. In this state he hears the judgments of God again" (HEIM-HOFFMANN).

Vers. 12, 13. The servants of our God have not merely His praise as a blessed prospect *before* them, but *behind* them also the cloud of witnesses which encompasses them resounds with the praise of His glory.—"All creation glorifies God; only the ungodly blaspheme Him" (STCK.).—A contrast to the people, who accused God of unrighteousness and severity, and thereby insulted His honour, just as when they imagined themselves to be the only people that was worthy and capable of knowing the Glorious One (after CALVIN).—"In His glory are comprehended all the perfections of God, which can ever be manifested to man, most of all the glory of His justifying grace (Jer. xxiii. 6; 1 Cor. i. 30). Hence the prophet had formerly seen the divine glory in the likeness of a man upon a throne. The Church wishes this only, that God's glory should be praised not merely in, but from its place, *i.e.* throughout the whole world, Mal. i. 5" (COCC.).—God's praise is the harmony in which heaven and earth, angels and men, all beings, agree.—One note, yet no monotony.—"By all these voices he might be encouraged and stimulated, as soldiers are by the sound of the trumpet and the drum" (L. L.).—Ver. 14. "How easy it is for God to bring a teacher to any place" (STCK.).—"To those who are younger the preacher's office appears sweeter than it does when, after due experience, the original sweetness is mingled with bitterness" (STCK.).

Ver. 15. "The silence of the prophets is the sign of God's wrath" (CHRYSOST.).—"Exactly so ought the people to sit in penitent sorrow and humiliation before their God; but their representative, the servant of Jehovah, is, at the same time, a sign of how ungodly the multitude surrounding him are, and how righteous the judgments which are descending upon the people" (HÄV.).—"The stillness of a sick-bed is often a means of salvation to ourselves and to others" (RICHT.).—Ver. 17. "It is a splendid misery to be obliged to stand on a height; those who encamp in the valley are decidedly more comfortable" (STCK.).—"That God has assigned him to that position, and placed him in it, ought to make the matter easy for him, and to make him careful in it" (B. B.).—"Jewels can be more easily watched than souls" (STCK.).—"God's word remains unspoken, partly from fear of man, partly from sloth, partly from desire to please man" (JEROME).—"The first step in salvation is the knowledge of our sins. Of comfort, the principal thing, nothing is said; the prophet is only to warn, for they became capable of comfort only after they had come to know their sin" (L. L.).—"The passage vers. 17–21 is a weighty lesson of doctrinal instruction, given in holy earnestness" (RICHT.).

Ver. 18 sqq. "If the prophet neglects his duty, that does not help the wicked; he dies because of his iniquity: hasn't he got Moses? Where the public ministry does not do its duty, still Holy Scripture is at hand; and it is every one's own blame if he does not allow himself to be called to repentance by its voice" (H.).—Those murderers who must die by the hangman's hand are far from being so bad murderers, in God's sight, as many thoroughly genial and very cultivated men, who look to their office simply as a fat living, and who, by their example, or even merely from their being dumb dogs, allow souls to go to destruction in hell.—The weight of the sin of omission in God's scale.—"Thou art every moment in danger of becoming a murderer, and of undergoing the judgment of the murderer: this is an effective stimulus for every one who is entrusted with the office of the public ministry" (H.).—God as the sinner's blood relation and avenger of blood. What an intensity about the divine love!—"The life lost is something lost, the soul lost is everything lost. Oh what folly, when a teacher is silent for the sake of a handful of earth, and over and above brings his own soul into danger!" (ST.)—"Plainly and diligently the warning is to be given, with earnestness and impressiveness, not with flattering words, nor half in joke, nor merely touching the skin, but setting forth the danger most carefully" (B. B.).—"God quickens, by means of grace, His servant through the instrumentality of the word of exhortation; the sinner quickens himself by the acceptance of the word. Without spiritual life and quickening here there is no life in eternity, but there also only death. Faith is spiritual life, and piety the sign of this life" (STCK.).—"We are not forthwith to despair of the salvation of the sinner, for at even also many still go into the vineyard (Matt. xx.); the malefactor was not converted till upon the cross. God must declare a man wicked and condemned; otherwise he is not so, although the whole world were to shut him out of heaven" (L. L.).—"For in God's sight nothing is more precious than our souls" (CALVIN).—Ver. 19. Every function in his calling is a saving of himself in the case of the servant of God. What need, then, has he to cast a side-look after reward, love, comfort, honours, etc.?—"There are men who do indeed gladly proclaim what God wishes, but who yet, when they see that their words have no entrance and are of no use, are thereby troubled, and, from fear of having deceived themselves, no longer wish to have anything to do with the word. But all who continue to act so are lovers of themselves. An honest servant of God bears the word so long as God will have it, and does not trouble himself about the good result" (B. B.).—That which is demanded of the sinner, viz. *return*, shows that the prayer finds audience: Turn Thou me, and I shall be turned.—Return is promised by God, but man would rather hold fast what is his own, viz. wickedness and the wicked way.—Progress on the bad road resembles standing still on the good one. —Ver. 20. "It is not enough to have been pious, but we must also have continued so. Be thou faithful unto death, and he that endureth unto the end shall be saved" (STCK.).—"Then does godliness shine most, when it has the opportunity of sinning, nay, is everywhere enticed thereto, and yet does it not; on the other hand, the man who turns away from what is good and from the way of righteousness is worse, and in a more dangerous condition than the man who has never known it, 2 Pet. ii. 21" (B. B.).—"He who does not admonish the sinner,—a duty to which even common love binds every man, when he sees another in danger, and can in any way help him,—is exposed to the judgment, but much more still, if he is specially appointed by God for the purpose, or pretends to be so" (B. B.).—Ver. 21. "A faithful teacher must care for converted and unconverted alike; for the latter, that they may awake out of the sleep of false security; for the former, that they may not again fall asleep" (ST.).—"Yea, even where parties are found who are willing to help sinners into the right way, there is still difficulty in finding one to offer his hand to the righteous, in order that they may advance with greater ease in the true way" (B. B.).—"We sin indeed daily, but let us beware of sinning knowingly. The man who hates sin flees from it, shrinks back with dread from it, does not sin" (STCK.).—"If a teacher does not seek with all earnestness the salvation of the hearers entrusted to him, it is a sure sign that he is not very much concerned about his own salvation; for if the latter be the case, he cannot neglect the former" (ST.).

Ver. 22 sqq. "Isolation is the condition of the receipt of divine communications. God makes Himself known to the mind only when it has been quite withdrawn from worldly influences. We must be in the *valley;* but we may be in the bustling town, and yet in the valley" (H.).—Ver. 23. "Although the saved will behold the glory of God eternally in heaven, yet they will never become satiated or wearied of it; for here below even the contemplation of the divine glory fills believers with hunger in all the fulness of enjoyment" (STCK.).—Ver. 24. "Those are the true children of God who are continually ruled by the Spirit of God, Rom. viii. 14" (STCK.).—Ver. 25. "*Bands* and trouble is the reward for the faithful labour of an unwearied teacher" (STCK.). Whoever is pleased with such a salary is fit for the kingdom of God.—"The bands wherewith believers are bound are of different sorts: misery, pains, the cross, temptations; but God has arranged it beforehand, and frees us from it" (STCK.).—"To feel at home in the world is to feel well in the midst of danger" (STCK.).—Vers. 26, 27. "God has His times and seasons. Well for him who gives heed to them" (TÜB. B.).—"It is no good sign God's hindering His servants when eager to speak, Acts xvi. 6" (LG.).—"God must give teachers and preachers a joyful opening of the mouth, if they are to teach profitably" (CR.).—To be silent to men and to speak from God is the right kind of preacher.—"How great is God's mercy, that He causes the sermon to reach dumb ears even!" (STCK.)

2. THE FOUR SIGNS, AND THEIR INTERPRETATION (CH. IV. 1–V. 17).

1 And thou, son of man, take thee a brick, and give [lay] it before thee, and
2 portray upon it the city, [viz.] Jerusalem. And give [lay] siege against it, and
build a siege-tower against it, and cast a mound against it, and make a camp
3 against it, and set battering-rams against it round about. And do thou take thee
a pan in [of] iron, and give [set] it as a wall in [of] iron between thee and the city;
and direct thy face against it, and it is in siege, and thou layest siege against it:
4 this is a sign to the house of Israel. And lie thou on thy side, the left one, and
lay the guilt of the house of Israel upon it; according to the number of the days
5 that thou shalt lie upon it thou shalt bear their guilt. And I have given thee
the years of their guilt, according to the number of the days, three hundred and
6 ninety days; and thou bearest the guilt of the house of Israel. And thou
accomplishest these, and liest upon thy side, the right one, a second time, and
bearest the guilt of the house of Judah forty days; a day for a year, a day
7 for a year, have I given it to thee. And toward the siege of Jerusalem thou
shalt set thy face, and thine uncovered arm, and thou prophesiest against it.
8 And, behold, I have laid bands upon thee, and thou shalt not turn from one side
9 to another, till thou endest the days of thy siege. And do thou take unto thee
wheat, and barley, and beans, and lentils, and millet, and spelt, and put them in
one vessel, and make thee bread thereof; according to the number of the days
that thou art lying upon thy side, three hundred and ninety days shalt thou eat
10 it. And thy food which thou shalt eat is by weight, twenty shekels a day; from
11 time to time thou shalt eat it. And water shalt thou drink by measure, the sixth
12 part of an hin; from time to time shalt thou drink it. And barley cake, that

shalt thou eat, and in [with] dung that cometh out of man shalt thou bake it
13 before their eyes. And Jehovah said, So shall the children of Israel eat their
14 bread defiled among the heathen, whither I will drive them. And I said, Ah,
Lord Jehovah! behold, my soul hath not been polluted, and neither carcase nor
what is torn in pieces have I eaten from my youth up till now; neither hath
15 abominable flesh come into my mouth. And He said unto me: Behold, I give
thee dung of cattle for dung of man, and thou makest [preparest] thy bread thereon.
16 And He said unto me, Son of man, behold, I break the staff of bread in Jerusalem,
and they eat bread by weight, and in anxiety; and water by measure, and in
17 anguish shall they drink; Because bread and water shall be wanting, and man
and his brother are struck dumb [from anguish], and pine away in their guilt.

Ver. 4. Sept.: . . . κατα ἀριθμον τ. ἡμερων πεντηκοντα κ. ἑκατον ἡμερας ἁς κοιμηθησῃ ἐπ' αὐτου· κ. ληψῃ τ. ἀδικιας αὐτων.

Ver. 5. . . . τας δυο ἀδικιας αὐτ. εἰς ἀριθμον ἡμερων ἐνενηκοντα κ. ἑκατον ἡμερας—

Ver. 8. Anoth. read.: מצוריך plur.

Ver. 9. . . . ἐνενηκοντα κ. ἑκατον—(Some MSS. חטים.)

Ver. 16. . . . κυριος—

Ver. 17. ὁπως ἐνδεεις γενωνται ἀρτου . . . (Anoth. read.: באחיו). Vulg.: *ad fratrem*—

EXEGETICAL.

What the silence of the prophet is intended to signify, in case their own bad conscience should not set it before them vividly, is now represented in emblem to their curiosity by *four symbolical actions*, of which three are contained in our chapter; the explanatory inscription at the end is always given in shorter or longer terms, according to the expressiveness and completeness of each separate picture. According to ch. iii. 24 sq., and as is clear from themselves, the carrying out of these symbolical actions takes place *in the house of Ezekiel. Next to his family*, and perhaps called in by them, we have to think of his *countrymen as spectators*. The sections vers. 1–3, vers. 4–8, vers. 9–17, have a connection with one another (vers. 7, 8, 9 sqq.), and supplement one another. While *the siege of Jerusalem*, as the theme in the first section, is at the same time carried into further detail, and made more graphic in the second and third, after the *inward, the outward condition* of the parties concerned is indicated to us. Hengstenberg again transfers everything to the "sphere of the subjective" (similarly HITZIG: allegory), on which account also (according to him) the carrying out of the prophet's instructions is not mentioned, and agrees with Ewald, with whom likewise the "literary activity" of Ezekiel is the principal thing, for which the objectivity (or not) of the symbolical action is a matter of pure indifference. Calvin, likewise, makes ver. 4 sqq. take place in vision. As regards the "almost childish impression" of the action in question as an objective reality, this has to be attributed to Hengstenberg's exposition itself; but that a publication of what takes place in the house of Ezekiel is not to be a matter of anxiety, follows from the well-known lively intercourse between those in exile and the great mass in the fatherland. ("Meanwhile, as the man of God, though full, is not permitted to speak, he is to employ the silent language of writing. But his writing is in symbol. His heart is with Jerusalem; there he portrays upon a brick the picture of the beloved city."—UMBREIT. "The heavy judgment which is to burst upon Jerusalem is announced, in harmony with the vision of ch. i., which already held out in prospect the approach of God to judgment."—HENGST.)

Vers. 1–3.—*The First Sign.*

Ver. 1. ואתה applies the foregoing special instruction to the prophet; and, at the same time, the imperative passes over into the description of what Ezekiel is to do, hence the perfects with ו consec. "Just the year before Zedekiah had journeyed to Babylon, for the purpose of testifying his submission to Nebuchadnezzar" (J. D. MICH.).—As to לְבֵנָה, comp. WINER, *Realw.* ii. p. 731 sqq. We are not to think of real stone, but of something baked from clay (white? chalky?), dried in the sun, or burnt white in the furnace. The walls of ancient Babylon were of bricks, and these Babylonian bricks are one foot long and broad, five inches thick and square. "Such bricks as the Assyrians and Babylonians, just in those districts where Ezekiel lived, filled so often with inscriptions" (EWALD). Besides, there is the significant allusion *to Egypt and the bondage* of Israel there, Ex. i. 14, v. 7 sqq. "In order to be able to engrave a delineation that will last," Hitzig requires the "clay-brick," which is likewise common in Canaan (Isa. ix. 10). Just so Keil: "white clayey substance." Others: a brick-shaped slate.—As is usual with those who are thinking about anything, he is *to lay* the brick *before him*.—חקק is neither more nor less than: to fix, which may be done just as well by drawing as by engraving. "First of all only **a city**; **Jerusalem** would be the last of all the cities of the earth to be thought of, when the subject in hand is a city to be besieged by the Lord. After Jerusalem we are to suppose, as it were, a mark of exclamation" (HENGST.).—But to the brick there belongs not merely, as Hengstenberg maintains, the picture of the city, but also (in accordance with Ewald's view) what follows, describing "how in all regular order, through all the steps from the beginning onwards to the end, one would open a siege against it." It would be to press the letter, to make the execution of it from the outset impossible or "childish," if one were to imagine the contents of ver. 2 to be outside the brick; and how does ver. 3 (comp. ver. 7) suit such a view? The stone itself is not Jerusalem! (HITZIG.)—Ver. 2. מצור from צור, to press, to straiten. HITZIG: siege-work in general. דיק is Aramaic (HITZIG: it thus belongs to a land whose masters were thoroughly acquainted with fortress warfare, Hab. i. 10; Isa. xxiii. 13) and modern Hebrew: to look out, to fix the eyes upon; whence the noun, probably a Chaldee technical term, דָּיֵק, watch-tower (except in Ezekiel, elsewhere only in 2 Kings xxv. 1 and Jer. lii. 4), for the most part collectively, and so also here for the (wooden) towers of observation equal or superior in height to the walls round about the city to be besieged, from which weapons were thrown and shot by means of the ballistæ, as well as in other ways. [J. D. MICH.: two lines of circumvallation, a mound and rampart furnished with palisades. W. NEUMANN: the all-prostrating storming-machine.] The plural מחנות, because several separate camps. כרים, from the iron ram's head in front of beams, which, hanging in ropes or chains inside a scaffolding to be moved upon wheels, were directed against the walls and gates in order to push them in. Hävernick traces back the word to כרר, כרה, כּוּר, "to bore through." Comp. besides, Josephus, *De Bello Jud.* iii. 7, § 19. (Others have understood by the expression, the "he-goats," *i.e.* the leaders of the army divisions in the different camps.)—If, then, the prophet, as commissioned by God, enters on such a siege, the real besieger of Jerusalem is the Lord God; and while the Chaldeans appear as mere instruments in the divine hand, Ver. 3—which brings to a close the first symbolical action—intimates what state of mind, on the part of the Lord, Ezekiel has to represent.—ואתה (just as elsewhere also) introduces a new element, put on a parallel with ver. 1 by means of קח-לך.—מחבת signifies something bent together, which may be flat for frying or roasting; in such saucepans the flat cakes were fried, Lev. ii. 5. As he is to set the *iron pan* as an iron *wall*, it is clear that he has to set it up perpendicularly; it is likewise clear, from the expression **between thee and the city**, that a relation of *separation*, of division, between Jerusalem as portrayed upon the brick and the representative of God is meant to be expressed. Only on the ground of such a relation between God and Jerusalem can we explain alike the hostile attitude of the prophet's face, and specially the clause, **and it is in siege**, and along with that vers. 1 and 2. But as the wall is to be after the manner of *iron* (ב), the iron pan cannot be taken as a fascine protecting the besieger, because such a thing, as a rule, was not of iron, and because certainly there could be no need of a protection for God the Besieger, but rather of a protection from Him; nor are we to think with Ewald (1st edit.) of the "very strong iron-like wall of Jerusalem" (RASCHI), since the suffix also in אליה does not refer to the pan, but to the city, and the strength of the city wall is not certainly to be made prominent. Ewald also in his very recent 2d edition approaches the view of Hävernick (who with Ephraem understands "the mass of misfortune which is coming upon Jerusalem"), inasmuch as he makes the prophet put "the merely painted siege more strongly and palpably by means of the picture of a wall, as it were, of iron." But in this way also the so express attitude of separation, which Hitzig recognises, is lost. The allusion to Jer. i. 13 for "the horrors of the siege" (HÄV.) is too far-fetched [A LAPIDE: the burning of the city; ORIGEN: the horrible tortures of the inhabitants, Jer. xxix. 22; 2 Macc. vii. 5; others: the army-fire of the Chaldeans]. Jerome (that the wrath of God is represented) nearly approaches the correct view, to which Kimchi points by referring to Isa. lix. 2. The pan, therefore, as a wall, symbolizes the strong (Jer. i. 18, alike in accordance with God's decree, and in consequence of the corruption of Israel) wall of separation, which finally explains everything, what precedes and also what follows. Vatablus and Grotius bring in, besides, "their hardness of heart and the blackness of their sins," just as Hitzig also, "the base metal" and (in accordance with ch. xxiv. 6) "the rust as a picture of defilement through sin." (HENGST.: first the refusal of divine help, then God Himself even the assailant.) Not so much the preparation of food which follows (KLIEF.), as the circumstance that such a pan (according to Ewald: "the nearest iron plate") was at hand in every household (KEIL), suggested the choice of the same. As the siege is described with the prophet as besieger, so "certainly it will be carried out, not hundreds of years afterwards, but in the lifetime of Ezekiel, during his labours" (KLIEF.). The significance of the iron pan would certainly disappear if we imagined that the prophet had grouped the siege in little figures round about the brick. Moreover, what is portrayed upon the stone, and is here spoken of as **the city**, is called in ver. 7 "the siege of Jerusalem."—The **house of Israel** is here the same as in ch. iii. Comp. on the other hand, ver. 5.—If the symbolical action is to be a **sign** (in the sense of foreshadowing), then the view, that it was also shown them, that, as it was for them, so it made its appearance objectively before them, is certainly more probable than Hengstenberg's subjective view, more probable than with Städlein, Hävern., Hitzig, to make the action one that was not really performed, but only discoursed about (Isa. xx. 3). KLIEF.: "an important action, even when besides it is a silent one, must be performed; although the text does not mention it expressly, a thing that quite explains itself in the case of one who has received a command from God."

ADDITIONAL NOTE ON CH. IV. 1–3.

[In regard to the part required to be played by the prophet himself, however it may have been understood in former times, we should suppose few now will be disposed to doubt that the successive actions spoken of took place only in vision, and are no more to be ranked among the occurrences of actual life than the eating of the prophetic roll mentioned in the preceding chapter. Indeed, such actions as are described here, though well fitted, when rehearsed as past, and read as narratives of things ideally done, to make a strong and vivid impression upon the mind, would probably have had an opposite effect if transacted in real life. It would have been impossible for ordinary spectators to see Ezekiel conducting a miniature siege with a tile and a saucepan, and such like implements of war, without a feeling of the puerile and ludicrous being awakened; and the other symbolical actions mentioned, especially his lying for 390 days motionless on one side, if literally understood, can scarcely be regarded as coming within the limits of the possible. And along with the physical impossibility of one part of the requirement there was the moral impossibility of another, since to eat bread composed of such abominable materials would have been (if performed in real life) a direct contravention of the law of Moses,—that law, respectful submission to which was ever held to be the first and most essential characteristic of a true prophet (compare Deut. xiv 3, xxiii. 12–14, with xiii. 1–5). Besides, we find the prophet (ch. viii. 1) represented as *sitting* in his house before the number of the days to be spent in a lying posture could have been completed. So that, on every account, it is necessary to consider the actions to have taken place in vision, as, indeed, was usually the case in prophetical actions, and uniformly so, as we shall find in Ezekiel. — FAIRBAIRN'S *Ezekiel.*— W. F.]

Vers. 4–8.—*The Second Sign.*

Once more a new appointment, which onwards to ver. 8, carrying into further detail the above indicated destiny of Jerusalem, gives us a more vivid picture of it as *respects the inner condition of the parties concerned*, after the manner of a *second* symbolic action on the part of Ezekiel. In the position of a prophet, it is implied that such an one may be the representative alike of God and of the people; and as, therefore, Ezekiel represents Jehovah in vers. 1–3, so now, and in ver. 9 sqq., he represents Israel. "Where in this way Jehovah Himself fights against His people, their downfall is certain; the prophet immediately assumes this position" (HÄV.). The mere circumstance, that he is to **lie** on the one side and the other ("to sleep," as the Sept. and Vulg. make it, plainly contradicts the context), is symbolical as regards those whom he represents, *a picture of the poli ical situation* (Isa. xxviii. 20, l. 11; Amos v. 2; Ps. xx. 8, xliv. 25); not "as a sick person who can lie only on one side, and must always without shifting lie upon it" (EWALD), not as a figure for a state of political languishing, but in contrast with standing upright, a lying down in consequence of a fall (HITZ.).—As the period fixed is **days** (which, however, mean **years**), *the reference generally to the besieged* ("the frightful constraint from without, during which one cannot move or stir," EWALD) is to be held fast in the first place; but then, farther, the *carrying captive which follows*, and the *sojourn in exile*, is at the same time to be kept in view. First the **left** side is made prominent when the reference is to the severed **house of Israel**,—according to Ewald, Hitzig, because of the geographical situation to the north of Judah (ch. xvi. 46), while the latter lay in the south,—according to Grot., Hävernick, Keil, because of the superiority of the latter over the former (comp. ch. xxiii.), Eccles. x. 2. MALDON.: it had the priesthood and the kingdom.—עון is the **guilt**, thus the sin in its consciousness of punishment; neither the former alone nor the latter alone, but the transition from the one to the other in process of being effected for the subjective consciousness. The consciousness of guilt on the part of the people is to be awakened.—Inasmuch as Ezekiel is to lay the guilt **upon it**, *i.e.* his left side, the side upon which he himself has to lie, the problem can only be solved when we regard *Ezekiel himself*, in virtue of his lying upon his left side, as the bearer of the guilt, which is also immediately said. According to Keil, he would come to lie upon the guilt, and not the guilt upon him! That נשא cannot here mean "to bear," as Hengstenberg asserts, one cannot see, because, if he is to lay the guilt upon himself, he will have to bear it also, and the matter in hand is not at all an official and mediatorial or atoning substitution, but only a symbolical bearing of a burden which has to lie heavily upon the people, whom he only represents. As many days as he shall lie upon his left side, so long will he represent the burden of guilt of the ten tribes. This is not certainly meant to signify the number of the years which they have sinned (ROSENM.). Is this, then, asserted by ver. 5? The **number of the days** of his lying means, of course, "*the years of their guilt;*" but what is carefully to be noticed, as a period *given him by God* (ואני נתתי לך), yet not surely as a period selected by God from their course of sinning for the purpose of being represented by him? is such a divine formulating of the period of *their sinning* well conceivable? but as the *guilt* measured by God, to be represented by Ezekiel, and thus to be announced in actual fact, which they have brought upon themselves, and have *to bear in years.* What comes upon them in years, Ezekiel is to represent to them in days, thus bearing **the guilt of the house of Israel.** This explanation, simply arrived at from the text, will have to be tested by the interpretation of the periods given. For Israel there are appointed 390 days, and the prophet **has accomplished these.**—Ver. 6. For his lying on his **right side, a second time**, to bear **the guilt of the house of Judah,** 40 days are appointed. The question, whether the 40 days are to be supposed as included in the 390 (with Cocc. and others), is expressly answered in the negative by the שנית ("for the second time"); there are 390 and 40, in all 430 days, which sum the text certainly does not add together. For the special reason, that the season of punishment has begun long ago in the case of the ten tribes, just as it is already touching Judah also, a division of time readily suggested itself, while the division of collective Israel into Israel and Judah presented itself historically. In getting the 390 years to correspond in respect of sinning, and especially the 40, if they are to be reckoned as actual years, and therefore exactly, even the most diverse modes of explanation have found themselves helpless. The whole kingdom of Israel did not last for 390 years; and we must therefore go back beyond the ten tribes, into the period of the judges, not to mention other modes of reckoning by means of omissions. Rosenm., therefore, made the distinction between Israel and Judah step into the background as regards the 390 years; and inasmuch as he gets at 386 years from the division of the kingdom down to the eleventh year of Zedekiah (the conquest of Jerusalem), he consoles himself for what is wanting with the poetic rounding off of prophetic language; but Judah's 40 years of sin are reckoned from the twelfth year of the reign of the pious king Josiah! Hengstenberg understands Israel as collective Israel, begins with 2 Chron. xii. 1 (comp. 2 Chron. xi. 17), *i.e.* from the fourth year of Rehoboam, "the year of the falling into sin of the whole nation," and supports himself in this view by Vitringa's reckoning of 430 years 6 months from the founding of the temple to the destruction of the state; and deducting 37 years of Solomon's and 3 of Rehoboam's, there remain 390 years; and Judah, according to him, is contrasted with the whole people, the 40 years being 40 from the collective 390: "the despising of the grace of God in the raising up of king Josiah (2 Kings xxiii. 25), and the frustration of the last attempt made by Jeremiah," beginning with the thirteenth year of Josiah, the first appearance of Jeremiah on the stage, whose labours down till the destruction of Jerusalem lasted 40 years. The connection with vers. 1–3 manifestly makes the time of *punishment* more probable than a time of sin; and the computation of the number 390 for *the days which the siege of the city* lasted, from the 10th day of the 10th month of the 9th year of Zedekiah down to the 9th day of the 4th month of the 11th year, can very simply be made to correspond by making a deduction for the temporary raising of the siege on account of the Egyptians (Jer. xxxvii. 5). On the other hand, every calculation of 390 and of 40 *years*—which is certainly involved—fails as a time of exile for Israel and Judah. In this state of matters, if one reckons by literal days and years, but still more considering the all-pervading symbolical character of the whole and of the details, the acceptance of *symbolical formulas of time* for the divinely-awarded punishment of the guilt alike of Israel and of Judah commends itself. For the number 390 in reference to Israel, Kliefoth, by comparing Deut. xxv. 3 with 2 Cor. xi. 24, in accordance with the number of the ten tribes, arrives at 10 × 39 years of punishment as just so many strokes of divine chastisement; and for Judah, on the other hand, as he does not treat it as two tribes, by a fair adjustment he arrives at the highest legal number of just 40 strokes, *i.e.* years. What Keil remarks in opposition to this view may be said, but is less decisive than the certainly surprising character of *such* a mode of reckoning for the prophetic symbolism of an Ezekiel. Klief. has been driven to his ingenious attempt at interpretation, because the number 390 baffled every other interpretation. But this number also, which stands for Israel, can claim no peculiar symbolism for itself. The ten tribes, as Klief. himself calls them "torn off branches, atoms of a nation," have, in view of the longer historical duration of their exile, as well as by reason of their greater liability to punishment, only in general a claim to be more heavily punished. In particular, they do not come into consideration as regards the siege in our verses which applies to Jerusalem, nor in any other way, save that the national prophetic spirit must include them in its conception of collective Israel, for which Judah with Jerusalem is the title. With such a historical *meaning* also for Judah, with which also the right side of the prophet standing for it corresponds, one need not be stumbled with Kliefoth, although the number 390 should be "in itself quite meaningless." It is the same as with the left side of Ezekiel, so quite peculiarly taking the lead in vers. 4, 5, for this reason only, because his misery as an exile, long ago begun, and already entered upon in part by Judah likewise, is fitted to exhibit before the eyes of the remnant of Judah what will not be wanting to them just as visibly. For the *symbolism* the number 40, which is applied to Judah, is the determining element. The relation of the 40 to 390 may be similar to the case in which Bähr (ii. p. 491) does not allow the numbers 33 and 66 as such to come into consideration, but only in their connection with 7 and 14, bringing them up to 40 and 80. As respects the number 40 itself, Bähr says convincingly, according to it, almost universally, such periods are fixed as bring with them a state of more or less constraint and oppression, and yet somehow at the same time a state having a bearing on religious affairs. Keil is right in basing the symbolical meaning of a definite term of divine visitation not simply on the 40 years' leading of the people through the wilderness (Num. xiv.), which properly amounted to 38 years only, but on the earlier passage Gen. vii. 12, 17 Comp., in order to determine the meaning of the number 40, Ex. xxxiv. 28 (Deut. ix.); 1 Kings xix. 8; Jonah iii. 4; Matt. iv. As in this way the 40 for Judah, which alone properly came under consideration, threw light on the 390, the summing up might be let alone; with some reflection it was done, as a matter of course, and this all the more that the number 390 in itself must of necessity appear meaningless. The possible connection with the actual period of the siege of Jerusalem, or a portion of it (comp. on ver. 9), may be regarded as a subordinate reference. "The sufferings of the siege will, in the general sense of severe constraint, certainly continue during the whole exile also," etc. (Ew.) The addition of 390 and 40 gives (according to Ex. xii. 40) the period of sojourn of the children of Israel *in Egypt*, 430 years, significant for all after periods of the nation, on account of the parallel of this period with the exile (Introd. p. 19), and in the law even (Deut. xxviii. 68), as well as in Ezek. ix. 3, 6, viii. 13, brought into significant prominence. That the sojourn in Egypt, which sprang from quite a different cause, suits badly as a type for a period of punishment (Klief.), cannot accordingly be maintained. Comp. besides, Gen. xv. 13 (Acts vii. 6), where we have it in round numbers! "The period of the first heathen tyranny over the people of Jehovah repeats itself in the history of the nation: the old, everlastingly memorable time becomes to the seer—himself already living amid heathen surroundings—a type of the oppressions rushing in anew upon them with irresistible violence; hence the punishment of the exile is intensified by the circumstance that it appears as the antitype of the ancient 430 years' Egyptian bondage" (Häv.). But here Klief. is right, when, against a special reference of the 40 years for Judah to the 40 years' leading of the people collectively through the wilderness (for which Häv. points to ch. xx. 13 sqq., 23 sqq., 35, 36), he raises the objection, that in this way another occurrence lying outside the 430 years is drawn in, while the 40 years must certainly lie within the 430. We must therefore either abide by the general symbolical character of the number 40, or like Keil, who very ingeniously draws attention to the circumstance, that the last 40 years of the Egyptian bondage furnished a reason for a division of the 430 into 390 and 40, find again in the 40 the 40 years of his exile which Moses spent in Midian. Comp. Ex. vii. 7 with Acts vii. 23, 30—not as Keil, Ex. ii. 11–iii. 10; Acts vii. 23–30. "These 40 years," remarks Keil, "were not only for Moses a season of testing and purification for his future calling, but doubtless for the Israelites also the period of their severest oppression by the Egyptians, and in this respect quite appropriate as a type for the future period of Judah's punishment; so that as Israel in Egypt lost in Moses her helper and protector, so now Judah was to lose her king, and to be given up to the tyranny of the heathen world-power." [See Additional Note at the close of the Exegetical Remarks.—W. F.] Instead of the Kethib הימיני (elsewhere only in 2 Chron. iii. 17) we must read, with the Qeri, הימני.—Comp. on ver. 5.—The suffix in נתתיו refers to עון. Hengst., who takes למספר as = for just as many days (KLIEF., KEIL: for the number of, for a number of), translates: so that for every day there comes a year, I give it thee. [The 190 of the Sept. for the whole, and 40 for Judah, Hävernick explains to himself by the bringing in of another type, viz. the deluge, Gen. vii. 24, 12. They read Ex. xii. 40 differently from the Hebrew text. Hitzig makes them reckon their 150 from the year 738 to 588.]

By means of ver. 7 our section goes back upon the first (ver. 3), and harmonizes the two symbolical actions. Inasmuch as the prophet represented the people before, and not so much Jerusalem, he can in representing Jehovah set his face **toward the siege of Jerusalem** (viz. as that was to be represented in vers. 1–3), fixedly, sharply, as an enemy. The **bared arm,**—(Isa. lii. 10) as of a warrior, for the purpose of fighting, stripping it of the garment up to the shoulder,—according to Raschi, prefiguring Nebuchadnezzar, is at the same time the *free* arm of the prophet, who is lying upon the other. As it must be the right arm for the warlike object in view, we shall have (as against Hitz.) to think of the 390 days in vers. 4, 5, during which Ezekiel lies upon the left side, with which ver. 8 also agrees. The arm outstretched in the same direction strengthens as well as gives effect to the permanence of the look; if it were to be understood as occasionally lifted up, then the על, which is certainly usual elsewhere also in the case of threatening announcements, would be explained still more definitely.—In accordance with ch. iii. 25, the expositors understand the *prophesying* as not so much orally in words, but virtually by means of this very symbolical acting. Comp. however, on ch. v. 5 sqq.—Ver. 8. והנה נתתי in contrast with הנה נתנו, ch. iii. 25; there in order to move him along, here in order to make him fast. The **bands** are not the same as there; but whereas those bands of men do not make the prophet obedient to them, a slave to their will, the bands here, on the other hand, which God throws over him, answer their purpose of fixing him according to God's will. The outward literal bands become in the divine speech a *figurative* expression for the *divine power* which will hold him down, and at the same time (KLIEF.) make him bear it with patience. [According to Häv., a new element is introduced by והנה; the prophet, in a vivid manner, is placed in the condition of the besieged. According to CALV.: indicating the stability and firmness of the divine decree.]—The turning which is hindered in such wise is that *from the left to the right side*, onwards till the accomplishment of the days of his besieging; so that he has to represent the siege of the city, which may in this way be specified as lasting 390 days (comp. on vers. 6 and 7), unless what follows was intended to suggest a still more special reference. [Klief. refers vers. 7, 8 to the whole period of 430 days; Hitz. refers the prophesying to the 40 days merely.]

Vers. 9–17.—*The Third Sign.*

Ver. 9. A new charge, as in ver. 4; a still more detailed amplification, now especially of the *outward condition; a third symbolic action*, by which also provision is made for the sustenance of Ezekiel while the above described state of affairs lasts; and thus in connection with it. A representation of the people. If already in ver. 8 "the state of restraint of the besieged" (HENGST.) were thought of, then an immediate transition would be made from this more general calamity to the more special want of sustenance.—חטין, a Chaldaic plural; ן instead of ם, **wheat** in grains (in the sing. especially wheat on the stalk, in the field). HENGST.: as wheat is the usual means of sustenance among the exiles, the Chaldaic form pushes itself forward. Manifestly from a better time (HÄV.: descending from what is better to what is worse and worse); for now there follows what,—however good and in part delicious the ingredients in themselves are,—when baked into bread, as is the case here, is prison-bread,—**barley** in grains, 1 Kings iv. 28 (Judg. vii. 13; 2 Kings iv. 42; John vi. 9), **beans** as well as **lentils**, a favourite dish (Gen. xxv. 34), of the latter of which down to the present day the poor in Egypt, in time of dearth, make use as food; דחן, **millet** (from דח, to swell in water, or from the dark colour, allied with דגן, "grain"), yielding a bad kind of bread; and כסמים, fitches, **spelt** (Ex. ix. 32), as being one of the poorest sorts of grain, which produces a dry and not very nourishing kind of bread.—The circumstance that Ezekiel is to take of all together does not indeed run counter to the law (Lev. xix. 19; Deut. xxii. 9), but comes very near the prohibition, *possibly indicating circumstances of a lawless character, where one is not so rigid.* More expressly it is suggested in this way, that the besieged *will in their distress be compelled to gather together everything that can possibly be turned into bread.* ("Απαντα γάρ τοι βρωτὰ πολιορκουμένοις.) This state of matters is represented yet more strongly by means of the **one vessel**, which shows that of each separate sort *not much more* is to be had (ver. 10).—The length of time (מספר הימים = as many days as there are) is given definitely as 390 days. It is therefore "inadmissible," with Keil, to get rid of this clear and definite statement by the supposition that the greater number merely is given (PRADO), and that the 40 days are to be understood with the rest, but (EWALD) are omitted for brevity's sake (in the case of Ezekiel!!). It is conceivable that for 390 days exactly the famine would make itself specially felt. (2 Kings xxv. 3; Lam. ii. 20, iv. 9, 10.) At all events, the prophet has to calculate his prison-fare for 390 days, for so many days is he to eat it. (390 loaves, JER.)—על־צדך is accordingly his *left* side (ver. 5), before he turned to the right one. Comp. on vers. 7, 8. Klief. is right as against the including of the 40 days in the 390, not, however, in the extended application which he asserts for these 390 days, viz. on to ver. 17, as will soon appear. It is a very good remark of Klief., that the prophet was not altogether prohibited from letting service be rendered to him.

Additional Note on Ch. iv. 9.

[At ver. 9, he is ordered to "make bread according to the number of the days that he should lie upon his side; three hundred and ninety days shalt thou eat thereof." Here the 40 days are left out, although during them also he was to lie upon his side—not, as commentators generally, and still also Hävernick, suppose, from the first period being by much the larger of the two, and as such standing for the whole; but to keep the reference clear to the distinctive character of the wilderness-period, which was the point chiefly to be had in view by the Jewish exiles. The eating of polluted bread as a symbol, properly implied a constrained residence in a Gentile country—an unclean region; hence, in the explanation given of the symbol at ver. 13, it is declared of the house of Israel, that "they shall eat their defiled bread *among the Gentiles.*" But in the wilderness Israel stood quite separate from the Gentiles, though still under penal treatment, and in a sense still connected with Egypt (hence "the wilderness of Egypt," xx. 36); and so they who were in a manner to return to that state again were merely to "eat bread by weight, and with care, and drink water by measure, and in desolateness:" a state of chastisement and trouble, but not by any means so heathen-like, so depressed and helpless, as the other.—Fairbairn's *Ezekiel.* —W. F.]

Ver. 10. His food is this bad mixed food (Ewald), not the definite portion which he will have to eat (Keil), for it is defined as portions only by what follows. Ezekiel is to have to eat, not as much as he likes, but, as usually happens in a time of scarcity during sieges, by weight (ver. 16). **20 shekels** (*shekel*, what is weighed, hence a definite weight, just as *mishkol* is weight in general)—according to Ewald, about 20 ounces; according to Keil, 22–23 ounces of bread; according to Philippson, equivalent to 400 beans in weight (Lev. xxvi. 26). Although in those warmer countries a man needs less than in our climate, yet here it is at most the half of what is usually necessary that is specified for each day. The definition **from time to time** strengthens the daily element, as distinguished from the hunger which is continually making itself known, never satisfied; he will not be at liberty to give heed to this latter, but will have to consider the time, that he has only 20 shekels for each day, hence—seldom, at long intervals, sparingly! [Keil supposes: at the different hours of the daily meal time. He makes Ezekiel provide himself with a store of grain and legumes, and prepare his bread daily therefrom. Precisely so Klief., who brings in, besides, the pan from ver. 3 for the purpose.] And as the food is by weight, so the drink—the water is by measure.

Ver. 11 (ver. 16). A whole **hin** is reckoned by the Rabbins at 72 egg-shellfuls; hence one-sixth the same as two logs = 12 egg-shells. Too much for dying, too little for living. As in this way food and drink are specified for the 390 days, the idea readily suggests itself, with Grotius and others, *of referring Ver.* 12 *to the* 40 *days that still remain.* The express mention of the number was not necessary *here*, because its symbolism (comp. on vers. 5, 6) in general sways the whole, and because in particular it is, of course, understood as the residue after the 390 had been so expressly made prominent (ver. 9). The description may the more readily dispense with the number, as from the facts of the case it becomes sufficiently clear, on the one hand, by means of the new element of uncleanness, especially after the divine explanation which immediately follows in ver. 13, and, on the other hand, by means of that freer movement on the part of the prophet which is demanded by ver. 12. The 40 certainly symbolizes (comp. on vers. 4–6) chiefly *the exile among the heathen*, as it was to begin for Judah after the taking of besieged Jerusalem. Hengst. excellently remarks: "the barley cake here has nothing at all to do with the pot in ver. 9; that is gone." Ewald finds in it an "exceptional sort of thing, as if for a feast;" certainly too much, and not in accordance with the character of the period of exile. עֻגָה, the warm cake of bread baked in the hot ashes, just as is usual down even to the present day in eastern lands, especially on journeys, is distinguished as something *more common*, what is more in order, from the preceding unusual and extraordinary mixed food. The *poor* standing of exiles causes it to be of *barley* (comp. ver. 9), unless such cakes baked in ashes were as a rule of barley, of which Keil has by no means proved the contrary, as against Hitzig. [Keil, Hitzig, and others translate predicatively: as a barley cake, prepared in that manner, shalt thou eat it. (Is the suffix neuter? is it to be referred to לחם in ver. 10?)] Since the important thing here, as regards the sense, is merely the emphasizing of the *uncleanness* of the food, and since the use of dry animal dung as fuel (ver. 15) is at least nothing unusual in the East, גללי צאת האדם was the strong term for it. As fuel (comp. for בגללי, ver 15: עליהם), unlike Isa. xxxvi. 12, it has nothing to do with the siege, beyond which, as regards the symbol, we have now come, as if it were pointing to a scarcity of wood; but at most, it refers to the harassing, immured condition of Ezekiel in his own house. Filth and misery round about on every side: what an overwhelmingly vivid sermon for his countrymen this situation before their eyes! Comp. besides, Deut. xxiii. 12–14. תעגנה from עוג, a technical word for עֻגָה, either: to make round, to curve, to bend, in reference to the form of these cakes, or: because they were surrounded with hot ashes. (Sept.: ὁ ἐγκρυφίας.)

Ver. 13. The divine interpretation, which is immediately annexed to this quite extraordinary demand, and just because it is so, lays stress (for the reference is not to the siege, but it is already the exile that is spoken of), not on the difficulty as to fuel, but on its uncleanness, and that not so much in a Levitical as in a moral point of view, as judged by the universal human instinct of decency. Man's dung signifies the profane sojourn in the heathen world in general with its idols (גלולים!). Comp. Ezek. ix. 3. The prophet raises his objection—in Ver. 14—in the sense: if I have never eaten that which is unclean according to the law of Israel, how should I have anything to do with a thing unclean generally! (GROT.)—אֲהָהּ, an exclamation of astonishment, fear, horror. **My soul**—not so much as: I myself; it expresses rather the living consciousness of the prophet in his feelings, alike as to his antipathies and sympathies (Matt. xxvi. 38). A lively expression of feeling, especially characteristic of a *priest!* Comp. as to the subject-matter, Deut. xiv. 21; Ex. xxii. 31; Acts x. 14, xi. 8; Dan. i. 8.—פִּגּוּל, according to Ges.: something made fetid, stinking; hence, on the one hand: unpalatable, on the other: forbidden to be used by the laws of food, something abominable, disgusting, or: something rejected, worthy of rejection (Lev. vii. 18); also without בשר, Isa. lxv. 4. According to HÄV.: especially characterizing the priest, inasmuch as in the case of the sacrificial meals flesh left over till the third day was reckoned פגול, Lev. xix. 7. God makes the concession to him—Ver. 15—with רְאֵה, corresponding to his הִנֵּה, of *cow's* dung (Kethib: צְפוּעֵי, Qeri: צְפִיעֵי), like camel's dung—a very common, odourless fuel. The objection and concession (HAV.: an impressive episode) give a distinctness of their own to the matter in hand; and thereafter Ver. 16 returns to the beginning, not merely of this third symbolical action (ver. 9 sqq.), but, in winding up, of the whole chapter (ver. 1 sqq.), and in this way to what is most closely impending, viz. to the siege of Jerusalem. And to this corresponds in point of form the בֶּן־אדם, and, as regards the subject-matter, the participial construction הנני־שבר, of what is as it were shown in the act of being broken in pieces.—As in Isa. iii. 1 bread and also water are named as that which supports (DELITZSCH), or more exactly, that on which one supports himself, so here the **staff of bread**, since bread supports, *i.e.* nourishes, strengthens, refreshes the heart of man, Ps. civ. 15; Gen. xviii. 5; Judg. xix. 5; Lev. xxvi. 26. This staff being broken on which the earthly man leans, he falls into the dust of death. Defined more exactly, and, at the same time, set forth vividly by means of ואכלו־לחם־. Comp. vers. 10, 11.—בשממון strengthens בדאגה, the anxiety about the means of subsistence (Matt. vi. 31, 32) rising up into silent, speechless pain, caused by the impending starvation.—Ver. 17. Either dependent on the principal thought in ver. 16: "in order that" (EWALD), or, as this is limited to bread, dependent on the amplification of the same there: **because**.—The **brother** also in Ps. xlix. 7.—In other respects, a quotation from Lev. xxvi. 39; Lam. ii. 12, 19 (Luke xxi. 26).

ADDITIONAL NOTE ON CH. IV.

[Jerusalem in a state of siege represents the covenant-people, as a whole, straitened and oppressed by the powers of this world, as the instruments of God's just displeasure. And the prophet being appointed to bear, during its continuance, the iniquity of the people, with stinted and foul provisions, points in another form to the same visitation of evil—only with a more particular respect to the cause from which it was to spring; and the penal character it should wear. That the time specified should have been in all 430 years, denoted that the dealing was to form a kind of fresh Egyptian exile and bondage to the elements of the world; but much more so in the case of the one house than in that of the other. The house of Israel having cast off nearly all that was distinctive in the position and privileges of the covenant-people, they had consequently sunk into a condition of greatest danger, one bordering on heathen darkness and perdition—nigh unto cursing. What they might expect was to be bruised and crushed to the dust, as if under the rod of Egypt. But Judah was not so far gone; she had the true priesthood to minister at her altars, and the house of David to rule by divine right over the heritage of God; so that her subjection to the powers of evil was only to be like the time of chastisement and trial in the wilderness, out of which she might again emerge into a state of peace and blessing. As the prophet also again declared, in a later prophecy, "And I will bring you into the wilderness of the peoples (not the wilderness merely, but the wilderness of *the peoples*, to show that it was to be the same only in character as of old, but not in geographical position), and there will I plead with you face to face; like as I pleaded with your fathers in the wilderness of the land of Egypt, so will I plead with you, saith the Lord God" (ch. xx. 35-38). A new time of chastisement, but mingled, as of old, with mercy; severe and earnest dealing, but for a gracious result—that they might be refined and purified, so as to become fit for enjoying the good which, as a redeemed people, was secured to them for a heritage of blessing. And if any hope remained for the other branch, the house of Israel—if they were ever to escape from their state of Egyptian darkness and bondage, it must be by their going to join their brethren of Judah in the wilderness, and sharing in their peculiar treatment and prospects. On which account, it is not the whole of the 430 years of the Egypt-state that is appointed toward the house of Israel in the vision, but this shortened by the 40 years of the wilderness sojourn, to teach them that a way still lay open for their return to life, but only by their having the Egypt-state merged into that of the wilderness; in other words, by ceasing from their rank idolatries and open apostasy from the way of God, and coming to seek, along with Judah, through God's covenant and ordinances, a restoration to righteousness and peace and blessing.

But why should the prophet, in thus announcing the future dealings of God, have thrown the delineation into so peculiar, so enigmatical a form? Why should he have presented it to the view as a returning again "of the years of former generations"? Not, certainly, on the principle of a bald and meagre literalism, as if he meant us to understand that the clock of Providence was actually to be turned back, and the identical ground trodden over again, the precise measures of time filled up anew, of which we read in the earlier history of the chosen race. He who would interpret in such a style the symbolical visions of an Ezekiel is incapable of entering into the rapt emotions of such a mind, and must necessarily flounder at every step. For here we have to do, not only with a lively and fervid spirit, which is ever breathing life, as it were, into the dead, but that spirit in a state of ecstatic elevation, in which the mind naturally served itself of the more remarkable facts and providences in the past; yet only as aids to the utterance of prophetic thought—appropriate forms wherein to clothe the new things concerning God's kingdom, that were through the Spirit imaging themselves to the prophet's vision. And, indeed, the very imperfection that usually appears in the *frame* of such historical visions, as compared with the past realities,—the partial mingling together here, for example, of the two great consecutive periods of past judgment and trial in the history of the covenant-people, so as to make the second begin *before* the first had ended,—this very imperfection shows, as it was doubtless intended to do, that an exact reproduction of the past was not in the eye of the prophet, and that the *nature* of God's contemplated designs, rather than any definite *bounds* and *limits* respecting them, were imaged under those ancient periods of tribulation in Egypt and the wilderness.

There were three reasons chiefly why the prophets in general, and this prophet in particular, might be often led to speak of the future under the form and image of the past. In the first place, as the meaning obviously did not lie upon the surface, it called for serious thought and inquiry regarding the purposes of God. A time of general backsliding and corruption is always a time of superficial thinking on spiritual things. And just as our Lord, by His parables, that partly veiled while they disclosed the truth of God, so the prophets, by their more profound and enigmatical discourses, sought to arouse the careless from their security, to awaken inquiry, and stir the depths of thought and feeling in the soul. It virtually said to them, You are in imminent peril; direct ordinary discourse no longer suits your case; bestir yourselves to look into the depths of things, otherwise the sleep of death shall overtake you.

Then, again, it conveyed in a few words—by means of a brief allusion—what the most lengthened description without it could scarcely have accomplished. It was employing a device which the most powerful and effective orators have sometimes resorted to with the greatest effect—as in the memorable words of Mirabeau, when, wishing to repel the thought of danger, he flashed out the pregnant interrogation: "Is Hannibal at the gates?" In like manner, the prophet here, seeking to impress upon his countrymen the certainty and the awfulness of God's impending judgments on account of sin, carries them back to the past; he brings up to their view Egypt and the wilderness as ready to renew themselves again in their experience. What thoughts of terror and alarm were these fitted to awaken in their minds! Centuries of bondage and oppression! A wearisome sojourn amid drought and desolation! And then this foreshadowing of the future, not only rendered more distinct, but also strengthened as to its credibility, *authenticated* by those stern realities of the past! It assuredly *has* been; shall it not be again?

But this suggests another and, indeed, still deeper reason for such a mode of representation having been adopted; for such renewed exhibitions of the past were among the means specially chosen by God for the purpose of enforcing on men's notice the uniformity of His dealings, and teaching them to regard the providential facts of one age as substantial predictions of what are to be expected in another. It told men then, and it tells us now (only it was more peculiarly adapted to those who lived in ancient times, as the revelations they possessed consisted, much more than now, in the records of history—yet it tells all alike), that the *forms* alone are transitory in which divine truth and righteousness manifest themselves, while the *principles* embodied in these forms are eternal, and can never cease, amid all outward varieties, to be giving forth similar exhibitions of their life and power to those which have already appeared. The eye that can thus look through the shell into the kernel, may see the future things of God's administration mirrored in the past—not, indeed, the exact copy and image of what is to be, yet its essential character and necessary result. Even those very periods of bygone tribulation and chastisement, which the prophet here represents as coming to life again in his day—have they not also a voice for other times? Are they not still reiterating their lessons, and perpetually renewing their existences, in the case of impenitent transgressors now, as well as formerly, in that of drooping exiles in the cities of the Medes, or on the banks of Chebar? One of these periods—the sojourn in the wilderness—the Baptist still finds prolonging itself to the era of his own ministry. His word of stern expostulation and solemn warning makes itself heard as "the voice of one crying in the wilderness;" for he sees everywhere around him trackless deserts where ways of God need to be opened up—elements of corruption working which require to be purged away by the searching application of divine righteousness, before the Canaan of God's inheritance can be properly entered and enjoyed. And the lukewarm and fruitless professor still—so long as he cleaves to the ways of iniquity, and refuses to yield a hearty surrender to the will of God—what else is his condition? He is in bondage to the elements of the world, and therefore can have no part in that good inheritance which floweth with milk and honey. The doom of Heaven's condemnation hangs suspended over his head; and if not averted by a timely submission to the righteousness of God, and a cordial entrance into the bond of the covenant, he shall infallibly perish in the wilderness of sin and death.—FAIRBAIRN'S *Ezekiel*, pp. 57–61.—W. F.]

DOCTRINAL REFLECTIONS.

1. In the case of a prophet of Ezekiel's peculiarity, it must be granted that the boundary between symbolic representation in mere forms of speech, and by means of action in real life, may be a movable one. Where, however, the prophet, just as in the case before us, is not to speak, but to be silent, what he relates as a series of facts can hardly be otherwise understood than as actually so. Preaching by means of things done as a mere form of speech is a contradiction in itself. He is to act as He who has sent him will also act. There is, in the first place, enough of words. And then it would perhaps be difficult to reconcile with the "honesty and uprightness of the prophet," which, however, Hengst. maintains, what he asserts of his symbolical actions, that they are "only pictures executed in a lively manner, calculated to make an indelible impression on the imagination." For example, vers 14, 15. [But see Note on vers. 1–3.—W. F.]

2. "If any one reads what Ezekiel reports here, it will perhaps appear to him like a childish play,

which it would also be, if God had not commanded the prophet to make it so. From this we may learn that the sacraments also are distinguished from empty illusions by means of the word of God alone. The authority of God for them is the mark of distinction, by which the sacraments are singled out, and have their meaning. It is not the outward appearance, but the Author that is to be looked at. So also the whole system of divine worship under the law differed almost in no respect from the ceremonies of the heathen; yea, these latter brought their sacrifices, and that even with the greatest possible pomp; but Israel had God's command and promise on their side" (CALV.).

3. The sinner will not get off so easily before God, however lightly he may appear to deal with his sin before men, and before the tribunal of his own conscience. Sin lies as guilt upon man's conscience, as a burdensome consciousness that one deserves punishment, has to expect punishment. Between the past, when the sin was committed, and the future, when punishment is deservedly to be expected, guilt is the painful, burdensome present of the sinner. Guilt is an abiding thing, even if punishment is a past thing.

4. If every one in himself has to bear his guilt, this moral side is supplemented by the specifically religious one, that a freeing from the burden of it, an exculpation—not the denial, nor the lessening, the explaining away, but the removal of guilt—has been provided for. Without this thought, by means of which the forgiveness of sins is accomplished, true religion is inconceivable. Such a removal of guilt took place mediatorially in Israel by means of the priesthood. What lay in this case in the office, as of divine form for the period of shadows, lay also in the sacrifice, as of divine substance for the same period of types; by means of the sacrifice, the removal of guilt took place in the way of substitution, of atoning acceptance of that guilt. Everything was in a manner like a bill of exchange, of which God meant to get payment (*realisiren*) in His own time. This divine realization in the fulness of the times will thus have the form of a priest and the essence of a sacrifice. The Servant of Jehovah in Isa. liii. is both, priest as well as sacrifice; but the prophet is not so, who has neither to mediate nor to make atonement, but who speaks God's word or embodies it in action—in our case here the latter; that is to say, he symbolically represents the guilt of the people in his own person, not so much, of course, by action as by suffering.

5. As Ewald already points out, the 40 years for Judah are parallel with the 70 years of the Babylonian exile in Jeremiah. What the latter are in a predominantly numerical point of view, the 40 of Ezekiel are in a purely symbolical.

6. Hävernick, in connection with the episode of vers. 14, 15, mentions the case of Daniel, who in deepest sorrow must eat the bread of affliction, and pine away in grief over the sins of his people, but an angel of God comes also, and comforts and strengthens him. So likewise here, as he says, Jehovah alleviates the punishment. The protest of Ezekiel not less closely resembles the εἰ δυνατόν of the Son of man in Gethsemane, and the strengthening by an angel from heaven.

7. The circumstance that they were to eat "their bread polluted" among the heathen, pointed at the same time, according to Cocc., to the entire want of the means of cleansing through sacrifice (Hos. ix. 4). The land of the heathen far from the temple was an unclean land, because there was no possibility of cleansing according to the law of the Sanctifier of Israel.

HOMILETIC HINTS.

Ver. 1. Similar *symbolic actions* we find performed by Christ also, who places a child in the midst of His disciples, washes their feet, etc. And so God wishes here also to say to Israel: "Thou wilt not hear; open thine eyes at least!" (H. H.)—God sometimes demands things which appear to men foolish, nay, silly. But in God's foolishness there is wisdom, while in all the wisdom of men there is mere foolishness in the end, 1 Cor. i. 25.—"Elisha in 2 Kings xiii. causes bow and arrows to be brought; Isaiah in ch. xx. walks barefoot; Jeremiah in ch. xxvii. wears a yoke, bonds, etc. The apostles shake the dust off their feet (Matt. x.), shake their clothes (Acts xviii. 6); Agabus binds Paul with his girdle (Acts xxi.). Let us recal to mind the bundle of arrows wherewith that heathen preached concord to his sons" (L. L.).—"Most of all art thou besieged, when thou supposest that thou art not at all besieged. There is a security of the Christian which is storm; for, according to Job, man's life upon earth is a warfare" (JER.).—"Besieged Jerusalem is the soul in its sins, against which all the works of the divine righteousness are directed; but as the unburnt brick is easily dissolved in pieces by water, so also the soul in its sins by the tears of repentance" (A L.).

Ver. 2. Titus confessed of the second destruction of Jerusalem, that the city was conquered more by the angry Deity than by means of the Roman weapons.—"Temptation may be called a spiritual siege" (STCK.).—The whole world round about us is, in the main, a siege of the soul; in the world we have tribulation. If only the iron pan does not stand between us and God! For if God be for us, who can be against us? But, on the other hand, if God must be against us, according to the testimony of our own conscience, what could peace even with all men help us!

Ver. 3. "Preachers frequently appear to their hearers as their enemies, because they proclaim to them their ruin, and depict the punishment of their sin vividly before their eyes; and yet they do not wish their ruin, but the salvation of their souls" (STCK.).—"The Jews might shake their heads and thrust out their tongues, but this fact they could not alter, that it was a *sign* for Israel" (CALV.).—To him who has his soul before his eyes, everything, even if it is not said so expressly as here, may be a sign.—All things must, and in fact do, work for good to those who love God.

Ver. 4 sqq. "Preachers are to grudge no trouble and inconvenience for the best interests of their hearers, 1 Thess. ii. 8, 9" (ST.).—"God does not always punish on the spot, when men deserve it with their sins" (O.).—Preachers are to preach not merely with the word, but by their example, in doing as well as in leaving undone, and also in suffering.—God's patience and His servants patience is a fine sermon.—"We, for the most part, reckon up only our days of sorrow, but for our days of joy, and especially for our days of sin, we have neither reckoning nor remembrance" (STCK.).—Ver. 7. How much longing, how much pain, but what righteousness also, lay in this look toward Jerusalem!—A prelude on Ezekiel's part to Luke xix. 41 sqq., but also a contrast—here the uncovered arm, there the weeping eyes of Jesus. —"Ah! if now Jerusalem and we who are in it were to judge ourselves, and were to look upon our sins and vices as our worst enemies, and to attack them; then it would not be necessary for God with those who are His to take up a position against us as enemies" (B. B.).—Ver. 8. "Diseases and afflictions of every kind are such *bands*, wherewith God binds His own, and not merely the ungodly" (STCK.).—"And now, behold, I go bound in the spirit," says Paul in Acts xx.—"Let us break their bands asunder, and cast away their cords from us," is a well-known watchword of those who are mighty according to the flesh in this world.—"We bind ourselves with our sins, and Satan knows how to hold us fast in these bands of our own" (STCK.).

Ver. 9 sqq. So the *bread* of misery is ever still of many sorts, and yet not much for each day.—"But our days also for the bread of misery are measured and numbered, and beyond them it is not to last" (B. B.).—Want of bread is to be endured, for man lives not by bread alone; but the want of God no man ought to be able to endure, not even for a single instant; and yet how many become old and grey without hunger on this account!—Vers. 10, 11. The high importance of bread and water in a bodily and spiritual point of view; and yet, for the most part, we are able to think only of prisoners in connection with bread and water.—Ver. 12. "Nothing can be so loathsome to men as sin is to God" (STCK.).—"But what else, pray, are those doing but eating dirt, who delight themselves in earthly things, and do everything for the sake of the belly or the flesh?" (B. B.)—And in what is the daily intellectual food of so very many men, consisting as it does of newspapers and pamphlets, of social intercourse and conversation—in what is it baked? Paul reckoned everything but dung for Christ, Phil. iii.—Ver. 13. Along with the Jews, all those, even at the present day, are eating defiled bread, who, like them, are despising the bread of life which came down from heaven.—Ver. 14. He who must *be silent* to men, may yet open heart and mouth to his God.—"There is full permission to ask God for the alleviation of the cross" (O.).—Ver. 15. "God is and remains gracious even in the midst of wrath; if He does not take the cross of His children entirely away, yet He alleviates it" (CR.).—Ver. 16 sq. "No one has less thought of it than the rich, that there was to be a possibility of the want becoming so great in their case, that bread and water were so easily to fail them, even although a famine should happen. But the rich man experienced it even in hell, and could not get a drop of water, however much he wished to have it" (B. B.).

CHAPTER V.

1 And thou, son of man, take thee a sharp sword; as a barber's razor shalt
thou take it; and thou causest it to pass over thine head and over thy chin, and
2 takest thee weighing-balances, and dividest them [the hair]. A third part thou
burnest in the flame in the midst of the city, as the days of the siege are fulfilled
[when they are complete]; and thou takest the [second] third part, with the sword
shalt thou smite round about it [the city]; and the [third] third part shalt thou
3 scatter to the wind; and I will draw out the sword after them. And thou takest
4 thereof a few in number, and bindest them in thy skirts. And thou shalt take
of them farther, and thou castest them into the midst of the fire, and burnest
them in the fire; therefrom shall fire go forth to the whole house of Israel.
5 Thus saith the Lord Jehovah: This [city] Jerusalem, in the midst of the [heathen]
6 nations I placed her, and the countries round about her. And she quarrelled
with My judgments more wickedly than the [heathen] nations, and with My
statutes more than the countries which are round about her; for they despised
7 My judgments, and walked not in My statutes. Therefore thus saith the Lord
Jehovah: Because ye raged more than the [heathen] nations which are round about
you, walked not in My statutes, and did not My judgments, and [also] did not
8 after the judgments of the [heathen] nations which are round about you. Therefore thus saith the Lord Jehovah: Behold, I am against thee, even I, and I
9 execute judgments in thy midst before the eyes of the [heathen] nations. And I
do in thee what I have not done, and the like of which I will not do any more,
10 because of all thine abominations. Therefore fathers shall eat sons in thy midst,
and sons shall eat their fathers; and I execute judgments in thee, and scatter
11 thy whole remnant to every wind. Therefore, as I live, sentence of the Lord
Jehovah: Surely, because thou didst defile My sanctuary with all thy detestable
things, and with all thine abominations, I also will cut off; neither shall Mine eye
12 spare, neither will I show pity. A third part of thee—of the pestilence shall

they die, and with the famine shall they perish in the midst of thee; and
the [second] third part—by the sword shall they fall round about thee; and the
[third] third part will I scatter to every wind, and the sword will I draw out after
13 them. And Mine anger is accomplished, and I cause My fury to rest upon them,
and I breathe again; and they shall know that I, Jehovah, have spoken in My
14 zeal, while I accomplish My fury on them. And I will give thee to desolation
and to mockery among the [heathen] nations which are round about thee, before
15 the eyes of every passer-by. And it is a reproach and a taunt, a warning and an
astonishment, to the [heathen] nations which are round about thee, when I execute
judgments in thee in anger and in fury, and in furious rebukes: I, Jehovah, have
16 spoken. When I send upon them the evil arrows of famine, which are for
destruction, which I will send to destroy you, and I will increase famine upon
17 you, and I break for you the staff of bread; And I send upon you famine and
evil beasts, and they make thee childless; and pestilence and blood press upon
thee; and a sword will I cause to come upon thee. I, Jehovah, have spoken.

Ver. 2. Sept.: Το *τεταρτον . . . , κ. ληψη τ. τεταρτον κ. κατακαυσεις αὐτο ἐν μεσω αὐτης, κ. τ. τεταρτον κατακοψεις*—

Ver. 4. . . . *πυρ.* Κ. *ἐρεις παντι οἰκω 'Ισρ.*

Ver. 6. Κ. *ἐρεις τα δικαιωματα μου τη ἀνομω ἐκ των ἐθνων, κ. τα νομιμα μου ἐκ των χωρων των κυκλω αὐτης·*

Ver. 7. Sept.: . . . *ἀνθ' ὡν ἡ ἀφορμη ὑμων ἐκ τ. ἐθνων*—(Anoth. read.: עשיתם without לא. Syr.)

Ver. 11. Anoth. read.: אגרע.

Ver. 12. Το *τεταρτον σου . . . κ. τ. τεταρτ. σου ἐν λιμω κ. τ. τετ. σ. εἰς παντα ἀνεμον . . . κ. τ. τετ. σ. ἐν ῥομφαια . . . κ. μαχαιραν*—

Ver. 14. . . . *ἐρημον κ. τας θυγατερας σου κυκλω*—

Ver. 15. Anoth. read.: בגוים; Sept., Arab., Vulg.: *in gentibus.*

Ver. 17. . . . *et bestias pessimas usque ad internecionem*—

EXEGETICAL REMARKS.

Vers. 1–4.—*The Fourth Sign.* Vers. 5–17.—*The Divine Interpretation of the same.*

What follows may be called a second sign, inasmuch as the three preceding symbolical acts fit into each other as parts of *one* symbolical whole. There is also the indication of the new section, just as in ch. iv. 1: **And thou, son of man.** Ch. v. 1–4, however, is not without reference to ch. iv. If, then, ch. iv. 13 already carried us beyond the siege of Jerusalem as such, so much the more readily may the (numerically) fourth sign which the prophet is to perform place us *in the midst of the conquest of the city.* For it is with this that ver. 1 begins. The whole of the lively action revolves round the **sword,** which now does its work victoriously; what follows is a threefold act of the sword. Comp. Deut. xxxii. 41. Ezekiel, just as in ch. iv., also represents therein both God and the people. What he is to take to himself is what God will take to Himself in the person of the king of Babylon, whose sword of execution is that of God, here that of Ezekiel. Comp. Isa. vii. 20. ("The mere image becomes a symbolically isolating action; where others only speak of shaving the head as a sign of deepest grief, Ezekiel takes a sword," etc.—UMBREIT.) Ewald's translation appears to invert the matter, where, namely, the razor is to serve as a sharp sword. Ezekiel is rather to take *a sharp sword as a razor.* (The purposely-emphasized *sharpness* of the sword ought to relieve Hengst. of the difficulty which the outward execution causes him. Of smooth shaving, so that no hairs at all are left, nothing is said; and what shall one say, when Hengst. makes the task still more difficult by adding: "especially for a man of predominant subjectivity, who is usually not skilled in such manipulations." Such a thing sounds ridiculous, but not what Ezekiel is to do.) חרב is the instrument that "devastates," "destroys," not (at all events, in the context of our chapter): a cutting tool in general, knife (HITZIG), although it has to serve as a barber's razor.—*Head* and *bearded chin* come into consideration, neither as being the capital nor as being the head of the nation, the king, in contrast with the land or the people, but *solely in reference to the hair,* which, therefore, we are also to understand in the clause: **and dividest them:** they mean *the innumerable* (Ps. xl. 12) *individuals of Israel,*—in its fulness (the flowing ornament, just as it is the manly strength, of the oriental) the ornament and the strength of a nation,—conceived of especially as inhabitants of Jerusalem. (In Lev. xxi. 5, the shaving off of the hair is specially forbidden to the priest, HÄV.)—The **weighing balances** (dual) symbolize the divine justice, as it weighs out the punishment (Isa. xxviii. 17), and render possible the division into three parts of equal weight which follows.

Ver. 2 puts us back into ch. iv.: the prophet is to burn a third part of his hair which he has cut off באור, in the flame of a fire kindled for this purpose. The **flame** as an emblem represents, not Jerusalem rising up in flames (as Hengst.), but, according to ver. 12, *the consuming violence of the pestilence and the famine* (Lam. v. 10). Hengst. gives himself unnecessary trouble to make the dead bodies be consumed by the flames. Keil correctly refers בתוך העיר to that Jerusalem which is portrayed upon the brick which Ezekiel is besieging (ch. iv. 1 sqq.). KLIEF.: he is to burn this third part upon the stone. The fourth symbolical action has a common sphere with the three preceding ones. The *fulfilling* of the days of the siege is thereby put in connection with (כמלאת, Jer xxv. 12) ch. iv. 6, 7, 8—comp. there—so that we have to think of the remainder of the time, specially the 40 days. In *this* period, as the 390 days of the siege are at an end, he has to perform what is here commanded him. The lying on the right side is therefore, according to this statement also (comp. on ch. iv. 12), to be understood in a looser sense.—סביבותיה refers to the portrayed city, round about which, as respects the second third part, Ezekiel is to smite with the sword (comp. ver. 12), in this way (while, for the first third part, the *siege* was still kept hold of) forming a transition to the subject which follows, viz. the capture of Jerusalem. Either in general: what is slaughtered at the capture in the environs of the city, when fleeing out of the same, or more specially: with reference to the flight of Zedekiah (Jer. lii. 7, 8) and his attendants (?). GROT.: during the various sallies of the besieged. HENGST.: while seeking for subsistence or attempting flight (?).—The action with the last third symbolizes (ver. 12) the scattering in the fullest sense, and that alike to all the four winds, and in such a way that the wind can make its sport therewith as it will (לרוח), Isa. xli. 16. —אריק אחריהם (Ex. xv. 9) *constructio prægnans*, a quotation from Lev. xxvi. 33, consequently not the hairs, but what is signified by them: the Jews, partly those who can flee, in still larger number those who are taken prisoners. EWALD: "even then still pursued by the sword, so that only very few after repeated testings (?) ultimately remain over, Isa. vi. 13." (Jer. xlii. 15 sqq., xliii. 10 sqq., xliv. 11 sqq.) The LXX. have from ver. 12—where pestilence, famine, sword, and wind occur—introduced a fourfold division here, against which both the text—that they had a better before them does not appear—and the symbolical meaning of the number *three* for the *divine* recompense testify, as also, besides, Zech. xiii. 8, 9; Rev. viii.

Vers. 3, 4 contain a continuation (KEIL) or rather the *completion* of the symbolical transaction. משם, "*from there*," because the last third, remaining as it does in life, is *conceived of as locally* somewhere in the figure and in the reality. It is the third part scattered to the wind that is spoken of, as in every case of such scattering, some part remains lying on the ground, another part comes to rest somewhere farther on. —**A few in number.** This even indicates a certain care, but still more the symbolic *binding* (not a collecting, but a preserving) of the hairs in the skirt of the garment. (Hos. iv. 19 does not belong to this category.) That "the Lord will gather the remnant of His people from their dispersion, and lead them back to their native land" (HENGST.) is not said: on the contrary, in ver. 4 there is also another (עוד) **taking of them** (ומהם), *i.e.* of those that were taken, the few, counted hairs; and, in fact, not only are those thus taken *cast into the midst of the fire* and *burnt* therein, but ממנו, *i.e. from the midst of the fire* (תוך), in which they are burning, there **shall fire go forth to the whole house of Israel.** Neither in connection with these words nor from ver. 13 sqq. can the thought arise of testings, of a fire of purification. Nor is it, as UMBREIT: "that the most pungent grief over the mournful lot of the besieged of Jerusalem shall seize all Israel." The *fire* symbolizes throughout the *judgment of the wrath of God*, at last annihilating the people as a whole. (Jer. iv. 4; Zeph. iii. 8.) Jer. xxix. 21, 22 is not to be quoted here as Raschi does; but we must rather go back with Grot. to Jer. xl. sqq.: these fugitives gathering together in the land may at least easily be compared to the hairs which fell to the earth immediately around the prophet (ver. 3); and their destiny also corresponds (Jer. lii. 30). Häv., Hengst. think of those brought back from Babylon down to the burning of Jerusalem by the Romans. It is still farther fetched, with Kliefoth, Keil, to drag in Luke xii. 49 here: where, pray, has a "cleansing, purifying, and quickening power gone forth from Christ over the whole house of Israel"? There remains certainly a remnant from vers. 3, 4, only it is neither characterized as a holy seed (Isa. vi. 13), no even as in Ezek. vi. 8 sqq.: *it is left between the lines.* [Ewald (1st edit.) translated: from me shall a fire, etc., as if it were ממני. Keil, after Hitzig, would refer it ("therefrom") to the whole transaction described in vers. 3, 4. But Hitzig makes the sin to be a fire (Job xxxi. 12), and also the prophecy threatening destruction a fire pent up (Jer. xxiii. 29), which breaks forth into flame at the moment of its accomplishment. To refer ממנו directly to אש is prevented, of course, by the feminine construction תצא אש. HENGST.: "from it, *i.e.* from them, the numerical multiplicity being combined into an ideal unity with reference to the uniting bond of the evil disposition." Have the LXX. with their ἐξ αὐτῆς thought of the city?] Comp. besides, Judg. ix. 15, 20.

Inasmuch now as in ver. 5 the *divine interpretation* begins with כה אמר, what is said in ch. iii. 26 (comp. ch. iii. 27), as well as a purely symbolical prophesying in ch. iv. 7, is thereby modified. "To prophesy" (comp. ch. xxxvii.) is also, primarily, to speak in the spirit, as that usually takes place by divine direction. But the divine interpretation begins with the *meaning* of Jerusalem. This city portrayed upon the tile, viz. Jerusalem, the word of Jehovah points out as placed by Him **in the midst of the heathen nations,** of course not in a local sense, like Delphi, the navel of the earth. Already the Chinese empire of the centre points as such to the maxims as to the ethical equilibrium prevailing in the Chinese system. But this is the central position as regards the history of salvation of Israel—represented by its capital, hence in local symbolism—for the history of the world, so that from it all the rays go forth to the world as a circumference. John iv. 22. (Lam. ii. 15.) In its position, so distinguished by God's grace, we get the measure of the *guilt* of Jerusalem, *i.e.* of those whom it represents, inasmuch as they have come so far short of the obligation therein implied, that—Ver. 6—in God's sight they appear even more wicked than the heathen (2 Kings xxi. 9). Ewald reads unnecessarily (because of מן) וַתָּמֶר, from יָמַר, מוּר, which in Hiph. is read with בְּ; and הֵמִיר, according to him, means originally: to cause to totter, hence: to exchange something against (מן) something else, so that it gives way before this latter. (RASCHI: "changed My judgments into wickedness." Similarly Chald. and Syr.) וַתֶּמֶר is simply imperf. apoc. from מרה Hiph. (an allusion to Ex. xv. 23 sqq., the first resistance of the newly-saved people.) Comp. Deut. i. 26, 43, ix. 7, 24, etc. Like a technical term for Israel's rebelliousness.—מן, in a comparative sense: more than, leaving the heathen behind them. לרשעה, unto wickedness; as an adverb: wickedly. (Hitz. infin.: so that they sinned more grievously.) לרשעה brings into prominence the condition which makes Israel appear worse comparatively than the heathen; hence מן is most connected with it. Unsuitably, Hengst. compares 1 Cor. v., where the question is not about the *what*, but about a *how*. Neither have Isa. ii. 6 and Jer. ii. 10 any connection with this passage. But the more wicked character of Israel is intelligible, partly as contrasted with the grace of God which they have experienced, partly therefore from the circumstance that they were acting contrary to the express will of God. The comparison is, in a general sense, possible, because the heathen also, by means of conscience, know about the divine will, have a law written in their hearts. Rom. ii. 14, 15. כי inasmuch as they so acted, they were rebels convicted by law and statute, apart from conscience, common to them with the heathen.

Ver. 7. לכן (on account of such things), as usual, at the beginning of a weighty, and, for the most part, of a threatening consequence. But before the *threatening of punishment* there is a second emphasizing of their greater guilt. [Instead of הֲמָנְכֶם Ewald reads הֲמֻנְּכֶם, from מנה, to count; HITZ.: it stands for הֲמְמְכֶם, "because of your driving;" Häv, after the Syr.: because ye were more careless than the heathen (?). Most simply, as also Ges., from הָמַן, or as Fürst, from הָמוֹן, going back to המה: "because of your raging," with significant reference to Ps. ii. 1.]—With בחקותי there is inserted an energetic parenthesis of direct address, taking up again the close of ver. 6 backwards, in which the מאסו (to push away, to reject) is changed into לא עשיתם, and in this way occasion is given for the following statement with לא. Ewald and others strike out the latter, and that also because of ch. xi. 12. If ver. 9 manifestly threatens Israel with a heavier punishment than ever before the eyes of the heathen, then it is but too plain we must understand vers. 6, 7 of a wickedness on the part of Israel greater than that of the heathen; and such acting more wickedly than the heathen is intensified in ver. 7 merely with respect to the natural law of conscience; in other words, this reference still left unexpressed in ver. 6 is expressly brought in afterwards. God's laws and statutes they rejected, neither did they act in accordance with the natural laws belonging to the standpoint of the heathen conscience. In yet another application, ch. xvi. 47. In ch. xi. 12 the connection and the reproof is a different one; there is nothing said there of a being worse than the heathen.

In ver. 8 we have, with לכן (ver. 7) repeated, the *threatening of punishment*, first of all *generally*, then, in what follows, in a form more and more concrete.—הנני עליך; comp. Amos vii. 9; Rev. ii. 5.—גם־אני marks out the interposition of God as being a retribution: hitherto, thou, now I, yes, even I, with a mode of acting corresponding to thine own (Matt. x. 33; 2 Tim. ii. 12).—As in ver. 7, so also here: עָשָׂה, illustrated by the fundamental passage Ex. xii. 12 (Num. xxxiii. 4).—Because Israel has not made itself a pattern to the heathen, an *example* in what is right and becoming (the negative side to ver. 6 is brought in afterwards), God on His part makes it a *spectacle* for the heathen. The *laws* (*Rechte*) of God become *judgments* (*Gerichte*) of God. This is the *one* element of retribution; the *other* in ver. 9: because Israel has gone beyond the heathen in wickedness, His punishment also will go beyond anything in the past or future.—בָךְ is the resumption of בְּתוֹכֵךְ (ver. 8).—כמוהו עוד = *the like of which I will not do again* (Matt. xxiv. 21).

Ver. 10. *A more concrete exemplification* of what is thus threatened. The thought thereby expressed is the breaking up alike of natural *family* ties and of the theocratic bond of Israel as a *nation*, this being what has never taken place in the past, and, having once happened, what is not to be repeated in the future. Comp. Lev. xxvi. 29; Deut. xxviii. 53; Jer. xix. 9; Lam. ii. 20, iv. 10; 2 Kings vi. 28, 29 (Luke xii. 53).—שפטים (ver. 15), *penal* judgments, more exactly defined as משפטים in ver. 8.—וזריתי; comp. vers. 2, 12.

Ver. 11. The repeated לכן is exceedingly impressive. חי־אני, the adjective being made to precede, properly: living I. Deut. xxxii. 40. He will show Himself to them as being the *Living One*. Corresponding to the climax of the discourse in the oath, there is the solemn earnestness of the נאם part. pass. constr. from נאם (המה נהם), low, secret speaking; therefore: utterance = "speaks," a parenthetical noun-clause.—The *desecration* with which Israel is charged in ch. viii. has respect to the *temple*, but to that as being the *abode of Jehovah's glory*. The avenging judgment (with a reference to ver. 1) holds out in prospect the *cutting* off (another reading: אגדע, Isa. xv. 2) of this noblest ornament of the people, where Jehovah meets with His people, and they with Him. [גרע, in this its simplest sense, too readily suggests itself for us to have recourse, with Hengst., to the fundamental passage Deut. iv. 2 (ch. xiii. 1): to take therefrom of that which God has promised to give them, or, like Häv.: I also will withdraw from the people what is theirs, or, with Ges., to supply the following עֵינִי: I also will draw off mine eye, or, like Ewald, to read, from xxiv. 14, לא אפרע: "I will not neglect." HITZ.: I also will sweep you away (גרף, 2 Kings xxi. 13), or (אפרע): I also will let myself alone, leave myself scope to do as I please. Keil, like Ges. (Job xxxvi. 7), takes ולא תחום adverbially: that it may not feel.

compassion, and understands the last וגם־עני accordingly.] אגרע stands emphatically without an object; if it is allowable to refer it to the temple, the following transition (Jer. xiii. 14) to vers. 12, 13 sqq. announces certainly something more general, more comprehensive. Comp. ch. ix. 6.—Ver. 12. After this reference to ver. 1, as already in ver. 10, we have now the more detailed divine interpretation of ver. 2. Comp. besides, Jer. xxix. 17, xvi. 4, xv. 7. By means of what is threatened, the anger of God is accomplished—Ver. 13—inasmuch as it is fully poured out. The full realization is its accomplishment. Up to the point of "causing it to rest *upon* them," and, at the same time, *in* them, so that they have the consciousness thereof, comp. John iii. 36. [To give vent to His fury *upon* them suits badly, after the anger is accomplished.] Comp. besides, ch. xvi. 42, xxi. 22 [17].—והנחמתי, perf. Hithp., by syncope for והתנחמתי. The meaning of the Niphal (to have compassion) does not suit the context, especially in what follows. נָחַם is properly: to take draughts of air, to draw in and send forth the breath, whence the Piel: to comfort, Hithp.: to comfort oneself (so also the Niphal). The meaning: "to be revenged," does not suit here. Comp. Isa. i. 24. The accomplishing of anger comes therefore to mean also the bringing of it to an end; one might say: grace recovers breath again. The extremely anthropomorphic style of our passage is a highly figurative mode of representing the personal life and acting of God.—וידעו, knowledge as the result of experience.—דברתי twice again (vers. 15, 17). In the word spoken in zeal we have a guarantee of the certainty of the deed. [The different division of the words by Ew., who takes בְּ־ as a formula of swearing, is unjustifiable.]

Ver. 14. Like חֶרֶב, the "devastator" (in this section of the sword of God), חרבה is the "devastation," the desert, wilderness. Lev. xxvi. 31, 33; Jer. vii. 34; Lam. ii. 1 sqq. Alliteratively therewith, חרפה: the tearing in pieces; in other words: the dishonouring, derision. Jer. xxiv. 9; Ezek. xxxvi. 34. The divine interpretation from here onwards touches on what is said in ver. 4—the national annihilation of Israel.—Ver. 15. והיתה, viz. Jerusalem, to which the discourse returns, as in ver. 8 (ver. 5). (Deut. xxviii. 37; Lam. v. 1.) Declamatorily in the third person.—ובתכחות חמה, rebukes in actual fact, from יכח, to reprove, to chastise. Comp. besides, Deut. xxix. 24.

Ver. 16. Famine is the predominating element. Because sent forth among them by the Lord, its operations are compared to the arrows of a bow. Deut. xxxii. 23, 42; Lam. iii. 12, 13.—As in ver. 15 היתה, so now בהם.—The **evil** arrows, because they are למשחית, from שחת, which is explained by what follows.—The description of the famine rises to a climax; first it strikes like single arrows—destruction is present; then it increases, accumulates—the arrows from all sides become thicker; at length the staff of bread is broken (comp. ch. iv. 16).—Ver. 17. The famine is again referred to, in order to connect with it what remains, after the manner of the Pentateuch and of Jeremiah; comp. ch. xiv. 15; Deut. xxxii. 24; Lev. xxvi. 22, 25; Ezek. xxviii. 23. Hengst. understands the evil beasts figuratively of the heathen. Isa. lvi. 9; Jer. xii. 9. **Famine and evil beasts,** in parallel with **pestilence and blood** (not = bloody pestilence, as Ew.). Correspondingly with the beginning of the chapter, it comes to an end at last with the **sword.**

DOCTRINAL REFLECTIONS.

1. It belongs to the prevailing aspect of *judgment,* that those who are to be saved appear like a minimum, which is indicated, indeed, but not described more fully. *This* also is characteristic, that their salvation is made dependent wholly on their being *concealed* and *spared* (ver. 4), without any reference to their subjective state. As judgment reigns on the one hand, so unconditional free grace on the other.

2. Judgment must prevail where the national standpoint is that of the law. This lies as a consequence in the character of the law. It is only his having a certain position towards, or betaking himself *to, the person* of the Lawgiver that can preserve the transgressor, the sinner, from the sentence of death pronounced by the law. But Israel as a whole stands in opposition to Jehovah, not merely with its unlawful outward conduct, but as regards its thorough ungodliness of heart. Thus *compassion* ceases, as is expressly mentioned in ver. 11. That Jehovah is engaged in the most personal way is attested by the very form of the expression in ver. 13.

3. The lost condition morally of the people as such is significantly brought before us, in ver. 11, in the profanation of the *sanctuary.* For this is the most express local symbol of the *personal* presence of Jehovah in the midst of Israel, with which, besides, the most perfect indwelling of God in the fulfilment (John ii. 19 sqq.) is identified.

4. The judgment threatens the *national* existence of Israel. But if the nationality of Israel is the holy nationality of *the people of God,* then it is as intelligible, that the peculiar form, the symbolical body, of this idea which is to be realized may perish in the judgment of God, as it is certain that the idea will be realized, in however few it may be; in reality, there has been but One Israel, that was alike sacrifice and priest, people and king.

5. Häv., Hengst., and others find in our chapter the announcement of yet a second penal judgment, viz. the last by the hand of the Romans, as already Theodoret, Jerome. The truth is, that the more complete (the expulsion of the ten tribes was a partial thing) unfolding of judgment involved in the Chaldean destruction of Jerusalem is not finished till the judgment of the world on the last day (Matt. xxiv. 21). The judgment which still farther diminishes the small number in the skirt of the garment in ver. 3 thus finds in the context—where a transition is made from the numerical element to the substance of the matter—its goal in the consuming of the whole of Israel (ver. 4). In the Chaldean judgment, Israel's nationality perished; at that early period, not first by the hand of the Romans. "We have no king but Cæsar" is the answer of the leading men of Israel already in John xix.

6. On ver. 9 Häv. remarks: "Alone of its kind, and to be compared with nothing else, is

the judgment of the Lord which runs through the history of the kingdom of God; it is a judgment continually rising higher and higher, as compared with which what goes before always appears an insignificant one, and in this its unceasing progress paving the way for the culminating point of the last judgment." Hengst. calls the judgment on Israel "a thing unique in the history of the world." Only one must not choose to read the true fulfilment in Josephus first, but as and because the Chaldean destruction of Jerusalem was the first judgment of the kind, so it remains, *as to its essence* also, the *only* one. For where is there a second nation, to which God has stood so near, driven forth in such a way from its land of promise since the days of the fathers, judged and, as being judged, preserved? But as this political mummification serves the world-purpose of the Anointed One, so it is in the same direction that we are to seek the meaning of the destruction of Jerusalem by the Romans, viz. not as a repetition, but merely *as an application* of the Chaldean judgment to the last period of the world beginning with Christ, to the last day. Hence the general eschatological character of the discourses of Jesus in the Gospels bearing on the subject.

7. For the central position of Jerusalem, in a theological point of view, Hengstenberg quotes "Jeshurun, the congregation of the upright, the pattern nation prepared by God, which was to send forth its light into the surrounding heathen darkness, to honour its God, and to draw others to Him. Deut. iv. 5, 6; Isa. xlii. 19. Comp. Matt. v. 14; 1 Pet. ii. 9."

8. Judgment is, in every decisive moment of the history of salvation (in the history of the world), the goal, the end. "Crisis" is the name given to it when one contemplates history from a remedio-pathological point of view.

HOMILETIC HINTS.

Ver. 1 sqq. "By means of the similitude of the hair, the Lord would intimate His exact connection with Israel, how they have received from Him all nourishment and supplies; from which fellowship He now cuts them off like hair" (B.B.).—"On account of its much hair, *i.e.* its great population, Jerusalem was so proud and full of vain confidence" (C.).—"And what an impression must it make, when Ezekiel, who was of the priestly class, contrary to Lev. xxi., shaved head and beard!" (L.)—"The judgments of God have their stages, and come at last, when the measure of sins is full, in a crowd, so that he who escapes the one falls into the other" (TÜB. B.). "Men and all creatures become sharp swords, when God makes use of them in judgment" (STCK.).—"Behold an example of divine providence! God does not strike blindly in His judgments, but, in the midst of the greatest confusion of human affairs, weighs, as it were with scales, all that is to happen to every one" (W.).—"Not even a hair shall be wanting to us; but neither shall a hair escape with the just God" (B. B.).—"God is just, but He is also merciful: let us betake ourselves to His mercy" (L.).—"If one does not himself in time cut off his vanities and bad habits, then must a razor belonging to another make the eyes water, and cut in such a way, that of skin and hair nothing remains" (B. B.).—"In the judgment learn God's justice, in the foretelling of it His goodness; but sin's loathsomeness brings on the judgment" (STCK.).—"If one does not fear before the sword of the Spirit or God's word (Eph. vi.; Heb. iv.), then must the sword of the enemy come and hew down the barren trees" (B.B.).—God's judgments: (1) sharp, (2) without respect of persons, but (3) just.—Ver. 2. "Exile is honourable if it happens to us for Christ's sake; the man who has to endure it because of sin cannot comfort himself therewith" (STCK.).—"These were certainly thoroughly scattered sheep, because they had forsaken their Shepherd! He that will not allow himself to be gathered under the wings of Jesus, will be carried away by the wind of the divine wrath down to hell. And let a man flee whither he will, if he wants a good conscience, then the vengeance of God follows; there is no possibility of escape from Him" (B. B).—Under the sword of God: (1) the man whom the flame in the inner man, the fire of conscience, does not consume, (2) is struck down by the outward calamities of life, (3) or he is carried away by every gust of wind—of pleasure, of opinion, etc., in the world, and so is lost.—Ver. 3. "Divine providence and goodness remembers mercy in the midst of wrath, because of the Messiah, who was to be born of this seed" (STCK.).—"Otherwise it would have happened as in the case of Sodom and Gomorrah" (L.).—Think how we are first bound up in the skirt of the righteousness of Jesus Christ! And no one will pluck us out of His hand.—Ver. 4. "This is not to be literal fire, but something much more real even than this, the fire of the wrath of God, when He gives them over to the curse, and to the everlasting torment of an evil conscience; and this fire is to take hold of all Israel, with the exception of those preserved in the skirt of the garment" (COCC.).

Ver. 5 sqq. The greater the benefit, the greater ought to be the gratitude.—"In the Church, greater sins are often committed than outside of it" (ST.).—After the manner of Jerusalem, those cities acted in later times, where most of Jesus' miracles were wrought (Matt. xi.).—Outward advantages, without the inward disposition to correspond, are tow for the fire.—"We have therefore to see to it, that we bear the pleasure (the burden) of prosperity with a strong mind" (C.).—To whom much is given, of him much may be required, and much is required; and yet there shall only be required faithfulness in stewardship, and that gratitude which is so easily understood of itself.—"He that knows his Lord's will, and does it not, sins more grievously, and has more grievous punishment to expect, Luke xii. 47" (O.).—"Perversion of the true doctrine and of the true worship and unholy living draw the judgments of God after them" (TÜB. BIB.).—Ver. 6 sqq. "The heterodox often show in their worship more zeal, earnestness, and stedfastness than the orthodox" (ST.).—"Their vices we often adopt from the heathen, and in what is good allow them the advantage. They ought to have learnt from us, and we may learn even from them" (B. B.).—Ver. 8 sqq. "As it is the comfort of the pious: if God be for us, who can be against us? so it is the terror of the ungodly: since God is against you, who will be for you?" (STCK.)—The divine judgments in the world are a mirror for the world.—Ver. 9. The individuality of the judgments of God an interesting historical theme.—Ver. 10. "Famine has no eyes, no ears, no hands, but teeth. It has no respect of persons, nor does it listen to anything, nor does it give, but is cruel and unmerciful" (STCK.).—Fathers often enough devour their children by the bad example which they give them. And children devour their fathers by their covetousness, want of affection, disobedience, by the grief which they prepare for them.—Ver. 11. In him that does not sanctify God, God sanctifies Himself.—I live, and ye shall live also. But it is a fearful thing to fall into the hands of the living God. These are contrasts.—How many profane the sanctuary of God by sleep, by extravagance in dress, by their distracted worldly thoughts!—Ver. 13. There thou seest how zealous love can be. This causes the jealousy of Him who is Israel's Husband.—Therefore we ought to hear betimes, lest we be compelled to feel when it is too late.—Ver. 14. How many such monuments of divine retribution stand on our life-path! We walk past, yes, alas! past them. Into the mirror of the judgments of God we look in vain, just as into that of the divine law.—"If love cannot improve us, then must we feel the iron sceptre" (B. B.).—Ver. 17. "All the creatures are ready for vengeance, and wait merely for God's command" (STCK.).—"If men do not terrify us, then there are the beasts" (STCK.).—Thus there is a chain of divine punishments; one takes the other's hand.—"In the end, it is God with whom we have to do. Be not, then, like the dog which bites the stone, and not the hand which threw it!" (STCK.)—"God subscribes the threatening with the royal monogram of His name" (A L.).

3. THE TWO DISCOURSES OF REBUKE (CH. VI. AND VII.).

CH. VI. 1. And the word of Jehovah came unto me, saying: Son of man, set
2 thy face toward the mountains of Israel, and prophesy to them. And say,
3 Ye mountains of Israel, hear the word of the Lord Jehovah. Thus saith the
Lord Jehovah to the mountains and to the hills, to the brook-channels and
to the valleys: Behold, I, even I, cause a sword to come upon you, and I
4 destroy your high places. And your altars are desolated, and your sun-
pillars are broken in pieces; and I make your slain to fall before your dung-
5 idols. And I lay the carcases of the children of Israel before their dung-idols,
6 and scatter your bones round about your altars. In all your dwelling-places
shall the cities be laid waste, and the high places become desolate, in order that
your altars may be laid waste and broken in pieces, and your dung-idols be laid
waste and done away with, and your sun-pillars be thrown down, and your handi-
7 works be rooted out. And the slain falls in your midst, and ye know that I am
8 Jehovah. And I leave a remnant, inasmuch as there are to you some that have
escaped the sword among the heathen nations, when ye are scattered in the
9 countries. And your escaped ones remember me among the heathen nations,
whither they are carried captive, when I have broken their whorish heart, which
hath departed from me, and their eyes, which go a whoring after their dung-idols;
and they feel loathing in their faces for the evil things which they have done in
10 respect of all their abominations. And they know that I am Jehovah; not in
11 vain have I said that I would do this evil unto them. Thus saith the Lord
Jehovah: Strike into thy hand, and stamp with thy foot, and say, Woe to all
the evil abominations of the house of Israel, who shall fall by the sword, by the
12 famine, and by the pestilence. He that is far off shall die by the pestilence;
and he that is near shall fall by the sword; and he that remained over, and he
that is preserved, shall die by the famine; and I accomplish My fury upon [in]
13 them. And ye know that I am Jehovah, when their slain are in the midst of
their dung-idols round about their altars, at every high hill, upon all the tops of
the mountains, and under every green tree, and under every thick terebinth, on
14 whatever place they did offer sweet savour to all their dung-idols. And I stretch
out My hand upon them, and make the land a desert and waste more than the
wilderness of Diblath, in all their dwelling-places; and they know that I am
Jehovah.

Ver. 3 Vulg.: . . . *rupibus et vallibus*—(Anoth. read.: אני הנה; is wanting in some.)
Ver. 5. Anoth. read.: לפני גלוליכם. Vulg.: *simulacrorum vestrorum.*
Ver. 6. . . . *ἐν πασῃ τ κατοικιᾳ ὑμων. Αἱ πολεις*—
Ver. 9. Sept.: . . . *ὁτι ὀμωμοκα τῃ καρδιᾳ αὐτων*—
Ver. 12. Ὁ *ἐγγυς ἐν ῥομφαιᾳ . . . ὁ δε μακραν ἐν θανατῳ τελευτησει, κ. ὁ . . . κ. ὁ περιεχομενι ἐν λιμῳ*—*relictus . . . et obsessus*—
Ver. 13. . . . *ὑμων*—

EXEGETICAL REMARKS.

The first discourse is not exactly a continuation, or even a farther elucidation of what precedes, but a word by itself, although with reference to what went before. Its resemblance to Jeremiah will be shown by manifold points of contact with the style of Jeremiah. According to Calv., Ezekiel turns now from Judah to Israel (?).—Ver. 1. Comp. ch. i. 3, iii. 16.—Ver. 2. שים פניך expresses the direction, and that simply: **toward**; the translation of אל by: "against," is stronger than is necessary.—The **mountains** of Israel remove, of course, the horizon of the prophet from Jerusalem, which was hitherto mainly the subject of discourse, to a greater distance; but the expression is used, not so much in order to characterize the whole land according to its peculiarity, as a land of mountains in the sense of Deut. xi. 11 (Hengst.), which in the connection here would be quite superfluous; but the mountains come into consideration, as the sequel shows, as Israel's *well-known, favourite places of sacrifice* (Jer. iii. 6). According to J. D. Mich.: "a prophecy against the remnant of the ten tribes in Palestine, which took part even in Hezekiah's and Josiah's passover." As in the case of words of speaking, אליהם might also mean: "to prophesy **of them**;" but they are—Ver. 3—formally addressed. Comp. 1 Kings xiii. 2.—אָפִיק may be a narrow valley, a defile, and equally well a river-bed, a brook-channel.—For וְלַגֵּיאוֹת we have in the Qeri: וְלַגֵּאָיוֹת. Not for the purpose of depicting the whole land, but in order graphically to set forth the mountains; or because defiles and valleys, on account of the growth of trees, are distinctively for idolatrous services (*e.g.* the valley of Hinnom, Jer. vii. 31, xxxii. 35). In the latter respect, the sword comes and destroys the high places, as high places of worship, self-chosen; hence **your**.—הנני אני energetically expressive. The sword-tone from ch. v. begins again to make itself heard.

Ver. 4. ונשמו perf. Niph. of שָׁמֵם, comp. ch. iv. 17; here of being rendered silent by devastation: to lay waste.—The **altars** where sacrifices are offered.—חַמָּנִים only in the plural, statues, images of the Phenician sun-god (Baal-Hamman); Raschi: "sun-pillars."—גִּלּוּלִים likewise only in the plural, certainly not: "stocks," from גָּלַל, "to roll" (?), but undoubtedly connected with גָּלָל and גֵּלֶל, "dung," unless: the "abominable," "horrible," from the original meaning: "to separate," "to divide." Häv.: stone monuments (contemptuously: loose stones), dead masses of stone. (Perhaps: "your excrements.")—לִפְנֵי, "in face of," lying before the face. Dust to dung.—Ver. 5. פגר is: something fallen, a dead body; comp. Lev. xxvi. 30.—עצם is "what is strong," hence: a bone. (Lav. remarks here, that perhaps also they made themselves be buried beside their idols, and that now the bones of the dead were to be brought out and scattered by their enemies seeking after the ornaments of the dead.) The discourse is addressed to the mountains; but as it is spoken *of* the children of Israel, so also in reality it is spoken *to* them.

In Ver. 6 the place of execution is extended by means of בכל מושבותיכם to the inhabited land, more specially to the **cities** (Jer. ii. 28).—תחרבנה, with significant allusion to חֶרֶב (sword).—למען: the extermination of the idolatrous worship therefore is the object.—ויאשמו. Hengst.: "and become guilty," be convicted as guilty by means of the destruction. אשם is "to demolish," "to break in pieces," and from that morally: to commit a fault, and consequently to become guilty, finally: to suffer punishment. Guilt appears a strange thought for our context here.—Ver. 7. **Slain** [sing.]; the individual instead of all who are like him, one here, another there.—Because the discourse reaches a pause, after the personal element (as in vers. 4, 5) has been added to the material, there is mentioned as the result the experimental knowledge of Jehovah,—not so much of His being God alone, as of His eternity; here in contrast with the idols which pass away. With such knowledge taken into view as the effect of later experience, the way is paved at the same time for Ver. 8. (Ew. converts והותרתי, which is to him "incapable of explanation" (!!), into דִּבַּרְתִּי, which he attaches to ver. 7.)—The remnant are such as have escaped so far as the sword is concerned, etc.; comp. ch. v. 2, 12, 3 (Rom. ix. 27, xi. 5).—בהזרותיכם, inf. Niph. with plur. suffix, for בְּהִזָּרוֹתְכֶם.

Ver. 9. Comp. Luke xv. 17 sqq. (Lev. xxvi. 41).—אשר: if, or when.—נשברתי Ges. understands in a middle sense: "I break for myself." Hengst.: "The passivity passes over, as it were, from those whose heart is broken to Him by whom, and in whose interest, it has been broken: I was broken, instead of: I have broken for myself." [Others: By whose whorish heart I am broken (with pain, Gen. vi. 6). Hitz.: their heart and eyes, which could not be satisfied with whoredom (ch. xvi. 28, 29), God will then "satisfy" with bitter feelings (הִשְׂבַּעְתִּי instead of נשברתי). Ew. reads, instead of אשר נשברתי, "more simply," וְנִשְׁבְּרוּ. The LXX. have read נשבעתי.] Is there an allusion to David in Ps. li. 17 (2 Sam. xi. 2), as Hengst. supposes?—זנה is found properly only of the woman, as here also in the application to the *marriage* relationship of *Israel* to Jehovah. The word means properly: to incline; but whether is it *towards* or *away from?* In the latter sense (Hos. ix. 1) we have it interpreted by means of אשר־סר מעלי; in the former by means of אחרי.—ונקטו (קוט) with Dag. euphon. in the last.—בפניהם, not of the idols =לפני, vers. 4, 5, but of the escaped, who feel loathing in their own faces ("not reciprocally," Hitz.). (Hengst.: to become a loathing to themselves. Rosenm.: so that their face shows the loathing.) Ch. xx. 43, xxxvi. 31.—אל־הרעות: "in reference to," as respecting, etc. Comp. besides, Jer. xxii. 22; Hos. iv. 19.—לְכָל, like אל, of which it is an abbreviation.

Ver. 10. Like ver. 7, a pause in the discourse, a repetition of the object in view. *He* remains what He is, but *they* must change, must away back to Him. In this experimental way they come to know Jehovah.—חנם (חֵן), *gratis, frustra*, in complete form אל־חנם. That the deed proves the word is not the special point of this second pause in the discourse, but (according to the accents) the eternity of Jehovah, as in ver. 7, in contrast with the idols that pass away, so now in contrast with those who change in Israel. —The words **"Not in vain have I said,"** etc. (comp. on ch. xiv. 23), show in general how it is possible, by means of the fulfilment of what has been said, that they can acquire from experience the knowledge of Jehovah; and they form, besides, the transition to Ver. 11: כה־אמר. Pain and displeasure, in general lively emotion (Num. xxiv. 10; Ezek. xxi. 19 [17], xxii. 13). Not like ch. xxv. 6 or 2 Sam. xxii. 43. But comp., as to the *first* gesture, ver. 14. Either: with the *hand* upon the thigh (Jer. xxxi. 19), or: one hand into the other. The gesture with the *foot* Hengst. takes in the sense of impatience, which cannot wait for the suffering following upon the sinful action. The prophet symbolizes in his own person the indignation of Jehovah.—אשר, according to Keil, a conjunction: *that*.

Ver. 12. Since the "house of Israel" (ver. 11) as a whole is interpreted by means of אשר in the plural, and since, in fact, more exactly it is those who fall by the sword, etc., the specification of our verse refers to the same parties. He that is **far off,** who may reckon himself far off from the sword, which is first named in ver. 11, **dies** by that which is last named in ver. 11, and hence relatively farthest off: **pestilence.** He that is **near,** who is near the death by famine, the second named, does not, however, perish by it, but **falls** by what is still nearer to him (according to ver. 11), the first named **sword.** He that **remaineth over,** viz. from the pestilence, and he that is **preserved,** viz. from the sword, **dies** nevertheless, as it were of himself, by the **famine.** The prevailing reference here, according to ch. iv., v., is to the siege of Jerusalem; but הנצור is not on that account: he that is besieged (Hitz.). Comp. besides, ch. v. 13.

Ver. 13. A third pause in the discourse; comp. vers. 7, 10. The point in hand is the eternity of Jehovah—the beginning being at the same time resumed in a supplementary way now at the close and termination of the discourse—in contrast with the land, consequently with what has been promised and given by Jehovah Himself! Thus the accomplishment of the divine fury just threatened (ver. 12) is brought about. Perhaps also the hearers of the prophet are addressed, who may be conceived of as acquiring such knowledge. Comp. besides, vers. 4, 5; 1 Kings xiv. 23; 2 Kings xvii. 10; Deut. xii. 2; Isa. lvii. 5 sqq.; Hos. iv. 13; Jer. ii. 20, iii. 6.—*Heights of hills and tops of mountains*, as being nearer heaven, the heavenly powers, as it were like *natural altars of the earth*, adapted *also for watching the progress of the sacrifice*, of the sacrificial *smoke* mentioned in what follows.—Not forests, groves, but *single green trees* found in the brook-channels and ravines.—אלה like אַלּוֹן, from its strength, a tree similar to the oak, ever-green, rich in shade, with fruit in clusters, *capable of reaching a great age*, hence also used for monuments, landmarks, and the like (Kimchi: our elms). In arboriculture the tree most preferred, *perhaps as being sacred to Astarte.* מקום אשר, *loco quo = ubi.*—The standing formula in the law of the offering in general, and in particular of the burnt-offering which is wholly consumed, ריח ניחח, "savour of rest," is a bitter *criticism*, where God must pronounce it of the worship of idols. ("The idea of *rest* is, like that of *peace*, synonymous with acceptability, pleasantness, so that the formula is intended to assert that the offering, when it rises up, is acceptable, well-pleasing to God," Bähr.) Comp. Gen. viii. 21; Ezek. viii. 11, xvi. 18; Hos. ii. 13.

Ver. 14. The exceedingly expressive gesture (ch. xiv. 9, 13) explains itself, in contrast with the foregoing spread of idolatry (ונתתי over against נתנו־שם in ver. 13).—שממה ומשמה is: **a waste and desolation,** *the greatest waste.* Comp. ch. v. 14; Jer. vi. 8.—A **wilderness of Diblah** is not known elsewhere, hence many have read Riblah, a city which lay on the northern boundary of Palestine (?), with ה local attached to it, in this sense: "from the wilderness (in the south and east) as far as Riblah." Besides the fact that the change of reading is without support from the ancient translators, there is so much against it in a linguistic and geographical point of view (comp. Deut. xxxiv. 11 and 2 Kings xxiii. 33; Jer. xxxix. 5, lii. 10), that certainly the simpler plan recommends itself, to take מ comparatively (מן) and "Diblathah" = Diblathaim (Jer. xlviii. 22; Num. xxxiii. 46), which is also in the inscription recently discovered at Dhiban, on the other side of the Dead Sea (comp. Schlottmann's *Osterprogramm*, 1870; Nöldeke, *Die Inschrift des Königs Mesa von Moab*, Kiel, 1870), the Moabite city on the margin of the great wilderness of Arabia Deserta. Comp. Keil on the passage. [Häv. takes "Diblathah" as a proper name formed by Ezekiel, whose appellative meaning (the form like תְּמֻנָתָה, side by side with תְּמוּנָה) is perhaps: "wilderness of ruin, of destruction" (Joel ii. 3; Jer. li. 26), analogously to "Babylon."]

Additional Note on Ch. v., vi.

[In the vision of the siege and the iniquity-bearing, a heavy burden of troubles, partly in progress, and partly still impending, had been announced by the prophet as determined against the covenant people. The afflictions of Egypt and the trials of the wilderness were, in a manner, to pass over them again. But even that was not enough; for as their guilt exceeded the guilt of their forefathers, so the chastisement now to be received from the hand of God was to surpass all that had been experienced in the history of the past. This more severe message is unfolded in the next vision, that recorded in these chapters.

The judgments themselves are distributed into three classes, according to the threefold division of the hair: the sword was to devour one-third of the people; famine and pestilence another; and that which remained was to be scattered among the nations. The strongest language is employed to describe the calamities indicated under these various heads, and everything is introduced that might have the effect of conveying the most appalling idea of the coming future. Amid the horrors to be produced by famine and pestilence, the dreadful words of Moses, that "their fathers should eat their sons in the midst of them," are reiterated, with the addition of the still darker feature, that "the sons should also eat their fathers" (ver. 10). The wild beasts of the field, too, were to embitter by their ravages the calamities produced by the evil arrows of famine; and the sword was to pass through the land in such fury, that none should be able to escape, rendering all a desolate wilderness (ch. vi. 14), destroying also their idols, and scattering around them the dead carcases of the people, so that the things in which they had foolishly trusted should only in the day of evil prove the witnesses and companions of their ruin (ch. vi. 3–6). Finally, in respect to those who should escape the more immediate evils, not only should they be scattered far and wide among the nations, but should there also meet with taunting and reproaches; nay, a sword should be drawn out after them, as had already been predicted by Moses (ch. v. 12; Lev. xxvi. 33); they, too, were to be for burning (so also Isa. vi. 13); for the anger of the Lord was still to pursue after them with "furious rebukes," until He had completely broken their rebellious hearts, and wrought in them a spirit of true contrition for sin and perfect reconciliation of heart with God (ch. vi. 9).

Nothing of a definite nature is mentioned as to time and place in this dark outline of revealed judgments. That the doom of evil was by no means to be exhausted by the troubles connected with the Chaldean conquest is manifest; for that portion of the people who were to go into exile and be dispersed among the nations were appointed to other and still future tribulations. There was to be a germinating evil in their destiny, because there would be, as the Lord clearly foresaw, a germinating evil in their character; and so long as this root of bitterness should still be springing up into acts of rebellion against God, it should never cease to be recoiling upon them with strokes of chastisement in providence. In this there was nothing absolutely singular as to the *principle* on which the divine government proceeded—only, as God had connected himself with Israel in a manner He never had done with any nation before, nor would with any other again, there should be a certain singularity in their case as to the actual experience of suffering on account of sin. In *their* history as a people, the footsteps of God's righteous judgment would leave impressions behind it of unexampled severity, according to the word here uttered: "And I will do in thee that which I have not done, and whereunto I will not do any more the like, because of all thine abominations."

But there is no caprice in the dealings of God. When He afflicts with the rod of chastisement and rebuke, it is only becaus the righteous principles of His government demand it; and the fearful burden of evils here suspended over the heads of ancient Israel sounds also a warning-note of judgment to all nations and all ages of the world. There have been, it is true, such changes introduced into the outward administration of God's kingdom, as render it, for the most part, impossible to trace the execution of His judgments with the same ease and certainty with which we can mark their course in the history of ancient Israel. But it is not the less certain that the principles which produced such marked effects then are in active operation still; and wherever Israel's guilt is incurred anew, there will infallibly be experienced a renewal of Israel's doom. For the gospel has brought no suspension of God's justice any more than of His mercy. It contains the most glorious exhibition of His grace to sinners; but along with this it contains the most affecting and awful display of His righteous indignation against sin. Both features, indeed, of the divine character have reached under the gospel a higher stage of development; and so far has the introduction of the new covenant been from laying an arrest on the severity of God, that not till it appeared did the Jews themselves experience the heaviest portion of the evils threatened against them; then only did the wrath begin to fall upon them to the uttermost, and the days of darkness and tribulation come, such as had not hitherto been known. This vision of woe, therefore, extends alike over both dispensations, and speaks to men of every age and clime; it is a mirror, in which the justice of God reflects itself for the world at large, with no further alteration for gospel times than such as is implied in the words of the apostle: "Of how much sorer punishment, suppose ye, shall he be thought worthy who hath trodden under foot the Son of God, and hath counted the blood of the covenant, wherewith he was sanctified, an unholy thing, and hath done despite unto the Spirit of grace?"—FAIRBAIRN'S *Ezekiel*, pp. 64, 65–67.—W. F.]

DOCTRINAL REFLECTIONS.

1. But what has Israel sought with all its idolatry? It has sought a strange righteousness instead of that offered to it in the law of God, viz. the heathen righteousness, which is that of the natural man in his self-will. Therefore God's righteousness in judgment breaks in pieces this self-righteousness in all its manifold forms.

2. It is therefore the first petition in the prayer which the Messiah has taught us: Hallowed be Thy name, of which the first step is thus expressed in the Heidelberg Catechism: Grant that we may rightly know Thee, a point to which this chapter also returns over and over again. And to glorify and praise God in all His works, as the catechism farther teaches, is exactly the opposite of the works of our own hands in ver. 6.

3. Without a remnant, the eternity of the divine covenant, and with it the eternity of Jehovah Himself, the essence of His name, would fall to the ground. The continuity of the Church of God is the defence of the divine covenant-faithfulness, the proof of the divine providence (government), the triumph of grace over all judgment. He who judges, sifts.

4. "But first must heart and eye be broken, and fallen man must feel a loathing of himself on account of his wickedness, before he turns to Him who has not spoken in vain. This is the only way to the knowledge of the living and true God; and we all must first with Israel learn to seek and find with broken whorish hearts and eyes the light of the gospel in the shame of captivity among the blind heathen" (UMBR.).

5. "One may certainly feel that he has to do with God, but not humble himself; just as Cain (Gen. iv. 6) was compelled to tremble before God, but always remained the same. So it usually happens with the lost. It is certainly a part of repentance to recognise God's judgment, but the half merely. To be displeased with oneself is the other half" (CALV.).

6. By consenting to God's judgment, by approving of it and of His righteousness with our whole heart, as the prophet is to smite with his hands and to stamp with his foot, let us judge ourselves, and then we shall not be judged. Our justification of God leads to our justification by God, in the way shown, *e.g.*, in Ps. li.

7. It is a specialty of the prophecy of Ezekiel, on the one hand, the prominence given to Jehovah, who speaks and will act accordingly (ch. v.), and, on the other, the emphasis laid on knowledge as the result of experience. Because Jehovah speaks in accordance with His nature, will, decree, He will be what He is, when what He has said comes to pass. In such knowledge of Jehovah, reached through experience of what comes to pass, there lies an eschatological, New Testament element. There is a reference to the fulness of the times, alike in the judgment on Israel, and as regards the salvation of the whole world. The judgment on the heathen element in Israel is, besides, the judgment on heathenism in general. Jehovah is the holy monogram of all the future, the divine motto for the appearing of eternity in time, the manifestation of God in flesh. (Comp. Hos. ii. 19 sqq.)

HOMILETIC HINTS.

Vers. 1, 2. So a son of man may be brought by God into such a position as to assail "mountains" even, *i.e.* those who tower like mountains above the level of the rest of men, princes and kings and the like, with the word (Ps. cxliv. 5).—"Sin not only pollutes man, but drags the rest of the creatures also into suffering along with him" (A L.).—Ver. 3 sqq. Against the sword of God idols are of no avail.—How many a place condemns many a man, and becomes his place of judgment!—There thou seest the manifold ways of men, in which they depart from the One Living God, and make to themselves broken cisterns, Jer. ii. 13.—In particular, a false worship does not remain unpunished, although it boasts a long time.—The power of strange gods over a heart which is not at home with God, and which follows unceasingly its strange lust: this, namely, that house and heart become desolate places of death.—Ver. 6. God first smites man repeatedly on the hand; at last He smites in pieces the works of his hands.—Ver. 7. "If, therefore, sin is committed in our midst, be not silent, laugh not, give no applause' (STCK.).—God is not less to be known in His judgments.—Vers. 1–7. God and idols: (1) how His word condemns them; (2) how His judgment annihilates them; (3) how those who serve them come to shame, spiritually and corporeally.

Ver. 8. "The Jews among the heathen nations—an example of the goodness, but also of the severity, of God, both leading us to repentance" (STCK.).—"God has and keeps for Himself at all times a little flock in the world, which can be overpowered by no one" (CR.).—"Yes, what is there that is not scattered over the earth! Only think of the many graves and gravestones!" (STCK.)—Ver. 9. "So long as it goes well with the sinner, he is usually deaf and blind amid all admonitions and judgments. What a benefit therefore conferred by God, when he opens his eyes and ears by means of evil days!" (ST.)—"Among the heathen" means grace in the strange land, where one was not to expect it.—The blessing of affliction.—In prosperity misery, in adversity salvation!—Remembrance a way to God.—"Affliction is, as it were, a hammer for our strong heart, and is able to force tears from the eyes" (A L.).—"Misery is the best preacher of repentance, when one will not listen to others. The majority are always like horses and mules; they are not to be brought to God otherwise than by bits and bridles, whips and rods" (B. B.).—In idolatry there is a whorish ardour, as the religious history of heathendom characteristically proves.—"For it is chastity of the spirit to serve God purely" (C.).—How must the good God thus go after us men, in order merely to bring back our heart and our eyes even from destruction!—"The sinner has nothing of his own, neither his heart, nor his eyes, nor his feet; everything belongs to the world, and is in the service of the devil" (A L.).—"The true grief for our sin begins in the heart, manifests itself through the eyes, and proves itself in the whole life and walk" (STCK.).—"Sincere repentance never comes too late, but has always access to the grace of God, Rev. iii. 17, 19" (W.).—"When it is right in the penitent heart, there is also *loathing* of ourselves, Luke xviii. 13" (after ST.).

Ver. 10. "The knowledge of God a fruit of repentance" (C.).—"Men make their boast with empty threatenings; but with God there is earnestness" (B. B.).—Ver. 11. Ezekiel's exclamation of woe has, as one may say, hand and foot. The whole man is wholly in it with his heart. Such excitement is not to be blamed in any servant of the Living God. The messengers of peace at least (Matt. x.) are to shake the dust off their feet. And He Himself, the Peaceful One, has in Luke xi. uttered one woe after another.—"God has many rods, wherewith He chastises evil-doers, but three especially, in which all the rest are gathered up" (L.).—Ver. 12. "No man can escape God" (STCK.).—Death overtakes us in all forms; woe to the impenitent!—"There are two kinds of flight from God: one which is of no use, and that by means of true repentance, which avails" (L.).—Ver. 13. "As is the case with Paul in Phil. iii., it causes the prophet also no annoyance to say the same thing repeatedly" (STCK.).—How sin can turn what is pleasing to the Most High into exactly the opposite!—Ver. 14. "When God has held His hand long enough stretched out to allure, to bless, then at length He stretches it out also to punish" (STCK.).—The wilderness shall blossom (Isa. xxxv.); but what was blossoming may also become a wilderness, and both from God.—"Jehovah is He who will be what He is; in other words, He who shows His eternity and power, and fulfils His word, and does not change, nor deny Himself" (COCC.).

CHAPTER VII.

1, 2 And the word of Jehovah came unto me, saying, And thou, son of man,
thus saith the Lord Jehovah: An end to the soil of Israel! the end comes
3 upon the four corners [borders] of the land. Now [comes] the end upon thee,
and I send Mine anger into thee, and judge thee as thy ways [are], and give
4 upon thee all thine abominations. And Mine eye will not restrain itself from
[have pity upon] thee, neither will I spare; for [but] thy ways will I give upon
thee, and thine abominations shall be in thy midst; and ye know that I am
5 Jehovah. Thus saith the Lord Jehovah, An evil, one evil, behold it cometh.
6 An end cometh, there cometh the end; it awaketh for thee, behold, it
7 cometh. The turn (?) cometh to thee, O inhabitant of the land; the time
cometh; the day is near, tumult and not joyous shouting upon the mountains.
8 Now will I shortly pour out My fury upon thee, and I accomplish Mine anger
upon [in] thee, and judge thee as thy ways [are], and give upon thee all thine
9 abominations. And Mine eye will not forbear, and I will not spare; as thy
ways [are] will I give upon thee, and thine abominations shall be in thy midst;
10 and ye know that it is I, Jehovah, that smiteth. Behold, the day, behold, it
11 cometh: the turn (?) springeth up; the rod sprouts; pride blossoms. The
violence riseth up into the rod of wickedness; not of them, nor of their
multitude, nor of their pomp; neither is there anything glorious upon
12 [in, among] them. The time comes, the day arrives; let not the buyer rejoice,
nor the seller mourn; for heat [of anger] cometh upon the whole multitude
13 thereof. For the seller shall not return to what is sold, even were
their life still among the living; for the vision is upon [against] the whole
multitude thereof; he shall not return, nor shall they—in his iniquity is
14 every one's life—show themselves strong. They blow the horn, and make all
ready, and there is none who goeth to the battle; for My heat of anger is
15 upon [against] their whole multitude. The sword without, and the pestilence
and famine within! He that is in the field shall die by the sword; and he
16 that is in the city, famine and pestilence shall devour him. And if their
escaped ones escape, they are upon the mountains like doves of the valleys,
17 all of them cooing, each one in his iniquity. All hands shall be slack, and all
18 knees shall dissolve into water. And they gird sackcloth about them, and
horror covers them; and upon all faces is shame, and baldness on all their
19 heads. Their silver shall they cast upon the streets, and their gold shall be
to them for repudiation. Their silver and their gold shall not be able to
deliver them on the day of the outpouring of the wrath of Jehovah: they
shall not satisfy their soul, neither fill their bowels; for it was a stumbling-
20 block of their iniquity. And the ornament of his decoration—for pride they
placed it, and images of their abominations, of their [their *accus.*] detestable
21 things, they made of it: therefore I give it to them for repudiation. And I
give it into the hands of the strangers for a prey, and to the wicked of
22 the earth for a spoil; and they profane her. And I turn away My face from
them, and they profane My secret; and violent ones come into her, and pro-
23 fane her. Make the chain; for the land is full of blood-guiltiness, and the
24 city is full of outrage. And I bring wicked ones of the [heathen] nations, and
they take possession of their houses: and I make the pride of the strong to
25 cease; and their holy places are profaned. Destruction cometh [came]; and
26 they seek salvation [peace], and there is none. Destruction upon destruction
shall come, and rumour shall be upon rumour; and they seek a vision from
the prophet; and the law [instruction] shall perish from the priest, and counsel
27 from the elders. The king shall mourn, and the prince shall put on blank
amazement, and the hands of the people in the land shall be slack: according
to their way will I do unto them, and according to their deserts will I judge
them; and they know that I am Jehovah.

Ver. 2. Sept.: . . . *ταδε λεγει . . . τη γη τ. Ἰσρ. περας ἡκει, το περας ἡκει ἐπι*—(Anoth. read.: קץ בא בא הקץ.)
Ver. 3. . . . *τ. περας νυν, το πέρας πρός σε.*
Ver. 4. Anoth. read.: כדרכיך.
Ver. 5. Anoth. read.: אחר.
Ver. 7. . . . *ἡ πλοκη . . . οὐ μετα θορυβων οὐδε μετ' ὠδινων*—*contritio super te . . . prope est dies occisionis, et non gloriæ montium.* (Anoth. read.: אליך fem.)
Ver. 10. Sept.: . . . *ἡμερα κυριου, ἰδου τ. περας ἡκει*—.
Ver. 11. K. *συντριψει στηριγμα ἀνομου, κ. οὐ μετα θορυβων οὐδε μετα σπουδης.* K. *οὐκ ἐξ αὐτων εἰσιν, οὐδε ὡραισμος ἐν αὐτοις.* (Anoth. read.: ולא נח. Vulg.: *et non erit requies in eis.*)
Ver. 13. . . . *ὁ κτώμενος προς τον πωλουντα . . . ὁτι ὁρασις . . . τ. πληθος αὐτης οὐκ ἀνακαμψει, κ. ἀνθρωπος ἐν ὀφθαλμοις ζωης αὐτου οὐ κρατησει.*
Ver. 14. . . . *κρινατε τα συμπαντα*—(Anoth. read.: תִקעוּ, Sept., Arab., Vulg.)
Ver. 16. *Ὡς περιστεραι μελετητικαι παντας ἀποκτενω, ἑκαστον*—
Ver. 22. . . . *εἰσελευσονται εἰς αὐτα ἀφυλακτως*—
Ver. 23. . . . *πληρης λαων*—
Ver. 24. . . . *κ. ἀποστρεψω το φρύαγμα τ. ἰσχυος αὐτων*—(Anoth. read.: עזם, Arab.)
Ver. 27. . . . Anoth. read.: וכמשפטיהם. Vulg.: *et secundum judicia*—

EXEGETICAL REMARKS.

According to Hengst., the first cycle closes here, and, in fact, with a song (?). But the "lyric" element (Ew.) is rather a rhetorical one. Neither is there any "solemn close, which corresponds with the solemn introduction," but simply a *second prophetic discourse* attached to the first in ch. vi. The prophet has in his eye the time of the breaking forth of the divine judgment. (Hitzig from ver. 3 onwards works himself into the idea of two defective recensions of the original text, for which there is no valid ground. Neteler lays the Hebrew text as a basis, so far as it is confirmed by the Greek translation, in order to obtain a "piece of four parts carried through with complete symmetry.")

Ver. 1. Comp. ch. vi. 1.—Ver. 2. ואתה, as so often, an address to the prophet in contradistinction from the people (ch. ii. 8, iii. 25, iv. 1, v. 1). The Sept. supplied אמֹר. A mark of exclamation is enough.—לְאדמת, not "of" (Hengst.), nor, as Ew. maintains against the accents: "thus saith . . . to the fatherland of Israel." אדמה is the soil of a country, for which afterwards הארץ; hence the total ruin. Comp. ch. vi. 14. The preceding discourse is brought to a point in this, under the motto of the **end.**—Instead of אַרְבַּעַת the Qeri gives the more usual form אַרְבַּע.—Ver. 3. בָּךְ, so that it finds its place in thee, where it can have vent.—**Ways** for walk. In accordance therewith will be the judgment. Their abominations come upon their own heads.—Ver. 4. חוּם, "to restrain oneself," hence "to spare" (ch. v. 11), to have compassion.—They are to see their abominations again in their midst, in their consequences, the divine punishments. Comp. besides, ch. vi. 7.

Ver. 5. רעה, what is *destructive, injurious,* here conceived of as being *so evil,* that it is spoken of as *one* standing alone, and not as a succession of evils. (Comp. ch. v. 9.) J. D. Mich.: "which makes an end at once, so that no second is necessary."—The curt, abrupt character of the discourse portrays the *sudden, violent* nature of the judgment.—The Chald. read perhaps אחר.

Ver. 6. הקץ הקיץ, a play upon words. After having apparently *slept* so long and so soundly, **the** end (not Jehovah) **awakes,** and therefore **it comes.**—אֵלַיִךְ, fem., because *Jerusalem* is in the background, as in ver. 3 also. ("The repetition indicates the certainty, the greatness, and the swiftness."—A L.)—בָּאָה (fem.) resumes the so strongly-emphasized רעה of ver. 5, or it stands impersonally (Häv., Keil), or it prepares for הַצְּפִירָה in ver. 7, which means "a crown" in Isa. xxviii. 5, a meaning which is not suitable here. It might be allowable to translate in our verse: "the turn comes to thee," inasmuch as צפירה from צפר may be something "arranged in a row together" with something else, where one thing follows another. But this certainly hardly suits יצאה in ver. 10. The interpretation most in favour, viz. "destiny" (Hitz.: the goddess of fate, properly: vicissitude of fortune, catastrophe), gives a suitable although heathenish sense; we would be compelled to admit a borrowing on Ezekiel's part from his Chaldaic surroundings, and yet the expression itself is not thereby explained. It is sought to be explained by the circle of fate, or its being shut up within itself. One might think of the *return of the sin in the punishment, wherewith it finishes its course;* comp. vers. 3, 4. (צפר in Judg. vii. 3 = to return circuitously.) Others hold fast by the meaning "crown," and understand by it the kingdom of the Chaldeans, or the king of the Chaldeans. Häv., who combats this meaning, asserting that in Isa. xxviii. it is a plait of hair that is meant, accepts a later Aramaism, צפירה = צפרא, "the dawn," viz. of the evil day (Joel ii. 1, 2). Grot. with reference to הקיץ in ver. 6, inasmuch as it was customary for judgment to be administered in the morning. Others in other ways. Was it intended, perhaps, to indicate something equivalent to: what is marked with the graver (צפרן), what is *determined,* established, as in Jer. xvii. 1?—אֵלֶיךָ, masc., because of what follows (Hos. ix. 7).—הַיּוֹם, artic.: *dies ille.*—**Tumult,** perhaps alarm of war, and in contrast therewith הֵד, *i.e.* הֵידָד (comp. Isa. xvi. 9, 10; Jer. xlviii. 33), cry of joy of the vine-dressers (?), or cry of *victory,* Isa. xl. 9 (J. D. Mich.), or *festival*-pomp of the idolaters, ch. vi. 3, 13 (Rosenm.). Hengst.: "joyful shout *of the mountains,*" because **the shout of joy is heard on them and called forth by** them (Ps. lxxxix. 13), in place of which will come the painful tumult of those who are seeking deliverance. Häv. takes הד for הוד, "brightness," so that the dawn rises without mountain-brightness (?), without irradiating the mountains which are first to be irradiated (!).

· Ver. 8. עַתָּה; comp. ver. 3.—מקרוב, in Deut. xxxii. 17 of place, here of time (Job xx. 5). Comp. besides, ch. vi. 12, vii. 3, 4.—Ver. 9. Comp. ver. 4. The added expression **smiteth** does not announce what follows, but meets beforehand a false interpretation of the same (the sprouting rod). Ver. 10. Comp. on ver. 7.—יצאה, because of what follows of the springing up, *like a plant*, from the *soil* of which the sinners are bragging.—The **rod** is for Israel, *in order to punishment*, in fact, the staff of the Chaldean ruler, Nebuchadnezzar's sceptre. What a contrast to Num. xvii. 2, 3! To the "*sprouting*" of power, which *can*, corresponds the "*blossoming*" of pride, which *will*. (זוד, to boil, to boil over.)

Ver. 11. Thus **the violence**, the violent acting which takes place, rises into the **rod of wickedness**, *i.e.* which punishes the wickedness of Israel; into the staff, sceptre, of the Chaldean, wherewith Israel's wickedness is smitten (Isa. x. 5). Other expositors interpret מטה already in ver. 10 of the tribe of Judah (GROT.), its royal sceptre (COCC.), and refer alike זדון there and החמס here to the complete sinful development of the kingdom (EW.), so that the rod of wickedness would be that rod wherewith wickedness smites itself. Grot. takes ל adversative; the violent Chaldean rises up against the wicked tribe of Judah. COCC.: Israel's violent conduct (Gen. vi. 11) brings upon them instead of God the sceptre of the Chaldean dominion of wickedness. It would be natural to understand the immediately following **not of them,** etc., in such a way that this "rod of wickedness," "of violence," would now be pointed out more definitely, in as far as it is not to spring forth from Israel (לא־מהם), *neither from their roaring* (המון, Isa. v. 13, 14, the noisy, politically-roused multitude), *nor from their humming* (by paronomasia, equivalent to: pomp), consequently neither of democratic nor of aristocratic origin (comp. 1 Kings xii. 11). הֵם or הֵמָּה, plur. המים (only to be found here); מהמהם for מהמיהם, GES.: of their possessions, KEIL: the multitude of possessions. [HENGST.: "nor of them, and them (yet again),"—like הם הם in Isa. lvii. 6,—however much they may hold up their heads; Jewish expositors resolve it into וְלֹא מֵהֶם אֲשֶׁר מֵהֶם, and understand it of their children (so the Chaldee); HÄV.: cares, anxieties, these are as useless as the multitude of the people themselves!?] The penal judgment will come from outside themselves. HENGST.: "It is a throwing contempt on the 'we,' which they had continually in their mouth, and repeated with great emphasis: we, we shall do everything, etc. (Jer. xxx. 21; Zech. x. 4)."—וְלֹא־נֹהַּ בָּהֶם, Ges. from נֹהַּ, Keil, from נָוָה, "to be prominent;" something **glorious.** [HÄV.: "and there is a want of beauty in them." (The word is found only here.)—According to the Jewish expositors, נֹהַּ for נֹהַה, from נָהָה, loud lament. HENGST.: "that wailing will be forgotten in deep despair." (Cocc. making it refer to the falling sceptre of David, they will be obliged to conceal their wailing on that account before the tyrant who conquers them!) EW.: "Nothing will remain of the wicked, neither of their proud, haughtily blustering, luxurious conduct, in prosperity as hitherto, nor of their sighing or even their discontented grumbling and murmuring in adversity." Similarly Calvin, of the root and branch destruction of them, their multitude, their possessions.] Accordingly ולא ולא לא are understood as short sentences descriptive of *the result of the stroke* of ver. 10 (KEIL), the effect of the repetition being heightened by the omission of the verb, as if they were exclamations. As for the rest, Hitz. remarks excellently: "unannounced ὡς κλέπτης the day will come, unexpectedly, and so much greater the shock of surprise."

After a second emphasizing in ver. 12 of the leading thought of the proclamation—comp. ver. 7—הגיע, בא, proph. preterites—**the buyer and the seller** are given as an exemplification from the dealings of ordinary life. The former is not to **rejoice** in the possession which he covets; he does not come into the enjoyment of it. The latter is not to **mourn** over the loss of a property he would fain retain, but which has been alienated from necessity; much else is at stake: for חרון, elsewhere חרון אף, comes upon כל־הֲמוֹנָהּ (the suffix agreeing with לאדמת ישראל, or referring to Jerusalem), the whole of the people is consumed. Comp. Ps. xxxix. 6. HENGST.: the multitude which makes so much ado about nothing.—The general reason is followed in ver. 13 by a more special one (as Hengst.), or by what is merely a specializing of חרון.—כי might also stand in the sense of: *but certainly, i.e.* the seller is not to mourn, *but certainly he shall not return to his property that is sold;* hence the possible return thereto must not be a motive for him not to mourn. That is to say, the *seller* would have,—and therefore is this specialty introduced, in order, at the same time, to mark the *national* ruin,—according to Lev. xxv., the prospect of the year of jubilee, the carrying out of which is thus attested here (HÄV.), or at least presupposed in its idea, and therewith the return to what he had sold remained open. (Philipps. thinks of the right of the seller at any time to buy back again what was sold, either himself or through the nearest kinsman, for the selling price, Ruth iv.; Jer. xxxii.) But although in other circumstances the man who has no possession, the vexed poor man, has a better chance of being left behind than the man who has a possession, the joyous rich man, in the case impending it will in general be otherwise, *i.e.* quite alike for the one and for the other. *Individuals,* indeed, will *remain alive.* ועוד, a conditional circumstantial clause (HÄV., KEIL), *so that the case is supposed,* that **their** (viz. the sellers') **life** is **among the living,** that they come out of it with their life. **The seller,** consequently, is used collectively for the individuals who as such **come** to be considered. The judgment applies to *the persons*—this is the leading thought—and not, as the expositors assert, to their possession. Hence כי־אל־כל־המונה is repeated from ver. 12, but instead of חרון we have by paronomasia חזון, the *glowing heat* seen in the prophetic *vision* (ch. i.). חזון might perhaps confirm the interpretation of הצפירה in ver. 7 as what is fixed, determined. In like manner לא ישוב is resumed from the beginning of our verse, and that in the same sense, so that it is certainly not to be translated: "for the prophecy against the whole multitude shall not return" (JER.), a thought which is too little in keeping with the exceptional earnestness of the context. Rather is the statement meant to be something additional *as to the persons*, appended to the special exemplification of the seller. Hence ואיש equivalent to: *since every one* has "his life in his iniquity," and it is therefore very questionable whether (as was parenthetically supposed above) "their life" might be "still among the living."—לא יתחזקו: **they shall not show themselves strong**, manifest strength, courage; the iniquity cripples their power of life, with which what follows agrees admirably. [Other expositions: EWALD: "But certainly they may become unfortunate or the reverse for a time: he who was compelled to sell his property may not even obtain it in the year of jubilee, or, on the other hand, the divine punishment may no longer light upon the rich brawlers, yet the former remain in their lust after a life of sense in the world, without coming to repentance through adversity (Ps. xvii. 14), and the latter do not suffer themselves to be drawn out of their sins by prosperity; all are irresolute, cowardly people," etc. Häv. explains the last clause also of the year of jubilee still, whose object is "to be strengthened in life" (חיתו, an accus. to be connected with the passive יתחזקו), so that one springs up into new life: there has been a restoration—a new birth. No one is to obtain a new strength of his vital powers by means of his sin; rather do those fearful Sabbatical years make their appearance, Lev. xxvi. 34 sq. The second לא ישוב has also been understood by some in the sense that no one "turns," although the prophecy summons all to repentance, which agrees just as little with the context. ואיש־ is interpreted on the part of some by an omission of the relative: "every one whose life is in his iniquity," while others take the first suffix pleonastically, in this way: "they shall not any of them strengthen themselves by means of (on account of) the iniquity of his life," so as to be able to stand against their enemies. The plural with the collective איש. HENGST.: "The seller will in no case return to the property which he has sold, so that he should be obliged to regard it with pain, for the whole land is stripped of its inhabitants; but it may also happen that he loses his life, and he has to account it good fortune if this does not take place, so that the thing sold cannot be a source of pain to him: and many a one (ואיש) will not retain his life because of his misdeed."] The LXX. read עין instead of עָוֹן.

Ver. 14. The predicted feebleness is placed before our eyes in a picture all but ironical.—בַּתָּקוֹעַ has nothing to do with Jer. vi. 1 (where Tekoa is a proper name). But an infin. absol., with preposition and article, is grammatically too bold. Neither are we to translate, as Hengst. does: "they blew with a loud blast," but (as also the Sept.) as designating the *instrument* wherewith the blast is made. The infin. absol. הָכִין (הָכֵין)—comp. Nah. ii. 4 [3] (a military term)—shortly for the finite verb (Ew. *Gram.* § 351, *c*).—למלחמה, Hitzig acutely: *to* the battle, not: into the battle.—Comp. besides, vers. 17, 12; Lev. xxvi. 17.—Ver. 15. Comp. ch. v. 12, vi. 12; Lam. i. 20. Comp. also Mark xiii. 15, 16. Instead of acting offensively, not even on the defensive; without resistance they fall victims, partly to the sword of the enemy, which, according to ch. v. 7, is the sword of God, partly to the pestilence combined with the famine.

Ver. 16. The fate of those of them who in any way escape is localized **upon the mountains** (אל for על, ch. vi. 13),—having fled thither (Ps. xi. 1; Mark xiii. 14; Luke xxi. 21, 22), they shall be there like, etc., their condition being compared to that of **doves of the valleys**, *i.e.* doves which, having lost their nests, are not like wild doves at home upon the mountains, and which, when frightened by birds of prey, make known their sorrow, their painful feeling.—כלם המות, rightly KEIL: figure and reality mixed up together; in form belonging to the comparison, in reality to the things compared. The stronger expression המה, not without reference to המונה in vers. 13, 14, and their tumult going before.—For איש בעונו, comp. ver. 13. As is their life, if they still save it, so is their expression of that life, and, in fact (by the individualization of the all, כלם), each one gives utterance to his sorrow **in his iniquity**, as a sorrow that is deserved, therefore as a penal sorrow. [The LXX. read perhaps המתי. But the text is not to be changed in accordance therewith, for certainly in what follows the farther description of these fugitives is given.] Hence ver. 17 is not to be understood of the whole people (KEIL, HENGST.); it is rather the interpretation of the melancholy cooing in ver. 16. A picture of the repentance which is wrung from them. The **hands** refuse to perform their office, nay, even the **knees** refuse to stand and keep firm. The expression for the latter (ch. xxi. 7) is intended to portray the *complete desolation of their strength;* comp. Josh. vii. 5 (Isa. xiii. 7; Ex. xv. 15). The LXX. too literally. (For תלכנה, comp. Joel iv. 18.)

Ver. 18. Along with such (negative) feebleness we have (as positive elements): mourning and horror, shame and grief. As the expression of the first, the cloth of coarse hair, which they girt about themselves with a cord (Isa. iii. 24). For the second, the strong expression כסתה פלצות (Ps. lv. 5): if mourning is their girdle, then horror is their covering. But as shame is upon (אל for על) all faces, so baldness is on the back part of the head of all, as the result of grief, or it must be supposed the custom in mourning (Job i. 20), or that they have plucked out their hair in their pain (Ezra ix. 3). Comp. besides, Jer. xlviii. 37; Amos viii. 10; and Deut. xiv. 1.

Ver. 19 speaks in the outset of the fugitives still, who cast from them everything that is burdensome. But what one casts away, that he also in a certain measure repudiates; hence נִדָּה, "detestable thing," "abomination." The renewed mention *together* of the two principal means employed in sinning (silver *and* gold), in the next place, *generalizes* the circle of the persons involved, so as to embrace the *people* generally. Of idols of silver and gold (Isa. ii. 20), however, there is no need as yet to think. It is rather *treasures* of that sort that are spoken of, which hinder one during a flight, which only provoke the booty-loving enemy still more, nay, which, now that the saving of life is aimed at, appear *like rubbish*. For that life might be purchased therewith is no longer the case, since the day of the overflowing (עֶבְרָה) wrath of the Eternal (Luke xxi. 22) is come (comp. Isa. xiii. 17; Zeph. i. 18; 1 Pet. i. 18). They have neither *enjoyment* (satisfaction) from it, nor even the *filling* of the bowels by means of it. Silver and gold are, alike for the *taste* and for *necessaries* (in a practical point of view, æsthetically and physically considered), without significance in this day of judgment; the element which comes in that case into consideration is the **stumbling-block** which they *made* of it, so that they fell into **iniquity** over it. In ch. iii. 20 we have a stumbling-block which is *given*. Their riches and their trust in them made them satisfied, so that they needed nothing. As a punishment, these riches do not now satisfy them, do not even fill their belly; nothing can be bought with them so that they may live.

The giving of a reason for the punishment drawn from the guilt leads to a *farther description* of this guilt in ver. 20. The וְ is explanatory. Because the riches wherewith Israel was *decked out*, and *might adorn herself* like a bride, of course ἐν κυρίῳ, were, on the contrary, misused for self-exaltation and pride. Comp. Isa. ii.—שָׂמָהוּ; the subject is the people, or: every one, or: one;—the suffix refers to the **ornament of his decoration** (HÄV., KEIL: elegant ornaments), by which *others* understand, not the gold and silver, but the temple. Hitz. reads שָׂמוּהוּ. From the self-exaltation resulted the will-worship, the diversified self-choice in divine worship.—שִׁקּוּצֵיהֶם, as frequently from Deut. xxix. 17 onwards; omitted by the LXX.—בוֹ, not: in the temple, but: of the *silver and gold*. Comp. Ex. xxxii.; Hos. ii. 10 [8], viii. 4, xiii. 2.—עַל־כֵּן נְתַתִּיו; the idea of retribution here explains the לְנִדָּה in ver. 19.—But as God gives it to them as a thing to be cast away and rejected, so He gives **it** to their enemies in ver. 21, who are described as in ver. 24 (Ps. lxxv. 8), for a prey. The victory of the wicked is God's penal victory.—הארץ is not Babylon, but we should rather say the **wicked of the earth** are the Babylonians. In defence of the Kethibh וְחִלְּלוּהָ, with fem. suffix (comp. ver. 12), where hitherto masculine, Ewald remarks: "a gradual transition from the masc. צבי to the holy city, which, strictly speaking, is meant, and even distinctly named in ver. 23." The Qeri is וְחִלְּלוּהוּ, which Hitzig defends. According to Häv. (LXX., VULG.), to be referred **to the** "elegant ornament;" according to others, to the objects of worship of gold and silver.

Ver. 22. מֵהֶם from those at Jerusalem, so that the enemy can get the mastery over it. Others: I will not look what the enemy shall do, but let them act.—From the "profanation" of what is holy an explanation is got of the preceding characteristic title of the "strangers" as the "wicked of the earth." צְפוּן is "something hidden," something concealed; according to Häv., of the place: the sanctuary, the holy of holies, where Jehovah dwells in sacred darkness; according to others: the holy land in general; according to Hengst., of the matter in hand: the church-treasure, which is secularized. [The LXX. read perhaps פְּקֻדָּתִי. EWALD: the treasure of My guardianship, *i.e.* of My country or My people.] The suffixes of בָהּ and חִלְּלוּהָ belong to *the city*, Jerusalem, which always stands in the background. Others prefer a neuter construction; KEIL: come "over it." For **violent ones**, comp. Matt. xi. 12 (which passage is to be understood in accordance with this).

Ver. 23. In form directed to the prophet, like the whole discourse; in substance equivalent to: pronounce the captivity to be ready. "As it were indignant at the profanation, Jehovah commands to put an end to the doings of the enemy by the deportation of those who were left behind" (HÄV.). By means of the article, the putting in chains is declared to be no longer a thing to be doubted, but certain, quite fixed, just as things generally known have the article. Others collectively. "In reality the king was carried away in chains and cast into prison" (BUNS.).—The plural דמים always means blood poured out; hence משפט דמים, a trial which is held with respect to such a case, a sentence which is pronounced upon it, a punishment which is decreed for it, all of which are unsuitable for the parallel חמס. Just as unsuitable here is: the right of blood-shedding. We are therefore to understand it of the case in law, the crime, the **blood-guiltiness.** Comp. Deut. xix. 6 (Gen. vi. 11). Häv. understands it of the judgment on blood-shedding ("hence: inexorable, relentless"), while he refers חמס to the violent enemies. Of course "blood-guiltiness" gives a reason for (כי) something more than putting in chains, viz. death; but perhaps captivity is thereby meant to be indicated as the *least* thing that can happen to them after guilt such as theirs.

Ver. 24. "*Wicked heathen*"—(ver. 21) so that they fall, besides, into *bad* hands of men (2 Sam. xxiv. 14). Comp. Ew. *Gram.* § 313, *c*; Hab. i. 6 sqq.—גאון, either as in ver. 20: pride (HÄV.: everything of which the mighty are wont to boast), or: ornament, decoration, glory, of the temple (ch. xxiv. 21).—They may be called **strong,** as well because of their *real* strength, when they preserved their fidelity to the Strong One who dwelt in their midst, as in accordance with their *imagined* strength (Lev. xxvi. 19). Ew. reads גְּאוֹן עֻזָּם, "their proud splendour."—נחלו cannot be the Piel of נחל, which would mean "to divide for a possession," but is the

Niphal of חלל.—מקדשיהם, according to Ew. (*Gramm.* § 215, *a*) from מִקְדָּשׁ, with vowel pushed back. Rosenm. reads: מְקַדְּשֵׁיהֶם; Häv. מְקַדְּשֵׁיהֶם. HENGST.: "those who sanctify them," hence partic. Piel without *Dagesch forte* of קדש, understanding the priests now no longer able to discharge their functions, whereby the means of reconciliation are withdrawn from Israel (Lev. xvi.; Isa. xliii. 26, 27). [Others: of unworthy Levitical service, inasmuch as the Holy One of Israel is also his only true Sanctifier, ch. xxxvii. 28.] "Ezekiel points to the cloud only, Jeremiah in ch. xxxiii. opens the view to the sun hidden behind it." By **their sanctuaries** are understood sometimes the buildings of the temple, but, as being no longer God's, sometimes the self-chosen ones of the Jews.

Ver. 25. קפדה only here (see GESEN. *Lex.*). According to Meier, not: destruction, but in accordance with the root-meaning ("to draw together"), as in the Syr., of the drawing together of the skin and hair from fright (*horror*). Exactly so Ew., HENGST.: contraction, in contrast with the expansion which is connected with all joyful prosperity, and which is founded in the nature of the people of God, Gen. xxviii. 14; Isa. liv. 3. [HÄV.: the conclusion, the close (קץ, vers. 2, 6).] For the gender and masc. verb comp. Ew. *Gramm.* § 173, *h*, 174, *g*. [Ros.: ה paragog.] בא, a proph. perf. (KEIL).—"Peace" is too narrow for שלום, as also attempts at peace with money-offerings with Nebuchadnezzar, of which some think. The attempts at salvation which they make in vain are specified in what follows.

Ver. 26. While the disasters are accumulating, and the rumours are multiplying (Matt. xxiv. 6), they **seek,** first of all, from the **prophet** (the generic idea). Comp. Jer. xxxvii. 17, xxxviii. 14. [Hengst. understands it of the false prophets, and compares for the priests Zeph. iii. 4; Jer. ii. 8; Ezek. xxii. 26.] What they seek, viz. **a vision,** is mentioned, but it is not said that they *find* it. That they do not becomes clear alike from ver. 25, and from the circumstance that instruction *perishes* from the **priest,** and counsel from the **elders.** Comp. Jer. xviii. 18 (Luke xxi. 25). To the threefold class in ver. 26 we have a corresponding parallel in Ver. 27, **the king—the prince of the tribe—the people in the land;** and to the want of counsel corresponds the failure in action. It is a *national* ruin. (As to יתאבל, see GESEN. *Gramm.* § 53, *Obs.*) לבש, a well-known figurative mode of expression for *being covered with and wrapt up in terror*, just as in the case of the king it is a *deep silent mourning* that is meant (אבל). For ידי׳ו, comp. ver. 17 (παρειμένας χεῖρας, Heb. xii. 12). Like their conduct will God's dealing with them be, drawn from it, regulated in accordance with it. As to אותם, see Ew. *Gramm.* § 264, *b.* ובמשפטיהם, HENGST.: "with judgments which correspond to their deeds," and so Ew. also and others. Better: according to *what is right in reference to them.* Instead of בְּ there is also the reading בְּ (ver. 3). With the well-known (ch. vi. 14, v. 15) refrain וידעו׳, the two discourses of rebuke in ch. vi. and vii. come to a close.

DOCTRINAL REFLECTIONS.

1. We have before us in this chapter an Old Testament pattern for the awe-inspiring *Dies iræ, dies illa*, the so-called "gigantic hymn" (comp. Zeph. i. 14 sqq.). What Fr. v. Meyer says of the latter may be uttered also of this chapter of our prophet: "With the man who is so insensible that he can read it without alarm and hear it without dread, I should not like to dwell under the same roof."

2. The contents are the same, ever the same. The drops fall without intermission on the stone, the heart of Israel. Unbelief has just the characteristic either that it believes in no punishment at all (2 Pet. iii. 3 sq.), or that its frivolous mind knows beforehand that what will come will certainly not be so severe nor last so long. And therefore God does not grudge to tell us over and over again our inevitable destiny, and also to push it ever nearer to us. The enduring meaning as well as application of our chapter may be expressed in this way, that the end of those things in which they place their trust, and in which they find their satisfaction, is to be held up before the false security of the men of this world on every side. *Respice finem.*

3. "Sin has an active and a passive history. When the latter begins, then what was formerly an object of pleasure becomes an object of dread" (HENGST.). "On the day of judgment the abominations stand in Israel's midst not in their alluring, seductive form, but with all the woe which comes in their train" (HÄV.).

4. "God does indeed punish the sinner from moment to moment in his conscience, but, so far as outward experience is concerned, He causes him to learn the error of his way at first only in omens of the most gently threatening character, so to speak, by means of passing, dimly visible angels of warning. In this way He gives him great scope for freely bethinking himself and for returning of his own free-will, or else for completing of his own free-will his experience of the ruin which lies on his path of bondage. But in this way the divine long-suffering is revealed, which gives the sinner time for repentance. The picture of this long-suffering of God is furnished by the three years of Christ's ministry. Then at the end of its lingering the long-suffering steps into the background behind the divine wrath" (LANGE).

5. The love of God and its ultimate aim in redemption is resisted in particular by the folly of the sinner, which pursues as its object deliverance from misery, and that the misery which at any time happens to be present, and in self-righteousness sets itself against deliverance from sin, sometimes by disputing the causal nexus of sin and misery as punishment, sometimes by the denial of sin altogether. The redeeming love of God, therefore, cannot make itself known, in opposition to man's vain imagination, in any way more practical and concrete than, first of all, by means of the zeal of divine wrath. In view of the aim, viz. redemption, and as being divine, **this zeal of wrath is not merely a thing of the**

O. T., but not less expressly belongs to the N. T. It is redemptive inasmuch as, through retributive visitation by means of punishment, not only does God, who has vanished from the consciousness of the self-righteous man — self-righteous although both a sinner and a debtor — reveal Himself, but man also by this means is to become free from the hurtful delusion of "envious gods," of a "blind fate," of an arbitrary "necessity of nature." Judgments like that on Judah and Jerusalem are therefore, besides being divine, of a redemptive character. There is an effort after salvation in such crises, and at all events in the biblical wrath of God there is more of the wisdom of love than in the common assertion that a God who is angry is a God who does not love.

6. The tragic truth of the history of the world, and especially of the history of the kingdom of God, celebrates in those epoch-making catastrophes, which are the emblems of the last judgment, the truth of the idea of God's zeal in wrath, of this fatal curse of sin.

7. Where God is seen angry in Holy Scripture, there we have no mere personification of divine righteousness, but the personality of the Holy and Just One revealing itself; there there can be no reference to human passion ; there, in fact, we have divine compassion. The form of sinfulness is just as little an essential and necessary element in wrath as in love.

8. However anthropomorphic the stamp it may wear, God's wrath is no less truly a part of His nature, by means of which the absolute antagonism of His spirit and will to sin is expressed from the innermost energy of His holiness. It is not the ebullition of an impure lòve for unrighteousness, as is the case with the wrath of man, but it is the necessary (unless God chooses to deny Himself) reaction and opposition of His holy love for righteousness. In the operations of divine wrath, therefore, the holy will of God is revealed in its character of righteousness by means of righteous judgment, which recompenses the sinner according to his own works.

9. The continuance of a nation depends not only on the usual material conditions, but on ideal powers of life, which, when despised, show themselves to be powers of death.

HOMILETIC HINTS.

Ver. 2 sqq. God's grace has indeed no end, is an everlasting grace, but its manifestation and our consciousness of it may come to an end, which at the same time announces a perfecting in what is evil.—"What had begun in the ten tribes was completed in the tribe of Judah" (B. B.).—"What is long hidden is not remitted. The longer God delays with punishment, the heavier it is" (W.).—"The end as respects God's long-suffering; then, in respect of the land, with which it had not yet come to the end; lastly, the completion of the punishments" (Cocc.).—*The end:* a *universal* end (not only of Israel, but as of Israel, so of every man and of the whole world); a *fearful* end (if under the wrath of God according to our abominations); an *inevitable* end (however safe we seem, however thoughtlessly we think and speak).—"God has his Now (Luke xix. 42), which is, of course, hid from our eyes and ruinous, if we have not regarded the Now of our merciful visitation" (Stck.).—"So also in respect of antichristianity, which has spread among the people of the New Testament, its end is fixed, when God will lay upon it all its abominations, and will pour out His vials of wrath" (B. B.).—He that is secure says: Soul, take thine ease; but God says: This night thy soul shall be required of thee (Luke xii. 19, 20).—What an awakening call for every sinner! The end comes, alike of pleasure and of life.—"If the sinner will not awake, then the punishment must awake" (B. B.).—Ver. 9. "It was not strokes of fate or the like they were to perceive therein, but God's hand and smiting" (Cocc.).—Every one must know the Lord in the end, if not as one that calls, allures, blesses, then as one that smites, is angry, punishes.—"Let the sinner know that he binds for himself the rod which will smite him" (A L.).

Ver. 11. "Tyrants are God's scourges" (O.).—Ver. 12 sq. "As for the pious an hour of help is promised, so for the transgressor an hour of destruction strikes" (Stck.).—God's judgments sometimes remove the distinction arising from prosperity and possession, and make men alike.—Ver. 14. "What avails the trumpet, and of what use all weapons and every preparation, if the Lord departs from a people, from a city, from an army?"—"Courage is also God's gift, as we see in the case of Gideon, Samson, David, and others."—"Where God's terrors are at work, there neither counsel, nor call, nor deed gives help" (Stck.).—"In vain do men blow the trumpet, if that of the Supreme Judge makes itself heard" (Umbr.).—Ver. 15. War, pestilence, famine, these three remain down even to the end, and are bound up with one another.—"The sinner would fain flee or hide himself" (Stck.).—"God can find thee everywhere" (B. B.).—Ver. 16. "Reflect that thou also must one day leave everything, and see to it that thou keep a good conscience" (Stck.).—"So, many kinds of sighs are heard in the world. But the best are the unutterable ones, wherewith God's Spirit Himself makes intercession for believers, Rom. viii. 26" (B. B.).—"Late repentance is seldom true repentance" (Stck.).—Ver. 17. "The hands and knees of believers also do indeed sometimes become weary, but they know where to strengthen them" (St.).—Ver. 18. If the inward return is wanting, God knows well how to enforce the outward; and that even as far as to bring about the public confession of the fault, as may be seen, surely, in the case of Judas.

Ver. 19. How can one have such eager desire after what he will at another time cast from him in such cold blood?—"God is the only true and abiding treasure which is to be sought" (Stck.).—"Oh, if one were only betimes to cast it out of his heart, that it might not make him unjust, covetous, and ungodly!" (B. B.).—"Would that this were written on the doors, yea, in the hearts of all the avaricious, and the rich, and those eagerly desirous of riches, that gold and silver will not be able to save in the day of wrath, and in the hour of death, and at the day of judgment! What has been sought after with so great pains, scraped together with much injustice, guarded with the greatest care, that leaves its possessor comfortless and helpless when he most needs help, and leaves him lying on his sick-bed in his pains, and can rescue him neither from the enemy, nor from the sick-bed, nor from death, much less make him blessed" (B. B.).—Vers. 19, 20. The danger of riches: in the false estimate of them, in the abuse of them.—The final judgment on riches: how it will take place (by means of the rich themselves, and before God and men); by what means it is incurred (through pride and idolatry).—"How many would have been happy in this world, and blessed in the world to come, if they had not been rich!"—Ver. 20. What adorns is also easily soiled.—What ought to humble man for the most part makes him so much the more proud.—Self-seeking the source of all abuse of earthly blessings, as well as of the neglect and contempt of heavenly blessings.—"This is ingratitude, to misuse such gifts of God for pride, for extravagance, for mere finery, and for idolatry" (H. H.).—Ver. 21. "Our worldly possessions are not ours, but God's, who can do with them how and what He will."—"God employs for the carrying out of His judgments heretics and ungodly men, in order that those whom He punishes by this means may be the more pained that they had falsely boasted of the true religion" (St.).—Ver. 22. The face of God the consecration of our life: our free upward look to it, its gracious look on us.—These are the critical turnings in the life of the individual and of whole nations, the turnings of the divine face.—The profanation by the enemy is, alas! always preceded by the profanation on the part of the friends.—God protects Himself against His friends by means of His enemies.—What a sign the profanation of Jerusalem and of the temple for all high-churchism, still so splendid and ostentatious!

Ver. 23. God makes various chains; even that of Paul had been made by Him.—"First transgression is linked to transgression; then comes the chain of the wrath of God; at last come the chains of darkness" (Stck.).—Ver. 24. Pride comes before a fall, and after the fall come the sufferings.—Woe be to us when our sanctuaries are nothing but *our* sanctuaries!—Ver. 25. "Men often delay so long till death comes, before they trouble themselves about their spiritual peace. Oh, how easily it may come about, that they are snatched away by death before they obtain that peace!" (St.).—The danger of the death-bed.—In order that we may be able to seek it early, God's salvation is there for us even before our birth.—Vers. 26, 27. "On God depends the weal and woe of states" (Stck.).—"Famine as regards the word of God is at such a time the heaviest punishment of all" (Cr.).—"That is the most terrible judgment, when God does not permit the light of His word any longer to shine, and allows us to sink into the darkness of ignorance, because it is a strong comfort, even in the greatest suffering, when the Lord sheds light upon us with His word" (H. H.).—"Therefore David prays: See if I be on any wicked way, Ps. cxxxix." (Stck.).—In the end, out of all the ways of men, and in accordance with their own desert, God's truth and righteousness come to light.—"This is life eternal, to know God and Jesus Christ, John xvii. 3" (Stck.).

III. THE SUBSEQUENT EXECUTION OF DIVINE COMMISSIONS.—Ch. viii.–xxiv.

1. The Vision (Ch. viii.–xi.).

1. *The Abominations in the Temple* (Ch. viii.).

1 And it came to pass in the sixth year, in the sixth [month], on the fifth of the
month—I was in my house, and the elders of Judah were before me, and there
2 fell upon me the hand of the Lord Jehovah. And I saw, and lo a likeness as the
appearance of fire: from the appearance of His loins and downwards, fire; and
from His loins and upwards, as the appearance of brightness, as the look of the
3 brightness of gold. And He stretched out the form of a hand, and took hold of
me by the front hair of my head, and the Spirit lifted me up between the earth
and the heaven, and brought me to Jerusalem in visions of God, to the opening
of the door of the inner [court] that points toward the north, where is the seat of
4 the [idol-] image of jealousy, which provoketh to jealousy. And, behold, there the
5 glory of the God of Israel, like the vision which I saw in the valley. And He said
unto me: Son of man, lift up now thine eyes toward the north. And I lifted up
mine eyes toward the north, and behold on the north at [northward of] the gate of
6 the altar that [idol-] image of jealousy at the entrance. And He said unto me:
Son of man, seest thou what they are doing? great abominations that the house
of Israel doeth here, in order to be far from My sanctuary! And yet again shalt
7 thou see great abominations. And He brought me to the opening of the court,
8 and I saw, and behold a hole in the wall. And He said unto me: Son of man,
break now through the wall. And I broke through the wall, and behold an
9 opening. And He said unto me: Come and see the wicked abominations that they
10 are doing here. And I came and saw; and behold every (every kind of) form of
creeping things and beasts, abomination, and of all the (all kinds of the) dung-gods
11 of the house of Israel, portrayed (painted) upon the wall round and round. And
there stood before them seventy men of the elders of the house of Israel, and

Jaazaniah the son of Shaphan standing in their midst, and every one his censer
12 in his hand, and vapour of the cloud of the incense rising up. And He said unto
me: Hast thou seen, son of man, what the elders of the house of Israel are
doing in the dark, each one in his chambers of imagery? for they say, Jehovah
13 seeth us not; Jehovah hath forsaken the land. And He said unto me: Yet again
14 shalt thou see great abominations that they are doing. And He brought me to
the opening of the gate of the house of Jehovah which was toward the north;
15 and, behold, there sat the women weeping for Tammuz. And He said unto me:
Hast thou seen, son of man? Yet again shalt thou see abominations greater
16 than these. And He brought me to the court of the house of Jehovah, the inner
one, and, behold, at the opening of the temple of Jehovah between the porch
and the altar about five-and-twenty men, their backs to the temple of Jehovah
and their faces toward the east, and they bowing themselves toward the east
17 before the sun. And He said unto me: Hast thou seen, son of man? Was it
[viz. ver. 16] a lighter thing for the house of Judah than to do the abominations
which they [vers. 5-15] have done here? for they filled the land with violence, and
returned to provoke Me to anger, and [there], lo, they stretch out the vine-branch
18 to their nose. And [but] I also will deal in fury; Mine eye shall not spare, neither
will I show pity; and if they cry in Mine ears with loud voice, then I will not hear.

Ver. 1. Sept.: . . . ἐν τ. πεμπτῳ μηνι—
Ver. 2. Sept. and Arab. read: כמראה־איש.—Anoth. read.: ולמטה כמראה אש.
Ver. 3. . . . του ζηλους του κτωμενου (Sept. and Arab. from קנה).—Anoth. read.: במראת, *in visione.* Sept., Vulg., Syr., Chald., Ar.
Ver. 6. . . . κ. ἐτι ὀψῃ ἁμαρτιας μειζονας.
Ver. 9. . . . ὡδε σημερον.
Ver. 12. . . . ποιουσι ὡδε, ἑκαστος—
Ver. 14. Vulg.: *plangentes Adonidem.*
Ver. 16. Anoth. read.: משתחוים.
Ver. 17. . . . μη μικρα τῳ οἰκῳ Ἰουδα του ποιειν τας ἀνομιας ἁς πεποιηκασιν ὡδε, διοτι ἐπλησαν . . . ; κ. ἰδου . ἐκτεινουσιν τ. κλημα ὡς μυκτηριζοντες.

EXEGETICAL REMARKS.

Of the abominations which come to be represented in this vision of our prophet there are *four:* (1) after an *introduction* (vers. 1–4), the *image of jealousy,* vers. 5, 6; (2) *the idolatry in the secret place of the chambers of imagery,* vers. 7–13; (3) the *mourning for Tammuz,* vers. 14, 15; (4) the *worship of the sun,* with a closing *threatening of God,* vers. 16–18. The common feature is the localizing of these abominations *at the temple.* That in this way a really existing state of things connected with the temple (EWALD) is meant to be reproduced—according to Häv. a feast of Adonis, which had been held in the 4th month (!) at Jerusalem in the temple—is just as little to be granted as it is to be denied that this or that allusion to the real state of matters may find a place here (2 Chron. xxxvi. 14). Disobedience toward Jehovah, in common with all Israel's idolatry, could not, at all events, find a more suitable symbolical expression. For sin is a profanation of the Holy One of Israel, and therefore since He has in the temple His palace in the midst of Israel, so much the more is it a profanation of this dwelling of Jehovah, if Israel's sin is idolatry, since the only place of worship for Israel was to be that connected with the worship of Jehovah in His temple-palace. Hengst. lays emphasis on the circumstance that the temple is "the ideal dwelling-place of the people" (Lev. xvi. 16), and thus "every sin polluted the sanctuary." "So, then, here also all that was present in the land of an idolatrous character is united in a single comprehensive picture, and placed in the temple, to cry thence to God and call forth His vengeance." Neteler admits also "four idolatrous symbols" as "a figurative delineation of the yet much more dangerous, more subtle idolatry: the first picture a representation of pride, from which the passions spring, which are reflected in the animal forms of the second picture." "As pride lays waste the soul, so sensuality lays waste the body—represented by the mourning of the women for Tammuz; and this lordship of nature over the spirit is completed in materialism, which holds lifeless matter to be the Absolute, and worships it accordingly." Hengst. thinks "not so much of idolatry springing from aberration of the religious instinct, as rather of a homage which was paid to the world-powers, for the purpose of attaining to safety through their help without God, nay, even against God." At all events it corresponds to the symbolical character of the whole, to recognise as symbolized in the number four the realm of heathenism as that of the natural world outside the kingdom of God. (KLIEF.: "that Israel has brought together its religious rites from all parts of the world, and spread them throughout the whole land.") The connection of our chapter with the two discourses of rebuke, in ch. vi. and vii., is clear, especially from the comparison with ch. vii. 20 sqq.

ADDITIONAL NOTE ON CH. VIII.

[A new stage of the prophetic agency of Ezekiel, and of his spirit-stirring communications to the captives on the banks of the Chebar, opens with this chapter, and proceeds onwards in an uninterrupted strain to the end of the eleventh. These four chapters form one discourse (as the preceding portion had also done, from ch. iii. 12 to the close of ch. vii.), and a discourse somewhat more specific in its character and bearing, than the revelations previously made. The vision of the siege, and of the iniquity-bearing, described in ch. iv., had respect to the covenant-people generally—including, indeed, the inhabitants of Jerusalem, yet so as also to comprehend the scattered portions of Judah and Israel. This, too, was the case with the vision of the shaven hair, and its foreshadowing desolations, contained in ch. v.-vii. The burden there delivered was an utterance of divine judgments against the whole covenant-people on account of sin; because, having been planted as the witnesses and heralds of God's truth in the midst of the nations, they had themselves fallen before the heathen corruptions, which it was their special calling to have resisted to the uttermost. Therefore, in just retribution for the betrayal of God's cause into the enemies' hands, the heathen were become His instruments of vengeance, to inflict on the whole house of Israel the various forms of a severe and prolonged chastisement. But now, in the section of prophecy which commences with ch. viii., the people of Jerusalem, and the small remnant of Judah, who, under Zedekiah, continued to hold a flickering existence in Canaan, form the immediate object of the prophet's message, not only as apart from the Babylonish exiles, but even as standing in a kind of contrast to them. And it is of essential moment to a proper understanding of the purport of the vision that we rightly apprehend and estimate the circumstances which led to so partial and specific a direction in the message now delivered.—FAIRBAIRN'S *Ezekiel*, pp. 81, 82.—W. F.]

Vers. 1-4. *The Introduction.*

The date in ver. 1: **in the sixth year, on the fifth day of the sixth month.** (August—September.) The year is that after the captivity of King Jehoiachin; comp. ch. i. 2. ("By means of such a reckoning He humbles the Jews," CALV.) The year of Israel (WINER, *Realw.* i. 530 sq.) is reckoned at 354⅓ days, each of the twelve months at 29-30 days. From ch. i. 1 sqq. to ch. viii. 1 there are 14 months = 413 days, as a medium between 406 and 420. But we need according to ch. iv.: 390 *plus* 40 days, to which, according to ch. iii. 15, seven days more are to be added, thus in all 437 days. As it is inconceivable (so also Hitz.) that with a date so precise Ezekiel should have been guilty of an inaccuracy so easily avoided, a *fourfold* solution is possible. (1) Either the symbolical actions in ch. iv. v. are subjective, or a mere rhetorical turn (HÄV., HENGST., HITZ., KEIL): in this case every difficulty disappears. (2) Or we may include the 40 days for Judah in the 390 (comp. on ch. iv. 6, 9), and get in this way the necessary days. (3) Or the fifth year of Jehoiachin was an intercalary year of 13 months, as such usually occurred every 3 years, sometimes also even with the 2d year (J. D. MICH.); and then there are reckoned for it (RELANDI, *Ant. Sacr.* iv. § ii.) 381-385 days *plus* 2 months (58-60 days), in all, 439-445 days. (4) Or, lastly, *our vision falls into the* 40 *days for Judah* (comp. on ch. iv. 12), as Kliefoth's view is, against which Keil's objections have no force. And not only the contents, but also the *circumstances* accord therewith. First of all the *place:* **in my house;** comp. on ch. iii. 24. יוֹשֵׁב does not necessarily indicate the posture as one of sitting, in contrast with lying in ch. iv., since ישׁב means radically: *to be fixed somewhere* (hence: to dwell, to tarry, to remain) and some*how;* hence: to sit, also: to lie, as well as: to stand (מושׁב, ver. 3). Then, farther, the representatives of the parties addressed, to whom the prophetic vision is directed (ver. 17), correspond: **the elders of Judah,** of the captivity. That it took place on the Sabbath, that they had come to hear a sermon, is not said. Comp. rather on ch. iii. 24. According to Ewald, they were seeking comfort and advice, especially on account of the bitter contempt of the poor exiles on the part of the proud, intoxicated capital.

ADDITIONAL NOTE ON CH. VIII.

[No express reason is assigned for their sitting there, though we can have little doubt that it was for the purpose of receiving from his lips some communication of the divine will. The Lord also was present, to impart suitable aid to His servant; but, lo! instead of prompting him to address his speech directly to those before him, the Spirit carried him away in the visions of God to the temple at Jerusalem, that he might obtain an insight into the state of corruption prevalent there, and might learn the mind of God respecting it. The message delivered to the elders who sat around him consisted mainly in the report of what he witnessed and heard in those divine visions; and it falls into two parts,—the account given of the reigning abominations contained in ch. viii., and the dealings of judgment and of mercy which were to be pursued toward the respective parties in Israel, as unfolded in the three succeeding chapters.

Now, what should have led the prophet to throw his message into such a form as this, but that some connection existed between the exiles of Chebar and the remnant in Jerusalem, which made the report of what more immediately belonged to the one a seasonable and instructive communication to the other? We formerly had occasion to notice, that among the exiled portion there were some who still looked hopefully toward Jerusalem, and, so far from believing things there to be on the verge of ruin, were persuaded that ere long the way would be opened up for their own return thither in peace and comfort. Among those also who were still resident in Jerusalem and its neighbourhood, it appears, there were some who not only looked upon themselves as secure in their position, but eyed their exiled brethren with a kind of haughty indifference or contempt, as if these had no longer anything in common with them! That it was this latter state of feeling which more immediately led to the present interview between the elders and the prophet, and the revelations which ensued, we may not doubtfully gather from the allusion made to it near the close of the vision (ch. xi. 15)—where the inhabitants of Jerusalem are represented as saying to the exiles, "Get you far (rather, Be ye far, continue in your state of separation and distance) from the Lord; unto us is this land given in possession." As much as to say, "It may well befit you to be entertaining thoughts of evil and dark forebodings of the future; your outcast condition cuts you off from any proper interest in God, and renders such sad anticipations natural and just. Abide as you are—but as for us, we dwell near to God, and by His good hand upon us have the city and land of our fathers in sure possession. It is not improbable that this taunting declaration of their own fancied superiority and assured feeling of safety had been called forth by the tidings reaching Jerusalem of the awful judgments announced in Ezekiel's earlier predictions; as, on the other hand, the express and pointed reference made here to that declaration leaves little room to doubt that the rumour of it had been heard on the banks of the Chebar, and had led the elders of Judah to present themselves in the house of the prophet. For, in their unhappy circumstances, the knowledge of such thoughts and feelings being entertained toward them at Jerusalem must have exercised a most depressing influence on their minds, and could not but seem an adequate occasion for their endeavouring to ascertain the mind of the Lord as between them and their countrymen in Judea.—FAIRBAIRN'S *Ezekiel*, pp. 82-84.—W. F.]

According to Hengst., the "rousing political intelligence" had arrived, that Elam and Media have joined the coalition! As to the rest, comp. on ch. i. 3, iii. 22, 14. KLIEF.: "the hand, etc., because, again, the matter in hand was not revelation in word, but action."—Ver. 2. The vision, going back and attaching itself to what goes before, begins, like ch. i. and iii., with a *theophany*. Comp. on ch. i. 4, 5. אש, from ch. i. onwards, characteristic, hence also the first impression which Ezekiel receives; comp. ch. i. 27. The Sept. read, or gave as an explanation, איש, of course from the mention of the **loins**, etc. It looked for the most part *like* (כמראה) fire, yet there was not wanting upwards זהר, the brighter splendour (Dan. xii. 3). (Ch. ix. 4.) As to the rest, comp. on ch. i. 4, 27.—החשמלה (EWALD, *Gram.* § 173, *h*, 1).—Ver. 3. From the fire-picture there is stretched the תבנית (from בנה, to build, to form) of a hand. As always, the *figurative* expression emphasized as contrasted with the spirituality of God. (JUNIUS: the hand is the Spirit, who proceedeth from the Father and the Son; comp. Matt. xii. 28 with Luke xi. 20.) Hence not in a corporeal sense (therefore רוח, not "wind" [KLIEF., KL.]; comp. on ch. iii. 12); ch. xi. 24; as also במראות אלהים, comp. on ch. i. 1. Clarius notices the difference between this passage and ch. xl. 1 sqq. Thus far the *manner* of the occurrence, now the *direction* taken: in general *to Jerusalem*, in particular to the spot where *the gate* of the inner *court of the temple* (the court *of the priests*, for which the "priest" Ezekiel uses merely הפנימית, viz. חצר, vers. 7, 16; the fem. gen. would agree neither with פתח nor with שער, whereas חצר is com. gen.) *opened* (פתח), *looking toward the north*. This court of the priests was (Jer. xxxvi. 10) on a higher level than the great court or the court of the people. The partition-wall between the two was (in order to allow of the people looking on), of so little consequence, that in 2 Chron. iv. 9 there is no mention of the gates in it. The *opening* of the gate is *not toward the court of the people*, so that the position of the spectator, as was also suitable for the priest, is taken *from the inner court.* צפונה (comp. on ch. i. 4), in *this* direction, hence northward we are to understand אשר־שם. HENGST.: "from the north the punishment was to come; this position was an actual summons to the north to send forth its avenging hosts; possibly also a reference to the sin already committed, the political adulteries of Jerusalem with the northern power Babylon, against which they alternately conspired and then again sought to gain it over, as Zedekiah, in the same year in which he had treated with Edom, Moab, etc., against Babylon, suddenly made off again to Babylon, Jer. li. 59." Or the expression northwards points out the principal tendency of Jewish idolatry (Hos. ii. 18 [16]), viz. towards Bel (Baal, of the Babylonians, who were, of course, in the north, or properly in the north-east. The **image of jealousy**, which, perhaps, on this very account is mentioned just here (comp. ver. 5), is, on the one hand, particularized by means of סמל (something covered over, an *idol*-image of that description, Deut. iv. 16), and, on the other hand, explained more generally by means of המקנה. The latter expression stands for הַמַּקְנִיא (from קנא), as is usually understood. Lightfoot thought of an image of Moloch. In the reign of Manasseh (2 Kings xxi. 7) we meet with the image of Astarte, which Ewald conjectures here, from the circumstance that love is allied to jealousy. Although with an allusion to an existing state of things (2 Chron. xxxvi. 14), yet, in accordance with the symbolic character of the whole vision, resting much more on the basis of Deut. xxxii. 16, 21, Ex. xx. 5 (comp. Ezek. v. 13, xvi. 38, xxiii. 25), and agreeably to the all-pervading representation of the relation of Jehovah and Israel, we may perhaps with Hengst. (WARBURTON) have to think of an "*ideal concentration of all idolatrous practices*," and these *as they* were in vogue, in the first place, *among the people in general;* hence the image in the court *of the people.* With this also corresponds admirably in ver. 4 the so characteristic antithesis of the **glory**, etc. Comp. ch. iii. 22, 23, i. 4, as well as in our chapter vers. 2, 5; farther, ch. i. 28, ix. 3, xliii. 3. שם, as before אשר־שם. The **God of Israel** He is called, in contrast with "the gods of the nations of the earth, the work of men's hands," 2 Chron. xxxii. 19.

Vers. 5, 6. *The Image of Jealousy.*

In addition to the foregoing virtual description of the image, we have the description in so many words in ver. 5; but so expressive is the thing of itself, that Jehovah needs only to summon the prophet to look. The direction repeatedly given is too plain to admit of there being any obscurity with respect to **the gate of the altar**. Because of this being named, the expression מ׳ ל׳ is used. For, coming from the north, as the "glory" (ver. 4) is to be supposed to do (ch. i. 4), this gate led into the court of the priests, where Ezekiel has taken up his position (ver. 3), and where the brazen altar of burnt-offering was, in reference to which (ch. ix. 2) the name "gate of the altar" (perhaps with an allusion to 2 Kings xvi. 14) is **explained; wherewith, at the same time, an anti-**

thesis of the image of jealousy might again be hinted at. Others (*e.g.* KIMCHI) have thought of the altar of the image (2 Kings xxi. 4, 5). **At the entrance** of the gate, thus in the outer court.—Ver. 6. מהם, an emphatic contraction in running interrogatory speech : מָה־הֵם (Qeri), sufficiently explained by what immediately follows (**the house of Israel**, etc.), so that there is no necessity for maintaining that some were actually engaged in worship.—**Great abominations**, ch. v. 11, vi. 9, is the motto, the ever-recurring refrain of the chapter, vers. 9, 13, 15, 17.—לרחקה, Ewald, Häv., like most of the ancients, supply the Speaker Jehovah: "in order that I may go far off from My sanctuary," may turn away from disgust (ch. xi. 23). HENGST.: "that they (those formerly mentioned) may be removed, as unworthy of dwelling with the Lord, may be driven out, as Adam once was from Paradise." HITZIG: "what ought to be far away." As רחק means "to be far off," why not render it by the bare infinitive: merely **in order to be far off from My sanctuary?** The construction with מֵעַל (ch. xi. 15; Jer. ii. 5) makes them appear as former members of the family, who in going away elevate themselves *above* Him who is enthroned in the sanctuary.

Vers. 7–13. *The Idolatry in the Secrecy of the Chambers of Imagery.*

Although at תוע' נד' in the preceding verse we cannot exactly carry out the comparison by supplying a מְאֵלָּה (as in ver. 15), yet there lies in the ועוד תשוב תר' the preparation for, the intention, the beginning of a climax in the thought. In the preceding section: the **house of Israel**, in this: its **elders**; this would be a climax. Comp., however, on ver. 11. Here: *in secret*, there: *openly*; this, at all events, is no climax.—Ver. 7. *Where the court opens*, the *inner* one into the outer, for אל־פתח החצר is manifestly the same as אל־פתח שער הפנימית' in ver. 3; thus neither the eastern principal door (LIGHTF., EWALD, HENGST.) of the court of the priests, nor the northern exit of the court of the people (HÄV., HITZ., KLIEF., KL.), in which case mention is made by some holding the latter view of porches with cells (2 Kings xxiii. 11; 1 Chron. xxviii. 12; Jer. xxxv. 4). In favour of the former view, the absence of any farther definition cannot be used as an argument; for while, after enough had been said in vers. 3 and 5, there was no need of any farther definition for the well-known פתח, there would certainly have been need of it, if all at once the intention was to speak of the eastern door, as is also expressly done in ch. x. 19, xi. 1. But as regards the other view, the **and He brought me** is no support, as the prophet certainly, who is in the inner court, is brought also farther (of course in vision) when he now gets to see the **hole** (Neteler translates: "a hole for one") **in the wall**, viz. *the gate portion of the wall which divided the courts.* As he is to go still farther, he is commanded in Ver. 8 **to break through**, to enlarge the hole which shows him the way (is not "as it were a model," HENGST.), so that his own person may get through. When this has been done, **an opening** shows itself, a door or window, or what opens up to him the glimpse which follows. When—Ver. 9—he has approached at the divine summons, idolatry once more reveals itself, and that the so peculiar *animal-worship of the Egyptians*, a fact which Klief. disputes without cause. According to him, the hole was in the wall of the outer court, and he makes the prophet break through and discover the pictures, etc., on the outside. In that case what was secret about it, as it is certainly represented to be? Hitzig maintains that the worship was in the interior of the gate-building, which contained chambers, but ch. xl. 36 is no proof for this temple. The entrance, Hitzig supposes, was built up during Josiah's reformation in worship.—Ver. 10. Comp. Gen. i. 24, ix. 3; Deut. iv. 17, 18; Rom. i. 23. שקץ (ch. v. 11) is construed by Ewald, Hitz., Hengst. in apposition with ובהמה: "beasts of abomination," "abominable beasts," since to them was paid the honour due to the Creator—according to Hitz., *e.g.* dogs, cats, etc.; Kl. takes it as in apposition with רמש also (according to Hitzig, beetles especially), inasmuch as the representation of both was made for the purpose of paying religious honours to the pictures. Best of all Bunsen: "every form of abominable creeping things and beasts." What follows might stand by way of explanation: *and, in fact*, of all, etc., or all idols *of this sort* are meant, as also birds, etc. (Hitz.: calves [Apis and Mnevis] and he-goats.) Klief., Kl. maintain that in this way all other possible varieties of idol-worship which had spread in Israel are subjoined co-ordinately with כל תב'. But the delineation or painting (מחקה, neut. sing.) of all upon the wall of the apartment into which Ezekiel looks through the opening is so characteristically Egyptian, that for one who is unprejudiced anything else is inconceivable. Ch. xxiii. 14 is not to be brought into comparison as against this view. As to the גל', so common with our prophet, see on ch. vi. 4; in Lev. xxvi. 30 first, in Deut. xxix. 17 expressly of the idols of Egypt. The **seventy** in Ver. 11, according to Ewald, "a round number to express the great strength of the Egyptian party among the nobles, which according to Jeremiah then existed"; according to others: the Great Sanhedrim, an institution, however, which first arose after the exile. According to our text, they figure either as a representation of the collective body of the elders, a committee (council of elders) drawn from (מִ) these official persons, or they represent the house of Israel, are a representation of the people. [By mentioning precisely this number of elders, the prophet sets before us a representation of the whole people,—an ideal representation, and of such a kind as to indicate the strong contrast that existed between former and present times—the original seventy (Ex. xxiv.) being employed in immediate connection with God's glory and covenant, while these here were engaged in an act which bespoke the dishonouring of God's name, and the virtual dissolution of His covenant.—FAIRBAIRN'S *Ezekiel*.—W. F.] The number 70 is chosen for symbolical reasons, 10 times 7 (BÄHR, *Mos. Kult.* ii. p. 660) resting on **Ex.**

xxiv., Num. xi., in reference to the *covenant* between God and Israel. In favour of the symbolical character of this number there is also the circumstance that Jaazaniah, the 71st, is not counted among them. The individual named as **son of Shaphan** is a different person from יאזניהו in ch. xi. 1. The name **Shaphan** we read also in 2 Kings xxii.; Jer. xxix., xxxvi., xxxix. He appears to have had a good reputation, so that for the symbolical meaning by the mention of him the contrast in conduct on the part of his son here might be rendered the more emphatic. Similarly BUNSEN, HENGST.: "who probably filled the same post as his father (as chancellor), was perhaps the soul of the negotiations with Egypt; partly on this account, partly because of his ominous name: the Lord hears, which involved the judgment on this procedure, introduced as a historical personality into this ideal company." Is the expression: **standing in their midst**, meant to indicate an official superiority as president, or his social consequence among them, or the circumstance that even the son of such a father, with whose name the memory of the pious destroyer of idolatry, Josiah, was united, could be found in the midst of such a company (Ps. i. 1)? לפניהם, *i.e.* the idol-pictures on the wall round about. עתר, according to Hengst.: "the prayer of the cloud of incense, because it was an embodied prayer, Ps. cxli. 2; Rev. v. 8, viii. 3, 4." "They say by the offering of incense before those miserable figures: Deliver me, for thou art my god (Isa. xliv. 17)." The Hebrew word means certainly: to press on any one with requests, but also: to press together so that there is a large quantity, to heap up, so that that which swells up, the vapour, may be indicated here. So richly that there was a **cloud**; comp. besides, Lev. xvi. 13. After Ezekiel has seen it, the interpretation is given him in Ver. 12. **In the dark, every one in his chambers of imagery,** contains everything necessary for understanding it. First of all, the *darkness* may certainly be regarded as a symbol of the darkened knowledge of God, but means still more that the procedure of the nobles of the people shuns the light, has its being *in secret*. In this way we have a complete explanation of the hole in the gate portion of the wall, in the wall of the court (ver. 7), of the clandestine manner in which the prophet gets access (ver. 8), etc. ("They had in Egypt, in the rocks on the banks of the Nile, deep underground passages, sometimes labyrinths, which led to underground vaults, whose walls were covered over and over with hieroglyphs, and, in fact, the entrance to them is, just as here, only a hole, at which no one imagines there is anything of consequence behind," etc.—J. D. MICH.) That **every one** does so proves the representative character of the 71 in ver. 11. חדר is that which is shut up, the interior of a tent, of a house; hence, a chamber. The **chambers of imagery** have idolatrous pictures painted on the walls. As it is represented (vers. 9, 10) in the wall of the court between the higher and the lower court, so it is done within the walls of their own dwellings by the elders of the people, who approached the priests in virtue of their official character. The *domestic* heathenism, as distinguished from the *public* in vers. 5, 6. Hengst. makes the direct participation in Egyptian idolatry step into the background. ("The people relied at that time on the help of the Egyptians, and looked to them as their saviours."—COCC.) Ewald maintains that Egyptian animal-worship was at the time really practised in deeply concealed apartments of the temple area, inasmuch as every idolater of that sort offered incense as his own priest, and prayed in a separate apartment (and hence so many of them are found in Egypt), comp. Amm. Marc. xvii. 7, xxii. 15. He points in proof of this to the Egyptian vassalage of King Jehoiachim. The pressure of the Chaldean party at the time upon the Egyptian explains, according to him, the expression, repeated in ch. ix. 9, of their deep despair of the affairs of the fatherland. Hengst. speaks in a predominantly political sense of the Egyptian fancies wherewith they occupied themselves in their inner man; the revolt from Babylon, undertaken in concert with Egypt, was still, he alleges, "a public secret." **For they say:** אין י'. This is their so-called right to do it, not meant as an excuse, perhaps. Jehovah shall have the blame. That He **seeth not** can hardly imply (Isa. xxix. 15) a dogmatic denial of His omniscient (Ps. cxxxix., xciv. 7) Godhead (Ps. xiv. 1), just as little as His having **forsaken the land** is meant to deny in so many words His omnipresent omnipotence; but their speech is practical ungodliness: when He has turned away His eye and presence from us and from the land, when we are no longer anything to Him, then nothing is left for us but to look out for the gods of other nations and lands, that they may dwell with us.—Ver. 13. Comp. ver. 6.

Vers. 14, 15. *The Mourning for Tammuz.*

In ver. 7 Ezekiel was between the inner and outer court; in ver. 14 he is brought to the opening of the gate **of the house of Jehovah.** Comp. **to the opening of the gate of the house of Jehovah which is toward the north** with ver. 3: **to the opening of the gate of the inner [court] that looketh toward the north**; thus the gate **of the house** and **the gate of the inner [court]** correspond with each other, the one as applying to the whole, the other as referring only to a part of the same. The **house of Jehovah** is the whole of the temple, consequently the opening of the gate of it can hardly be anything else than the place where the outer court of the temple opens to the outside altogether. The northerly direction of the gate also corresponds best with the movement of the prophet hitherto. There, then, are **the women,** viz. those who are **weeping for Tammuz,** for this reason sitting on the ground, as was the custom of mourners (Matt. xxvii. 61). [According to Hitzig: the female population represented in the individuals, who are exactly at the place assigned to the women.] First, the people in general; then, the elders of the people; now, the female sex. This is like a climax. The publicity also of the proceedings of the women (as distinguished from the elders) makes the occurrence in so far parallel with the first in vers. 5, 6. MEIER: the name probably signifies: possessor of power, mighty one, ruler; **Tammuz**=*dominus*, properly: tamer, lord. יהוה and תמון, a contrast! According to Häv., a contraction from תְּמֻזוֹן (מוז=מסס, to melt away), or from תַּנְמוּז (נָמַז), of persons or things in reference to the "disappearance" (dying, the ἀφανισμός in contrast with the εὕρεσις) of the Greek "Adonis," who (אָדוֹן, *i.e.* "lord" with the Phœnicians) is the Syrian Tammuz (Θαμμούζ, Θαμμούς). According to the fable, the beautiful favourite of Venus, killed by a boar in the chase, but afterwards rising to life again, in whose honour the fourth month (June—July) was called "Tammuz." At his feast the kinnor (a sort of lyre) was played; hence Cinyras, the father of Adonis, just as Myrrha, from the incense (מֹר) usual thereat, was his mother among the Greeks. It was a funeral-feast in the East, for it celebrated the death of the beautiful life of nature about the time of the greatest summer-heat (תקופת תמוז). Byblos in Syria, where the swollen waters of the river Adonis assumed a red colour about this time, when the snow melted on Lebanon, was the principal seat of the god. (Comp. Häv. against Movers, who makes the oriental celebration of the festival approach nearly to the Greek, in autumn. But comp. also Hitz. on the passage, and Winer, ii. 601 sqq.; Herzog, *Realencycl.* xv. 667 sqq.) According to Preller (*Griech. Mythol.* i. p. 219), the disappearance of Adonis was at first expressed allegorically (ἀφανισμός), after which they sought him (ζήτησις), until at length they found him (εὕρεσις), and now bewailed him as dead, by means of the exhibition of his picture, with gloomy elegies and the usages of a funeral. The solemnity ended with the cry: Adonis lives and has risen; hence with the comfort of his return. Pain for the lost beauty of the year, dread of winter, the ray of hope connected with spring. Sappho already sang of the death of Adonis and of the lamentation for him. BUNSEN: "seven days long the women gave themselves up to their lamentations, and were obliged **to shave their** hair or to sacrifice their chastity" (J. D. MICH.). Hävernick, as no trace of the worship of Adonis can be found in earlier times among the Hebrews, brings forward the view: that under Josiah's successors such idolatrous worship obtained a footing, especially through Zedekiah's political alliance with the Phœnicians against Babylon; that the seductive charm of this worship, which is attested by its wide diffusion, is to be taken into account; and that the gloomy direction of the popular consciousness at the time (ver. 12, ch. ix. 9) was in sympathy with nature's mournful mood. "The Adonis-myth was thus a picture of the history of the people, as the natural consciousness arranged it for itself and arbitrarily interpreted it (ch. xi. 2, 3)." Hengst. lays emphasis on the northern origin (between Tripolis and Berytus) of the worship, the characteristic wailing women, and finds the real import in the seeking of political aid among the Phœnicians. (Others have thought of a kindred Egyptian worship. Hitzig makes the worship of Adonis come from Egypt; Adonis = Osiris.)—Ver. 15. Comp. vers. 12, 13. The climax, up till now merely hinted at, is plainly expressed with respect to what follows. Vers. 6 and 13 keep what goes before in a co-ordinate relation.

Vers. 16–18. *The Sun-Worship* (vers. 16, 17); *the Closing Threatening of God* (ver. 18).

Now comes in conclusion the culminating point of the abominations, introduced by the *locality*, viz. the court *of the priests.* It takes place in the inner part of Jehovah's house,—thereby placed in contrast with the publicity going before, and parallel with the actings of the elders in ver. 7 sqq.,—and in fact (והנה) where the temple (the holy place) opens into the inner court, indicated still more minutely because of the significance of the locality. **The porch,** 1 Kings vi. 3. **The altar,** the brazen altar of burnt-offering. Comp. Joel ii. 17. (Matt. xxiii. 35; 2 Chron. xxiv. 20, 21.) Accordingly there can be no doubt that *the persons*, the 25 men,—as most expositors along with Lightfoot believe, *the presidents of the* 24 *orders of priests* (1 Chron. xxiv.) with *the high priest* at their head,—represent the priesthood. כְּ "asserts the fact expressly, but only in a subjective way" (HITZ.), as what appeared to be the case, the prophet, as it were, not trusting his own eyes. In this way the abomination to be described is **greater** than what has hitherto been related of the kind. But then, farther, the description of the posture assumed (comp. 1 Kings vii. 25, xiv. 9; 2 Chron. xxix. 6; the antithesis of **their backs** and **their faces,** the contrast of אל-היכל י' with קדמה, "toward sunrise") sets forth what is abominable in the highest degree. The sanctuary of the Eternal is a thing going down behind them; they turn to the new light. For מִשְׁתַּחֲוִיתֶם, which is probably an error in transcription, almost all read מִשְׁתַּחֲוִים (partic. from שחה, GES. *Gram.* § 74, 18), as an abbreviation of אַתֶּם, "ye," could not tally with הֵמָּה. According to Häv. an ironical alteration of the usual form, with an allusion to שַׁחַת in the Hiphil (to destroy, to do evil). HENGST.: an anomalous form, just as the abnormal certainly cannot surprise us in Ezekiel; the form a *quid pro quo,* like the conduct indicated by it; by inserting ת, the prophet gives a criticism after the manner of a quotation from Ex. xxiv. 1; Deut. xi. 16; as much as to say: they worship, whereas it is said in the law of God: Ye shall not worship. If Tammuz is the sun-god, then an easy transition from what goes before is accomplished, without our being obliged here also on that account to look with favour on Hävernick's worship of Adonis. It is the primitive *Sabæism;* comp. Deut. iv. 19, xvii. 3. (2 Kings xxiii. 5, 11.) EWALD: sun-worship in accordance with Zoroastrian superstition (Job xxxi. 26). Hengst. takes the 25 as princes of the people (ch. xi. 1), an ideal representation of the ruling class,—2 from each of the 12 tribes, besides a president (!). Because of the absence of the definite basis in the Mosaic books, which in contradistinction the 70 in ver. 11 had, כְּ stands here, "nearly," "about" (!). The gradation in ver. 15 points to the **sin,** at present just in full bloom (?). The project of a league with Medo-Persia (already mentioned in Isaiah as the destroyer of the Chaldean universal monarchy, ch. xiii. 17, xxi. 2) had perhaps called forth the inquiry of the elders in ver. 1, especially as the Diaspora was the appropriate instrument for such a coalition, etc.—Ver. 17: vers. 15, 12, 6. Hitherto the question was followed by something else of a different kind, *i.e.* of a worse kind. This time a new question winds up: *was it a light thing* (a small thing—Niph. of קלל; comp. 1 Kings xvi. 31) for Judah *more than* (מֵעֲשׂ') = *was that which thou hast seen* a lighter (smaller) thing than the committing of the abominations? *i.e.* embracing in one vers. 5–15. A *negative* answer is supposed, since, according to ver. 15, *what is seen in ver.* 16 *is to be the culminating point of all*, more burdensome than all else. And as in ver. 12 a כִּי introduced the alleged justification (in a parallel case) of the elders of the people in their acting by God's mode of procedure, so God furnishes the reason (כִּי) of the negative answer expected to His question, *so that Judah can have nothing more heinous to be put in the opposite scale* from what they have done: **for they,** etc.; comp. ch. vii. 23. (It looks quite like a parallel to the "for they," etc. of ver. 12.) And instead of turning to the Eternal, they have returned merely for the purpose of provoking Him to anger. The thought taken in connection with ver. 12 would accordingly be: the land of which they say that Jehovah has forsaken it, they have filled with violence, so that there remained no room in it for the Holy One; but their acting in the temple shows (a climax) that, as regards the Eternal, they are seeking not the expiation for their guilt, but His wrath. He seeth not, say they,—**and, lo, they,** etc. (the highest point of the climax), so that שׁלחים את' is either to be understood of a specially provoking gesture in idolatrous worship, or must be interpreted from the context as a proverbial mode of speaking. [Ewald translates: "is it too small a thing for the house of Judah to practise the abominations which they practised here, that they filled the land with injustice and exasperated Me repeatedly, and that now they even put the twig to their nose?" having in view the twig of the sacred tree held before the mouth during prayer (so already J. D. Mich. and many expositors), "as if there were not yet enough in the more ancient revolting idolatries as well as in the already depicted (ch. vii. 23) roughness of their everyday life, and as if, besides, this most recent superstition must now be added."] The climax in the thought and the reference to Parseeism lies in the context, but the "Barsom" (a bundle of different kinds of twigs) does not correspond with הזמורה (a vine branch, ch. xv. 2; Isa. xvii. 10), neither does the solemn holding before the mouth with the left hand correspond much with שׁלח אל־אפם. Hengst. assigns as a reason for "the vine-branch" its being "a quite pre-eminent product of the sun"; and, according to him, the nose is mentioned ironically instead of the mouth. A gesture in worship is demanded by the expression והנם. Klief. confesses himself unable to explain the idolatrous custom. The thyrsus-staff of the worshippers of Bacchus has also been suggested. Keil finds the climax in the acts of violence as compared with the abominations,—the moral corruption shows the full measure of their guilt; but the proverbial mode of speaking has not yet been sufficiently cleared up. Israel himself has been suggested here as the vine-stock (Jer. ii. 21), אַף, translated by "anger" (their anger, viz. which they have provoked on God's part, or which they cherish towards God and His prophets), and the interpretation given as if the meaning were: to pour oil into the fire, to bring brushwood to the flames. HÄV.: "and, lo! they send forth the mournful ditty (about Adonis, זמורה for זְמִיר, זְמִרָה) to their anger" (that which falls upon them). Hitzig renders זמורה: pruning-knife ("they put the pruning-bill to their nose"), wishing to provoke Me, they provoke themselves (Jer. vii. 19; Hab. ii. 10; Prov. xxiii. 2), in connection with which he quotes the scene in Auerbach's cellar from *Faust*, etc.—Ver. 18. Comp. ch. v. 11, vii. 4, 9, ix. 5, 10, threatening with corresponding retribution on the part of God. (Ch. xi. 13; Isa. i. 15; Jer. xi. 11).

DOCTRINAL REFLECTIONS.

1. As the idea of salvation is especially dominant in the history of Israel, and draws from it the most manifold types, so in a pre-eminent degree prophecy is ruled by the idea. In verbal prophecy the idea, and especially the Christian idea, of the future, clothes itself at one time in accordance with what is peculiar to the prophets as individuals, at another by making use of allusion to the form of the present, and of the forces, persons, occurrences, etc. moving it, but in general entirely within the sphere of the Old Testament mode of representation; so that what is meant to be just the most striking expression for the idea shows itself, through the later realization of the idea exactly in this form, to be at the same time a prediction, apart from the express predictions of the prophets. (Comp. on this subject THOLUCK, *die Propheten*, ff. p. 105 sqq.) Now what the figurative word accomplishes as regards the object aimed at, that, as regards deepening our views of the truth, appears to be the task of symbol in prophetic action, in dramatic vision. The vision of the abominations in the temple here in Ezekiel is a theologizing one of the apostasy of Israel, now ripe for judgment.

2. The living God of revelation is the measure of the dead idols of the heathen, alike as regards the pantheistic slumping of them in the world, and as regards their polytheistic separation according to the different lands and peoples. He is, and whatever wanders to those others and is falsely attributed to them belongs to Him. On the same deep basis of truth theologically, our vision brings the idolatry of Israel into view in the temple of Jehovah, and therewith into condemnation. The temple becomes the standard for judgment of every heathen worship.

3. It was condescension in the sphere of history on the part of the idea of revelation, that for so long a period a fixed nation, like Israel, was to be the bearer of it, and that, after the general analogy of heathen nations, church and state covered each other. Only with the expansion of the church into its ideal, *i.e.* into the kingdom of God among mankind as a whole (Rev. xxi. 3), have "state religion" and "state church" as ideas become effete. They are merely existing realities of a wretched kind; their ideas, if one chooses to speak of them, are antiquated; they are reproductions of the past, Judaism, if not

heathenisms. Progress, and by no means "radical" progress merely, but much more still religious, *i.e.* Christian progress, points away beyond them.

4. The distinction made between "abominations" and "violence" recalls the difference between the two tables of the law,—sins against God and sins against men. Over against violence in the latter respect, there makes its appearance what God must abhor. As the former fills the land and becomes the fashion, so the latter provokes the anger of God. Ungodliness and immorality in their connection here bear witness to the connection between faith and morals.

5. Superstition and unbelief—the one acting, the other speaking—present themselves together in ver. 12 in *one* sentence, just as these forms of the self-originated theology of the sensuous self-consciousness touch each other from opposite sides. Unbelief, which Holy Scripture never knows absolutely, since to it faith is the original godliness in the nature of man, appears here also as one that "speaks" (Ps. xiv., liii.) and has gods. Superstition draws its reason from unbelief. As Nitzsch describes the process: "in the depraved working of passive piety man attempts first of all to deny the facts of the religious conscience, wholly or in part; but yet, in so far as the consciousness of God compels him, he leaps over from unbelief into superstition, *i.e.* he defines for himself the divine as a thing that is human, sensuous, worldly, analyzes for himself the feeling of God into the sensuous, out of which, in the next place, arise fanatical imaginations, sometimes slavish, sometimes audacious, Rom. i. 21–25." When Plutarch, in his well-known treatise *περὶ δεισιδαιμονίας*, gives the preference to unbelief, he underestimated it as a source of superstition; he winds up, moreover, with the converse, viz. that many fall from superstition into unbelief. Jean Paul, on the contrary, who calls superstition "faith with a *but*," would "rather live in the densest malarious atmosphere of superstition than under the air-pump of unbelief," where in the former case one breathes with difficulty, in the latter he is suffocated.

6. Augustine raises the question: why should the Romans, who paid divine honour to all the gods of all nations, as they showed by having a Pantheon, yet have continually refused to honour the God of Israel? and found the reason in the exclusiveness wherewith Jehovah claims to be honoured alone, as being the true God in contrast with the false gods.

7. The mourning for Tammuz reminds us of the sorrow "of the world" in 2 Cor. vii. Is it unintentional that only this side of this idolatry is indicated in Ezekiel? It worketh death, says the apostle of the sorrow of the world. Over against the pleasure of life in the rites of Tammuz on its mere natural basis, the prophet has to take his stand on the divine sentence of death of the spirit; as there is no repentance on the part of any one, the other side in the worship of Tammuz cannot possibly prophesy of salvation. (As against BAUER, *Rel. d. A. T.* ii. p. 234 sq.)

8. The front of the temple looked to the east, the back, therefore, to the west. And such is the case, moreover, with most of the ancient nations; and so it meets us again also, for the most part, in Catholic church architecture. But a universal rule it is not (according to Vitruvius, the opposite is the rule for heathen temple-architecture), just as little as the turning of the face toward the east in Christian prayer is a universal rule; sometimes the front, sometimes the apsis, is turned to the east. Some have wished to find the reason for the holy of holies being turned toward the west in the antithesis to heathenism. MAIMONIDES, *More Neb.* iii. 45: "Superstition generally at that time worshipped the sun; therefore Abraham turns to the west on Moriah, so that he turned his back to the sun." Comp. on the other hand, BÄHR, *Symb.* i. 212. When the Catholic church architecture built the choir towards the east, the alleged anti-heathenish design of the opposite course was set aside, inasmuch as Christ, as the Sun of Righteousness, now determines the direction; it was imagined also that paradise was there, etc. etc.

9. There is a gradation in wickedness, for there is a development towards ripeness for judgment. And as the greatness of the sin is determined according to the person and circumstances, so the corresponding greatness of the punishment is determined according to the knowledge of and opportunity for what is good. But the Judge and Avenger is God.

HOMILETIC HINTS.

Ver. 1. "We may be assured everywhere, whether at home or from home, of the presence of God; hence also we have to fear God everywhere" (STCK.).—The pulpit for the exiles in the house of the prophet.—"Elders also ought to hear and learn God's word" (STCK.).—Ver. 2. Comp. on ch. i. 27 sq.—Ver. 3. "The saints in mortal flesh are between heaven and earth, for they are not yet indeed completely above, but still they have already forsaken what is below" (GREGORY).—"As here by the hair, so by the smallest thing the pious are lifted upwards by God" (JUN.).—"God's children and servants are led and guided not by the spirit of the world, but by the Spirit of God" (ST.).—"Yea, if this body could follow the spirit, it would lead it into heaven with itself."—"God was Master of the house at Jerusalem, and they brought in to Him another idol: that displeased Him justly" (RANDGL.).—See how jealous love can be! the jealousy of Israel's Husband.—"So God is provoked also by all who admit into their heart passion, pride, arrogance, debauchery, avarice, and other idols" (B. B.).—Ver. 4. Christ and Belial.—God in His jealousy is likewise God in His glory.—"In another way also God lets His glory be seen, when He causes a peculiarly powerful testimony to be borne in His Church, by means of which He unveils the abominations in all ranks, and causes them to be punished through His witnesses, since there also, as here, public worship especially is wont to be assailed."—To perceive God's glory in spite of all abominations is the privilege of His faithful servants, of His children, who do not cast away their confidence. Our faith is the victory which hath overcome the world.—"Such a strengthening was needed by the prophet, in order that he might fearlessly withstand the raging audacity and stubbornness of the people: God equipped him in this way with a suit of armour" (C.).

Ver. 5. "God places our sins before His eyes, and in like manner also before ours" (STCK.).—"So sits the envious Pharisee also, who has merely an outward righteousness, like an image of jealousy in the doorway, and will not let the simple people enter through the fear of the Lord into the faith and love of Christ, and thus takes away the key of knowledge (Matt. xxiii. 13)" (B. B.).—Ver. 6. "Whoever opens door and gate to sin, falls from sin to sin" (St.).—"Whatever man does, he does it before God's face, although the blinded sinner thinks God blind" (Stck.).—"God's people also may fall into great darkness and blindness" (St.).

Ver. 7 sqq. God's eye sees also through the wall, and He can give His servants a hole in the wall as well as eyes, so as to see what is between the walls.—"Guilty consciences love what is concealed" (Stck.).—Occasionally an Ezekiel comes across those concealed ones.—"Thy heart is to be God's temple. But how does the Lord find this temple? Just as here. Only dig through the white-washed wall of thy self-love and hypocrisy, then shalt thou perceive in the light of God all sorts of monsters and abominations, which the enemy has gathered together in thee, to the disgust of the Master of the house. Enough of unclean reptiles shalt thou find behind the wall of thy flesh, only dig through!" (B. B.)—"Assuredly, as soon as the true worship of God is forsaken, men have no longer any limit; from one they pass to a myriad" (C.).—Idolatry is not merely of the gross kind; nor is that which Christians practise merely of the refined kind.—Yea, everything which is on earth may become an idol to man.—I count everything but dung, Paul testifies in Phil. iii.—Ver. 11. "Those who ought in this way to take the lead of others in showing a good example, are often the worst" (St.).—"The elders before the idols, men before beasts, the living before mere pictures!" (B B.)—May all assemblies of churchwardens take an example by them!—Ver. 12. God is to blame for our guilt!—Thus many make for themselves a blind God, like Fortune.—Ver. 13 sqq. What a corruption must be among a people where the old and the female sex are infected!—On ordinary days, the lust of the flesh; on fast-days, repentance and sorrow.

Ver. 15 sq. "Nothing is so absurd as that a man might not be brought to it, Rom. i." (St.)—"Daniel turned in his prayer toward Jerusalem" (B. B.).—"All the ungodly turn their back on God" (St.).—"But who will count those who in our time turn their back on God?" (B. B.)—Ver. 18. They turned their back on God, and so He turns His back on them.—The eye and ear of God shut, what a picture!

2. *The Judgment on the Guilty* (Ch. ix.).

1 And He cried in mine ears with a loud voice, saying, Near are the visitations
2 of the city, and every one [has] his weapon of destruction in his hand. And,
behold, six men came from the way of the higher gate, which looketh toward the
north, and every one his weapon for breaking in pieces in his hand; and a man
in their midst, clothed in linen, and an inkhorn on his loins: and they came and
3 stood beside the brazen altar. And the glory of the God of Israel rose up from
the cherub, over which it was, to the threshold of the house; and He called to
4 the man clothed in linen, which had an inkhorn on his loins. And Jehovah said
unto him, Go through the midst of the city, the midst of Jerusalem, and mark a
[cross-] mark upon the foreheads of the people that sigh and that groan for all
5 the abominations that are done in the midst thereof. And to the others He said
in mine ears, Go through the city after him, and smite; your eyes shall not
6 spare, neither shall ye show pity. Old man, young man, and maiden, and child,
and women shall ye slay to destruction, and [yet] no one upon whom is a [cross-]
mark shall ye touch; and ye shall begin at My sanctuary. And they began with
7 the men, the elders, who were before the house. And He said unto them,
Defile the house, and fill the courts with slain; go ye forth. And they went
8 forth, and slew in the city. And it came to pass, when they had slain, and I
was left, that I fell upon my face, and cried, and said, Ah, Lord Jehovah!
destroyest Thou the whole residue of Israel, whilst Thou art pouring out Thy fury
9 upon Jerusalem? And He said unto me, The guilt of the house of Israel and
Judah is exceeding great, and the land is full of blood, and the city full of
wresting of judgment; for they say, Jehovah hath forsaken the land, and Jehovah
10 seeth not. And I also, Mine eye shall not spare, neither will I show pity; their
11 way I give upon their head. And, behold, the man clothed in linen, which had the
inkhorn on his loins, gave answer, saying, I have done as Thou hast commanded me.

Ver. 1. Anoth. read.: כלי plur., Sept., Syr., Arab. In ver. 2, also, the Syr. and some *codd.* have the plural.
Ver. 2. . . . *ἐνδεδυκως ποδηρη, κ. ζωνη σαπφειρου ἐπι της ὀσφυος αὐτου.*
Ver. 4. . . . *δος το σημειον*—Vulg.: . . . *et signa Thau super*—
Ver. 5. Instead of על anoth. read.: אל.
Ver. 6. . . . *κ. ἀπο των ἁγιων μου ἀρξασθε . . . οἱ ἠσαν ἐσω ἐν τ. οἰκῳ.*
Ver. 7. . . . *πληρωσατε τ. ὁδους . . . κ. κοπτετε.*
Ver. 8. Other read.: בהכותם, ונשאר, ואשאר.—ואזעק קול גדול, Syr.
Ver. 9. (For דמים they read חמס.) Sept.: . . . *ὁτι ἐπλησθη ἡ γη λαων πολλων, κ. ἡ πολις . . . ἀδικιας κ. ἀκαθαρσιας*
Ver. 11. Anoth. read.: ככל אשר (Talmud Babyl., Targ.).

EXEGETICAL REMARKS.

The iniquity (ch. viii.) is now followed, in accordance with God's threatening (ch. viii. 18), by the *punishment* as the carrying out of the threatening, and that as regards the execution of judgment on *the guilty inhabitants* first. But in the midst of destruction there is *at the same time preservation.*

Ver. 1. **He**; the same as in ver. 4. **With a loud voice,** not without allusion to ch. viii. 18; just as also: **and He cried in mine ears.** The loud voice does not correspond to "the greatness of the abominations which cry to God" (HENGST.); rather is "the strength of the emotion" thereby portrayed (HITZ.)—"the loud outburst of indignation" (JUN.)—at the same time an energetic act of the Lord.—קרבו (ch. xii. 23), most simply with Hengst. perf. Kal, as in Hos. ix. 7 'בָּאוּ, an announcement meant alike generally and for Ezekiel,—HENGST.: for the special executioners of what has been announced ('ואיש), viz. that it is now the time. קרב in Kal: to press on, to come near, to be near; in Piel, transitively: to cause to approach, to admit, to offer; intransitively (and at the same time intensively): to be very near, to approach with the greatest haste. (Hitzig reads קָרְבוּ. HÄV., KL.: imper. Piel intransitively: "hither ye," etc.)—פקדה, as almost always: penal visitation (Hos. ix. 7). The plural is not out of place either as regards the meaning of the word or in the connection. A plurality is implied in ch. v. 12, 15 sq. [HITZ.: "authority" for: those who have received orders against the city, so that פקודות is particularized by means of איש. HÄV., KL.: "overseership," the guard, the heavenly watchers of the city, who, as an authority appointed by God, are to execute the punishment on the ungodly.] Hitzig asks: to whom is the summons addressed? Cocc. answers: not so much to those entrusted with the visitation, as to the watchers of the city, who have hitherto kept off the former. In the meantime, however, no summons at all is issued, but with express reference to the prophet the approaching punishment is proclaimed by God,—as regards the substance of the thing, expressed in general terms, and as respects the form of its execution, in such a way that it is only in ver. 2 that a more detailed definition follows. What sort of persons are to be understood by איש may, of course, be conjectured from their equipment: 'כלי, according to the context (comp. also ch. v.): each one his sword; against which Häv.: "no common earthly weapon is suitable in the hands of such a host." A hint as to who the persons are is contained, perhaps, in the expression: משחתו; comp. Exod. xii. 23; 2 Sam. xxiv. 16. [BUNSEN: "the judges of the city, the punishing and destroying angels."]

Ver. 2. They are **men** also in Gen. xviii. 2, but none the less angels. [According to KLIEF.: men, as such, execute the judgment on Jerusalem; according to CALV.: the Chaldeans; according to GROT.: the generals of Nebuchadnezzar, who from six sides besieged and took the city (?). According to Cocc.: signifying the angelic hosts together with the Babylonian army-corps.] An explanation of the divine judgment makes itself clear (ch. i. 4). The number **six,** whose interpretation has been attempted even to desperation, needs no explanation, since it is rather the number *seven* that lies before us with the **one man in their midst,** etc., the *specially sacred number;* consequently: how, on the basis of God's covenant with Israel, punishment and exemption take place. [HITZ.: "the dogma of the seven archangels in germ."] As Ezekiel is to be supposed in the court of the priests (ch. viii. 3, 5, 16), the **higher gate** will be the gate indicated there. Comp. that passage.—מפצו, Jer. li. 20 sqq. He who is in the midst of the destroyers proves that in the midst of destruction there is also to be something else. What? His clothing tells us partly, his equipment partly. קסת הספר, only in our chapter, is: a writer's utensil; not a writing-tablet, but: an inkhorn, such as writers were accustomed to carry hanging in their girdle or on it. From this, however, we are not to infer, with Keil, that he is "a chancellor among the other officials," for such is not the character of the six; but from that wherewith he is provided we are to infer what he has to do: he is not like those others to destroy, to break in pieces. He has an inkhorn, whereas they have each a sword! [The Sept. read הַסַּפִּיר, and translated: a sapphire girdle.] From the destroyers he is distinguished likewise by his clothing, which is certainly not in conformity with an appointment of that kind. **In linens** (plural) is explained by Hengst. of the collective linen (Lev. xvi. 4, 23) garments of the high priest, whose antitype is the Angel of the Lord, the Angel of the covenant (Mal. i. 3), who, according to Zech. i. 12, gets from the Lord good comfortable words for the covenant-people, just as the high priest appears in Zech. iii. as the type of Christ, as the figure of the Angel of the Lord. So already Hävernick. Keil, on the other hand, only admits that the one man in relation to the six "stands somewhat like the high priest in relation to the Levites." According to Hitz. the garment of byssus marks him out as the highest in rank; he appears to be the same in whom, with Zechariah and the author of the Apocalypse, the spirit of prophecy assumes personality, the so-called *par excellence* Man of God, Gabriel of the book of Daniel and of the Koran; similarly the πνεῦμα in ch. viii. 2, 3 appears to have assumed angelic form (!). According to Cocc. the Spirit of God is likewise symbolized here, who produces the mark upon the foreheads of believers,—their confession. According to Calvin it is an angel, who is distinguished by the ornamental character of his dress from the men, the remaining six. Keil admits in addition the comparison with Dan. x. 5, xii. 6, 7 (Rev. i. 13 sqq.), but holds that the view of the Angel of the Lord is not thereby established, inasmuch as "the shining white robe" is peculiar not merely to this angel or Christ, but the seven angels also in Rev. xv. 6 appear in shining white linen, and the shining white colour symbolizes in general divine holiness and glory (Rev. xix. 8). In the first place, however, by the expression: **clothed in linen,** nothing at all is said as to brightness of colour, but it is simply the *material* of the clothing that is given, which, if it points to anything, points to the clothing of *the high priest.* Now, as the linen garments of the priests (comp. ch. xliv. 17 sqq.) mark them out "as the mediators of sanctification," whose "entire calling had for its aim the sanctification of Israel by Jehovah, and the sanctification of Jehovah by Israel" (BÄHR, *Symb.* ii. 89), the **in linen** is admirably appropriate in our context. The sanctification of Israel is limited here, of course, to the separation of certain parties in order to their being spared, as it is given in commission to the man by Jehovah (ver. 4); but the sanctification of Jehovah takes place in the case before us not merely through, but on Israel. Ever and always it is a *priestly act*, in the midst of destruction, to make the mark on what destruction does not touch (ver. 6). If, accordingly, it is not so clear from the clothing and equipment who the party in question is, as what he is to do, for what he is designed, yet it is generally acknowledged that his being in the midst of the six is the place of *leader*, of chief among them. Only after he has marked or not have they to smite; they go after him (vers. 4, 5); he answers in their name likewise (ver. 11). To a position of such distinction, if the six are *angels, the Angel of Jehovah* thoroughly corresponds. Comp. Zech. i. 11 sq.; Josh. v. 14; Gen. xviii. By their taking up their position at the brazen altar is by no means asserted their taking up their position before Jehovah, *i.e.* because the glory of God is there, as Keil, Klief.; but the meaning is: *where the guilt has reached its climax* (ch. viii. 16), *from that point also the punishment must go forth.* [HÄV.: as the coming from the north stood in relation to the sin committed there, so now the heavenly beings appear "as it were looking after and protecting the rights of the altar." "As a heavy accusation, the forsaken and despised brazen altar stood there;" comp. Amos ix. 1. GROT.: they stood there as those who would prepare many victims for God! Isa. xxxiv. 6; Jer. xii. 3, xlvi. 10.] The high-priestly man in linen also corresponds therewith. Comp. besides, Ex. xxxii. 35 sqq. (HENGST.: "the protection of the pious is his privilege; but the work of vengeance also is under his control." "The angels *stand,* waiting for God's beck and command. He whose spiritual eye was opened could only look with deep horror on the people filled with joyful hopes of the future. They appear at the place of transgression, in order to glorify God in the downfall of those who would not glorify Him by their life.")

Ver. 3 makes **the glory,** etc. (which is there conceived of as the Shechinah-cloud) move *out of the holy of holies* (HÄV., HENGST.), and that not merely as far as "the gate of the sanctuary, near which the altar stood" (HENGST.), for, "in order to give commands to His servants," it is not necessary for Jehovah to go to the place where they are standing; **and He called** suggests rather a greater distance. As to **the house,** comp. on ch. viii. 14, 16. Accordingly, by the **threshold** of it will not be meant, as Keil supposes, the threshold of the temple porch, through which one entered into the holy place (ch. viii. 16), but the outermost point, *where the exit was from the court of the people into the city*—quite in accordance with the direction which follows in ver. 4 sqq. That the glory of Jehovah, according to ch. viii. 16, stood over the cherub between the porch and the altar (KEIL), is not said in ch. viii. 16; and Klief. says at first also merely: "where the vision of God and the prophet had for the moment their station." We do not forget that the characteristic of Ezekiel is the prophecy of glory (see Introd. to ch. i. 4–28), and that therefore everything comes forth to the prophet always from the glory of Jehovah; but the vision of that glory changes alike as regards the locality and as regards the form of manifestation, so that sometimes this, sometimes that other feature steps into the foreground, and the rest into the background. For this there was a thorough appropriateness in the "variable hieroglyph," as v. Meyer has happily called the cherub. (BÄHR, i. 312.) The word הכרוב appears in Ezekiel for the first time here, and that in reference to the arrangements of the holy of holies, specially of the ark of the covenant. As the chajoth in ch. i. are the same as the plural כרובים, used by Ezekiel also in ch. x., and common elsewhere (הַכְּרוּב collectively, not: for the "ideal unity of the cherubim" (HENGST.), but: for *the well-known double ornament of the sacred chest*), the converting of the chajoth into cherubim in its application here (Doctrinal Reflections, 12, p. 55) may be looked upon at the same time as a prophetic interpretation of the employment of the cherub in worship, especially over the ark of the covenant, on the basis of the vision in ch. i. As to the disputed etymology, see GES. *Lex.* and *Thes.*; KURTZ, in Herzog, ii.; LANGE, *Genes.* p. 241. For the prophetico-historic employment of the cherub in ch. x. in respect of its movement (p. 40), the conjectural derivation from the converting of רְכוּב (Ps. civ. 3, xviii. 10) into כְּרוּב commends itself more than any other, as hinting at the passing of the chajoth of ch. i. into the cherub. The chariot-element (as against Kurtz) has in the representation of Ezekiel something essential; and if the form is not carried out perfectly as regards the copy in the tabernacle and temple, yet, as far as the idea is concerned, there can be no hesitation about it, as Jehovah may also remove His abode from the midst of Israel, inasmuch as He (אלהי ישראל) is no national God in the heathen sense. As to the rest, see Doctrinal Reflections.—With ver. 3 is still to be compared ch. x. 4, 18; Ex. xl. 36 sqq.; Num. x. 11 sq. The rising up of Jehovah already prefigured the abandonment of the temple to the enemies of Israel for judgment on them.—**Over which it was,** from the setting up of the ark, in accordance with the idea of the symbol, for threatening and promise, not always visible, but (as here) making itself so in a given case (Ps. lxxx. 1).

Ver. 4. The divine command runs: "Away into the city." Yet grace shall go before justice. But nothing is said of marking in the temple; and, on the other hand, certainly in vers. 6, 7 smiting is spoken of. תָּוָה = to make a תָּו, which last letter in the Hebrew was in the ancient Phœnician alphabet, in the Egyptian writing, as also upon the Jewish coins, of the form *of a cross* (T). Hence as in general תוה (1 Sam. xxi. 13) is "to mark," and תו "a mark" (Job xxxi. 35), so perhaps here והתוית תו is used on purpose of the marking *of this particular mark.* "A cross was just as natural for a mark as for a signature" (HITZ.). Häv., who (as also Vitringa) conversely derives תו from תוה, holds the indefiniteness as required by the circumstance, that the mark was not intended for men. But an indefinite thing is certainly no mark, not even for angels, who are conceived of here in human form; and if it was to be a mark of any kind you like, this certainly would be somehow expressed. KLIEF. (VULG.): a Tau as mark. The deeper significance, that a cross was to be the mark for sparing, Christian exegesis has perceived from of old (TERTULLIAN, ORIGEN, CYPRIAN, JEROME). As to the rest, comp. Rev. vii. 3, ix. 4, xiv. 1; Ex. xii. (Gen. iv. 15). "By this mark one is separated from the mass" (HENGST.). Consequently, if the mass is dedicated to destruction, he is preserved. **Upon the foreheads**, according to most: because there it is most easily seen; according to others: as there slaves bore the names of their masters (*inscripti, literati servi*). Comp. also Ex. xxviii. 38 (BÄHR, ii. 143).—**Men**, because of what precedes: **the city, Jerusalem**: inhabitants, citizens. The qualification for the mark is twofold, expressed in words of similar sound. אנח inwardly, אנק also uttering it; consequently those who are not only not like-minded, but also audibly make known their pain. (The Niphal, which commonly stands in the case of reflex influences on the mind.)

Ver. 5. עַל, Qeri אֶל; as also the singular עֵינְכֶם, which is unnecessary. Comp. Ex. xxxii. 27; Ezek. viii. 18, v. 11.—Ver. 6. Deut. xxxii. 25; Ezek. v. 16. The command is not merely to knock them down, but to make **an utter end** of them. Because of ch. viii., the beginning (supplementary to ver. 5) is made with the **sanctuary**; and this is immediately explained of **the courts**, which are before **the house** in the narrower sense, as men (ch. viii. 16), elders (ch. viii. 11), women (ch. viii. 14) were in them. [Keil, following Klief., supposes: "they were in general old men, well stricken in years, who had come into the court to sacrifice, but yet all the while were liable to the judgment." HITZ.: it was just the Sabbath! ROSENM.: "at My sanctuary," *i.e.* at those who have sinned there. SEPT.: as if וּמִמְּקֻדָּשַׁי = at My holy ones, the priests. "When the Sept. read: 'inside the house,' this is manifestly incorrect," Ew.] Comp. for this **beginning** 1 Pet. iv. 17. (Consequently not like 2 Kings xi. 15.)

In ver. 7 what has already been done is not approved in the form of a command (HENGST.), because the **Go forth** is to follow; but as in this way the beginning is called good, so the order is given to continue onwards till the end. Comp. Num. xix. 11 (Lev. xi. 24). The defiling of the house takes place in accordance with ver. 6, inasmuch as the courts belonging to it as a whole (which explanation of הבית is given by means of החצרות, so that **house** here = "sanctuary" in ver. 6) are filled with corpses. It is only now they go into the city. He pushes them on, as it were, with military abruptness (HENGST.).

In ver. 8 Ezekiel only is left remaining in the court of the priests of the temple, for it is there **the prophet is**. (Against KIMCHI, HITZ., KEIL.) **Impressive solitude!** (1 Kings xix. 10.) It is not as being spared that Ezekiel, speaking as he does of his own accord as a mere spectator, comes into consideration, just as also the preserving mark is not made upon him. His objection is meant, therefore, to be read *as occurring between the execution in the courts* of the temple *and that in the city*. נֵאשְׁאַר, ROSENM., HENGST.: third pret. Niph. with א epenthetic for the first = "and he remained over," viz. "I," where we are to supply in thought אֲשֶׁר. HENGST.: "taking the place of the noun: a he-remained-over." It is at all events surprising, in order to arrest attention, to emphasize the result. BUXTORF: expressing the consternation and perplexity of the prophet by means of the confused form of the word. Keil, following Hitz.: a "malformation, a blending together of the partic. and the imperf., and manifestly a slip of the pen, to be read as a partic. נִשְׁאָר, and to be connected with כְּהַכּוֹתָם." See other attempts at explanation in Häv. Ew. reads simply: וָאִשָּׁאֵר. Comp. Num. xvi. 45; Josh. vii. 6. His anguish vents itself in this cry to God (ch. xi. 13; 1 Sam. xv. 11). For the question, comp. Gen. xviii. 23 sqq., xx. 4. This question is not: "from the soul of those upon whom the judgment has just fallen" (HENGST.), whose representative Ezekiel cannot be, but: *from the feeling of his fellow-exiles*, of whom therefore no mention is made. That his question is not hindered by his having heard of the pious being spared (HITZ.), shows either his fear in this respect, that in Jerusalem there will be nothing at all to be spared, or that the sparing in comparison with the destruction does not at all come into consideration. Hence כל. The **residue of Israel** is that which still remains (especially at Jerusalem) of Israel collectively after the previous (the Assyrian and the Chaldean) catastrophes. Comp. besides, ch. vii. 8. Here the outpouring of fury, elsewhere the outpouring of the Spirit.

Ver. 9. As the prophet, on account of the greatness of the destruction, makes no mention of the sparing in his question, in like manner God also does not do so in His answer, because of the greatness (במאד מאד, in a superlative sense) of the guilt alike of Israel and of Judah (ch. iv. 4 sqq.). Comp. Gen. iv. 13; Lam. iv. 6.—Ezek. viii. 17, vii. 23.—מטה, Ew.: perverseness; HENGST.: declension; HITZ.: identical with מוטה, Isa. lviii. 9. Hoph. of נטה, perhaps (as such testimony in favour of what is right on God's part is necessary): of the *perversion*, the setting aside *of the right* (Deut. xxvii. 19; Amos v. 12). Apostasy from God does not lie in the context, and would also be more definitely expressed (1 Kings xi. 9). As in ch. viii. 12 their idolatry is explained in this way from their own mouth, so here their moral corruption. Here also the question is not about God's being and essence, but about His will and acting. The clauses are inverted to correspond with the present context: in ch. viii. 12 it is the "not seeing" that is spoken of first, here it is the "having forsaken." The filling of the land and city with lawless conduct shows how they imagine they have free scope, and fancy that no one is taking the oversight of them. And with the "not seeing" there is connected in ver. 10 a partial confirmation of their saying as regards the eye, which, however, on the other hand, so fearfully demonstrates God's presence in the land by means of righteousness and judgment (aposiopesis). Comp. ver. 5, ch. viii. 18, v. 11, vii. 9. The **way** is the bent, and in general the manner, of life. But what they suppose they are treading under their feet comes as iniquity to be punished upon their head (1 Kings viii. 32).—Ver. 11. Already the answer of God gave an affirmative reply to the question of the prophet; but still more is this the case with the announcement of the accomplished fact made by the leader of the mysterious avengers in their name,—an announcement which certainly includes in it also the possible sparing. Comp. on ver. 2. Comp. Gen. xxxvii. 14; Num. xiii. 26. Comp. Luke xiv. 22; John xvii. 4. The Qeri כְּכֹל אֲשֶׁר is unnecessary.

DOCTRINAL REFLECTIONS.

1. It is a peculiarity of what our prophet sees in vision, that, however much the vision of glory (ch. i.) remains at the foundation, and however much on this basis the unity of Him who speaks to the prophet and transacts with him is in substance preserved, yet sometimes the one or the other element of the form of manifestation retires into the background, *e.g.* in ch. viii. 2 sqq. the throne-chariot and the chajoth; and that sometimes, as in the chapter before us (ver. 3), a change of view takes place, corresponding to the sphere of the revelation, which is here the sanctuary of Jehovah. The thought which is to be expressed at the time supplies of itself the reason of the distinctive form of expression in vision, while at the same time there is no want of retrospective reference showing that it is one and the same thing, so that, as has been said, amid all the diversity the unity continues. In this way it is the same Jehovah who is seen in His glory in ch. i. that lays hold of Ezekiel in ch. viii. 3, and that everywhere speaks to him and acts as his Guide. And so He who lifts him up, the Spirit (ch. viii. 3), certainly controls the movements of the chajoth also in ch. i. 12, 20 sqq. And in the seven men of ch. ix. 2 it is merely the glory of Jehovah that is again unfolded.

2. Our chapter also furnishes a prelude to the last day, the "evening of the world" (as Lange calls it at Gen. xviii.), approaching for the inhabitants of Jerusalem. Thus the appearance of angels on the scene is not merely natural by reason of this parallel, but so much the more as the judgment on Jerusalem in Holy Scripture—much more than the destruction of Sodom and Gomorrah—is a foil, nay, a constituent element for the last judgment.

3. In the vision of glory (ch. i.) we have noticed repeatedly (comp. especially on ch. i. 28), along with a predominantly judicial character on the whole, the bright splendour, the sun-bright element, and lastly the rainbow. Thus the priestly form in white linen in the midst of the avengers cannot surprise us. The "one man" in their midst is a vivid allusion to "the likeness as the appearance of a man" in ch. i. 26.

4. Although conceived of executively in a historical form of expression for the immediate object of the vision in ch. ix., yet the group of seven represents substantially the same thing as what ch. i. set before the eyes of the prophet, in reference, first of all, to Israel. Comp. in this connection especially what is held as established as to the Angel of the Lord in relation to the glory of Jehovah (LANGE, *Genesis*, p. 386 [T. & T. Clark], and our Doctrinal Reflections on ch. i. 4–28). The Son of man, when He shall come in His glory, and all the holy angels with Him, as it is said in Matt. xxv. 31, likewise separates (just as here the mark is the dividing element) the assembled nations one from another. Quite in accordance with the difference of times, of the last day from the time when it is called to-day, just as expressly does the judgment devolve upon Him then as does the sparing in our chapter.

5. It is not "Hebrew poetry," as was the opinion of the ofttimes more æsthetic than theological Herder (*Geist der hebr. Poesie*, ii.), that is to be credited alike with the priestly element in the angel-leader of Ezekiel, and with the angelic element in the priesthood in general. But neither does the "symbolic cultus," as Bähr and Umbreit maintain on the other hand, furnish the only ground for it. But it lies in the nature of the calling of the angels (*nomen officii*) to be the mediating element, mediators of the divine revelations; hence to be in general what constitutes the prophetic office also (Hagg. i. 13), but quite specially what belongs to the employment of a priest (Mal. ii. 7). If, however, according to Num. xvi. 5, the priests are those whom Jehovah permits to come near to Him, are called the קרובים (an explanatory designation having the same letters as the cherubim), and if their proper work is the bringing near of the sacrifices, then their mediation lies especially in the direction from Israel to Jehovah; while, on the other hand, the mediation of the angels has its sphere in the other direction, and that exclusively, viz. from God to man, and so they are called "messengers, ambassadors," and in accordance therewith a doctrine is framed with regard to them in Heb. i. 14. The perfection of the idea of mediation, where the two directions met, was brought about through Him in whom the divine sending is a self-manifestation of God, and the priestly character is a self-sacrifice of humanity (1 Tim. ii. 5). Now Jehovah appears in His angel κατ' ἐξοχήν, just as on the other side the priestly order represents Israel, the nation of priests, and its head, the high priest, represents the Israelitish order of priests. There would thus be a prefiguration in vision of the perfected mediation in the Angel of Jehovah here in priestly office as well as priestly clothing ("the noble white form of peace," UMBREIT).

6. "We must consider this as beforehand probable," remarks Hengstenberg, "because the Angel of the Lord is represented elsewhere also as the leading personality in the great divine judgments, which are executed in the interests of the kingdom of God. He it was, *e.g.*, who as the destroying angel slew the first-born of Egypt, Ex. xii. 23." "There lies at the foundation the old picture of the Egyptian passover, but transfigured in the prophetic spirit. As there the destroying angel appeared as the Deliverer of the covenant-people, so here he appears as the Shield

of the ideal theocracy, of those truly faithful to God among His people (ch. ix. 4 sqq.), as the Avenger of ungodliness on the apostate theocracy (ch. x. 2, 7). Both things serve *one* object, the true welfare of the covenant-people" (HÄV.).

7. For the typical allusion to Christ the following points are enumerated by the ancients: (1) The human form, as having respect to the incarnation as well as to His powerful mediation; (2) that He is "one," 1 Tim. ii. 5; (3) that He is found in the midst, as it were as a prince, pointing to the kingly majesty and dignity of Christ; (4) the linen garment, the symbol of innocence, purity, of priesthood, etc.; (5) that He carries no weapon of destruction, but inscribes the elect in the book of life. In reference to the last, Hengstenberg expresses himself as follows: "It admits of question whether the inkhorn serves at the same time for inscribing the names in the book of life, of which mention is first made in Ex. xxxii. 32 (Ps. lxix. 28; Rev. xx. 12). It is, of course, probable, especially taking into account the fundamental passage, Isa. iv. 3. According to this view, the inscribing the names in the book of life is to be looked upon as the primary thing, the marking of the foreheads simply as a consequence."

8. Bähr (ii. p. 75) explains the priestly linen garment as symbolizing at once salvation and life and righteousness, which appears to suit only the commission to spare (ch. ix. 4), just as he explains the garment of purity as referring to those who had kept themselves pure from the defilement of Jerusalem's trespass.

9. The well-known Shechinah of Jewish tradition is equivalent to the glory of Jehovah (John i. 14). If the former is to be regarded more strictly as a cloud, and the latter more as a brightness of light or fire, yet the latter is to be conceived of in closest connection with the former. That this symbol of the presence of Jehovah was a permanent thing above the ark of the covenant in the holy of holies, as was for the most part the view of the older theology along with the Jewish tradition, cannot be drawn from the Scripture passages referring to the subject. Lev. xvi. 2 is not indeed to be explained, with Bähr (i. 395 sq.), Winer, and others, by ver. 13, but neither does it fix (as HENGST., KEIL) such a wonderful manifestation of the divine glory for the great day of atonement, and in fact also for the whole after period of the Solomonic temple; but it is to be understood simply in connection with the cloud of guidance during the journey through the wilderness, Ex. xiii. 21 sq., xiv. 24; Num. xiv. 14; Neh. ix. 12, 19; Ex. xl. 36 sqq., xxxiii. 9; Num. xii. 5; Deut. xxxi. 15; Num. ix. 15 sqq.; Ex. xix. 9, xxv. 22. The phenomenon on the occasion of the consecration of the tabernacle and of the temple (Ex. xl.; 1 Kings viii.) was an extraordinary one. Comp. the reasons against a permanence of such a presence of God in Bähr (i. 397). Comp. also Herzog (xiii. p. 476 sq.); and as to the controversy during last century, see the literature in WINER, *Realw.;* KEIL, *Archäol.* § 21, i. p. 115.

10. The idea which was symbolized by the ark of the covenant in the most holy place is indisputably that of a throne, however much the immediate object was in reality to be an ark (chest) for the law of the covenant. The purpose of the ark was accomplished with the two tables of stone. The idea of the throne was illustrated by the two cherubim. The two cherubic ornaments correspond with the two tables of the law, as these latter, with the capporeth, represent the dualism of the righteousness and mercy of God, which finds in the blood of the sacrifices (Lev. xvii. 11) its typical divine institution and promise of adjustment and harmony. The fact of the cherubim being joined in the closest manner to the capporeth strips it of the mere signification of a "cover" for the ark-chest, which already, apart from the destination of the capporeth, receives no countenance from its composition as being a plate wholly of gold. Delitzsch compares with it the heavenly רקיע in ch. i. 22. [כַּפֹּרֶת from Piel כִּפֶּר, in a causative sense: to make to cover (Gen. vi. 14), or intensively: to cover entirely, thoroughly, does not signify that the law of God was covered up, which would mean the covering up of God's rights and righteousness, which are meant to be protected rather, but, as is at once understood of itself: that that sin which becomes manifest through the law finds covering before God, atonement on the capporeth (Lev. xvi. 14).] It may certainly be admitted that the view, as it were, of a covering on the ark might have figuratively its point of transition to the idea of atonement. As, then, the ark guards the tables of the law, so the cherubim with their wings protect the capporeth, Ex. xxv. 20. The manifested presence of Jehovah in righteousness and mercy as holy love is shiningly clear. Understanding the cherubim as the chajoth, as is the case here in Ezekiel, we have in them, in the shape of an ornament, the symbolization of the life of creation (Doctrinal Reflections, 12, p. 55), as it appears in a state of heavenly rest engaged in the worship of God, yet none the less ready always, in the way of active service, to glorify Him alike in judgment and in mercy. In actual fact they acknowledge the heavenly King in Israel, the Holy One of Israel, Jehovah, as the living Elohim of revelation (p. 40), the Most High over all. And when Delitzsch defines the difference thus: that the ark of the covenant as מֶרְכָּבָה (1 Chron. xxviii. 18) is not so much a moveable, travelling throne, as the throne that is stationary and at rest, with this, of course, accords the circumstance that the double cherub on the capporeth as it were surrounds Him who is enthroned (Ex. xxv. 22); but yet the circumstance is not to be overlooked, that the staves intended for removing the ark of the covenant were continually to remain in it (Ex. xxv. 15). As regards the etymology of the word, we must reject that which has been attempted, after the analogy of the root *gribh* in the Sanscrit, from "*greifen*" (Eng. to grip, grasp) (DELITZSCH: as those who lay hold of and carry forward the divine throne; or FÜRST: like the Greek griffins and the Egyptian sphinxes as guardians), because a laying hold of is nowhere ascribed to the cherubim; and the fact that in Gen. iii. 24 they have to keep the way to the tree of life, is not to be derived from a peculiar quality as guardians, just as also we cannot, with Kurtz (Herzog, ii. p. 655), deduce therefrom a "task," according to which paradise was "entrusted" to the cherub, and that he gave it back "into the hands of man, its original possessor," having also "preserved beyond the flood its proper essence, the paradisiacal powers," etc. Nothing of this has any place in Holy Scripture. What is said in Rev. xxi. and

xxii. reminds us (ch. xxii. 1 (?), 2) in some respects of what belongs to paradise, but is by no means paradise, but the holy city, New Jerusalem, the tabernacle of God with men (ch. xxi. 2, 3), which by new creation (ver. 5) comes down from God out of the new heaven to the new earth. The cherubim do not inhabit (Gen. iii. 24) paradise, but "on the east of the garden of Eden," consequently outside of it is found the Shechinah (וַיַּשְׁכֵּן), which exhibits Jehovah Elohim. The meaning of this is, that for man henceforth the glorious presence of God is outside paradise, and hence also the approach to the tree of life in the midst of paradise is denied to man. For Israel, life before God and God's glorious presence are symbolized, as regards worship in the most holy place, specially by means of the atonement on the capporeth and the double cherub, as well as by means of the cloud during the journey in the wilderness, and on occasion of the dedication of Solomon's temple. In reality, the life is restored for mankind when He whose body is the temple (John ii. 21, i. 14) could say on that great all-accomplishing day of atonement on Golgotha to the thief: "Verily I say unto thee, To-day shalt thou be with Me in paradise" (Luke xxiii. 43). Moreover, we have to distinguish the historico-symbolic cherub, the cherub of worship, the cherub of prophetic vision, and the rhetorico-prophetic (Ezek. xxviii.), as well as the cherub of poetry (Ps. xviii.).

11. If the mark of the cross is the simplest exegesis of the תו, we must not merely say with Schmieder, that "this coincidence in any case remains ever memorable for the thoughtful observer of the ways of God, whose counsel has planned everything beforehand," but it will also be interesting to mention what is analogous in different quarters. The Egyptian Apis was denoted by a white triangle (or square), the characteristic mark of the power of nature (or of the world). On the brow of the Indian Shiva is the picture of the fertilizing stream of the Ganges. Shiva's or Vishnu's mark is made on the brow of the Hindoo who has been cleansed in the holy water. The Japanese pilgrim to the temple of Tensjo Dai Sin gets as a token of indulgence a small square box, on which, in large characters, the name of the god is written, and which he carries home upon his forehead. If, according to the ancients (and the more recent mystics also), the four quarters of heaven, the flying fowl, the praying, the swimming, even the walking man, the rowing ship, the ploughing peasant, etc., the Egyptian key of Isis, the hammer of the god Thor, not to speak of the preparation of the paschal lamb,—if all these furnished a "silent prophecy pointing to Christ," "the providential element may at all events (says Merz in Herzog, viii.) be acknowledged, that the putting to death of the world's Redeemer must be accomplished by that very instrument of torture, which is capable, as no other is, of being made, represented, set up, and looked upon as a *sign* before all the world, and in all the world," etc.

12. It is not Grotius, as Hengst. erroneously asserts, but Junius, who has already remarked that in Egypt it was the doorposts, here it is the foreheads, and that consequently while in the former case it was still families, houses, here it is merely single individuals that come into consideration. As contrasted with Egypt, it is Israel which in this crisis of the world stands the test, in virtue of a cleansing by means of blood, of a purification from sin. For if God will impute sin, who shall stand? Here in Jerusalem, on the other hand, the question is as to the Israelite (Deut. vi. 8), who is so after the spirit and not after the flesh, as it is not all Israelites who are the true Israel. It is a crisis in a narrower sense, consequently a separation. Hence, also, over against the persons comes the person of the Lamb, just as in Matt. xxv. 12 the "I know you not" is the decisive element. His mark brings about exemption from punishment in Jerusalem (Joel ii. 32), while in Egypt it is the blood of the lamb (Ex. xii. 13, 7). Whoever has not the Spirit of Christ is none of His. For, finally, the Spirit is the mark wherewith we are sealed, whereby we cry, Abba, Father (Rom. viii. 15; Rev. xiv. 1).

13. "The marking" (observes HENGST., as already J. H. MICH.) "does not secure against any share in the divine judgment, for this would not correspond with the nature of the divine righteousness, as even the elect are affected in many ways by the prevailing corruption; it is merely a security against their being carried away with the wicked (Ps. xxviii. 3), against an evil death, and everything which would stand opposed to the rule that 'all things work together for good to them that love God' (Rom. viii. 28). Jeremiah is an example." Comp. also Jer. xxxix. 16 sqq., xlv. 5.

14. One may, with Häv., find in the description of those to be spared (ver. 4) a characterizing of fidelity according to its negative side merely. They are the Protestants from the bottom of their hearts in Jerusalem. Moreover, the circumstance that they are described in such a way shows how oppressed they are by the corruption universally prevailing, so that their being spared in the judgment is at the same time a deliverance from the wicked (Ps. i. 4 sqq.; Luke xviii. 7 sq.).

HOMILETIC HINTS.

Ver. 1. "Each one is to have his weapon in his hand, not merely by his side or on his shoulder, in order that he may strike out on every side immediately. The Chaldeans were as it were the executioners, the Jews the criminals, and the appointed time was come. When they shall say, It is peace! and reckon the evil day far from them, destruction shall come upon them swiftly" (B. B.).—"The visitation of grace brings salvation for the pious (Luke i.), while the visitation in wrath is the portion of the ungodly (Ps. vi. 1, 2)" (STCK.).—Ver. 2. "Those who admonish are followed by the executioners, the prophets by the soldiers, the friends by the enemies" (STCK.).—"Although the Lord sends forth His angels of vengeance, yet the Angel of the covenant is with them, who watches over the children of God" (TÜB. B.).—"From this we deduce, in the first place, the effective threatening for the ungodly, that God has always servants who stand ready to obey Him; in the second place, the comfortable conviction, how even the unbelieving Chaldeans wage war under God's commands, and must act in accordance therewith; and lastly, we see that God spares His elect. This is just God's secret providence" (C.).—"The small number of believers need not surprise us; they have often been only few" (L.).—Thou seest how the Son of God at all times gathers for Himself by His word and Spirit a church chosen to everlasting life, and protects and upholds it (HEIDELBERG CAT. *Qu.* 54).—A contemplation at the altar, which is fitted to *alarm* us (by reminding us of our sin, by the thought of retributive punishment), which is meant to *comfort* us (by means of the atonement, by the act of sparing in the midst of the judgment).—Vers. 1–3. The six and the seventh in their significance for the judgments of God.—The severity and the goodness of God.—Punishment and grace along with one another.

Ver. 3. "The Jews imagined that God was, as it were, bound to the visible temple; but He shows them and us something different. If we imitate the Jews, our pretence of pure doctrine will likewise avail us nothing" (L.).—Ver. 4. "The Holy Spirit is properly the true seal and mark wherewith believers are marked by God, and then the cross, so long as they are still in the Church militant" (B. B.).—"In Rev. xiii. we find also a mark of the beast on the right hand or on the foreheads!" (L.)—How many a man bears his mark on his forehead!—We are not to make ourselves partakers of other men's sins by our looking on with indifference, or by our silence even.—And yet, what power the example of a corruption that is universal exercises!—"If thou art a person in office, cease not to admonish; if thou art merely a private individual, then show at least thy displeasure at what is evil! Noah and Lot did not follow the fashion" (L.).—Fear of man and desire to please man influence many men.—First the eye looks, then the mouth smiles, then hands and feet act.—O what a characteristic mark the sighing of the heart is, of whose child one is! Comp. Rom. viii. 22, 23, 26.—But how is it that here there is no mention of prophesying, of casting out devils, or of mighty signs, no mention of men of singular sanctity? Well, in the case of such it may happen that the Lord does not know them, never has known them, as He knows His own. Mention is made only of souls who are in earnest alarm in such a world as this, or even in a Jerusalem. Let these be comforted.—"When the apostle (2 Pet. ii. 7, 8) commends the patience of Lot, he says that his soul was vexed so long as he lived in Sodom. He could not as a single man, one who was besides still a stranger, bring those who were so thoroughly depraved to bethink themselves. He did not, however, himself become hardened amid the shamefulness of so many horrible deeds, but he sighed constantly before God, and was in continual sorrow. On the other hand, it is certainly a proof of great lethargy when we see that the holy name of God is despised, and yet feel no pain. Hence it is no wonder if we are involved in the punishments of those sins which we foster by our connivance. For that admonition is to be considered well, that the zeal of God's house is to eat us up, and that the reproaches of those who reproach God fall on us" (C.).—Those who are spared—a picture for the cabinet. Their outward and inward mark, according to ver. 4.

Ver. 5 sqq. Where God's grace is followed by God's judgment, and where the former has been turned into lasciviousness, there the discoveries which we must make in ourselves or in others have something exceedingly strict, harsh, severe about them. Neither the remainder of life, the helplessness and weakness of age, nor the blooming freshness of youth in its vigour, nor its grace and beauty, nor even childlike innocence or honourable appearance, is spared.—The unsparing character of God's judgments on the despisers of His grace, of His word (comp. ver. 10).—"The old take precedence of the young in the judgment, because they did not go before those younger ones in good example," 2 Chron. xxxvi. 17 (B. B.).—But the beginning is made with the temple, which Christ also cleared first, before the Jewish land was cleared of the Jews.—On ministers, princes, lords, the rich, the distinguished, and on those whom foolish people are accustomed to regard with most envy,—on these God's sword of justice when drawn falls first of all, or even most of all.—To stand near the house of God is a blessed and also a safe position; but it is also the most dangerous position if it is hypocrisy. Certainly in this case religion is no lightning-conductor, but what the tree is in the storm; those who are under it are sure to be struck dead.—A lie in God's face, or under the name of truth, is a lie of the worst kind, bringing with it eternal death.—Those who go about with fire lose certainly the dread of fire, but so much the more readily perish by the fire.—"Ye shall not touch any one of those who have the mark on them, is certainly no small testimony on God's part and no small privilege, of which one stands very much in need at the time of visitation in general judgments, or when God in a special way strikes all around us, since the heart very easily becomes desponding and timorous, distrustful and afraid. But believers must not use it for self-exaltation above others, but rather for true humiliation before God, and for joyful confidence toward Him in trouble and death" (B. B.).—Ver. 7. "In other cases, those who hope to be spared flee for refuge to the temples and places of worship; but here this avails nothing; on the contrary, the slaying just begins there" (L.).—"First the teachers, then the hearers" (B. B.).—Ver. 8. "Ah, Lord! is the voice of His servants, as they look at rampant ungodliness; at the approach of God's judgments; while they call to repentance; as they make their daily supplication for the Church" (STCK.).—"However cruel the prophets might appear to the Jews because of their threatenings and rebukes, yet they were anything but their enemies, inasmuch as they not only felt intense solicitude, but also made fervent intercession for their people. Such was the case with Moses, with Samuel, with Jeremiah (ch. ix.)" (L.).—"So the hearts of believers are full of love, as we see in the case of Paul in Rom. ix." (C.)—Ver. 9. "Ungodly men come to know God only after His judgments, but not in the right way of conversion" (LANGE).—"God does not answer all his doubts. For God does not free us from all the difficulties in which we are involved, but puts our modesty to the test. We are, however, to learn here not to weigh the judgments of God in our scales, because we usually extenuate our sins; it is God's business to sit in judgment on sin" (C.).—"We never sufficiently comprehend the justice of the divine judgments. We always overlook something in God's judging, however just and right it is. Here the secret providence of God is to be taken into consideration" (L.).—When the cup is full, it runs over.—Ver. 11. It is also an "It is finished" that closes the priestly as well as the judicial work, John **xix. 30** **(ch. iv. 34).**

3. *The Coals of Fire on the City* (Ch. x.).

1 And I saw, and, behold, on the expanse that was above the head of the
cherubim,—as it were a sapphire stone, as the appearance of the likeness of a
2 throne was seen [appeared] over them. And He spake unto the man clothed in
linen, and said, Come hither between the wheels, hither under the cherub, and
fill thy two hands with coals of fire from between the cherubim, and scatter over
3 the city. And he came before mine eyes. And the cherubim stood on the right
of the house, at the coming of the man; and the cloud filled the inner court.
4 And the glory of Jehovah rose up above the cherub, over the threshold of the
house; and the house was filled with the cloud, and the court was full of the
5 brightness of the glory of Jehovah. And the sound of the wings of the cherubim
was heard as far as the court, the outer one, as the voice of the Almighty God when
6 He speaketh. And it came to pass, at His giving the command to the man clothed
in linen, when He said, Take fire from between the wheels, from between the
7 cherubim; then he came, and stood beside the wheel. And the cherub stretched
forth his hand from between the cherubim unto the fire that was between the
cherubim, and lifted it, and gave it into the two hands of him clothed in linen;
8 and he took it, and went out. And there appeared in the cherubim the form of
9 a man's hand under their wings. And I saw, and, behold, four wheels beside the
cherubim, one wheel beside one cherub, and one wheel beside another cherub;
10 and the appearance of the wheels as the look of the stone of Tartessus. And
their appearance: one likeness to them four, as it were a wheel in the midst of a
11 wheel. When they went, they went toward their four sides; they turned not in
their going, for whither the head turned, they went after it; they turned not in
12 their going. And all their flesh, and their backs, and their hands, and their
wings, and the wheels, were full of eyes round about; they four had their
13 wheels. As regards the wheels attached to them [or: As regards the wheels, regarding
14 them], it was cried in mine ears, O wheels. And four faces were to every one:
the face of the one was the face of the cherub, and the face of the second the
face of a man, and of the third the face of a lion, and of the fourth the face of an
15 eagle. And the cherubim mounted upwards: this was the living creature that I
16 saw by the river Chebar. And when the cherubim went, the wheels went beside
them; and when the cherubim lifted up their wings to mount up from the earth,
17 the wheels also turned not from beside them. When the one stood the other
stood, and when the one mounted up the other mounted up; for the spirit of the
18 living creature was in them. And the glory of Jehovah went forth from above
19 the threshold of the house, and stood over the cherubim. And the cherubim
lifted up their wings, and mounted up from the earth before mine eyes, when
they departed, and the wheels beside them; and it stood at the opening of the
gate of Jehovah's house, the east [gate]; and the glory of the God of Israel was
20 over them above. This was the living creature that I saw under the God of
21 Israel at the river Chebar; and I knew that they were cherubim. Every one
had four faces, and every one four wings, and the likeness of the hands of a man
22 under their wings. And [as regards] the likeness of their faces, they were the faces
which I saw by the river Chebar, [as regards] their appearances and themselves;
they went every one straight forward.

Ver. 2. Sept.: . . . τ. ἐνδεδυκοτα την στολην—
Ver. 6. . . . τ. στολην την ἁγιαν—
Ver. 9. . . λιθου ἀνθρακος.
Ver. 11. . . . εἰς ὀν ἀν τοπον ἐπεβλεψεν ἡ ἀρχη ἡ μια—*ad quem ire declinabat quæ prima erat*—
Ver. 12. . . . πληρεις ὀφθαλμων κυκλοθεν τοις τεσσαρσιν τροχοις αὐτ.—*plena . . . oculis in circuitu quaš. rot.*
Ver. 13. *Et rotas istas vocavit volubiles*—
Ver. 19. . . . K. ἐστησαν ἐπι τα προθυρα—
Ver. 21. Sept.: . . . κ. ὀκτω πτερυγες.

EXEGETICAL REMARKS.

What follows is to be regarded as a second act in this dramatic vision, for the first woe closes with the report in ch. ix. 11. That the vision makes a new start is shown immediately in ver. 1: **And I saw, and, behold** (ch. viii. 2); and we shall be preserved from manifold perplexity if we mix up nothing from the previous chapter with this.—Comp. first of all on ch. i. 22, 25. By this express reference to chapter i. it must already be clear (comp. ver. 20) that הכרבים are the chajoth known from that passage. Comp. farther on ch. i. 26. The throne making its appearance prepares for the command of Him who is enthroned; but nothing appears except the throne, for the glory of Jehovah is conceived of as above the cherub, from which it moves in ver. 4. KEIL (KLIEF.), following the punctuation, takes נראה עליהם as an independent sentence: He (Jehovah) appeared above them.

Ver. 2. Comp. on ch. ix. 1, 2.—The vision in ch. i. corresponds with the temple-vision, an application of what was seen there to the case in hand (Matt. xxii. 7).—בוא, as usual, in contrast with הלך.—בינות לגלגל is the *intermediate space in the wheelwork*, hence: *between the four wheels on the ground*. For although גלגל does not mean "whirl," yet neither is it quite = אופן (wheel), but it combines at the same time what was implied in the *wheel* with the idea of swiftness *in rolling*, of repeated, frequent motion. Comp. in the meantime for illustration, on ch. i. 15 sq.—אל-תחת לכרוב confines within narrower limits the more general expression which precedes; hence כרוב here is neither the double cherub on the ark, nor the whole of the cherubim, but the definite (ver. 7) individual cherub.—We are not certainly to think of any hearth for material fire as being **between the cherubim**, nor is the altar of incense (Isa. vi. 6) to be dragged in for explanation; but it is *the wrath of God* (comp. ch. ix. 8), which destroys Jerusalem, that is symbolized, in accordance with the description in ch. i. 13. [Ew.: the punishment, as in Gen. xix. 24, the worst. Calv. adopts the view of a silent antithesis to Lev. vi. 12, 13.] Herewith properly everything is already said as regards the judgment *on the city*; the statement ויקח ויצא in ver. 7 brings merely in addition the execution of it, which is immediately followed up by allusions (also to the vision in ch. i.), mostly of an explanatory character, which are meant to illustrate the matter with all fulness and circumstantial exactness.

Ver. 3 begins to supplement by telling us *where* the cherubim (vers. 1, 2) in this second act appeared to the prophet as standing, where they had taken up their position: **on the right of the house** [on account of the inner court (of the priests) which follows, to be explained of the temple proper]; according to most: on the *south* side or *south-east*wards (ver. 19, ch. xi. 23), in contrast with ch. viii. 5 sq., 14 (Ew.: because the south is the place of fire and death, just as the Indian Jamas dwells there and comes thence); according to others: on this very account, and because of the execution of judgment by the Chaldeans, on the *north* side. Along with the cherubim the whole vision is transferred from ch. i., although first of all it is merely the cloud that is mentioned, which is certainly also the first thing in ch. i. 4 (comp. there). The circumstance that it fills the court of the priests is an impressive contrast to 1 Kings viii. 10 sq.

Ver. 4 is almost a verbatim repetition of ch. ix. 3, and accordingly the expression מעל הכרוב is to be understood as there of the double cherub on the ark, so that, as in ch. ix. in connection with the judgment on the citizens, so here in connection with the burning of their city, *the abandonment of the temple on the part of Jehovah is prefigured*. The prophet explains *how* the connection in the latter case was made clear to him,—how, namely, *outside* the temple-edifice *the cherubim* (chajoth) stood ready *with the coals of fire*, and the cloud threateningly filled the inner court, *when at the same time in the most holy place the glory of Jehovah rose* from its old resting-place, which the worship Sabbatically celebrated, so that it *mounted up* (וירם) *over* (על, which may of course be for אל, but rather stands here in contrast with אל in ch. ix. 3) *the threshold of the whole, visible* as well as *raised high* above all; "cherubim" and "cherub" balancing each other in this way, that the **house** (in the narrower sense) became full of brightness from the **cloud** which filled the inner court, the (inner) **court** became so from **the glory of Jehovah** taking its departure out of the most holy place. Comp. on the "cloud" and the "brightness," Doctrinal Reflections, p. 117. And as the brightness in this way attended the glory of Jehovah visibly through the court of the priests, so in Ver. 5 **the sound of the wings**, etc., ready for movement, accompanies it audibly; comp. on ch. i. 24. The mention of its being heard **as far as the** (outer) **court** proves the correctness of the exposition given of ver. 4, as being parallel to ch. ix. 3. Comp. besides on ch. i. 24 (Ex. xix. 16, 19, xx. 1, 18 sq.).

Accordingly, after the adjustment of the relation of cherub and cherubim (the explanations of ver. 3 sq. are attached to the latter), Ver. 6 returns to ver. 2, resuming the command to the man clothed in linen. The execution of what is there commanded is described as it began. אצל האופן, *i.e.* beside the one definite wheel to which he went; not "an ideal combination of the wheels," as Hengst., or = plural (SEPT. [ENG. VERS.]).

Then Ver. 7 tells us *how he obtained the fire* (the coals of fire of ver. 2). The cherub next to that wheel (ver. 9) took it and gave it to him. Thus the band of avengers (ch. ix.) under his leadership, in whom we recognised a setting forth of the divine glory, is parallel with the cherubs of the vision; one hand grasps the other (Rev. xv. 7, viii. 5). The character in which the priestly man appears as mediating exemption from judgment (ch. ix.) has thus (quite in accordance with the departure of Jehovah on the throne of grace out of the most holy place, where also no sacrificial mediation is possible any longer) assumed the form of a mediation of pure judgment. This abandonment of the temple on the part of Jehovah, which is much more prominently connected with the judgment on Jerusalem than in ch. ix. 3, prefigures the ויצא of the man (comp. ch. ix. 7), who thus takes his departure from the court of the priests for the city. But the mention of the hand of the cherub in ver. 7, as well as of the wheel in ver. 6, gives occasion for the continuation of explanatory additions which follows.

First comes Ver. 8. Ch. viii. 3; comp. on ch.

i. 8.—Then in reference to the wheel, Ver. 9; comp. on ch. i. 15 sq., i. 4, 16. A distributive repetition of the statement.—Ver. 10. Comp. on ch. i. 5, 13, 16. As the **appearance** of the wheels is described in two aspects, the expression is repeated, just like מראה in ch. i.—Ver. 11. Comp. on ch. i. 17, 8, 9. **The head,** according to Hengst., is: "what is upmost, highest, most excellent, *i.e.* the wheel which for the time had the direction, and which the others required to follow." HITZ.: "This is also the case with ordinary vehicles; but where each wheel has a fourfold movement, there are also four heads, consequently: the head which begins the movement and carries the other three heads along with it." KEIL: "whither the foremost turned." All these explanations keep aloof from any reference to the cherubim, while in ver. 9 the wheels stand beside them, and the following ver. 12 mentions the cherubim first. Comp. ver. 14. הראש is therefore = פנים in ch. i. 15, to which also יפנה seems to point. Consequently it is the *primus motor,* the *face* of the cherub *giving the direction,* which they followed as their head (comp. on ch. i. 11).

Ver. 12. **And all their flesh,** etc., can only refer to the cherubim, which accordingly are described (Rev. iv. 6) additionally to ch. i. 18 (comp. there). לארבעתם אופניהם expressly specifies the connection between the cherubim and wheels thus characterized.—Ver. 13. Hengst. translates in a meaningless way: "the wheels were called the whirl in my hearing." Comp. for גלגל, ver. 2, and for באזני, ch. ix. 1. The verse does not so much wind up as prepare for what follows. The call (הַ, the sign of the vocative) is not, however, addressed to the wheels, as KEIL: "to the wheels, to them it was cried in my hearing, O whirl"; but it contains *what* was cried, as giving the signal for departure, *in reference to them* (as Ver. 14 also shows), *with a view to the cherubim,* which are described according to their faces, which give the direction (comp. ver. 11). Comp. first on ch. i. 6, 10. The description of the faces in detail makes prominent only one of each of the four cherubim. (Is it that which is directly in front of the prophet?—KEIL.) [Kimchi incorrectly: the first, second, etc., of the four faces of each.] The face **of the one** (first) was פני הכרוב, *i.e.* simply of the one definitely referred to in vers. 2, 7 (KLIEF.). That it is *the ox's* face is proved from the connection. If the north side is taken for it (see on ch. i. 10), then the definition in detail of the faces, significant as it is for the quarter from which the judgment breaks forth (ver. 3), may possibly be according to the quarter of the heavens, and not according to the standpoint of the beholder, so that on all four sides *of the vision as a whole,* one face would be made prominent. [Hence it is vain to connect with this the etymology of the word כרוב, which is still spoken of as worthy of notice by Kurtz, and accepted by Schmieder, viz. כרוב = *arator,* according to the Syriac; which would lead, as Umbreit assumes on grounds purely conjectural, to an "ox-form as specially prominent in the whole phenomenon of the cherub, particularly on the ark of the covenant." Hitz., following the Sept., makes the whole verse disappear as a gloss.]

Ver. 15. Now comes the soaring aloft of the cherubim, thus prepared for (Isa. xxxiii. 10); and in this connection already (ver. 20) we have the identification with the vision in ch. i. Comp. there, ver. 20.—Ver. 16. The connection of cherubim and wheels in their harmonious movement, repeated just as in ch. i., with the mention, however, here of their **wings,** which were not mentioned there. Comp. ch. i. 19 (x. 11).—Ver. 17. Ch. i. 21, 20.

Ver. 18. ויצא corresponds with ויצא in ver. 7. It was really the last moment before the complete departure from the temple! The glory of Jehovah, after it had risen up "from above" the cherub in the most holy place, had shown itself aloft above the threshold of the temple-edifice as a whole (ver. 4); now it betakes itself *thence,* so as to be **over the cherubim** (ver. 3); and in Ver. 19 the now (as in ch. i.) united (ויעמד) whole—cherubim, wheels, and glory of Jehovah—completes *the abandonment of the temple as a whole.*—בצאתם (comp. their standing-place in ver. 3), corresponding with ויצא in ver. 18.—'פתח ש—where the court of the people opened toward the city, at the east gate of the temple-edifice.—(הקדמוני, comp. Gen. iii. 24: מקדם.)

Ver. 20. A repetition in completed form of ver. 15. There the cherubim were the living creature; here the living creature is the cherubim. *The recognition of the chajoth as being cherubim is the explanation of the vision of ch. i. as referring to Jerusalem, and it was brought about by means of the double cherub on the ark of the covenant.* The cherubim must certainly have been well known to the *priest*-prophet from that quarter. The circumstance that they had appeared to Ezekiel (ch. i.) *as the living creature,* threatened therefore alike the *dead worship* in the most holy place, and the service of the *dead idols* everywhere in Israel, with the wrath of the *living* God ('אלהי־יש), with infallibly certain judgment. Their appearance by the Chebar predicted already the departure of the glory of Jehovah from the most holy place, and the abandonment of the Holy City; it had predictions at the same time for those who were in exile, as ch. xi. will show. Thus it appears important to Ezekiel to recapitulate in vers. 21, 22 the common features which serve as proof.

DOCTRINAL REFLECTIONS.

1. It is much less to the judgment on the city, of which the account is a very brief one, that the prophet directs his attention, than to the showing of the coincidence with ch. i. If the vision there was that of the glory of Jehovah, as Ezekiel expressly says in summing up (ch. i. 28: הוא 'מראה), its relation to the glory of Jehovah above the cherubim, in the most holy place of the temple at Jerusalem, remained an open question. Has the glory of Jehovah, therefore, forsaken the temple, or will it? is it about to depart from thence, that it appears by the Chebar amid the misery of the exile? We know from the Introduction to our book how important this matter is for Ezekiel's mission and labours. The question, then, which had remained open, is answered by ch. x.; and this the prophet does not merely by repeated allusion, running throughout the whole of ch. x., to ch. i. in the description, but **also by the quite definite statement in ver. 15,**

and still more expressly in ver. 20: היא החיה. The removal of the presence of Jehovah (vers. 4, 18) from the ark of the covenant (already in ch. ix. 3), the corresponding manifestations in vers. 1 sq., 5, etc., to the well-known vision of ch. i. (already in ch. viii. 4), form the exceedingly dramatic, and at the same time the characteristic element of our chapter, which consists in the identity of the symbol of the divine presence for purposes of worship in the most holy place of the temple with that seen in vision by the Chebar, having so important a bearing on the downfall of Jerusalem as well as on the prophetic task of Ezekiel and the prospects of his companions in exile.

2. Bunsen remarks: "Hence the glory of God in the temple was none other than that which is reflected on the spirit of the pious man from the created universe. But this implies also that to the prophet, the law, or the ark of the covenant in the most holy place of the tabernacle, and afterwards of the temple, was a temporary phenomenon, and that the time for the spiritual knowledge and worship of God was approaching. It is a foreshadowing of what is announced in John iv. 21, shortly before the destruction of the temple at Jerusalem. But this latter already wanted the ark of the covenant and the glory of the Eternal bound up therewith. We must, moreover, compare the departure to the Mount of Olives (ch. xi. 22 sq.), and the entrance into the new temple (ch. xliii. 2 sq.)." Cocceius says: "God's proper dwelling-place is not between the cherubim made of gold, in which there is no life, no energy, no motion, but between the cherubim which are chajoth, *i.e.* living creatures, who have eyes to see, who possess the light of truth and the fire of love in themselves, God's life in them, and who therefore glorify God: where this is the case, there is God's dwelling, His holy temple, His glorious presence."

3. If (ver. 14) it is just to the ox-faced cherub that the dispensing of the fire (vers. 7, 2) is assigned, then, in fact, we have an approximation to Lange's interpretation of the bullock as the "suffering and bleeding life-form" (*Lebensgebild*), the "tragic-sacrificial animal." LIGHTFOOT: "When the high priest approached the ark in the holy of holies, the cherub, which of necessity first met his eye on his right, was turned to him with its ox-face."

4. The approach of the man clothed in priestly linen garments has, according to the representation of the prophet, not only something which reminds us of the entrance of the high priest into the holy of holies on the great day of atonement, but, in the fire of the divine wrath being handed out to him here, has a significant Christological feature in it, where the aspect of eternity at the fearful moment and the noble simplicity of the transaction have an overawing effect. Comp. Deut. xviii. 15, 16.

5. "The holy fire of God cleanses every creature which it touches; but in the case of the pious, the burning coal is a gracious power of cleansing, as in Isa. vi.; for those who are thoroughly corrupt, it is a consuming fire of judgment" (SCHMIEDER).

6. In the harmony wherewith the glory and cherubim and wheels are represented as moving, there is mirrored, as Hävernick remarks, the ideal character of the heavenly world.

(For the rest, see Doctrinal Reflections on ch. ix. and i.)

HOMILETIC HINTS.

Ver. 1 sq. "By this it was meant to be shown that Christ's majesty and power are higher than the heavens (Heb. vii. 26),—not, indeed, in respect of a residence in space, but in respect of the greatness of His glory" (ST.).—"How great is the glory of the Lord, the great God, and how terrible is His majesty, when He rises up to punish sinners! Nah. i. 2" (TÜB. B.).—He who formerly made the mark for sparing, behold, he now scatters coals of fire upon the city. So the Son of man is likewise the Judge of the world (John v. 22, 27).—"Christ the Messiah was the Judge not only in the destruction of the last Jerusalem, but also in the destruction of the first (Luke xix. 44)" (TÜB. B.).—The exact counterpart in the New Testament to this judgment with fire on Jerusalem in the Old Testament is the day of Pentecost at Jerusalem, fiery though it also was: instead of the coals of fire, tongues of fire.—Ver. 3. "So oughtest thou also to be prepared and to stand prepared to execute the divine will; as in heaven, so on earth ought it to be" (STCK.).—"That every one, therefore, should execute his office and calling as willingly and faithfully as the angels do in heaven" (HEIDEL. CAT. 124).—"For the last time, when the glory is already on the way to take its departure. But also a beautiful type of the incarnation of the Word" (B. B.).—Ver. 4. This is to be forsaken indeed, when God prepares to forsake us. Lo! then more than ever darkness comes over all the powers of man's spirit and over his life, and even trusted, loved countenances of friends go into shadow. Good thoughts grow ever fewer, impulses to prayer ever more rare; admonitions of conscience cease; the holy of holies in the man becomes empty down to the four walls and the usual pious furniture, etc.—Ver. 5. "The wings of the cherubim were heard in the confession of believers and in the executionary troops" (B. B.).—So also in the announcement of the shepherds (Luke ii. 15 sq.), as well as in the declaration of the wise men from the East, and then later and specially in the preaching of the apostles, was this rushing to be heard.—The thunder of the Almighty will make itself be heard more distinctly at the end, where He has hitherto spoken tenderly to draw the miserable out of the world.—Ver. 6 sq. "In the execution of important works, one ought to offer his hand to another (Ex. iv. 28, 30)" (ST.).—"Willingness and ability to perform the divine will is the meaning of the man's hand; its being concealed under the wings shows the servants of God in their mysterious dependence on God's beck and command" (ST.).—Ver. 9 sq. Comp. Homiletic Hints on ch. i.—"By this repeated and still plainer description the 'galgal' is to be made very clear to us" (COCC.).—Ver. 10. "In the kingdom of Christ everything stands in a close union and beautiful harmony" (ST.).—Ver. 11. "Now so ought it also to be among God's children and servants. Not the one thing here, and the other out there. At the same time, one may be in front, whom the others follow; this detracts nothing from the equality" (B. B.).—"Dear friend, take no long counsel with flesh and blood, but follow after" (ST.).—

Ver. 12. "The expression: 'full of eyes,' points to the enlightenment for looking to the ways of the Church, for watching that the church wheels may always be on the way of righteousness" (LAMPE).—Ver. 13. It may also be cried: Revolution! that everything must be turned topsy-turvy. Evolution is better. But if the people, princes, and potentates will not themselves turn, then the Spirit of God in judgment causes them to be turned in manifold ways, so that the foremost comes to be hindermost.—"Oh, revolution and change of all things in the world, until the kingdoms of this world shall become the kingdom of God and of His Christ!" (B. B.)—"The believer is always in motion; there is no standing still in the Christian life, but continual progress in virtue and purity" (STCK.).—Ver. 14. "Laboriousness, humanity, heroic courage, and depth of insight into the mysteries of God are especially the gifts of grace wherewith God is wont to endow men for the spread of His kingdom" (LANGE).—Ver. 15. "So ought it to be with us also, Col. iii. 1 sq."—"Where God departs, His angels go with Him" (B. B.).—Ver. 16 sq. Repetition makes it the more certain.—Ver. 20 sq. The prophet also grew in knowledge.—Ver. 22. "Like them ought we, none the less keeping our goal in view, to go after Him."

4. *The Leaders of the People* (CH. XI.).

1 And the Spirit lifted me up, and brought me unto the gate of the house of
Jehovah, the east one, which looketh eastward; and behold, in [at] the opening
of the gate five-and-twenty men; and I saw in their midst Jaazaniah the
2 son of Azur, and Pelatiah the son of Benaiah, the rulers of the people. And
He said unto me, Son of man, these [are] the men that devise mischief, and
3 that counsel evil counsel in this city; That say, [it is] not "near," "building
4 of houses"; it [is] the caldron, and we [are] the flesh. Therefore prophesy
5 upon them, prophesy, son of man. And the Spirit of Jehovah fell upon me,
and He said unto me, Say, Thus saith Jehovah: Thus said ye, O house of
6 Israel, and the things which rise up in your spirit, I know it. Ye have
7 multiplied your slain in this city, and filled its streets with slain. Therefore
thus saith the Lord Jehovah: Your slain, whom ye have laid in its midst
[the city's], they [are] the flesh, while it [is] the caldron, and one brings you
8 forth out of its midst. A sword ye feared; and I cause a sword to come
9 upon you: sentence of the Lord Jehovah. And I bring you forth out of its
midst, and give you into the hands of strangers, and execute judgments on
10 [among] you. By the sword shall ye fall; on Israel's border will I judge you;
11 and ye know that I am Jehovah. It will not be the caldron for you, so that
12 ye should be the flesh in its midst; on Israel's border will I judge you. And
ye know that I am Jehovah, ye that walked not in My statutes, neither
executed My judgments, and [but] did after the judgments of the heathen
13 which were round about you. And it came to pass, as I prophesied, that
Pelatiah the son of Benaiah died; and I fell upon my face, and cried with a
loud voice, and said, Ah, Lord Jehovah! art thou making an utter end of the
14, 15 remnant of Israel? And the word of Jehovah came unto me, saying: Son
of man, thy brethren, thy brethren [are] the men represented by thee as
kinsman, and [yea] the whole house of Israel, it wholly, to [of] whom the
inhabitants of Jerusalem say, Be far from Jehovah; unto us was it—the land
16 —given for a possession. Therefore say, Thus saith the Lord Jehovah,
Because I removed them to a distance among the heathen, and because I
scattered them in the countries, I become [became] to them for a sanctuary for
17 a little in the countries whither they came. Therefore say, Thus saith the
Lord Jehovah, And I gather you out of the nations, and assemble you out of
the countries in which you were scattered, and give you the land of Israel.
18 And they come thither, and they take away all its detestable things and all
19 its abominations out of it. And I give them one heart, and a new spirit will
I give in your inward part, and I take away the heart of stone out of their
20 flesh, and give them a heart of flesh. That they may walk in My statutes,
and keep My judgments, and do them, and may be to Me for a people, and
21 I may be to them for a God. And [as for them] whose heart walketh after the
heart of their detestable things and their abominations, their way give I
22 upon their head: sentence of the Lord Jehovah. And the cherubim lifted
up their wings, and the wheels [were] beside them, and the glory of the God

23 of Israel over them above. And the glory of Jehovah rose up from over
the midst of the city, and stood over the mountain which is on the east of
24 the city. And the Spirit lifted me up, and brought me to the land of the
Chaldeans, to the exiles, in the vision, in the Spirit of God; and the vision
25 which I had seen rose up from above me. And I spake to the exiles all the
words of Jehovah which He showed me.

Ver. 1. Sept.: . . . *τ. ἀφηγουμενους του λαου.*
Ver. 3. . . . *οὐχι προσφατως ὠκοδομηνται αἱ οἰκιαι;—Nonne dudum ædificatæ sunt domus?*
Ver. 7. Anoth. read.: אוציא. Sept.: K. *ὑμας ἐξαξω*—and all the Versions.
Ver. 13. כהנ׳; anoth. read.: בהנבאי.
Ver. 15. The second אחיך is omitted by some Codd., Sept., and Arab.—Sept.: . . . *και οἱ ἀνδρες τ. αἰχμαλωσιας σου κ. πας . . . συντετελεσται, οἱς εἰπαν*—
Ver. 16. . . . *εἰς ἁγιασμα μικρον—in sanctificationem modicam*—
Ver. 17. . . . *αὐτους*—
Ver. 19. . . . *καρδιαν ἑτεραν κ. πνευμα καινον . . . ἐν αὐτοις*—(Anoth. read.: לב חדש—ונתתי לכם, Syr.—בקרבם, בקרבהם, Syr., Sept., Arab., Chald., Vulg.—מבשרכם, לכם in some Codices.)
Ver. 21. Instead of ואל־לב, there is a reading ואל כל.
Ver. 24. . . . *κ. ἀνεβην ἀπο της ὁρασεως*—

EXEGETICAL REMARKS.

The execution of judgment on the guilty inhabitants of Jerusalem is followed, as a second act, by the fire of wrath on the city, in connection with the departure of Jehovah from the temple (ch. x.). The vision is brought to a close by means of a striking occurrence. But, as in ch. ix. in the midst of destruction there was at the same time the exercise of forbearance, so here also comfort and promise are joined with it. In the outset we have in Ver. 1 (comp. at ch. iii. 12, 14, viii. 3) a new ecstatic commencement as regards the prophet. The locality to which (from where it is not said, and ch. viii. 16 is not the rule for it; comp. on the other hand, ch. x. 5) he is transported is that mentioned in ch. x. 19. As in ch. viii. 16 we have קֵדְמָה from קֶדֶם, so here קָדִימָה from קָדִים. The express repetition of the quarter of the heavens has something which points to ch. viii. 16, without thereby identifying the five-and-twenty here with those mentioned there; it is only the similar turning away from the God of Israel towards an east, rich in hope, as they imagine, that can be hinted at therein. Comp. on ch. viii. 16. "At the opening of the temple" is not = **at the opening of the gate.** Moreover, those mentioned in ch. viii. 16 cannot (in accordance with ch. ix. 6 sq.) be conceived of as any longer alive. The **Jaazaniah** (יַאֲזַנְיָה = יַאֲזַנְיָהוּ) **in their midst**, who is first mentioned by name, accords in name and appositional statement with ch. viii. 11: "and Jaazaniah . . . standing in their midst," but without the possibility of their being the same person, as their fathers are different; only their parallel disposition (we shall be able here also to notice it) might have been meant to be hinted at. There is some allusion to ch. viii. in the expression. We know nothing more otherwise, either of the first named or of the second. [Hengstenberg extracts symbolically from the names of the men themselves and of their fathers the concentration of their thoughts: "all was full of joyous music to them." "God-bears, the son of the Helper, and God-helps, the son of God-builds," are to him "excellent names for men who promise themselves salvation without repentance, the direct opposite of the name Jeremiah: God-casts-down."] The fact that the two who are named are designated as "princes of the people," as it is commonly translated, does not at the same time assign this position to the remaining twenty-three, as the expositors admit; on the contrary, they appear thereby to be distinguished above the rest of the men; and the reason for it seems to be given in their importance, which immediately follows (ver. 2). The שָׂרֵי הָעָם, however, are by no means נְשִׂיאֵי הָעֵדָה; but the more general meaning of שַׂר admits of the sense *demagogues*, those having sway over the people, rather than of elders (זְקֵנִים), or presidents of parts of the city, or members of the Sanhedrim, or presidents of the classes of priests, or of our thinking of the twelve princes of tribes and the twelve royal officials (colonels), with the king himself (KLIEF.) or commander-in-chief of the army. In their quality as bearing sway over the people they come into consideration, not as representing the civil authority of Israel, as those in ch. viii. 16 represent the spiritual chiefs of the covenant-people (KEIL). In this way, also, it might be explained why the two are mentioned by name. The number given (25) may be intended to express a parallel with ch. viii. 16, just as a parallelizing tendency to ch. viii. seems to belong to the expression here at the close of the vision. With the patriarchically representative constitution of Israel, where the influence of the elders and heads of families easily pervaded the whole nation (SAALSCHÜTZ, *Archäol.* ii. 432, § 4), the two individuals named may nevertheless also be, if not princes of tribes, yet elders of the people, although they are not here designated as such officially. It is no ordinary sitting of a college, as Hitzig alleges, but an assemblage of persons like-minded (officials, notables, individuals out of the mass) that is represented; perhaps, however, in order to represent the "house of Israel" (ver. 5) amply, designedly in the form of two for every tribe, and one more besides.

Ver. 2. **Son of man**, ch. ii. 1.—אָוֶן, with no

fixed boundary between cause and effect, stretching from the moral to the physical, from the subjective to the objective,—**mischief**, as it results from injustice. Their **evil counsel** turns out ill. Their manner of speaking in Ver. 3 is the popular-rhetorical, which makes an impression on the sensuous mass by its striking, figurative character, and is easily remembered. How they think, and what corresponding counsel they give, is shown first of all by the statement: **It is not near, building of houses**,—their reply, namely, to the prophets of this period, who supplement one another, Ezekiel and Jeremiah. The distinctive expression in the case of the former—comp. ch. vii., especially vers. 7, 8 (עָתָּה מִקָּרוֹב)—is met by the bold denial לֹא בְקָרוֹב, and at the same time, בְּנוֹת בָּתִּים (**building of houses**) ridicules the letter of Jeremiah to the exiles (ch. xxix. 5), beginning with בְּנוּ בָתִּים ("build ye houses"), which threatened those at Jerusalem with sword, famine, and pestilence, etc. [Other explanations of these words are either hardly justifiable linguistically,—such as Luther's, those of the Sept. and Vulg. (Ewald takes לֹא as a question, *Gram.* 324*a*),—or give a far-fetched sense, such as Hitzig's.] Positively their meaning is expressed to this effect, that Jerusalem will keep its inhabitants, as the caldron keeps the flesh; and therefore their counsel is, to remain and to trust to the secure walls, instead of trusting the word of the prophets. [According to Hävernick, with allusion to Jer. i. 13; according to Kliefoth, alluding to Jer. xix. ?] BUNSEN: "We sit here in Jerusalem warm and protected, like the flesh in the caldron."

Their reply to the prophetic word is answered in Ver. 4: **therefore**—the repeated **prophesy**; and in Ver. 5 we have Ezekiel's immediate carrying out of the command in virtue of the divine equipment; comp. ch. viii. 1. The **Spirit**, instead of **the hand of Jehovah**, because of the revelation in word (אֱמֹר). Jehovah knows what rises up in their spirit (ch. xx. 32), as His Spirit also goes forth to meet their spirit. Thus there is a return to their saying. [יָה־ refers to מַעֲלוֹת (Deut. xxxi. 21; Hos. v. 3; Ps. cxxxix. 2; John ii. 25), or it is a collective feminine.] The expression: **house of Israel**, emphasizes almost ironically the contrast of what they pretended, what they also ought to be. Their mischievous devising, their bad counsel (ver. 2), is set before their eyes in Ver. 6 in its ultimate effect in actual fact, by means of the result to which it will lead when they are brought forth (ver. 7). Not that their deeds hitherto are to show the wickedness of their plots,—neither from "the epoch of Jeconiah" (HITZ.), nor, in accordance with a more general interpretation, of murder in a refined and gross sense (HÄV.),—which would lie outside the context, but the **slain** (חָלָל, properly: "to pierce through," as happens in the case of those who are put to the sword) are those to be slain by the Chaldeans, already slain from the standpoint taken up in the discourse of God. They are by their wicked counsels the authors of their death (HENGST.). חָלָל, comp. ch. vi. 7; Ew. *Gram* 278*a*.

Ver. 7. A retributive (לָכֵן) interpretation of their proverb in accordance with such a result of their counsel. It is fulfilled, but how? Not for themselves. Inasmuch as they—in contrast with their remaining in the city, which they have strongly asserted (ver. 3)—are brought forth, they remain alive, as distinguished from those slain as the result of their counsel. Yet comp. ch. v. 2. (Like the Sept. and Vulg. [Eng. Vers. also], Ewald reads אוֹצִיא instead of הוֹצִיא.) [J. D. MICH.: "Many citizens misled by you shall perish in the city, for whom it will be the caldron, and they the flesh which is cooked therein; only ye yourselves shall not be the flesh in this caldron, but shall be dragged forth and cut in pieces elsewhere."]

Ver. 8. From fear of those who are able to kill the body (Matt. x. 28), but not from fear of God (otherwise they would have hearkened to the word of His prophets), they took the walls of Jerusalem as a "caldron," which was to enclose them securely as the "flesh." ("Ye would not give yourselves up to the Babylonians, as Jeremiah advised you, because ye were afraid of being put to death by them," etc., A LAP. "Their revolt from the Chaldean king, the coalition and Egypt, will not save them from the sword of Babylon, on the contrary will bring it upon them," HENGST.) Ch. vi. 3. Comp. also at ch. v. 11.

Ver. 9. Now comes the question how it will be with the bringing of them forth (ver. 7). First of all, Jehovah (not Babylon, as it may appear outwardly) is He that brings them forth. Then farther, there is along with that His design, His aim; comp. ch. vii. 21, v. 10, 15.—Ver. 10. Ch. v. 12. Comp. the fulfilment, 2 Kings xxv. 18 sq.; Jer. xxxix. 6, lii. 10, 24 sq.—עַל־גְּבוּל, or אֶל גְּ׳, in Ver. 11 (Ew. *Gram.* 351*a*), removes the judgment not merely outside Jerusalem, which was to be a "caldron" for them, but outside Israel, which they have represented so badly (ver. 5).—Ver. 12 explains more definitely what is meant by the experimental knowledge of Jehovah in ver. 10,—that where they have not made themselves known before the heathen as Israel by doing what is right, He will make Himself known to them as Jehovah by means of His judgment, which deprives them of city and land. Comp. ch. vi. 7, 13, v. 7.

The sudden dying of Pelatiah takes place literally within the sphere of the vision merely, although in his case there may have been a corresponding reality at the same time, or at least about this time. As the prophet had to predict to the individual in question, as well as to his fellows, their being brought forth out of Jerusalem for judgment by the sword, but not their immediate death (ver. 4 sq.), this incident, whose awful character (Acts v. 5) is attested to us by the impression upon Ezekiel, symbolizes prophetically the certainty in actual fact of the judgment of death on the others also (comp. besides, Jer. xxviii. 17). And so Ezekiel sees them all already dead, and ch. ix. 8 repeats itself. Comp. there. Just as there, so here also it is the portion of the people still remaining at Jerusalem, in the land of Israel, and the standpoint of feeling is likewise (as against Hengst.) that of the exiles. For כָּלָה עָשָׂה, comp. Jer. iv. 27, v. 10, 18; Ezek. xx. 17. According to HÄVERN.: a juridical term for the carrying out of the final sentence. [Hävern. and Hengst. find an allusion besides to the name of the individual in question,—that the "help of Jehovah" is at an end, that with him, as it were, all salvation for Judah fell to the ground (?).]

But while ch. ix. 9 sq. emphasized guilt only, and God's justice only as confronting it, Ver. 14 introduces, and that solemnly, God's mercy.—Still Ver. 15 does not on that account form any "antithesis" (as Hävernick), but rather confirms what is announced in ch. ix. 9. For those in reference to whom remark will be made, and not merely of their being spared, but more positively even of their being preserved in an extraordinary manner, are different from those for whom Ezekiel interceded. He did so from a brotherly heart, and, because speaking from the standpoint of feeling of the exiles, characterized these also at the same time, in accordance with Jer. xxiv. **Thy brethren, thy brethren,** namely, those who are so in truth, and not merely according to the flesh (Matt. xii. 48; Rom. ix. 3). The repetition in the first place lays emphasis on this, but then farther, at the same time, puts in his right place the prophet of the glory of God in the midst of the exile, as we have seen Ezekiel to be (see the Introd.) in this his calling. For the designation of the exiles as "men of thy גְּאֻלָּה" (predicate, not subject) is not = thy kinsmen (GESEN.), which after such emphasizing would be equivalent to a weakening of the idea, but it reminds the prophet of his duty. [The Sept. read גּוֹלָתְךָ.] גְּאֻלָּה embraces the whole duty of the גֹּאֵל (the brother or nearest kinsman): redemption of goods and property, of liberty and life, the avenging of blood, the marriage obligation, and thus the entire representation of, giving of assistance to, and attorneyship for him who was reduced to poverty, slain, or dead. The expression: **and the whole house of Israel,** just as little adds "the laity" (HITZIG) to the others, as by the expression: **the men,** etc., is meant the priests only, as Hävernick also understands, in accordance with his view of the twenty-five in ver. 1; but the discourse sets over against the title (ver. 5) the thing itself, over against the name the reality, and at the same time deals with the (as in ch. ix. 8, so here in ver. 13) so-called "remnant of Israel," inasmuch as, corresponding to the repetition ("thy brethren," etc.) at the beginning of our verse, the **whole house of Israel** (ch. ix. 8), by being repeated through means of: **it wholly,** is made emphatic. (Ch. xx. 40; Rom. xi. 26.) HENGST.: "The contrast is, of course, such only on the whole; otherwise Jeremiah even would be no true Israelite. According to ch. ix., even in Jerusalem there is an election under the Lord's sheltering protection, although it cannot prevent the downfall of the city; and according to ch. xiv. there is also among the exiles much refuse." [John i. 47 (ch. xlviii.); Rom. ii. 28, 29, ix. 6; Jer. vii. 4; 1 Tim. iii. 15; 1 Cor. iii. 9.] The idea which is expressed by כָּלָה stands forth still more prominently by means of the contrast, so far as appearances go, to which those who are still for the moment the inhabitants of Jerusalem (ch. xii. 19) give expression, in accordance with their Pharisaic, hypocritical self-exaltation. Their characteristic dictum is quoted. For the imperative רַחֲקוּ, comp. on ch. viii. 6 and John ix. 22. What they themselves are inwardly in reality, the appearance of that—its outward realization—they cast to those in exile. "They fall into a kind of holy zeal. In this position which they assumed toward their brethren, they themselves bear witness that they are not in the true sense brethren" (HENGST.).—לְמוֹרָשָׁה, Ex. vi. 8.

Over against such a saying (ver. 15) on their part, Ver. 16 places the retributive saying of Jehovah: **Therefore say, Thus saith the Lord,** etc. And what is retribution towards Jerusalem is at the same time promise towards the exile. But there are two things said and therewith promised by God. The first, which is in reply to that saying: "Be far from Jehovah" (ver. 15), which made a declamatory use of their being outwardly far from the temple at Jerusalem, is the declaration so rich in promise: **I become a sanctuary to them,**—a thought which must from the first in ch. i., along with other things, have been indicated by the vision at the river Chebar, but which especially the vision in ch. viii. sq. has brought as a compensation for the symbol of the presence in the outward temple of Jerusalem. The older Jewish expositors think of the synagogues. כִּי, not before the direct speech, like: Yea, etc., and therefore impressively repeated (HITZ.); but in fact granting the reality, although tracing it back to Jehovah expressly, it begins like a protasis which gives the reason, or at least in the sense of: "if," "although," or the like. [מִקְדָּשׁ, according to Gesen. "asylum," which is too narrow.] מְעַט, either the length of time, or in the sense of measure (in some measure), which does not suit the context so well, and a promise of God, as here, still less.—(Isa. viii. 14; John ii. 19; Rev. xxi. 22.)

The second answer to the saying of the inhabitants of Jerusalem has reference to the statement: "to us was the land given" (ver. 15). Hence Ver. 17, with **therefore,** parallel to ver. 16, and continuing the promise by means of וְ, in the *oratio directa.* **I gather you** (Jer. xxiii. 3)—comp. John xi. 52—for which the return from Babylon was merely the outward substratum. In how spiritual a sense the return is conceived, namely, as at the same time an inward return to Jehovah (Jer. xxiv. 7), and therefore into the land promised by Him, is shown immediately by Ver. 18. **And they,** etc., *i.e.* the parties addressed, the parties mentioned. The history of the Jews after the exile proves the purification of Palestine from the previous idolatry (ch. v. 11).—To the gathering corresponds the divine bestowal in Ver. 19, just as it explains the reformation (ver. 18). [HITZIG: אַחֵר, "another" heart, like the Sept.] **The one heart** (Acts iv. 32) and the **new spirit in the inward part** are parallel. The old spirit which ruled them inwardly did not permit the harmony and concord which now ensue. But with the gift of a new spirit, the **heart of stone,** the *unnatural* element, is at the same time removed out of the flesh, and the *natural* element —**an heart of flesh**—is given. It is therefore no antithesis of Holy Spirit and flesh, as elsewhere,—not the contrast of nature and grace, but "a new spirit" and the opposite of the "one heart" that is to be given, *i.e.* the old spirit, that confront each other,—nature and the unnatural. The manner of expression is peculiar to Ezekiel. As they take away (הֵסִירוּ) all the detestable things and abominations out of the land, so Jehovah takes away (הֲסִרֹתִי) the heart of stone out of their flesh. The "stony heart" stands in relation to the idols; so also the "heart of flesh," "the new spirit," the "one heart," stands in relation to the only true God (1 Kings xviii. 21; Ps. lxxxvi. 11; James i. 8, iv. 8). Comp. the opposite in ver. 21. [Commonly the heart of flesh is taken as a soft heart, receptive of the impressions of divine grace, and the stony heart as the human heart in its natural condition.] Comp. ch. xxxvi. 26; Jer. xxxi. 33, xxxii. 39; Ps. li. 12 [10]. Israel, by her apostate, polytheistic conduct, has fallen entirely out of what was natural to her as a people,—that she should be the people of the one true God, the people of His holy law. This unnatural element of her conduct as a nation is to cease by means of the divine gift and working, and so לְמַעַן in Ver. 20 fits in quite simply as defining the purpose. Comp. besides, ver. 12.

Ver. 21. In contrast, either those at Jerusalem who have filled the land with their idolatry (ver. 18), or those among the people of God to be restored who shall prove worthless (comp. ch. xiv. 3), or the latter as well as the former. (In a grammatical point of view, comp. Ew. *Gr.* 333, p. 820.) Just as one may take up idols into his heart, so a heart may be ascribed to them. It is only the practical side of his becoming one with them, so that one is represented as one heart (ver. 19) and one soul with them, when his heart walketh after their heart, instead of walking in Jehovah's statutes (ver. 20). Comp. besides on ch. ix. 10.

Ver. 22. The closing scene of the vision of ch. viii.-xi. Comp. the previous scenes connected with the movement and departure of the glory of God out of the most holy place of the temple, as equivalent to and parallel with the vision of glory in ch. i., viii. 4, ix. 3, x. 3, 4, 18, 19.—Comp. ch. x. 19.—Ver. 23. The expression: **from over the midst of the city,** points at the same time to this circumstance, that the execution of judgment and the exercise of forbearance within the city (ch. ix.), as well as the throwing of the coals of fire over the city (ch. x. 2), were a manifestation of glory. The position in ch. x. 19, xi. 1 ("inasmuch as the city stretches to the north and south beyond the temple," HITZ.), indicates also the middle of the city. Such an abandonment of the temple, therefore, is at the same time an abandonment of the city (Hos. v. 15). While the vision still lasts, the glory of Jehovah stands over the Mount of Olives (2 Sam. xv. 30; Zech. xiv. 4), as is the view of ancient and modern expositors alike. Its situation and height are suitable ("the commanding point in reference to Jerusalem, which is overlooked from it in its whole extent," HENGST.). (Comp. Luke xix. 37, 41 sq., xxi. 37, xxii. 39; Acts i. 12.) Comp. ch. xliii. 2. Whether for the purpose of there presiding over the judgment on Jerusalem and the temple, or whether for the purpose of going back from thence to heaven, it is not said. This is objectively the end of the vision, but likewise subjectively as regards the prophet, Ver. 24; comp. on ver. 1, ch. viii. 1, i. 1, iii. 11 (Acts x. 16). The fulness of the description lays emphasis on the divine superhuman as well as non-human character of the revelation made to him, with a view specially to those to whom he in Ver. 25 communicates it. דְּבָרִי, as throughout Holy Scripture. Yet the word, in a pre-eminent sense (John i.), is finally the deed, the Word of God κατ' ἐξοχήν.

DOCTRINAL REFLECTIONS.

1. Demagogism in Israel is characterized in Num. xvi. as a laying stress on the universal priesthood of Israel, as opposed to the special office of Moses and Aaron. In our chapter its seductive skill in words is turned against the prophets of the period, Jeremiah and Ezekiel, inasmuch as the popular orators harangue their public on the possession of Jerusalem and the dwelling in the promised land. If, therefore, in Num. xvi. the argument is borrowed from the idea of Israel,—what she is to be according to Ex. xix. 6,—it is argued in our case from the existing reality of Jewish affairs at the moment; hence, in comparison, also a degenerate demagogism, just as everything in Israel's case points downwards. Perhaps we may compare the relation of social demagogism to the old republican demagogism, which latter at least still inscribed the ideas, liberty, equality, fraternity, on its red banner, while socialism agitates merely in reference to the actual relations of society for the moment.

2. Hävernick admits the "remarkable literal fulfilment" of vers. 9-11, but refuses, on the other hand, with Grotius, to understand them as "a prediction." The idea of the threatening in our prophet here "lies much deeper, in the nature of the subject itself; the extent of its application accordingly is also much wider." Hengstenberg remarks: "The prophecy cannot have been framed merely after the event; Ezekiel laid his book before his contemporaries, who were able to put him right. And the guarantee for the predictions which were fulfilled in the lifetime of the prophet lies in those which did not come to be fulfilled till long after his death. The confidence of Ezekiel is a sufficient proof that there is a supernatural element," etc. Certainly neither the canon of Nitzsch, that the prediction must not destroy the history, nor the limitation of Tholuck, that the detailed prediction must not be expressed before the subjects who are actors in the history, can suffice for regulating the prophetic gift of divination. Alike the psychologico-anthropological and the specifically theological elements are deprived of an adequate scientific basis.

3. "It is lamentable if we must gain the knowledge of God (vers. 10, 12) by our own destruction—if He in whom we live, and move, and have our being, is known only by the strokes

which break our own head. The knowledge has in this case, moreover, no moral import. It is a mere passive knowledge, forced also upon the ungodly, unconnected with repentance" (HENGST.).

4. Although the prospect which the divine promise (ver. 16 sq.) opens up regarding the captives of Israel is expressed everywhere in forms of Old Testament life as it appears under the law, yet the New Testament background, the "Messianic salvation" (EWALD), shows itself behind it. The realization of the covenant into which God entered with Israel for the human race, that they should be to Him a people and He should be to them a God, remains a theme down even to Rev. xxi. 3. With this the fulfilment also coincides, as it brought the return from the exile. The exiles were gathered out of their banishment to be a people again, and that on the "recovered soil of Israel," under Zerubbabel, Ezra, Nehemiah; just as those who had continued to dwell in the heathen countries solemnly professed by their visits to the feasts at Jerusalem (Acts ii.) that they belonged to the nation of the Jews. The reformation of the religious condition was an energetic one, as directed against the heathenish lusts after idolatry on every hand which prevailed before the exile. Comp. also the period of the Maccabees. Monotheism became the purifying fundamental dogma of the Jewish nation. And there was also developed a scrupulous legality, down even to Pharisaism, in the trivial actions of life. It was "a new spirit," and proved to be in general, and in comparison with the previous "stony heart," which God's judgment had broken in pieces, an "heart of flesh;" but yet it was merely an heart of flesh. The New Testament interpretation must not as a matter of course be put upon ver. 19 sq., as is done by Cocceius and the most of believing expositors. The prophetic words do not affirm this; but the prospect into the New Covenant does not open till at the close, where God gives the assurance that He will make Himself known as their God to those who have become His people. For this took place when He εἰς τὰ ἴδια ἦλθε, John i. 11. Only ὅσοι δὲ ἔλαβον αὐτὸν, ἔδωκεν αὐτοῖς ἐξουσίαν κ.τ.λ. (ver. 12). The renewal *for that* is not contained in ver. 19 sq. Cocceius, indeed, interprets מִקְדָּשׁ מְעַט (ver. 16) by: *sanctuarium paucorum*, i.e. *Deum per inhabitationem suam in aliquibus, paucis, eos sanctificare*, and finds therein the antithesis to Isa. liii. 12 and Rom. viii. 29!

5. What the vision of the glory of Jehovah which Ezekiel had at the Chebar already signified, but still more in accordance with its supplementary confirmation as well as renewal by means of ch. viii. sq., that obtains in the statement: "I become to them for a sanctuary" (and that not merely in a rhetorical sense, as it may be understood in Isa. viii. 14, and hence as an emblem of protection and also of blessing), its retrospective, but, at the same time, preparatory (as regards ch. xl. sq.) expression, and, in general, one that is predictive and rich in promise. The saying in ver. 15 does not indeed affirm anything expressly of the temple, but would make the presence of Jehovah be decided as a matter of fact by the possession of the land. But so much the more does the divine reply, in contrast with the material possession of the land, draw attention to the "sanctuary," by means of which Jehovah's presence in the land is brought about, and in which one is able to draw near to Jehovah (קָרַב, as opposed to רָחַק). Since, then, Jehovah promises to be to them a sanctuary, *i.e.* a temple in this connection, the priestly-prophetic office of Ezekiel is brought specially to light, by means of which the exiles approach God, and God makes Himself known to them, and in addition to which there is the glorifying of the name of Jehovah in and through Daniel; but along with that in general, there is promised a presence of God in spirit and in truth, as John iv. 20 sq. expresses it in respect of worship. Thus the exile might be to the Jews a school as regards the indwelling of the Word in flesh among men full of grace and truth, as regards the revelation of glory as of the Only-Begotten (John i. 14), as regards the temple which appeared in Jesus Christ (John ii. 19 sq.).

["The dispersion, besides being a just chastisement on account of sin, and a salutary discipline to lead the heart of the people back to God, had an important end to accomplish as a preparatory movement in Providence for opening the way for Messiah's kingdom. It was very far from being an unmixed evil. As a mere external arrangement, it was destined to be of great service in diffusing the knowledge of God, and providing materials for the first foundations of the Christian Church, by giving the bearers of God's truth a place and an influence in many of the most commanding positions in the heathen world. But still more important and necessary was the end it had to serve, in spiritualizing the views of the better part of the Jews themselves, and training them to the knowledge and service of God, without the help of a material temple and an earthly kingdom. Practically it had the effect of indefinitely widening the bounds of Canaan, or of giving to the world at large somewhat of its distinctive characteristics, since the devout worshipper at Babylon, Alexandria, Rome, or wherever he might be placed, found himself a partaker of God's presence and blessing as well as in Jerusalem. What a mighty advance did the kingdom of God thus make toward the possession of the world! And in rendering the dispersion of His people instrumental to the attainment of such a result, how strikingly did the Lord manifest His power to overrule a present evil for the accomplishment of an ultimate good! Nor were it, perhaps, too much to say, having respect to the issues of things, that the dispersion of the Israelites among the nations was fraught with as much blessing for the Church and the world as even their original settlement in Canaan."—FAIRBAIRN'S *Ezekiel*, p. 114.—W. F.]

"For a little," it is said in ver. 16, Jehovah Himself will be a sanctuary; in view of the destiny of the Jewish people, the state in exile could only be of a provisional character, only preparatory. For salvation is of the Jews, and the destiny of the people—and this must be upon its own soil—is the building of the temple of the kingdom of God (ch. xl. sq.). Palestine became the cradle of the incarnation of God in Christ, and thus of the Church on earth. But now, when the exile of the Jews has become a long period, the Jews must have fallen out with their destiny, as in such a case they have neither recognised their temple in Christ, nor built themselves as a people for a temple of God (Eph. ii. 21; 1 Cor. iii. 16 sq.; 2 Cor. vi. 16; comp. John xvii. 19 sq.).

6. "How different the Babylonian exile from the present! In the latter case, no proof of the presence of God; the people can keep only feasts of commemoration, and dream of the future; between the distant past and the distant future an immense empty space, a complete Sahara. In the former case, for him who looks more deeply, in the deepest humiliation there are everywhere traces of the loving care of God, pledges of the enduring election, of the future glorification" (HENGST.).

7. As against Keil, who quotes Hengstenberg for his view, we must assert that the passage Deut. xxx. 6 does not lie at the foundation of the promise in ver. 19, as was held already by Cocceius, who quoted in addition Col. ii. 11 sq., and the Epistle to the Hebrews. The "*one*" heart can only mean in the case of the individual a *united* heart,—a heart, therefore, which does not in its thoughts go from one thing to another, which does not through its lusts scatter itself on outward things, but is held together by the fear of God in its bent towards Him; which comes to the same thing as לֵב שָׁלֵם, *i.e.* a *whole* heart, not divided between God and any other (Deut. vi. 5, x. 12). But here it is the people as a whole and generally that are spoken of. Their σκληροκαρδία is well known (Matt. xix. 8); it has come to light by means of their history, that even the best, the noblest of this people shared in it (Mark xvi. 14). We call attention to the passages in our prophet, ch. ii. 4, iii. 7. Comp. Isa. xlviii. 4 (and this, too, with reference to idolatry); Jer. v. 3. They have hardened themselves in such a way (Deut. x. 16, like Pharaoh under the plagues) in opposition to the law, that God's law, which was written on tables of stone, is written as it were, with its penalties and its curse, upon stony Israel. But whatever their hardness may be, there is confronted with it (Deut. ix. 27) what they are in Abraham, and Isaac, and Jacob; in other words, that they are as flesh, that is their nature, and hence to be the Lord's servant. And that God says He will give back, restoring what originally belonged to their nature ("an heart of flesh"), in contrast with the unnatural and that which is against nature which has grown up in them ("the heart of stone"). Comp. on the other hand, John i. 13.

8. There is generally more said than ought to be said according to God's word, that "in its natural state man's heart" *is* "hard as a stone" (HENGST., KEIL). It becomes the "heart of stone" only by hardening. By nature it is rather "an heart of flesh," which grace confronts with spirit of Spirit (John iii. 6). Even in the case of Pharaoh there comes forth on repeated occasions the fleshy element of his heart (Ex. viii. 4, 21, 24 [8, 25, 28], ix. 27, etc.). And with the fleshy state of the heart manifold gifts of God are conceivable, as was the case with Israel from their fathers (hereditary blessing).

9. The "heart of stone," which has become such by hardening, God breaks *in pieces.* Thus it happened to Pharaoh. He does not *break* it; in that case it must have been an "heart of flesh." But this is done in Zech. xii. 10. Or, as in our chapter, God takes away the "heart of stone," and gives "an heart of flesh." The keeping apart of flesh and stone is as important as that of flesh and spirit.

10. "In a threatening (ver. 21) the whole terminates in a remarkable way. The idols are in themselves dead—mere reflexes and objective representations of the popular spirit; but even as such they exercise an enormous power over individuals. What power has Mammon now, as a Jewish (?) national god, over Jewish minds, although he is in himself a mere shadow?—Jehovah even may be an idol. With the idol-images the idols themselves do not yet disappear from a land" (HENGST.). "Little children, keep yourselves from idols," the disciple of love still says to us (UMBR.).

11. The Messianic significance of the Mount of Olives, which is not denied by the Jews even, has its Christological fulfilment in the Gospels; but in addition, the whole movement of the glory of Jehovah in ch. x., xi. has its meaning for the life of the Son of God in the flesh. Jerome remarks: "By degrees the glory of the Lord takes its departure from Jerusalem. After it leaves the temple, it stands first on the threshold, thereafter at the entrance of the east gate, finally over the Mount of Olives, whence the Saviour ascends to the Father." Comp. the beginning in Luke ii. 46, the continuation in John ii. 14 sq., along with the New Testament passages already quoted in the exposition; and for the end, still farther, Matt. xxi. 12 sq., xxiv. 1 sq. (ch. xxvii. 5, 51). One might say, Ezekiel has seen beforehand the life of Jesus in its elements of judgment in reference to the Jewish people.

12. Baumgarten (*The Acts of the Apostles,* on ch. i., Clark's Trans.) remarks on the glory of Jehovah in relation to the Mount of Olives: "It was therefore a departure, and yet a remaining in the neighbourhood; if the outward protection and blessing of Jehovah should be withdrawn from His people, the invisible power of His Spirit will remain near them, and perhaps manifest itself the more gloriously. It is the very same Ezekiel, who has afterwards brought vividly before us this side of promise and hope even in the departure of the glory of Jehovah; it is just Ezekiel who has beheld, represented, and described in the most impressive way the awakening, creative power of the Spirit of Jehovah for the whole nation of Israel (ch. xxxvii.). In like manner, Jesus, in whom dwelleth the divine glory bodily, withdraws from the Jews (John viii. 21); but His standing on the Mount of Olives is a sign that He remains invisibly and blessedly near them, Acts iii. 26."

HOMILETIC HINTS.

Vers. 1–3. "Do thou also give thyself up to the drawing of the Spirit of God. Wherever He may lead thee, it will be to a joyful end at last. But beware of the leading of the evil spirit" (STARCK).—When those who bear sway over the people are not able even to master their own wicked thoughts and words, but rather strive against God's thoughts and words, it must certainly turn out ill both for themselves and for the people. The beautiful names of such leaders avail nothing, just as little as the voice of the people is, as is said, the voice of God, unless it be that God's judgment is made known by it.—"We learn from this chapter how great a blessing from God it is for a people to have pious leaders."—"That the prophet names only two may show us how it is the few who draw so many after them: so it is in the senates of princes, so it is in the free states" (LUTHER).—Thus God reveals the thoughts of men, 2 Cor. v. 10.—Ver. 3. "They allude to Jer. i. 13, and insinuate that the prophet contradicts himself. What! thou threatenest us with captivity, and yet thou sayest this city is the caldron, and the Chaldeans will be the fire! If it is God's pleasure to cook us, then we shall remain in the caldron! Just as abandoned and profane men are always in quest of subtleties wherewith they may put down the heavenly doctrine, so they turned what was said by the prophets into the opposite: Well, then, we shall be thoroughly cooked, and shall therefore remain in Jerusalem onwards to extreme age" (CALV.).—"Impenitent sinners delight themselves in their sins, and do not suffer themselves, in the midst of their ungodly conduct, to dream of anything but pure good fortune, Jer. v. 12" (O.).—"In this way reason is accustomed always to drive all judgments out of the mind, or to comfort itself with the thought how it is quite able to withstand them by means of the flesh" (BERL. BIB.).—"Now-a-days still there are certain men who love to make the word of God contradict itself" (LUTHER).

Ver. 4. They are against the prophets, and therefore prophecy is against them, and that without regard of their persons, or of the multitude at their back. Our prophet mentions the ringleaders even by name. How indelicate! how imprudent! how defiant! Is it not? But with God's word at our back, we have the Almighty Himself at our back, and God's servants are neither to be dumb dogs nor flatterers of men.—"Son of man" the prophet remains notwithstanding; his is the weakness, the power is God's.—"God does not suffer Himself to be mocked, Gal. vi. 7" (STARCK).—Ver. 5. "It is not the commissioned servants that speak, but the Spirit of their Father, Matt. x. 20. He is the Preacher, they are merely the voice, John i. 23" (BERL. BIB.).—What rises up out of the heart of man (Matt. xv. 18, 19) is of such a nature that God must put a bridle on it; and this is just God's bridle, that the darkness is dragged to the light, and reproved by the light, Eph. v. 13.—"It is of no use, therefore, to make a show in the theatre of the world, even if the matter obtains the applause of men, because it goes at last before the heavenly tribunal, where God alone will be Judge. He knows our thoughts, and will not accept our subterfuges, nor allow Himself to be mocked by our subtleties. What men have held to be the highest wisdom, God will show them to be a vain conceit, and worthless" (CALV.).—Ver. 6 sq. God is in word and deed a righteous Judge. To that very point to which the counsel of the ungodly brings those who follow them, God brings the ungodly themselves in the end. He judges them according to their words, although not as they mean them.—The irony in the divine retribution.—The "caldron," the coffin.—The "flesh" is slaughtered; the "caldron" broken in pieces.—The retribution of God (1) attaches itself to the form of the sin, but (2) changes the substance of the sin into the substance of the punishment.—Ver. 8. "The sword, therefore, does not come by chance where it comes, but God's hand is in the matter" (BERL. BIB.).—Vers. 9–12. "He who will not bend his heart before God must bend his head to strangers" (STARCK).—"They had not chosen to know God from His word, and so they were now to learn to know Him, according to His word, from His works. If God's law does not enlighten so as to impart a knowledge that is saving, then must God's righteousness in judgment enlighten so as to impart a knowledge which is not saving" (LUTHER).—Vers. 13, 14. "If one will not listen to words, then God must speak by means of examples, which in that case call to us, Luke xiii. 3, 5" (BERL. BIB.).—"A sudden death in the case of the ungodly is the most terrible thing that can happen, 1 Thess. v. To the pious, on the other hand, who are always living in sight of death, even the most sudden death does not come unexpected" (LUTH.).—"Although the pious do not find fault with God's sentence, yet they look on the ruin of the ungodly with a sigh" (O.).—"When an angry father is going about in the house with a rod, even a dutiful child is afraid, falls at his feet, and pleads for his brothers and sisters: this a believer also does for the ungodly when God punishes them, Ex. xxxii." (STARKE).

Ver. 15. It is not the word "brother" that is of consequence, but what the word expresses, and therefore it is repeated; and just as little is it the dwelling together that is of consequence, but their being one with each other (ver. 19) is the reality of brotherhood.—1 John v. 16: There is a sin unto death, for which one is not to pray.—What the inhabitants of Jerusalem say reminds one of the manner of speaking of many in the "only-saving" Church, as well as of many who fancy that they are "the community of the faithful."—Comp. the Pharisee, Luke xviii. 11.—But the meek shall inherit the land, Matt. v.—"There is a passage here which is worth noting, that we may learn not to estimate the state of the Church according to the common judgment of men, nor according to the glitter, which for the most part dazzles the eyes of the simple. For thus it comes about that we suppose we have found the Church where there is no Church, and are in despair when it does not present itself before our eyes. Rather are we to hold fast by this, that frequently the Church is preserved in a wonderful way in secret; and farther, that members of the Church are not those puffed-up people who impose upon fools, but rather the common people, whom no one regards" (CALV.).—Ver. 16. The exile a Jewish school, in which the Jews (1) may learn the spirit of the temple, (2) may be prepared for the Spirit of Christ, (3) might have been educated in the spirit of true Christianity.—Vers. 17–20. True return home is return to the true God.—Ver. 18. "The true cleansing of the Church has taken place under the New Covenant; the perfect cleansing will take place on the day of harvest, at the last judgment."—"True reformation of life must show itself by earnest hatred of what is evil, Ps. cxix. 128" (STARCK).—Vers. 19, 20. "To the one heart belonged the outward union of the tribes under *one* name (Jews), the unity of endeavour on the part of all to return to Canaan, the unity in the doctrine of Moses, their unanimity against all idolatry, etc. From the stone we may take the following properties: that it is hard, deaf, fixed, etc. The flesh, on the other hand, is soft, moveable, receives impressions, feels pain and blows" (STARCK).—The grace of God makes man again natural, human; before he is unnatural, inhuman.—"For true Christianity it is not enough to perform this and that other act of outward worship, at times even to do what is good, but one must become another man" (STARKE).—"It is not merely gross idolatry that is to be rejected, but everything that is at variance with the word of God" (LUTHER).—Ver. 21. "The walk after the heart of the idols stands opposed to the walk after the heart of God" (HENGST.).—"The fountain of all evil is to be sought nowhere else but in the innermost depth of the heart, Matt. xv. 19" (STARKE).

Ver. 22. Jesus lifts up His hands (Luke xxiv. 50), and departs in the act of blessing; here, on the other hand, the uplifted wings announced the outpouring of the curse. The Mount of Olives on both occasions, the contrast and the predictive type.—The life of Jesus in decisive moments, and the glory of the Lord in Ezekiel.

2. THE SIGNS (CH. XII. 1-20).

1. *The Sign of the King's Departure* (vers. 1-16).

1, 2 And the word of Jehovah came unto me, saying, Son of man, thou dwellest
in the midst of the house of rebelliousness, who have eyes to see, and they see
not; and they have ears to hear, and they hear not: for they are an house of
3 rebelliousness. And thou, son of man, make thee [therefore make thee, thou son of man]
baggage of the emigrant, and remove by day before their eyes. And thou shalt
remove from thy place to another place before their eyes,—perhaps they will
4 see?—for they are an house of rebelliousness. And thou shalt bring forth thy
baggage as baggage of the emigrant by day before their eyes. Yet thou shalt
5 go forth at even before their eyes, like the removals of the emigrant. Before
6 their eyes break thee through the wall, and bring forth thereby. Before their
eyes shalt thou lift up upon thy shoulder, in the darkness shalt thou bring
forth; thou shalt cover thy face, and thou shalt not see the land: for as a
7 wonder-sign have I given thee to the house of Israel. And I did so as I was
commanded; my baggage brought I forth, as baggage of the emigrant, by
day, and at even I dug through with my hand; in the darkness brought I
8 forth, I lifted up upon my shoulder before their eyes. And the word of
9 Jehovah came unto me early in the morning, saying, Son of man, said they
not unto thee, the house of Israel, the house of rebelliousness, What doest
10 thou? Say unto them, Thus saith the Lord Jehovah: The prince is this
lifting up [ver. 7] in Jerusalem, and the whole house of Israel that [are] among
11 them [or, therein]. Say, I am your wonder-sign; as I have done, so shall it be
12 done unto them; into banishment, into captivity they shall go. And the
prince who is in their midst, to his shoulder shall he lift up, in the dark, then
shall he go forth; through the wall shall they break to bring forth thereby;
he shall cover his face, because he shall not see with his eye, he [shall not see] the
13 land. And I spread My net over him, and he is taken in My snare; and I
bring him to Babylon, the land of the Chaldeans; and he shall not see it,
14 and there shall he die. And all that are round about him, his help and all
his forces, will I scatter toward every wind, and a sword will I draw out after
15 them. And they know that I am Jehovah, when I disperse them among the
16 nations, and scatter them in the countries. And I leave over of them men
of number, from the sword, from the famine, and from the pestilence, in order
that they may declare all their abominations among the heathen, whither they
come; and they know that I am Jehovah.

2. *The Sign of Bread and Water* (vers. 17-20).

17, 18 And the word of Jehovah came unto me, saying, Son of man, eat thy
bread with quaking, and drink thy water with trembling and with anxiety.
19 And say unto the people of the land, Thus saith the Lord Jehovah of the
inhabitants of Jerusalem on the soil of Israel: They shall eat their bread with
anxiety, and drink their water in pain, that her land may become waste

20 from its fulness, because of the violence of all the dwellers in it. And the cities, the inhabited ones, shall be laid waste, and the land shall become desolate; and ye know that I am Jehovah.

Ver. 2. Sept.: . . . ἐν μεσω των ἀδικιων αὐτων—
Ver. 3. Sept.: . . . ὁπως ἴδωσιν διοτι —
Ver. 6. . . . ἐπ' ὠμων ἀναληφθησῃ κ. κεκρυμμενος ἐξελευσῃ—
Ver. 7. . . . κ. κεκρ. ἐξηλθον, ἐπ' ὠμ. ἀνεληφθην—
Ver. 10. Sept.: . . . ταδε λεγει . . . εἰπον τῳ ἀρχοντι κ. τῳ ἀφηγουμενῳ ἐν . . . κ. παντι οἰκῳ—
Ver. 11. . . . εἰπον· ὁτι ἐγω τερατα ποιω ἐν μεσω αὐτης. (Another reading: יעשה לכם, Syr.)
Ver. 12. . . . ἐπ' ὠμων ἀρθησεται κ. κεκρ. ἐξελευσεται δια τ. τοιχου, κ. διορυξει του ἐξελθειν αὐτον δι' αὐτου—
Ver. 19. For ארצה there is a reading: ארצם and ארץ without the suffix. For מְמל' there is a reading: ומלאה.

EXEGETICAL REMARKS.

The visions in ch. viii.-xi. have the connection we have seen with the vision in ch. i. Ch. xii. now, in the first place, takes up what is said in ch. ii. and iii., in order afterwards to give us, in close connection with ch. iv. v., the continuation of the prophet's discourse in the language of signs. If we take ch. viii. sq. along with ch. iv. sq., then we get information about the siege, the taking of Jerusalem, and we are made acquainted, not only generally, but in detail, with the destiny of the inhabitants. The fate of the distinguished popular leaders (ch. xi.) offers the most natural transition *to the person of the king in its meaning for the whole.* If, moreover, what has hitherto been referred to from ch. iii. 24 onwards was transferred *inter parietes*, then so much the more strikingly does the prophet now step *abroad.*

Ver. 2. Comp. on ch. ii. 5 sq., iii. 26 sq. The description of the state of the exiles is kept in accordance with what they have seen (especially ch. iv. v.) and also heard (ch. xi. 25). Thus it is with them at the time, while at another time, which the promise has in view, it is to be as in ch. xi. 16 sq. Comp. Isa. vi. 9, 10; Jer. v. 21. The reason given is the universal and all-pervading rebelliousness (different from Deut. xxix. 3 [4]). Hence in Ver. 3, "*perhaps* they will see;" and because of this possibility, which would not be supposed in the case of hardening in consequence of judgment, Ezekiel is to perform the sign in question **before their eyes** (repeated). כִּי' is, just because of the parallel close of ver. 2, not to be rendered by "that" (HITZ.). The thing meant also is merely "seeing" (*i.e.* in the sense of hearing how it will happen to them), and not by any means comprehending what they are. We are to think of a question implying doubt, whose doubtful purport, and along with that (or merely in general) the action commanded, is supported by a reason. — גּוֹלָה, "emigration" (HENGST.: "the emigrants," an ideal gathering into one of the emigrants), consequently utensils such as are usual in a case of the kind,—not simply travelling gear, as hat, staff, bag (Matt. x. 9, 10), but rather vessels for food and drink, household furniture, as distinguished from personal apparatus for a journey. Hence עָשָׂה is not: "to make," or: "to furnish oneself with" (KLIEF.), but equivalent to: "to put together" (comp. ver. 4). גּוֹלָה (Jer. xlvi. 19) is immediately explained, **but,** as the more detailed definitions which follow show, the explanation is kept general. Comp. on ver. 6. The emigration is specified as regards its starting point and goal.—In favour of the objective reality of the action to be performed, the remarks made on ch. iv. v., as against HÄVERN., HITZ., HENGST., have a still more pointed application in the present case.

Ver. 4. The bringing forth of his household stuff, so far as it can be taken with him, describes more fully the "make thee," etc. of ver. 3; and it becomes clear at the same time how the expression there, וּגְלֵה יוֹמָם, must be understood, viz. of the beginning of the emigration, of the first preparation for it. Lastly, יוֹמָם is explained, by means of בָּעֶרֶב, as meaning the daytime in its most proper sense; and the prophet's own migrating from his dwelling-place is characterized in the most definite way, in contrast with a mere journey, by the expression כְּמוֹצָאֵי גוֹלָה (comp. on ver. 6), a comparison which Hävern. considers applicable to the time of departure alone. Comp. Hengst. on Mic. v. 1. His rendering here is: "as emigrants go forth," in the costume and garb of emigrants, combining, as he does, "bag on shoulder, staff in hand," with their being "sad, and their heads drooping" (Num. xxxiii. 2).—Ver. 5 describes more minutely the bringing forth of the stuff in question (ver. 4). The prophet is to break for himself a hole for the purpose (וְהוֹצֵאתָ, as in ver. 4) in the wall, *i.e.* of course, of his house, perhaps a clay wall; for were it to be the city wall of Tel-Abib, as Hengstenberg, in the interest of his "subjectivity" of the symbolic action, asserts, thereby throwing into confusion the occurrence and the text, then it must, especially with this detailed description here, have been expressed more definitely. Hengstenberg makes Ezekiel bring his baggage as far as the city wall, and when the darkness came on, break a hole through it, etc. The text, on the other hand, makes the breaking through of a hole in the house wall (instead of the usual exit by the house door), for bringing forth the stuff, take place, like the bringing forth itself (ver. 4), before their eyes, consequently in clear daylight, since the taking up upon the shoulder (ver. 6), though happening also "before their eyes," has to take place (comp. ver. 4) "at even," both as distinguished from בַּעֲלָטָה (עֲלָטָה, from עָלַט, the restrained light), *in thick darkness* (Gen. xv. 17). It may be taken for granted that Ezekiel, with this breaking through, for which he is not forbidden to use a tool, will have the whole day to do it. Neither Klief. nor Keil has correctly apprehended the course of the action. As Ver. 6 portrays sufficiently the departure of Ezekiel himself, when he puts his goods and chattels on his shoulder, there is no need for understanding the Hiphil תוציא intransitively, or for supplying נַפְשְׁךָ. Moreover, by the expression is meant the emigration with bag and baggage from his own place to "another" (ver. 3); hence the complete departure, as distinguished from וְהוֹצֵאתָ, like תֵּצֵא and וְהוֹצֵאתָ in ver. 4. It corresponds to the darkness about him that he is to cover his face besides; and in this way the expression כְּמוֹצָאֵי גוֹלָה (ver. 4) is explained for us, inasmuch as emigrants' departures usually take place with shame and sorrow, which do not allow themselves to be seen, and which will no longer cast a look on the home that is to be forsaken (2 Sam. xv. 30). Yet the land which he is not to see (comp. vers. 12, 13) is perhaps still more that to which he is going forth. Hence vers. 5 and 6 are two parallel (לְעֵינֵיהֶם—לְעֵינֵיהֶם) and more minutely descriptive statements as regards ver. 4.—מוֹפֵת (either from יָפָה, "something shining," similar to the derivation of the German "Wunder" (miracle), or from an assumed root יָפַת, what is suddenly "turned," singularly "twisted," "turned away" from what is usual), therefore, not merely אוֹת, simply a significant sign, but specially a sign of a *divine* sort, and that, in the sense of our context, equivalent to τύπος, Ps. lxxi. 7. In this word there meet together the superhuman (miraculous) character alike of the purport and of the cause, the surprising character of the spectacle, as well as the manner of working of the astonishment and the typical object in view.

In Ver. 7 Ezekiel reports as to his execution of the divine command, whose objective reality Keil admits in the case before us. The report of the prophet is a recapitulation, in which the points of *time* (**by day, at even, in the darkness**) form the salient points, to which, without keeping up the order of succession as to the rest (since this is certainly contained in the preceding command of God, according to which Ezekiel acted), the detail *with reference to the interpretation* (of the symbolical action) *which follows* is attached. As in what follows the double reference—to the people as a whole, and to the prince in particular—comes out, so Ezekiel makes prominent in his report, (1) what is the thing which is impending over them in general (**my baggage,** etc., **as emigrants' baggage, by day**), and (2) in what way the prince personally gets out, viz. by breaking through in the night-time. Accordingly, because of the significance attached to the digging through the wall, which may possibly be indicated even in ver. 5 by the expression חֲתָר־לְךָ, and which becomes complete only when the prophet himself comes through the hole in the wall, he connects his day's work with his own departure at even. בְּיָד is meant to express in general the idea: *with my own hand*, as contrasted with the help of others. The emphasis lies on the personal element in the action. As distinguished from: **I brought forth . . . by day,** the expression: **I brought forth in the darkness,** refers to the removing from out of the dwelling-place. לְעֵינֵיהֶם at the close adjusts the execution of the command to the object in view, and at the same time to the explanation which follows; and for this reason the thing which lies nearest and is still visible, although occurring before the complete "darkness" of the departure properly so called, viz. the taking up upon the shoulder at even, is mentioned. The transaction is (and this is also Umbreit's view) to be conceived of in this way: the elders (ch. viii.) might have left the house of the prophet. In accordance with what has been remarked at the commencement of the chapter, the impression made by Ezekiel's disclosures (ch. xi. 25) may have been but slight, or not lasting. Just then a hole is opened in the wall of his house, ever growing wider and wider. It is easily understood how the multitude gathers from curiosity. Perhaps late in the afternoon of the day, what a man can carry of household furniture is brought out through the opening in the wall. At even the prophet himself steps forth, loads himself with the emigrant's baggage, and takes his departure, with his head covered, in the midst of total darkness, etc., from Tel-Abib for some other place.

Ver. 8 assigns the divine word of interpretation to the early morning of next day. Comp. 2 Chron. xxxvi. 15.—Ver. 9. הֲלֹא (as against Klief., who does not admit a question at all) presupposes that they have asked Ezekiel for the meaning of what he has done. By means of the expression: **house of Israel**, the exiles are put on an equal footing with those in Jerusalem; just as by means of the expression: **the house of rebelliousness** (see on ver. 2), they are at the same time characterized as regards their disposition while putting the question. Therefore Ezekiel is, in reply to what they have said unto him, in Ver. 10 to say unto them what Jehovah says. He has answered them the evening before by silence (ch. iii. 27), and has merely done as he was commanded (ver. 7).—הַנָּשִׂיא, either passively: "he who has been lifted up" or: "he who lifts himself up."—Hengst.: "one on whom something is laid, who is burdened with the government, which he bears, as it were, on his shoulder," Isa. ix. 6 (?)—as בִּירוּשָׁלַם shows, the king (ch. vii. 27) Zedekiah. There is an unmistakable play upon the word הַנָּשִׂיא in הַמַּשָּׂא, which (likewise derived from נָשָׂא) means: **the lifting up**, and, without our being obliged with all the expositors to think of the meaning "sentence" (judicial utterance of God) or "burden" (threatening prediction), as elsewhere, refers simply to the statement (ver. 7): עַל כָּתֵף נָשָׂאתִי, which paves the way for the interpretation. Comp. the Syriac translation. Hence the meaning is: this lifting up on the shoulder of emigrants' stuff on my part means the prince. The meaning is not (as Hengst.): "prince and burden, as it were, cover each other," so that he is wholly swallowed up by misfortune, the crushing burden leaves nothing of him remaining; but this: the prince is what the prophet represents by his action. The exalted personage in Jerusalem, still seated on a regal throne, and this lifting up of mere emigrants' baggage, impressively confront each other. Thus a day, an evening, a night changes everything! [Commonly (and so Eng. Vers.): the prince is the subject of this burden or of this sentence. HITZIG refers to Jer. xxiii. 33; but KLIEFOTH: this burden-bearing, undertaken as a sign, concerns the prince and the house of Israel (as accusatives!). EWALD: "O thou crown-bearer of this burden in Jerusalem, and those of the whole house of Israel who are in its midst!" הַנָּשִׂיא being imagined to be in the construct state to what follows.] Because emigration is to be the common lot, the people are added to the king, and in fact **the whole house of Israel** (according to the older expositors: those out of the ten tribes who had fled to Jerusalem), among whom, especially as having already emigrated, the fellow-exiles of Ezekiel are included (בְּתוֹכָם, like אֲשֶׁר, referring to the **house of Israel**); or better, because of what follows, as Hengstenberg does, referring the suffix to Jerusalem or its inhabitants, inasmuch as there was yet another house of Isrel, ch. xi. 15.—Quite evidently he speaks now of the fate of the whole in Ver. 11. With the expression: "*your* wonder-sign," the exiles (in conformity with ver. 6), for whom it is meant in the first place, are addressed; while לָהֶם refers to those at Jerusalem, hence also, perhaps, הֵמָּה in ver. 10.—כֵּן יֵעָשֶׂה לָהֶם might also mean: so will it be done by them. In any case it is an explanation of what precedes. בַּגּוֹלָה בַשְּׁבִי, an emphatic asyndeton: it will be no voluntary, but a compulsory emigration.

Ver. 12. The king specially. אֲשֶׁר בְּתוֹכָם, the reference being undoubted, confirms the interpretation we have preferred of אֲשֶׁר־הֵמָּה בְּתוֹכָם. So also אֶל־כָּתֵף יִשָּׂא confirms our view of וְיָצָא.—הַנָּשִׂיא הַמַּשָּׂא הַזֶּה, **then**, etc., lingering over the picture of the moment. Keil, like Klief., against the accents: "he will lift it up in the darkness and will go forth." יַחְתְּרוּ, *i.e.* the attendants, his suite. (ROSENM.: in order to bring him forth.) The prediction of what is recorded as having happened some years later (Jer. xxxix. lii.; 2 Kings xxv.). As the lifting up upon the shoulder of the baggage does not necessarily indicate any selfish grasping at the valuables, but may symbolize the emigration, so the breaking through the wall does not necessarily mean this in a literal sense but the haste and hurry of the flight by the speediest available route; and just as little have we to prove the covering of his face to be historical. Besides, the latter was among the circumstances, as is understood of itself, suggested by prudence even; pain or shame is not to be thought of at all. Comp. on ver. 6. Certainly there was yet another object in view beyond that, which had influence, as is expressed in Ver. 13. לַעַיִן and the הוּא placed after it draw attention to something peculiar, and אֶת־הָאָרֶץ is the land of the Chaldeans. (Ver. 13.) The being taken prisoner,—in addition to the emigration (ver. 11),—which the prophet had not prefigured, is depicted by means of the figurative mode of speech borrowed from the catching of fish, from the chase (Isa. xix. 8; Jer. xvi. 16). In spite of his hasty, violent flight, he does not escape his fate; like the darkness of night, the holy penal order of the Judge and Avenger in heaven is laid around him. Umbreit, who views the breaking through the wall as a breaking forth from the city perforated by the enemy, finds in the circumstance that the king shall not see the land of the Chaldeans, his full and complete imprisonment expressed.—**To Babylon**, etc., is the "other place" of ver. 3.—In how far the king would not see the land where he was to die, must remain incomprehensible for so long, until the blinding (a common punishment with the Persians, and probably also with the Babylonians, for the dethroned) of Zedekiah at Riblah, after he had been caught in his nocturnal flight not far from Jericho, by the Chaldeans, made it palpable to the senses.

Ver. 14. What is **round about him** may be the attendants fleeing along with the king, and **his help** may perhaps be the hoped-for Egyptian help. עֶזְרָה (עֶזְרוֹ) is a play upon words with אזרה. אֲגַפִּים, only in the plural, and peculiar to Ezekiel; according to Gesen.: "wings" (Isa. viii. 8); according to Hitzig: "bands," the whole military power, with which a king stands or falls. Comp. Jer. xl. 7, 12, lii. 8. We may compare besides, ch. v. 2, 10, 12.—Ver. 15. Ch. v. 13, vi. 8.—Ver. 16. Ch. vi. 8. **Men of number**—HITZIG: that may be counted. Few in comparison with ver. 14.—Comp. on ch. v. vi.—Narrators of their guilt with the knowledge gained from experience of the holy punitive justice of God. [Rosenm., Hitzig, and others refer the refrain thus repeated to the heathen! Klief. translates: "count," that they shall ponder their sins one by one thoroughly!]

The *second* and connected *sign* which is introduced in Ver. 17, like the preceding one in ver. 1, but which has along with it its divine interpretation without an introduction, as is the case in ver. 8, depicts (with an allusion to ch. iv. 16) *the misery of the inhabitants*, just as the interpretation by the word of Jehovah (similarly to ch. vi. 14) announces *the misery of the land* inhabited by them.—Ver. 18. **Bread** and **water**, not exactly scanty food (KLIEF.), but merely the food that is necessary. The significant thing, however, is the **quaking, trembling**, and **anxiety** which the prophet's expression of countenance, appearance, and demeanour must have expressed during the carrying out of the divine command (which is not indeed narrated, because understood as a matter of course). **The people of the land** in Ver. 19, those addressed, are the poor, wretched Jewish people in Chaldea (vers. 12, 13); according to Cocc., the message is meant for the heathen, that these might not ascribe the fate of the Jews to their Bel, inasmuch as Jehovah has caused it to be represented three years before by Ezekiel.—Comp. besides ver. 10. **The inhabitants of Jerusalem** may possibly be (in accorddance with ch. xi. 15) those who at the time were still there, although in the condition during the impending siege (so Hengst.). But in connection with the preceding sign they are rather the poorest remnants of the people still remaining **on the soil of Israel** (אֲדָמָה, comp. on ch. vii. 2) after the flight of the king and the leading captive of the people, Jer. xxxix. 10, lii. 16. And such an explanation corresponds also with what follows. לְמַעַן (ch. iv. 17) is meant (according to Hitzig) to be a particle assigning the reason: because their land, stripped of its fulness, will become stiff; that is to say, their torpid amazement mirrors forth the motionless stiffening of the land. Certainly with more correctness, and more in accordance with the context: their misery will cause the land's also (אַרְצָהּ, *i.e.* Jerusalem's), which is the design of Jehovah; they will in their anxiety and anguish content themselves with mere necessaries (bread and water), and not cultivate its fruitfulness, etc. According to the other explanation, the invasion of the enemy will leave the land waste behind them. Comp. besides ch. vii. 23, viii. 17.—Ver. 20. Ch. vi. 6.—Cocc. (comp. above) refers the clause: "and ye know," etc., to the heathen, the Chaldeans, just as in ver. 16.

DOCTRINAL REFLECTIONS.

1. When Stephen (according to Acts vii. 51) brings the charge against the Jews, that they were always resisting (*ἀντιπίπτειν*—using this strong and, in the New Testament, unusual expression) the Holy Ghost, that they, like their fathers, were stiffnecked and uncircumcised in heart and ears, we need not, with the expositors since Hävernick, fall back upon Deut. xxix. 3 [4]; and this the less, as the meaning is certainly somewhat different in this so-called fundamental passage. In Isa. vi. 9, 10 it may be made use of as a text; Ezekiel, like Jeremiah (ch. v. 21 sq.), has to do with the bad national character of the Jewish people. The "perverse will" is brought into special prominence by both prophets, as Hävernick remarks, continuing as follows: "a feature which runs through their whole history, down to the appearance of the Redeemer." But who will be able to deny that in this way, in the bad character of the Jews as a nation, the corrupt nature of fallen humanity as a whole is portrayed? This people have merely exhibited it carried to its farthest consequences, inasmuch as they were placed in a position, by means of the law and the prophets, and lastly God's Son, where they must either let their wills be broken or ruin themselves. But then, farther, as the Jews are a standing historical decision with respect to natural men, so, on the other hand, in contrast with their national character (here also: "perhaps they will see?"), we have mirrored forth all the riches of divine longsuffering and patience. "Ye would not,"—this on the one hand; but on the other: "how often would I have gathered thy children together!" (Matt. xxiii. 37.) The mirror of human perversity is at the same time the mirror of divine grace, Rom. v. 20.

2. "If any one is so far enlightened that he is able to see and understand what is necessary, then it may be said that he has eyes to see, etc. The natural (unregenerate) man perceiveth not, etc. (1 Cor. ii. 14). But any one may also be so far enlightened that he sees much, and by this means he may be brought to see what is necessary to be seen; and especially that he recognises the word which contains the true wisdom as being God's word. Those who have come this length may, however, neither see nor hear what is necessary to be seen and heard, in so far as they cannot rightly judge of what they see and hear, through the opposition of their fleshly wisdom, which perverts God's words. Such parties no longer err in the usual way, but are hardened, so that they fancy their error is God's word. They are also difficult to cure. The cause of one's not understanding God's word is disobedience. For fleshly wisdom and the love of it is in truth disobedience" (Cocc.).

3. From the importance which is attached in the history of the Jews, in a good as well as a bad sense, yea, in the highest sense (*i.e.* the Messianic), to the king, in asking whom (1 Sam.) the people at first expressed their wish to be "like the other nations," we can understand the express symbolical representation, in this special and preeminent way, of the fate of Zedekiah. "The mass of mischief is concentrated first of all in the king," for which Hävernick adduces as a farther reason "the existing circumstances," among which "the political faithlessness and dishonesty of the king, as well as his anti-theocratic conduct, his idolatry, his mockery of all prophetic warnings and threatenings," were prominent, "although he was in Jerusalem and among the exiles the idol of trust." Hengst. in this connection designates the king as "the centre of their dreams of the future, which were preventing repentance."

4. The prediction in our chapter—of which Tholuck (*The Prophets and their Predictions*, p. 108) gives the following estimate, that "against the prophetic character of the passage no critical objection is raised from any quarter; the genuineness of the book and the integrity of the passage are beyond a doubt; that divergent interpretations found no place; and that reference is made merely to its fulfilment according to the authentic testimony of history"—ought properly to have been removed from all the attempts at half or wholly naturalistic interpretation, by the repeated divine explanation that it is a "mopheth" (see the explanation of the word at ver. 6). Nevertheless, while Eichhorn and Hitzig decree simply a prophecy after the event, and while Ewald makes it out that the prophet had happy presages, correct foresight, Umbreit attempts as far as possible to keep the text free from what might press us to the acceptance of a supernatural prediction. On the other hand, Josephus even (*Antiq.* x. 10. 11) has in his mind our prophetic testimony when he tells us how Zedekiah may not have been able to give credence to Ezekiel, because he said that the king would not see Babylon, whereas Jeremiah had prophesied to him that he would be carried captive thither. To Nitzsch, the prediction of occurrences resting on divine communication is neither so impossible as Cicero asserted it, nor so useless or even hurtful as Kant attempted to

show. The prediction sustains interest in this way, by announcing a result which could not have been known beforehand by any human means. Even in the case where the foreknowledge is of no use, it may yet awaken a wholesome attention, and, confirmed by the result, it may, by producing a testimony for persons and affairs, come to serve important ends in other directions. J. D. Michaelis holds the view that the exact announcement beforehand was of service against the *communis sensus* of polytheism at the time, when even among the Jews the faith in one God alone kept its ground only in a sickly way, as being to every one an easily understood and irrefragable confirmation of the true religion. One may have recourse to the genius of great minds, their far-reaching historical glance in certain cases; may lay stress upon the secret power of divination in the human mind, the connection of the human conscience with the judicial steps of the moral order of the world (HERZOG, *Realencycl.* xvii. 640 sq.); but what Ezekiel here expresses in symbol, he knows he has received from Jehovah's mouth, and every criticism of this consciousness runs the risk either of accusing the prophet of self-deception, or even of making him a hypocritical deceiver, especially where a chapter like the 13th follows.

HOMILETIC HINTS.

Ver. 1 sq.: "We ought not, therefore, to allow ourselves to be deterred either by the view that we ourselves and the doctrine which we teach would be rejected, or even by the impression that we would be engaged in something ridiculous" (CALV.).—"Rebelliousness does not spring from weakness, but from wickedness" (STCK.).—"How many there are who are sharpsighted in earthly and temporal things, and who know how to turn everything prudently to their own advantage, but who, on the other hand, in what is spiritual, are found to the last degree blind and stupid, as well as incapable of faith! Hence they have ears likewise to hearken to what pleases the flesh, and to the talk and lies of the false prophets, but they have no ears to hear God's voice. They hear and hear, but not with obedience and faith" (BERL. BIB.).—"They had ears to hear, because from youth up they were instructed in the law of God, and the threatenings were held up before them by the prophets" (CALV.).—The natural blindness and deafness of man in spiritual things causing God to proclaim His word. The wilful blindness and intentional deafness of him who yields to God with suffering and affliction. The blindness and deafness which God hangs as punishment over the hardened sinner. —Ver. 3 sq. "Perhaps they will see?" Thus God leaves nothing untried: this is the exercise of His long-suffering and patience.—"When we see that others are falling into misfortune, trouble, adversity, we ought to reflect: This is a sign to me, and ought to apply it to our own improvement, Luke xiii. 2, 3" (WÜRTEMB. BIB.).—Ver. 5. "What fear can do! For it no door was high enough or broad enough; in their flight they ofttimes squeeze themselves through the most miserable wretched hole" (STCK.).—Ver. 6. The earthly mind will see only the earth—nay, such an one will at length become earth; yet, when the eye is darkened, and the gloom of death covers everything, he will no longer see even the earth. —Ver. 7. "Such things would call to mind the days of Noah and Lot" (CALV.).

Ver. 8. God's grace is new every morning. They who seek Him early find Him; and those who ask after Him will be answered by Him.—Ver. 9. There is something precious about a right question.—Ver. 10. "Princes are called exalted, but certainly not because they are to exalt themselves; for He that is enthroned in heaven knows how to humble princes even" (STCK.).—"Every ruler, prince, or king, however little he may have taken up upon his shoulders, will at least be compelled to bear the burden of his sins and the wrath of God, which will fall heavily enough upon him, provided the burden of his duties has been sitting easily upon him" (BERL. BIB.).—"God does not overlook the mighty even when they sin, but makes them feel His heavy hand" (STARKE). —God's judgment on a land embraces prince and people alike, although a people may also have God's judgment already in their prince, and a prince may have it in his people.—Ver. 12. "The ungodly walk about with a bold countenance, but in the judgment they will conceal it" (STCK.). —Ver. 13. First the net of pleasure and vanity, then the net of death and hell.—"He that lives wildly is hunted and taken like the wild beasts" (STCK.).—God a fisher and hunter.—Ver. 14. "Of what avail to the sinner all his imagined succours and pretended helpers?" (STCK.)—We will by and by withdraw our confidence from all creatures.—The Eternal blew, and the Armada was scattered to all the winds of heaven.—"If God is our enemy, we have no friend in heaven or upon earth" (STCK.).—Ver. 15. Alas that we should become wise only by injury, and should come to know God only from experience of punishment, instead of tasting and thus seeing how good the Lord is!—Ver. 16. Thus it is that God receives honour because of His righteousness, when His grace is despised.—"God blesses the chastisements which He sends forth upon His people to unbelievers also" (STARKE).

Ver. 18. "Only those who have their standing in grace can eat their bread without fear and carefulness" (STARKE).—It is not in vain that Christ has taught us the petition: Give us this day our daily bread.—"A verse which we may read with profit in the midst of plenty" (STCK.). —Ver. 19. "That one is able to eat and drink in rest and peace is a great benefit from God, but one that is not known by the thousandth part of men" (STARKE).—"Jerusalem and her inhabitants are eloquent orators, and preach with unction" (STCK.).—Ver. 20. "If one will not learn to know God from His benefits, then he must often do so in the midst of punishment, Dan. iv. 30, 31" (STARKE).—Thus the wilderness was Israel's school, and became Israel's judgment.

3. The Near Execution of the Punishment (Ch. xii. 21—xxiv. 27).

1. *The Repeated Preliminary Announcement* (ch. xii. 21-28).

21, 22 And the word of Jehovah came unto me, saying, Son of man, what [meaneth]
this proverb of yours upon the land of Israel, saying, The days are pro-
23 longed; and every vision comes to nought? Say unto them therefore, Thus
saith the Lord Jehovah: I will make this proverb to cease, and they shall no
more use it as a proverb in Israel: but speak unto them, The days are at
24 hand, and the word of every vision. For there shall be no more any vision
25 of deceit nor flattering divination in the midst of the house of Israel. For
I, Jehovah, will speak whatever word I will speak, and it will [shall] come to
pass; it shall be no more prolonged, for [but] in your days, O house of rebel-
liousness, I will speak a word, and perform it: sentence of the Lord Jehovah.
26, 27 And the word of Jehovah came unto me, saying, Son of man, behold the
house of Israel, who say, The vision that he seeth is for many days, and he
28 prophesieth for [of] times afar off. Therefore say unto them, Thus saith the
Lord Jehovah: There shall none of my words be prolonged any more; the
word which I shall speak shall be done: sentence of the Lord Jehovah.

Ver. 24. Sept.: . . . *και μαντευομενος τα προς χαριν.*—(Another read.: ומקסם חדל, and divination shall cease. בני יש', all the versions.)

EXEGETICAL REMARKS.

Announcement of the end as one that is near, and that repeated (ver. 26 sq.). For after the wind-up, as it were, which precedes, with the misery coming upon land and people, there remained only the announcement of the same, preliminary to its near occurrence. Hitherto it has been a going back upon ch. vi., now we have a return to what was said in ch. vii.

Ver. 22. Derived as it is from a verb meaning: to go before, to lead, to preside,—to represent something, to signify,—to pronounce a sentence, etc., מָשָׁל is equivalent to "maxim," the form being always that of similitude, proverb, derisive verse (Isa. xiv. 4). Here also not without the derisive element. The common saying, in which the current sentiment among those still dwelling in the land of Israel (ver. 19) had found for itself suitable expression (*beati possidentes*), derided the Eternal in His prophets by means of the comfort of the time, that the time is passing away, and what was alleged to be seen in vision is passing away with it; as nothing is coming out of it, so neither shall there be anything in it. The days that are being prolonged may refer to Jeremiah's long ago uttered prediction of ruin; comp. too on ch. xi. 3.—לָכֶם combines the prophet with the mockers, as being his people. On such fellowship of the servants of God with their people is based at last in a pre-eminent sense the relation of the incarnate Son of God to the human race (Ex. xvi. 28).—Ver. 23. הִשְׁבַּתִּי, prophetic preterite: "to bring to rest;" after the trouble they give themselves, their inventive labours, comes the Sabbath of Jehovah (Gen. ii. 1 sq.).—**Are at hand** (ch. ix. 1, xi. 3), in contrast with the preceding: "are prolonged."—וּדְבַר כָּל חָזוֹן, the verbal contents of every vision of His prophets,—the word, and the thing meant by the word. Keil rightly: the days in which every predicted word shall be realized. (Hengst: "as against a merely partial fulfilment, as if the prophets had exaggerated somewhat," etc.)—Ver. 24. As there is also a false (2 Pet. ii. 1) prophecy (שָׁוְא),—mere divination (מִקְסַם), which deceives in the way of flattery with its smoothness,—the divinely inspired prophecy is distinguished first of all from it, as the following contrast shows, and as will, of course, be shown still more in ch. xiii. **There shall be no more**, etc., is parallel with: "and they shall no more use it as a proverb in Israel" (ver. 23): that mocking proverb had taken shape with the help of the false prophecy in Israel. Hence in Ver. 25 a co-ordinate or resumed כִּי. The disjunctive accent (*rebii*) over יְהוָה makes "I Jehovah" a sentence by itself, so that the Author of true prophecy sets *Himself* face to face with the false. In like manner, *pashta* at the end of אֲדַבֵּר acts as a disjunctive, while the conjunctive *telisha-kethannah* with אֵת connects what follows. Jehovah reserves for Himself uncontrolled power to speak, and almighty power to make it good. And with this is joined the statement that there will be no farther delay, no longer postponement (with reference to that proverb): **in your days** (Matt. xvi. 28, xxiv. 34), therefore with a subjective, personal application. Such a fulfilment of the divine prediction will at the same time be the end of the false divination, which by this very means is covered with disgrace. In some sense also the **I Jehovah**, *as being Messianic*, is contrasted with preceding prophecy in general. Comp. besides on ver. 2, ch. xi. 8.

In Ver. 27 there follows the more objective application, referring to the matter itself. The statement that if there is a prophecy at all that will yet be fulfilled, it at all events refers **to times** that are far off (Dan. viii. 26, 17), is rejected by the Lord as regards Ezekiel. Before it was a mockery of Jehovah, here we have a mockery of His prophet rather in the words quoted.—Ver. 28. See as to the feminine תִּמָּשֵׁךְ here, as in ver. 25, EWALD, *Gram.* § 295*a*.

DOCTRINAL REFLECTIONS.

1. The significance of prophecy and its fulfilment for the divine credibility of the prophetic testimonies, and thus of Holy Scripture generally, has been understood by Apologetics from the beginning. See Keith's *Evidence of the Truth of the Christian Religion derived from the Literal Fulfilment of Prophecy.* Besides, already in Deut. xviii. 21, 22, the fulfilment of what has been predicted is put as a characteristic mark of genuine prophecy.

2. If the absolute and almighty power which God attributes to Himself in the section before us, as contrasted with false divination, is our creed, then the word of prophecy ranks with the word of creation, and what serves as an argument for the divine sovereignty in the latter connection is not less an argument in the former. By the word of the Eternal were the heavens made, and all the host of them by the breath of His mouth (Ps. xxxiii. 6). The living God is also the law of prophecy as regards its fulfilment.

3. What is accepted as true of the divine power in Creation comes to be applied for the fulfilment of prophecy still more by faith in Divine Providence, the co-operation and government of God. The Eternal ("Jehovah," ver. 25) is not merely the God of the beginning and the end, of the origin and the goal, but also He who is co-existent with the life of the world and specially of mankind. It is the divine element in and mixed up with the history of the world with which prophecy has to do. But this is not merely the eternal idea, which is continually realizing itself anew, so that what refers to time and place would in comparison with it have to be regarded as the mere form of representation, but this divine element is alike the real which is predicted, and the necessary which is prophesied. As respects the divine decree, which because of sin has developed itself from the world-plan of the Creator into the counsel of salvation in Christ for the world, things small and great may be distinguished; but because both are serviceable in carrying out the decree of God, both alike are divine, and therefore suitable for prophecy.

4. It is of importance, however, as respects the delay, as respects the postponement, *e.g.* of the realization of the prophecies of judgment, that there is a correspondence between the prolonging of the days and the divine long-suffering and forbearance (2 Pet. iii. 9), as in the case before us in Ezekiel. The prophecy of judgment is besides a preaching of repentance, so that if it produces the repentance which it preaches, the fulfilment of the prophecy may be hindered. But even apart from such conditionality lying in the thing itself, other circumstances, always, however, willed by God, may give to a prophecy the character of perspective foreshortening.

5. "Prophecy was an act of faith; it likewise demanded faith. And as what true prophecy insisted on above all was conversion of heart, it resisted the sinful consciousness and life of unbelief, and was resisted by it (Amos vi. 3). It is the nature of sin to reckon itself to be no sin, and hence as far as possible to break up the connection and separate between sin and punishment" (HÄV.).

ADDITIONAL NOTE.

["We cannot but think with wonder, when we look back upon the times of these Old Testament prophets, of the obstinate incredulity and measureless content in which so many of the people seem to have shut themselves up, alike in defiance of the most solemn warnings of God, and in spite of several lowering appearances in Providence, which seemed to give no doubtful indications of a coming storm. . . . But it is well for us to bear in mind, that the spirit of unbelief and false security, which prevailed so extensively then, is ever springing forth anew, and is plainly announced in New Testament Scripture as destined to form a distinguishing characteristic of the last times. It was a significant question of our Lord, and evidently pointed to the great defect in this respect that should discover itself before the consummation of all things, 'When the Son of man comes, shall He find faith in the earth?' Such faith, namely, as He had been speaking of,—faith realizing in firm confidence the certainty of the Lord's manifestation to put a final end to the evils that afflict His Church, and in this confidence waiting, hoping, praying to the last. The apostle Peter also still more distinctly intimates in his second epistle what might be looked for: 'There shall come in the last days, scoffers, walking after their own lusts, and saying, Where is the promise of His coming? For since the fathers fell asleep, all things continue as they were from the beginning of the world.' It will readily be understood that the danger from this source to this faith of God's elect will always be the greater, the more the time is lengthened out that is to intervene between the first and second coming of the Lord. For time, which is justly said to try all things, in this respect also tries faith, that it silently impairs in men's minds the foundation on which faith rests—the word of God. In common with other things of meaner value, this, too, seems to wax old as time proceeds, and to become, the longer it is in use, the less in power and value. Even already it is looked upon by many as comparatively antiquated, out of date; the facts of which it testifies are but faintly descried in the distant past; centuries have rolled away since they took place and were put on record; and the record itself has been so long in existence, so frequently handled, and so fully discussed, that, with those to whom nothing is interesting but what possesses the freshness of novelty, the sacred volume, so far from being able to nourish and support a living faith, has itself become stale and dead.

"Thus it is that natural men judge of God's word, as if, like their own productions, it were subject to wasting and decay. They know not that this word of God, being the expression of His own eternal nature, has in it what lives and abides for ever,—what is as new and fresh to the heart of faith still, as the very moment when, ages ago, it proceeded from the lips of those who spake as they were moved by the Holy Ghost. Then, along with a prevailing ignorance or forgetfulness of this great truth, there is the fascinating influence which is apt to be wielded over men's minds by the onward movements of society in knowledge and civilisation. Here they find an attractive contrast to the stationary character of the ground and objects of faith. For everything in this lower field seems constantly in progress, and big with hope for the future. It is deemed incredible, that while such vital powers are at work, and such a career of advancement is in prospect, God should lay a sudden arrest on the vast machinery, and wind up the affairs of the world by bringing in the fixed and final issues of eternity. Nay, the belief of a personal God, separate from the workmanship of his own hands, and capable of suddenly introducing a state of things altogether new, is, in many quarters, fast giving way. In a new and peculiarly subtle form, the old carnal and idolatrous tendencies are reviving, impiously commingling the divine and human, identifying the creature with the Creator. And, judging from present appearances, there is too much reason to conclude that, precisely as before Christ came to execute judgment upon Jerusalem, a rage for *worldly saviours* was one of the reigning delusions of the time, so, as the period draws on for His coming to execute judgment upon the world, a like rage will prevail for a *worldly gospel*,—one that will seek to confound heaven and earth, God and man, and, in a manner, possibly even more daring and presumptuous than in the Papacy, will dispose man to 'exalt himself in the temple of God, and show himself that he is God.' What need, then, for those who would escape the condemnation of the wicked, to look well to the foundation of their faith, and to see that this stands not in the wisdom of man, but in the word of God! How careful should each be to dwell beside the fountain of Israel! For times of trial manifestly are coming, in which they only who are taught of God, and kept by the power of His Spirit, can expect to resist the swelling tide of delusion, and maintain even the appearance of godliness."—FAIRBAIRN'S *Ezekiel*, pp. 124-126.—W. F.]

HOMILETIC HINTS.

Ver. 22. "God spares the ungodly, and thereby invites them to repentance. But what is it they do? They scoff at the servants of God, and reckon their words to be idle tales" (HEIMHOFF.).—"Thus they despised the riches of divine goodness and forbearance and long-suffering, and instead of allowing themselves to be led thereby to repentance, after their hardness and impenitent heart they treasured up unto themselves wrath, etc., Rom. ii. 4, 5; 2 Pet. iii. 4" (COCC.).—Ver. 23. The Sabbath which awaits the proverbs of the world, when every tongue which has not suffered itself to be hallowed to the Lord shall be hallowed to the Lord by the judgment of condemnation. To be *compelled* to confess that Jesus is Lord is indeed a terrible Sabbath, if one has not otherwise hallowed Him.—The lying mouths which God's word cannot stop are removed by God's deeds.—Ver. 24. "*Prophecy* and *roughness*, these go hand in hand among a sinful people" (HENGST.).—"If Jesus, who came after the Babylonian captivity, had been a false prophet, or His disciples, as the Jews assert, then must the promise of this verse have been false" (COCC.).—"And so also shall all flattering representations of a flourishing state of the Church, which have sprung from reason and fleshly learning, come to an end" (BERL. BIB.).—Vers. 27, 28: "What God says we are not to separate from its fulfilment, because God who speaks is not in Himself divided; when He opens His mouth, He stretches out His hand at the same time to the work, so that the hand itself is in a manner included in the word" (CALV.).

2. *The Discourses against the False Prophets and Prophetesses* (ch. xiii.).

1, 2 And the word of Jehovah came unto me, saying, Son of man, prophesy
unto the prophets of Israel that prophesy, and say unto the prophets out of
3 their own heart, Hear ye the word of Jehovah; Thus saith the Lord Jehovah:
Woe unto the foolish prophets, who walk after their own spirit, and that they
4 have not seen! Like foxes in the ruins have thy prophets become, O Israel.
5 Ye have not gone up into the gaps [breaches], nor built a wall round the house of
6 Israel, to make a stand in the war in the day of Jehovah. They beheld deceit
and lying divination who say, Sentence of Jehovah,—and Jehovah sent them
7 not,—and expect confirmation of a word. Saw ye not a deceitful vision, and
spake ye not a lying divination, and [that while] saying, Sentence of Jehovah, and
8 I have not spoken? Therefore thus saith the Lord Jehovah: Because ye speak
deceit, and see a lie, therefore, behold, I am upon you: sentence of the Lord
9 Jehovah. And Mine hand is [comes] upon the prophets that see deceit, and that
divine a lie: in the assembly of My people shall they not be, and in the register
of the house of Israel they shall not be registered, and into the land of Israel
10 shall they not come; and ye know that I am the Lord Jehovah. Because, even
because they seduced My people, saying, Peace [salvation], and there is no peace;
and they [*i.e.* the people] build a wall, and, lo, they [*i.e.* the false prophets] daub it with
11 a coating. Say unto them which daub with a coating: And it shall fall: there
comes a pouring rain; and ye, O hailstones, shall fall, and stormy wind shall
12 [thou, O stormy wind, shalt] break forth. And, lo, the wall falls; shall not one say unto

13 you, Where is the daubing wherewith ye daubed? Therefore thus saith the
Lord Jehovah: And I cause stormy wind to break forth in My fury, and pouring rain shall fall in Mine anger, and hailstones in My fury, unto utter destruc-
14 tion. And I break down the wall that ye daubed with a coating, and cast it to
the ground, and its foundation is uncovered, and it [Jerusalem] falls, and ye perish
15 in its [Jerusalem's] midst; and ye know that I am Jehovah. And I accomplish
My wrath upon the wall, and upon them that daubed it with a coating, and I will
16 say unto you, The wall is not, neither are they that daubed it; The prophets
of Israel who prophesied upon Jerusalem, and who saw for it a vision of peace,
17 and there is no peace: sentence of the Lord Jehovah. And thou, son of man,
set thy face toward the daughters of thy people, who prophesy out of their own
18 heart; and prophesy thou concerning them, And say, Thus saith the Lord
Jehovah: Woe to those who sew together for themselves coverings upon all joints of My hands, and who make the veils upon the head of every stature to hunt [catch] souls! Ye will hunt the souls among My people, and ye will save souls
19 alive among you! And ye will profane Me in face of My people for handfuls of
barley and for bits of bread, to slay souls that should not die, and to save souls
20 alive that should not live, by your lying to My people that hear lies! There-
fore thus saith the Lord Jehovah: Behold, I am against your coverings, wherewith ye there [where ye hunt] hunt the souls when flying, and I tear them out of
21 your arms, and let the souls go that ye hunt,—souls in their flying. And I tear
in pieces your veils, and deliver My people, and they shall be no more in your
22 hand as prey; and ye know that I am Jehovah. Because of troubling the
heart of the righteous falsely, and [when] I did not make him sad, and that ye strengthen the hands of the wicked, that he should not return from his wicked way,
23 to remain alive: Therefore ye shall no more see deceit, nor divine divinations;
and I deliver My people out of your hand; and ye know that I am Jehovah.

Ver. 3. Sept.: . . . *προφητευουσιν ἀπο καρδιας αὐτων, τ. πορευομενοις ἀπο τ. πνευματος αὐτ.*—

Ver. 5. . . . *κ. συνηγαγον ποιμνια, κ. ἐπι τ. οἰκον τ. Ἰσρ. οὐκ ἀνεστησαν οἱ λεγοντες ἐν ἡμερα κυριου*,— Vulg.: *Non ascendistis ex adverso neque opposuistis murum pro domo*—

Ver. 6. . . . *κ. ἠρξαντο του ἀναστησαι λογον.* Vulg.: *et perseveraverunt confirmare sermonem.*

Ver. 9. . . . *ἐν παιδεια τ. λαου μου οὐκ*—

Ver. 10. Vulg.: . . . *liniebant eum luto absque paleis.*

Ver. 11. Sept.: . . . *κ. δωσω λιθους πετροβολους εἰς τ. ἐνδεσμους αὐτων, κ. πεσουνται, κ. πνευμα ἐξαιρον, κ. ῥαγησεται.*

Ver. 14. . . . *ὃν ἠλειψατε, κ. πεσειται* . . . *κ. συντελεσθησεσθε μετ' ἐλεγχων*,— Vulg.: . . . *linistis absque temperamento . . . et cadet et consumetur in medio ejus*—

Ver. 15. . . . *κ. πεσειται, κ. εἶπα προς ὑμας*—

Ver. 18 . . . *ἐπι παντα ἀγκωνα χειρος* . . . Κ. *αἱ ψυχαι διεστραφησαν τ. λαου μου, κ. ψυχας περιεποιουντο*, Vulg.. . . . *Et cum caperent animas* . . . *vivificabant animas eorum*,

Ver. 19. Another read.: שמע—דברי כזב, *audienti mendacium.*

Ver. 20. . . . *τ. ψυχας αὐτ. εἰς διασκορπισμον*, Vulg.: *animas ad volandum*; (Sept., Syr., Hexapl., the Targum read: נפשם.)

Ver. 21. . . . *ἐν χερσιν ὑμ. εἰς συστροφην.* Vulg.: . . . *ad prædandum*; (Other readings: יהיה—בידכם, מידכם *erit*,—וידעתם.)

Ver. 22. . . . *το καθολου μη ἀποστρεψαι*—

EXEGETICAL REMARKS.

Now that the text has been given in ch. xii. 24, there follows in two parts (vers. 1-16, and 17-23)—in each case first the characteristics with which they are reproached (vers. 1-7, vers. 17-19), and then the penal sentence (vers. 8-16, vers. 20-23)—the sermon upon the text, a detailed treatment of the theme, viz. *false prophecy* in Israel, as the same was in vogue both at home and in the exile (comp. Jer. xxix.), and cannot be overlooked as an element in the interchange of false hopes and expectations in either case, and of mutual intercourse (Introd. p. 9). While the second part is usually understood of false prophetesses, Hengst. makes the false prophets the subject here also, merely "on account of their feeble nature, like women" (!). He brings forward as an argument for this Oriental and poetic exegesis the "designedly interspersed masculine pronouns (vers. 19, 20)," whereby the prophet "all but expressly says that he has to do with women in men's clothes;" and farther, that in the whole of the Old Testament "a false prophetess is nowhere mentioned," "so that so serious a punishment as we have here would have been out of place." Comp. as against both statements, the exposition of the section in question below. Neteler sees in the prophetesses "striking representatives of the synagogues," with their interpretations, sayings, commentaries.

Ver. 2. אֶל indicates the destination of the prophetic discourse which follows, which, as regards its tendency and contents, is directed *against* **the prophets of Israel**. Who are meant, הַנְּבִאִים.

tells us, viz. *those who prophesy*—who, from the fact of their prophesying, and consequently being in authority, are (alas!) the prophets of Israel. "Jeremiah in Jerusalem, and Ezekiel among the exiles, stood as oddities there, and had the government and the spirit of the age and of the people absolutely against them" (HENGST.). A more exact definition follows as regards the source whence their prophecy flows or is drawn: **out of their own heart**; and thus out of what is their own (Neh. vi. 8), in contrast with the true prophet, who utters God's word from God. And in this way their pretended office, their dignity in Israel, is already gone, and an ironical light falls upon the title, **prophets of Israel**. It fits into the contrast indicated with the true prophet, that they are to hear **the word of Jehovah**.—Ver. 3. **Woe**, already announcing the due punishment inevitably awaiting them, an exclamation of grief; telling at the same time with mingled pain and anger (as in Isa. i. 4; Matt. xxiii. 13 sq.) what ought not to be, but is the case with prophets of what is their own. הַנְּבָלִים, a *paronomasia* with הַנְּבִיאִים. Why they are called fools is clear from Ps. xiv. 1, liii. 1. To exhibit themselves as prophets, and not to be so from God, was a practical denial of God, especially of His avenging justice; was ungodliness, and at the same time stupidity in the highest degree. Where wisdom is wanting in this way, and where God is not the source, man "walks after his own spirit." The "heart" with its lusts is the source, the **spirit** the guide, *i.e.* instead of the Spirit of God, the thoughts, which take shape as they come out of the heart, make themselves master of the man; the man goes after his imaginations, fancies, himself at last believing in them. According to Hävern., therefore, the two necessary conditions are wanting, the right starting-point and goal. וּלְבִלְתִּי רָאוּ, usually taken as a relative clause: "and after that which they have not seen" (?). For the woe, at all events, a positive as well as negative reason is given. Comp. Doct. Reflect., p. 54.

They are compared to the **foxes** in Ver. 4, as destroyers in a general sense, because the foxes are hurtful creatures; and there is no need for us to think specially of the undermining of the ground, hence of the "sapping of the moral foundations of the state" (KEIL), or of depasturing the vineyard (of Israel, Isa. v.; Jer. xii. 10), Cant. ii. 15 (ROSENM.), or of injuring the game (HENGST.); and, least of all, have we to think of what is proverbial with us, the cunning of the fox. Comp. besides, Luke xiii. 31, 32; Matt. vii. 15; Acts xx. 29. The **ruins**, on the one hand, indicate the favourite haunt of foxes and similar animals, and on the other, point to the ruin of Israel. [KLIEF.: "The ruins of the theocracy are undermined by the false prophets besides, inasmuch as they take up their abode in them." HENGST.: "At no time were the false prophets rifer than in the last days of the Jewish state." KIMCHI: "*Thy* prophets," which are not Jehovah's.]—Their conviction, however, in the form of an energetic address in reference to Israel's welfare, turns in Ver. 5 not so much on what they have done, as on what they have neglected to do as regards the "ruins." As prophets, as men of God, they had to place themselves in the gap, or to build a wall, etc. Both images are chosen with reference to the siege of Jerusalem. (According to Hävernick, the thing meant is the watching of the vineyard against thieves and wild beasts!) **To make a stand in the war** has reference both to what is required of the person and to what the state of affairs requires. The **day of Jehovah** is the time fixed by Him with reference to the reckoning to be given in to Him. Although the case is only as yet impending, yet it is spoken of as if it were an accomplished fact. It cannot happen otherwise with them, considering what they are (ver. 5), and how they are acting (ver. 6). [EWALD: "But what follows from such internal perversity has already taken place long before, while they, when wrath breaks forth as in the divine assault, and the helpless people are panting all the more after prophetic help, withdraw from cowardice, speaking flatteringly where it causes them no danger," etc.] Comp. ch. xxii. 30 (Ps. cvi. 23; Isa. lviii. 12; 1 Sam. xxv. 16); Amos v. 18, 20; Mal. iii. 23 [iv. 5]. For the meaning of the figurative language in ver. 5, we must think with the older expositors of intercessory mediation, of the awakening of Israel to repentance, the putting a stop to their wickedness, the building of them up in newness of spirit, etc. **In the day**, etc., and **in the war**, throw light on each other, so that he who wages war against Israel is Jehovah in the day of His wrath (ch. vii. 19; Isa. lxiii. 10; Job xxxviii. 22, 23). The "breach" is the sinful condition of the people. (HITZ., HENGST.) [Häv., like Cocc., understands לַעֲמֹד of the house of Israel (others: of the wall). The day of the Lord means, according to Cocc., the day of Christ's appearing!]—Ver. 6. Jer. xxiii. וְיִחֲלוּ, according to others, is dependent on שְׁלָחָם: that they might hope, etc. Inasmuch as they believe their own lie, they wait (in vain) for its becoming true by being realized, that I would confirm it. Instead of this, in Ver. 7, just as in ver. 5, guilt is brought home in a direct address on God's part. HENGST.: a question of conscience.

Ver. 8. The retributive punishment. הִנְנִי אֲלֵיכֶם is the explanation of the אֶל in ver. 2. After the purpose has been expressed generally, there follows in Ver. 9 a carrying out of it in detail. סוֹד, abbreviated from יְסוֹד (יָסַד), "a taking together," is: **an assembly**, a council, and also a confidential circle; here the former.—כְּתָב, the roll of citizens, and that the new one that is to be drawn up.—The exclusion from the people, just as their assembling, taking note of their condition, and afterwards returning home,—implying, of course, an advance,—refer to the (ch. xi. 17 sq.) promised restoration. Comp. Ps. i. 5, lxxxvii. 6; Ezra ii. 62.—יַעַן וּבְיַעַן, in Ver. 10, formally and solemnly, in the style of judgment (Lev. xxvi. 43). In this way an additional and special retribution is introduced; the unauthorized announcement of salvation (Jer. vi. 14, viii. 11; Isa. xlviii. 22), which is expressively compared to *the daubing of a wall*, beneath which the slim and worthless building material, as well as any gaps that may exist, disappear from the eye, is to be punished with the manifestation in actual fact of the misleading activity of the false prophets. **And they build**, viz. the people, not the false prophets. Compared with ver. 5, instead of the wall which the prophets were to build, the people left to themselves in their self-help are reduced to a clay wall (חַיִץ) merely, which they erect for themselves with their wishes and hopes. (HENGST.: the political effort made by the coalition, to which the false prophets gave the appearance of a higher sanction.) The daubing which masks the unstable handiwork is provided by those prophets with their announcement of salvation. תָּפֵל, not טִיחַ, as in ver. 12, because the sense, the meaning, breaks forth from the figure. EWALD: "elsewhere what is absurd intellectually, what is inconsistent with itself; here the mortar that does not hold together, clay without straw, or dry clay." They spread their dull, stupid coating of words of salvation over it. HENGST.: absurdity (Jer. xxiii. 13; Lam. ii. 14). Comp. also Acts xxiii. 3; Matt. xxiii. 27.—The fall of the wall in Ver. 11 is in fact the special sentence on the daubers, יִפֹּל having a resemblance in sound to תָּפֵל.—הָיָה, as it were beginning a narrative, after the manner of a parable (EWALD).—A lively address (**and ye**) to the powers of nature. The circumstance that the description proceeds in this physical strain is perhaps intended to suggest the thought, how much as a matter of course it lies in the very nature of such a wall that it should fall, in spite of all the art of the daubing and coating.—אֶלְגָּבִישׁ, peculiar to Ezekiel, is **hail**, an expansion of גָּבִישׁ, "something stiffened" (ice), with א prosthetic and *dagesh forte* following אֶגְּבִישׁ = אֶלְגָּבִישׁ, a Chaldee form. EWALD: probably from אֵל גָּבִישׁ, "a mist of hail," *i.e.* thickest hail frozen together. Gesenius summons to his help unnecessarily the Arabic article; Hävernick regards the whole word as Arabic, as the crystal came to the Hebrews from Arabia. Comp. Ex. ix. 18; Josh. x. 10 sq.; Isa. xxx. 30; Ps. xviii. 13, 14 [12, 13]; Job xxxviii. 22; Matt. vii. 25, 27; Rev. xvi. 21. Hail, though rare in Palestine, is a thing well known in its devastating effects.—סְעָרוֹת, because of the violent rushings. תְּבַקֵּעַ may also be the second person, but can hardly as an address apply to God: a stormy wind thou shalt rend (!), as Hengstenberg. Expositors have also thought of a breaking through the wall. [So the Eng. Vers.: "a stormy wind shall rend it."]—In Ver. 12 now הַקִּיר, which it ought to be, **the wall**, instead of חַיִץ in ver. 10. The daubing was meant to give it the appearance of a solid wall.—Ver. 13. Ch. viii. 18, xi. 13.—Ver. 14. Breaking down to the foundation. בְּתוֹכָהּ, the feminine suffix pointing from the figure to the thing itself, **the city to be** destroyed, viz. Jerusalem, as נָפְלָה already does.—Ver. 15. The discourse plays upon the כָּלָה; comp. vers. 13, 14. There is a bringing to an end (ch. v. 13, vi. 12, vii. 8), and hence an application in Ver. 16 to the false prophets, against whom this first part of the discourse is directed. In ver. 15 we need not read with Ewald: וְאֹמַר, "that it is said of you." What is impending will be a *sermo realis*.—Ver. 16. An apposition which brings the reference to the false prophets to an end.

Ver. 17. *The False Prophetesses.*—Peculiar to Ezekiel, and so much the more interesting, and none the less accordant with the actual condition of those last days of a life ever more and more mixed up with heathenisms. The prophetess Huldah appears, however, in 2 Kings xxii. 14, as a divinely inspired woman on the side of the living God. In caricature of her, in connection with idolatries like ch. viii. 14, the class of false prophetesses, against whom Ezekiel is to bear testimony, may have been formed. Hävernick mentions the old Arabian legendary history.—**Set thy face toward**, etc., ch. vi. 2.—עַמּוּךְ, as it were: to this has it come with them! Comp. on ver. 2. The Hithpael perhaps more sharply emphasizes their betaking themselves thereto, their conducting themselves as such, their female vanity. עַל indicates therefore the correspondingly superior prophetic commission of Ezekiel.—Ver. 18. Comp. ver. 3. Like the false prophets, the false prophetesses also prophesy out of their own hearts, but quite in womanly fashion "sewing together for themselves (Ew. *Gr.* § 120*b*, with bad assiduity) *kĕsathoth*, and making *mispachoth*." (1) The **literal** interpretation of these words: Ewald makes both things be placed on the body of these divineresses as ornament, so that while thus employed they were wont to look as upon a magic mirror upon the "knobs" which were sewed firmly on the wrist or arm, and with their mantles hanging over their heads they imitated the mantles of the prophets. Far-fetched; especially "the children's heads," which Ewald brings forward in addition to the sorceries. —According to Calvin, a kind of sleepy condition was aimed at in this way, whereby they carried themselves and others away in transport from the earth.—[Old expositors explained the expressions in question of armlets for the purpose of divination; more modern ones, like J. D. Michaelis, explained them of magic fillets on the hands and head, which preserve the life of the wearer, but which bring death to the enemy.] Hävernick notices, first of all, the contrast of the luxurious, wanton life (Isa. iii. 16 sq., xxxii. 9 sq.) with the pretence of being prophetesses, and then compares for the catching of souls, Prov. vi. 26; ch. vii. 21 sq. The unusual form כְּסָתוֹת is, according to him, a technical term for a definite kind of coverlets, rugs, which are sewed together for cushions, sofas. יְדֵי he takes as an abbreviated dual form, and understands by אַצִּילֵי the joints of the hand in the wider sense (Jer. xxxviii. 12), so that every joint of the arm has its rug. Thus they lie on a comfortable couch (Prov. vii. 16), in luxurious clothing besides—*instar omnium* מִסְפָּחוֹת, a word which (Isa. iii. 22; Ruth iii. 15), as a designation of the upper garments, the large shawls of the women, is put by Ezekiel for מִסְפָּחוֹת, with an allusion to מִסְפַּחַת (scab, Isa. iii. 17); taken in connection with עַל־רֹאשׁ, hence coquettish wearing of veils over the head for every stature. That rugs were not laid over or upon (עַל) the joints, elbows, shoulders, cannot certainly be maintained by Keil as against Hävernick, since עַל may here as well as afterwards be rendered by "for" of the standard.—Hitzig thinks of the analogy of the תְּפִלִּין, which one fastened during prayer on his left hand, and of the טַלִּית, a long and broad piece of cloth with which the suppliant covered his head. (2) The *figurative* interpretation: According as יָדַי is referred indirectly or directly to God; in the former case, so that: "upon all joints of My hands"= those of My people, hence that Jehovah regards Himself as injured in His people;—they impede the free movement, cover the eyes of every one (UMBREIT) by their lies and flatteries (usually: they lay the people in a bed of deceitful rest, cover them with all sorts of excuses, high and low alike); in the other case, as Klief. has it: it is brought as a charge against the prophetesses, that they cover by their false divination the word of God and the threatening hand of the Judge therein, and that they veil, exactly according to the stature of the individual, men's hearing and seeing.—There is a correspondence between the analogy of the preceding discourse to the false prophets, which is certainly to be held fast, and the *figurative* interpretation, to which Hengstenberg and Keil also have given in their adhesion. What in the former case is daubing with a coating, is here covering and veiling. [כָּסָה is: "to cover;" סָפַח, to draw together, to envelope closely. עַל־רֹאשׁ, however, is not meant of the standard by which one is regulated, but is simply "over," inasmuch as they know how to counsel every קוֹמָה (height, stature) of those who trust them.]—Jewish expositors have unnecessarily taken הַנְּפָשׁוֹת as a question. The contrast with חַיָּה shows what צוּד has in view. Hence what tends to destruction in the one case, is meant to turn out for preservation in the other. Such a result cannot possibly occur where the living God and these women confront each other (**among My people** and **among you**), and where He would be profaned. [HÄV.: לְ= those belonging to the people—those belonging to you, *i.e.* your own souls. Others draw the distinction between members of the people and adherents of the false prophetesses, to the former of whom they threaten destruction; to the latter, on the other hand, they promise prosperity. EWALD: souls of honest men they render gloomy and sickly, and thus they bring them down to death; souls of sinners they strengthen in their sins, in order that they themselves also through their gratitude may be the better able to live along with them. LUTHER: when ye have caught them among My people, ye promise them life. KLIEF.: they steal from the people of God their life, and take care of their own.]—Ver. 19. In contrast with the intended profanation of Jehovah, specially of His name by their lying (**in face of My people**, as afterwards: **to My people**), the price is emphasized sharply, the wretched life of the body (Mic. iii. 5; Tit. i. 11; Rom. xvi. 18). Those that **should not die** are the souls of the people of Jehovah (ch. iii. 17 sq.); those contrasted with them are the souls of the prophetesses themselves (Deut. xviii. 20). According to others: the former are the pious, the latter the wicked. Comp. ver. 18. בְּכַזֶּבְכֶם, the masc. suffix, embracing at the same time the false prophets along with them, or an inaccuracy of Ezekiel's (HÄV.). Comp. on ver. 20. Comp. besides, Mic. ii. 11.

Thereafter, in Ver. 20, *the judgment*, as in the case of the false prophets (ver. 8 sq.). **There**—the coverings are, as it were, the ground on which the hunt takes place, according to Hengstenberg. According to others: there, at Jerusalem (ver. 16).—לְפֹרְחוֹת (from פָּרַח, to break through (בָּרַךְ), like בָּרַח, to flee) is rendered by HÄV.: "to rejoicings (excesses)." Prov. vii. 18. NETELER: "in their bloom." Others: "to blooming pleasure-gardens"; others still: "in order that they may blossom," according to your prophecy. PHILIPPSON: "to flutter in the net." HENGST.: "like birds." EWALD: "as if they were birds of passage." פֹּרְחוֹת, Aramaic, means "flying ones"; so it is acknowledged by most in what follows, and so it is here likewise, only that the connection makes the difference,—that here they are hunted, *caught, as such*, but instead of this, in what follows, with piquant repetition, they are *let fly*. The very sameness of the expression, amid opposite surroundings, is the point. Because the false prophetesses are conceived of here (Ps. xi.) *as fowlers*, who are usually men, the masc. suffix preceding the comparison is easily understood. The **souls** are torn out of the arms in question; according to the usual interpretation: the coverings are torn away from the arms of the false prophetesses.—וְשִׁלַּחְתִּי, as in Deut. xxii. 7 (Ex. xxi. 26).—Ver. 21. With the feminine suffix the address returns again to the women. While hitherto ver. 18 was kept in view, with Vers. 22, 23 the reference is to ver. 19. While they threw suspicion on the pious among the exiles, and made them sad, etc., they strengthened those in Jerusalem in their pride of expectation. They did evil to the good, and to the bad they did no good. And so shall all their doings come to an end. By the events shall they be put to shame, and they shall perish in them.

DOCTRINAL REFLECTIONS.

1. Cocceius gives the name of false prophecy to the doctrine which is contrary to God's word, to the false exposition of Scripture, as well as to prophesying without having seen and heard God's word, as well as, above all, to the imagination of,

or the laying claim to, possessing such divine revelation.

[2. "Here, then, lay the grand characteristic of the true prophet, as distinguished from the false. There was exhibited objectively to his soul, through the operation of the Spirit of God, a thought, or succession of thoughts,—an action, perhaps, revealing the mind and will of God; and then taking up this in the apprehension of his mind, he went forth to declare it to others, as from his own inward consciousness, clothed in such words as fitly expressed what had been seen within. With the false prophet, on the other hand, even supposing him to be perfectly sincere in what he uttered, all proceeded from the impulse of his own inflated imagination or excited feelings; the whole was from within merely, nothing from without, from above. Yet, with this distinction so clearly traced, and traced for the express purpose of drawing the line of demarcation between the true and the false in prophetic utterances, we are still presented with views and theories of inspiration, which, in the case of inspired men generally, prophets as well as evangelists and apostles, if they do not altogether discard the objective, render the subjective alone prominent,—make so much account of the internal consciousness or intuitional sense of the subject of inspiration, as necessarily to throw into the background the divine communication made to him from above. But in the two classes of prophets here presented to our notice, the one could lay claim, as well as the other, to the internal consciousness of some spiritual thought or idea; the only question was, whence came the idea? Did it spring up from within, as of itself? or was it presented there by the Spirit of God? Was the mind's consciousness of the thoughts and feelings it experienced of its own awakening, or was it awakened by a divine and formal communication from above? If we lose sight of this important distinction, we virtually make no account of what constitutes the fundamental element of a divine revelation, and leave ourselves without a fixed landmark between the movements of God's Spirit and the capricious workings of human fancy. And confounding thus things that essentially differ in regard to the *origin* of a revelation, we lay ourselves open to the farther error of disparaging the *value* of a revelation, when made; we totally change it, indeed, and lower its character, and assign it only a kind of higher room among the views and cogitations of men's own imagining."—FAIRBAIRN'S *Ezekiel*, pp. 133, 134.—W. F.]

3. "False prophecy does not believe in any day of judgment of Jehovah's" (HÄVERNICK).

4. "Because God will never be separated from His word, while He is in Himself invisible, He manifests Himself only in His word. Hence in the case of false prophecy, making constant use as it did of the expression: 'The Lord hath said,' all the attributes of the divine nature necessarily ran the risk of being denied or profaned" (CALVIN).

5. Prophecy in Israel was a gift of the Spirit, and already, as being so, had no restriction as to sex. But when it came to be upheld by the Spirit of Christ, in whom there is neither male nor female (Gal. iii. 28), this overlooking of all sexual distinctions of necessity still more characterized it.

6. It is a symptom of dissolution of all social bonds when women are in power in such fashion as we find them here in Ezekiel. The French Revolution and the most recent so-called emancipation question [emancipation of women] are proofs of this.

7. On the other hand, in the sister of Moses, in Deborah, in the mother of Samuel, during the time of the Old Covenant even, we have illustrations of what was to be set forth in the highest degree by the blessed among women, viz. the religious capabilities of the female sex. The caricatures of the holy are also its foil.

8. Inspiration is essentially a thing belonging to women. If the apostle (1 Tim. ii.; 1 Cor. xiv.) prohibits the female sex from teaching, yet he shows, even in the former of these passages (comp. 2 Cor. xi. 3), how receptive woman is for the spirit-world, for all that is transcendental in word and deed, in form and substance; and not less must we take into account the influence of the female sex, and the art (so easy to them) of deception, of seduction.

HOMILETIC HINTS.

Ver. 2. "Prophecy against prophecy, the prophecy from above against the prophecy from beneath: this is the everlasting ordinance in the kingdom of God" (HENGST.).—"But when he says that God is coming against the false prophets, he by no means intends to excuse the people. For the people had the law and likewise true prophets. In Deut. xiii. the distinguishing marks of the true and false prophets were given. Theirs was blindness in clear day. And therefore God suffered the arrogance and disobedience of the people to be punished" (CALV.).—"Satan's power is especially very great in the case of teachers and preachers, 1 Kings xxii." (LANGE.)—"Thus prophet came into collision with prophet. And now-a-days still God will in this way test the faith of His own, and disclose the hypocrisy of many (1 Cor. xi. 19). It is not in vain that He permits the servants of Satan to rise up against sound doctrine, and that the Church is torn in pieces by divergent opinions, and that vain conceits are able to attain such strength that the truth must have the worst of it. For in this way the stedfastness of the pious comes to light, and equally the lightmindedness of the hypocrites, who suffer themselves to be carried away by every wind" (CALV.).—The presence of false prophets a sign of dissolution, as well as of the judgment of God.—The false prophets involve the people in guilt; the people are to blame for the false prophets, 2 Thess. ii. 11.—The word of God, that which is to be heard by all, in all things, and at all times.—Ver. 3. Self-deception and the deception of others go together.—"From this we see how it stands with man's spirit, for God presupposes here a standing controversy between man's spirit and the revelation of His Spirit" (CALV.).—And yet, for the most part, it is just the wise people that are found among these fools.—The wisdom of the world and folly before God.—"Whoever will open the eyes of others, let him see to it beforehand whether he himself has an eye open Godwards" (STCK.).—Ver. 4. "The spiritual foxes flourish the better, the more degraded the condition of the people" (HENGST.).—"The people in the wilderness of the exile were very much exposed to the false prophets" (LUTH.).

Ver. 5. False prophets cannot pray.—The intercession of the prophets steps into the breach. —"Right doctrine is the right wall, just as it also teaches right living" (CALV.).—"There is no better wall than reformation of life" (BERL. BIB.).—Vers. 6, 7. Without being sent by God, no one ought to enter a teacher's office.

Vers. 8, 9. We have to give an account of our words even.—God convicts sinners sometimes out of their own mouth.—Ver. 9. "It is a fearful thing to fall into the hands of God; a king's hands we may escape, but not God's" (STCK.).—"Because the Jews have refused to become Christians, they have not been enrolled in the register of Israel" (COCC.).—"It is not enough that men should reckon us members of the Church. We must know in our own hearts whether we have the inward marks whereby the children of God are distinguished from those who do not belong to His family" (CALV.).—Ver. 10. "Ungodly teachers preach to their hearers of good days merely, and comfort them into hell, Jer. viii. 11" (STARKE).—"The wall is the mere external service of God; and yet all the while the false prophets flatter them, treat them as pious persons, all without exception saints in Christ" (BERL. BIB.).—The world, too, wishes peace, but not the peace of God through Jesus Christ.—"God proclaims peace to us, it is true. But we must wage war with ourselves and with our vices" (CALV.).—There are among preachers those who build without a foundation, and, alas! also mere outside-daubers.—[SCOTT: "Some teach men to expect safety from a comparative decency of moral character; some on account of formal or superstitious observances; some because they belong to an orthodox part of the Church, and have got some notions of certain important doctrines; some because of their impressions and enthusiastic reveries; and others even by a direct abuse of the gospel, and making Christ the minister of sin. Men of learning and ingenuity employ themselves in daubing these tottering walls with untempered mortar, to prevent their weakness from being discovered. But they are all alike distant from Christ, the true foundation: they build not on Him by a penitent faith, that worketh by love, and produceth obedience; they either leave out His merits and atonement, or the work of His new-creating Spirit, or the substantial fruits of righteousness; and in different ways endeavour to varnish, paint, and repair the old building, instead of erecting a new one on a new foundation, for 'an habitation of God through the Spirit.'"—W. F.]—"We believe much more readily those who preach to us of glory, riches, and peace, than those who promise us nothing but the cross. And yet the words of glory are deceitful words, and the devil can very easily mix himself up with prophecies of that sort, and does it too; but the cross abides and remains" (BERL. BIB.).—False hope of life is a sign of approaching death.—Ver. 11 sq.: "Every building of which faith has not laid the foundation helplessly gives way when God's storms come" (UMBREIT).—"No doctrine of mere human reason can stand in the time of trouble and temptation; but he who is built upon the doctrine of the holy apostles and prophets has built his house firm and sure, Eph. ii. 20" (CR.).—Man's work, slim work; God's storms, bad storms.—Vain conceits, hypocrisy, and deceit do not stand in the divine judgment.—Ver. 14. "The foundation is the important thing in building, and even when the wall falls. For one may (1 Cor. iii. 12, 15) build on the true foundation all sorts of things, which are consumed in the fire, yet so that the builder himself is saved. Here, on the other hand, the foundation is false, and therefore building and builder alike disappear" (COCC.).—"It is besides a peculiarity of the judgments of God, that they are a revelation, and make manifest to all the world what was deceit and falsehood" (LUTHER).

Ver. 17 sq. "False prophets for the most part rear for themselves false prophetesses" (COCC.).—"The woman Jezebel speaks (Rev. ii. 20), alleging that she is a prophetess, by false interpretation, application, and perversion of Scripture, whereof each one chooses for his own use what suits him best. Of such cushions there are enough in the present day still, and God's mercy itself is so perverted. But whenever one would hunt and would fain catch something, it is commonly the destruction and death of the object that he has in view. And so here one seeks his gain and advantage with and from the destruction of other people" (BERL. BIB.). — "What Satan cannot accomplish by means of the male sex, he attempts by means of the female, Acts xvi. 16" (STARKE).—"Effeminate is all accommodation theology. It is its nature to set aside, as in general all that is uncomfortable for the old Adam and gives him pain, so especially the energy of the requiring and punishing divine righteousness—the *severity* of God, Rom. xi. 22. Where Ezekiel puts the cushions, there we put perhaps the icy glove. Besides the cushions for the hands of the Lord, which touch [men in their natural state] very ungently, they make coverings for the heads of their penitents, that the hand of God may not touch them ungently, and indeed for heads or people of every stature, always according to the greatness of the reward to be expected—the greatest for the king. The higher any one is placed, the more zealously do they endeavour to clear his conscience, as Jesuits before the Jesuits, differing from their successors in this, that the latter had in view the interest and power of the Church, while the former serve merely their own belly" (HENGST.).—Ver. 18. "It is a striking, awful word, that a lie has the power to catch and to kill souls" (UMBREIT).—A heart, indeed, for every head, for the wrong-headed even, the servant of God ought to have, but not pious caps for all heads.—"Satan keeps a large richly furnished store of rugs and pillows, such as cherished habits, the example of others, the way of all the world, church-going even, partaking of the Lord's Supper," etc. (STCK.)—"God is angry with them, for they prop up souls, hinder them, lay under their deeds a pillow of reward, teach them to place their reliance in their own thoughts and imaginings, instead of in the truth. But they become still worse through a certain emotional power, which flatters them with a semblance of life in the midst of death. The prophets who know how to produce this feeling of life with their promises are more readily accepted as true prophets than those who cut off all supports, and bring about death. A true prophet announces nothing but destruction—war, famine, and death (1 Kings xxii. 8). And the reason is this, that the prophesying of death must precede the prophesying of life" (BERL. BIB.).—Ver. 19. The prophetic spirit of lying, a spirit of murder, and also of blasphemy, putting an end alike to men's fellowship with one another and to their fellowship with God.—"God is the truth; with it He too vanishes, becomes the ghost of one that is dead. But it was a special pledge of His love that God gave them prophets, that He had promised the gift of prophets to Israel. With the prostitution of the name of prophet God's own gracious name must of necessity in a special way have been put to shame, and that among His own people, as distinguished above all other nations" (CALV.).—"They profane God among His people, by making Him take up a friendly position toward sin" (HENGST.).—To cast away the living God for the means of sustaining this earthly life, what self-murder!—"Mark it, ye brethren of Gehazi, what hateful leprosy, 2 Kings v." (STARKE.)—"The true and faithful servants of God also kill souls and make them alive; for the word of God is life, and brings salvation to lost men; and not less does it become a savour of death unto death to those who are lost, 2 Cor. ii." (CALV.)—"Whoever wishes to live, let him betake himself to the living God, to whom the word of life of all true prophets points us. Every soul must die that does not tread this way of life" (CALV.).—"Those who have no pleasure in the truth, must, in accordance with the righteous judgment of God, believe a lie" (O.).—"They would so fain have it, that the false might turn out truth" (Cocc.).

Ver. 20 sq. That they do not remain unpunished is no special act of judgment on God's part, but nothing else save the revelation of judgment contained in the third commandment.—The ten commandments are full of judgment-seats for God.—"It is the everlasting comfort of the poor human race, exposed as it is to that spirit who is a liar and a murderer, that the almighty God of truth rules as a defender and protector of souls. The Lord will also save and set free captive souls from the hands of their deceiver and seducer; for in truth they are not irrational birds, destined for fluttering and flying, but images of their Divine Creator" (UMBREIT).—"Pious hearts are filled with fear of God's name, and hence they are easily vexed and taken captive with false doctrine, delivered to them in God's name" (RANDGL.).—Ver. 22. "It is nevertheless sin not to comfort or to trouble still more those who are troubled, as well as to strengthen the stiffnecked in their wickedness, Isa. v. 20" (CR.).—The unlawful "trouble" caused by certain preachers of repentance.—Rightly to divide the word of God, a gift and distinguishing mark of a true teacher.—False doctrine makes wounded hearts, but also hard hands.—Ver. 23. False prophecy also was to cease until the appearance of the Great Prophet, the Son of God.—"Thus God was resolved to save His people under the New Testament; so that brother should no more need to teach brother, because the fulfilment would be in their midst. The Word Himself would in very deed become flesh" (Cocc.).

3. *The Testimony against the Idolatrous Seekers after Oracles* (CH. XIV.).

1 And there came unto me men from the elders of Israel, and sat before me.
2, 3 And the word of Jehovah came unto me, saying, Son of man, these men
have caused their filthy idols to go up upon their heart, and the stumbling-
block of their iniquity have they given before their face; shall I indeed
4 allow Myself to be inquired at by them? Therefore speak with them, and
say unto them, Thus saith the Lord Jehovah: Every man of the house of
Israel that shall cause his filthy idols to go up to his heart, and shall put the
stumbling-block of his iniquity before his face, and comes to the prophet, I
5 Jehovah, do I answer him in that,—in the multitude of his filthy idols? In
order to take the house of Israel in their own heart, who have departed from
6 Me in all their filthy idols: Therefore say unto the house of Israel, Thus
saith the Lord Jehovah; Repent, and turn from your filthy idols, and from
7 all your abominations turn away your face. For every one of the house of
Israel, and of the stranger that sojourneth in Israel, if he shall separate him-
self from Me, and shall cause his filthy idols to go up to his heart, and shall
put the stumbling-block of his iniquity before his face, and comes to the pro-
8 phet to inquire in Me, I Jehovah answer him in Myself, And set My face
against this man, and make him desolate, for a sign, and for proverbs, and
cut him off from the midst of My people; and ye know that I am Jehovah.
9 And the prophet, if he shall let himself be enticed, and speaks a word, I
Jehovah have enticed that prophet, and stretch out My hand upon him, and
10 destroy him from the midst of My people Israel. And they bear their
iniquity; as the iniquity of him that inquires, so shall the iniquity of the
11 prophet be; That the house of Israel may go no more astray from Me, and
may no more be polluted [defile themselves] in all their transgressions; and
that they may be to Me a people, and I may be to them a God,—sentence of
12, 13 the Lord Jehovah. And the word of Jehovah came unto me, saying, Son
of man, if a land shall sin against Me, so that it acts very treacherously, and

I stretch out mine hand upon it, and break for it the staff of bread, and
14 send upon it famine, and cut off from it man and beast; And there are in
the midst of it these three men, Noah, Daniel, and Job,—they shall deliver
their own soul [life] by their righteousness,—sentence of the Lord Jehovah.
15 If I shall cause evil beasts to pass through the land, and they bereave it, and
it becomes a desolation, because no one passes through because of the beasts;
16 These three men in the midst of it—as I live, sentence of the Lord Jehovah
—they shall deliver neither sons nor daughters; they alone shall be delivered,
17 and the land shall be a desolation. Or if I shall bring a sword upon this
land, and I say, A sword shall go through the land, and I cut off from it man
18 and beast; And these three men are in the midst of it—as I live, sentence
of the Lord Jehovah—they shall deliver neither sons nor daughters; for they
19 alone shall be delivered. Or if I shall send a pestilence on that land, and
20 pour out My fury upon it in blood, to cut off from it man and beast; And
Noah, Daniel, and Job are in the midst of it—as I live, sentence of the Lord
Jehovah—they shall deliver neither sons nor daughters; they shall deliver
21 their own soul [life] by their righteousness. For thus saith the Lord Jehovah;
How much more when I send My four sore judgments—sword, and famine,
and evil beasts, and pestilence—upon Jerusalem, to cut off from it man and
22 beast! And [yet], behold, therein is left an escaped portion, who are brought
forth, sons and daughters; behold, they come forth unto you, and ye see
their way and their doings, and ye are comforted concerning the evil that I
23 have brought upon Jerusalem, all that I have brought upon it. And they
comfort you, when ye shall see their way and their doings; and ye know that
not without cause have I done all that I have done in [upon] it,—sentence of
the Lord Jehovah.

Ver. 1. Another read.: ויבאו.
Ver. 3. Sept.: . . . ἔθεντο τα διανοηματα αὐτ. ἐπι τ. καρδιας αὐτ. κ. την κολασιν τ. ἀδικιων αὐτ ἔθησαν προ—
Ver. 4. Other read.: בא, בי? Sept.: . . . ἀποκριθησομαι αὐτω ἐν οἱς ἐνεχεται ἡ διανοια αὐτου,
Ver. 5. ὁπως μη διαστρεψωσιν τον οἰκον τ. 'Ισρ. κατα τ. καρδιας αὐτ. τας ἀπηλλοτριωμενας ἀπ' ἐμου—
Ver. 7. . . . και ἐκ των προσηλυτων—ἀποκριθησομαι αὐτω ἐν ᾡ ἐνεχεται ἐν αὐτω,
Ver. 15. Sept. read.: ושכלתיה, *et orbavero illam.*
Ver. 21. Sept.: 'Εαν δε και— Vulg.: *quod et si.*
Ver. 22. . . . ὑπολελειμμενοι ἐν αὐτῃ οἱ ἀνασεσωσμενοι ἐξ αὐτης, οἱ ἐξαγουσιν υἱους—
Ver 23. Some add: אל; there is a reading: אל חנם.

EXEGETICAL REMARKS.

Vers. 1–3. *The Occasion.* The outward occasion for the divine testimony in this chapter is first mentioned, and then the inward occasion is set forth plainly.

Ver. 1. The outward occasion is furnished by a deputation—in this way we explain the singular of the verb (וַיָּבוֹא), which surprised the old commentators. More certainly is meant than *il vient des hommes.* Grotius supposes ambassadors from Palestine, on occasion of the embassy of Zedekiah to Babylon (Jer. li.). They were certainly from the exiles (Keil); to be distinguished, however, from those of ch. viii. 1. Those latter are already with the prophet; the former first come to him. It is not, however, merely because of the different expressions used,—"elders of Judah," in ch. viii. 1, while here we have: **men from the elders of Israel,**—but rather because of the keeping apart as well as putting together which follows in ch. xvi., that we shall have to think of ambassadors from the exiles of the kingdom of the ten tribes (comp. Introd. pp. 7, 8); whether they were themselves elders is not exactly said, but simply that they came from the elders of Israel, out of **their midst.** Comp. ch. xx.—That they **sat** down before the prophet, seems to show that they were waiting to see whether they might not hear something from him, of course concerning Judah, concerning Jerusalem, for in this direction was the interest of all who were in exile turned (Introd. pp. 8, 9).

["For what purpose they came—whether to ask counsel from the prophet regarding some point of difficulty that had occurred to themselves, or to hear what he might be prompted by the Spirit to communicate of seasonable instruction—we are not expressly told. But that they came in the character of inquirers may be almost certainly inferred from ver. 3, where the Lord at once proceeds, through His servant, to repudiate the idea of His being inquired at by persons of such a character—persons who had 'set up their idols in their heart, and put the stumbling-block of their iniquity before their face.' After this it is scarcely possible to doubt that they came in the character of inquirers: though what might be the precise object of their inquiry is nowhere indicated in what follows, unless we can suppose (what is in the highest degree probable) that the message of the prophet was so framed as in some part to meet the proposed subject of inquiry, and thus incidentally to discover what the subject itself really was. This supposition is confirmed by the fact, which strikes us the moment we glance over the contents of the chapter, that it falls into two parts,—the first (vers. 3–11) referring to the preliminary point respecting the character of the inquirers, and the remaining portion addressing itself to a subject entirely distinct—God's method of dealing with a land and people when they have reached a state of hopeless corruption and depravity. It is more than probable, therefore, that while God refused to give any formal answer to such inquirers as those who now sat before the prophet, He yet, in this latter portion of the message, gave a substantial deliverance on the question about which their anxiety had been raised."—FAIRBAIRN'S *Ezekiel*, pp. 143, 144. —W. F.]

He was able certainly to anticipate their question—as is actually done in Ver. 2 sq.—inasmuch as, by means of divine revelation, the still unexpressed design of their coming is made known to him, and in this way they are made manifest before him. They wish, according to Hengst., "to make an experiment, whether they cannot obtain a more favourable answer through the prophet, whose fearfully threatening announcement they have heard not without shuddering" (grace without repentance); but from the text we can only learn that the older portion of the exiles put themselves in an exactly similar position toward Ezekiel as that which, alike in the exile and at Jerusalem, the people assumed toward the false prophets. Hence, Ezekiel treated like the false prophets,—that is the immediate connection, the connection with what precedes. The meaning is not (as Häv., and also Cocc.), that the guilt of the people in general, who so willingly hearken to the lie (ch. xiii. 19), is to be brought out in detail, by way of supplement to the guilt of the false prophets already handled; nor does Ezekiel intend by his own example to make clear and prominent the contrast between true and false prophets. But by the example of these men from Israel, while he speaks to their conscience, he predicts the impending divine judgment upon Judah and Jerusalem. The internal necessity of it, from the connection of sin and punishment, is justified to their consciousness. This is the more remote connection, the connection with what follows. Hence Ver. 3, giving what forms the inner reason for the divine testimony.—On גִלּוּלֵיהֶם, see at ch. vi. 4.—The statement: **these men have caused their filthy gods to go up,** etc., as bearing on the object of the discourse we have just indicated, is expressed more exactly by what follows: **and the stumbling-block of their iniquity,** etc. (see on ch. vii. 19); inasmuch as their idols are up **upon** their heart (ch. xi. 5), the occasion taken therefrom (to fall into sin) is given or put **before their face** (ver. 4). ["Anything which, in consequence of the inward disposition of mind and will, is conceived of also as an object of attention outwardly, and as the immediate occasion of corresponding actions, is spoken of as coming up or put upon the heart, Isa. lxv. 17; Jer. iii. 16, li. 50; 1 Cor. ii. 9; Jer. vii. 31, xix. 5, xxxii. 35; 2 Kings xii. 5 [4]; 2 Chron. vii. 11; Acts vii. 23. — Dan. i. 8; 2 Sam. vii. 3; 1 Chron. xvii. 2; Acts v. 3."—BECK.] They are portrayed accordingly as persons whose spirit cleaves to the old idolatrous memories; they are sinners against Jehovah, they have already even been punished by Him, but in heart, just as before, they are not freed from their idols. This, of course, is the explanation of the strongly negative character of the question. הַאִדָּרֹשׁ, inf. abs. Niphal, for הִדָּרֹשׁ, ה being changed into א, according to Kimchi, because of the doubling of the ה. In דָּרַשׁ there lies an element of urgency or zeal, with which one seeks in order to find—in the case before us, asks in order to get an answer.

Vers. 4–11. *A further Disclosure of the Divine Mind,* with a *more general* reference, and in ver. 9 sq. a *special* application *to the prophet.*

Idolatrous oracle-seekers, as Ver. 4 a second time portrays them, generalizing the case before us (אֶל-לִבּוֹ, although merely **to** the heart; אִישׁ אִישׁ, without exception), have therefore (לָכֵן, see ver. 4 at the end) to expect what corresponds to their state. For אוֹתָם, comp. on ch. ii. 1. **I Jehovah,** in emphatic antithesis to the **filthy idols.** Hence, as well as because of ver. 3, where an answer is absolutely refused, נַעֲנֵיתִי is a question without any particle of interrogation, which after ver. 3 is unnecessary (HENGST.). The Niphal of עָנָה means: to be inclined, to show oneself willing to answer. [EWALD: "I am become bound to answer him in Myself, for," etc., *i.e.* I can no longer remain in a mere state of indifference toward him, but must treat him at the right time as he deserves (!). Castel also, without the form of a question: I answer him, as is becoming in the case of such idols. Cocc. refers to this category such an answer on the part of the prophet, that the inquirer remains fixed in the multitude of his idols, does not repent, 1 Kings xxii. 23.] בָהּ (Qeri, בָא), because of the antithesis to Jehovah, a pregnant announcement beforehand of what follows: בְּרֹב', indicates the condition in which the inquirer is. [Others: according to it. The fem. instead of the plural; while others have taken it as בֹּה, referring to רֹב, or as a neuter: for it, for this coming to the seer, or (like Hitz.) read בִּי (Jehovah will answer in actual fact).]—Ver. 5 is understood by most of a good intention on the part of God in such answering, which is to correspond to their idolatry, and is to be given first in ver. 8. KEIL: not merely to move and to benefit them, but to bend their heart by means of judgments, etc. Hitz. on the other hand: in order to take them in their state of mind, as their acting is perhaps legal. According to Hengst., giving the reason for refusing an answer: in order that they may attain to a knowledge of sin, to touch their conscience. Rather does לְמַעַן place in the foreground the ruling purpose in the call which follows. It is their heart God means to reach, just as it is there their idols live (vers. 3, 4). אֲשֶׁר, a pronoun, not a conjunction.—נָזֹרוּ, as in Isa. i. 4, Niph. reflexive of

זוּר, expressing deliberation; where we have in that case אָחוֹר for מֵאֲחוֹרָיו, here we have מֵעָלַי, corresponding to what follows: וְהָשִׁיבוּ קְעַל.—כֻּלָּם is taken by others as a repetition of the subject: all of them together.—Ver. 6. וְהָשִׁיבוּ, namely: פְּנֵיהֶם; not: your heart, as Hengst., Rashi. (Others: your wives, children, etc.)—Ver. 7. Comp. Lev. xvii. 8, 10, 13, xviii. 26, xx. 2. If it is the rule for the **stranger**, much more for every one of Israel.—לִדְרָשׁ־לוֹ בִי, HÄV.: to apply to the prophet (as organ) for counsel from Me (so that at bottom he inquires of Me). Similarly HENGST.: to inquire of him in Me = to inquire of Me through him. ROSENM.: inasmuch as he pretends faith in Me. KEIL: to seek Me for himself (לוֹ reflexively, or *dat. commodi* of him who inquires). בִי forms the antithesis to 'בָהּ בְּרֹב (ver. 4) or בְּגִלּוּלֵיהֶם (ver. 5). The case is—after the demand being made by the prophet (ver. 6), as is presupposed—one of aggravated hypocrisy, that is, no longer mere coming to the prophet with idolatrous hearts (vers. 3, 4), but an express appeal to the Lord in spite of inward cleaving to idolatry; hence, a putting of trust in Him, although one is away from Him (ver. 7). Hence 'אֲנִי is no longer (as Hengst.) a question, a refusing to answer, but in this case Jehovah reveals Himself as giving an answer. But how?—Ver. 8. The divine answer demanded turns out to be one in actual fact; the word of God is God's judgment. Comp. Lev. xvii. 10, xx. 3, 5, 6; Deut. xxviii. 37. In the **face** we have the revelation of wrath. In the individual the land is already personified (ver. 13 sq.). וַהֲשִׁמּוֹתִיהוּ from שָׁמֵם, "to be desolate" (ch. xx. 26); according to others in the meaning: to put in a state of dumb terror. Ew.: from שׂוּם, as also the ancient translators [and Eng. Vers.] (Ps. xliv. 15 [14]). 'לְאוֹת, so that he becomes a sign, etc.—Comp. on ch. xii. 22.

With a special application to the prophet, Ver. 9 sets forth the case of one to whom one has come to inquire in the name of the Lord (ver. 7). That a prophet like Ezekiel was thought of, is not to be inferred from the occasion (ver. 1); at most we may say with Hengst.: "Let not one make demands on the true prophets which they are not able to fulfil, appealing to the utterances of the false prophets." Hitzig certainly maintains that the case of a prophet is supposed in the future who really has, or in good faith imagines that he has, a word of God. But that the prophet supposed is a false prophet is shown by the result. First of all, פָּתָה itself means: to talk over a credulous person; and hence the person meant here is one who, from his own want of true faith, is not himself acting rightly in a religious point of view, and therefore cannot judge rightly what such acting is, and what is not. Of a desire for gain, honour, or such like, nothing is said; we are not o think of Balaam. Then, farther, there is the expression: וְדִבֶּר דָּבָר, being talked over he gives himself to talk, **speaks** where he ought to have been silent (ch. iii. 27), or was at least bound to demand repentance (ver. 6), or else to announce judgment—consequently, speaks in a way to flatter the sinner. The case is made quite evident by the explanatory apodosis; what has already happened is God's judgment on the prophet, punishment, since Jehovah rather speaks to His prophets, gives them His word; and the result which follows in the case of this prophet is therefore merely the completion of the divine judgment. Comp. ch. vi. 14. (1 Kings xxii., where we have demoniac elements, does not properly belong to the category before us). From fear of man, or from desire to please man, the prophet suffers himself to be persuaded to speak. Because he so depends on men, men get the mastery over him, but in these men the hand of God shows itself against him. His leaning to men is his divine judgment; the conjuncture brought about by God, the prophet in this conjuncture left to himself and to men. According to J. H. Michaelis, Hengst., it is intended in this way to obviate the objection drawn from the solitary position of Jeremiah and Ezekiel.—Ver. 10 combines vers. 8 and 9. By the equality of punishment, the equality of the offence is proved. The oracle-seeker and the oracle-giver thus, by means of their punishment, expiate their guilt, with which they have burdened themselves in consequence of their sin; and as the punishment of the one offence corresponds to that of the other, it is thus clear that the guilt in both cases is alike in God's sight. The divine intention therein—Ver. 11—is, in respect to all Israel, to prevent their going astray, their defilement or polluting of themselves, on such devious paths (in all sorts of transgressions); for Israel's destination continues to be the holy one of being Jehovah's people, even as Jehovah's promise continues to be the glorious one of being their God. Comp. ch. xi. 20. With this reference, so general in its character, the special case of the prophet comes to an end.

Vers. 12–23. *The Application to Jerusalem* (ver. 21), *and the Justification thereof* (vers. 22, 23).—In accordance with what, from the outset, has formed the expectation of those who had come to Ezekiel, viz.: that they should know the fate of Judah (of Jerusalem), and in accordance farther with what has been expressed, in a general way, by the divine discourse of the prophet in the shape of judgment on false oracle-seeking and false oracle-giving,—in accordance therewith the section (ver. 12 sq.) closes, inasmuch as there is an application of the judgment pronounced, first to an unfaithful land, and then to Jerusalem expressly; an application which is seen to be the more justifiable, as the going astray and the pollution, which God designs to put away for the future by means of the judgment, still characterize the miserable remnant (vers. 22, 23).

Ver. 13. **A land**, indefinitely; not, however, for the purpose of giving utterance to a general proposition as a rule (KEIL), but because the nearer definition is expressed by means of the character of the land, and that as a character attaching to it as a whole. The "sinning" in general is specialized as: לִמְעָל־מַעַל, which is to be understood therefore in the strict sense which it everywhere has when it is a special expression. Comp. Lev. v. 21 [vi. 2]; Num. v. 12; Deut. xxxii. 51; Josh. xxii. 20; 1 Chron. x. 13. There cleaves to the word a contrast between the inward and the outward; it speaks of secret unfaithfulness, of concealed acting, and the like. And so it stands here also, quite in accordance with ver. 3 sq., where the subject in hand was the duplicity of oracle-seekers, false prophets, and at the same time paving the way for ch. xv. 8. (Ewald sees in מַעַל the treachery of Zedekiah, as a vassal bound by oath to his liege-lord of Babylon, by his leaning toward Egypt.) After such definiteness in the description of the sin of the land, the indefiniteness of the land itself can occasion no difficulty. What is thus kept indefinite rouses the hearers the more to think for themselves what land it will be. The indefinite expression presupposes, in particular, that those "men" (ver. 1), from their own conscience, might easily supply what was wanting. There is also an element of retribution—a certain measure of secrecy on the part of God, in return for their secret state of heart. Would that they would only ask! We find ourselves in the act of applying what has gone before to that land for which Jerusalem is the title (ver. 21). Hence the expression: **and I stretch out**, etc., literally the same as in ver. 9. As to the rest, there is a retrospective reference to ch. iv. 16, v. 16, 17. **Cut off**, as in ver. 8.—Ver. 14. As the description up to this point is an appeal *ad hominem*, to reflect and to determine the land for themselves, so this number: **three**, might perhaps draw attention to the difference at Gen. xviii. 32. There it is promised that there will be no destruction if there are ten righteous. Here it is only three that are supposed, belonging to quite different periods, nay, not even mentioned in chronological order. The case supposed is therefore, after all, an inconceivable one, to show at once the impossibility of the land being delivered; or, if the thought were admitted that three men like these were in it, yet the deliverance of the land is meant to be denied, since the three would save their own life merely. The judgment on the land, and that as a judgment that is all-embracing, corresponding with the character belonging to each and all, is to be set forth in all four directions (comp. ch. v. 17) in which it is pronounced, as one that is unalterable, that stands fast for that land. That is the thought. That the elders who had come to the prophet, as well as the people, had cherished the hope (Keil) that God will, for the sake of the righteous, avert the destruction of Judah and Jerusalem, is certainly nowhere even hinted. [True, indeed, there is no express statement to that effect. But why is the prophet's message thrown into this particular form? Why should he so emphatically declare—once and again, and again, and even a fourth time—that the presence of these three righteous men in the land could not avert its destruction, if no such thought was lurking in the minds of the elders and of the people generally? Keil's view, which is also that of Fairbairn, is of course a conjecture, but a conjecture that has not a little probability.—W.F.] As the diminution in number from ten in the fall of Sodom to three here is noticeable, so as regards **Noah, Daniel, and Job** personally, a lowering in the thing itself is to be observed. For these parties come into consideration here neither as regards their righteousness, as being patterns of it, nor even as examples of those who had been themselves spared, as is commonly supposed. בְּצִדְקָתָם (also in ver. 20) gives the reason for their deliverance merely, and לְבַדָּם, in vers. 16 and 18, isolates them merely for the case in hand. According to their history, which is related to us along with their names, all three, in fact, not merely saved their own lives, but exercised influence in the direction of saving others along with themselves. In addition to Noah himself (Gen. vii. 13 sq.), his family was saved in the ark, and even a selection of the creatures. Daniel not only saved himself and his companions, but also arrested the execution of the wise men of Babylon (ch. ii. 18). The representation of Hävernick, and of those who follow him, is in this matter as incorrect as in respect to Job, to whose intercession for his friends Jehovah certainly has respect (ch. xlii. 8 sq.). The climax, also, which Klief. and Keil still concede to Hävernick, has therefore no existence. In the parallel passage in Jer. xv. 1, Moses and Samuel are not supposed to be inhabitants of the land, like those here named; who are also not so specially Israelitish personages, but of a more general historical character, in harmony with the indefinite mode of conceiving the land. (But comp. also for the connection with what precedes, Jer. xiv.) Daniel figures between Noah and Job, not certainly in order to his being canonized by means of the two primeval personages (Hengst.), but—if this lifting into prominence of a still youthful contemporary by the insertion of his name between theirs is not to be reckoned mere flattery—because of his universally (and especially by the exiles) recognised real and high importance for the faith of Israel at the royal court. Comp. also ch. xxviii. 3. According to ch. viii. 1 (comp. with ch. xx. 1), we are in the sixth year of Jehoiachin's captivity. Thirteen or fourteen years earlier, in the reign of Jehoiakim, Daniel was carried into exile in his youth. The divine discourse, therefore, makes rhetorical use of them as three personages universally known for preservation against destruction, in order to represent the state of affairs here in question as the more hopeless; for Noah, Daniel, and Job will save nothing but their own life, *i.e.* as the repeated assurance in the three following cases expresses it with pathetic emphasis, neither son nor daughter, not to speak of others, or even friends; whereas Noah was able to save beasts even, Daniel Chaldean magi, Job such as were actually outside the community of Israel. The apodosis begins with הֵמָּה.

[Fairbairn: "The two most powerful and honoured intercessors, Moses and Samuel, could not prevent or rectify the evil by their intercession, Jeremiah had said. No, responds Ezekiel from the banks of the Chebar; nor could three of the most righteous men that have ever lived, either in past or present times, do it by their righteousness. Though Noah, Daniel, and Job were all at this moment in the land, they could not stay the judgment of God from proceeding."—W.F.]

Ver. 15. לוּ, with the imperf., used of things not now actually existing, but perhaps possible.—

The wild beasts of prey conceivable in connection with every kind of devastation (comp. ver. 21), here placed between famine and war. (HENGST.: "In the usual sense or in human form.") Comp. ch. v. 17; Lev. xxvi. 22; 2 Kings xvii. 25.—Ch. xii. 20.—מִבְּלִי, because of the want of, because there is not, or: so that there is not = Ver. 16: אִם־וָאִם, they shall not do so, quite certainly.—Ver. 17. Ch. vi. 3, xi. 8.—Ver. 19. Ch. v. 17, ix. 8. בְּדָם, not: because of blood shed, blood-guiltiness, but: so that the outpouring of divine wrath manifests itself in the shedding of human blood, *i.e.* either generally: through dying, or more specially: through violent death, hence: as in war, or that (HENGST.) the epidemic is represented as an execution as it were with the sword, or (HITZ.) that a peculiar epidemic, which should make itself known by a vomiting of blood or the like, would be meant.—Ver. 20. A winding up, and therefore a repetition of the three in the form of ver. 14.

Ver. 21. כִּי does not introduce the application, for all that precedes was already that; but gives the reason why for the whole deliverance is not to be thought of, only destruction, **Jerusalem** being now named, as we shall see, in order to justify such procedure with it. אַף כִּי, a climax, inasmuch as the separate judgments given above as examples are now all four together, and with definite certainty (שִׁלַּחְתִּי, perf.) pronounced upon Jerusalem. (HENGST.: How much more must it manifest itself in the servant who knew his master's will, and did it not!) The number **four** may possibly symbolize the completeness of the judgment, as one on all sides (KLIEF.). Formerly famine was first; here it is the **sword**, because the calamity of war lay immediately before them. In consequence of it the other three judgments came after one another, and side by side with one another. War brings famine into the cities, corpses outside, which attract the beasts; and from all there follows the pestilence. It is superfluous in Hengst. to point to ch. xix. 2 for figurative beasts. Jerusalem is thus the "land" formerly spoken of, represents it.—Ver. 22. It is exceedingly striking (וְהִנֵּה), that after all a number **escape** the judgment, who are carried captive to Babylon (**to you**); but they are not those who save their life by their righteousness, but those who are to justify Jehovah's righteousness *ad oculos* (הִנָּם), and that by means of their **way**; not in the sense of lot, or what happens to them, but in the connection here, where עֲלִילוֹתָם gives the more exact explanation, as designating their walk, just as עֲלִילוֹתָם itself indicates their habitual actings, and, indeed, their bad way of acting. Ye shall convince yourself with your own eyes that these escaped ones might rather be regarded as an irony, a caricature of these three men. אֵת כָּל־: "as respects all that." Still more clear is it in Ver. 23 that it will be a comfort through the persons themselves, and that it will consist in the knowledge that such corruption had deserved such destruction. לֹא חִנָּם, comp. ch. vi. 10. There of speaking, here of acting. Hence, as it is there said in reference to the consequence, the result, so here in reference to the cause—not without being deserved. Chap. vi. of the remnant themselves; in our passage of those to whom they are added as exiles. We see that there is not much hope of conversion for the former as a whole. That, even in the case of a relentless extermination of the bad, "there should yet be left a remnant of good" (NETELER), is certain, but is not said here. It is thus opposed to the context when Hitzig, appealing in a singular way to Num. xiv. 31, understands by הַמּוּצָאִים the younger race who had not grown old in sin, who shall conduct themselves in an irreproachable way, just as they have by their blamelessness saved themselves merely, not their parents also; whereby, however, compassion will be only the more stirred; they will be a pleasing spectacle in their inoffensive and God-pleasing life. The right knowledge is therefore to be this, that God has exterminated the wicked, has saved the innocent, consequently has judged righteously (with good cause). Just as little have we here an asseveration (really, truly), as Hävernick understands אַף כִּי, announcing a new, unusual judgment besides the four.

DOCTRINAL REFLECTIONS.

1. Not merely in view of the dangerous position of Israel in the midst of the heathen nations, but as flowing from the peculiar relation of Jehovah to His people as chosen from mankind, there is a prophecy under the Old Covenant mediating that covenant. For the Holy Ghost was not yet present, John vii. 39. God speaks and manifests Himself in demonstration of the Spirit and of power by the mouth of His holy prophets. Extraordinary gifts of the Spirit assert a place for themselves; things perceived in vision, disclosures by means of the dream, profoundly significant utterances and signs occur even in the service of individual needs. But prophecy becomes a prophetic office and formally an order of prophets, and that especially the more the priesthood sinks, and the commonwealth of Israel is secularized by means of the kingdom. Ever stedfast to Jehovah, and regulating itself by His law, this prophecy preserved its genuine character and proved its genuineness; just as it continued to uphold, with the force of constitutional law and with a reformer's energy, the sovereignty of Jehovah against every power which rose up against it. As, however, in spite of this, the national life sank to the verge of dissolution, there appeared, in opposition to the divine ordinance of true prophecy, an order of false prophets, devoted to idols and to the court, which enjoyed the sympathies of high and low. It cultivated the rhetoric of a phraseology at once yielding and heroic, in other respects having manifold affinities with the journalism of the present day as it is exhibited by the French press. In itself thoroughly ungodly, it affects outwardly the appearance of a species of religiosity, which certainly desires to know nothing of sin, and consequently also nothing of punishment. It brands with the suspicion of fanaticism and hypocrisy

the zealous prophecy of the law, which, in opposition to the ridicule as well as blandishments of the spirit of the age, has to proclaim the reformer's call to repentance, and along with that, in ever louder tones, the prophecy of judgment.

2. As Jer. xxix. 13 explains the zealous seeking (דָּרַשׁ) with the whole heart, the seeking (בִּקֵּשׁ) which finds, it is a standing requirement from all who would draw nigh to God that they believe that He is (Heb. xi. 6). The idolatrous practical atheism corresponds neither to the one nor the other. Thus there can be no talk of finding or letting oneself be found. The answer of God, which is therefore no answer, as the parties in question also have not yet inquired, is consequently a declinature; and that of a special kind, to allow of its being got by inquiry. But it is the nature of idols to be able neither to hear nor to answer. Accordingly, if Jehovah is not to wear the semblance of an idol, He must not only show Himself as one that hears, but as one who tries the heart and reins, and understands the thoughts afar off; and His silence will have to be regarded as speaking, in the same way as His speaking as it passes over into the virtual answer of punishment, of judgment.

3. In the heart the stream of our life is gathered up, alike in its outflow and inflow. To it the Bible assigns the central place, both in a corporeal and spiritual point of view. Comp. BECK, *Umriss der bibl. Seelenlehre*, 3 Aufl. p. 74 sq. Its hidden depths are known to God alone, who at the same time takes hold of man in his conscience, when He takes him in his heart. In this way He makes the unanswerable witness speak of guilt and punishableness; and alike for faith and for love, the whole heart, the full activity of man's reason and emotional nature, as it has its sphere in the moral self-determination of the personal consciousness, is claimed. In accordance with such a meaning of the heart must the call to turn from their idols be understood as a taking hold on God's part of the heart of Israel.

4. The case of the prophet who allows himself to be persuaded, to be enticed, illustrates to us the course of punishment. It is not merely that God permits the temptation, the misleading,—although it proceeds originally from the indwelling sin (Jas. i. 14),—for every following sin is at the same time a punishment of that which goes before. "In virtue of a divine law, the man is compelled either to take back the sin with regret, repentance, conversion, to its commencement and its principle, or to continue in its path towards his punishment" (NITZSCH). "God has no inactive part in the development of sin; He knows how to guide the matter throughout, so that sin attains its full maturity, and brings on punishment. He takes care that there can be no standing still, no halting at an intermediate stage; He makes the occasions and removes the hindrances" (HENGST.). Thus God gives up the sinner to his sin, but reveals Himself at the same time in His power, whereby there is always given along with the sin corruption, and that as punishment; and in this way He causes the righteous reward to come upon him.

5. As the false prophets appear in connection with national corruption as a definite stage in the development, so likewise they are put in relation to Jehovah, and in this relation are recognised as a dispensation of God, as a divine judgment, although at the same time meant for separation and decision in Israel. To this we must refer the "testing," for which provision is made in Deut. xiii. "The fact that false prophecy sprang up with quite peculiar energy about the period of the exile, appears accordingly not to be accidental and devoid of significance. The process of separation between the pious and the ungodly was thereby accelerated. But that period is only the bringing to light of a truth which retains its import onwards to the end of the world, 2 Thess. ii. 9 sq." (HÄV.) ["The point chiefly to be noticed in this deliverance of the mind of God is the connection between the self-deceived people and the deceiving prophet; regarding whom it is said, in peculiarly strong language, 'I the Lord have enticed (or deceived) that prophet.' It is an example in the highest sphere of the *lex talionis*. If the people were sincere in their desire to know the mind of God, for the purpose of obeying His will, the path was plain. They had but to forsake their idolatries, and the Lord was ready to meet them with direction and blessing. But if, on the other hand, they were bent on playing the hypocrite, professing to inquire concerning Him, while their hearts in reality were cleaving to corruption, punishment was sure to overtake them, and that, too, in the first instance, after the form of their own iniquity. God would chastise their sin with a corresponding sin; and as they had rejected the safe direction of the true light, he would send the pernicious delusion of a false one. Prophets would be given them, who should re-echo the deceitfulness that already wrought in their own bosom, so that their iniquity should prove their ruin."—FAIRBAIRN'S *Ezekiel*, p. 147. —W. F.]

6. "In the juxtaposition of Daniel with the exalted figures of Noah and Job, we have a solid support for the historical character of the book of Daniel. Besides, the connection with eminent wisdom in ch. xxviii. is exactly the characteristic feature in the personality of Daniel, as it is represented in his book" (HENGST.).

HOMILETIC HINTS.

Ver. 1 sq.: "Hypocrites may indeed deceive men, but not God, Ps. xii. 2, 3" (CR.). Acts v.—"So also the scribes and Pharisees came to Christ in the gospel: not that they wished to learn of Him, but for the purpose of tempting Him" (LUTHER).—As the prophet is here warned of God, set right through the Spirit, so Jesus knew what was in man (John ii. 24, 25).—"We learn from this how false men are; for who could have supposed this of old men, who were near the grave?" (LUTHER.)—To listen to God is to get clear insight as to men.—"It is not wrong for one to ask counsel of teachers in doubtful cases; but those teachers are to give it not according to the imaginations of their own heart, but according to the leading of God's word" (STARKE).—"Those parties do not judge rightly who do not wish to put the images out of the temples until the idols are away out of men's hearts. We ought rather to give testimony against both, because God in His word rejects images and idols alike. For if the former are not removed from the eyes of men, there remains the danger that one may again worship them. From the adulterous woman, the clothes, rings, letters of her paramours must be taken away, that she may not again be reminded of her lovers. This holds good also of the spiritual adultery of superstition" (LUTHER).—"Such a filthy idol is one's own righteousness, the high opinion which a man has of his own works, Phil. iii. 7, 8" (COCC.).—"Most men have something on which their heart's dependence is placed, and in this way are chargeable with a refined species of idolatry. Hence it is no wonder if God does not hear their prayer, John ix. 31" (STARKE).—"From the despisers of the truth the word of God is taken away, Acts xiii. 46" (O.).—The speaking and silence of God here, as in the case of Jesus before the Sanhedrim and before Pilate.—"Answering as well as greeting is a sign of good-will and friendliness; and so God shows His indignation when He does not answer, or does not answer as one desires. As *e.g.* happened to Saul" (LUTHER).—Ver. 4. "God leaves sinners without answer and help, in order that they may come to the knowledge of their sin" (HENGST.).—Ver. 5. God aims at the heart of man.—Ver. 6. Conversion is a step backward, but one which is also a step forward, and that from idols to the living God.—Vers. 7, 8. As with respect to whole lands, so with respect to the individual man, visitation ends at last in utter destruction. He that wooed to repentance adjudges to perdition. The heart which has become stone is rejected.—Lot's wife, for example, is a sign; proverbs are such as Sodom and Gomorrha, Dathan and Abiram, Judas, etc.—The cutting off from Israel often takes place inwardly, so that only the individual himself knows about it.—"Although God does not always cause hypocrites to be publicly put to shame, yet the testimony of their own conscience is often punishment enough" (CR.).—"Because God sees, hears, knows all, He will one day also give an answer as respects all, not only to pious hearts, but also to the ungodly, although such an answer is long delayed" (W.).—Vers. 9, 10. "When the men of the world do not hear from the true prophets what they would like to hear, they are wont to seek out the false prophets. In this way they have already fallen into the judgment of God, for there are no false prophets without God's will. But now they are expressly said to share also the judgment on the false prophets" (LUTHER).—"Such miserable men, who themselves lie under the destiny of God, are led by Him whither they will not, and are hastening to meet the judgment, cannot possibly furnish a staff for others" (HENGST.).—He who does not wish the truth—and truth for man consists first of all in the knowledge of sin—is brought to ruin at last by the lie, notwithstanding all his asking after truth and speaking of truth.—God manifests Himself therefore to hypocrites also, but as righteousness.—"God plants the pious, but roots out the ungodly, hearers and teachers alike" (STARCK).—Ver. 11. And yet all at last turns out for the good of His children.—"If the flourishing of the false prophets serves to test the faith of the pious, their fidelity in confession, their stedfastness, the judgment on them and on those who follow them confirms the pious in their piety" (LUTHER).—Even the burning houses of the wicked are a light on the way of the pious.—The universal approbation which apostasy from God enjoys in the world would lead, if it were possible, to the very elect being seduced in such days as ours. And therefore not only must the world pass away with the lust thereof daily before the eyes of those who, blessed be God, can see, but striking judgments of God as well must confirm to those that hear God's word the fact that it alone abideth for ever.—"How merciful is God, who reclaims the wanderers, and cleanses the polluted, and in His judgments still fulfils His promises!" (LUTHER.)—Ver. 13. Land and people,—the former suffering for the sake of the latter, the latter through the former.—Sin the destruction of the people.—"Although public calamities have their natural causes, they stand under God's government" (STARKE).—Ver. 14. "The Jews in all likelihood placed much reliance on the commandments and the intercession of the saints, and supposed that on this account they need not be afraid of the threatenings of the prophets. But such empty hope Ezekiel dismisses" (LUTHER).—Ver. 15 sq. "If the godly in such judgment cannot be heard when they pray for the ungodly, how much less will the latter find audience for their own persons!" (LUTHER.)—Godliness has the promise of this life also.—"The cause of wars is sin, which God means to punish; but He means to test the godly also in their patience, and to visit them" (LUTHER).—Vers. 21-23. "In a similar relation with the people of the Old Covenant stand the Christian nations, only that in their case the responsibility appears enhanced" (HENGST.).—God's righteousness is clearly manifested in those that perish, as well as by means of those that escape.—"The ungodly man, so long as he remains unconverted, at most keeps in check, but never changes, his disposition" (LUTHER).—"Comfort lies in the justification of the ways of God. Knowledge of the greatness and depth of sin—this is in all cases the chief foundation of the theodicy" (HENGST.).—Even these miserable ones may be an apologetic.—"So long as we do not understand that God on just grounds acts sternly, so long are our souls distressed and tormented" (CALV.).

4. *The Parable of the Vine Tree for the Burning* (ch. xv.).

1, 2 And the word of Jehovah came unto me, saying, Son of man, what shall
the wood of the vine be more than any wood? the vine-branch which was
3 among the trees of the forest! Is wood taken thereof to do any work? Or
4 do they take a peg of it to hang any vessel thereon? Behold, it is [was]
given to the fire for fuel [food]; its two ends the fire consumed, and its middle
5 is scorched; is it fit for any work? Behold, in its uninjured state, it will not
do for any work; how much less, when the fire hath devoured it, and it is

6 scorched, will it still do for any work? Therefore, thus saith the Lord
Jehovah, As the wood of the vine among the wood of the forest, which I
have given to the fire for fuel, so have I given the inhabitants of Jerusalem.
7 And I have set My face against them; from the fire they went out, and the
fire shall consume them; and ye know that I am Jehovah, when I set My
8 face against them. And I have made the land a desolation [a wilderness],
because they have committed treachery: sentence of the Lord Jehovah.

Ver. 2. Sept.: . . . *τι ἀν γενοιτο*— Vulg.: . . . *quid fiet.*

Ver. 4. Παρεξ ὁ πυρι δεδοται . . . την κατ' ἐνιαυτον καθαρσιν αὐτης ἀναλισκει—

Ver. 6. For בעץ there is a plural reading: בעצי.

EXEGETICAL REMARKS.

A figure (vers. 1–5) and its application (vers. 6–8). The former is carried out in detail; the latter follows in the shape of interpretation. With much plausibility, Neteler (comp. ver. 7 with ch. xiv. 22 sq.) refers what follows specially to "the remnant left over," in support of which the connection with what precedes might be pleaded; but it must not be forgotten that this remnant are the justification of the judgment on the whole; and hence, that the reference generally to Judah and Jerusalem is to be maintained.

Ver. 2. The figure of the **vine** or vineyard is in current use for Israel (Deut. xxxii. 32; Isa. v.; Hos. x.; Jer. ii. 21; Ps. lxxx. 9 [8]; Matt. xxi. 33 sq.) in manifold shades of meaning,—sometimes the noble vine, sometimes the degenerate, sometimes the wild vine. The latter is perhaps the idea lying at the foundation, no stress, however, being laid upon it; but the vine in general, as compared with other wood, is meant to be spoken of, so that the figure of the vine furnishes merely, as it were, the customary title of Israel. What superiority has Israel, although the so-called "vine," as a nation over other nations? Culture makes the vine a vine, just as it causes it to bear noble fruit. Now, however, instead of the despised culture, there manifests itself the judgment of God! Hence, also, 'עֵץ: the **wood** of the vine.—מַה־יִּהְיֶה, not so much: what superiority has it? as rather: what will be its fate? how will it fare with it? as judgment is hinted at.—מִכָּל־עֵץ. Every other wood can be made use of; the vine, on the contrary, is of no service except for its fruit. The answer supposed for the question, therefore, not merely denies the claim to a better fate, but even makes the wood of the vine inferior to other wood, that is to say, when it fails of its aim. This is the intermediate thought, which the apposition (corresponding as it does with the accents): 'הַזְּמוֹרָה אֲשֶׁר, explains. Differently the Sept. and Vulg. זְמוֹרָה (commonly so called from paring or pruning; according to others, from intertwining; or, "that which shoots;" זָמַר is used to express a process—that of nipping off—derived from vine-culture) is the plant of the vine (Isa. xvii. 10), which accordingly has been removed from its original habitat in the wilderness, in order to be planted, to be cultivated. The masc. הָיָה refers to **wood**, as being the connection in which the זְמוֹרָה is thought of. So also in what follows. If it has not repaid the planting, and this is the case here—but it is not expressly said that it had become degenerate, had borne no fruit at all or bad fruit (HENGST.: "the vine-shoot which is among the trees of the forest" = the vine which corresponds with the forest-trees in barrenness, as it is mere wood; the wild vine does not occur at all in Scripture),—the questions that follow naturally suggest themselves in this connection.—Ver. 3. For use its diameter even unfits it (HITZIG); while its appearance is too paltry for ornament, and it is too weak to bear anything except fruit.—Ver. 4. Useless as wood, because it is of service merely for its fruit, it falls of right to the fire (John xv. 6; Matt. vii. 19). But still less is to be thought of it, and therefore, just as at the beginning (ver. 2) a question was put as to its fate, the question is renewed in view of the effect of the fire. The **two ends** are in the application perhaps not so much the kingdom of the ten tribes and Judah, as rather those tribes of Israel on the one side and on the other; so that the **middle** piece, which may still come in question, is Judah with Jerusalem, or the latter alone. נָחָר partic. Niph. of חָרַר. Figure and reality running into one another. What is in prospect is in part realized fact, on the ground of which a further question is put (Matt. iii. 10; Heb. vi. 8).—Ver. 5. הִנֵּה resumes the parallel הִנֵּה of ver. 4. What could not even be in its uninjured state, can much less be when the case stands with it as in ver. 4.

The carrying out of the figure already indicated its reference generally; the application now interprets it expressly of the inhabitants of Jerusalem.—Ver. 6. אֲשֶׁר־נְתַתִּיו, such a destiny as has just been made to take effect. HENGST.: "which I give" by a law of nature with regard to the vine.—Ver. 7. Ch. xiv. 8.—**From the fire**, etc., that is to say, in the sense of vers. 4, 5. Already burnt, they would have required to be on their guard against the fire. But in this way that is only "the beginning of the end" (HENGST.). Many expositors point specially to the experiences of the divine wrath under Jehoiakim and Jehoiachin. But comp. on vers. 4, 5. (Grot. proverbially: coming out of the one, the other will fall upon them.)—Ch. v. 4, x. 2.—Ver. 8. Ch. xiv. 15, 16, 13.

DOCTRINAL REFLECTIONS.

1. The temple of Herod even was decked off with the "distinguishing mark" of Israel, the vine and its clusters (JOSEPHUS, *Wars of the Jews*, v. 5. 4).

2. What is here called the "wood," Paul would express by the words: "after the flesh."

3. "The chosen people of God, if they deny and profane the Holy Spirit of heavenly fruitfulness, who works in them, are, as regards the barren wood of their original stock, less than all other nations" (UMBREIT).

4. "A nation or an individual to whom God has made Himself known, and who turns His grace into lasciviousness, sinks far beneath those who have not known God. Heb. vi. 4 sq." (HENGST.)

5. "The Church is not to be a wilderness, but a vineyard; is not to bear flowers only, or leaves and twigs merely, but fruit. She is not an apple-tree or fig-tree, but a vine. Wine cheers, inspirits, enlivens. Outwardly insignificant, there is the noblest power within. The grace of Christ working through poor apostles" (A LAPIDE).

HOMILETIC HINTS.

Ver. 2 sq. The question as to superiority was called forth by the vainglory and self-complacency of Israel. They boasted of being superior, and therefore what they are to become is held up before them; for it is not what we seem to ourselves to be that constitutes our superiority over others, but it is what has come out of us that will ultimately show whether we are to go to the right hand or to the left. The end decides the matter. It is not: the beginning good, everything good.—"Our faith constitutes our superiority, proving itself as it does in our conduct and edifying others" (STARCK).—If thou hast, why boastest thou thyself, seeing thou hast received it? Keep what thou hast, that no man rob thee of thy crown.—"The intention of the prophet is to humble the foolish self-confidence of the people, who boasted themselves of the gifts of God's grace, as if they were mere natural excellences. On the ground of His benefits they took a stand against God" (CALV.).—"The comparison with plants and trees is in many respects a suitable one for man" (STARCK).—"Believers have but a mean appearance before the world; but in Christ, the True Vine, they are fruitful, John xv." (STARKE.)—"He who looks at the vine as regards its wood will scarce reckon it among the trees. It lies at the feet of the trees of the forest. Their wood far surpasses its wood. But because God had planted Israel, he came forth from the wilderness of all the nations. Out of Egypt God brought him (Ps. lxxx. 9 [8] sq.). Other nations, on the contrary, flourished by means of arts, riches, population, capacity for war, etc. These were lofty forest trees, which drew the eyes of all upon them. Israel stood and fell with God's grace" (CALV.).—To the Jews the law was given very much as a vine-dresser's knife, that they might bring forth more fruit.

Ver. 6 sq. "God is always punishing; but the punishment is unto destruction when He sets His face against the sinner" (LUTHER).—"The fact that one evil is past makes men secure without reason, for another comes after it" (STARCK).—"Let us learn from this chapter to beware of fleshly security" (LUTHER).

5. *The Story of the Lewd Adulteress* (ch. xvi.).

1, 2 And the word of Jehovah came unto me, saying, Son of man, cause Jeru
3 salem to know her abominations; And say, Thus saith the Lord Jehovah unto
Jerusalem: Thy origin [extraction] and thy birth is of the land of the Canaanite;
4 thy father was the Amorite, and thy mother a Hittite. And [as regards] thy
birth, in the day that thou wast born, thy navel was not cut, neither wast
thou washed with water for cleansing; and thou wast not rubbed with salt
5 at all, nor wast thou wrapt in swaddling-bands at all. No eye had pity upon
thee [looked upon thee compassionately], to do one of these things for thee, to bend
over thee; and thou wast cast out upon the face of the field [upon the open field],
6 in contempt of thy soul [life], in the day that thou wast born. And I passed
by thee, and I saw thee stamping [or, trampled] in thy blood, and said unto thee,
7 In thy blood live! and [yea] said unto thee, In thy blood live! Ten thousand
[myriads] like the bud of the field I made thee [to be, to become]; and thou didst
increase [didst grow up] and wax great, and camest to most excellent ornament;
thy breasts became firm [rose up], and thy hair grew, yet thou wast naked and
8 bare. And I passed by thee, and saw thee, and, behold, [it was] thy time, a
time of movements of love, and I spread My wing over thee, and covered
thy nakedness; and I swore unto thee, and entered into covenant with thee
9 —sentence of the Lord Jehovah—and thou becamest Mine. And I washed
thee with water, and rinsed thy blood from off thee, and anointed thee with
10 oil. And I clothed thee with broidered work, and shod thee with tachash,
11 and wrapped thee round with byssus, and covered thee with silk. And I
decked thee with ornament, and put bracelets upon thy hands, and a chain
12 about thy neck. And I put a ring in thy nose, and earrings in thine ears,
13 and a splendid crown upon thy head. And thou didst adorn thyself with
gold and silver, and thy clothing was byssus and silk and broidered work
fine flour, and honey, and oil didst thou eat; and thou wast [becamest] exceed

ingly beautiful, and didst prosper into [attain unto] a kingdom [kingly authority or
14 dignity]. And thy name went forth among the heathen for thy beauty; for
it was perfect through My adornment, which I put upon thee—sentence of
15 the Lord Jehovah.—And [yet] thou didst trust in thy beauty, and didst play
the harlot upon thy name, and didst pour out thy fornications upon every
16 one that passed by; his it was. And thou didst take of thy garments, and didst
make for thyself high places, spotted [patched] ones, and didst play the harlot
17 upon them: they should not come, neither should it be. And thou didst
take articles of thy splendour [thy splendid jewels] of My gold and My silver,
which I had given thee, and didst make for thyself images of men, and didst
18 play the harlot with them. And thou didst take thy broidered garments,
and didst cover them; and My oil and My incense thou didst set before them.
19 And My bread which I gave thee, fine flour, and oil, and honey I gave thee
to eat, and thou didst set it before them as a sweet savour: and it was so—
20 sentence of the Lord Jehovah. And thou didst take thy sons and thy daugh-
ters, whom thou barest unto Me, and didst sacrifice them to them to devour;
21 was it less than thy whoredoms? And thou didst slay My sons, and gavest
them up, in causing them to pass through [the fire] for them [i.e. for the idols].
22 And with all thy abominations and thy whoredoms thou didst not remember
the days of thy childhood [youth], when thou wast naked and bare, wast
23 stamping [trampled] in thy blood. And it came to pass after all thy wicked-
24 ness—woe, woe unto thee! sentence of the Lord Jehovah—That thou didst
build for thee a vault, and didst make for thee a high place in every street.
25 At every head of a way [crossway, parting-way] thou didst build thy high place,
and didst put to shame [didst abhor] thy beauty, and didst spread out thy
26 feet to every passer-by, and didst multiply thy whoredoms. And thou
didst whore after the sons of Egypt, thy neighbours, great of flesh, and
27 didst multiply thy whoredoms, to provoke Me to anger. And, behold, I
stretched out My hand over thee, and diminished thy allowance, and gave
thee to the soul of them that hated thee, the daughters of the Philis-
28 tines, who were ashamed of thy lewd way. And thou didst whore after
the sons of Asshur for want of being satisfied; and thou didst whore with
29 them, and still wast not satisfied. And thou didst increase thy whore-
dom unto the land of Canaan, Chaldea, and even with this wast not satis-
30 fied. How exhausted [spent with longing] is thy heart—sentence of the Lord
Jehovah—when thou doest all this, the doing of an imperious whorish woman.
31 When thou didst build thy vault at the head of every way, and madest thy
high place in every street, thou wast not like the harlot, to scorn the hire.
32 The woman that committeth adultery under her husband receiveth strangers!
33 To all harlots they give [are accustomed to give] a present [a gift], and [yet] thou
gavest thy presents to all thy lovers, and didst make presents to them, to
34 come to thee on every side for thy whoredoms. And there was in thee
the contrary of women; in thy whoredoms they did not follow after thee for
whoredom, and in thy giving of hire when no hire was given to thee; and
35 [so] thou wast the contrary.—Therefore, O harlot, hear the word of Jehovah.
36 Thus saith the Lord Jehovah: Because thy brass was poured out [emptied out],
and thy nakedness uncovered in thy whoredoms with thy lovers, and with all
the filthy idols of thy abominations, and according to the blood of thy sons,
37 whom thou hast given unto them; Therefore, behold, I am gathering all
thy lovers, to whom thou wast pleasant, and all whom thou hast loved, with
all whom thou hast hated; and I gather them against thee from round about,
38 and uncover thy nakedness unto them, and they see all thy nakedness. And
I judge thee with the judgments of adulteresses and of those who shed blood;
39 and I make thee into blood of fury and jealousy. And I give thee into their
hand, and they throw down thy vault, and demolish thy high places; and
they strip thee of thy clothes, and take the articles of thy splendour [thy splendid
40 jewels], and leave thee naked and bare. And they bring up a company against
thee, and cast at thee with stones, and hew thee down with their swords.

41 And they burn thy houses with fire, and execute judgments upon thee before
the eyes of many women; and I make thee cease from being a harlot, neither
42 shalt thou give hire any more. And I make My fury rest in thee, and My
jealousy departs from thee; and I take rest, and I will no more be angry.
43 Because thou hast not remembered the days of thy childhood [youth], and
didst rage against Me in all this, behold, I also have given thy way upon thy
head—sentence of the Lord Jehovah—and hast thou not committed lewdness
above all thy abominations?
44 Behold, every one that deals in proverbs shall utter a proverb against
45 thee, saying, As is the mother, so is her daughter. Thou art thy mother's
daughter, that spurneth [casteth off] her husband and her children; and
thou art the sister of thy sisters, who spurned their husbands and their
46 children; your mother is a Hittite, and your father an Amorite. And
thy great sister is Samaria, she and her daughters, that dwell at thy left;
and thy smaller sister than thou, that dwelleth on thy right, is Sodom and
47 her daughters. And [yet] thou didst not walk in their ways, nor didst after
their abominations; as only a little, thou wast more corrupt [didst act more cor-
48 ruptly] than they in all thy ways. As I live—sentence of the Lord Jehovah—
if Sodom thy sister hath done, she and her daughters, as thou hast done and
49 thy daughters! Behold, this was the iniquity of Sodom thy sister: pride,
fulness of bread, and rest free from care [tranquil security], were to her and her
daughters; and the hand of the poor and needy she did not take hold of
50 [strengthen]. And they were haughty, and committed abomination before Me;
51 and I removed them when I saw it. And Samaria hath not committed the
half of thy sins; and thou didst multiply thy abominations more than they,
52 and didst justify thy sisters by all thy abominations which thou didst. Thou
also bear [take upon thee] thy disgrace [shame], which thou didst adjudge to thy
sisters; by thy sins, wherein thou hast done more abominably than they, they
will be more righteous than thou; and [yea] also be thou ashamed, and bear
thy disgrace, because thou didst justify thy sisters.
53 And I turn back their misery, the misery of Sodom and her daughters, and
the misery of Samaria and her daughters, and the misery of thy miseries
54 in the midst of them. That thou mayest bear thy disgrace, and be
55 ashamed of all that thou hast done, in that thou comfortest them. And thy
sisters, Sodom and her daughters, shall return to their first estate, and Samaria
and her daughters shall return to their first estate, and thou and thy daugh-
56 ters shall return to your first estate. And Sodom thy sister was not for a
57 report in thy mouth in the day of thy haughtinesses, Before thy wickedness
was discovered, as at the time of the scorn of the daughters of Aram, and of
all her [Jerusalem's] surroundings, the daughters of the Philistines, who despised
58 thee round about. Thy lewdness and thy abominations, thou hast borne
59 [bearest] them—sentence of Jehovah. For thus saith the Lord Jehovah: And
I did with thee as thou hast done, who didst despise the oath to break the
60 covenant. And [yet] I remember My covenant with thee in the days of thy
61 childhood [youth], and establish unto thee an everlasting covenant. And
thou rememberest thy ways, and art ashamed, when thou receivest thy sisters,
those greater than thyself along with those smaller than thyself; and I give
62 them to thee for daughters, and not by thy covenant; And I establish My
63 covenant with thee; and thou knowest that I am Jehovah. To the end thou
mayest remember, and be ashamed, and there may be no more opening of thy
mouth because of thy disgrace, when I cover for thee all that thou hast done:
sentence of the Lord Jehovah.

Ver. 4. Sept: . . . *οὐκ ἐδησας τ. μαστους σου . . . οὐκ ἐλουσθης του χριστου μου*— Vulg.: *non es lota in salutem*—Sept., Syr., hex., and Arabic read: שדך, *ubera tua.*

Ver. 5. . . . *ὀφθαλμος μου ἐπι σοι . . . τουτων, του παθειν τι ἐπι σοι . . . τη σκολιοτητι της ψυχης σου*—.

Ver. 6. . . . *πεφυρμενην ἐν τω αἱμ. . . . ἐκ του αἱματος σου ἡ ζωη σου, κ. πληθυνου* (ver. 7.)—For חיי, there is a reading חייך, *vita tua.*

Ver. 7. . . . κ. εἰσηλθες εἰς πολεις πολεων— Vulg.: *Multiplicatam quasi germen . . . et ingressa es et pervenisti ad mundum muliebrem; . . . nuda et confusione plena.*—For שדים, there is a reading: שדיך.

Ver. 8. . . . ὡς καιρος καταλυοντων. Vulg.: *tempus tuum, tempus amantium.*

Ver. 12. κ. ἐδωκα ἐνωτιον ἐπι τον μυκτηρα σου . . . κ. στεφανον καυχησεως—

Ver. 13. For ומלבושך, there is a reading: ומלבושיך, *et vestimenta tua;* Sept., Syr.

Ver. 15. . . . ὁ οὐκ ἐσται— Vulg.: . . . *ut ejus fieres.*—Sept. reads: תזנותך, in the sing.

Ver. 16. . . . κ. οὐ μη εἰσελθης οὐδ' οὐ μη γενηται. Vulg.: . . . *sicut non est factum neque futurum est.*

Vers. 19, 20, 21. . . . κ. ἐγενετο μετα ταυτα . . . κ. ἐλαβες . . . Ὡς μικρα ἐξεπορνευσας, κ. ἐσφαξας τ. τεκνα . . . ἐν τω ἀποτροπιαζεσθαι σε αὐτα ἐν αὐτοις. (Many Codices and the Complut. have the plural: מתזנותיך; see also vers. 25, 26.)

Ver. 27. Ἐαν δε ἐκτεινω την . . . κ. ἐξαρω . . . κ. παραδωσω σε εἰς ψυχας . . . τας ἐκκλινουσας σε ἐκ τ. ὁδου σου ἡς ἠσεβησας. Vulg.: *et auferam justificationem tuam.*—(Another reading: ואגדע.)

Ver. 28. . . . θυγατερας Ἀσσουρ . . . κ. ἐξεπορνευσας κ. οὐκ ἐνεμπιπλω,

Ver. 29. κ. ἐπληθυνας την διαθηκην σου προς γην Χαν. κ. Χαλδ.— Vulg.: . . . *in terra Chan. cum Chaldæis*—

Ver. 30. Τι διαθω την θυγατερα σου . . . ἐν τω ποιησαι σε . . . κ. ἐξεπορνευσας τρισσως ἐν ταις θυγατρασιν σου— Vulg.: *In quo mundabo cor tuum . . . cum facias omnia hæc . . . ?*

Ver. 31. . . . κ. ἐγενου ὡς πορνη συναγουσα μισθωματα. Vulg.: . . . *nec facta es quasi meretrix fastidio augens pretium, sed* (ver. 32) *quasi mulier adultera*—

Ver. 32. Ἡ γυνη . . . ὁμοια σοι, παρα τ. ἀνδρος αὐτης λαμβανουσα μισθωματα πασιν (ver. 33) τ. ἐκπορνευουσιν αὐτην προσεδιδου μισθωματα. Κ. συ δεδωκας . . .

Ver. 34. . . . ἐξεστραμμενον παρα τ. γυναικας ἐν τ. πορνεια σου, κ. μετα σου πεπορνευκασιν ἐν τω προσδιδοναι σε μισθωματα κ. σοι μισθ. οὐκ ἐδοθη— Vulg.: *et post te non erit fornicatio*—

Ver. 36. For וכדמי, the Sept., Chald., Arab., Vulg. read: ובדמי.

Ver. 37. . . . κ. ἀποκαλυψω τ. κακιας σου προς αὐτους—

Ver. 40. . . . ἀξουσιν ἐπι σε ὀχλους—

Ver. 42. . . . κ. οὐ μη μεριμνησω οὐκετι.

Ver. 43. . . . κ. ἐλυπεις με . . . κ. οὑτως ἐποιησας τ. ἀσεβειαν σου ἐπι πασαις τ. ἀνομιαις σου. Vulg.: . . . *provocasti me . . . et non feci juxta scelera tua in omnibus abominationibus tuis.* (For בראש, there is a reading: בראשך, which also that of Syr. and Arab.—Sept., Syr., and Arab. read: עשיתי, without the negation.)

Ver. 46. . . . ἡ πρεσβυτερα . . . ἡ νεωτερα—

Ver. 47. Κ. οὐδ' ὡς . . . οὐδε κατα . . . παρα μικρον κ. ὑπερκεισαι— Vulg.: *fecisti pauxillum minus; pene sceleratiora fecisti.* (Another reading: מהם.)

Ver. 49. . . . κ. ἐν εὐθηνια οἰνου ἐσπαταλων αὐτη—

Ver. 50. Vulg.: *sicut vidisti.* (Another reading: כאשר ראית.)

Ver. 51. Another reading: ממנה, *præ illa.*

Ver. 53. Vulg.: *Et convertam restituens eas conversione Sodomorum c. filiabus . . . et conversione Samariæ . . . et convertam reversionem tuam*—

Ver. 55. . . . ἀποκατασταθησονται καθως ἠσαν ἀπ' ἀρχης—

Ver. 56. κ. εἰ μη ἠν Σοδομα—

Ver. 57. προ του . . . ὁν τροπον νυν ὀνειδος εἰ— Vulg.: *Palæstinarum*— (Another reading: בנות אדם (*Edom*), Syr.)

Ver. 61. κ. δωσω αὐτας σοι εἰς οἰκοδομην—

EXEGETICAL REMARKS.

The humbling prophetic discourse passes from the designation of the vine to that other, where Jerusalem specially is spoken of as the "daughter" of Zion. At the basis of such a conception of the people, *i.e.* of Judah as a woman in their still standing capital city, the leader of fashion, there lies the mystery of Jehovah's covenant as a marriage. To the course of sinning stretching over centuries, and with special reference to מָעַל מַעַל in ch. xv. 8, there corresponds the detailed picture, which borrows its colours and therewith obtains its justification from the thoroughly sensual idolatry into which the people had fallen. It is spoken after the manner of the East, and must be translated into the language of the West,—in other words, traced back to its spirit and the ideas lying underneath. The story which is therein related is in so preponderating a degree a story of *sin* (vers. 2–34), and the *punishment* of sin (vers. 35–52), that the glimpse of *grace*, with which the long chapter concludes, only occupies the verses 53–63. ("The whole representation runs on like a progressive drama, which in an earthly picture sets forth so vividly the conflict of the holy love of God with man's unfaithfulness, that many a reader certainly, with feelings of shame, will exclaim: My soul has been the faithless spouse of God!"—SCHMIEDER.)

Vers. 2–14. *The Grace at the Beginning.*

In this way (comp. Deut. xxxii.) the abominations (ch. vii. 3, 4, 9) of Jerusalem—representing the people in their own land—are to be the more affectingly brought home to her consciousness, are to be held up before her in so much the more shameful a light ("the abominations of Canaan," HÄV.). "He first loved us," is the golden background for the dark and gloomy picture which follows, but which even in Ver. 2 is kept in view, and already in Ver. 3 hints at Jerusalem's Canaanitish origin. Of such a nature are those abominations of hers which the prophet is to make known to Jerusalem, that such an inference seems justifiable, and one that may be drawn. (Kimchi, Grotius, have supposed an announcement by means of a letter!)—As in the figurative expression: מְכוּרָה (from כָּרָה, to dig), the reference is to the place where metals are found (comp. Isa. li. 1), or to the source (Häv. compares ch. xxi. 35 [30], and understands: "place of generation," corresponding to the **father**, just as the place of birth corresponds to the **mother**), so also מוֹלְדוֹת, which is likewise in the plural, means something belonging to the sphere of nature. The higher divine origin of the people is, in fact, lost sight of; they **are conceived of as regards the land of their** natural development, where their capital city is situate. The intermediate thought is the implied accusation, that they have not dealt with the inhabitants of the land in accordance with the promise (comp. Ex. xxiii. 32 sq.; Deut. vii. 1 sq.), but have become degenerate like them, and therefore themselves ripe for extermination. Just as in John viii. 44, in contrast with Abraham, "the devil" is spoken of as the "father" of the Jews, so here the **Amorite** (Gen. xv. 16; Josh. x. 5), who by himself, or also along with the **Hittite**, is elsewhere named instead of the Canaanite in general, either because these two were the most distinguished of the Canaanitish nations, or because with them more than the rest of the Canaanites the earliest reminiscences of the fathers of the Jewish people were connected (Gen. xxiii., xxvi. 34, 35, xxvii. 46, xxviii. 1, 6, 8). Where, as here, the reference was to the land, it was the Canaanite (in Greek: the Phœnician) who principally came into consideration with the Jews (Gen. xxxviii. 2). What is implied in the expression **Canaanite** might be seen already in Gen. ix. 25, were not the Hamitic corruption of this people (comp. in what follows the different hints of this) a fact established from profane literature even. The close intercourse with the Semitic tribes, already carried on in earliest times, is reflected especially in the Semitic character of the language of Canaan; it was the overpowering spirit of the Semitic to which almost all the Hamitic dialects have succumbed: so much the more ignominious must the spiritual dependence of the degenerate Jews, with which Ezekiel charges them, appear. (Comp. Zeph. i. 11.)—Ver. 4. The circumstances connected with the birth, of which the description is still continued in ver. 5, point to Egypt, where the nation first saw the light of day.—הוּלֶּדֶת, inf.: the being born. The dagesh after shurek is unusual.—כָּרַּת and שָׁרְּךָ, both times ר with dagesh: *shorrech, chorrath*.—The bandaging and cutting of the navel-cord, as is necessary after the birth for the independent life of the child. And just as in this way there is expressed what is necessary, so in the washing with water we have what is customary and fit. מִשְׁעִי only here; probably a Chaldaic form for מִשְׁעִית. Other derivations from שָׁעַע or שָׁעָה: *ad lenimentum*, JARCHI: "for brightness," COCC.: *ad jucundum aspectum meum*.—What was done elsewhere to new-born infants (according to Galen), and is still done in the East down to the present day, in order to harden the tender skin, according to Häv. and Hitz., because of the symbolic meaning of salt, in order to express the hope and wish for a vigorous life.—Augusti derives from this the usual sprinkling of salt in baptism,—is perhaps at the same time intended to serve for a more thorough cleansing, or (according to others) for healing the wound of the navel. It was not fostering care that fell to the lot of Israel's national life in the times that succeeded Joseph, when they grew from a family into a nation, but envy, persecution, contempt on the part of the Egyptians; so that they must have looked like an exposed Bedouin female infant (foundling) abandoned to its misery (a heathen custom prevailing in many quarters), given over to perish.—Ver. 5. Those who had looked up to Joseph did not even look down with compassion on thee.—"The existence (soul) of Israel as a nation was an object of abhorrence to the Egyptians. The image of a child the more suitable, as Moses, the type of his people, was actually exposed," etc. (HENGST.) [Others: inasmuch as thou wast to them an object of loathing; or: in the loathing which thou hadst of thine own life.] Such outward misery is not conceivable without a corresponding inward misery. Hengst. makes the wretched condition in Egypt to be a punishment of the evil tendencies dwelling in Israel from of old (Gen. xv. 13, 14).

In contrast with such neglect (ver. 4) and such treatment (ver. 5) on the part of man, the divine compassion rises up into greater prominence in Ver. 6. Jehovah is portrayed after the similitude of a king (as so often in the German legends a king's son finds a deserted maiden), who passed thereby, perhaps on the chase.—In the **blood** still adhering from the time of birth (JUV. *Sat.* 7: *adhuc a matre rubentem*). But by this expression is at the same time meant to be signified the danger to the life of the child, and not merely its impurity (*quanquam fœda es sanguine, volo te vivere*). [TARGUM and RASHI: of the blood of circumcision and of the passover lamb; the verse *Blessing* in the ritual of circumcision.] As in this way from the very commencement בְּדָמָיִךְ is connected in thought with the desperate movement or situation of the child, in like manner it is afterwards to be joined both times with חֲיִי. It is from the first the word of promise (וָאֹמַר לָךְ twice), but as being seriously meant and certain, and hence continued without interruption, rendered more vivid by means of the repetition. מִתְבּוֹסֶסֶת, Hithpalel of בּוּס, GES.: given up to be trodden under foot. The root-meaning is "to tread down," "to trample." ("This child was able to survive such trampling." HENGST.) HÄV.: "despised," in a derivative signification. The continued promise of life in the midst of danger continually threatening, makes us think besides of Ex. iii. 2.—In Ver. 7 there follows the mightily efficacious blessing in the increase of the people, a visible confirmation and realization of the word of promise (Ex. i. 7, 12). According to Hitzig, we have by this means a transition from the figure to the thing signified. According to Hengst., the subject in hand is an ideal child, that comes to view in a multiplicity of separate existences; רְבָבָה is not one myriad, but a numerical measure, an ideal unity, embracing a multitude of actual myriads (Num. x. 36; Deut. xxxiii. 17).—בַּעֲדִי עֲדָיִים, either: into the age when maidens think of dress and finery (when would that be?), or, from the fact of her being naked, of the highest charm of youthful beauty, which would quite fit into the context. [HÄV.: "the most distinguished morning-time of life, the most beautiful season of youth." And just as he appeals in support of this view to Ps. ciii. 5 [4], so Hitzig at the same time appeals to Ps. xxxii. 9 for an explanation in the sense: "and thou wentest along in the ornament of cheeks."] —The sprouting hair about the *pudenda* as a sign of becoming marriageable. Indecent (HÄV.) nakedness is not the subject in hand, but merely nakedness in contrast with clothing and ornament.

Ver. 8 brings to view a significant act of grace on Jehovah's part, parallel to that in ver. 6. The parallel is not, that after "the founding of the city" there comes now "its passing into the hands of Israel, and that for the dwelling-place of Jehovah;" nor that in the one case we have "the wandering horde," and in the other "the covenant at Sinai" (HITZ.); but it consists in this, that as Jehovah's mercy was shown to the people by their preservation and increase in Egypt, so it was shown by their deliverance from Egypt, which reached its immediate close in the giving of the law at Sinai; in the former case more outwardly, in the latter for the most part in an inward way.—**Thy time**, connected by means of the "seeing" with what goes before, is defined by the following עֵת דֹּדִים (wooing-time), as meaning that the marriageable one has become ripe for love.—The spreading of the corner of the upper garment and the covering of the nakedness symbolize in general, that He took the miserable, helpless one under His protection, interested Himself in her; specially, however, with the thought of conferring the honour of betrothal, marriage—comp. Ruth iii. 9 (in which connection Cocc. makes mention of the covering cloud at the departure from Egypt and the passage through the Red Sea); a thought which is solemnly carried out in the swearing and entering into covenant, by means of which Israel, grown into a nation, now became the peculiar people of Jehovah. Comp. ch. xx. 5, 6; Ex. xix., xx. 2, 5, xxiv.; Deut. v. 2; Eph. v. 32.—Ver. 9 in part resumes ver. 4, in order to make the cleansing appear as thorough as possible; even what still cleaved to Israel from his birth was to be put away, the reason being that they were sanctified by God to be wholly and entirely His people, to occupy a priestly place among the nations. This peculiar destiny of Israel as a nation is symbolized by the washing. [HÄV.: cleansing in the solemn covenant-sacrifice, Ex. xxiv. Hitz., as already older expositors: of the laws of cleansing, *e.g.* Lev. xv. 19.] At the reception into the royal harem, lengthened preparations, especially purifications, are customary in the East; comp. Esth. ii. 12; Ruth iii. 3. To the same category belongs also the anointing. We are not debarred from thinking of spiritual benefits—the gifts of the Spirit in Israel.—Ver. 10. After the cleansing and anointing comes the clothing, in view already of the kingly character of Israel generally, Ex. xix. 6; Ps. xlv. The Egyptian colouring of the painting is at the same time, perhaps, not unintentional.—רִקְמָה, from רָקַם (to puncture), is embroidered work, specially of variegated colours; here with gold and silver, figures, flowers, etc. The art of working in various colours is even at the present day very much developed among the Egyptians.—תַּחַשׁ, elsewhere only in the Pentateuch, of the outermost covering of the tabernacle and of the sacred furniture; here manifestly an article of luxury. Some have thought of the seal, the dolphin, the fox, a species of hyena, etc. (WINER, *Realw.* ii. p. 596 sq.), of whose skin the shoes were manufactured. The old translations, on the contrary, leave out of view the material, and lay stress upon the colour of the leather; not exactly blue, but of a dark colour, red, violet. BYNÆUS, *De Calc. Hebr.*: scarlet. HENGST.: morocco. Niebuhr heard in Arabia, from a learned Jew, that *tachash* is the red-coloured skin of the ram. To tanning and colouring the root-meaning of the word may possibly have some reference.—שֵׁשׁ, Egyptian *shens* or *shenti* (comp. ch. ix. 2), means, like βύσσος, cotton, of which splendid garments were worn, but also linen, which is fine like cotton. Here the finest linen headband (turban) must be meant (חָבַשׁ), Ex. xxviii. 39.—וָאֲכַסֵּךְ (comp. ver. 8) in no way necessitates the meaning of covering with a veil (HITZ.), but ver. 13 uses the word מֶשִׁי of the clothing, which is, according to the tradition of the Jewish commentaries, silk (τρίχαπτον = threads fine like hair), but according to Hitzig, coloured cloth. Comp. BRAUNIUS, *De Vest.* etc. At all events, it is meant to be the highest degree of splendour, where the clothing even is like ornament.—Vers. 11 and 12. Plainly the bride's ornaments, by the detail of which the rich and splendid era of Solomon is still more vividly set before us. Comp. besides, Gen. xxiv. 22, 30, 47. But if even the **chain** about the neck is something peculiar (Gen. xli. 42), so above all is the **crown** (Lam. i. 1; Isa. lxii. 3; Jer. xiii. 18).—Ver. 13. In consequence of the divine adorning, Israel could adorn herself (שֵׁשִׁי וּמֶשִׁי, one of Ezekiel's paronomasias), and nothing was too costly; and to such riches corresponded the maintenance, the rest of the living, as the husband has to provide it for his wife, above all in the East. The choice delicacies appear to form the contrast to the usual food of the people in Egypt. By the word לִמְלוּכָה there is now expressed what was hinted at already, along with the priestly elements in what goes before. By means of their kingdom the kingly character of the people in general was suitably represented before the heathen nations also, but so much the more gloriously as the Messianic idea was symbolized thereby. Besides, there is also a preparation for ch. xvii. Comp. in addition, Cant. vii. 7 [6]; Lam. ii. 15.—The extraordinary beauty of Israel is their law (Deut. iv. 6 sq.) and their Messiah (Ps. xlv. 3 [2]).—Ver. 14. Already exemplified in Ex. xv. 14 sq.; still farther in 1 Chron. xiv. 17; 1 Kings x. Let it be noted that Israel is thus spoken of as perfect through Jehovah, of grace, not by nature or by reason of merit. Faithfulness, therefore, would have kept them in this glory. (Hos. ii. 10 [8]; Mic. ii. 9.)

ADDITIONAL NOTE.

["The second stage of this allegorical history, exhibited in vers. 8–14, represents the singular honour and glory conferred on the ideal virgin in her exaltation to the rank of a spouse to the King of Zion, and her decoration with apparel suited to her elevated station. . . . The description presents a vivid and impressive image of the singular goodness of God to Israel, from the time that He visited them in Egypt, and raised them from the low and depressed condition which they held there, to the nearest fellowship with Himself, and the highest place among the kingdoms of the earth. The relation formed between Jehovah and Israel at that interesting period had already been more than once represented under the image of the marriage-union." See Isa. l. 1, liv. 1; Hos. i.–iii.; Jer. ii. 2. "Indeed, no earthly relation could so fitly have been employed as that of marriage to exhibit the nature of that hallowed union, in virtue of which the Lord not only conferred upon them the rich dowry of temporal good, but also graciously condescended to maintain with them a most intimate and endearing interchange of love. . . . It is the internal relationship established between them and God, and the spiritual blessings immediately growing out of it, which are here primarily and chiefly referred to. Even the outward temporal blessing secured in the covenant, and in part also realized, should never have been viewed as an ultimate and independent good, but rather as the expression and emblem of something higher and better. They were not properly blessings at all, except in so far as they were held in connection with the favour of Heaven, and bespoke the fellowship of love that subsisted between Jehovah and His people. . . . But considering the state in which they were found in Egypt, they much needed to undergo a process of purification, to fit them for bearing aright so high and ennobling a character. That many rites of cleansing should have been prescribed to them, and a long course of preparatory discipline appointed, only betokened the Lord's earnest desire to have them qualified for the exalted state and destiny He wished them to fill. And throughout, nothing was wanting of tender compassion and faithful dealing on His part. From the first He crowned them with marks of His goodness. A fulness of power and glory rested on them far surpassing what their numbers alone might have warranted them to expect. And when the kingdom at last rose to meridian splendour, and received the confirmation and enlargement given to it, especially in the days of David and Solomon, the surrounding heathen were compelled to own that there is a great reality in the favour and blessing of Heaven. They saw in Israel, as a people, living monuments of the mighty efficacy of divine grace, how it can exalt the feeble, and lay the powers of the world, as well as the bounties of nature, under contribution to the furtherance of its beneficent designs."—FAIRBAIRN's *Ezekiel*, pp. 166–168.—W. F.]

Vers. 15–34. *The Horrible Unfaithfulness.*

Ver. 15 is in the form of an introduction, which announces two parts of what follows: (1) the *nature*, (2) the *extent* (ver. 23 sq.) of the people's sinning. The inmost nature of it is represented as being a trusting (בָּטַח) in the gift, conceived of apart from the Giver, hence as self-righteousness, pride, security. The way in which such a self-pleasing disposition expressed itself is portrayed, in accordance with the image of a wife, as **fornication,** alike in a political and in a religious point of view, from the time of Solomon. עַל־שְׁמֵךְ (in connection with ver. 14), on the ground of the report, the fame of thy beauty; on that ground, relying thereupon as upon a charter, that thou certainly hadst the name above others, as if nothing could rob thee of thy privilege (Jude 4; Rev. xviii. 7). [Others: "because of" (so Eng. Vers.); or: "notwithstanding," forgetting the name which thou hadst received from thy husband; or: against, *i.e.* against thy husband, so that adultery would be specified, which is dragged in from ver. 32.] Deut. xxxii. 15; Hos. xiii. 6.—The flowing forth of unrestrained desire, the extent to which the degeneracy reached, is expressed in the strongest way in the words **and didst pour out,** etc. (ch. xiv. 19).—לוֹ יֶהִי. HENGST.: "his be it," as if the words of the adulteress, that is to say, to him will I yield myself. HITZ.: יָפְיֵ, though at some distance, is the only possible subject; properly וַיְהִי, but the copula has fallen away because of לוֹ going before. KLIEF.: his it became, indefinitely: what thou hadst to bestow. A contrast to וַתִּהְיִי לִי: "and thou becomest mine," in ver. 8. (Comp. Ps. xlv. 12 [11].)

Ver. 16. A description in detail of the idolatry and the idolatrous worship as an abuse of the gifts and blessings of Jehovah, and a more and more heinous robbery of Him.—The worship of the high places was still a worship of Jehovah, but was already a self-willed degeneracy from the command that there should be one sanctuary (Deut. xii.), a divergence according to fancy and foreign examples. The בָּמוֹת are in themselves **high places,** natural heights set apart for worship, meant as they were to help the lacking elevation of heart, affecting as they did the high flight of the imagination; here, in connection with the **garments**: tents, made of variegated stuffs for garments, or provided with curtains of the same, or—shall we say?—laid out with variegated carpets, seeing that such things were woven by women for the Punic Venus (2 Kings xxiii. 7). HENGST.: "small idol-temples for domestic use." EWALD: small altars (vers. 24, 31). The worship of Astarte (?). Because of the epithet: טְלֻאוֹת, Hitzig makes mention of "smaller pieces of cloth also," but rejects the interpretation: "patched" high places; referring, however, to Gen. xxx. 35 sq. ("the sensuous piety became wanton over the party-coloured rags!")—עֲלֵיהֶם, masc., referring to בֶּגֶד, the עַל pointing to the "high places," *i.e.* to the high places thus clothed. [HENGST.: to be referred to the paramours, in the sense of: "with them." Others: on the carpets (?) in the tent-temples.]—בָּאוֹת, a paronomasia with בָּמוֹת. לֹא בָאוֹת, *i.e.* according to the law of Israel. They ought not to find entrance. [COCC.: which do not come from God to you, like the ark and the temple, but are inventions of your own heart!] וְלֹא יִהְיֶה, in reference to the clause: "and didst play the harlot upon them." [Others: the like has not come to pass, nor will it ever be. HENGST.: the like shall not come nor happen, as denoting unprecedented shamelessness.]

Ver. 17. A contrast between what was taken and the purpose for which it was taken. At the same time there now comes into view (וַתִּקְחִי in ver. 18 for the third time) the robbery of Jehovah. **Images of men**—(idolatry in general) because of the figure of a woman the idols are represented as men. [HÄV.: images of the *membrum virile* (*phallus*). EWALD: penates (teraphim), covered with ornament, set up in the house, honoured with *lectisternia.*]—Ver. 18. The "covering," according to Hitzig, is meant of the clothing of the idols with splendid drapery; MOVERS: of the wrapping up of the *phalli*, when they are placed in the shrine. The "setting before" them took place in sacrifice (Lev. ii. 1, 2).—**My**, not only as being from God, but still more as being destined for Him (Ex. xxx. 23–25). Ch. vi. 13, viii. 11.—Ver. 19. As for the erection of sanctuaries (ver. 16) and the making of idols (ver. 17), so for the honour paid to the same, Israel deprived herself not only of her clothes, but even of the divine food (ver. 13). The rich heathen worship of Hither Asia!—וַיֶּהִי, not interrogatively, but the simple shocking fact.—Ver. 20. The last step of apostasy, even their own children!—וַתִּקְחִי once more, as in vers. 18, 17, 16.—The worship of Moloch, as it existed from the time of Ahaz. זָבַח is: to slay in sacrifice; and the same thing is expressed by לֶאֱכוֹל, with which שָׁחַט in ver. 21 is to be connected, in order to explain to us בְּהַעֲבִיר as a lustration in the shape of burning; 2 Kings xxiii. 10; Jer. xxxii. 35, vii. 31. HENGST.: "The passing through was the mode of slaying, and the devouring was the consequence of it. The idol was supposed to be present in the fire."—To the question: הַמְעַט מ׳, a negative answer is expected, as in ch. viii. 17: Was it (the sacrificing of the children) less than, etc.? On the contrary, it far exceeded them. [HÄV.: Was there still too little of your whoredom? namely, to stop with vers. 15–19. HENGST.: Hadst thou too little of thy whoredoms?] Instead of: "thy," we have in Ver. 21: **My**; what was in the former relation inhuman, was in the latter not only a robber's, but also a murderer's outrage against God.—Ver. 22. Where there is now a transition to the extent of the idolatrous actings, we have a very suitable retrospective glance in recapitulation (כָּל), and, corresponding to the worst degree of outward idolatry, the forgetfulness of God in the inmost heart. The recollection of the first condition (vers. 6, 7) would necessarily have become the remembrance of Jehovah. Self-pleasing (ver. 15) did not allow it to come to this, but such non-remembrance was the parent of such gratitude.

Ver. 23. The *extent* to which, with such aggravation, the unfaithfulness reached. The picture, hitherto having reference to religious matters, now assumes a political hue. It appears that the representation given in vers. 15–22 is now used as a clothing for the thought in a figurative way. **After all**, etc. Hengst. understands the expression of time: with the oppression by the world-powers the apostasy became properly national. In that case the **wickedness** would require to be taken as calamity, and the misery that has come to Israel in consequence of such sins against Jehovah would have to be read between the lines, or the: **woe**, etc. would have to be connected with וַיְהִי. But the repeated exclamation seems rather to be a preparation for something future, the judgment still to come, and hence to be conceived of as a parenthesis, and וַיְהִי to be introductory to ver. 24; and therefore it seems necessary to interpret אַחֲרֵי, not indeed in the way of climax (HÄV.: even beyond, etc.), for ver. 20 sq. closed with the highest degree of guilt, but rather of the moral consequence. Such apostasy from Jehovah could not fail to be followed by the inner (political) decline of the theocracy, and the falling away to all possible world-powers.—Ver. 24. גַּב, in a collective sense, related to רָמָה, perhaps as altar to temple-height. Both are constructed, and thus רָמָה is distinguished from the natural בָּמוֹת. The actual idolatry, or the national decline set forth under this figure, showed itself in the midst of the bustle of the city. (According to others: גַּב = *fornix*, in the service of those religions of nature; farther defined by means of רָמָה as in an elevated situation, striking the eye.) Comp. ch. vi. 13.—Ver. 25. Comp. Prov. viii. 2.—וַתְּתַעֲבִי, as if thou thyself hadst an abhorrence of thy national glory (vers. 13, 14). [Others causatively: to make an object of loathing.]—Israel lay on the path for manifold intercourse with the world, especially between the Asiatic and African world-powers.—Ver. 26. **The sons of Egypt** are not its gods, and therefore the reference is to political whoredom. Let it be remembered how in express terms intercourse with Egypt was forbidden to Israel, how return thither is threatened them rather as the worst punishment (Deut. xxviii. 68); and let one compare, from the days of Solomon onwards, 1 Kings iii. 1, ix. 16, x. 28; 2 Kings xviii.; Isa. xxx., xxxi. 1, xxxvi. 6; Jer. xxxvii, 5, 7.—(2 Kings xvii.) But גִּדְלֵי בָשָׂר is characteristic for the licentious character of Egyptian worship (Mendes!). בָּשָׂר, the *membrum virile.* Comp. HENGST. *Authentie*, i. p. 119 sq.; *Mos. und Egypten*, p. 216. This expressive mode of designating them is, according to Hengst., intended to mean great of power. It marks rather the brutal lowness of having dealings with a state of such a character, religiously considered, of longing after it. In accordance therewith we have the provoking of Jehovah to anger, and what follows in Ver. 27 (ch. vi. 14, xiv. 9, 13). The "diminishing" is in contrast with the "increasing."—חֹק. HENGST.: "law;" in general: what accrues of right to the wife in respect of sustenance, clothing, lodging (Ex. xxi. 10); here in particular: what is destined for Israel by Jehovah in respect of maintenance, nurture, adornment, increase (ver. 9 sq.); only not exactly with Häv.: "the destined inheritance." As regards the thing meant, we may compare what the nation lost in land, and people, and influence, and splendour, or the like, especially indeed through Egypt, 1 Kings xi. 18, 21, 40, xiv. 25. (Joel iv. [iii.] 19.)—**Gave thee to the soul**, etc., usually interpreted, with an unwarranted quoting of such passages as Ps. xxvii. 12, xvii. 9, xli. 3 [2], lxxiv. 19, of a giving up to the desire, rage, bloodthirstiness, as if it were like נָתַן בְּיַד, whereas here at least the disposition of soul of the **Philistine** cities or states is expressly said to be different.—"Haters" they were already, but they became despisers.—מִדַּרְכֵּךְ זִמָּה is kept too closely to the figure by Hitz.: "because of thy profligate conduct, which is a disgrace for her also, because for the whole female sex;" while Häv. interprets too definitely of the thing meant, and has besides mistaken the meaning: they themselves brought back the ark (1 Sam. v., vi.).—זִמָּה, craftiness, baseness, (Lev. xviii. 17) most shameful uncleanness. Either a descriptive genitive or an emphatic apposition: thy conduct pure lewdness. The Philistines, who are introduced rather as spectators than as parties actively engaged, to whose contempt Israel was given up by Jehovah, turned away with shame from Israel's heathenish policy, inasmuch as they, in pleasing contrast thereto, stuck by their gods. Comp. Jer. ii. 10 sq. (GROT.) [Hävernick's view is that the Philistines are named *instar omnium*, in the sense of outward violence inflicted by fiercest enemies. Hitz. puts out of view the period of the judges, and refers to 2 Chron. xxviii. 18; Joel iv. [iii.] 4, 5; 2 Chron. xxi. 16; comp. besides the article in Winer, ii. p. 252 sq.]—Ver. 28. Having got no satisfaction in the African, they betake themselves now to the Asiatic world-power. Hitz. lays stress rightly upon the difference between זָנָה אֶל (already in ver. 26) and זָנָה with the acc., where in the case before us the two are contrasted with each other: first longing after, and then no satisfaction even when the longing is realized. (Comp. 2 Kings xvi. 7; 2 Chron. xxviii. 16; Jer. ii. 18; 2 Kings xxiii. 29.) And with this Ver. 29 connects the Babylonians. Ever more and more (vers. 25, 26) of insatiable lust.—כְּנַעַן is taken by most in an appellative sense, as meaning commerce, trade; hence: the land of traders, Chaldea (ch. xvii. 4; Isa. xxiii. 8; Job xl. 30 [xli. 6]), a view which is suggested by no kind of hint in the passage. Then, certainly, to translate: "with the land of Canaan," and to think of Canaanitish (Phœnician) idolatry (Ps. cvi. 38) "as far as Chaldea," or "at the same time turned to Chaldea," *i.e.* while taking in addition the Babylonish worship of Belus and Mylitta, is still less suitable. But כְּנַעַן means simply: "low ground" (low land); why not keep by the proper name in this sense? With an allusion to this, this downward step would be held up before the elevated Judah-Jerusalem, when in Chaldea, in the longing after political fellowship with the Babylonians, it hoped at the same time to get **the land of Canaan,** *i.e.* to get the Promised Land kept through such help of Asia herself against Asia. כַּשְׂדִּימָה, with ה parag., is the explanation which is added, to show in what sense אֶרֶץ כְּנַעַן is meant. Hengst., referring to ch. xxiii. and Isa. xxxix., and to the want of satisfaction spoken of here, points to the fact that they had at this very time turned back again to the Egyptians. Their new "Canaan" came to stand them in still worse stead than their intercourse with Assyria; Chaldea's friendship showed itself to be pure selfishness.

Ver. 30. By means of the exclamation (surprise, complaint?) a pause is introduced; what has been said (ver. 15 sq.) is forcibly summarized.—EWALD: "how languishing is thy heart!" biting sarcasm; how great must be the languishing of love! Similarly GES.: "How thy heart languished from lust!" HENGST.: "how withered," etc.; designedly the form לִבָּה, not elsewhere occurring in the sing.: a womanish heart, which has lost its sap and vigour in the world. אֲמֻלָה, likewise only here as partic. Kal. — **Imperious**, instead of being under thy husband, bold, unruly.—Ver. 31. בִּבְנוֹתַיִךְ, inf. with plur. suff. for בִּבְנוֹתֵךְ. Comp. vers. 24, 25. The "doing" mentioned in ver. 30 is exemplified, and then its imperiousness is unfolded: **thou wast not like the harlot,** namely, in that, as a thoroughly genuine harlot does, who wishes merely to play the whore at any price, thou thoughtest little of, scornedst the harlot's hire. Ver. 33 will show that she rather paid such hire to her lovers, purchased some for herself therewith. וְלֹא־הָיִיתְ is to be taken along with לְקַלֵּס' = thou scornedst not, etc. Commonly: in that thou scornedst, etc. [Others: not like the harlot, who despiseth, scorneth her hire, that is to say, wishes to extort more, because it appears to her too small; but thou didst accept everything, because the only object with thee was to satisfy thy lust. Others still: like the harlot who boasteth of her hire.]—As the people are portrayed from ver. 8 onwards as the spouse of Jehovah (comp. אִשָּׁה in ver. 30), we have in Ver. 32 very suitably, just as also in ver. 30, the exclamation (HÄV.: "O adulterous woman, who taketh!"), which lays stress upon the adultery involved in this policy with the foreign world-powers. תַּחַת, while she was under the authority of her husband (Rom. vii. 2), *i.e.* was legally and morally bound to be faithful to him. Others [as Eng. Vers.]: "instead." The horrible unfaithfulness is set forth as the whoredom of a married woman. Going back upon ver. 31, Ver. 33 portrays her whoredom, explaining fully the לְקַלֵּס' there. נֵדֶה, here merely instead of אֶתְנַן. HÄV. thinks of נִדָּה, *res fœda*. The **lovers** are not the heathen gods,—although not without reference to them (comp. ver. 36), in contrast with Jehovah,—but the strange nations (ver. 26 sq.): and these as bought. Comp. 2 Kings xvi. 8; Hos. viii. 9 sq., xii. 2 [1]; Isa. xxx. 5, 6. HITZIG: the presents through ambassadors, the yearly tribute, etc. As she was still always drawing upon her Husband's resources, she might well give presents. That she did so with such a view, for such an object, how horrible!—Ver. 34. **The contrary** or the reverse, so that from among all women thou standest forth alone of thy kind. What nowhere else finds an imitator among women, when a woman has done it before! In general there was no following after thee **in thy whoredoms**; but in particular (ver. 33) there was no one imitated thee in such giving of hire for whoredom.

Vers. 35–52. *The Punishment.*

Ver. 35. As if in a public judicial process, the indictment is read out.—Ver. 36. To **pour out** comp. ver. 15 ; here **brass** (GESEN.: copper, the art of tempering which was known), either used for metals of all kinds ; or goods and chattels generally (comp. ver. 10 sq., ver. 16 sq.) ; or money in particular, in which case it admits of question whether copper money was in use, not to speak of being common. (Matt. x. 9 ; Mark xii. 41.) It is put instead of the "whoredoms" of ver. 15, because according to ver. 33 these were purchased by means of presents ; and this the more appropriately, as in Deut. viii. 9 (comp. this Comm. *in loco*), and in ch. xxxiii. 25 of the same book, in the blessing of Moses, the richness in brass of the Promised Land is significantly referred to. Hence (1) the misuse and squandering of the dowry of the people, as it was given them in their own land. [HÄV.: brass as an ignoble and impure (?) metal, because of the disposition and the use made of it. BUNS.: "because thy kettle ran over," to denote the overflowing of lustful desire.] —(2) Shameful self-prostitution in national and religious respects, as contrasted with ver. 8, and visited with retribution in ver. 37.—Policy led at the same time to the introduction of the gods of the world-powers (ch. viii. 10). Ver. 16 sq. וְעַל is taken by many in the same sense as יַעַן: "and because of," unnecessarily ; but וּכְדְמֵי must be so taken. As respects idolatry, the sacrificing of their own children even. Ver. 20 sq. Hence (3) murder. These are the separate counts of the indictment. — Ver. 37. The public judgment. First of all, the assembling of the lovers as witnesses. She who has dishonoured and brought herself to shame becomes now, by the interposition of God, to the one party an object of loathing, to the other an object of mockery. The last attraction, and what might still have been an object of regard, vanishes. Hävernick refers to the procedure in the case of a married woman suspected of adultery, Num. v. 18.—Ver. 38. The sentence, which is one of death, because for adultery and murder ; the **jealousy** referring to the former, the **fury** to the latter.—**Into blood,** *i.e.* so that thou shalt be dissolved into that in consequence of such fury and jealousy ; ch. v. 13, 15. —Ver. 39. Those who before were witnesses now appear as executioners of the sentence. Grotius thinks of the temple. But it is the annihilation of the national life, which had fallen away from Jehovah, and not so much the plundering of Jerusalem, as generally the stripping of Israel of all her glory as a nation, that is the thought, expressed figuratively in accordance with the foregoing representation (vers. 24, 7).—Ver. 40. קָהָל, in accordance with the procedure in the case of adulteresses, as it were a "local community." Most interpreters make the stoning, which is merely a keeping up of the figure, refer to the *ballistæ* of the besiegers. The murder (vers. 36, 20 sq.) is punished with the **swords.**—Ver. 41. Comp. Deut. xiii. 16 ; 2 Kings xxv. 9. The **many women** are the numerous spectators, and these are the nations. Israel becomes a spectacle to the world. The opportunity and means for political intercourse with the heathen will disappear with the political independence.—Ver. 42. Comp. on ch. v. 13. The divine justice comes to an end in its character of **jealousy** ; in other words, as the injured faithfulness and love of Israel's Husband.—The **departing** of the jealousy might perhaps, by comparison with Isa. xi. 13, show grace in the background ; but the connection with what follows requires rather a thought like Hos. ii. 4 [2]. Jehovah gives up the adulterous whorish wife. **No more**—in wrath there is certainly love still !

Ver. 43. זָכַרְתִּי, with appended י, as in ver. 22, and frequently in Ezekiel and Jeremiah.—2 Kings xix. 27 sq. HENGST.: "thou wert angry with Me in all this," *i.e.* notwithstanding all the benefits, etc. ; Isa. viii. 21. Better at all events than : "thou didst provoke Me to anger by all this," for the Kal stands firm.—Ch. ix. 10. —עָשִׂיתִי is usually taken in the second person, either in the sense : "and [that] thou shalt not commit a deed of shame in addition to all," etc., that is to say, the measure is full, and in the place of the sin the punishment shall enter ; or in the sense : "for thou hast not taken thought (הַזִּמָּה) to thyself = hast not repented concerning all," etc. ; or interrogatively : "hast thou not committed this great transgression in addition to all," etc. ? Others have taken the verb in the first person, alleging that the clause was to be understood as meaning that Jehovah repelled from Himself the charge of having borne with the whoredom of the people, and hence of having Himself committed it, inasmuch as he had not punished it,—a very singular thought, surely. הַזִּמָּה is emphatic, and with a reference back is the same as in ver. 27 ; and the clause can scarcely be understood otherwise than as an interrogation, inasmuch as certainly the peculiar unfaithfulness of the people, depicted so prominently in ver. 30 sq., is elsewhere distinguished from all their abominations.

Ver. 44. Comp. on ch. xii. 22. The poet, perhaps also he who makes use of such proverbs, takes them into his mouth, utters them, for he can do it rightly.—אִמָּה, either for אֵם, like לִבָּה for לֵב in ver. 30, here also betokening the effeminate, womanish character, or for אִמָּהּ: "as is her mother," etc. Not the Jerusalem of former days, but (comp. ver. 3 with ver. 45) the style of Canaan.—Ver. 45. The **husband** is God, who can only be one and the same, either with reference, *e.g.*, to Melchizedek, who could point back to a better primeval time, or generally, because all idolatry is adultery, apostasy from God ; Acts xvii. 24 sq. ; comp. Isa. liv. 5.—The aversion for their children was shown in the worship of Moloch ; Lev. xviii. 21, 24 ; Deut. xii. 30, 31.—אֲחוֹתֵךְ, according to Ges., a plural ; according to Rosenm., "the dual, comp. ver. 46 ;" according to Hengst., an ideal person, the sisterhood.—Ver. 46. As "their husbands" were spoken of, because the relation in the case of Samaria was certainly different from that in the case of Sodom, Jehovah in the one, Elohim in the other, so Samaria and Sodom—**sisters** of the Jewish kingdom, because belonging to the same mother-country, and at the same time homogeneous in character—are still farther distinguished as to their size, in respect of the number of the tribes and cities, which are the **daughters,** and also as to their northern and southern position. Both come significantly into consideration as regards Judah, as being already judged.—Ver. 47. כִּמְעַט קָט, according to GES.: "it would be only a little;" Ewald: "only a little while;" Hengst.: "it wanted a little" (a softened "almost"); Häv.: "for a short time it caused thee loathing, disgust" (! ?). The meaning is perhaps: as if it were only a little, how Samaria and Sodom have conducted themselves, and what they have done, thou even wentest beyond them. [So Eng. Vers.] Others connect it with what goes before: "thou didst not walk, etc. a little merely, but thou wast," etc. Some have even taken לֹא=לוּא: "yea, hadst thou only, etc., but," etc. Comp. besides, Luke xii. 48; Matt. xi. 24.—Ver. 48. A solemn denial, as regards the more notorious of the two sinners (Sodom), that she has done like Judah. Hence in reality her acting was "as it were only a little" in comparison with thee! For she had neither Moses nor the prophets.—Ver. 49. It was the ordinary natural man who in Sodom ripened himself for judgment, in presence certainly of the riches of divine goodness, but not of the clearest revelation of truth. For the close of the verse, comp. the inhospitality in Gen. xix.—Ver. 50. Comp. Gen. xviii. 20, 21.—Ver. 51. The specification is wanting in the case of Samaria, not only because the remembrance too readily suggested itself, but also because the thought was a familiar one from Jeremiah; Jer. iii. 11. Judah had the temple, the royal house of David, at all events, with a longer season for repentance, not only Sodom's, but also Samaria's judgment before her eyes.—The **justification** is a comparative one: in relation to thee, Sodom and Samaria must appear as righteous. There is perhaps also the thought, that this relative justification so much the more demands the divine judgment upon Judah-Jerusalem.—Ver. 52. The mention of the judgment upon Samaria is wanting, as well as the mention of the details of her sinning; the inference is immediately drawn in its application to Judah. The **disgrace** is the judgment, the punishment, to those with whom she agreed, which she recognised in reference to the others as being righteous. Comp. Rom. ii. 1. [EWALD: "thou who hast called in question thy sisters." HENGST.: "thou who didst judge" [so Eng. Vers.]. Older expositors: "because thou hast been intercessor," hast virtually absolved.] She reviled them; now she must revile herself, or at least she is reviled, and this all the more as through Judah's sins they are more righteous than she.

Vers. 53–63. *The Return of Grace.*

Ver. 53. Just as there is grace at the beginning, so the end is grace.—For שׁוּב שְׁבוּת or שְׁבִית, comp. this Comm. on Deut. The fundamental passage is Deut. xxx. 3. A standing, as it were, proverbial phrase, but not necessarily of the bringing back from exile, rather Messianic in sense; for the abstract שְׁבוּת, from שָׁבָה, means in general: destiny, misery, as here a state of punishment. Of an exile of Sodom certainly nothing can be said! In form there is a paronomasia, but we are not to explain in this way the putting of the Kal for the Hiphil; the phrase requires a meaning like "to restore," a putting an end to and turning of the misery for this purpose. See Job xlii. 10. The transitive use of שׁוּב must thus be admitted as against Hengst.—Before Judah's restoration is mentioned, that of Sodom and Samaria is promised,—of the former as being the greatest sinner, of the latter as being the next to Judah. Thus Judah appears in the middle between the punished sinners,—just as in the New Testament publicans and Samaritans,—and her misery is not superlative, in the sense "misery of miseries" (HENGST.: deepest misery, such a misery as displays itself as misery even in the midst of misery; HÄV.: heaviest, most fearful); nor is the expression to be taken as a pleonastic explanation in the sense of "misery which is thy misery," in order to emphasize the idea "thy own" (KEIL); still less as = the captives of thy captivity [Ewald in perplexity reads: 'וְשִׁבְתִּי שׁ]; but summing up (ver. 58): of all thy great and manifold misery, the special one, that which is wholly and entirely so. Placed in the midst of such sinners by means of such penal misery—Ver. 54—Judah shall (this is the divine intention, the object which it is meant to serve) amid her disgrace be compelled to be ashamed of all her sins, while she "comforts" the others, *i.e.* because restoration was the leading thought which goes before in ver. 53, and which is immediately resumed,—inasmuch as she furnishes them in her own case with an illustration, real though only in the third place, of grace. [Rosenm. takes the clause ironically, as meaning that Judah has been found still worse than themselves (ch. xiv. 23). KEIL: inasmuch as they learn from the punishment endured by Jerusalem, God's righteousness, etc. Others: by means of fellowship in misfortune, and that a misfortune so much greater. EWALD: in order that Jerusalem may never again reckon herself better, but may rather through her suffering with them comfort the others.]—Ver. 55. קַדְמָה is the *status ante*, but is not to be more closely defined. Not as before the punishment, for then Sodom and Samaria were wicked, and Judah full of pride (ver. 56); in that case the idea would be the possibility of conversion, so that they might be converted. But they are certainly not to return to the state before punishment, in order perhaps to be converted, but at most, conversion might perhaps be conceived of as the implied condition of such restoration. Matt. xi. 23 does not refer to a restoration, but to the possibility of Sodom's having remained in the state in which she was. An earthly and physical restoration, alike of Sodom with the cities and inhabitants of the Jordan valley and of Samaria, and also of Judah-Jerusalem, has been thought of, just as in Acts iii. 21 the universal renewal of the world to its original glory before the entrance of sin, the palingenesia (Matt. xix. 28; Rom. viii. 18 sq.; 2 Pet. iii. 13), has been thought of; or at least such a resurrection of the dead to life has been taken to be the clothing, the colouring of the thought of their being made partakers of pardoning grace. But as in ver. 45 sq. it is merely moral relations that are spoken of, which of course have to do with persons, the inhabitants of the cities in question, an ethical *restitutio in integrum* suggests itself as the meaning of the text (comp. Mal. iv. 6; Matt. xvii. 11). If, therefore, a restoration of the divine image (in Christ) should not be thought of, then certainly the **return to the first estate** must be understood as a symbolical way of expressing the idea of bestowing pardoning grace. Cocc. fixes his view upon the descendants of those who had survived the destruction of Sodom. So also Neteler: In Gen. xiv. two expeditions against Sodom are spoken of; the captives of the first expedition came to Elam, and their descendants are destined to enter the Church; just as also it was merely the descendants of the captives of Samaria and Jerusalem that could return. "The beginning of the return ensued on the day of Pentecost, perhaps even earlier through those that sprung from the captives of Sodom that went to Elam (proselytes)," etc. Hengst. suggests "a continuation of the means of grace after death for those to whom on earth salvation did not present itself in its highest completeness, for the inhabitants of Sodom swept away by the judgment," appealing to 1 Pet. iii. 19, 20, iv. 6. (Matt. xii. 41, 42.) Comp. on the other hand, ver. 60 sq. The symbolical view (comp. ch. xxix. 14, xlvii. 8 sq.; Jer. xlviii. 47; Amos ix. 14; Isa. xix. 23, 24) will not certainly commend itself by such assumptions as that Sodom represents the two and a half tribes on the other side of Jordan, or that it represents the Ammonites and Moabites, or that it is a type of that heathendom which is morally allied to it. Against such assumptions there is the parallel with the two definitely historical conceptions, Samaria and Jerusalem, comp. vers. 49, 50; and the Ammonites and Moabites in particular are just as little Sodomites as Lot was. But this much will be clear from the way in which Jerusalem is placed side by side with Sodom precisely and Samaria,—in other words, with the most notorious sinners (Deut. xxxii. 32; Isa. i. 10; Jer. xxiii. 14; Rev. xi. 8); sinners, too, from whose judgment in long bygone days Jerusalem seemed to herself far removed, just as she despised those most nearly related to herself in lineage who had been carried into exile;—this much will be clear, that over against the sin and the judgment spoken of here, grace and favour are manifestly to be taken in a Messianic point of view, and are meant to be set forth in a way that is full of promise. Comp. Rom. xi. 32. The promise "soaring far above the censure," as Hitzig says of the section vers. 53-63. The solution of the difficulty, as it is attempted by Calvin, by means of assuming a *comminatio a conditione impossibili* (John xv. 20), —if Sodom and Samaria, then also thou; but the former not, therefore thou also not,—is supported neither by the letter nor by the connection; we have promise before reaching ver. 60 sq. "The restoration is, as in the case of Job, a lifting up to a stage of existence far surpassing the former, —admission into the kingdom of God and participation in all its blessings" (HENGST.).

Ver. 56. Such a prospect stands out the more prominently, as the retrospect hinted at in ver. 54 appears by its side. שְׁמוּעָה—what is heard, and ought to be marked; hence: tidings, report, what may at the same time serve for instruction, for warning. Sodom had not been taken, either in her sins or in her punishment, by Israel as an intimation to herself, which is to be heard and pondered whenever the topic appeared in her mouth; she merely talked it on its way, without drawing from it instruction or warning for herself, giving herself up as she did at the time to her Sodom-like (ver. 49, ch. vii. 20, 24) proud boastings. [HÄV.: "was not for instruction, so that thy mouth was full of the impression." Others: "she was not heard in thy mouth; thou didst not think of her, didst not speak of her." ROSENM.: thou didst not take Sodom's name at all into thy mouth from mere pride (!?). KEIL: "Sodom was not a discourse in thy mouth, that thou didst talk of her and lay to heart her fate." EWALD: "although Sodom had no reputation in thy mouth, was defamed by thee, somewhat as thou thyself now art by thine enemies," etc. Others take the sentence as a question. So HENGST.: "Was not Sodom evil spoken of in thy mouth?" HITZ.: "Was not Sodom a discourse in thy mouth? a theme which thou didst handle in an edifying manner?" Others still, as Luth., Cocc., Klief., take it as a future, against the grammar.]—Ver. 57. A more exact determination of the time of בְּיוֹם. It was before the punishment, to which, and not merely to the sin, the retrospect is directed, just as in ver. 53 "miseries" are spoken of in the plural. By means of the punishment the discovery (vers. 37, 36) of her wickedness took place, her wicked pride came to shame and dishonour; namely, by means of the impending judgment from the direction of Babylon, which can be looked back to as a thing already accomplished in the past, and that all the more as Jehovah speaks from the standpoint of the promised favour following thereupon. [Ewald translates: "just as thou art now the scorn," etc. The expression: **as at the time**, is commonly referred to Isa. ix. 11; 2 Kings xv. 37, xvi. 6; 2 Chron. xxviii. 5, 18 sq.; Keil adding 2 Kings xxiv. 2.] Her own experience of punishment, that Sodom in reality came to be heard and felt by her, therefore humbled even earlier the pride of Judah, if not in her own eyes, yet in those of strangers. If, therefore, Sodom was of no use before, if her own experience did her harm, yet by means of the impending discovery of her wickedness, something else is to be brought about. (HENGST.: "By that which she suffered she learned what she had done; she no longer spoke in pride of Sodom with a 'God, I thank thee,' but laid her hand upon her own heart.") The Aramaic (Syrian) cities and nations are to be looked upon, according to Hengst., not as the destroying powers—"in that case Asshur and Babylon would be mentioned"—but as mocking neighbours. Häv. takes them and **the daughters of the Philistines** to be instruments of the divine avenging justice,—but not with reference to any single occurrence, but in regard to the whole history of the covenant-people, as the north-eastern and southern neighbours of the theocracy; and says that not for them alone, but for **all her surroundings**, the same thing lay in store,—a multitude of punishments, which corresponded at the same time to their hard-heartedness.

Ver. 58 is taken by others as future. Hitz.: "in the mouth of Jehovah of the certain future: thou must bear." It is, as already remarked on ver. 57, the standpoint of the certain bestowment of grace, from which the last punishment also is looked upon as one that has already taken place. The aim, the divine intention of ver. 54, is reached. Comp. on ver. 43.—With the mention of the punishments already over (ver. 57) there is connected this summary sentence, which, pointing to the impending culmination of punishment, brings the matter to a conclusion, in order with Ver. 59 to make the transition to the opposite.—כִּי gives the reason with divine attestation why it must be so, that it is according to righteousness; not merely, however, in reference to punishment, but (ver. 60) looking beyond to grace as well.—וְעָשִׂית, the וְ therefore (also in ver. 60) a continuation of the discourse in ver. 58. Others: "yea." The Qeri rightly: וְעָשִׂיתִי, in the first person. Others take it as the second person: thou didst to thyself what thou didst; comp. Rom. ii. 5.—**Oath**, Deut. xxix. 11 [12].—Comp. ver. 8.—Ver. 60. Faithfulness as opposed to unfaithfulness. Lev. xxvi. 42. See Ex. xix., xxiv.—Comp. Isa. liv. 8, 10; Jer. xxxi. 31, xxxii. 40.—Ver. 61. In addition to Jehovah's remembering, we have now the people's remembering. He remembered His covenant, His faithfulness; they had to remember their ways, their unfaithfulness. The being ashamed is that already alluded to in ver. 54 after their experience of penal chastisement; here, however, still more expressly in view of the grace to be experienced. Israel may well **receive** what is **given** her. Comp. vers. 46, 53, 55. The plural, however, stretches beyond Samaria and Sodom to the greater and smaller national communities of mankind. **For daughters** — ROSENM., HITZ.: Jerusalem therefore the metropolis, the capital of the new theocracy. KEIL: "because the heathen nations are engrafted in Israel as their stem." The position of daughter, as it regards the maternal relation of Israel, is clear from John iv. 22. Comp. besides Ps. lxxxvii.—The expression: **and not by thy covenant**, is made perfectly clear by John x. 16. Hengst. explains the short, but so much the more forcible, addition from ver. 59: "not because the fulfilment of thy covenant obligations gave thee any claim to it." Similarly most expositors. But the covenant is always God's covenant; expressly so in ver. 60, as also immediately again in ver. 62. Hence "*thy* covenant"=*My* covenant *with thee* in the days of thy childhood, ver. 60. The parties in question are designated as "without law," *i.e.* as not springing from the law, although not as standing outside the promise. Comp. on ver. 8; Rom. ii. 12, 14. And so in ver. 62 the **everlasting covenant**, again resumed with emphatic אֲנִי from ver. 60, is represented as pure gospel, as a most gracious fulfilment of promise, as well as, of course, of the law of Israel ("My covenant with thee," ver. 60). But the relation under the law was always temporary, and also local, national, one that passed over into the fulfilment; which indeed drew forth from the law even the latent gospel, and realized it, but which in divine faithfulness brought about the fulfilment of promise in a more general sense (*e.g.* Gen. xii. 3), and which accordingly stretches from eternity to eternity, and for this reason the knowledge of **Jehovah** is significantly connected with it. (Ex. iii. 14.)

Ver. 63. לְמַעַן reminds us of ver. 54, while at the same time ver. 62 is resumed. **Remember** thy "ways," the sins thou hast committed.—**Be ashamed**, comp. ver. 52; that is to say, instead of her former pride, which shut her eyes to her deepest corruption and apostasy, but opened her mouth the more shamelessly for self-justification as well as for bringing charges against God.—As the covenant springs from pure mercy and faithfulness, so in its inmost essence it consists in forgiveness of sins.

DOCTRINAL REFLECTIONS.

1. The scene with the adulteress in John viii., whom the scribes and Pharisees brought to Jesus, might perhaps appear still more significant resting on the background of our chapter. Let it be supposed that Jesus wrote Ezek. xvi. with His finger on the ground, and on the basis of that put forth the well-known challenge of John viii. 7.

2. If in respect of the temporary garb this chapter is kept to the Old Testament, it is essentially New Testament in its spirit and design. Paul has not more sharply assailed the Jews, nor more thoroughly stripped them of all their own righteousnesses. Comp. Rom. ii. 3. The prophet does not even once bring into view their descent from Abraham. That and everything else for him lie sunk in pure sin and misery. Justification by works is here held up even to irony, inasmuch as the greater sinner "justifies" the lesser ones by means of her deeds of abomination. At the close comes salvation.

3. And just as salvation is reached at the close, so our chapter shows itself at once as a way of salvation, from the fact that the actual sin in all its ingratitude and inconceivability, but along with that the natural corruption cleaving to the people of God, is disclosed. For in what blindness does a man live with regard to himself, so long as he lives to sin! The greatness of my sin and misery must ever be the first thing for me to know, if I am to live and die happily in the consolation of the gospel.

4. Inasmuch, however, as the form of the prophetic discourse exhibits in detail a whore and adulteress of the most abandoned description, in order to hold up before the people in the picture a mirror of themselves inwardly, we are, as Cocceius very truly remarks, to make matter of reflection (for this is the object of the description) the much more shameful spiritual unchastity as regards God, even while there may be outward fleshly decency before men. And this all the more as the ordinary judgment of mankind falls so unmercifully upon the fleshly form of manifestation, while it is wont to form a liberal and tolerant estimate of the apostasy from God and the yielding up of the spirit to idols. Cocceius, in this connection, points to Rev. xiv. 4, and explains the "virgins" spiritually of the true and faithful followers of Jesus.

5. "Our chapter is, by the keeping up throughout of the figure therein, one of those Scripture passages which vindicate for ever the truth of the so-called mystic interpretation of the Song of Solomon" (KLIEF.).

6. For the Hebrew nation, which is more essentially a nation than any other, inasmuch as it "does not consist of more or fewer disparate, heterogeneous, and mutually foreign conglomerates, and more or less accidental aggregates, united by accretion from without, but is pre-eminently one individual, one family" (ZIEGLER). Egypt was the heathen foil, and still more the proper birthplace. There it grew to be a nation from the twelve heads of tribes. The natural potencies,

which in this case come likewise to be considered, such as the great fruitfulness of this land, its climate so extraordinarily adapted for population, etc., are still more than met by the antithesis—on the one side monotheistic, on the other side polytheistic — which here lay open, and which prevented a dangerous mixture, and by what sprang from it in the shape of a "great spiritual antipathy and idiosyncrasy of the two nations," through which a preparation was made for the pregnant development of religio-moral individuality as a nation at Sinai.

7. It is worthy of notice, and the after-effect is always visible in the history of the Jewish people, that they became a nation in a foreign land, in misery, and hence were already a nation before they took possession of the Promised Land.

8. It is one thing, Israel's becoming a people (ver. 6); it is another, Israel's becoming the people of Jehovah (ver. 8). In the latter respect the introductory declaration, "I who have brought thee out of the land of Egypt, out of the house of bondage," gives the right key-note for the law of the covenant. In accordance with that it was to be understood as the will of one who was gracious, whose commandments, rightly understood, cannot be grievous. They led to grace, even when they led to the knowledge of sin.

9. Although "the whole of the development of Israel" (HENGST.) is surveyed by the eye of the prophet in the divine discourse, and although Häv. should not deny that regard is had at the same time "to the later history of the nation under David and Solomon," yet it is principally the first season of youth that is here apostrophized, so that we get a pendant for what is said in Rev. ii. 4 about the "first love." (Comp. especially ver. 8 in our chapter.)

10. HÄV.: "The departure from Egypt, the giving of the law, the covenant of God with Israel, are facts which, comprehending as they do the choosing and preparation of the people to be a people of God, are of such a kind that they include at the same time the later blessings in germ; these are only the farther realization, confirmation, and development of those divine manifestations of grace there deposited in germ in the midst of the people."

11. Hengst. asserts that "we are not to think of spiritual benefits," that "the prophet abides by what is palpable, which the ungodly even, whose consciences he wishes to touch, would necessarily recognise,"—a view against which Häv. rightly remarks, that the material, outward blessings are special, just because they "have in them a spiritual significance,"—because they are "symbols, the concrete embodiment of spiritual verities and heavenly blessings." This "is clear even from the nature of allegory itself."

12. The covenant-people are portrayed for us both in their priestly and in their kingly character as a people. The more clearly they appear in this way as chosen out of the world—and thereby in their task, in their destination, for the world—the deeper feeling of ignominy and pain must their identification with the world, nay, in consequence of that, their sinking far below the heathen world, produce as a warning example to Christendom!

13. Marriage and religion here run so much into one another, that the vesture of the thought, the figure, becomes, as it were, the thing itself; and from this ideal hallowing of the institution of marriage there springs a religious and thus a very profound conception of its nature on the Old Testament ground (comp. Mal. ii. 14), just as in Eph. v. 32 we have the New Testament view.

14. Israel's identifying himself with the world is thorough unfaithfulness, as Israel was offered in the covenant relationship with Jehovah grace to withstand, to ward off, temptation through the world-powers, —is an unfaithful misapplication not only of the gifts of grace and blessings which have come to Israel, but of his state of grace. But he who forgets what manner of man he was, he who has a high opinion of himself, has no desire for grace; and the more he trusts in himself, the more quickly will he squander gifts and blessings. "If once this direction is taken, the wickedness advances farther and farther, unceasingly, with unabashed countenance; it spares no gift of God which it would not bring as an offering to its self-made gods, to itself, and to its sinful lust" (HÄV.).

15. Self-exaltation leads from grace, just as self-knowledge leads to grace.

16. With the self-annulling of the relationship to God is bound up the annulling of a nation's self in its different relations. Where there is no religion, there may be manners, but no morality; neither is there any historical nationality, however much of self-praise it may receive. Godliness is always the true policy, having the promise of the life that now is, as well as of that which is to come. With its religion a people's nationality is bound up. (The honouring of God and the national honour. The significance of the religious character of a people as it regards their ethical and national side.)

17. "In the Hebrew worship there was found a theocracy elsewhere unexampled. Originality and independence in the domain of natural religion was wanting in the case of the Hebrews; the fundamental bias produced by the worship of Jehovah left room merely for a pressing in of natural religion, dependent for the most part on outward circumstances. Striking proof how original and deeply rooted monotheism is in Hebraism" (HÄV.). Comp. the development of this idea in SAALSCHÜTZ' *Archäol.* ii. p. 382 sq.

18. With this national character of hers as a people of Jehovah, Israel's polytheistic aberrations are quite as much sins against herself, her true, essential, proper self, as against the Lord her God.

19. The punishment of death is inflicted by the law of Moses either in the shape of burning (? perhaps only of the corpses, after previous stoning), Lev. xx. 14, xxi. 9,—Gen. xxxviii. 24 appears to be a pre-Mosaic legal usage,—or by stoning, or by the sword. Hanging is not a Mosaic punishment.

20. Grotius drew the inference from our chapter (vers. 38, 40), that after Moses' time the severer punishment of stoning was introduced in the case of adultery; without ground, as Meyer on John viii. rightly decides. It was the legal Mosaic punishment of adultery, perhaps in general, as Häv. on Ezekiel *in loco* makes very probable, and not merely in cases like Deut. xxii. 20 sq., 23 sq., to which Meyer limits it; although the figurative language used by our prophet in reference to the punishment would have its emphasis if the law had been to decree stoning only in cases so peculiar. (Israel conceived of as

betrothed in marriage! Her obligation as a people to virgin-like purity!)

21. It is a fearful development that of Israel—the more grace, the more sin. And yet grace would display itself the more mightily, the more mightily sin had developed itself. "What a great, free kingdom of grace," says Umbreit, "which the prophet builds up, in which Sodom, Samaria, and Jerusalem stand before God in a line connected in the closest way!"

22. The key to the interpretation of the restoration held out in prospect for Sodom and Samaria and Jerusalem is the undeniably representative character of all three. As this representative character of Judah-Jerusalem is clear in our prophet,—that is to say, the Jewish people is represented in this, its characteristic remnant,—so it is no less to be admitted in reference to Sodom and Samaria. The addition at the outset in every case, "and their daughters," by means of which three groups are formed, strips the cities named of their individuality. But it is not the Jordan valley and the land of the kingdom of Israel, and just as little is it the respective inhabitants, that are to be represented thereby, as it is plain from the connection that no special reference of any kind, either to local circumstances as such, or to persons as such, exists. Both Sodom and Samaria come into view with the prophet merely as regards sin and judgment, and with respect to grace and favour. As regards sin and judgment, they belong to history, and are specialized as regards this historical side of theirs, especially Sodom (ver. 49 sq.); with respect to grace and favour, they are received into the promise concerning the Jewish people, not merely to throw important light on that promise, but to characterize it Messianically as a world-wide prospect for humanity in general. We are not at liberty to say with Hengst.: "Sodom represents the entire heathen world standing in similar circumstances with her." For what would Samaria represent, as distinguished from her and from Jerusalem? But if sin and judgment indisputably constitute the historical element of Sodom and Samaria, we shall require to express ourselves in this way: Sodom and Samaria set before us, symbolize in general, two sinful states of mankind, which are specially distinguished from each other in this way, that Sodom has sinned and been judged without having the law of the covenant, while Samaria has fallen away from the law of the covenant and exposed herself to judgment. It is not as representing heathendom that Sodom comes into view, but as standing outside the covenant of law; and the difference between Samaria and Jerusalem in respect of the covenant of law, out of which Samaria has fallen, is attested by the mercies which have maintained within Jerusalem and for her the covenant and the law so much longer. If Paul writes in Rom. ii. that they who have sinned without law perish also without law, and that they who have sinned in the law are judged by the law, the statement is illustrated by Sodom and Samaria as to the prospect for Jerusalem. But because, with Ezekiel, grace and favour shoot up their beams behind and beyond the judgment, the fact that Sodom and Samaria, in connection with their sinning, are lost, serves indeed the purpose, in respect of righteousness, of placing Jerusalem—exceeding both as she has done in sin and corruption—even lower than them, and consequently of humbling her more deeply; but the deeper the humiliation, the deeper shall be the sense of shame, since grace and favour form the last prospect. A thought such as that expressed by Hengst.: "If God has compassion on the most notorious sinners among the heathen, how should He not have compassion on all?" lies outside our text. In accordance with our text the thought would need to run: If grace lies in prospect for Jerusalem, so much the more must this be the prospect for Sodom and Samaria, how greatly soever Jewish Pharisaism might set its face against it. The fact that the favour held out in prospect is expressed as a "return to their first estate," explains the "turning" of the captivity, or more generally of the misery, as שׁוּב שְׁבוּת, as a "bringing back," inasmuch as it is a "returning," and both alike are figurative modes of speech. As the one takes its colour from Sodom's judgment, so the other takes its colour from Samaria's punishment. Sodom must be restored, since she is destroyed; while Samaria would have to be brought back from her misery, since she is in exile—if favour, notwithstanding judgment and after judgment, were to be the thing spoken of. But it is just such favour of which God means to speak to us by the mouth of His prophet. This favour is in the case of Jerusalem assigned indeed to the last time, in so far as the Messianic period is the last time; nothing, however, being said of transferring it to the world to come or to the last judgment, nor of its being delayed till the general restitution of all things. The same must hold good of the parallels, Sodom and Samaria. But ver. 61 makes it perfectly clear, inasmuch as the grace lying in store is spoken of there as a receiving into the fellowship of the everlasting covenant with Jerusalem; and Sodom and Samaria, just as they appear manifestly as types of humanity to be made partakers of grace, so far as they themselves are concerned, step into the background. When Stier wishes to explain Ezekiel by means of Matt. xi. 24 in reference to Sodom, he drags into the words of our Lord what does not necessarily lie in them. The last day, which according to Stier's interpretation is to manifest "ways of grace still open" even "in the world to come," does indeed make manifest those who are saved by grace through faith, as it likewise justifies the righteousness of God in its judgments before the whole world. That it will be more tolerable for Sodom on this day is explained simply enough from the circumstance that her guilt, as also that of Tyre and Sidon, when compared with the guilt of others, will appear as less heinous. But that Sodom will be restored is not said by our Lord in Matthew, any more than He says that Tyre and Sidon will repent. Where Ezekiel speaks of Sodom and Samaria (just as also of Jerusalem), as cities, localities, Sodom is removed from the face of the earth, Samaria lies waste, the style of expression as to "returning to their first estate" is merely colouring. The motto with the prophet, which runs through the Old Testament, in gospel terms is this: I am come to seek and to save that which was lost. This is the Messianic world-wide prospect for mankind, as it is symbolized in Sodom, Samaria, and Jerusalem.

23. "The prosperity and safety of the olden time is the immediate form under which the pro-

phet beholds also the future,"—just as to be in paradise = to be in heaven; "but presently this future appears also in so ideal a splendour, that that very form bursts asunder, and in truth a new world presents itself to his eye. It is the old God, with the old gifts of His love; but the subjective condition has become a different one, and hence the old blessings also are of a new kind, and the whole state in consequence has become one far more exalted, far more glorious than the old" (HÄV.).

[" It is as if an assurance were given to a child, whose family had become enveloped in misfortune, that he should live to see the former prosperity return again; but meanwhile he himself springs up to manhood, and, having now other wants to satisfy, and higher relations to fill than formerly, the revived prosperity must bring new and nobler gifts within his reach, to place him in the same relative position he originally occupied. In short, the bringing back of the captivity, and returning to the former state, as applied to the covenant-people, indicates nothing as to the outward form of things to be enjoyed, but points only to their *nature* and *character*, as similar to what had already been" (FAIRBAIRN).—W. F.]

24. Hengst. wishes to find, in the circumstance that in vers. 53 and 55 (just as also in Isa. xix. 23, 24) Israel takes only the third place, a hint that the heathen world will attain sooner to salvation, and a preparation for Rom. xi. 25 (?). Again, the "comforting" of ver. 54 is to be explained from ver. 61, and is meant to signify the preaching of the gospel (Isa. xl.), which will come at first from an election of Jews (the apostles) to the heathen. The high honour of this mission to the heathen world will fill with deep shame, because of the earlier apostasy. There is no question, at all events, as to the remark that the kingdom of God "can only for a time be limited to a single nation, and the limitation must be the means of removing the limitation."

25. HÄV.: (1) "The old covenant appears as the foundation, the presupposition, of the new, so that the latter rests on the former. The new institute of salvation is not the dissolution, but the fulfilment, the confirmation, and completion of the old. (2) It is characteristic of the new covenant that it is to be an everlasting covenant. But the eternity of duration already promised to the old covenant nevertheless stands fast, inasmuch as the old covenant rises into and passes over into a covenant of such a kind that its dissolution is not to be thought of." Comp. besides our exposition of ver. 61 sq.

26. "Vain is the boast which Rome takes up against Jerusalem. For it is not from Rome that the gospel has gone forth, but from Jerusalem; just as it is also not to the Romans alone that it has forced its way. We are children of Jerusalem, but not of Rome. If Rome will be saved, she must become a daughter of Jerusalem; and this means that Rome must in this case accept the law which has gone forth from Jerusalem, and dare not accept or deliver aught else. But Jerusalem has begun to show herself as a mother, inasmuch as the apostles and believers from Jerusalem have preached the gospel to us" (COCC.).

HOMILETIC HINTS.

Ver. 1 sq. "As a physician, when he wishes to heal a wound thoroughly, must probe it to the bottom, so a teacher, when he wishes to convert men thoroughly, must first seek to bring them to a knowledge of their sins" (CR.).—"The man is thoroughly sick who does not wish to hear how sick he is, lest he should be compelled to know and believe it. But such is the sinner, who reckons himself as righteous" (STCK.).—"Without the knowledge of sin, repentance and conversion are not to be thought of. We know indeed already by nature that we ought not to kill, to steal, etc.; but because through inborn defect our natural knowledge is very much obscured, God has given the ten commandments, to set the law of nature in a clearer light; and the prophets are the expounders of the ten commandments. In other men we perceive at once the sins which we do not discover in ourselves. To ourselves we are indulgent, especially if we err in the service of God, since we are always clinging to the view that what we did with a good intention cannot possibly displease God. So much the more must the prophets drag our sins to the light" (LUTHER).—Ver. 2. "Those who are in the Church, and yet live an ungodly life, are to be considered the same as the heathen before God, Matt. xviii. 17" (TÜB. BIB.).—Ver. 3. "What Jerusalem had to listen to in the passage before us! And yet what would have to be said of our extraction, as to who we are, and from what heathen we are sprung?" (JER.)—Ver. 4. The abuse of benefits increases guilt. Hence the preaching of those conferred by God on the Jewish people, as here by Ezekiel, is a thorough carrying out of the original commission: Cause Jerusalem to know her abominations.—Ver. 5 sq. It is above all as seen in contrast with our natural corruption that we come to understand the grace of God the Father in Jesus Christ, His only-begotten Son, through the Holy Spirit.—"How did it stand with ourselves, before God stretched forth His hand to us, and brought us out of the filth of our sins? We are born children of wrath; we lie under guilt for our sins; we must have died eternally, had we not been quickened through Christ, Eph. ii. 4, 5; 1 Cor. vi. 12" (LUTHER).—Where none helps, God is our help.—"Priest and Levite pass by; God does not. He not only will, but He also can help. His looking upon us is already help" (STCK.).—Remembering a good preparation (for the table of the Lord also): (1) let us remember what we are by nature; (2) let us remember still more God's grace.—Ver. 8 sq. "This is the second gracious visitation of God; the first is in ver. 6 sq." (SCHMIEDER.)—Ver. 9 sq. "With such grace God comes to meet us, when as the compassionate Father He comes to meet His prodigal sons (Luke xv.), embraces them, and by His promises and so many proofs of His love takes away our unbelief, and enters into covenant with us. This takes place when He forgives us our sins, imparts to us His Spirit, and frees us from the bondage of sin. But as those who have the gift of freedom bestowed upon them change their clothes, so we put on our Lord Jesus Christ, and are numbered with the royal priesthood (Col. iii. 12, 13)" (HEIMHOFF.).—"Observe that God not only washed, but also anointed; in other words, He not only forgives our sins, but at the same time sanctifies us by His Spirit" (COCC.).—"Do you wish to know what articles of clothing these really are? Compassion, kindness," etc. (JER.)—"But the adorning of godly women is not to be that which is outward, but the new man inwardly, 1 Pet. iii. 3 sq.; Gal. v. 22" (STARKE).—"The kingdom of glory is reached by those only who keep the faith to the end" (STCK.).—Ver. 14. "A name of renown is no small favour from God, but one ought not to pride himself in it, Matt. iii. 9" (O.).—"There is no name of greater glory and renown than to be a child of God. Strive to bear this name with truth, Hos. i. 10" (STARKE).

Ver. 15. "The divine gifts, so soon as we cease to recognise them as such, inevitably become a snare. The heart that has grown proud by means of them becomes the sport of all lusts and passions" (HENGST.).—Ingratitude is the reward of the world; it was so even in the case of the nation placed in so splendid a position in the heathen world, and that in reference to the Lord. What a mirror for Christendom!—"How many a one has been corrupted by beauty!" (STCK.)—"Beauty, whence comes it? is it not also a divine gift? Who can make himself beautiful? And should it not serve to keep what is unbeautiful, to keep vice far from us? And how soon is beauty gone!" (LUTHER.)—Prosperity without piety, in nine cases out of ten, leads to corruption.—"This is a worm which gnaws and destroys the most precious souls, and renders the commandments of no effect, when the man is content with the praise of men, and boasts himself as if his own doings were enough for him. Beware, therefore, of trusting in thine own will, because it is nothing without God's assistance. When you have done all, say, We are unprofitable servants. 'It is not of him that willeth, nor of him that runneth, but of God that showeth mercy' (Rom. ix. 16). It is the Lord's will that we should place our confidence in this, that our names are written in heaven" (HEIM-HOFF., after CALV.).—"The name of a Christian is not enough, if the walk of a Christian does not go along with it" (STCK.).—"The more distinguished thou art among men, the more watchful over thyself thou shouldst be" (LUTHER).—Ver. 16 sq. "What is there that men do not spend upon sinful objects, and especially upon false worship!—All that thou offerest to the idols: tell us, then, earthly-minded man, what hast thou offered in thy life to God?" (STARKE.)—New patches upon an old garment; here, as so often, upon the old idolatry!—"Observe that those who fall away from the true religion are accustomed to walk at the head of processions, and would fain even excel others through their superstition, so that the latter are even displeased" (LUTHER).—Ver. 17 sq. There is a systematic theology, professing to be biblical, after this pattern, where the gold and silver of Holy Scripture are wrought up into doctrinal statements and practical inferences according to one's own liking, under splendid wrappings (phrases), and by means of an eloquence that reminds one of better times.—"The true God clothes and feeds His own; but the false gods must be clothed and fed by their worshippers, and for this purpose God's gifts are to serve" (STCK.).—Ver. 20 sq. "God's right not only to the grown up, but also to their children, is not merely in virtue of creation and preservation, but in virtue of the covenant" (STARKE).—"The extent of the grace which was promised to Abraham must be recognised in the Church of Christ also. Christ imparts the sparks of His Spirit to whom He will; and hence many in the first years of childhood have a purer fear of God than those who are grown up. And therefore in the worship of the Church, and especially in baptism, the grace of the new birth for children of God is ascribed to little children even, in dependence on the promise: I am thy God, and the God of thy seed" (HEIM-HOFF.).—"Thou darest not, O false, hypocritical Christian, hold thyself to be righteous as compared with the Jews, because thou hast an abhorrence of what they did; for the rearing of thy children for the devil and the world is certainly not better" (BERL. BIB.).—"God retains His right over our children; and so He does thee no wrong when He summons them away from thee into heaven" (STCK.).—Ver. 22 sq. The ungodly and idolatrous have a bad memory. It is the memory that the devil seeks first to steal from man. When memory comes back to us through grace, how our eyes are filled with tears! Sometimes the dying hour draws aside the veil from our memory. Oh, let it not come so late!—Ver. 25. "The beauty is the national honour, a noble boon bestowed by God, which not to esteem, but to prostitute, is a sign of deep degeneracy and alienation from God" (HENGST.).—Ver. 26. "Ofttimes neighbours entice one another to sin" (STARKE).—Ver. 27. Even upon Israel's most wicked ways God's hand is ever discernible still.—Ver. 28 sq. There is an insatiable hunger in sin.—"With God's word, on the other hand, men become so quickly satiated" (STCK.).—"Without repentance we go from sin to sin" (JER.).—"Our heart has no rest until it rests in God" (AUGUSTINE).—"If we are too intimately connected with the ungodly, it is just as if we went near a fan, and made it blow up our evil desires, which without that are already burning sufficiently in our soul. It is difficult to keep the favour of those with whom we are on terms of friendship, if we do not agree with them" (HEIM-HOFF.).—Ver. 30. "A withered heart, a heart that has lost its sap and vigour (Ps. xxxii. 4), is the heritage of those who seek in the world what God alone can impart. Hope always disappointed is the enemy of life."—Ver. 31. Where wickedness has grown into a habit, everything becomes a means to the end, for its only wish is to gratify its lust.—Ver. 32. "Those who serve God and Mammon, Christ and Belial, are in the same condemnation" (STCK.).

Ver. 35 sq. The punishment of God begins with the holding up before us of our sins; and thus our evil conscience is the announcement of yet another condemnation.—God's word and Spirit never flatter, but call sinner and sin by their right name.—Such is the relation in which God stands to whoredom; how different the position taken up by states and cities toward it, that still wish to be called Christian!—To hear while it is yet time, to hear the voices of grace, saves us from being compelled to hear the sentence of punishment.—Ver. 37. False, sinful love readily passes over into fierce hate, which is also a judicial sentence of God, even in this life.—Such is the case also with boon companionship, gambling companionship, and similar worldly friendships.—This is the curse of sin, that those with whom we have sinned make common cause with our enemies for our punishment.—"The penal uncovering of the nakedness is the righteous retribution for having done so voluntarily" (HENGST.).—Friends may in certain circumstances be the most painful rods in God's hand.— Keep me, O God, from friends who are not Thy friends.—Ver. 38 sq. The history of the world, still more the history of the Church, most of all the history of the Jewish people, shows a retribution at work, and proves at the same time the existence of a Judge.—To be in the enemy's hand does not, in the case of faith, exclude the comfort of knowing that we are in God's hand ; but for the ungodly it is a sign that God has given them up.—Those are the most awful scenes of burning, in whose ruins we see ourselves pointed away beyond man altogether to the righteous God. In this way Jerusalem has become a parallel to the Dead Sea. — He who refuses to obey God must in the end obey men. —Ver. 40. The sin public ; the shame public ; the judgment public.—Ver. 41. "God can easily bring it about that we shall sin no more ; in other words, that even if we wish it as before, we shall be able to go no farther" (STCK.).—Ver. 42. If the sin ceases, the wrath ceases, it rests over the sinner ; and so the nationality of Israel has ceased among the nations.—God's resting, His being no longer angry, may be hell.—The extremity of judgment is such indifference on the part of God. Ver. 43 sq. All sin becomes still worse from its being a crime against God's grace. "Against Thee, Thee only," is the so thoroughly damning element in sin.—"The sins and bad habits of parents do not excuse the children, but render them the more guilty, because they have not shunned ways so wicked" (STCK.).—Ver. 47 sq. When sin has grown to madness, the most horrible depths of corruption disclose themselves just in the case of those who have had most to do with God's word.—A man of the world cannot possibly sin like one who has formerly been a "Christian." —What sinner in Israel did not reckon himself a pious man, if not a saint, as compared with Sodom! How different is God's judgment from men's judgment upon others and upon themselves!—Ver. 49 sq. Good days may become bad weeks, a bad eternity. — Unmercifulness shows that we ourselves have not obtained mercy.—If we are to be ashamed before Sodom and Samaria, how much more before the penitent thief upon the cross!—Ver. 51 sq. The mote and beam, as in Matt. vii.—In judging of sins, many a thing has to be considered which God alone can know. Hence we should not wish to judge, but should leave the judgment to God.— Justification before men, and justification before God ; justification from men in word, through their praise, or in actual fact, through their greater guilt; and justification from God, in His word, through Christ's work.

Ver. 53 sq. "Teachers and preachers must preach not only the law, but also the gospel" (O.). — However great our sin and misery may be, there is a redemption from all.—"What the prophet here predicts has been fulfilled in the Church, and is being fulfilled still daily" (JER.).—The gospel proclaims and promises return from captivity, and restoration of the divine image alike to the grossest sinners, and to the apostates who have fallen away from the truth, and also to those who boast themselves of Moses and the prophets, yea, of Christ and the apostles, but who shall the more righteously fall under judgment if they do not repent. —"In the case of spiritual captivity we must think of the jailor, of the chains, and of the bondage. But from Satan's yoke, and the chains of darkness, and from wicked works, Christ leads us to freedom" (STCK.).—Ver. 54. "This is a beautiful revenge and a blessed retribution on God's part, the shaming of the sinner by means of grace" (COCC.).—To be ashamed of salvation, and to be ashamed because of so great salvation, how different are these two things!—Ver. 55. It is a bringing back, the restoration of the nations to a united humanity in the Son of man, the new heavens and the new earth, the creation of redemption.—Ver. 56. "How many rejoice in the calamity of others, and do not reflect that perhaps a still greater one hangs over their own head! Prov. xxiv. 17" (STARKE).—The stones of the temple at Jerusalem cry loud enough in the ear of Christendom!—Ver. 57. The day of judgment makes bare.—"In this life much remains hidden, but the last day will make manifest thoughts as well as words and actions" (STCK.).—In the end, and — if one looks deep enough — already even, he who despises God and is cast off by Him is despised by men likewise.—Ver. 58. "He who seems to bear sin lightly will find the punishment so much the heavier."—Ver. 59. God deals with us according to our works, and He does not deal with us according to our works ; both already in this world, but thoroughly only in the world to come.—God's remembering His grace produces the everlasting covenant.—"Believers have no right to assume or imagine that they have been reconciled to God from any other cause than from the grace of the covenant" (CALV.).—Ver. 61. Our remembering is never without shame on our part.—God's grace awakens, sharpens memory also.—"The remembrance of our former state of sin ought to humble us thoroughly, but at the same time to awaken us to the gratitude we owe to God for having shown us so great mercy, 1 Cor. xv. 9, 10" (STARKE).—Ver. 63. "God is willing to remit not one and another sin merely, but all our sins" (LUTHER).—"In this chapter, as in Rom. i. sq., God makes a complete disclosure of the abominations of sin, but for the purpose in grace of also covering them up wholly" (RICHT.). —"The justification of grace takes away from those who have come to know their sin thoroughly all boasting of their own merits, Rom. iii. 24" (STARKE).—Our being struck dumb in judgment, our being struck dumb from grace.

6. *The Riddle about the Royal House of David* (ch. xvii.).

1, 2 And the word of Jehovah came unto me, saying, Son of man, put forth a
3 riddle, and speak a parable unto [for] the house of Israel. And say, Thus
saith the Lord Jehovah, The great eagle, with great wings, with long wing-
feathers, full of feathers, which had divers colours, came unto Lebanon, and
4 took the topmost branch [leafy crown] of the cedar. The topmost of its shoots
he cropt off, and brought it to the land of Canaan; in a city of merchants he

5 set it. And he took of the seed of the land, and put it in a seed field; took
6 it to many waters, set it as a willow. And it sprouted, and became a spread-
ing vine, of low stature, so that its branches might turn toward him [the
eagle], and its roots should be under him; and it became a vine, and produced
7 branches, and shot out leafy twigs. And there was another great eagle with
great wings and many feathers; and, behold, this vine turned languishingly
in its roots toward him [the other eagle], and shot forth its branches toward him,
8 that he might water it, from the beds of its planting. In a good field by
many waters was it planted, to produce leaves and to bear fruit, to become a
9 splendid vine. Say, Thus saith the Lord Jehovah: Will it thrive? will he
not pull up the roots thereof, and cut off the fruit thereof, that it wither?
In all the leaves of its shoots it shall wither; and not by a great arm or by
10 many people will it have to be lifted up from its roots. And [yea], behold, it
is planted, will it thrive? will it not utterly wither as soon as the east wind
11, 12 touches it?—And the word of Jehovah came unto me, saying, Say now to
the house of rebelliousness, Know ye not what this is? Say, Behold, the
king of Babylon came to Jerusalem, and he took its king and its princes, and
13 he brought them to himself to Babylon. And he took of the royal seed, and
made a covenant with him, and caused him to enter into an oath; and the
14 rams [strong ones] of the land he took: That it might be a kingdom of low
condition, that it might not lift itself up; that his covenant might be kept,
15 that it might stand. And he rebelled against him, so that he sent his mes-
sengers to Egypt, to give him horses and much people—Shall he prosper?
shall he escape that doeth this? And he broke the covenant, and should he
16 escape? As I live—sentence of the Lord Jehovah—surely in the place of
the king that made him king, whose oath he despised, and whose covenant
17 he broke, with him in the midst of Babylon he shall die. And not with great
power and much people shall Pharaoh act with him in the war [battle], in cast-
18 ing up a mount and in building a siege-tower, to cut off many souls. And
[yea] he despised the oath, to break the covenant; and, behold, he gave his
19 hand: and all this he did; he shall not escape. Therefore thus saith the
Lord Jehovah, As I live, surely My oath which he despised, and My cove-
20 nant which he broke, I give upon his head. And I spread My net upon him,
and he is taken in My snare, and I bring him to Babylon, and I contend with
him there because of his treachery which he hath committed against Me.
21 And all his fugitives in all his squadrons, they shall fall by the sword, and
those that remain shall be scattered to every wind; and ye know that I,
Jehovah, have spoken.

22 Thus saith the Lord Jehovah, And I take of the topmost branch [of the leafy
crown] of the high cedar, and set [give]; from the topmost of its shoots will I
23 crop off a tender one, and I plant it upon a mountain high and exalted. On
the elevated mountain of Israel will I plant it, and it bears leaves and pro-
duces fruit, and becomes a glorious cedar: and under it there dwell all birds
24 of every wing; in the shadow of its branches shall they dwell. And all
the trees of the field know that I, Jehovah, brought down the high tree,
exalted the low tree, made the green tree wither, and made the dry tree to
flourish; I, Jehovah, spake and did.

Ver. 3. Sept.: . . . *ὀς ἐχει το ἡγημα εἰσελθειν εἰς τ. Λιβανον*—

Ver. 4. . . . *εἰς πολιν τετειχισμενην*— Vulg.: . . . *in urbe negotiatorum*—

Ver. 5. . . . *ἐπιβλεπομενον ἐταξεν αὐτο.* Vulg: . . . *et posuit illud in terra pro semine . . . in superficie posuit illud.*

Ver. 7. . . . *ποτισαι αὐτην συν τω βωλω της φυτειας αὐτης.* (Another reading: כנפה, *alarum instar produxit.* מערנח, *ab areola.* Syr. and Arab.; see ver. 10.)

Ver. 9. Another reading: התצלח, interrog.

Ver. 10. . . . *συν τω βωλω ἀνατολης αὐτης ξηρανθησεται.*

Ver. 17. . . *ποιησει προς αὐτον Φαραω πολεμον*—

Ver 20. . . . *κ. ἁλωσεται ἐν τη περιοχη αὐτου.*— (Another reading: בכועלו, *propter scelus ejus.* על מעלי, Syr.)

Ver. 22. . . . *καρδιας αὐτων ἀποκνιω κ. καταφυτευσω . . . ὑψηλον,*

Ver. 23. K. *κρεμασω αὐτον ἐν ὀρει μετεωρω του Ἰσρ. κ. καταφυτευσω . . . κ. ἀναπαυσεται ὑποκατω αὐτου παν θηριον, κ. τα πετεινα ὑπο την σκιαν αὐτου ἀναπαυσεται κ. τ. κληματα αὐτου ἀποκατασταθησεται.*

EXEGETICAL REMARKS.

After the preparatory hints in the preceding chapter, *e.g.* vers. 13, 26, the discourse, as in ch. xii., turns specially to the subject of the kingdom.

Vers. 1–10. *The Riddle.*

Ver. 2. חוּד חִידָה, always in this connection (Judg. xiv. 12, 13, 16) means: to tie a knot of speech, which is to be loosed; according to others: from חָדַד, a sharp saying; but in how far sharp? (Comp. Doct. Reflec. 1.) What requires sharpened wits to understand it, is certainly too remote from the connection. חִידָה is in general the figurative speech, and therefore used in parallel with מָשָׁל (comp. ch. xii. 22); which may be, and for the most part is, in this form, especially as contrasted with the plain, literal statement. Designedly veiled, it is meant to rouse us to remove the veil, and thus with the process of reflection so much the deeper an impression is made. As the discourse is to be addressed to the house of Israel (ver. 12), there is no need for quoting, as Hitz. does, ch. xvi. 44.—Ver. 3. The **great eagle** is Nebuchadnezzar, as ver. 12 shows; and the same figure is employed in Jer. xlviii. 40, xlix. 22, so majestic and powerful as well as strikingly appropriate, without for that reason being a specially Babylonian title, or an animal form appearing in the armorial bearings of the Babylonian rulers. The points of comparison are the royal character, the robber-conqueror element, the power of rapid flight, the sharp vision from which nothing can be concealed, the power of stroke; perhaps also Matt. xxiv. 28. **With great wings**, points to the extent of dominion; **with long wing-feathers**, to the energy, especially of the military power; **full of feathers**, to the multitude of subjects; the **divers colours**, to the diversity of the subjugated nations in speech, customs, dress.—**Lebanon**, if it stands for Judah, does so because the latter represents the whole of Israel, and in this case, according to Hengst., "because the mountains in Scripture language mean kingdoms;" but rather, perhaps, inasmuch as for the king of Babylon Lebanon is the boundary of the land, the first sign of the Jewish land. More correctly, however, in connection with what follows, and in accordance with ver. 12, it is taken as a symbol of Jerusalem; and that not so much because of the temple and the other palaces, as because of the king's house, constructed of cedar beams, on Mount Zion, for which comp. 1 Kings vii. 2, x. 17, 21; Jer. xxii. 23.—צַמֶּרֶת, a word peculiar to Ezekiel for the topmost foliage of the cedar, by which is meant in general what stands out prominently, namely, what stands out prominently in the house of David; so that from the generality of the expression we may include in the exposition "the princes" of vers. 12, 13. Hengst. happily: "the then royal court." The more special statement follows in ver. 4: **the topmost of its shoots**, etc. The tip, the highest of the shoots which together form the topmost branch, with an allusion at the same time to his youthful years, means king Jehoiachin. **Canaan**, here the same as in ch. xvi. 29. Comp. there. Ironically: yea, into a new Canaan! a low land as contrasted with the lofty Lebanon! Similarly Häv. The **city of merchants** does not necessitate our interpreting the "land of Canaan" as a land of merchandise, as most expositors take it, but side by side with the ironically so-called "Canaan" = Babylonia, there is placed in addition a special feature, for which comp. Introd. p. 19. *The market of commerce in contrast with the king's house!* As in Babylon all possible products of commerce were huddled together, so in a manner also were huddled together the most diverse crowns and princes. Hengst. supposes that the Chaldean diplomacy is meant as being a policy of interests, as we also speak of international intrigues. "Self-interest is the point of comparison between politics and trade" (Rev. xviii.).—Ver. 5. The **seed of the land** denotes, as contrasted with a foreign ruler, and specially with a Babylonian viceroy, one of the native royal family (ver. 13), namely, Zedekiah (Introd. p. 6). But in the difference between the "top of its shoots" (ver. 4) and the "seed of the land," there is set forth prominently a difference between Zedekiah and Jehoiachin (Matt. i. 12). It is not so much, perhaps, the policy of Nebuchadnezzar, as Hengst. puts it, "in order to secure for him the sympathies of the people," as rather the considerateness, the clemency of the procedure, that is meant to be brought out.—בִּשְׂדֵה זָרַע, **in a seed field**, which is described more particularly in what follows. What is meant is the as yet favourable circumstances, as Judah was neither a "sterile land," nor even an exhausted soil.—קָח with kametz (Hos. xi. 3), see Häv. on the passage, a resuming of the preceding וַיִּקַּח. The **many waters** portray the fertile situation, in harmony with צַפְצָפָה, a word peculiar to Ezekiel, which Gesenius derives from the inundated, well-watered soil which the willow loves. There is no need for supplying a comparative כְּ, as the accusative is an apposition. The LXX. derive it from צָפָה: he caused it to be watched over. So also the Syriac Version.—Ver. 6. If a humiliation is implied in the illustration used: "as a willow," the statement that **it became a vine** may possibly be meant to make up for this. But however luxuriantly the vine stretched out, yet it was no longer the Davidic cedar, as is specially indicated by the **low stature** (ver. 14); which at the same time forms the transition to the intentional לִפְנוֹת, that it was to continue turned toward the Babylonian ruler, and subject to him with all its growth and with the roots of its existence and vigour. (Klief.: it was not to stretch out its branches toward its own post, etc.) וַתְּהִי לְגֶפֶן, a short repetition, to prepare for what now follows (ver. 7), as being the opposite of what was intended. The "carefully selected" (Häv.) form of expression (בַּדִּים and פֹּארֹת) brings out in strong colours the overweening self-conceit.—Ver. 7. נֶשֶׁר־אֶחָד, **another**, as distinguished from the one pointed out emphatically in ver. 3. Comp. ver. 15. The description is similar to that in ver. 3, but more meagre, corresponding to the inferior position of the Egyptian king in respect of power. In כָּפְנָה there is a certain play upon the word גֶּפֶן. The meaning is (comp. ver. 6) plainly to turn strongly in some particular direction,—is it to wind because of hindrance from the soil in which it had been planted? or is it to languish, to thirst after, portraying the vehement self-willed longing?—The "watering" is probably not without allusion to the process of irrigation peculiar to Egypt by means of the overflow of the Nile.—**From the beds**, etc., *i.e.* from the spot where it had been planted by Babylon, went forth its leaning toward Egypt, which marks already the discontent, the ingratitude, the unfaithfulness, and thus paves the way for Ver. 8. Comp. besides ver. 5.—אַדֶּרֶת, according to some, from a root "to be wide" (to have it comfortable); according to others, from a root "to be strong."—Ver. 9. The difficulty of the riddle is presented for solution; the consequence to be foreseen from such conduct is put as a question. According to Häv., with an expression of displeasure; according to others, ironically. But the prophet does not in this case utter his own sentiment, but what the Eternal says. The divine sentence may be learned from the riddle. From the additional question annexed to it, it follows that the first question is to be answered in the negative. (Comp. Matt. xxi. 40 sq.; xx. 15 sq.) צָלֵחַ is: to force a way in, to force a way through, to come forward. Keil in his exposition takes it as a neuter: will it succeed, prosper? and what follows, in his translation also, indefinitely: will they not pull up? etc., instead of referring it to Nebuchadnezzar. The **roots** have respect to his existence as king; the **fruit** is the produce, the result of this royal existence by Nebuchadnezzar's grace; there is no special allusion to Zedekiah's children (2 Kings xxv. 7). **All the leaves of its shoots** = the whole productive energy and vital force which such a kingship in any way showed. The subject is the vine, as also in ver. 10. The common interpretation is, Nebuchadnezzar will not need for this purpose his whole power, specially his whole military forces. But לְמַשְׂאוֹת (a feminine infinitive form), in accordance with the interpretation of ver. 17, is rather to be understood of the lifting up again from the roots, into which it has sunk down withered. [HÄV.: And without great power and without much people, *scil.* it will parch up (?), when one pulls it up from ts root, that is to say, without the expected help of Egypt he will sink. HENGST.: Nebuchadnezzar, who did indeed, according to Jer. xxxiv., lead a numerous army against Jerusalem, did not require to make so great preparations (Deut. xxxii. 30; Lev. xxvi. 8). The taking away with the roots = the total annihilation of the national existence, Mark xi. 20; Matt. iii. 10; Luke iii. 9.]—Ver. 10. A strengthening repetition (ver. 9) to produce greater attention. Comp. besides ver. 8. The **east wind**—very appropriate for the Babylonians, dwelling in the east, as well as in the figure, because it is dangerous for plants—is employed in conclusion to disguise for the second time, quite after the manner of a riddle, the instrument of punishment.—With a mere touch, and on the spot of his ungrateful pride, he will find his judgment.

Vers. 11–21. *The Interpretation.*

Ver. 12. Because now "the house of Israel," to whom the riddle was proposed, are to know the meaning, are in any case to have the riddle interpreted to them by the prophet, although they are called a **house of rebelliousness** (ch. ii. 5, 6), the case before us is a different one from that in Matt. xiii. 10 sq., and from that in Isaiah, to which Jesus there refers back. We are to think of the exiles as favourably distinguished from those at Jerusalem.—For the interpretation, comp. ver. 3, and 2 Kings xxiv. 11 sq.; Jer. xxiv. 1, xxix. 2.—The **princes** of Jerusalem along with the king, the "topmost branch" in the riddle of which Jehoiachin is the top-shoot (ver. 4).—Ver. 13. Comp. ver. 5; Jer. xli. 1; 1 Kings xi. 14; 2 Kings xxiv. 17 (Introd. p. 6). In reference to the vassal's oath of fidelity, see 2 Chron. xxxvi. 13.—The אֵילֵי cannot perhaps be taken as a simple resumption of the "princes" of the preceding verse, yet they may be understood as included. But the expression is to be interpreted especially from 2 Kings xxiv. 14, 16. HITZ.: the owners of property, rich proprietors, artisans, and warriors. The intention (ver. 6) is clearly expressed in Ver. 14; the parties in question were not so much meant to be hostages.—KEIL: "that he might keep his covenant, that it might stand."—Ver. 15. Comp. ver. 7; likewise 2 Kings xxiv. 20. The Egyptian was to support him with that which was peculiar to Egypt (Deut. xvii. 16), and which Zedekiah needed. Did the latter wish to appoint the riders for the horses?—The **much people** refers back to ver. 9, and likewise to the question of ver. 10, which is at the same time explained.—The answer is given in Ver. 16 in a divine utterance, such as we have in ver. 9, only that the terms are still stronger, taking the well-known form of an oath.—Comp. ch. xii. 13.—Ver. 17. **And not with great power**, etc., refers back to the "horses and much people" of ver. 15, and is meant to explain the statement in ver. 9. Pharaoh is the subject. The meaning is, either that he will not be willing to render Zedekiah the expected help, or that he will not be able. Comp. Jer. xxxvii. 5, 7. The "acting," on which it depends, turns out insignificant—nothing more than a feeble demonstration on the part of Egypt. [HENGST.: Pharaoh will leave his protegé in the lurch, when he is hard pressed by his enemies. That the Chaldean needs no great military force against Jerusalem (ver. 9), finds its explanation here in the circumstance that the Egyptians, against whom alone such a force was necessary, do not come to its help with such a force.]—The march of the Egyptian auxiliary army took place when Jerusalem was besieged by the Chaldeans. Comp. in this connection on ch. iv. 2. **To cut off**, etc., draws attention to the fact of how necessary powerful help would be in such a situation.

Ver. 18. The riddle is interpreted, but the divine discourse lingers still over the breach of oath and covenant, because such acting on Zedekiah's part, with what is implied in it, is still to be judged and to have sentence pronounced upon it by Jehovah.—Ver. 19, just like ver. 16. It is not only that every oath, and hence also this oath, is of a religious character, and that the despising of it necessarily compromised the God of Israel in the eyes of the heathen; but still farther, considering the clemency of Nebuchadnezzar in making such a covenant, as Jehovah's instrument, Jehovah's goodness was turned into lasciviousness.—Comp. besides ch. xi. 21, ix. 10. —Ver. 20. See on ch. xii. 13. The "contending," the going into court with him, involves the punishment.—Ch. xv. 8.—Ver. 21. Instead of מִבְרָחוֹ (Qeri: מִבְרָחָיו), **fugitives**, the Chaldee reads: מִבְחָרָיו, "chosen ones" (ch. xii. 14). So also Hitzig. He who thinks to save himself by flight —hence the whole military forces of Israel are driven into flight—shall be slain by the sword. But for the people left over, for all the remnant generally, the fate in store is the same as in ch. v. 10, 12. Bitter experience brings them to know and understand, although, alas! too late, that God had spoken by the mouth of His prophet.

Vers. 22–24. *The Prediction.*

With a very beautiful variation the close of our chapter, which follows, takes the form of the theme of the riddle at the beginning. The threatening colours there are exchanged here for those rich in promise.—Ver. 22. וְ, marking a continuation; but as the לָקַח is that of Nebuchadnezzar, there is rather an antithesis. Ingeniously Hitzig: "Jehovah, who is Himself in Deut. xxxii. 11 and Ex. xix. 4 compared to an eagle, appears upon the scene, confronting the former one (ver. 3)." And He who asserts His dignity in opposition to him, whom neither Jerusalem nor Egypt is able to oppose, can really do so: אָנִי, with emphasis. He does as Nebuchadnezzar does, and yet He does so quite differently! He brings low that which would fain be high; He exalts that which is apparently reduced to nothing (ver. 24). **Of the topmost branch,** etc. Thus the illustrious original house of David (the cedar) is still in existence; and not only the royal family, but its royal position as well (the topmost branch). And thus the statement is modified, that (ver. 3) the great eagle took *the* topmost branch of the cedar. The הָרָמָה here, which is wanting in the former case, is not without significance. Thus the matter presents itself to God's eye. His taking is really "giving" (וְנָתַתִּי).—In ver. 4 we have אֶת־רֹאשׁ, here מֵרֹאשׁ; so that in spite of the taking away of Jehoiachin, his kingdom is still supposed to continue. The definition added: **a tender one,** may be interpreted of the planting, shoots of this kind being generally used; still better, perhaps, of a child (Luke ii. 12). The Chaldee paraphrases: of his children's children a little child. At all events, it cannot here mean a thing small and insignificant, as Hengst. supposes, nor something weak. [Hitzig takes "tender" as = youthful; but this idea lies already in the word "shoot." Comp. on ver. 4. Tender youth, which is just childhood, is indicated by the stronger expression.]—אֶקְטֹף, *decisio significat mortem*, Isa. liii. 8; Dan. ix. 26 (Cocc.).—The contrast lying at the foundation is a twofold one,—to Jehoiachin too (ver. 4), but much more to Zedekiah (ver. 5), in whose case "planting" is spoken of. In the same direction chiefly the contrast of the **mountain** also is kept. It is the contrast to the low country generally,—on the one hand to the Canaan of Babylon, on the other to the Canaan of Jerusalem (ch. xvi. 3). The partic. pass., תָּלוּל (only here), adds to the natural height an extraordinary exaltation besides, whether it be to serve as a powerful counteractive to the depression that has taken place, or whether it be to hint already at the approaching glory of ver. 23. A farther designation of the mountain is given in Ver. 23. **The elevated mountain of Israel** is not Zion directly as such, nor Zion in the wider sense, as embracing also Mount Moriah, as must of course be the view taken if appeal is made to ch. xx. 40 (Isa. ii. 2; Mic. iv. 1); but Jerusalem is here meant, in the same way as in ver. 3 it was spoken of as "Lebanon." Comp. there. (Ch. xxxiv. 13, 14.) Hence restoration (in accordance with ch. xvi.), and that with increased splendour. Because such restoration of Jerusalem, of Judah, is brought about by means of the royal child of David's line, in thought the reference to Zion may predominate, Ps. xlviii. 3 [2], ii. 6, lxviii. 17 [16]. That the kingdom of God, the kingdom of heaven, springs from the Jews for the whole world, is aptly symbolized by the planting of the royal shoot in the royal city, and by what now follows. It is to be observed that the mountain is a mere foil, the typical substratum, and that it neither "comes into view as the seat and centre of the kingdom of God," nor does it even "denote this kingdom itself;" but the kingdom and all its glory are conceived of as *in the shoot of David*, and represented as proceeding from him, behind whom all else steps into the background. Klief. alone correctly: "the person of the Messiah will grow into His kingdom, which becomes the spiritual home of all the nations of the world." However historical, yet the promised personality is in this respect kept in an ideal shape. Fulfilling what is typical, becoming the full embodiment of what was shadowed forth by Israel, he attains to what he is meant to be; he realizes completely his idea, which has to do with mankind generally. The **foliage** is in order to the **shadow**. The **fruit**, as being a tree, as it must be, perhaps also one which yields nourishment to those to whom it gives shelter (Isa. xi. 1). As in ver. 8 we had אַדֶּרֶת, so here אַדִּיר: what Zedekiah had not become as a "vine," that He who is here meant is as a "cedar," so as to fulfil the promise given to David regarding his posterity. For the clause: **and under it there dwell,** etc., comp. ch. xxxi. 6; Dan. iv. 9 [12]; Matt. xiii. 32. An emblem of the universal sovereignty, to which all submit themselves, but in which also they rejoice and put their confidence (**in the shadow**, etc.).—The expression: **all birds of every wing,** points to Noah's ark of safety, Gen. vii. 14. The meaning is: all the different nations and families of men upon earth, ch. xxxi. 6, 12; see also Ps. viii. 7, 9 [6, 8], lxxxiv. 4 [3]. A contrast alike to ver. 6 and ver. 7!—Ver. 24. **All trees,** etc., are the collective ruling powers of this world, the princes and kings of the earth.—הַשָּׂדֶה looks back perhaps to ver. 5 (8); other than mere *earthly* kingdoms Nebuchadnezzar and his compeers are able neither to found nor to rule.—The **bringing low** of the **high tree,** just as correspondingly the **exalting** of the low tree, refers specially to Jehoiachin; while the making **the green tree to wither**, and the **making the dry tree to flourish**, in accordance with ver. 9 sq., point back to Zedekiah, inasmuch as through him the kingdom in Judah came to ruin. The revivification of this kingdom, the sending forth of shoots from that which withered with Zedekiah, and the raising up again of the seed of David from the humiliation of Jehoiachin,—all this is accomplished by Jehovah through the Promised One (**I, Jehovah, spake and did**). Hitzig, like most, takes the sentence as a general thought (1 Sam. ii. 7). In form it is kept general, but its import is certainly special, referring to what lies before us. Only the thing to be considered is the right interpretation. According to Hengst., of course, the high tree is the worldly sovereignty; the low tree, David or his family; the green tree, Nebuchadnezzar's sovereignty of the world at the time.

DOCTRINAL REFLECTIONS.

1. The form of the discourse here, just as in the case of our Lord, who has developed the parable into one of His ordinary modes of teaching, is to be explained chiefly from the object in view,—partly as it was designed for a circle of hearers, or rather or readers, which, although mixed up in all sorts of ways with higher interests, is yet to be thought of as living mainly in the world of sense, and especially as bound fast in the misery of the exile, and sympathizing in the false and faithless policy prevailing at the time in Jerusalem; partly as it might recommend itself to the prophet in the political circumstances by which he was surrounded. The *mashal* before us in Ezekiel goes, therefore, far beyond mere popular illustration. Still less is it to be explained away from the æsthetic standpoint, as merely another rhetorical garb for the thought.

2. As in the parable the emblematic form preponderates over the thought, so also here. What the prophet is to say to Israel is said by the whole of that mighty array of figurative expression, for which the animal and vegetable worlds furnish the figures. But the eagle does what eagles otherwise never do; and what is planted as a willow grows into a vine; and the vine "is represented as falling in love with the other eagle" (J. D. MICH.). The contradictory character of such a representation, and the fact that in the difficulties to be solved (ver. 9 sq.) the comparison comes to a stand, and the closing Messianic portion in which the whole culminates, convert the parable into a "riddle." A trace of irony and the moral tendency, such as belong to the fable, are not wanting.

3. As to the predictions in this chapter, see what is said on ch. xii., Doct. Reflec. 4, pp. 136, 137. As respects the time, ch. xvii. stands between the 6th month of the 6th year and the 5th month of the 7th year of Jehoiachin's captivity; and its contents, therefore, would probably be spoken from four to five years before the destruction of Jerusalem.

4. Not only does Ewald call vers. 22–24 "a short and beautiful picture of Messianic times," but Hitzig gives a still more definite exposition: "the passage is an actual prediction, and in fact a Messianic one." Bunsen makes our prediction be "partly fulfilled" in Zerubbabel ("the prince of the Jews after their return from the captivity, Ezra i. 8.; 1 Chron. iii. 19; Matt. i. 12; Luke iii. 27"), adding, however, that the glory of the new king as here described "goes far beyond that of Zerubbabel." Similar is the view of Hengst., viz. that as Zerubbabel "in a certain sense did everything which God did generally for the re-establishment and maintenance of the civil government in Israel," he also might be regarded as included under the terms of the prediction, because Ezekiel has before his eye, "not the Messiah as an individual," but "the whole family of David." As against this view, Hävernick points (1) to the image of the cedar-shoot as a descendant of the house of David; and (2) to the context, where only personalities are spoken of (Jehoiachin, Zedekiah, Nebuchadnezzar). The oldest Jewish exposition understood the passage of King Messiah.

5. The kingdom of Judah, even although it had become idolatrous, yet could not (as Ziegler remarks) all at once be cast off—for David's sake. The house and family of David appear like a stay and support in Judah. "For David, Jehovah cherishes an unceasing and solicitous regard throughout the whole history of this kingdom, just because this kingdom itself was to be nothing else than the link of connection between David and his Son κατ' ἐξοχήν. David is the point always referred to in the history of this kingdom; he is the factor ever present and ever working in that history, just as the Son of David is the factor at work beyond."

6. Hävernick has already pointed out the inner connection between the Messianic announcement here and that in the preceding ch. xvi. 53–63. What is to be understood there by the turning of the misery and the *restitutio in pristinum* becomes quite clear to us by means of the prediction as to Messiah in our chapter.

7. The Church of God is not destined to disappear in the kingdoms of this world: but all the kingdoms of this world shall become the kingdoms of God and of His Anointed.

8. "Among the manifold predictions of the Lord's Anointed and of His kingdom in the world, this of our prophet stands forth like a cedar; in this similitude, so grand, and yet so simple, he has most strikingly portrayed the future salvation in its most universal significance and verity" (UMBREIT).

9. Hengst. draws attention to the fact that at the close the interpretation of the symbol is not added,—"for the same reason that in Ezekiel there is no prophecy against Babylon, while the whole of the prophecies of Jeremiah find their close in such a prophecy. The prophet prophesied in the land of the Chaldeans, and had to exercise caution in view of the surrounding heathen."

HOMILETIC HINTS.

Ver. 1 sq. "Formerly, how they have broken God's covenant; here, how they have not kept faith with men" (LUTHER).—Ver. 3 sq. "Princes also have no security against misfortune; those who are nearer the clouds are nearer the lightning also. They should not forget that they also are men, and that God alone is the King of kings" (STCK.).—"The eagle is an emblem of empire and dominion: he is called the king o birds. Pyrrhus, when saluted as an eagle by his soldiers, was much pleased, telling them that they had raised him on high with their weapons, as it were with wings" (À LAP.).—The important eagles in the history of Israel: Nebuchadnezzar, Pharaoh, Rome.—Ver. 4. "Thus many a one suffers in a strange land for the sin he has committed in his own" (STCK.).—Ver. 5. The soil is often better than the seed which is sown in it. —Ver. 6. Prosperity turns out for the advantage of but few men. Most grow on all sides and produce leaves, but bear no fruit, or bad fruit.—Ver. 7. Ingratitude makes no situation better, does not render dependent circumstances more pleasant, and brings to shame every one who is guilty of it, let the object of it be who he may.—It is not easy to rest contented with God's ordering and leading; the discipline of the Spirit of God is needed for it: let my ways be pleasing in Thine eyes. We must give up our heart to the Lord, and keep it directed toward Him—our heart, with all the thoughts which come out of it, and which would fain be as God, yea, wiser than God. —Keep me in Thy paths, in the way which Thou Thyself showest me.—Ver. 8. Discontentment has driven many a one from a snug spot.—Ver. 9 sq. "When God wishes to punish the wickedness of men, He needs no great warlike host for the purpose" (O.).—Unfaithfulness beats its own master.—Those who have not God on their side, who have only their own wits, can be driven to flight in thousands by one.—"It is a bad thing to trust in man's wisdom; take thou counsel with God, open His word, look to thy calling, ponder thy duty, and think of the end" (STCK.). —Ver. 10. The east wind of divine judgments.—Thus the place of fortune becomes the place of misfortune; the scene of wickedness, the scene of punishment; the theatre of ingratitude (toward God also), the theatre of ruin.

Ver. 11 sq. It is not all riddles that are interpreted to us; we are guessing away at many during our whole life; but we also make far too little use of the key of self-knowledge.—Misfortune it is said to be, while it is only crime.—Ver. 15 sq. The oath is to be kept to every one and by every one. Even by the emperor Sigismund to the "heretic" Huss!—"Kings, and those in high position generally, ought to be a good example to others. How much their example can build up as well as pull down!" (STCK.)—"If the Lord humbles one, he must bear the tribulation with patience, and not seek by forbidden means to extricate himself from it, Heb. xii. 7" (TÜB. BIB.).—"God avenges and punishes perjury with the greatest earnestness" (O.).—"For God is the truth, and will see to it that fidelity is upheld among men, and hence abhors all deceit and perjury. Even if we have promised anything by constraint which is in other respects unjust, we are not to break our word, because the name of God is to be dearer to us than all earthly advantages, Ps. xv. 4" (HEIM-HOFF.).—"The humiliations as well as the exaltations of earthly kingdoms are certainly foreseen and appointed by God" (STCK.).—How many a one is the architect of his own misfortune at least!—"The chariot of Israel, and the horsemen thereof!" said Elisha of Elijah.—Ps. xxxiii. 17.—"Think not to whom, but remember by whom, thou hast sworn an oath" (JER.).—Why is there so much oath-breaking and perjury in Christendom itself even yet!?—Ver. 16. God lets man's righteousness too get its rights, just because it means to be righteousness.—What Babylon has made, Babylon also destroys.—This is security, to be a plant of the heavenly Father's planting, Matt. xv. 13.—"The earth is everywhere the Lord's, but to be laid with one's fathers is certainly more pleasant."—Ver. 17. The help of man is of no avail when God means to destroy. God's help, on the other hand, avails even against man's help: Zedekiah with Egypt, Nebuchadnezzar with Jehovah. Look at the copartneries for thyself, and bestow thy confidence accordingly. The latter firm is the more reliable.—Cursed is the man that trusteth in man, Jer. xvii.—Men promise, and break their promise; God promises, and does not break His.—Ver. 19. God's oath as against Zedekiah's perjury.—God does not swear, and then fail to keep His oath: that shall be learned by experience by those who swear falsely, or who do not keep their oath.—If thou appealest to God as a witness, thou summonest Him also as a judge, as an avenger!—We have never to do with men alone.—Ver. 20 sq. No one can escape God.—"The enemy's sword is sharp; God's sword is sharper still" (STCK.).—Comp. what is said to the Hebrews of the word of God.—God's judgments are always meant to lead to the knowledge of Himself as well, and not merely of ourselves.

Ver. 22 sq. The riddle of Israel is the riddle alike of the human heart in its perversity, and of the heart of God in Christ.—The omnipotence and love of God join hands, and the result is the grace of God.—"Whosoever laid up this promise thoroughly in his heart would thereby be delivered from the region of vain political hopes and intrigues. The saying of Augustine applies here: 'That which thou seekest is, but it is not where thou seekest it'" (HENGST.).—"Because the Church of Christ has been planted by God Himself, it shall certainly remain" (CR.).—"The planting on Golgotha" (WITSIUS).—Ver. 23. "Babylon, and with it the whole series of the old world-powers, are dried up; David flourishes and bears fruit, and under the shadow of his offshoot the fowls of heaven dwell" (HENGST.). —Ver. 24. The history of the world is to be recognised as God's government.—The divine government of the world culminates in Christ.—Everything turns out in the end according to God's word.—(Fr. W. Krummacher preached in 1852 on vers. 22-24: "The Tree Christ, which God has prepared for us, (1) as to its nature, (2) as to its destiny.—Summer and winter the cedar is green, and never loses its leaves nor its verdure. The everlastingly green Tree of Life is Christ. No wood is more durable; so Christ is the indestructible foundation for our hopes, etc.—We are the branches in the Cedar of God. Our fruits are Christ's, who produces them in us and by us. John and Peter, Paul and James, what boughs in that Cedar! and the Fathers and the Reformers, and all believers since, what a Tree! What a green, flourishing, fruit-laden array of branches that which sways around it! What a mighty, densely-foliaged, far-shadowing crown! and in the crown what gales, and zephyrs, and rustlings of holy life and divine love! Here there is promised to Christ and His cause nothing less than final triumph over the whole world.—The pompous glory of Babylon, Egypt, Rome, and Athens, where is it to be found?")

7. *The Laws of the Divine Punitive Righteousness* (ch. xviii.).

1, 2 And the word of Jehovah came unto me, saying, Why do ye use this
proverb upon the land of Israel, saying, The fathers have eaten sour [wild]
3 grapes, and the teeth of the sons are set on edge? As I live—sentence of the
Lord Jehovah—if ye shall have occasion to use this proverb longer in Israel
4 [ye shall no longer use this proverb]. Behold, all souls to me they [belong]; as the soul
of the father, so also the soul of the son is mine. The soul that sinneth, it
5 shall die. And if any man be righteous, and do judgment and righteousness:
6 Has not eaten on the mountains, nor lifted up his eyes to the idols of the
house of Israel, nor defiled his neighbour's wife, nor drawn near to his wife
7 in her uncleanness; And oppresses no one, restores his debt-pledge, robs not,
8 gives his bread to the hungry, and covers the naked with clothing; Gives
not on usury, and takes not increase, withdraws his hand from injustice,
9 exercises true judgment between man and man; Walks in My statutes and
keeps My judgments, to do truth,—he is righteous, he shall surely live,—
10 sentence of the Lord Jehovah. And should he beget a violence-doing son, a
shedder of blood,—and he [the father] did towards his brother each of those
11 [things]:—And he [the son] does none of all those things, for [but] he has eaten
12 upon the mountains, and defiled his neighbour's wife; The poor and needy
he has oppressed, he has robbed, he restores not the pledge, and to the idols
13 he has lifted up his eyes, he has done abomination; Has given on usury and
taken increase, and shall he live?—He shall not live. He has done all these
14 abominations; he shall surely die. His blood shall be upon him. And, lo,
should he beget a son who sees all the sins of his father which he hath done,
15 and sees and does not the like:—He has not eaten upon the mountains, nor
lifted up his eyes to the idols of the house of Israel; he has not defiled his
16 neighbour's wife, Nor oppressed any one, nor taken pledge in pledge, nor
robbed; he has given his bread to the hungry, and covered the naked with
17 clothing; From the needy he has turned away [withheld] his hand, usury and
increase he took not, he executed My judgments, he walked in My statutes:
18 he shall not die in [on account of] his father's iniquity; he shall surely live. His
father, because he practised extortion, committed robbery against his brother,
and did that which is not good in the midst of his people, lo, he died in his
19 iniquity. And ye say, Why has not the son borne the iniquity of the father?
Because the son has done judgment and righteousness, kept all My statutes
and done them, he shall surely live. The soul that sinneth, it shall die.
20 The son shall not bear the iniquity of the father, and the father shall not
bear the iniquity of the son. The righteousness of the righteous shall be
upon him [the one], and the wickedness of the wicked shall be upon him [the
21 other]. And if [because] the wicked shall turn from all his sins which he hath
done, and keep all My statutes, and do judgment and righteousness, he shall
22 surely live, he shall not die. All his transgressions which he hath done shall
not be remembered to him; in [on account of] his righteousness which he hath
23 done, he shall live. Have I any pleasure at all in the death of the wicked?
Sentence of the Lord Jehovah. Not when he turns from his way [ways] and
24 lives!? But if the righteous turn from his righteousness, and commit iniquity,
and do according to all the abominations which the wicked commits, shall he
live?—All his righteousness which he hath done shall not be remembered;
in [on account of] his faithlessness which he hath practised, and in [on account of]
25 his sins which he hath sinned, in [on account of] them shall he die. And say ye,
The way of the Lord is not equal!? Hear now, O house of Israel, is My way
26 not equal? Are not your ways unequal? When the righteous turns from
his righteousness, and does iniquity, and dies thereby; in his iniquity which
27 he hath done he dies. And when the wicked turns from his wickedness which
he hath done, and does judgment and righteousness, he shall save his soul
28 alive. And should he see and turn from all his transgressions which he hath

29 done, he shall surely live, he shall not die. But they of the house of Israel say,
The way of the Lord is not equal! ? Are My ways not equal, O house of Israel?
30 Are not your ways unequal? Therefore I will judge you, each man according
to his ways, O house of Israel,—sentence of the Lord Jehovah. Return,
and turn [you] from all your transgressions, and iniquity shall not be your
31 ruin. Cast away from you all your transgressions, in which ye have gone
astray, and make you a new heart, and a new spirit; and why will ye die,
32 O house of Israel? For I have no pleasure in the death of him that dies,—
sentence of the Lord Jehovah; therefore turn ye [be converted] and live!

Ver. 2. Sept.: . . . *τι ὑμιν ἡ παραβολη αὑτη*—

Ver. 4. . . . *αὐτη ἀποθανειται, κ. του φαγοντος τον ὀμφακα αἱμωδιασουσιν οἱ ὀδοντες αὐτου.*

Ver. 7. Vulg.: . . . *pignus debitori reddiderit*—

Ver 10. Sept.: . . . *κ. ποιουντα ἁμαρτηματα*, (11) *ἐν τῃ ὁδῳ τ. πατρος αὐτου του δικαιου οὐκ ἐπορευθη*,— Vulg.: . . . *effundentem sanguinem, et fecerit unum de istis*, (11) *et hæc quidem omnia non facientem*— (10. Some codices read: מאחת fem.)

Ver. 14. Sept.: . . . *κ. ἰδῃ . . . κ. φοβηθῃ*— The Chald. only translates: *et vidit; Sept., Vulg., Arab.: et timuerit.*

Ver. 17. *κ. ἀπο ἀδικιας ἀπεστρεψεν τ. χειρα*— Vulg.: . . . *a pauperis injuria averterit manum*—

Ver. 18. Vulg.: *Pater ejus quia calumniatus est et vim fecit fratri*—.

Ver. 22. *Omnium . . . non recordabor*—

Ver. 23. Sept.: *Ὁτι οὐ βουλομαι τ. θανατον . . . ὡς το ἀποστρεψαι αὐτον ἐκ τ. ὁδου . . . κ. ζην αὐτον.* (For מות there is a reading: במות; for מדרכו, מדרכיו in plur.)

Ver. 24. Vulg.: *Si autem averterit . . . et fecerit iniquitatem secundum omnes abominationes quas operari solet impius, numquid vivet?*—

Ver. 29. Another reading: דרככם, sing., Sept., Arab.

Ver. 30. Sept.: . . . *κ. οὐκ ἐσονται ὑμιν εἰς κολασιν ἀδικιας.* Vulg.: . . . *et non erit vobis in ruinam iniquitas.*

Ver. 31. Sept.: *κ. πνευμα καινον, κ. ποιησατε πασας τ. ἐντολας μου.*

EXEGETICAL REMARKS.

Vers. 1–4. *The Principle of the Divine Punitive Righteousness.*

Ver. 2. Comp. ch. xii. 22. A popular expression, arrogating to itself the authority of a divine voice, has established itself in Israel in opposition to the word of God.—The **land of Israel** should emphatically not be the place for such language, as it is the scene of God's holy justice as well as His gracious mercy.—The question is not one of mere surprise, but of solemn anger, as befits divine speech.—**Fathers** taken generally, so that it is left to each to consider for himself who are particularly designated (2 Kings xxiv. 3; Jer. xv. 4). Our chapter at the same time links itself on thereby to what has gone before (especially ch. xvi.). The proverb took the prophet, as it were, at his word.—יֹאכְלוּ corresponding to the general form of statement: to be accustomed to eat.—The **sons**, on the other hand, are the definite persons who are exposed to suffering in the existing state of things. In the most thoughtless and frivolous manner the popular criticism of God's way,—of the history of Israel, expresses itself. What those did wrongly must be visited on us! There is no sense of sin, nor acknowledgment of guilt, and just as little reference to divine judgment and retributive righteousness. Hävernick refers rightly to the "heathenish" disposition of the people, who, "destitute of faith in a living God, were driven to the delusion of a blind Nemesis," a natural necessity. "Accordingly repentance seems useless" (HENGST.). They could thus shield themselves against the ever-repeated call to radical repentance. The divine answer sets itself over against the people's word, energetically, in the form of an oath, Ver. 3, in which, according to the two-sided tenor of our chapter, it remains undecided whether the impending judgment, or the Messianic redemption, embraced in conversion, shall bring this style of speech to an end in the future. —בְּיִשְׂרָאֵל, a thing unbecoming even "upon the land of Israel" (ver. 2), above all, unbecoming among the people to whom (Rom. iii.) the oracles of God are committed.—After the *form* has thus been found fault with, the substance, Ver. 4, is objected to; and since the question actually touched is the retributive righteousness of God, its ground-principle is first of all stated, from which its individual laws naturally proceed. **Behold** points to an undeniable fact, and therefore presupposes universal assent.—**All souls**, sq.: "perhaps an allusion to Gen. xviii. 25" (HÄV.). In other respects, as Calvin: not merely would God here maintain His paramount authority and lordship, but, still more, evince His fatherly love towards all mankind as their Creator. HENGST.: "God would surrender His property if souls suffered punishment for the guilt of others; since they are in the likeness of God, souls cannot be degraded into servile instruments." HITZ.: "I am not under the necessity of punishing another, —the son,—as if I could not lay hold of the guilty father." PHILIPPS: "Before God all souls are equal, so that each man represents himself only." All these explanations are insufficient to meet the thought. The proposition is in reality a fundamental principle, for it goes back to the origin of things, according to which the souls of men, created by the breathing of the divine Spirit of life into corporal matter, breathe supernatural, spiritual vital energy, in a sentient form of life and activity. This divineness of men, at least in respect to their souls, which, on the other hand, they possess in common with the lower creatures as animal life, is opposed to every form of dependence on nature, whether on a heathen fate, or, in particular (which is here the immediate contrast), on bodily parents, therefore to the dependence of the son on the father. God's exclusive property-right (emphasized by the repeated לִי) in persons could not be maintained, if any man required to suffer death from the fact of being his father's son. **Die,** the end of a process,—the separation of the soul from its life-source, the Spirit of God. (Deut. xxx. 15; Jer. xxi. 8; Prov. xi. 19.)—Comp. on ch. iii. 18. This cannot happen without an act of God's retributive justice, so that the punishment inflicted by God must correspond to man's guilt. **The soul that sinneth** —disloyalty to the living influences of the Spirit of God, considered as a continuous present—**it shall die.** Through this latter, as a judicial utterance, the general proposition as to God's possessory-right is more specifically expressed in reference to His authority to judge. Comp. Jas. iv. 12.

Vers. 5–9. *The Law of the Righteous Man.*

Ver. 5. The first application of the principle is made to the righteous man. Comp. ch. iii. 18 sq. He is described according to *Being* and *Doing,*—essentially and actually; in particular, doing **judgment,** in general, **righteousness:** his doing is then more precisely depicted, not without a tendency to antithesis.—Ver. 6. Even kings who were otherwise loyal to the law, were unable to abolish the worship of the "high places." [Usually the expression is made to refer to the gross forms of idol-worship (1 Cor. viii. 4–10, x. 7); and what follows, to the more refined.]—The feasts referred to are sacrificial feasts which were not observed in the sanctuary, Deut. xii.—The second thing, singled out in reference to the first table of the **law,** is the undoubtedly rare case of complete apathy and indifference towards the popular idols of Israel. Hitzig understands it of supplicating, worshipping, Job xxxi. 26 (Ps. cxxi. 1). Hävernick, of inward longing. Comp. ch. vi. 4. —The natural transition, after ch. xvi., to the marriage relation singles out from the second table of the law not ordinary adultery (the word is neither נָאַף, nor even חָמַד, Ex. xx.), but the more precise and **deeper** defilement (טִמֵּא) of the neighbour's wife, in order, through the selected expression, to throw a clear ray of light on their own marriage relation and its mysteries (domestic purity). Comp. Lev. xviii. 19, xx. 18. —Ver. 7. **Oppression** in general, in its more peaceful as well as its directly violent (גָּזֵל) form (Lev. xix. 13).—חוֹב, according to Hengst., the accusative of restriction: debt-pledge; Hävernick, on the other hand: his pledge, a debt, *i.e.,* along with the pledge, the obligation, softening the always rather offensive signification of חֲבֹלָה (from חָבַל, to bind, to tie), so that just demands are referred to. Hitzig makes the word a participle: "restores his pledge to the debtor (GESEN.: for debt)." Compare besides at Ex. xxii. 25; Deut. xxiv. 12. Following this, more positive benevolence.—Ver. 8. Comp. Lev. xxv. 36, 37; Deut. xxiii. 20.—The close of the verse probably refers to the special activity of a judge or arbiter.—Ver. 9. Concluding summation corresponding to the introduction in ver. 5,—the apodosis to the protasis. Righteousness before God in contradistinction to its semblance (לַעֲשׂוֹת אֱמֶת). The Septuagint read אוֹתָם.—חָיֹה יִחְיֶה, **live** in the fullest, deepest sense of the word.

Vers. 10–13. *The Law of the Unrighteous Son.*

A second application of the principle deals with the case of an unrighteous man,—the son of the righteous man. Personally there is a connection (**should he beget**), essentially, the greatest contrast, as פָּרִיץ, etc., immediately shows. But the actual contrast shall become still more decided, and shall, for that reason, appear as a personal one,—therefore וְעָשָׂה, etc.—Ver. 10. The description of the father reduced to a minimum: if there was any one of these forementioned just and righteous things, he did it,—in short, he was righteous. [אח Hengst.: in relation to his brother, as the antithetic parallel in ver. 18 decidedly recommends. So also the Chaldee version. Rosenm.: *simile quid.* According to others, it is the apocopate form of אֶחָד. Others, again, have omitted it. את has also been proposed as a reading. Hitzig., Ewald: = אַךְ, "only."]—The contrast follows more at length in Ver. 11, in the description of the son. **And he does none of all those things,** which are then mentioned in detail. Comp. ver. 6.—Ver. 12. **Poor and needy** illustrates the undefined object of ver. 7. Compare in other respects with ver. 6.—Ver. 13. See ver. 8.—וָחָי, the apodosis. The facts oppose every other issue; the emphatic divine negative only adds confirmation. His deeds adjudge him to death,—yes, he himself is to blame. With the judicial form of expression (מוֹת יוּמָת, not as in Gen. ii. 17) comp. Lev. xx. 9; only that in this case the son curses his righteous father virtually by his life!

Vers. 14–20. *The Law of the Righteous Son.*

Third application of the principle, in which, as in the first case, the reference is to a righteous person,—the son of the forementioned unrighteous man,—who takes warning from his father's sins. Always father and son, corresponding with the proverb which was being answered.—Ver. 14. Comp. ver. 10. He **sees,** repeated for the sake of emphatic description. The reading וַיִּרָא, followed by the Sept. and Vulg. in the latter part of the verse, is to be rejected.—Ver. 15. Comp. ver. 6.—Ver. 16. Comp. ver. 7.—("He allowed himself even less than he might," in contrast to the conduct of his father—Hitzig.)—Ver. 17. **From the needy,** etc. Not only doing him no violence, but, as described, showing him compassion. Ewald reads מֵעָוֶל from ver. 8. Comp. as to further details, vers. 8 and 9. Here and in Ver. 18, עָוֹן, in anticipation of ver. 19. In order to separate and contrast father and son as decidedly as possible, the former is once more briefly described.—Ver. 19. There is here no allusion, as most suppose, to Ex. xx. 5. Nothing necessitates this. Since the proverb (ver. 2) in its frivolous rude form was at once disregarded, and since the divine reply to it immediately made it more profound, and, especially from ver. 17, applied it to the question of guilt and perdition on the ne hand, righteousness and life on the other—so with the inquiry as to the why, a perception of the deeper signification of its contents generally may therefore be attributed to the people. This not only recommends itself on rhetorical grounds, since in the case before us the conclusion is introduced by it,—and the thought can hardly be introduced in a more lively manner than by the deduction of a general maxim from the foregoing concrete examples,—but the moral presumption that the people are so far interested in the profound gravity of the subject, requires that they also should contribute the "why," which was altogether so natural (not merely with reference to the law), and which sounds so full of meaning, because by what has gone before the unity of Israel must seem shattered, nothing being taken into account but the individual. "Have ye (supposition) said: **Why,**" etc. The individual facts answer you. So say ye; so did he! Comp. further, vers. 5, 9.—Ver. 20. A quotation from ver. 4, which is impressively extended, concludes the paragraph with a statement which so sharply contrasts righteousness and wickedness, that a new solution, to wit, through the action of the one or the other, *i.e.* through a change of disposition, must come into view.

Vers. 21–32. *The Principle of Grace, as against the Principle of Retribution, expressed in the Call to Repentance.*

Ver. 21. Comp. ch. iii. 18 sq. Return from wickedness to God's righteousness, evidenced by facts, ensures true life instead of death. The principle of divine retribution affected the case of persistent, continued sinning only. Whoever abandons sin is left untouched by the retributive righteousness of God.—Ver. 22. In such an event, viz. of return, the past, however full of sin, is left out of account; one is not required to bear the penalty of one's own, much less of another's sin. Righteousness is done. But the principle thus contrasted with the previously explained law of retribution proclaims itself in the plainest way as the principle of grace and divine compassion.—Ver. 23. If the retributive righteousness of God—the law of His government—must occupy itself with the sin of the sinner, the sinner himself is God's property (ver. 4), and to the profoundest law of the Divine nature (חָפֵץ) not death, but life corresponds, although for righteousness' sake, the right of the divine Possessor must exhibit itself in the case of the sinner who continues in sin, or who apostatizes, as the might of the Judge.—Hengst. translates הֲלֹא, "Should he not live if he returns," etc.?—Ver. 24. The foregoing strengthened and confirmed by a counter-proof, as it were, and that the strongest imaginable, by a caricature of the holy—the reverse of conversion. The previous sentence is still in a manner continued by בְּ, yet so that with the contrasted case the appropriate negative is also understood; then it breaks off, and the matter of fact which is adduced brings in the question which must naturally be negatived,—וָחָי, as in ver. 13. The usual translation is: "but if the righteous turn, etc., should he live?"—"All his righteousness," etc.—The antithesis to ver. 22. Comp. ch. iii. 20, xv. 8, xvii. 20.—Ver. 25. תָּכַן, to measure, weigh; to be equal. Comp. 1 Sam. ii. 3. The assumed objection presupposes, like ver. 19, that the people have intelligently followed the exposition up to this point. "And (supposed) say ye," etc. Measure your own ways! Hitzig rightly refers the questioned "way of the Lord" to a procedure, such as has just been described in regard to an apostate righteous person, which would leave all his righteousness unweighed. The counter-accusation, contained in the divine answer, is in complete harmony with the scope of our chapter, since it points at self-examination, and thereby at the sense of sin. For the argument finally occupies itself with each individual man, and with the way which each chooses, and continues in.—Ver. 26 is therefore a recapitulation from ver. 24, as Ver. 27 from ver. 21.—But as the conclusion of the whole is to be the call to repentance, the case of ver. 27 is again introduced with this in view.—Ver. 28. Comp. ver. 21.—Ver. 29. Renewed remonstrance, with the object of inducing them to seek self-knowledge by means of trying their own ways—see ver. 25. (Not: "and ye say," but: **and they of the house of Israel say.**) יִתָּכֵן, the singular, according to some: each of your ways, thus individualizing them; or, the actual diversity of the way comprehended in the ideal unity of the walk; or better, what they had said of the Lord's way (it is not equal) adopted as a motto which is far more applicable to their ways.—Ver. 30. לָכֵן points, in the first place, as a reason for judgment, to the equity of God's way as compared with Israel's; then, as a reason for every one being visited according to his ways, to the principle of ver. 4 sq. Finally, however, vers. 27, 28, as **Return,** etc. shows, also come in with the greatest emphasis. Comp. ch. xiv. 6.—לְמִכְשׁוֹל עָוֹן, rendered by Hitzig and most others as in ch. xiv. 3; sin as a stumbling-block, whereby one falls into guilt and punishment. This is right in point of fact, but not in this connection (nor according to the accents), according to which iniquity, even their own, does not prove their ruin, and this because Israel shall abstain from everything which entails guilt. Hengst.: "let not iniquity be your ruin."—Ver. 31. **And make you,** to be understood agreeably to ch. xi. 19, and therefore without difficulty. The divine gift of grace stands as it were ready, and Israel only requires to cast away sin (ch. xi. 18; Heb. xii. 1) and to lay hold of it, while death is equally in their choice (Matt. xxiii. 37)! Comp. Phil. ii. 12, 13. And as this readiness of divine grace here, so in Ver. 32 the statement of ver. 23 is made as intense as possible. Instead of רָשָׁע we have הַמֵּת (Deut. xvii. 6),—the wicked being represented as already the victim of death. ("The prophet unveils to us the nature of the divine retributive righteousness in its most glorious light. Here no one but the unrepentant sinner dies unblessed. Whoever repents, and does what is good in God's sight, receives the gracious promise of life. The Living One can have no pleasure in death," UMBREIT.)

DOCTRINAL REFLECTIONS.

1. Proverbs reflect the moral and religious mood of a people in any particular period.

2. The proverb cited here and in Jer. xxxi. 29 is usually regarded as containing a reference to Ex. xx. 5 (xxxiv. 7). The words of the proverb do not require this, nor does the surrounding context involve the slightest allusion. Neither is its substance, nor, corresponding to that, the divine controversy against it, of a nature to lead us to infer that a misunderstanding of the passage of the law in question, regarding the visitation of the sins of the fathers on the children, is to be combated. The idea that Ezekiel here and Jeremiah in ch. xxxi. announce the repeal of the retribution-doctrine contained in the law of Moses, is quite foreign to the sense and connection of the passage. Ezekiel appears here neither as improver nor yet "simply as expositor of the law" (HENGST.). Hitzig is of opinion that Ex. xx. 5 "leaves the question undecided (!) whether children, who are themselves guiltless, also bear the sin of their fathers," and that "the fact that the son is often quite unlike his father morally, has at last gained recognition, and subjectivity received its due at the hands of Ezekiel." The assumed indefiniteness of the teaching of the decalogue would place the law of God (Gen. xviii. 25) upon the same level with 'the righteousness of men in the east," from which, as from heathen retributive justice universally, the judicial practice which should obtain in Israel is expressly distinguished (Deut. xxiv. 16). Comp. also 2 Kings xiv. 6; 2 Chron. xxv. 4. The jealousy of the holy and righteous God which subscribes the two first commands (Ex. xx. 5) is illustrated and made more conspicuous by the well-known words, "visiting the iniquities of the fathers," etc.; the words only say that sin, especially the sin of hating God, shall certainly be overtaken by divine vengeance, even if not till the third and fourth generation, although it was not punished judicially in its own time, nor even appeared to incur divine retribution. Moreover, the national character of the ten commandments is also to be taken into account, and the fact that Israel's national life rested essentially on the family, and especially the relation between parents and children. But the defence of the truth and equity of such retribution is foreign to our purpose, for the proverb which the prophet uses as the text of his discourse has nothing to do with Ex. xx. 5, xxxiv. 7; Num xiv. 18; Deut. v. 9 (comp. also Jer. xxxii. 18; Lam. v. 7). For this style of criticising the national circumstances which had taken the form of a proverb never once touches the question of sin and chastisement—into this region the proverb is first carried by the divine address—but merely the question of the natural result of an insipid craving being visited upon those who yet "will not eat sour grapes," who consider themselves too prudent to do so (Matt. xxiii. 30). Only when one perceives the levity (the gallows-humour) of the self-satisfaction and self-righteousness which display themselves in the proverb, will one be in a condition to recognise the thunder of the Eternal in Ezekiel's treatment of it.

3. According to Jeremiah, the proverb ceases to be used contemporaneously with the dawning of the Messianic epoch. The connection in Ezekiel is to be similarly interpreted, especially with ch. xvii. 22 sq. It should, however, be peculiar to the Messianic redemptive-period, that while Israel as a people would reject the Messiah, the individual would be brought to account for himself, according to his personal guilt, for his unbelief, the result of his outward, seeming, hypocritical work-righteousness. One supposes oneself planted among statements like John iii. 17 sq. The question is not one of outward family or national weal and woe, but of life and death in their most pregnant and individual sense. The case before us is just as little that of teeth set on edge in regard to the children, as of sour grapes in regard to the fathers. (Comp. ch. xvi. 17.) The moment of judgment decides as to the soul's salvation and blessedness, but it is a self-determination, a self-judgment. "To every man will be given the opportunity of turning to God, the door will stand open to all; he only who persists in wickedness through his own unbelief shall die" (COCCEIUS).

4. As in the law, even the taking of a pledge is difficult, almost impossible, so according to it, whatever could be properly called interest or usury falls aside. What was permissible towards a foreigner, the duty of benevolence towards the fellow-Israelite, as well as the fellow-inhabitant of the land, even though he were a stranger, forbade. Lending in these circumstances could only aim at relieving sudden, personal, domestic necessities. (Israel was not a mercantile people, at least in an inland sense.) ["The tendency of usury is to oppress one's brother, and hence it is to be wished that the very names of usury and interest were buried and blotted out from the memory of men," CALVIN.]

5. If ch. xvi. depicted the Jewish people as it were in their ancestral sin, according to their Canaan-nature, the turning to grace, repentance, which is wholly in Christ, exonerates from the ancestral sin. Liability to death, increased by each actual sin, issues in the punishment of death in his case only who does not flee from it in the appointed way of God's righteousness (judgment and grace). "Thereby a contrast is indicated between nature's order, and the supernatural order of grace" (NETELER). "Dying, according to our prophet, means more than returning to the dust of the ground, for that happens to all, even to the repentant. Still the latter do not die, but live. The reference is not to the judgment of God which follows sin, but the reference to divine grace is to be held fast" (COCCEIUS).

6. Israel's question (ver. 19) must not be narrowed by referring it solely to Ex. xx. 5. It is a "why" from the Old Testament view-point as a whole; and in so far as in the answer to it the significance of the individual becomes more prominent, so far also is another view-point, viz. that of the New Testament, placed in opposition to that of the old, which is emphatically abandoned. The matter could not have been settled in this way from a merely Old Testament standpoint.

7. "The expression of the prophet has rightly been reckoned as a *dulcis exhortatio ad peccatores* for all times. God has no pleasure in the death of the wicked, is a dictum of itself sufficient to refute the charges of a modern heathenism (Feuerbach), which professes to discover its own cold, unfeeling God in the Old Testament. The God of the Old Testament has a heart: Himself the essence of all blessedness, and mirroring Himself in the blessedness of the creature, He has a heart for every being who has fallen away from Him, and who is exposed to death. The fundamental feature of His character is holy love: He delights in the return of the sinner from death to life" (HÄV.).

8. "How deeply and clearly our prophet sees into the nature of redemption! Here are crowded together, the law with its demands, God's rigour in executing its sentences, His boundless grace and compassion, the conversion of the sinner to God, the laying hold of that divine grace which obliterates all guilt, and the proof of repentance in sanctification of life" (HÄV.).

9. As the sinner who persists in sinning, rather than sin, comes into view in this chapter,—sins are treated of in so far as they bring to light the sinful personality of the sinner,—so righteousness also is here that which the man who was previously righteous, or who becomes so by conversion, manifests in his life and walk. To be in the law as in the covenant of God, through faith, or to return to the law of the covenant God full of grace and compassion, by repentance; this is righteousness. The law was there for the knowledge of sin, so also the righteousness of the law is a mirror, that Israel, recognising itself in its distance from God, may seek the righteousness of God which is His grace. (See Introd.)

10. Manasseh, son of Hezekiah, may be regarded as an example of a godless son (ver. 10 sq.) of a God-fearing father, as Hezekiah, son of Ahaz, of the opposite case (ver. 14 sq.). Manasseh (see 2 Chron. xxxiii. 11 sq.) may also illustrate the case of ver. 21 sq.

HOMILETIC HINTS.

Ver. 2. "It is the way of the old Adam never to acknowledge sin, but always to put the blame on others, Gen. iii. 12, 13" (O.). "There is no greater folly than a man's murmuring against God on account of chastisement, and exculpating himself before this all-seeing and most righteous Judge" (TÜB. BIB.).—"The insolent sinner has neither shame nor sorrow, but must boast and proclaim himself before the whole world" (STCK.).—"The teeth are set on edge only when a man himself eats sour grapes" (B. B.).—"Men lay hold of and quote bad proverbs more readily than good" (ST.).—The end of all the words we have spoken will be that for each useless word we shall require to give an account.—"The cause of its cessation is the severity of the divine judgments. When these appear, the fig leaves fall off, the slumbering conscience awakens and cries out, It is I and my sins! There is a multitude of theorems and theological dogmas which are possible only in certain times, and slink away abashed when the thunders of divine judgment begin to roll" (HENGST.). Either one recognises in judgment—in the self-judgment of a believing repentance—his guilt before God, or God makes the whole world recognise it in us, through the judgment which overtakes us, even when we would deny our guilt.—God swears by His life; for where His righteousness is called in question, His life in this world of sin and death is assailed.—Ver. 4. If God is the father of all souls, other fathers cannot destroy souls. Each man is his own self-destroyer through unbelief.

Ver. 5 sq. "Righteousness of life is necessarily associated with the righteousness of faith, Rom. vi. 22" (ST.). Righteousness is defined by the law of God, but the end and fulfilment of the law is Christ; whosoever believes in Him is righteous.—There is a righteousness in works which is a mere semblance, but one is not justified by it. The justified man must be righteous.—Ver. 6. "God's table and the devil's do not agree" (STCK.).—"What the idols are here, creatures to whom one cleaves idolatrously are now-a-days" (LANGE).—"God abhors these three, atheism, indifferentism, syncretism" (STCK.).—Our conduct towards our neighbour, towards the nearest of all also, who is one flesh with us, reflects our relation to God.—Ver. 7. "Covetousness is a root of all evil, and a vice which is too little accounted of, 1 Tim. vi. 10" (ST.).—Ver. 8. "Not without reason is that which is said of usury coupled with compassion and gentleness towards the poor; Christ also connects giving and lending, Matt. v. 42" (COCC.).—Ver. 9. "Were it possible for a man to abandon all that is evil, and yet do nothing positively good, should he fulfil the will of God? Isa. i. 16 sq." (ST.)—By conduct it is made clear of whose spirit one is the child. If the fruits are wanting, where is faith?—Ver. 10 sq. The apple often falls far from the stem. Nothing has so much power as children, to bring shame and disgrace on their parents.—That struck at the hope and boast of the Jews, that they were the children of Abraham, who was justified by faith.—Ver. 11 sq. "Sins are linked together; whoever plunges voluntarily into one sin will not shrink from another when the temptation comes. This is to be noted, for when Satan entices us at the beginning, we believe that we are always free to turn back as soon as it seems good to us. But we are presently entangled in this sin and that, and when we are now taken in the snares of Satan we no longer desire to become free. Since one can make such progress, let each be careful lest he fall into any sin" (H.-H.).—Ver. 15 sq. "It does no harm to pious children that they have had godless parents, provided they walk not in the same footsteps" (ST.).—"The righteousness of the works of the children of God is no doubt but halting, although they are at pains to fashion themselves according to the directions of God's law; yet it is regarded by God as perfect, because He does not impute to them their sins, and their works are pleasing to Him because His Spirit operates in them. Sanctification of life proceeds doubtless from faith alone. Yet God also recognises the hidden faith of those who have not yet come to clear knowledge of His saving grace, but who sincerely fear Him, and commit themselves to the discipline and guidance of His Spirit" (H.-H. after CALV.).—Ver. 19. "Men are more concerned about the question of God's equity than with searching into their own sins" (STCK.).—Ver. 20. "Sinner, see to it that thou thyself sinnest not!" (TÜB. BIB.).—Ver. 21. "If a man turn honestly to God, he must resolve to forswear all sins: here no reservations can be made, 1 Pet. iii. 11" (ST.).

—"The true turning consists in this, that one gives his sins their dismissal, and consecrates himself to God for obedience. One sees a half conversion in many: they join virtues with transgressions, and imagine that their guilt will be removed when they do something praiseworthy. But that is as if a servant should bring to his master spoiled wine, for God will not so save men as to abolish the distinction between good and evil" (H.-H.).—How do we escape death, and enter into life? By passing over from the sin which is our own to the righteousness which is God's.—Ver. 22. "To the truly penitent sins are so forgiven as if they had never been committed, Isa. xliii. 25" (O.).—He who turns does righteousness.—Ver. 23. The immediate element in the turning is faith in God's mercy.—"A word of comfort which can and should encourage every forlorn sinner to turn" (SCHM.).—The question from heart to heart.—It grieves God when the wicked perish.—Life is not on our way, when our way is not God's.—Ver. 24. The bad and the good turning.—One can fall from righteousness, but that he can fall from grace is not here said.

Ver. 25 sq. Jehovah's way, and the ways of Israel.—Accusations enough, only no self-accusation!—God must be weighed by sinners!—Ver. 26. "As thou leavest this life, so must thou appear before the judgment-seat" (B. B.).—Ver. 27 sq. Turning from iniquity a defence against death.—The true life assurance.—The sinner is blind; but he who repents receives eyes to see.—Ver. 30. Iniquity brings ruin when it is not removed through forgiveness, as in the case of the repentant.—The thought of divine retribution a motive to repentance.—Ver. 31 sq. "God, who is rich in love, as it were meets the sinner's soul wandering under its burden of sins on the way which leads to perdition. Although it will not recognise Him, yet in beseeching love and compassion He unceasingly addresses it" (SCRIV.).—"David made himself a new heart when he entreated God to create it within him, Ps. li." (COCC.).—"Give what thou requirest, and require what thou wilt!" (AUG.) Why will ye die? Again a question from heart to heart.—"As a worthy forerunner of the great apostle, the prophet exhorts us, not only to put off the old filthy garment of sin, but to put on an altogether new man" (UMBR.).

8. *The Lamentation over the Kingdom of Israel* (ch. xix.).

1, 2 And do thou take up a lamentation for the princes of Israel. And say:
How has thy mother lain down—a lioness among lions [lionesses], among young
3 lions she reared her whelps! And she brought up one of her whelps; he became
4 a young lion, and learned to catch prey; he devoured men. And the heathen
peoples heard of him, he was taken in their pit, and they brought him in chains
5 to the land of Egypt. And she saw while [when] she waited, her hope had
6 perished; then she took one of her whelps, made him a young lion. And he
went up and down among the lions [lionesses], he became a young lion, and
7 learned to catch prey; he devoured men. And he knew [knew well] his widows
[palaces], and he laid waste their cities; and the land and its fulness were deso-
8 lated by the noise of his roaring. And the heathen nations round about
from the provinces set against him, and spread their net over him; he was
9 taken in their pit. And they put him in ward in chains, and brought him to
the king of Babylon, brought him into a stronghold, that his voice might no
10 more be heard upon the mountains of Israel.—Thy mother [is, was] like a vine,
in thy blood, planted by the waters; fruitful and full of branches was it,
11 from many waters. And it had strong rods for staves [sceptres] of rulers; and
its growth was high, up among the clouds, and was conspicuous in its
12 height, in the multitude of its branches. And it was plucked up in fury,
cast to the ground, and the east wind dried up its fruit; broken and withered
13 were its strong rods, fire consumed [devoured] them. And now it is planted in
14 the wilderness, in a land of drought and thirst. And fire went out of a rod
of its boughs, consumed [devoured] its fruit, and there was not in it [more] a
strong rod, a staff [sceptre] for ruling. This is a lamentation, and shall be for
a lamentation.

Ver. 1. Sept.: . . . ἐπι τον ἀρχοντα—

Ver. 3. K. ἀπεπηδησεν εἰς των—

Ver. 5. K. ἰδεν ὁτι ἀπωσται ἀπ' αὐτης κ. ἀπωλετο ἡ ὑποστασις αὐτης, κ. ἐλαβεν ἀλλον—

Ver. 7. . . . κ. ἐνεμετο ἐν τ. θρασει αὐτου, κ. τ. πολεις αὐτων— Vulg.: *Didicit viduas facere, et . . . in desertum adducere—*

Ver. 9. . . . ἐν κημω, κ. ἠνεγκαν αὐτον ἐν γαλεαγρα— (For מלך בבל other copies read ארץ בבל.)

Ver. 10. . . . ὡς ἀμπελος, ὡς ἀνθος ἐν ῥοα ἐν ὑδατι— Vulg.: . . . *quasi vinea in sanguine tuo super aquam—* (For בדמך there is a reading: ברמך *in celsitudine tua.*

Ver. 11. κ. ἐγενοντο αὐτη ῥαβδος ἰσχυος ἐπι φυλην ἡγουμενων, κ. . . . ἐν τω μεγεθει αὐτης ἐν μεσω στελεχεων— Vulg. *statura ejus inter frondes—*

Ver. 14. Sept.: . . . φυλη εἰς παραβολην θρηνου ἐστιν, κ. ἐσται εἰς θρηνον.

EXEGETICAL REMARKS.

The parallel to ch. xvii. shows itself clearly in substance and form: that also referred to the kingdom of Jerusalem; this has the same enigmatic style, the same borrowing of figurative expressions from the plant and animal world, and agrees partially in general, and in particular expressions.

Ver. 1. וְאַתָּה, introducing a partial contrast, so that the "proverb" of the previous chapter, from the side of the people, is now confronted by the **lamentation,** from the side of the prophet. It is an elegy (possibly on the model of songs like 2 Chron. xxxv. 25, HÄV.), a lament, whose occasion is contemplated as an existing reality. That which hangs over the kingdom is already an accomplished fact; one only requires to summon what has happened into the present, in order to anticipate easily what is about to happen. Comp. ch. ii. 10.—The **princes** (ch. vii. 27, xii. 10, 12) are evidently the existing kings, Jehoahaz and Jehoiachin, as royal types for the future of the Israelitish kingdom. According to Häv., the lament was devoted to the Davidic royal race in general. Purposely **of Israel,** because David's house alone was legitimate over all Israel (HÄV.).—שָׂא, paronomasia with נְשִׂיאֵי.

Vers. 2–9. *The Kings.*

Ver. 2. The address is directed to the people. According to Hengst., to the tribe of Judah, the people of the present. [Ewald makes Ezekiel sing beforehand, in the spirit of prophecy, a lament over Zedekiah, and his inevitable overthrow. Hitzig even alters the plural, *princes*, into the singular, *prince* (following the Sept.), for the sake of this interpretation. Rosenm. makes Jehoiachin the subject, who, like Ezekiel, was in exile.]—The **mother** of the people is Jerusalem (ch. xxi. 25 [20]). Comp. Gal. iv. 25 sq. [EWALD: the ancient church. HITZIG: the people of Israel. HÄV.: ancient Israel in its earlier glory. KLIEF.: Israel as a historical people. HENGST.: the people *per se.*] Perhaps an allusion to Isa. xxix. 1 sq. Jerusalem-Judah, as in ch. xvi.—The retrospective reference of the figure employed to Gen. xlix. 9 sq. is evident, recommends itself also by the allusion to Judah, and is not gainsaid by Klief.; just because the figure is here turned *in malam partem*, all the more would the contrast suit as a set-off to the promise in Gen. xlix. Comp. Num. xxiii. 24, xxiv. 9. The royal nature is meant to be depicted ("of equal birth with other independent and powerful nations, as this royal nature was historically displayed, especially in the times of David and Solomon," HENGST.): Jerusalem the royal city (Rev. v. 5). The complaint fairly begins with מָה. [Klief., on the other hand, assumes a double reproach, that Israel conforms itself to the heathen world-powers, and that it thus destroys its kings (!). Hence it is rather a complaint against the Israel of that time.]—That she **lay down** among the neighbouring royal states betokens majestic repose and conscious security,—the fearless one exciting fear by imposing power. (Comp. further ch. xvi. 14.)—The simple result is, that **among young lions** (כְּפִיר is the young lion which already goes after prey, גּוּר is any young creature which is still with its mother, in particular the young of the lion) Jerusalem brought up her royal children in royal splendour, for a kingly destiny. Perhaps also a hint at the first establishment of the kingdom of Israel, which would be "like all the nations" (1 Sam. viii. 5–20)!

Ver. 3. **She**—the royal mother-city (Lam. i. 1).—The **one** of her young ones, so that in רִבָּתָה may be included the idea of the increase of the family, is described entirely from the natural side as a real young lion. טָרַף is: to snatch away; hence: to acquire as booty; also: to tear asunder, into which sense the clause, **he devoured men,** immediately passes over. Comp. as to Jehoahaz, 2 Kings xxiii. 32. What is there said (ver. 30) of the "people of the land" in reference to the anointing of Jehoahaz is taken by Hengst. in connection with this verse. **He became a young lion,** can also be equivalent to: became a king; and what follows may betoken the political development of kingly power.—Ver. 4. **Heard of him:** as when the rumour of the proximity of a devastating lion spreads, and the hunt ing of the ravenous beast now begins; or, that their attention was directed towards him by his roaring, so that they proceeded to hunt him. As to the fact, see 2 Kings xxiii. 33, 34.—חָח is a hook, a ring, which one puts through the nose of animals that require to be restrained (2 Kings xix. 18), to attach to it the bridle by which they are led, by which also their power of breathing can be lessened.

Ver. 5. Up to this point, Egypt; now the other world-power, Babylon (2 Kings xxiv. 7). Comp. ch. xvii. Pharaoh Necho had appointed Jehoiakim king, who is left out of account in the lament, because death had deprived him of his crown, 2 Kings xxiv. 6. For the connection, he is omitted as Egyptian, and therefore not answering to the representation of ver. 3 (comp. ver. 6). After Jehoahaz only Jehoiachin can come into view.—נוֹחֲלָה, Niphal from יָחַל (חוּל), to expect; Ewald: to be in pain, to feel feeble, hence to despair; she saw that she was deceived—her hope lost. Häv. as Gen. viii. 12: and she saw that her hope was deferred and had come to nothing, to wit, the hope entertained at first of possibly procuring the deliverance of Jehoahaz through the humiliation of Egypt. Expectations from the other world-power, to which the eye could turn, are here most appropriate, since the Babylonish world-power was forming itself at that very time. כִּי is simply: **while (when) she waited, she saw;** her hope touching the one royal son had perished. **Then she took,** etc., 2 Kings xxiv. 8 sq. כְּפִיר answers perfectly to the youthful age of Jehoiachin.—Ver. 6. Jehoiachin conducted himself as a king, exactly like other kings; comp. ver. 3. If אֲרָיוֹת is to be translated lionesses, then the idea might thereby be made prominent that he acted after the manner of his mother, ver. 2.—Ver. 7. וַיֵּדַע. Against the sense which Häv., Hengst., and others adopt, it may be said that **the figure would be abandoned, and that**

2 Kings xxiv. 9 refers to nothing so special as the defilement of widows. HÄV.: *their* (collective: of the slain, ver. 6); HENGST.: *his* (whom he as king was bound to protect), at the same time the people's widows, the *personæ miserabiles.* Others: he observed his widows (whom he had made so by devouring their husbands). He had them before his eyes. אַלְמְנוֹתָיו can hardly signify here "widows" in the ordinary sense, it would be so entirely against the parallelism (וְעָרֵיהֶם). The passage remains figurative; although the king referred to breaks through the figurative drapery, he is spoken of in a still more appropriate pictorial manner. As in Isa. xiii. 22, the word in question is used poetically of widowed palaces, *i.e.* forsaken of their inhabitants, so here ironically. Jehoiachin is described (2 Kings xxiv. 9) as altogether like his father (Jehoiakim), which must not be overlooked; while (2 Kings xxiii. 32) it is said of Jehoahaz, more generally that he did as "his fathers." If we were entitled to colour the portrait of Jehoiachin from our knowledge of Jehoiakim, then Jer. xxii., especially ver. 13 sq., offers, in what is said of his despotic passion for building, all that is necessary for a good understanding of our passage. ידע is therefore: he perceived, *i.e.* was anxious about (Gen. xxxix. 6), knew—his palaces, built by his father, which so soon (after three months) became widowed palaces. And as that was the object of his anxious thought and longing, his conduct corresponded, inasmuch as, for his palaces, he devastated the cities of others (**their**). [Ewald (like the Chald.) reads וַיָּרַע, from רעע: "shattered their palaces."] The words 'וַתֵּשַׁם describe the disorder of the land. Ch. xii. 19.—Ver. 8. The object of וַיִּתְּנוּ is completed from what follows. The **heathen peoples round about,** etc. EWALD: The gay Chaldean host (ch. xvii. 3). HENGST.: "The provinces are the surrounding countries, as parts of the Chaldean empire; comp. 2 Kings xxiv. 2, according to which the Syrians, Ammonites, and Moabites were summoned against Jehoiakim, the father of Jehoiachin."—Comp. ver. 4; ch. xii. 13.—Ver. 9. "It is customary to transport lions in large and very strong cages" (J. D. MICH.).—The heathen-world thus made an end of the dominion. וַיִּתְּנֻהוּ recalls ver. 8. **In chains,** as ver. 4. **To the king of Babylon,** counterpart to "to the land of Egypt." As to further parallels, see the verses. **Stronghold** (Heb. pl.), an indefinite, poetic, general term (Judg. xii. 7). **That his voice,** etc., points back to ver. 7. 2 Kings xxiv. 12 could not be expressed otherwise, by means of the foregoing figure, than in terms parallel to ver. 4. The more special element of the history is concealed by the poetic veil.

Vers. 10–14. *The Mother of Kings.*

Just as in ch. xvii., a transition to another figure, namely, to that which is there (ver. 5 sq.) used as to King Zedekiah, the subject still remaining the kingdom.

Ver. 10. The address, as in ver. 2, and the **mother,** who is compared to a **vine,** is also, as there, Jerusalem (Ps. lxxx. 9 [8]). **In thy blood;** Ewald: in his likeness, like thee (Zedekiah!):—analogous to *in thy name.*—HENGST.: "it concerns thee" (דם=דְּמוּת, comp. ἐν παραβολῇ, Heb. xi. 19), *i.e.* what is here said of the mother applies pre-eminently to the people of the present—*tua res agitur*, etc. Kimchi and Rashi fix on בִּדְמוּתְךָ, others derive דם from דָּמָה, or read נִדְמָה; whereas Piscator, Häv., and others adopt דום, דָּמָה, *in silentio tuo*, in thy rest, the happy peaceful time (Isa. xxxviii. 10), which hardly suits the line of thought, and doesn't at all fit into the figure of the vine. Gesen. reads: בְּכַרְמְךָ, "in thy vineyard." The Sept. reads: בְּרִמּוֹן, "by the pomegranate tree," because vines and pomegranates were often found together (Num. xx. 5). HITZIG: He had thus a support in contradistinction to ch. xvii. 4. The simplest rendering is "in thy blood," *i.e.* in the life of the stem of Judah. Ver. 2 looked back to Gen. xlix. 9 sq., and this verse looks back to ver. 11 of the same chapter, where the figurative allusion to the blood of the grape (Deut. xxxii. 14) suggests the point of connection with the vine figure. Comp. further at ch. xvii. 8, 5.—Ver. 11. There grew up in Jerusalem-Judah strong shoots of David, able to rule (Gen. xlix. 10).—קוֹמָתוֹ, ch. xvii. 6. The singular suffix refers not to גֶּפֶן, but rather to מַטֵּה, either to the one who was before their eyes, *i.e.* Zedekiah, or better still, with Hengst., to the sceptres conceived of as one, and thus to the royal race as a whole. The plural עֲבֹתִים, which is peculiar to Ezekiel, has made many think of "thickets,"—a profuse growth between the thick branches, rising above them. According to Ewald and most moderns, it stands for thicket-clouds and darkness. HENGST.: "among the clouds, through and over them."—**And was conspicuous:** subject מַטֵּה.

Ver. 12. Without the intervention of anything farther, there follows its splendid growth, like a lightning flash from the clear heavens, the complete overthrow of the vine, *i.e.* of Jerusalem-Judah, the birthplace of kings, and therewith the Davidic kingdom. Answering to it, there is here the Hophal of נָתַשׁ, its only instance. Only one must not assume, with most interpreters, that the banishment of the people is what is meant (Ewald also makes "the whole congregation fall with the king"). The distinction between the two paragraphs is merely this, that while vers. 2-9 bewailed the existing kings, both as bearers of the Davidic royalty, and at the same time as suggestive, by their fate, to the actual king; now Zedekiah, as he with whom the Davidic kingdom is subverted, becomes the subject of the lament, just as if everything had already happened. (Comp. Deut. xxix. 27; 1 Kings xiv. 15; Jer. xii. 17.)—Ch. viii. 18. Through the anger of God. **To the ground,** etc. Pictorial, but not indicating the expatriation to another land.—Ch. xvii. 10, 9.—'מַטֵּה, collective; comp. with ver.

11. The singular, construed with the plural of the verb, comprehends the strong rods in a single view, with reference to Zedekiah. The suffix הָ- refers to מַטֵּה, not to גֶּפֶן. Comp. ch. xv. 5, 7. The **fire,** the divine judgment in its consuming character, as is explained by ver. 14.—Ver. 13. **And now,** spoken in presence of the circumstances of the exile, concerning the remnant of the Davidic royal line. Hence "planting" after the withering and burning can still be spoken of, and this not on account of the people, but because the residue of the Davidic royal line is likewise in exile.—**The wilderness** (figurative)—without any allusion to Israel's passing through the wilderness (HENGST.), which was altogether different—simply describes, in contrast to ver. 10 sq., a condition of chastisement in which the vine, Judah's kingdom, cannot prosper.—**Drought,** objective; **thirst,** subjective.—Ver. 14 adds to (1) the wrath of God, and to (2) the Chaldeans as instruments (ver. 12), the explanation of the fire (ver. 12), to wit, (3) Zedekiah's offence (according to ch. xvii. 15 sq.). Comp. ch. v. 4; Judg. ix. 15.—**Rod of its boughs** (ch. xvii. 6) is the rod which the boughs made, which the strong vitality of the royal vine caused to shoot.—The closing sentence appropriately includes both parts of the chapter,—that which has happened and that which is to happen. וַתְּהִי, prophetic perfect. ("It is not the fancy of a gloomy seer, but the prediction of a lamentation which will actually flow in a thousand voices from the mouth of the people," etc., HENGST.) HÄV.: "And it was for," etc.; as historical notice of the subsequently written prophecy, to attest its true fulfilment.

THEOLOGICAL REMARKS.

1. Hävernick describes the fundamental character of this chapter as lyrical, prophetically elegiac. Ewald calls it "the model of an elegy"—"artistic as to the construction of its lines,—the finest and most touching of all in the Old Testament." As to the form, he says: "The long line prevails, but it is almost always divided in the middle into two complete halves, so that the second half abruptly broken off follows the first only like a brief, transient, sighing echo. And thus, what the construction of the whole song is, as to its two directions, is repeated in the line."

2. It is a song of three kings; or of two broken, and one breaking sceptre.

3. In regard to the historical relations, the carrying away of Jehoahaz to Egypt is parallel to that of Jehoiachin to Babylon. The intermediate Jehoiakim is left out; but because he is the more important and the characteristic person, for the beginning of the Babylonian servitude, Jehoiachin is retained in his true colours. (As similarly Zedekiah in Jer. xxvii.)

4. In the lion-figure, the nobler passes over into the less noble aspect, on which Hengst. remarks: "By the constitution of human nature, arrogance is inseparably connected with high rank, and therewith a rude barbarity towards all who are barriers in its way. He only who walks with God can escape this natural consequence, and the walk of faith is not the attainment of every man. It should, however, be the attainment of every one of the people of God; and where it is wanting, so that the corrupt nature unfolds itself without opposition, there the divine vengeance takes effect. Jehoahaz showed himself a barbarous tyrant towards his own subjects, whereas the kingdom of Israel was designed to exhibit a heroic energy against the enemies of the people of God. On this account he was punished."

5. The Messianic hope was bound up with the Davidic kingdom, whose subversion is here illustrated from ch. xviii. 22 sq., and its fulfilment is shown in this, that He who appeared in the world, declared, not without a reference to our chapter, "I am the true Vine."

HOMILETIC HINTS.

Ver. 1 sq.: "In all times the sorrowful and the joyful have been expressed in poetry" (L.).—Sacred poetry a companion on the heights and in the depths of life and feeling. See the Psalms.—"Princes should be pious people, who care for the eternal as well as temporal welfare of their subjects, who judge equitably, avoid tyranny, and corrupt none by their example. But when subjects do not pray for their princes, and descend everywhere to the level of beasts in their habits, God gives them beasts as princes. For the sins of a people tyrants rule over them" (L.).—Ver. 2. "So long as the Jewish people acted according to the law of God, they rested in safety and without fear" (SCHM.).—"Judah brought up, in its princes, the rods of God's chastisement" (RICHT.).—"The society of bad men only makes one become more wicked" (STCK.).—Ver. 3. "A royal up-bringing, when it is merely that, makes royal sinners. Great lords, alas! frequently bear lions and such like not merely on their escutcheons. That they also do, who drain men of everything, even to their blood" (B. B.).—There are men-eaters who yet devour no men.—Ver. 4. Violence is always topped by greater violence or cunning.—Many a court, though it be the prince's own, is the pit in which the lion is taken!—There are also chains for kings—their minions.—Ver. 5 sq. In the place of one tyrant a second can come.—Ver. 7. Through a prince, his land also suffers.—"The king's voice should be terrible to the wicked only, never to the good" (L.).—To the lion's roaring belong cabinet orders, royal edicts.—Ver. 8 sq. What a network is woven about princes by court intrigues!—"The fate of tyrants has usually been a sad one. God has pits, nets, hunters, and cages for them even in this world, but certainly in the next" (L.).—"He who lives like a beast, shall be requited like a beast" (STCK.).—At last the lion's roaring on the mountains dies away.

Ver. 10. In Judah there was royal blood,—the lion and the vine together.—"Apply that to the blood of Christ!" (RICHT.)—"He who can count the drops of water, may count the number of God's acts of love" (B. B.).—"It is of God's unmerited grace that some royal houses are blessed beyond others, and for this He will be honoured and praised, 2 Sam. vii. 18" (ST.).—Ver. 11 sq. "The higher the ascent, the deeper the fall; God remains the highest, the highest over all."—The night before destruction is sometimes full of happiness and splendour.—The bloom of princely houses, as of great cities and famous trading houses, is of a tender and easily withered nature.—Ver. 13. "Where God's gracious presence with His word and Spirit is wanting, there a desert is;

and the whole world is a land of drought, which can give no refreshment to the soul which hungers and thirsts for God" (B. B.).—The prosperous soil for princes and also for people is true religion.—Where God's word is despised, kingdoms themselves become a waste.—Ver. 14. "Each man supplies the fire for his own burning" (STCK.).—"The fire of one's own unrighteousness kindles the wrathful judgment of God, Isa. i. 31" (SCHM.).—"Men first become parched, then the fire consumes them" (STCK.).—"A little spark, a single sin apparently, and at first really a little one, can cause a great fire" (STCK.).—"Till Christ no other king from David's stem" (RICHT.).—"Every sin ends in lamentation, even here, but certainly there" (STCK.).

9. *The Survey of the Leading of the People from of old* (ch. xx.).

1 And it came to pass in the seventh year, in the fifth [month] on the tenth
[day] of the month, that men of the elders of Israel came to enquire of
2 Jehovah, and sat [down] before me. And the word of Jehovah came to me,
3 saying: Son of man, speak to the elders of Israel, and say unto them, Thus
saith the Lord Jehovah, Do ye come to enquire of Me? As I live, if I will
4 be enquired of by you! Sentence of the Lord Jehovah. Wilt thou judge
5 them? Wilt thou judge, son of man? Make them to know the abominations
of their fathers. And say to them, Thus saith the Lord Jehovah; In the day
that I chose Israel, then I lifted up My hand to the seed of the house of
Jacob, and made Myself known to them in the land of Egypt, and lifted up
6 My hand to them, saying, I [am] Jehovah [am] your God. In that day I lifted
up My hand to them, to bring them out of the land of Egypt, into the land
which I had sought out for them, flowing with milk and honey,—which is a
7 glory [ornament] to all lands. And I said to them, Cast ye away, every man,
the abominations of his eyes, and defile not yourselves with the idols of
8 Egypt. I, Jehovah your God. And they rebelled against Me, and would
not hearken unto Me; they did not cast away every man the abominations
of his eyes, nor forsake the idols of Egypt. And I said that I would pour
out My fury upon them, that I would accomplish My anger in them, in the
9 midst of the land of Egypt. And I wrought for My name's sake, that it
might not be polluted before the eyes of the heathen, among whom they
were, in whose sight I made Myself known to them, to bring them out of the
10 land of Egypt. And I led them out of the land of Egypt, and brought them
11 into the wilderness. And I gave them My statutes, and made known to them
12 My judgments, which, if a man do, he shall live in them. And I also gave
them my Sabbaths, to be a sign between Me and them, so that it might be
13 known [they knew] that I Jehovah do sanctify them. And the house of Israel
rebelled against Me in the wilderness; they walked not in My statutes, and
they despised [cast away] My judgments, which if a man do, he shall live in
them, and they grievously profaned My sabbaths. And I said that I would
14 pour out My fury upon them in the wilderness to destroy [uproot] them. And
I wrought for My name's sake, that it should not be polluted before the
15 heathen, in whose sight I brought them out. And also I lifted up My hand
to them in the wilderness, that I would not bring them into the land which I
had given, flowing with milk and honey—which is a glory to all lands,—
16 Because they despised My judgments, and walked not in My statutes, and
17 profaned My sabbaths, for their heart went after their idols. And [yet] Mine
eye pitied, instead of destroying them, and I did not make an end of them in
18 the wilderness. And I said to their sons in the wilderness, Ye shall not walk
in your fathers' statutes, nor observe their judgments, nor defile yourselves
19 with their idols. I am Jehovah, your God; walk in My statutes and keep
20 My judgments, and do them. And hallow My sabbaths, and they are for a
sign between Me and you, that ye may know that I am Jehovah your God.
21 And the sons rebelled against Me; they walked not in My statutes, and they
kept not My judgments to do them, which if a man do, he shall live in them;
they profaned My sabbaths; and I said that I would pour out My fury upon
22 them, that I would accomplish My anger in them in the wilderness. And

[yet] I turned My hand, and wrought for My name's sake, that it should not
23 be polluted before the heathen, in whose sight I brought them out. I also
lifted up My hand to them in the wilderness, that I would scatter them
24 among the heathen, and disperse them in the countries; Because they
executed not My judgments, and despised My statutes, and profaned My
25 sabbaths, and their eyes were after their fathers' idols. And I also gave them
statutes that were not good, and judgments in which they could not live;
26 And I polluted them in their gifts, inasmuch as they caused all that openeth
the womb to pass through, that I might desolate them, that they might know
27 that I am Jehovah. Therefore speak to the house of Israel, son of man, and
say to them, Thus saith the Lord Jehovah; In this again your fathers mocked
28 [blasphemed] Me, in dealing faithlessly with Me. And I brought them into the
land, which I lifted up My hand to give them, and they saw every high
hill, and every thick [dark] tree, and there they offered their sacrifices, and
gave there the provocation of their offering, and there they presented their
29 sweet savours, and there they poured out their drink-offerings. And I said to
them, What is the high place to which ye go? And its name was called
30 "Bamah" to this day. Therefore say to the house of Israel, Thus saith the
Lord Jehovah; In the way of your fathers do ye pollute yourselves, and do ye
31 go wantonly after their abominations? And in the offering of your gifts, in
making your sons to pass through the fire, do ye pollute yourselves according
to all your idols to this day, and shall I be enquired of by you, O house of
Israel? As I live,—sentence of the Lord Jehovah,—if I shall be enquired of by
32 you! . . . And that which has come up in your mind shall not at all happen,
that ye say, We shall be as the heathen, as the families of the countries, to
33 serve wood and stone. As I live,—sentence of the Lord Jehovah,—if I shall
not rule over you with strong hand, and with outstretched arm, and with fury
34 poured out! . . . And I will lead you out from the peoples, and gather you
out of the countries in which ye have been dispersed, with strong hand, and
35 with outstretched arm, and with fury poured out, And I will bring you into
36 the wilderness of the peoples, and contend with you there face to face. As I
contended with your fathers in the wilderness of the land of Egypt, so will I
37 contend with you,—sentence of the Lord Jehovah. And I will cause you to
pass under the staff [sceptre], and bring you into the bond of the covenant.
38 And I will purge [separate] out from among you the rebels, and the transgressors
against Me; out of the land of their wanderings [strangerhood] will I lead them
forth, and [yet] he [they] shall not come to the land of Israel, and ye shall
39 know that I Jehovah. And ye, house of Israel, thus saith the Lord Jehovah,
—Go, serve every one his idols. Yet afterwards,—if ye will not [now] hearken
unto Me, ye shall not further pollute My holy name with [in] your offerings
40 and with [in] your idols. For upon My holy mountain, upon the high
mountain of Israel,—sentence of the Lord Jehovah,—there shall they serve
Me, the whole house of Israel, the whole of it in the land; there will I accept
them graciously, and there will I require your [heave] offerings, and the first-
41 fruits of your oblations, with all your holy things. As a sweet savour will I
accept you graciously, when I lead you out from the peoples, and gather you
out of the countries, in which ye have been dispersed, and sanctify Myself in
42 you before the eyes of the heathen. And ye shall know that I am Jehovah,
when I bring you to the land of Israel, to the land which I lifted up My hand
43 to give to your fathers. And there shall ye remember your ways, and all
your doings, in [with] which ye have been defiled, and loathe yourselves in
your own sight, for all your wicked things [evil deeds] which ye have done.
44 And ye shall know that I am Jehovah, in My dealing with you for My name's
sake, not according to your wicked ways, and your corrupt doings, O house of
Israel. Sentence of the Lord Jehovah.

Ver. 3. Sept.: . . . ζω ἐγω εἰ ἀποκριθησομαι ὑμιν . . . εἰ (4) ἐκδικησω αὐτους ἐκδικησει.—(Another reading, 3: אל זקני.)

Ver. 5. . . . ἀφ ἧς ἡμερας ἡρετισα . . . κ. ἐγνωρισθην τω σπερματι . . . κ. ἀντελαβομην τη χειρι μου αὐτων—

Ver. 12. The LXX. add: K εἶπα προς τ. οἰκ. τ. 'Ισρ. ἐν τ. ἐρημω· 'Εν τοις προσταγμασιν μου πορευεσθε κ. τ. δικαιωματα μου φυλασσετε του ποιειν αὐτα, ἁ ποιησει αὐτα ἀνθρωπος κ. ζησεται ἐν αὐτοις.

Ver. 18. . . . μη συναναμιγνυσθε κ. μη μιαινεσθε.

Ver. 22. K. οὐκ ἐποιησα, ὁπως το ὀνομα μου—

Ver. 26. K. μιανω αὐτους . . . ἐν τω διαπορευεσθαι με παν . . . ὁπως ἀφανισω αὐτους.—Vulg.: *Et pollui . . . cum offerrent omne quod—*

Ver. 27. . . . 'Εως τουτου παρωργισαν με—

Ver. 28. . . . κ. ἐθυσαν ἐκει τοις θεοις αὐτων—

Ver. 30. Sept.: Εἰ ἐν τ. ἀνομιαις τ. πατερων ὑμων.—

Ver. 31. κ. ἐν τ. ἀπαρχαις τ. δοματων ὑμων κ. ἐν τ. ἀφορισμοις υἱων ὑμ. ἐν πυρι—(Another reading: בניכם ובנתיכם.)

Ver. 32. κ. εἰ ἀναβησεται ἐπι τ. πνευμα ὑμ. τουτο. K. οὐκ ἐσται ὁν τροπον ὑμεις λεγετε—

Ver. 36. Another reading: אשפוט את'. Sept., Vulg., Arabs: *judicabo vos.*

Ver. 37. . . . κ. εἰσαξω ὑμας ἐν ἀριθμω. (*Targ. et versiones.*)

Ver. 38. Another reading: לא יבאו.

Ver. 39. Sept.: . . . ἑκαστος . . . ἐξαρατε, κ. μετα ταυτα εἰ μη ὑμεις εἰσακουετε μου, κ. τ. ὀνομα—

Ver. 40. . . . ἐκει δουλευσουσιν μοι . . . εἰς τελος—

Ver. 43. . . . τ. ὁδους . . . κ. τ. ἐπιτηδευματα ὑμ. ἐν οἱς ἐμιαινεσθε.—Vulg.: . . . *et displicebitis vobis in conspectu vestro—*

Ver. 44. . . . ὁπως τ. ὀνομα μου μη βεβηλωθη κατα τ. ὁδους ὑμ. . . . κ. κατα τ. ἐπιτηδευματα ὑμ. τα διεφθαρμενα—

EXEGETICAL REMARKS.

Vers. 1–4. *The Occasion and Theme of the Discourse.*

Ver. 1. A date is prefixed to the occasion of the following prophetic discourse, which points us back to ch. viii., and which at the same time applies to ch. xxi.–xxiii. [KLIEF. reckons 11 months 5 days since ch. viii. 1; 2 years 1 month 5 days since ch. i. 2 (adhering to the captivity of king Jehoiachin); and 2 years 5 months before ch. xxiv. 1.]—The parallel to ch. xiv. 1 is evident. There, indeed, we have וַיָּבוֹא אֵלַי, and here only בָּאוּ. But they are called **men of the elders of Israel** in both places. That they were the same persons (KLIEF.) is questionable; probably not. Rather can they be considered as the successors of that deputation, and they may be distinguished from it by the fact that they mentioned the purpose of their visit, **to inquire**, etc., although what they asked is not stated, while the former deputation can be depicted as sitting before the prophet in speechless amazement. That a middle, a turning point in Ezekiel's labours is indicated, as Klief. thinks, by the fact of a spirit of inquiry being excited in the minds of his hearers, is too much to draw from the words. Hengst. sees in the men "representatives, not of the totality of the exiles, but of the great mass of those only externally fearing God, while internally addicted to the spirit of the world and of the age," as in ch. xiv., and conjectures a special occasion in a favourable turn which the affairs of the coalition had taken.(?) Owing to the interest felt in Judah and Jerusalem by all the exiles, nothing prevents us understanding here also, as in ch. xiv., envoys (if not elders themselves?) from the elders of the exiles of the ten tribes. As these had been so long in a state of exile, the existence of the elder-organization is the more intelligible. That the divine message of the prophet is addressed to the whole people, does not prevent its being coloured with a special regard to the ten tribes, as the details of our exposition may possibly show.—Ver. 3. Comp. ch. ii. 1, xiv. 3.—Ver. 4. The repeated question, **Wilt thou**, etc., is connected with the appearance of the men of Israel, who are thereby represented as if standing before a tribunal, but at the same time destitute of an advocate, and of any ground for self-justification. Hitzig rightly perceives in the repetition evidence of the emotion which the presence of unworthy persons had excited. "The form of a question makes apparent the impatient wish that the thing should happen, and so includes a command." Therefore the imperative: **Make them to know the abominations**, etc. The theme of the discourse is a review of the objective [leading], and over against that, the subjective [behaviour] conduct of the people from the days of old (ch. xxii. 2; xxiii. 36). The reference to the fathers points to an ancient and deep-rooted evil which demands a radical cure (HENGST., CALVIN). Matt. xxiii. 32; Acts vii. 51; ch. xvi. 2.

Vers. 5–9. *Israel in Egypt.*

Ver. 5. בָּחַר with בְּ, as Israel is subjected to examination, so Israel remains the object of the divine election. "Choosing in the sense of divine, prevenient love and grace, Deut. vii. 6, xiv. 2" (HÄV.).—The lifting up of the hand, as the gesture of one making oath (Deut. xxxii. 40; Ex. vi. 8), assured and confirmed the choosing of Israel as the people of God (Deut. vii. 6, xiv. 2) with reference to Canaan (vers. 6, 15, 28).—**Israel** is significantly interchanged with **Jacob**. The former points to the grace of their election to the position of Jehovah's warriors; the latter points to their natural origin.—As interpreted by the clause: **and made myself known**, etc., the **day** was the period when Jehovah in point of fact revealed Himself to the people in Egypt as that which He had called Himself to Moses (Ex. iii. 14, etc.) by signs and wonders, as by an actual, renewed oath (therefore the very significant repetition of the lifting up of the hand).—Ver. 6. A sort of conclusion. Once again, **I lifted up**, etc., and emphasizing of the **day**, in order to mark God's solemn determination, as well as what had taken place. The imaginations of priests and vain sayings of the people are not the point in question. The object was "bringing out," therefore freedom, redemption, which is described according to its issue and goal.—**Sought out** (comp. Num. x. 33), ere ever they had spied it out.—Ex. iii. 8.—The לְ in לְכָל, either, datively, **that all lands reckon it so; or with respect to**

or, above all lands (?).—Ver. 7. The Sinaitic law also said this plainly, as it rested expressly upon the 'אֲנִי יְהוָה, Ex. xx. 2. But from the beginning the same was proclaimed by the fact of election, which involved a reciprocal obligation on the part of the people.

["The very form given to the commission of Moses to go and vindicate the children of Israel for God, that they might come forth and serve Him, was itself a proof how much the worship of Jehovah had fallen into abeyance, and how generally the people had allowed themselves to sink into the prevailing idolatries. They must go out of the polluted region, where other lords, spiritual as well as temporal, have had dominion over them, that they may stand free to worship and serve Jehovah. And so the whole design and purport of the commission of Moses might be regarded as a protest against their connection with the abominations of Egypt, and a call not only to Pharaoh, to let the people go, but also to the people themselves, to come out and be separate, as a seed whom the Lord had chosen."—P. F.—W. F.]

Of the **eyes,** not merely which the eyes see, but whereon they fix, with which they become familiar, etc.—Ver. 8. Israel's further rebelliousness in the wilderness would even justify a similar inference as to their behaviour in Egypt. Compare further Josh. xxiv. 14; Ex. xxxii. 3; Lev. xvii. 7 (Ps. cvi. 7).—**And I said**; not to them, nor to Moses, but to Myself. It corresponded to the character of God and the actual condition of the people. Comp. Ex. xx. 5, xxxii. 10.—Ch. vii. 8, v. 13, vi. 12; and besides, Ex. v. 3.—Ver. 9. **And I wrought,** forms a contrast to: "and I said;" consequently the thing contrasted with what was said,—the object of the verb "wrought,"—which can be gathered from what follows, may also be assumed as known.—**For My name's sake,** etc. (Ps. cvi. 8); they were unworthy of it, had not merited it. But the revelation which I had given of Myself **before the eyes of the heathen among whom they were** was not to be desecrated before these same eyes, especially before the Egyptians, as if to wish well to My name were present with Me, but not the power of performance (regard being had at the same time to the heathen, as Israel was placed in a peculiar position in regard to humanity as a whole). Comp. Num. xiv. 13 sq.; Ex. xxxii. 12 (Num. xxiii. 19).

Vers. 10–24. *Israel in the Wilderness.* Vers. 10–17, *The First;* 18–24, *The Second Generation.*

Vers. 10–17. *The First Generation in the Wilderness.*

Ver. 10. Transition from the foregoing to the following.—Ver. 11. The giving of the law on Sinai, as introduction to the present leading of the people, after being brought out, Ex. xx. sq.—**Statutes** and **judgments,** as often, comprehending the general idea of the law. **Live** includes prosperity and blessedness, bodily and spiritual, temporal and eternal. Comp. Deut. iv. 1.—The law was given for life, Rom. vii. 10; Matt. xix. 17; Ex. xx. 12, etc. **Which if a man do.** The leading through the wilderness served to test them as to this. [KEIL translates: "Which a man shall do in order to live through them."]—Ver. 12. Ex. xx. 8, xxxi. 13. **A sign** must denote something, so the Sabbath repeating itself (therefore the plural with each week's close betokened the rest of God, into which the people of God are to enter after all their works, Heb. iv. This is a common element to Jehovah and Israel on the ground of the covenant. As the Sabbaths of Jehovah are to be hallowed by Israel, and to be separated from the other days of the week, it would thereby be made evident that Jehovah sanctifies Israel, and separates them from the world-peoples to be His own peculiar people. This is the reciprocal relation of the Sabbath to Jehovah and Israel. Therefore the Sabbath was so characteristic for Israel.—As the prophetic sense of the law, and of the Sabbath-law in particular, reaches far beyond a formal, outward observance of it, so the prophet is speaking not of the mere letter of the law as a whole, nor in ver. 13 of merely external desecration of the Sabbath (Isa. lviii. 13, 14). Compare further Ex. xvi. 27 sq.; Num. xv. 32 sq. Also ch. v. 6, 7.—Ver. 11.—Ver. 8.—With Ver. 14 comp. ver. 9.—Ver. 15. **And also** = and even; for after the contrast to: "and I said," in ver. 13 has been expressed in ver. 14 by: "and I wrought," 'וְגַם resumes the thread. The thought as to the destruction of the rebellious expressed itself even in the oath which excluded the first wilderness generation from Canaan; Num. xiv. 11 sq.; Ps. xcv. 11, etc. [Hengst. interprets 'וגם of retribution; so they, and I also!]—Ver. 6.—Ver. 17 carries out the idea of ver. 14 (ch. xvi. 5).—Ch. xi. 13. The sequel shows what is meant.

Vers. 18–24. *The Second Generation in the Wilderness.*

Ver. 18. The contents of the fifth book of Moses belonged peculiarly to the **sons** (children)—the spared second generation in the wilderness. The **fathers** in question are represented in their constant disobedience to the laws which Jehovah gave (which even necessitated their repetition and renewal in Deuteronomy), as in some sort lawgivers according to their own ideas and on their own authority.—Ver. 7.—Ver. 19. But!—Comp. ver. 11.—Ver. 20. Comp. ver. 12.—Ver. 21. Num. xv. 16, 17.—Vers. 8, 13.—Ver. 22. Contrast to ver. 21; Num. xvi. 21 sq., ch. xvii. 9 sq.—Vers. 14, 9.—Ver. 23. **I also,** as in ver. 15, here in relation to ver. 21.—Ch. xii. 15, vi. 8. The threatening with exile, Deut. xxviii. 30; Lev. xxvi. 33 sq.; and as an oath, Deut. xxix. 13, 18.—Ver. 24. As ver. 16.

Vers. 25–31. *Israel in Canaan.* Vers. 25–29. *The Fathers.* Vers. 30, 31. *The People of the Present.*

Vers. 25–29. *The Fathers in Canaan.*

Ver. 25. Transition, linked to the foregoing with 'וְגַם, as in ver. 23 'גַּם hinted at what succeeds. The threat of exile, the fulfilment of which had begun in the people of the present, could be denounced against the second generation in the wilderness, because they were brought into Canaan, and along with the following generations, in so far as they could come into account as "your fathers" (ver. 27), they are set over against the existing people. The second generation in the wilderness was therefore the medium of transition to, and at the same time became, Israel in Canaan. Therefore, although it was not executed against the second generation in the wilderness, the threat of exile remains in its original force and form. The reference to Canaan, which ver. 28 formally makes, determines the peculiar forms of expression in vers. 25 and 26. Such a progress in sin is made, that at last God makes sin its own punishment. Thus—ver. 7. They are warned against idolatry in Egypt, which is followed up in ver. 11 sq. by the Sinaitic legislation in the wilderness.—In ver. 18 sq., over against their own law-making, of which the first generation was guilty, there is the renewal of the Sinaitic law with reference to Canaan, but even already under the threat of exile (ver. 23). Finally—in Canaan as a beginning of the judgment of God, there were given to Israel for chastisement the wicked statutes and the death-bringing judgments of Canaan. Because they would not have My good law, I gave them Canaan's law, which is not good, etc. Thus the force of: **I gave,** etc., is to be maintained, and by no means to be weakened to *permission* or any similar idea, as Jewish and Christian interpreters wish.—**Not good** is sufficiently explained by לָהֶם going before, and by the parallel לֹא יִחְיוּ'.—Ver. 26 shows clearly what sort of "statutes" and "judgments" are meant, from the result which they produced, more precisely describing: "I gave," as: **I polluted them.** The pollution of Israel was very notably exhibited in that which they did with their first-born male children, who in virtue of Ex. xiii. 12, 13 required to be redeemed. This ordinance, according to the connection in Ex. xiii., being characteristically associated with the redemption of the people from Egypt, the allusion in our verse is most significant. Comp. also Ex. xiii. 11, which introduces the statute in question. As a guide to the understanding of בְּהַעֲבִיר, לַיהוָה, which is associated with הַעֲבַרְתָּ in Ex. xiii., is here omitted, and בָּאֵשׁ is added in ver. 31, so that the Canaanitish Moloch-worship is undoubtedly meant. (Lev. xviii. 21, comp. ver. 3; Deut. xviii. 10, 9.) Comp. ch. xvi. 21. So the life, the continuous life which the people of Israel should have enjoyed in their sons, became its opposite, death. How could these be good statutes! [Cocceius also connects הַעֲבַרְתָּ with Ex. xiii. 12, and understands the pollution of Israel as a *declaration of the uncleanness* of the people (Häv., on account of the heathenish turn which had been given to the law), since Aaron and the Levites had been installed by Jehovah in the sacred office instead of the first-born, Num. iii. 45!] Comp. as to the whole, Rom. i. 24 sq.; Acts vii. 42; 2 Thess. ii. 11.—As to the "desolation," comp. ch. xiv. 8. Others render it: *to be benumbed, shocked,* so that if possible they might be brought to reflection from what was so abhorrent to parental feeling. According to our rendering of the word, preparation is here made for the idea of the wilderness, which is afterwards so prominent in the chapter: they came to resemble a wilderness-people even before they were brought into the wilderness of the peoples (ver. 35).—Ver. 27. The people of the present are addressed, although the matter itself still concerns the fathers in Canaan. Ver. 30 sq. will define more precisely the meaning of this address.—**In this again** (ch. xvi. 29), besides what was formerly adduced. The thing meant is first of all indicated more generally as mockery and faithlessness (ch. xv. 8, xiv. 13), and is then in Ver. 28 stated more in detail. Comp. with ch. vi. 13, xvi. 16.—כַּעַס' refers to the forementioned mockery, whereby they aroused the displeasure and wrath of Jehovah (Deut. xxxii. 16, 21); רֵיחַ' (comp. ch. vi. 13, xvi. 19) to the faithlessness which could present **sweet savours** of various kinds to idols.—Ver. 29. **And I said,** etc. By the question there is recalled to mind God's ever-repeated opposition to and condemnation of the worship of the high places (therefore the collective singular: הַבָּמָה, in contrast to the one sanctuary—the temple), with all that He had said against it. [Häv. adopts the explanation of Kimchi, who refers it to the high place at Gibeon, 1 Kings iii. 4; 2 Chron. i. 3.]—וַיִּקָּרֵא', the thing itself, as well as its name, continued to this day.

Vers. 30, 31. *The People of the Present.*

Ver. 30. לָכֵן, resuming the strain of ver. 27, and substituting אֱמֹר for דַּבֵּר, directly addresses the people of the present, *i.e.* the inquirers of Israel who had come to the prophet in the interest of those who still remained in Canaan.—Ver. 31. The note struck in the question of ver. 29 is still maintained, not merely to express astonishment, but still more to compel self-reflection. I ask what further communication you would have?—Comp. ch. vii. 20.—Ch. vi. 9.—Ver. 26.—Comp. ch. xiv. 3.

Vers. 32–44. *Prophetic Survey of the yet Future Dealing with the People.* Vers. 32–38. *In Judgment.* Vers. 39–44. *In Mercy.*

Vers. 32–38. *The Impending Judgment.*

Ver. 32. Transition to what follows.—Comp. ch. xiv. 3, xi. 5.—However much the people had become like the heathen, yet they were not to become heathen, which the inquirers of ver. 1 may have said to themselves, with a feeling of satisfaction or of despair, Deut. iv. 28, xxviii. 36, 64. Such was not to be the end of the people of God. But Jehovah will manifest Himself to them as their King.—Ver. 33. Backward glance at His mighty, royal dealing in former times, when they were redeemed from Egypt (Deut. iv. 34; Ex. vi. 6, etc.). Comp. ch. vi. 14. But it is immediately added, in order to point to retributive judgment (see Ex. vi. 6): **and with fury poured out,** which is repeated in ver. 34 in connection with the "leading out," and "gathering," by which the aforesaid (ver. 33) royal authority will also manifest itself, so that these too must be regarded as acts of divine judgment. A future leading into Canaan (against which see also ver. 35), after the conversion of all Israel, is thereby strictly excluded. But: **out from the peoples,** and: **out of the countries,** when rightly taken, namely, in contrast to: "into the wilderness of the peoples," by no means excludes a reference to the existing Babylonish captivity. That Israel was then dispersed in one land only, and among one people (KLIEF., KEIL), is not in the least to the point, when the empire of the king of Babylon could be described in such a manner as, *e.g.*, in Jer. xxvii. 5 sq. ! The exile, says Jehovah, the King whose supreme power they were to experience, shall not be mere dispersion among "peoples" and in "countries" (different from the fatherland, Canaan), where the external relations of life may be to some extent of an agreeable character, as was the case (see Introd.). I will lead you thence and conduct you into another exile, for—Ver. 35 —**I will bring you into the wilderness of the peoples,**—an expression whose deepest interpretation is immediately added, viz.: **and contend with you,** etc.; a change of condition is meant—an intensifying of exile to "a wilderness of the peoples," which must be taken figuratively (comp. Hos. ii. 16), like the leading out and gathering of the previous verse, and the "wilderness" in ch. xix. 13. (Häv. compares ch. vi. 14.) In the form of the word, the previous expressions (ver. 34): "countries," and: "peoples," coalesce. As "the bringing into" corresponds to: "the leading out," so Jehovah's "contending" corresponds to the "gathering." The "dispersion" becomes a gathering **face to face,** *i.e.* person opposite person —the people opposite the King who contends with them. In such a connection the idea of Hitzig and others is weak. They refer the expression to the great wilderness which separates Babylon from the lands on the shore of the Mediterranean, which lay in the way of the exiles who ultimately returned. It is almost analogous to the word "world" in the New Testament. Although Keil explains the "leading out," etc. of ver. 34 as neither local nor material, yet we do not understand it with him "of a spiritual separation from the heathen world" (to which they are immediately brought, ver. 35), "lest they should be absorbed in it," etc., but of an aggravation of their exiled condition, a spiritual experience of it, so that they should know and feel that they as the people of God were once more in the wilderness, but not at all in the same sense as before (Deut. viii. 15, xxxii. 10). [Cocceius with perfect right here points still farther forward to the Roman period.] The future "contending" (comp. ch. xvii. 20) is compared in Ver. 36 to a former contention with their fathers **in the wilderness of the land of Egypt.** As the **fathers,** according to ver. 27, are the second generation, which reached Canaan from the wilderness, the "contending" with them is to be referred not to Num. xiv. 28 sq., but rather to such judicial scenes as Num. xvii. 5, 6, 10. The Babylonish exile was formerly called "wilderness of the peoples," in relation to the "peoples" from among whom Israel (ver. 34) was to be led thither; in like manner the Arabian wilderness, to which the expression "wilderness of the peoples" alludes, is called the wilderness of the land of Egypt, because the people had been led out into it from Egypt. They were not led thither as a punishment, although on account of their disobedience it often became a place of punishment; but the divine intention was to try them (to prove, Deut. viii. 2 sq.), from which resulted separation of individuals, purification, which was so strongly urged upon them in reference to Egypt, whither they were always looking back (Num. xx. 5, xxi. 5). While, therefore, the "contending" of ver. 36 also includes chastisement, yet in the application of it to the future, Ver. 37, the idea of the separation—the purification of the people through divine chastisement is the prevailing one. The judgments which God brought on Israel (Num. xvi. 17, 20, affecting even Moses and Aaron!) were only purifying separations. The question is not that of a possible re-entrance into Canaan, so that, with reference to this result, the future guidance of Israel is represented as a repetition of their former guidance (KEIL), nor with Neteler can we understand by: "the wilderness of the peoples," Palestine (?); but ver. 33 as well as ver. 36 point back to Egypt, to the exodus thence, which Keil also on the other hand admits. [Hengst. supposes that the part taken by the exiles in the political intrigues of the home country brought upon them also severe sufferings (Jer. xxix. 21, 22); but that by true repentance many may have been freed from participation in the punishment here threatened!!] They shall go out of the state of exile (ver. 38), but this going out shall be a **passing under the staff** (the "contending," in ver. 35 sq., is here viewed in a new way). The underlying figure is that of the shepherd (Lev. xxvii. 32; Mic. vii. 14; Jer. xxxiii. 13), under whose staff the sheep were required to go individually in order to be inspected and numbered (HITZ.); but its application is here to be understood of the royal sceptre of Jehovah, agreeably to the expression: "rule over," in ver. 33. Comp. further Ex. xiii. 12; 1 Sam. xvi. 8. The meaning of the figurative expression is neither subjection to the government of God (HENGST.), nor a special guardianship of God (KEIL), nor anything similar, but choice, with a very narrow inspection of individuals, the idea distinctly expressed in ver. 38 as to separation and purification being the prominent one. The result intended by this royal inspection, as the parallel sentence: **and bring you,** etc., brings out more fully, alludes to the giving of the covenant-law at Sinai after the passage of the Red Sea (comp. Ex. xiv. 16). Under the **bond** (קָסֹרֶת, contr. for קַאֲסֹרֶת, from the root אָסַר) is a much preferable rendering to: under "the discipline (יָסַר?) of the covenant," whether the penalties of the covenant only, or its promises also, be thought of. The law, which must not be conceived of apart from its promises and penalties, and which may be either a bond of love or an oppressive chain according to one's personality, became, from the fact of men turning to it and observing its statutes, a medium of separation between heathenism and Judaism, and also between the people themselves. The extent to which this was the case is shown especially by the history of Pharisaism since the exile, both on its bright and its shady side.—Ver. 38 now states explicitly what end is contemplated by the impending leading forth of the people in judgment. Hävern. notes a paronomasia in וּבָרוֹתִי and הַבְּרִית.—Comp. ch. ii. 3.—**Land of their wanderings,** *i.e.* wherein they were strangers, Canaan is elsewhere called, Gen. xxxvi. 7; Ex. vi. 4. Here, with a fine antithesis, it is the land of their exile.—לֹא יָבוֹא,

Hengst.: "the rebels are here collected into one ideal person." Keil, who understands the "leading forth" as an utter sweeping of them away, takes the singular in a distributive sense: not one of the transgressors shall enter in. It accords better with the context to regard: **I will lead them forth,** as containing a retrospective reference to ver. 34, so that the rebels and transgressors in the close of the paragraph are again taken together with the whole people. **Yet not to the land of Israel,** would then say negatively what the "wilderness of the peoples" in ver. 35 said positively, consequently that Jehovah will enter into judgment with them all (ver. 35). The singular subject to לֹא יָבוֹא can therefore from אַדְמַת יִשְׂרָאֵל be Israel. (Possibly even, with an eye to the inquirers of ver. 1, with a reference to the always doubtful question of the return of the ten tribes! ?) With: **and ye shall know,** etc., the message is again directed to the persons who spoke to the prophet; if not to Israel in a special sense, at least to Israel in general.

Vers. 39-44. *The Promised Mercy of God.*

Ver. 39. Since judgment, as has been stated, approaches the house of Israel, every man who will not do otherwise may be commanded to go and serve his idols. The impending judgment will make a separation, and the future will belong to the people of God. Comp. Rev. xxii. 11. The holy irony of Him who knows that mercy is laid up for the future.—וְאַחַר is not to be translated: "also afterwards," and coupled with **serve,** nor yet can it be joined with what follows imperatively, but it stands by itself, as if with a —. אִם־ can be simply a conditional particle: **if ye will not hearken** (in the present) **unto Me,** then (וְ takes up וְאַחַר again) **ye shall not farther,** etc. The majority of expositors take it as a particle of swearing, introducing with the negative (אִין, with *Part*) an affirmative sentence, so that the sense would be: and afterwards ye will surely hearken unto Me, and ye will no longer profane My holy name, etc. (comp. ch. xxxvi. 20).—Ver. 40. The positive ground. Comp. Ps. ii. 6, and ch. xvii. 23.—**They shall serve Me,** in contrast to: "serve . . . . idols," ver. 39.—כֻּל, and again כֻּלֹּה, point to the healing of the breach between Judah and Israel. Comp. also ch. xi. 15. The emphatically repeated: **there,** just as in the contrasted ver. 38, remains within the horizon of the Old Testament (comp. the New Testament expansion, John iv. 20 sq.), as the form and clothing of the thought in the rest of the verse maintains the phraseology of the Old Testament worship.—Ver. 41. The previous steps are now recapitulated. Through the leading out and gathering already brought into view in ver. 34, the people, purified by judgment, shall be acceptable to Jehovah as a **sweet savour** (comp. ch. vi. 13), and in them as a holy people, anew consecrated to God, shall be exhibited to the heathen the holiness of Jehovah. —Ver. 42. But then shall they also, as was assumed in ver. 40 ("in the land"), return to the **land of Israel** (ver. 38).—Ver. 43 finally adds a portrait of the inner condition of the people—the complement to ver. 40. Comp. ch. vi. 9, xiv. 22, 23 (ch. xvi. 61).—Ver. 44. Conclusion. The knowledge of Jehovah from an experience of His gracious dealings with them for His name's sake (comp. vers. 9, 14).

DOCTRINAL REFLECTIONS.

1. The prophet may judge (ver. 4), for Jehovah will manifest Himself as King to His people. Prophetic activity in interpreting and applying the divine law was always based on the royal might of God in relation to Israel.

2. The exile was a political and a religious question of the day. The former might easily be confounded with the latter. Therefore in the chapter before us the history of the people is simply opened up, and the exile is exhibited to their conscience as the righteous result of their own conduct.

3. The experience which succeeded to Egypt was the wandering in the wilderness, where the people were purified. The exile which followed Canaan was designed by God to accomplish a similar result, only deeper and more essential in its character, as an ever-increasing corruption had fastened upon Israel's inner being. If, therefore, the wilderness of Egypt was especially an external experience, and the testing came from without, the exile was to be more decidedly an internal exile—a wilderness of the peoples—to the people of God, in order to give them a felt experience of the "world," and of "anguish" in the world.

4. Since the still existing kingdom of Judah, and the people as a whole, were to be upbraided with sin, the kingdom of Israel, which had already sunk into the condition of exile, supplied the most appropriate materials for colouring the accusation. It had from the beginning adopted the way of the heathen, and maintained it almost without interruption. Because it had become like the heathen, it at last fell completely under the dominion of the heathen. And thus there was at hand a course pursued up to the point of judgment, from which a demonstrative argument could be deduced.

5. Already, with their self-willed abandonment of the sanctuary at Jerusalem, but above all with their enforced removal from the Holy Land, the kingdom of Israel became the "Diaspora," *instar omnium*, the "dispersed among the Gentiles," and "scattered in the countries."

6. That which the history of the people testifies regarding their conduct is stated in the ever-repeated refrain of our chapter: "and they rebelled against Me," etc. (vers. 8, 13, 21). God's leading (the objective in opposition to the subjective conduct just mentioned) shows itself throughout, on the other hand, as law according to ver. 37, *i.e.* as a judicial statement (ver. 7), as a formal enunciation of law (ver. 11 sq.), as a recapitulation of the law which had been given (ver. 18 sq.). Therewith threatening is connected (vers. 8, 13, 21, also 33 sq., 38). God's threat strengthens itself to an oath (vers. 15, 23, 31, 33), had even been fulfilled as punishment (vers. 15, 23, 25 sq.), and still remains to be similarly fulfilled (vers. 34 sq., 38). But the patience and long-suffering of God (vers. 9 sq., 14, 22, 28), His mercy (ver. 17), walk side by side with the law from the beginning to the end; and just as life was promised to the people in the law itself (vers

11 sq., 21), so mercy promises the ultimate purification of the people (vers. 32, 35, 37, 38), so as to make them a sanctified "all" Israel, well-pleasing to God (ver. 39 sq.). As Ewald expresses it: "In order to bring the redeemed to a proper recognition of their former great transgressions, and thus to confirm the other and still greater truth which lies in the ancient history, namely, that in the end, grace is still the deepest and the all-surviving element in Jehovah."

7. "I am Jehovah, your God."—On this the law is based, and this underlies the whole history of the people from the beginning to the end. (Vers. 5, 7, 9, 14, 19, 20, 22, 44.) The history of God's people is the evolution of the name of Jehovah, the people of God being in regard to it after the flesh, what the Son of God was after the Spirit.

8. "Not the old race, adhering to idolatry, but a race spiritually new, devoted to Jehovah in profound love and dependence, was to leave Egypt" (Häv.).

9. The divine discourse of the prophet does not draw its materials from tradition apart from the Pentateuch, as from very different standpoints has been assumed by a Vitringa and a Vatke, in order to explain what the prophet states as to the condition of Israel in Egypt. Criticism would fain show therein a conflict between Ezekiel and the Pentateuch. But the evident dependence of the prophetic statements on the Pentateuch is made prominent throughout, and here also in ch. xx. We note, besides what has been brought out in our exegesis, that the spirit of the prophets knew how to read "between the lines" of the history, while criticism attempts, at the most, to import its own spirit into the Holy Scriptures.

10. For the theological understanding of the chapter, the emphatic reiteration of the expression "wilderness" is important. Neteler has entitled the passage: "The people in two wildernesses." Hengst. and Häv. define the idea of the wilderness as "calamity, spiritual and bodily need." As to the kernel of the matter, this, however, would be better: alone with God, when the judicial character of the leading of the people in question would not so distinctly refer to experiences of which the heathen peoples could be eye-witnesses.

11. "The precepts which God gave His people also imply, above all things, that they shall confess their sins, and seek forgiveness in the blood of atonement. This is required by the laws concerning the sin-offerings, which in the Mosaic law form the root of all the other offerings; the passover, which so strictly requires us to strive after the forgiveness of sins, and connects all salvation with it; the great day of atonement" (Hengst.).

12. "The fundamental feature of life through sincere devotion to the law is holiness, and God, as the sanctifier of Israel, is therefore the law's centre. This idea of the sanctification of the people through their God comes notably to the front in the Sabbath. It is the sign of God's creative activity, as well as the expression of man's relation to God: rest in God after life's toil" (Häv.). The life of man is therefore a divine one,—the life of God, just as the justifying righteousness which appeases the conscience and satisfies the law is also the righteousness of God. See Bähr's *Symbolism*. ("From the expression: 'and also My Sabbaths,' they could learn that the commands as to works in which the man lives who does them were not given with the view of making them attempt to live by works, but that they might renounce their own righteousness after learning what kind of a righteousness is essential to life; and since God had declared that it was His will to sanctify them, that they might believe that He who cannot make void His own law (the reward of life is connected with the doing of the commandments, to show that an obedience of this sort is required in order to gain life) would provide an offering by which their conscience could be cleansed, and a priest through whose obedience they could be made righteous, so that they might keep God's commands, hate and avoid all that is opposed to them, from a spirit of grateful love," Cocc.)

13. "Only those who truly fear God celebrate the Sabbath in a right sense, so that all that in the books of Moses attests the want of true godliness among the people in the wilderness involves at the same time the charge of desecrating the Sabbath" (Hengst.). "The Jews were careful to observe the Sabbath, but they missed its meaning and end" (Calv.), "for they perverted it to their corrupt, dead righteousness" (Cocc.).

14. [The command as to the Jewish Sabbath "must have been, and it was, intended not only to separate the people from their worldly employments, but also to call out their hearts in suitable exercises of faith and love to God, and in brotherly acts of kindness and good-will toward those around them. On no other account could its faithful observance be represented as indicative of a sound and healthful state of religion generally. And we might ask, without the least fear of contradiction, if the same practical value is not attached to the careful observance of the Lord's day now by those who have an enlightened regard to the interests of religion? When this day ceases to be devoutly observed, all experience and observation testify that there never fails to ensue a corresponding decline in the life and actings of religion."—P. F.—W. F.]

15. "God has so constituted human nature, that revolt from Him must be followed by total darkness and disorder; that no moderation in error and sin, no standing still at the middle point, is possible; that man, however willing he may be to stand still, must, against his will, sink from step to step. Revolt from God is the crime, excess in error and moral degradation the merited doom, from which all would willingly escape if it were in their power" (Hengst.).

16. The temptation (Gen. xxii.), in which Abraham, as representing all his descendants, the people who were to settle down in the land in which he wandered as a stranger, was taught experimentally the difference between Jehovah and Moloch, did not influence them as it ought to have done—they surrendered their first-born to the bloody cultus of the land; Abraham's temptation became Israel's judgment.

17. That Israel should become like the heathen would be repugnant to the nature of God, especially to His name Jehovah. The very reverse would be much more in harmony with it, namely, that the heathen should become like Israel. For the idea informed in this people, and for which it was chosen out of all peoples, is the idea of the people of God, with God as King and Lord (the idea of the theocracy), whereby Israel is at the same time the bearer of the idea of humanity as a whole; and just as this idea, conformably to

creation, is, to be of God (τοῦ θεοῦ, Luke iii. 38), so is it realized through the restoration of man to God by redemption, whereby God becomes all in all (1 Cor. xv. 28), and men become His willing subjects as He becomes their God (Rev. xxi. 3). Now, as the realization of this idea of Israel, and of humanity generally, takes place in the fulness of time in the One Man, who is both Israel and "the Son of Man," so His historical appearance is linked, according to the flesh, to Israel (this is the meaning of the genealogies of Jesus); but according to the Spirit there is developed out of Him the new humanity, which He Himself is in Spirit and truth, and which it was the office of Israel to prefigure. The pouring out of the Spirit promised by Him, shows that Israel had not become heathen (unless in so far as the languages were concerned), but that the heathen had been incorporated in Israel, Acts ii. Only this can be the spiritual fulfilment of ver. 40, according to the idea of the "all" Israel (כלה). Every other would apply to a privileged nationality, and therefore to the flesh. That for a long time after the dissolution of the kingdom of Israel, Judah gave the tone to the Old Testament people of God; that from the very first the theocratic elements of the kingdom of Israel were attracted to Judah (2 Chron. xi. 13 sq.); that, like Benjamin, many from the other tribes returned with Judah from exile, so that it thereafter furnished a name for the whole people,—all that was a transient historical manifestation, as it was nothing more than that when the kingdom of Israel, on account of its size, its greater population, and in the consciousness of more fully representing the whole people, appropriated the name of the whole, and called itself Israel, under which name it was acknowledged by King Mesa on the recently discovered Moabitish stone. Ver. 40 sq. is undoubtedly Messianic, and in this sense apocalyptic. Klief., who includes in the idea of the Babylonish exile the present dispersion of the Jews, seeing in this the real wilderness of the peoples, makes vers. 40-44 prophesy the gathering of the Jews, their conversion to Christ, and their return as a Christian people to their own land, and holds that God, after the θλῖψις μεγάλη of the end (Rev. xii.) shall have intervened, will separate this believing Israel, together with all other believers, from the wicked, and openly establish them in the life everlasting.

18. "The heathen stood under the divine long-suffering (Rom. iii. 25); not so Israel, to whom God had so gloriously made Himself known. Wherein the heathen prosper, therein must Israel decline" (Hengst.).

19. Cocceius remarks on our chapter, that, "when the Jews had returned from Babylon under Zerubbabel and Ezra, along with those who adhered to them from all the tribes, they formed a unity, possessed a temple at Jerusalem, and became a single people under the same presidency. Thus matters continued under the rule of the Persians and also of the Greeks. But God freed them from all foreign authority, so that He alone was their King, and made them greater than in the days of their fathers, and the Asmonæans ventured to assume the royal diadem," etc.

20. Calvin's prelections on Ezekiel end with the twentieth chapter, as to which Schipper says: "After he had completed this last prelection, that distinguished man Dr. John Calvin, who was previously ailing, began to feel himself much worse, which is the reason that he left off at the end of the twentieth chapter, and never finished the work so well begun."

HOMILETIC HINTS.

Ver. 1. "Here we see that the people of God, even in exile, did not repair to magi, star-gazers, enchanters, and such like, but to the prophet, Deut. xxx. 12 sq." (C.)—"The fifth month is our month July. Thus the Spirit of God notes day and date" (Stck.).—It is enough to say merely that they came to inquire, for from the prophet's mode of answering them we see that they made no inquiry as to deliverance and the way of salvation; they were troubled as to political things, the duration of the exile, the end of the Babylonish power, the issue of Zedekiah's faithlessness. We too ask, Watchman, what of the night? rather than, How shall I find grace? —Why are we so concerned about the future? It will be like our past. We should be deeply concerned on account of the past.—"In our approaches to God, humility and reverence should be combined with a strong and assured faith, which must acquiesce in the authority of the one God, and yet must not object to hear God speak through His servants" (C.).—Summon thyself to the study of the prophets and apostles through whom God has spoken!—God will be inquired of, but still more should His will, which is sufficiently known to us, be done.—"To call on God, and yet not to obey Him, is an abomination in His sight. He heareth not sinners, John ix. 31; Isa. i. 15" (Tüb. Bib.).—Ver. 2 sq. God's suggestive silence, and His more suggestive answer. —God in the mouth, and idols in the heart, a most critical condition.—God speaks not the smallest word of comfort to hypocrites. "For hypocrites there is in the heart of God, and in the Holy Scriptures, no other counsel but to sincere repentance, Isa. lv. 7" (St.).—"Thus they were not in a condition to hear God's word. God hides Himself from those who hear His word with their gaze fixed only on their idols. They have no part in God's word" (Cocc.).—Ver. 4. That is an upbraiding grounded on their ancestral sin, which therefore (ch. xviii.) cannot be denied.—One should not merely touch (ch. xx.) ulcers, after the manner of the moral preacher, but cut them out according to the law of God. The former tickles, the latter causes pain. Here God impels to judge, and in the new covenant the word is always, Judge not! But the Son of God Himself, who yet was not sent into the world for judgment, becomes to the unbelieving a self-judgment. Here Ezekiel sets in motion God's, and not man's, judgment.—Fathers are judged in their sons, but sons may also be judged in their fathers.

Ver. 5 sq. Three witnesses against Israel,—Egypt, the wilderness, Canaan.—"God anticipates men with His grace" (O.).—God's election in relation to merit and demerit; not resting on the one, nor hindered by the other.—Circumcision was the sign of the election. The substance consisted in God's willingness to be their God. The result of Israel's election was the whole leading of the people; the choosing of a people for the preparation of humanity to be a praise to God's glorious name,—an Israel out of all peoples.—

"By no act of God's good-will do we acquire desert, but by each we come under obligation" (STCK.).—If God is to be anything to a man, He must give him an experimental knowledge of Himself. The first experience of God is the recognition of His revelation in the word: the various experiences of His requiring, chastising, forgiving love, follow.—"Oh how many are the ways in which God makes Himself known to men as a gracious God! Acts xvii. 27, 28" (ST.).—"God lifts up His hand to swear; one day His hand will execute what He has sworn, the threatening as well as the promise" (C.).—"We call God our God by faith" (STCK.).—"The time when faith in Christ is bestowed on us, and we as it were hear the assurance, I, the Lord, am your God, is the day of our election. He who is assured of his election by God is sufficiently armed against flesh and blood. There is no other way of throwing off the abominations of sin, but by being assured of the love of God. Through faith alone is the heart cleansed from idols" (H. H.).—Vers. 6, 7. Men are chosen of God not to uncleanness, but to redemption from sin and the power of the devil.—"God must be our God, else we make a god of ourselves, or serve the devil as God" (C.).—"God is indeed the God of all men; but by promise, covenant, and grace, He becomes our God, that our faith may embrace Him as such" (B. B.).—Ver. 6. "God is ever mindful of His promise, but we forget it" (STCK.).—"Once an ornament, now a desert" (B. B.).—Ver. 7. The idolatry of the eyes. We never merely contract guilt by sinning, we pollute ourselves at the same time; just as, on the other hand, forgiveness and sanctification always go together.—Ver. 8. "In Ex. v. 21 only their repute in the eyes of Pharaoh and his servants is in question. Had they believed in the name of Jehovah, they would have rendered a better obedience. But they were infected with the Egyptian idolatrous spirit, as all of us are naturally inclined to idolatry, and they were anxious to stand well with the Egyptians" (C.).—"A worse yoke for Israel than that of the Egyptians was the yoke of their idols" (COCC.).—Note the increased oppression, and in the end the persecution of Israel by the Egyptians, as a sign of God's anger.—Ver. 9. "God's honour and the welfare of the Church are bound together" (C.).—With God, word and deed, promise and fulfilment agree, Num. xxiii. 19.—The holiness of God's name our safety.—Ver. 11. The law is designed for life, not only according to its idea as the revealed will of God, so that he who should keep it would live a divine life, but also in reality, for in him who is led by the law to the knowledge of sin and conversion unto God, it does not tend to death, but rather to life, as our conversion is God's will, and results in life; the law is therefore the will of God, and the medium of its fulfilment.—"He makes mention of the promise along with the law, where He might justly have made mention of the law alone; this shows His fatherly love" (C.).—Ver. 12. The Sabbath pointed directly to the life which the law promises, to the rest of God, that man should be in God, and that God desires to be in man. It pointed beyond the works of the law, as such, to the rest of faith which is in Christ.—"But we rest from our works, when, self being dead, we allow ourselves to be led by the Spirit of God; thus the Sabbath when rightly observed involves the death of self" (C.).—The Sabbath the key of the whole law, according to its highest intention.—The lighting up of the Mosaic law by the ante-Mosaic Sabbath.—Ver. 13 sq. Idleness and good cheer are neither Sabbath-sanctification nor Sunday-observance.—"Let it be observed that the disobedience happened in the wilderness, where they were wholly dependent on God every moment! Usually men revolt from God in the arrogance of prosperity; here it happened when Israel had death before their eyes" (C.).—"What will become of those who in Christian times spend their Sabbaths in drinking, amusement, and such like!?" (B. B.)—Ver. 15. "It depends on the will of every one what position he will take towards God; but he must be prepared for this, that his act will be attended by a corresponding divine act" (HENGST.).—Ver. 17. The lifted-up hand and the compassionate eye of God.

Ver. 18. "The one standard of our whole life should be, not human opinion and ancient custom, but the word of God, Ps. cxix. 105" (ST.).—"Godlessness has such authority that it is respected as a law. For the devil and the world have also their statutes and ordinances, which are more accounted of than God's command" (B. B.).—"If the Church is to be truly reformed, a beginning must be made with the youth" (ST.).—Ver. 23. The threatening with exile a set-off to the wilderness.—The scattering threatened amid outward gathering, and carried out to the inward gathering of the people.—How fruitless love, suffering, and everything else may be!

Ver. 25. He who makes himself like the world is punished by God through the world.—"The true doctrine of God is peace, joy, and life in the Holy Ghost. Man's doctrine is nothing but unrest, pain of heart, and death. For it gives the consciences of men neither rest nor peace, although they do great things, making even their loved children pass through the fire," etc. (RANDGL.)—"That which brings evil on them, and is fraught with death and ruin, has nevertheless the greatest attraction for men" (STCK.).—Ver. 26. To be forsaken of God means to be compelled to recognise, in the state of desolation into which one falls, who God is, and what He is.—He who will not present his offerings to God must present them to the devil.—Religious desolation is a judgment from God.—Ver. 27 sq. A self-invented religious worship pretends to be something lofty, and yet it casts down the glory of God, and exalts man's unreason only.—In departing from God, one never rests with the first, nor yet with the second step, but step follows step. To combine God and idols in one's religion is blasphemy.—Faithlessness to the word of God in our worship.—Mockery of God in many an act of adoration.—Ver. 28. Even Canaan may become a place of corruption, if we there seek high places, and if God is not to us the highest and the only high place.—"If one will present to God a sweet savour, one must offer up to Him heart, soul, and spirit, feeling and desires, otherwise prayer is offensive to Him" (B. B.).—Let one neither add to nor take from the word of God, and thus avoid lighting on dubious high places!—Ver. 29. The irony of all our high places.—God's laughter on hearing His enemies without, and perceiving their earnest proceedings. Not on the heights of human philosophy, but in the high and holy place dwells the

Lord, who abides with him who is humble and of a contrite spirit (Isa. lvii. 15).

Ver. 30 sq. Why does God hide Himself from us when we profess to seek truth? Because the truth which we seek is only an idol-picture. God reveals not Himself to those who serve idols. —Idolatry gradually obscures man's natural knowledge of God.—"How powerfully men are influenced by bad examples! how easily the sensuous pomp of false religions stirs them! How soon the heart is carried captive by the outward, forgetting the true, inward worship of God!" (St.)—Ver. 32. "The world of the heathen was to them an object of greater interest than the exiled Church, just as in our days also many regard an irreligious condition as preferable to the struggles of a religious life. To others, God's sincere solicitude for His house appears as hardness and severity, and therefore they prefer freer relations with less control. Thus Israel thought of its redemption when among the heathen" (C.). —Let us leave the heathen to their heathenism, and not only that, but let us ourselves become like the heathen, has all been already desired, said, and carried out in action. Our modern method is no new wisdom.—Dreadful as it sounds, a child of God can be reduced to the melancholy condition of exclaiming, Oh that I had never known God!—"The despair of the Jews was their unbelief,—that they did not believe that Christ would arise from among them" (Cocc.).—Vers. 33-35. God will not withdraw from His obligations. He watches over us, and leads us out of the world when He leads us into it, *i.e.* gives us an inner experience of it, that it may be known if we will still be as the heathen.—"God withdraws the sinner from the opportunity of sinning" (Stck.).—"Oh how good it is for men when God compels them to obedience, and brings them by means of affliction when they will not come of their own accord!" (B. B.)—"To bring the Jews under His own authority, God must needs gather them out of the peoples, as they were there scattered in exile. This He did, not without anger, as the house of his master seems to a recaptured slave like a sepulchre because he is either thrust into a deep dungeon or there is required of him threefold more than he can bear. And so, after they were brought back from Chaldea, they lived a lonely life as if they were in a corner of the earth, or in a desert in the midst of the peoples; and the great majority wandered about virtually in the wilderness, as only a small proportion returned to the fatherland. He led them forth as King, He ceased not to reveal Himself to them as Judge. Then He showed His wrath to them" (C.).—"The wilderness of the peoples was their incorporation with the Roman Empire,—a wilderness in contrast to the vanished Canaan-glory under the Maccabees. In this wilderness, Canaan now lay" (Cocc.).—"Among great crowds one may feel oneself lonely and desolate, as, on the other hand, one may feel in waste places as if he were in a circle of friends" (L.).—"Face to face indicates confidential discourse, for God can come nearer the heart in the wilderness, Hos. ii. 14" (B. B.).—As to the "contending," read also the books of Nehemiah and Ezra.—Ver. 36. "Ancient examples of chastisement are not written in vain" (St.).—The wilderness a type and picture of the exile.—Egypt and Babylon in their significance for the people of God.—Ps. lxxxii. 1.—Rev. xi. 8, xvii. 3.—Ver. 37. "Points to Christ, John x. 14. He came for the sake of the sheep of the house of Israel, but they only are Israel whom Christ reckons so, touching them with the point of His staff and numbering them" (Cocc.).—Jehovah, who spoke to Israel face to face through Moses on Mount Sinai (Deut. v. 4), who appeared to Ezekiel (ch. i.) in the form of man, would plead with them in the flesh when He came to the lost sheep in the wilderness of the land of Judah (Matt. iii.), where the Baptist had prepared His way. Comp. Isa. lii. 8.—"They may have thought in the state of exile, that they would become free and uncontrolled, if they could obliterate from their souls the name of Jehovah; but He, on the other hand, is mindful of that which is His own, that not even one should be snatched from Him, since He claims authority over all without exception" (C.).—"His covenant stands, His love is for ever." God had left the heathen to go on in their own way, Israel's way was always brought back again to the covenant.—Still Christ asks that His yoke be taken, Matt. xi. 29.—"For the docile, who patiently bear the yoke, the bands are cords of love, Hos. xi. 4" (Schm.).—Ver. 38. Transgressors stand not in the judgment, nor sinners in the congregation of the righteous, Ps. i.—This purifying process with Israel foreshadowed the still severer process which was to succeed, when Christ appeared and the gospel was preached. This purification was the sanctification of the Church from among the Jews.—Israel so-called did not inherit the land, which is promised only to the meek (Matt. v. 5), who learn of the Meek One (Matt. xi. 29).—Ver. 39. Decision; to this all God's leadings point.—However many run after idols, God has still a people. "Thus God gives them up to a perverted mind" (B. B.).—In the end, all tongues, even involuntarily, must hallow His name.—"Go! is sounded out by God's voice, as the condemned shall one day hear" (St.).

Ver. 40 sq. "When a renewing of the gracious covenant is in question, God first sifts His Church, and casts out the hypocrites. This needs no external force" (Schm.).—The spiritual worship of the New Testament can be well described in the phraseology of the Old Testament worship, by which it was symbolized and prefigured. We still speak of the heavenly "Jerusalem."—There is high place and high place. Here the high mountain of Israel; in ver. 28 sq. the high places on the mountains of Canaan.—Ver. 41. In Christ we are made acceptable to God.—Ver. 43. "When believers are admitted to the grace of God, and lovingly treated by Him, they remember their transgressions with shame, and perceive for the first time their real greatness and enormity. After his conversion, Paul regarded himself as one born out of due season, as the least of the apostles, because he had persecuted the Church of God. This remembrance gives birth to the song of grateful praise, 'By the grace of God I am what I am.' Thus our sins exalt the glory of God. Comp. Deut. viii., ix. Hence it follows that Christian life is a perpetual repentance, from which the life of grace received from God shines forth" (H. H.).—Ver. 44. Not unto us, not unto us, but to Thy holy name be praise and glory!—"All salvation is founded on God's grace and the forgiveness of sins, but not without repentance" (Schm.).

10. *The Approaching Judgment* (ch. xxi.).

1, 2 And the word of the Lord came to me, saying, Son of man, set thy face
toward the right, and drop toward the south, and prophesy against the forest
3 of the field in the south; And say to the forest of the south, Hear the word
of Jehovah. Thus saith the Lord Jehovah, Behold, I am about to kindle in
thee a fire, and it will devour every green tree in thee, and every dry tree.
The flaming flame shall not be quenched, and all faces shall be scorched in it
4 [by it], from the south to the north. And all flesh shall see that I, Jehovah,
5 have kindled it; and it shall not be quenched. And I said, Ah! Lord God,
6 they say to me [of me], Doth he not speak parables? And the word of
7 Jehovah came to me, saying, Son of man, set thy face toward Jerusalem,
and drop toward the holy places, and prophesy toward the land of Israel,
8 and say to the land of Israel, Thus saith the Lord Jehovah, Behold, I am
against thee, and I have drawn My sword out of its scabbard, and will cut off
9 from thee the righteous and the wicked. Because I cut off from thee the
righteous and the wicked, therefore shall My sword go forth out of its
10 scabbard against all flesh from south to north. And all flesh shall know that
I, Jehovah, have drawn My sword out of its scabbard, nor shall it return
11 again. And thou, son of man, sigh with breaking of loins, and with bitterness
12 shalt thou sigh before their eyes. And it shall be, when they say to thee,
Wherefore dost thou sigh? that thou shalt say, For the tidings, because it
cometh; and every heart melts, and all hands hang down, and every spirit
faints [is dulled], and all knees are dissolved into water. Lo, it comes, and has
13 happened: sentence of the Lord Jehovah. And the word of Jehovah came
14 to me, saying, Son of man, prophesy and say, Thus saith Jehovah; say, A
15 sword, a sword, sharpened and also furbished [is it]! To kill with slaughter
it is sharpened; furbished [is it], that it may glitter as lightning! Or can
16 [shall] we rejoice over the staff [sceptre] of My son, despising every tree!? And
He gave it [it is given] to be furbished, that it may be taken into the hand; it
is a sword sharpened and furbished, that it may be put into the hand of the
17 slayer. Cry and howl, son of man, for it shall be upon [against] My people,
upon all the princes of Israel; they are given up [thrown] to the sword along
18 with My people, therefore smite upon the thigh. For it makes trial [trial is
made]. And how?—If also the despising staff [sceptre] shall not be!—Sentence
19 of the Lord Jehovah. And thou, son of man, prophesy, and smite hand
against hand, and the sword shall be doubled to the third time; it is the
sword of the pierced-through, the sword of one pierced through, of the
20 mighty, that penetrates to them. In order that the heart may faint, and the
stumbling-blocks be multiplied at all their gates, have I given the threatening
21 of the sword. Ah! made for flashing, drawn for slaughter! Unite thyself,
turn to the right; direct thyself, turn to the left, whither thy face is appointed.
22 And I also will strike My hands together, and I will cause My fury to rest.
23 I, Jehovah, have spoken. And the word of Jehovah came to me, saying,
24 And thou, son of man, set thee two ways for the coming of the sword of the
king of Babylon; out of one land shall they both proceed; and make a finger-
25 post—at the head of the way of a city make [it]. Thou shalt set a way for
the coming of the sword to Rabbah of the sons of Ammon, and to Judah in
26 Jerusalem, [the] inaccessible. For the king of Babylon stands at the mother
of the way, at the head of the two ways, to use divination; shakes the arrows
27 together, inquires at the teraphim, inspects the liver. In his right hand is
the divination "Jerusalem," to place [battering-] rams, to open the mouth in
slaughter, to lift up the voice in the war-cry, to place rams against the gates,
28 to cast a mount, to build siege-towers. And it is to them as lying divination
in their eyes that have sworn oaths for themselves; and [yet] he remembers ini-
29 quity, in order to take [them]. Therefore thus saith the Lord Jehovah, Because
ye shall remember [bring to remembrance] your iniquity, since your transgressions are

made bare, so that your sins are seen in all your doings, because ye are come
30 to remembrance, ye shall be taken with the hand. And thou, pierced-through,
wicked one, prince of Israel, whose day has come at the time of the iniquity
31 of the end, Thus saith the Lord Jehovah, Remove the head-band, take off
the crown. This [is] not this. The low is [to be] exalted, and the high [to be]
32 brought low. Overturned, overturned, overturned will I make it. Yea, this
[also] is not, till He comes to whom the judgment belongs, and I will give it to
33 Him. And thou, son of man, prophesy and say, Thus saith the Lord Jehovah
concerning the sons of Ammon, and their reproach; even say, A sword, a
34 sword, drawn for slaughter, furbished sufficiently to glitter! While they
see vanity for thee, while they divine a lie to thee,—to lay thee upon the
necks of the pierced-through, of the wicked, whose day has come at the time
35 of the iniquity of the end. Let it return to its sheath. In the place where
36 thou wast formed, in the land of thy origin will I judge thee. And I will
pour out My indignation upon thee, with the fire of My wrath will I blow
upon thee, and will give thee into the hand of consuming men, forgers of
37 destruction. Thou shalt be for fuel to the fire; thy blood shall be in the
midst of the land; thou shalt not be remembered, for I, Jehovah, have
spoken.

Ver. 7. Another reading: אל מקדשם, *ad sanctuarium eorum.* Syr. Sept. et Arabs. have the suffix.

Ver. 14. Sept.: . . . ὀξυνου κ. θυμωθητι, (15) ὁπως σφαξης σφαγια, ὀξυνου ὁπως γενη εἰς στιλβωσιν, ἑτοιμη εἰς παραλυσιν· σφαζε, ἐξουδενει, ἀπωθου παν ξυλον.—Vulg.: *Qui moves sceptrum . . . succidisti omne lignum.*

Ver. 17. . . . κροτησον ἐπι την χειρα σου,— Vulg.: . . . *Israel qui fugerant—*

Ver. 18 ὁτι δεδικαιωται. Και τι εἰ και φυλη ἀπωσθη;— Vulg.: . . . *quia probatus est. Et hoc cum sceptrum subverterit, et non erit—*

Ver. 19. . . . ἡ τριτη ῥομφαια τραυματειων ἐστιν, ῥομφαια τραυματειων ἡ μεγαλη, κ. ἐκστησει αὐτους,—*ac triplicetur gladius interfectorum: hic est gl. occisionis magnæ, qui obstupescere eos facit,*— There is a reading: החרדת, *perterrefaciens*). Another reading: לכם.

Ver. 20. . . . K. πληθυνθωσιν οἱ ἀσθενουντες ἐπι πασαν πυλην αὐτων. K. παραδεδονται εἰς σφαγια ῥομφαιας, εὐ γεγονεν εἰς σφαγην, εὐ γεγονεν εἰς στιλβωσιν.— *et multiplicat ruinas. In omnibus . . . conturbationem gladii acuti et limati ad . . . amicti ad cædem.*

Ver. 21. Another reading: התאחרי, *retro ito vel: mora, retarda.*

Ver. 24. *Et manu capiet conjecturam, in capite . . . conjiciet.*

Ver. 26. Sept.: . . . τ. ἀρχαιαν ὁδον . . . ἀναβρασαι ῥαβδια κ. ἐπερωτησαι ἐν τοις γλυπτοις—

Ver. 27. 'Εκ δεξιων αὐτου ἐγενετο . . . στομα ἐν βοῃ . . . *Ad dexteram ejus facta est . . . os in cæde—*

Ver. 28. K. αὐτος αὐτοις ὡς μαντευομενος μαντειαν ἐνωπιον αὐτων, κ. αὐτος ἀναμιμνησκων ἀδικιας αὐτων μνησθηναι. *Eritque quasi consulens frustra oraculum in oculis eorum, et sabbatorum otium imitans; ipse autem recordabitur iniquitatis ad capiendum.*

Ver. 29. For בכל, read וכל.

Ver. 30. . . . βεβηλε, ἀνομε— Vulg.: *profane . . . dies in temp. iniquitatis præfinita,*

Ver. 31. 'Αφειλου . . ἐπεθου αὐτη τον στεφανον, οὐ τοιαυτη ἐσται· ἐταπεινωσας το . . . ὑψωσας.— Vulg.: . . . *nonne hæc est, quæ humilem sublevavit—*

Ver. 32. 'Αδικιαν . . . θησομαι αὐτην, οὐ τοιαυτη ἐσται . . . ὡ καθηκει— Vulg.: . . . *ponam eam; et hoc non factum est, donec—*

Ver. 35. 'Αποστρεφε, μη καταλυσης . . .

Ver. 36. . . . βαρβαρων— Vulg.: . . . *insipientium.*

EXEGETICAL REMARKS.

To join vers. 1–5 with ch. xx. (as is done in the Eng. Ver.) would be against the connection; while, as the first part of ch. xxi., it both admirably introduces the whole, and in particular, by ver. 5, paves the way for the explanation in ver. 6 sq.

Vers. 1–5 [ch. xx. 45–49].—*A Picture.*

Ver. 2. Comp. ch. ii. 1.—vi. 2 (xiii. 17); Luke ix. 51. **The right**, according to ver. 7, is Jerusalem. **Drop** is after Deut. xxxii. 2 a very common expression for prophetic discourse. It is suggested by the rain or the dew, and points to the place of its origin,—above, and also to the beneficial influence which it is intended to exert, and is used even when the discourse does not contain promises merely, but also threatening and judgment, as is the case here exclusively, and to a large extent also in Deut. xxxii. May it not also hint at the concise, abrupt style of composition adopted in the chapter? דָּרוֹם, the bright, sunny **south**, in ver. 7 the expression is: the "holy places."—נֶגֶב (either "dryness," or also from "brightness") defines the **forest of the field**, more precisely, as situated in the **south**, pertaining to the south country (ver. 3), as Judea is often described. The threefold direction symbolizes perhaps the divine element in his commission. For **field**, comp. ch. xvii. 5; "land of Israel" in ver. 7 corresponds to it—the fruitful native soil of the whole people; Hengst.: because an agricultural people are here treated of. **Forest,** figurative for people, on account of the density of the population, but by no means with any reference to the degeneration of the noble vine (Isa. v.) to a wild forest (UMBR.), or the impending reduction of the land to an uncul tivated and forest condition, nor yet on account of its forest stretches; just as the southern definition of the direction from the standpoint of the exiled prophet is not to be taken in a precisely geographic sense. Besides, that which is said of the north in ch. i. 4 is here confirmed.—Ver. 3. Ch. vi. 3.—The **fire** suits both the forest-figure and the idea of Jehovah's avenging wrath. Comp. ch. i. (ch. xv.) Comp. ch. xvii. 24. **Green** and **dry** become in ver. 8 "righteous" and "wicked" (Luke xxiii. 31).—לְהֶבֶת שַׁלְהֶבֶת, assonant ascending climax, to which the result corresponds. Endeavouring, in a far-fetched way, to conform to the figure, Hitzig interprets **faces** of the outside, as that which the fire first consumes. A similar view is maintained by Schnurrer in a special dissertation on the previous chapter,—"on all sides—out and out."—Ver. 4 explains "all faces" by: **all flesh**—all Israel; and so וְרָאוּ also can be understood as: seeing to their own hurt (vers. 9, 10). Hengst. makes the "faces" stand for the persons, as the material which the fire is to consume. Comp. ch. v. 10. [Cocc. refers it to the judgment on Babylon, which was to follow the judgment on Israel.]—**All flesh**, equivalent to: every man. What does not pass speedily away, but endures to completion,—that which abides, makes on short-lived, fading man the impression of eternal duration.—Ver. 5. Is it a complaint, owing to experiences following on what has just been propounded, or to his experience generally as a prophet? Perhaps an indirect petition for a less figurative message; as Hitzig, following the Chald.: "accept my petition."—Comp. ch. xvii. 2 (2 Cor. iv. 4).—Transition to ver. 6 sq.

Vers. 6-12 [1-7]. *The Interpretation (through the Sword).*

It is noteworthy that the foregoing figure is explained by another (Matt. xiii. 10).—Ver. 7. Comp. ver. 2.—**Holy places** (comp. ch. vii. 24). Hengst. refers the plural to the glory of the one sanctuary, and understands it of "the spiritual abode of the people." Others have thought of the individual buildings of the temple, its two or three parts. [Cocc.: "because many buildings were erected by men in addition to those authorized by God, or because Ezekiel prophesies not only of Solomon's, but at the same time of Zerubbabel's temple."]—Ver. 8. **The land of Israel**, equivalent to: "the forest of the south," ver. 3. What follows is also parallel. The explanatory figure is the well-known one (ch. v., vi.) of the sword. —**The righteous and the wicked** (comp. at ch. iii. 18 sq.). According to Hengst., not in contradiction to ch. ix. 4, "for if two suffer the same, yet it is not the same (Rom. viii. 28)." The contrast is to be taken like young and old, rich and poor, similarly to Matt. ix. 13. Those whom you call righteous and wicked,—all, fall under the power of the sword. With which Ver. 9 harmonizes; for **all flesh**, etc., points to the whole extent of the Jewish territory as the field for its exercise. ["As is manifest from the whole nature of the representation, it is the merely external aspect of the visitation which the prophet has in his eye. The sword of the Lord's judgment, he announced, was to pass through the land, and accomplish such a sweeping overthrow, that all, without exception, would be made to suffer in the fearful catastrophe. This did not prevent, however, but that there might be, in the midst of the outward calamities which were thus to burst like a mighty tempest over the land, a vigilant oversight maintained, and special interpositions of Providence exercised in behalf of the pious remnant who still continued faithful to the covenant of God. It was this distinguishing goodness to some, even amid the horrors of a general desolation, which, as we showed before, was the real object of that sealing of God's servants on the forehead in a former vision; while here, on the other hand, it is merely the general desolation itself which is contemplated by the prophet. And the very circumstance that he should now have looked so exclusively on the outward scene of carnage and distress, which he descried in the approaching future, seemed to say that this was to be the grand feature of the time, and that the special interpositions which were to be put forth in behalf of the better portion would be so few that they scarcely required to be taken into account."—FAIRBAIRN'S *Ezekiel*, pp. 233, 234.—W. F.]—Others: on the ground of this certain universal destruction in Israel, a still more extensive judgment shall take place, *e.g.* on the Ammonites. [Cocc. thinks of all wars, etc. up to the subjugation of the nations to Christ.]—Ver. 10 recalls, however, ver. 4. There: "it shall not be quenched," here: **nor shall it return.** In other words, a full end. Some see the distinction between this and earlier judgments indicated here.—Ver. 11. Symbolical description of intensest expression of sorrow. **With breaking,** etc., when the prophet sinks down like one whose loins are broken, and who is unable to stand upright (Deut. xxxiii. 11). [Others: a pain which can break the seat of man's strength; or as spasmodic pains; or as in travail-pangs; or with girdle burst asunder, etc. EWALD: smiting on the thigh.] Quite conceivable, without any hypocrisy, owing to Ezekiel's sympathy with his people. Comp. Rom. ix. 1 sq. In **bitterness**, the pain at the same time audibly expresses itself. They shall become aware of it (**before their eyes**).—Ver. 12. Ch. vii. 26, 2 sq. That which to others is merely **tidings**, is to the prophet already coming, or it is to him a "thing heard" (Umbr.: a revelation made at an earlier time), which is passing into fulfilment; therefore his pain. But they shall be compelled to experience in themselves what they perceive in him. In all, courage gives place to terror, activity to prostration, counsel to perplexity. No one holds out any longer; as to which comp. ch. vii. 17.—It is not merely coming, *i.e.* on the way, but that which the tidings bode, which they actually are (ver. 13 sq.), is as good as already accomplished.

Vers. 13-22 [8-17]. *The Sword.*

The prophet's bitter pain (ver. 11) is audibly expressed in this sword-song, as it has been called.—Ver. 14. The subject of the tidings emphatically repeated as **a sword.**—(הוּחַדָּה, perf. Hophal from חָדַד.—מְרוּטָה, partic. pass.)—Ver. 15. It shall slay, and even before it proves its sharpness, **terrify** (הֱיֵה, infinitive). בָּרָק, from its gleaming brightness. (Deut. xxxii. 41.) מֹרְטָה, partic. Pual for מְמֹרְטָה, with the euphonic *dag. forte.*—The close of the verse is a *crux interpretum.* The abrupt statement of the contrary to that which was demanded of the prophet by Jehovah in ver. 11 is intelligible, and all the more so as an inquiry as to the reason for his exhibition of pain of heart has been already presupposed in ver. 12. **Or can [shall] we rejoice,** etc.? In this case the prophet can associate himself with Jehovah, while "crying," etc., again (ver. 17) remains his occupation alone. The latter is made all the more prominent by the clause: "Can we rejoice?" The **staff,** in accordance with ch. xix. 11 sq., is to be understood of the sceptre, and thus of the kingdom (comp. ch. xvi. 13). **My son** must be the same as "My people" in ver. 17—namely, Judah; which is all the more appropriate, as there is before us the promise of Gen. xlix. 8 sq. (see ch. xix.), which was also confirmed to David, 2 Sam. vii. 23. The sceptre of Judah, on account of this promise to bless Israel,—Jehovah regarding it as His own,—is perpetual. **Despising every tree,** conformably to ch. xvii. 24,—every other prince and king. (May not, conformably to ver. 3, allusion be also made to the man-despising wickedness (ver. 30) of the last Jewish kings, so as to yield the very striking sense: Or could we rejoice in the reigning wickedness which the sword makes an end of!?). The construing of the masculine שֵׁבֶט as a feminine (which Rosenm. calls the supreme difficulty of the passage) is sufficiently explained by the underlying idea of lordship. (See Häv. and Rosenm.) Therefore: in respect of the sword, is there room for any feeling but pain? Could there be joy over the kingdom, which shall not depart from Judah, according to the blessing which rests on it, and the promise made to David,—joy that Judah still survives, while the princes of Israel's kingdom have long since passed away?! Should we be able to rejoice? Even this kingdom is about to fall beneath the sword, etc. Ver. 17 sq., 19, 30 sq. But doubtless the Messiah will also come, ver. 32. The connection decidedly recommends this interpretation. One must remember what the kingdom and the last remnant in Jerusalem were, even in the lament of Jeremiah (Lam. v. 15). [Other interpretations: "Shall we rejoice, namely, over this sword, which despises the stem (?) of My son Israel, and every tree?" Or שֵׁבֶט is taken as the chastening rod (?) of Israel, which this sword is, and which rod in hardness and solidity surpasses every other wood (RASHI). HENGST.: the punishment hanging over Israel exceeds in rigour all other punishments, according to the law set forth, Luke xii. 46. ("We—I and thou—spoken from the soul of the people.") Hävern. takes אוֹ ironically: "or should (נָשִׂישׂ=נסים) (projecting) with a play on נָשִׂיא) the sceptre of My son be haughty (Ex. iv. 21; Hos. xi. 1; Gen. xlix. 9; comp. therewith 1 Kings xxii. 11; Deut. xxxiii. 17), despising every tree (with reference to all other powers)?" UMBR.: "The rod of My Son—that which concerns Him—despises every (feeble) tree, has transformed itself into unbending iron."[1]]—Ver. 16. The most probable subject of וַיִּתֵּן is the "son,"—Judah itself prepared the Chaldean sword of vengeance. Comp. ch. xix. 14. Or indefinitely: it was given.—Ver. 17. As the joy was groundless (ver. 15), so all the more is the emotion of ver. 11 enjoined, ch. ix. 8, xi. 13.—That which הָיְתָה בְ would say both as to the people and the princes of Israel is expressed by מְגוּרֵי (part. pass. Kal of מָגַר). Others: "Terrors (מגורים from גּוּר) because of (אֶל) the sword being upon (אֶת) My people." Which, however, says too little in this connection.—**Upon the thigh,** as women upon the breast; pain, terror.—Ver. 18. **For,** resumes what is said in the previous verse.—בֹּחַן, proving, trying; or, impersonal perf. Pual, trial is made. HÄV.: "for there is a proving" in relation to the judgments of God. Too far-fetched. HENGST.: "for (it is) a trial." A brief statement of the threatening character of the impending period. PHILLIPS: "for a purification must take place." Consequently, either of the past (as Rashi), of the sufferings whereby the people have already been tried, or with reference to the future. According to the connection, the trial, if not spoken directly of the sword, must be thought of in relation to its terrible murderous violence, as shown in ver. 17.—וּמָה, briefest continuation, but rather an exclamation than a thought. What, in fine, when people and prince are doomed to the sword,—when even the scornful (become inhuman in its arrogance, comp. ver. 15) kingdom of Judah shall now be brought to an end? [RASHI: And what will happen to My son when the sword overtakes him? He shall perish. KIMCHI: The sword will be for trying. And what if that sword, despising the stem of Israel also, should not smite it? There would be no trial. HÄV.: "And how? if the sceptre is still so arrogant, it shall not stand." HENGST.: "And how? should the despising rod (the punishment that far outstrips all other punishments) not be?" KEIL: When even the sceptre of Judah fails to show the might expected from it, what shall then be? NETELER: "And how? if also the sceptre of the despiser (Jerusalem) shall not be!"]—Ver. 19. Comp. at ch. vi. 11. The gesture here is the sign of an impending energetic action (HENGST.). To say that it expresses lively excitement of feeling is little; rather it arouses the sword to demand redoubled slaughter, which immediately follows. One stroke shall not be enough, but the strokes are repeated. Not that Ezekiel shall call out the following words, repeating them three times; nor yet is threefold doubling (?) nor threefold multiply-

[1] The greater number of Schroeder's bracketed "other interpretations" have been omitted, as being destitute of probability, and quite unworthy of notice. Dr. Fairbairn's rendering: "perchance the sceptre of My son rejoiceth,' is grammatically inadmissible, for נָשִׂישׂ is not a participle, but the 1st plur. imperf. But could we not adopt his translation of the last clause and render the passage: "Or shall we rejoice over the rod [sceptre] of My son?" as if it at least were safe, come what will? Nay, that cannot be, for "it (the sword) despiseth every tree [all wood]," the sceptre of Judah not excepted.—W. F.

ing meant (as doubling is the thing in question). But once, twice, and yet a third time a double sword-stroke, to wit, with reference to the people, princes, and king, so that what is stated before (vers. 17, 18) is compressed. [KLIEF.: For the third time the sword is a slayer, after it had previously come doubled (twice); the number three is symbolical.] It is called **the sword of the pierced-through,** from the multitudes whom it pierces. HÄV.: the sword of the slain.—**Sword of one pierced through, of the mighty.** The subject is indefinite, but becomes definite in the adjective. "Among the crowd of the slain there is also one pierced through, made altogether like to them, who is the great one" (HÄV.). As the sword-song throughout keeps the kingdom in view, the king (ver. 30) is undoubtedly referred to, to wit, Zedekiah. The fact that his sons were slain before his eyes, that his own eyes were put out (2 Kings xxv. 7), that he died in bonds in Babylon (Jer. lii. 11), especially when one considers how the context as well as other passages point, sufficiently justifies the application of the "pierced-through" one to him; so that it is not to be referred to "the great" collectively, nor to the wicked Chaldee king (! ?), nor to "the great sword of the slain which surrounds them." (Comp. Keil in opposition to Hitzig.) הַחֹדֶרֶת, from חָדַר. GESEN.: *to surround, to besiege,* "lies in wait for them." **That penetrates to them,** with an allusion to חֶדֶר, the inner chamber. The old translations: which puts them in terror.—Ver. 20. **In order that;** that which will abundantly come to pass is also abundantly expressed. The intention made prominent by being placed in the forefront. אִבְחַת is found here only=threatening, or quivering, or shaking, or destroying, etc.; or a misprint for טִבְחַת (shambles of the sword). But whatever the precise meaning of the word be, it qualifies the sword, so that by means of it the courage of the people fails, and **at all their gates** obstructions lie on which they stumble, —either "crowds of corpses hard by the gates where the besieged made their sallies," or circumstances which exposed them to slaughter. The **flashing** explains the fainting, etc.; the **slaughter** points to the **stumbling-blocks.**—Ch. vi. 11. Abrupt exclamation of the prophet.—מְעֻטָּה, ἅπ. λεγ.; meaning: polished, sharpened (GESEN.); MEIER: whetted; HÄV.: drawn; others the very opposite: covered, still in the sheath.—Ver. 21. Address to the sword. Up to this point no more than one sword has been spoken of, so that the one must be summoned to ally itself with all other possible swords. But the concentration of the thrice-repeated double stroke in a single stroke, which would better correspond with ver. 19, could be the meaning. Or it is to collect its energies for the directions which are to be presently given it. [Hitzig reads: "turn thyself backwards," and completes הַשִׂימִי by supplying פָּנַיִךְ; "turn thyself forwards," in order to procure the two additional directions to **right** and **left.** Ew.: "Collect thyself southwards, assail northwards, whithersoever thy points are appointed."] Häv. connects: "Turn thyself with all vigour to the **right,"** and (corresponding to this): "direct (thy face, thy edge) to the left!" There are, however, four words which depict the activity and rapidity of the individual sword-strokes; perhaps they are also military commands? If הַשִׂימִי and הִתְאַחֲדִי correspond, then the rendering must be: "attention," "to your post!" (GESEN., HENGST.) Besides, it is perhaps preparatively to the following paragraph as to Jerusalem and Ammon that only a twofold direction, "right" and "left," is specified. The destination **whither,** etc. concludes the passage. [Cocc. is not amiss in regarding אָנָה as an interrogative; Hitzig does the same.]—Ver. 22. Comp. ver. 19. Jehovah makes the gesture of the prophet His own. Comp. further ch. xvi. 42, v. 13. What a rest, and, going before it, what an agitation!

Vers. 23–29. *The King of Babylon against Jerusalem.*

A symbolical action, as in ver. 11 (17, 19). Hengst., as always, makes it belong to the internal world; but what would have been the meaning of a command of this sort, were it not to be carried out externally? The whole point lies in its external representation. It is a demonstration *ad oculos* (ch. iv. 1 sq.). Ezekiel is to place before himself on a table or tablet a sketch of the nature mentioned, by means of cutting or engraving, as may be surmised from בָּרֵא, Ver. 24.—The **two ways** already point to another reference besides that to Jerusalem.—**The sword of the king of Babylon** is the "tidings" which come (ver. 12); into his murdering "hand" (ver. 16) this approaching sword is given.—The **one land** (or land of one, namely, the Babylonish king) from which both ways shall proceed, owing to the manner in which it is emphasized, leads one already to suppose that both ways were originally one, which at a later point was parted into two.—יָד, the finger-post which here points the way to a (still indefinite) **city.** At the **head of the way,** *i.e.* where the way in question begins, the hand shall be formed.—Ver. 25. More particular description of the way, according to which it appears as two ways (hence: **for the coming of the sword,** as in ver. 24), with the finger-post for guide. As to Rabbah, the capital city of the Ammonites, see Deut. iii. 11. The city at the head of whose way the finger-post stands can properly mean Rabbah only, from the fact of its being first mentioned; and this points it out as the place lying nearest on the way of the coming sword, so that (as Hengst. rightly remarks) the human probability was that the vengeance of the king of Babylon would begin with Ammon, which had provoked it by adhering to the same anti-Chaldean coalition (Jer. xxvii. 3). As if less exposed, behind it appears Judah, more precisely defined by Jerusalem; which supports our way of taking Judah-Jerusalem in ch. xix. (See Doct. Reflec. there.) **In,** because Judah exists essentially in Jerusalem; and the way of the sword goes thither, so that the sword rests there. Its strength, its **inaccessible** elevation, shall be merely nominal (Deut. xxviii. 52).—Ver. 26. Even the king of Babylon is uncertain which way to choose.—**Mother of the way,** is immediately explained by: **the head of two ways,** to be the point whence they branch off like two daughters from the way which had previously been one. [Häv. avails himself of the Arabic idiom, according to which "mother of the way" means the great military road, along (אֵל) which Nebuchadnezzar is about to proceed, which then divides into two ways.]—The tacit contrast between: **to use divination**, and: to "prophesy" (vers. 19, 14, 7, 2) is interesting; they are nevertheless unified by the divine will. (Comp. at Deut. xviii. 10.) Perhaps on account of this divine element in the background, it is carried out in a threefold manner, according to the symbolism of numbers.—Does the arrow-oracle refer to the significations of קלל, "light," or "gleaming," so that the divination is founded on the fact of the one flying more swiftly than the other, as being the lighter, or on the fact of its shining more brightly? It is the simplest way, however, to think of two arrows, the one marked "Rabbah," the other "Jerusalem," being put into a vessel, perhaps a helmet, when the decision is made according as the one or the other is first drawn or shaken out; unless the quarter to which the head of the lighter arrow points on falling out, either right or left, be the ground of the decision. Comp. Häv. on the passage.—It is impossible to decide as to the method of consulting the teraphim. See Winer, *Realw.*; Herzog, *Realencycl.* xvi. 32. Israel brought them out of Chaldea, Gen. xxxi. 19, 34. According to Häv.: gods of fortune; Hengst.: intermediate gods, serving for the investigation of the future. Häv. supposes a transference of the Hebrew popular faith to Babylonish divinities analogous to Gad and Meni. Hitzig: his household gods, private idols (θέραπεις). As to the inspection of the liver, see Hävernick's *Commentary*. Such circumstances were taken into account as its condition, size, whether large, with inwardly bent lobes, etc., whether dry, defective, ulcerated, etc.—Ver. 27. **In his right hand is the divination**, requires to be understood neither as: into his right hand came, etc., nor yet, with Hitzig, of the arrow-lot in particular, which pointed to Jerusalem, if it be only stated that Jerusalem was designated by the divination ceremony as the object to be attacked,—therefore, the "right hand." "The right hand is employed; he has the decision spiritually therein; is determined in his actions by the decision given for Jerusalem in its three forms" (Hengst.). Hence there immediately follows: לָשׂוּם'. Comp. at ch. iv. 2. **To open the mouth**, etc., either: the battle-cry calling and exciting them to destroy, or (with Jun.): to open a mouth (breach) in the wall by destroying and piercing it. [Hengst.: "with slaughter," which is virtually contained in the slaughter-cry. Häv.: here, the cry of the besiegers according to its intention, afterwards according to its outward expression.] As the siege is the thing in question, the expression: **rams**, is repeated, with special reference to the **gates**. As to the rest, comp. at ch. iv. 2 (xvii. 17).—Ver. 28. While the oracle determines the Chaldeans to proceed in this way, that which the prophet proclaims on the point is, to the Jews, as a **lying divination in their eyes**, inasmuch as they rely on the visible fact that Jerusalem still stands before their eyes.—שְׁבֻעֵי, שְׁבֻעוֹת, apposition clause: "who have sworn oaths" (Gesen.), and these for themselves (לָהֶם). And this circumstance, owing to their consciousness of infidelity towards the king of Babylon (comp. ch. xvii.), must make the near approach of his unlingering vengeance in the highest degree probable. The latter (**and he remembers**) therefore assists their faithless memory in an active way (עָוֺן, ch. xviii. 30), so that they are taken and crushed by punishment (ch. xiv. 5). [Other interpretations:—Kimchi: Because the Chaldeans had sworn oaths to them (or: the Chaldeans were to them, as the oath of oaths, the most sacred oath), they were bound by oath to them, so that Nebuchadnezzar must first remember their treachery against him. Cocc. refers לָהֶם in both cases to the Babylonians, to whom the oracle appeared delusive, because they remembered the strength of Jerusalem and the fate of Sennacherib; whereupon the Chaldean divines made repeated protestations, and some one then called to mind the guilt of the Jews, who, having fallen away from their God, were given into the hand of the king of Babylon. There is a whole story on the subject, as to which see Targ., Rashi,—namely, that Nebuchadnezzar inquired at the oracle forty-nine times, and always received the answer, Besiege Jerusalem. (Similarly Eich., Schn.) Häv.: "Oaths of oaths are to them," namely, from God; so that the Jews relied on God's most holy promises, which were assured to them (!). To which, however, the sin of Judah stood in opposition, which Jehovah, as her husband, would bring to remembrance (Num. v. 15). Hengst.'s view, who translates similarly, is at all events better: "that which was sworn to them by oath," so that "the sworn of the oaths" is the announcement of destruction, sworn to them by oath ("as truly as I live") in various ways, which they repelled as a delusion, while the prophet, behind whom the Almighty stands, makes known to them anew His irrevocable decree. "In this way Judah brings to remembrance (ver. 29) the iniquity, which it was its duty to atone for by sincere repentance." Umbr.: But the inhabitants of the city live on in blind confidence, in spite of the most sacred protestations of God, etc. Yet Jehovah brings guilt to remembrance, so that Jerusalem shall at last be overtaken by punishment. Ewald: "They thought they should have weeks upon weeks," while He (as their adversary—God) "recalls the (their) guilt (faithlessness towards Him), as a sufficient cause for allowing them to be besieged and taken."]—Ver. 29. It seems most appropriate to the previous context to regard them as brought to remembrance, and thus everything else stands in close connection with that fact.—Ch. xvi. 57.—Ch. xx. 43.—Ewald: "Because ye come to remembrance, ye shall be taken by the hand." Phillips.: "Because He hath brought sin to your remembrance, since, etc., because they are brought to your remembrance, ye shall be taken by His hand." Rosenm.: Because ye are remembered—before Me.—בַּכַּף is equivalent to: violently (ch. xii. 13, xix. 4). Usually it is understood of the minister of divine vengeance (HENGST.). — Nebuchadnezzar, with reference to ver. 16.—Ver. 29 in connection with ver. 28 forms the transition—the introduction to the following paragraph.

Vers. 30–32 [25–27]. *The Prince of Israel.*

ADDITIONAL NOTE.

["By a lively and energetic turn in the discourse, the prophet passes from the people at large to address himself immediately to Zedekiah, and styles him not only wicked, but also pierced through, although, it is well known, he was not actually slain in the calamities that ensued. But it is not exactly what was to be done by the external sword of the Babylonians that comes here into view; it is the execution of the Lord's judgment, under the same form and aspect of severity as that which had been presented in the former part of the vision—the terrors of His drawn sword. The sword is but an image of the judgment itself, precisely as the devouring fire had been in the vision immediately preceding; and it is not the less true that Zedekiah fell under its powerful stroke, though he personally survived the catastrophe. Driven ignominiously from his throne, doomed to see his family slain before his eyes, to have these eyes themselves put out, and to be led as a miserable and helpless captive in chains to Babylon, he might with the most perfect propriety be regarded as the grand victim of the Lord's sword — already, in a manner, pierced through with it; for, to the strongly idealistic spirit of the prophet, the wickedness and the sword, the sin and its punishment, appear inseparably connected together. The overthrow to which he was destined seemed to the prophet's eye at once so inevitable and so near, that he could speak of it no otherwise than as a thing already in existence.

"But it was to be no merely personal loss and degradation; the overthrow to be accomplished on Zedekiah was to draw along with it the complete subversion of the present state of things. Therefore, while the prophet represents the day of visitation as coming upon him, he also speaks of it as being at the time when sin generally had reached its consummation, and the completeness of the guilt was to have its parallel in the complete and terminal character of the judgment. All must now be made desolate; the mitre of the high priest (the emblem of his official dignity and honour, as the representative of a consecrated and priestly people), as well as the crown of the king, was to be put away, and everything turned upside down. Such a convulsed and disorganized state of things was approaching, that, as it is said, 'this should no longer be this;' in other words, nothing should be allowed to remain what it had been, it should be another thing than formerly; as is presently explained in what follows: 'The low is exalted and the high is brought down,'—a general revolution, in which the *outward* relations of things should be made to change places, in just retaliation upon the people for having so grossly perverted the *moral* relations of things. Yet the agents and participators in these revolutions are warned not to expect any settled condition to come out of them; 'this also,' it is said, 'shall not be,' it shall not attain to permanence and security; and so, overthrow is to follow overthrow; 'nowhere shall there be rest, nowhere security; all things shall be in a state of fluctuation, until the appearing of the great Restorer and Prince of Peace.'"—FAIRBAIRN'S *Ezekiel*, pp. 242, 243.—W. F.]

Ver. 30. One is specially singled out and apostrophized (comp. ver. 19).—חָלָל is not: "profane," or "sacrilegious," as רָשָׁע (we recall the contrast to צַדִּיק in ch. iii. 18) stands beside it. The Chaldee gives: "worthy of death."—Comp. at ch. xii. 10.—The **day** is the time of judgment, of punishment, of overthrow (1 Sam. xxvi. 10; Ps. xxxvii. 13; Job xviii. 20).—**The time of the iniquity of the end** (ch. vii. 2) is when iniquity (breach of oaths) brings the end (generally). [SCHN., COCC.: The end-guilt as the last and utmost.] In what sense the end is to be taken, how far Zedekiah's guilt, who is therefore the subject of address, brings it about, Ver. 31 shows.—The infinitive denotes the mere action, without stating from whom it proceeds (HENGST.), more expressively than the imperative מִצְנֶפֶת, from צָנַף (Isa. xxii. 18: "enwrap"), denotes in the Pentateuch (11 times) the head-band (turban) of the high-priest. As עֲטָרָה, from עָטַר (to surround), denotes the royal crown, and thus stands for the kingdom in contradistinction to the high-priesthood, so הָרִים (from רום) could also be taken in as absolute contradistinction to הָסִיר,—as Hitzig interrogatively renders it: "lift," "raise," or "maintain in elevation." But that the kingly dignity should remain untouched, cannot, in the light of the context, be a matter of uncertainty, and even in Hitzig's opinion Jehovah's negative to such a question is undoubted. צְנוֹף מְלוּכָה, in Isa. lxii. 3, combines the royal and priestly, not merely in a figurative sense, but on the ground of Ex. xix. 6. Besides, Ezekiel is speaking of the end as a whole, not of the subversion of the kingdom merely; although it comes to pass specially by means of the iniquity of the king who is apostrophized, and **the judgment** (ver. 32) points to the priesthood as well as the royalty. Thus nothing remains but to interpret הָרִים as synonymous with הָסִיר, even without a מִיִּשְׂרָאֵל, which can be easily supplied from the context (Zedekiah is expressly designated "Prince of Israel" in ver. 30). Consequently, "sentence of death is pronounced on the theocracy," according to its existing form, which the history of the people subsequent to the exile confirms. Comp. Keil on the passage. [COCC. takes both as designating the kingdom as a whole, not merely Zedekiah's; and then understands the following as referring to the elevation of the Asmonæans, whose crown, however, would not be the Messianic one promised. In reference to this latter, Ewald remarks: "This corrupt earthly kingdom is not this Messianic kingdom which is to come."]—זֹאת לֹא־זֹאת (neuter) indicates, according to most interpreters, the complete subversion of the existing state of things (ver. 32), so that the low is to be elevated, and the lofty made low, as ver. 32 shows, by Jehovah. Israel having abased herself by sin, God thoroughly abases her by punishment. Häv. takes הַשְּׁפָלָה — ה as: "turned towards the low," a *constructio prægnans*, betokening the condescension of God. Compare at ch. xvii. 24. Then 'זֹאת would be understood thus: This (what has just been brought low) is not this, namely, what it should be (according to its ideal), but a "not this." And with this is connected elevation (ch. xvii. 24), namely, through the Messiah, as is seen in what follows; whereupon the bringing low of the high, which is more forcibly depicted in ver. 32, returns again to the existing condition of things under Zedekiah; and "this also," merely recapitulating = Yea, this cast-down priesthood and royalty is not (namely, according to ver. 31) what it should be, and thus in reality is not, and this condition endures till its elevation in the Coming One (**till**, ideal terminus, like Gen. xlix. 10).—Ver. 32. The thrice-repeated **overturn** (found here only) accords with the well-known symbolism of the divine. Usually taken as emphatic, to denote total destruction. [According to Abarbanel, it refers to the three last kings, Jehoiakim, Jehoiachin, and Zedekiah; according to others, to the three destructions—the Babylonish, the Greek under Antiochus, and the Roman.] Comp. Isa. xxiv.—שָׂמְתִּנָּה goes back on זֹאת, or means the land (?).—According to most, **this also** indicates an additional overthrow; it is more natural to regard it as betokening the present overthrow. הָיָה, masculine, being construed with it, shows זֹאת to be neuter. But this inverted state of things is not to be for ever. עַד, according to its root-signification, includes the future, so that the Person in question brings to an end the overthrow, or the abasement to "nothing," since He completes it, .e. makes it complete in form; but at the same time, through realization of the idea in the "overthrown" or "brought low," effects the fulfilment.—The **judgment** is God's, Deut. i. 17, therefore here also Jehovah gives it. The expression speaks of a re-establishment of "the judgment" by means which include chastisement; it embraces the royal and priestly office (Ex. xxviii. 29; 1 Kings iii. 9 sq.). Comp. besides, Gen. xlix. 10; Ps. lxxii. 1; Isa. ix. 6, xlii. 1; Jer. xxiii. 5, xxxiii. 17; John v. 22; Acts vii. 14.

ADDITIONAL NOTE ON VER. 32.

["We can have no hesitation in understanding by this person the Messiah, whether we translate, 'Till he comes to whom the right is,' or, 'Till he comes to whom the judgment belongs;' 'and I give it to him.' It is not expressly said what was to be given him, and should stand waiting for its proper possessor till he should come; but the context plainly forbids us to understand anything less than what was taken away—the things represented by the priestly mitre and the royal crown. The true priestly dignity, and the proper regal glory, were to be gone for a time into abeyance; some partial, temporary, and fluctuating possession of them might be regained, but nothing more; the adequate and permanent realization was only to be found in the person of Messiah, because in Him alone was there to be a fitting representation of the divine righteousness. It is true there was something like a restoration of the standing and honour of the priesthood after the return from the Babylonish exile; and if the ideas currently entertained upon the subject were correct, there might appear in that a failure of the prophecy. But there was no right restoration of the priestly, any more than of the regal dignity at the time specified; it was but a shadow of the original glory. For there was no longer the distinctive prerogative of the Urim and Thummim, nor the ark of the covenant, nor the glory overshadowing the mercy-seat; all was in a depressed and mutilated condition, and even that subject to many interferences from the encroachments of foreign powers. So much only was given, both in respect to the priesthood and the kingdom, as to show that the Lord had not forsaken His people, and to serve as pledge of the coming glory. But it was to the still-prospective, rather than the present state of things, that the eye of faith was directed to look for the proper restoration. And lest any should expect otherwise, the prophet Zechariah, after the return from Babylon, took up the matter, as it were, where Ezekiel had left it, and intimated in the plainest manner, that what was then accomplished was scarcely worth taking into account; it was, at the most, but doing in a figure what could only find its real accomplishment in the person and work of Messiah. Especially at chap. vi. 14: 'And he (the branch) shall build the temple of the Lord, and he shall bear the glory; and shall sit and rule upon his throne, and he shall be a priest upon his throne.' Thus the mitre and the crown were both to meet in him, and the temple in its noblest sense be built, and the glory be obtained, such as it became the Lord's Anointed to possess. Meanwhile all was but preparatory and imperfect."—FAIRBAIRN'S *Ezekiel*, pp. 244, 245.—W. F.]

Vers. 33–37 [28–32]. *Against Ammon.*

As the prince of Israel had his counterpart in the Messiah, so the declaration "against Jerusalem" in vers. 21–24 sq. finds its counterpart in this paragraph; hence also the analogous expressions.—Ver. 33. **Reproach** is injuring by words: directly,—reviling; or indirectly,—self-glorification. Thereby the mention made of the Ammonites is illustrated. When Babylon first of all inflicted punishment on Jerusalem, Ammon took occasion to boast over the besieged (ch. xxv. 3, 6; Zeph. ii. 8; Lam. i. 2, iii. 61), and to applaud the conquerors. Ammon's self-exaltation had exhibited itself practically by their seizing a portion of the trans-Jordanic territory of the former kingdom of Israel (Jer. xlix. 1 sq.).—Comp. vers. 14, 19, 15, 20. לְהָכִיל, according to Gesen., for הַאֲכִיל (from אָכַל), *to cause to consume* (?). Others; from כּוּל, *holding, containing* (ch. xxiii. 32); almost adverbially: *as much as possible*, or (יָכֹל) *as much as can be.* HENGST.: *abundantly.* HITZIG: *to dazzle;* properly: *to make the eyes dull of vision.* (Oxymoron.)—That it may glitter, ver. 15.—Ver. 34. בְּ, equivalent to: "notwithstanding that," and to be taken as parenthetic. Even in Ammon, therefore, false prophets and false confidence! Ch. xiii. 6, vii. 9; Jer. xxvii. 9, 10

KLIEF.: The oracles of Nebuchadnezzar, ver. 26, while they pointed to Jerusalem, showed Ammon false. See Keil in opposition to this notion.—לְתֵת, HITZ.: the occasion of the sword's being placed (reading אֹתָהּ) on the necks. (Of the pierced-through? Wherefore this again?) Others: that I may lay thee; or: that one (the enemy) may lay thee; or, as Ewald (*History of the People of Israel*): as it is falsely prophesied to thee that thou shalt be laid on the necks of the Jews to destroy them, I will return thee to thy sheath,—namely, the sword of the Ammonites which is addressed. It depends rather on the foregoing verse: The **pierced-through of the wicked**—from among the Jews; comp. vers. 30, 19. They have received the death-blow of the sword on their necks, which are brought into prominence for the sake of pictorial description. Thus Ammon is judged like the prostrate Judah, which it mocked. Comp. ver. 30.—Ver. 35. Address to Ammon. The sword, which is to be supplied, is not mentioned, because it does not come into account in contrast to the sword of God's vengeance against Ammon. The gender (הָשַׁב, with Patach, masc. imper.) alternates with feminines, the sword-bearing men with the nation as a feminine idea. [Ewald, infin. absol. as in ver. 31.] Therefore all resistance is vain. (Matt. xxvi. 52!) It receives its sentence from Jehovah,—its end where it originated. Comp. Joseph. *Antiq.* x. 9. 7.—Ch. xvi. 3.—Ch. xi. 10. [Should one, with Jerome, in ver. 35 (Rashi, ver. 34) regard the Babylonians as the persons addressed, so that with the: "against Ammon," an: "against Babylon" is joined, but which from intelligible reasons is simply implied, then ver. 10 would not be opposed to this view. A separation of Jehovah's sword from that of Babylon, which as such scarcely comes still into account, especially in reference to that which follows, has nothing inconceivable in it; and since Jehovah judges Babylon, His sword would remain drawn. The scabbard does not therefore require to be understood as meaning the land, but the meaning would be, that after the completion of the judgment against both Jerusalem and Ammon, by means of war, Babylon's sword should be sheathed, and should await the judgment of God in its own land. The execution of it by the Persians would be characteristically depicted in the following verses, while in relation to Ammon the statement seems rather strong; and the supposition of Häv. that Ammon represents heathenism generally, or, according to Hengst., "the world-power hostile to the kingdom of God," is very suggestive of perplexity.]—Ver. 36. שָׁפַךְ (ch. xiv. 19) makes a *paronomasia* with שְׁפָט, immediately before. עֶבְרָה, "outpouring;" hence used of wrath as poured out. בְּ may also be translated by: **blow upon**, as, when fire is blown upon or against any one, the fire itself is blown on. Hitzig, however: "with the fire of My fury I will breathe upon thee." In the end the subject passes over from the sword to the fire, as in the beginning, from the fire to the sword. **Consuming men** are those who prepare this fire; HENGST.: "burning men are those who are filled with glowing anger." [In the explanation which points to the Persians, an allusion to their fire-worship!] HÄV.: fierce, cruel; GESEN.: foolish, brutish, Ps. xciv. 8. So also Hitzig, in relation to the language of the Chaldeans, which was unintelligible (stupid) to the Ammonites.—Ver. 37. Ch. xv. 4, 6.—**Thy blood,** etc., in which the figures of fire and sword are unified,—**in the midst of the land**, as in ver. 35: "in the place," etc., "in the land," etc. It will fall on them in their homes, so that weapons of defence shall be of no service. Contrast to a war of offence. Others: "flowing everywhere in the land" (?). Ewald: "Thy blood shall remain in the midst of the earth, and thou shalt not be made mention of."—HENGST.: "From the times of the Maccabees, the Ammonites and the Moabites have quite disappeared from history." Their subversion is complete, while Israel has still something to look forward to.

THEOLOGICAL REMARKS.

1. The bitterest and most painful plaint finds expression in poetry. A truly spiritual grief and the poetic form readily combine. This is the psychological truth of the chapter. The unusual forms of expression, the rapid transitions, and the idiomatic difficulties which this chapter presents, are accounted for by its poetic construction. This subjective-logical, abrupt-dithyrambic text has been marred by a Philistine criticism which tramples on psychology and æsthetics.

2. Fire and sword are the two figures in which divine judgment clothes itself. The latter is, however, more than a picture, if the significance of war in the history of the kingdom of God among men is not overlooked.

3. Every judgment of God keeps in view the establishment of the right on earth, and is unimaginable apart from grace and mercy.

4. It is to be noted as to the Jewish kingdom, now ripe for destruction, that it "despised every tree;" whether that means that which was subject to it, or mankind generally. It thus became inhuman, lost sight of Israel's essential relation to humanity, and became faithless to the fundamental significance of the people of God.

5*a*. Justice will be done to the text by regarding the manifold Chaldaic divination as nothing more than a highly dramatic representation of the idea of Providence. Hävernick, indeed, since he makes the agreement of soothsaying and prophecy—brought about, of course, by divine guidance—subservient to the carrying out of God's will, goes still farther; so far, indeed, as to maintain that there is in Ezekiel, notwithstanding his "otherwise markedly Levitical character," "a decided recognition of divination." He finds the occasion in the exile-period, when "Hebraism was so remarkably tinctured with the soothsaying of heathenism;" as appears also in Daniel, etc.

5*b*. ["What a sublime proof of the overruling providence and controlling agency of Jehovah! The mightiest monarch of the world, travelling at the head of almost unnumbered legions, and himself consciously owning no other direction than that furnished by the instruments of his own blind superstition, yet having his path marked out to him beforehand by this servant of the living God! How strikingly did it show that the greatest potentates on earth, and even the spiritual wickedness in high places, have their bounds appointed to them by the hand of God, and that however majestically they may seem to conduct themselves, still they cannot overstep the prescribed limits, and must be kept in all their operations subservient to the higher purposes of Heaven!"—P. F.—W. F.]

6. In his oft-cited work, *The Prophets and their Prophecies*, Tholuck calls attention to the distinction between "subordinate" divination, which, "resting upon a natural substratum, divines the future from this" (interpreters of oracles, diviners, augurs, *haruspices*), and the "higher" method of the "revealer of the future who is immediately impelled by God" (Divination, Prophecy). PLUTARCH, *Vita Homeri*, ch. 212; CICERO, *De Divin.* i. 18. After giving a sketch of the views of the fathers, Tholuck comes to the conclusion: "Whatever we may ascribe to the agency of priestly fraud and superstitious self-deception, it is now universally acknowledged by philologists, and investigators into antiquity, that at the foundation there was a reality." He then refers more particularly to the insight gained, since the end of last century, into a middle territory between the divine and the non-divine agencies of divination (the phenomena of magnetism and somnambulism, which are ranked by medical men and philosophers as physiological and psychological facts).

7. "There is a natural divination," says Beck, "inasmuch as the course of the world developes itself according to certain original and standing fundamental laws in exact regularity, which we are taught by our conscience to regard as the moral order of the world. As, by means of a definite consciousness of this standing divine order, conscience often gives a man, in relation to his own doing and suffering, very clear indications of his own future; so a living and vigorously aroused conscience can lead him to a perception of how the past and present must have come about in virtue of that moral order, and partly of what must farther emerge from it. Where, however, this prophetic conscience is intensified by especially profound experiences, or earnest investigation of history, the moral connection between past, present, and future may often become clear even to the smallest details. But this divination extends only to the world-bond already existing under the universal government of God, and to the historical bond regulated and limited by internal and eternal moral laws. Into new determinations of the course of the world, which first became manifest by special governmental acts of God which reveal them,—the proper divine order and development of the kingdom,—mere divination cannot penetrate, for it is destitute of the necessary preliminary conditions."

8. As to the relations between divination and prophecy, see Tholuck in the treatise referred to, § 8, and Herzog's *Realencycl.* xvii. p. 641 sq. In regard to the substance of the matter, the difference proves itself to be, that while, at most, room is made for the former by the providence of God as the principle of world-government, redemption, *i.e.* Christ's redemption, lifts the latter to its post of elevation. Then also divination must always be estimated in relation to the physical region in which it moves, and according to whose laws it is excited; while prophecy finds its sphere not only in the soul, but also in the spiritual life, and, though dealing in some measure with individual, national, human interests, ever stretches beyond to eternal truth as the object of its supreme interest.

9. It is to be observed that the Davidic king, by whose means the ruin of Israel is brought about, on the other hand also serves here as a medium for the Messiah. Not only did David's family furnish in point of fact the last "prince (king) of Israel," but the idea of an everlasting royalty in Israel was bound up by God's promises with David's house. The contrast between sin and grace, despair of all and hope for all, death and resurrection, is concentrated in the last representative of David's family. It is peculiar to our prophet to have so strongly emphasized this contrast, vers. 30–32.

10. Israel ought to have been a kingdom of priests to Jehovah. As Israel fell away from this position with the fall of the priesthood and the kingdom, so on the other hand, with the renewed bestowal of priesthood and royalty in the Messiah, Israel is also reinstated in Him as that which it ought to be, 1 Pet. ii. 9, 10.

11. The high-priesthood, indeed, still continued after the exile. But in that period it fared with the priesthood as with the temple. "Both," says Häv., "bound together in the closest way by divine arrangement, fell short of that which they had been before the exile. There was only a shadow of the ancient glory, as the temple was only a provisional one for an abnormal state of things. This was outwardly apparent, for there was no ark of the covenant in the temple, and the high priest was denied the right of consulting by Urim and Thummim, Ezra ii. 63. As, then, the high-priesthood was totally in abeyance so far as the exiles were concerned, and as after the exile only its shadow was provisionally set up, so in the eye of prophecy the exile and the appearance of the Messiah are closely connected facts."

12. As to the kingdom, Zerubbabel, the leader of the people after the exile, although of David's line, was no king on David's throne. But Herod, who becomes king over Israel, is of Edomite origin.

13. "In the remarkable passage of the *Tract. Sota*, p. 1069, ed. Wagenseil, it is said: The Urim and Thummim, and the king from David's stem, had ceased with the destruction, and their restoration is to be expected only when the dead are raised up, and the Messiah, David's Son, appears" (HÄV.).

14. The old versions, with great unanimity, have made use of the Messianic passage here in Ezekiel for the explanation of "Shiloh," Gen. xlix. 18. Hengst. complains, in his *Christology*, that instead of an allusion, they have mostly assumed an explanation; to him the relation of Ezekiel to the passage in question seems unrecognisable. But while the prophet supplements Gen. xlix. from Ps. lxxii. 1–5, where righteousness and judgment are the basis of the peace introduced by the Messiah, we do not find in Ezekiel that which we might expect,—to whom the "peace," but "to whom the judgment," belongs. In Ezekiel, however, the peace is also in the background, for the advent of Him whose is the judgment makes an end of destruction. That dangers would threaten the sceptre of Judah before the coming of Shiloh, even Jacob intimated by the stress which he put on: it "shall not depart

from Judah till," etc. Kurtz, however, in his *History of the Old Covenant* (vol. ii. pp. 87, 88, Clark's Trans.), maintains too much when he asserts that the two passages are entirely different. The completion of the glory of Judah is here, as there, kept in view, and in both cases in a Messianic sense. The distinction is, that what concerns Judah as Judah is taken ideally in Gen. xlix., and really in Ezekiel. Therefore, here a temporary "is not," and there a (definitive) "not depart."

15. Obscurity, ambiguity, and difficulty of interpretation are characteristic of the Messianic prophecies. Comp. 1 Pet. i. 10, 11.

HOMILETIC HINTS.

Ver. 1 sq. [xx. 45 sq.] The sentence of burning; the Judge who pronounces it; the avenger who executes it; the judgment whereby it is accomplished.—The forest in the south—a picture, a history, an example.—"In nature descends now a gentle, now a dashing rain-shower" (ST.).—"The word of God is rightly likened to rain. Like rain, it descends from above, and not according to man's will; it is also, like it, useful and beneficial; as rain flows down from rocks upon the fields, so the word of God upon the godless, and, on the other hand, into pious hearts; and, like the rain, it is not equally acceptable to all," etc. (FESSEL.)—"That which is bitter to the mouth is wholesome to the heart. The word of God, even when it is sharper than a two-edged sword, is like the quickening rain" (HENGST.).—Ver. 3 [xx. 47]. A wood bends beneath the storm of the Almighty, and rustles while it waves; but we men harden ourselves more and more.—"God will turn us from the instruments whom He employs against us to Himself, that we may learn whom we have sinned against, and by whom therefore we are punished" (ST.).—The tree, which in spite of everything is unfruitful, is ripe for the fire.—"When the green tree does not stand, how will it go with the dry?" (STCK.)—The fire which is not quenched.—Ver. 4 [xx. 48]. "If we see that all human plans and devices, even the most promising, come to nothing, we are led to the confession that we have to do with personal Omnipotence and Righteousness, against which the battle is unavailing" (HENGST.).—Contemplation of the judgment of God.—God's judgments permit no malicious or even idle spectators.—Knowledge of the holy and righteous God from His judgments in this world.—Ver. 5. "The godless never want for excuses: if one preaches by analogies, it is too dark; if by plain statements, it is too simple, blundering, etc., 1 Kings xxii. 15" (CR.).—"The world cries out against preachers who touch their conscience; that which is hateful to the world, many are ashamed to confess" (SCHM.).—"The sighing of preachers over their hearers."—The bad style of criticism of preaching.—"Nothing remains but to flee to Him by whom they were sent to preach" (STCK.).—How do so many sermons meet such opposition?—The fault is the hearer's. Thus many a sermon is a judgment to many people.—"The disciples, Luke viii., asked, 'What might this parable be?'" (STCK.)

Ver. 6 sq. [ver. 1 sq.] The sword-word over Judah—a word of God, and a word of destruction.—"Jerusalem," the address of a sword, and what a sword!—Ver. 7 [2]. Thither the Jews turned their face when they prayed in war or in a foreign land, 1 Kings viii. 44, 48 (B. B.).—Ver. 8 sq. [3 sq.] "In national chastisements the pious suffer along with others" (ST.).—But there is a difference even when the suffering is outwardly the same.—"All men are, besides, unrighteous of themselves, and according to their nature have deserved nothing better than the godless. But during judgments they separate from the fellowship of the wicked, from which they may not before have held themselves sufficiently aloof" (L.).—The sword is God's. God is in the swords, although men bear them.—"Let us learn to judge rightly of war. God oversees it from beginning to end" (L.).—"The sheath in which God's sword is put is His forbearance" (THEODORET).—"Man's sword we may escape, but not God's" (STCK.).—The axe was even then laid unto the root of the trees. The sword of the Romans at last followed that of the Chaldeans.—"So it proceeds till the last Antichrist and his desolation" (B. B.).—Ver. 11 sq. [6 sq.] "The judgments which hang over the wicked world are so dreadful, that a believer may well sigh over them, Dan. ix. 4 sq." (ST.)—"A preacher who wishes to move and teach others must himself feel similar emotions" (CR.).—The sighing of the servant of God over that which men can and yet will not hear, and over that which they will require to hear and see.—He who will not hear must feel.—"Just as we, when we read that the Saviour wept over Jerusalem, lightly ask why He wept" (RICHT.).—"How insolent and confident the godless are in prosperity; in adversity they are equally faint-hearted and desolate! Then they are in terror of a falling leaf; much more of a destroying sword" (L.).—"Ah, it is not good when God's witnesses merely weep in secret (Jer. xiii. 17); much more when God's messengers and angels of peace weep bitterly (Isa. xxxiii. 7), and are obliged to fulfil their office with sighing (Heb. xiii. 7), because it is too much for them; and usually there follows thereupon a mighty outpouring of wrath" (B. B.).

Ver. 13 sq. [8 sq.] The sacred, terrible sword-song. See Körner's *Song of the Sword*.—The prophets doubtless treated politics both on their outward and inward side, but only the politics of the kingdom of God.—Ver. 14 [9]. "God shows us the sword, and waves it over our heads, so that we should be timeously and profitably alarmed" (STCK.).—"God can use every creature as His sword; it is always prepared to execute His command" (ST.).—"War as a divine judgment, therefore for the punishment of evil-doers; but it is also a preaching of repentance, when God sharpens the sword and makes it glitter" (L.).—"He who will not submit to the sword of God's word (Heb. iv. 12) will be overtaken by the sword of the enemy" (STCK.).—Ver. 15 [10]. God Himself takes the offering which men will not give Him voluntarily. The personal offering—the free and the constrained.—"He fares as a brute who lives brutishly, Ps. xlix. Wickedly have I lived, wickedly died, shall be the epitaph of the godless" (STCK.).—There can be joy amid the deepest suffering, but not over another's suffering, especially when it is punishment for sin.—"But they obey God only who are obliged to slay such offerings for Him" (L.).—Ver. 16 [11]. "The executioner with whole armies" (B. B.).—The sin of the people presses the sword into the hand for war.—Sin was also interwoven with the conquering chaplets of the victors, as the dew upon these chaplets was innumerable tears and drops of blood.—Which is ever to be remembered amid songs of triumph!—Fortune of war, as men call it, what a sad fortune!—God is the judge, behind and in the conqueror.—Ver. 17 [12]. Like people, like prince, the sorrow of the prophets.—"Even the great have no privilege to sin" (B. B.).—"Pain, but not murmuring" (STCK.).—Ver. 18 [13]. "Trial is a terrible word to a people that suffers the deepest calamities. When the trial comes, nothing remains undisclosed, nothing unrequited; every varnish disappears, and all glitter vanishes" (HENGST.).—A tried sword is a dreadful thing when it turns against a people whom God has given up to judgment.—If a king or a people should never have regarded men, they must regard the man who bears God's sword.—One day an end will be made of all despisers of God and man.—A kingdom's, inhumanity its death-sentence. God relieves men from the sceptre of tyrants. Rehoboam had formerly despised Israel, 1 Kings xii.; Zedekiah regarded neither God nor Nebuchadnezzar in his perjury; Judah had long lightly esteemed God's prophets.—Ver. 19 [14]. The history of the world as the fulfilment of prophecy.—Symbolical prophecy.—The emblems of punishment.—Some must prophesy judgment who would so willingly speak of redemption, and redemption alone; men will not have the blessing, and therefore the curse must be exhibited.—"Where sin is doubled, there also is punishment doubled" (STCK.).—God's sword draws not back from human elevation; it reaches the dwellers in the valley, and those also who sit on lofty seats.—No earthly throne is a protection from the sword of God; the history of the world is filled with proofs of this.—The last mighty pierced-through one is Antichrist.—"Alas, who can hide from the wrath of God!" (B. B.)—Ver. 20 sq. [15 sq.] Every heart melts under judgment, why not under God's mercy?—God is always as a stumbling-block to the ungodly. How terrible is judgment in times of peace, but how much worse in times of war! With the severer judgments of God, the ungodliness of the sinner comes wholly to light.—Walls are no defence to sinners, when God is not their defence.—The terror of a servant at the judgment which will certainly overtake the world.—The troubled heart of those who proclaim peace, and say, Be ye reconciled to God!—Those whom nothing amazes will at last be amazed by God's judgment.—God's sword on all sides.—"Mountains fall on us," etc., Luke xxiii. 30; Rev. vi. 15 sq.—"God has still a king of Babylon, who shall destroy the false Jerusalem" (B. B.).—Ver. 22. The fearful hands of God, Heb. x. 31.

Ver. 23 sq. [18 sq.] The ways of the sword of God. Its manifestation.—God knows how to find sinners.—Just as Ezekiel sketched to the Jews, as if with chalk on the table, that which was to happen to them.—Everything proceeds according to the divine will, whether we will it or not. When God judges, everything becomes a finger-post to the avengers whom He sends. On many a life-way the finger-post which will direct punishment is already erected.—Ver. 25 [20]. "By God's arrangement, judgment shall begin at the house of God" (HENGST.).—"Let us not reckon ourselves guiltless when others are found guilty! God spares us still in His long-suffering" (STCK.).—Sins scale the best fortified cities.—Ver. 26 [21]. Prophecy and divination in their resemblance and difference.—Divination under the omnipotence and wisdom of God, as to which comp. Matt. ii.—The Egyptian enchanters and the Chaldean magi in their significance for the kingdom of God.—Ver. 27 [22]. To-day, Jerusalem; to-morrow, thou!—"God makes use even of divination for prophesying, but in doubtful circumstances we should apply to Him; His word will direct us and divine for us" (STCK., ST.).—"Unbelief is punished in the Ammonites, ver. 34" (RICHT.).—Ver. 28 [23]. "Unbelievers always believe that they are far from judgment" (STCK.).—His own evil conscience, and not merely the judgment of God which bursts upon him, ought to lead the unbeliever to belief,—at least that a righteous God lives, and will not be mocked.—"The nearer God's judgments, the more callous the ungodly are wont to become" (STCK.).—Ver. 29 [24]. "Their own sins cry out against the ungodly, and call for God's vengeance, Gen. iv. 10" (ST.).

Ver. 30 [25]. "Thus God gives various titles; comp. Ps. lxxxii. 6" (W.).—"The ungodly is already judged; a couple of years' respite, which are still left to him, are not accounted of. Before the eye of faith, the sinner, who is still in reality set on high, lies already in his blood" (HENGST.).—"From whom He will, God can take away, and on whom He will, bestow kingdoms, Dan. iv. 29. Therefore stand in awe of this great Lord, ye princes of the people, and serve Him with trembling in the presence of His holy majesty, Ps. ii. 10, 11" (TÜB. BIB.).—"Unrepentant wickedness, which has been often warned and chastised, which has witnessed many examples of judgment, and been long borne with, is the iniquity of the end" (B. B.).—Ver. 31 [26]. "In the kingdom of God there are no promises, but such as resemble those streams which alternately flow above and under ground, as surely as all the bearers of the promises are infected with sin" (HENGST.).—The lifting up of Jehoiachin, the casting down of Zedekiah.—"Of this Mary also sang, Luke i. 52" (STCK.).—"David's line proceeds through Zerubbabel to Christ" (L.).—Ver. 32 [27]. The royal sinner, and the royal Saviour.—Since royalty and priesthood shall both be given to Him (Ps. cx.), these can only be spoken of spiritually, as in this sense they pertained to the Anointed with the Spirit. His kingdom was not of this world; and the Epistle to the Hebrews is to be read in reference to His high-priesthood.

Ver. 33 sq. [28 sq.] There are doubtless race-types, prophetic national physiognomies.—In Ammon there are the manner of Edom and the mocking of Ishmael.—To defer is not to revoke.—Ammon's mocking of Israel was at the same time a deriding of its true and future King; in other words, of Jehovah and His Anointed, Ps. ii.—Jerusalem's punishment should be traced back, not to God's impotence to defend them, but to His righteousness, which Ammon also is to experience.—The judgment of sinners never happens for the self-justification of other sinners.—Ver. 34 [29]. Divination, looking beyond sin and the righteousness of God, is at all times false and deceptive.—But men prefer lies to truth; for the lie flatters, while truth does not spare. We love the joys of the present, and therefore we hate the painfulness of truth.—"Divine punishment has a day, which is not deferred when the measure is full" (W.).—False doctrine is punished as well as an evil life. —Ver. 35 [30]. The place of the sin is often also the place of punishment; but God knows how to find the guilty everywhere. How can our sweet home become so bitter? Thy own heart is thy judgment.—We all have our sentence of death in Adam.—Besides, it also comes to Babylon's turn. For the sword continues to be God's, although it glittered for a while in Babylon's hand.—Ver. 36 [31]. How consoling to die in the Lord! How dreadful to be destroyed by God!—The world, men, one's own heart, can becom a hell.—Let me not fall into the hands of men!—The wicked the executioners of the wicked.—Ver. 37. The memory of the righteous is blessed, and endures, but the name of the ungodly perishes. "Well for him who obtains a new name from God, Prov. x. 7; Rev. iii. 12" (St.).—God's words of mercy and of judgment are alike sure.

11. *The Conviction of Ripeness for Judgment: (a) Of Jerusalem's in particular* (ch. xxii.); *(b) and of Judah's and Israel's as a whole* (ch. xxiii.).

(a) Jerusalem ripe for Judgment (ch. xxii.).

1, 2 And the word of Jehovah came to me, saying, And thou, son of man, wilt
thou judge? Wilt thou judge the city of blood [blood-shedding]? Then make
3 her to know all her abominations. And say, Thus saith the Lord Jehovah,
A city that sheds blood in the midst of it, that her time may come, and has
4 made idols for [over] herself that she may be defiled! In thy blood which
thou hast shed thou hast become guilty, and in thine idols which thou hast
made thou art defiled; and thou hast caused thy days to draw near, and art
come to thy years: therefore have I given thee for a reproach to the heathen,
5 and for a mocking to all lands. Those that are near, and those that are far
from thee, shall mock at thee as one polluted in name, and full of confusion.
6 Behold, the princes of Israel, every one according to his arm, were in thee in
7 order to shed blood! Father and mother they lightly esteemed in thee;
with [in relation to] the stranger they have acted unjustly in the midst of thee;
8 the widow and the orphan they have oppressed in thee. My holy things
9 thou hast despised, and hast profaned My sabbaths. Men of slander have
been in thee to shed blood, and in thee they have eaten upon the mountains;
10 they have committed lewdness in the midst of thee. In thee, one has uncovered
a father's nakedness; in thee they have humbled her that is unclean in
11 her separation. And one has committed abomination with his neighbour's
wife; and another has lewdly defiled his daughter-in-law; and another has
12 humbled [ravished] his sister, his father's daughter, in thee. They have taken
bribes in thee to shed blood; thou hast taken usury and increase, and hast
overreached thy neighbour by extortion, and thou hast forgotten Me: sen-
13 tence of the Lord Jehovah. And, behold, I have smitten My hand at thy
gain which thou hast made, and at thy blood-shedding which was in thy
14 midst. Will thy heart endure [be stedfast]? or will thy hands be strong for
the days when I shall deal with thee? I, Jehovah, have spoken, and will do
15 [have done]. And I will scatter thee among the heathen, and disperse thee
in the countries, and will consume [make to cease] thy filthiness out of thee.
16 And thou shalt be profaned in thee [through thee] before the eyes of the heathen;
17 and thou shalt know that I am Jehovah. And the word of Jehovah came to
18 me, saying, Son of man, the house of Israel has become to Me dross; the
whole of them are brass, and tin, and iron, and lead, in the midst of the
19 furnace; they have become the dross of silver. Therefore, thus saith the Lord
Jehovah, Because ye have all become dross, therefore, behold, I will gather
20 you into the midst of Jerusalem. [As] a gathering together of silver, and
brass, and iron, and lead, and tin, into the midst of the furnace, to blow the
fire upon it that it may be melted, so will I gather you in My anger and in
21 My fury, and I will leave you and melt you. And I will collect you, and will
blow upon you in the fire of My wrath, and ye shall be melted in the midst
22 thereof. As silver is melted in the midst of the furnace, so shall ye be melted
in the midst of it; and ye shall know that I, Jehovah, have poured out My
23, 24 fury upon you. And the word of Jehovah came to me, saying, Son of man

say to her, Thou art a land that is not cleansed, that has no rain in the day
25 of indignation. The conspiracy of her prophets [is] in her midst; like a roar-
ing lion ravening the prey they have devoured souls, taken treasure [property]
and precious things [jewels]; her widows they have multiplied in the midst of
26 her. Her priests have done violence to My law, and profaned My holy things;
they have not distinguished between holy and unholy, nor discerned between
clean and unclean; and they have hidden their eyes from My sabbaths, and I
27 am profaned among them. Her rulers [princes] in the midst of her were like
wolves ravening the prey, to shed blood, to destroy souls, and to make gain.
28 And her prophets have daubed for them with whitewash, seeing vanity and
divining lies for them, saying, Thus saith the Lord Jehovah, when Jehovah
29 hath not spoken. The people of the land have practised oppression, and
committed robbery, and have vexed the poor and needy, and oppressed the
30 stranger against the right. And I sought for a man among them that might
build up a wall, and might stand in the breach [step into the gap] before Me for
31 the land, that I might not destroy it; and I found none. So I poured [pour]
out upon them My indignation, in the fire of My wrath I consumed [consume]
them; I have recompensed [recompense] their way upon their head: sentence
of the Lord Jehovah.

Ver. 3. Sept.: . . . κατ' αὐτης— Vulg.: . . . *contra semetipsam.*

Ver. 4. . . . κ. ἠγαγες καιρον ἐτων σου. (The Oriental Jews, etc. read: עת שנותיך.) Many codices: בגוים.

Ver. 5. . . . πολλη ἐν ταις ἀνομιαις— Vulg.: . . . *sordida, nobilis, grandis interitu.*

Ver. 6. . . . ἑκαστος προς τους συγγενεις αὐτου συνανεφυροντο ἐν σοι—

Ver. 9. . . . 'Ανδρες λησται—

Ver. 11. . . . την νυμφην αὐτου—

Ver. 12. . . . κ. συνετελεσω συντελειαν κακιας σου την ἐν καταδυναστεια σου, ὁτι ἐμου ἐπελαθου—

Ver. 16. κ. κατακληρονομησω ἐν σοι— Vulg.: *possidebo te.*

Ver. 18. . . . ἀναμεμιγμενος χαλκω . . . ἐν μεσω ἀργυριου ἀναμεμιγμενος ἐστιν.

Ver. 19. . . . παντες εἰς συγκρασιν μιαν—

Ver. 24. . . . γη οὐ βρεχομενη, οὐδε ὑετος καταβησεται σοι— Vulg.: *immunda et non compluta—*

Ver. 25. Οἱ ἀφηγουμενοι αὐτης . . . ὡς λεοντες ἐρευγομενοι . . . . ἐδυναστευσαν ἐν δυναστεια, δωρα ἐλαμβανον ἐν ἀδικια— Sept. and Arab. read: אלמנותיך.

Ver. 27. Sept.: Οἱ ἀρχοντες . . . αἱμα, ὁπως—

Ver. 28. . . . πεσουνται—

Ver. 29. Τον λαον . . . ἐκπιεζουντες—

Ver. 30. . . . ἀνδρα ἀναστρεφομενον ὀρθως κ. ἑστωτα . . . το ὁλοσχερες ἐν καιρω της ὀργης μου, του μη εἰς τελος ἐξαλειψαι αὐτην·—

EXEGETICAL REMARKS.

["This chapter stands closely related to the last chapter, and may fitly be regarded as supplementary to it; the former having presented a striking delineation of the Lord's purpose to execute the severity of His displeasure upon the people of Jerusalem, while this returns to lay open the fearful mass of corruption on account of which such severity was to be inflicted. In what is written here there is nothing properly new; in its general purport, it is a repetition of the charges which were urged in ch. xx.; and so the chapter begins much in the same way,—with a call upon the prophet to judge the people, and set before them their iniquities. There, however, the charge took the form of a historical review for the purpose of connecting the present state of wickedness with the past, and showing how continuously the stream of corruption had flowed through all periods of their national existence. Here, on the other hand, the prophet looks exclusively to the present, and brings out in fearful array the many heinous and rampant sins which were crying in heaven's ear for vengeance."—FAIRBAIRN'S *Ezekiel*, p. 249.—W. F.]

Jerusalem becomes especially prominent at the very beginning of the chapter; and to the close, the fundamental reference of the divine discourse is to Jerusalem, in its significance for Judah and the land.—The oft-repeated: "in the midst of," points significantly to Jerusalem as the place where sin had been, and in which punishment would be, concentrated. Jerusalem was the Paris of the land of Judah.—The chapter comprises three sections.

Vers. 1–16. *Jerusalem's Abominations, which had made it ripe for Judgment.*

Ver. 2. Comp. at ch. xx. 4.—The plural, דָּמִים (comp. at ch. vii. 23), points to bloody acts, and tells of blood-guiltiness (ver. 4). The explanation of this title of Jerusalem follows in ver. 3 (ch. ix. 9). To such a pitch of violence have the **abominations** reached. (Comp. at ver. 3.) Comp. ch. v. 11, xvi. 2. A summary statement of her abominations is a judging of Jerusalem. Ch. xx. speaks especially of the abominations of their ancestors, this of the abominations of the existing generation, as facts visible to every one,—proving their ripeness for judgment.—Ver. 3 speaks of shedding *blood*, as ver. 22, on the other hand, of shedding (pouring out) *fury*. It may refer to murderous deeds generally; specially to judicial murders, consequently to the shedding of the innocent blood of righteous, God-fearing men, prophets, etc. Comp. Matt. xxiii. 37. The city which had its name from "peace" has become a city of death to those who require true peace.—לְ, *de eventu;* it is the inevitable result; while it so acts, it also brings **its time,**—the final day of judgment (ch. xxi. 30, 34). The **making of idols** (comp. at ch. vi. 4) explains the "abominations" of ver. 2.—עָלֶיהָ simply means the lifting up of the idols over those who worship them. [KEIL: as it were, covering the city therewith. HÄV.: Jerusalem, as it were, laden with idols, as of an intolerable burden and debt. HENGST.: so that it heaps upon itself defilement with its consequences. HITZ.: "For itself," in order to make the idols gracious. Others: "Against itself," *i.e.* to its hurt, or: "beside itself."]—Ver. 4. The deeds of blood are Jerusalem's blood-guiltiness; the abominations of the idols which have been made are its defilement. The one is rooted (בְּ) in the other. But therewith and thereby the sinful city has herself brought near her **days** (comp. vers. 14 and 3), thus wantonly shortening the respite of grace; she is the more quickly ripened for judgment (ch. ix. 1, xii. 23). PHILLIPS.: "As the punishment is first introduced by the **therefore**, it is intimated that Jerusalem has squandered all her days and years in bloodshed," etc. (?) According to Hengst., the days and years are those of decision, of the crisis which she brings on by her violent dealing. **And art come to thy years,** is evidently parallel to the previous sentence; at least the "years" cannot be those of chastisement and judgment (KEIL); and Hitzig rightly opposes the idea that there is any parallelism with Jer. xi. 23 (ch. xxiii. 12). The figure of a person ripe for death (not exactly aged) underlies the expression, as Hitzig puts it: that has arrived at (עַד) their full measure.—**Reproach;** comp. ch. xxi. 33; so that what Ammon is there to be punished for, appears here as deserved. (Ch. v. 14, 15.)—Ver. 5. Fuller explanation of "mocking to all lands," which are more precisely described as the near and the far. They mock, since Jerusalem must seem to them sullied, so far as its name is concerned; which is not to be understood morally,—of the sins of the "holy" city, but of its fate, which dooms the city of God to fall into the hands of the heathen. What they themselves have done by sin (ver. 3 sq.) is requited to them in a corresponding punishment. The **confusion** may be internal (through fear) and external overthrow and ruin (Deut. vii. 23, xxviii. 20); also tumult, like ch. vii. 7. [HITZ.: Inward moral and religious confusion.]

Ver. 6. Instances are now stated; and since violence was first of all referred to, the finger is, as it were, pointed to the example of the **princes,** as a something patent to the eyes of all. The **arm** alone was taken into account by them: not right, but might; neither equity nor duty—not even the responsibility of their position. Israel's princes **were** princes "according to the arm,"—each according to his own power, not *ex gratia Dei.* This connects "princes" with "were." It has also been by some coupled with what follows: "to be there with the intention," etc. Each, according to his power, strove; and then follows the שְׁפָךְ דָּם, which is constantly repeated in relation to the "city of blood-shedding" (comp. ch. xix.).—[HÄV.: Directed towards his arm. EWALD: Each according to his own authority, *i.e.* arbitrarily. HITZ.: Were helpful the one to the other (Ps. lxxxiii. 8).]—Ver. 7. To the disorder in the higher circles corresponded the complete dissolution of those bonds of subordination between children and their parents (Ex. xx. 12; Deut. xxvii. 16), which must underlie the obedience of subjects to their princes. At all events, as the princes carried it towards the people, so the people carried it towards those who were entitled rather to demand consideration and protection,—as the stranger, the widow, and the orphan, ch. xviii. 18, 7. Comp. Ex. xxii. 20 sq.; Deut. xxiv. 14 sq.—Ver. 8. And, finally, Jerusalem became towards God what it was towards men. Comp. farther, ch. xvi. 59, xx. 12, 24.—Ver. 9. A second group of sins. A comparison with Lev. xix. 16, to which it is parallel, leads one to think of false witnesses like those mentioned in 1 Kings xxi. 10 sq., who acted as informers in subserviency to the princes. רָכִיל, properly: the slanderer, which fits in admirably with the foregoing. HENGST.: "the slanderer as an ideal person." A clique of this nature had formed itself into a corporation in Jerusalem. Comp. also ver. 6.—Ch. xviii. 6. The relation to God is coupled therewith,—the falsity of the worship of false gods, with lying against one's neighbour (**in thee**, to be understood of the inhabitants of Jerusalem), with which worship, "lewdness" (ch. xvi. 27) of every kind was naturally bound up.—Ver. 10. Mother or step-mother; comp. Lev. xviii. 7, 8, xx. 11 (1 Cor. v. 1). An אִישׁ is to be supplied as the subject of the verb.—Ch. xviii. 6. In consequence of child-bearing, as well as during the monthly period. Comp. at Lev. xviii. 19, xx. 18.—Ver. 11. אִישׁ—אִישׁ—וְאִישׁ. There were such cases! Impurity in every form. A specimen of the moral atmosphere as a whole.—Ch. xviii. 6.—Lev. xviii. 15, xx. 12.—Lev. xviii. 12 (2 Sam. xiii. 12). TACITUS, *Hist.* v. 5.—Ver. 12. Third group of sins. As false witnesses (ver. 9), so also unrighteous judges, served the "princes." The corruption of the higher classes is emphasized,—it proceeded from above downwards,—so that the prominence of the rulers of Israel for the judgment of God (ch. xxi. 17) is justified; while in a sense so very different, all good should have come to Israel from those in authority, and especially through God's representatives. Comp. Ex. xxiii. 8 (1 Sam. viii. 3).—Ch. xviii. 8; Lev. xxv. 36. The discourse now gathers itself for the direct form of address; hence the brevity and the energetic close. Self-seeking, which makes one ignore one's "neighbour," finally abolishes the remembrance of God, which is the soul of all moral relations.

Ver. 13 passes over to the subject of punishment for such conduct. As the guilt is apparent ("Behold," ver. 6), so also is the judgment (**Behold**), when there is such ripeness for it.—**I have smitten My hand**, is usually regarded (like ch. xxi. 22, 19) as an indignant gesture **at** (on account of) **thy gain**, etc. (EWALD: as a signal **that the last hour should come**); which neither the words nor the connection can recommend. Hitzig, far more appropriately: Jehovah is indignantly occupied with the matter of their gain; as being unrighteous, it is brittle, and He shall smite it with the hand, etc. בָּצַע means: to *cut off*, to *plunder*, also: to *break;* so that in the "lightly come," there may already lie the "lightly go."—The avenging hand of retributive righteousness strikes the **gain** first, because this was mentioned first in ver. 12; but at once a return is made to the (collective) "shed blood," עַל very appropriately alternating with אֶל. [Hengst.: הָיוּ, a *pluralis multitudinis:* "of which there is much in thy midst."]—Ver. 14. The judgment is not yet come, hence the future; but the result is absolutely sure, therefore the interrogative forms, which are equivalent to negatives. Comp. therewith ch. xxi. 12, 20, vii. 27, vi. 59, xvii. 24.—Ver. 15. Ch. xii. 15, xx. 23.—The complete extinction of Jerusalem's uncleanness can only be understood as the extinction of its polluted inhabitants, ver. 3 sq. Others compare it with Isa. iv. 4, and think of a purification of the people during the exile.—Ver. 16. וְנִחַלְתְּ בָּךְ, if from נָחַל, either = "thou possessest thyself,"—while formerly thou wert My inheritance, the heathen shall see that thou art so no more (!); or = "thou art possessed," either by the heathen who rule over thee; or = I inherit thee, take thee in possession, as all the heathen shall perceive. Altogether forced. Therefore the more recent interpreters derive it from חָלַל; comp. ch. vii. 24.—**In thee.** Hengst.: So that thou must experience in thyself the desecration as punishment for ver. 8. Häv.: "Then Jerusalem stands out as an unholy city, which has profaned itself by its own conduct, and as such has received its recompense before the eyes of all peoples, vers. 4, 5." [Hitz.: Through all those who belong to her, who through her mournful fate shall tend to her dishonour; thus is she her own spot, Deut. xxxii. 5.] Comp. at ver. 18.

Vers. 17–22. *The Judgment in Jerusalem a Melting in the Furnace.*

Ver. 18. The figure (as to which see Introd. p. 18) in which the discourse clothes itself, in order to rouse and occupy the attention of the hearers all the more, takes its theme from the immediately preceding verses, 15 and 16. According to ver. 15, annihilation shall accomplish the cleansing of Jerusalem. Things have come to such a pass with the holy city, that there is for it no other purification. Those who think of any other purification, from what is spoken of in ver. 15, must regard it as taking place outside Jerusalem, to wit, in the exile. **The house of Israel,** as far as it comes into account, has become dross (סוּג here only, elsewhere סִיג, refuse of metals). סִגִים כֶּסֶף (the reverse order: כֶּסֶף סִגִים, in Prov. xxvi. 23—silver dross which is not yet purified) is not even ore containing silver, but means (Prov. xxv. 4) dross which has been separated from the silver. The figure indeed employs a noble metal, but nothing of it save the ignoble (comp. at vers. 20, 22) dross—of which a clearer idea is presently given by: **the whole of them are brass and tin and iron**—continues to exist in Jerusalem (Isa. i. 22; Jer. vi. 27 sq.). Thus —would God say—thus has Jerusalem, anticipating the impending judgment, shown itself as a smelting furnace. Light is hereby thrown on the peculiar phrase of ver. 16, וְנִחַלְתְּ בָּךְ: That which Jerusalem shall completely become, through divine punishment, it has already become in itself through its sins; it is already profaned in itself,—according to the figure, it has become the ignoble dross of noble silver. It appears as nothing else to Jehovah (הָיוּ־לִי); it only remains that the fact of its guilt should become evident as a fact, to the eyes of the heathen, through the judgments of God. For this purpose Jerusalem, which had ministered to sin, now becomes the **furnace** which is employed for its punishment, and the ignoble dross-community is completely consumed; in other words, annihilated. If the text be viewed in this way, no objection can be made to the figure, and all the earlier and later misunderstandings of it may be corrected.—Ver. 19 clearly expresses the thought underlying the figure employed. As the individual persons are to be thought of as scattered here and there, and as seeking protection in the fortified city on the approach of the enemy, the **gathering together** of all into Jerusalem by Jehovah is not to be understood in a merely figurative sense—even though in Ver. 20 the expression is again employed in accordance with the figure of the furnace. The כְּ of comparison (קְבֻצַת) is dropped for the sake of euphony. That **silver** is still spoken of in regard to the impending judicial process partly arises from the necessities of the figure, as ver. 22 shows still more plainly ("as silver is melted"), and partly from the fact that the word contains a significant and painful reminiscence of that which Israel had been, and of that which it could become in the crucible of God-sent tribulation! In the brass, etc. there is still some silver, interpreters say; but this idea is entirely excluded by the "dross" of ver. 18. The meaning of the comparison is rather this, that while in other cases there is also silver along with the brass, etc., or that which is cast into the furnace is only silver ore, from which art and skill then extract a noble metal (Mal. iii. 3), so here a similar process takes place in **anger** and **fury,** resulting no more in purification (Umbr. finds the purifying judgment of God prefigured in the complete melting)—at least neither the text nor context points to such an issue—but in complete annihilation. Keil, like Hitzig, is obliged to admit that the "melting" is here regarded as punishment only, and the separation of the ignoble portions is not taken into consideration.—Ver. 21. Ch. xxi. 36.

ADDITIONAL NOTE ON CH. xxii. 17–22.

["In modern metallurgy lead is employed for the purpose of purifying silver from other mineral products. The alloy is mixed with lead exposed to fusion upon an earthen vessel, and submitted to a blast of air. By this means the dross is consumed. This process is called the cupelling operation, with which the description in Ezek. xxii. 18–22, in the opinion of Mr. Napier (*Met. of Bible*, pp. 20–24), accurately coincides: 'The vessel containing the alloy is surrounded by the fire, or placed in the midst of it, and the blowing is not applied to the fire, but to the fused metals. . . . And when this is done, nothing but the perfect metals, gold and silver, can resist the scorifying influence.' And in support of his conclusion he quotes Jer. vi. 28–30, adding, 'This description is perfect. If we take silver having the impurities in it described in the text, namely, iron, copper, and tin, and mix it with lead, and place it in the fire upon a cupell, it soon melts; the lead will oxidize and form a thick, coarse crust upon the surface, and thus consume away, but effecting no purifying influence. The alloy remains, if anything, worse than before. . . . The silver is not refined because "the bellows were burned," there existed nothing to blow upon it,'" etc. (SMITH, *Dict. of the Bible*, art. "Lead.")—W. F.]

Vers. 23–31. *Jerusalem's Ripeness for Judgment extending to all Classes.*

This third section runs parallel with the first, vers. 1–16. Thus the end returns to the beginning, and the whole is rounded off. There the character of the prevailing corruption is described, here its extent, as one which has penetrated to all classes in Jerusalem.—Ver. 24. Many interpreters unnecessarily refer לָהּ to אֶרֶץ; HÄV.: The pronoun is placed before the noun to which it refers for the sake of emphasis. The whole **land** is named because the far-reaching extent of their sin is borne in mind. It will be quite sufficient if לָהּ (as is the case throughout the chapter) be referred to Jerusalem. For Jerusalem is constantly taken for the whole land and people, so that this relation scarcely requires, at least here, to be made specially prominent. In that case אַתְּ אֶרֶץ is evidently a figurative form of address; Jerusalem = Judah, is likened to **a land** in the manner then following. Finally, it can be all the more regarded as a "land" from the fact that everything which is in the land is to be collected into Jerusalem. The land is called **not cleansed**, namely, from the weeds, briars, and thorns with which it is overgrown; comp. Heb. vi. 8. [Not, as Hävernick puts it: "unclean, stained with sin," which lies outside the figure.] לֹא גֻשְׁמָהּ must contain a corresponding statement. That which best harmonizes with the context is: whose rain is not, *i.e.* appears not in the day of judgment—namely, the rain belonging to it, and which should have made it fruitful (Heb. vi. 7). In the words of the Epistle to the Hebrews: found good for nothing, it is nigh unto cursing, and its end is to be burned. [Other interpretations:—HÄV.: "Its rain shall not descend on the day of indignation," namely, that which, as a gracious pledge (Lev. xxvi. 4; Deut. xi. 14, xxviii. 12), was promised to the people. Comp. Joel ii. 23; Hos. vi. 3; Jer. v. 24; Zech. x. 1; Ezek. xxxiv. 26; Rev. xi. 6, etc. Thus no trace of grace will appear in the judgment. HENGST.: "that has no rain," etc., that finds no grace, because impurity is not removed. The rain could extinguish the flame of divine indignation. Or, with Kimchi, גֻּשְּׁמָה is taken as the 3 *fem. pret. Pual*: that "is not rained upon." This reading Keil adopts, and (because rain is not a purifying medium according to Hebrew ideas) he makes מְטֹהָרָה = "that is not shone on by light;" so that, enjoying neither sunshine nor shower in the day of wrath, the land falls under the curse of barrenness. Ewald, again, thus gives the sense: While in other cases fire can be mitigated and extinguished, on the day when the land is overtaken, ver. 22 (31), by the fire of God's indignation, it shall not be freed from its glowing heat nor made fruitful by rain from heaven.]—Ver. 25. **The conspiracy** (Isa. viii. 12; Jer. xi. 9) **of her** (false, comp. at ch. xiii.) **prophets,** indicates that they acted not merely as separate individuals, but as a corporation, made strong by combination and unity, so that they were careful not to contradict each other's lies. They appear as a sort of inquisition, everywhere prepared to denounce the servants of God to the animosity of the great, and to hand them over to the sword of the princes. [HITZ.: As the prophets appear again in ver. 28 (but comp. there!), as ver. 27 says almost the same thing (as ver. 25) of civil dignitaries (which, however, is no reason for supposing the same class to be referred to!), while what is said of prophets and priests, vers. 26 and 28, is totally dissimilar (which, however, proves nothing),—on these grounds Hitzig reads נְשִׂיאֶיהָ, conjecturing that Zeph. iii. 3 is the original of our passage. He also lays stress on the fact that ver. 6 began with the princes, so that instead of the prophets he understands in our verse the royal family, together with the great officers of the crown.] The first section of the chapter, with which the last runs parallel, made prominent, violence on the one hand, and godlessness on the other. To this twofold division there corresponds a twofold class-personification—in vers. 25, 26, prophets and priests; in vers. 27, 28, civil officers and prophets. The significance of false prophecy (comp. at ch. xiii.) is indicated by the fact that it is here referred to at the beginning and at the end. All which is swept away by Hitzig's unnecessary alteration of the text, to which even Keil assents, in opposition to old authorities. The portraiture of the prophets in regard to their violent dealing, as **soul-devourers,** is founded on the figure (ch. xix. 7) of the "roaring lion" (collective, or each of them). With this compare 1 Pet. v. 8, and also ch. xiii. 18, 19, which is not very foreign to the subject, and to which the **ravening the prey** (ch. xix. 3) may also contain an allusion. They enrich themselves with the possessions of the pious, whom they surrender to death, thereby increasing the number of the **widows** of Jerusalem.—Ver. 26. **Her priests.** The reference is to godlessness; the transition is made by the word **violence.** The law of God is violated by the priests in regard to those very things from which it was the duty of the priesthood to debar the people. Laxity in doctrine, as well as laxity in life, was a violation of God's authority in Israel. (Zeph. iii. 4; comp. also Mark vii.

9.) HITZ.: "Not content with making the law a sham, they went in the very teeth of it."—The very comprehensive expression: **holy things** (ver. 8), is unfolded (*a*) with a retrospective reference to Lev. x. 10, 11; (*b*) with reference to the Sabbaths (ch. xx. 12). In regard to the former, they should have watched lest the **holy** should become profane, as it was also their duty to teach how the **unclean** could be cleansed; with which latter the mention of the Sabbath is suggestively coupled. The two sets of opposites are not simply placed in contrast, and בֵּין־לְ is not chosen without design; for, besides the matter of their differences, the change of the one into the other is in question. הוֹדִיעוּ (**discern**) is to a certain extent a judicial expression, since, in relation to the "clean and unclean," it points to their official determinations (Luke xvii. 14).—**From My Sabbaths**, etc., not only means that they saw them desecrated by the people without offering any opposition, but that they did not wish to do so, since they themselves had forsworn, and lived in neglect of, the Sabbath law.—Ver. 27. שָׂרֶיהָ can also be: her princes, but in ver. 6 the word is the precise נְשִׂיאֵי. Comp. at ch. xi. 2. It means properly the heads of tribes, families, etc., on whom lay the obligation of administering the laws. [HENGST.: "the political authorities and officials."] They are described in relation to their "violence." Comp. Zeph. iii. 3. As to the rest, comp. with ver. 12. The authorities of Jerusalem, the judges of the people (this follows from the similar conduct, ver. 25), act on the same principle as the false prophets. This is again expressly confirmed in Ver. 28, where לָהֶם must be referred to what goes immediately before. The false prophets are here mentioned in relation to their godlessness. [BUNSEN: "They are depicted in ver. 25 principally on the side of their selfishness, and here as the responsible watchmen of the people (ch. iii. 17 sq.), appointed by God to prevent them being lulled to sleep."] Comp. at ch. xiii. 10, 9, 7.—Ver. 29. The common people resemble the dignitaries and authorities at Jerusalem. Comp. ch. xviii. 18, xvi. 49. (Ex. xxii. 20; Deut. xxiv. 17.)—Ver. 30. According to the significance of false prophecy (comp. at ver. 25), **among them** is to be referred to the false prophets; ch. xiii. 5 makes this certain. [HITZ.: Not by intercession, but as a righteous man. But where, then, was Jeremiah? And how is this consistent with ch. xiv. 12 sq.?] As Jerusalem stands for the land, so one of its prophets ought to have been found, who would intercede **for the land**, and thus avert its destruction by Jehovah.—Ver. 31. Ch. vii. 8, 4, ix. 10, etc.

THEOLOGICAL REMARKS.

1. Here, as in ch. xviii., Ezekiel shows an understanding of the law according to the spirit of the Messiah, who is in him, *i.e.* in Christ's manner. See the Sermon on the Mount. The connection between God's obligations and human duty is treated quite according to Christ's spirit and manner of apprehending it.

2. "The distinction between religion and morality is a fiction opposed to experience" (HENGST.).

3. The loosening of the bonds of filial obedience, disrespect to the rites of religious worship, a disordered condition of the relations between the sexes, open licentiousness, adultery, a social opinion which tolerates or recognises it, bribery, extortion, the arrogance of wealth, oppression of inferiors, and such like, are in all times the cloud-streaks presaging the gathering storm which will burst on a people.

4. False prophecy leans on civil authority, and therefore flatters and serves it. In God and His law, in human conscience and personal faith, it has neither root nor support. That is always the civil position of false theology, as of every court clergy, however orthodox it may otherwise be.

5. The dissolution of a nation's life takes place when false doctrine comes into vogue. Going hand in hand with the passions, it banishes conscientiousness from official life. Priests become worldly courtiers, who aim at making a career for themselves; judges become dependent and open to influences, and take their cue from the reigning power and from public opinion. When the Church and the bench take their tone from party spirit, then, along with sound teaching and civil rights, the religious and moral foundations of national life are swept away. The ruling principle becomes mere caprice, which undermines the penal code with frivolous distinctions, shallow conceptions of law, alleviation of penalties, lax views as to responsibility, etc.

HOMILETIC HINTS.

Ver. 1 sq. "Thus God's complaint against His people is ever renewed; and our times are not unlike those. But one should not be weary of administering reproof" (STCK.).—Ver. 2. Comp. at ch. xx. 4.—"The prophets are judges through God's word, the apostles through the Spirit, who convinces the world of sin, John xvi. 9. The saints judge the whole world, 1 Cor. vi. 2 sq. The spiritual man judgeth all things, 1 Cor. ii. 15. This judgment-seat is better than a worldly one. This is the employment of the keys in binding and loosing—the 'power of the keys'" (H. H.).—"A Jerusalem may become a Sodom, a holy city a den of murderers. Let no one think himself so secure as to be in no danger of falling, Rom. xi. 20, 21" (W.).—Ver. 3. "God has meted out to sinners the time of forbearance, the day of grace" (COCC.).—The sinner imagines that he can go on without end, and so hastens on all the faster to the end.—Ver. 4. He who wantonly wages war makes himself blood-guilty.—"They made idols for themselves, which is even worse than cherishing the ordinary superstition of the idolatry which has been handed down to us" (L.).—Whoever mocks God, is mocked by God in His own time, through men.—Ver. 5. "We bear the name of evangelical, we believe that we possess the pure doctrine; therefore we should be the more careful to keep the gospel before our eyes, and to remain far from pollution and false doctrine" (L.).—"Every one shrinks from a polluted name, but not from a polluted life, which makes one dishonourable before God" (B. B.).—Sin brings the best order into confusion.—Ver. 6. "See how it is laid on the conscience of teachers and preachers to condemn the sins even of those who are high in station" (Tüb. Bib.).—Since their example is so much taken notice of, princes should look more intently to God's word and law than to their own authority.—Civil power should be for a terror to evil-doers, but should not minister to the gratification of the flesh.—Blood-stains may be seen even upon the purple.—Might goes before right—even an Old Testament experience.—Ver. 7. Parents are themselves to blame for the disobedience of their children, but at last a whole people is required to bear the blame.—God is assailed in the persons of the stranger, widow, and fatherless; they are God's wards.—A man should be most on his guard against, and especially sensitive to, that which most easily leads him astray. — Ver. 8. Jehovah's holy things were places, things, persons, times, etc.—"The idea of the sanctuary is as wide as that of the Jewish religion" (Hengst.).—Comp. at ch. xx. 12.—He profanes the Sabbath who does not celebrate it, who celebrates it ill or who consecrates it to the service of sin.—Ver. 9. "The slanderer is a thief" (Stck.).—Where the ruler is wicked, false tongues are plentiful.—Where there are wicked judges, false witnesses are not wanting.—False speech is base coin. Compare at ch. xviii. 16, xvi. 16.—Impurity and idolatry in their combination.—Ver. 10 sq. Custom and morals go together.—Impurity ruins the individual, the family, and the state, in body and soul. — God sees when we suppose ourselves unseen.—Though the ruler be still, God is not silent.—There are sins which sink man, who was made in the image of God, lower than the beasts. Parents, watch over the members of your families from earliest years.—Ver. 12. Every man has his price, for which he can be bought.—"Men in authority, counsellors of kings, take heed of covetousness, of gifts, of violence and misuse of your office, otherwise God's vengeance will surely smite you and your houses!" (Tüb. Bib.)—Jewish tradition ascribes the destruction of Jerusalem to covetousness, because it is the root of all evil.—"Not only he who demands more than is just, but he also who shows no forbearance, oppresses his neighbour, Matt. xviii. 28 sq." (Stck.)—"Avarice spares neither friend nor foe, its rule is self-interest" (Stck.).—He who loves not his neighbour as himself has forgotten God.—"Forgetfulness of God opens the window to every wicked action" (H. H.).—Ver. 13. How God's hand in the end strikes upon all the hands of men!—Ver. 14. In sin and in the time of God's judgment how different is the bearing of men!—When God is against us, heart and hand, courage and power, fail.—"God speaks not in vain, and will do more than terrify" (B. B.).—Ver. 15. Awful cleansing—the extirpation of the ungodly!—When we make no end, God makes it.—Ver. 16. God hides His own from men, but here sinners are given up to the heathen.

Ver. 17 sq. Threefold smelting furnace: Of sin, in which one can become dross;—of trial, where the silver is tested;—of judgment, where even the dross is consumed.—The dross-communities.—"Oh that a salt may still continue among us, that we may be preserved from utter corruption!" (Tüb. Bib.)—Ver. 18. The dross does not typify hypocrites; but where what one had, has been taken away, there the past may have been very noble.—Ver. 19. The heaping up of sins, and the gathering of sinners for judgment.—Ver. 20 sq. God's anger and fury—sad smelters! Unsavoury salt is trodden under foot, Matt. v. 13.—Ver. 23 sq. The judgment-day considers whether cleansing has taken place and fruit been brought forth.—Not merely the soil, but much more the heart of man, yields all manner of weeds. God has denied rain to no soul, His word has been richly bestowed on us.—Ver. 25. It should not impose on godly men that false prophets keep together; falsity must be aided by falsity.—Satan the great conspirator to the end of time.—The avarice and worldliness of false theology.—"A hireling is never a soul-seeker" (Stck.).—Ver. 26. Not only by direct transgression, but also by false explanation and interpretation of the law of God, is violence done to it.—The sacred boundary-guard between Christ and Belial.—"The teacher who does not make a marked difference between the godly and ungodly in applying saving truth, profanes the name of the Lord in the sanctuary" (St.).—Ver. 27. No one is placed so high as to be beyond the reach of divine punishment. The loss of a single soul over against the gaining of the whole world.—Ver. 28. Comp. at ch. xiii.—Ver. 29. Where prophecy does no good, a people must become a waste.—Ver. 30 sq. The pious are the lightning-conductors of God's judgments.—"The want of pious people is a terrible want, the premonition of judgment" (Cocc.).

(*b*) *Judah and Israel's Ripeness for Judgment* (ch. xxiii.).

1, 2 And the word of Jehovah came to me, saying, Son of man, there were
3 two women, the daughters of one mother; And in Egypt they played the
wanton; in their youth they wantoned, there were their breasts pressed, and
4 there were the teats of their virginity bruised. And their names were
"Oholah," the great [greater], and "Oholibah" her sister; and they were
mine, and bare sons and daughters; and their names were Samaria—Oholah,
5 and Jerusalem—Oholibah. And Oholah when under me played the wanton,
6 and doted upon her lovers,—on Assyria, her neighbours, Clothed in
purple, captains and rulers, all of them comely young men, knights riding on
7 horses. And she bestowed her wantonness upon them, all the choice of the
sons of Assyria; and with all on whom she doted, with all their idols she
8 polluted herself. And her whoredoms brought from Egypt she did not
leave; for they lay with her in her youth, and they bruised her virgin breasts,
9 and poured their whoredoms upon her. Therefore I gave her into the hand

of her lovers, into the hand of the sons of Assyria, upon whom she doted.
10 These discovered her nakedness [shame]; they took her sons and daughters,
and herself they slew with the sword, and she became a name to women, and
11 they executed judgment upon her. And her sister Oholibah saw it, and
made her wantonness more corrupt than she, and her whoredoms more than
12 the whoredoms of her sister. She doted on the sons of Assyria,—captains
and rulers, her neighbours, clothed gorgeously, knights riding upon horses, all
13 of them comely young men. And I saw that she was defiled; they had both
14 one way. And she still added to her whoredoms; and she saw men portrayed
15 upon the wall, likenesses of the Chaldeans, painted with vermilion, Girdled
with a girdle on their loins, flowing turbans on their heads, all of them having
the appearance of leaders, the likeness of the sons of Babylon, of the Chal-
16 deans in the land of their birth. And she doted upon them as soon as her
17 eyes saw them, and sent messengers unto them to Chaldea. And the sons of
Babylon came to her into the bed of love, and defiled her through their
whoredoms; and she was polluted with them, and her soul was estranged
18 from them. And she discovered her whoredoms, and discovered her naked-
ness; and My soul was estranged from her, as My soul had been estranged
19 from her sister. And she multiplied her whoredoms, so that she remembered
the days of her youth, when she played the wanton in the land of Egypt.
20 And she doted on their paramours, whose flesh is the flesh of asses, and their
21 issue the issue of horses. Yea [and] thou didst seek after the lewdness of thy
youth, when the Egyptians bruised thy teats on account of thy youthful
22 breasts. Therefore, Oholibah, thus saith the Lord Jehovah, Behold, I will
stir up thy lovers against thee, from whom thy soul is estranged, and I will
23 bring them against thee from every side; The sons of Babylon, and all the
Chaldeans, Pekod, and Shoa, and Koa, all the sons of Assyria with them,
comely young men, captains and rulers all of them, leaders and men
24 of renown, every one riding on horses. And they shall come against
thee with weapons, chariot and wheel, and with an assembly of peoples;
target and shield and helmet they shall set against thee round about;
and I will set judgment before them, and they shall judge thee with their
25 judgments. And I will set My jealousy upon thee, and they shall deal
with thee in fury; they shall take away thy nose and thine ears, and thy
remnant shall fall by the sword; they shall take thy sons and thy daughters,
26 and thy remnant shall be devoured by the fire. And they shall strip thee of
27 thy clothes, and take away thy fair jewels. And I will make thy lewdness
to cease from thee, and thy whoredom from the land of Egypt; and thou
28 shalt not lift up thine eyes to them, nor remember Egypt any more. For
thus saith the Lord Jehovah, Behold, I will deliver thee into the hand of
those whom thou hatest, into the hand of those from whom thy soul is
29 estranged. And they shall deal with thee in hatred, and shall take away all
thy earning, and leave thee naked and bare; and the nakedness of thy
whoredoms shall be discovered, and thy lewdness and thy wanton courses.
30 This shall be done unto thee because thou hast gone a-whoring after the
31 heathen, because thou hast defiled thyself with their idols. In the way of
32 thy sister thou hast gone, and I give her cup into thy hand. Thus saith the
Lord Jehovah, The cup of thy sister, the deep and wide, thou shalt drink;
33 it shall be for laughter and mockery according to its measure. Thou shalt be
filled with drunkenness and sorrow; a cup of wasting and desolation is the
34 cup of thy sister Samaria. And thou shalt drink it and suck it out; and
thou shalt gnaw its sherds, and tear off thy breasts; for I have spoken,—
35 sentence of the Lord Jehovah. Therefore thus saith the Lord Jehovah,
Because thou hast forgotten Me, and hast cast Me behind thy back, do thou
36 also bear thy lewdness and thy whoredoms. And Jehovah said to me, Son
of man, wilt thou judge Oholah and Oholibah, then show them their abomi-
37 nations. For they have committed adultery, and blood is in their hands, and
with their idols they have committed adultery; and also their sons whom

38 they bare unto Me they have made to pass through the fire to them. This
besides they did to Me; they defiled My sanctuary in the same day, and pro-
39 faned My Sabbaths. And when they had slain their sons [children] to their
idols, they came to My sanctuary on the same day to profane it; and lo!
40 thus have they done in the midst of My house. Yea, they sent even to men
coming from afar, to whom a messenger was sent; and, lo, they came, for
whom thou didst wash thyself, paint thine eyes, and deck thyself with orna-
41 ments; And thou satest upon a stately bed, and a table was laid before it,
42 and My incense and My oil didst thou set upon it. And the voice of a loose
crowd [was] in her [Jerusalem], and to people of the multitude were brought
drunkards from the wilderness, who put bracelets on their hands, and a
43 beautiful crown upon their heads. And I said of her worn out with adul-
44 teries, Will they now commit her adulteries? And she [also]? And they
went in to her as they go in to a harlot. Thus they went in to Oholah and
45 to Oholibah, the lewd women. But righteous men, they shall judge them
with the judgment of adulteresses, and the judgment of those that shed
46 blood; for they are adulteresses, and blood is in their hands. For thus saith
the Lord Jehovah, I will bring up a company against them, and give them
47 to maltreatment and spoiling. And the company shall cast stones upon
them, and cleave them with their swords; their sons and their daughters
48 they shall slay, and burn their houses with fire. And I will cause lewdness to
cease out of the land, so that all women shall be warned, and shall not do
49 after your lewdness. And they shall recompense your lewdness upon you,
and ye shall bear the sins of your idols, and ye shall know that I am the
Lord Jehovah.

Ver. 3. Sept.: . . . ἐπεσον οἱ μαστοι . . . διεπαρθενεύθησαν.
Ver. 12. . . . ἐνδεδυμενους εὐπαρυφα— Vulg.: *indutis veste varia*—
Ver. 13. . . . μεμιανται ὁδος μια—
Ver. 15. διεζωσμενους ποικιλματα . . . τιαραι βαπται . . . ὀψις τρισση.
Ver. 20. κ. ἐπεθου ἐπι τους Χαλδαιους, ὡν ἠσαν ὡς . . . αἰδοια— Vulg.: *insanivit libidine super concubitum* . . .
Ver. 21. Sept., Vulg., Syr. read: במצרים.
Ver. 23. . . . παντας τρισσους κ. ὀνομαστους— *nobiles, tyrannosque et principes . . . duces et magistratus . . . principes principum et nominatos*—
Ver. 24. . . . ἀπο βορρα, ἁρματα κ. τροχοι, ἱπποι, μετα . . . κ. βαλει ἐπι σε προφυλακην κυκλω.
Ver. 29. . . . τους πονους σου κ. τους μοχθους σου—
Ver. 31. Sept., Syr., Arab. read: בידיך.
Vers. 32, 33. . . . το πλεοναζον του συντελεσαι μεθην, κ. ἐκλυσεως πλησθηση— *Eris in derisum . . . subsannationem, quæ est capacissima . . . repleberis, calice mœroris et tristitiæ*—
Ver. 34. Sept.: . . . κ. τας ἑορτας κ. τας νουμηνιας αὐτης ἀποστρεψω—
Ver. 37. . . . δι' ἐμπυρων;
Vers. 41, 42. . . . προ προσωπου αὐτης . . . ἐξευφραινοντο ἐν αὐτοις, κ. φωνην ἁρμονιας ἀνεκρουοντο— *vox multitudinis exultantis . . . in ea et in viris qui de . . . adducebantur et veniebant de deserto*—
Ver. 41. Vulg. reads: לפניך. Syr., Chald., Arab. read: לפניהם.—42. Some codd.: ידיהם; some also: ראשיהם.
Ver. 43. K. εἰπα· οὐκ ἐν τουτοις μοιχωνται; ἐργα γυναικος πορνης ἐποιεις; Vulg.: *ei, quæ attrita est in . . . Nunc fornicabitur in fornicatione sua etiam hæc.*
Ver. 44. Another reading: ויבאו.
Ver. 46. Many codd.: עליהן.
Ver. 47. . . . λιθοις ὀχλων.
Ver. 49. Codd. and Syr.: ונתתי.

EXEGETICAL REMARKS.

The allegory in which the ripeness for judgment of Judah and Israel is represented, is closely allied to that of ch. xvi. The remarks made on it are to be compared with the present chapter. In contradistinction to ch. xvi., which gave prominence to the love borne to the faithless one by her lawful husband, ch. xxiii. directs our attention rather to the seductive power and splendour of the lovers for whom Jehovah was forsaken. The prospect of pardon presented by the earlier chapter here disappears behind the penal judgment.

[FAUSSET: "The imagery is similar to that in ch. xvi.; but here the reference is not, as there, so much to the breach of the spiritual marriage-covenant with God by the people's *idolatries*, as by their *worldly spirit*, and their trusting to alliances with the heathen for safety, rather than to God."—W. F.]

Vers. 1–4. *Preface.*

Ver. 2. The **one mother** may be presupposed from ch. xvi. as the Hittite. Comp. at vers. 3, 44 sq. As, however, it is not the present object to give prominence to the ancestry in the sense of ch. xvi., the word simply describes the original unity of the people. This also explains what is said in ver. 3 relative to Egypt. The two kingdoms which form the theme of the chapter are assumed as already two in Egypt; but in point of fact, what is said holds as to the yet undivided people. [Hengst., indeed, appeals to Gen. xlix., in which the two tribes of Judah and Ephraim appear as two independent powers.]—On account of the legitimate relation in which the nation stood to God from its very origin, namely, of a marriage-covenant, the political and religious departure of both kingdoms from the principles laid down in the law, appears as wantonness (זָנָה), ch. xvi. 15 (Jas. iv. 4).—Here also (comp. ch. xx. 7 sq.) they are said to be tainted with the spirit of Egypt. Comp. also at ch. xvi. 26. **In their youth**, points (comp. ch. xvi. 22, 43) to their innate corruption, showing itself early in sinful lust.—Even when still unwedded (ch. xvi. 8), as Jehovah's betrothed, the conduct of the people was to be judged according to Deut. xxii. 23. Comp. farther, ch. xvi. 7; Hos. ii. 4 [2].—עִשּׂוּ, the Egyptians (ver. 8). Egypt was the means of exciting the first carnal impulses of the youthful people to a heathenish mode of feeling and action, whereby they were robbed of their virgin purity. The Sept. explains **their virginity** according to Deut. xxii. 20. Hitz. repels the idea of any allusion to idolatry, and makes the reference to be to the oppression by the Egyptians.—Ver. 4. **Oholah** = *her tent, i.e.* either generally (HENGST.): that has a house of her own, an independent existence, or (on account of the contrast to Oholibah): who possesses her wilfully erected sanctuary (1 Kings xii. 28 sq., 16), which makes it unnecessary to think of an abbreviation of אָהֳלָהּ־בָּהּ, *her tent in her*. Häv., while maintaining the Hittite reference, ch. xvi. 3, etc., makes prominent the allusion found in it to the history of Esau, and explains Oholibah relative to Gen. xxxvi. 2, inasmuch as Aholibamah [Oholibamah], who is called Judith in an earlier passage (Gen. xxvi. 34), could most appropriately represent the kingdom of Judah. While Aholibamah merely means (*tent of the high place*): *My tent* (house, family) *is a height* ("I have a high tent"), in the name Oholibah—*My tent* (namely, Jehovah's, who speaks) *in her*—the reference is taken from the tabernacle; whereby one is reminded of the habit which prevailed among the exiles of naming their children from the temple and similar objects (1 Chron. iii. 20; Ezra ii. 43, 59), to express their yearning for restoration. (Moreover, the members of a family in the East often bear the same or like-sounding names.) The kingdom of Judah had also the advantage of possessing the one true sanctuary, which, however, made its guilt the more aggravated. **The great** is to be rendered, as in ch. xvi. 46, and not with Hengst.: the elder, with an allusion to Joseph's precedence, Gen. xlix. 26, to that of Ephraim in the time of Joshua and the judges, and to that of Benjamin which belonged to the ten tribes in the time of Saul, while Judah attained supremacy only in the time of David (Ps. lxxviii.). Häv. combines with the political importance of Samaria, owing to its greater extent, its priority in sin as well as in punishment.—Comp. ch. xvi. 8, 20. Häv. translates וַתִּהְיֶינָה לִי: "And they belonged to me as wives," with emphasis.—The explanation of the names as those of Samaria and Jerusalem (representing Judah as hitherto) closes this introduction.

Vers. 5–10. *Oholah's Adulterous Wantonness* (vers. 5–8) *and Punishment* (vers. 9, 10).

Vers. 5–8. *The Harlotries.*

Ver. 5. Comp. at ch. xvi. 32. HITZ.: "When she turned her back on me" (?). So also the Chaldee. But rather is the marriage relation pointed to, in the line of ver. 4 (Hos. iv. 12). UMBR.: "While she rests under her husband, her thoughts run wantonly after others."—עָגַב, found only in Jeremiah and Ezekiel, means: to *desire*, to *burn*. The description of the Assyrians begins with קְרוֹבִים. It is in apposition, like all that follows. The nearness is to be taken neither locally, nor yet morally—of inward relationship, but it brings into prominence the historical element, the time when the Assyrians became neighbours of Israel; comp. 2 Kings xv. 17 sq., xvi. 9, xvii. 3. [The supposition of a loose connection of the words = "and neighbours," who were somewhere in her neighbourhood, is not consistent with what follows. Others: Who came near her lustfully (Gen. xx. 4). HÄV.: "So closely related, intimate, trusted friends," that alliances were made with them, and their favour courted, until, from being bosom friends, they became deadly enemies. There is nothing of all this in the context, which only states that on the first opportunity, namely, when the Assyrians approached, Israel was captivated by the carnal glory of the world-power, which is then portrayed with greater minuteness.]—This political power is Assyria, which does not come into view, in the first place, on the side of its idolatry; but when Israel wantoned after it from political motives, this infidelity to the idea of their complete dependence on God could not fail to issue, from the first, in apostasy from God, and the other natural consequences of the forbidden relationship.—Ver. 6. Description of the Assyrians from the view-point of Israel's apostate heart, to whom this world-power seemed most imposing, as Hengst. remarks: "with a touch of irony." The impressions are entirely such as are made on the mind of a carnal woman, whereby the previously mentioned doting gaze is accounted for.—תְּכֵלֶת, either from its thick, hard shell, or from its dark colour, is the name of a mussel (*helix ianthina*) with a purple shell, from which a blue or violet purple was made.—פַּחָה is a foreign word, denoting the military governor of a province. Similarly סָגָן (סֶגֶן) = the representative of the prince, commander-in-chief. (Something like governors and generals.)—The special mention of **horses** is intended to distinguish the noblest and proudest class of riders from those riding on asses and camels.—Ver. 7. מִבְחַר briefly resumes ver. 6, in order, perhaps, to suggest, besides the "choice," etc., those who were of less account; at all events, she doted also on others, as the Egyptians, who are presently mentioned. — וּבְכָל־בְּכָל, the one illustrating the other; the political confederation with the heathen led to idolatry. (HENGST.: The idols of the world-powers are not beyond and above them, but themselves made objective.)—Ver. 8. Thither Jeroboam's calf-worship pointed back, so that their ancient deliverance from Egypt, instead of remaining a fact, had become a mere tradition. As to the political application (Rashi), 2 Kings xvii. 4 is to be compared. Hitzig takes it in an exclusively political sense.

Vers. 9, 10. *The Punishment.*

Ver. 9. The recompense for ver. 7: "And she bestowed," "Therefore I gave." Comp. 2 Kings xvii.—Ver. 10. The shame of her wantonness is succeeded by the shame of punishment, executed by her paramours themselves. Comp. besides, ch. xvi. 37. So in the figure; as to the fact, it was accomplished by the captivity of the people, the slaughter of those on whom the existence of the kingdom depended, of the men who were able to bear arms, so that Israel became notorious among the nations on account of its shameful overthrow, ch. xvi. 41.

Vers. 11–35. *Oholibah's Guilt* (vers. 11–21) *and Punishment* (vers. 22–35).

Vers. 11–21. *The Guilt.*

Ver. 11. She saw both the transgressions and their recompense. The former should have filled her with loathing, by the latter she should have been warned. But her corrupt conduct was still worse than that of Samaria (ch. xvi. 47).—Ver. 12. Comp. 2 Kings xvi. 7 sq.; 2 Chron. xxviii. 19 sq.—Comp. at vers. 6, 5.—מִכְלוֹל (in ver. 6, תִּכְלֶת) means: *perfection*, therefore: *splendour;* not exactly (Sept.): "with beautiful (purple) fringe," as Hitz. EWALD: "clothed in martial coats of mail."—Ver. 13. **And I saw,** counterpart to וַתֵּרֶא, ver. 11. (Comp. Jer. iii. 8.) The way and end of both sisters were the same. — Ver. 14. The description of Judah's baser conduct follows. Her relations with the Assyrians were similar to those of Samaria. They had in reality approached the kingdom of Judah, as they had the kingdom of Israel. In regard to the Chaldeans, on the other hand, the relation to them was brought about by means of **likenesses,** which Judah saw,—מְחֻקֶּה, partic. Pual, *something engraven* or *sketched, painted* (HÄV.: probably coloured bas-reliefs), in vermilion (which would be all the more appropriate for warriors); or perhaps in ochre, as frescoes of this description for the glorification of the Chaldean commanders and their victories were sufficiently common in Ezekiel's neighbourhood. The representation here, therefore, may possibly be the mere drapery of the thought, that the bare report of the military prowess of the Chaldeans had inflamed the imagination and the senses of Judah. So Hengst. Owing to the undeniable intercourse between nations in the Old World, which certainly obtained between Palestine and Babylon, it is not in itself unimaginable that such wall-pictures of representatives of foreign nations may have existed in the royal palaces of Judah. Hitz. here takes note of "the influence (of pictures) on a woman's imagination," under which figure Judah is personified. Häv. cites ch. viii. 10, and thinks of "pictorial representations from the circle of Chaldean mythological ideas." The Chaldean embassy of 2 Kings xx. 12 sq., 2 Chron. xxxii. 31 (comp. Delitzsch on Isa. xxxix.), shows that the Chaldeans kept up intercourse with Judah, even when Assyria was still the dominant world-power. May not this embassy have been perpetuated by a painting as the occasion of an alliance with the Chaldeans against Assyria? Ewald supposes: "beautiful idol-pictures, which, as *e.g.* Mithras, were represented in the human form," and cites ch. viii. 16.—Ver. 15. The **flowing turbans** are such as may be seen on the monuments of ancient Nineveh, with which the following descriptions correspond throughout. See Layard's *Nineveh and Babylon.* [טְבָל refers not so much to the colour (gay), but rather means originally to *twist round.* Layard remarks, by the way: "The general was clothed in embroidered robes, and wore on his head a fillet adorned with rosettes, and long tasselled bands." Probably, waving head-bands. The Kurds, who still preserve the most ancient Eastern customs, wear on their bright-coloured turbans, appendages which hang over their neck and shoulders.]—שָׁלִישׁ in the plural betokens the charioteers, of whom there were three in each chariot, one driving, one bearing the shield, and a third fighting. (**Appearance and likeness;** see ch. i. 5.) The emphasizing of: **the land of their birth,** according to Hengst., is intended to form a contrast to the Assyrians, whom Judah saw in her own land,—to point perhaps to Ur (Gen. xi. 28) of the Chaldees (Abraham's native land), so that the original blood-relationship may have been alluded to in this political intercourse (?). HÄV.: "The Chaldean's fatherland theirs," which sarcastically places side by side, the original home of the once fierce and warlike people, and the idolatrous pictures, which resemble them, but not the existing *fainéant* Babylonians. The statement made by the sentence is simpler: that even they were not farther removed than Abraham, the founder of the Jewish people,—"whose fathers served strange gods in Ur of the Chaldees (Josh. xxiv. 2), so that he was called thence," etc., as Cocc. remarks.—Ver. 16. Apodosio to ver. 14: "And she saw," resumed by: **as soon as her eyes saw.** The **messengers** mentioned here can scarcely be those of Jer. xxix. 3. "They were probably," says Hengst., "the occasion of the embassy sent from the Chaldeans, who were to take a view of the resources of the people proposing an alliance." This side of the history of Judah is not described elsewhere. Enough that Judah, as is in itself probable, made the first advances (ch. xvi. 29).—Ver. 17. The political alliance led to religious defilement—was itself, in fact, religious defection; and after the defilement was effected, it led again to political hostility. Judah found that it had only changed its masters, Jehoiakim and Zedekiah rebelled against Babylon, 2 Kings xxiv.—In נָקַע (the weaker form is יָקַע,

from which the fut. is derived) there lies the idea of satiety and loathing; in this sense the meaning of the verb is: to *push away* any one, to *break a relationship*, to be *alienated* from any one. Comp. 1 Cor. vi. 16; ch. xviii. 6, 11.—Ver. 18. Yet the satiety was not absolute. Others take the connection thus: "and when she had discovered," etc., "then was," etc. But more is meant to be stated as the ground of Jehovah's estrangement, for Judah's alienation from the Chaldeans might also have led her back to Jehovah. More general prostitution, however, was the result, by which is especially meant alliances with the lesser states against Babylon, and at the same time breaches of faith towards men, ch. xvii. 15. Jehovah's estrangement from Judah is a suggestive parallel to Judah's from the Chaldeans.—Ver. 19. Comp. vers. 3, 8, ch. xvi. 51. But Judah **multiplied**, etc. Instead of remembering the misery of her youth, and the grace then shown (ch. xvi. 22, 43), she thought only of renewing quite another "first love" than that of Jehovah.—Ver. 20. עַל is unjustifiably pressed by some interpreters ("beyond," more than the neighbouring people of Egypt, or, "together with," ch. xvi. 37), as its construction with עָגַב in the chapter sufficiently shows. Nor does this single masculine form of פִּלֶגֶשׁ, which is elsewhere fem., justify the interpretation of Kimchi, that Judah wished to be the concubine of the Egyptians. It is rather a derision of the Egyptian eunuchs, *i.e.* courtiers and officers who mediated the alliance with Egypt. (פִּלַגְשֵׁיהֶם does not mean the men-concubines, which the Egyptians are, nor is it to be taken in the sense of *eunuchus imbellis*, or *puer mollis*, or polyandry.) The representation which follows is sufficiently explained by the particularly lecherous character of the animals mentioned, and describes the obscene character of the Egyptians (ch. xvi. 26). HENGST.: "The falling power of Egypt sought to provide a prop for itself by diplomatic art."—Ver. 21 sums up. "The sudden transition to the address in ver. 21 is explained by this, that the prophet has the actual state of affairs (the union with Egypt) before his eyes" (HENGST.).—בְּ explains זִמַּת in accordance with ver. 3, to which the inexperienced sensuousness and carnality of the youthful people presented the inducement.

Vers. 22–35. *Oholibah's Punishment.*

Ver. 22. She is punished by those with whom she had wantoned. Comp. ver. 9. The following verse shows who are meant. Those from whom she would (ver. 17) escape out of loathing, will not allow her to escape punishment.—Ver. 23. **The sons**, etc., are more definitely personified. Ewald regards the three names as the proper names of three subordinate Chaldee tribes, which are placed together from similarity of sound. As there is no proof of this, nor even of their being *nomina propria*, modern interpreters for the most part regard them as the titles of Chaldee dignitaries (Hengst.: "Pekod = supremacy; Shoa = the chief; Koa, of uncertain meaning"), or three classes of the people, three branches of the military force, or three ranks in it (Hitz.: "noble and prince and lord"). From the description, the assembly which is to be gathered together to execute punishment, shall be great and imposing. The Assyrians figure as part of it, and are ironically represented in the manner of ver. 12 (6). —אוֹתָם, therefore the שָׁלִשִׁים from ver. 15 are named. קְרוּאִים, Ew.: *renowned*, which Hitz. questions. For the purpose in hand, the word is either formed after Num. i. 16, xvi. 2: formally "appointed," or means generally: "summoned."—Ver. 24. The assembly was not more conspicuous for its numbers than for the completeness of its equipments. הֹצֶן (חצן) ἁπ. λεγ. (something hard, cutting, sharp), signifying indefinitely: weapon, so that a threefold equipment is specified. [MEIER: *battle-axe.* HENGST.: *sabre* (a Chaldee military word). EWALD: "with shoulder, bridle, and wheel," as the three modes in which soldiers advance,—shouldering (with bent arm), riding, and driving.] The missing בְּ is easily understood; but it is not required, as the three expressions standing for the concretes, foot, horse, and chariots, could be the subject to וּבָאוּ.—וּבִקְהַל (ו *explic.*), since the **assembly of peoples** in the manner of the Israelitish congregation (ver. 23) supplies the proper element for the judgment which is to be held. To indicate that they (while on Jehovah's mission) are secured against any anxiety as to the result, three pieces of exclusively defensive armour are now mentioned, which correspond to the above threefold description,—the shield which covered the whole person, the smaller shield of the light-armed soldier, and the helmet. They received from God the right to judge according to **their judgments**, their ideas of judgment. Thus it was a divine judgment. They were judges in God's stead. But with a reference, at the same time, to the fact that Judah had been in fellowship with them politically, religiously, and morally.—Ver. 25. The jealousy of God was turned against Israel; in consequence of it the judgments of the heathen were fierce. The mutilation is to be understood in conformity with common Asiatic and Chaldee usages, but, in the present connection, of the "severing of portions of the national body-corporate" (HITZ.), or with Hengst., of the annihilation of their military strength, which is to a people what "nose and ears" are to a woman. The older interpreters understood Judah's royal splendour, or (KIMCHI) kingdom and priesthood. The **remnant** is defined the first time by "nose" and "ears," so that there is pronounced, on the one hand, mutilation, and on the other, slaughter; the meaning of the expression in the second instance is defined by the carrying away of the children, so that it can only refer to the empty houses (ch. xvi. 41).

[HENDERSON: "Vers. 25, 26. Punishment by cutting off the nose and ears was inflicted for adultery, not only among the Chaldeans, but also among the Egyptians, Greeks, and Romans. It was therefore most appropriate to represent that which adulterous Judah was to suffer, under the image of such ignominious and cruel treatment. They were also to be stripped of what lewd females set most value upon—their rich dresses and costly jewels, by which they attract the notice of their paramours, ch. xvi. 39."—W. F.]

Ver. 26. Ch. xvi. 39, 17. The plundering is either symbolical or actual.—Ver. 27. The **lewdness** is made to cease by God as to subject and object.—Ver. 28. Comp. ch. xvi. 37.—See vers. 17, 22.—Ver. 29. Hatred (ver. 28) and counter-hatred instead of all the former intimacy. Despoiling by the Chaldeans till she is reduced to her original condition in Egypt (ch. xvi. 7), from which results the discovery of her guilt and accumulated infamy (ch. xvi. 37).—Ver. 31 (ver. 13). The figure of the **cup**, to represent the final issue, under the idea of drinking out.—Ver. 32. **The cup** described as containing much: תִּהְיֶה is the 3d, not the 2d pers., and the subject to it, is either the cup or מַרְבָּה (*amplitude, wideness*); but the former is preferable, with the latter as epexegetical. The cup, from its capacity, occasions the derisive laughter of the enemies,—that the person, formerly so wide-mouthed and haughty, now become so insignificant, requires to swallow so much.—Ver. 33. What the cup contains for those who have to empty it, and hence what cup it is. Stupefaction with sorrow and woe, until they are distracted by the **wasting and desolation!** (The verse begins with שִׁכָּרוֹן, and ends with שֹׁמְרוֹן.)—Ver. 34. Not so much an intensification of the figure (Keil), as of the drunkenness, arising from the anguish of thought. In the madness of her pain she licks up the last drops of the cup. Her affliction is her thirst. —The **sherds** point to an earthen cup—nothing is gilded or splendid in this Nemesis-song—and presuppose a breaking in pieces, which is incidentally set forth in the madness which follows; but the word is especially intended to fit in with תְּגָרֵמִי, which expresses the idea of crushing or gnawing the sherds with the teeth, in order to suck out the last drops of moisture left in them. (Hengst. says merely: "Thou shalt break the sherds thereof, as one who, having taken a very disagreeable potion, shatters the vessel in ill-humour.") The tearing of the breasts is placed beside the breaking of the sherds, as if it were done by means of the sherd-fragments. Or it may even have been done in frenzy by her own nails. See vers. 3, 8, in reference to the **breasts.** "We find a historical illustration of this in the treatment they gave Gedaliah, the Chaldean governor, for which they were compelled to suffer, Jer. xli." (Hengst.)—Ver. 35. Ch. xxii. 12.—She followed after the heathen and their gods (ver. 30).—Ch. xvi. 43, 52, 58.

Vers. 36–49. *Oholah's and Oholibah's Abominations together.* Vers. 36–45. *The Abominations.* Vers. 46–49. *The Judgment.*

Vers. 36–45. *The Abominations.*

Ver. 36. Ch. xxii. 2, xx. 4. Since the ripeness of both of them for judgment is evident, this refrain is most appropriate.—(Ch. xvi. 2.)—Ver. 37. Adultery with the idols, and blood-shedding, as in ch. xxii. 3, etc. Ch. xvi. 38. The latter illustrated by the bloody sacrificing of children. (Ver. 4. Ch. xvi. 20, xx. 31.)—Ver. 38. Ch. xx. 27.—Ch. v. 11. (2 Kings xxi. 4, 5, 7.) **In the same day,** makes the shocking contrast more obvious. Desecration of the sanctuary and Sabbath, as in ch. xxii. 8.—Ver. 39. (Ch. xvi. 21.) **To their idols,** explains "to them" at the close of ver. 37.—The doing of the one and the other,—this was the special affront to Jehovah. Not that children were sacrificed in the temple, but Jehovah was repaired to after Moloch, each in their several places. That which was "defilement" of the sanctuary in ver. 38, when the idea of offering to Moloch was included, is here called "profanation," when both are treated separately. **To profane it,** however, seems to mean something more, namely: that they came to the temple to profane it also by alien rites of all sorts, as the clause: **and lo . . . in the midst of My house,** evinces (ch. viii. 3 sq.). The immediately following change from the plural to the singular shows that the background is here supplied by the period subsequent to the destruction of Israel; Judah appears before the prophet's eye for Israel, partly on account of the temple, but also in consideration of all Israel's relations to Judah both before and after (2 Chron. xv. 9, xxx. 11).

Ver. 40. Climax, a *non plus.*—תִּשְׁלַחְנָה is not the 2d plur. (address), but is said of both, although it could also be the 3d sing. The signification of the imperf. shows the conduct as continuous; not once and again, but they were wont to do so. Ew.: "They sent repeatedly." Unless it be merely a repetition of ver. 16 from a new point of view? The point of the **coming from afar** is not in its contrast to the near (vers. 5, 12), but in the exertions which it presupposes, so that it is expressly added: **to whom a messenger was sent,** although this was already involved in: **they sent. And, lo, they came,** seems to say this, that those who were far off were at last moved, and actually came. Which may apply to others besides the Chaldeans. To this correspond the special exertions she makes to prepare herself for those whom she has addressed, as "washing;" then painting the eyes (כָּחַל, *to make dark*)—staining the eyelashes and eyebrows with a powder, so as to make the glance of the eye more brilliant (comp. Winer, *Realw.*); and finally the attire in general, 2 Kings ix. 30; Jer. iv. 30.—Ver. 41. "Sitting" is the most natural rendering with מִטָּה, *couch, cushion;* with which also the rest harmonizes. The placing of the **table** betokens the preparation of a meal (according to the prevalent custom). Hengst.: "Eating and drinking play an important part in harlotry, either in the usual or the spiritual sense." (לָהּ, to be referred, not to שֻׁלְחָן, which is masc., but to מִטָּה.) Every effort was made to fill the heart's emptiness in relation to Jehovah, by other and remote associations. For this purpose she placed even Jehovah's holy **incense** (Ex. xxx. 1 sq.) and **oil** beside herself on the couch, so that nothing was any longer sacred to her. Comp. ch. xvi. 18. [Hengst.: The bed is made fragrant by the incense and oil; whereby are meant the rich gifts by which Judah sought to purchase the favour of the heathen sovereigns, Isa. xxx. 6, lvii. 9 (?). Hitz.: The oil is used at table for anointing, and the incense kindled to excite sensuous feeling. Adultery through commercial intercourse is meant, so that it can be the merchant's table, where oil could be exchanged for incense. Häv. understands it of the lascivious worship of the Babylonish Mylitta. The wanton Israel is described as preparing herself for one of the high festivals of this goddess, and as abandoning herself to strangers like the young women of Babylon; incense and oil, therefore, for the purposes of a religious ceremony.]—Ver. 42. הָמוֹן (הָמָה), a *humming;* hence, from the sound of the noise it makes: a **crowd. Loose,** in a bad sense. **In her,** pointing away from the figure to the fact. [HENGST.: "Secure murmur," arising from the self-confident intercourse of the adulterers with the adulteresses, from the festivals which were held for the sealing of political friendship. Ew.: "While a godless shouting resounded thereat." KEIL: "The loud noise became still" (!?). Häv. recalls the reckless wantonness which characterized the worship of Aphrodite in the East.] The loud, dominant **voice,** which is alone heard in Jerusalem, is further explained as **loose,** from the fact that it is the voice of the great (godless) multitude, rich and poor, high and low, with whom those **brought from the wilderness** (ver. 40, "men coming from afar") associate themselves (מוּבָאִים, Hoph. makes a paronomasia with סוֹבָאִים). By this the coalition against Nebuchadnezzar, already frequently referred to, must be meant, not (as Hengst.) "the great anti-Assyrian coalition in the time of Hezekiah," which can be no element in the ripeness for judgment referred to in this chapter. [According to Hengst., סוֹבָאִים is a mixed form that signifies both Sabeans and topers, loose barbarians, besides many others from all the world; and the verse should be referred to political connections with Ethiopia. (Isa. xxxvii. 9, xliii. 3, xlv. 14; 2 Kings xix. 9; Isa. xviii.)] That the **people of the multitude,** who are the same as the "men coming from afar" of ver. 40, represent the Assyrians (KEIL) cannot be evidenced by Isa. xxxix. 3, since those mentioned there are Babylonians, therefore Chaldeans; nor can the **drunkards from the wilderness** (here Keil makes מִמִּדְבָּר correspond to מִמֶּרְחָק (!)) be the Chaldeans, who are afterwards called "righteous men." The addition: "from the wilderness," does not (as Häv.) refer to the Arabian-Syrian wilderness, which separated Babylon from Palestine, but must be taken as an antithesis to בָּהּ,—from the region outside Jerusalem. Jerusalem accordingly appears as a political harlot-house, in which the counterpart to the native multitude, with their noisy watch-cry, is formed by the foreign dissolute rabble, the political sots of the coalition against Babylon. [Hitz. supposes the Arabians, Dedanites, and Sabeans, who had in their hands the commerce between the Persian Gulf and the Mediterranean. But commercial relations are not in question, apart from the fact whether such could be depicted as harlotry. As the commercial highways did not pass through Jerusalem, they must have been induced (according to Hitz.) to go thither by special circumstances. Ew. regards סוֹבָאִים as a pathetic repetition of מוּבָאִים, since he translates: "And for men . . . brought from the wilderness, they laid bracelets," etc.] The giving of the **bracelets** and the **crown** suggests how the combination against Nebuchadnezzar, referred to, promised to reunite Judah and Israel as one kingdom (therefore "crown," in the singular), and generally, as the expressive parallel in ch. xvi. 11, 12 shows, to restore them to their ancient glory. Such was the harlot-reward given to the adulterous women on this side. [According to Häv., the words betoken the self-adornment of the women with an eye to the crowd (?). Jerome supposes that the women had so adorned their lovers, that even men wore bracelets. Hitz. finds in it that both lands had become not only rich, but also luxurious, through commerce.]

Ver. 43. The judgment-boding sentence of God upon such abominations. If וָאֹמַר be taken with לַבָּלָה, the translation would be: And I said *to,* or *of,* etc. The older translators connect the latter word with נִאוּפִים, and supply בְּ, *in adulteries;* the more modern take it in the same connection, but accusatively: *In relation to, no more capable of,* etc. Hitz. as a question: "Does the faded one prosecute adultery?" So also Hengst.: "Are adulteries to the faded? *i.e.* shall her adulteries still go on to the worn out?" The subject to יִזְנֶה (for which the Qeri reads: עַתָּה יִזְנוּ) is, according to some, the woman in question (?); as Ewald: "Now she also prosecutes her whoredoms," *i.e.* Judah is as Samaria; according to others: תַּזְנוּתֶיהָ, taken generally as adulterous character and conduct; and וְהִיא personifies her still surviving, indestructible lewdness, although the woman herself has become shrivelled: "Now shall her lewdness itself go a-whoring" (HITZ.). It is less forced to assume a question, which applies the resultant בָּלָה נִאוּפִים to paramour, adulteries, and adulteress, which expresses what should be the consequence of sin, even before judgment decrees and executes punishment. [HENGST.: "Shall adulteries be still committed even with her?" The Lord cannot possibly suffer this, He must at length make an end (ver. 45). Philippson renders וְהִיא: "when she is so (withered)!" RASHI: "Yet she continues to play the wanton."]—Ver. 44. וַיָּבוֹא justifies our exposition of יִזְנֶה in the previous verse. On this account, therefore, judgment is influenced to descend upon those who are ripe for it. Jerusalem, as stated, and as is expressly added, represents the whole people. Comp. also ch. xvi. 30.—אִשֹּׁת, a unique plural.—Ver. 45. The judges and executioners are called **righteous**—comp. at ver. 24—because they carry out God's judgment conformably to the judgment appropriate to such women (Isa. xlix. 24). A moral comparison between the Chaldeans and the Jews is not intended, nor are prophets and righteous men among the people themselves to be imagined.—Comp. ch. xvi. 38.—Comp. at **ver. 37.**

Vers. 46–49. *The Judgment.*

Ver. 46. According to Hengst. and many others, an address to the prophet: "Bring up" in the might of prophecy. Others suppose the infin. absol. to stand either for the indefinite 3d pers. fut., or (Hitz.) the 1st pers. (ch. xxi. 31).—The **company** retains the character of the previous description of the Chaldeans as "righteous," ch. xvi. 40. The heathen are thus solicitous about that which Israel, as a congregation, had neglected to do (Judg. xx.).—As in the previous verse, the masc. suffix interchanges with the fem., the reference passing over from the figurative to the actual—the men in question. Comp. besides, ch. vii. 21, and at Deut. xxviii. 25.—Ver. 47. The **company**—the Chaldeans—again made specially prominent. **Cleave** (comp. at ch. xxi. 24) is here used in its natural sense.—Comp. ver. 25. —Ver. 48. Ver. 27, ch. xvi. 41.—וְנוּסְּרוּ, according to Gesen., for נִתְוַסְּרוּ, if the Rabbin. punctuation be maintained; otherwise it could be read: נוֹסְרוּ, Niph. instead of a mixed Nithpael. Deterrent beacon for all peoples, as ver. 10; ch. v. 15.—Ver. 49. וְנָתְנוּ, according to some: the women, namely, with their tongues; according to most: the avengers noted in ver. 45,—in very deed. [Hitz.: "the heavenly powers."] In consequence of this recompense, those who are thus judged bear in their punishment the **sins of the idols**, those occasioned by them, committed with, *i.e.* by means of them. (Vers. 7, 30, 37.) —Ch. xvi. 58.

["The closing part of the description represents the two women, and especially the one that personated the people of Judah, as persevering to the last in their wicked and profligate courses. Like persons in the final stages of abandonment, they went on rioting in the ways of evil, unchecked by all the troubles and humiliations they had experienced in the past; and now, therefore, as utterly reprobate and hardened and hopeless, they must be adjudged to the doom appointed against such incorrigible and shameless offenders. So the doleful story ends. The prophet looks only, from first to last, to the course of crime and its deserved recompense; and he allows the curtain to drop without one gleam of hope as to the future. He sees that the hammer of the law in its strongest form is needed to break the hard and stony heart of the people. So urgent was the call for a work of conviction, and so great the danger of that not being effectually wrought, that he would not drop a word which might lighten the impression of guilt upon their minds, or afford the least excuse for delay. His message was, Now or never. Judged by the sense of right and wrong current among men, your conduct toward God calls for judgment without mercy. And if there be not immediately awakened the contrition of sincere repentance, you have nothing to expect but the most unsparing visitations of wrath."—Fairbairn's *Ezekiel*, p. 257.—W. F.]

DOCTRINAL REFLECTIONS.

(See Doct. Reflec. on ch. xx. and ch. xvi.)

1. As contrast is an inherent element in all human development, so through the people κατ' ἐξοχήν, among the peoples, a dualism immediately accompanies the evolution of the triad of the patriarchs to the dodecad, in its relativeness (of the 3 to the 4) to the world as a permeating influence. The two foci of the ellipse illustrate for us the history of the chosen people in their orbit. Even in Gen. xlix. (comp. therewith Deut. xxxiii.), Joseph, as against Judah, is prominent compared with the others. If the first position in the camp was allotted to Judah, and a signally large extent of territory in Canaan bestowed on it, to Joseph (and Ephraim took precedence of Manasseh, Gen. xlviii.) belonged the distinction of furnishing the nation with Joshua, the leader of the host and conqueror of Canaan, as well as of long retaining the tabernacle in its midst. (For the independence of Ephraim in the time of the judges, comp. Judg. viii. 12; Ps. lxxviii.) The jealousy which obtained between the two appears, after Saul's death, in the kingdom of Ishbosheth. Only the centralizing personality of a David was capable of unifying the existing dualism. Yet the fire of discord, which continued to smoulder beneath outward harmony, nourished the rebellion of Absalom and the revolt of Sheba. Under Solomon, it is true, the glory of the nation silenced for the time the variance of the two tribes; but Solomon's polytheistic aberration from the monotheistic path introduced an additional element of division. When sin, including that of Rehoboam and the seceding tribes, had in this way accomplished the division into the two kingdoms of Judah and Israel, this result of sin was at the same time a judgment of God; for which, however, the foundation was laid in that original dualism between Judah and Joseph-Ephraim, and the way paved, in the course of history. The form of the representation in our chapter rests on this view of the subject.

2. One may regard Solomon's polytheistic aberrations (*e.g.* 1 Kings xi. 5) as a refined pantheism, or a more universal, more cosmical Jehovism; yet his marriage with Pharaoh's daughter, at the very beginning of his reign, must have exerted some influence on the religious attitude of the kingdom of the ten tribes. And how could the calf-worship of Jeroboam have been introduced without meeting universal opposition, unless previously, during Solomon's reign, religion and politics had taken a decided outward bias? Note also Solomon's commercial relations with different countries, Syria, Arabia, Egypt, and especially his alliance with the Phœnicians. Thus a toleration sprang up under the influence of trade and intercourse, which necessarily became a religious toleration, and which was still farther defined by politics as a doctrine. The example of the king acted on the people, and it is not surprising that Solomon's connections with the world, and his heathen culture, found their echo in the craving of Ephraim and her associates for a heathen-worldly, revolutionary, anti-theocratic government. Solomon is herein to be compared to the church-father Augustine, to whom Roman Catholicism links itself, as the Reformation also falls back on him; so with Solomon are connected the Song of Songs and the form of the apostasy of the ten tribes.

3. The Egyptian bias of Solomon, which gained national expression in the worship of the calves, was seconded by the policy of Jeroboam, who, imitating the example of Aaron at Sinai, transplanted to Israelitish soil the worship which he had seen at Memphis and Heliopolis, 1 Kings

xii. 26 sq.; 2. The Egyptian animal symbolism, which was thereby applied to Jehovah, was a new growth from old roots. Comp. ver. 8 in our chapter. This corrupt worship of Jehovah moved on the same line as ordinary idolatry (1 Kings xiv. 9), so that the one was as closely related to the other, as the second commandment to the first. Hengst. remarks very justly: "By the introduction of the worship of images, a breach was made for heathenism, through which it rushed irresistibly."

4. As Egypt has a very ancient, original significance for the sacred history, so on the Egyptian monuments, even at a very early time, the Assyrians, under the name "Shari," are represented as in conflict with the Egyptians. The Assyrians, who first broke into the kingdom of Israel under Menahem, are, no doubt, to be considered in historical connection with that ancient kingdom; but their military valour, which they made Israel feel, and which excited its longing for association, appears, however, to point to a recent fresh revival of the ancient Assyrian glory. Pul, to whom Menahem was tributary, was succeeded by Tiglath-Pileser, who led into captivity a portion of the inhabitants of the kingdom of the ten tribes; to him Shalmaneser succeeded, who conducted a still more comprehensive deportation to Assyria, which became complete under his second successor, Esar-haddon, so that the Israelitish kingdom was then made a full end of.

5. The subversion of the kingdom of Israel under its last king, Hosea, whom Shalmaneser had made tributary, took place, besides, on account of the hankering of the people after alliances with Egypt, which one might call the hereditary sin of the whole people (ver. 8); the attempted combination with Egypt against Assyria had provoked a new expedition by Shalmaneser. The destruction of Israel was for Judah a "Remember whence thou art fallen," a *memento mori* (ver. 10). But even before this, Ahaz, the Ahab of the kings of Judah, as he had offered one of his sons to Moloch, so also he regarded the might of the Assyrians as better than the help of Jehovah. Comp. the passage of Isaiah relative to him, and ver. 11 of our chapter. "Thy servant and thy son am I," he had said to Tiglath-Pileser; "come up and deliver me."

6. The Babylonian-Chaldean power, which, like Judah, was dependent on Assyria, affected the imagination of Jerusalem so seductively in the time of the pious son of the godless Ahaz, that even Hezekiah succumbed to the temptation. The expectations entertained from Egypt had faded away, and the Lord had overwhelmed the Assyrians by His hand before Jerusalem (2 Kings xviii. 19); yet Hezekiah's imagination lingers upon his treasures, and upon the embassy which the then vice-king of Babylon had sent to him (perhaps also, as Bunsen conjectures, ver. 14, frescoes of Babylonish heroes and warriors). The preponderating world-power seems to incline from Nineveh to Babylon. Perhaps the destruction of the Assyrian army under Sennacherib incited the Babylonians to revolt from Assyria. Niebuhr (*The History of Assyria and Babylon*) says concerning the relation of Babylon to Assyria: "Assyria was by no means the foremost and most ancient people. The inhabitants of Shinar, the Babylonians, were so. The Ninevites had elevated themselves above them through bravery and good fortune, and the older race, to whom belonged the religious metropolis, the most fertile soil, the origin of history, was compelled to submit to the younger. Their constantly repeated attempts at revolt showed how bitterly the Babylonians felt this disgrace," etc. Ezekiel confirms what Isaiah had formerly predicted to Hezekiah, to cool his carnal expectations from Babylon. The Chaldeans, after destroying Nineveh in combination with the Medes, "stepped into the place of the Assyrians for Judah as well as generally, and this also on the same arena" (HITZ.). Egypt maintained the same attitude toward Assyria as toward Babylon, and the kingdom of Judah, like that of Israel, was subverted through its political harlotries (vers. 19 sq., 27) with Egypt.

7. Through this fatal significance of Egypt for the whole people, that motive of the Decalogue, "Who brought thee out of the land of Egypt, out of the house of bondage," acquires a striking political prominence.

8. When the people which had come out of Chaldea in Abraham, in the end returns to Chaldea, the circle of their natural history is completed. The beginning is also the end. "Moreover it is noteworthy," says Ziegler, "that as the dispersion of mankind into all lands proceeded from Babylon, now the Jewish people, or at least the kingdom of Judah, is carried away to Babylon." "The whole history, from the exodus till now, was a constant provoking of God; therefore it must at last drink a cup full of indignation."

HOMILETIC HINTS.

Ver. 1 sq. "We are called Christians, children of the one heavenly Father; but do we also bear ourselves worthily of the name?" (STCK.)—The two women, Oholah and Oholibah, in their resemblance and difference.—"Oh that all young women from their youth up would deport themselves modestly and chastely! What honour and peace of conscience it would procure for them in old age! Job xxvii. 6" (STCK.).—"One can fall from the greatest light into the greatest darkness and folly, if one be faithless to the grace which has been received" (TÜB. BIB.).—"That is spiritual adultery, when souls fall away from the Creator to the creature" (LUTHER).—"Since body and soul are the temple of the Holy Ghost, He wills that we should preserve both pure and holy, and forbids all unchaste deeds, gestures, words, thoughts, desires, and whatever may excite one thereto" (HEID. CAT., quest. 109).—The youth of a people in its charm and perils.—Harlotry, in all its forms, stains before God, burdens the conscience, and also brings disgrace before men.—The allurements of Egypt for Israel.—The coarseness of apostasy from God amid all the refinement of so-called culture.—For the sake of truth, God's word speaks of fleshly things as they are, and as men practise them; discloses hidden things, and shows them in their naked deformity.—Plain speaking is not attractive; flowery ambiguities are of the devil.—True religion leads to fellowship with God.—"A Christian congregation is a spiritual mother, which should honour God through its sons and daughters" (CR.).

Ver. 5 sq. "Under the guise of piety they committed the worst abominations. As adulteresses foist the children which are the fruit of adultery upon their own husbands, so would Jeroboam also serve the true God under the calf-image" (STCK.).—"To yield oneself unreservedly to God is not to throw oneself away" (HENGST.). — "To expect help from men, to rely on them, to depart from God for the sake of profit, honours, etc., is adultery or harlotry in religion" (STCK.).—"To fear God is the true politics."—Ver. 6. "He who forsakes God is easily carried away by semblances, dress, splendour, honours, and such like" (STCK.).—"How highly the earthly and carnal mind values the friendship and favour of the rich and great!" (B. B.)—Ver. 7. He who holds fellowship with the world must also go after its idols.—The friendship of the world is enmity with God, is idolatry.—Ver. 8. "Behold the power of youthful habit! What has been instilled into one in the years of youth usually remains with one all life through" (HEIM.-HOFF.).—[M. HENRY: "This corrupt disposition in the children of Israel, when they were first formed into a people, is an emblem of that original corruption which is born with us and is woven into our constitution, a strong bias towards the world and the flesh. This sinful tendency of theirs was bred in the bone with them, and would never out of the flesh, though Egypt had been a house of bondage to them. Thus the corrupt affections and inclinations which we brought into the world with us we have not lost, nor got clear of, but still retain them, though the iniquity we were born in was the source of all the calamities which human life is liable to."—W. F.]—Ver. 9 sq. "God excites those against us for punishment, to please whom we have sinned" (O.).—Lovers and scourges.—Honour makes a name for one, so also does dishonour.

Ver. 11 sq. Judah must therefore have been more corrupt, since she did not take warning by Israel's punishment, and since she misused, or at least neglected to use, so much greater grace, which would have enabled her to resist.—"Those who go the same way also reach the same place" (STCK.).—The dangerous power of the imagination.—"Worldly glory seduces the worldly mind" (STCK.).—Ver. 14 sq. Seeing and longing.—"So men now-a-days are chiefly enamoured of that which is nothing; for what is all our honour, delight, external prosperity, nobility, dignity, and glory, our power and strength, but a picture in which there is no reality!" (B. B.)—Ver. 16. "So it comes to pass, unless one makes a covenant with his eyes not to look on worldly glory, and that which is alien to him, that he is presently absorbed in it, and turns away from God" (B. B.).—Ver. 17. One must not paint the devil on the wall.—Love becomes passion, and passion becomes satiety, yea, hatred.—"Estrangement is the usual end of impure love, of the selfishness concealed under it" (HENGST.).—"Friendship and fellowship in sin are of short duration" (ST.).—Ver. 18. He who gives himself up to false friends often loses thereby the true Friend, the Lord.—Ver. 19 sq. It is sad when one goes back to his earlier sins.—"When one lives bestially, he cannot be pictured otherwise than as a beast" (B. B.).—Ver. 21. "The falling back into the old sin is like a visit which is made to her whom one should hate and avoid" (HENGST.).

Ver. 22 sq. The wicked are punished through the wicked.—At a death-bed there is often a great gathering from bygone days. Our sins, and those with whom we have sinned, surround us on every side.—Ver. 25 sq. "The ungodly have no power over God's people, unless they are given up to them by God" (ST.).—Dreadful judgments presuppose dreadful sins.—"We should not wait till God drags us away from sin with violence" (O.).—Ver. 27. "What God's goodness and patience could not accomplish, that the wickedness and tyranny of men shall bring about" (STCK.).—Every one receives at last his due.—Ver. 28 sq. He who surrenders himself to sin shall be surrendered to punishment. Hate spares not.—What love covers, hate discloses. The unclothing through punishment shows well what the clothing through grace is.—Ver. 30 sq. Yea, he who expects to cleanse himself otherwise than through the blood and Spirit of Christ, pollutes himself still more by idolatry.—"Like sins, like punishments" (TÜB. BIB.).—"Him whom thou hast followed in life, thou shalt also follow in death" (STCK.).—"He who accepts not the cup of salvation, must drink the cup of wrath" (ST.).—Ver. 34. It must be drunk out. As we have sided with lust, God sides with punishment.—The dreadful nail-test.—"In righteous judgment God causes sinners to be punished in the members in which they have sinned" (ST.).—Ver. 35. "To remember God is the summary of all godliness, as, on the contrary, to forget God is a summary of all ungodliness; therefore God comprehends all in this one, at the close of the catalogue of sins" (JABLONSKY).—"The sieve of man's memory retains only husks—that which is useless" (ST.).—["Men need no more to sink them than the weight of their own sins; and those who will not part with their lewdness and whoredoms must bear them."—M. HENRY.]

Ver. 36 sq. Comp. at ch. xx. 4.—God is not silent with His sentence, and even the judgments of God hasten like His grace. That which seems to be delay is long-suffering; but during it, sin ripens all the more quickly for judgment.—Ver. 37. As they literally shed blood, so also in the services of idolatry, fleshly impurity found place.—Judah and Israel as Medea.—He who serves Venus and Bacchus offers to them also his children.—Ver. 38 sq. How largely profanation of the Sabbath is the fashion now-a-days also!—"To run from the harlot-house to God's house, from murder to the place of prayer, from sin to singing, is not pleasing to God" (STCK.).—"Self-invented, hypocritical worship of God dishonours Him, more than love of the world" (RICHT.).—From sin to sin,—thus ruin is reached; that was the way of Oholah and Oholibah.—"What holy thing is there which the sinner does not profane!" (STCK.)—"They considered neither place nor time" (JEROME).—Ver. 40 sq. "The society of the ungodly should not be wished, still less sought for" (STCK.).—"Those who are separate from God go in quest of men" (STCK.).—"The sinner wishes in all things to be pleasing to men; why not to God?" (STCK.)—Washing themselves for men, remaining unclean before God: thus hypocrites act.—How much of the activity of social organizations is here literally described!—Ver. 43 sq. "The longer a man continues in sin, the more shameless he becomes" (ST.).—Ver. 45. God's righteousness makes even of the Chaldeans "righteous men."—Ver. 46. "When the judgment-hour strikes, judge and executioner are found so ready that they only require to be called" (STCK.).—Ver. 48 sq. "Even still, although men will not depart from sin, they must depart from life" (L.).—Bad examples, through God's overruling, may serve a good end

12. *The Marking down of the Event that has taken place* (*the Symbolical Discourse and the Virtual Sign*) (ch. xxiv.).

1 And the word of Jehovah came to me in the ninth year, in the tenth
2 month, on the tenth [day] of the month, saying, Son of man, write [register]
thee the name of the day, this same day; the king of Babylon has assailed
3 Jerusalem on this same day. And utter a parable against the house of
rebelliousness, and say to them, Thus saith the Lord Jehovah, Set on a caldron,
4 set it on, and also pour water into it. Gather its pieces into it, every good piece,
5 thigh and shoulder; fill [it] with the choice of the bones. Take the choice
of the flock, and also a wood-pile under it for the bones; let it boil and boil,
6 so that its bones be sodden in the midst of it. Therefore thus saith the Lord
Jehovah, Woe to the bloody city! the caldron in [on] which its rust is, and
whose rust hath not gone out of it! piece for piece bring it out; no lot has
7 fallen upon it. For her blood is in the midst of her; on the bare rock she
has put it; she poured it not upon the earth, that it might be covered with
8 dust. To make fury to ascend, to execute vengeance, I have put her blood
9 on the bare rock, that it should not be covered. Therefore thus saith the
Lord Jehovah, Woe to the bloody city! also I will make the pile great.
10 Heap on wood, kindle the fire, make ready the flesh, and let the fat be
11 melted, and let the bones be burned up. And set it empty upon its coals,
that it may be hot, and its brass glow, and its uncleanness in the midst of it
12 be melted, and that its rust should cease. It has wearied labours, and its
13 much rust went not forth from it; into the fire its rust! In thy filthiness is
lewdness; because I purged thee, and thou wast not purged, thou shalt no
14 more be purged from thy filthiness until I cause My fury to rest on thee. I,
Jehovah, have spoken; it comes, and I do; I will not slacken, nor spare, nor
repent; according to thy ways, and according to thy works, they shall judge
15 thee: sentence of the Lord Jehovah.—And the word of Jehovah came to me,
16 saying, Son of man, behold, I take away from thee the desire of thine eyes
with a stroke; and thou shalt not mourn nor weep, neither shall thy tears
17 flow. Groan, be still, make not mourning for the dead, bind the tire of thy
head about thee, and put thy shoes upon thy feet, and cover not the beard,
18 and eat not the bread of men. And I spake to the people in the morning,
and in the evening my wife died; and I did in the morning as I was com-
19 manded. And the people said to me, Wilt thou not tell us what this [imports]
20 to us that thou doest [it]? And I said to them, The word of Jehovah came
21 to me, saying, Say to the house of Israel, Thus saith the Lord Jehovah,
Behold, I will profane My sanctuary, the pride of your strength, the desire
of your eyes, and the pity of your soul, and your sons and your daughters
22 whom ye have left shall fall by the sword. And ye shall do as I have done;
23 ye shall not cover the beard, and the bread of men ye shall not eat. And
your tires shall be upon your heads, and your shoes on your feet; ye shall
not mourn nor weep; and ye shall pine away in your iniquities, and sigh one
24 to another. And Ezekiel is unto you for a portent; according to all that he
hath done shall ye do; when it cometh, then ye shall know that I am the
25 Lord Jehovah. And thou, son of man, shall it not be, in the day when I
take from them their stronghold, the delight of their glory, the desire of their
26 eyes, and the wish of their souls, their sons and their daughters; That in
that day he that is escaped shall come to thee, to cause the ears to hear it?
27 On that day thy mouth shall be opened [at the same time] with him that is
escaped, and thou shalt speak, and shalt be no more dumb; and thou shalt
be to them for a portent; and they shall know that I am Jehovah.

Ver. 4. Sept.: . . . *ἐκσεσαρκισμενα ἐκ των ὀστεων*— Vulg.: . . . *electa et ossibus plena*—
Ver. 5. *ὑποκαιε τα ὀστα ὑποκατω αὐτων*— *compone strues ossium*—
Ver. 10. Some codices read: יחרו, *adunentur.*
Ver. 12. Vulg.: *Multo labore sudatum est . . . neque per ignem.*

Ver. 13. . . . κ. τι ἐσται ἐαν μη καθαρισθης ἐτι ἑως— *Immunditia tua execrabilis, quia . . . et non . . . Sed nec mundaberis prius*—

Ver. 14. . . . Δια τουτο ἐγω κρινω σε κατα τα αἱματα σου, κ. κατα τα ἐνθυμηματα σου κρινω σε, ἡ ἀκαθαρτος, ἡ ὀνομαστη κ. πολλη του παραπικραινειν. All the ancient versions read: שפטתיך.

Ver. 16. ἐν παραταξει.

Ver. 17. Στεναγμος αἱματος, ὀσφυος πενθους ἐσται αὐτη . . . ἐν τοις ποσιν σου· οὐ μη παρακληθης ἐν χειλεσιν αὐτων—

Ver. 18. K. . . . το πρωι ὀν τροπον ἐνετειλατο μοι, κ. ἀπεθανεν—

Ver. 19. ויאמר, Sept.: κ. εἰπεν . . . ὁ λαος— For כי, אשר is read.

Ver. 22. . . . ἀπο στοματος αὐτων οὐ μη παρακληθησεσθε—

Ver. 23. . . . κ. παρακαλεσετε ἑκαστος τ. ἀδελφον—

EXEGETICAL REMARKS.

The threatened judgment of Jerusalem and Judah is now a fact. The whole previous preparation for it, and therewith the first part of the book—the prophecy of judgment—close with this chapter. Looking back from this point, the detailed division with respect to the symbolism of numbers which was stated in the Introduction justifies itself. 1. Under the divine mission of the prophet (ch. i.–iii. 11) there was shown first of all, in the *two* sections (ch. i. and ch. ii.–iii. 11), the mutual opposition between God and the people. 2. The first carrying out of his divine commission (ch. iii. 12–vii. 27) fell, through the determining influence of the more special relation to God, into the *three* sections (ch. iii. 12–27; iv. 1–v 17; ch. vi. vii.). 3. The succeeding instances of his fulfilment of his commission (ch. viii.–xxiv.), on the other hand, in passing over to the subject of the secularized people, made the number *four* significant in the first section (ch. viii.–xi.), the *two* of contrast in the second (ch. xii. 1–20), and—as this whole third division, like the second, is also governed by the number three—after prominence had been given to the fact that the people of God had become like the world, and after their opposition to Jehovah had been emphasized afresh, there followed, in the third section of the third division of this first part of the book, *twelve* sub-sections, according to the number of the tribes of the whole people, with a notification, in the eleventh of these, that Judah and Israel were parted from each other, ch. xii. 21–xxiv. 27.

Vers. 1, 2. *The Accomplished Fact.*

Ver. 1. To the accomplished fact corresponds the date, with which are to be compared the previously-mentioned dates, ch. i., viii., xx., and therewith 2 Kings xxv. 1; Jer. lii. 4, xxxix. 1; Zech. viii. 19. The synagogue still observes the day as a fast.—Ver. 2. After formal prominence has been given to the day by Ezekiel's being required to write down not only its **name**, but the day itself (עֶצֶם, comp. ch. ii. 3), its historical substance, or that which happened in it, is stated as the beginning of the siege of Jerusalem by Nebuchadnezzar. סָמַךְ is: *to lie hard upon* (Ps. lxxxviii. 7), as כָּבֵד is used in Ps. xxxii. 4 of the hand of God.

Vers. 3–14. *The Symbolical Discourse.*

Ver. 3. As what follows is expressly denoted as a מָשָׁל (comp. at ch. xii. 22, xvii. 2), and the **caldron** is merely that of ch. xi. 3, of course no external symbolical action is to be supposed here, but thereby the supposition of such action in the other passages is made all the more probable (comp. ch. xii., iv., v.). Comp. besides, ch. ii. 5, etc.—The repeated demand, expressing urgent haste, **set on**, is at the same time sarcastic; fetch their caldron (ch. xi. 3): Nebuchadnezzar has planted himself before their walls; presently it may become apparent how far their proverb was a true word. The "pouring in" of the water will, as it were, prevent a possible oversight by which the caldron could be injured. Don't forget the water; the next and chief concernment is with the inhabitants. They are the **pieces**, Ver. 4. It is possible that there is an allusion in אסף ("to sweep together," comp. therewith ch. xxii. 19) to those who fled before the Chaldeans from the country into the city, and in נתח ("to cut in pieces") to the sword which hung threateningly over all. The ה‍ָ— relates to those who come into consideration (ch. xxi. 17) for the caldron (Jerusalem). They are described as the marrow and strength of the population, as the best who are still in the land, as the **choice** even of the **bones**. Many interpreters distinguish the people of quality, the wealthy, the princes, the king, as the bones. It is perhaps more correct to regard the expression as hinting at the high opinion of themselves, entertained by the natives of Jerusalem (ch. xi. 15).—Ver. 5 specifies the whole by **the choice of the flock**, to wit, sheep or goats, of which those pieces are made; and then mentions the fuel, דּוּר, a round piled-up heap, composed of wood (like *strues*), as is evident from the connection, and especially from ver. 10, so that the genitive, as is also immediately explained, betokens the destination; for as the bones likewise (which were even brought for the special purpose) are to be sodden, the wood-pile under the caldron (with reference to the investment of the city round about) must therefore be requisite. [Fairbairn translates the clause in ver. 5: "and also pile the bones under it," and adds in explanation: "What the prophet means is, that the best, the fleshiest parts, full of the strongest bones, representing the most exalted and powerful among the people, were to be put within the pot and boiled; but that the rest, the very poorest, were not to escape: these, the mere bones as it were, were to be thrown as a pile beneath, suffering first, and, by increasing the fire, hastening on the destruction of the others. דּוּר is properly a noun, a pile; literally: And also let there be a pile of the bones underneath. The expression cannot signify, with Häv., a pile of wood for the bones; for דּוּר is simply a pile, not a pile of wood, and when coupled with bones can only mean a heap of these."—W. F.]

רְתָחֶ, "the boiling," found here only, and that in a plural form, strengthens the idea of the verb in this interest. בָּשֵׁל = "to be cooked."

Ver. 6 introduces with לָכֵן the explanation, but at the same time a something additional, a new element. In the previous part of the similitude, the fate of the city is symbolized with regard to those who are present in Jerusalem; the actual fact of the commencement of the siege by the Chaldeans (ver. 2) is also brought into view—therefore woe, etc. (ch. xvi. 23)—ch. xxii. 2. The mention of the blood leads to the new feature in the amplification of the similitude, namely, the **rust,** חֶלְאָה, by which can be meant a stain made by burning, or, still better, the rust-stain formed on metal by the influence of damp, whereby it is eaten away; comp. Jas. v. 3; the ruddy colour being well adapted to represent blood. [Homer sometimes nods. Who ever heard before of the "ruddy colour" of verdigris!? Schroeder must have forgotten that "the caldron" is a caldron of brass.—W. F.] Thus judgment is motived by the guilt of the inhabitants of Jerusalem. The destruction from without merely completed that which had begun long before, from within. That such rust is not done away, means that the shed blood having remained unavenged (ver. 7), punishment must therefore be executed on the inhabitants of Jerusalem as a body (Deut. xxi. 7, 8).—The siege is not a testing which leads to repentance, so that ch. xi. 3 sq. could be fulfilled, but, as Ewald also understands the passage: "the pieces as many as there are pieces," in other words, the inhabitants without distinction or exception shall be fetched out; and as the blood-rust adheres properly to the inhabitants, and only in the figure to the caldron, which however is also employed figuratively in relation to them, so ה— doubtless refers in point of fact to the inhabitants; but it can be referred, so far as the figure is concerned, to the caldron, *i.e.* the city, although the most natural method would be to refer it to the rust, with which also harmonises the verb, which is twice used in regard to it—יָצְאָה and הוֹצִיאָהּ. The rust thus goes out of the caldron, only when all the inhabitants go out at the same time, which may either be when they are led captive or when they are destroyed. The statement as to there being **no lot** only confirms this result; comp. 1 Sam. xiv. 42; John i. 7. Under Jehoiakim and along with Jehoiachin, the choice of the people had been carried away.—Ver. 7 passes from the figure to the reality, namely, to the city, as representing the inhabitants, and states to what extent the rust continues unremoved (ch. xxii. 13, xxiii. 37). Comp. Lam. iv. 12 sq. HENGST.: Judicial murders perpetrated by the dominant party, *e.g.* Jer. xxvi. 20 sq. צְחִיחַ (צחח), from the idea of solidity rather than of dryness, which would have made it drink in that which was poured out; either the smooth and non-porous, or the glancing white rock is meant. [Ew. obscures the simple line of thought by taking the close of ver. 6 interrogatively: "Is not the lot fallen upon it, because her blood was in the midst of it?" and still more by reading, with the Sept., the first person: "Upon the sunniest rock have I placed," etc.] The shed blood is nothing hidden,—nothing which is covered over with dust (Lev. xvii. 13), but, Ver. 8, notorious wickedness, which is made manifest under the rule of Divine Providence, and which calls down the vengeance of God, Gen. iv. 10, 11; Job xvi. 18; Isa. xxvi. 21. "God would make sin manifest, so that His judgment might be recognised as righteous" (HÄV.). Jerusalem was distinguished by the openness and audacity with which it sinned; but the upshot of it all was simply, the bringing near of its judgment. The bold openness of the blood-shedding provoked the **fury**; the fact of its having remained unpunished provoked the **vengeance** of God.

Ver. 9, like ver. 6, explanation, and a new, third element. As the prophet in the similitude (ver. 5), so **also** Jehovah in fact. Or גַּם־אֲנִי now adds to the permitting of guilt to become ripe, the corresponding execution of punishment (ch. xvi. 43). As God takes the matter in hand, מְדוּרָה alternates with דּוּר (ver. 5), Isa. xxx. 33. But as the similitude is to be carried still farther, the prophet, Ver. 10, is enjoined to carry out the divine purpose (ch. xi. 6, xxi. 20). As to the **fire,** comp. ch. v. 4, x. 2, xv. 7.—With הָתֵם, from תָּמַם, comp. ch. xxii. 15.—רַקַּח can mean: "to spice;" Hengst.: "put in the spice" (sarcastic), which, however, fits into the connection with difficulty. The word means properly: to make soft. KEIL: to thoroughly boil the broth. Others, from its also meaning: "to make ointment," translate it by: "stir the mixture."—Ver. 11. The new element. We know from ch. x. 2, i. 13, what **its coals** are. That the caldron, *i.e.* the city, is also overtaken by the judgment, is a fact so natural, that Keil, in opposition to Hitzig, required to point for proof merely to ch. xxiii. 25, xvi. 41. The **empty** caldron, moreover, points back to ver. 6, as ver. 9 to ver. 5, so that with the renewed reference to the rust, the similitude is rounded to a conclusion. **Its uncleanness is its rust,**—the blood-guilt, in which are especially included the polluting Moloch-offerings, ch. xxii. 3, 4, 15, 21, 22. As that which is before the inhabitants is not a time of testing, so that which the city is to experience is not the burning out of evil, or purification.—Ver. 12. תְּאֻנִים הֶלְאָת Gesen. translates: "With hard labour it (the caldron) wearies me." Many render the close of the verse: "in the fire," or: "through the fire its rust." Fruitless efforts (comp. ver. 13) at purification are meant. According to Hitz.: "through such extreme heat to remove the rust" (Jer. vi. 29); so that a pause of expectation requires to be imagined between vers. 11 and 12, which, however, is arbitrarily assumed. J. D. MICH.: "When verdigris has eaten very deeply into it, copper is made red-hot in the fire, and cooled in water, when the rust falls off in scales, etc. It can be partially dissolved by the application of vinegar. Only one must not think of a melting away of the rust by the fire, since in that case the copper would necessarily be melted along with it. Also through the mere heating the greater part can be loosened, so that it can be rubbed off." Hengst. mentions the severe labour of the true servant of the Lord, Isa. xlix. 4. [DUTCH ANNOTATIONS: "*She hath wearied* (me with) *vanities*, making such a continual stir by her idolatries, heathenish covenants, intestine oppression, lying, hypocrisy, and all manner of wicked devices, whereby she would underprop her ruinous condition and keep off threatened destruction, instead of repenting and turning unto me, whereunto I exhorted them by my prophet with such patience and forbearance, and admonished them so faithfully and frequently with sore threatenings, that I am even grown weary of it, they being not (in the least) bettered, but grown still more obstinate and hardened thereby."—W. F.] While the **much rust** is destined for the fire, so that the caldron, in contrast to it, does not come into account, the fate of the caldron at the same time becomes evident.—Ver. 13, departing from the figure, addresses Jerusalem. HITZ.: "on account of thy unchaste uncleanness." So also most interpreters. The degeneracy of the people is described as one in which the death-deserving crime of **lewdness** forms the characteristic element.

[HENDERSON: "The impurity of the inhabitants of Jerusalem was of the most atrocious character. זִמָּה, *crime*, deliberate *wickedness*, is a term employed to denote a criminal act, perpetrated on set purpose. Root, זָמַם, *to think, devise, purpose*; mostly used in a bad sense. Jehovah had used a variety of means, both physical and moral, to restore them to purity, but they had produced no effect. It remained now only for the Chaldeans to do their work. The decree was irrevocable, and the execution inevitable."—W. F.]

Comp. ch. xxiii. 44, 48, xvi. 27, 42, etc. (Lev. xviii. 20.) While they degenerated to such an extent, both politically and religiously, they withdrew themselves from the influence of the efforts made by Jehovah, who by word (promise and threatening) and deed (chastisements and deliverances) was all the while bent on the purifying of Israel. All promulgation of law was designed to effect the separation of the people from the heathen world, and their purification from innate corruption (2 Chron. xxxvi. 15). The judgment which has overtaken them brings to an end these fruitless efforts for their purification, and every prospect of their being cleansed. Henceforth—that is the immediate future of Israel—the **fury** of God **rests on** them. Comp. at ch. v. 13 (Jer. xiii. 27; Isa. iv. 4).—Ver. 14. The close of the symbolical discourse. Comp. ch. xxiii. 34, v. 13.—Ch. xxi. 12.—Ch. xvii. 24.—Ch. vii. 3, 8, 27.—פָּרַע, either with reference to persons: to let the guilty go free (GESEN.), or in a neuter sense, which is the preciser idea: to depart from My word through a procedure not conformable to it.—(Ch. xx. 44.) Ch. xxiii. 24, 45.—The words which are here added by the Sept. (were they following a different version?) are inserted by Hitz. and Ew. as conformable to the text.

ADDITIONAL NOTE ON VERS. 6–14.

["After having briefly given the ground of the parabolical description, the prophet proceeds, in vers. 6–14, to make special and pointed application of it. His leading object is to show that it was the excessive and inveterate wickedness of the people which provoked, and even rendered necessary, the severe dealing to which they were subjected.

"All measures of a less extreme kind had been tried in vain; those were now exhausted; and as the iniquity appeared to be entwined with the whole fabric and constitution of things, nothing remained but to subject all to the crucible of a severe and overwhelming catastrophe. This is represented by keeping the caldron on the fire till its contents were stewed away, and the very bones burnt. And as if even this were not enough, as if something more were necessary to avenge and purge out such scandalous wickedness, the caldron itself must be kept hot and burning till the pollution should be thoroughly consumed out of it. The wicked city must be laid in ruins. It is the very same thought which occurs in Isa. iv. 4, where the filth of the daughters of Zion is said to be washed away, and the blood of Jerusalem to be purged from the midst of it by the spirit of judgment and the spirit of burning; only, after the manner of our prophet, the image is extended to many minute and particular details. In plain terms, the Lord was no longer going to deal with them by half-measures; their condition called for the greatest degree of severity compatible with their preservation as a distinct and separate people, and so the indignation of the Lord was to rest on them till a separation was effected between them and sin."—FAIRBAIRN'S *Ezekiel*, pp. 261, 262.—W. F.]

Vers. 15–27. *The Virtual Sign* (*the Silence of Ezekiel*).

Ver. 16. מַחְמַד, what the eyes desire, 1 Kings xx. 6, what they rest on with affection.—מַגֵּפָה, from נָגַף, *to smite*, can be: overthrow, calamity, and means here sudden death. So much the more natural would those gestures and expressions of feeling be which were forbidden to him. סָפַד is almost always used of lamentation for the dead. Even the tears which were so natural (**thy**), not to speak of "weeping," were not allowed to him, 1 Cor. vii. 29.—Ver. 17. The feeling of grief God does not forbid, only its loud, outward expression; the pain felt in regard to a private experience shall be dumb, just as the universal experience symbolized by it must absorb every private sorrow. The opposite of the **mourning** which was made **for the dead** (מֵתִים is placed expressively at the beginning of the clause) is described in detail. פְּאֵר is a "head-ornament" (Isa. lxi. 3) in general (ver. 23), not exclusively that of the priest; people laid it aside in times of mourning, and went bareheaded—comp. however, Deut. xiv. 1; strewed ashes upon their heads, Lam. ii. 10; went barefooted, 2 Sam. xv. 30; covered, as did lepers, the lower part of their face, Mic. iii. 7—the beard, as man's adornment; obtained food from other people, as from neighbours, who sent it to the house, in contradistinction to the food prepared by themselves at other times, Jer. xvi. 7.—Ver. 18. As Ezekiel **spake to the exiles in the morning**, namely, ver. 3 sq., **and his wife died in the evening**, the directions which he received for his behaviour in regard to this event, and which he complied with on the morning after the death, were communicated to him on the same day with the symbolical discourse. [Hengst. refers the "speaking" to the communication of the divine command to the people, and makes the prophet appear before them on the succeeding morning with the intelligence that his wife had died the previous evening, when he acted in the already-mentioned symbolical manner.]—Ver. 19 (ch. xii. 9) assumes that the death of the prophet's wife has become known to the people, since their question is occasioned by the inconsistency of his behaviour with that fact. As it is inexplicable when considered in relation to himself, the inquiry as to its bearing on them springs to their lips.—כִּי either stands for אֲשֶׁר, or is to be explained thus: For thou doest it for us; in relation to thyself thou wouldst necessarily have acted otherwise. [The expressions which Hengst. has not hesitated to employ may be quoted on account of their singularity: "The prophet appears merely as a holy actor" (!); "We have to do with a mere figure," with a "fact of the holy phantasy;" Ezekiel may have had "no wife at all," etc.]

Ver. 20. The explanation of his conduct follows, as he was divinely commissioned to give it, —Ver. 21—namely, that what had happened to himself, whereby he is placed before them in a more impressive manner as the representative of the **house of Israel**, as the exiles' "companion in tribulation," was a type of that which was about to happen to them. As the expressions show, the wife of Ezekiel must typify the temple; her death represents especially its desecration, when Jehovah allows it to fall into the hands of the heathen (ch. vii. 22), whereby the symbol of his marriage-relation to Israel, the dwelling together, disappears. If this relation between the wife and the temple is established—comp. ver. 16—by the expression: מַחְמַד עֵינֵיכֶם, then the temple on its part symbolizes all the possessions and power of Israel. To its existence in their midst they appealed against their brethren, ch. xi. 15; and to this they trusted amid all their wickedness and apostasy, ch. viii. 6; Jer. vii. 4. **Pride of your strength**,—since they took pride in it as their strength. Comp. Lev. xxvi. 19.—Note the alliteration in מַחְמַל and מַחְמַד; according to Hengst.: "the sympathy of your soul," since the soul that is inwardly united with it suffers with it (?); Gesen.: "what your soul desires, loves." The following would correspond better with its signification elsewhere (ch. vii. 4), namely: that your soul would spare,—pledging life itself for it. (*Dutch Trans.*: the sparing of your souls.)—In the symbolical significance of Ezekiel's wife for Israel, next to the special relation to the temple, the people come into consideration,—the **sons** and **daughters**; in the symbol, sudden death; as to the people, death by violence. (Hitz.: "On the occasion of the expatriation, many parents may have been obliged to leave their children with relatives, from their being of too tender age to accompany them." Perhaps also they could be left behind in expectation of better times.)—Ver. 22. In regard to both the relations referred to, the exiles addressed shall imitate Ezekiel; comp. ver. 17.—Ver. 23. Vers. 17, 16. The direct application of what has gone before, which is made by the prophet to his companions in exile, gives a symbolical character to what has been said, which becomes all the clearer, as what is exactly meant is immediately expressed, namely: **Ye shall pine away in your iniquities**, etc. (ch. iv. 17), which describes a state of inward and personal woe which is destitute of all comfort (Isa. l. 1, lix. 2).—נָהַם is the pressing out of the breath in lowing and also in roaring; here it corresponds to what is said of Ezekiel in ver. 17,—a sighing with groans, and that of the one to the other, instead of the former mutual interchange of complaints, wishes, and hopes. [Häv. and others understand it as: pain and sorrow on account of sin, which is said neither here nor in Lev. xxvi. 39; Eich.: dull indifference at the downfall of Jerusalem in consequence of the misery of banishment; Ew.: a stupified, unrepentant state of mind; many: fear and shame before the Chaldeans among whom they dwelt. Hitz. makes them growl one to another like bears, discontentedly seeking the source of their misfortune in others instead of in themselves; Hengst.: despair.] As, in the prophet' case, the misfortune of his wife's death disappears in the deep shadows of the overthrow of Jerusalem and Judah, so all the personal feelings of the exiles shall be absorbed in this destruction of the last remnant of the kingdom and city. One and another shall be benumbed with pain, so that no comfort shall come from any quarter; on the contrary, a desolating feeling of guilt shall be general,—such shall be their knowledge of the Lord.—Ver. 24. Comp. at ch. xii. 6.—Ver. 14. הָ— is referred by many to ver. 26. The introduction of Ezekiel's name completes the personal type.

["It appears to us almost unaccountable how any person of ordinary discernment should understand the prophet here to mean, that those Jews were to receive the coming catastrophe in a callous and indifferent manner, sullenly yielding to their fate, but without any sensible movement of the springs of sorrow and regret. Yet such is the view taken of the passage by some leading commentators abroad (in particular, by Eichhorn, Ewald, Hitzig), although the express declaration at the close, and the whole character of the representation, plainly lead to an opposite conclusion. In the typical part of the delineation, it was not because the prophet was insensible to the loss he sustained by the death of his wife that he was to abstain from the habiliments and usages of mourning; but because there was another source of grief behind, of which this was but the sign and presage, and in itself so much greater and more appalling, that his spirit, instead of venting itself in expressions of sorrow at the immediate and ostensible calamity, was rather to brood in silent agony and concern over the more distressing evil it foreshadowed. And in like manner with the people, when all their fond hopes and visions were finally exploded—when the destruction of their beautiful temple and the slaughter of their sons and daughters came home to them as dreadful realities, they could only refrain from bewailing the loss of what had so deep a hold on their desires and affections, by having come to discern in this the sign of what was still greatly more dreadful and appalling. And what might that be but the blood-stained guilt of their iniquities, which had brought on the catastrophe? Had it been that portion of the people who dwelt at Jerusalem that the prophet here more immediately referred to, there might have been some room for supposing (with Pradus and others) that he pointed merely to the overawing terror of the enemy, and to the breathless horror and astonishment connected with the capture of the city, when he spake of such an arrest being laid on the common outgoings of grief. But it is the captives at Chebar of whom he more immediately speaks, who, he well knew, would be living in outward quiet, far removed from the scene of uproar and destruction. It could not, in their case, be the presence of a Babylonian host, or the turmoil and consternation caused by the success of the Babylonian arms, which should check the customary expressions of grief; it would be the overwhelming sense that should then break in upon them of the iniquities to which they had clung with such fatal perverseness, absorbing their spirits, and turning their moanings into a new and higher direction. The agonies of bereavement would be in a manner lost under the self-inflicted pains of contrition and remorse (comp. ch. vii. 16).

"Yet, while this seems obviously the meaning of the prophet's announcement,—of the not mourning in one way, and still pining away with distress and sorrow in another,—the description must be understood with certain qualifications, and indeed is to be viewed as the somewhat ideal delineation of a state of things that *should* be found, rather than the exact and literal description of what was actually to take place. The representation would otherwise stand in palpable contrariety, as well with undoubted facts as with statements elsewhere made both by Ezekiel and by his great contemporary in Judea. That many, on the fall of Jerusalem, did really exhibit the usual signs of mourning, and give the fullest vent to their feelings of distress, may be inferred with the utmost certainty from what is written in the Lamentations of Jeremiah, where we read of all the common symptoms and appliances of grief: 'elders sitting upon the ground, casting dust upon their heads, girding themselves with sackcloth;' and the prophet himself—though he had been told not to lament or bemoan (ch. xvi. 5)—weeping till 'his eyes failed with tears, and his liver was poured on the earth, for the destruction of the daughter of his people.' Nay, while Ezekiel here speaks as if all the indications of mourning should be restrained at the destruction of Jerusalem, he had previously spoken of the people being so filled with distress on account of it, that 'they should gird themselves with sackcloth, and have baldness upon their heads' (ch. vii. 18), and had himself also been instructed to howl and cry in contemplation of the approaching troubles (ch. xxi. 12). There can be no doubt also, on the other side, that the conscience of sin, however powerfully it might work in some bosoms, and absorb other feelings, would be very far from being universally felt as it ought to have been. The prophets were by no means disposed to cherish exaggerated views on the subject. Jeremiah had even spoken of the people carrying their iniquities with them into other lands, and there serving other gods day and night (ch. xvi. 13). And Ezekiel himself, in ch. xx., represents them as still needing, after they had been all scattered among the nations, to be brought as into the wilderness, that they might there be dealt with for iniquities not yet forsaken, and purged from still remaining abominations.

"It is clear, therefore, that the description in the passage before us must not be understood in the absolute sense, as if it were intended to portray what was certainly to be realized among the people at large on the taking of Jerusalem. It is what should have been realized in all; but what, in point of fact, was to have its realization only in part. The people should, on the occurrence of such a fearful catastrophe, have sunk under an overpowering sense of their guilt and folly, and, like the prophet, turned the tide of their grief and mourning rather against the gigantic evil that lay behind, seen only in the chambers of imagery, than what outwardly appeared; they should have bewailed the enormous sins that had provoked the righteous displeasure of God, rather than the present troubles in which that displeasure had taken effect. Their sorrow should have chiefly flowed in this more inward and spiritual direction, for it was here pre-eminently that the evil stood. And such, undoubtedly, was the case with the better and more enlightened portion of the people; but many still cleaved to their idols, and would not receive the instruction given them, either by the prophet's parabolical example, or by the reality of God's afflicting dispensations."—FAIRBAIRN'S *Ezekiel*, pp. 266–268.—W. F.]

Ver. 25. The prominence given to the person of the prophet leads now to the announcement of a sign which is to be given him hereafter, and to the giving of an instruction for his procedure thereupon. **And thou,** etc. The statement is interrogative in its form, but assumes an affirmative answer. It is equivalent to: I ask thee, shall it, can it be otherwise? The time is expressed as a definite **day**. A year and a half elapsed before then, ch. xxxiii. 21; comp. Jer. lii.—The **delight of their glory** means: that in whose glory they delighted, ver. 21.—**The wish of their souls**, that to which they looked with longing and yearning. According to others: "the burden of their souls," namely, that which oppresses them. The **sons and daughters** are named along with the temple, without a connecting word, but as in ver. 21.—Ver. 26. **The escaped** is a definite person. [According to Hengst.: an ideal person, comprehending in himself the whole host of those carried away; others: a fugitive, one of their number.] As an eye-witness of what had been passed through, he will place the fact before the exiles as one which cannot be doubted.—Ver. 27. As he (which is also a virtual sign, namely, for the prophet) opens his mouth, Ezekiel does the same, who consequently has had to keep silence up to that time. The opening of the prophet's mouth at the same time with that of the fugitive takes place in ch. xxxiii.; comp. vers. 21, 22. The word of Jehovah, however, comes to the prophet in the interval, ch. xxv.–xxxii. As these prophecies are directed against non-Israelites, the silence of the prophet, which is introduced with ch. xxiv., must be regarded as relative, and be understood in reference to his discourses to Israel only: to them he will not speak in the present period; he will do so only (ch. xxxiii.) when, with the renewal of his divine mission, a "new period for prophetic speech" (HENGST.) **shall open,** comprehending the second part of his book. Comp. at ch. xxix. 21. As, now, this second part, containing the prophecies of divine compassion, sets itself over against the first part which contains the prophecies of judgment, and the retrospective reference of ver. 27 (ch. xxxiii. 22) to ch. iii. 26, 27 is unmistakeable (comp. there); so Ezekiel's becoming dumb can be taken in relation to prophesying of mercy as distinguished from prophesying of judgment, so that the meaning would be: Thou shalt then speak of mercy, and no more of judgment, which has become an accomplished fact. But therewith the prophet's becoming dumb appears as a becoming silent touching mercy, and as a speaking concerning judgment, just as speaking, of this nature, was characteristic of the first part of the book; so that the dumbness of Ezekiel affects, in the first place, the period up to the appearance of the fugitive from Jerusalem with the news of its downfall; but further, on its close, looks back on the whole period of the first part of the book, which it concludes. Thus it is evidently to be understood as a prophetic dumbness, not as silence in a general sense. The prophet speaks of judgment to foreign peoples, during the time which is to be assumed from our chapter, exactly as in the first part of the book,—the time of his silence as to mercy, he spoke to Israel. Thus his becoming silent is here also a virtual sign to Israel, just as it was so at an earlier time, ch. iii. 26, 27.—Through all this speech and silence (thus many refer it to the whole activity of the prophet), and in other ways, he is shown to have been a significant symbol to his fellow-countrymen. [DUTCH ANNOTATIONS: *In that day*, etc.; "As if God should say, Thou hast now sufficiently foretold my people of the miseries that are at hand, be now silent for a while till all things be clearly fulfilled and plain before their eyes; then shalt thou speak to them again for their comfort and instruction, that thou mayest thus be unto them and to My whole church in sundry ways a wonderful token of great things to come."—W. F.] HENGST.: "When the eye-witnesses report that all has happened as announced by him, he will become to them an object of wonder, they will recognise the Lord behind the son of man." It is more natural, however, to regard it as a simple repetition of ver. 24, as Ezekiel's dull pain (ver. 17) prefigured not merely the feeling and behaviour of the exiles, but also God's pain: it could be regarded, if one might so speak, as a striking symbol of the silence of the Judge in regard to Israel, after the sentence had been passed, which is now being executed,—of His still continued silence towards His people concerning mercy.

DOCTRINAL REFLECTIONS.

1. With the prediction of our chapter, comp. Doct. Reflec. on ch. xii. No. 4. "This discourse is peculiarly important," says Häv., "owing to the definiteness of its prediction." "The place on the Chebar where the prophet lived was distant from Jerusalem more than a hundred German miles; it was therefore impossible for Ezekiel to know by human means that the siege of Jerusalem had commenced on that very day; and when it was afterwards ascertained that the prediction had exactly corresponded with fact, it would be regarded as an invincible proof of his divine mission" (J. D. MICH.). Ew. makes the prophet act on that day "in an altogether animated way, as if the siege of the distant city had been set in array against himself." He supposes also that the anticipation of soon losing his wife by a sudden stroke was a "presentiment." Umbreit interprets the matter in almost the same way, by regarding the wife of the prophet as "prostrated by a severe illness," so that he foresaw her speedy death. Hitz. admits that "anything fortuitous is not to be imagined; and all the less, from the fact that we have here nothing to do with premonition, since the certainty of the tone, and the definiteness with which Ezekiel speaks of the subject, must rest on a proper knowledge of the fact." With his decision in favour of a *vaticinium post eventum*, not only the prophetic, but also the moral character of Ezekiel falls to the ground.

2. "The earth drinks in the blood which is righteously shed, or covers it, so that it is not avenged on him who shed it; on the other hand, it is said of the blood which is to be avenged, that the earth covers it not, or discloses it in its season, Job xvi. 18; Isa. xxvi. 21" (Cocc.).

3. ["As to the principle of dealing, there is no essential difference between what God did then with Israel, and what He still does with those who stand in a similar relation to Him, and pursue a similar course. Where there is the profession of a belief in God's word, and a regard to God's authority, though intermingled with much that is false in sentiment, or unrighteous in conduct, there must still be dealings of severity and rebuke, to bring the professor, if possible, to a sense of his sinfulness, and lead him to renounce it; but, failing this, to vindicate concerning him the righteousness of God, and leave him without excuse if his iniquity should prove his ruin. In the case of sincere, God-fearing people, the severity exercised will always be attended with salutary results; for they have the root of the matter in them, and are sure to profit by the chastening of the Lord. But with those who have the profession only, without the principle of true godliness, the iniquity is clung to in spite of all the severity that is exercised, until the wrath falls on them to the uttermost. There is enough in New Testament Scripture, and the experience of men under the present dispensation, to warrant us to expect *so far* a similarity in God's method of procedure to the representation here given of His conduct toward Israel. But, on the other hand, a difference may also be expected, in so far as His dealings now, in accordance with the genius of the new dispensation, respect men more as individuals, less as public communities, and bear more immediately upon their inward state and spiritual relations. He who would regard aright the operations of the Lord's hand, and profit by the corrections of His rod of chastisement, must keep a watchful eye upon the things that concern his own experience and history. There may be signs of the divine displeasure sufficient to startle the tender conscience, and call for deep humiliation of spirit, while nothing appears outwardly wrong, and all may even wear a smiling aspect as far as regards social and public relations. Should there be a restraining of divine grace within, an absence of spiritual refreshment, a felt discomfort of mind, or an obvious withdrawal of spiritual privileges, there is beyond doubt the commencement of a work of judgment; and if such marks of God's displeasure are slighted, others of a more severe and alarming kind may assuredly be looked for

But as men's tempers and circumstances in life are infinitely varied, so there is a corresponding variety in the methods employed by God to check the risings of sin, and expel its poison from the heart. And it is the part of spiritual wisdom to seek for the wakeful ear and the discerning eye, which may enable one to catch even the earliest intimations of God's displeasure, and so improve these as to render unnecessary the heavier visitations of wrath."—FAIRBAIRN'S *Ezekiel*, pp. 262, 263.—W. F.]

4. Hengst., in denying the reality of the death of Ezekiel's wife, states the proposition that "a moral relation like marriage cannot be degraded to a mere mode of representation;" as if this would less be the case if we had before us "only a vividly drawn figure!" This death is just as little a "mere mode of representation" as anything else which, ordained by God, happens specially to His children and servants. But the moral significance of the event for Ezekiel was altogether subordinate to the prophet's significance for the people. That which was merely purifying trial to him was to be punishment to them. "He endures," says Schmieder, "the pain, like other sufferings of his prophetic office, as the servant and instrument of God for Israel, in order to lead the people to saving repentance." "God by no means spares His servants, and they endure willingly, because they know that the Lord in His own time makes all things work together for good, and because they are always ready to offer up to Him in love and confidence whatever He requires." We must not forget that Ezekiel was set as a "portent" for the people; comp. at ch. iv. (Doct. Reflec. 4), ch. xii. Thus, according to the individuality of his official position, for which his loving sympathy with his people is the psychological medium, he is a type in virtue of a personal symbolical substitution or representation. Ezekiel prefigures, in a most painful domestic experience, the judicial punishment which is ordained of God for the people, with whom he is joined by personal sympathy, as well as by the fact of being equally an exile. It might be said that a Messianic element here makes itself apparent in the prophet. The symbolism of marriage in relation to Christ and the Church (Eph. v. 32) harmonizes with this theological explanation of the case. Consider, besides, the reference to Jer. xvi., on which Hävernick lays stress.

5. The instructions received by Ezekiel in connection with the death of his wife are very remarkable. They suggest various inferences, both as to his own character as the servant of God, and as to the nature of the prophetic office. While the prophet was frequently one of the most gifted, and always one of the most honoured of men, he was at the same time one of the most severely tried. Like all places of honour in the kingdom of God, the position of a prophet involved the bearing of burdens which were exceptionally heavy. The closeness of his fellowship with God had two sides—a dark as well as a bright. For his high degree in the kingdom of God he had to pay a great price, by being preeminently a cross-bearer. He was taught, and often by painful experiences, that it was necessary to "count all things but loss" for God; "to hate father and mother and wife and children and brethren and sisters, yea, and his own life also," in order to fulfil the duties of his high office. Only in so far as he had learned this truth did he attain to the character of the ideal prophet. A perpetual spiritual law was enunciated by our Lord, when He said, at least in effect, to the ambitious sons of Zebedee, that drinking of His cup and being baptized with His baptism, were the conditions of occupying places of honour in His kingdom. This law held in the Old Testament period no less than in the New. The man who was distinguished from his fellows by receiving power to inherit all the ages, to dip into the future and comprehend the near and the remote in a single gaze of his divinely opened eye, to understand and proclaim the eternal moral principles according to which God determines the order of world-history, to be, in short, a prophet, was also distinguished from them by profounder experience of sorrow, suffering, and self-abnegation. The words which were spoken by God in reference to Paul, when he was about to be introduced to the apostolic office, might have been applied, with scarcely a verbal change, to Ezekiel, or to any of the ancient prophets, when they were called to their life-work: "He is a chosen vessel unto Me to bear My name before the Gentiles, and kings, and the children of Israel; . . . I will show him how great things he must *suffer* for My name's sake."

Self-consecration was an essential condition to the proper fulfilment of the duties of the prophetic ministry. The prophet was required to devote to God the energies of his mind and soul, the treasures of his heart,—all that he prized most; for God regarded them as His own, and might use any, or all of them, as instruments for the carrying on of His work. The tasks which God enjoined presupposed this complete surrender on the part of His servants. Their accomplishment would have been impossible otherwise. The prophet was often asked to do things difficult, disagreeable, or even unnatural, in order that effect might be given to his divine message. For, when the spoken word was not regarded as sufficient, it was supplemented by the acted word or the symbol, in the choosing of which, regard was had, not to the comfort, convenience, or private feelings of him whose duty it was to set the symbol forth, but only to its power to teach and impress. Often, indeed, the symbols chosen were of such a kind that the employment of them did not necessarily involve self-denial; but the case was altered, when acts and experiences of the private life of the prophet which touched his deepest feelings, were regulated and controlled so as to transform him into a personal symbol. Thus, for the sake of perfecting him as a teacher by signs, Hosea was commanded to form peculiar domestic ties, to which natural feeling would have disinclined him. And whatever view be held as to the Divine *intention* in taking away Ezekiel's wife by a stroke, her death was used as a symbol of a great public calamity, whose character was further symbolized, by the prophet's deportment under his affliction, in which he was influenced by a regard to his mission only. When he went forth to the people on the morning after his bereavement, he could have said in a double sense, "The *burden* of the Lord."

The fact of God imposing upon Ezekiel the command to repress all signs of feeling, and, notwithstanding the suddenness and severity of the stroke, to be calm and self-controlled, proves that the servant of God must lead a life of self-sacrifice, that individual feeling must be merged in the higher claims of duty; while the promptness and perfection of his obedience show how well he had learned to subordinate all things to the fulfilment of his ministry, and how all-absorbing was his desire to arouse his people to a sense of things spiritual and divine. That the affliction which came upon him was most crushing, may be inferred from the nature of the case and from the narrative. To one who could be described as "the desire of thine eyes," the prophet must have been knit in tenderest love, and he would feel the bereavement all the more because his nature was intense and lonely, his soul, one which dwelt apart. Deep must have been the sense of desolation which filled his heart, when he knew that he was to be for ever deprived of the sympathy which was so grateful because so rare, so helpful because so loving, and so trusted because it had never failed. But the manner in which God communicates His purpose, and the use which He asks the prophet to make of the bereavement, assume his possession of the intensest spirituality of mind and devotion to his prophetic mission. The bereavement is regarded entirely as to its possible bearing on public utility, and not once as to its bearing on private happiness. The prophet's private feelings are ignored, except in so far as their natural expression is forbidden; God foretells him of his affliction, not so much that he may be prepared to bear, as that he may be prepared to use it for the fulfilment of his ministry. No compensation for the desolation of his human heart is hinted at except this —that he shall enjoy, on account of his affliction, the opportunity of preaching by new symbols of unusual impressiveness—of becoming himself an eloquent symbol. What he suffers as a man may be counterbalanced by what he shall accomplish as a prophet. For the anguish of bereavement, for the pain of self-repression, of abstinence from every expression of grief, from even the sweet solace of tears, he may find some compensation in being enabled, by means of his own circumstances, to place the future before the minds of his people, in a way fitted to make them realize the coming woe, and to arouse them to repentance. His great sorrow hidden in his heart, Ezekiel, the servant of God, proceeds to the work which God gave him to do. The shadows which appeared to rest on his soul proceeded, less from the recollection of his own bereavement, than from foresight of the calamities of his people. His private sorrow seemed to be overlaid by an anticipation of the greater sorrow which was to affect them. His manner seemed to say, "Weep not for me, but weep for yourselves and for your children." As he was a "portent" to Israel, so, by his beautiful, self-forgetting devotion to prophetic duty, which was made possible to him, not merely by the grace of God which accompanied the command of God, but also by the powerful sympathies of his own sanctified nature, Ezekiel is an example to the servants of God in every age.—W. F.]

HOMILETIC HINTS.

Ver. 1 sq. "Ch. xxiv. is to be regarded as a farewell" (HENGST.).—One goes on speaking till the last moment. "As the hour for bringing help to the pious is fixed, so also is the hour for executing God's vengeance on the wicked" (STCK.). —"This happened in our month of December" (L.).—That which is carried out at Jerusalem is written down at Babylon.—"He who is condemned to death knows not the day, which his Judge, however, knows well" (STCK.).—Our calendar should be a very different one were the days noted according to God's bidding.

Ver. 3. "God loves to say to man what He means to say to him by means of intelligible figures; therefore preachers should avoid obscuring His word with ambiguities" (L.).—In the wrath of God, because it is His despised love, as in the love of God, there are intensity and vehemence.—In the time of God's judgment all the excuses of men will fall to the ground.—Ver. 4. God is already gathering to His judgment-seat those whom He will judge.—Ver. 5. Divine punishment overpowers even the strongest.—Even the best is not too good for God's chastisements.

Ver. 6 sq. Man's sentence and God's sentence upon cities.—A woe follows on shed blood.—The rust on the caldron.—"Sin is the rust which cleaves to us all" (STCK.).—Ver. 7. "On account of the blood of Christ, shed at Golgotha, Titus at length burned the city" (À LAP.).—Ver. 8. God's leading and governing apparent amid the sins of men.—Ver. 9 sq. The ascending climax in the judgments of God.—He who will not hear must feel.—"God easily finds wood in abundance" (STCK.).—The ungodly shall not stand in the judgment.—"An evil conscience is a small caldron above a great fire" (À LAP.).—Ver. 12. God's fruitless efforts, what an awful prelude!—The abuse of divine grace.—"Thus also it was not cleansed by Christ, who had wearied Himself in labours for Jerusalem even to hot tears" (JEROME).

Ver. 15 sq. God takes away,—this should never be forgotten in any case of bereavement.—The Lord has taken away,—Job's words, Ezekiel's experience. "God wills that we should give up, at His command, all that is dear to us in this world" (TÜB. BIB.).—Not lost, but gone before. "Righteous people are often snatched away from the evil to come" (L.).—The children of God are not therefore insensate stones, but they desire to observe the God-appointed limits in their grief.—The Jews laid great stress on pomp in their mourning; and with how many Christians that is the whole or the principal part of mourning!—"No one should do as Ezekiel did unless commanded by God" (STCK.).—Ver. 18 sq. "In all things, even in what is hard for us, we should obey the divine command" (TÜB. BIB.).—"That which is impossible to our own natural power can become possible through the power of grace. Obey, then, even when it seems impossible to thee, and believe that the needed help will be given thee" (ST.).—Ver. 20 sq. "Oh, the punishment, when God Himself profanes His sanctuary, and takes away the light of true religion!" (TÜB. BIB.)—Sorrow without comfort is great sorrow.—Ver. 24. "Preachers of repentance must be signs to the unrepentant, and teach them not only with words, but also with their whole life" (CR.).—Ver. 26. The lame post from Jerusalem.—"Carnally-secure men believe a human messenger sooner than a messenger of God" (STCK.).—Who believes our preaching?—"Now the thunders of God's judgment began to speak" (HENGST.).

THE TRANSITION FROM THE PROPHECY OF JUDGMENT TO THE PROPHECY OF COMPASSION, OR THE PROPHECIES AGAINST THE ADVERSARIES.

A–B. CHAPTERS XXV.–XXXII.

THE TRANSITION FROM THE PROPHECY OF JUDGMENT TO THE PROPHECY OF COMPASSION, OR THE PROPHECIES AGAINST THE ADVERSARIES.

THE prophecies against the heathen nations are put here into one collection, as is the case also in Jeremiah and Isaiah (Introd. pp. 10, 11). The common character of their contents admits of their standing thus together, whilst they are also distinguished from each other by occasional chronological notices. From ch. xxix. 17, it is probable that the prophet made up at that time the preceding smaller collection, if not the greater one, of his whole book; comp. ch. xl. 1. According to most, however, these prophecies actually lie between ch. xxiv. and xxxiii.

"The prophecies (Kliefoth remarks) against foreign nations, that is, against heathenism and the heathen world, against the worldly power as opposing the kingdom of God and its development, form continually, since the prophecy of Balaam (Num. xxiv. 17–24), a separate chapter of prophecy." So is it first of all in Obadiah, then also in Joel, Amos, etc. The later prophets in this lean upon their predecessors, whose prophecies they partly employ by citation, partly supplement and expand.

The thought which dominates the collection of Ezekiel is that of judgment, as seen in the burning of Jerusalem, the flight-fire. Ezekiel, in consequence, limits himself in the survey he takes of the heathen, as that is also still further limited, that no reference is made in it to the Chaldeans.

Only the idea of judgment connects exactly with ch. xxiv. The discourse of judgment as now to go forth upon the adversaries was, as the silence of compassion had been, "an astonishment," in respect to its being appointed to the prophet for this particular time. If the prophecies are viewed as an appendage to the first main division, the connection can scarcely be conceived of more precisely.

The judicial character of these chapters, however, still keeps within the historical position,—the recompense which actually takes place in the world's history. Among the peoples that here make their appearance, there occur the heathen members of the coalition against Babylon, those who partook in Judah's breach of oath and fidelity, denounced in ch. xvii. The prophets are "the divinely-authorized conscience-preachers," as Tholuck designates them, "the directors of conscience whether wished for or not," who stand among the people, "as the wakeful eye of the God of Israel." The judgment of Judah must go forth from them upon these heathens; for that in human affairs there prevails a holy ordering of retributive righteousness is the general theme of prophecy.

The limitation in Ezekiel's predictions to judgment is not to be regarded as an exclusion of the heathen from Messiah's salvation. For out of the judgment, as for Israel, so also for the heathen, comes forth the great salvation of the future destined to embrace both. Ezekiel stands in no antagonism to the other prophets as regards their prophetic announcements on the heathen nations. It is enough to compare ch. xvi. There is merely a certain difference between him and them in this respect. "But he still holds by the right landmarks; temporal subversion alone, the loss of their political and civil existence, is what he threatens them with; but that a remnant of them should survive, according to the word of the earlier prophets, and that this might spiritually attain to blessing, he leaves open, without contradiction" (Kliefoth).

That the idea of judgment specially controls the following collection of Ezekiel has its explanation in his prophetic mission. It is so precisely adapted to this, that, in consequence, we find in this collection no prophetic judgment against Babylon. The explanation which is given, even by Hengstenberg, that "no reason existed for his braving the danger," can afford little satisfaction; must "the personal relations" have been pleasantly adjusted for an Ezekiel? If ch. xxi. 30 sq. is not to be understood as directed against Babylon (see, however, at the passage), the silence of Ezekiel generally respecting the judgment upon Babylon, and in particular the absence of any prediction of judgment in the section ch. xxv.–xxxii., finds its explanation simply in his position and calling in the exile. That Ammon, Moab, Edom, the Philistines, Tyre, Sidon, Egypt, were accessaries to the judgment upon Judah, to Judah's faithless breach of oath towards Babylon,—this of itself would have made Babylon's place in the midst of them fit badly. In that respect alone it would have injured the moral nexus. Still more, however, in another respect was silence upon Babylon's judgment ordered. It may be enough for this to point to ch. xxiii. 45; for that other decisive respect is the circumstance that Babylon had, in God's name, to execute judgment as well upon the nations in question as upon Judah-Israel. Ezekiel's prophetic mission we have recognised to be that of the prophet of Jehovah's glory in the exile; and likewise, the revelation of the glory of Jehovah meets us immediately in the 1st chapter as primarily taking effect in judgment and through righteousness. Hence it follows that it was also very suitable to the prophetic mission of Ezekiel, since it accords with the glory of Jehovah as now manifesting itself, that Babylon, its instrument, should directly appear only as such, in the light of the divine judgment and the divine righteousness upon Israel, and upon the related heathen nations. The exile in its primary aspect was judgment, the judgment of God, which Babylon inflicted. With this did not suit a prophetic judgment also upon Babylon. [More especially as one of the prevailing tendencies of the time was to overlook the hand of God in the present elevation of Babylon to its high ascendency, and to fret against the dominion which God had for a season given her over the nations.—P. F.] It should necessarily, too, have obscured the more direct impression to be produced. "Whosoever," says Hengstenberg, "obtained an insight into the whole of God's judicial acts, must have been powerfully drawn away from politics to repentance."

That the announcement of judgment, and of judgment alone, upon the heathen was done for the sake of consolation, which was implied therein for the exiled,—that such a consoling must here already be regarded as the prophetic mission of Ezekiel, is without warrant, according to ch. i.–xxiv., and is certainly not agreeable to the manner in which ch. xxv.–xxxii. are connected with that principal portion of our book.

It becomes, then, a matter of special importance to justify *the position* of this collection of predictions here against the heathen after ch. xxiv., with the contents, design, etc., of these predictions. The question of *place* goes first; the question of *time* follows as the second. For as their fulfilment took place later than the downfall of Jerusalem-Judah, so their announcement also took place, and consequently the reading of them, first at the time of the second main division, so that they might also serve as a foil for this. Considered from the point of view of the later publication, we may therefore conjoin with the mode of connecting this collection relatively to the first main division, a transition-character to the idea of the second main division of our book, as scattered and occasional indications of such a transition are to be found in ch. xxviii. 24 sq., xxix. 21. "These prophecies present themselves as forerunners of cheering intelligence, in so far as the downfall of the heathen powers here announced is throughout total and definitive, whereas hope is still always left to Israel" (Hengst.). This is also to be considered in accordance with the same, that the injury done to Israel is brought prominently forward among the causes of the divine judgment upon the heathen, ch. xxv. 3, 8, 12, 15. Ewald remarks, besides, that the punishment of Edom was expected from Israel, and for the Philistines immediately from Jehovah Himself, which would connect more closely with the manner in which the prophet, onwards from ch. xxxiii., is going to speak of Israel (comp. also Introd. § 6).

In agreement with the general considerations affecting the whole, which serve to justify the position and character of the following collection, there is also to be noticed this and that individual trait in the particular parts, which belong alike to the form and to the substance of these predictions.

There are *seven* separate prophecies; and to this number, says Hitzig, "he very persistently adheres." With a *symbolic* tendency, the Philistines are reckoned in the number, who do not appear as members of that coalition in Jer. xxvii.; and so, too, Tyre and Sidon are kept quite apart from each other, as in Jeremiah. "The placing together also of four nations immediately at the beginning, while three follow, indicates the clear consciousness with which the author is minded to make out a seven number" (Hitzig). This intentional form should be reckoned as belonging to the transition-character of the portion ch. xxv.–xxxii.: *On the ground of the covenant of the Eternal with Israel*, the judgment upon their open and secret enemies goes forth. In these judgments, therefore, Jehovah brings to remembrance His covenant with Israel.

Ewald delineates the particulars of the prophetic series geographically as beginning on the north-east from Judah with Ammon, thence turning southwards toward Moab, going down with Edom entirely to the south, thereafter bending in a western direction to the Philistines, then in the west stretching again to Tyre and Sidon, lastly to Egypt. Hävernick finds a beautiful harmony in the following connection between the individual predictions:—First, peoples that were in open enmity to the theocracy, ch. xxv.; then, in Tyre and Sidon, haughtiness, fleshly security, ch. xxvi.–xxviii.; finally, their combination in Egypt, ch. xxix.–xxxii. Keil has with good right perceived a distinction between Egypt and the other nations; but to suppose a formal twofold division on that account of six and one, destroys the symbol of the number seven, and is not warranted by that distinction, which lies much deeper than Keil has indicated (comp. Doct. Reflections, ch. xxix.–xxxii., 3). The idea of the coalition rather appears to have been distributed after this manner: first the four nearer are mentioned, then the two more remote members, whereupon the proper fulcrum of the whole conspiracy discovers itself according to its real significancy. The coalition could as such also historically have been one first against Babylon, and the last Egypt alone (comp. at Jer. xxvii.), and so giving play to the sequence in respect to time. With this agrees the just remark of Keil, that, as well in ch. xxviii. 24 sq. as in ch. xxix. 21, a prospect full of promise for Israel forms a *cæsura* in the heroic measure of the members.

According to the specific chronological statements (see Introd. § 6), there result, as successive series of prophecies against the heathen, since the indeterminate, if special reasons to the contrary do not exist, become determinate through the immediately preceding chronological indication:—1. Ammon, Moab, Edom, the Philistines, ch. xxv.; 2. Egypt (first and second word), ch. xxix. 1–16, xxx. 1–19; 3. Tyre (first, second, third, and fourth word) and Sidon, ch. xxvi.–xxviii.; 4. Egypt (third word), ch. xxx. 20–26; 5. Egypt (fourth word), ch. xxxi.; 6. Egypt (fifth word), ch. xxxii. 1–16; 7. Egypt (sixth word), ch. xxxii. 17–32; 8. Egypt (concluding word), ch. xxix. 17–21.

1. Ammon, Moab, Edom, and the Philistines (Ch. xxv.).

1, 2 And the word of Jehovah came to me, saying: Son of man, direct thy face
3 to the sons of Ammon, and prophesy upon them. And say to the sons of
Ammon, Hear the word of the Lord Jehovah: Because thou sayest "Aha"
to My sanctuary, for it is profaned, and to Israel's ground, for it is desolate,
4 and to the house of Judah, for they have gone into banishment: Therefore,
behold! I give thee to the sons of the east for a possession, and they place in
thee their enclosures, and make in thee their dwellings: they shall eat thy
5 fruit, and they shall drink thy milk! And I have given Rabbah for pasture-
ground [stable] of camels, and the sons of Ammon for the lair [resting-places] of
6 flocks; and ye know that I am Jehovah. For thus saith the Lord Jehovah,
Because thou didst strike the hand [in the hand], and with the foot didst stamp,
and didst rejoice thyself in all thy despite in the soul upon the ground of
7 Israel; Therefore, behold! I have stretched out My hand against thee, and
have given thee for food [booty] to the heathen; and I root thee out from
among the peoples, and make thee to perish from among the lands: I will
8 destroy thee! and thou dost know that I am Jehovah. Thus saith the
Lord Jehovah: Because Moab says, and [as] Seir: Behold, as all the heathen
9 is the house of Judah. Therefore, behold, I open the shoulder of Moab,
from the cities, from his cities, from his end, the ornament of the land, Beth-
10 Hajesimoth, Baal-Meon, and toward Kirjathaim, To the sons of the east, to
the sons of Ammon; and I have given it for a possession, that the sons
11 of Ammon may not be [any more] a remembrance among the heathen. And
12 on Moab will I do judgment; and they know that I am Jehovah. Thus saith
the Lord Jehovah: Because Edom exercises vindictive revenge upon the
house of Judah, and they made themselves guilty and guilty, and avenged
13 themselves upon them; Therefore, thus saith the Lord Jehovah, And I have
(there have I) stretched out My hand upon Edom, and I root out from him
man and beast; and I have given it for salvation; from Teman and to Dedan
14 shall they fall by the sword. And I have given My vengeance on Edom by
the hand of My people Israel; and they do on Edom as My wrath and My fury
15 is; and they know My vengeance—sentence of the Lord Jehovah. Thus saith
the Lord Jehovah: Because the Philistines act in revenge, and vengefully
revenged themselves in disdain, in the soul, for destruction, everlasting enmity;
16 Therefore, thus saith the Lord Jehovah, Behold, I stretch out My hand
against the Philistines, and root out the Cherethim, and destroy the remnant
17 by the coast of the sea. And I do on them great revenges, in punishments
of fury; and they know that I am Jehovah, in that I give on them My revenge.

Ver. 7. בגוים; Sept. Arabs.
Ver. 8. Sept.: . . . ὁ οἶκος Ἰσραὴλ καὶ Ἰουδα.
Ver. 9. . . . ἀπο πολεων ἀκρωτηριων αὐτου, ἐκλεκτην γην, . . . ἐπανω πηγης πολεως παραθαλασσιας.
Ver. 12. . . . και ἐμνησικακησαν κ. ἐξεδικησαν δικην, . . .
Ver. 13. και ἐκ Θαιμαν διωκομενοι ἐν ρομφαια— . . .
Ver. 15. Sept.: . . . του ἐξαλειψαι ἑως αἰωνος,—*implentes inimicitias veteres*—
Ver. 16. Vulg.: . . . *et interficiam interfectores.*

EXEGETICAL REMARKS.

Vers. 1–7. *The Ammonites.*

The time is not specified in ver. 1. As will be seen from what follows, however, the final execution of judgment on Jerusalem is presupposed. If the actual fact is assumed, the prediction would have its proper place after ch. xxxiii. (JEROME). The presupposition, however, is that only of anticipation, the position of the prophecy being taken from the idea of the connection with ch. xxiv. As the prophet foretells how it is going to be with Ammon, there is a pointing backwards also to what Ammon has been. It cannot behave itself otherwise than it has been perpetually manifesting itself. See Doct. Reflections, i. 3.—Ver. 2. Comp. ch. vi. 2, xxi. 2, xiii. 17. With eye and hand.—Comp. for the following prophecy that already pronounced against Ammon in ch. xxi. 28 sqq.—Ver. 3. Ch. vi. 3, xiii. 2. Where parties look merely at results that are pleasing to them, they ought assuredly at the outset to be called upon to hear, and, indeed, what Jehovah says, not what they may themselves think, and approvingly give one another to hear.—The current speech of Ammon (אמרך)—feminine as a nation, the popular community—significantly places itself directly over against **My sanctuary.** In the judgment of it His people vanish, as in His compassion their sins vanish; He meets on behalf of this people the **Aha,** the malignant joy, of their enemies.; comp. ch. xxiv. 21. At the same time, the enmity of Ammon is thereby, from the first, marked as blasphemy of the Spirit who ruled over and in Judah-Israel. It is not merely injury to the land and people (ch. xxi. 28), that their national, human form of existence should be shattered to pieces, although there should be this also, in accordance with what follows. In the latter respect, the neighbourly relation has to be thought of, which, in point of space, was relationship of the nearest kind, to say nothing of what there was of blood-relationship, in consequence of the derivation through Lot.—בגולה, HENGST.: "went as exiles;" comp. ch. xii. 11.—Ver. 4. The offence draws after it the punishment, wherein Nebuchadnezzar entirely falls into abeyance. Jehovah comes forth; and **the sons of the east**—according to Grotius and others, undoubtedly the Chaldeans; according to that which is here declared of them, and always elsewhere, the Arabian tribes—descendants of Ishmael, the Bedouin, especially as in the text it is not properly the execution that is assigned to them; but they, after the judgment took effect, only gave conclusive evidence of the completed fact. They are in a sort of way classical for this, since "they always appear where fire and sword have wasted a country" (HENGST.), or generally where a place has become desert. "The old Ammonitis, the ruin of which began in the time of Nebuchadnezzar, and continued thenceforward without interruption, is abandoned to the Bedouin Arabs to this day" (HENGST.).—HITZIG translates: "**and** settled in thee shall be their pens;" but ישבו is probably Piel, though only here. טירות are the enclosures (for cattle) of a nomad village.—The repeated המה impressively dismisses the Ammonites from their territory, because others have taken their place.—Besides the fruit of the ground (פריך), there is mentioned exhaustively the produce from the cattle-tending.—Ver. 5. There is here still an especial signalizing of the old Ammonite capital city, Rabbah, ch. xxi. 20 (later, Philadelphia). HENGST.: "the name (the populous) in melancholy contrast to what follows, as camel and wilderness go inseparably together;" comp. Amos i. 14; Jer. xlix. 2. **The sons of Ammon,** parallel for "their other cities" (Zeph. ii. 9). [Surely a somewhat peculiar parallel: the sons of Ammon are just the Ammonites; men, not cities or places. But they were to be given "for the couching of flocks"—flocks for men, and not that merely, but flocks in a state of perfect repose. In plain terms, the agricultural parts of the country were to become pastoral—where men were wont to be seen labouring, there should only be found sheep browsing or resting.—P. F.] In the present day, Rabbah, while it has great ruins, for example, of a theatre belonging to the Roman period, yet it is wholly destitute of inhabitants. Arabians with camels met Seetzen in the neighbourhood, dangerous people for a visit to these ruins. When Buckingham spent a night among the ruins, an Arab was pitching there; and the traveller could not sleep for the bleating of sheep, the neighing of horses, and the barking of dogs.—The transition to the Ammonites themselves is prepared for ver. 6 (וידעתם).

Ver. 6. Comp. for the gestures, ch. xxi. 14, 17, vi. 11. The undoubted import is given by the **and thou didst rejoice.** The malicious joy is strengthened, marked, and deepened, since, as hand and foot were not wanting in it, nothing failed of despite; it was whole and entire: *in the innermost soul.* (HITZIG: "So that one is therein with the soul, with passion; therefore with the whole heart's contempt of which you are capable.")—Ver. 7. Hand **against** hand. Instead of לבג, *for food*, the Qeri has לבז, *for booty.* But "booty" expresses too little, where an "allotment," a portion had been explicitly assured, and in the comparison at ver. 4 is so very suitable. HITZIG only objects that "the book of Daniel is not contemporaneous with Ezekiel;" for in Dan. i. 5, 8, etc., פתבג is used of court-food [this latter word being thought by Hengst., Häv., and others to countenance the text against the Qeri here.—P. F.]

Vers. 8–11. *The Moabites.*

The association of Edom, by means of the mountain (Seir), with Moab in this affair, implies that the sentiment uttered was one that had a much more extensive prevalence, and already provides a ground for the later judicial sentence upon Edom. What they say amounts to disavowal and blasphemy of the Spirit in Judah. Comp. with Ammon (= where is now their God?).—Ver. 9. The punishment is, as in the case of Ammon, that the land is opened to the nomadic Arabians (ver. 10), and primarily, indeed, with an eye to the fortified cities. The portion contemplated therein, because it was the upper north side which leant on Ammon, is called **the shoulder of Moab**, on account of the position, which is more clearly indicated in what follows, probably not without respect to the gradually ascending or sloping ground; but hardly, with Grotius and Hengst.: "because there blows and sword-strokes are most easily applied," of which nothing is said. **From the cities** (the מִן on no account to be taken in a privative sense, with Hitzig: "bare of cities") commences the opening very intelligibly; then occurs the strongest opposition, and, indeed, from the cities, which are designated as **from the end** (not: "to the last," for to how far has not yet been said), that is, as border cities in the extremity of the land, according to the supposed side; so must the rest of the land assuredly lie open, as it is called **the ornament of the land**, therefore that which is brilliant by its fruitfulness, or perhaps by rich pastures. After some cities, mentioned by way of example, there is expressed in **to Kirjathaim** the point how far, and the intended compass is marked off.—בית הישימות, south or south-east from Jericho, on the Dead Sea (Bethsimuth, Besimoth), signifies *house of the wastes*—might it be Suaime, on the north-east border of the Dead Sea?—**Baal-meon**, now Mæin, the considerable ruins of which Seetzen saw from a distance, lying on the east of Attarus, where there are said to be springs.—**Kirjathaim**, west of Medaba, el Teym (?). These cities clearly point to the ancient inheritance of Reuben (Josh. xiii.); but when the Assyrians led into captivity the transjordanic tribes, the Moabites obtained possession of them. Comp. on ch. xxi. 36 [28] sq. (EWALD: "Therefore I now loose Moab's crown from the cities.")—Ver. 10. עַל, *on to*, upon Ammon and also Moab (ch. xvi. 37). HÄVERNICK: "primarily upon Ammon, then pouring itself forth upon Moab." The Ammonites still stand forth directly before the Moabites. Comp. on ch. xxi. 37 [32].—Ver. 11. When the land of the Ammonites should fall into the enemy's hand, then would similar divine judgments be executed on Moab, ch. v. 10. (Comp. besides, Isa. xvi. 6; Jer. xlviii.)

Vers. 12-14. *The Edomites.*

The charge in respect to sinning mounts up; for as Edom appears in ver. 8 as the ringleader against the people of the Lord, so is it as to intellectual supremacy.—Ver. 12. The old spirit of revenge, in which he had acted from the olden time, still keeps by his side. While in the more distant relationship of Ammon and Moab, malignant joy is the expression of hostile feeling, with Edom, in his much nearer relationship, the same feeling vents itself in actions of revenge (עשות־בנקם נקם): hence the charge of sinful procedure as the incurring of guilt; comp. besides, Gen. xxxvi. 31 sq., xxvii. 17 sq.; Obad. 10 sq.; Amos i. 11; Ps. cxxxvii.—Ver. 13. In such dealings the stretching out of the hand is plain enough (ver. 7). The ו, **and**, denotes continuation of the foregoing punishments, which form one chain.—Ch. xiv. 13, 17.—Ch. v. 14.—*From Teman to Dedan* designates the land of the Edomites from south to north.—Ch. xxiv. 21.—Ver. 14. Revenge for revenge. So also **My people Israel** is set over against Edom, without, however, thereby referring to the mode of the execution. Since Israel is here so expressly announced as the executor of the divine vengeance, Nebuchadnezzar cannot possibly be thought of in connection with it; but we must think of the times of the Maccabees (John Hyrcanus). The Messianic interest must not be brought into view. The compulsory reception into Israel, whereby the Edomites ceased as a people, is plainly to be regarded as the proper execution of judgment, as this national annihilation.

Vers. 15-17. *The Philistines.*

The Philistines are in ver. 15 joined to Edom on the side of their *doing* (ver. 12 sq.); to Ammon-Moab on account of their *contempt* of the people of God. The latter was the inmost feeling, hostility the impelling force, wherein the distinction from Edom lay. **For destruction**, this is the design, the abiding tendency. The **everlasting enmity** reaches back to the earliest days. A perpetually enduring war is the standing feature of the relation, while fixed hostility was the root of it.—Ver. 16. The outstretched hand, as in vers. 13, 7.—The effect of the action on the Philistines is the extirpation of the Cherethites, a name manifestly given, not to a part of this people, but to the whole of the Philistines, for the sake of the paronomasia. HENGST.: "The name Philistines probably signifies the emigrants, those from the regions on the Black Sea, from Colchis and the adjacent Pontic Cappadocia, Kaphtor. Of substantially the same import with this name is *Kretim* (Eng. form: Cherethites), that is, the extirpated, namely, from their native country. These Kretim are now to become a second time Kretim; their name shall verify itself anew."—The annihilation is announced as total, including the remnant also by the coast of the Mediterranean Sea. To this also corresponds the closing word, ver. 17: **in punishments of fury**, as at ch. v. 15. "Jehovah Himself, never again ceasing" (HITZIG).

DOCTRINAL REFLECTIONS.

1. Ammon and Moab share together, not merely the incestuous nature of their origin (Gen. xix. 30 sq.), but the juxtaposition of their residences, their historical outcome, in particular their hostility toward the people of God, which, having respect to what is said of them in the time of Moses (Deut. ii. 9-23), was the more unjustifiable in its manifestations. (See Doctrinal Reflections, 4, at the passage.) There is nothing to be alleged in vindication of it, for its root is to be traced to the strife, in Gen. xiii. 6 sq., which led to the separation from Israel,—a separation which was kept up by the latter with the utmost care and vigilance. It is therefore the natural contrast of the

carnal spirit against the Spirit of God—haughtiness its manifestation on the one side, injurious treatment on the other, blasphemy of the Spirit in all. The prescription in the law (Deut. xxiii. 3) is already a significant one as to the relation which existed between Israel and Ammon-Moab.

2. In the dark contrast, however, between Israel on the one side and Ammon-Moab on the other, the analogy is not to be overlooked; here also the elder (Moab), as there Esau, is the one that falls into the background. The younger (Ammon), on the other hand, bears the sword, and is named before the other. Both, as distinct tribes, disappear wholly at last in the Arabians.

3. Ammon and Moab, the demoniacal counterpart to Judah-Israel.

4. The people of God must undergo the experience which the man of God undergoes. Matt. x. 36; Mic. vii. 6. Out of his blood-relationships there springs a hostility even to blood. While this revolves around the Spirit that wrought in Israel, it could not but finally array itself against the Messiah, as He has Himself said that we shall be hated for His name's sake.

5. Edom might be the bad conscience of Israel. Esau himself, however, after Israel's night-conflict, met him in a gracious spirit, and parted from him in peace (Gen. xxxiii.). He who has wrestled with God, and has obtained mercy, has also overcome man. Thus it was only the respect paid to the kin-relationship, which in the case also of Ammon and Moab came into consideration, but was specially made mention of in regard to Edom (Deut. ii. 4), that determined the holding aloof on the part of Israel. But the nearer the affinity was in Edom to Israel, so much the more horrible appears the spirit of revenge, which will even avenge, because grace has been shown to the other, because to him on that ground precedence has been granted, in order to compensate for the disadvantage on the territory of nature. The revenge of Edom, which was just a relapse into the feeling of Esau (Gen. xxvii. 41), could not endure that Israel should be a separate, and what was called God's chosen, people. "Edom holds his ground constantly as the bitterest denier of the right of the first-born, of the divine preference of Israel" (KLIEFOTH). The vengeance of God could not in a more marked retribution manifest itself upon Edom than by the extirpation of his nationality, and that precisely in the form of an absorption by Israel.—Robinson delineates a scene in the land of Idumæa as it has come to be, *Res.* ii. p. 502: "We were now upon the plain, or rather the rolling desert, of the 'Arabah; the surface was in general loose gravel and stones, everywhere furrowed and torn with the beds of torrents. A more frightful desert it had hardly been our lot to behold. Now and then a low shrub of the Ghudâh was almost the only trace of vegetation. The mountains beyond presented a most uninviting and hideous aspect: precipices and naked conical peaks of chalky and gravelly formation rising one above another without any sign of life or vegetation."

6. "The revenge of Edom on account of the precedence granted to Israel by God, his superiority, viewed in respect to its deep religious significance, is nothing else than the constant resistance, the permanent protest raised against the higher dispensation established by God, His method of salvation; and in that is mirrored a fundamental characteristic of heathendom generally" (HÄV.).

7. As in Ammon, Moab, and Edom there appear three degenerations toward heathenism, so the whole picture is fitly closed in by the heathenish Philistines (the Ἀλλοφυλοι of the Septuagint and the Apocrypha). Heathendom was round about Israel; it was the background, the soil from which his relief comes out so much the more distinctly.

8. "The four number (remarks KLIEFOTH) points to the four regions of the world, and so to mankind at large; it indicates that it will not fare otherwise with collective heathenism throughout the whole earth, alike inimical to the people of God, than it did with those hostile tribes which on all the four sides surrounded that people."

HOMILETIC HINTS.

Ver. 1 sq. "The fall of Jerusalem was in a religious point of view a catastrophe for the world. The subjection of the covenant-people under heathenish ascendancy is therefore no victory of heathendom over the true theocracy. Exactly the reverse: the apparent annihilation of Israel leads to a new resurrection of it. Out of its death-conflict there breaks forth a new glorious life, salvation in its world-overcoming power. Precisely now on this account does the period always more decidedly approach when the worldly power will discover itself as a broken one, when the kingdoms of heathendom, with all the splendour of their earthly glory, shall appear as evanescent powers of the past. Accordingly, the judgment upon the theocracy and the heathen on the one side stands in inseparable connection; on the other side, it is an essentially different one" (HÄV.).—"Judgment indeed begins at the house of God; but if the Father of the household does not spare the sons, how soon must it alight upon the others! This doctrine first of all shines forth from the connection of this chapter with the preceding chapters. Then, also, we see here how, with all the special solicitude wherewith God interested Himself in Israel, He still by no means let the heathen out of His sight, since He must show Himself to be a God also for the heathen" (L.).—"If thou wilt not rightly apply the gifts and loving-kindnesses of God, God can take them from thee and give them to another" (ST.).

Ver. 3. Hear: Ah, yes, it depends on the hearing! Give right ears, O God, to hear! He who suffers the damage need not care for the mockery; but sit not where the mockers sit: their seats, however festive they may be, have nothing to make them fast.—Ver. 4 sq. The Arabians, through Mohammed, were executors of punishment of quite another sort.—Ver. 7. "Thou canst think of no man so poor as thou thyself mayest actually become" (STCK.).

Ver. 8 sq. However degenerate Christian people may become, Christian truth can never be as one ring among the well-known three rings.—"But we must watch that we do not cause the adversaries of the Lord to blaspheme" (W.).—What unites the world, separates it from the kingdom of God.—The Almighty God is in possession of a universal passport.—Grace makes friends, but also enemies; God, however, is expert with His enemies.—"It is best to learn to know God from His benefits" (STCK.).

Ver. 12 sq. Edom's revenge his special hereditary sin.—"Revenge is God's, and not man's, whosoever, therefore, anticipates Him in this, on him will He be again avenged. Let no one, then, recompense evil for evil" (TÜB. B.).—"When relatives by affinity or blood become inimical to one another, they are much more embittered against each other than strangers" (O.).—Even the oldest grudge that nations have toward one another must be turned to peace through the power of the gospel; else God will place Himself between them, and finally root out the haters, who will not abandon their hatred.—Disdain and frivolous scorn may stalk on before; so much the more surely will God's judgment come after.

Ver. 15 sq. "It is an essential part and property belonging to the judicial administration of God, that He exercises vengeance on the ungodly; therefore He will have the same also preserved as an especial royalty, Deut. xxxii. 35" (CR.). Above all else, survey the old world—where remain those who were enemies to God and His kingdom? Their places know them no more. But God's word remains, as it has been verified in them.—The depopulated places of the ancient historical world.—"Israel was hated of all those nations, not on account of his sins, but for the sake of his religion. Thus the cause of Israel was God's cause. Blessed people, whom men cannot hate and slander without hating and slandering God Himself! The malignant contempt was recompensed with the extirpation of the remembrance, the hostile revenge with a divine revenge," etc. (KEITH).—"If these prophecies of judgment only came into complete fulfilment after the lapse of centuries, one still sees their fulfilment to this day before the eyes of travellers" (RICHT.).—[It is still to be remembered, however, that, as the prediction had respect not simply to the land of Edom (and the same applies equally to the other predictions of judgment), but to the land as connected with the Edomite race, "these desolations of later times have no direct relation to the Edom of Scripture; and if they are to be taken into account at all, it should only be as affording a collateral (or supplementary) proof of the judgment that was to befal the children of Edom. But it is the desolations of an earlier period, and above all, the utter extinction of Edom as a people, and *that* by the hand of Jacob, in which the more direct and proper fulfilment of the prophecy is to be sought. . . . At the present day there are, in certain parts of what was the territory of Edom, 'wadys full of trees, and shrubs, and flowers,' and the eastern and higher parts are extensively cultivated, and yield good crops' (Robinson). Still the Edom of prophecy—Edom considered as the enemy of God and the rival of Israel—has perished for ever: all, in that respect, is an untrodden wilderness, a hopeless ruin; and *therein* the veracity of God's word finds its verification."—P. F. on *Prophecy*, p. 219 sq.]

2. TYRE AND SIDON (CH. XXVI.-XXVIII.).

CH. XXVI. 1. And it came to pass in the eleventh year, in the first of the month,
2 that the word of Jehovah came to me, saying: Son of man, because Tyre
[Heb. Zor] says upon Jerusalem, Aha, broken is [has become] the gate of the people;
it turns itself [or, is turned] to me; I will be [become] full; she is [has become]
3 desolate. Therefore thus saith the Lord Jehovah, I am against [over] thee, Tyre,
and I bring up upon thee many nations [heathen peoples], as the sea mounts up by his
4 waves. And they destroy the walls of Tyre, and break down her towers; and I
5 sweep her dust out of her, and give her as a mere [bald] rock. A spreading of
nets shall she be in the midst of the sea; for I have spoken—sentence of the
6 Lord Jehovah—and she is for a booty to the nations. And her daughters which
are in the field shall be slain with the sword: and they know that I am Jehovah.
7 For thus saith the Lord Jehovah, Behold, I bring against Tyre Nebuchadnezzar
king of Babylon, out of the north, a king of kings, with horse, and with chariot,
8 and with riders, and company, and much people. Thy daughters in the field he
will kill with the sword, and he gives against thee a battering-tower, and casts up
9 a wall against thee, and places against thee a buckler. And the thrust of his
breaker will he give against thy walls, and break down thy towers with his
10 swords. From the abundance of his horses their dust shall cover thee; from the
sound of the rider, and the wheel, and the chariot shall thy walls shake, at his
11 entering into thy gates, as one cometh into a broken city. With the hoofs of
his horses shall he tread all thy streets: thy people shall he slay with the sword,
12 and the pillars of thy strength he shall throw down to the earth. And they
plunder thy wealth, and despoil thy merchandise [thy commercial goods], and break
down thy walls, and the houses of thy pleasure shall they pull down, and shall
13 lay thy stones and thy timbers and thy dust in the midst of the sea. And I
make to cease the noise of thy songs, and the sound of thy harps shall no more
14 be heard. And I give thee as a mere [bare] rock: a spreading of nets shalt thou
be; thou shalt be built no more: for I, Jehovah, have spoken it—sentence of the
15 Lord Jehovah. Thus saith the Lord Jehovah to Tyre, Shall not the isles shake
at the sound of thy fall, of the groaning of the pierced-through, at the murder and

16 murder in thy midst? And all the princes of the sea descend from their
thrones, and lay aside their robes, and shall put off their embroidered garments:
in terror shall they clothe themselves: upon the ground shall they sit and tremble
17 every moment, and are astonished at thee. And they raise over thee a lamen-
tation, and say to thee: How art thou destroyed, inhabited, out of the seas,
renowned city, which wast strong in the sea, she and her inhabitants, which
18 gave their terror to all her inhabitants! Now shall the isles tremble in
the day of thy downfall, and the islands which are in the sea shall be amazed at
19 thy disappearing [lit., going out]. For thus saith the Lord Jehovah, When I give
thee as a desolate city, as cities [are] which are not inhabited, when I make the
20 flood to come over thee, and the waters, the many, cover thee; and I make thee
to come down with those that go down to the pit, to the people of ancient time;
and I cause thee to dwell in the land of the depths, in wildernesses from of old,
with those that go down to the pit, so that thou mayest not be inhabited: there
21 have I given beauty in the land of the living. For a terror will I give thee,
and thou art not [any more]; thou shalt be sought for, and shalt not be found any
more for ever. Sentence of the Lord Jehovah.

Ver. 1. Sept.: . . . *μια του μηνος του πρωτου*—

Ver. 2. . . . *συνετριβε, ἀπολωλεν, τα ἐθνη ἐπεστραφη προς με, ἡ πληρης ἠρημωται*—Sept. read: נמלאה; so also Chald., Ar., Syr.: *desolata est.*

Ver. 4. . . . *πυργους σου, και λικμησω τον χουν αὐτης ἀπ' αὐτης.*

Ver. 6. Sept.: . . . *αἱ ἐν τω πεδιῳ*—

Ver. 7. . . . *και συναγωγης πολλης ἐθνων σφοδρα.*

Ver. 8. . . . *προφυλακην κ. περιοικοδομησει, κ. περιποιησει ἐπι σε κυκλῳ σου χαρακα κ. βελοστασεις ὁπλων, κ. τας λογχας αὐτου ἐπι σε δωσει.* (9) *Τα τειχη σου κ. τους πυργους*—Vulg.: *Et vineas et arietes . . . destruet in armatura sua.*

Ver. 10. Sept.: . . . *ὡς ὁ εἰσπορευομενος . . . ἐκ πεδιου.*

Ver. 11. . . . *κ. την ὑποστασιν τ. ἰσχυος σου ἐπι . . . καταξει.*

Ver. 13. K. *καταλυσει . . τ. μουσικων σου . . . των ψαλτηριων σου*—

Ver. 16. . . . *ἐκ τ. ἐθνων τ. θαλασσης . . . τ. μιτρας ἀπο τ. κεφαλων αὐτων . . . και ἐκστασει ἐκστησονται . . . φοβηθησονται τ. ἀπωλειαν αὐτων.*—Vulg.: . . . *auferent exuvias suas . . . et attoniti super repentino casu tuo admirabuntur.*

Ver. 17. Sept.: . . . *και κατελυθης ἐκ θαλασσης . . . ἡ δουσα τ. φοβον αὐτης.*—Vulg.: . . . *quos formidabant universi.*

Ver. 18. Vulg.: . . . *eo quod nullus egrediatur ex te* (other read. האיים).

Ver. 19. Sept.: . . . *ἐπι σε τ. ἀβυσσον*—

Ver. 20. . . . *προς τ. καταβαινοντας εἰς βοθρον . . . ὡς ἐρημον αἰωνιον μετα καταβαιν. . . . ὁπως . . . μηδε ἀνασταθης ἐπι γης ζωης.* (Some Codd. have אל יורדי.)

EXEGETICAL REMARKS.

Ver. 1. *The Starting-point of the Prophecy.*

The year indicated in this verse is that of the conquest and destruction of Jerusalem (Jer. xxxix. 2); therefore the parallels suggested are: Tyre *against* Jerusalem, Tyre *as* Jerusalem. The blank month (as also at ch. xxxii. 17) some (for example, HENGST.) would supply out of ch. xxiv. 1, therefore the tenth, as pointing back to the beginning of the siege; others, and of these already the Sept., by taking the number given for the day (**on the first**) as applying also to the month. If we do not resort to a slip of the scribe (KEIL), we may as well suppose, with Hävernick, the **fifth month** suggested by the specified year as that of the destruction of Jerusalem, as, with Kimchi, the fourth month of the same year for the conquest of the city (Jer. lii. 5, 6, 12). With both suppositions ver. 2 agrees, where the hostile utterances might well enough have proceeded on the ground of what, if not actually done, was certainly in the course of being done.

Vers. 2–6. *Outline of the Judgment in the general.*

Ver. 2 (ch. xxv. 3). צֹר; צוֹר=צוּר, that is, *flint-stone, rock* (sarra)—the Greek designation *Τύρος*, from the Chaldaic form טֻר—was that Phenician city which for a long course of time possessed the supremacy that had previously been exercised by Sidon. In the present time it is pronounced by the Arabians *Ssur*. On account of its connection with the coalition, Tyre forms the more clamant an occasion for God's judgment, as, being, according to Hävernick, "on the summit of external splendour, it then deemed itself to be invincible;" and according to Hengst., it was, "along with Egypt and Babylon, the most glorious concentration of the worldly power."

דלתות, plural, the *gate-leaves*, for the gate, hence with the sing. of the verb. Jerusalem was not thus spoken of by Tyre, because many people were generally going and coming there, which also would not have been expressed by העמים (**the peoples**), but either with reference to the messengers of the coalition, who assembled there (Jer. xxvii.), or, as Hitzig supposes, as a centre of foreign commerce, a business-mart, for which a natural jealousy could speak, since Solomon had established the commerce of Palestine. Hengst. looks upon Jerusalem as a "world-city, because it regarded the true religion as the highest good," and makes the Messianic expectations of Zion to have been known in Tyre, and to have awakened bad blood in the proud queen of the seas (?). The streaming of the peoples thither, on account of which the gate was said to be broken, is to him the Jerusalem for the future brought to view

(Isa. ii. 2; Mic. iv. 1), as Jerusalem was at all times a magnet for the minds in heathendom that sought after God.—נסבה, Niph. from סבב, fitly spoken of a gate (comp. Prov. xxvi. 14). If with reference to Jerusalem it was broken down, then with reference to Tyre it is turned towards him; that is, the commerce of the people is open to him; he has that alone now which hitherto he had to share with Jerusalem. [KLIEFOTH: into Jerusalem's gate, hitherto shut to the peoples, on religious grounds, Tyre might now especially draw in, turn it to account (?). Hitzig derives the subject from what follows, and translates: "her fulness turns itself to me."]—The **being full** (ch. xxvii. 25) has respect to traffic and the wealth which flows from it.—Ver. 3 (ch. xiii. 8, 20)—the **many nations** correspond as well to the general comprehensive outline of the prophecy in this first section, as they answer to the outspoken scorn of Tyre and his malicious arrogant speculations (ver. 2).—The pictorial representation is derived from the marine situation of Tyre. Hitzig, who thinks of the particular bands of the host to be brought up, makes **the sea** the accusative, supplies the subject from the context, and takes לְגַלָּיו distributively; as the sea in regard to its waves, one after the others, and over the others. According to Ewald, לְ denotes the accusative. Hengst. explains according to ver. 19: "as if I brought up the sea and its waves." This representation already suggests the younger Tyre (Φοινισσα νασος in Euripides), which stood upon the island-rock hard by the coast, that is now united to the land. The **walls** and **towers** in ver. 4 appear to be quite in accord with the general character of the prophecy, and to go farther beyond the time of Nebuchadnezzar than some have supposed (CURTIUS, iv., ARRIAN, ii.), although the five years' siege which it sustained against Salmanassar seems to imply the existence then of walls and towers (JOSEPHUS, *Antiq.* viii. 5). Hiram II. not only built the temple of Melkarth, and formed both the islands into one, but also added an entirely new quarter to the city (Eurychoron), and surrounded the city with a strong wall. A second harbour was besides added by him, and a palace erected for him, while old Tyre fell more into the background. What is here said, however, of the fortifications might equally, if not rather, be said of the old city, which was built upon the land; since insular Tyre came into consideration pre-eminently on account of the Melkarth temple, the old national sanctuary of the "Tyrian Heracles," which stood upon its north side, on a second small island somewhat farther to sea, on account also of the maritime power of the state, what belonged to it as a fleet-station. Whence the name very specially reflected its insular position; so that insular Tyre must here be regarded *as a pregnant title for the whole*.—Her **dust** is the rubbish of the demolished buildings. סחיתי, **I sweep**, only here, from סחה, to sweep, forms a paronomasia with שחתי, and prepares for the following, in which Tyre, that in ver. 2 had boasted it over the desolated Jerusalem as being full, should be reduced to its original bare condition. A **papyrus roll, which has preserved to us an** account of an Egyptian officer's journey, describes insular Tyre in its beginnings as a village, which lies on a rock in the midst of the sea: people bring water to it in wherries, and the place abounds with fish.—Ch. xxiv. 7, 8. *Nomen omen.*—Ver. 5. מִשְׁטַח denotes a place where something is spread out, here: *the fishermen lay out their draw-nets to dry*. So precisely did Robinson find it.—Ch. vii. 21.—Ver. 6. The **daughters of** Tyre **in the field** are manifestly to be regarded as distinguished from insular Tyre, but, according to the general style of the section, in correspondence too with the plural, such as, if not dependent on her, submitted to the supremacy of Tyre, and then had under the ascendency of Assyria withdrawn from this relationship—as the insular city Aradus (Arvad), on the coast Antaradus (Tortosa), and Marathus (Amrit), Simyra (Sumra), Botrys (Batrun), Gebal (Byblos, Dschebeil), Beryton (Beirut), Sidon (Saida), Ssarpat (Sarepta), etc.; so, too, Palætyrus, the old city, where still exists the great old aqueduct, the Khan, and the smithy of Ras Al Ain.

Vers. 7–14. *The Execution by Nebuchadnezzar.*

In these verses the general outline is exhibited in a detailed description suited to the time of Ezekiel, as it was to be carried into execution by Nebuchadnezzar. Here and elsewhere he is named Nebuchadrezzar (Greek: Nabuchodonosor, Nabuchodonosorus, Nabukodrosoros), upon the old Persian inscriptions at Bisutun: Nabuqadratschar, Nabuqudratschar, a name compounded of Nabu (Nebo), the name of God, Zar or Sar (prince), and Kadr (in Arab. might). According to Niebuhr, the form given here in the text would come very near to the native one. That he should be represented as coming **out of the north** points to the way by which he was to come on Judah.—**King of kings**, on account of the vanquished princes, along with *Great King*, a common title in the inscriptions.—The rhetorical delineation of the army is not to be pressed. **Horse** and **chariot** look away in the first instance from the manning; they fetch up the **riders** for horse, for chariots, perhaps **company** (קהל), in order to close with the great multitude of people on foot. Hengst. understands by the **riders** the chariot-warriors (ver. 10). According to others, the company consists of **much people** (עם־רב); comp. ch. xxiii. 24.—Ver. 8. The population of the towns on the land fall under the enemy directing his attack from thence, chiefly put to the sword; and so ver. 6 is fulfilled.—Ch. xxi. 27, iv. 2.—**Buckler** designates the long bucklers held close together, so that in a siege men could work under their cover, and get near to the walls. On account of the distinction indicated by **thy daughters in the field**, the expression **against thee** is used, and it must consequently be the insular Tyre against which the siege conducted by Nebuchadnezzar was directed.—Ver. 9. מחי from מחה is the thrusting. קבל must, according to Gesenius, be that which lies over against, therefore, with מחי, *percussio oppositi*, for **wall-breaker** (battering-ram). קבל without doubt indicates a besieging instrument in general, if not some one in particular. (Chald. *percussio tormentorum suorum.*)

Meier thinks of what envelopes, protects, covers (קובע, buckler), hence of the protecting cover under which men attacked with the battering-ram, similarly as צנה in ver. 8. "The thrust of his protecting cover," that is, what he effects under the same, etc. Hävernick translates מחי by extirpation, and קבל by defence (?). Hengst.: "The destruction of his battering-ram, or engine." [" מחה, from which מחי comes, is always used in the sense of destroying, extirpating, etc.; and so, not thrusting or striking, but destruction is the natural meaning of the noun. קבל is anything in front of, or opposition to, another; **hence kaballo** is a general designation of what the enemy was to put in hostile array against the walls of Tyre—his enginery. And the two words together may be fitly expressed by, his enginery of destruction."—P. F.]—The **swords** kill the defenders of the towers, in consequence of which the towers are torn down. As Häv. justly remarks, the unusual, the superhuman, the fact that God Himself was in the work, is meant to be represented. [This idea, however, is found by Häv., not in the swords killing the defenders of the towers, but being said to break down the towers—as if the swords had imparted to them a supernatural force, to do a work not proper to them.—P. F.] Most, however, generalize the expression בחרבותיו into: "through his iron," thinking of iron hooks, which were driven in, cutting into the hook-work (J. H. MICHAELIS: *securibus*).—Ver. 10. The expressions here are of a poetico-rhetorical character. The land moves into the sea, as it were, with its dust, through the excessive number of cavalry moving into the island-city. **Wheel** and **chariot** are distinguished with reference to the **sound**, which is ascribed to them, rolling and rattling. As the siege already described, so now the pressing into the taken city presupposes silently, because quite self-evidently, a connecting mound between the land and insular Tyre, which, according to Hengst., must already have existed, but probably was thrown up by Nebuchadnezzar for the purposes of the siege. It is made perfectly clear by the 'כמבואי that Tyre as well as every other (land-city) was vanquished. ("The uncommon sea-fortress must sink down before this power into a common stronghold.") מבקעה, Hitzig: "more exactly, one burst open, taken by storm."—Ver. 11. מצבה, from נצב, is something set right up, a **pillar**, not to be thought of as applying to memorial pillars of heroes or kings, but monuments of national strength in the temple of Hercules, such as the two mentioned by Herodotus (of gold [chrysolith] and emerald). Sepp.: "At the entrance into the temple of Melkarth stood two pillars (like Boaz and Jachin at Jerusalem), as the well-known boundary-pillars or sun-stadia in front of all the temples of Hercules, which should set a bound to deluges and conflagrations—water and fire." According to others: the gods of Tyre go down in the dust. Hengst.: "These pillars were symbols of the power and glory of Tyre."—Ver. 12. רכל of going about, trafficking. Treasures and wares.—ובתי חמדתך, Hengst.: "Thy beautiful houses," corresponding to palaces, Isa. xxiii. 13. Hitzig: "More exactly after which one has desire, which please one." **Ewald**: "The beautiful turreted dwellings and summer towers of the rich merchant-princes." Häv.: "On account of the limited space, very high houses, such as did not exist even in Rome" (Strabo, xvi.). These were to the home-returning merchants the object of their longing desire; as in Isa. xxiii., it is with the impression upon such home-voyagers that the prophecy opens. Arsenals and wharfs, the buildings adapted for marine trade, might also be meant. — **Stones, wood, dust**, point to the entire ruins; comp. ver. 4.—Ver. 13. So comes the constrained Sabbath upon song and lyre, noise and pleasure. Nothing remains but the silent rocks and the desert sea.—Ver. 14. The resumption (as already at ver. 12) of vers. 4, 5 conducts back what was accomplished by Nebuchadnezzar to the general outline at the beginning, just as what is said in Isa. xxiii. 15 sq. is to be thought of episodically in the Epos on Tyre. To this latter point matters were tending with Tyre, and Nebuchadnezzar was a force in regard to it.

Vers. 15–18. *The Impression made by the Fall of Tyre.*

Ver. 15. הלא, in the form of a question we have the sure prognostication of what would, on the spreading of the report of Tyre's fall, be the impression made by it in the colonies. The same enemy, indeed, did not harass them; but what can now any longer be placed aloft above others? What can still be secure before others? —The **fall** must be rendered palpable by the **groaning**, etc.—איים are the seaboard regions as well as the isles.—Hitzig notices the excellent choice of the expression, as the coasts and islands of the Mediterranean are precisely those which have been commonly visited by a shaking (earthquake, רעש). —Ver. 16. We must call to mind the settlements of the Phœnicians in the Sidonian and Tyrian period along the various coasts, in Cyprus, Rhodes, Malta, in Spain, Sicily, Sardinia, the Baleares, and think of Utica, Gades (Cadiz), Kalpe (Gibraltar), Malaka (Malaga), etc. On the **princes of the sea**, comp. Isa. xxiii. 8. One can imagine the princely might and pomp of the chief men in these places of commerce, the aristocratic style of their public appearances. — What follows is a description of the Eastern way of mourning.—Jon. iii. 6; ch. xxi. 31 [26].—מעיל, outer garment, wide for display.—Ch. xvi. 18.—Instead of all glory, which they lay aside, they clothe themselves in **terrors**.—Ch. vii. 27; Job xii. 13.—וחרדו repeats חרדות.—לרגעים, **at moments**, so that the trembling, like a fever, never for a moment leaves them (Hitzig).—Ver. 17; ch. xix. 1.—The catastrophe and ruins ask, How could so peculiar, wonderful, famous, powerful a place have met its overthrow? —Häv.: "Ah! how art thou condemned to the ground, thou inhabitress of the seas!" since מימים is = upon the seas there; but the city that dwelt away upon the seas is that whose inhabitants spread themselves over the seas, settled down there. Others: inhabited, peopled from the seas, that is, sea-dwellers, sea-peoples. Hitzig: "Thou populous in the sea," properly, forth of the sea, or more exactly, from out of the sea. "Bearing a human population, it jutted up immediately above the surface of the water, as if it had sprung from the lap of the sea."—Ewald reads, after ch.

xxvii. 34, נִשְׁבֶּרֶת, *shattered out of the seas.* Some have also read מִיָּמִים = from days (of old), from everlasting inhabited.—הַהֻלָּלָה from הלל, to make shining, to praise.—She is called **strong in the sea** (בים); Hitzig: through the sea, her maritime position. More correctly: in the sea, in the strong element it was a strong city; therefore not only a sea-power, but a power in the mighty sea.—חתיתם is the **terrors** ascribed to Tyre and its inhabitants. These terrors of her name she gave far and wide through the sea (in consequence of her wealth, her greatness, and power), **to all her inhabitants**, which would point to Venice similarly situated, if therewith it were meant that the city with its population inspired before it fear into all its individual inhabitants, held them over against one another in fear and trembling (Cocc.). It must rather be meant that the terror of the Tyrian supremacy stuck and adhered to every Tyrian, as later something of the same sort to every Roman. Comp. Hitzig. [Hengst.: "Tyre had a double class of inhabitants—her citizens, and her connections in the colonies, who, ideally taken, dwelt in Tyre, because the roots of their existence were there. The inhabitants in the one sense were the terror of the inhabitants in the other. They must bow before them, and obey their commands." So previously Hävernick. (Isa. xxiii. 2.) Ewald refers the second יושביה to the inhabitants of the sea, which is hardly feminine. The Syriac supplies הארץ, *omnibus habitatoribus terræ.*]—Ver. 18. Hitherto Tyre had frightened all; now all are frightened over Tyre. אשר בים sharpens the idea of island, and intensifies the preceding האין.—Comp. ver. 16.—If Tyre fell, what issue then awaits even islands in the midst of the sea? The issue, **outgoing**, is more nearly defined by the **fall**. Others have thought of emigration, flight in the ships.

Vers. 19–21. *The End and—a Beginning.*

An epilogue in these verses.—נחרבת looks back to החרבה in ver. 2.—בהעלות parallel to בתתי, but containing the thought of destruction in an image, which at the same time prepares for vers. 20, 21. The flood rises out of the depth to fetch down the city covered with many waters, with its rubbish and its corpses.—תהום, from הום (המה), is the swelling-depth, the boiling mass of water up from the sea. [According to Hengst., it is ideal: the overflowing of the nations—for which ver. 3 supplies no ground.]—Ver. 20. The city goes along with it, as with the dead generally, אל־עם עולם, either general: to the people among the hidden, in the darkness of the realms of death; or more special: to the people of ancient time; or quite special: to the people covered, buried by the deluge (Hengst.: the ancestral guests of hell, Gen. vi. 4).—תחתיות, **the lowest depths**, pictured out by בחרבות מעולם, **in the uninhabited places from everlasting**, by means of which "the image of the destruction, the annihilation of all human greatness, is thoroughly completed" (Häv.). As the going down, so also the dwelling is coloured by the fellowship of the dead, in parallel sentences.—למען לא תשבי, some, so that thou dwellest not, namely, longer where thou dost dwell; Hengst: "that thou sit not," but mayst lie down. The intention is perhaps to be understood of the entire disappearance from among the dwelling-places of men; comp. at ch. xxix. 11.—ונתתי, unless dependent upon למען, introduces a new sentence, and then fitly a conclusion. Or ver. 20: "Then I make thee go down," sq., "then I make thee dwell," sq., "then give I thee," sq. Over against the ruin of Tyre comes **beauty** (ornament, ch. xxv. 9)—(with that בארץ תחתיות, with this בארץ חיים)—the land of the living, earth with its life-hope, life-development, over against the lower world separated by death; Ps. xxvii. 13. [Hitzig: "And that thou shed not forth renown in the land of the living." Ewald reads ולא תִנָּצְבִי, and translates: "that thou remain not, nor exist in," etc. Kliefoth: "that thou be not inhabited, and I do not make glorious (namely, in respect to thee, Tyre (?)) in the land." The negative ought to be applied to both clauses of the verse: not be inhabited, and not set as an ornament. The Chaldee and those who followed it understood the last clauses of Judah, and hence took it positively. But the Sept. properly understood both clauses of Tyre, and took both negatively.—P. F.]—Ver. 21. Close of Tyre. בלהות, of frightful judgments, and indeed of sudden destruction. Therefore to be made an example of such. Gesenius concretely: I will make thee for the down-going, that is, into something that goeth down. Philippson: "I suddenly annihilate thee."—The נתתי צבי is met by this בלהות אתנך.—Comp. besides, Ps. xxxvii. 10, 36.

CHAPTER XXVII.

1, 2 And the word of Jehovah came to me, saying: And thou, son of man, raise
3 over Tyre a lamentation. And say to Tyre that dwells at the entrances of the
sea, trafficker of the peoples in many islands [coasts]: Thus saith the Lord
4 Jehovah, Tyre, thou sayest, I am perfect in beauty. In the heart of the sea
5 is thy territory, thy builders have perfected thy beauty. Of the cypresses of
Shenir they have built for thee all thy boards; cedars of Lebanon they have
6 taken to make a mast for thee. Of the oaks of Bashan have they made thy
oars; thy rudder they made of ivory, inlaid in larch, from the isles of Chittim.

7 Byssus in embroidered work from Egypt was thine outspread [flag], to be for a
sign to thee; purple-blue and purple-red from the islands of Elishah was thy
8 covering. The inhabitants of Zidon and of Arvad were thy rowers; thy
9 skilled men, Tyre, were in thee, they were thy pilots. Gebal's masters and
its wise men were in thee; they fastened [repaired] thy leaks. All the ships of
10 the sea and their mariners were in thee to carry on thy traffic. Paras, and
Lud, and Phut, were in thy [marine] force, thy men of war: the shield and
11 helmet they hung in thee; they gave thy ornament. The sons of Arvad and
thy force were on thy walls round about, and Gammadim (?) were in thy
towers: their shields they hung upon thy walls round about; they completed
12 thy beauty. Tarshish traded with thee because of the fulness of all kinds of
wealth [goods]; in silver, in iron, in tin and lead they paid for thy wares.
13 Javan, Tubal, and Meshech, they were thy merchants; in souls of men and
14 articles of brass they made thy traffic. From the house of Togarmah
they paid with steeds [horses], and riders [steeds], and mules were thy wares.
15 The sons of Dedan were thy merchants; many islands [coasts] were the traffic
of thy hand; horns of ivory and ebony they brought as thy barter-payment
16 [to thee as exchange in value]. Aram was thy trader because of the abundance of
thy works; in carbuncle, red purple, and embroidery, and byssus, and corals (?),
17 and rubies they paid for thy wares. Judah, and the land of Israel, they
were thy merchants; in wheat of Minnith, and pastry, and honey, and oil,
18 and balm they made thy traffic. Damascus was a trader with thee on account
of the abundance of thy works; on account of the abundance of all riches, in
19 wine of Helbon and white wool. Bedan and Javan from Uzal, for thy
wares they paid wrought iron; cassia and calamus were among thy goods.
20, 21 Dedan was thy merchant in broad coverings for riding. Arabia and all the
princes of Kedar, they were dealers of thy hand in lambs, and rams, and he-
22 goats: in these they were thy dealers. The merchants of Sheba and Raamah,
they were thy merchants: in the best [the chiefest] of all spices, and all sorts of
23 precious stones and gold, they bought thy wares. Charan, and Khanneh, and
24 Eden, the merchants of Sheba, Asshur, Chilmad, were thy dealers. These
were thy merchants in ornaments, in mantles of purple and embroidery, and
in treasures of many-threaded [many-coloured] yarns [rich damask], bound with
25 cords, and firm, in thy market. The ships of Tarshish were thy caravans,
thy traffic; and thou wast very glorious [mighty] in the heart of the sea.
26 They that rowed thee have brought thee into great waters; the east wind
27 broke thee in the heart of the sea. Thy riches and thy wares, thy mer-
chandise, thy mariners and thy pilots, the repairers of thy chinks, and the
traders in thy merchandise, and all thy men of war that are in thee, also
with thy whole company which is in thy midst, they shall fall into the heart
28 of the sea on the day of thy fall. At the sound of the cry of thy pilots the
29 suburban grounds shall shake. And from their ships shall come down all that
handle the oar, the mariners and all the pilots of the sea, that are in thy
30 midst, they shall stand upon the land. And they shall make their voice
heard over thee, and shall cry bitterly, and cast dust upon their heads:
31 they shall strew themselves with ashes. And they shave themselves bald for
thee, and gird themselves with sackcloth, and weep upon thee in bitterness of
32 soul with bitter lamentation. And they raise over thee in their wailings a
lamentation, and lament over thee: Who is like Tyre? as the destroyed one
33 in the midst of the sea! When thy wares went forth out of the seas, thou
didst satisfy many people with the abundance of thy riches and thy merchan-
34 dise; thou didst enrich the kings of the earth. At the time thou wert broken
by the seas in the depths of the waters, thy merchandise and thy whole
35 company fell in the midst of thee. All the inhabitants of the isles are
astonished at thee, and their kings shudder greatly, their countenances
36 tremble. The merchants among the peoples hiss over thee; terrors shalt thou
be, and shalt be no more for ever.

Ver. 3. Sept.: . . . τῳ ἐμποριῳ τ. λαων, ἀπο νησων πολλων . . . ἐγω περιεθηκα ἐμαυτη καλλος μου,—

Ver. 4. . . . θαλασσης τῳ Βεελειμ, κ. υἱοι σου (other read.: בָּנַיִךְ, גבולך, כלב, thy sons,) Arabs, Syr., Hex.).

Ver. 5. . . . ᾠκοδομηθη σοι, ταινιαι σανιδων κυπαρισσινων—other read.: באו לך; Syr.: adduxerunt. Hexapl.: ædificata est tibi, as Sept.

Ver. 6. . . . (ἱστους) ἐλατινους, ἐκ . . . ἐποιησαν τ. κωπας σου. Τα ἱερα σου . . . οἰκους ἀλσωδεις ἀπο νησων—(other read.: קדשך, Arabs as Sept. in plur.—Sept. read בתי אשרים).

Ver. 7. . . . του περιθειναι σοι δοξαν κ. περιβαλειν σε ὑακινθον . . . και περιβολαια ἐγενετο σοι.

Ver. 8. Κ. οἱ ἀρχοντες σου οἱ κατοικουντες Σιδωνα—

Ver. 9. . . . Οἱ πρεσβυτεροι Βιβλιων . . . οὑτοι ἐνισχυον τ. βουλην σου . . . ἐγενοντο σοι ἐπι δυσμας δυσμων. Vulg.: . . . habuerunt nautas ad ministerium variæ supellectilis tuæ.

Ver. 10. . . . ἐκρεμασαν ἐν σοι —

Ver. 11. Sept.: . . . φυλακες ἐν τ. πυργοις . . . ἐπι των ὁρμων σου—(other read.: וגמרים, et Cimmerii. Sept. read ושמרים); Vulg.: . . . sed et Pygmæi—

Ver. 12. . . . Καρχηδονιοι ἐμποροι σοι . . . και χρυσιον κ. χαλκον . . . ἐδωκαν τ. ἀγοραν σου. Vulg.: Carthaginenses.

Ver. 13. Ἡ Ἑλλας και ἡ συμπασα κ. τα παρατεινοντα. Vulg.: advexerunt populo tuo.

Ver. 14. Other read.: תורגמה.

Ver. 15. Sept.: Υἱοι Ῥοδιων . . . ἀπο νησων ἐπληθυναν τ. ἐμποριαν σου ὀδοντας ἐλεφαντινους, κ. τοις εἰσαγομενοις ἀντεδιδους τ. μισθους σου,

Ver. 16. ἀνθρωπους ἐμποριαν σου . . . του συμμικτου σου, στακτην κ. ποικιλματα ἐκ Θαρσεις κ. Ῥαμμωθ κ. Κορχορ ἐδωκαν (other read.: אדם, Edom, Sept. in the sense of *man*, followed by Arabs, Syr., Hexapl.).

Ver. 17. . . . ἐν σιτου πρασει κ. μυρων, κ. κασιας, κ. πρωτον μελι . . . εἰς τ. συμμικτον σου (ופנג, *nonnulli per: "et balsamum," alii* ופנג, *"et ficus, grossulos," vel ex Arab. "angurias, pepones Indicos"*). Vulg.: . . . *in frumento primo: balsamum . . . et resinam* (Sept. ῥητινην) *proposuerunt in nundinis tuis.*

Ver. 18. Sept.: . . . κ. ἐρια ἐκ Μιλητου (19), κ. οἰνον εἰς τ. ἀγοραν σου ἐδωκαν. Ἐξ Ἀσηλ σιδηρον . . . σπαρτιον κ. τροχιας ἐδωκαν· ἐν τ. συμμικτῳ σου ἐστιν. Vulg.: . . . *in vino pingui, in lanis coloris optimi. Dan et Græcia et Mosel*—(other read.: הדן).

Ver. 20. . . . μετα κτηνων ἐκλεκτων—Vulg.: . . . *in tapetibus ad sedendum.*

Ver. 21. . . . δια χειρος σου, καμηλους—(other read.: בפרים, *in tauris vel juvencis.*—Chald.).

Ver. 23. . . . και Δαιδαν . . . κ. Χαρμαν. (For חרן it is read הרה, and for וכנה a reading exists וכלנה.)

Ver. 24. . . . ἐν μαχαλιμ κ. ἐν γαλιμα ὑακινθον κ. πορφυραν κ. θησαυρους ἐκλεκτους δεδεμενους σχοινιοις ἐν κυπαρισσινοις (25) πλοιοις ἐν αὐτοις. Καρχηδονιοι ἐμποροι σου, Θαρσεις ἐμποροι σου ἐν τ. πληθει ἐν τ. συμμικτῳ σου, κ. . . . κ. ἐβαρυνθης.—Vulg.: . . . *multifariam involucris hyacinthi et polymitorum gazarumque pretiosarum . . . cedros quoque habebant in negotiationibus tuis. Naves maris principes tui in negotiatione tua*—

Ver. 26. Div. read.: כמים.

Ver. 27. Other read.: וכל. Sept.: ἡσαν δυναμεις σου, κ. ὁ μισθος σου ἐν τ. συμμικτῳ σου . . . και οἱ συμβουλοι σου και οἱ συμμικτοι σου ἐκ τ. συμμικτων σου, κ. . . . πασα ἡ συναγωγη.—

Ver. 28. . . . της κραυγης σου οἱ κυβερνηται σου φοβῳ—Vulg.: . . . *conturbabuntur classes.*

Ver. 29. . . . και οἱ ἐπιβαται κ. οἱ πρωρεις της θαλασσης.

Ver. 32. Sept., Arabs, Syr. read בניהם, "their sons." Και ληψονται οἱ υἱοι αὐτων . . . κατασιγηθεισα ἐν μεσῳ θαλασσης;—

Ver. 33. Ποσον και τινα εὑρες μισθον ἀπο τ. θαλασσης; Ἐνεποιησας ἐθνη ἀπο τ. πληθους σου κ. ἀπο τ. συμμικτου σου . . . παντας τας βασιλεις—

Ver. 34. Νυν συνετριβης ἐν θαλασσῃ, ἐν βαθει ὑδατος ὁ συμμικτος σου. Vulg.: . . . *contrita es a mari; in profundis . . . ceciderunt.*

Ver. 35. (Ἐπεσον) παντες . . . και οἱ κωπηλαται σου ἐστυγνασαν ἐπι σε . . . κ. ἐδακρυσαν τῳ προσωπῳ αὐτων ἐπι σοι. Vulg.: . . . *tempestate perculsi mutaverunt vultus.*

Ver. 36. Sept. add λεγει κυριος ὁ Θεος.

EXEGETICAL REMARKS.

Vers. 1–25. *The Glory of Tyre.*

The lamentation over Tyre is closely connected with the prophecy in ch. xxvi., and is prepared for by the 17th verse of that chapter.—Ver. 2. For **that** the overthrow of Jerusalem was the prophetic prolepsis, for **this** the overthrow of Tyre. With the lamentation, expression is at the same time given to the righteous pain occasioned by the misuse of the fulness of divine gifts, which Tyre had enjoyed.—ואתה, J. H. Michaelis makes: *tu etiam, ut alii.*—Ver. 3. מבוא is the entrance into a city, the entrance of the gate; and so here מבואת, the openings or **entrances of the sea,** into which people entered from the sea, and again went out into the sea—therefore the harbours or ports (*porta* and *portus*). Hävernick refers to Strabo xvi. 2, Arrian ii. 20, 21, who make mention of a northern and southern harbour of Tyre, and at the same time of the deficiency elsewhere of proper harbours on the Syrian coast. HENGST.: "from whence the sea is readily accessible on all sides, in the centre of the then civilised world: thus Tyre went forth for purposes of trade to visit the nations."—For הַיֹּשַׁבְתִּי (to be thus pointed) the Qeri has הַיּוֹשֶׁבֶת.—On רכלת, comp. at ch. xxvi. 12.—אל־איים, which for the sake of merchandise frequents many coasts.—The address to Tyre holds up to her, as previously in ch. xxvi. 2 her scornful malicious joy, so here her complete self-satisfaction. **Perfect in beauty** is as much as: perfectly beautiful, that is: of perfect beauty, but not as well: the completion of beauty. Observe the parallel with Jerusalem in Lam. ii. 15. What is indicated thereby appears from ver. 4: for the "**I am perfect in beauty,**" in the mouth of Tyre is the theme of the detailed descriptions that follow.—**In the heart of the sea** = in the midst of the sea, surrounded on every hand by the same. J. H. Michaelis cites the words of Alexander the Great to the Tyrian ambassador (CURTIUS, iv. 2): *Vos quidem fiducia loci, quod insulam incolitis, pedestrem hunc exercitum spernitis.*—A strait of four stadia separated the city from the continent.—The boundaries, the strict meaning of גְּבוּלַיִ, are the **territory** enclosed by these.—Hence the perfectness of its local position; hence, also, this perfectness under the notion of the beautiful, which certainly comprehends not merely the architectural (though this primarily), but also generally the civic beauty of Tyre.

Ver. 5. In this further look Tyre is allegorized by our prophet—after his own peculiar manner—under the image of a state-ship. The **builders** (in ver. 4) mediate the transition; not less (as Hitzig acutely remarks) was the image suggested by the local position of Tyre,—in the midst of the sea, surrounded by a wilderness of masts, the city had the appearance of a sea-ship.—Because a state-ship, hence the finest kinds of wood for material (accusative).—(Häv. remarks, that in reality the palaces of Tyre were made of cedar from Lebanon, JOSEPH. *Antiq.* viii. 5.)—שְׂנִיר (= שריון, Deut. iii. 9), the Amorite name for Hermon, though from this in the stricter sense distinguished, was renowned for its cypresses (Sir. xxiv. 17), which were recommended by the firm, durable nature of the wood (VIRGIL, *Georg.* ii. 444).—The framework of the vessel, with which the delineation commences, presents itself as dualistic (לחותים),—the **boards** or timbers both right and left, especially where the whole is meant, as here. The mast (main-mast), in accordance with its representative character (comp. ver. 7), is of wood of the nobler kind, cedar, Ps. xxix. 5.—Ver. 6. **Bashan,** on the farther side of Jordan, from Jabbok to Hermon, and eastward to the outermost limits, on the south-west mountainous—so called from its **oaks.** It belongs to the world-embracing character of Tyre that all lands contributed to her glory.—מִשּׁוֹט = מָשׁוֹט, ver. 29, from שׁוּט, to row. The oars must be of heavy, in particular of firm, wood.—קֶרֶשׁ is "board" or plank, from קָרַשׁ, to split; here collectively, either of the benches for rowers (vers. 2, 3) over each other, or of the deck (HITZIG). HÄV.: the thick plank-work as stays, the scaffold of the mast. MEIER: table-work, wainscoting, for the laying out of the ship. RASHI: the helm; which recommends itself more than the others, on account of its importance for the vessel, and its suitableness in respect to the adorning that follows. The strange שֵׁן, **ivory** (elephant's tooth), is anyhow modified by בת־אשרים, **daughter of** —what? אשור is "step," from אָשַׁר. A kind of wood, however, must be meant. As it is more nearly indicated by **the isles of Chittim,** and by these are to be understood in the larger sense the islands and coasts of the Mediterranean, Rosenmüller thinks of Sardinia and Corsica, and, with many, supposes the box-tree to be meant, which **is** quite common in the latter island (VIRGIL, *Æn.* x. 137). The expression, however, more particularly denotes the islands and coasts of Greece. Recent expositors understand it of Cyprus, on account of the old Phœnician city in it, Κίτιον, Κίττιον (Chethi), and of the islands and coasts in the neighbourhood. Häv. is in favour of the Cyprian pines (THEOPHRAST. *Hist. pl.* v. 8)—very suitable; Cyprus was particularly famous for its excellent ship-building materials. The regularly successive compact growth of the pine would agree well with אשר, also its firm, sure position, and its thick wood. Gesen. takes the word as = תְּאַשּׁוּר, **Sherbin-cedar.** Hitzig throws the two words together, and reads בַּתְּאשרים; which is unnecessary, since בת denotes simply the subordinate dependent relationship—more exactly expressing that which is enclosed by another (בת עין, the pupil: also in Lam. iii. 13, בת אשפה, the arrow), and indicating that the ivory formed only the costly article inlaid in the wood mentioned. This wood itself was the material; of it was the helm made, and the handle and other parts were ornamented with ivory.—Ver. 7. Comp. on ch. xvi. 10. Out of Egypt, with its famous looms, went forth "embroidered linen" (HITZ.), "embroidered byssus" (HENGST.), with flowers and figures.—The more immediate destination: **to be to thee for a sign** (נֵס, visible from afar), leads one, with מפרשך, to think either of sails provided with emblems and devices, after the Egyptian fashion, or rather of the flag placed by the ancients on the fore-part of the ship.—ארגמן is the red purple, purple-red cloth, from a shell-fish (πορφύρα) found on the Syrian and Peloponnesian coasts. **The islands of Elishah,** according to Jerome, were the islands of the Ionian Sea; according to Bochart, the Peloponnesus, in which was Elis (Hellas). As derived from so great a distance, this purple figures here as a foreign commodity, and does so, indeed, by means of its finely coloured fabric; its splendid colour was much prized.—תכלת; comp. at ch. xxiii. 6.—מכסה (part. Piel of כסה) is the covering of the ship above deck, against the heat of the sun.

Ver. 8 forms a transition to the manning, not of the ship, but of the Tyrian state-constitution. **Zidon,** the oldest city of Phœnicia, on this account designated "the mother," and **Arvad,** the island Aradus, entirely covered by the city of the same name,—hence a second Tyre, which, as did also Zidon, always possessed its own kingdom,—serve to illustrate the commonwealth represented by Tyre, each contributing its share of help; but illustrate also the relation of the several parties, the oarsmen being from those places, but the helmsmen (captains), those skilled in navigation, were Tyrians, so that Tyre stands forth as the guiding intelligence. And so also in ver. 9 figure **the ancients;** they were the experienced, approved masters and skilled architects from **Gebal** (where was the burial-place of Adonis, whence the name), in Tyre, employed in its marine force. Comp. 1 Kings v. 32 [18]. For the allegory of the ship, their expertness in healing breaches, renovating, instantly repairing what was decayed, is drawn into consideration. (May there not, however, withal be meant to be conveyed an impression of the supremacy which Tyre in this position exercised upon the other Phœnician states?) But the sentence that follows introduces the principal point, for which all that precedes was merely preparatory, namely, that Tyre was a **mercantile** power.—מלח is, in the general, seamen, so designated from the "salt," for sea (ἁλιεύς, from ἅλς). Tyre included, as it were, all navigation in itself; the sea-world was its fleet. (HITZIG: foreign merchant-vessels lie here at anchor. HENGST.: all the Tyrians with their colonies are, as it were, in this one giant ship, as the jolly-boats in an ordinary large ship, and are sent out from it.)—ערב, "to exchange," hence: "to trade."

Ver. 10. Before the main tendency indicated was given way to, the representation turns back from the image of the ship, through an emphasizing of the military weapons of defence and offence, in which Tyre prided herself, to the beginning, and so to the city.—פרס (Pares, Fares, Fars, in the cuneiform inscriptions Pâraça) must be Persia. Hitzig contends for those who, in primeval times, settled in Africa. Hengstenberg, as also Häv., holds firmly by their Asiatic character, and as having even then probably entered into connection with the anti-Chaldaic coalition in a relation to Tyre,—the first germ of their later victorious lifting of the shield against the Chaldean ascendency; comp. at ch. viii. 16. **Lud** and **Phut** are African populations: the former, not the Semitic Lydians, may well enough be the Hamitic Ludim (Gen. x. 13); the latter, the Libyans of antiquity—both well known as soldiers in the Egyptian army (Jer. xlvi. 9). Either to picture the far-extending relations of the Tyrian mercantile power are they named, or because the most foreign among the foreign; as in Rome, in Byzantium, they were purposely taken into pay, whether for display or as a security against internal tumults. We learn the existing relations best from Carthage. Rich enough to pay the costs, the mercenary army secured for the Tyrian merchant ability to ply his traffic; he found in it military protection for his settlements, and advantage also for prosecuting new undertakings. If the **hanging up of shield** and **helmet** is not a poetical expression,—their arms were thy arms, their conquests thine, or such like,—we must think of a military custom, as to-day still the armour is hung up when there is no service. The garrison of the city they did not likely form (HITZIG), as Ver. 11 shows that the protection of the city was committed to domestic and allied troops. But what were the **Gammadim?** Hävernick explains the word from the dialects by "valiant," "audacious," and thinks that it was the favourite expression for the national militia, as there was among the Carthaginians a "sacred host." The latter, however, would not be designated the proper troops, in contrast to the mercenaries! Hence HENGST.: "bold champions"—a Tyrian designation for a select band. HITZ.: "deserters from the neighbouring countries, to whom the rich republic offered more favourable conditions than the kings,"—if there may not have been the marring of the original גִּבֹּרִים, with reference to Cant. iv. 4! [Jewish expositors made out of the word pigmies—from גֹּמֶד, an *ell*, therefore ell-high—because they appeared such in the towers. Others conjectured a particular Phœnician allied people to be meant by it (Gamale); the Targum: Cappadocians. Meier, with an eye to עמד, explains it: "as posts." We must then render: "The sons of Arvad and thy force were on thy walls round about, and posts in thy towers."]—It is to be remarked that שֶׁלֶט is a noble shield, while in ver. 10 only common armour is mentioned. So, too, the language rises; while it is there תלו־בך, here it is 'תלו על־חום; the home element is heightened. Hence, also, instead of נתנו הדרך, which is as much as: **it ornamented thee** (ch. xvi. 14) thus to have distant ones, foreigners, in thy pay, to do thee service, now it is: כללו יפיך, **they completed thy beauty,** forming at the same time a close of the detailed theme.

Ver. 12. The mercantile glory of Tyre begins here; comp. v. 9.—**Tarshish,** the most renowned mart of commerce in the West, a city and district of Spain, Tartessus, between the two mouths of the Bætis (Guadalquivir). It traded with Tyre not so much by means of things brought thither, as because the fulness and variety of the Tyrian wares, the costly, rich articles which the Tyrian vessels brought, were given (נתן) in payment for the abundance in precious metals for which Tartessus was renowned in antiquity (DIODOR. v. 35 sq.; STRABO, iii.; PLIN. *Hist. Nat.*). But **trader** agrees better with that than merchant. It was a barter-dealing, as was very commonly the case in antiquity.—עזבון (only in plural), from עזב, to let go; and hence better, with Hitzig, taken as equal to **wares,** than, with Ewald, as "sale."—Ver. 13. **Javan** is the land of Greece (Ionia); **Tubal,** often joined with **Meshech,** are together the Tibareni and Moschi of the ancients, in Lesser Asia,—the former to the west of the latter, who were the inhabitants of a mountainous region between Iberia, Armenia, and Colchis. The enumeration of the traders in Tyre's merchandise turns now, therefore, northwards.—**In souls of men,** slave-traffic; if we have not a special case in Joel iv. 6 (Eng. V. iii. 6), then it was reciprocal. Häv. is of opinion that female slaves from Greece were of old highly estimated in the East, and, on the other side, male slaves (?).—For the copper (or **brass**) **articles,** Hitzig makes account of the name Tibareni, as well as the neighbours of the Moschi, the Chalybes, and remarks that to this day the Colchian mountains in Trabosan contain unexhausted mines of copper. Häv. notices that in the hilly Caucasian region inhabited by Tubal and Meshech, the people have been ever distinguished for their beauty, and that through all time they have been noted for commerce in slaves (see BOCHART, *Phaleg.*). Comp. besides, at ver. 9.—Ver. 14. **Togarmah** is Armenia. —**From the house,** either out of the region, or the race of people from it (?). Armenia was distinguished for its breeding of horses. Herodotus speaks of its asses (i. 194).—סוסים ופרשים, usually draught horses and riding horses.—Ver. 15. **The sons of Dedan,** occasioned by מבית going before, are the Cushite Dedanites (Gen. x. 7), as middlemen in the trade. As such, and as representatives of the land-trade with their caravans, yet as identical with those in ver. 20, since Scripture knows only of one Dedan, the Arabian one, they are regarded by Hengst.; but he admits of no connection on the part of Dedan directly with **the many islands.** On the other hand, Häv., following Heeren's guidance, thinks of a south Arabian tribe, and the three Bahrein islands (GESEN.: "perhaps the island Daden"?), on the west side of the Persian Gulf, where were the "many coasts" of the East Indies, with which the articles mentioned of ivory and ebony very well suit. With Hitzig, also, the Dedanites are the traders with Tyre in the south-east, from the Persian Gulf (Isa. xxi. 13). If we should understand by איים islands, we must suppose it to be said, that what the caravans transported had also by Tyre been conveyed by sea. According to Philippsen, it is meant that those caravans of the Indian wares contained others also from distant sea-coasts unknown to us.—סחרת, according to Hitzig to be pointed as a participle (?), is merchandise or **traffic,** in the sense of the abstract for the concrete. The addition: **of thy hand,** marks the dependence, the intermediate sort of traffic; they were agents for Tyre.—The **horns,** used of **ivory,** since it was the teeth of the elephant, must be understood by way of comparison. Pliny recognises it as *dentes,* and yet names it *cornua elephanti.* It is commonly connected with **ebony** (*Diospyros Ebenum,* which has white bark, dark green leaves, and medlar-like fruit). For both, Ethiopia was famous in the old world.—אֶשְׁכָּר (שָׁכָר, שֶׁכֶר)—comp. Hupfeld on Ps. lxxii. 10—might, with השיבו (to bring back, restore), be understood in the sense of a sort of tribute, since Tyre would represent herself as having, through her merchandise, made the products of all lands, as it were, tributary to her. It suits with אשכר (payment), however, as with השיב, to think of barter, in which the value of the goods purchased is brought back, restored.

Ver. 16. Those who read Edom [that is, instead of Aram, which was done by the Sept., exists also in several codices, and is preferred by Ewald, Hitzig, etc.] conceive that Aram lay too far out of the way from Dedan, in the direction of Israel (!); also, that first in ver. 18 it comes in regular order. Edom, however, and in particular Petra, was important as a goods emporium. And not less so was Aram, *i.e.* Syria, in the wider sense Mesopotamia, for an agency-traffic. The Syrians, according to Jerome, were born merchants, madly intent on its gains. [*Usque hodie permanet in Syris ingenitus negotiationis ardor, qui per totum mundum lucri cupiditate discurrunt, et tantam mercandi habent vesaniam,* etc.] —מרב מעשיך, for which, at ver. 12, there is מרב כל־הון, designated as (artistic) work, manufactured goods. **Carbuncle** (נפך), a precious stone; see at Ex. xxviii. 18. On the rest, comp. at ver. 7.—בוץ appears to designate the Syrian, in contradistinction from the Egyptian byssus (שֵׁשׁ)—the finest white cotton?—Babylon was renowned for its weaving, as it was also a market for precious stones.—רָאמוֹת, part. act. plur. for רמות; Hengst.: precious things, what stands high, is valuable. In particular, red (dark) corals or pearls, have been thought of.—כדכד, a gem of glittering splendour (GESEN.); jasper has been suggested, also garnet, crystal, **ruby.**—Ver. 17. Palestine gave **wheat** in merchandise **to** Tyre (חטים, in grains).—**Minnith** (מנית), a place in the territory of the Ammonites (Judg. xi. 33); comp. 2 Chron. xxvii. 5; 1 Kings v. 25 [11]; Acts xii. 20.—פנג, according to Meier, might be: "the rubbed off," "the shaved off" = *κασια,* קְצִיעָה; or more generally: "something soft" = sweet, which dissolves itself. R. Parchon in his Lexicon makes it = חלות דבש, *placenta mellis.* Some have referred to פנק, *deliciari,* and combined therewith several operations. Comp. Rosenmüller. Balsam, however, has also been given as an interpretation, but צרי is the term for that, namely, the resin from the balsam-powder (*opobalsamum*), Jer. viii. 22. Hitzig recurs to *pannaga* (serpent), a Sanscrit word for a healing aromatic wood.—דבש, the **honey** of bees, as well as grape-syrup (dibs) and fruit-syrup generally—a great article of merchandise in Palestine, ch. xvi. 13; Deut. xxxii. 13.—On **oil,** comp. Deut. viii. 8, xxviii. 40; 1 Kings v. 25 [11]; 2 Chron. ii. 10; Hos. xii. 2 [1].—Ver. 18. **Damascus** is here specialized, because it was a particularly important mart of commerce for Tyre; comp. vers. 16 and 12. Hengst. remarks on the **riches,** that they must therefore have paid for wares also with gold.—**Helbon,** now Aleppo, famous for its wine, the wine of the Persian kings, still a notable city (STRABO, xv.). Instead of **white wool,** Ewald has "wool of Sachar," a Syriac town, where was then the best wool. But צחר expresses the shining white wool, as wool of that sort was especially derived from the pasture-lands of Syria and Arabia (HÄV.). "The finest and most silky, because the sheep pasturing in the deserts were always under the open heaven" (J. D. MICH.). The Sept.: Milesian wool.—Ver. 19. ודן can neither be a third Dedan (EWALD), nor "and Dan," but it must be taken for an unknown Arabic district; according to Movers, it would be the trade-renowned Aden. Javan, too, is perhaps to be taken for a Greek settlement in Arabia, and to be distinguished, as Arabic, from that in ver. 13; and מאוזל may serve as a nearer determination of it—only not as part. Pual from אָזַל, to turn, wind (a thread); in the Talmud: to spin, מְאוּזָּל, that is, "the spun" yarn (GESEN., MEIER)—such a mention of a particular sort of ware being scarcely suitable here, but as מֵאוּזָל, agreeably to Gen. x. 27 = out of Sanaa, the capital of Yemen. It accords with this that a Javan in Yemen is mentioned, and the articles which are referred to likewise agree. Tuch very properly calls to remembrance, in connection with ברזל עשות, wrought iron, the sword-blades of Yemen, along with the Indian so famous through all the East.—קדה, the Arabic **cassia** (a kind of cinnamon), and קנה, a reed, *acorus calamus,* likewise native to Arabia; according to others an Indian product, which Yemen traded in from there.

Ver. 20. Dedan—ch. xxv. 13; Gen. xxv. 3—Semitic—comp. ver. 15—in Northern Arabia. בגדי־חפש לרכבה, GESEN.: *tapetes stratæ ad equitandum;* from the verb חפש, to stretch. Others: "robes," "garments of the nobles," which would be expressed through the meaning "setting free." Häv. questions the signification of spreading out (comp. Hupfeld on Ps. lxxxviii. 6 [5]); holds "to cover," "to bind," "to wind round," as the radical meaning; and as to the matter, compares Judg. v. 10. The allusion probably is to the splendid riding or horse apparel, which in the East (like the stirrups, for example) are marks of distinction and luxury.—Ver. 21. **Arabia** (ערב; comp. ערבה, a steppe), here together with "**all the princes of Kedar**" (Gen. xxv. 13)—in Pliny, *Codrei*—a particularizing of the small trafficking nomadic tribes in the interior of Arabia; comp. ver. 15. Their large property in flocks is well known; comp. also Jer. xlix. 28 sq.—Even the roving, unsettled Bedouins of the desert were Tyre's ready instruments for his merchandise.—Ver. 22. **The merchants of Sheba and Raamah** (רעמה), that is, Sabæa, in Arabia Felix, and the Cushite Ῥέγμα, on the Persian Gulf.—ראש, the head, for the highest of their kind; here of the foremost, most excellent perfumes (בֶּשֶׂם, or בֹּשֶׂם, of the balsam-shrub), if the genuine balm is not meant by it. The mountains of Hadramaut and Yemen yield all sorts of precious stones, and the latter was esteemed among the ancients as a very rich gold region.—Ver. 23. **Haran** (Gen. xi. 31, Κάῤῥαι, the Carræ, noted in later times for the defeat of Crassus) comes into view as on the cross-way of the caravans when they were passing through Mesopotamia. **Khanneh** (כנה, contracted for כַּלְנֵה), the later Ctesiphon, as a commercial city on the Tigris. **Eden** (עדן) is the Mesopotamian, as distinguished from the Syrian, town, which has been sought in the delta of the Euphrates—Maadan?—By the **Sheba** here Rosenmüller understands another Sabæa than that mentioned in ver. 22. Häv. translates: "Haran and Canneh and Eden are the merchants of Saba; (on the other hand) Asshur, Chilmad are thy customers" (?). Keil and Movers understand the meaning to be, that the Sabæans, who held a yearly market in Carræ, were named as negotiators between the districts of Mesopotamia and Tyre.—**Asshur** must, according to Keil, not be Assyria, but (MOVERS) the emporium of Sura (Essurieh), on the Euphrates, above Thapsacus, in a caravan road which branches off toward כלמד, Charmande. Häv. sees in Chilmad a Tyrian emporium for the trade with Assyria.—Ver. 24. מכללים, from כלל, **ornaments**, perfectly fine articles, finished productions; by which may be understood, with Häv., works of art of tasteful, perfectly beautiful workmanship, or, with others, of splendid garments. (EWALD: full equipments.)—גלום (from גלם, to roll, wind up) is a mantle, a wide garment, well-nigh corresponding to the Chlamys; comp. ver. 7.—גנזים, **treasures**, which signification Hengst. firmly retains; but what were "treasures of damask"? The word must specify the preceding more general objects of beautiful workmanship. Häv. takes it for a Persian word, intended to designate a foreign object, and naturalized in Syriac; either girdles, or pouches, or trousers. (GESEN.: chests for packing and preserving in; HITZIG: "and in cords." גנז, what is twined, wound up. EWALD: pouches of Damascus.)—ברומים; GESEN.: a kind of cloth with a many-coloured wool, the πολύμιτα of the Greeks, damask. Häv.: garments of peculiar sorts of weaving (διπλοΐδες?). The Tyrians then dyed silk-yarn, silk, and cotton wool.—בחבלים' Häv. translates: "with threads wound round and firm," as a nearer description, partly in respect to the costly threads with which the cloth in question was inwrought, and partly in respect to its durability.—ארזים the ancients mostly connect with אֶרֶז, cedar, and understand by it chests of cedar. PHILIPPSON: packed in cedar. חבלים must be taken for **cords** or strings. חבש, to bind. HENGST.: "bound with cords and fastened." "Ezekiel describes the bales of such stuffs probably according to his own view." HITZIG: "with many-threaded, tight-drawn cords."—Ver. 25. The sum from which the tendency of the whole representation clearly appears. Häv. unsuitably connects this verse with ver. 26. Tarshish alone points back to the commencement of the representation, in ver. 12. **Ships of Tarshish**, however, were those prepared for distant voyages generally, as we speak now of "Indiamen," "Greenlanders."—שרות, according to Häv., must mean "walls," as if the Tarshish fleet had formed, in a manner, the breastwork of Tyre—had been the security of the Tyrian commerce. According to other explanations, "singers," who celebrate thee on account of thy merchandise; HITZIG: שְׂדוֹתַיִךְ = thy fields, thy lands. It probably comes from שׁוּר, Chald. שְׁיָרָא, **caravan**; and the sense will be: they moved off caravan-like to drive your traffic (GES.). HENGST.: "The ships of Tarshish visit thee, thy wares; these were the special object of the visit." But this made nothing for the aim of the representation; and the sentence that follows stands better, if the ships are conceived of as trading towards Tartessus, and then always bringing back their gains from the distant world, which filled Tyre, and lent to it its singular importance in the midst of the sea. Comp. on ch. xxvi. 2.—מערבך can be the accusative: in respect to thy merchandise; as to the sense, much the same as: navigation, on a grand scale, was thy business; it was his lever.—Ver. 4.

Vers. 26–36. *The Overthrow of Tyre.*

In ver. 26, already introduced by ver. 25, the lamentation upon Tyre resumes the image of a ship, which was dropped at ver. 10. Häv. justly draws attention to the contrast, since Tyre received his deathblow in the midst of his glory, and to the impressive repetition of בלב ימים, **in the heart of the sea.** "The overthrow of the city was its shipwreck" (HITZIG). במים'; comp. Ps. lxxvii. 20 [19]. Therefore like a vessel that was brought upon the high sea by its rowers, who moved it;—which, indeed, did not bespeak a policy that adventured into danger, but might well enough indicate the proud self-sufficiency which inspirited the whole. Hengst.: "The many waters an image of great dangers and sufferings."—The **east wind** (ch. xvii. 10, xix. 12), exactly as at Ps. xlviii. 7. Peculiar to it are strong, continued blasts; if the vessel strengthens itself to the storm, then the danger becomes very great. "In the midst of the sea" is no deliverance, it now becomes the grave for all and of all. —Ver. 27. A recapitulation; comp. vers. 12, 18, 19, 22, 9, 17, 8, 10—ch. xxvi. 15.—Ver. 28. Cry of the **pilots,** which depicts the perfect hopelessness of deliverance.—מגרש, from גרש, a separate piece of ground: a common, pasture-ground, but this as the environs of the city, so that the continent with its adjoining territory will be meant. The death-cry on the high sea finds its echo on the continent,—Palætyre?—The sensation upon the land is connected in Ver. 29 sq. with a prolonged representation of the same on the sea. Very fitly those who stood in a marine relationship to Tyre took up the lamentation over her. Whether it might be to give a strong impression of the general insecurity since Tyre had fallen, or to add solemnity to the lamentation, in the one way or the other is the coming down of the persons concerned to be understood; either all will as quickly as possible find deliverance on the land, or sympathy makes them come nearer to the scene of the disaster.—Ver. 30. Comp. ch. xxvi. 16 sq. A collection of all sorts of expressions of mourning, with the view of representing the grief as at once great and general.—Ver. 31. Comp. ch. vii. 18.—Ver. 32. ני, contracted from נהי, suited for the yelling, sharp wail-cry (HAV.); against which, Hitzig gives as an emendation: בְּפִיהֶם, raised up in their mouth = took upon their lips.—מי כצור, Hitzig quite correctly grounds in vers. 33, 34: from so great a height so deeply sunk down!—כדמה (GESEN.: דֻּמָּה, destruction, that which is destroyed; KEIL, part. Pi. with מ dropt off: "as the annihilated in the midst of the sea"; HITZIG, part. Pual) is the destination suitable to a place like Tyre. Hengst.: דמה is not the participle, but the perf. Pual, which, as often with the perf., stands in place of the participle: "like one that is destroyed." EWALD: "like her in the midst of the sea." HÄV.: "who is, like Tyre, become so still!"—compared with the earlier noisy bustle of the city. In the בתוך הים there sounds again בלב ימים.—Ver. 33. **When thy wares went forth.** HENGST.: "from the seas they were brought into all the harbours of the world." ROSENMÜLLER: out of all seas to Tyre. HITZIG: like the productions, the fruits of the field from all soils.—**Satisfy is:** to meet the desire, the demand, the necessity. Tyre, on the one side, satisfied the world's need; on the other, it enriched those of whom it bought or trafficked in respect to gold or costly goods. The "Suri" or Tyrian gold pieces were well known in antiquity.—Ver. 34. The contrast. עת נשברת, indication of the time, which so far is specified as to be identified with that of Tyre's overthrow. Others: now. (Ewald improves thus: עַתְּ נִשְׁבַּרְתְּ, "now art thou shattered.") **The going down of a vessel, where all goes down.**—Ver. 35. The closing chorus in a manner: those who were friendly to the commerce; and in ver. 36, the co-operators and rivals in it. Amazement, terror, but also malicious joy. The close agrees with ch. xxvi. 21.

CHAPTER XXVIII.

1, 2 And the word of Jehovah came to me, saying, Son of man, say to the prince
of Tyre, Thus saith the Lord Jehovah, Because thy heart is high, and thou
sayest, I am God, the seat of the gods I occupy in the heart of the seas; and
thou art man, and not God, and thou makest thy heart as the heart of the
3 Godhead: Behold, thou art wiser than Daniel; nothing concealed is dark to
4 thee: In thy wisdom and in thy prudence thou hast made for thee wealth,
5 and makest [procurest] gold and silver in thy treasures: In the fulness of thy
wisdom in thy traffic thou didst increase thy wealth, and thy heart was high
6 in thy wealth: Therefore thus saith the Lord Jehovah, Because thou makest
7 thy heart as the heart of the Godhead; Therefore, behold, I bring strangers
upon thee, the violent of the heathen; and they draw their swords upon the
8 beauty of thy wisdom, and they dishonour thy shining beauty. To the grave
they will bring thee down, and thou diest the death of the pierced-through
9 in the heart of the seas. Wilt thou say and [still] say, I am God, in the
presence of him that slayeth thee? and thou art man, and not God, in the
10 hand of him that pierceth thee through! Deaths of the uncircumcised shalt
thou die in the hand of strangers: for I have spoken: sentence of the Lord
11, 12 Jehovah. And the word of Jehovah came to me, saying, Son of man, raise
a lamentation over the king of Tyre, and say to him, Thus saith the Lord
Jehovah, Thou confirmedst the measure, full of wisdom, and perfect in beauty!
13 In Eden, the garden of God, wast thou; every precious stone was thy covering,
sardine, topaz, and diamond, Tarshish-stone, onyx, and jasper, sapphire,
carbuncle, and emerald, and gold: the work of thy kettledrums and of thy

pipes was with thee; in the day that thou wast made they were prepared.
14 Thou cherub of the anointing, that covered; and I have given thee [therefor, thereto]; upon the holy mountain of God wast thou, in the midst of fiery stones
15 thou didst walk. Blameless wast thou in thy ways from the day that thou
16 wast made, till perverseness was found in thee. In the abundance of thy merchandise they filled thy midst with mischief, and thou sinnedst; and I will profane thee from off the mountain of Godhead; and I will destroy thee,
17 covering cherub, from the midst of the stones of fire. Thy heart was high in thy beauty; thou didst corrupt thy wisdom on account of thy shining beauty; to the earth will I throw thee down; I give thee before kings, that
18 they may look upon thee. From the multitude of thy iniquities, in the corruptness of thy traffic, thou hast profaned thy sanctuaries; and I will make fire go forth from the midst of thee, which burns thee up; and I will give thee
19 to ashes upon the earth in the eyes of all who see thee. All who know thee among the people are amazed at thee; for terrors thou art become, and thou art no more even to eternity.
20, 21 And the word of Jehovah came to me, saying, Son of man, direct thy
22 face toward Zidon, and prophesy upon it, And say, Thus saith the Lord Jehovah; Behold, I [come] upon thee, Zidon, and glorify Myself in the midst of thee: and they know that I am Jehovah, when I do judgments in [on] her,
23 and sanctify Myself in her. And I send pestilence into her, and blood into her streets; and the pierced-through fall in the midst of her by the sword upon
24 her round about; and they know that I am Jehovah. And there shall no more be to the house of Israel a pricking thorn and a smarting sting from all round about them, who despised them; and they know that I am the Lord
25 Jehovah. Thus saith the Lord Jehovah, When I gather the house of Israel from the peoples among whom they have been scattered, then I sanctify Myself in them before the eyes of the heathen, and they dwell upon their
26 ground which I have given to My servant Jacob. And they dwell upon it in security, and build houses, and plant vineyards, and dwell in security, when I do judgments on all who despised them of those round about them; and they know that I, Jehovah, am their God.

Ver. 3. Sept.: *μη σοφωτερος εἰ συ; . . . ἡ σοφοι οὐκ ἐπαιδευσαν σε ἐν τη ἐπιστημη αὐτων;*
Ver. 4. *μη ἐν τη ἐπιστημη σου; . . .*
Ver. 5. *ἡ ἐν τη πολλη; . . .*
Ver. 7. Sept.: *ἀλλοτριους λοιμους ἀπο ἐθνων . . . ἐπι σε κ. ἐπι το καλλος . . . και στρωσουσιν το καλλος σου εἰς ἀπωλειαν.*
Ver. 8. *Και καταβιβασουσιν σε,*
Ver. 9. Sept., Vulg., Syr., Ar. read: הורגיך and מחלליך.
Ver. 12. Sept.: . . Συ εἰ ἀποσφραγισμα ὁμοιωσεως . . . κ. στεφανος καλλους—חוֹתַם, or in stat. const.—For תכנית some codices read תבנית.
Ver. 13. Another reading: כעדן=*quasi Eden.* Sept.: *ἐν τη τρυφη τ. παραδεισου . . . κ. ἀργυριον κ. χρυσιον κ. λιγυριον κ. ἀχατην κ. ἀμεθυστον κ. χρυσολιθον κ. βηρυλλιον κ. ὀνυχιον, κ. χρυσιον ἐνεπλησας τους θησαυρους σου, κ. τας ἀποθηκας σ. ἐν σοι. Ἀφ' ἡς ἡμερας ἐκτισθης συ.*—Vulg.: *In deliciis paradisi . . . aurum opus decoris tui; et foramina tua in die*—
Ver. 14. Sept.: *μετα Χερουβ, ἐθηκα σε ἐν ὀρει . . . ἐγενηθης ἐν μεσω.*—Vulg.: *Tu Cherub extentus et protegens,*—
Ver. 15. *(Ἐγενηθης) ἀμωμος ἐν ταῖς ἡμεραις σου*—
Ver. 16. *Ἀπο πληθους . . . ἐπληθυνας τ. ταμιεια σου . . . κ. ἐτραυματισθης ἀπο ὀρους . . . κ. ἡγαγεν σε το Χερουβ το συσκιαζον.* Vulg.: . . . *repleta sunt interiora tua*—
Ver. 17. Sept.: . . . *διεφθαρη ἡ ἐπιστημη . . . μετα του καλλους σου δια τ. πληθος τ. ἁμαρτιων σου ἐπι τ. γην*—
Ver. 18. . . . *και ἀδικιων τ. ἐμποριας.* Vulg.: *polluisti sanctificationem tuam*—(Some codd. read.: עונך sing. and מקדשך.)
Ver. 19. . . . *ἀπωλεια ἐγενου*—*nihili factus es*—
Ver. 22. . . . *και γνωση*—Sept. for בה read twice בך; Chal., Ar., a few, בם.
Ver. 23. Sept.: . . . *ἐν σοι περικυκλω σου*—
Ver. 24. *Και οὐκετι ἐσονται σκολοψ πικριας κ. ακανθα ὀδυνης*—
Ver. 25. . . . *και συναξω . . . ἐκ τ. χωρων οὐ . . . ἐκει . . . ἐνωπιον τ. λαων των ἐθνων.* Sept. read שם.
Ver. 26. . . . *ἐν ἐλπιδι . . . ὁ Θεος αὐτων, κ. ὁ Θεος τ. πατερων αὐτων.*

EXEGETICAL REMARKS.

Vers. 1–10. *The Prophecy on the Prince of Tyre.*

Ver. 1. There is first, therefore, a prophecy of judgment, as in ch. xxvi., with reference to Tyre.—**Ver. 2.** נגיד; **Meier**: one who holds together, a governor, director. In Ethiopic, *Nĕgus* is king. Gesen.: he who goes before, duke, doge. The special prominence given to this person, designated **king** in ver. 12, was natural from the marked parallel with Jerusalem; comp. ch. **xvii. 19.** But there was expressed in the **kingdom, and**

especially in the case of Tyre, also a characteristic state-constitution. Small as many of the Phœnician cities were, each still had its king, and Tyre, in particular, kept by a hereditary kingdom, so that even in the latest times only those related to the old royal house were admitted to the throne. This kingdom combined with a rich and powerful aristocracy the mercantile interest, the gains of commerce, which founded it (ver. 16). After the analogy of Carthage, a senate stood by the side of the king, of the old families, which must in many respects have limited him, so that the Oriental despotism could not develope itself here. According to Josephus, it was Ethbaal II.; but not the person, only the position comes into consideration, and especially as in him the mercantile power of Tyre had its proud, secure representative.—As elsewhere also (ch. xxv.), so here the sinning goes first on to ver. 6.—The self-exaltation which is ascribed to him has respect, on one side, to the high opinion entertained of himself; on the other, to the same in connection with his dwelling-place. What is to be made account of in the latter respect is plain from the assertion, **I am God,**—to be distinguished from the likeness of the Most High (אדמה לעליון) in Isa. xiv. 14, also from Acts xii. 22; it expresses the heathenish-mythological consciousness. The rock on which Tyre was built is at the same time to be viewed in its connection with the oft-mentioned temple. The Phœnician myth represented the two islands as moving about in the sea, until an eagle was sacrificed as an atonement. Down to the third century Tyrian coins exhibit the two islands, with the inscription, ἀμβρόσιε πέτρε (immortal rock). According to Sanchoniathon, Astarte, when wandering through the world, consecrated a star that fell down before her eyes to the island Tyre. The foundation of the temple to Melkarth was represented by its priests as contemporaneous with that of the city—about 2750 B.C. So Herodotus relates; and Arrian calls it the oldest sanctuary known in the annals of mankind. Thus מושב אלהים is sufficiently explained; while Hengst. still thinks of an "absolute inaccessibleness," and Hitzig of the circumstance that this kingly residence "sprang up out of the water, as the palace of God out of the heavenly ocean." ["Sanchoniathon expressly calls it 'the holy island'; and it is known that the Tyrian colonies all reverenced it as the mother-city of their religion, not less than the original source of their political existence. It was only in the spirit of ancient heathenism to conclude, that a state which was not only strong by natural position, and by immense maritime resources, but also stood in such close connection with the divine, might be warranted in claiming, through its head, something like supernatural strength and absolute perpetuity of being."—P. F.]—**In the heart of the seas** is an echo from ch. xxvii. 4, 25, 26.—The rejoinder, **and thou art man,** etc., is sharp, yet at the same time sober—the simple contrast between **man** and **God** (El).—**And thou makest thy heart,** etc., continues the **thou sayest,** as well explaining גבה לבך, as giving forth the speech that naturally flowed from it, the thoughts, the ebullitions of a heart which was **the heart of Godhead.**—HITZIG: נתן indicates what is made.

Ver. 3 begins an interlude, which, however, does not picture forth the imagination of his being God, to which the mention of Daniel would as little suit as what thereafter follows; but rather proceeds on the ground of the admitted manhood, and so does only the more feelingly censure the loftiness of spirit. It needs not be understood either as a question, or as spoken ironically. **Behold,** what exists, according to thy mistaken notion; it shows the **being wiser than Daniel** to be merely an imagination. There hence arises, at the same time, a clear confirmation of the book of Daniel (comp. Hengst. here), since Daniel's wisdom was at any rate well known in the circle of Ezekiel, one also recognised at the Chaldean court, and therefore to be held up against the Tyrian sovereign. On the כל־סתום, that to him nothing concealed, secret, was unknown, comp. Dan. ii. 10, 11, 19, iv. 6. Here also, indeed, is only a man, but with a generally admitted superhuman, truly divine wisdom, which God had in reality given (that is the main element in the comparison with Daniel), which he has not, as thou hast done, in his imagination appropriated to himself. Hengst. lays stress also upon the statesmanlike, the really princely position of Daniel, which so excellently grounded the kind of counter-position assigned him in relation to the king of Tyre.—Ver. 4 goes a step deeper still, namely, to the real standpoint of the Tyrian prince,—his wisdom and prudence in the matter of worldly riches (1 Kings iv. 29). In connection therewith, one naturally thinks of the traditions according to which an ancestor of the royal house was the first sailor, who was borne to the island in the hollow trunk of a tree, and there erected pillars to the wind and fire; that the forefathers of the Tyrian kings alleged they had found purple on the island (the Tyrian colour, scarlet, the lack-dye of Sor).—חיל is presently specified in **the gold and silver.**—אוצר is: provisions, treasure, treasury (Zech. ix. 2, 3).—Ver. 5. However great this wisdom might be, however much and varied its manifestations, it centred in the merchandise; and with the growth which accrued to the wealth, the heart also became swollen, as its self-elation found in that wealth its proper element.

Ver. 6 connects itself in a summary way with ver. 2, and prepares for the conclusion in Ver. 7, which joins the punishment to the course of sin that had just been described.—עריץ, terrible, powerful and violent: those who are so pre-eminently above others—the Chaldeans (ch. xxvi. 7). HITZIG: "Against (why not **upon**?) **the beauty of thy wisdom.**" What is meant is: that the beauty of the mercantile state of things in Tyre was the offspring of the wisdom which distinguished its king. יפי and יפעה are almost the same, the latter, however, indicating more the shine or glitter of the beauty. The shine of the beauty may be referred especially to the princehood of Tyre. [EWALD: "they draw their swords upon thy most beautiful wisdom."] חלל, to pierce through, Pi. to dishonour, to make common.—Ver. 8. שחת = בור, ch. xxvi. 20.—The plural ממותי, **deaths,** admits of explanation partly from the representative character of the Tyrian princehood, partly from the feeling therewith connected, of his dying in the death of every Tyrian that was slain. Hengst. compares ch. xxix. 5; Gen. xiv. 10. Others: as the pierced-through dies of many death-wounds (ch. xxi. 30, 19 [25]). Even without rendering חלל, "profane," there is a pointing back to וחללי in ver. 7 in this way, namely, that the princehood should at last share the fate of every one who was pierced through, and, stripped of all splendour, should be cast into the grave.—Ver. 9. The word here goes still farther back than ומתה in ver. 8, and transfers the scene to the very moment of being killed, and confronts the vaunting discourse (in ver. 2). לפני הרגך, ch. xxi. 16 [11].—The extremely cutting argumentation, **and thou art man**, etc.—מחללך, Pi. = מחולל, Poel (Isa. li. 9).—Ver. 10. מותים, plur. from מות, comp. at ver. 8.—ערל is **uncircumcised** (comp. ch. xliv. 9; Isa. lii. 1); for Jews, on account of the sacramental import of circumcision, it designates the heathen world as outside the covenant of God (1 Sam. xvii. 36, xxxi. 4, *barbari?*). The opposite in Num. xxiii. 10: "the death of the righteous." Also for the Tyrian, as here, it is hardly to be understood without the circumcision reported by Herodotus of the Phœnicians (II. 104). Earlier, in ver. 8: as every one that is pierced through; here there is an ascension: as a non-Tyrian through strangers.

Vers. 11–19. *Lamentation over the Prince of Tyre.*

Now ver. 11, as ch. xxvii.—Ver. 12. The lamentation is in fitting adaptation to the person who was just killed. Comp. at ch. xxvii. 2.—In the connection with מלא חכמה and כליל יפי, which in themselves, and after what has preceded, are quite clear, חותם תכנית cannot possibly be rendered, with Hitzig: "thou art a curiously wrought seal-ring." Ewald has: "O thou seal of the completion." חותם means: to cut in, to impress with a seal, to seal; therefore partic.: **thou wast sealing**. Also חוֹתָם, the seal-ring, is properly the impressor. The transferred signification: to seal, that is: to attest, to confirm, to verify, recommends itself through תכנית (from תכן, to determine exactly, to weigh), the measure, the determinate, that which must have a certain amount (ch. xliii. 10); accordingly: **thou confirmedst the measure,** thou fulfilledst, madest the right measure good; therefore a threefold thing is boasted of the Tyrian kingdom: **measure, wisdom,** and **beauty.** The first of these may be said against despotism; comp. at ver. 2. ["According to the present text and punctuation, the expression plainly means: thou art the one sealing exactness (the noun חותם denoting anything that is of an exact or perfect nature). To say of the king of Tyre that he sealed up this, was in other words to declare him every way complete: he gave, as it were, the finishing stroke, the seal, to all that constitutes completeness; or, as we would now say it, he was a normal man—one formed after rule and pattern. Hence it is immediately explained by what follows: 'full of wisdom and perfect in beauty'; in this stood his sealing completeness."—P. F.]—Ver. 13. **In Eden**; comp. ch. xxxvi. 35; Isa. li. 3. And the delightsome land, wherein the garden for primeval man lay, brings up the garden of God (El, not Jehovah); ch. xxxi. 8, 9; Gen. xiii. 10. As the Tyrian king himself was certainly not God, but what was said of him in ver. 12, so his dwelling was unquestionably not מושב אל, the habitation of God; it might, however, be named paradisiacal, since all fulness of what was pleasant, and all possible magnificence, surrounded the same, covered it (מסכתך). Hitzig freely: "every precious stone was thy figure-work;" because out of the stones the figuration of the ring must be composed! The transition to **every precious stone** brings to remembrance Gen. ii. 11, 12. The distribution of the particulars forms three groups, each having three precious stones, rounded off by the gold, which makes ten (the symbolical number of completeness). This emblematic representation of kingly greatness and glory, therefore, carries no respect to the breastplate of the high priest and its twelve stones, where also they are ranged in a different order; comp. however, on the signification of the particular names, at Ex. xxviii. 17 sq., xxxix. 10 sq. Comp. also here at ch. i. 16, 26, xxvii. 16.—מלאכה may signify business, performance, work, also goods. Manifestly *music* is meant by it here, as the older expositors have rendered, an ordinary accompaniment of the pomp of royalty (comp. Dan. iii. 5)! תף is therefore the (hand) kettledrum, as a specimen of all instruments that were struck (תפף); and נקב will be the pipe (from נקב, to push through, bore through), for the wind instruments as they were then constructed. [Ges. takes תף for the socket in which the gem is put, and נקב as ring-socket. Ewald: "were appointed for thy oracle and soothsaying work on the day of thy creation." He would take it ironically: the man—who might be called the seal, that is, the consummation, etc., was once certainly as the first of all men in paradise (Job xv. 7), so that he has a completeness beyond any other person—took, doubtless, for his holy ornament, which covered him from the first day of his life, all the twelve stones of the high priest's oracle-sign, and was doubtless made by God a cherub upon the mountain of the gods, and was also, doubtless, unblameable from his birth—only, alas! till his guilt was discovered! Others thought of נְקֵבָה, the female (woman). So Häv.: "the service of thy kettledrums and of thy women was ready for thee on the day of thy creation," which (by a reference to Gen. i. 27) must indicate the king's entrance on his government, and the ladies of his harem, who surrounded him with dance and song.]—On the הבראך, comp. ch. xxi. 35 [30]. With the creation of this princedom, as it took in Tyre precedence of the still older Zidon, there forthwith existed all sorts of parade and glory, such as could be found only in kings' courts. (כונן, Pual from כון?). Firm and well prepared did this kingdom start into being.

Ver. 14. As the colour given to the representation has already, with its kettledrums and its pipes, forsaken Eden and paradise, and "the day of creation" does not quite constitute the Tyrian king a second Adam—as the whole representation generally appears to take into account only the very ancient origin on which this kingdom prided itself, perhaps also not without some touch of irony—so certainly **the cherub** here has little or nothing at all to do with paradise (comp. at ch. i., ix. 3, 10); for it is unnecessary for the following context to think of the history of the Tyrian kingdom after the analogy of the history of the fall. Rather may we suppose that the designation of cherub points simply to the temple at Jerusalem, and especially to the most holy place there. There is thereby symbolized out of the history of this kingdom that historical epoch when it came through Hiram II. into connection with David and with Solomon, so important, in particular, for the design of the temple-building, and important also for the commerce of Tyre. Already, as architect of the temple of Solomon (and that Hiram was a connoisseur as well as a promoter of the building art is testified by Josephus, in addition to what is said in the Bible, from the fragments of Dius and Menander in his possession), the king of Tyre takes beside Solomon in this respect a position which makes his appearance under a name borrowed from the architecture of the holy of holies, the cherub, not unsuitable. That cherub is applied to him only symbolically is rendered plain by the otherwise incomprehensible addition of ממשח, that is, of the anointing, which imports as much as: anointed cherub, therefore: who is king. What Hengst. concludes from Ex. xxx. 22 sq., that "anointed" = holy, because all the vessels of the temple were anointed, to impress on them the character of holiness, runs out to this result, that the king of Tyre, as king, was *res sacra*, because God had communicated to him of His greatness—therefore, that he is said to be anointed because **he was king.** Since הסוכך, "the covering," repeated in ver. 16, refers to Ex. xxv. 20, and we know (comp. Doctrinal Reflections on ch. ix.) that the cherubim, screening with their wings the ark of th covenant, symbolized the life of creation, confessing, as it actually does, the heavenly King, the Holy One in Israel, the Most High over all, so it is not out of the way if the king of Tyre, who has shown himself to be, along with Solomon, the protector of the temple,—a building which unquestionably culminated in the most holy place,—should, agreeably to this testimony, be honoured as "the anointed cherub that covereth." Yea, as the whole creation serves the eternal King of Israel, so also has the Tyrian kingdom served Him in His house at Jerusalem (on which also Isa. xxiii. 18 leans), and thus a proper contrast to the self-elevation in vers. 2 and 5 is brought out, as is expressly said through the immediately following נתתיך, **I have given thee. Upon the holy mountain of God** is here, therefore, as always, to be understood of the temple-mount at Jerusalem (2 Chron. iii.), where He right truly was, as architect of the temple. And because there the sanctuary for the ministrations of the priestly service in Israel was executed through him, and in the high priest of Israel the whole Israelitish priesthood culminated, it might be said, with reference to the high-priestly Urim and Thummim, of the Tyrian king, that "**he walked in the midst of stones of fire.**"

[*Other Explanations.*—Häv. thinks that the king of Tyre was named cherub as the ideal of a creature (so, too, Bähr previously in his *Symbolik*); ממשח is with him to be distinguished from משיח, an anointed object (Ex. xxx. 26), and הסוכך is as much as: a reflection of the divine glory. He thinks of a holy gods'-mountain (Isa. xiv. 13), wherein the king of Tyre, as one of those mighty mountain-gods (1 Kings xx. 23) whom the Tyrians honoured, was located; and the fiery stones were, according to Häv., those in the temple of Herculus as the fire-god, which may have been illuminated. Hengst. takes the cherub, with Häv., as a representation of the earthly creature-life in its highest grade, and in its highest perfection; which, however, cannot be conceived of as proper to the Tyrian king. As "covering," he covered Tyre so long as God's favour was with him and his people. The mountain of God must be his elevation to the holy mount of God, a participation in the divine greatness (Ps. xxx. 8); and the fiery stones correspond to the walls of fire, which indicate the divine protection (Zech. ii. 9). EWALD: "thou—into the wide-covering cherub, into that I make thee;" and from the holy mountain of the gods rush down the sparkling stones of fire, namely, thunderbolts against the wicked (!). Hitzig, like the Sept., takes אַת as אֵת, **with**: "beside the cherub, etc., so have I set thee;" then: "cherub of the width of the covering." But he is in some doubt; he thinks by the mountain of God might be meant Horeb; but it might be the Albordsch of Asiatic mythology, and in the stones of fire there lies at bottom the idea of a Vulcan. One sees the despair which attaches to every rationalistic exposition.]

[The rationalistic explanations of this singular passage are certainly bold and unsatisfactory enough; but our author's own appears to make greatly too much account of the historical relation of Hiram to the temple at Jerusalem, and too little of the poetical element which pervades the representation. "It is one of the most highly figurative representations of prophecy, and is only to be compared with Isaiah's lamentation, ch. xiv., over the downfall of the king of Babylon. It characteristically differs from this, however, in that, while it moves with equal boldness and freedom in an ideal world, it clothes the ideal, according to the usage of our prophet, in a historical drapery, and beholds the past revived again in the personified existence of which it treats. It is a historical parable. The kings of Tyre are first personified as one individual, an ideal man—one complete in all material excellence, perfect manhood. And then this ideal man, the representative of whatever there was of greatness and glory in Tyre, and in whom the Tyrian spirit of self-elation and pride appear in full efflorescence, is ironically viewed by the prophet as the type of humanity in its highest states of existence upon earth. All that is best and noblest in the history of the past he sees in imagination meeting in this new *beau-ideal* of humanity. It was he who in primeval time trod the hallowed walks of paradise, and used at will its manifold treasures, and regaled himself with its corporeal delights. It was he who afterwards appeared in the form of a cherub—ideal compound of the highest forms of animal existence—type of humanity in its predestined state of ultimate completeness and glory; and, as such, had a place assigned him among the consecrated symbols of God's sanctuary in the holy mount, and the immediate presence of the Most High. Thus, occupying the highest spheres of created life, and familiar even with the sight of the divine glory, he knew what it was to dwell amidst the consuming fire, and to walk as on burning stones of sapphire (Ex. xxiv. 10). So thou thinkest, thou ideal man, thou quintessence of human greatness and pride—thou thinkest that manhood's divinest qualities, and most honourable conditions of being, belong peculiarly to thyself, since thou dost nobly peer above all, and standest alone in thy glory. Let it be so. But thou art still a man, and, like humanity itself in its most favoured conditions, thou hast not been perfect before God: thou hast yielded thyself a servant to corruption, therefore thou must be cast down from thine excellency, thou must lose thy cherubic nearness to God, etc. . . . So that the cry which the prophet would utter through this parabolical history in the ears of all is, that man in his best estate—with everything that art or nature can bring to his aid—is still corruption and vanity. The flesh can win for itself nothing that is really and permanently good; and the more that it can surround itself with the comforts and luxuries of life, the more only does it pamper the godless pride of nature, and draw down upon itself calamity and destruction."—P. F.]

Ver. 15. To wish to bring תמים into connection with Adam's sinless constitution, has against it the expression בדרכיך, **in thy ways**. It is simply the contrast to the expression: **perverseness was found in thee**; therefore: blameless in thy walk. One might suppose, after the exposition given of the walking in the midst of the fiery stones in ver. 14, an allusion to the וְתֻמִּים! The earlier procedure of the kingdom of Tyre, as seen in the fellowship it then maintained with the David and Solomon of Israel, must be viewed as set over against the corruption into which it latterly fell (ch. xxvi. 2, xxvii. 3, xxviii. 2 sq.). A dogmatic antithesis, such as Hengst. supposes, is not to be imagined.—Ver. 16. Here now follows the origin of the perverseness that was found in him, namely, in his vast commerce (ver. 5); and so one has to think of the Tyrian kingdom as carrying on and plying merchandise, and that in all sorts of ways, by which it fell into pernicious and sinful courses. —מלו, indeterminate as to its subject, or (HENGST.): thy inhabitants (?); more properly: fellow-citizens, subjects, if they are not to be regarded as the merchants from all countries. Rosenm. preferred the intransitive signification of the verb: "through the multitude, etc., was thy interior filled." [HITZIG: מָלוּ = מָלוֹא, "the filling of thy interior was injustice."] Thus, in place of the former blamelessness, there has come to be a ground for punishment. Hence for the punishment there must now, through God, be a withdrawal from the relations once held to Israel, the most elevated reminiscences of its history, as through God it had been introduced to these. This lies in מהר; and that it is contemplated as a holy downfall, with a view to the building up of the sanctuary in Israel at the time, we perceive from the ואחללך—ch. vii. 21, 22. [HITZIG: "and thou, covering cherub, art quite rooted out"!!]—For the rest, comp. at ver. 14.—Ver. 17. The discourse here, with גבה, again reverts to the subject announced at the very beginning (ver. 2), the corruption of the Tyrian kingdom: the proud self-elation in or on account of his beauty; comp. at ver. 7. The higher man raises himself, so much the poorer does he become as to his wisdom. A proud man, a fool; so it is said in common life, for this special reason, that the splendour of wealth, the whole attractive display of its outward position, so apt to bewitch strangers even and to beget envy, brings the possessor so much the sooner and the more to a self-pleasing condition. This is distinctly involved in the על, **on account of**, which does not need to be taken as = with, together with. EWALD: "thou hast lost thy wisdom upon thy splendour."—The self-destruction and annihilation (שחת) of such self-elation corresponds, as to time, with the casting down effected by God (על־ארץ), and, with respect to the preceding glory, with the abandonment to the astounded and at the same time malicious gaze of those who were companions as to rank and position. Hengst. remarks that ראה, with ב, marks the affecting contemplation, especially with a joyful participation. לראוה, the infinitive form, like לדאבה, לאהבה.

Ver. 18. מרב עוניך is parallel with ברב רכלתך in ver. 16, and בעול רכלתך throws light on עוניך.—The profanation proceeded from the moral offence; the unrighteous mammon in commerce brought along with it sin and guilt. After what is said in ver. 16 in reference to God as to the **profaning**, the words חללת מקדשיך can occasion no difficulty. The **sanctuaries** of the Tyrian kingdom are those holy reminiscences regarding the mountain of God and the sanctuary of the Lord, and of Israel's high-priesthood. One cannot possibly serve God and mammon. (Others have thought of the temple, which Tyre made on his holy island (?!). With Hengst. every sort of greatness ordained by God, or of glory distributed by Him, is a sanctuary.)—The **fire**, according to Hitzig, must be the perverseness with which his interior was penetrated, as fire bound up in him (!!). Some, too, have under it thought of a traitor, who would pass over to Nebuchadnezzar. Vatke has also mentioned the phœnix, giving itself to be burnt. It is a biblical form of speech, frequently used, for the punishment of divine wrath which comes from sin, and which, as is evident from the term **ashes**, was to annihilate the kingdom of Tyre (ch. xix. 12).—ואתנך, contrast to ונתתיך in ver. 14.—The **seeing** once more emphasizes the spectacle, which will be presented to every one in the subject so judged.—Ver. 19. Here at last is the conclusion. With the seeing with the eyes there is conjoined the knowing, the understanding with the spirit.—Comp. ch. xxvi. 16. They are prophetic preterites.—Ch. xxvii. 36, xxvi. 21.

Vers. 20-26. *The Prophecy on Zidon.*

Vers. 20, 21. The brief and supplementary

manner in which this prophecy respecting Zidon is introduced arose from the backgoing character of this city, though it was more ancient than Tyre (hence sung of by Homer, while Tyre is not), and, according to such tradition, still very commonly represented the Phœnician state (for example, Isa. xxiii. 4, 12); comp. Gen. x. 15, xlix. 13. On coins, as among the Greeks, Zidon is called the metropolis of Tyre. On account of its still always preserved independence, whence it took part in the coalition against Babylon (Jer. xxvii.), —one may say, the Genoa of the old world,—there was due to it a word, however short, especially since, as a representative of Canaan, with which no such relations were maintained as between Tyre and Israel under Hiram and Solomon, it formed most fitly the contrast for the promise which bore respect to the people of God. Comp. Judg. x. 12.

Ver. 21. צִידוֹן, that is, "fishing," which indicates the earliest employment of its inhabitants, lay in a plain, which resembled an orchard, several hours' walk along the sea, and had a summer and a winter harbour; at present a small, insignificant place. Of the old fortress there still remains a square tower. Fishing and traffic in fish are still practised there.—Ver. 22. הִנְנִי עָלַיִךְ, as at ch. xxvi. 3.—וְנִכְבַּדְתִּי; comp. Ex. xiv. 4, 17, 18. May a preparation have been intended, through this reference to Egypt, for what follows in ch. xxix.? In such a being sanctified, or in God sanctifying Himself, as is done by means of a judicial punishment, there is presupposed the certainty that Zidon would not have sanctified Him. The impressive transition from the second to the third person makes the fact appear, in a manner, as already accomplished, so that one speaks of Zidon as of such a person.—Ver. 23. For which sort of judgments see ch. v. 17. Pestilence in connection with war,—that in the houses; this as the shedding of blood in the streets, as is presently brought vividly out.—וְנִפְלַל, Pil. equivalent to Kal, but strengthening, enhancing, as also alliterating; producing a resemblance of sound which has in it something graphic (HÄV.). Continually, as it were, the pierced-through fall.—The **sword**, through which God will act upon them, comes upon Zidon from **round about**, so that there is no escape.—The representation of the predicted judgment is kept general. With Zidon the analogous prophecies respecting judgment first reach their end. And thus also can the following be joined to it the more fitly.

Ver. 24. The point of contrast is presented by the idea of neighbourhood—the nearer (ch. xxv.), or the more remote, as was the case with Tyre and Zidon; it is said expressly: **from all round about them**. On סִלּוֹן, comp. at ch. ii. 6. GES.: "like the young shoots and twigs of the palm."—מַמְאִיר, partic. Hiph. from מָאַר, to thrust; intransitive: to be sharp, bitter. GES.: "raising bitter pain." קוֹץ is something cutting, stinging.—כָּאַב, to bend oneself for pain, hence Hiph.: to cause pain. —The promise, accordingly, amounts to this, that the sensible pain which the people of Israel must have experienced through the contempt of their neighbours shall cease in the future. The figurative representation is a marked repetition of Num. xxxiii. 55; the pain experienced was punishment; comp. Gen. xv. 18 sq.; Josh. xiii. 19; Judg. i. 31, 32, iii. 3. But now the Lord accomplishes what His people had slightingly neglected. Comp. also ch. xvi. 57.—The negative side is followed by the positive in Ver. 25; the scornful heathen go down, but the people in whom the Lord sanctifies Himself, in contrast to them, come gloriously up. Comp. ch. xi. 17, xx. 41.—The change, also, from **Israel** to **Jacob**, is to be noticed, and the relation of **house of Israel** to **My servant Jacob**.—Ver. 26. In consequence of the added definition: לָבֶטַח, in security, it is repeated that they should dwell upon their home-soil. בָּטַח, according to MEIER: to stretch forth oneself, *i.e.* give away oneself, confide; hence: to be careless, secure. GES.: the same derived from a primary meaning, "to be void, empty."—But also the secure possession in the confidence of faith is in this comforting promise repeated, and finally, such grace of God is again, and still more expressly than before, set over against the divine judgments. Comp. besides, Isa. lxv. 21. HITZIG: "the first וְיָשְׁבוּ preceding the building and planting is inchoative: they settle down; the second: they are established, dwell, or abide." Hengst. remarks: "It is designed to meet the despair which, after the opening of the siege of Jerusalem, had become the most formidable enemy. So that here, in the onesidedness which so commonly adheres to prophecy, because everywhere connecting itself with definite temporal relations and issues, only the light side of the future of the covenant-people is brought into view. Along with that there was also a shady side, which is supplied by the successors of Ezekiel, Zechariah and Malachi. A great national judgment was destined to follow the Chaldean." Häv.: "This is the eternal blessing which rests upon Israel, that it shall one time attain to a blessed peace, while the heathen powers shall lie under the penal judgment of God." He calls to mind the gathering through the gospel. That here, as in ch. xxvi. 20, in the shape of a brief glance into the future, there are traits of Messianic colouring, is manifest. Comp. also at Amos ix. 14.

DOCTRINAL REFLECTIONS.

1. The time for the fulfilment of these prophecies against the aliens, where no dates of a definite nature are to be found in the prophecies themselves, depends on the kind of realization applied to them. Tholuck admits of a wide interval "in the relation between truth and reality in the prophecies." But when he presently, again, limits the principle, that "the mode of realization may be to us a matter of indifference," since "the simply religious spirits" are to be distinguished from divine seers, nothing is gained but the arbitrary definition that the prophets, "though not uniformly, yet in great part, saw the truth of the future not merely *in abstracto*, but under the concrete veil of their historical realization." And what is meant by "seeing the truth *in abstracto*"? Is there not a self-contradiction in this as applied to the prophets, to whom the ideas presented themselves as matters of fact, and these facts in this or that actual form? There must, first of all, be admittedly something of human weakness,

especially in the subsequent reproduction of the previously received divine communications and visions. Many an intermediate link in this way was lost; but thereby the end came so much nearer to the beginning, the ultimate background to the foreground. In this and other respects there is the dust of finiteness on these prophetic paintings, which but so much the more furnishes a pledge of their divine origin. With this agrees what is said in 1 Pet. i. 10–12,—said, indeed, with reference to the time of the Christian salvation, yet admitting also of a more general application,—where there is ascribed to the prophets an "inquiring" and "searching into,"—a matter of study, therefore, also for them, since, when the meaning had not been expressly made manifest to them, they sought for traces [of the fulfilment], and made trial of them in regard to the times which lay near at hand. If their prophecies had been the product of their own spirit, such want of knowledge in regard to the cases in question, and their procedure in consequence thereof, must have been strange; but in this way we have, with their searching concerning their prophecies, perhaps the proper soul of their so-called literary activity.

2. In the prophecies of judgment contained in the earlier chapter [*i.e.* ch. xxv.], the execution of the judgment rests wholly in the hand of God. So upon Ammon, upon Moab, upon the Philistines; only in respect to Edom was it said that the accomplishment would be made specially through Israel. The divine sentence speaks throughout of the extirpation of the very name. As regards place and time, no other fulfilment could lie nearer to the prophet and his contemporaries than that through Nebuchadnezzar. That this was only the beginning of the end could not be concluded without some insight into the divine patience, and the manifestation of Christ in the flesh. Still more clearly do these relations discover themselves in the case of Tyre.

3. The transition to Tyre is made by our prophet through the Philistines. Considered generally, this has its ground in the heathenish character of the race. More specially, for their appearance in this connection, account has been made of a notice (see Movers, *Phœn.* ii. 313), according to which the Zidonians, after they had (B.C. 1209) been brought into subjection by the Philistines, laid the foundation of the island-city of Tyre. Lenormant (*Manuel d'Hist. Anc. de l'Orient*), and, leaning upon him, M. Busch, have woven thence the story, that a Philistine fleet, sailing from Askalon, had surprised Zidon, and put an end to the hitherto Zidonian supremacy. Thus would the Philistines, as having furnished the occasion for the origination of Tyre, have had their proper place assigned them, in a historical-genetical respect, at the close of ch. xxv. and before the beginning of ch. xxvi. of Ezekiel. M. Duncker (*Hist. of Antiq.* i. 519) merely says: "In the year B.C. 1254, a number of the Zidonian race emigrated from Zidon, and over against Old Tyre, upon an island-rock, beside the temple of Melkarth, founded New Tyre. This New Tyre grew into a commonwealth with the old city on the land. The strengthening which Tyre hereby received put it in the position of setting up a rivalry with the commerce and the colonization of Zidon. From B.C. 1100 Tyre saw herself at the head of the Phœnician cities."

4. Tyre, as very commonly happens with commercial states, and still more with commercial cities, presents, in the few and disconnected things that we know of its history, an image of ups and downs, and inversely. Commonly it is said, in connection with our chapter, that Tyre was then at the summit of its power. But this might rather be said of the times of David and Solomon (DUNCKER, p. 520). For the period under consideration it comes nearer to the truth to say, that Tyre had again revived, and continued to maintain a certain precedence among the Phœnician cities. For though the revolt of Kition in Cyprus had been suppressed, and the island stronghold of Tyre had under King Eluläos successfully withstood the Assyrians (Salmanassar), yet the dependent relationship of the Phœnician cities toward Assyria from the year B.C. 900 became more and more marked, and Tyre had to stretch all her powers to preserve her position, or again to make it good. During the Assyrian siege it lost its last colony in the Thracian seas, namely, Thasos; and an Assyrian fleet ere long robbed it anew of the island of Cyprus, which it had again reconquered. A memorial stone in the Berlin Museum commemorates this success of Salmanassar against Tyre. According to Lenormant's representation (ii. p. 313; Busch, p. 247 sq.), while Salmanassar, B.C. 720–15, had been successfully resisted, there were, about B.C. 700, decided failures against Sennacherib, who conquered the island Tyre, and set up there a vassal (Toubaal) as king. The bas-reliefs in the rocks of Nahr el Kelb, around Beirût, even to the present time, according to Lenormant, bear witness to the complete subjection of Phœnicia by Sennacherib (? Sargana-Salmanassar!), and the overthrow of the Tyrian supremacy. (If this French representation were to be trusted, the prophecy of Isaiah in ch. xxiii. would have to be applied to it, though the Chaldeans were already to be descried in the distance; and Ezekiel would connect with the restoration which intervened (Isa. xxiii. 15 sq.) the prophecy of a new judgment upon Tyre by the hand of the Chaldeans, as generally the judgment upon Tyre. But also in the otherwise general representation, which knows only of the unsuccessful siege of the island-city by Salmanassar, is the reference thereto of the prophecy of Isaiah in its first aspect to be held fast. What Isaiah predicts in ch. xxiii. accords quite well with the Assyrian issue of things. For Salmanassar did subject the Phœnicians to himself, and also Old Tyre (JOSEPH. *Antiq.* ix. 4. 2), so that Salmanassar could cause himself to be glorified at Lykos beside the monuments of the Egyptian Ramses. The five years' siege assuredly did not pass without inflicting serious injuries; and it is anyhow matter of fact, that King Eluläos recognised the sovereignty of Assyria, for he henceforth took the title of Pha (פחה), that is, governor, vassal. As the Chaldeans and the siege, through Nebuchadnezzar, emerge behind the Assyrian, the prophecy of Isaiah certainly has a much more distant background, precisely as is the case also with Ezekiel.) That the catastrophe at Jerusalem should have inspired new courage into Tyre, called forth words that were expressive of new hopes (ch. xxvi. 2), is sufficiently explained not through any position she occupied on the height of power, but rather through the relations which arose out of events in connection

with Assyria. (As Lenormant mentions (ii. p. 314), if the Tyrian ascendency had been ill borne by the other Phœnician cities, since Tyre in many ways abused her position (comp. at ch. xxvii. 8 sq.), there would hence, on this side, have been no farther interest for Tyre; also, at the end of the Assyrian period, it is rather Zidon which appears at the head of an insurrectionary movement against the son of Sennacherib, Esarhaddon, as is testified by an inscription. That Zidon was worsted in the affair is shown by an inscription found in the British Museum, which represents Tyre, indeed, as among the tributaries of Assyria, but takes no notice whatever of Zidon.) In consequence of the decay of the Assyrian power, Egypt also, through Pharaoh Nechoh, attained to the position of making the Phœnician states subject to it. This took place at the period to which belongs the circumnavigation of Africa, through Tyrian mariners in the employ of the king of Egypt. During this whole time, however, and in spite of the Assyrian supremacy, the merchandise of Tyre flourished, and there was no diminution of the resources and wealth which it brought to the hand of Tyre. The place, so favourably situated, always raised itself anew; its walls were rebuilt. so that, in its re-established condition, it was able to offer resistance to Nebuchadnezzar.

5. The determination respecting the issue of the thirteen years' siege of the island Tyre by Nebuchadnezzar has been, on one side, made dependent on ch. xxix. 17 sq., while on another, Gesenius, Winer, Hitzig have turned to a wrong account the silence which is observed upon the consequence of the siege in question, in the passages quoted by Josephus regarding it (*Antiq.* x. 11, *con. Ap.* i. 21).[1] They thence draw the conclusion that the Chaldeans did not get the city into their power, nor inflict any damage upon it. The silence, however, observed in this respect, especially when it is practised by Phœnician historiographers, speaks rather for the opposite view. For if the siege had really been without any result, how should it have made for the side in question, that no notice was taken of Nebuchadnezzar's leaving his affair with Tyre in an unfinished state? The very honourable report for Tyre, of its having withstood a thirteen years' siege, which is given by Josephus from the original sources, does not exclude the supposition that the siege ended in a capitulation (in 573), but involves the assumption of a corresponding pressure through Nebuchadnezzar; although in this Chaldaic siege of Tyre, as in the Assyrian, a much wider and more comprehensive view must be taken (as already said) of the prophetic announcements pointing in that direction. The evidence for the subjection of Tyre to the sovereignty of Babylon may be seen in Movers, ii. 1, p. 448 sq., 461 sq.; comp. Häv. *Comm.* p. 429 sq. On King Ethbaal being obliged to abdicate, or however the act may be designated, Nebuchadnezzar brought in Baal in his place. The royal family was carried away to Babylon. Berosus says that all Phœnicia became subject to Nebuchadnezzar. At all events, we see the Tyrians, and Phœnicians generally, in a still more marked state of dependence upon Babylon than formerly on Assyria. Twice, as we learn from Assyrian sources, did the people of Tyre receive their king from Babylon—with which Hitzig compares 1 Kings xii. 2 sq.; but Delitzsch rightly judges 2 Kings xxiv. 12, 14, Dan. i. 3, more worthy of comparison, for the quite undoubted supremacy of the Persians over all Phœnicia appears plainly as the taking over of a subject-relationship which had already existed under the Chaldeans. "How also should princes have been brought back by the Tyrians, who had not long before sought refuge in a court so hostile to Tyre as Babylon was?" (HÄV.) As Lenormant represents the matter (ii. p. 318 sq.), the city on the mainland was first attacked by Nebuchadnezzar, taken, and wholly destroyed. Thereupon came Nebuchadnezzar in person (B.C. 574), to press forward the slumbering work; and now the island-city was taken by storm, sacked, and partly destroyed. A number of the people had previously escaped by sea to Carthage. Tyre henceforth merely vegetated; Carthage was her heiress.

6. Tyre, in the prophets, comes into consideration not in a political respect, but as the representative, the might, of the world's commerce. Jehovah and Mammon is the counterpart to Jerusalem and Tyre. "This last" (says Delitzsch) "gained as peacefully as possible the treasures of the nations, and secures for itself the advantage it won by means of colonies and factories."

7. The judgment upon Tyre is history—an entire development of judgment even to utter extinction, as is now most clearly manifest. Assyria is in this judgment-history one chapter, Nebuchadnezzar also one, and Alexander the Great still another: Assyria the type of the Chaldeans, the Chaldeans the type of the Macedonians—each one surpassing the other in the power of inflicting judgment, like wave upon wave of the sea, till the flood had overwhelmed all (comp. ch. xxvi. 3, 19). "The deeds of

[1] The point which Josephus, in the first passage, confirms from different authors is, that Nebuchadnezzar had been "a more energetic, more enterprising, and more prosperous man than the kings who had been before him." Thus Berosus, in the third book of his Chaldean History, writes of his deeds—that with a part only of his father's host, and while himself but a stripling, he had vanquished those who were in a state of revolt—*τεταγμενος σατραπης ἐν τῳ Αἰγυπτῳ και τοις περι την Κοιλην Συριαν και την Φοινικην τοποις, και την χωραν ἐκ ταυτης της ἀρχης ὑπο την αὐτου βασιλειαν ἐποιησατο.* On the report of the death of his father, *και καταστησας τα κατα την Αἰγυπτον πραγματα κ. την λοιπην χωραν*, and after entrusting the Jewish, Phœnician, and Syrian prisoners to certain of his friends, to convey them to Babylon, together with the heavy-armed soldiers and baggage, he himself went thither and assumed the government. Megasthenes, also (Book III. of his Indian History), is cited by Josephus, and Diokles (Book II. of his Persian History); finally, Philostratus, by whom it is said, as well in his Indian as his Phœnician History, that Nebuchadnezzar besieged Tyre thirteen years. If this long siege was to serve as a proof of Nebuchadnezzar's practical energy, and, in particular, of his extraordinary prosperity, Josephus could not have been of opinion that Nebuchadnezzar had been obliged to withdraw from Tyre without result. That Josephus was convinced of the agreement of the profane writers with the historical accounts of his own people in the point under consideration, is still more clear from his work against Apion. He there repeats from Berosus, what he had elsewhere said upon Nebuchadnezzar, that the latter, after the revolt of Egypt and Judea, obtained the mastery over all—Egypt, Syria, Phœnicia, Arabia; and that he surpassed all the Chaldean and Babylonian kings who had been before him by his deeds, for which he again quotes the words of Berosus, and in the following section (20) adds, that in such things "the Chaldean history must be deemed trustworthy,"—*οὐ μην ἀλλα κἀν τοις ἀρχαιοις των Φοινικων συμφωνα τοις ὑπο Βηρωσσου λεγομενοις ἀναγεγραπται, περι του των Βαβυλωνιων βασιλεως, ὁτι και την Συριαν και την Φοινικην ἁπασαν ἐκεινος κατεστρεψατο.* With this, also, he says, Philostratus agrees, in the place where he makes mention of the siege of Tyre, and Megasthenes; so that that siege is throughout to be understood in the light of the result stated, that "he overthrew all Syria and Phœnicia."

Nebuchadnezzar rank with the prophet for more than an isolated fact. In the conquest by that monarch, he beholds from the historical ground of the present the whole mass of destruction concentrated, which links itself in history thereto as a closely connected chain of events. The might of Tyre, broken by Nebuchadnezzar, coincides in his view with the entire annihilation of the same. This was demanded by the internal theocratic significance of that fact in relation to the destruction of Jerusalem. The conquest of Tyre by the same hand which struck the city of God has the counter signification of a future glory (ch. xxix. 21, xxviii. 25, 26). Nebuchadnezzar inflicts on Tyre the death-wound, and its whole subsequent existence is a struggle with death" (HÄV.). The Macedonian conqueror first destroyed Old Tyre; then out of the ruins he constructed a mound to the island—the idea having been suggested to him, it is said, by Hercules appearing in a dream, and from the temple in the island stretching out the hand to him; and at last, by means of treachery, he conquered the island-city in the seventh month, and dealt with it so severely, that what remained of it was but the ashes of the Tyre which had formerly existed (comp. ch. xxviii. 18). After this manner is prophecy and fulfilment to be made out. That Tyre still, even in Jerome's time, was an active place of trade, he had no difficulty in understanding, because he took into account, on the other side, the ancient world-wide ascendency of the Tyrian state. From the time of Alexander the island Tyre continued to be united to the mainland: its sacred position in the sea had reached its end. A pathway conducted every one quietly over to the once splendid harbour of ships, and the alluvial deposits from the sea continually added to this connecting mound, while on the other hand the waves wasted the rock (PLIN. *Hist. Nat.* v. 17; POMP. MELA. i. 12; PTOL. v. 15). Alexandria became the centre of the world's commerce. From the hands of the Seleucidæ the city passed under the sway of the Romans; and it is known as still existing in the Gospels, and in the book of Acts (Acts xxi. 3 sq.). In the early times of Mahommedanism it fell into the hands of the Arabians. The crusades in the 12th century again lent to it a sort of poetic glimmer; but at the end of the 13th century it was brought to desolation by the Saracens. "Where once waved the forest of the ships of Tarshish" (says Sepp, *Jerusalem and the Holy Land*, ii. p. 409), "there scarcely now rise out of the water two well-rigged keels of English merchants; commerce has found another centre. The lucrative trade in purple cloth passed over to the Jews, who as merchants and dyers pervaded the Lebanon, and in the Greek cities, as at Thebes, founded purple-dyeing establishments. Venice transplanted to itself from Tyre the manufacture of glass. The rocky part of the old island actually serves, according to the prophetic word, as a place merely for the spreading of fishing-nets. Under the sand of the old island there are still discovered traces of streets, etc. Thus has the pride of the old sea-princess been humbled, and she wears now none but a beggar's attire. From the time of Abulfeda onwards into the 17th century, all travellers represent Tyre as a heap of ruins, with broken up arches and vaults, towers cast down, and shaky walls, so that the inhabitants had to shelter themselves in the hollow places that remained between portions of the rubbish. Maundrell did not find a single dwelling-house in good preservation, but only a couple of fishermen occupying a sort of vaults. To the present time it is not frequented by Jews, so little is there now of chaffering and trading in the old merchant-city. Something is done in corn and tobacco, which grows upon the western side of the place. The earthquake of 1837 drove into flight those who were not destroyed by it. Only the knowledge of ancient times and a number of waving palms lend an interest to the Tyre of the present day." Comp. HENGST. *de Rebus Tyriorum*, p. 88 sq.

8. Cocceius makes application of Tyre spiritually to the great city which commits fornication with all nations, and desires to install herself in the place of Jerusalem, and interprets the prince of Tyre as a hieroglyph of the Pope. He does not deny the historical basis, but it is to him an allegory.

9. The special prophecy upon the Tyrian kingdom, and the lamentation in ch. xxviii., receive also a light from particular points in the history of Tyre—not so much through the revolt which, in the twenty-sixth year after the death of Hiram II., drove the legitimate dynasty from the throne, and the horrors which led a part of the old Tyrian race to emigrate with Elissa (Dido), and found Carthage—as rather through the translation of the government, after the death of the king introduced by Nebuchadnezzar,[1] to judges, who were chosen from among the priests and considerable men of Tyre. Hävernick is of opinion that the appearance of judges in the midst of a regular succession of Tyrian kings might only be regarded as a Chaldaic arrangement for the punishment of insubordination or the like; just as Tyre was deprived by Alexander of its ancient constitution, in the way of punishment. For, as ch. xxviii. shows, the kingdom belonged to the pride of Tyre, as generally, according to the Oriental mode of contemplation, and especially would it do so with a race of such old renown as the Tyrian. Internal factions might readily enough have called into existence rival kings, but never the removal of the kingly state altogether.

10. The prophetic collocation, Tyre and Zidon (Joel iv. [iii.] 4; Zech. ix. 2; Isa. xxiii.; Jer. xxv. 22, xxvii. 3, xlvii. 4; here in Ezek.; comp. on the other hand, 1 Chron. xxii. 4; Ezra iii. 7), —not a geographical or political point of view,—determines the New Testament allusion to both in this order. From its antiquity alone the mention of Zidon would admit of explanation. In the Pentateuch, as in Homer, notice is taken only of it; its name stands for Phœnicia at large. The ups and downs, also, experienced by Tyre occasionally brought Zidon to the summit, or, at least, placed Tyre at her side; so, too, it is in the highest degree probable, that the governors of Syria and Phœnicia, who succeeded one another, would probably in their own interest not allow the old rivalry between Zidon and Tyre to remain untouched. While the Chaldean conquest humbled

[1] This person, called in the Phœnician sources from which Josephus draws in his *con. Apion.* § 21 (where he mentions for the third time the siege of Tyre), Baal—succeeding, and in connection with the siege, Ithobal, was most probably made, or at least confirmed as king by Nebuchadnezzar; whereupon, after ten years, "judges were appointed, who judged the people"; after them "reigned Balatorus"; and "after his death they sent and brought Merbalus from Babylon, who reigned"; lastly, "after his death they sent for his brother Hirom."

Tyre, Zidon appears to have from the first bowed to the conqueror, and still more so afterwards. But anyhow, under the Persian rule, Zidon appears as "the first city of Phœnicia, and its kings take precedence of those of Tyre, and of the other states" (DUNCKER, ii. p. 738; HERZOG, *Real-encyc.* xi. p. 626). About the middle of the 4th century, when, in the self-consciousness of its position as at the head of the Phœnician States, it had revolted under Artaxerxes Ochus (B.C. 351), it was again destroyed by the Persians, and required to be built anew—whereupon it readily submitted to Alexander the Great. We learn from Diodorus, that at the fall of the city 40,000 perished; and Artaxerxes also sold the burnt ruins for the sake of the gold and silver they contained. Under the Macedonians and Romans, Zidon was nothing but a provincial city; at the time of Cæsar pre-eminently a Jewish city. After coming into view in the time of the crusades,—being destroyed again and again by the Saracens, Crusaders, Mongols,—it still exists, and has some exports of silk, cotton, and gall-nuts. This survey of Zidon also confirms with reference to Ezekiel the far-reaching view of his prophetic word.

11. Neteler remarks on our chapter: "Through the most extraordinary wonders God placed His covenant-people on such a height, that all the Chaldeans must bow before the giant spirit of Daniel, and Nebuchadnezzar himself proclaim to the whole world that there is no god who can deliver as the God of Israel. Nebuchadnezzar and his Chaldeans consequently had the calling, as heroes standing in the service of God, to overthrow the Hamitic worldly power, and to prepare the way for the kingdom of God."

12. Schmieder says, that the threatening of the Lord against the historical Tyre was as little accomplished to the full through Nebuchadnezzar as the similar one against Babylon (Isa. xiii. 20), and many other threatenings, which were proclaimed for the very purpose that they might not need to be executed. Certainly God promises only to conversion the removal of the threatened punishment (Jer. xviii. 7, 8); but He sometimes also mitigates the punishment, where the measure of sin has not been so full, or the means for conversion may have been exhausted (Matt. xi. 21, 22). The historical Tyre is only an imperfect type of the spiritual Tyre, on which account the severest threatening was uttered against it, though still not in its entire severity was it executed. This early denunciation of judgment, this sparing alleviation as to the execution, begins already at Gen. ii. 17, etc. In ch. xxviii. the prophet exhibits, first, the highest glory of the true king, who has been set up by God, as it can alone perfectly appear in Christ (vers. 12-15); and second, the deep fall of the king, who would make himself a god, as such fall shall only be completely manifested in the Man of Sin, and in the Prince of this world. The king of Tyre is a type of both,—of the King of the kingdom of heaven by his office, of the prince of darkness by his misuse of the dignity, his pride and fall. Thus does Ezekiel teach us to understand and explain the history of the world.

HOMILETICAL HINTS

On Ch. xxvi.

Vers. 1-6. Tyre, the home of the first learned jurist, Ulpian, is the burial-place of the gifted theologian Origen; and the ruins of its once gorgeous cathedral cover the bones of the Emperor Frederick Barbarossa. — "Selfishness is a very great sin, especially when one seeks to become rich through other people's hurt" (CR.).—Tyre against Jerusalem: a study for the times.—"The prophet would check the despondency which a sight of the world shining in its glory can so readily evoke in the people of God when sighing under the cross" (HENGST.).—The loud triumph of the world over the Church is still only an apparent triumph.—The Church may be brought down, but the world with all its lust must utterly go down. — Ver. 3. Yes; many nations shall come; God took Tyre at her word, but how?—Against the high wave-stroke of the towering heart, there come the high beating waves of retribution.—"God serves Himself of men in executing punishment, where an angel might rather have done it (Sennacherib), in order that we may become more sensible of our impotence" (STCK.).—The sea, which had been the hope of Tyre, now its terror.—God, the Leader of the enemies of His enemies.—Ver. 4. Walls, towers, all is nothing, if God is not all.—What survives if God falls upon us?—The comforting and the terrible faithfulness of God to His word.—All things and persons are included in the annihilating judgments of God.

Vers. 7-14. Nebuchadnezzar, a servant of God: in Egypt the insects were such.—The world-conqueror and the world-ruler.—The king out of the north is, above all, death; and if he draws up in array, he has a multitude also for his host, and there will be pain for the soul as well as for the body.—No fortress stands so secure and so firmly guarded that God's judgment cannot reach and enter it.—Every power is broken at last.—"Whosoever does not tremble before the divine law will be only the more affrighted before the divine punishment when it alights" (STCK.).—Ver. 12. The spoiling of our goods is the final end of all upon earth; therefore should we lay up for ourselves treasures in heaven, which remain for ever. *Sic transit gloria mundi.*—Vers. 13, 14. The lust of the world shall be one day suffering; the suffering of the pious eternal glory.—Let not thy heart be so stunned by the noise which the world makes as not to mark the bare rock which lies beneath; be not deceived by the merry songs and lively instruments of music: upon the graves even of the rich and the great all is still.—Here the fishing-net, elsewhere the cobwebs.

Ver. 15 sqq. The interest in the downfall of others, arising from the consideration of the nothingness and perishableness of all earthly things, from the feeling of one's own impotence and weakness, from the consciousness of sin and guilt.—The echo of misery.—"When God punishes, He does it not merely on account of the ungodly, who must feel such punishment, but also on account of other ungodly persons, that they may become better by such examples" (ST.).—Herakles, the strength of Tyre, the might of commerce (comp. the Heb. word *rakal*).—The fall of Tyre an impressive preaching of repentance.—"The downfall of the ungodly is more readily mourned and bewailed than the tribulation of the righteous" (ST.).—"That may be accomplished in a moment which was not expected to take place in years" (STCK.).—The Bible also represents tragedies, in which whole peoples may weep and kings take their place in the dust. —"When earthly well-being departs, the world complains—only its eternal perdition troubles it not" (STCK.).—The fall of the great should make us shy of seeking after such perishable greatness. —The unrighteous grief of the world, and the righteous lamentation of the world.—The terror before Tyre, and the terror upon Tyre.—If thou art frightened at sin in time, thou shalt not need to be frightened at its punishment when it is too late.

Vers. 19-21. "These three verses hang together. The overthrow of the great city, and the glorification of the church. The one is the consequence of the other. There was a time when Rome was desolated, and the peoples covered it like water. At last it also went down to the dead in the Council of Trent, where, by its anathemas, it cut itself off from true believers. God has delivered His church, the land of the living, from Babylon, and adorned her with peace and manifold gifts" (COCC.).—Tyre in the going down, Zion in the rising up again.—"He who has such hope may well let the scorn of Tyre pass—*respice finem*" (HENGST.).—"Just as God overthrows the proud antichristianism, so much the higher will He one day raise His church" (TÜB. BIBLE).—"Even in the hardest threatenings there is an under-current of promise for the children of God" (ST.).—Ver. 21. As there is a seeking and not finding, so also shall there be a being sought and not found.—"This is likewise said of every ungodly one who has been prosperous, Ps. xxxvii. 36. He is not to be found in heaven for ever, and in hell none cares to seek or to be found" (B. B.).

On Ch. xxvii.

Vers. 1-10. "When Tyre rejoices over Jerusalem, then the prophet raises a lamentation over Tyre: this is the recompense of the pious" (STCK.).—If we must not repay evil with evil, there still is with God a recompensing of evil with evil.—"All human and earthly things go out at last in lamentation" (STCK.).—This is the lamentation of the Spirit, that the world sows to the flesh, and of the flesh reaps corruption.—With kettledrums and flutes the world begins, but it ends with wailing and misery.—"We must profoundly know the *gloria mundi*, if we are to take to heart the *sic transit gloria mundi*" (HENGST.). —Vers. 3, 4. "Let no one boast of his strength or worldly elevation; how soon can the Lord, if His judgments should break forth, bring all to the dust of desolation! Jer. ix. 23, 25" (TÜB. B.). —There is a perfection of beauty which is nothing else than ripeness for judgment.—Beauty is a transient splendour, but the knowledge of the Eternal leads from glory to glory.—"In boasting one sees what things the heart is full of" (STCK.). —The contrast between Tyre and the daughter of the king, Ps. xlv., who is all beautiful within.—"The security is very different: one is of faith, since we know that we are reconciled through Christ, and, even if the world should fall in ruin, can remain in peace; the other proceeds from unbelief, which has respect to men, walls, etc., and relies upon these" (L.).—"There are many kinds of beauty, but none perfect without godliness" (STCK.).—"We shall also have to think of that woman who, Rev. xviii., says, I am it" (B. B.).—The buildings of men and the building of God, namely, His church, against which not even the gates of hell can prevail.—Vers. 5-9. Comp. with the splendid ship Tyre the heavenly Jerusalem, Rev. xxi.—"When people once surrender themselves to pride, pomp, and dissipation, they can hardly lay them aside again; nay, they often know not, from inconsideration and wantonness, what they should do, Deut. xxxii. 15 sq." (O.) —Trim the lamps!—Every land has its peculiar gift from God, and the gifts of God must thus shamefully minister to the vanity of men!—God forbids the misuse of His gifts as an unprofitable waste.—It is quite right to take into one's service and pay qualified persons, but woe to him who makes flesh his arm, and whose heart departs from the Lord!—Ver. 10. The best defence is after all another thing than soldiers, Ps. xxxiii. 16, 17.—The angel of the Lord encamps round about those who fear Him, Ps. xxxiv. 8 [7].—God's camping host for believers, Gen. xxxii.; 2 Kings vi. 17.—We must, according to Eph. vi. 10 sqq., put on the divine armour, which protects land and people.

Vers. 12-25. Men run through the wide world for the sake of merchandise, while the word of God, which makes rich without trouble, and imparts treasure which neither moth nor rust corrupts, nor can thieves steal, is so near us!—The one pearl of great price Tyre did not make an article of traffic.—What advantages it to gain the whole world if the soul suffers damage?—"Ezekiel writes as little from the point of view of a minister of commerce, as Isaiah in ch. iii. does from that of a milliner" (HENGST.).—Covetousness must serve all.—"O how many gifts of God are in the service of sin!" (RICHT.)—"Great merchant-cities, great cities of sin" (TÜB. B.).—Ver. 13. How often and in how many ways are men's souls the object of buying and selling!—Ver. 24. "With things perfectly beautiful man was certainly to occupy himself. But where are they to be found in the earthly sphere? Col. iii. 2" (B. B.).—Ver. 25. "That Tyre was so full and honoured, while Zion became always poorer and poorer, and sunk miserable—this formed a stumbling-block to the people of God. But what has become of all the fulness and glory of Tyre? Zion, on the other hand, has gloriously blossomed anew" (HENGST.).

Vers. 26-36. "The glory of the earth shall become dust and ashes."—The higher we reach, so much the more precipitous, and so much the deeper will be the fall.—The element of our security can so easily become the element of our misery: here the sea, elsewhere gold, one's position, etc.—A person of high estate when cast down is lower than one who has always been in a humble position.—The wind does not always fill our sails; it often also, and suddenly, tears them short and small.—In prosperity men so rarely consider how vain it is, that in adversity they cry out the more loudly; but, alas! only upon the vanity of earthly things, and not upon the vanity of their earthly hearts.—It is with that which men build for themselves, such that if one stone should fall out of the wall, all the other stones will follow it.—Remember that thou art dust, and bethink thyself that thou hast a soul!—Fear is salutary, but there is also a fear which we again shake off, and which we do not suffer to warn us. —The loss of earthly things gives such trouble and for the loss of heavenly goods men will laugh! —A Christian should not so mourn, but should smite his breast alike in prosperity and in adversity.—Ver. 32. Michael and Tyre.—Who is as thou? This it is proper to say only of God in reference to glory. In respect to nothingness, on the other hand, one of us is as another.—Mournful times should be times of repentance.—The holy sense of the *nil mirari.*—Ver. 33. Our striving should be to become rich in the knowledge of the truth, and to make rich in regard to such knowledge should be our purpose in life.—Ver. 34. The end of earthly things, their scale, value, and true estimation.—All this world is nothing; how surely must there be what is something!—But faith cries out of the depths to God.—The glory of the children of God, and the world's glory.—Formerly and now, two resting-points for the consideration of Tyre.—Vers. 35, 36. Fear and shame have their limit only at a throne, that is, where the king reigns, who represents us.—"So one at length becomes an object of the world's mockery with his pride and his sins" (TÜB. B.).

On Ch. xxviii.

Vers. 2–11. "The prophet had the more reason to bring forward the king of Tyre in his fall, as he thus obtains a counterpart to the glorious rise of the kingdom of Israel in Christ" (HENGST.).—"God resisteth the proud, 1 Pet. v. 5. Whoever, therefore, is proud has God for his enemy" (STCK.). "I am God—many, indeed, will not speak plainly out; but they bear themselves so as if no one had the right to say anything to them. God may well enough call governors gods, but they are not themselves to assume anything on that account, else their divinity will soon come to a disgraceful end with Dagon, 1 Sam. v. 3, 4" (B. B.).—"The new wisdom teaches, man is God, and there is no God except in man—which points to the man of sin, 2 Thess. ii. 4, whose typical foreshadowing the king of Tyre was" (SCHMIEDER).—"It belongs to the nature of God to be and have everything out of Himself; to the nature of man, to derive all from the fulness of God" (HENGST.).—"Nothing is more foolish than when a man forgets his human condition" (STCK.).—Thou sayest, I am rich, etc., see Rev. iii. 17.—Ver. 3. The fear of the Lord is the beginning of true wisdom.—"Our wisdom puffs us up, when love fails" (H. H.).—"Imaginary wisdom hinders prayer for the true wisdom" (ST.).—The worldly wisdom of Daniel, as compared with that of the prince of Tyre.—Ver. 4. The husbandman, also, gathered much into his granary; yet he was a fool, whose soul was that night to be required of him, Luke xii.—Ver. 5. God demands the heart; mammon lifts it up, that it may not betake itself to God.—No one can become happy by means of riches.—Ver. 6. The king of Tyre and the king of Babylon, Dan. iv. 27.—"The punishment for pride is humiliation" (H. H.).—"To come from a pit to a high position is an agreeable change, as with Joseph and David; but the coming for the ungodly is in the opposite direction" (STCK.).—God must bring us to the height, and keep us in the height, if we are not to fall from all real and imaginary heights into the depths of the abyss.—Ver. 9. "In the day of trouble men employ quite another language than in prosperity, nay, learn then what they would not learn throughout their whole life" (STCK.).—Ver. 10. "Balaam desired to die the death of the righteous" (STCK.).—The death of the ungodly is death manifold—bodily, spiritual, eternal.

Vers. 11–19. Even this lamentation shows that God has no pleasure in the death of the wicked.—"Impress of the original, therefore the image of God, Heb. i. 2. More exactly: he who not only in himself, but also in all his works, expresses the prototype. This Jesus testifies of Himself, John v. 19, 36" (SCHMIEDER).—Ver. 13 sq. To whom much is given, of him also shall much be required.—The great spirits, who think the law was not given for them, in the judgment.—"So also we must regard as precious stones Christ and His name, the Holy Spirit, faith, the prophets, God's word, the sacraments, the virtues, the patience of the saints, the forgiveness of sins, etc.—with which a false Christ seeks to bedeck and to adorn himself, Rev. xvii. 4" (B. B.).—"Ungodly people have their Eden in this world, but believers seek it in heaven" (ST.).—Ver. 15. "On the common ground of hereditary corruption, there still are in the life of individuals and of whole nations differences, times of comparative innocence as well as of deep declension, provoking the judgments of God. As a rule, youth is the better time; the older the worse. Sin, when not combated, is continually on the increase," etc. (HENGST.)—"It does not always happen that they who promise well in youth shall be the same in advanced life, for many change their habits" (ST.).—"Every man flatters himself, and every king is flattered by his Tyre" (SCHMIEDER).—Ver. 16. The perils of merchandise for entire peoples, and for individuals.—"They who aim at being rich fall into dangerous snares" (STCK.).—Ver. 17. "The foundation of wisdom is humility, which sees things as they are, has an open eye for one's own weaknesses and the excellences of others, and is on its guard against dangerous undertakings, Ps. cxxxi. 1. The 'brightness' received into the heart blinds the eye, so that one regards himself alone as great, everything else as little, and rushes wantonly into dangers for which he is not prepared, adventures upon paths which lead to perdition—as the combat (of Tyre) with the flourishing Chaldean monarchy. But haughtiness itself works its own ruin. This is the rock on which all the heathen powers of the old world were wrecked" (HENGST.).—"But God-fearing kings will thence derive the instruction that the king, not less than the meanest subject, has to pray daily to God on his knees for a wise and humble heart" (SCHMIEDER).—The dust of kings appears and is treated exactly as the dust of the very poorest. *Sursum corda*, but in the right sense!—Our heart should be a sanctuary of God.—Vers. 18, 19. "The fire of lust and covetous desire draws after it the other fire of judgment" B. B.).—"A destruction like that of Sodom in the olden time, in which the sin-root of Canaan first came to full development, while the judgment upon Tyre forms the close of the long series of judgments upon the Canaanites" (HENGST.).—"On the other hand, he who does the will of God abides for ever, 1 John ii. 17" (STCK.).—"Where thou wilt not be for ever, there seek for thyself no fixed abode" (B. B.).

Ver. 20. "In the judgments of God shines forth His glory, so that men are obliged to confess that He is righteous, and that His judgments are righteous" (STCK.).—Ver. 24. "God's judgment on the ungodly tends to the good of His church" (CR.).—God sets His own free at length.—"How easily is a thorn drawn out!" (STCK.)—"How well is it to be under the protection of the Lord Messiah, and under His gracious wings to dwell securely!" (TÜB. B.)—"Hence has it been fully made good through Christ, as Zacharias says (Luke i. 74 sq.), that we are redeemed from the hand of our enemies to serve Him without fear," etc. (H. H.)—"Then do believers first come to their true and perfect rest, when all their bodily and spiritual enemies have been rooted out" (O.).—"This prophecy is fulfilled in the Christian Church, which is the true seed of Abraham, Isaac, and Jacob. Those born under the Old Covenant were in bondage, while believers under the New Testament are free" (COCCEIUS).

3. EGYPT (CH. XXIX.–XXXII.).

CH. XXIX. 1. In the tenth year, in the tenth [month], on the twelfth of the month,
2 came the word of Jehovah to me, saying, Son of man, Set thy face upon [against]
3 Pharaoh, king of Egypt, and prophesy upon him, and upon all Egypt! Speak
and say, Thus saith the Lord Jehovah, Behold, I [come] upon thee, Pharaoh, king
of Egypt, the great dragon that lieth in the midst of his streams, who saith, To
4 me [belongs] my stream, and I, I have made myself. And I give rings in thy
jaws, and hang the fish of thy streams on thy scales, and draw thee out of the
midst of thy streams, and every fish of thy streams [which] hangs on thy scales;
5 And I set thee free [drive thee] into the wilderness, thee and every fish of thy
streams; upon the plains of the field shalt thou fall, thou shalt not be picked up,
and not gathered; to the beast [living creatures] of the earth and to the fowl of the
6 heaven I have given thee for food. And all the inhabitants of Egypt shall know
that I am Jehovah! Because they were a staff of reed to the house of Israel,—
7 When they take hold of thee by thy hand, thou art broken, and splittest to them
every shoulder [the whole shoulder]; and when they lean upon thee, thou art shattered,
8 and lamest for them all loins,—Therefore thus saith the Lord Jehovah, Behold,
9 I bring upon thee a sword, and root out of thee man and beast. And the land
of Egypt is [shall be] for desolation and a waste, and they know that I am Jehovah!
10 Because He said, The stream [belongs] to me, and I, I have made it, Therefore,
behold, I am against thee, and against thy streams, and I give the land of Egypt
for deserts of waste of desolation, from Migdol to Syene [Seveneh], and even to
11 the borders of Cush. Foot of man shall not pass through it, and foot of beast
12 shall not pass through it, and it shall not be inhabited forty years. And I have
given the land of Egypt [for] desolation in the midst of desolate lands, and its
cities shall be desolate forty years in the midst of desolate cities, and I disperse
13 Egypt among the heathen and scatter them in the lands. For thus saith the
Lord Jehovah, At the end of forty years will I gather Egypt out of the peoples
14 whither they were dispersed: And I turn the misery of Egypt, and bring them
back to the land of Pathros, to the land of their birth; and they are there a low
15 kingdom. Lower than the kingdoms shall it be, and it shall not lift itself up any
more above the heathen; and I diminish them, so that they do not rule among
16 the heathen [have dominion over them]. And it shall no more be for confidence to the
house of Israel, a remembrancer of iniquity, when they turn after them; and they
17 know that I am the Lord Jehovah. And it came to pass in the seven and
twentieth year, in the first [month], on the first of the month, the word of Jehovah
18 came to me, saying, Son of man, Nebuchadnezzar the king of Babylon has
caused his army to serve a great service against Tyre: every head became bald,
and every shoulder peeled; and there was not reward for him and his host out of
19 Tyre for the work, which he has wrought against it [the city]. Therefore thus
saith the Lord Jehovah, Behold, I give Nebuchadnezzar the king of Babylon
the land of Egypt, and he takes away its tumult, and plunders its spoil, and
20 seizes its prey; and it is a reward to his host. As his hire for which he has
wrought against it [Tyre], I have given him the land of Egypt, because they did
21 [it] for Me—sentence of the Lord Jehovah. In that day will I make a horn to
bud forth to the house of Israel, and I will give thee the opening of the mouth in
the midst of them; and they know that I am Jehovah.

Ver. 1. Sept.: . . . μια τ. μηνος—
Ver. 2. . . . στηρισον τ. προσωπον—
Ver. 3. . . . ἐμοι εἰσιν οἱ ποταμοι και ἐγω ἐποιησα αὐτους.
Ver. 4. . . . τας παγιδας . . . ταις λεπισιν σου προσκολληθησονται.
Ver. 5. και καταβαλω σε ἐν ταχει κ. παντας—
Ver. 7. Sept.: . . . τη χειρι αὐτων, ἐθλασθης, κ. ὀτε ἐπεκροτησεν ἐπ' αὐτους πασα χειρ κ. ὀτε ἐπανεπαυσαντο ἐπ' αὐτους συνετριβης κ. συνεκλασας αὐτων.—Vulg.: . . . *te manu* . . . *et lacerasti* . . . *et dissolvisti omnes renes eorum.*
Ver. 10. . . . και ἐπι παντας τ. ποταμους σου . . . εἰς ἐρημον κ. ῥομφαιαν κ. ἀπωλειαν ἀπο Μ. κ. Συηνης—Vulg.: . . *in solitudines, gladio dissipatam a turre Syenes*—
Ver. 12. . . . εἰς ἀπωλειαν ἐν μεσῳ τ. ἐρημου, . . . ἀφανισμος ἐσται—
Ver. 14. Sept.: . . . και κατοικιω αὐτους . . . ὀθεν ἐληφθησαν—*in terra nativitatis suæ*—
Ver. 15. παρα πασας τ. ἀρχας. Οὐ μη . . . του μη εἰναι αὐτους πλειονας ἐν—
Ver. 16 . . . εἰς ἐλπιδα ἀναμιμνησκουσαν ἁμαρτιαν ἐν τῳ αὐτους ἀκολουθησαι ὀπισω τ. καρδιων αὐτων—*docentes iniquitatem, ut fugiant et sequantur eos*;—
Ver. 17. . . . μια τ. μηνος τ. πρωτου—
Ver. 19. . . . τ. πληθος αὐτης—
Ver. 20. Ἀντι τ. λειτουργειας αὐτου ἡς ἐδουλευσεν—19 . . . *exercitui illius* (20) *et operi quo servivit*—
Ver. 21. . . . ἀνατελει κερας παντι τ. οἰκῳ—*pullulabit cornu.*

EXEGETICAL REMARKS.

In reference to the anti-Chaldean coalition, Egypt, as the mainstay of the undertaking, justly forms the conclusion of those prophecies toward such as were without. But even apart from this, the significance of Egypt, as well in its antagonistic position to the Chaldean monarchy as in its relation to the people of God, and therewith to the world in general, demanded an adequate treatment at the close.

Vers. 1–16. *Outline of the Prophecy as a whole.*

Vers. 1, 2. As to time (B.C. 588 ?), this first prophecy upon Egypt goes before ch. xxvi. (two months, eighteen days, SCHMIEDER). That notwithstanding it is placed later, shows the position of Egypt at the close is to be regarded as an intentional one; comp. also vers. 18, 19. Hengst. remarks: "The prophecy, as appears from ch. xxiv. 1, was delivered during the siege of Jerusalem. The occasion is the hope of recovery through Pharaoh." (SCHMIEDER: six months, except three days, before the taking of the city (Jer. xxxix. 2), one year and two days after the prophet's mouth had been shut for his people.)—Ver. 2. שׂים פניך על, elsewhere with אל; for example, at ch. vi. 2.—פַּרְעֹה, the title of all the native kings of Egypt down to the Persian times; according to Josephus and the Coptic, as much as *king* (comp. פֶּרַע; prince); Jer. xliv. 30, Hophra. The prophecy, in accordance with its general character, stretches over king and people, or more precisely, the land.

Vers. 3–6*a*. This portion has respect to the king of Egypt.—תנים, only here, according to Gesen. a mere corruption for תנין; according to Hengst. intentionally the *plur. majestatis* from תנין=תן: "since this dragon blows himself up so much, sets himself forth as the ideal of all dragons." What is meant by it is no great sea-fish or great serpent, but what was so distinctive of Egypt, as also suitable for the description in ver. 4, **the crocodile**; Job xl., xli. 25, 26. For a farther symbolical application of the idea, comp. Isa. xxvii.; Ps. lxxiv. 13, 14; Rev. xii. (תנה—תנן—τεινω, to stretch, of the long-stretching body; also of the long-protracted sound, the jackal.)—The consciousness of power on the part of the Pharaohs, their pride of sway, is visibly expressed by רבץ (**ch. xix.** 2), the secure rest, the undisturbed comfortable lair; after the manner of the crocodile, and by the nearer designation: **in the midst of his streams.** יְאֹר (יאור) GESEN.: an Egyptian word, on the Rosetta inscription, *jor*—here of the (seven) arms of the Nile (Isa. vii. 18), elsewhere of its canals, when those are called נהרות. The Nile is "the heart of Egypt," on account of which divine honours were of old paid to it, in particular by the kings, with devout regard, "as the vivifying father of all that exists" (CHAMPOLLION). As he already says **my stream** (ch. xxviii. 2), the לי may not merely import that it belongs to him, is his property, but: it belongs to me of right, or so that it cannot be taken from me—therefore lawfully and inalienably. It gives expression to the loud boast on the ground of natural might as from primeval time and for ever; in which lies the heathenish contrast to Jehovah, who alone is unchangeable, eternal, gives and takes according to His will.—עשיתני, *either* (ואני, nom. absol.), that he had made himself, which, apart from the fact that the Egyptians boasted of being the oldest men (HEROD. ii. 2; DIODOR. i. 10, 50; PLATO *in Tim.*), accords well with the Egyptian deification of the kingdom. So upon the monuments the priests ever are represented as kneeling in the dust before the kings. The Pharaohs—and this is peculiarly Egyptian—were not merely sprung from the gods, but were themselves gods of the land (DUNCKER, *Hist. of Antiquity*, i. 150). Therefore, as the king of Tyre (ch. xxviii. 2) with his gods'-seat asserts his divinity, so does the king of Egypt with his stream at least his independence of any other origin = what I am, that am I of myself. *Or*, we may take the suffix as equivalent to לי, for which, however, ver. 9 cannot be adduced, and which cannot be understood with Häv. as meaning: "I have secured for myself its blessings," or, as still more strongly put by Hitzig: "I have made it for me in a right condition," with its canals, embankments, sluices, etc., as the Dutch also have been named the creators of their land. [Targum Jonathan: *meum est regnum, et ego subjugavi illud.*] JEROME: He trusts in the peculiar overflowings of the Nile, which belongs to him; the rain of heaven is of no moment for him. Thus also the old expositors of Homer understood the διιπετεος of the "Aigyptos," *i.e.* the Nile, of the annual overflowings (*Odys.* iv. 477). In its application to Pharaoh Hophra (Apries), the notice of Herodotus is characteristic, that he thought neither the power of men nor of gods could destroy his kingdom (ii. c. 169).

Ver. 4. The sin referred to is followed by a corresponding punishment, as the threatening is given forth, that from both king and people the ground of their pride and prosperity should be taken away.—The "behold I am against thee" of ver. 3 explicates itself.—חַחִיים, Qeri חחים, from חַח, ring, such as is put into the nose of beasts, or about the most tender and susceptible parts of the head, for taming them. HENGST.: "a double ring," in the Dual, like לְחָיַיִם, so that both halves join together in the mouth (comp. ch. xix. 4). Rosenm. understands it of the hooks, by which, according to Herodotus, the crocodiles were taken (Job xli. 2).—The **fish** of the arms of the Nile signify the living and well-conditioned Egyptians in general, who had felt themselves like fish in the water, but were now to be placed upon dry ground. HITZIG: specially Pharaoh's men of war; JONATHAN: the princes and nobles.—הדבקתי, ch. iii. 26.—For תדבק, supply אֲשֶׁר.—As to what historical signification is to be put upon the image, which is of a quite general kind, no indication whatever is given. But see the Doctrinal Reflections, No. 2.—Ver. 5. The **wilderness** forms, as to the sense, the contrast to might and pomp and all sort of abundance; as to the figure, it is a contrast to the Nile, which formed an oasis in the midst of the wilderness, being secured by the heights on the west against the quicksands and storms of the great desert, and separated by the mountains on the east from the rocky cliffs, the desolate plains, and sand downs. The irrigation of the ground in consequence of the abundant waters of the Nile, especially at the season of the yearly overflowing, the cooling of the atmosphere precisely at the time when the heat is greatest, are the more important, since the blue and shining heaven is never troubled by rain-clouds, the heat is strong, and the south-west gales sometimes drive the sand and dust of the Sahara over the Libyan mountains as far as the Nile. ("Egypt is a land without rain, without springs, without refreshing winds, without alternating seasons. Instead of these, however, it possesses a fertile stream, which has not its like upon earth. In the far-reaching expanse one sees only the dead wilderness; but on approaching the Nile, all is life and prosperity. The camel of the desert scents the fresh Nile air at the distance of half a day's journey. The Arabs call it Bachr, the sea; it is, however, one of the greatest and longest rivers of the earth, to be compared with the Amazon, Mississippi, and Yenisei."—SEPP.) Hence, for the very reason that it reckons itself distinguished, as forming a green oasis of luxuriant fertility and coolness in the midst of a boundless waste, Jehovah brings it into that wilderness condition. A deeper parallel, however, also lies in this relegation to the wilderness, in respect to the divine guiding of Israel into the wilderness when Israel came out of Egypt.—"Upon the face of the field" means the same as "the wilderness;" according to Hengst.: "the open field as contrasted with the splendid mausoleums in which the Egyptian Pharaohs were buried in the times of their glory." Not even an honourable burial would be given him (TARGUM). At all events, in the place where he falls, there he remains lying; and, indeed, what previously were separate from each other, **thee and every fish**, now come to be united in the representative person of the king. "Every one of his deceased subjects was, as it were, a part of Pharaoh, as in the retreat from Moscow Napoleon was seen in every dead Frenchman" (HENGST.). They are simply abandoned to the wilderness; hence there is found no gathering up and carrying away (אסף), no bringing together (קבץ).—Comp. Matt. xiii. 47 sq.—Ver. 6*a*. A knowledge which is the very reverse of what was distinctively Egyptian, according to which the Pharaohs were honoured, on the monuments, as "the dispensers of life," the "ever-living," and such like. (Comp. the Rosetta inscription.)

Vers. 6*b*–12. This section has respect to the land. The words: **all the inhabitants of Egypt,** mediate the transition from the king to the land.—The יען can scarcely be the reason for the fact of the Egyptians knowing God; but this sentence properly breaks off here, and a new sentence begins, to which ver. 8 forms the conclusion; so that ver. 7 comes in parenthetically (KL.).—The image of the **reed-staff** is derived from Isa. xxxvi. 6, the more suitably as it is there found in the mouth of the Assyrian king, whose heritage passed over to the Chaldeans; and to repeat with the fact the addition of **broken,** used there by him, was, as a judgment already openly pronounced upon Egypt, so much the more a ground of shame for Israel. What had discovered itself even in the Assyrian time should have needed no fresh proof.—Ver. 7. It means that a reed-staff is not only no support, but a hurtful support; it carries with it a show and deceit of a dangerous kind. It is not, however, to be forgotten, that there is a characteristic allusion involved in the figure to the prolificness of Egypt in reeds and bulrushes (Isa. xix. 6).—Instead of בְּכַפְּךָ, the Qeri has בַּכַּף, as if the personified Egypt, or this as addressed in its king, could have no hand! In order to hold fast by the image of the reed, which is certainly continued by the רצץ (Isa. xxxvi. 6), Kliefoth translates: "by thy twig"; but who would lay hold thus of a reed if he means to support himself upon it?—That Israel promised himself support from Egypt is evident from the result of the breaking of this reed-staff; while the wounded, torn shoulder leant upon it, the splinters of the reed ran thereinto.—KLIEF.: "the staff of reed pierced through the hand and arm, up even to the shoulder." The שׁען expressly says this, at the same time strengthening the "laying hold of" to a resting thereon with the whole body.—והעמדת, GESEN.: only the Hiphil, transposed for וְהַמְעַדְתָּ (Ps. lxix. 24 [23]), "and makest shake." HENGST.: sarcastically, "a pretty staying, which was, in fact, a casting down." If the root-meaning of עמד is to draw together, it might stand here as = laming: "and drawest together for them the whole loins" (MEIER). "To make to totter," or shake, certainly says very little, and "to make to stand," so that they must use their own loins, without any stay, can hardly be the right explanation. KLIEF.: it pierced through their shoulders, and made these, by injuring their muscles, ligaments, and joints, stiff and rigid, so that they could but stand, and move no more. ("So fared it with the kingdom of the ten tribes under Hosea in connection with Egypt, and likewise with the kingdom of Judah under Zedekiah." —J. D. MICHAELIS.)—Ver. 8. Solemn conclusion, with feminine suffixes, on account of the reference to the land. The **sword** indicates war; ch. xiv. 17.

Ver. 9. The consequence of this desolation of the land.—יען, as in ver. 6.—Comp. at ver. 3. Because Pharaoh, regarding himself as all Egypt, in his lordly spirit asserts for himself the right and power of all,—ואני points back to כי אני; עשיתי, not so properly the Nile as generally what is to be made (Isa. x. 13), always, however, with reference to the arms of the Nile,—therefore, in Ver. 10, Jehovah falls upon this pompous "I," as well as its supports, the streams which it calls its own, and gives the land of Egypt, with which this "I" had identified itself, to a state of most complete desolation. The heaping together of the synonyms, and the double genitive, express a superlative. Here, as at ver. 5, the wilderness in contrast to the Nile. [Hitzig points לְחָרָבוֹת, "for deserts, desolation of the waste." Schmieder remarks on it, that definite pre-intimations of inevitable chastisements are commonly milder, and draws attention to an unmistakeable softening in what follows (vers. 12–16), which might be still more lightened in the execution of the punishment.] **From Migdol**, a similar bounding to that in ch. xxv. 13 (Sept.: ἀπὸ Μαγδώλου); placed over against **Syene** (Aswan), the most southerly boundary, on the cataracts of the Nile, and to be taken as the boundary on the north. It was, as the name imports, a "fortress," perhaps the border-watch toward Syria; on account of which Jerome: *a turre Syenes.* סונה, according to Champollion, from *ouen*, to open, and *sa*, through which it acquires the sense of "the opener," the key (of Egypt). Here rise the mighty terraces of reddish granite (Syenite), which formed the building material of the Egyptian kings. The determining expression 'ועד does not go beyond, but fixes Syene as the boundary on the Ethiopian side.—Ver. 11 paints the desolation (vers. 9, 10), corresponding to ver. 8. Neither traffic nor travel. —ולא תשב, HENGST.: "and it shall not sit" (!); therefore it shall lie down. The forty years are (according to him) historical, to be branched off from the seventy of Jeremiah, ch. xxv., xxix., which began in the fourth year of Jehoiakim, when, with the slaughter at Circesium on the Euphrates, the power of Egypt was for ever broken. Thirty years had it continued, till the war passed over to the proper head of the anti-Chaldean coalition, and Egypt was laid waste. Hitzig takes the number for a round one (1 Sam. xvii. 16; Ex. xxiv. 18, etc.), after the analogy of ch. iv. 6 (but see there). The parallel already indicated at ver. 5, as well as the general character of the prophecy, Nebuchadnezzar not being named here, recommend the *symbolical* import of the number: Israel, when delivered from Egypt, forty years in the wilderness; Egypt, with respect to Israel, forty years a wilderness; there a proving, here a judgment, punishment. [Tholuck is of opinion that the number is indeed a round one, but still of an approximate nature as regards the probable reckoning, about 36 or 37.]—On תשב, comp. ch. xxvi. 20. ישב signifies: "to be master of something," to possess, therefore: to tarry somewhere, and so here: to occupy house, be at home. We are not to regard it as a poetical phrase for being inhabited (KLIEF.), but rather to consider it as spoken with reference to the scattering, etc., of the inhabitants in ver. 12.—Ver. 12. *As an absolute contrast to Israel in the wilderness, corresponds in a symbolical respect the repeated delineation of the like total desolation of Egypt* (ch. xii. 20, xiv. 15). *In reality, this can only be understood relatively, as compared with Egypt's former flourishing condition as a land.*—The twice repeated בתוך points to the neighbouring lands, with their cities, or to the provinces of Egypt, or to the members of the coalition against Babylon (HENGST.). Häv. regards it as purely ideal, since otherwise the article must have stood before ארצות. According to HENGST.: "the desolation is not so precise a fact as the supremacy, which was decided by a single battle. It is sufficient if the beginning of the desolation took place within the fourth decennium from its end (?). The end of the forty years, at all events, coincides with that of the seventy years in Jeremiah, of which the first seventeen had elapsed at the time our prophecy was published—seven under Jehoiakim, ten under Zedekiah. Therefore there still were thirteen years to expire before the beginning of the forty years. In ch. xxix. 17 the prophet has himself expressly determined the beginning of the four decenniums." —By the scattering of the Egyptians is meant the deportation of the young and the noble, as such was then associated with every hostile occupation, Nah. iii. 10 (THOLUCK). Also those scattered through terror are not to be forgotten. HÄV.: "Almost the same expressions here of Egypt, which elsewhere are used only of the dispersion and gathering again of Israel." "Egypt the caricature of Israel."

Vers. 13–16. **The end.**—Ver. 13. The כי assigns a reason for the forty years, by pointing to what is to take place thereafter. But that by the **end of** this period respect is had to the end of the Chaldean supremacy, as in Jeremiah, is not indicated in the text, nor would it have been according to Ezekiel's style (comp. Introd. to ch. xxv. sq.; comp. also Jer. xlvi. 26).—The promised gathering of Egypt, in Ver. 14, is restitution (comp. at ch. xvi. 53), indeed, to their original condition, but not to the height which it had then reached.—**Pathros** is what belongs to the south; South or Upper Egypt, Thebes, which (as Ewald remarks) "was not, according to the Manethonian dynasties, precisely the oldest seat of royalty, yet still a Southern Egypt older than Memphis; but after the time of the Hyksos, all the power of Egypt departed from Thebes."—Comp. HEROD. ii. 4, 15; DIODOR. i. 50.—מכורתם, see at ch. xvi. 3 (xxi. 35 [30]).—On the expression: **a low kingdom,** comp. at ch. xvii. 14. HENGST.: "This is no mere prediction, but an indirect practical advice (Isa. xli. 28), to dissuade from a foolish confidence in Egypt." The parallel, besides, with Israel has already been noticed.—Ver. 15. **Comparison with other kingdoms.** Such it had **often** made, and therein gone to excess. Now God makes the comparison, and certainly with another result.—Ver. 16. למבטח, compare therewith the repeated לבטח, ch. xxviii. 26.—יהיה, masc., while formerly תהיה, a kingdom being thought of, but here it is conceived of as a people, or as king.—That the Egyptian people (as the אחריהם might indicate) could inspire Israel with confidence, so that the latter should lean upon them, support itself on them, especially as against Babylon—in that respect they were a remembrancer of iniquity (comp. on ch. xxi. 28 [23]). This is what is plainly expressed by פנה with אחרי, namely, "to turn oneself to any one, in order to follow him"—on which comp. ch. xvii. 6, 7; Ps. xl. 5 [4]. (HENGST.: "Whosoever beguiles into iniquity brings iniquity to remembrance, or to the knowledge of him under whose cognizance it falls. For the iniquity which is committed cannot remain unmarked by 'the Judge of the whole earth,' nor unpunished." HÄV.: "Now Egypt comes forth as an accuser of the covenant-people before God, as a witness in respect to their want of confidence in Him, their idolatrous admiration of worldly, external power, therefore of their falling away from God." Ewald translates: "Still further the house of Israel had a Satan for their confidence.") The knowledge of Jehovah as Lord and Ruler, as in judgment, so in compassion, is the perpetual refrain; it is for Israel and for the heathen the end of the ways of God.

Vers. 17–21. *The appended key for understanding the prophecies concerning Egypt.*—Not merely the relation to what went before, but the relation also to what follows, calls for consideration. In the former respect, the section is an appendix; in the latter respect, and generally, it is a key for the understanding of the prophecies respecting Egypt. We have to regard it as a sort of parenthesis, since the announcement of time in ver. 17 expressly shows it was above 16 years later than ver. 1, later even than ch. xl. [SCHMIEDER: exactly 16 years, 2 months, 17 days after the preceding prophecy; not quite 17 years after the destruction of Jerusalem, two years after Ezekiel's vision of the new temple. HITZIG: the new-moon day of April 572 B.C.] It consequently stands quite apart from the preceding prophecy, but so does it also from the one that follows, ch. xxx. 1–19, by its closing verse. Ch. xxx. 1–19 stands related to ch. xxix. 1–16, as ch. xxvi. 7–14 to ch. xxvi. 2–6; so that the indication of time in ch. xxix. 1 holds good also for ch. xxx. 1. Hengst. denies the number seven for the prophecies upon Egypt, because the necessary chronological specification is wanting at ch. xxx. 1. This reason cannot avail against the consideration that the significant number, which rules the whole, in a way that perfectly accords with its symbolical import as well as with the relation of the close (of Egypt), reverts with this close to the whole, and thereby connects the whole together. The chronological specification has been omitted at ch. xxx. 1, because it would have been the same as that at ch. xxix. 1; and the verses 17–21 are interjected here precisely on this account, that ch. xxx. 1–19, being contemporaneous with ch. xxix. 1–16, might form a separate prediction and so complete the seven number of prophecies upon Egypt.

Ver. 18. The thirteen years' siege of Tyre furnishes the key for the more immediate understanding of the prophecy upon Egypt; the breaking off of the siege in question rendered possible the approaching fulfilment of the anti-Egyptian predictions.—Ch. xxvi. 7.—The **work** against Tyre, consequently the siege of the city, is designated **great**, and this not without respect to the consequences which it involved for the host of the king of Babylon. Of the bearing upon the head and shoulder, with reference to helmet and burdens, קרח and מרט are used, which presuppose long and heavy toil. According to HENGST. the works had to do with the erecting of besieging towers, and especially the casting up a rampart (ch. xxvi. 8); but they suit decidedly better when viewed with respect to the mound running over to insular Tyre, as indicated by Ewald (ch. xxvi. 10). Hitzig makes the ingenious remark, that the shallowness of the sea-strait in Alexander's time, mentioned by Arrian, may have been occasioned by the efforts of Nebuchadnezzar to construct this mound. However, it is not in such respect, therefore, as to what concerns the greatness of the work, that 'ושכר לא is to be understood of a like great reward corresponding to it. שָׂכָר, according to its root-meaning, is "a something made fast,"—either subjectively, what any one held fast by himself or had made fast with another, or objectively, what for material considerations must be held fast. It is in a general way denied that Nebuchadnezzar and his host had received from Tyre hire or reward for their work. As the siege was the work, the hire must mean the booty, especially with respect to the host. The separate mention of **him** and **his host** seems to point to a distinction between Nebuchadnezzar and his host in reference to the hire. Jerome affirms simply, though he does not say on what grounds, that the nobles and rich men of Tyre made away from it in ships, carrying with them their treasures over the sea, and Nebuchadnezzar's host could find no spoil. Ewald accepts this; and Häv. cites in support of it Isa. xxiii. 6, and what happened at the siege of Tyre under Alexander (DIODOR. xvii. 41; CURT. iv. 3). Probable, at all events more probable than the supposition of Hitzig that the money of the Tyrians was spent in the war, must be the consideration that the besiegers of Tyre also had an interest in sparing the city, and refraining from plundering it. Only the prophet does not say this, but makes the Chaldee host come to Egypt to its hurt. With the conquest of the city, however, whether it was or was not effected, our verse has nothing really to do, as Movers justly remarks. Ver. 19 rather suggests another reference. For Nebuchadnezzar, at least, the consequence of the siege of Tyre, "his hire," could only be Egypt, if the great work was not to remain without reward. First with the punishment of Egypt did the recompense become complete which must strike the anti-Chaldean coalition. Egypt also would otherwise have remained the spark which was ever ready to inflame a new Phœnicia and Syria. If the overthrow of Tyre was to yield profit to Nebuchadnezzar, not merely must Jerusalem be laid prostrate, but Egypt also, the pillar of all opposition, as against Assyria so against Babylon, be brought down. It is from such points of view in Babylonian policy that we are to understand what is meant by his hire not having been given him. But what naturally mediates the result, what forms the consequence of the evil, this is in truth, spiritually considered, the divine punishment; and hence the **therefore,** etc., in ver. 19. The policy of the divine recompense as against Egypt (the prop of Israel's unfaithfulness and treachery to the covenant), sc for Nebuchadnezzar's work ("which they did for Me," ver. 20), in the service of Jehovah, is primarily the key of the prophecies touching Egypt.—המון is noise, and from that "a noisy multitude;" here, on account of the connection, and because נשׂא merely is used: **the great mass of things,** therefore: **the riches.** [EWALD: "its noisy pomp."]—As Herodotus and Diodorus report, certainly after the quite untrustworthy tradition of Egyptian vanity, Hophra had besieged the Phœnicians and Cyprians by land and sea, and returned with rich booty to Egypt. There were assuredly no lasting results of such a thing; for after the defeat at Carchemish, and the miscarrying of the relief of Jerusalem, the position of Egypt was not adequate to that; although still, as also Duncker thinks, the Egyptians might have brought home spoil and trophies. There was a glimmering of Egypt's early splendour in the circumstance of its being given for a reward to Nebuchadnezzar.—Hitzig takes as the subject to והיתה the land of Egypt (ver. 20).—Ver. 20. פְּעֻלָּה, as in Ps. cix. 20, that which is wrought for, the fruit of labour. EWALD: "as his pay." —בה is perhaps, after the expression in ver. 18, אשר עבד עליה, to be understood of the city of Tyre. It is commonly rendered: for which he wrought. Hitzig justly remarks: "that Nebuchadnezzar had besieged Tyre in the service of Jehovah could have been declared by the prophet only then, if the city had been conquered;" but since, according to Hitzig, this could not be, he applies עשׂו to the Egyptians (!), as was already done in the Targum of Jonathan, and necessarily imposes on אשר the signification: in regard to that which; that is, for that which.

Ver. 21. This verse vividly represents the character of the whole section. It is a close which corresponds to the subsidiary character of the section, vers. 17–20, in relation to the general prophecy upon Egypt, by the generalness of the style in which it is given, as thereby also it accords with the design that this section should serve as a key to the Egyptian prophecies generally. Comp. the analogous ch. xxviii. 25, 26. In the latter respect it is indicated to us in ver. 21, that although the immediate fulfilment of that which concerned Egypt should be accomplished through Nebuchadnezzar, yet Egypt opens a farther prospect still, since it is to be regarded, in these prophecies of Ezekiel upon foreign peoples, as heathendom generally in its close coming into regard for Israel's destruction. From this point of view, the ביום ההוא certainly connects itself with the moment of the fulfilment through Nebuchadnezzar; but it at the same time conducts farther, expands this day to "an ideal day" (HENGST.)—the day of the Lord (ch. xxx. 3)—to the Messianic time, as Ewald has properly recognised. [SCHMIEDER: "every annihilation of a national power, which bent itself against the Lord, is to the prophet a type of all human power which rises against God—a type of the world's judgment. Therefore also the promises, which were given Israel for the last time, connect themselves therewith, and now revive again."] According to Hitzig, the attack upon Egypt was to Ezekiel the pledge of the then also beginning salvation announced in ch. xx. 40 sq., xvii. 22, xvi. 60.—צמח, used of gradual growth out of small beginnings and constant burstings forth again, new shoots, with reference to the צמח in Jeremiah and Zechariah.—**The horn,** as very commonly derived from horned beasts, in particular the bull, a biblical expression for strength, and the courage resting thereon; not so properly with reference to pushing (HENGST.), for which the context affords no occasion; as in contrast to the impotence of Egypt (heathendom), the power and pomp of the flesh—therefore another sense of power, the consciousness of the victory which overcomes the world. Ps. lxxv. 5, cxxxii. 17; Lam. ii. 3; Luke i. 69; comp. also 1 Sam. ii. 1 with respect to the following פתחון־פה.—**The opening of the mouth** points expressly to ch. xxiv. 26. (See there.) What was said in that place upon the symbolical import of the dumbness of the prophet determines also his speaking here in the midst of Israel as a prophetical one. Only, "the house of Israel" must not be resolved into the community of the Lord, and the mouth of Ezekiel into the word of prophecy, agreeably to Joel iii., as Theodoret already explained the matter; but we have to cleave to the second chief part of the predictions of our prophet, for which the opening of his mouth to Israel is, according to ch. xxiv. 26 sq., the characteristic, in contradistinction to the first main portion of his book. But in so far will such opening of Ezekiel's mouth have place as his prophecy of the compassions of God shall then have found their confirmation.

CHAPTER XXX.

1, 2 And the word of Jehovah came to me, saying, Son of man, prophesy and
3 say, Thus saith the Lord Jehovah, Howl! alas for the day! For near is the
day, and [indeed] near is the day of Jehovah, a day of cloud; a time of the
4 heathen nations shall it be. And the sword comes into Egypt, and there is
anguish in Cush at the fall of the pierced-through in Egypt; and they take
5 his tumult, and his foundations are pulled down. Cush, and Phut, and
Lud, and all the strange people, and Kub, and the sons of the covenant-land,
6 shall fall with them by the sword. Thus saith Jehovah, And they that

uphold Egypt fall; and the pride of his strength comes down: from Migdol
to Syene shall they fall in him by the sword, sentence of the Lord Jehovah.
7 And they shall be desolate in the midst of the desolate lands, and his cities
8 shall be in the midst of the wasted cities. And they know that I am Jehovah,
9 when I give a fire in Egypt, and all his helpers shall be shattered. In that
day shall messengers go forth from before Me in ships, to frighten Cush the
secure, and there is anguish among them, as in the day of Egypt; for,
10 behold, it comes. Thus saith the Lord Jehovah, And I make the tumult of
11 Egypt to cease through the hand of Nebuchadnezzar king of Babylon. He
and his people with him, the violent of the heathen, are brought to destroy
the land, and they draw their swords upon Egypt, and fill the land with the
12 pierced-through. And I give [make] the streams for drought, and sell the land
into the hand of the wicked, and lay the land and its fulness waste by the hand
13 of strangers: I, Jehovah, have spoken. Thus saith the Lord Jehovah, And
I destroy the foul idols, and make the idols to cease out of Noph; and there
shall be no more a prince out of the land of Egypt: and I give fear in the
14 land of Egypt. And I make Pathros desolate, and give fire in Zoan, and do
15 judgment in [on] No. And I pour out My fury upon Sin, the stronghold of
16 Egypt; and cut off the tumult of No. And I give fire in Egypt: Sin shall
writhe [for pain], and No shall be for conquest [broken], and Noph—besiegers
17 [have] by day. The young men of Aven and Pi-beseth shall fall by the sword,
18 and they [these cities] shall go into captivity. And in Tehaphnehes the day
shall be dark, in that [when] I break there the yokes of Egypt, and the pride
of its strength ceases in it: a cloud shall cover it, and its daughters shall go
19 into captivity. And I do judgment in Egypt, and they know that I am
Jehovah.

20 And it came to pass in the eleventh year, in the first [month], on the seventh
21 of the month, the word of Jehovah came to me, saying, Son of man, the
arm of Pharaoh, the king of Egypt, I have broken; and, behold, it is not
bound up, that one might apply healings [means of healing], that one might lay
on a fillet to bind it, that it may become strong, that it may take hold of the
22 sword. Therefore thus saith the Lord Jehovah, Behold, I [come] on Pharaoh,
the king of Egypt, and I break his arms, the strong and the broken, and make
23 the sword fall out of his hand. And I scatter Egypt among the heathen, and
24 disperse them in the lands. And I strengthen the arms of the king of
Babylon, and give My sword into his hand, and shatter the army of Pharaoh,
25 and he groans the groans of the pierced-through before him. And [yea] I take
firm hold of [hold strong] the arms of the king of Babylon, and the arms of
Pharaoh shall fall; and they know that I am Jehovah, in that I give My
sword into the hand of the king of Babylon, and he stretches it out against
26 the land of Egypt. And I scatter Egypt among the heathen, and disperse
them in the lands; and they know that I am Jehovah.

Ver. 2. Sept.: . . . ὠ ὠ ἡ ἡμερα, (3) ὁτι—Vulg.: . . . *væ, væ diei!*

Ver. 4. . . . και πεσουνται . . . το πληθος αὐτης κ. συμπεσειται τα—

Ver. 5. Sept.: Περσαι κ. Κρητες κ. Λυδοι κ. Λιβυες κ. παντες οἱ ἐπιμικτοι ἐπ' αὐτην . . . διαθηκης μου ἐν αὐτῃ μαχαιρᾳ—Vulg.: *Aethiopia et Libya et Lydi et omne reliquum vulgus* (Another read: וכנוב; Arab: *Nubienses.*)

Ver. 6. Vulg.: *superbia imperii ejus: a turre Syenes—*

Ver. 9. . . . ἀγγελοι σπευδοντες ἀφανισαι . . . ἐν τῃ ἡμερᾳ—(Another read.: ביום, Syr., Ar., Targ., Vulg.)

Ver. 11. αὐτου κ. του λαου αὐτου. Λοιμοι ἀπο ἐθνων—Vulg.: . . . *fortissimi—*

Ver. 13. . . . κ. καταπαυσω μεγιστανας ἀπο Μεμφεως κ. ἀρχοντας Τανεως ἐκ γης Αἰγυπ. κ. οὐκ ἐσονται οὐκετι—

Ver. 14. Sept.: . . . ἐκδικησιν ἐν Διοσπολει. Vulg.: . . . *in Alexandria.*

Ver. 15. . . . ἐπι Σαϊν . . . το πληθος Μεμφεως : . . *Pelusium . . . multitudinem Alexandriæ.* (Another read: מעון.)

Ver. 16. Συηνη . . . κ. ἐν Διοσπολει ἐσται ἐκρηγμα κ. διαχυθησεται ὑδατα. Vulg.: . . . *quasi parturiens dolebit Pelusium et Alexandria erit dissipata et in Memphis angustiæ quotidianæ.*

Ver. 17. . . . Ἡλιουπολεως . . . κ. αἱ γυναικες—*et ipsæ captivæ—*

Ver. 18. . . . ἐν Ταφναις . . . τα σκηπτρα Αιγ.—

Ver. 21. Vulg.: . . . *non est obvolutum ut restitueretur ei sanitas—*

Ver. 22. Sept.: . . . κ. τους τεταμενους κ. τ. συντριβομενους—

Ver. 24. . . . και ἐπαξει αὐτην ἐπ' Αἰγ. κ. προνομευσει την προνομην αὐτης κ. σκυλευσει τα σκυλα αὐτης.

Ver. 26. . . . ἐπιγνωσονται παντες οἱ Αἰγυπτιοι—

EXEGETICAL REMARKS.

Vers. 1-19. *The Day of Judgment.*

As this section is without any chronological preface, this may be understood if it justifies its place by the fit position of its contents. Thus the **day in ver. 2** appears as the **time of the heathen nations** in ver. 3; hence it is quite suitable as an appendix to the outline of the prophecy taken as a whole (ch. xxix. 1 sq.). So, too, the sword coming upon Egypt (ver. 4) is more definitely indicated in ver. 10 sq., as through the hand of Nebuchadnezzar, and so ver. 20 sq. is prepared for. Not that "the naked thought expressed in the introduction to the prophecy (ch. xxix. 17–21), of the great catastrophe hanging over Egypt, assumes flesh and blood in the main body of the prophecy (ch. xxx. 1-19)," as Hengst. expresses himself; but the prophecy upon Egypt in ch. xxix. 1–16, primarily coloured by its reference to Israel, is now again coloured by the respect had to the heathen, in particular to the Egyptian covenant-associates.

Ver. 2. **Howl**, Isa. xiii. 6 (ילל, to sound). The sound is expressed by הָהּ,—like אֲהָהּ (ch. iv. 14), especially with לַיּוֹם,—in the word-sound. The **day**, therefore the time, when that takes place which is contained in ver. 4 sq., gives the reference (לְ) of the mournful howl. The persons addressed will presently become plain.—Ver. 3. Why they were called to howling had its ground in the *nearness* (ch. vii. 7), which, however, has no chronological determination, except in the very near approach of the day. This is primarily designated as יוֹם לַיהוה, *i.e.* the one proper to the Lord, His day in particular, not only determined, fixed by Him; also not that alone which comes from Him; but, as the standing formula: "And they know that I am Jehovah," readily suggests, **the day of the manifestation of Jehovah**. It is, as the comparison with Obad. 15, Joel i. 15, Isa. xiii. 6–9, Zeph. i. 7, 14, shows, the becoming manifest in judgment. (Klief.: judgment, punishment, slaughter-day.) With this also agrees the designation of it as "a day of cloud;" comp. ch. i. 4. The symbolical import is obvious, since, when the clear light of day comes to be veiled, there is a threatening of storm (ver. 18, ch. xxxiv. 12; Joel i. 15, ii. 2; Zeph. i. 15); therefore one has to think of the wrath of God, and, in consequence thereof, a calamity which will break forth. Accordingly, עת גוים יהיה (without article) is self-determined, as meaning the *time when heathen nations*—they, consequently, are the parties addressed in ver. 2, spoken of generally as contradistinguished merely from Israel, but more definitely indicated in what follows—*shall experience their judgment;* not precisely "their end" (as Hitzig), but Jehovah's manifestation in the judgment of wrath pregnant with calamity to them. Comp. besides, ch. xxii. 3; Isa. ii. 12. [Not "identical with the day of Egypt, ver. 9," as Hengst. thinks, however similar, for the heathen were not simply the Egyptians. But still less, with Vatabl., Münst., and others, are we to think of the Chaldeans as executors of the judgment.]

Ver. 4. The way and manner of the predicted judgment is here represented: **the sword comes; and the heathen peoples, who are addressed in** ver. 2, are now named, viz. **Egypt**, in which war or bloody uproar so frightfully raged, that **in Ethiopia** the impression made by it was חַלְחָלָה, the corporeal state of convulsive writhing, for: anguish, terror, and woe. Nah. ii. 11 [10]; Isa. xxi. 3.—Upon כּוּשׁ, see the Lexicons.—Hitzig: חלל alludes to חַלְחָלָה.—The subject to: **and they take**, is naturally: the enemies, considered indefinitely.—הֲמוֹנָהּ, see at ch. xxix. 19. Hengst.: "this is here the prosperity of Egypt bringing with it active life."—יְסוֹדוֹת, the **foundations**, figuratively of the state as a house, not to be understood literally of the Egyptian chief cities. The figure, however, must not be limited (as שָׁתוֹת in Isa. xix. 10) to the higher classes, who bear immediately the state-building: nor must it (as Hitzig) be understood of the mercenaries, who only support Egypt (vers. 5, 6), and could hardly be represented as the foundations of its existence as a state. The representation must undoubtedly be (as well remarked by Hupfeld on Ps. xi. 3) of that which bears the civic society and holds it up—ordinances and laws; so that, if formerly it was the *well*-being of Egypt which was concerned, it is now the *being*, the very existence of it.

Ver. 5. **Ethiopia**, as already at ver. 4, *instar omnium*, named as the neighbour and political associate of Egypt, opens the array of Egypt's supporters (ver. 6). Upon **Phut** and **Lud**, see at ch. xxvii. 10.—עֶרֶב is: "joining-in," "mixing," "immigration," therefore: **strange people**; scarcely (as the Syrian translates) could "all Arabia" be meant. Ex. xii. 38; 1 Kings x. 15; Jer. xxv. 20, 24, l. 37; Neh. xiii. 3. Häv. distinguishes these from the covenant-associates of Egypt. But what else could Cush be?—**Kub**, only here, is by some regarded as written instead of לוּב, which Ewald reads, though he translates Nubia; while Kliefoth thinks of the Lubim in Nah. iii. 9, 2 Chron. xvi. 8, the Libyægyptii of the ancients; or taken instead of נוּב, so Gesenius and the Arab. translation, "Nubians;' and Hitzig also supposes לוּב to have been the older Heb. form for Nubia (?);—by others it has been understood (Häv.) of a people *Kufa* frequently occurring on the monuments of Egypt—according to Wilkinson, an important Asiatic people lying farther north than Palestine, with long hair, richly clothed, and with parti-coloured sandals; the tribute which they are represented as bringing bespeaks not a little of wealth, civilisation, and skill. **Hengst.** combines Kub with ch. xxvii. 10, and makes it correspond to the Persians, who had entered in consequence of the coalition into the service of Tyre, and whose appearance here cannot be thought strange; everywhere where there was a struggle against the tyrants, mercenaries were to be found of this powerful aspiring people. The name was a domestic one—"Kufa" in old Persian = mountain; the particular region, as appears to Hitzig, to be sought in Kohistan.—**The sons of the covenant-land** are understood by Jerome, Theodoret, the Sept., the Arab. trans., also by Hitzig, of the Jews who had taken refuge in Egypt (Jer. xlii.–xliv.); the covenant-land (with the article), that promised to Abraham and his seed according to God's covenant, is Canaan. The Syriac translation, on the other hand, points to the associate in the league, which the expression certainly does not clearly justify. Hence Hengst., understanding by the covenant-land Cush, makes the beginning turn back to the close; while Schmieder, with whom Kliefoth agrees, conjectures a tract of land unknown to us, but near to Egypt, and in a state of league with it (!).

Ver. 6. ונפלו סמכי', either as Ewald: "there fall Egypt's supporters"; or, after it has been said in ver. 5 that the anguish in Cush shall become a falling with Egypt, there is in ver. 6 a more comprehensive general statement: as well as, etc. [Hengst.: "a new break, new touches to be given to the picture."] Comp. Ps. xxxvii. 17, liv. 6 [4]. When the one party falls, the other sees itself necessitated to go down from its self-conscious height. On **pride**, etc., see at ch. xxiv. 21; comp. besides, ch. xxix. 10. They who shall fall **in him**, or it, are those who would support it. Too far removed are the idols and princes of ver. 13, which are brought in by Schmieder as the supporters; also the fortified cities in ver. 15, and the warriors in ver. 17.—Ver. 7. Comp. ch. xxix. 12. Where Egypt is the principal subject, there can be no question of its being so also here.—Ver. 8. The practical knowledge of experience is made in the **fire**, which Jehovah causes in Egypt, that is, at the breaking forth of His anger, with which also most fitly suits: **and they shall be shattered**, etc., so that they must know the judgment of God to be upon them. According to others, the war-fire; according to the Chald. paraph., a people violent as fire; according to Cocceius, it must mean the consuming, desolating result of the war.—All the **helpers** of Egypt are those who give support in ver. 6, both those who are named (ver. 5), and those who are not named.

Ver. 9. With manifest allusion to Isa. xviii., **messengers in ships** are made to announce to Ethiopia the fate of Egypt. (In Isa. it is papyrus-skiffs, which people were wont to roll together when they passed the cataracts of the Nile, and then open out again. The צי here, from צוה, to set up, according to Häv. certainly with reference to the existing sea-force of Egypt: war-ships, which suits neither with fugitives nor with messengers.) The business-mart and commerce on the boundaries of Upper Egypt and Ethiopia readily provide the image of such messengers at command,—represented as going forth **from before** Jehovah sitting in judgment upon Egypt,—so that one does not need to think either of the Chaldeans, or of Egyptian messengers formally sent by the Egyptians, or of Egyptian fugitives. —Since there is חלחלה בכוש, according to ver. 4, so this is only explained here by להחריד את־כ'; hence also והיתה חלחלה is repeated; therefore not a joyful message, as in Isa. xviii. with reference to Assyria.—כיום, *either*, a definite fixing of time (Isa. xxiii. 5), as also ביום is read, but which would plainly be a repetition of ביום ההוא; *or*, better perhaps, with Häv., pointing to that old period of punishment in the history of Egypt which filled neighbouring regions with dread of Jehovah (Ex. xv. 14 sq.).—Ch. vii. 5, 6, 10, xxi. 12. The coming is that which had been threatened, to be supplied from the context.—Ver. 10. Comp. ch. xxvi. 13.—Ch. xxix. 19.—The **tumult** comprehends as well the dense population characteristic of Egypt, as the moving of goods and chattels hither and thither. Kliefoth: "the turmoil of the people in the possession and enjoyment of their goods."—The **hand** of the Judge, His instrument and executioner, is to be **Nebuchadnezzar** (comp. at ch. xxvi. 7).—Ver. 11. Ch. xxviii. 7.—xxiii. 42. Hengst.: "they come not of themselves, but the Almighty brings them, hence they are irresistible," etc.—The destruction of the land by the sword is more nearly given, since it is represented as being filled with the slain. Comp. ch. xii. 14, xi. 6.—Ver. 12. Ch. xxv. 5, xxix. 10, 3. The destruction of its prosperity, since its natural springs and the land become the property of others, like a slave that has been sold by his master. Hitzig: "God assists the instruments of His will, taking an immediate part in the work of destruction, and, at the same time, displacing a hindrance to their advance and a bulwark of the Egyptians."—Since רעים is parallel with זרים, the **wicked** can only be interpreted from the feeling of the Egyptians, and in accordance with the hurtful action of the **strangers**, as רעע is to beat down, to destroy. The general wickedness of mankind (Matt. vii. 11) lies here as far out of the way as a special application to the Chaldeans, as being also not better than the Egyptians. Comp. however, ch. vii. 24, xxviii. 7.

Ver. 13. A carrying out of the judgment by special traits, which for Egypt especially are characteristic. Thus, as regards the גלולים (see at ch. vi. 4), the אלילים (chiming with the "nothings"), Lev. xix. 4, xxvi. 1, and often (1 Cor. viii. 4), so that there is no need for supplying from Isa. xix. 1; they are neither the images of the gods, nor the worshippers of them (as the Chald. paraph.): it is simply the idol-gods.—**From Noph** (מנף, sometimes also מף), that is, from Memphis; to-day, unimportant ruins on the western side of the Nile. The name in Plutarch is explained as ὁρμον ἀγαθων, and as ταφον 'Οσιριδος; in hieroglyphics, "Mam-Phtah"; that is, the place of Vulcan. The lower valley of the river honoured as the highest god Phtah (fire-god), the oldest and first of the gods, according to Manetho, ruling 9000 years before the others, as he is named in the inscriptions: "the father of the fathers of the gods," "the heavenly ruler," "the lord of the gracious countenance," "the king of both worlds," "the lord (the father) of truth." As god of the beginning, he has the form of a naked child, of a dwarf; at other times wrapped round mummy-like, standing by a rod, with a flagellum and mace and the Nilometer in his hand. As he was called Tatamen (the former), as world-creator, so he commonly has before him an egg upon a potter's wheel ("the weaver of the beginnings moving the egg of the sun and moon"). The Egyptian scarabæus (beetle) was sacred to him, which was sometimes shown upon his shoulders in the place of a head. His great sanctuary at Memphis, which was said to have been as old as Egypt itself, was adorned and extended by the Pharaohs down to the overthrow of the kingdom. Cambyses, when admitted into this temple, exhibited his disdain toward the image of the god.—Since Memphis was at the same time the old royal **city**, the transition from the service of idols to the נָשִׂיא was natural, especially as the connection of the gods and kings is genuinely Egyptian. Comp. on ch. xxix. The history of Egypt is that of its gods, and the names and deeds of its kings, as they are painted upon the walls of its temples. —That there was to be no more a native prince is not necessarily said with 'מאר, but only that as prince there should no more be one like the old Pharaohs and the Egyptian gods, out of Egypt, as contradistinguished from other lands, whose princely power would, as hitherto has been the case, obtain legitimation. Therewith also agrees the **fear**, which seems to point to a foreign ascendency that was to carry it over all.

Ver. 14. From Lower to Upper Egypt, the description gives prominence especially to the mother-land (see on ch. xxix. 14), the birth-land of the people.—Comp. ver. 8.—**Zoan**, however, is, again, in Lower Egypt, the old Tanis, on the branch of the Nile which bears that name ("Dschane," Egyptian: low ground),—a chief city, Num. xiii. 22; Ps. lxxviii. 12, 43.—Ch. v. 10.—**No** (נא) leads back to Upper Egypt; when fully read No-Amon, it is Thebes (Vulg., anticipating, Alexandria), the very ancient Upper Egyptian chief city, with the Greeks Diospolis. ("Noh," Egyp.: surveyor's chain; hence: inheritance; therefore: seat of Amon—see GESEN. *Lex.*) In the Upper land there reigned as divinity Amun (Amen), probably = "the concealed," the reigning god in the height, whose colour is blue on the monuments. He was for Upper Egypt what Phtah was for Lower Egypt. He is represented as standing, or sitting enthroned, with two high feathers upon his kingly head-dress. According to Manetho, the union of Egypt under a great dominion was effected by Menes from This, below Thebes, therefore proceeding from the Upper land—although this state-life had its centre in Memphis, in the Lower land; and during its flourishing period, another dominion, the territory of which stretched beyond the cataracts of Syene, had been founded at Thebes. Princes of Thebes afterwards ruled over all Egypt, took their seat at Memphis, and the kings of Egypt were now called "Lords of both Lands" in the inscriptions. Upon the monuments the red higher crown is that of Upper Egypt, the lower white one that of Lower Egypt. So that the prophetic representation takes into view the whole of Egypt, repeats Thebes for Upper Egypt, yet knows, at the same time, to mention names mostly from the more extensive, as well as more important and more powerful, Lower country.—Ver. 15. Ch. xiv. 19, xxi. 36 [31], ix. 8, vii. 8.—סִין, the "mud-city," Pelusium (πηλος), a border city on the east, in a swampy region, which the sea now overflows. Egypt, according to Strabo, was here difficult to be attacked, and Suidas designates Pelusium the key of Egypt for ingress and egress.—מָעוֹן, ch. xxiv. 25.—וְהִכְרַתִּי, ch. xxix. 8.—אֶת־הֲמוֹן נֹא (ver. 10), comp. ver. 14. An allusion undoubtedly to Amon, whence No derived its surname (Jer. xlvi. 25). Amon is incapable of preserving to the city its *Hamon* (**tumult**), HENGST. The mention of the multitude of people in No Hitzig finds to be suitable, since the population of the Thebaid crowded principally into the far-extending chief city. (Comp. *Iliad*, ix. 381 sq.) —Ver. 16, vers. 8, 14.—Instead of: תָּחִיל, the Qeri has: תָּחוּל, from חול, whence חַלְחָלָה in vers. 4, 9.—The repeated mention of Sin, No, and Noph gives emphasis to the boundaries, Upper and Lower Egypt.—תהיה להבקע = תִּבָּקַע, in ch. xxvi. 10.—צָרֵי יוֹמָם is clear so far, as צור is plainly to be understood of a pressing, closing-in siege; on the other hand, יומם may signify **by day**, as in the well-known juxtaposition with ולילה, but also what this juxtaposition paraphrastically expresses, namely: *always*, unceasingly, therefore: *daily* = כל־יום, or "the day over," also "the whole day long" = כל־היום (comp. Ps. xiii. 3 [2]). [Michlal Zophi interprets: "and against Noph come the enemies of day," that is, openly, not as thieves of the night. Similarly Hitzig: "enemies will be in broad daylight," meaning that it will be filled by them. KLIEFOTH: of the enemy not fearing an open assault. Also Hengst., who, from Jer. xv. 8 and Zeph. ii. 4, understands it of a state of deep humiliation, in which the enemy disdains, in the consciousness of his absolute superiority, to surprise by night (Obad. 5). "Enemies (besiegers) by day, a concise expression for: such an one as has to deal with enemies by day."]—It might be also an affecting exclamation. [Abendana (after Job iii. 5) = their day will be distress (VULG.). The Chaldee paraphrase: enemies compass her daily. Peculiar are the renderings of the Sept. and of the Arabic, which understand it of a breaking down of the Nile dams, and a rushing in of the waters; the Syriac: "will give way into fragments." EWALD: Memphis will be for perpetual rust (צְדִי)! HÄV.: Memphis shall become a constant splitting, that is, shall be for ever shattered; it shall now be, in a manner, called צרי יומם, in allusion to the local name of Memphis, מצור!]

Ver. 17. בַּחוּרֵי, the choice young men of war (Mark xiv. 51); rightly HITZIG: the garrison (warrior-caste), as contradistinguished from the inhabitants.—**Aven** (אָוֶן), the purpose in the change of the name אוֹן, אֹן, must, according to Hengst., point to the cause of the divine judgments which were coming on it (comp. Hos. iv. 15, x. 5). **Aven** is nothingness, vanity, with respect to the worship of idols. [HENGST.: "vileness," that people serve the creature more than the Creator.] It was the Greek Heliopolis, Jer. xliii. 13, "House of the Sun;" Kopt. On; Egyptian, Anu,—a city in Lower Egypt on the east bank of the Nile, and was from of old the proper seat of the Egyptian sun-worship; a centre of idolatry, with a numerous learned priesthood; the principal city in this respect, and that where Plato and Herodotus received instruction; mentioned in Gen. xli. 45, 50. Now there are only some ruins beside a village, with an obelisk seventy feet high of red granite. Here, in a famous temple, was Ra, the god of the solar disc, worshipped ("the father of the gods"), the second ruler of the world. His symbol was the sun's disc borne by two wings; the beasts sacred to him were the sparrow-hawk, the light-coloured **bull**, and the cat. From Ra, their original and type, the Pharaohs derived their power over Egypt, as "sons of Ra," the name given to them. See, besides, in Duncker, i. p. 39 sq.—**Pi-beseth**, only here; at present existing merely as ruins; Kopt.: Poubast, "the cat," on account of the goddess Pacht (Basht, Pascht), commonly represented with a cat's head, who was worshipped at Bubastis, in Lower Egypt, on the Pelusian branch of the Nile. (She was also named "the Mistress of Memphis," and also "Mother.") To her joyous service, according to Herodotus, was devoted the most pleasant of Egyptian temples. At her festival, to which men and women came in boats from all places, amid song, playing of flutes, clapping of hands, and striking of rattles, more wine was drunk than in all the rest of the year.—If the guardians, the protectors of the sanctuaries, fall by the sword, then also by the same must the gods themselves fall. Herodotus designates the Bubastic Nome as the region where especially resided the Calastrians, that is, the young recruits of the army. Comp. also vers. 5, 6, ch. vi. 11, 12. The וְהֵנָּה are not the women (SEPT.), but the cities named, their inhabitants (comp. ver. 18); see also ch. xii. 11.—Ver. 18. Not far from Sin comes the border city (toward Syria) תְּחַפְנְחֵס, Tehaphnehes, in Jeremiah (xliii. 9) תַּחְפַּנְחֵס, Tahpanhes, where, as we there learn, was a royal palace, Daphnoi (Taphne); the name, according to Jablonski, Egyptian: T'aphe-eneh, as much as, Land's End.—חשך היום, HENGST.: "the day spares, withholds as a miser." Therefore, from חָשַׂךְ, which in substance, however, is the same as: darkens itself; from חָשַׁךְ, to be darkened. There, for those of Israel who had fled thither (Jer. xliii. 7 sq., xliv. 1 sq.), the pre-intimations of the day of judgment begin (Kl.); or generally: there changes the prosperity and splendour of Egypt; according to others: there will be mourning. HÄV.: "here had Jeremiah spoken his powerful word of threatening against Egypt; here, through the settling down of the Jews at that time, the idea of Egyptian oppression toward Israel springs up afresh; and hence a calling to remembrance of Lev. xxvi. 13." Hengst. compares with "the breaking of the yokes of Egypt" ch. xxix. 15 and xxx. 13, "no prince," etc.; the yoke formerly lying upon Israel, latterly also upon other nations, was now to be for ever broken.—שָׁם refers to the border-place, with which the land opens, and with the broken land "the yokes" which Egypt had imposed, consequently its dominion (comp. vers. 21, 22, 24), should be broken. (UMBR.: "All order and discipline shall be dissolved in the ruled and strongly-curbed land: an end shall be made to its old renown and pride.")—בָּהּ, like גְּאוֹן עֻזָּהּ, is to be understood of the whole land. [Cocceius thinks of the death of the king with reference to the king's seat at Taphne (Jer. xliii. 9). Rosenm. reads מַטּוֹת, also Ewald and the Sept.; while Hitzig supposes to be meant, not the spears indeed (Hab. iii. 14; 2 Sam. xviii. 14), but the supporting staffs, ver. 6, which in ver. 8 are also represented as going to be broken.]—היא, not Daphnai, but Egypt, on which account it precedes emphatically; as also **her daughters**, namely, the cities, could only be referred to Egypt; if referred to Daphnai, too much would be said for it (ch. xvi. 27, 31, 46, xxvi. 6).—עָנָן (ver. 3). The Chaldee Paraphrast makes the cloud mean the host of the king of Babylon.—Ver. 19 concludes with Egypt generally.—Ver. 14.

Vers. 20-26. *Pharaoh and the King of Babylon.*

Ver. 20. As to the time, almost a quarter of a year later than ch. xxix. 1 sq.; KLIEFOTH: "in the second year of the siege of Jerusalem," as is clear also from ver. 21, after that Hophra had been defeated by the Chaldeans (Jer. xxxvii. 5, 7). (That ch. xxix. should contain no notice or allusion to the attempt of Pharaoh to bring help to Jerusalem, etc., may be controverted from what is said there in ver. 6.) HENGST.: about three months later followed the conquest of Jerusalem (Jer. xxxix. 2). As at ch. xxix., so also here, the look of the exiled toward Egypt is to be turned back from it.—Ver. 21. זְרוֹעַ is certainly for the most part the forearm, as here also the expression "to hold the sword" proves, and so help, too, assistance, is expressed by it; so that, with Häv., Ewald, and others, one might think of the Egyptian attempt for the relief of Jerusalem: on the other hand, however, Hengst. is right when he explains the breaking of the arm of Pharaoh of a "great overthrow," such as was only to be found in the well-known disaster at Carchemish, seventeen years before our prophecy, as this battle, in fact, destroyed the power of Pharaoh to make war, struck his might with a blow (comp. Jer. xlvi.); while what respects the retreat of the Egyptians from Jerusalem, which became a matter of necessity to them, is nowhere reported. So that, as Hitzig in particular recognises, from the manifest contrariety of ver. 22, which announces the future, שברתי is a full preterite, and presupposes a longer interval in connection with the indication of time in ver. 20 than could be the case with that retreat before Nebuchadnezzar, if this should have to be thought of generally as a thing already accomplished. Hengst. remarks: "After it (*i.e.* the retreat of the Egyptians from Carchemish) our prophecy would have been unnecessary; it must have been delivered at a time when, humanly speaking, there was hope from the Egyptians."—וְהִנֵּה, having respect to the existing state of Egypt since the battle of Carchemish, introduces the following description, in which "the binding" forms the principal statement on which the infinitives are dependent. **Bound up** is the first, the most immediate thing which has to be done after wounding, and the intention or aim thereof is to apply the **means of healing** (cures); in particular, since the chief means consist in the band which holds together the broken parts, that a bandage be applied (לחבשה resumes חבשה again) so that the arm be strengthened, and, as the consequence, be again rendered capable of "taking hold of the sword."—Ver. 22. **Therefore** refers to the foregoing principal announcement, that Pharaoh's might is broken without the prospect of restoration, and accordingly what is farther impending can only be a complete overthrow; and this is introduced by הנני, a parallel to ver. 21, and then summarily pronounced (זרעתיו).—The **strong** (החזקה, with a reference to לחזקה in ver. 21) signifies: what still existed unbroken as to power in Egypt, particularly in the land itself; the **broken** (ver. 21), that which must still be broken, with allusion to the shattering at Carchemish; especially the impotent attempt to turn aside to the help of Jerusalem, which must therefore be thought of as still in immediate prospect. [Cocc. explains the two arms of Hophra, and the small Egyptian kingdom which followed. They have been also explained of the supremacy over Syria and that over Egypt.] —The might, power, and dominion of Pharaoh are to become incapable of attack and resistance.

Ver. 23. Comp. ver. 26, ch. xxix. 12, xxii. 15. —Ver. 24. וְחִזַּקְתִּי, Piel (strengthening; anyhow, still another חזק than is to be supposed in the לחזקה of ver. 21); for the **sword** also is not that which has fallen out of the hand of Pharaoh, but Jehovah's, whence the following explains itself, and at the same time what is said in ver. 22.—לְפָנָיו, before the king of Babylon, who and his arms, here and in ver. 25 placed in opposition to Pharaoh and his arms, are the antithesis which forms the substance of this section.—Ver. 25. וְהַחֲזַקְתִּי, Hiphil, for distinction in respect to the Piel in ver. 24, which, on account of the failing יָד, is explained by Hitzig, not through "seizing," but with a reference to Ex. xvii. 11, 12, and by way of contrast to תִּפֹּלְנָה through "holding upright," "holding above," so that he retains the upper hand. But the slight difference between "holding strong" and "strengthening," endowing with power, is of itself enough. Hengst. compares Gen. xlix. 24, in respect that the arms of the king of Egypt, left to his own impotence, sank down powerless.—Since the arms of both are named, the words: **and they know,** etc., may easily be referred thereto, but principally to the king of Babylon; yet also to the land of Egypt, against which the sword of judgment in the hand of that king was stretched out. אוֹתָהּ may be referred to יד, also to חרב.—Ver. 26. Repetition of ver. 23 at the close.

CHAPTER XXXI.

1 And it came to pass in the eleventh year, in the third [month], on the first of
2 the month, that the word of Jehovah came to me, saying: Son of man, say to
Pharaoh, the king of Egypt, and to his tumult, To whom art thou like in thy
3 greatness? Behold, Asshur [was] a cedar tree upon Lebanon, beautiful of foliage,
and a shadowing thicket, and high of stature, and between the clouds was his
4 top. Waters made him become great, the flood made him high, with its streams
it went round about its planting, and it sent forth its canals to all the trees of
5 the field. Therefore his stature became higher than all the trees of the field,
and his branches became many [great], and his foliage-branches [boughs] became
6 long, from many waters in his spreading himself forth. In his branches nested
all the fowls of heaven, and under his boughs every living thing of the field
7 brought forth, and in his shadow dwelt all the many nations. And he became
beautiful in his greatness, in the length of his twigs [shoots], for his root was on
8 many waters. Cedars darkened him not in the garden of God; cypresses were
not like his branches, and plane trees were not like his foliage-branches [boughs];
9 all wood in the garden of God was not like him in his beauty. Beautiful had I
made him in the multitude of his shoots; and all the trees of Eden, which were
10 in the garden of God, envied him.—Therefore, thus saith the Lord Jehovah,
Because thou becamest high in stature, and he gave his top even to between the
11 clouds, and his heart raised itself in his height; Therefore will I give him into
the hand of the mighty one of the heathen; he will do, do to him: in [on account of]
12 his wickedness I drove him out. And strangers hewed him down, the violent
ones of the heathen, and left him upon the mountains; and in all the valleys his
shoots fell, and his foliage-branches [boughs] were broken in all hollows of the
earth; and all the nations of the earth went down out of his shadow and left
13 him. On his ruins all the fowls of heaven alight, and on his boughs is every
14 living creature of the field. To the end that none of the trees of the waters
become lofty in their stature, nor give their top up between the clouds, and that
no drinkers of water should remain standing by themselves in their height; for
they are all given to death, to the underground, among the children of men, to
15 those who go down to the grave. Thus saith the Lord Jehovah, In the day of
his going down to hell [Sheol] I caused to mourn [I made a mourning]; I veiled on
account of him the flood, and stayed its streams, and there were many waters held
back; and I made Lebanon dark over him, and all the trees of the field sank in weak-
16 ness over him. At the sound of his fall I made the heathen quake, in that I made
him go down to hell with those that go down to the grave; and all the trees of Eden,

the choice and good of Lebanon, all drinkers of water, comforted themselves in the
17 underground. They also went down with him to hell, to be pierced through with
the sword, namely, those who, his arm, dwelt in his shadow among the heathen
18 nations. To whom, then, art thou like in glory and in greatness among the trees
of Eden? And thou art cast down with the trees of Eden to the underground;
in the midst of the uncircumcised shalt thou lie with those pierced through by
the sword. This is Pharaoh and all his tumult. Sentence of the Lord Jehovah.

Ver. 1. Sept.: *μια του μηνος—*
Ver. 2. . . . *ὡμοιωσας σεαυτον . . . ὑψει σου*; Vulg. . . . *similis factus es—*
Ver. 3. . . . *κυπαρισσος . . . ἐγενετο ἡ ἀρχη αὐτου.* Vulg. . . . *et inter condensas frondes—*
Ver. 4. . . . *κυκλω των φυτων αὐτου—fluinina ejus manabant in circuitu radicum ejus . . . ligna regionis.*
Ver. 5. Other readings גבהה, גבה.
Ver. 6. Vulg.: *Cumque extendisset umbram suam, in . . .* (Anoth. read.: יֵשְׁבוּ.)
Ver. 7. Sept.: . . . *ἐν τ. ὑψει αὐτου δια το πλ θος—*
Ver. 8. *Κυπαρισσοι τοιαυται οὐκ ἐγενηθησαν ἐν τ. παραδεισω τ. Θεου, κ. πιτυες*—Vulg.: *Cedri non . . . altiores . . . abietes non adæquaverunt summitatem ejus*—(Another read.: כפארתיו, or with ב.)
Ver. 9. Sept.: *δια τ. πληθος τ. κλαδων αὐτου.* K. *ἐζηλωσαν . . . της τρυφης τ. Θεου.* Vulg.: *quoniam speciosum feci . . . et multis condensisque frondibus . . . omnia ligna voluptatis—*
Ver. 10. . . . *ἐδωκας τ. ἀρχην σου . . . κ. εἰδον ἐν τω ὑψωθηναι αὐτον.* Vulg.: . . . *sublimatus est . . . summitatem suam virentem atque condensam.*
Ver. 11. *κ. παρεδωκα αὐτον . . . ἀρχοντος ἐθνων, κ. ἐποιησεν τ. ἀπωλειαν αὐτου.* (Other read: כרשעו איל.)
Ver. 14. Vulg.: *Quam ob rem non elevabuntur . . . inter nemorosa atque frondosa.* (Other read.: אֲלֵיהֶם, *fortes eorum: sibi, super se,* עליהם. For אל יורדי, there is a reading את י׳.)
Ver. 15. Sept.: . . . *ἀδου, ἐπεστησα ἐπ' αὐτον τ. ἀβυσσον—induxi luctum, operui eum abysso*—(Anoth. read.: וכל חית.)
Ver. 16. . . . *εἰς λακκον.* K. *παρεκαλουν αὐτον . . . τ. ξυλα της τρυφης κ. τ. ἐκλεκτα—qui descendebant in lacum. Et consolata sunt . . . ligna voluptatis egregia et præclara—*
Ver. 17. . . . *ἐν τραυματιαις μαχαιρας, κ. το σπερμα αὐτου παντες οἱ . . . ἐν μεσω τ. ζωης αὐτων ἀπωλοντο. Nam et . . . descendent . . . et brachium uniuscujusque sedebit sub*—(Another read.: יֵשְׁבוּ, יָרְדוּ.)
Ver. 18. . . . *ὡμοιωθης; Καταβηθι κ. καταβιβασθητι . . . ξυλων της τρυφης . . . κ παν τ. πληθος της ἰσχυος αὐτου—Cui assimilatus es, O inclyte atque sublimis inter ligna voluptatis? Ecce . . . cum lignis voluptatis—*

EXEGETICAL REMARKS.

Egypt (Pharaoh) and Assyria.

The whole chapter is taken up with this prophetical allegory, which the indication of time in ver. 1 places not quite two months later than ch. xxx. 20 sq. (SCHMIEDER: therefore one month and eight days before the conquest of Jerusalem). In accordance with the antithesis there, a highly poetical parallel now follows, which might work in a more powerful manner upon hearers and readers, as it was taken from the still fresh experience of his contemporaries; for in 606 Nineveh had been laid prostrate by the combined attack of the Babylonians and Medes, and the kingdom which had domineered in Asia above five centuries had reached its end. The year after that was the year of the battle at Carchemish; and thus had the fate of Assyria become palpable shortly before the calamity which was threatening Egypt. Comp. besides the juxtaposition of Assyria and Egypt elsewhere, Isa. vii. 18, xxvii. 13; Jer. ii. 36; Hos. xii. 2 [1]; Zech. x. 10.

Ver. 2. The commencement is made properly by the question which is addressed to Pharaoh and his tumult (הָמוֹן, see at ch. xxx. 10, xxix. 19), in the answer to which the prophet sets forth a prognostication for himself and his people. HENGST.: "The matter has respect not to an opinion, but to a real resemblance." Hitzig limits the reference to the "official Egypt," being that "which made tumultuous noise in the land, which had something to say and to order; the governing classes and ranks (Isa. iii. 2, 3), in contrast to the quiet people in the land (Ps. xxxv. 20), who keep silence and obey." According to Schmieder, the question calls for the answer: No one! "Thou art incomparable, alone of thy kind. This was also the feeling of Pharaoh Hophra. But Ezekiel," etc.—גֹּדֶל (along with כבוד in ver. 18), not = "strength," but also not precisely: fancied greatness, huge self-elation (RASCHI), as at Isa. x. 12 of Assyria, for Egypt's very ancient culture already gave him still a real precedence, and in other respects also placed him before Assyria.

Vers. 3–9. *Assyria's Glory.*

Ver. 3. **Behold,** a call to attention, introducing the answer which the divine word has to give. HENGST.: "the future in a historical dress, as at ch. xix. the history of Jehoahaz and Jehoiachim."—אַשּׁוּר (comp. ch. xxvii. 6) is taken by Ewald for a definite kind of cedar, the highest of its kind; against which compare the convincing proof of Hitzig. Häv. also justly remarks against the construction of the word as an adjective, that the most distinguished characteristic for a cedar tree is the accompanying designation: **upon Lebanon**; comp. besides, ch. xvii. 3. It is a common image for people of great might, princes. The Sept. renders אֶרֶז by *κυπαρισσος*.—Because חֹרֶשׁ, "thickness," may signify a forest, Hengst. translates here (taking מצל as partic. Hiphil from צלל), "shading the forest" or wood. The representation is carried out farther by עֲנָף, as well as by **between the clouds,** etc.; also by קוֹמָה (from קום, "stature") גָּבַהּ.—Upon עֲבֹתִים, see at ch. xix. 11; on צַמֶּרֶת, comp. ch. xvii. 3.

Ver. 4. *Explanation of such growth.*—What is said of the **waters,** that they **made him become great,** fits too well to the image of the cedar for one to be able to get something still better by a reference to the description of paradise (as Häv.), or by bringing into account the situation of Nineveh, which was important for the history of Assyria, with the Tigris on the west, the Zabatos (Lykos) on the south, with its neighbouring stream Bumodus on the east, and the brook Khosr on the north.—Still more, **the flood** (not the rain: comp. Isa. xliv. 14) contributed to the prosperity. The designation, therefore, previously, of the Lebanon was *epitheton ornans.* תְּהוֹם is the water-treasure in the depths pouring itself forth in springs, etc. HITZIG: image of the multitude of men flowing together into Assyria, on the basis of which the political power rose. More correctly HENGST.: "the water and the flood denote what the world calls good fortune, the divine blessing."—אֶת־, either: *with*, or taken accusatively: *what concerns.*—Hence תהום is here kept feminine; the **streams** are those of the flood, and the masculine הֹלֵךְ, which is likewise to be referred to the flood, is justified after this manner, that תהום can also be used as a masculine; and the masculine in the present case, as Hengst. remarks, is the more suitable, being preceded by מים.—The **planting** (ch. xvii. 7) can scarcely be referred, with Hengst., through the fem. מַטָּעָהּ, to Assyria as a tree; but is conceived of with reference to the flood, whether it might be because this had a share in the prosperity spoken of, or, which the הלך סביבת recommends, because it streams around this cedar-planting, the place on which it grows. The תְּעָלוֹת, first coming into consideration in the second line, are to be understood of the overflowings of the water-fulness that rises up (עלה), just as the **all trees of the field** are distinguished from the cedar tree described; and this, in ver. 5, is raised into prominence over against them. Hengst. takes the subjects to be designated by the expression; Hitzig applies it to other lands and princes. Of the inhabitants of Egypt we are as little to think as, with Rosenmüller, of the Nile.—Ver. 5. עַל־כֵּן, from his overflow of water his greater height than all the trees finds its explanation, ch. xix. 11 (גבהא, Aram. for גבהה)—(סרעפה, Aram. for סעפה, with ר inserted).—פֹּארֹתָיו, under which must here especially be understood the fruit-bearing ones, ch. xvii. 6.—בְּשַׁלְּחוֹ, HENGST.: "because in his time of shooting he had many waters." [HÄV.: "at his sending forth, namely, the twigs on all sides." Tautology. Vulg. connects it with ver. 6.]

Ver. 6. Ch. xvii. 23. The closing words give the signification of the figure (Dan. iv. 9). "Bird" and "living thing," in contrast to domestic creatures, the Assyrians themselves. The imperfect יֵשְׁבוּ expresses, in contradistinction to the preceding perfects, the incomplete, the continuous, the progressive. [EWALD: "sat gladly all the many," etc.]—כל־גוים רבים, BUNSEN: all great peoples (?); KEIL: all sorts of great nations; ROSENM.: the entirety of many peoples.—Ver. 7. בְּ, through, on account of.—Ch. xvii. 6.—Ver. 8 carries still higher the preeminent glory brought prominently out in ver. 5, through the diversified comparison and the designation "in the garden of God," on which comp. xxviii. 12. That לֹא־עֲמָמֻהוּ (to "darken" = excel) separates this nearer designation from ארזים, is very impressive (HÄV.): even such as were found in paradise. HITZIG: "in an eminent sense, planted by God, Gen. ii. 9; Num. xxiv. 6." What still has not been expressed is more distinctly indicated in ver. 9, that what God had done to Assyria even transcended the trees of paradise, therefore the eminent divine planting was even more marked in the case of Assyria. The paradise-creation was, after all, only nature, symbolizing grace, consequently might be the similitude for a *state*-creation, without, however, being like the latter, as little as also the most glorious trees themselves. **Every tree,** namely in this, in a natural respect, so that the tree of life and the tree of knowledge (Gen. ii.), as being of a spiritual nature, are exempted, and the simply parabolical allusion to Eden and to the garden of paradise is clear. [Hengst. makes the totality of the great men of the earth as stately trees in the garden of God as a counterpart of paradise, since all human greatness has its origin in God. Klief. (Raschi) regards the garden of God directly as "the world-planting," since all peoples and kingdoms of the world have been planted as trees by God. GROT.: in Babylonia, where formerly paradise stood. OSIANDER: no king of the people of God was like him!]—["This parabolical representation, as formerly in the case of Tyre, ch. xxviii., combines the historical with the figurative. While the cedar that represents the king of Babylon is called a cedar of Lebanon, it is presently transferred in the prophet's imagination to the land of primeval beauty and perfection, the Eden in which was the garden that God had planted. There this cedar is described as growing and flourishing, till it overtopped in magnificence and beauty all the trees around it. . . . But it was only that it might afford another specimen of that instability and transitoriness which belong to all on earth, when the good bestowed by Heaven is abused to purposes of selfishness, and the creature begins to thrust himself into the place of his Creator."—P. F.]—Ver. 9. This "beauty" is here explained as having been made by God, as a historical creation-act (עשיתיו), and expresses, while at the same time bringing the similitude to a close, the impression which the striking elevation of the Assyrian grandeur was fitted to produce.—That **the trees of Eden,** as in the larger sense they are called (in respect to local position), should be designated as those which belonged to **the garden of God,** distinguishes them still more; it is an ascension. Kliefoth takes "trees of Eden" freely, as equivalent to "trees of beauty," lovely trees. That more is meant by the expression, while still paradise is thought of merely in the way of similitude, appears from ver. 16.

Vers. 10–14. *The Judgment executed on Assyria.*

Ver. 10. This verse transfers us into the midst of the things already in fact brought to pass. We might render כה אמר: thus said to him, etc.—לכן: He who made the Assyrian so beautiful, even He, announced to him the overthrow that should take place, because of what he made out of himself.—The whole passage expresses the cause of the judgment of Jehovah upon Assyria, namely, that with such a glory from God (vers. 5, 3) the position of the heart was not in correspondence; there was not humility in all the greatness, but high-mindedness on account of it. The commencing address, **Thou**, in the life-like character of the representation, becomes changed into a declaration respecting him—**and he.**—'וְרָם, Deut. viii. 14. Only in conformity with the gift, not in accordance with the grace. Comp. ver. 14.—Ver. 11. Here the sentence of judgment, as just going to be pronounced for the first time, is, by the use of the imperfect, placed more distinctly before us. HENGST: "which was the more suitable, as the like in Egypt was shortly to be repeated."—אֵל גּוֹיִם is Nebuchadnezzar, "the mighty" (אוּל), not God. [HITZIG: אַיִל, ram, for prince, champion, under which Cyaxares is to be thought of.]—What he will **do** to him discovers itself in what follows; it will be **nothing but doing**; for Asshur it remained merely to suffer. —גֵּרַשְׁתִּיהוּ, Piel, with reference to his paradisiacal glory (Gen. iii. 24). The perfect agrees with the quieter mode of speech.—Ver. 12. As what was said last has taken place, there is now by means of the historical tenses a narration; consequently the execution of the pronounced judgment carried out. (Others make it future, with application now to Egypt, now to Assyria.)—Ch. xxx. 12, 11.—נטשׁ is: "to let go," therefore either: to let him lie (HENGST.), or: to push away, to throw down (ch. xxix. 5). Throwing down is already indicated in the hewing, and is expressed through the "falling;" and on the other hand, "the leaving" is again resumed at the close, while it is extended to "all peoples." The "mountains" prepare for the "valleys," and the "falling," the "being broken" in all hollows (ch. vi. 3). Still, in its overthrow, the greatness as well as lofty elevation of this cedar tree is vividly displayed.—וַיֵּרְדוּ abides closely by the image, according to ver. 6, partly of birds which had nested in its branches, partly also of beasts which had brought forth under its boughs, which, according to ver. 12, had its place on the mountains, so that in both respects the "going down out of his shadow" is clear, and there is no need, with Hitzig, to read וַיִּדְּדוּ, from נדד, to fly, for which עַמִּים would otherwise present no obstacle; but here, as at ver. 6, the reality at the close breaks through the figure.

Ver. 13. If מִקּוֹל מַפַּלְתּוֹ in ver. 16 refers to עַל־מַפַּלְתּוֹ here (ch. xxvi. 15, 18, xxvii. 27), there is no necessity, with Raschi, Kimchi, and later expositors, to think of the substitution of the image of a corpse (carcase, Judg. xiv. 8), and of eagles, ravens, and other beasts of prey which rend and gnaw the members of Assyria, signified by his boughs (HITZIG); but מַפֶּלֶת, from נפל, is with Gesen. simply: the fallen or hewed-down stem, which is, as it were, a living ruin (HENGST.). —יִשְׁכְּנוּ, otherwise than at ch. xvii. 23, as is shown also by the immediately following **and on his boughs is;** since those who had nested and brought forth there (ver. 6) now betook themselves away from him, taking, perhaps, whatever they could of his fruit, reaping the greatest possible advantage from the mighty catastrophe.—Ver. 14, by way of conclusion, expresses the divine intention, the practical aim, the moral, and that with respect to Egypt. **To the end that** (since vers. 12, 13 may be regarded as parenthetical expansions) can be connected with ver. 11.—עֲצֵי־מַיִם signifies primarily: those standing on the waters, what afterwards is more nearly indicated by שֹׁתֵי מַיִם (שׁתה, just as Sanscr. "padapa," designating the tree as drinking with its foot, through its root): those which attain to height and glory from the position granted to them by God—of which description was Egypt, from its relation to the Nile (ch. xxix.). HENGST.: "the great of the earth, to whom God gives joyful prosperity."—Comp., on ver. 10. As there: "and his heart raised itself," etc., so it is said here: וְלֹא־יַעַמְדוּ אֲלֵיהֶם, therefore to be understood of self-assumption, as in Sept. אֵלֵיהֶם instead of אֱלֵיהֶם is no hindrance; as is also Keil's ultimate conclusion, since אֵלֵינוּ is common, and אֵלִימוֹ poetic, Ps. ii. 5.—[Other expositions: "and their strong ones do not continue in their high-mindedness all water-drinkers"; or, "and their oaks (terebinths, Isa. lxi. 3) do not stand there (remain standing) in their elevation, all," etc. ROSENMÜLLER: "and stand not to them, that is, *allied to them* in their height, where they had grown so high, all, namely, the other water-drinkers, that is, powerful and rich princes." KLIEF.: "and that henceforth among all their strong trees that drink water no one may remain in his height." EWALD: "and no water-drinkers assail (!!) their gods in their pride" (!), which he afterwards more particularly explains: So that trees, beings who might raise themselves ever so high, are still always dependent on their nourishment, and cannot live of themselves in a spirit of contempt toward their Creator, nor, again, arrogantly war with their superior (their Creators, gods), since they still are all destined to go down as common men to the lower world.] Comp. ch. xxvi. 20. They could give themselves nothing, since they themselves were given away, as such were already appointed; therefore also could not remain standing where they were standing, and assumed the airs of continuing to stand, but must go down to the lower world, therefore be brought low, be humiliated, though not before humble, come to stand on a footing with the children of men. The expression: **among the children of men,** is to be regarded as parallel with: **given to death**; and: **to those who go down to the grave,** with: **to the underground. Those that go down,** men continually dying, even the highest; or, "those that have gone down," as EWALD: those sunk into the grave.

Vers. 15–18. *The Impression and Close.*

As at ch. xxvi. 15 sq. Ver. 15. (רֶדֶת, inf. constr. of ירד.) The connection is made with what immediately precedes, so that the reference is not (as Hitzig) to ver. 13. Upon שְׁאוֹל, see

Doct. Reflect.—The "mourning" is immediately defined more nearly without כִּסֵּתִי being asyndetically joined to it, as HÄV., EWALD, HENGST.: "to cover with mourning," "to veil in mourning," "I made it veil itself for mourning." The mourning which Jehovah effects through His judgment upon Assyria touches primarily **the flood**, in thorough accord with ver. 4, as that which in the first line contributed to the cedar its increase. Therefore עָלָיו, "on his account." That the flood was covered upon him, as the Syriac, Arab., and Vulg., is at least not indicated in what precedes (ver. 12). Comp. on the contrary, ch. xxvi. 19. We must (it was thought) suppose a historical reference, since the siege of Nineveh was protracted to two years, while in the spring of the third year, in consequence of a sudden swell in the Tigris, raised by excessive falls of rain, the mighty flood in one night tore down the wall next the stream, and so laid open a wide breach to the enemy (Duncker, i. p. 806; Nah. i. 8, ii. 7 [6]). However, in this passage the discourse is not properly of the overthrow of Assyria in process of accomplishment,—ver. 15 giving no representation of the judgment itself, as Häv. maintains,—but of the impression of the same as one already accomplished; and כסה as "to veil" is, even without שַׂק, perfectly intelligible, but how it is meant in respect to the flood is made sufficiently plain by the וָאֶמְנַע (not future). HITZIG: "In mourning, people commonly draw themselves in and hold back, the loose garment is changed into the narrow שק; and so the flood also withdraws its waters into itself, which it had hitherto joyfully poured forth and spread abroad"—which Hitzig applies to the influx of people come to a standstill. Theodoret: to the refusal of tribute. Comp. on the figure, ver. 4. מַיִם רַבִּים points back to vers. 5, 6, 7.—The mourning produced by Jehovah next affects Lebanon (comp. ver. 3), therefore the height as well as the depth. אַקְדִּר עָלָיו, parallel with כסתי עליו, Hiphil from: to be "dark," "black," therefore: to darken, as much as: to make sad, to cause to mourn. **Lebanon** is otherwise the *white* mountain. [According to Hitzig, the other princes must be indicated by this; according to Hengst., the kingdoms of the heathen.]—**The trees of the field** (ver. 4) are the third party whom the mourning affects, which is therefore also represented as far and near. עֻלְּפֶה, in Pual, "to be covered;" transferred to the consciousness: to become powerless. עֻלְפֶּה has been explained as a verbal from Pual with derivative ה—, "languishing," or instead of עֻלְּפָה, fem. of the preterite Pual, since from the connection a perfect seems to be required (EWALD), the plural construed with the feminine singular.—Keil, as Umbreit, makes all nature (?) be painfully moved by Assyria's fall, whereas the impression of this fall is merely kept **in the figurative style** of vers. 3, 4.—Ver. 16. Ch. xxvi. 15. Since that is the same expression (מפלתו) as in ver. 13, and in ver. 15 his going down was spoken of, so we are carried back to ver. 12. The "going down of the peoples out of his shadow" in that passage is explained; at the same time, however, the רִדְתּוֹ of ver. 15 is comprised in the בְּהוֹרִדִי, and referred to the Sheol.—Now, according as וַיִּנָּחֲמוּ is translated "comforted themselves," as reflexive of Piel, since here still another feeling than in ver. 15 may be expressed; or the Niphal "and they sighed" is what is to be understood (EWALD, HENGST.), we have either a distinction between the lower world and the trembling people of the upper world, or the two are parallel the one to the other. For the first interpretation speaks the comparison of Isa. xiv. Hitzig understands by **the trees of Eden** princes carried down with Assyria; in particular the Assyrian war-princes, who feel themselves comforted because the much more powerful one for whose cause they have fallen, their murderer, shares their fate; while Hengst. more correctly understands by them the former great ones of the earth, those who resembled the trees of paradise in glory. As paradise was itself a thing of the past, those who were likened to the trees of its region were contemplated as now existing in the realms of the dead. The allegorical character of the expression is proved by the exegesis: **the choice and good.** Besides, comp. at ver. 14.—Ver. 17. **They also** are not those last named in ver. 16, but the parties presently going to be described more closely—already, indeed, indicated in ver. 16 as those with whom Jehovah made Assyria go down to hell (את, not אל, as in ver. 14). "And his arm" defines more exactly the "they also" as the subject of "the going down,"—his help, his assistant, the vassals, subject-kings, commanders, and such like, to whom the words: **who dwelt in his shadow among the heathen,** very well suit, and not less that they are associated with those pierced through with the sword. Assyria was not only a political, but also a military power among the nations. [If הֵם must apply to "all the trees of Eden" in ver. 16, so must "with him" be made equal to "not less than he," just as Hengst., looking away from simultaneousness, views them as already in Sheol when Assyria arrives there. Therefore: they also, like him, went down before, etc. Ewald reads with the Sept.: וְזַרְעוֹ, "and his seed" (!).]

Ver. 18. This verse gives the conclusion, pointing back to ver. 2; it makes the application to Pharaoh, who is the party addressed.—כָּכָה, Hitzig: "in such a fashion, in circumstances of such a kind," when this cedar after such a manner went down. The reference **among the trees** belongs to the **to whom.**—Comp. at ch. xxviii. 10. From this passage, also, there appears to emerge the opposite of what is commonly found in it, viz. that the Egyptians appear as uncircumcised with our prophet. According to Herodotus, the practice of circumcision was actually of Egyptian origin. Origen confines it to the priesthood among the Egyptians. The kings certainly were not uncircumcised; so the *vis* of our passage shines clearly out: **This is Pharaoh,** sq. HITZIG: so shall it **happen to Pharaoh.** הוּא is the predicate.

CHAPTER XXXII.

1 And it came to pass in the twelfth year, in the twelfth month, on the first
2 [day] of the month, the word of Jehovah came to me, saying: Son of man, take
up a lamentation over Pharaoh the king of Egypt, and say to him: Young lion
of the heathen peoples thou didst imagine thyself [thou didst compare thyself to such an one],
and thou [wast] as the dragon in the sea [in the seas], and brakest forth in thy streams,
and didst trouble the water with thy feet, and didst trample their streams!
3 Thus saith the Lord Jehovah, And I spread forth My net over thee in the
4 assembly of many peoples, and they pull thee up in My draw-net. And I set
thee free into the land [push thee away thither], upon the plains of the field will
I sling thee; and I make all the birds of heaven to sit down on thee, and let the
5 living creatures of the whole earth satisfy themselves with thee. And I give thy
6 flesh upon the mountains, and fill the valleys with thy high heap [thy height]. And
I cause the land of thy overflowing to drink out of thy blood, even to the moun-
7 tains; and the hollows shall be full of thee. And I cover [veil], while I extinguish
thee, the heaven, and darken its stars; the sun will I cover with a cloud, and the
8 moon will not make her light to shine. All luminaries of light in the heaven, I
will make them dark over thee; and I give darkness upon thy land: sentence of
9 the Lord Jehovah. And I vex the heart of many peoples, when I bring thy
breach [destruction] among the heathen peoples, to lands which thou knowest not.
10 And I make many peoples astonished over thee, and their kings shall shudder
shudderings over thee, when I brandish My sword before their face; and they
tremble every moment, each one for his soul [life], on the day of thy downfall.
11 For thus saith the Lord Jehovah: The sword of the king of Babylon will come
12 to thee. By the swords of heroes will I make thy tumult to fall; the violent of
the heathen [are] they all, and they lay waste the pride of Egypt, and all its
13 tumult is destroyed. And I extirpate all the beasts thereof from many [the great]
waters, and foot of man shall not trouble them any more, nor shall the hoofs of
14 beasts trouble them. Then will I make their waters to sink, and make their
15 streams go as the oil: sentence of the Lord Jehovah. When I give [to] desola-
tion the land of Egypt, and the land is wasted away from its fulness, when I
16 smite all that dwell in it, then they know that I am Jehovah. This is lamenta-
tion, and as lamentation they intone it, the daughters of the heathen peoples will
intone it as a lamentation; upon Egypt and upon all its tumult shall they intone
17 it as a lamentation: sentence of the Lord Jehovah. And it came to pass in the
twelfth year, on the fifteenth [day] of the month, the word of Jehovah came to
18 me, saying: Son of man, wail for the tumult of Egypt, and cast it down, it and
[as] the daughters of the glorious heathen peoples, to the land of the depths, with
19 those that go down to the pit. Whom dost thou surpass in being lovely? Go
20 down, and lie with the uncircumcised! In the midst of those pierced through
with the sword shall they fall; sword is given; they drag it [Egypt] and all its
21 tumults away. The strong of the heroes from the midst of hell [Sheol] shall speak
of [to] him with his helpers: they go down, they lie, the uncircumcised, pierced
22 through with the sword! There is Asshur and his whole company; round about
23 him his [their] graves; they all pierced through, fallen by the sword: Whose
graves were [are] given in the innermost of the pit, and his company was [is]
round about his grave; they all pierced through, fallen by the sword, who gave
24 terror in the land of the living. There [is] Elam and all his tumult round about
his grave; they all pierced through, fallen by the sword, who are gone down,
uncircumcised, to the land of depths, who gave their terror in the land of the
25 living, and henceforth bear their shame with them that go down to the pit. Amid
the pierced through they gave him a couch with all his tumult; round about him
his graves; they all uncircumcised, pierced through with the sword; for their
terror was given [spread] in the land of the living, and they henceforth bear their
shame with those that go down to the pit; among the pierced through is he
26 given [laid]. There [is] Meshech, Tubal, and all his tumult; round about him his

[their] graves; they all uncircumcised, pierced through with the sword; for they
27 gave their terror in the land of the living. And they do not [they shall not] hence-
forth lie with the heroes, the fallen of the uncircumcised, who went down to hell
in [with] their weapons of war; and they gave their swords under their heads, and
their iniquities were upon their bones, for terror of heroes [were they] in the land of
28 the living. And [also] thou among the uncircumcised, thou shalt be broken, and
29 shalt lie with the pierced through by the sword. There [is] Edom, his kings
and all his princes, who have been given in [with, in spite of] their strength with the
pierced through by the sword; they lie henceforth with the uncircumcised, and
30 with those that go down to the pit. There are the princes of the North, they all
and all the Zidonians, who went down with the pierced through, in their terror
[the terror before them] from their strength [proceeding from their strength] come to shame;
and they lie henceforth uncircumcised with the pierced through by the sword,
and bear from this time onwards their shame with those that go down to the
31 pit. Them will Pharaoh see, and will comfort himself over all his tumult; pierced
32 through are Pharaoh and all his host: sentence of the Lord Jehovah. For I gave
his terror [that which is before him] in the land of the living, and Pharaoh and all his
tumult is laid [now] among the uncircumcised with the pierced through by the
sword: sentence of the Lord Jehovah.

Ver. 1. Sept.: . . . *μια τ. μηνος*—(Anoth. read.: בעשתי עשרה, *undecimo anno.*)

Ver. 2. . . . *Λεοντι . . . ὁμοιωθης . . . κ. ἐκερατιζες τοις ποταμοις . . . τ. ποταμους σου.* Vulg.: *Leoni assimilatus es et draconi . . . et ventilabas cornu in*—(Other readings: ותרפס and בנהרתַיך.)

Ver. 3. . . . *και ἀνξω σε ἐν τ. ἀγκιστρῳ μου*; so too the Vulg.

Ver. 4. . . . *Πεδια πλησθησεται σου*—(Anoth. read.: כל חית הארץ, Syr.)

Ver. 5. . . . *ἀπο τ. αἱματος σου πασαν γην.* Vulg.: . . . *colles tuos sanie tua.* Anoth. read.: רמותיך, *excelsa tua*; רמתיך, *projectionibus tuis* (Targ.), v. *vermibus tuis* (Syr.).

Ver. 6. . . . *ποτισθησεται ἡ γη ἀπο τ. χωρηματον σου κ. ἀπο τ. πληθους σου . . . φαραγγας ἐμπλησω ἀπο σου.* **Vulg.**: *fœtore sanguinis tui*—

Ver. 8. Vulg.: *mœrere faciam super te*—

Ver. 9. Sept.: . . . *ἡνικα ἀν . . . αἰχμαλωσιαν σου . . . εἰς γην ἡν*—Vulg.: *irritabo contritionem tuam*—

Ver. 10. Sept.: . . . *προσδεχομενοι την πτωσιν αὐτων ἀφ' ἡμερας πτωσεως σου.*

Ver. 12. *ἐν μαχαιραις γιγαντων, κ. καταβαλω τ. ἰσχυν σου. Λοιμοι ἀπο ἐθνων*—

Ver. 14. *Οὑτως τοτε ἡσυχασει*—Vulg.: *Tunc purissimas reddam . . . adducam*—

Ver. 15. *cum dedero . . . deseretur autem*—(Anoth. read.: ומשמה in Hophal.)

Ver. 17. Anoth. read.: בעשתי עשרה, Syr. and interlined Bible. Sept.: . . . *ἐν τ. πρωτῳ μηνι*—

Ver. 18. Sept.: . . . *και καταβιβασουσιν αὐτης τας θυγατερας τα ἐθνη νεκρας εἰς το βαθος τ. γης προς τους* . . . (ver. 19: *Ἐν μεσῳ τραυματιων μαχαιρα πεσουνται μετ' αὐτου, κ. κοιμηθησεται πασα ἡ ἰσχυς. κ. ἐρουσιν σοι οἱ γιγαντες· Ἐν βαθει βοθρου γινου, τινος κρειττων εἰ; κ. καταβηθι κ. κοιμηθητι*—). Vulg.: *gentium robustarum ad terram ultimam*—(Other read.: והורידו, and אל ארץ תחתית, and אל יורדי, Sept.)

Ver. 19. *Ἐξ ὑδατων εὐπρεπους καταβηθι, κ. κοιμηθητι μετα*—

Ver. 20. . . . *πεσουνται μετ' αὐτου, κ. κοιμηθησεται πασα ἡ ἰσχυς αὐτου.* (Other read.: המונה.)

Ver. 21. Sept.: . . . *σοι οἱ γιγαντες. Ἐν βαθει βοθρου γινου, τινος κρειττων ει; Καταβηθι κ. κοιμηθητι μετα*—Vulg.: *qui cum auxiliatoribus ejus descenderunt et dormierunt*—

Ver. 22. . . . *συναγωγη αὐτου, παντες τραυματιαι ἐκει ἐδοθησαν· ἡ ταφη αὐτων ἐν βαθει βοθρου, κ. ἐγενηθη ἡ συναγωγη αὐτου περικυκλῳ τ. μνηματος αὐτου, παντες*—

Ver. 23. *οἱ ἐδωκαν τ. ταφας αὐτης ἐν μηροις λακκου*—

Ver. 25. The words כי־נתן are not represented in the Sept.

Ver. 26. Sept.: *Ἐκει ἐδοθησαν . . . κ. Θοβελ . . . περικυκλω τ. μνηματος αὐτου, παντες τραυματιαι αὐτου, παντες ἀπεριτμητοι τραυματιαι ἀπο μαχαιρας, οἱ δεδωκοτες*—Vulg.: . . . *interfectique et cadentes gladio*—

Ver. 27. *Και ἐκοιμηθησαν μετα τ. γιγαντων . . . ἀπ' αἰωνος, οἱ . . . ὁτι ἐξεφοβησαν γιγαντας*—Vulg.: . . . *et incircumcisis*—(Anoth. read.: עונם, Syr.)

Ver. 29. Sept.: *κ. οἱ βασιλεις αὐτης κ. . . . οἱ ἀρχοντες Ἀσσουρ οἱ δοντες τ. ἰσχυν αὐτων εἰς τραυμα μαχαιρας, αὐτοι ἐκοιμηθησαν μετα τραυματιων μαχαιρας, ἐκοιμηθησαν μετα*—

Ver. 30. . . . *παντες στρατηγοι Ἀσσουρ, οἱ . . . τραυματιαι συν τ. φοβῳ αὐτων κ. τ. ἰσχυι αὐτων*—Vulg.: . . . *et universi venatores, qui . . . paventes et in . . . confusi*—(Anoth. read.: וכל צדונים, Chald., Syr.; or they read סרני, satraps. Instead of אשר, Sept. read אשור.)

Ver. 31. Vulg.: *Vidit eos et consolatus est*—

Ver. 32. *Quia dedi terrorem meum . . . et dormivit*—

EXEGETICAL REMARKS.

Vers. 1–16. *The Lamentation over Pharaoh.*

Hitzig justly finds the date, as also the place of this section, quite correctly given. He likewise abides, for the more exact determination of the time, by the Hebrew text of ver. 1; while the old translations read, some the tenth, others the eleventh year, some the tenth, others the twelfth month. It was twenty-one months after ch. xxxi. 1, almost two months after that the prophet had received intimation of the destruction of Jerusalem; and to this time also belongs the flight of the remnant of Judah to Egypt, which was prohibited through the mouth of Jeremiah. [SCHMIEDER: "The first of these two death-songs (vers. 1–16, 17–32) is dated on the day of the new moon, the second on the day of the full moon." Hengst.: "The occasion of this lamentation was probably the circulation of the Lamentations of Jeremiah among the exiles. Ezekiel delights generally to follow that prophet as his leader.

The double lamentation-song of this chapter accompanies, by way of consolation, the lamentation-songs among the people of God."]

Ver. 2. Comp. ch. xix. 1.—As ch. xxvii. 2 upon Tyre, and ch. xxviii. 12 upon the prince of Tyre, so here it is first upon Pharaoh, and afterwards, ver. 17 sq., upon Egypt.—The designation as **young lion** (ch. xix. 2) of the heathen nations (meaning of them not in the sense of being among them, but in that of showing himself to be such toward them), כְּפִיר גּוֹיִם, as in ch. xxxi. 11 אל גוים, an antithetical reference, very fitly applies to the personality of Hophra. The youthful, rapacious, conquest-loving spirit of this prince may have been characterized.—נִדְמֵיתָ, Niph. (from דמה), "to make one's self like" (the subjective of Pharaoh's to the objective of Jehovah's, ch. xxxi. 2, 18).—אֶל dropt, perhaps, on account of the immediately preceding אֵלָיו, or to be construed accusatively; anyhow, perfectly plain as to the meaning, since בְּתנים immediately follows. That Pharaoh could not be found "like a lion and also a dragon," as Hitzig alleges, has this only as a ground of offence, that it overlooks the distinction, the contrast, between the two resemblances. As a young lion Pharaoh is conscious of what belonged to him out of himself, whereas the other image rather represents the customary, perhaps also the limits to be kept by the Pharaohs of Egypt. ("With the third Ramses," says Duncker, "Egypt had ceased to be the first power of the old world. About the same time, when the warlike ambition of Assyria began to display itself, Egypt returned to a peaceful mode of life, and remained quiet within its old natural boundaries.") PHILIPPSON: "Pharaoh, who belonged only to Egypt as crocodile, would also as a lion seize upon other lands." So also Raschi. [Hitzig translates נדמית: "thou art a dead man" (COCCEIUS); HENGST.: "thou art undone; נדמה never means: to be made like, always: to be silent, undone." According to him, ver. 2 is a short outline which must be afterwards filled up.]—The representation generally is not that of the glory of the fallen king (KEIL), and the image of the dragon in particular will not explain that of the lion (HENGST.); though it is right to say that the bearing of Pharaoh is meant to be set forth, only not so properly among the peoples as in his own relation. For **in the sea** is neither the sea of the peoples (Hengst.), nor to be taken along with what precedes = on land and in water (ROSENM.), but a reproduction of the Nile-situation (ch. xxix. 3, "**in the midst of his streams**") corresponding to the self-elation implied in the "young lion of the heathen," as (comp. Isa. xix. 5) in Homer the Nile is called ὠκεανός, and the native designation speaks of the white, blue seas. The counter-position (וְאַתָּה) is this: To the heathen nations thou wouldst show thyself as a young lion, and thine own people thou didst destroy, didst ruin—as is presently brought out in the prophet's delineation. To the יַמִּים correspond the נַהֲרוֹת; וַתָּגַח, from גּוּחַ (גִּיחַ?), is, according to Kimchi, the Kal; who, however, allows it also as Hiphil, which Fürst takes to be the form, wishing, however, to understand it transitively: "and broughtest forth thy waters through thy streams;" but of Hiphil, as of Kal, is only the intransitive signification known. [Hitzig, who holds that the breaking forth of the crocodile is not meant to be expressed, would fain make it: "thou causest thy streams, namely, out of thy nostrils, to break forth;" but the streams and בְּ are against him, and he hence reads with Ewald: נְחִרֶיךָ, who translates: "since thou art as the crocodile in the waters, and with thy nostrils dost splutter (Job xli. 20)." Hengst. cites, for the mischief which Pharaoh did among the nations, the North American crocodiles ("thou brakest forth with thy rivers")—how, while breathing with the most frightful noise, they spurt forth streams of smoke and water, like a torrent in a hurricane, through their jaws and blowholes.] The sense, however, is much simpler: while in ch. xxix. 3, Pharaoh, the great dragon, lies in the midst of his streams at his ease, he is now represented as breaking forth in the same ("thine," as he there pretends); that is, not precisely with his hosts, but in this, his national-Egyptian pride of power, rising up, elevating himself—which elevation of Pharaoh (as indicated by Jerome, Vulg., and Sept.) troubled the waters of Egypt (דלח, comp. ver. 13), while he with his feet trampled their streams or caused a muddy jumbling. [SCHMIEDER: "With his restless ambition for war he stirred up the slumbering passions (the mire) among his peoples."] Very good PHILIPPSON: "brought his people into agitation, guilt, and danger;" while the heterogeneous intermingling of the figure of the dragon with that of the lion, and in consequence thereof the explanation with reference to the nations, occasions misunderstanding and needless attempts at interpretation—as when Ewald, who is followed by Hävernick, speaks of the crocodile foully wallowing with mouth and feet in the fresh waters and life-sources of the nations—as troubling all that was pure.

Ver. 3. See ch. xii. 13, xvii. 20.—בִּקְהַל׳, on comparison with ch. xxiii. 24, can scarcely be understood of mere spectators, since they **pull up**, therefore, as helpers, associates, servants, carry the matter into effect. The **peoples** punish the sin of Pharaoh committed on his own people. Under the **many** we may think of the Chaldean army as composed of many races (Dereser), or also of the diverse peoples that followed the Chaldeans in making war upon Egypt.—Comp. ch. xxvi. 5, 14, xxix. 4. In Siam, people often spread nets upon the river to catch the crocodile. Comp. ÆLIAN, *Var. Hist.* x. 21.—Ver. 4. Comp. ch. xxix. 5.—בָּאָרֶץ, **land**, in contrast to the water; while in ch. xxix. it is the "wilderness."—טוּל, "to throw down," Hiphil, strengthens נָטַשׁ, as בָּאָרֶץ is pictured out by עַל פְּנֵי׳, "on the plains (face) of the field."—Ch. xxxi. 13. It is acutely remarked by Bunsen, that in the description, as it passes over into the monstrous, the prophet comes to do with the matter, touches less upon the image.—Ver. 5. As the guilt, so the punishment takes place within the land, which is represented by **mountains** and **valleys** (ch. xxxi. 12). Pharaoh is laid there as to his flesh, together with his warriors.—רָמוּת, Gesen. from רוּם, "a high heap of corpses." Hengst.: "with thy height," in contrast to the valleys as low ground, "with the proud corpse." It were better to read רִמָּתְךָ, from רִמָּה, collective, "worms." Hitzig thinks of the blood which should flow down from the mountains into the valleys. Others take it, after the plural reading, of the hosts of which Pharaoh was proud, their corpses; Raschi, from רמה, "to throw away": thy thrown away, that is: thy fallen.—Ver. 6. Here צָפָה (from צוּף, "to overflow," "to inundate") with אֶרֶץ is not "the land of thy swimming" (GESEN.), in which thou as crocodile hast swimmed, but Egypt—only not as HENGST.: "the land which thou formerly didst overflow with thy rivers." At least ver. 2 cannot be adduced for this sense, except in so far as the Nile, which Pharaoh in ch. xxix. had in a manner claimed for himself, overflows Egypt, and thereby provides the ground of prosperity and strength to Pharaoh. That God "causes the land to drink" (Gen. ii. 10) is placed over against the boasted overflowing of it through Pharaoh's Nile; besides, however, the closer determination of the meaning by "out of (with) thy blood" (Ex. vii. 17 sq.), which Hitzig explains as a gloss of רָמוּתֶךָ in ver. 5. (Keil takes צָפָה as the "outflowing," and construes הִשְׁקֵיתִי with two objects, so that מִדָּמְךָ announces whence the outflowing comes, and wherein it consists. SCHMIEDER: "Pharaoh's life-juice, which flows with his blood from his wounds, the most precious, most peculiar possessions of his home-power." HÄV.: "I saturate the earth with thy current, on occasion of thy blood-covering the mountains." HITZIG: "the soil of the earth with thy outflow." Kimchi takes צפה as a fem. part.: "thy land over which the waters swam." Others: the land which from thee was overflowed, namely, by thy blood. Attention has been called by Kimchi also to צָפָה, "to spy out"—the land of thy spying out—so that the high places thereof might be meant.)—**Even to the mountains** signifies: to as far as the overflowing of the Nile usually extends.—Ver. 7 (ch. xxx. 18). The covering of the heaven, in its symbolic character, fitly enough regarded as analogous to the judgment-day of God (ch. xxx. 3; Joel ii. 4), need not, however, be conceived of from this point of view, but may remind us of Ex. x. 21 sq., while still it is expressly thought of in connection with Pharaoh's extinction, who in his glory must not be contemplated merely as a bright shining light (HENGST.), but, according to the Egyptian style of thought, as the light of the world for his subjects, beaming forth upon the land and imparting prosperity and blessing (comp. at ch. xxix. 6*a*, xxx. 17; see also Duncker, i. p. 150). It is unnecessary, therefore, for Hitzig to fall back upon Dereser, who, under the expression: "when thou art extinguished," makes the constellation of a dragon follow here upon the image of a sea-dragon, as then the zodiac might be of Egyptian origin. Keil regards Ezekiel as leaning upon Isa. xiv. 12; but the discourse is not at all of Pharaoh as a star of the first magnitude (DERESER), but with his extinction the heaven (the heaven, namely, of Egypt), the higher, the governing supremacy and glory, one may say, is veiled, which in what follows is more nearly defined and expressed. Comp. ch. xxxi. 15. The heaven comes into consideration as to its **stars**, and as such are specified (in place of all) **sun** and **moon**, which, again, appear in ver. 8 as מְאוֹרִים,—the sun, with כִּסָּה pointing back to כִּסֵּיתִי; the moon, with negative reproduction of the הִקְדַּרְתִּי. That with what is said, mourning, condolence should be expressed (as at ch. xxxi. 15), does not lie in the words; and just on that account vers. 9, 10 do not give, as Hitzig would have it, the import of the figurative speech here in vers. 7, 8. Finally, neither kingdoms, nor peoples, nor individual men of distinction are indicated by the stars.—Ver. 8. Gen. i. 14.—עָלֶיךָ, agreeably to ver. 7 (בְּכַבּוֹתְךָ): on account of thee, or as **upon thy land.**—**All the luminaries** resume the "stars" in ver. 7; אַקְדִּירֵם repeats הִקְדַּרְתִּי there, and the **darkness**, sq., combines what is said of sun and moon together in the effect. Through "thy land" light falls upon the "land of thy overflowing," in ver. 6.

Ver. 9. The vexing of the heart is to be understood according to ver. 10. Sorrow; not sympathy, but, in consideration of themselves, and of that which might still also be done to them, grief. It is not hard words only which vex us, but there are also hard fates which cause us vexation, especially the more we would live and would let live. שֶׁבֶר (and with Segol twice), probably: the report (but not necessarily to be read, as Ewald, with an Aramaic signification, שׁברך) of the destruction; that such a world-power was broken could not but cause many heart-breakings in the world. The addition: **which thou knowest not,** however, points to more than simple knowledge, namely, to persons who become acquainted with that of which they had hitherto been entirely ignorant, regions utterly unknown to them. (Targum of Jonathan: those broken through the war; HÄV., with a reference to the Sept.: the prisoners, who, as ruins of the old glory of Egypt, are themselves the heralds of the misfortune among the nations.) Comp. ch. xxx. 9.—Ver. 10. See ch. xxvii. 35, xxviii. 19.—שַׂעַר, so that the hair stands on end.—עוֹפְפִי, Pilel from עוּף, to make to fly. The sword, while they see how it flies to and fro over Pharaoh, is swung before their face, that they may with shuddering take a warning from it to themselves.—On וְחָרְדוּ לִרְגָעִים, comp. ch. xxvi. 16.—Ch. xxxi. 16.

Ver. 11. Since Jehovah's sword which is brandished is that of the king of Babylon, the coming of this king can now be fitly spoken of. תְּבוֹאֶךָ for תָּבוֹא לְךָ. Comp. also. ch. xxx. 10. There is a similar break in the discourse.—Ver. 12. Comp. on ch. xxxi. 2, 12, xxviii. 7.—כֻּלָּם, in their collective character; עָרִיצֵי, from עָרִץ, properly: spreading terror.—On אֶת־גְּאוֹן Hitzig remarks: "not that of which Egypt is proud, but what is proud in Egypt, what raises itself up, pushes into the height." Comp. ch. xxx. 6, 18. —Ver. 13. The extirpation of the beasts is explained by Schmieder figuratively of the potentates of Egypt, beside the crocodile Pharaoh, who stir up the population. As to the reality, Hitzig thinks of the grassy banks of the Nile, whither large herds of cattle were driven to get drink and to pasture (Gen. xlvii. 6, xli. 2 sq.; Ex. ix. 3). Rosenm. brings also to remembrance the Egyptian horse-training. The **beasts**, however, appear rather as embellishment, for the Nile with its waters forms the chief feature, as it also had led the inhabitants of the land of Egypt at an early period from shepherd life to agriculture, and had consequently given rise to the prosperity of the country. The desolation of the greatness and glory of Egypt, the annihilation of all its tumult (ver. 12), is represented by the extirpation of the beasts; in which the not unintentionally repeated לא תדלחם, in the transition to the מים רבים, points back with a certain irony to ותדלח־מים in ver. 2, while such a ruinous result for the land through the punishment of Pharaoh is rendered still more remarkable. The **not any more** does not import that it should no more at all happen, but only in comparison with the earlier—no more in such a sense, that the earlier ascendency of power should again have place. Foreign dominion, inflicting mischief, causing man and beast to disappear (ver. 12), should bring to a stand the native pernicious rule of Pharaoh. [According to the interpretation of others, it is to be understood with respect to other nations—as HENGST.: "in part also of the seductive glitter of Egypt"—of the ambitious military expeditions of Pharaoh (COCC., GROTIUS), or generally of the pushing character of Egypt as a worldly power (KEIL).]

Ver. 14. אז, when this takes place. What follows is explained by Hitzig to mean, that the Nile's fulness of water, which hitherto had overflowed the land and made it fruitful, should no longer have any aim (ch. xxx. 12); KLIEFOTH: that God Himself would change the nature of these streams. But this would imply too much, while the words—though not to be understood as Hävernick thinks, who applies ver. 13 improperly to troubling through hostile armies—would still express nothing more than the reference back to ver. 2 already indicated in ver. 13; namely thus: that instead of "the breaking forth in thy streams" there, now a depression takes place, **their waters sink,** that is, those waters which in the former state of prosperity man and beast troubled, but which in particular Pharaoh's haughtiness rendered turbid; *i.e.*, the well-being of Egypt, as this is represented by its Nile, is now gone, and shall no longer give occasion for abuse. The position of Egypt as to power must henceforth be of another description. ונהרותם (ver. 2), "their," of the "waters," which through Pharaoh go in a confused manner—כשמן, HITZIG: flowing softly and slowly, keeping within the prescribed path. The latter does not lie in the comparison, after the manner of oil; and that they do not as hitherto rush forth in impetuous volumes of water is not the contrast; although the citation in Hitzig from Isa. viii. 6 corresponds, for, as with Asshur there, so was the case here with Pharaoh. Hengst. rightly: that the comparison with oil has respect to the *soft* flowing. Comp. ch. xxix. 14. There needs only the **sentence** of the Lord, and then the proud waves subside, and that which fancies itself so high becomes low. (Now, inasmuch as such a state can be taken as a contrast to the ruin of ver. 13, some modern expositors, after the example of earlier ones, have found a promise here in relation to other peoples; TARGUM; GROTIUS: that they should be left in peace; HÄV., KEIL: that for Egypt a time of divine blessing shall follow, the Nile shall flow with oil; Ewald even: "then first might the Messianic times come also upon Egypt, where the waterfloods should no longer be desolating and troubled, by reason, namely, of the true knowledge to which the chastisement conducts.")—Ver. 15. Here is combined together, through a double parallel, ב, the divine judgment and its result,—the giving up of the land of Egypt to desolation, and the realization of what this implied instead of its former fulness (ch. xii. 19).—Rosenm., Hengst., translate ונשמה: "and the land wasted." It might also mean: when I give, etc., then the land is wasted.—The killing of *all* the inhabitants, and the knowing of Jehovah. According to Hitzig, בהכותי must be subordinated to the declaration.—Ver. 16. Comp. ch. xix. 14. The lamentation (ver. 2) comes here to a close. Its female singers, as this was laid upon women (Jer. ix. 16 [17]), will be the heathen nations themselves represented as such (**daughters**), or the mourning women of those nations mentioned in ver. 9. So certain is the matter.

Vers. 17-32. *Dirge upon Egypt.*

Ver. 17. The indication of the month is wanting here; according to Hitzig and others, from oversight. Comp. on ch. xxvi. 1. Hengst. and many derive it from ver. 1, therefore the twelfth month, so that what here follows falls only fourteen days later. It is the last word upon Egypt, save one after the conquest of Jerusalem, for ch. xxix. 17 sq. is absolutely the last; consequently a conclusion with respect to Egypt, and indeed in the manner of a *d'outre tombe.*—Ver. 18. Here we have a נהי, distinguished from the קינה going before, in particular, through its character ("gloomy, sorrowful grave-song," EWALD), and its six windings, its strophe-form.—What is meant by the **tumult** has been already said in vers. 15, 16: it is those who dwelt in Egypt, and are now slain. Besides, in what follows there is a leaning on ch. xxxi. 16 sq.—To wail over any one after the manner of our section is as much as to throw him down with the word. By such a juxtaposition, also, we prevent a false explanation of the נהה, confounding the prophet with hired howling women, after the manner of Egyptian funerals, when as such even the daughters of mighty nations should figure. (EWALD: while the same are let down; as a grave-song, therefore, at the interment. HÄV.: identity of the divine will with the prophetic announcement.)—The fem. אותה does not resume again the regular masc. המון, nor is it shown from the question in ver. 19 that we are to take it as אַתָּה (Hitzig, Ewald); but it is very simple, grammatically correct, and logical,—an impressive ranking of Egypt, as a land, beside the **daughters**, etc. What Hitzig says to the contrary is not worthy of consideration. Egypt, as the party referred to, is the more natural, as it also was what in the preceding context determined the המון.—The **daughters of the glorious heathen peoples** must, according to Dereser, Ewald, Hitzig, be those meant in ver. 16—a view that will scarcely commend itself; according to Rosenm.: the populations subject to the Egyptians, or in league with them—of whom there has been no discourse here; according to most: those specified in ver. 22 sq. If these last are already in Sheol, as in reality is the case, then is וּבְנוֹת' to be understood as if it stood thus: like those, etc., who have gone down conformably to the prophetic word. The process must in no way, as Hengst. expresses himself, be repeated anew; for, according to ver. 21 sq., the parties concerned speak out of hell to the Egyptians, therefore are not sent down with these "as it were a second time." The representation on occasion of the throwing down, which plainly has respect to Egypt, includes those already thrown down ("the daughters," etc.) in order to render the certainty of the fate of Egypt the more indubitable by patent facts, with which also the immediately following question in ver. 19 accords. The designation of the peoples as daughters is the more appropriate, as adornment and attractiveness, splendour and grace, would shine forth in them. For the rest, comp. at ch. xxvi. 20, xxxi. 14.

Ver. 19. The question with which our dirge begins—to supply לֵאמֹר or נְהֵה is superfluous, the address is more energetic without such an addition—is spoken either to the tumult of Egypt (ver. 18), or to Pharaoh and all his tumult (ver. 32). The נָעַם, "to be lovely," is indeed conceded, but it is held from the first to be a vain conceit that it was beyond any other, namely, the glorious heathen peoples, more lovely, therefore, than one of them. Ewald translates: "before whom wert thou more prosperous?" Which would not be so suitable as his allusion to the meaning of "uncircumcised" for Egyptians, and even also for Tyrians (ch. xxxi. 18, xxviii. 10). (Hitzig declares himself in favour of the Sept. on the weakest grounds.)—Hence, as they, so also thou, "go down"—in which remembrance is made of the "cast down" of the prophet in ver. 18, as also of those "going down" with whom Egypt must go down. Besides, comp. ch. xxviii. 10, xxxi. 18.—Ver. 20. Of the sword it was already spoken, ver. 11. They who should fall are the Egyptians, Pharaoh and his tumult. Targum Jon. takes נִתָּנָה as אוֹתָהּ of Egypt, but understands that it is given up to the sword.—מָשְׁכוּ, either 3 pret. or imperat. for מִשְׁכוּ. Of whom it speaks or to whom it is addressed is clear from חֶרֶב נִתְּ'; they are those to whom the sword is already given. And since they must fall, must fall in the midst of the pierced through, the seizing and dragging away is not to be regarded as of evil-doers to the judgment-seat; but if the death-blow is to be considered, and if there is a carrying out of the falling among the pierced through, still there remains as that to which they are to be dragged, indirectly as well as directly, if not precisely, Sheol, at least the grave.—Ver. 21. To the question above corresponds the speaking below. What they speak is not said, and confessedly with דָּבָר does not need to be said. If לוֹ is "to him," as Hengst. thinks, then the speaking is as much as: they greet him (Häv., with malignant welcome) as a colleague (comp. Isa. xiv. 10, 11); and "his helpers" is to be viewed as connected with "to him"—together with his helpers. Rosenm. connects "his helpers" with "the strong of the heroes," so that also his helpers address him. If לוֹ is to be translated "of him," then the discourse takes place with the helpers, who, besides, are the parties that remained to the last with him—ch. xxx. 8, 5 sq.—אֵלֵי גִבּוֹרִים—comp. ch. xxxi. 11—which Gesen. renders: "the strongest of the heroes." Ewald calls to remembrance in how high consideration a quiet natural death stood, with a correspondingly quiet burial, accompanied by the proper solemnities.—The words: "they go down," etc., might serve less as a closer description of the strong heroes (Hengst.), than as a ground for their being in the midst of Sheol. But if they are taken as the address of the strong heroes, for which also the tone of the words speaks, treating scornfully the Egyptians like other heathens, then "the uncircumcised" must be applied to the Egyptians; and it will hence be understood that they fall in the midst of the uncircumcised (their helpers), appear like these. By ver. 19 we are not obliged to take the speakers from hell as the uncircumcised. In Ver. 22 follows their mention by name. **Asshur**, primarily on account of the comparison in ch. xxxi., but especially on account of its so great, still recent experience, which also gave occasion to the beginning of the Chaldean ascendency, ever in Ezekiel appearing as the foil of the other, and, finally, on this more general account, from its importance as compared with the other nations to be named, opens the dark muster-roll.—In respect to gender, the *kingdom*, which is feminine, interchanges with the *king*, masculine, because in point of fact the one runs into the other.—The ruler, or his grave, is surrounded by the graves which might be called **his**, because they are those of members of his people; or קִבְרֹתָיו refers to קָהָל. This will import: Asshur is only a field of graves, and thereby indicate that the sword which threatens Egypt has already fallen upon it.—Ver. 23. In order, however, to bridge still more completely the contrast between this *hereafter* and the preceding *here*, the graves of Asshur (אֲשֶׁר, perhaps a play upon אַשּׁוּר; anyhow, not: *because*) are still more particularly characterized. יַרְכָתַיִם, dual, the two divergent sides, therefore the extreme part, here by means of בּוֹר determined to be the innermost—the point, namely, to which the pit turns off with its two walls. (Gesen.: the hindermost, farthest.) As much as: buried in the deepest place.—The graves are in Sheol; the latter, therefore, comprehensive of the former.

The distinction is a fluctuating one.—Again אֲשֶׁר, certainly a play of words.—נָתְנוּ, antithesis to נִתְּנוּ, for that which was given to them, that which they previously had given! The **land of the living,** as at ch. xxvi. 20, contrast to their deepest graves.—Ver. 24. **Elam** appears in the earliest times among the inhabited countries lying on the farther side of the Tigris, to the east of Babylonia—a Semitic people, nearly related to the Assyrians. On this account alone it might here be made to follow immediately after Asshur; comp. Gen. x. 22, xiv. 1 sq. From the commencement warlike, ambitious of conquest, the Elamites continued to the last true to this character. Strabo makes mention of their expeditions against Susiana and Babylonia. Originally settled in the valleys between the Zagrus range and the mountains which bound the Assyrian plains on the east, they are mentioned along with other marauding tribes. The Assyrians subdued Elam, so that its dreaded bowmen (Jer. xlix. 35) figure in the Assyrian army (Isa. xxii. 6). This explains Elam's position immediately after Asshur. And agreeably to such a relation to Asshur, the utterance concerning Elam is almost entirely similar.—The designation "**their** terror" makes it more expressive: the terror before them. With such a past their future laden with shame contrasts quite as expressively, just as the description: "those that go down to the pit," stands related to: "in the land of the depths."—Ver. 25. The "couch in the midst of the pierced-through" is an ignominious one, because implying their conquest, their fall by the sword. And after all the tumult this idle *lying* now!—נָתְנוּ, the subject undetermined; or if any one is to be thought of, then Asshur lies not less near than Nebuchadnezzar, by whom Hengst. maintains that Elam was vanquished (comp. at ch. viii. 16, xxx. 5).—בְּכָל', in company with.—Round about the king (**him**) the graves of Elam (ה as in לָהּ previously).—**For,** wild lovers of the sword, a terror to the living, their end consequently becomes associated with terror, their state in death takes the form of like to like.—נִתָּן against נִתַּן. Elam himself now, not: his couch. He is laid by the sword with the dead, while formerly the terror before him and his would not be allayed among the living.

Ver. 26. For similar reasons, probably, as in the case of Elam, the Moschi and Tibareni now follow—comp. at ch. xxvii. 13—linked as by a hyphen into *one* power. According to Hitzig, these represent the Scythians, whose numbers had recently been much reduced. Ewald takes the Chaldeans to be meant by the Scythians (!); Keil, here as in ch. xxxviii., understands by them a northern power, that should succumb, and here prophetically represented as having already succumbed.—The description as formerly, only כִּי־נָתְנוּ' instead of previously כִּי־נִתַּן', which Hitzig refers to God. The ground of procedure here turns more expressly on the guilt of the parties.—Ver. 27. Corresponding to such a presentation of the matter is וְלֹא', which by many expositors is taken for a question indicated merely by the tone, as often in lively discourse: "and should they not," etc.; that is, they especially could expect no better fate, among whom the significant custom prevailed of burying their fallen warriors with their slaughter-weapons, so that guilt and punishment are still combined together in the grave! (HENGST.: to the dead is ascribed what took place by their order, since they, like the race of Cain, placed therein their honour, saw in the murder of their brother a piece of bravery.) Others take it differently, as indicating that they were not to participate in the honour of resting with those for whom, because they had fallen gloriously, their armour was deposited in the grave. With the interrogatory mode of explanation the affirmative rendering of the Sept. seems to agree; but the other mode has this decidedly in its favour, that manifestly there is meant to be expressed, only in a different way, what was expressed in ver. 23 respecting Asshur by the humiliating words: "whose graves were given in the innermost of the pit," and in vers. 24, 25 regarding Elam, through the repeated: "and they bear their shame"—namely, that they are the conquered, pierced through by the sword, ignominiously fallen under the victor's hand, as was always again declared. With this agrees the mention of the **heroes** (comp. vers. 12, 21), in particular the latter passage, where these in a manner boast themselves over the Egyptians. The meaning therefore is: that their hereafter is not that of heroes, though these also have fallen from among the uncircumcised, and hence were likewise guilty.—אֲשֶׁר', therefore not the Moschi and Tibareni, as Hengst. thinks, "they who," etc., but a description of the "heroes."—בִּכְלֵי, **in their weapons of war,** in armour of defence and offence, that is, as conquerors of whom one can win no triumph, such as is done by those who carry forth in triumph the equipments of the vanquished.—**And they gave,** etc., as much as: "and men gave"; the survivors honoured their heroes after such a manner.—**And their iniquities were,** etc., is undoubtedly a continuation of the immediately preceding context, since to the marks of honour and judgment given on the part of men, there is very fitly added the judgment of God,—that "their iniquities were upon their bones," or "came upon their bones," though their swords were no longer on but under them, as also is presently said. To suppose, with Keil, that there is here a continuation to יִשְׁכְּבוּ will scarcely do, as they were not to lie down with the heroes, nor could they be named "terror of heroes." Hengst. translates: "heroes of terror." Ewald, with a threatening reference to the Chaldeans: "because the terror of tyrants reigns in the land," etc. (?). Häv. makes Gen. vi. 4, x. 9 sq. swim before the eyes of the prophet. Hitzig accepts *simpliciter* the translation of the Sept. But it may be regarded as a question whether Ezekiel did not think of the mode of burial among the Scythian princes, which has been similarly described by Herodotus.

Ver. 28. An address to Egypt (HITZIG: the tumult of Egypt); but certainly without an underlying word of threatening to the Chaldean king, as Ewald supposes. (HENGST.: "thou art broken and liest down," etc.)—תִּשָּׁבַר for תִּשְׁבֹּר.—Ver. 29. שָׁמָּה either = שָׁם, as a sort of variation, or "thither," which Häv. takes prophetically ("in like manner belong") of such as it stands before. Hengst. on the other hand, as he makes Meshech and Tubal to have been probably conquered with the Assyrians, supposes that the Chaldean storm had swept over Edom immediately after the downfall of Judah, certainly as to the beginning only.—The **kings**, who were elective, are distinguished from **all his princes** (comp. Gen. xxxvi. 15 sq., 40 sq., 31 sq.), the tribal heads or chiefs of the greater race-stems, who according to Keil probably chose the kings.—בִּגְבוּרָתָם, "corporeal strength," "bravery;" very suitable where "heroes" had just been spoken of. We might understand: in proof and trial of the same, or: notwithstanding it. Hitzig points to the olden time (Num. xx. 14 sq.; Gen. xxxvi. 35), and the wars with David.—Ver. 30. נְסִיךְ, from נָסַךְ, to pour out, scarcely to be understood as = anoint, hence: "anointed," as מָשִׁיחַ, but, according to a derived signification: to inaugurate, or to place forth, the former in the sacrificial libation (drink-offering), the latter through a casting of metal.—**The princes of the north**, who are conjoined with כָּל־צִדֹנִי, a collective singular, are thereby, according to Hävernick, more exactly defined as the many rulers of the biblical Aram (Damascenes, Syrians). In Jer. xxv. 26 we have: "all the kings of the north, near and afar off." Comp. ch. xxviii. 20 sq. The Zidonians, therefore, may have already fallen. Tyre is not mentioned, so (Hengst. thinks) it still stood, although the siege had commenced. The mention of the Zidonians appears obviously designed to suggest that by "the north" is meant not the high far north, but that in relation to Palestine, therefore distinguishing them from Meshech and Tubal, formerly noticed. Perhaps also the significant number of seven must be made out for the peoples.—**In their terror**, etc., merely as much as, notwithstanding the terror before them, which their strength produced.—בּוֹשִׁים, so that they bear their shame (vers. 24, 25).—Ver. 31. There is now the express application to Pharaoh. Hitzig gives וְנִחַם עַל: "and will make himself be sorry for all his host," namely, that those in vers. 27–30 still have on their clothing and equipment, as contrasted with those who had gone down with himself naked!! HENGST.: "he sighs." It is here the case of ch. xxxi. 16. Hav. thinks it is spoken ironically.—Ver. 32. The reason assigned has respect to the overthrow of the military force of Pharaoh, in so far as he could inspire terror only after God's will. He was not by reason of his own power an object of dread for a time on earth, but through the operation of God's providence, which made use of him as its instrument. In conclusion Kliefoth remarks very well: "People are wont to visit the pyramids of Egypt or its catacombs for the purpose merely of seeing that the glory of the Pharaohs is one that has its abode in Sheol; even to the new Ptolemaic Egypt, the old Egyptian existence was a complete riddle, a thing forgotten and incapable of being understood."

DOCTRINAL REFLECTIONS.

1. Although the prophecy in ch. xxix. is of a general character, yet by the reference to Nebuchadnezzar, and especially from ver. 17 onwards, it gets a more specific character. We have therefore to hold by a fulfilment through the Chaldeans, and, indeed, in connection with what is said respecting Tyre. Apart from the circumstance that we have here to do with a prophet of God, we could not judge otherwise simply on this account, that a little reflection upon the inevitable disgrace of such a self-deception as would have been the case in respect to Tyre must alone have kept Ezekiel—instead of merely suppressing the prophecy in question while the book was still in his own hand—from wishing now to compensate for the mistake by awakening like inconsiderate and rash expectations concerning Nebuchadnezzar in regard to Egypt. For one to whom the prophet is nothing but a writer must still at least credit him with this much of worldly prudence in respect to his literary honour. And if Ezekiel must needs prophesy *ex eventu* (as Hitzig, for example, conceives), then prophecies like those contained in ch. xxvi. and some following ones are purely unthinkable, so far as they remained unfulfilled; since it cannot but be supposed, that when our prophet closed his book, matters must have stood before him widely different from what they are presented in his prophecy. The "dogmatic criticism," however, cannot once admit now that a prophecy has been fulfilled,—a limitation of the standpoint which is not improved by the circumstance that the truth of the divine word (2 Pet. i. 21) is made dependent on the statements or the silence of profane writers, and even of such as have given notoriously imperfect reports. The false prophet, he whose word did not come to pass, has by God's word (Deut. xviii. 22) been as clearly as possible excluded from the canon.

2. The reward for work, which, as Hitzig rightly enough says, had still to be given to Nebuchadnezzar, raises no question as to the conquest and, as could not fail to happen after a thirteen years' siege, the destruction of Tyre. If the booty might have been thought of for the army, for Nebuchadnezzar it is necessary to think of Egypt. The song of triumph demanded by Hitzig for the fulfilment of the prophecy against Tyre is the double lamentation which we find in ch. xxvii. and xxviii. Every one has his peculiar manner. But as regards the so-called "historical witnesses," who should speak the decisive word on the fulfilment or non-fulfilment particularly of the prophecy of Ezekiel in respect to Egypt, they are "the Greek historians, at the head of whom stands Herodotus, and they know absolutely nothing of a Chaldean invasion of Egypt—nay, their narration is opposed to anything of the kind" (HITZIG). This is imposing; let us reflect, however, that Herodotus had also learned nothing from his Egyptian informants of the defeat at Carchemish. We need only mention farther, that this Greek historian himself reproaches the priests of Egypt, and precisely in regard to this particular time, with embellishing the history of their country. Now, according to

Herodotus, Pharaoh Hophra—in consequence of the defeat which his army sustained from the Cyrenians, against whom it was to have rendered help to the Libyans, and of the revolt which in consequence thereof, and of the foreign mercenary troops retained in Egypt, broke forth on the part of the Egyptian warrior-class against Amasis, who, instead of bringing back the rebels to obedience, suffered himself to be proclaimed king by them—lost freedom and his throne, and by the infuriated people was even murdered. Tholuck, who, "if the cattle with the ark of the Lord should once turn aside, would not obstinately drive forward," remarks that as a witness Herodotus alone comes into consideration; before whom, however, the testimony of Ezekiel, himself a contemporary of the events, has no need to be abashed. "If Herodotus readily received intelligence of the prosperous battle fought by Necho at Megiddo, but none respecting the much more important defeat sustained by him on the Euphrates from the Chaldeans, should it be thought strange if the priests observed silence also regarding the irruption of the Chaldeans into their own land? yea, if the miserable end which Hophra suffered through the foreign conqueror should have been rather represented by them as the deed of his own people?" (So also Rawlinson's *Herod.* B. ii. appen. c. 8.) With a fair appreciation of the historical representation of Herodotus, the cause there assigned, especially the revolution among the warrior-class of Egypt, might suffice for the overthrow of Hophra. Yet the hatred of the Egyptian people, not only expressed in Herodotus, but confirmed by monumental evidence (Rossellini points in this connection to a by-name of Hophra on the monuments: "Remesto")—such a hatred as is described in Herodotus toward Hophra (ii. 161–169), manifested in respect to a native ruler, is scarcely to be explained from what is stated, if it did not come into some sort of connection with a Chaldean invasion of Egypt, whereby the haughtiness of Hophra might well appear all the more hateful to the Egyptian people, as the misery of the land and the inhabitants, occasioned by him, stood in sharpest contrast to the previous prosperity and splendour. The grudge of the Egyptian warrior-class against the foreign mercenaries could not be of such moment as some have supposed, since even Amasis, who thereafter held possession of the throne till his death (forty-four years), and was succeeded in it by his son, took Ionians for his bodyguard, and generally granted to the Greeks still greater favour and privileges than his predecessor. Besides, as generally held, there is also the outline of the prophecy against Egypt in ch. xxix., which exhibits a distinction between ver. 6 sq. and ver. 4 sq.—in the one, the sword constitutes the figure (ver. 8); in the other, overthrow with reference to the wilderness. Especially if Hitzig's interpretation of "the fish" (ver. 4) as denoting Pharaoh's men of war is accepted, and under "the wilderness" there is couched an allusion to Libya, what is said in ver. 4 sq. might be explained by the narration which is reproduced by Herodotus, and ver. 6 sq. would, with the sword of Nebuchadnezzar, be such a supplementing as the conquest of Tyre to the siege of that city, also given elsewhere. Out of the miserable condition in which Hophra perished, Amasis would then have raised Egypt. Anyhow, as Tholuck brings out, the death of Hophra falls exactly into the time in which the occupation of Egypt by Nebuchadnezzar must have occurred; and thus the position of matters approaches to that which is wont to be extracted from Josephus in confirmation of our prophecy—*contr. Ap.* i. 19. It is there stated that Berosus reports of the Babylonian (Nebuchadnezzar) that he "conquered Egypt, Syria, Phœnicia," etc. Again, in ch. 20, he states that Megasthenes placed Nebuchadnezzar above Hercules, since he had subjected to himself a great part of Libya and Iberia (comp. *Antiq.* x. 11. 1, and Strabo xv. 1. 6; see also HÄV. *Comm.* p. 435, against Hitzig's remarks). In the 10th book of the *Antiq.* ch. 9. 7, Josephus expresses himself to this effect, that "in the fifth year after the destruction of Jerusalem, which was the twenty-third of the reign of Nebuchadnezzar, he made an expedition against Cœlesyria; and when he had got possession of it, he made war against the Ammonites and Moabites; and when he had brought these nations into subjection, he fell upon Egypt in order to overthrow it, and did indeed slay the king who then reigned, but set up another; after which he took those Jews that were there captive, and brought them to Babylon," etc. The ten years' time, which Hitzig doubts as the period of the earlier warlike expeditions, is maintained by Tholuck. The fifth year after the taking of Jerusalem would be 581; the thirteen years' siege of Tyre would fall into the period 586–572 or 573. For the different actions which were in part parallel as to time, we have only to suppose various divisions of the army employed, so that the whole might of Nebuchadnezzar did not at the same time lie before Tyre. The forty years of the Egyptian oppression, Tholuck, like Niebuhr, extends over the entire space that lies between the disaster at Carchemish and the overthrow of Hophra (thirty-six years), "during which Egypt, through the continued and in great part unfortunate warlike enterprises of Hophra, must have been much depopulated and extremely weakened, till at length the inroad of the Chaldeans consummated the oppression." Tholuck thinks that, "as the prophets in the beginning of the fulfilment comprehended the future (Jer. xiii. 18; Ezek. xxx. 24), in the last and completed fulfilment they also comprehended the earlier incomplete ones." The symbolical explanation of the forty years is not thereby denied (see the exposition). The worth of the statements of Josephus may be questioned, as is done by Hitzig; but for the relation of profane history to our prophecy, it suffices that Hophra miserably perished (ch. xxix. 4 sq.; Jer. xliv. 30 sq.), and that Egypt again revived, as took place under Amasis, although as a kingdom it was fit to be compared neither with its ancient glory nor with other great monarchies (ch. xxix. 13 sq.). As regards the resuscitation of Egypt, Duncker mentions that, according to a return of the priests, it then reckoned 20,000 country towns and cities (HERZOG'S *Realencyc.* i. p. 150), though it was "the last period of Egypt's glory;" and Lepsius says of the same, that Egypt succumbed to the first pressure of the Persian power, and remained from 525 to 504 a Persian province; that afterwards it became again for a short time independent, until in 340 it was reconquered by the Persians, and in 332 fell under Alexander the Great, etc.

3. Upon the importance of Egypt for the revenge of Nebuchadnezzar, see the exposition of ch. xxix. 18. Also generally for the Chaldean policy the transition to Egypt is rendered plain to us from ch. xxix. 17 sq. (HÄV.: "if Nebuchadnezzar would make the possession of Phœnicia once for all sure, Egypt must be completely broken.") Of the importance of Egypt by itself, its characteristic importance, some notice has already been taken, toward the close of the introductory remarks to ch. xxv.; as also of the distinction, indicated with correct feeling by Keil, between Egypt and the other nations mentioned by Ezekiel. But what Egypt signifies in its connection here, this must be discerned from its relation to Israel. It is quite true that the charge laid against Ammon, Moab, etc., also against Tyre, for spiteful joy, hostility, envy toward Israel, is not mentioned in respect to Pharaoh and Egypt. It may be said that Egypt's guilt in regard to Israel was that rather of a false, treacherous friendship. If, on the other hand, the excess of proud self-sufficiency must be regarded as the characteristic of Egypt, the same sort of self-elation meets us in the king of Tyre (ch. xxviii.); and in this respect Tyre formed a fitting transition-point to Egypt. The distinction between Tyre and Egypt might perhaps be found in this, that while in particular the kingdom of Tyre had had its time of sacred splendour and past greatness, as we have seen, in its former connection with the kingdom of David, Egypt on its part acquired importance on account of the sojournings of the pilgrim-fathers, Abraham, Isaac, and Jacob, and still more on account of the formation of their descendants into a people. Above all, the idea of redemption was associated with the land of Egypt. Here, therefore, the inverse relation holds good: Tyre has gone with Israel to school; Israel, on the other hand, was at school in Egypt, as was evidenced in manifold agreements and contrasts exhibited in their peculiarity as a people, without our needing on that account to ride off on the Spencerian principle [namely, of a servile borrowing from the institutions of Egypt]. More than from anything else, may be understood from Israel's reminiscences as a people, and the impress of Egyptian style and manner even upon their sacred things, their abiding sympathetic turning back toward Egypt. That Israel could not let Egypt go out of sight had its root in human nature; we must learn even from the children of this world (Luke xvi.). But it had also its dangerous side. It was Israel's worldliness, relapse, since Israel had been delivered by Jehovah from this world, and Jehovah had through Moses threatened them in connection with Egypt with the greatest evils (Deut. xxviii. 68). We have tribulation in the world, and we may have fear before the world; such fear, however, may be salutary in its operation. But dangerous is the stay that is sought in Egypt, trust and confidence therein. In this respect Egypt is designated a remembrancer of iniquity (ch. xxix. 16), since for Israel it had, and not as of yesterday, but from of old (comp. also ch. xvi. 26, xxiii. 8, 19), the fatal significance of a pride which resists Jehovah and leads away from Him, of a consciousness of worldly power, which amid the characteristic Pharaonic arrogance expressed itself just as distinctly (ch. xxix. 3, 9) as in Ex. v. 2, and had this the more seductively, as a self-conscious abiding worldly power is in fact fitted to impose on people. Friendship with Egypt is the most contemptuous relation in which Israel can be thought of, on account of the indifference which it necessarily implied on the part of the Israelitish people not only in regard to their former house of bondage, but also to the mighty deliverance obtained from it, and generally in what concerned their relation to Jehovah, on whom, as their own and their fathers' God, they had been thrown from their state of childhood. To make account of this specific historical position in respect to each other, according to which the growth, bloom, and decay of Israel were closely interwoven with Egypt, the prophecy of Ezekiel "dwells at greater length on Egypt than on the other nations" (HÄV.). Still more, however, it serves to explain the representation of the judgment upon Egypt as strikingly parallel with that on Israel, and to the last carried out (comp. ch. xxix. 5, 9 sq., 12, 13, etc.). Not less remarkable, because singular, is the prospect and declaration in regard to the resuscitation of Egypt, and of it alone, which have been introduced into the prediction of our prophet; by this also is Egypt quite expressly kept parallel with Israel. The reminiscence which brings up Egypt so distinctly is not simply that of the house of bondage, or of iniquity, but it is Joseph's post of honour, and the corn granaries of Jacob, together with his family. Comp. also Deut. xxiii. 7.

4. The interpretation of Neteler strikes out what is certainly a quite different path, strikingly reminding one of Cocceius, only with a specially Catholic tendency. According to him, the prophecies against the foreign nations constitute four groups, each of which contains four pieces: the first, ch. xxv.; the second, the overthrow of the Canaanitish culture-development, standing in contrast to the higher calling of Jerusalem, and reaching its culmination in Tyre. The prophecy against Sidon he severs from Tyre, in the interest of this fourfold division; it belongs to the Egyptian group, inasmuch as "Sidon's bloom falls into the time in which Egypt was the bearer of the Hamitic power and culture," and "the Sidonian development was a shoot of the Hamitic-Egyptian." The promises for Israel in this third section (ch. xxviii. 20–xxx. 19) must stand parallel with those of the same kind in the first group, wherein punishment is threatened to the four nations with reference to Israel; as the first group, "through ch. xxi. (Ammon), is placed in connection with the first destruction of Jerusalem," so "the third stands, through the opening of the mouth which occurs in it, in closer relation to the symbol of the second destruction of Jerusalem." The four last prophecies against Egypt are "mere symbols," according to Neteler. As Ammon "drove the surviving remnant, after the destruction of Jerusalem, out of Judea," so had "Moab decoyed Israel into gross idolatry before their entrance into Canaan;" and so, in the prophecies against Ammon and Moab, the beginning and end of Israel in regard to Canaan are connected together. The punishment of Edom and the Philistines must point to the "re-establishment of the house of David." In regard to Tyre Neteler expresses himself thus: "The command

given to Israel to root out the Canaanites, but by them neglected to their destruction, God will execute on Tyre through Nebuchadnezzar;" and this command must stand in a noteworthy relation to the historical development of the last period of 800 years before Christ, in which "those to the west (Carthaginians, Greeks, Romans) brought a real advance, while those to the east (the Hamitic kingdoms of Ethiopia and Egypt, the Semitic kingdoms of Assyria and Chaldea, the Japhetic Medians and Persians) repeat the development of the two earlier periods in smaller measure, yet as if thereby the problem of the western circle should be solved." He says: "If Israel, through the extirpation of the Canaanites, according to Num. xxxvi. 6–9 (!), had entered into the place of the Phœnicians, it would have formed the first member in the development of this period, and would have shown the right path to the Greek culture which came forth in the second third of it." To retrieve as much as possible that which was neglected (! ?), "Nebuchadnezzar must subject the Hamitic Tyre, even to the pillars of Hercules, and unite the eastern circle to the monstrous Chaldean kingdom, so that the externally insignificant Israel might be set in the centre of this gigantic Semitic power, which extended its sway even over the Turanian tribes in the high north." This contrast between the Semitic and Hamitic races (already occurring in the prophecy of Noah) must be of great importance for the understanding of the symbolical representation of Ezekiel in the prophecies relating to Tyre and Egypt. Upon the third group which Neteler distributes, and which reaches to ch. xxx. 19, we learn that, first of all, in the prophecy against Sidon, "the second possession of the land is associated with the first, as in ch. xx. the first deliverance from Egypt is made parallel with a deliverance in a higher sense." "As Israel did not fully carry out the extirpation of the Canaanites, whose place, according to Num. xxxiii. 54, it was their part to occupy, these were turned for them into thorns and briers. With the second possession, on the other hand, the servitude of Canaan, which was announced even by Noah, was after a sort realized, since the Canaanitish history becomes extinct. The second piece in this section, namely ch. xxix. 1–16, connects the end of the first Israelitish sojourn in Canaan, brought about by Egypt's iniquity, with the end of Egypt; and the humiliation of Egypt is such an elevation of Israel, that Christianity will not be under temptation to lean upon a decaying heathenism." The forty years occurring at ver. 11 sq. must not be distinguished from the forty years of Judah, for which the prophet had to lie forty days upon his right side; that is, as Neteler remarks on ch. iv., "a symbolical designation of the time, reaching from the destruction of the temple to the return from exile, derived from the sojourn in Kadesh." "The two first pieces, ch. xxviii. 20–xxix. 16, set forth the world-historical ideas, which were to be realized by the introduction of Christianity, but give, as to the way and manner in which the realization should be prepared for, begun, and carried forward, no information—this being first introduced by the prophet in the third piece (ch. xxix. 17–21). The might of Shem, through which God conquered Canaan in the world's history, must also carry forward the work in regard to Egypt. In the interest of Israel, whose service to God stands in contrast to Canaanitish industry, God will turn the Semitic world-power against Egypt, by which Israel was compelled to do Canaanitish work, and establish for them, on account of their labour in respect to Canaan, claims for compensation, which God would render valid because of the bondage laid by Egypt on the Israelites. The booty which God took from Egypt after the conflict, on occasion of the first deliverance, was only a type of a later plundering, which in a preparatory manner was begun by Nebuchadnezzar, and after the second deliverance from Egypt, that is, after the redemption achieved by the sufferings of the Servant of God was realized, when all power in heaven and on earth was committed to the *episcopate* of the Church (!!). The consequence of this victory over Egypt (ch. xxx. 1–19) is given in the form of a judgment upon Egypt, in which is delineated its desolation and the annihilation of its idols and yokes; but the sons also of the covenant-land are smitten by the judgment, which points to a fall that should take place among them." The continuation of this Catholic-theological-historical explanation and interpretation of Ezekiel will be given in No. 9.

5. Cocceius remarks on ch. xxix. 21: "Evil Merodach gave Jehoiachin freedom, and the first place of honour among the kings. Farther, Daniel was great in the kingdom of Nebuchadnezzar, and under the Persian dominion. Cyrus was called by God to give command to lead the people back, that they might rebuild the temple. Still higher grew the horn of Israel when they became free, and their priests assumed the diadem, as a sign of the freedom of the people, and the Israelites had become greater than their fathers, as announced in Deut. xxx. 5. But most especially was it so, when out of David's house the horn grew, which set the people free from all slavery, which subdued their enemies, and rendered the Gentiles subject to Israel, Ps. cxxxii. 13–18."

6. The day of Jehovah, Kliefoth remarks, "is not judgment in *one* point of time and destruction over the whole heathen world;" and then he continues: "The day of Jehovah is a period of indefinite duration, in the course of which God will punish with judgment and destruction all heathen nations in succession, just as they have shown their hostility to the people of God, and He sees that their time has come. From this point of view, also, is the announcement always to be understood, that this day of Jehovah is at hand. The day continues so long, that it lasts till, in the final judgment, the whole world, in so far as hostile to God, shall be destroyed; but it constantly begins anew, when any particular people, on account of their malevolence manifested to the people of God, falls under the righteous doom of perdition. Hence the day of Jehovah upon the heathen nations has, in the several prophecies, a different *terminus a quo*, according as they refer to this or that kind of relations." Only it must not be overlooked, that in ch. xxx. 1 sq. not indeed Egypt alone is contemplated, but Egypt in its connection with heathen nations; and yet, that it is not the day of judgment upon all anti-theocratic powers that is to be understood, as already Hävernick makes the prophet see this general idea obtaining realization; but as the time of Jerusalem was come, the time

when judgment had begun at the house of God, so the time must now be near when this judgment of God shall go forth upon the heathen. Hengstenberg finds here the fundamental passage for Luke xxi. 24, and points to the overthrow of the Roman Empire,—the "mountain" which was to be cast into the sea after the fig-tree of the Jewish people was withered (Matt. xxi.), the "mulberry-tree" which was to be plucked up and removed into the sea (Luke xvii.).

7. As in the kingdom of Tyre, ch. xxviii., allusion was made to a time of sacredness upon the holy mount of God, so there was also found there, by way of similitude, a bringing to remembrance of Eden, and especially of the garden of God. This retrospect of paradise furnishes the *beau-ideal*, the standard for the Old Testament world generally; hence with Assyria, and in connection therewith in reference to Egypt, which had not the same historical position as Tyre, it appropriately comes back again in ch. xxxi. As in the New Testament all is measured with heaven, so in the Old Testament what is or was glorious upon earth is made to hold of Eden and paradise.

8. On the derivation of the word "Sheol" there confessedly prevails a great diversity of opinion. For the biblical idea, especially the signification of the word in the Old Testament, this only is to be learned from this matter of etymological controversy, that as well the derivation from שָׁעַל, to be hollow (therefore for שְׁעֹל), since it points to "hollowing," and in so far to the grave, as the derivation which Hupfeld adopts from: "to sink down," and: "to go apart from one another," therefore: sinking down, depth, abyss, and: cleft, hollow, empty space—since the burying and the being in the sepulchre can be thereby expressed—both alike avail for the affirmation, that Sheol and the grave more or less run together. The derivation, on the other hand, from שָׁאַל, to demand, expresses as to Sheol only what constitutes generally the power and manner of death to demand for itself with insatiable desire all living beings (comp. Isa. v. 14; Hab. ii. 5; Prov. xxvii. 20, xxx. 16). As to form an infinitive verbal substantive, the use of the word belongs predominantly to the poetic language of the Old Testament, whence also is to be explained the circumstance that it never stands with the article. Sheol appears as the aggregate of all graves. Who could venture to deny this aspect of the matter, at least for the 31st and 32d chapters of Ezekiel? It is the universal grave, which calls down to itself all earthly life, how high soever it may have reached, however magnificent it may have been, however valiantly it may have fought. But much, also, as Sheol and the grave (בּוֹר) sometimes appear to approach (comp. also Isa. xiv. 11, 15), to cover one another, it must still not be overlooked that the grave, more exactly considered, is only the entrance into Sheol (Ps. xvi. 10), which certainly, as it is commonly represented, keeps the hue of the grave, in generals as well as in particulars (ירכתי בור, ch. xxxii. 23); it is the carrying over of the grave to the future state (while the grave as such is still always something here). It is quite reconcilable with this representation when Sheol is conceived of as a locality, and indeed as a deep abyss, just as the standing form of speech: "to go down," "to be thrown down," is thence explained as equivalent to being consigned to the dead. The occasional poetic delineation of this future must only not be formally dogmatized into an actual under-world with gates, rivers, etc. (Job xxxviii. 17; Ps. xviii. 5 sq.) The going down of the company of Korah (Num. xvi. 30) is often what is floating before the writer's mind; and not so much the locality of Palestine, which was rich in grottoes and caverns, or the darkness of the Hebrew family tomb-vaults, the stillness of the Egyptian catacomb-world. The interior and inmost part of the earth (ch. xxvi. 20, xxxii. 18), however, is not the earth's inner region as such, but שְׁאוֹל תַּחְתִּיָּה is the Sheol "beneath" (the underground, ch. xxxi. 14); that is, partly the contrast to heaven as the region of the divine life, partly the distinction from the surface turned toward heaven, the face of the earth. Out of that contrast, in which, however, the earth also and its life have their place, and still more in accordance with this distinction from the earthly life, must Sheol and what is connected therewith be understood. The death to which one is surrendered (ch. xxxi. 14) is not simply a going down, not annihilation, but as punishment for sin, the necessary consequence of the negation of God. Considered as a state, it is the contrast in respect to God, as curse, as judgment upon the sinner; hence the contrast in respect to life as divine, as salvation and blessedness, even to eternal perdition; and so Sheol posits a concrete, individual prolongation of life: the dead are represented in Ezekiel (ch. xxxi.) as living on individually and in space. Passages such as Ps. civ. 29, cxlvi. 4, and others, certainly have respect to the earthly life in the body, with its purposes and undertakings, doing and thinking, knowledge and wisdom together, Eccl. ix. 10 (so our Lord Himself in John ix. 4 makes account of it for His diligence in working while in the flesh). As life on earth in a mortal body is for all men a troublesome, poor, and sorrowful thing, so certainly the advancing decay of the powers of life, with the dissolution of the union between soul and body, necessarily becomes quiescence, impotence, and withdrawal of their life-energy in regard to the appointed sphere of action. But passages like Job xxvi. 5 sq., xxxviii. 17, Prov. xv. 11, Ps. cxxxix. 8, testify to the presence of the living God, through whom the subsisting and passing away of all beings is conditioned, as is said also in the אֲבַדּוֹן made parallel with Sheol (comp. Mark xii. 27; Luke xx. 38). The contrast, therefore, to the heavenly upper world as the proper region of the divine life is not that of not-being and being; and just as little is the continued existence in Sheol an unconscious shade-existence, at least not according to Ezekiel's representation: the heroes in Sheol speak and know themselves as such over against others, feel, etc. As the designation of shades (רפאים) for the dead in the Old Testament times cannot be proved, so the appearance, for example, of Samuel (1 Sam. xxviii.), so entirely accordant with the spirit and address of Samuel as he actually lived, is not at all brought forward as an exception, somewhat after the manner of the Theban seer Tiresias (*Odyss.* x. 492 sq.). In

the Old Testament, also, we read nothing of an instinctive repetition and continuation of the past life connected with the possession of blood. The representation of Sheol, into which there has often been greatly too much imported of heathen elements, is in no respect the localizing of the image, which, as Meier says, "remains like a blanched, bloodless, shadowy form, in the spirit of the living, of their dead and buried fellow-men." Life in Sheol cannot, indeed, run counter to the conditions that prevail in respect to human life. Man is soul, but he has spirit, which for him constitutes the power wherein the life of the individual consists; while the soul is plainly the seat of that, as the body is its organ. If the life connected with the body appears as life in the flesh, when separated therefrom it will become an existence of the spirit, and departed men will necessarily have to be thought of as spirits, and can only in so far be termed "souls" as a retrospective sense of the earlier corporeal life has place. On this side the description of Sheol is certainly, and especially as contradistinguished from the earthly upperground life, kept in due regard to the state of things existing there. With the going down into the grave, the bright joyful sunlight vanishes for men; hence Sheol is the land of darkness and of the shadow of death (Job x. 21). While the world of light is an organized one, the midnight region of Sheol appears as a confused intermingling of substances, chaotic (Job x. 22). Busy life, so repeatedly designated "tumult" in this chapter of Ezekiel, becomes motionless in the grave; so in Ps. cxv. 17 the dead go down to silence, to stillness (comp. Ps. xciv. 17, xxxi. 18). The expression, however, of "land of forgetfulness," Ps. lxxxviii. 12, must not be overstretched, though the reference is to be held fast in which it is said that, as God has given the earth to the children of men (Ps. cxv. 16), so the manifestation of His wonder-working power and righteousness is promised to them on the earth while they are in the flesh. Not in the heathen materialistic sense, but Christologically, however still on the temporal side, the thought as to its form was presented in the Old Covenant. And thence are such passages as Ps. vi. 5, xxx. 10 [9], lxxxviii. 10, 11, cxv. 17, Isa. xxxviii. 18, to be understood. The dead, accordingly, are done (Ps. lxxxviii. 5); their state, Sheol, is without a history (on the other hand, comp. 1 Cor. xv. 19). But to complete our knowledge of the Old Testament Sheol, the ethical side is not to be overlooked, that is, the idea of recompense comes therein likewise into consideration (comp. ch. xxxii. 23 sq.). The godly are there gathered to their fathers (Gen. xxv. 8, xxxv. 29, etc.). It is a mode of representation which incidentally receives a very touching illustration in Luke xvi. 22 for the poor, who has no brother in the world, who is an abject, forlorn, when he is said to be received into Abraham's bosom. The righteous snatched away enters into peace, and rests therein upon the foundation of the grave (Isa. lvii. 1). How far with the soul, when unclothed of the body, there takes place "an ineffectual tormenting effort to consolidate itself corporeally" (Beck)—the spirit, however, being incapable of being contemplated apart from the soul, which conditions its individuality, therefore also not to be thought of "as sunk after death into the corruption of the flesh"—may be left undecided. It is enough that the rich man found himself "in torment." With justice, however, Lange presses the thought that for the wicked Sheol is still not hell.

9. Neteler (comp. 4) maintains concerning ch. xxx. 21 to xxxii. 32, that is, the fourth of the groups set off by him, that "through four symbols the overthrow of a power standing in antagonism to the Church is exhibited," and that what is said is to be taken "eschatologically in a wider sense." Egypt is considered by him as "a symbol of the power of Magog," and under the Chaldeans is found "a combination of Romans and Germans." And here Neteler's book dwells on the "Russian Panslavism." The two last symbols must be fulfilled in the overthrow of Magog "only provisionally," so that "their complete fulfilment belongs to a still later future."

HOMILETIC HINTS.

On Ch. xxix.

Vers. 1–5. The close is made with Egypt, as Egypt was the beginning in respect to Israel.—"Egypt is with Ezekiel the oldest country of his people's disgrace" (Umbr.).—How clear is what God causes to be said to us! The address is plainly written, and can occasion no doubt to whom the word is directed; and not less clearly does it shine forth whose subscription stands under it, and who, therefore, will look after the punctual execution of the things spoken. It will not proceed according to man's sayings and opinions, but as God the Lord has said.—The prophetic word so much the surer as the fulfilment of it now lies completely before us.—What still survives of the Pharaohs lies in the midst of the wilderness; they are ruins to which the sand has still refused burial!—"Where can a mortal say: This is mine, or: This remains to me? But prosperity, where it is not understood as God's blessing, makes people stupidly proud. See there, too, the blessing of tribulations, which demonstrate before our eyes, that nothing is our right, and nothing our abiding property" (Stck.).—Those who do not seek after the things which are above regard the Nile, which flows on the earth, with precisely such eyes.—"But that there is also a spiritual Egypt may be seen from Rev. xi. 8, and that is a people, kingdom, and dominion which holds in fetters the people of God and makes them slaves. Now, as under the great dragon in the sea Antichrist also comes to be considered, together with his scales and members that stick to him, and are in a manner innumerable, so shall this power also after the prince of Tyre receive his doom, with all his adherents, who by overbearing conscience have done so much wrong to the faithful. Then also will appear the vain help which the house of Israel has sometimes assumed as belonging to the reed of the fleshly arm" (B. B.).—"Satan says to Jesus: All this will I give thee, all the kingdoms of the world and their glory, though still there was not an atom thereof in reality his" (Luther).—"Oh how vain is man in prosperity!" (St.)—Vers. 4, 5. Higher still than the highest is the Most High. He who comes from heaven is higher than all.—"It is bad when only amid loss people come wisely to learn that they had all of God, of which they were so proud and boasted themselves" (STCK.).—Pharaoh in the wilderness, and Jesus in the wilderness.—They who set themselves up above others may readily observe that they are thrown off and away before they are themselves aware of it!—The judgment of Jehovah upon the Pharaohs!—Jehovah at the Pyramids, a very different object from Napoleon before them.—The overthrow in the wilderness an image of a desolate ruin.

Vers. 6, 7. God punishes not those only who rely upon flesh, but those also who are flesh and yet wish others to find comfort in them.—No knowledge of God and no knowledge of self—this is what gives false self-confidence, and false confidence in man.—The love of God in discovering the false and rotten props.—"A reed is everything that is in this world, as man's favour, temporal prosperity, beauty, yea, the corporeal life itself; from without it appears like a staff, and as if many were walking with it, but within it is hollow and brittle" (STCK.).—But for none is such a reed more suspicious than for the people to whom God has pledged Himself, and therewith all His wisdom and His omnipotence.—It is certainly the same with the deceit and show of one's own righteousness, good purposes, and pious works. One cannot keep hand and shoulder far enough from these.—How many a one has such like splinters in his conscience!—The false reed-splinters in our bones, which make our going so feeble and our holding so insecure.—"The soldiers give to Christ a reed in mockery, Matt. xxvii." (LUTHER).

Vers. 8-16. The judgment of God by the sword in its significance for enemy and friend, warrior and conqueror, land and people.—Desolation is always a mark of punishment. First men become waste, then their place is laid waste.—Where the people become waste as regards God, there God causes the land to be waste of its people.—Whosoever will have it that he has made himself to be what he says that he is, with him God must make an end, so that he may learn what he himself is, and how still God can do all.—The mine and thine, as the grand controversy which moves the world's history.—So the sin of the people is their ruin; but though ancient history is full of examples, those who now live are not disposed to profit by them.—"Should one not be ashamed of such a speech, since it must so soon be changed into a past—it has been mine; and this often with much sorrow?" (B. B.)—The description of the earth is also a description of divine justice.—By means of fragments and arrow-heads in the yellow sands of the desert, and obelisks which still point heavenwards, people now read the names of men, of kings, and such like; but the *feci* of God is likewise to be read there.—The divine seasons of respite.—The years of humiliating in their significance for Egypt and for us all as punishments and deliverance from high-mindedness.—To stand low is to stand more secure than to go beyond bound and limit.—"All changes in the world have their bearing ultimately on the Church" (ST.).—God knows how to withdraw from the eyes of His own what dazzled their eyes and held them captive.—"Such is the aim of all the judgments that are inflicted, to withdraw the body of the faithful from confidence in what is human, and to supplant it by a firm trust in God" (B. B.).

Vers. 17-21. Warrior service hard service. He who serves God does not serve without pay.—The recompense of our works is never made on the ground of merit, but is always of grace.—"The downfall of the world is the deliverance of the chosen" (H. H.). Therefore lift up your heads, for your redemption draweth nigh (Luke xxi. 28).—When the world becomes poor, then the bones of the righteous flourish.—The new life out of ruins.—Upon silence to speak is better than to be silent upon speech.—It is God who must open the mouth for us, and He also can do it.—Immortality in the world and the eternal life in the sanctuary, Ps. xxiii. 6.

On Ch. xxx.

Vers. 1-9. "The judgments of God pass from His own people to other peoples; hence the day of the heathen could not be far off" (COCC.).—Despair howls, hope waits.—A day in clouds is also the day of death; the earth is shrouded from the eye, and especially when first the heaven has been covered to the spirit. Darkness then reigns below and above. How dark, then, is the grave!—Bad times are met by watchfulness; howling merely goes before them as the loud blast before the outburst of the thunderstorm.—Vers. 4, 5. Many others are carried along with the fall of one. In every judgment that takes place in the world, behold a type and prelude of the judgment which is to be executed on the world.—If not with the sinner immediately, yet on the sinner, and therefore through the sinner his companions shall be punished.—Where God strikes the blow, there not only is the stir which a people makes, and with which it makes such a noise, its work and gain brought down, but also law and order and that whereon all rests are overthrown.—Vers. 6, 7. How helpless with all his appliances may one that was helpful to us prove in a night! May God be our help, who has made heaven and earth.—Ver. 9. Everything does service as a messenger for God; in particular His word, which hence cannot be bound, but accomplishes that whereto it is sent.—God's seat of judgment stands always among mankind, and the world's history is God's judgment.—The terrors in the history of the world.—As there is a false security in individual men, so is there also a bad security with whole peoples.—The national security a national loss.

Vers. 10-19. When men do not sanctify God on holidays, God makes their bustling activity to keep holiday.—When God wills, a man's name can cause terror to the world. But only One Name is given under heaven to men wherein we can happily exult before all terrors.—Upon deeds of violence come still more violent ones, and tyrants are precipitated through tyrants.—"Whosoever sells himself to sin has already in doing so sold himself to his enemy" (STCK.).—God's blessing fills, His curse impoverishes a land.—Ver. 13. The hand of God alights some time upon all idols.—From the overthrow of heathenism is seen the vanity of idols.—"Where are the famous cities of the olden times? Why do they lie buried in disorderly stone-heaps? Sinner, behold what sin may effect" (ST.),—how it may build very high indeed, yet not for continuance, and still more may destroy.—Gods and princes combined the common delusion of idolatry, at first in splendour, so afterwards in ruin!—Terror is the opposite of courage, but not the fear of the Lord.—Where God kindles a fire, it is always for judgment; the old is consumed therein, but a new springs forth out of the ruins.—Without casting down, no progress in the life of humanity. —Ver. 16. Must not man always be engaged in conflict?—Ver. 17. With its youth the human future of a people goes down. Even the youth should be "the chosen" of God; instead of this, Satan at no period has so much of his nature in men as in the season of youth.—Vers. 18, 19. Walk in the light while ye still have the light, —we, that is, who have the knowledge of God in the face of Jesus Christ.—The judgment of God may, through the dogmas of men and a false philosophy, veil to us also the sun of truth, and wrap in darkness to men's view heaven and eternity.—When at length, with the authority of God, the authority also of the law over men gives way, then, where superstition gives place to unbelief, there falls upon them yoke for yoke, one in the room of another; there is only an exchange of tyrants.—How much old and high renown have the gravediggers of the world's history already buried under the sod among other sweepings! What is *gloria mundi?*—a *transit*.—The new plagues of Egypt.—The spirit of Pharaoh continued to be the spirit of the Pharaohs.—Self-heights are no heights—none, at least, that stand in the judgment of God, and remain above though all else should go down and disappear; but a height in the true sense is that simply whereof it is said, As high as heaven is above the earth, Ps. ciii. 11. This ought to be recognised, and that not merely at the last, amid howlings and gnashings of teeth, but betimes, when it may still serve for peace, with the calm open eye.—"The most wretched of all thoughts is that of having no part in God. How many an evil-doer has readily presented his head to the sword, in the conviction that through the punishment he should become a partaker of God!" (H.)

Vers. 20–26. How many the things are that men prize as an "arm," and how easily these arms are broken!—The arm of the Lord (Isa. liii.), and the arm of man, and the armies of princes.—"More easily is an arm broken than healed; but now first of all the conscience, how painfully does it sting, and how long is it in healing!" (STCK.)—What God has broken, God only can heal.—Ver. 22. But man never has enough by a fracture; so long as he can still move and stir otherwise, he must show himself. Therefore shall there come to be a destruction without mercy, if we will not submit to God on the footing of grace.—"Sickness breaks one arm, death both arms" (STCK.).—Every breakage which we must suffer is a call to repentance.—Ver. 23. "He who will not fear God in his fatherland has no injustice done him, if in a foreign land he is made to experience all sorts of misfortune" (ST.).—Vers. 24–26. "Strength and weakness come both from God" (W.).—"Upon whose side Jehovah stands, that man prevails in the conflict; to him there is prosperity in life; he enjoys a blessing with his work. But this favour has the Lord promised to the righteous. Without God all ends unfortunately, mournfully, and in perdition" (STCK.).—What serves God, that serves also the kingdom and the power of the Spirit; just as at the last, all the kingdoms of this world shall become God's and His Christ's.

On Ch. xxxi.

Vers. 1, 2. "The greatness of Egypt was the presumption against the warnings of the prophet. But greatness is no security against destruction; no greatness upon earth can withstand the strokes of God" (H.).—"With justice are kingdoms compared in Scripture to trees, as well on account of their form, the protection and shadow they afford to men and beasts, as also on account of their fruits; and still farther in this respect, that kingdoms, like trees, flourish and again cease to exist, torn up by the wind, or cut down by the hatchet of man" (L.).—It is very well for people to compare themselves with others, though not for the purpose of thinking better of themselves than others, as the Pharisee in the temple over against the publican, or in order to envy others; but humbly to learn that we are a part of mankind, and that what is human may befall us, and shall at last take place without exception. Also to make each one more contented with his lot, a comparison with others is, as a rule, fitted to be serviceable.—"Both the one and the other inference is right: As God has elevated that humble one, so can He, in His own time, elevate me; as God has abased that proud one, so may it also be done with me" (STCK.).

Vers. 3–9. "The histories of the world might teach great lords much, that they should not rely upon their own powers" (LG.).—Rulers and princes should be shady trees to the righteous. —"God has done good also to the heathen, that they might seek Him, if haply they might find Him, Acts xvii. 26, 27" (STCK.).—"Oh, what streams of grace flow upon the unthankful, if they would only perceive them! The waters are indeed not of one sort—one portion swims in pure felicity, another in tribulation and adversity; but the aim is uniform, and the divine loving-kindnesses which are concealed under the latter are certainly greater than the former, in the eyes of those who know to estimate things aright" (B. B.).—But their favourable condition and the friendliness of God only serve with many to puff them up, and render them proud and arrogant,—an end for which certainly all this was not given. —He with whom it overflows should make it trickle over upon others.—Ver. 7. To be radical in the proper sense is a good thing, namely, that one should know that his root is in God.—"The true comeliness of a prince stands in comely virtues, which adorn every man, especially a prince,—clemency and justice above all; to afford protection and solace to the persecuted; to spread forth as it were his branches to the miserable; to have about him servants resplendent with his own virtues, so that, as in every branch the nature of the tree, so in every servant the character of the prince, may appear reflected. He and they must not be terrible to the good, nor oppressive to his subjects. The love of the people is a good root for a race of princes" (COCC.).—Ver. 8. Better to be envied than commiserated. God makes man beautiful, as He alone also makes him good; the latter is the divine nature, the former the divine form, of a man.

Vers. 10–13. I have given thee into the hand of such and such an one—this explains much darkness.—The haughty spirit going before, the key to the fall afterwards.—"Now, however, we are all in Adam inclined to pride of soul; and the perishing things of this world, riches, honour, splendour, beauty, knowledge, etc., nourish our natural inclination, being all things which we overestimate. However, even a plain smock-frock often covers a repulsive arrogance. But kings are through their flatterers nourished in this vice, which is the root of all others" (L.).—One must grow in order to be able to lift the top so high; this is not so quickly reached;—on the other hand, to arrive at the lowest depth there needs only one overthrow, which may take place in a single moment.—One falls more quickly down a stair than one mounts up again.—God cannot suffer pride; I am meek and lowly in heart, it was said by Him who was God manifest in the flesh, Matt. xi. 29.—Out of the heart of man proceed also all high things that are offensive to God, which need not always wear a crown, but may have merely a pen behind the ear, or a pair of spectacles on the nose.—Vers. 12, 13. From the foreign land comes much suffering—first foreign sins, then punishment through foreigners.—A shameful fall into sin, and a frightful fall into misfortune—both invite to study.—There must also fall into the valleys branches that have been broken off, that poor people may not think the great ones of the earth are freed from death and judgment.—When the punishments of God break forth, then such as can flee gladly make off, while they were not to be enticed out of the shadow of sin, in which they delighted themselves.—God shakes the luxurious tree from top to bottom, and then all that stuck to its branches fall off; and so they are struck off, since they did not allow themselves to be warned off.—"How does the shadow of the rich vanish with the sun of prosperity, and with the shadow depart also the flatterers and panegyrists!" (STCK.)—He who chooses to be forsaken must become poor.—Fate can keep up the interest, but a rich man who has become poor is a woe-begone phenomenon for the world.—"How often do the goods of a rich man become scattered over the world after his death!" (STCK.)—Discern false friends in adversity!—To cut, and peck, and aid in plundering the very person in whose prosperity men formerly basked, and whom they hardly knew how to laud highly enough!—"So deeply is the friendship of the world rooted, and its caresses. So long as all goes well, friends and worshippers are readily found. But when that changes, all goes otherwise" (B. B.).

Ver. 14. Precautions must be taken that the trees do not grow into the heavens.—All are born naked—no one comes in purple into the world; but that is far from working so powerfully as the thought that the king must die as the beggar.—Death the moral of the human fable.—"A mighty lesson for our time" (RICHT.).—Somewhat for people who would see clearly upon the death of Napoleon.—That there is to be a general judgment after this life is evident alone from death, which strikes all, even great men.—"The consideration of the inevitable exit of all who live should beget moderation in pretensions. We take nothing with us of that which so many desire with such eagerness" (L.).—Vers. 15-18. Great fates cast forth also great shadows.—If our terrors did but lead us to the knowledge of our misery, as well as of the glory of God!—The grave unites all at the last.—"The glory of the earth must become dust and ashes," etc.—But who believes our report? may be said also here: he who exalts himself shall be abased, and he who humbles himself shall be exalted.—"Thus God throws the loftinesses of men into one heap" (B. B.).—"And so circumcision makes a distinction in death—not, of course, that which is done in the flesh, but the circumcised heart; so that a circumcised person may have his place also among the uncircumcised, as, on the other side, uncircumcised persons, who are not so in heart, may be counted as circumcised. At the close, however, the prophet writes the name 'Pharaoh' on the lid of the coffin" (COCC.).

On Ch. xxxii.

Vers. 1, 2. How far otherwise have the court poets ever and anon elegized!—The comparison with lions and dragons withdraws much that is human in respect to Pharaoh.—"This robber-fish (?) and dragon, which with his feet troubles the streams, is like the beast that should ascend out of the sea (Rev. xiii.). Pharaoh is hence the enemy of the chosen, a roaring lion, which troubles the waters of heavenly wisdom with the slime of human additions, so that they provide no proper drink for those who thirst for salvation" (H. H.).—"Should Christian kings be like lions and dragons? They ought to be the fathers of their country, caring day and night for the welfare of their subjects" (ST.).—"Tyrants and the covetous are insatiable, and cannot be at rest" (STCK.).—"Ah! how much misfortune can be brought about by a restless ruler! Therefore pray for a peaceful government of the kingdom" (ST.).

Vers. 3-10. "The godless hasten to meet their destruction, without being afraid of it, but often secretly driven thereto by God" (H. H.).—"God is the supreme hunter and fisher; He can throw upon the lions His toils, and upon the whales His net, to catch and destroy them" (W.).—"God knows how to tame the untamed, to humble the proud, and to curb the fierce; who can resist His power?" (STCK.)—To be rejected, if not thrown entirely away, is the end of the mighty after the flesh.—Corruption the last strophe also in heroic poetry.—"How mournful is it to be cast away by God!" (STCK.)—Even the ass will plant his footstep on the wounded dying lion.—What the rich boast themselves so much of is but a carcase, which those who live after them will divide among themselves.—"After death, shame and reproach overtake the wicked and shameless" (H. H.).—Vers. 5, 6. Overflowing for overflowing; for the waters of Egypt, now the blood of the hosts of Pharaoh.—"They who formerly swam in pleasures, shall by and by swim in their own blood" (STCK.).—Ver. 7. "The greatness of the calamity is described by the prophet from the sense of those whom the tribulation affects, to whom it seems as if the whole world were enveloped in darkness" (H. H.).—"The lights of heaven truly shine only for the happy; the sun exists not but for the sunlit eye" (H.).—"The godly sustain themselves in such circumstances by the thought that the Lord is their light, and therefore will not suffer the light of their heart to go out" (L.).—"But he who despises the light of grace, for him the light of glory also shall not shine" (STCK.).—It is also dark, and the stars even fall from the heaven, when great, noble, important, eminent men, heroes, sages, lawgivers, governors, teachers, are carried off by death—or worse, when they fall away into superstition or unbelief, ungodliness, injustice, and violence.—Ver. 9. "Many a fall leads to the elevation of others" (ST.).—To be frightened is still not to be awakened, and awakening without enlightenment is spiritual tumult without spiritual life.—The grave, too, is an unknown land, and thither we are all journeying. Yet for faith there is a sun which rises upon it, that never goes down.—"So the Lord loves to inspire terror, that He may break fleshly confidence" (H. H.).—Happy for him whom a sincere conversion has made secure against the terrors which seize upon the whole earth!—He who still has to fear for his soul, let him consider that the whole world can profit him nothing!—Every moment are we in danger of death, and consequently in sight of eternity.

Vers. 11-16. If no other cure proves effectual, then God betakes Himself to the sword.—The method of salvation through blood and iron; but what is the state of society presupposed in connection with it!—The guillotine and the sword both do their work quickly, and bring what is before as it were under them.—Ver. 13. "It touches a miserly man much more nearly if his beast dies, than if his children are taken from him by death" (ST.).—A stock of cattle a state of peace.—Vers. 14, 15. The stillness of the desert is indeed stillness, but it is not peace, any more than to flow "like" oil is the soft nature of the spirit.—There is rest in the grave, but much unrest thereafter, yea, more unrest, and of a worse kind than existed before.—"There go the waters softly, as in mourning" (UMBR.).—But God knows how to set at rest a land and its creatures which have been plagued and misused by men. Where have the oppressors gone? They also lie still.—Lamentation does not take away the pain, but in the lamentation it lives on.

Vers. 17-32. Whoever would gain a thorough insight into the dominions and powers of the earth, he must look down into hell.—The instructive glance into hell.—The song of hell.—*La divina comœdia* of Ezekiel.—The doctrine of Sheol as the doctrine of the state after death.—What does the Sheol of the Old Testament signify? (1) According to its name, the demand of death on all persons and things, therefore the power of death over every individual person and thing; therefore that death is the wages of sin, the judgment of God's wrath which takes effect on the flesh. (2) As to the thing, it is the state after death as existence in a spacious grave; that is, notwithstanding the dissolution of the body and the separation of soul and body, a continuous life of the spirit, and that with consciousness and recollection—hence, according to the character of this, in peace or disquiet.—Woe to him whom the doom of death precipitates into condemnation in death!—One can strike up no song to the living more unacceptable, yet at the same time none more profitable, than one about dying; should any one refuse to accompany it, it will still be sung upon him.—He to whom the earth was all, when he sinks into the grave, all sinks with him. It is thus easily comprehensible how death stretches into the future, even into the grave, and how all appears as grave and graves.—People and princes, Sheol demands both.—"Only to the pious is the tomb a chamber where they softly sleep, a resting-place without pain and commotion, a mother's bosom (as we are from the earth), a place of repose to lie down in" (STCK.).—Ver. 19. It will be so much the worse if one has been nothing but fleshly, for death seizes in a rough and frightful manner.—Ver. 20. The sword cuts into the life, severs from life, sadly if also from God. For to die is what still goes on, to corrupt also; but to become lost for ever, that is the death without end, to die for evermore.—Ver. 21. The salutation of the dead toward the living when they die.—Ver. 22 sq. "What is received into the human heart, finds its grave also there; so round about the prince of death are his grave-places, wherein after a spiritual manner he is buried" (GREGORY).—The grave for the unconverted, the condemned, the perspective of the future world.—"The grave is very deep, even though in a material point of view it may be but a few feet down; it is deep enough to shroud all glory" (H.).—"Powerfully seizes the mind and humbles the pride the ever-recurring *There*, when the subject of discourse has respect to a fallen king and his hosts. . . . We look upon a limitless field of graves, and it is remarkable and peculiar to our prophet, that he transfers the graves also to the lower world" (UMBR.).—"As the elect come from the east and the west, and sit down with Abraham, Isaac, and Jacob in the kingdom of God, so the cast off find their way to the uncircumcised, to the pierced by the sword, in the depths below" (H. H.).—Here many graves, in the house of the Father many mansions.—The counterpart of the fellowship of believers upon earth, of the elect in heaven.—The lowest Sheol and the heavenly Jerusalem.—The earth is everywhere indeed the Lord's, but not all the dead die in the Lord.—Ver. 27. Men take with them into the state of the dead their knowledge, and along therewith the judicial sentence due to their manner of life.—Nothing is forgotten before God which is not forgiven.—The wrath of God remains on them, it is said in John.—Ver. 31. "It is a wretched consolation which is derived from the circumstance that people see in others the same torments which themselves experience. And yet misguided mortals do really comfort themselves with it. It is a common necessity, they say; others have experienced the same, and are experiencing it daily," etc. (H. H.)—The word of God, however, brings home to every man at last the application: this is such and such an one; as we find written on the tombstones: Here lies N. N.—"The Pharaohs prepare to swallow up without mercy: Jacob's Shepherd laughs at them," etc. (HILLER.)

B. SECOND PRINCIPAL PART.—Ch. XXXIII.-XLVIII.

THE PROPHECY OF GOD'S MERCIES TOWARD HIS PEOPLE IN THE WORLD.

I. THE RENEWAL OF EZEKIEL'S DIVINE MISSION.—Ch. XXXIII.

1, 2 And the word of the Lord came to me, saying, Son of man, speak to the
sons of thy people, and say to them, When I bring a sword upon a land, and
the people of the land take a man from their borders, and set him for
3 their watchman; And he sees the sword coming upon the land, and blows
4 the trumpet, and warns the people; And any one hears the sound of the
trumpet, and does not take warning, and the sword comes and takes him
5 away, his blood shall be upon his own head. He heard the sound of the
trumpet, and took not warning; his blood shall be upon him, since, letting
6 himself be warned, he would make his soul [his life] escape [would deliver it]. And
the watchman, when he sees the sword coming, and does not blow the trum-
pet, and the people are not warned, and the sword shall come and take away
a soul [a man] from among them, he is taken away in his iniquity, but his blood
7 will I require at the watchman's hand. And thou, son of man, [as a] watch-
man have I given thee to the house of Israel, and [so] thou hearest the word
8 out of My mouth, and thou warnest them from Me. If I say to the wicked,
Wicked man, thou shalt surely die, and thou dost not speak to warn the
wicked from his way, he, the wicked man, in [on account of] his iniquity shall
9 die, but his blood will I require at thy hand. But if thou dost warn a
wicked man of his way, that he turn from it, and he does not turn from his way,
he shall die in [on account of] his iniquity, but thou hast delivered thy soul.
10 And thou, son of man, say to the house of Israel: Thus ye say, saying, If our
transgressions and our sins are upon us, and we pine in [on account of] them,
11 how shall [can] we then live? Say to them, As I live, saith [sentence of] the Lord
Jehovah, if I should have pleasure in the death of the wicked! but in the
turning of a wicked man from his way, that he may live. Turn ye, turn ye
12 from your evil ways; and why will ye die, O house of Israel? And thou, son
of man, say to the sons of thy people, The righteousness of the righteous
shall not deliver him in the day of his transgression, and through [in the]
wickedness of the wicked shall he [the wicked] not stumble [fall] in the day of
his turning from his wickedness; and a righteous man shall not be able to
13 live thereby [namely, because he is a righteous man] in the day of his sin. When I say
of the [to the] righteous, He shall surely live, and he trusts in his righteousness
and commits iniquity, all his righteousnesses shall not be remembered, and in
14 his iniquity which he does, in it shall he die. And when I say to the wicked,
Thou shalt surely die, and he turns from his sin, and does judgment and
15 righteousness: If the wicked shall restore a pledge, shall repay what he had
robbed, if he walks in the statutes of life, that he do no iniquity—he shall
16 surely live, he shall not die! All his sins which he sinned, they shall not be
remembered to him; he does judgment and righteousness; he shall surely
17 live! And the sons of thy people are saying, The way of the Lord is not
18 right—but they, their way is not right! When a righteous man turns from his
19 righteousness and commits iniquity, then he shall die thereby: And when a

wicked man turns from his wickedness, and does judgment and righteousness,
20 thereby shall he live. And ye say: The way of the Lord is not right? Every
21 one as his ways [are] will I judge you, O house of Israel.—And it came to pass,
in the twelfth year, in the tenth [month], on the fifth of the month of our cap
22 tivity, the escaped from Jerusalem came to me, saying, The city is taken. And
the hand of Jehovah was upon me [came upon me] in the evening before the
coming of the escaped, and He opened my mouth, until he came to me in
23 the morning; and my mouth was opened, and I was no longer dumb. And
24 the word of Jehovah came to me, saying, Son of man, the inhabitants of those
ruins on the ground of Israel are saying, Abraham was one, and he got the
land for a possession, and we [are] many, and the land is given us for a posses-
25 sion. Therefore say to them, Thus saith the Lord Jehovah, Ye eat upon [with]
the blood, and ye lift your eyes [continually] to your abominable idols, and shed
26 blood, and shall ye possess the land? Ye stand upon your sword, ye do
abomination, and pollute every one his neighbour's wife, and shall ye possess
27 the land? Say thus unto them, Thus saith the Lord Jehovah, As I live, if
they who are in the ruins shall not fall by the sword! And him that is in
the field will I give to the beasts to be eaten, and they that are in the forts
28 and in the caves shall die of the pestilence. And I give the land to waste
and desolation, and the pride of its strength ceases; and the mountains of
29 Israel are waste, that no one passes over them. And they know that I [am]
Jehovah, when I give the land to waste and desolation, because of all their
30 abominations which they have done.—And thou, son of man, the sons of thy
people talk of thee beside the walls and in the doors of the houses, and
speak one with another, each with his brother, saying, Come now, and hear
31 what the word is which proceedeth from Jehovah! And they will come to
thee as a people comes, and will be before thee [as] My people, and they hear
thy words, and they will not do them; for [but] in their mouth they are prat-
ing loves [ever making love-songs, have wanton pieces in their mouth]; their heart goes after
32 their gain. And lo! thou art to them as a wanton song, beautiful of sound
[voice], and one striking the chords well; and they hear thy words, and do
33 them not. And when it comes—lo! it comes, then they know that a pro-
phet was in the midst of them.

Ver. 2. Vulg.: *de novissimis suis—(licet ex infimis suis*, ROSENM., *vel de excellentioribus*, LYRA).
Ver. 3. Sept.: . . . *καὶ σημανη τ. λαῷ*,
Ver. 4. . . . *και μη φυλαξηται – et non se observaverit—*
Ver. 12. Sept. . . . *ἀνομια ἀνομου οὐ μη κακωση αὐτον . . . δυνησεται σωθηναι—*
Ver. 16. . . . *ἐν αὐτοις ζησεται.*
Ver. 21. Sept. . . . *ἐν τ. δωδεκατω μηνι*—Vulg.: *vastata est civitas!* (Another read.: בעשתי עשרה, Syr.)
Ver. 22. . . . *κ. συνεκλεισθη ἐτι.*
Ver. 25. Another read.: רעיניכם, fully.
Ver. 26. . . . *και ἀνηρ τον πλησιον αὐτου ἐμιαινετε*—(Another read.: עשיתם.)
Ver. 28. Sept.: . . . *δια το μη εἶναι διαπορευομενον.*
Ver. 31. . . . *ὁτι ψευδος ἐν τ. στοματι αὐτων κ. ὀπισω τ. μιασματων αὐτων*—Vulg.: *quia in canticum oris sui vertunt illos et avaritiam suam—*
Ver. 32. *Και γινη αὐτοις ὡς φωνη ψαλτηριου ἡδυφωνου εὐαρμοστου*—Vulg.: *quasi carmen musicum, quod suavi dulcique sono canitur;—*
Ver. 33. . . . *ἐρουσιν Ἰδου ἡκει—*

EXEGETICAL REMARKS.

It is a question whether the last division of our book opens with this chapter. Kliefoth denies it from the contents, which point back to what precedes, ch. iii. 17 sq., xviii. 20 sq. The third part must begin with ver. 21. In contrast to the foreign nations, ver. 2 associates this word of threatening against Israel with the words of threatening against foreign nations previously given, as is done also in Isaiah and Jeremiah. Ch. xxv. 1–xxxii. 32 numbers thirteen words of God; thereto belongs ch. xxxiii. 1–20 as a fourteenth, in order to make out the number 2 × 7. The contents, threatenings and warnings, are not suited as an introduction to the promises of the third part; while, on the contrary, they are quite proper as a conclusion to the preceding portions. Hengstenberg also regards ch. xxxiii. 1–20 as the author's conclusion, but to the whole of what precedes, namely, ch. i.–xxxii. The text does not show the impossibility of Ezekiel having delivered a prophecy to his people before the arrival of the escaped; but the admitted *résumé* out of the preceding is no argument against the supposition of an introduction to the following, as we shall see, just as little as the want of a specification of time. For with reference to the latter point,

Hitzig justly points to the historical notice standing in the middle, vers. 21, 22. Its importance for the present chapter, in fact, makes any farther indication of time superfluous; as was remarked by Häv., who in this only goes too far, that he makes the revelations on to ch. xxxix. to have been imparted to the prophet in *one* night—the portion vers. 1-20 forming the somewhat earlier introduction revealed to him, and vers. 21-33 attaching itself to the other very closely as a new introduction.

This chapter has first of all its relation to the transition portion, ch. xxv.-xxxii. In this respect it likewise has a transition character, which on one side gives indication of itself in this, that it, as also ch. xxv.-xxxii., points back to the earlier part. For as the predictions of judgment upon those without are in some sense an appendage to the repeated, always increasingly definite prophecy of the destruction of Jerusalem, so ch. xxxiii. 2 sq., in what it says of the watchman-agency of Ezekiel, attaches an admonition for Israel to try themselves, in presence of this activity of the prophet, whether Ezekiel had not dealt faithfully with his obligation, or Israel with his warning; but especially as regards the exiled, the verses 10 sq. render conspicuous, in contrast with the despair of these, God's will and procedure, and verses 17 sq. set forth these as being the right way. If people will not renounce every kind of a connection, for which there is no foundation, they will find—where now what was announced in ch. xxiv. 26 sq. begins to enter—the supposition of a close to the past prophetic activity of Ezekiel, the prophecy of judgment, quite deserving of acceptation. It was a close proceeding out of as well as with that which had preceded. But by reason of the relation of this chapter, as now indicated, primarily to ch. xxv.-xxxii., is farther expressed its relation to the first main division, ch. i.-xxiv. On the other side, however, the transition character of the section ch. xxv.-xxxii. (pp. 11, 12) is proved by that which is contained in these chapters of a preparatory, introductory nature to the second main division of the book. This is the case also with our present chapter. It might already be regarded as a preparation for something new, that at the close with what precedes the call of Ezekiel is formulated out of it, and Israel is challenged to self-examination, as also to an acquittal of the prophet and a justification of God. The in part verbal reference of this chapter to ch. iii. and xviii., in vers. 2-20, certainly does not (as Keil supposes) set forth the call of Ezekiel for the future, but it contains a *renewal* of his divine mission. The connecting together of the two halves of the chapter is on no account to be regarded as "merely accidental." "The two verses 25 and 26, just as ver. 15, alike point back to ch. xviii.; and on the other hand, that ver. 10*b* is in accord with ch. xxiv. 23, cannot be overlooked" (HITZ.). The full-toned charge in ver. 2: "Speak to the sons of Israel, and say to them," suits well as a commencement, while ver. 24 looks only like a continuation. What Ezekiel must say to the sons of his people (ver. 2) prepares for the opening of his mouth (ver. 22), and so introduces what is to be said in ver. 25. There can be no doubt that what is stated in vers. 21, 22 is the fulfilment of ch. xxiv. 26, 27; so that the new, to which the verses 2-20 form the preparation and introduction,—the prophecy of God's mercies toward His people in the world,—is the second main division of the book. The passage, also, ver. 10 sq. explicitly directs the despairing to grace, while in the parallel passage, ver. 24 sq., the stout-hearted are, on the contrary, pointed to the judgment; so that the section ver. 23 sq. speaks just as much of threatening as of the opposite.

Vers. 1-20. *What kind of a sending of Ezekiel that was which is now renewed.*

Ver. 1. On what occurred in the twelfth year, after the taking of Jerusalem, on the evening or during the night before the escaped made his appearance, comp. at ver. 22. The address being to **the sons of thy people** (ver. 2), shows that he was now to turn from foreign nations to Israel again—although עַמְּךָ is still used, not עַמִּי, as at ver. 31 for the first time. There is already a preparation made for the great turn which divides the book.—If an application to the fellow-exiles of the prophet is primarily to be understood, there is still a more general one indicated in what follows,—that to the Israel of the captivity the Israel at home were to be added, that Israel generally were to be contemplated. For with this also agrees "the house of Israel" in the application of the similitude (ver. 7), according to which the children of the people of the prophet were thought of in common, as those who were entering into one and the same condition (בּוֹא), just as in the similitude itself "land" is spoken of, and אֶרֶץ placed quite absolutely (comp. xiv. 13).—The idea is first expressed figuratively, vers. 2-6, before Israel is put into the frame and hung on the wall (vers. 7-9).—אֶרֶץ כִּי־אָבִיא, spoken generally, but not altogether hypothetically; so, however, that the hearers should think of a case before them which had either actually occurred or was in the act of doing so. The enemy was on the way (HITZ., GROT.), was standing at the cross-way (ch. xxi. 26 [21], xxiv. 2). The turning of the matter into a similitude is peculiar to our passage, as distinguished from ch. iii. 16-21. Peculiar, also, is the trait in a manner necessitating a certain experience on the part of the hearers, that the people of the land in question, the men, were themselves to appoint the watchmen, whence, in case they did not give heed to him, they withstood and strove against themselves, and so should be the more convicted of their guilt and folly.—מִקְצֵיהֶם, singular, but in a plural sense: from the end on all sides, the entire territory of the land; according to the suffix, to be understood of the whole community, with reference to לָקַח and נָתְנוּ לָהֶם (Gen. xix. 4; 1 Kings xii. 31). Häv., Tuch decide for an ellipsis וְעַד קָצֶה.—On צֹפֶה, comp. on ch. iii. 17.—Ver. 3. Corresponding to the fundamental idea of צֹפֶה, וְרָאָה.—שׁוֹפָר of the clear resounding tone. That we are to think of a horny sort of instrument, if not one simply of horn, is evident from its being exchanged with קֶרֶן, in Josh. vi.

for example. תְּקַע שׁוֹפָר is distinguished as a signal for the calling together of the people, in Num. x. 6, 7, from the sounding of an alarm at a breaking up. Here it is manifestly applied to the announcement of the enemy, for a warning or advertisement to the people (comp. ch. iii. 17, and pp. 72, 73). — Ver. 4. וְשָׁמַע הַשֹּׁמֵעַ, who hath ears to hear (Rev. ii. 7, 11, etc.).—נִזְהָר for נִזְהָר.—**And the sword comes,** when the sword is a-coming, and what is to be feared cannot be a matter of doubt. EWALD: "so that the sword came and carried him away, then his blood," etc. According to HENGST.: because people are wont to carry on their heads; according to others, the image is derived from sacrifice, in which the offerer transferred his guilt to his victim by the laying on of his hand (Lev. i. 4, xxiv. 14; Matt. xxvii. 25).—Ver. 5. The alone self-guiltiness of the individual is here made still more manifest. An explication without any need of the כִּי, **for.** —בּוֹ, as much as בְּרֹאשׁוֹ, ver. 4.—HITZIG: "Because he let himself be warned, he has delivered his soul." נִזְהָר is here the participle.

Ver. 6. The similitude has hitherto proceeded on the supposition that the watchman does his duty, because this is really the case in hand. But now the other supposition is made, that he has neglected what belonged to his calling.—הוּא, masculine, referring to נֶפֶשׁ.— Since only the soul which continues in sin is liable to death (ch. xviii. 4, etc.), a wicked person is presupposed (as at ch. iii. 18) as the one that should be carried away; it should be through his guilt, on account of it and in it. But while previously the guilt of his blood was simply his own, the blood-guilt of his disobedience in respect to the intended warning is now, without regard to his guilt otherwise and generally, sought at the hand of the watchman. It is to be observed that for this דָּרַשׁ is used here, while we have בִּקֵּשׁ at ch. iii. 18, 20.—That the case supposed is only a possible, by no means a real one, appears from the application made of it at Ver. 7 to Ezekiel—for the πρoτασις the ἀποδοσις (comp. Heb. xiii. 17). At the same time is his installation as watchman to the house of Israel taken out of human hands, —in that case, when men appoint for themselves a watchman, the last-named possibility (ver. 6) might all the more readily take place,—and Jehovah carries back the watchman-office of Ezekiel expressly to Himself (**I have given thee**).—וְשָׁמַעְתָּ׳, such literally was the expression used of the call given in ch. iii. 17, so that we must think of supplying to the words marks of quotation; therefore not importing that the prophet must thereby be instructed with respect to the future.—Ver. 8. The same as before, only with a still more emphatic address than at ch. iii. 18.—Ver. 9. So here again; comp. at ch. iii. 19 (Acts xx. 25, 26).

Ver. 10. Since nothing of the neglect of duty which had taken place is charged upon the prophet, only the original direction given him is again literally repeated: the guilt must be sought among the people, as was really the case, and indeed is clear from their own lips, as stated here. —לֵאמֹר, *their* saying is set over against that which had been said to the prophet in divine direction, according to which he must speak; *their* doing also in regard to the Lord, as they had known it from the prophet's behaviour toward them, set over against his doing and acting. —Of what nature the divine mission of Ezekiel was from the first has been repeated (vers. 2-9) in the similitude and its explanation, and now (hence אֱמֹר׳ repeated in ver. 11) there follows in what manner this mission of his is renewed to the prophet. A reference is made back to ch. xviii., but the difference between what is said there and here must not be overlooked. While there no consciousness of guilt, no confession of sin, appears (xviii. 2), the predominantly recriminative work of Ezekiel has still produced so much effect that they now say: **Our transgressions and our sins are upon us.** But this consciousness and this confession tinges in the darkest manner the feeling of despair in regard to life. It is by no means for the purpose of excusing themselves that the people appeal to the passage Lev. xxvi. 39. Consequently, the **upon us** is not to be understood as meaning: "testify against us" (ROSENM.), but as of a burden under which they are sinking (וּבָם׳ נְמַקִּים, comp. on ch. xxiv. 23, iv. 17). Those who represented themselves in ch. xviii. as expiatory sufferers for their ancestors, here are pining away under their own burden, and that with reference to the prospect of life, likewise repeatedly opened up in ch. xviii. (vers. 23, 32). We must, therefore, take into account the pressure, were it only of the evil forebodings, the foreshadows of the event mentioned in ver. 21, if not the actual knowledge of the taking of Jerusalem; so that in this also may be seen preparation, an introduction to what was to follow.

Ver. 11. What for this despair in respect to life (*i.e.* deliverance, salvation, favour) was the declared mind and will of Jehovah in ch. xviii. 23, 32, the same is here emphasized in the peculiar protestation: **As I live,** while there it is only: "Have I any pleasure?" or: "for I have no pleasure"—see there also ch. xviii. 30, 31.—Ver. 12. We learn, however, that the question is about conversion: "He combats despair only in so far as it is a hindrance to repentance. To afford mere tranquillity is not the aim of the prophet" (HENGST.). Comp. on ch. xviii. 20, where in like manner with reference to conversion we have this antithesis: "righteousness of the righteous," and: "wickedness of the wicked." Through this antithesis to לֹא תַצִּילֶנּוּ, the expression לֹא יִכָּשֶׁל becomes clear (Niphal); GESEN.: "he shall not be unfortunate." His own righteousness no means of deliverance, so soon as he falls into transgression; and wickedness, again, no necessary destruction, so soon as a change to the better comes. (פִּשְׁעוֹ is likewise infinitive.) Because presently the case of the righteous was to be spoken of, it is said by way of introduction thereto: **And a righteous man, etc.** בָּהּ, in, through, on account of his righteousness.—Ver. 13. **To** the righteous man who continues such, assurance of life is promised. Confidence in one's own righteousness (singular, as an actual quality), when one does unrighteousness (ch. iii. 20), may be on the one side, but on the other side there will be no remembrance of the earlier **righteousnesses.** Comp. ch. xviii. 24, 26.—Ver. 14. The contrast with the wicked. Here an address to such, because this is what is wished for; comp. ch. xviii. 21.—Ver. 15. A lively form of speech, hence without the copula, an exemplification. Comp. in reference to it, ch. xviii. 7, 12, 16, 21, 28, xx. 11.—Ver. 16. Comp. ch. xviii. 22.

Ver. 17. Comp. on ch. xviii. 24 sq. The immediate occasion for blame is formed here by such a representation of the wicked (ver. 14 sq.) who repented, over the righteous who does unrighteousness. The fact alone that "a righteous man" could be spoken of before them in such a manner, more especially that turning, turning, is what they are called to, while they had placed their confidence upon "the righteousness of the righteous" (ver. 12)—if not their own, yet that which belonged to them, descended to them as the people of God from their pious forefathers—that is the stone in the way of the Lord which the divine address takes away, in order to throw it to the quarter to which it belongs, namely, to the false way of Israel, which they had chosen for themselves with their outward carnal self-righteousness in such and such religious observances. Vers. 18, 19, however, do not simply repeat vers. 13, 14, but the two cases of the righteous and the wicked return again in the form which is the most appropriate for setting forth clearly and distinctly the way of the Lord, and in which it strikes at first sight, and at the same time with reference to the command given: "Return, return." Hence not וְהוּא־בָטַח עַל־צִד', as at ver. 13, but בְּשׁוּב־צַדִּיק מִצִּד' (ch. iii. 20), and with nothing farther וּמֵת בָּהֶם, namely, by these two parts: turning from his righteousness, which is left unnoticed, and doing unrighteousness. (ROSENM.: עָוֶל, collective.) Comp. ch. xviii. 24, 26. The **wicked** throws light on this caricature of turning—a *turning* it also is, indeed, only to what is evil—by his, on the contrary, turning **from his wickedness** (in ver. 14 it is from "his sin").—Ver. 20, as also ch. xviii. 29, repeats the charge for the purpose of making a suitable close. Comp. ch. xviii. 30 (ch. vii. 27).

Vers. 21, 22. *The fresh turn.*

The fact is now an accomplished one—Jerusalem is taken (ch. xxiv. 25); and therewith we have, as had been foretold at the close of ch. xxiv., not only the arrival of the escaped, but as the main thing the opening of Ezekiel's mouth, that he might no more be dumb. This historical notice in the middle of the chapter is therefore the kernel of the whole: the renewal of the divine mission of the prophet, over against the completed acts of judgment, now gives to his prophecy the expression of God's compassions toward His people in the world, with which the second main division of the book is occupied.

The indication of time which was to mark the turning-point for the prophet (for Jerusalem was overcome on the 9th of the 4th month of the 11th year) teaches us to understand the expressions: "in the day," in ch. xxiv. 25, or: "in that day," vers. 26, 27, of what was to take place more than sixteen months afterwards. Hitzig regards it as "very improbable that Ezekiel should first have received in January 586 the report of what had happened to Jerusalem in July 588;" and in place of considering that the text could not mean to speak of the report, he makes the prophet over and above "contradict himself," inasmuch as, according to ch. xxvi. 1, 2, he had already in the eleventh year heard the report of the matter—which, however, is not necessarily rendered clear by ch. xxvi.—and then at the close he changes the twelfth year into the eleventh, which is supported by the Syrian translation alone. Hengst. justly remarks that the notice does not refer to the first report concerning the taking of Jerusalem, and then proceeds: "The news of such events spread with amazing rapidity. The intelligence, doubtless, arrived in eight, or at the most fourteen days at the abode of Ezekiel; so that the difficulty is not removed by assuming most arbitrarily an error in the text, and putting the eleventh in place of the twelfth year." The meaning of what was announced beforehand in ch. xxiv., and according to our verse had now actually occurred, is that in place of all reports—so fitted to awaken hope, yet traversing the way of the Lord with His people, always again paralysing their necessary conversion—which up to the last had arrived, a certain fugitive shall now speak, and, as an eye-witness, place beyond all dispute what had actually happened. The matter-of-fact voucher given into the hand of the exiled with this escaped one must have removed out of the path of safety what at least the strong walls of Jerusalem threw in the way of their turning to the Lord. For the meaning ascribed to הִפָּלִיט, to make one's escape, get off through flight (Gen. xiv. 13), it is not necessary, with Hengstenberg, to suppose an ideal person, a collective, that is, "a band of exiles," as Ezekiel had already intimated, ch. xiv. 22, 23, that a whole host of such fugitives would come to the exiles, "so that these by their miserable plight should be a living proclamation of the frightful catastrophe through which they had passed." Hitzig thinks that "the fugitive may have escaped immediately after the bloodshed at Mizpah from the band of Ishmael (Jer. xli. 10); if not, which is improbable, only after the flight which ensued into Egypt." J. D. Michaelis explains out of the remoteness of Ezekiel's place of residence the so late arrival of the fugitive, especially considering the frightful disorder that took place.

Ver. 22. **And the hand of Jehovah,** etc.; comp. ch. xxxvii. 1, i. 3. The effect of it was *the opening of the mouth.* But this latter can be virtually and actually distinguished. In that respect the opening of the mouth of Ezekiel took place when it was commanded him that he should speak to the sons of his people, in respect to whom he had been dumb from the time indicated in ch. xxiv. He began to do so at ver. 1 of this chapter, to which, therefore, the expression concerning "the hand of Jehovah" brings us back—namely, that this hand had now removed from him his previous dumbness, so that he might henceforth again speak to Israel, and should do so. J. D. Michaelis remarks quite correctly: "the prophet fell into ecstasy," and the word contained in vers. 2-20 was imparted to him. In regard to the time, it is more precisely stated that the divine cause comes into operation on **the evening before the coming of the escaped**; and parallel therewith was the effect, the opening of the prophet's mouth, עַד־בּוֹא אֵלַי, therefore in the interval between the evening and the morning. It was hence independently of the escaped that the prophet got a renewal of his commission, and, indeed, while there was combined with the removal of his previously enforced silence a direct positive revelation and communication. Through a divine movement and working, everything was thus prepared and introduced for that which was going to take place on the fugitive's arrival. For the circumstance that on his actual arrival Ezekiel's mouth was opened (וַיִּפָּתַח פִּי is not to be regarded as an emphatic repetition for the purpose of connection with what follows, but in contradistinction to וַיִּפְתַּח אֶת־פִּי), adds to what was done *potentia*, as it now also took place *actu*, so that the divine word, vers. 2-20, given with this aim, for this particular moment destined, **was now also spoken to the people by the prophet**; and in proof that he was no more dumb, *he immediately proceeded to give the continuation of it* (ver. 23 sq.). In ch. xxiv. 27 it was said Ezekiel's mouth should be opened "with" the escaped. In the wider sense, namely, at the same time, about the time, when the escaped should come, it took place in the evening; literally, it took place with him in the morning, and the renewed prophetical mission of Ezekiel began then in fact. ["One may designate the following prophecies as the prophetically represented victorious history of Israel, of the kingdom of God among men. The wonderful, truly great, and divine is set forth here as a contrast to the present. In the presence of death only resurrection and life! The deepest humiliation of the covenant-people, their apparent annihilation is the path to their true greatness, nay, to their eternal glory."—HÄV.] Hengst. remarks: "On the night before the arrival of the exile-band, which was doubtless announced the day before, took place the opening of the prophet's mouth, the removal of the seal as it were from it. The impulse to speak to the people again asserted itself. The prophetic activity itself first commenced after the exile-band appeared, the arrival of which was to form the ground for the receiving of the new disclosures. Only after the complete death exhibited before their eyes, the annihilation of all earthly hopes, could the announcement of the joyful resurrection be made." Comp. besides on ch. iii. 26, 27, and xxix. 21.

Vers. 23-33. *The Renewed Mission of Ezekiel in view of the State of Heart of those in Canaan* (vers. 23-29), *and then of those in the Captivity* (vers. 30-33).

What sort of a mission that of Ezekiel's was which was renewed to him, namely, to do the part of a watchman, to warn the people, we have already seen in vers. 2-9. Hence in the connection of the following section with vers. 1-20 things stand in their proper order, and it entirely corresponds with a continuation of the divine discourse, that such a position of the prophet at the renewal of his divine mission first of all comes to an explanation with those who are still to be warned, to be threatened. The beginning of the divine word made known to Ezekiel corresponds very closely with that contained in vers. 8, 9. It is a complete misunderstanding on the part of Kliefoth, when he would not find "the inhabitants of these waste places," as he renders, in the desolated Jerusalem, or in the desolated cities of Judah, or in the desolated land of Canaan, *i.e.* in the remnants of the people who still remained there, but drags into the text the exiles in "the certainly not too well cultivated regions on the Chaboras." חֳרָבוֹת with the article implies demolition, **ruins** of cities and houses. HITZIG: "these wastes," less Jerusalem itself than the other cities which had been stript of their inhabitants (Jer. xxxiii. 13, 10), in which those who were without possessions (Jer. xxxix. 10) shared with the returned fugitives (Jer. xl. 12), having all at once come to great wealth of land, and were puffed up. Things were lying in a comfortless state; how do the hearts adjust themselves to the comfortless position of things? "That there were people who still, ever giving themselves up to illusions, thought that the judgment would not inexorably run its course, was proved by the revolt in which Gedaliah, the Chaldean governor, was slain" (HENGST.). Comp. also the representation in Neh. i. of the desolate condition of things, though an interval of upwards of a century had meanwhile elapsed!—As even in the time of Jesus they were always throwing themselves back on Abraham (for example, John viii., Matt. iii. 9), so was it the case here. An *argumentum a minori*. Since to Abraham, an individual man, in his posterity the land was given for a heritage, the less they conceive could it possibly fail to them—namely, to keep the land; not so properly with HENGST. to receive it again, for they do not give it up as lost—when in point of number they were many, and still more in the feeling of their souls they were without the knowledge of sin and the sense of guilt. In the words of Hengst: "they held themselves to be the true continuation of Abraham's being, the bearers of the promise given to him" (Gen. xv. 7)—the posterity in whom Abraham inherited it, to whom therefore it "was given." "They overlooked the wide gulf that stood between them and him; if they were Abraham's children, they would have done his works." (Comp. at ch. xi. 15.)

Ver. 25. To eat **upon the blood** is explained by Keil as eating of flesh which has not been cleansed of the blood; comp. Lev. xix. 26. "A fundamental law of the theocracy" (HÄV.). The prohibition was given so early as at Gen. ix. 4. There with respect to the shedding of blood, as the infliction of death, murder; so that it was aimed against the spirit of murder (HENGST.). TARGUM: "You eat upon innocent blood." From the blood a transition is made to the eating. In Lev. xix. it appears in connection with the service of idolatry, as also here.—Ch. xviii. 6, 15, ch. xxii. 3, iv. 27.—The question is repeated in Ver. 26. To stand or place one's self is = to support one's self, therefore to place his confidence thereon, which carries farther the shedding of blood.—עֲשִׂיתֶן תּוֹעֵבָה, feminine; hence it has been understood of the women, with reference to immodest idolatrous worship. Hengst. points to ch. xiii. 17 sq. ("The feminine character of the sinner is already indicated in Gen. iv. 7, where it appears unmanly to let sin conquer, instead of ruling over it.") HITZIG: ן stands for ם on account of the ת following. Ch. xviii. 12, xvi. 50, v. 11. The **abomination** must, according to Hengst., be adultery; ch. xviii. 6, 11.—In ver. 27, three punishments are placed over against 2 × 3 sins. The parallel to ver. 10—here referring to presumption, there to despair—is confirmed by: "As I live" (ver. 11).—בֶּחֳרָבוֹת (ver. 24) בַּחֶרֶב, a play of words.—Ch. v. 17, xiv. 15, 21; 2 Kings xvii. 25.—מְצָדוֹת, the mountain-tops, difficult of access; hence asylums, mountain-fastnesses, to which (as deeps to heights) the **caves** correspond on the other side, and which come into consideration as refuges from the sword and ravenous wild beasts, but not from the pestilence. (1 Sam. xiii. 6; Jos. *Bell. Jud.* i. 16. 4.) Ch. v. 17, xiv. 21.—Ver. 28. Ch. vi. 14.—(Niph.) ch. xxx. 18, vii. 24.—מֵאֵין עוֹבֵר, ch. xiv. 15. Cleared of men, even of passing travellers.—Ver. 29. Ch. xxxii. 15.

Vers. 30–33. The reference in the preceding verses to the accomplished fact of Jerusalem's overthrow is followed in Ver. 30 by a glance into the immediate surroundings of the prophet, as they stood related to his fresh mission. The position of matters was here full of consolation; the consolatory work of Ezekiel must begin, the announcement of salvation is going to proceed. How do the hearts of the exiles feel in regard to this? The prophet cannot speak comfort by means of Abraham, after the manner in which they comforted themselves in Canaan (ver. 24). He is "no servant of sin, but of the living God" (HÄV.). A putting of the prophet right, therefore, with respect to the men, such as that which fell to his lot at the outset of his mission, is entirely suitable also here for the new beginning and for the continuation even to the end.—**And thou** corresponds to the application, ver. 7.—הַנִּדְבָּרִים ("who talk among themselves;" they are presented to the prophet, as it were, with a: See there!—HENGST.). Hitzig makes the matter too pointed when he expounds: "Not who confer together upon thee, but who converse about thee as about a matter that is of no great interest to them." On the contrary, בְּךָ indicates a continuation of the discourse and a sense of interest, which Häv. thinks cannot be understood otherwise than with a hostile feeling. Still less, however, accords with such an interpretation the regular assembling of the people about the prophet, and above all, the impression which the fulfilment of his predictions will probably have made upon them. He hence forms the beloved standing object of their plaudits—must have done so, we may rather say. אֵצֶל', *sitting down by the walls* ("**upon** the divan," HENGST.)—as much as: in secret, or within their houses. (Scarcely, as Häv.: "the sons, etc., who speak against thee in the **house**, are thy opponents secretly, and in the doors of the houses, in public, there every one acknowledges thee.") בְּפִתְחֵי, *without*, namely, standing under the gates or doors of the house. **And speak**; this continues the action of the previous clause. The full form of expression likewise imports more than Hitzig will concede to them.—The words: **Come now**, etc., appear also to intimate that they must now expect something new, different from what they had been hitherto always hearing. But is it as at Hos. vi. 1? Would they only **hear**, as they say, and not also obey? not return to the Lord?—The prophet must not deceive himself on this account, that his person is their daily theme within and without, nay, that they come in a manner to the word of the Eternal, as is described in Ver. 31, namely, "as the coming of people," that is, like streaming multitudes, in vast crowds ("as on great solemnities," HÄV.)—to which is parallel עַמִּי, in an emphatic manner designating either: "My people" ironically, those who *should* be Mine—hear, but do not; or: "as My people," that is, as if they would be My people, and still are not. EWALD: "as if they were the true community." Or may it not be as HENGST.: "so respectful, attentive, and apparently earnest and willing"? What they will not do is clear from ver. 11; the words of the prophet aim at the heart's conversion.—כִּי־עֲגָבִים, HITZIG: "for the lovely is according to their taste;" but הֵמָּה עֹשִׂים? and עֹשִׂים is certainly suggested by לֹא יַעֲשׂוּ. "Lovely things" were such as they liked, desired, longed for; hence they are only about the doing of that which is pleasant in their mouth, smacks agreeably to them. Gesenius, however, puts it: "For with the mouth they do what is well-pleasing (to God), but their heart goes after their unrighteous gain." Hengst. declares the meanings of "loveliness" and "well-pleasing" to be without foundation, and renders: "they deal tenderly with their mouth," properly: "they show ardour, affect in words an ardent love to God and His word, while the real inclination of their heart goes quite another way, is turned to mammon, the god of the Jewish old man." HÄV.: "for lewdness they follow with their mouth." עגב with Ezekiel (comp. at ch. xxiii.) and Jeremiah unquestionably denotes impure love, passionate desire, especially unchaste fleshly desire, whether as akin to ἀγαπάω, or to "gaping after" (*gaffen*), looking after, or to "snatching at" (Germ. *happen*), hoping for, earnestly expecting. So much is clear as to the meaning of the word; all besides is imported, or arbitrarily connected with it. עֲגָבִים (only in the plural), however, occurs not merely in ver. 31, but also in ver. 32 connected with שִׁיר, song. What else, then, can it signify but "love-songs" (songs of impure love)? To the fact that they do not the words of the prophet, which according to their own confession proceed from Jehovah (ver. 30), the עֲגָבִים בְּפִיהֶם הֵמָּה עֹשִׂים form a restriction: certainly they also **do**, they are at the doing **in their mouth**: as much as, with words, with the tongue. What is received by the ear, this in the mouth becomes love-**songs**; **the** "doing" of that they make out of the words of God spoken by the prophet. Hence, after that in ver. 31 the expression עֲגָבִים has been explained, or more exactly defined, the statement: "and they hear thy words," etc., is again resumed. So that their doing remains in the mouth; the heart does not participate in it, as is presently indicated when it is said that their heart goes after its covetous, fraudulent gain (בֶּצַע from בָּצַע, to make a cut; ch. xxii. 27, 12). Nay, they take such advantage of the words of God, which Ezekiel announces to them, that they turn them to their own account; whence it is not so much their warm regard for Jehovah, as Jehovah's for them, which here comes into consideration. In some such way they treat the divine promises as loving declarations of a hot paramour. We are not, however, on this account obliged to interpret עֲגָבִים by: "frivolous jokes," "words of mockery" (with the Targum), or: "falsehood," "deceit," with the older translations. Not that they would "only amuse themselves," but more, they *turn grace into wantonness* (Jude 4). With them also, therefore, the matter concerns the *substance* of things, not so much "the lovely form;" and they were perverting it to excess according to their heart's lust.

Ver. 32. According to Hitzig, שִׁיר must signify not song, but "lovely singer." יְפֵה קוֹל does not necessitate that, for it may be referred to the fine tones of the song. But if it applies to the fine voice of the prophet, then it is to be understood that, after he has in שִׁיר been coupled with his prophecy (to which, however, the reference according to the connection must chiefly be made), he is thought of apart, and מֵטִב נַגֵּן continues the reference to the prophet, without therefore constraining us by this personal reference to understand שִׁיר also directly and simply of him. הֵיטִיב (Hiph. of יָטַב), with נַגֵּן, signifies either to play well, beautifully, or to do so vigorously, bravely. Junius refers what is said to the prophecies of doom upon those who are without (ch. xxv.–xxxii.). Hengst., in a manifestly modern fashion: "they rejoice amid the national impoverishment at the admirable rhetorical gifts of the new classic" (!).—Ver. 33. This verse joins to the repetition of their not doing the prediction of their unfailing and so different knowledge of the prophet.—**And when it comes**, in a general sense, what he speaks; not the more special utterance in vers. 27–29, which at least does not sound like a song of loves, rather the prophecies which were now going to follow. Thus the tone with which this second main division of the book commences is different; not: they shall know that I am Jehovah, but as at ch. ii. 5, where the language employed was still of a general kind. (See there.)—The: **behold it comes**, points back to the circumstance that the judgment on the people has actually come; and as such a thing has come, so certain also shall the following discourses be seen to be as to their fulfilment. (Hitz.: the matter shall certainly come to pass which is the object of thine address. Häv.: "And lo! it is already fulfilled; this must signify, Jerusalem is fallen, and the truth of the predictions perfectly established.") The experience is, however, a painful one, because the people's impenitence will exclude them from the future salvation. What far-reaching and, at the same time, true prospective vision, even to the days of the Son of man! It had already been declared to them through the prophets in the midst of them; so much the more, when He Himself actually came and spoke to them, did every pretext for their sin fall away, John xv. 22.

DOCTRINAL REFLECTIONS.

Compare the Reflections at pp. 72, 73, *and on* ch. xviii.

1. "Woe is me," exclaimed the apostle, "if I preach not the gospel!" (1 Cor. ix. 16.) This is a lesson which belongs to all those who have had the care or oversight of others committed to them. With that is not to be confounded the circumstance, that each individual has his particular gift from God, by means of which he can be profitable to his neighbour. The general love demands that we should seek the salvation of each other, Jude 21–23 (Cocceius).

2. In the office, calling, service which belongs to preachers, two things unite,—namely, the appointment through men, that is, in the present case, through the Church, as is implied in the similitude ver. 2 sq.; and that the Lord gives preachers to Jerusalem, as is said at ver. 7. Where this latter is not regarded, there the other also cannot be considered. If the civil magistrate, hence the State, or private individuals to whom the patronage belongs, will assert for themselves the *vocatio ministrorum*, they thereby ignore the Christian rights of the Church, just because they do not acknowledge the supreme right of God over His people. For it belongs to the Church to choose and ordain her servants, according to the order of Christ and His apostles; and a particular community, although it may be locally formed, does not at all stand related to the whole Church after the manner that a single commune, as a section of the civic commonwealth, stands related to the State; but it is in respect to constitution the Church itself, which has its representation in the community as regards its full possession of life. Not otherwise appear to us the communities of the Acts of the Apostles and of the apostolic epistles. Hereditary relations might well enough beget a temporary legal right of a historical kind, but really destitute of foundation, in so far as it is at variance with the fundamental rights of the Church, and can be proved to be the remnant of an antagonistic claim of rights, an unjust usurpation. We are not to speak with the Remonstrants of rights conferred upon the Church by the State in the matter of the *vocatio ministrorum*, since the State has no right to confer, because possessing none. And so the Reformation, if it found itself very much in the position, could not have the right, to erect a throne for the Cæsareo-papal government of the Church, since the Church, having the right to govern itself, renounces itself when it gives up to the State, or to the persons in whom the civil power concentrates itself, rights which are absolutely the Church's own, which therefore the civil power cannot possess, unless these rights are to

be turned to foolishness. In every tyranny exercised on the conscience, foolishness plays its part. But the claim of right, which, since the Reformation, has crept in for the conferring of rights which are against right, is of a piece with that of *summus episcopus*—whence the Papistical leaven of this title clearly appears. For it is Papistical doctrine in the general to ascribe the right of vocation to the bishops, if the Roman chair should not have granted special exceptions in regard to the election of pastors. When the limits of State-power have been formulated in this way, that it has to do with things *circa sacra*, but not *in sacris*, it certainly does look odd enough that "a supreme bishop" should indeed inspect the walls of the sanctuary, but must not tread upon them. The experience of upwards of 300 years, however, has shown much else than the absurdity of the formula in question—has proved the neglected, though oft-repeated and powerfully expressed, warnings of Luther and of the symbolical books, against the intermingling of the spiritual and civil jurisdictions, to have been only too well grounded. And when the Reformed theologian Heidegger, in his *Medulla Theologiæ*, with the view of smoothing over the folly of that formula, would not have the oversight and power of the State limited to the *circa religionem et ecclesiam*, but apostrophises the magistrate as *ὁμοπιστος et ecclesiæ membrum excellens*, thereby giving him to participate in the power which belongs to the Church, and then ascribing to him the obligation of serving Christ and His kingdom, and of advancing this kingdom with the authority lent him by God;—or when Burmann, also a Reformed theologian, enumerates the offices of the magistrate *circa sacra*, and among these reckons not merely the appointment and ordering of the acts of public worship, so as to secure that all be done according to the word of God, and the providing a safeguard against ecclesiastical arbitrariness, and the interposition on behalf of oppressed fellow-believers, and so forth, but also the suppression of errors, of heretics and heterodox, the reformation of the Church when it has become corrupt, etc.;—in all this we have a glance afforded us into a state of things which has actually existed, but which, and along therewith the alleged ground for such civil interferences, in spite of the so-called "Christian State," has long since passed away. But what is to be matter of controversy with the State will, above all, have reference to the so-called church patrons, for patronage is really of Romish-heathenish origin, and has never at all, in conformity with its proper sense, been Christianized as a juridical advocateship; at least a good part of the Germanic feudal lordship has infused itself into this assumption of a right of private domination. Now if, in opposition to all of this nature that is at variance with the self-government of the Church by means of the organization peculiar to her, a stand is to be made, and, in particular, the choice and calling of pastors are effected in this way through men, there still is, as the other factor, the Lord, whose body the Church of God is, and the right of the Church in its last source is the constitution granted by her sole Head, Christ. In consequence of this *regimen principale*, all are brethren who *serve* one another, the Lord alone has the supreme authority (theocracy or Christocracy); so that the Church, in respect to its inner spiritual form, is no democracy, neither is it an aristocracy any more than a hierarchy, but a monarchy in the highest sense of the word. Through the Holy Spirit, and by dint of such supreme invisible sovereignty, was Ezekiel sent to Israel, just as in ordinary circumstances the humblest village pastor is sent from the same quarter, whether it may be for grace or for judgment. For it is God's good pleasure that through such service on the part of men the divine will in respect to men should be accomplished (Eph. iv. 11 sq.); and the calling of a minister in any particular case will be perfect, where the *internal* through the Spirit corresponds with the *external* through the Church or its organs.

3. Ewald maintains that "the ultimate ground of all possibility of a true conversion stands in this, that in connection with the divine grace, which is ever working for good, a genuine prophet never fails, who, in perilous times announcing the pure truth, informs and warns all with dauntless, clear words." Against enthusiasts and Schwenkfeldians it has not, indeed, been denied by the teachers of the Church, that God, if such had been His will, could also immediately as from Himself have converted and saved men; yet still the Church has always held fast the conviction, that the public ministry and vocation to it in the Church is requisite by a hypothetical necessity, namely, with reference to the good pleasure and purpose of God.

4. The prophets are to be reckoned among the "extraordinary ministers." In the old Reformed theology, the extraordinary vocation was represented as threefold:—(1) When God effects it directly through His voice, as in the case of Abraham, Moses, the prophets under the Law, John the Baptist, and the apostles; (2) when it takes place by announcement through a human instrumentality, as in the case of Aaron and the tribe of Levi, by means of Moses as the mediating agency; (3) when the internal impulse of the Spirit drives in one direction or another, as was the case, for example, with the deacon Philip.

5. Death is the wages of sin, and sin is the destruction of people; and so, by reason of the universal sinfulness, quite apart from particular charges of guilt, an absolutely sinless extinction of life is not to be thought of; only relatively heavier or lighter will the guilt weigh in particular cases. But beside one's own guilt, that of each individual man, there stands upon the tablet of the Judge, as fellow-partakers thereof, human society in the general (through education, instruction, customs, etc.), and in particular its chiefs, as governors, princes, lords, teachers, etc., who should serve not merely as possessors of the dignity and of office, but also as examples to be looked up to in whatever place they may be.

6. "This is, however, the brightest and most glorious distinction of the prophetic calling, to proclaim the joy of the Creator in connection with the life of the converted sinner" (UMBREIT).

7. We have not on this account to despair of life, because knowing that we are in the midst of death. For this knowledge of death excludes only the thought of life, as that which might still be in ourselves, and could proceed out of us; but such knowledge by no means takes from us, it rather brings nearer, the prospect of life out of ourselves, namely, in the living God. The con-

version from sin to God, as also from all dead works of a simply legal nature, or of self-righteousness, is hence a burying in regard to the life which is merely man's, while in reality it is the way of that life which God gives, and which He Himself is.

8. "Conversion, internally considered, is the change of a man's state of mind into conformity with the will of God—a change, therefore, in which his internal feeling cannot be alone operative, but in which that effects his transformation in the power of God, which is the moving impulse from a higher power in respect to what he is going to be. But outwardly it appears as the complete reformation of his behaviour, since he turns from a direction toward the world into a direction toward God. The change which takes place in his state of mind in all the elements conditioning it becomes manifest in the transformation of his life. This change of mind is as to its nature a single decisive and deeply conscious act—the act of the whole inner life; but precisely on this account not the isolated occurrence of a single hour, of a particular frame or deed, though it frequently also comes to its highest manifestation in a particular hour, frame, or deed. It is not an abstract single change, but a revolution resting on a concrete single change, on a definite turning-point, an always renewed and always more deeply penetrating and pervading revolution, which is quite fitly designated by the term conversion. It is the everlasting deed of the man in the power of his God with reference to the old life" (LANGE, *Pos. Dogmatik*).

9. "Evil ways are not only the bad ways of wicked works, but also the false ways of righteousness. Nay, it is above all important, that whoever will live should turn from his own wisdom and fancied power, as if he could sanctify himself to God, and give Him the glory, and receive from Him justification by grace" (COCC.).

10. Because conversion of heart, sincere conversion, can at any moment savingly interrupt the course of development of sin, which would otherwise run on to its consummation in the judgment of death, so the disobedience of *unbelief* toward the alluring word of grace must be regarded as the sin unto death.

11. "When it is said that God has no pleasure in the death of the wicked, it must be understood after this manner, as if He were not inclined to give pardon to the penitent. God does not delight in judgment in such a way as not to delight in the justification of him who repents; as if repentance in faith on the word which promises grace to the sinner were of no account with God, or as if there were no righteousness of God available through which the penitent might obtain salvation. This word very clearly shows that there was no necessity for Israel pining away in their own sins, or in those of others, if they were but themselves in the right way. For whenever they turned from their evil way, life was thenceforth prepared for them. Whence it follows, that for that life neither a temple nor a state was requisite, so that those only should pine away of worldly sorrow who have their glory in these carnal and earthly things; whereas for such as would bend their hearts to believe in God, there should be no wasting away in their own or their fathers' sins, or in those of the people, but they should have life in hope, and should not feel the want of state-support or temple or priesthood, and carnal things of that sort, but should find all laid up for them in God, who would be mindful of His covenant with Abraham, and provide the Seed in which the Gentiles were to be blessed" (COCC.).

12. "The greatest danger that can arise out of suffering is that a man should misunderstand his Maker; one of the hardest problems for the servants of God is to bring reason into the suffering" (HENGST.).

13. The law in the Old Covenant directed its chief attention upon sin. The knowledge of sin must be for men the result that came out of all those imperatives, "Thou shalt not," and "Thou shalt." Hence the prophets in their relation to the law could, in the first instance, pursue no other aim than to set forth men as sinners. Sin remains as the mark of interrogation behind the righteousness of the righteous. As the conflict between the law and the carnality of man is not closed by the law, the doing of what is right according to the law may acquire for any one the predicate of a righteous person, but it will always only in particular cases be done aright according to the law; the righteousness out of the law must be "righteousnesses," specific ἔργα νόμου—such as, for example, are mentioned in ver. 14 sq. (and in contrast therewith ver. 25 sq.). So that there is a righteousness of the righteous, vers. 12, 13, 18, while still man does not see himself placed through the law in the position of a perfectly happy relation to God, freed from guilt and the curse of the law. It is not, however, knowledge alone of his sins and knowledge of himself as a sinner which the law gives to man, but along therewith the knowledge that the righteousness, the reality of which corresponds to God, which is the righteousness of God, must come as a revelation outside the law from God Himself through grace.

14. That with the completed fact of the overthrow of Jerusalem the silence of Ezekiel should be brought to an end, and he should be no more dumb—this circumstance lent to the fact in question a special character, caused it to appear so much the more in a peculiar light, as a parallel must be provided for it. Accordingly, it not merely seems as if Jerusalem must have fallen, so that salvation might with open mouth be prophesied, as the starry orbs of night disappear before the rising sun, but it was in reality so; and parallel with this first destruction, the last destruction of the Holy City, and the total dispersion of the people throughout the Roman world, on the one hand, made room for the fulness of the Gentiles at the table of Abraham, Isaac, and Jacob, and on the other, caused the gospel salvation to be preached to every creature. Jerusalem became then thoroughly desolate; but John saw a new Jerusalem coming down out of heaven. The Jews have been scattered abroad everywhere, but the Israel of God are being gathered meanwhile from all the ends of the earth, on the ground of the prophetic word, rendered more certain through the fulfilment certified by the apostles.

15. "Neither danger, or, more correctly, the anxious concern and dread about danger, such as we can well imagine to ourselves, nor any other hindrance, must be permitted to throw itself like an insuperable wall in the way of a servant of

God. This is no apology worthy of a prophet, 'I labour in vain; I preach to deaf ears;' but in season and out of season is the work to be carried on, and sinners to be admonished. No one must bury his talent (Matt. xxv.). And this holds equally with respect to magistrates and heads of families" (LAVATER).

HOMILETIC HINTS.

Ver. 1. "We men are daily and always anew to be reminded of our obligations, for individually and collectively we are slothful and negligent men" (STCK.).—Vers. 2, 3. "How profitable in dangerous times is the guardian care of watchmen! They must not, however, betray the confidence of the community, and must have open eyes, in order that the people of the Lord may not be taken by surprise. But when the Lord does not keep the city, the watchman waketh in vain, even though he does not fall into sleep" (LUTHER).—"The sword is the judgment, but the trumpet the holy gospel; the man who spies and watches is the bishop, whose part it is to preach and testify of the future judgment" (CLEMENT).—*Sollicitudo officium prælati est, non celsitudo* (BERNARD).—"The calling to the office of preacher is twofold—one immediate, the other mediate; the former is from God, the latter from man, Acts xxvi. 15, 16, vi. 5" (CR.).—"Who would choose a blind man to be the watchman of a city? How could he see the danger and give warning of it? How unreasonable is it, therefore, to appoint a spiritually blind or unconverted man to be a teacher! He does not at all see the danger, and how can he give warning? Isa. lvi. 10, 11; Matt. xv. 14" (STARKE).—The office and work, the service and fidelity of a right bishop or overseer of the community.—The profitableness and blessing of fidelity; on the other hand, the injury and curse of unfaithfulness.—"The importance and responsibility of the prophetic calling" (UMBR.).—"Although in the present day ministers are chosen and ordained to church employment by men, yet may such human choice, when it is rightly gone about, be also termed divine. But since it is God who assigns ministers their place, He ought to be entreated to send true and good ministers to His people" (LUTHER).—"What sort of a watchman would he be who should keep silence about the breaking out of a fire, because he would not rouse people out of their sleep? And so, what sort of teacher would he be who should remain silent at the sins of the ungodly, that they might not be disturbed in their sleep of security?" (ST.)—"No blind man, nor dreamer, nor drowsy sleeper, is fit for an office which takes its name from wakefulness" (BERL. BIB.).

Vers. 4–6. To let one's self be warned, what a profitable, serious, and yet very much neglected prescription!—"Ask those who have gone to hell; they will in a body give thee for answer, We would not take warning" (STCK.).—The disregarded or despised warnings from youth up.—Men can but warn, they cannot deliver.—The power and the weakness of our love.—"I hear the message well enough, but I want faith."—Ver. 6. Of the watching which is enjoined upon ourselves: "Watch, for ye know not," etc., we are not relieved by the obligation which lies upon the watchman. Hence he who is overtaken unwarned still does not fall guiltless, for his security, carelessness, etc., were the occasion of his fall.—Contempt of danger is therefore no true courage.—Every one must carry his soul as in his hand.—"What a mournful condition is it, when the Church does not watch, the State does not protect, the house does not admonish!" (STCK.)

Vers. 7–9. "Natural life and soundness of health are indispensably necessary to an ordinary watchman, and not less necessary are life and strength in the inner man to a spiritual watchman, Lam. ii. 14" (LANGE). "With a spiritual watchman there must be found a spiritual life, a spiritual light, a spiritual wakefulness, and dutiful fidelity in all parts of his office" (ST.).—As the prophet on the mouth of God, so the preacher is dependent on the word of God. He has by this to prove every word of man; on this last his office has no dependence.—The apostle pleads in the stead of Christ, 2 Cor. v. 20.—"Mark, Christian hearer! For God's sake, and because God wishes it, thy teacher must warn thee. Therefore be not wroth with him; if thou shouldst be so, then be assured that it is not with him, but with God, that thou art enraged, Gal. i. 6, 10; Deut. xviii. 19" (ST.).—Sympathy may be cruelty; everything at the right place and at the right time.—Love can cover the sins which are committed against us, but never can call evil good.—Whosoever despises him that is sent, fails in respect also to Him that sent him.—But they are no servants of God who flatter the ungodly.—(Comp. Homiletic Hints on ch. iii. 17 sq.) "The warnings which teachers have failed to give afford no justification to the wicked before God, for God warns them Himself in His word, Luke xii. 48" (ST.).—"A more intolerable judgment comes upon Chorazin and Bethsaida than upon Tyre and Sidon" (HEIM-HOFF.).—"The position of the servants of God is certainly not a comfortable one, since they have to dwell among those who are called briers and scorpions, and are likened even to lions; whence they do not get off without pricks and wounds" (STCK.).—"But the preaching is not enough which consists simply in the word. An evangelical watchman must teach conscientiously and live holily" (H. H.).—Even when the preacher's conscience is free from guilt in regard to the ungodly who perish in their sins, what a sorrow does it occasion in the life of the preacher when he has to see the impenitent die in their sins!—The pain connected with the preacher's office, which the world understands not.—"I would not willingly be saved without you" (AUGUSTINE).

Ver. 10. All in the end feel sin, but they hate it not.—"The way of the unconverted in this respect is to look rather to the temporal than to the eternal life" (ST.).—To despair, instead of turning to God, is but another form of the pride that is in the human heart.—Despair is another kind of impenitence.—How contrasts touch one another! The godly also are sometimes on the brink of despair—David, Ps. xxxviii., and Cain, Gen. iv.—"That punishment should always be heavier to us than sin!" (STCK.)—He who would justify himself would perhaps throw the blame even upon God.—God always deals unfairly with the wicked, as they think.—"When God's judgments break forth, then men readily remember their sins" (STCK.).—"One must hate sin before one can live" (B. B.).—He whose sin keeps him away from God, loves his sin more than his life. Why will ye die? God, therefore, always asks again.—"We must not despair of God's compassion, but turn ourselves toward it" (STCK.).—When the Holy One swears, He lets Himself down to the lies, the faithlessness, and fickleness which prevail on the earth. He comes before the judgment-seat of men, and bears His testimony against sinners who would die.—Unbelief must be ashamed and dumb, or be compelled to pass sentence on itself.—"He does not swear by His love, of which the smaller number only have some feeling; but that He lives all know" (B. B.).—Indubitable as the love of God is, yet not the less necessary is conversion for men.—Seek no back-doors, no bribery of the saints, no hushing up of the conscience with pious forms of speech; but go straight into the heavenly kingdom, as the prodigal son made for his father.—"We can think nothing good of ourselves; our whole salvation is hence a divine work" (H. H.).—The living God wills life, and also gives it to those who will; but unless men also wish it, He certainly does not give. To work this will, to lay the will of the flesh to sleep under God's word—this is the aim of the universal grace, *i.e.* the grace which God offers to all men through His word. But where the will has been wrought, there will also the performance be made good, according to the good pleasure of God; so that our conversion is not only His requirement, but also His working, although the deed is man's.

Vers. 12, 13. (See Homiletic Hints on ch. xviii. 24, 21 sq., 26, 27 sq.)—Righteousness from works does not preserve and save men.—It is not the righteousness of the righteous that is the question, but the righteousness of God, which is manifested indeed in the law, but does not come out of the law.—The righteous who are such by faith will live, and will live in their faith.—One must begin, but one must also continue to the end.—Unfaithfulness smites its own Lord.—The truly righteous also know of failings, but not of falling away.—Not that we are evil by nature is what finally condemns us, but that we remain evil in spite of the goodness of God, which seeks our conversion.—"No true penitent needs despair on account of his old sins, nor faint because of them, Ps. xxv. 3; Matt. ix. 2" (CR.).—"In true conversion it is not enough that there be a breaking off of some sins, but of all, Isa. i. 16; Jas. ii. 10" (STARKE).—"But this is the true life, if one can say with Paul: I live not, but Christ liveth in me, Gal. ii. 20" (STCK.).—Trust upon one's own righteousness is not faith, but trust upon the righteousness of God in Christ. Not assuredly the letter of our righteousness, but the spirit of that imputed to us, brings the assurance that we are children of God, and shall also remain such.—Ver. 14 sq. The voucher for the reckoning here furnished by means of the thief on the cross.—Conversion of heart, of conduct, of life.—The separation from sin is effected not only by the forgiveness of all our sins and of our sinful state, but also by a walk in all goodness after the Spirit, who now begins His ascendency.—"Man becomes free when in his conscious want of freedom he gives himself up to the free-making God" (LANGE).—The improvement of the life shows that things have become better with a man, that God has taken an interest in his soul, in order that it might not perish.—Ver. 17 sq. (Homiletic Hints on ch. xviii. 25–29.) "More than five years intervened [viz. between this and the similar utterance in ch. xviii.], and the people had still not got a step farther. Thus God Himself, by His example, teaches all parents, guardians, etc., patience. And we should much more exercise patience when we think of our own sins and of God's patience with us, but should also not be weary of watching and warning" (SCHMIEDER).—"An honest man has still much more faith in the world than God Himself, Gen. xix. 14" (ST.).—God's way is right even when He, nay, just because He does not allow the righteous to be righteous, and does not leave the sinner to perish.—Let him who thinks that he stands take heed that he do not fall!—Do this, it is ever again said, and thou shalt live.—Good works are productions of God, in consequence of the will having been set free by Him from the doing of evil to the doing of good.—The last day will make it clear that God's way has been right.

Vers. 21, 22. "The opened mouth of a servant of God is his frankness, the contrary is trimming and flattering; and it is also distinguished from sarcastic witticisms, evil speaking, and insult. The servants of God should be frank in speech; yet not like insolent fellows, who believe they may say everything because no one can contradict them, at least when in the pulpit" (LUTHER).—God's word will take effect at last; woe to him who then finds that he is a stricken man, who should have long ago recognised himself to be in that case!—"At last it comes, what men would not believe" (BERL. BIB.).—Our silence and our speaking are both of God.—"In the time of God's long-suffering, which sinners abuse, the righteous must often be silent till the judgments actually take place" (B. B.).—Ver. 24 sq. The deceitful conclusions of self-love.—The hereditary nobility in its foolish pretensions.—"Of" Abraham matters nothing, but to be like Abraham is what is needed.—*Noblesse oblige.*—Walls, cities, go to ruin, but a fool will still plant himself on the ruins, Prov. xxvii. 22.—"What is promised to faith, unbelievers will often be found appropriating to themselves" (STCK.).—The hope of the ungodly must come to shame.—When the mask falls from the hypocrites, then will the beast of prey which lay behind become manifest; and we shall all be made manifest before the judgment-seat of Christ; then the masquerade will be out.—There have not only been persons bearing merely the name of Jew, but there still are, and always have been, plenty of nominal Christians.—Our life must not belie our profession, else in our claim to the inheritance of the saints we shall reckon without our host.—Holy ruins are relics on which there is no inheritance.—Ver. 26. The natural man stands upon nothing else than his sword.—"In relation to sin men ought not to be womanish, but women to be manly" (HENGST.).—Ver. 27. The divine vengeance does not need to rush upon its victim from behind in order to lay hold of him, nor does it require to make a long and laborious search after him; but where he has fled to and fancies himself hidden, whether it be in the heights or in the depths, there the vengeance of God lies in readiness, and has been expecting him to come to it.—In the end we all come to God—alas! that so few should fall into His arms, while so many fall upon His sword!—If the wild beasts of passion do not tear a man, the pestilence of his natural corruption will gradually consume him.—Ver. 28 sq. Desolate shall it be at last about every ungodly man; for as the heart is, so is the life. First of all sin desolates; then come desolations through death; finally, we pass into the desolation of an eternity without God.—The knowledge of the Eternal many times the most terrible humiliation in what is temporal.—Ver. 30 sq. "It is suspicious when people praise the fineness of a preacher's voice, address," etc. (RICHT.).—Ezekiel shows that this is what may happen even with earnest and godly preachers, for what is there from which man cannot suck sugar?—"Externally to hear God's word, men will often encourage themselves, but not through God's grace to reduce it to practice, Jer. xlii. 1, 2" (ST.).—Merely to hear, without doing, makes all preaching unprofitable.—How many unwashed mouths wipe themselves clean on the servants of God!—Strange that sermons of rebuke should be more attractive than grace-sermons! It shows that the gospel requires a much greater earnestness of spirit than the law. But men would still always rather be smitten than caressed; they think, perhaps, that in the love there is too much of design. If one has been struck by the cudgel, it is still possible to preserve one's heart and head; but love leaves nothing to one's self, it demands all—the whole man, and the whole life.—"Shun the society of mockers, for nothing that is good can come of these" (STCK.).—"They only praise the eloquence, they do not trouble themselves about the matter, unless it be that it does not directly concern them, but the heathen, ch. xxv. sq." (B. B.).—A measure for judging of the flocking to mission festivals.—"There will always be hypocrites, who hear, indeed, but do not—yea, do quite differently from what their hearing should lead them to do. But God knows the thoughts of the heart, and looks upon all the ways of all men, and in His own time will avenge the despite done to His servants upon their despisers. Finally, we should not suffer ourselves to be entertained with God's word as with music. God does not play in His word that we may dance" (LUTHER).—To hear, but also to obey, that is the main thing.—Mere habit as regards the hearing of sermons makes people indifferent, and at last stupid.—The Lord preserve us from empty pews, but still more from stupid hearers, who only wish to show their Sunday clothes, and to have been in church!—How readily may a preacher deceive himself regarding his hearers!—God read here to Ezekiel a lecture on homiletics.—Pious sentimentalism, also, is spiritual adultery.—So must God to-day still be Love, since thus only can the world quietly remain the world, which He has loved so much.—The "dear God" (*liebe Gott*) the love-song of people of the world.—Satan goes with us into church.—Edification and the capacity for it are two different things.—A true prophet will always leave behind him the impression of a true prophet.

II. THE DIVINE PROMISES.

1. AGAINST THE SHEPHERDS OF ISRAEL, OF THE SHEPHERD KINDNESS OF JEHOVAH TOWARD HIS FLOCK, AND OF HIS SERVANT DAVID (CH. XXXIV.).

1, 2 And the word of Jehovah came to me, saying: Son of man, prophesy
upon the shepherds of Israel, prophesy, and say to them, to the shepherds,
Thus saith the Lord Jehovah: Woe to the shepherds of Israel, that were
3 feeding themselves! Should not the shepherds feed the flock? Ye ate the
fat, and clothed yourselves with the wool; ye killed what was fed; ye fed not
4 the flock. Those which became weak ye have not strengthened, and the sick ye
have not healed, and the wounded [broken] have ye not bound up, and the driven
away have ye not brought back, nor looked after that which was lost [perishing],
5 and with rigour have ye ruled them, and with oppression. And they were
scattered, because [there was] no shepherd, and were for food to all living crea-
6 tures [for meat to all beasts] of the field, and they were scattered. They wander,
My flock, upon all mountains, and upon every high hill; and upon the whole
face of the earth have they been scattered, My flock, and there is none that
7 seeks after, and none that looks after. Therefore, shepherds, hear the word
8 of Jehovah. As I live—sentence of the Lord Jehovah—Because My flock
has become for a prey [for booty], and they have become, My flock, for food to
all living creatures of the field, because [there was] not a shepherd, and My
shepherds have not sought after My flock, and the shepherds fed themselves,
9 and fed not My flock: Therefore, ye shepherds, hear the word of Jehovah;
10 Thus saith the Lord Jehovah: Behold, I [am] against the shepherds, and
demand My flock from their hand, and cause them to cease from feeding the
flock; and the shepherds shall no more feed themselves; and I deliver [snatch]
My flock out of their mouth, and they shall not henceforth be for food to
11 them. For thus saith the Lord Jehovah: Behold, I, I [am there], and seek for
12 My flock, and inspect [scrutinize] them. As a shepherd inspects his flock, in the

day that he is amongst his flock, the scattered [sheep], so will I inspect My
flock, and deliver [rescue] them out of all the places whither they were scat-
13 tered in the day of cloud and darkness. And I lead them forth from
among the peoples, and gather them from the lands, and bring them to their
ground, and feed them upon the mountains of Israel, in the valleys, and in all
14 the dwellings of the land [the earth]. On good pasture will I feed them, and in
[on] the high mountains of Israel shall their walk be; there shall they lie
down in a good walk, and on a fat pasture shall they feed upon the moun-
15 tains of Israel. I will feed My flock, and I will make them lie down: sen-
16 tence of the Lord Jehovah. I will look after the perishing, and the driven
away will I bring back, and the broken will I bind up, and will strengthen
the sick, and the fat and the strong I will destroy; I will feed it with judg-
17 ment. And ye, My flock, thus saith the Lord Jehovah, Behold, I judge
18 between sheep and sheep, the rams and the he-goats. Is it too little for you
that ye feed on the good [best] pasture, and ye tread down the rest of your
pasture with your feet, and drink the sunk water, and with your feet trouble
19 the residue? And My flock, must they feed on what your feet have trodden,
20 and of what your feet have troubled must they drink? Therefore, thus
saith the Lord Jehovah to them: Behold, I, I [am there] and judge between
21 fat sheep and lean [impoverished] sheep. Because ye push with side and with
shoulder, and thrust with your horns all those which have become weak, till
22 ye have scattered them abroad: Therefore I help My flock, and they shall no
23 longer be for a prey, and I will judge between sheep and sheep. And I appoint
[raise up] over them one shepherd, and he feeds them, My servant David; he
24 will feed them, and he will be to them a shepherd. And I, Jehovah, will be
to them a God, and My servant David prince in their midst. I, Jehovah, have
25 spoken. And I conclude for them a covenant of peace, and cause the evil
beasts to cease out of the land, and they dwell securely in the wilderness,
26 and sleep in the woods. And I give them and the environs of My hill [for a]
blessing, and cause the rain to come down in its season—showers of blessing
27 there shall be. And the tree of the field gives its fruit, and the land shall
give its increase; and they are safe upon their ground, and they know that I
am Jehovah, when I break the bars of their yoke, and I deliver [rescue] them
28 from the hand of those whom they served [who wrought through them]. And they
shall no more be a prey to the heathen, and the beasts of the field shall not
devour them, and they dwell secure, and there is none to make them afraid.
29 And I raise up for them a plantation for a name, and they shall no more be
swept away from hunger in the land, and no more bear the reproach of the
30 heathen. And they know that I, Jehovah, their God, [am] with them, and
they [are] My people, the house of Israel: sentence of the Lord Jehovah.
31 And ye My flock, flock of My pasture, men [are] ye; I [am] your God: sen-
tence of the Lord Jehovah.

Ver. 2. Sept.: . . . Ὦ ποιμενες . . . μη οἱ ποιμενες βοσκουσιν ἑαυτους;—
Ver. 3. Ἰδου το γαλα κατεσθιετε—
Ver. 4. . . . και το ἰσχυρον κατειργασασθε μοχθῳ. (Anoth. read.: האבדות.)
Ver. 5. . . . του ἀγρου κ. τοις πετεινοις του οὐρανου.
Ver. 6. Και διεσπαρησαν τα προβατα μου . . . (παντι) προσωπῳ (πασης) κ. γης . . . οὐδε ὁ ἀποστρεφων. (Anoth. read.: ועל פני כל.) Vulg.: *et non erat qui requireret, non erat, inquam, qui requireret.*
Ver. 8. Sept.: . . . εἰ μην ἀντι του γενεσθαι . . . εἰς προνομην κ. γενεσθαι τ. προβατα μου—
Ver. 10. . . . του μη ποιμαινειν τ. προβατα μου . . . ἐτ. οἱ ποιμενες αὐτα—
Ver. 12. . . . ἐν ἡμερᾳ γνοφου κ. νεφελης ἐν μεσῳ—
Ver. 14. Sept.: . . . ἐν τ. ὀζει τῳ ὑψηλῳ, ἐν τ. ὀρει Ἰσραηλ. Και ἐσονται αἱ μανδραι αὐτων ἐκει κ. κοιμηθησονται, κ. ἐκει ἀναπαυσονται ἐν τρυφῃ—
Ver. 15. . . . και ἐπιγνωσονται, διο τι εἰμι κυριος. Ταδε λεγει—
Ver. 16. . . . ἰσχυρον φυλαξω· κ. . . . αὐτα μετα κριματος. For אשמיד all read אשמיר (?אשמור) except Chald
Ver. 21. Sept.: . . . τ. κερασιν ὑμων ἐκερατιζετε, κ. παν το ἐκλειπον ἐξεθλιβετε.
Ver. 22. K. σωσω . . . κριου προς κριον.
Ver. 25. . . . τῳ Δαυιδ διαθηκην . . . κ. κατοικησουσιν ἐν τῃ ἐρημῳ—
Ver. 26. . . . αὐτους κυκλῳ τ. ὀρους μου, κ. . . . τ. ὑετον, ὑετον εὐλογιας αὐτοις.
Ver. 27. . . . ἐν ἐλπιδι εἰρηνης . . . τ. ζυγον του κλοιου αὐτων—
Ver. 28. Sept.: . . . ἐν ἐλπιδι—
Ver. 29. . . . φυτον εἰρηνης—
Ver. 30. Sept. Syr. Arab. add הגוים, and omit אתם.
Ver. 31. K. ὑμεις προβατα μου κ. προβατα τ. ποιμνιου μου ἐστε, κ. ἐγω—

EXEGETICAL REMARKS.

Vers. 1–10. *The Shepherds of Israel.*

Ver. 1. Hengstenberg regards the prophet with this **word of Jehovah** as meeting the trouble which arises from the loss of civil government: the seeming loss, he contends, is real gain, since the existing government was so bad. Keil excellently designates the turning against the bad shepherds as a foil for the ensuing promise. What the relation to the first part of the book, the natural sequel to the same already suggests, namely, a vivid representation of the past,—this will now show itself to be the more appropriate, since in the second part of the book the promise of God is what gives the prevailing tone. The future salvation cannot be better set off and characterized than upon the past distress; just as upon the dark background of our misery, redemption generally appears the brighter, and also so much the more a necessity; and John viii. 10 ("Woman, where are those thine accusers?") conveys an import of a similar kind with reference to a still more distant time than what is here referred to.

Ver. 2. עַל (comp. אֶל, ch. xiii. 2), agreeably to the tenor of what follows, as much as: *against;* but as the controversy has respect to positions of eminence, it carries a certain reference to that. Kliefoth undoubtedly views the **shepherds** rightly, when he understands thereby generally the entire body of officials who had committed to them the leadership of the people. At least the following description, bearing as it does the shepherd form, is capable of comprehending all, and admits of application to all. Hence some have taken it with reference to the kings, and also to the priests; others have thought merely of the kings, or of the collective order then holding the reins of government (as Hengst.); others, again, have found here the false prophets and teachers of the people. The reference to Jer. xxiii., which has been leant upon, decides nothing; it only shows how, in the second part also of his book of prophecy, Ezekiel kept himself in unison of sentiment with his predecessor and companion. Nothing can be proved here by the "biblical idea of the shepherd" (KEIL), since it is just the image of a shepherd which is set before us; and the fact that in ver. 23 sq. David forms the antithesis, and that in the character of prince, finds its explanation in the Messianic idea, thereby symbolized and historically exhibited, which, as in our prophet, is viewed pre-eminently in its kingly aspect (pp. 23, 24). So, on the other hand, by means of the contrast with the anointed, it leaves, under the image of the shepherd, the complex of official life to be understood. All the offices—hence He is called *Christ*—and princes also (comp. on ch. xii. 10) must, the more they had been guilty, culminate in him.[1] In order to retain the king and the great (שָׂרִים, the magnates, HITZIG), Hengst. notices the circumstance that Jehoiachin and Zedekiah, and likewise many of the chiefs, were still in life; that the announcement therefore might extend into the future. But he holds that what the prophet here announces as having as to its main part already taken place, must be simply an explanation of the judgment in the form of an announcement of it!—לָרֹעִים, the address repeated, *pleonasmus emphaticus,* whereby the shepherd-idea at the same time is prominently brought out, while, on the other hand, the threatening attached and description of the reality comes thus into more marked contrast.—**That were feeding themselves**; this already indicates all (אוֹתָם, reflexive, EWALD, *Gr.* p. 788), the selfishness that merely seeks its own, instead of what belongs to the flock. (צֹאן, small cattle; especially sheep, but also goats.) Comp. Phil. ii. 21; 2 Cor. xii. 14; Jude v. 12; Acts xx. 28; 1 Pet. v. 2.

Ver. 3. Here a detailed description is given of the "not feeding," to which the "feeding," the obligation involved in the relation of shepherd to flock ("should not the shepherd," etc., ver. 2), stands opposed; and the picture is drawn so as to make *enjoyment* merely take the primary place on the side of the shepherds. Such was their habitual acting. Instead of **fat**, Hitzig reads with the Sept. חָלָב, *milk,* as also Rosenmüller, so as thereby to avoid the anticipating and repeating as regards the killing in the third clause. Certainly the milk would suit well with the "wool," and the "eating" (1 Cor. ix. 7) should occasion no difficulty. There must not, however, be supposed the lawful use of the flock, but from the first the greed which appropriates to itself the best of the animal; at length the best animal itself is what appears in the representation—from which, however, nothing arises for determining more closely what office is meant, since it is applicable to each office ["but manifestly most strictly applicable to the kingly or ruling office," P. F.].—To the greedy misappropriation for one's own use, there is a companion picture in Ver. 4; the words: "ye fed not the flock," farther declaring, on the one hand, the want of care for the flock, the contemptuous neglect of them, nay, on the other hand, the merciless energy with which what should have been protection had turned into simple domination. נַחְלוֹת, partic. Niphal from חָלָה, are those which had become **weak,** wretched, whether it may have been through sickness or overdriving. חוֹלָה is the **sick** itself. The Niph. pass. of שָׁבַר denotes what is wounded, what has been somewhat broken—corresponding to which is: "to bind up," to wrap up firmly. Comp. Matt. xii. 20.—נִדַּחַת is the **driven away,**

[1] [The style of interpretation here does not seem quite satisfactory. It is true, the representation is given under the image of a shepherd, and under that image all official administrations *might* be in a sense included. But the question is, what in Old Testament scripture, especially prophetical scripture, is actually included in it? In Jer. ii. 8 the shepherds are expressly distinguished from both prophets and priests; they are named as a distinct class, and can only be understood of kings and rulers. These also are what are most naturally understood by shepherds in Jer. xxiii. 1–6. It was, in fact, the case of David which gave rise to this metaphorical language, who was taken from the humble office of feeding his father's sheep "to feed God's people Israel, and to be a captain over Israel" (2 Sam. v. 2; Ps. lxxviii. 70, 71); and this gave the tone to future use. The actions here also ascribed to the false shepherds favour the same view; they are such as belong not to faithless and corrupt teachers, but to bad rulers—violence, selfish disregard of the weak and oppressed, wrongful dealings with their goods, etc. This also is the view taken by Henderson: "not ecclesiastical rulers or teachers, but the civil governors."—P. F.]

the exiled, in consequence of harsh treatment (comp. 1 Pet. ii. 25). אָבַד, to lose one's self, to be lost, to perish (comp. Matt. x. 6, xv. 24, xviii. 11; Luke xv. 4, 6, xix. 10). The two last expressions prepare the way for the רָדָה (to domineer, to trample on) with חָזְקָה, and with פֶּרֶךְ (tyranny). Comp. Ex. i. 13, 14; Lev. xxv. 43, 46, 53; Judg. iv. 3; 1 Sam. ii. 16; 1 Pet. v. 3.—Ver. 5. There is here, finally, given the closing feature, as it is likewise involved in the verb רָעָה, the *keeping together;* while they did not discharge the shepherd-obligation, did not feed the flock, they also failed to keep them together, which is expressed by the Niphal of פּוּץ in respect to the sheep, which also had already been prepared for by הַנִּדַּחַת and הָאֹבֶדֶת (ver. 4). The description now applies to the flock, not to single sheep merely. The first תְּפוּצֶינָה Hengst. understands of the internal dissolution of the people, in consequence of which the power of resisting was lost in regard to those without; the second he understands of the exile. Both expressions, however, are fundamentally the same. When Israel was not held together in the name of Jehovah through the theocratic offices, the scattering, the self-abandonment, and surrender to the worldly powers was the natural, necessary consequence.—רֹעֶה מִבְּלִי, from the want, the non-existence of a shepherd; because no shepherd who had discharged his duty according to his office was there; comp. Jer. x. 21; Zech. x. 2; Matt. ix. 36. In consequence of the scattering of the flock—this first of all—they became food to the nations round about; the other—and on this account is וַתְּפוּצֶינָה repeated—overtook them to the full in their state of exile—as previously in the ten tribes, so now also in Judah, as set forth in Ver. 6. (Num. xxvii. 17; 1 Kings xxii. 17; John x. 12.) The representation in the image should plainly be understood as a pictorial delineation; so that: **upon the whole face of the earth,** by which the preceding: **upon all mountains,** and: **upon every high hill,** may be regarded as thrown together, must be taken to mean not their own land, as some have thought (THEODORET), viewing it in connection with the heathen worship practised there, but also the earth, without reference to heathen lands. The יִשְׁגּוּ, however, should be distinguished from נָפֹצוּ [that is, the "wandering" from the "scattering"], and possibly, therefore, the heathenizing tendency and the punishment borne among the heathen may be indicated. The repeated and emphasized **My flock** prepares for the resolutions of Jehovah that follow. There being none to search is explained by the preceding: "because there was no shepherd." Upon דָּרַשׁ and בִּקֵּשׁ, see at ch. iii. 18. According to Häv., דָּרַשׁ signifies to inquire farther, to search for, to concern one's self about, while בִּקֵּשׁ signifies the seeking for the lost.—Ver. 7. There is now, on the ground of such unfaithfulness to duty, pronounced the "woe" of ver. 2, under the form of hearing the word of Jehovah.—Ver. 8. The manner of proceeding, however, as commonly with Ezekiel, is first of all again to rehearse the guilt of the shepherds, and so to resume the charge that the flock, which Jehovah had committed to these shepherds as His own, had been taken away by the stranger, given up to the stranger, turned into a "booty,"—a contrast of such a kind that all, in a manner, was said by it. **A prey** is more exactly defined by: **for food**, agreeably to ver. 5; and the expression: **because there was no shepherd,** after ver. 6, is explained by: **have not sought after My flock.**—Ver. 9. This verse, with the **therefore,** renews the demand on the shepherds (ver. 7).—Ver. 10. Instead of חַי־אָנִי we have here כֹּה־אָמַר, and הִנְנִי instead of אִם לֹא.—Ch. xiii. 20, 8.—וְדָרַשְׁתִּי, antithesis to וְלֹא־דָרְשׁוּ. Comp. ch. xxxiii. 8; Zech. ix. 16.—The flock must be demanded of the officials, and these made to cease—which was fulfilled up to the time of Christ. With reference to the flock, such a seeking is a deliverance (הִצִּיל), considering the character of the shepherds; and because the circumstance of their feeding themselves goes immediately before, which points back to ver. 3, מִפִּיהֶם is put instead of מִיָּדָם, and לֹא־תִהְיֶיןָ forms the parallel to וְלֹא־יִרְעוּ עוֹד, previously used (ch. xiii. 21).

Vers. 11-22. *Jehovah in His Shepherd Tenderness toward His Flock.*

Ver. 11. This verse grounds (**For**) the ceasing of the past relation of shepherd and flock through the all-expressive personal addition: הִנְנִי־אָנִי, which the Targum Jona. renders by: "Behold, I will manifest Myself." As it is said in John i. 10 sq.: "He was in the world," and: "He came unto His own."—**I seek for My flock,** a contrast to: "there is none that seeketh for," in ver. 6, and to: "they have not sought for," in ver. 8. Instead of בִּקֵּשׁ, however, there stands the more inward בִּקֵּר, **inspect,** consider, by means of which the following expansion is introduced, which has respect exclusively to the flock,—"the community, on whose preservation everything depends" (EWALD).—Ver. 12. There must be the inspection (GESEN.: properly, Aram. inf. Poël) of a **shepherd;** Jehovah will therefore discover Himself not only as proprietor, whose proprietorship is of another kind, but specially as shepherd, which He really is, in contrast to the merely titular officials, nay, as if He alone were shepherd (Ps. xxiii.). Hence also עֵדֶר, where formerly there was צֹאן; comp. Jer. xiii. 17 (Isa. xl. 11; Jer. xxxi. 10; Luke xv. 4).—**In the day that he is amongst his flock** describes more fully what is implied in the brief though energetic and significant: "Behold, I, I," of ver. 11. The epithet נִפְרָשׁוֹת to צֹאנוֹ indicates the assumed condition, however much, as a characteristic apposition, it is at variance with the meaning and nature of a flock. One has to think of the day that succeeds a nocturnal storm and tempest, and all the dangers arising from wild beasts, etc., when, after that the selfish shepherds had in a body proved faithless to their calling, now at length the true shepherd of the flock presents himself. So that: "in the day that he is amongst his flock," evidently forms a contrast to: **the day of cloud and darkness**, at the close of the verse; which words are, therefore, improperly connected by Hitzig (KLIEF.), with an allusion to ch. xxx. 3, xxix. 21, and especially to Joel ii. 2, with: **and deliver them** (וְהִצַּלְתִּי). For the day "of cloud and darkness" (עֲרָפֶל, combination of "cloud" and darkness, yet not by a throwing together of עָרִיף and אֹפֶל, but an extended form, like כַּרְמֶל, from כֶּרֶם), as also the derivation of the formula from the lawgiving on Sinai (Deut. iv. 11; Heb. xii. 18) might indicate, is not the day of God's judgment upon all the heathen—also, not "the dark showers of the birth of a better time," as Ewald puts it, connecting the expression with ver. 13, but the day of the dispersion of His people,—the punishment which, according to the law of God from Sinai, befell them by the instrumentality of the heathen. Accordingly, בְּיוֹם עָנָן' belongs to the immediately preceding relative clause אֲשֶׁר־נָפֹצוּ', a connection which is usual.—The rescuing, delivering out of, whereby the inspection of the flock accomplishes the kind of salvation indicated, presupposes in the general: a dangerous position,—in particular: imprisonment, servitude, oppression, tyranny, etc. That it was to be **out of all the places**, etc., besides being in accordance with the preceding figure (ver. 6), arises from the form of the salvation, which is represented as primarily a gathering (ch. xxviii. 25), especially a bringing back out of exile to the land of their home, as is shown in Ver. 13 (Ex. vi. 6, vii. 4, 5; Acts ii. 9-11). Comp. also ch. xi. 17; John xi. 52. But at the same time, as Hengst. has said, "other glorious gifts and benefits, which, however, all pointed forward to the true fulfilment, and called forth desire for it," are indicated by: **and feed them** (וּרְעִיתִים).—Ch. vi. 2, 3.—**And in all the dwellings of the land** are, primarily, all the parts adapted for occupation, for inhabiting; might not הָאָרֶץ, however, have a farther reference?—Ver. 14. An explanation is here given of the "feeding" by Jehovah with regard to the fodder (מִרְעֶה), to which also נָוֵהֶם corresponds, but, at the same time, with reference to lairs, reposing, resting, dwelling. It lies, besides, in the thing itself that the pasture-ground was, at the same time, a lair and resting-place, fold, Ps. xxiii.; Song i. 7.—וּבְהָרֵי מְרוֹם', PHILIPPSON: "upon the mountains of the height of Israel;" comp. at ch. xvii. 23, xx. 40.—Ver. 15. A bringing together of what has been said in both respects; comp. on רָבַץ, ch. xxix. 3; Ps. xxiii.

Ver. 16. An explanation is here given, and in contrast to the denounced faithlessness (ver. 4) of those who had hitherto held the shepherd-office, of the "feeding" as that is understood by Jehovah, of a much more internal nature, and indeed with an eye to right and righteousness. As the contrast in **strong** and **strengthen** (comp. for that Luke xxii. 32) may of itself indicate, but as the words: **I will feed it with judgment**, put beyond doubt, and the sequel shows, the feeding by Jehovah is also a judging, which does not mean simply a right dealing, or treatment according to right and equity, but involves, as we shall see, a separation. **With judgment** is sufficiently explained by the: **I will destroy** (אַשְׁמִיד)—Ps. xxxvii. 38; comp. also ch. xiv. 9; Luke i. 51, 52. The ironical turn given to the אֶרְעֶנָּה (the suffix does not relate to the flock) may easily be understood from the visible antithesis to the: "and with rigour have ye ruled them, and with oppression," in ver. 4; comp. also the distinction between הַשְּׁמֵנָה and הַחֲזָקָה in the comparison with הַבְּרִיאָה in ver. 3. The Chaldee paraphrase interprets: "godless and sinners," while the Vulg. translates: *custodiam*, as does Luther also, as if it had stood שָׁמַר. Comp. also Rev. ii. 27; Ps. ii. 9.

Ver. 17. As a confirmation of the sense put upon the last part of ver. 16, this verse introduces by way of contrast the (remaining) flock: **And ye, My flock.** The officials are with ver. 10 discharged and gone; the persons concerned can therefore only come into consideration according to their personal qualities, not according to their official rank; consequently, as one sheep merely with another, in other words, as "fat" and "strong," or such like (Deut. xxxii. 15). Hence the: **Behold, I judge between sheep and sheep**, explains the: "in judgment," of ver. 16 as a judgment between one kind of sheep and another, individual members of the flock; therefore, that לְשֶׂה expresses the judicial separation in regard to those previously named fat and strong, and וְלָעַתּוּדִים (עָתַד, to urge, push; the he-goat עַתּוּד, properly: "pusher") לָאֵילִים is an enlarging apposition. HITZIG: "against the rams and the he-goats." Beside the pushing and pressing (ver. 21) there sounds distinctly forth the leading and guiding of the flock; so that the older expositors were right in thinking of the shepherds in ver. 2, yet not in that character, but simply as individuals. (As, in another respect certainly, the Servant of Jehovah, the Deliverer, is represented as a sheep, as a lamb (Isa. liii. 7), so in Ezekiel are the destroyers.) The fat and the strong among the sheep are therefore regarded as like the rams and he-goats, and placed on the one side—the situation, therefore, not at all so dissimilar to that in Matt. xxv. 32, as Keil repeats after Hitzig, who merely gives this explanation: "The separation of the sheep from the goats in Matt. xxv. 32 has nothing to do here." As belonging to the sheep-flock, he-goats and rams are also, in the general sense, sheep (small cattle), and they are expressly so called in the words: "between sheep and sheep"; but undoubtedly sheep and sheep (ver. 20) forms a distinction, namely, that those which Jehovah designates His are not like the he-goats and rams, from which He sets them apart. They are certainly not, as excellently remarked by Kliefoth, "represented as the righteous and innocent, but they are called the strayed, the driven away, the wounded, the weak: but they are the penitent, who hear the voice of God; therefore will He first seek them, and bring them back, and heal and strengthen them, but afterwards also will redeem them from the oppressions which the others, the he-goats, have exercised upon them." According to Hitzig, these latter are with the fat and the strong "the rich and noble, who in manifold ways wrest from the humble by force and rigour their worldly goods." But Kliefoth quite rightly: "a poor man can just as well be a he-goat as a rich man a sheep." Only with the poor man the sphere is very limited; while for the rich and noble, power and the right to exercise it sit upon the very rim of their cradle. The "robber-knights," as Hengst. calls them, are born in castles. The haughtiness, however, engendered by fatness and the misuse of their resources is to be taken into account. "David, even upon the throne, designates himself poor and needy" (HENGST.). The thing referred to, therefore, in the case of the rams and he-goats, is the wickedness which exhibits itself as violent procedure in superior positions of life. "God procures for the suffering sheep justice against the malicious" (HENGST.). — Ver. 18. The unjust behaviour of the one portion toward the other is here exposed. HENGST.: "The address extends to the tyrants of the future"—that is, to the Scribes and Pharisees of our Lord's time, whom it exactly suits.—Comp. on הַמְעַט מִכֶּם, ch. xvi. 20. Are ye not content with your own enjoyment, but must ye also disturb that of others? Thus fatness and strength might have enjoyed themselves at smaller cost. (Rev. iii. 17?) But now, as they left over to no one what they would not or could not use as pasture, but wantonly trampled it under foot, so did they also with respect to drink. מִשְׁקַע, from שָׁקַע, ch. xxxii. 14, "sinking of water," is commonly interpreted as: "water clarified through sinking," so that the clarifying is rather the main thing, the impurities have gone to the bottom. HENGST.: water of sinking, settled water; interpreted by Hitzig as: water on the ground, to be found at the bottom—that is, the coolest water. But as רָפַשׂ (promiscuously רָפַס, ch. xxxii. 2)—by treading with the feet to make confused and troubled—shows, what perhaps most readily suggests itself is, that the water which was sunk, which had become little, and so threatened want, they in their wickedness had made undrinkable. (Luke xi. 52?)—Ver. 19. וּצֹאנִי, with Athnach! Is this right?—Ver. 18.

Ver. 20. **To them** applies, according to ver. 17, to the last mentioned, the flock of Jehovah, and not to the evil and good together,—to the one for terror, and to the other for comfort (ROSENM.).—Ver. 11.—בִּרְיָה only here, with the view probably of distinguishing from ver. 3 (comp. at ver. 16). Usually בְּרִיאָה is read for it, also בְּרִיאָה.—רָזָה, to be thin, impoverished (comp. Mark ii. 17, xiv. 38; 1 Cor. ix. 22).—Ver. 21. Here follows an address to the others, as ver. 18 does on ver. 17. The point of view is not, with Hitzig, to be confined to the pressing of a flock to the fountain. Comp. at vers. 4, 5 (Jer. xxiii. 1, 2).—Ver. 22. וְהוֹשַׁעְתִּי, more general and comprehensive than וְהִצַּלְתִּי, vers. 10, 12.—Ver. 8; vers. 17, 20.

Vers. 23-31. *The Servant David.*

The **and** here gives the immediate sequence, without indicating anything remarkable in what was coming, as this indeed formed the abiding anticipation of the religious thought of Israel; so that since here the removal of the offices and the judgment upon the persons has been effected, he who was now to be looked for must at length come,—the course of events has plainly reached him as the last member in the series, according to which the: "I raise up" (הֲקִימֹתִי), will have to be understood. No special forthcoming effected by God for the good of Israel, as in Deut. xviii. 15 יָקִים לְךָ, in the more peculiar might and grace of the Spirit, but simply the official (mediately divine) appointment of the shepherd in question is announced, although with a reference to 2 Sam. vii. But what is said there at ver. 12, וַהֲקִימֹתִי ("I will set up thy seed"), was in ver. 11 illustrated beforehand by the: "I commanded to be over My people" (צִוִּיתִי), said with respect to the judges. These, therefore, appear as only provisional arrangements, as temporary, through God's command interjected into the disorder for putting an arrest on the same, while for the seed, of which ver. 12 speaks, a permanent introduction and settlement was to be made. In spite of this diversity in the use of צִוִּיתִי, however, there lies nothing in וַהֲקִימֹתִי to suggest the fable of the Gilgul, as was done already by particular Rabbins, and recently has been resumed by Strauss, Hitzig, and others. At all events, Ezekiel would have expressed himself otherwise, if we were here scientifically to find the exegetical idiosyncrasy of a corporeal return of the historical David, by a resurrection from the dead. It is a desperate consolation, such as could have been imagined by no good exegetical conscience, to feel obliged to refer for such like fancies to Rosenmüller—even to the Zoroastrian doctrine of the return of the Paschutan.—On רֹעֶה, see the Doctrinal Reflections to our chapter.—אֶחָד signifies here certainly not "one," one generally; also it can scarcely mean "only," and has nothing immediately to do with the union of the two kingdoms under his sceptre, because there was nothing said of this previously; but the contrast is with the former shepherds and the sheep of the flock scattered through their guilt—this **manifoldness** on the one side, on the other has set over against it the **oneness** of this shepherd, who is the complex embodiment of shepherd watchfulness, as of all the duties of the shepherd office,—the divine realization of the idea of all that is involved generally in the nature of the office, as service toward the community for the sake of God, as sacred service in behalf of God's people. [KLIEFOTH: "This shoot of David comprehends in his one person the whole shepherd-offices of Israel, and fulfils them; they are to be done away with him, but no other king over the people of God shall relieve him."]—On account of the com. gen. of the "flock," the fem. alternates with the masc. in the suffix.—He comes to his destination as a **shepherd** through the: **and he feeds**; the name is realized in his doing, with a reference to David's former life and procedure; see Ps. lxxviii. 70, 71.—**My servant David**, who, on account of his attitude of obedience as Jehovah's servant, showed himself to be one peculiarly fitted for serving the community, over which he was placed officially for the performance of such service, namely, as His servant not only chosen by Jehovah (objectively), but also called, but also anointed, but also in every way confirmed. As **David** "after the flesh," so **My servant** "after the Spirit" points back genealogically in connection with the dynasty. There will be a Davidic person, and he will be in accord with the kingly pattern of David, so that Jehovah's servant David will revive in him to the consciousness of every one. Therefore, in fact, a return of David, and indeed in the seed of David (Jer. xxiii. 5); therefore also different from the return of Elias in John the Baptist. Application is to be made to Christ, but to derive the exposition of the words from this presently fails, as when Kliefoth interprets "My servant" thus: "because he, as God's instrument, will accomplish what is written in vers. 11–22." One must be at home in the style of representation which is given throughout Scripture of David, but more especially in the prophetic style of representation concerning him, in accord also with the pregnant prophetic self-consciousness which discovers itself in his own psalms, in order rightly to understand these and similar descriptions of the Messiah. See the Doctrinal Reflections on the chapter, and comp. Hos. iii. 5; Jer. xxx. 9, xxiii. 5; Luke i. 32, 33. Besides, the respect had to the fundamental passage 2 Sam. vii. itself leaves no doubt as to the proper understanding.—How much the comprehensive ideal, just because figurative, notion of the shepherd preponderates, is clear from the expressly and intentionally repeated: **He will feed**, etc. (Rev. vii. 17).

Ver. 24. When it is said in 2 Sam. vii. 14, in reference to the immediate posterity of David: "I will be a father to him," there is here what corresponds to it in the words: **And I, Jehovah, will be to them a God.** Comp. ch. xi. 20. "Father" to him, "God" to them, as the Father of our Lord Jesus Christ is our God. In like manner: **and My servant David** points back to 2 Sam. vii. 8, where this appears in the form of an address, along with the promise there given; but נָגִיד is there, while here נָשִׂיא is used. That through the government of David Jehovah was going to be in truth the God of His people Israel, etc. (KEIL), is not expressly said, but the grand ideal, the eternity of the Davidic elevation and loftiness, is certainly set forth (2 Sam. vii. 13, 16; comp. Eph. i. 22). But that Jehovah is He who thus speaks must dispose of all opposition from the present aspect of things.

As the whole service of David the prince in their midst is appointed for the salvation of the people, there is expressed in Ver. 25 the establishing for them the covenant—that which always, when so peculiarly said in the technical phraseology, proceeds from the Highest in relation to the lower, that is, from Jehovah (Jer. xxxi. 31 sq.). The reason is, that the in itself ambiguous notion, yet corresponding to the covenant-relation originally in like manner established by God, manifests itself for the people as a revelation of such relationship, namely, as an attestation of offered grace, presenting itself, and giving assurance of God's readiness to enter into fellowship with men. Comp. at Isa. lv. 3 (Heb. viii. 10; Acts iii. 25).—**Covenant of peace** (Isa. liv. 10), since in consequence of the covenant relationship of God there is guaranteed to the people this security, happy condition, salvation (Rom. xiv. 17), of which the "ceasing of evil beasts" symbolizes the negative, and "the dwelling securely" the positive side. Comp. Lev. xxvi. 6 (Hos. ii. 20 [18]). According to Häv. and Hengst., the evil beasts are the hostile human potencies (ver. 5), and the driving of the heathen world from its hitherto domineering position must be meant. According to Hitzig, the public security in the land is pledged. But security (לָבֶטַח, ch. xxviii. 26) the **wilderness** itself must have offered to those dwelling in it, which is sufficiently explained by the parallel בַּיְּעוֹרִים (Qeri: בַּיְּעָרִים), surrendering themselves carelessly to sleep in the thicket of the woods. [Häv. finds an allusion to Solomon's time of peace and blessing; but Kliefoth a literal return of the paradisiacal state after a materialistic manner.]

Ver. 26. To the *personelle* (**them**) are annexed, in a local form of expression, the **environs**, by which, therefore, could not be meant men, with reference to the image of sheep, or the adjacent places for the persons inhabiting them. But the prominence given to **My hill**, that is, the temple-mount, or, with reference thereto, Jerusalem (Isa. xxxi. 4, x. 32), carries over the representation of the people's associates to the land. Comp. also ver. 14: "And on the mountains of the height of Israel." The words: **And I give . . . for a blessing**, chiming in with Gen. xii. 2, could not possibly (as Cocc. and Hengst. suppose) allow of our interpreting "the environs" as meaning the heathen joining themselves in the time of salvation to the old covenant-people (ch. xvii. 23, xvi. 61, xlvii. 8), which is quite remote from the connection here. "And thou shalt be a blessing," in Gen. xii. 2, is certainly explained thus in ver. 3; but here the expression: to "give for a blessing," as the immediately following explanation of "rain in its season" shows us (Deut. xi. 14; Joel ii. 23), adhering to the preceding reference to the land, will mean probably more than to bless. Yet still nothing essentially different, though giving utterance to it in a very marked manner.—*The people shall be bodily a blessing through their land*, to which Jehovah's hand of blessing will mightily testify; hence **showers of blessing** (which mediate the blessing, in distinction from ch. xiii. 13; Prov. xxviii. 3; comp. also Deut. xxxii. 2; Isa. lv. 10, 11; Rom. xv. 29; Eph. i. 3)—shall be so primarily on no other account, but simply for their own experience and their own personal enjoyment. But comp. ver. 29. [Rosenm. brings to remembrance how far superior Palestine was to Egypt in regard to such blessings of the material heavens.] Accordingly, Ver. 27 continues and portrays (comp. Lev. xxvi. 4) the fruitfulness thence arising in the field and land, in order presently to come back to the inhabitants settled again upon their home-soil—on which comp. ver. 25, ch. xxviii. 25, 26.—עֹל (from עָלַל, to join, make fast, bind) is generally the yoke of draught-cattle, in order to fasten them together or to the plough. מֹטוֹת are the two ends of the cross-piece of wood which forms the chief strength of the yoke; hence in ch. xxx. 18 = yoke. The cross-piece of wood laid upon the neck of the animal was fastened by a cord or thong to the pole of the plough, and passing under the neck of the animal (see Delitzsch on Isa. lviii.). As the allusion to Lev. xxvi. 13 and what follows here will show, it is to be understood figuratively—not in general of the endurance of sufferings, but specially of slavery, as in Egypt formerly, which should be broken. For parallel with בְּשִׁבְרִי stands 'וְהִצַּלְתִּים and הָעֹבְדִים בָּהֶם (Ex. i. 14), of the laying on of slave labour. עָבַד with בְּ is to work with or through any one, so that the working stands out in him, he appears purely as an instrument (Matt. xi. 28, xxiii. 4; John viii. 36; Acts xv. 10; Rom. viii. 2; 2 Cor. xi. 20; Gal. ii. 4).

Ver. 28. Comp. vers. 22, 8.—Vers. 25, 8 (ch. xxix. 5).—Lev. xxvi. 6; also Micah iv. 4. Those whom they are said, in the preceding verse, to have served, are therefore the **heathen**, and the two other promises resume again the same two sides as ver. 25, while the words: **and there is none to make them afraid**, portray still farther the secure peaceful rest, almost reminding us of the opposite picture at the close of ver. 6.—Ver. 29. **And I raise up for them** is parallel to ver. 23; the promise there begun in these terms reaches here its conclusion, for the whole of what has gone before relates to one and the same Messianic character.—According to Hitzig, מַטָּע can only mean a plant-place or ground; the plant-land should become to them for renown; what they planted should grow and prosper so as to be a glory for them. According to the older style of exposition it is the "plant," Isa. xi. 1: the Sept. and others read with it שָׁלוֹם. Simpler, certainly, is the rendering **plantation** (agreeably to ver. 26 sq., and as at ch. xvii. 7), and it is also explained by the: "no more sweeping away by hunger," etc., by reason of the fruitfulness of the country, and in contrast to the state of destitution mentioned elsewhere (ch. v. 12, 16, vi. 11, 12). So, too, לְשֵׁם (**for a name**) has its explanation in their having no more "to bear reproach from the heathen." [The exposition which, by a reference to Gen. ii. 8, 9, would understand it of "a renewal of the paradisiacal plantation" (HENGST.), is far-fetched, there being nothing in the connection for it; nor can it be understood how such a renewal, under comparison of ch. xxxvi. 29 sq., would consist "in the rich distribution of harvest blessings." According to Kliefoth, the plantation, like that of the first paradise, must be the suitable thing for holy men.] Instead of the contempt with which the heathen scoffed at the fallen, prostrate, ruined condition of the people, those same heathen should now be convinced, from the blessing upon Israel, that the children of Israel, those who really were such, were also in reality the blessed of the Lord. Hitzig merely: it should no longer be said among the heathen, "The Israelites are hunger-bitten, they have nothing to bite and chew." Comp. on the other hand, Matt. v. 6; John vi. 27, 35; Rev. vii. 16, 17; Matt. xiii. 43.

Ver. 30. Jehovah will be **their God**, and as such will be **with them**, will show Himself to be such toward them (Rev. xxi. 3). To this corresponds the other side of such a relationship, indicated by: **My people**, as also by: **the house of Israel** (2 Cor. vi. 16).—Ver. 31. This verse does not, of course, mean that what was said of the flock has its application to men; but rather is it God's design to testify that His promise in respect to both sides, as well what He is to them to whom He gives it—therefore against doubt and feeble faith—as what they are taken for by Him, and so equally against all undue self-exaltation, keeps in view *Adam*, the man, or: **men**, which also fits in exactly with the immediately preceding designation of the people as: "the house of Israel."—וְאַתֵּן, comp. ver. 17.—**Flock of My pasture** (Jer. xxiii. 1; Ps. lxxiv. 1); not: "which I tend" (GES.), but because Jehovah had given Israel the fruitful land of promise for a pasture-ground. The exposition of **My people** by **men**, and still more the repetition, notwithstanding that, of: **I am your God**, entirely corresponds to the character of the second main division of our book, to the prophecies respecting God's compassions toward His people in the world (Ps. xxxvi. 8 [7]), and the rather so, if, with Hävernick, the fundamental prophecy in relation to what follows is to be seen here.—That the Sept. should have omitted אָדָם is not to be commended, although the Targum and the Arab. translation have done the same. The Syriac, however, has retained it, and it is scarcely to be explained how it should have been brought in, where (after ver. 30) the solemn remark, that not real sheep and goats were meant, would have to be called more than superfluous and flat. HENGST. translates: "And ye are My flock, My pasture-sheep are ye men," etc.; KEIL: "And ye are My flock, etc., ye are men"; HÄV. explains: "Indeed ye, who are called to what is so great, are weak creatures; but where the Lord acknowledges to men that He is their God, He is strong in their weakness; no glory is too great that it might not come to be manifested in them." Kliefoth, who finds the translation of Hengst. against grammar, and calls Hävernick's exposition a superimposed one, carries forward his misunderstanding of the paradisiacal reference: those belonging to the people of God would, through the Branch of the house of David, be as Adam was when he received from God this name after creation. J. F. Starck, with an emphasis on the general grace: "And ye, etc., ye men, I am your God." ["And ye, My flock, My pasture-flock, men are ye, I am your God." There is evidently an emphasis on **men**: "men are ye, remember your place, you are merely human; but remember, at the same time, that I am your God; so that without Me nothing, but with Me all."—P. F.]

DOCTRINAL REFLECTIONS.

1. We should admit, on the one side, that the term "shepherd," as is also so natural from the fulness of the references which the image includes, has application to the guiding of the people in general, consequently to every office of that nature; yet we should not deny, on the other side, that "shepherds" especially and primarily signified "kings." Only the rendering of the word by "overseer," and in particular when the overseers or elders of the exile come into consideration, is very wide of the mark. However, the notion also of civil magistracy, which Hengstenberg attributes to the shepherds as kings, is an abstraction which is not appropriate to the image. In relation to the theocratic people primarily, in which relation we must seek for the more immediate reference of the biblical expression "shepherd," the feature of leading will naturally assume the more prominent place, as it does in John x. 3 sq., which gives us an interpretation from the fulfilment of what is contained in this chapter. That the shepherd is the leader finds, then, its culmination in the protection, which the giving of his life for the flock provides for it, John x. 11. The other features in the image do not therefore fail; they only fall behind the one more peculiarly brought out, such as discipline, tender care, which belong to the spiritual import of the image (comp. John x. 9, 10). The prophetic or teaching office is therein expressed, as in the self-surrender of the shepherd for the flock the priestly office is indicated. The notion of the "shepherd," accordingly, comprises generally the official form and representation of the Old Testament theocratic life, and likewise pre-eminently the kingly office, giving prominence to the kingly government (pp. 23, 24), as is the case with the Messianic idea under the Old Covenant, with that of "Christ" under the New Testament, so that "shepherd" and the "anointed" come near and mutually supplement each other. In the Messianic character of the shepherd, there comes out, along with the relation to the theocratic people, the other relation, that, namely, to Jehovah, the Lord of the theocracy, according to which the shepherd appears as the representative of Jehovah among His people. If in this respect Messiah is the term for the relation in question as regards equipment, or internal power of the Spirit, so in that of "shepherd" there is given, we might say, the fulfilment, the realization of the same relation by means of a corresponding government. On account of what they had not done, the shepherds of Israel are manifestly the unrighteous, the wicked ones. On account of that which He does who makes Himself known in John x., He proves Himself to be the Good Shepherd. But as there the Jews (John x. 20) supposed Him to be actuated not by the Spirit of the God-anointed, the Messiah, but to have in him an evil spirit (δαιμόνιον ἔχει), so they misunderstood also His unbosoming of Himself on that occasion as the Shepherd, and turned away from Him.

2. "In this chapter" (says Cocceius) "the office of shepherd is taken from the shepherds of Israel, and promise is made of the kingdom of Christ, the Chief Shepherd. The shepherds of Israel are of a threefold order, Zech. xi. 3, 8. The three shepherds there are *vigil, et respondens, et offerens munus* (Mal. ii. 12); that is, elder, prophet or doctor, and priest. They are called 'gods,' but in Ps. lxxxii. 6 sq. their abolition is pronounced. Therefore the apostle, 1 Cor. ii. 6, says of the princes of this world, that they are come to nought."

3. "The prophecy in ch. xxxiv. is kept very general, and does not connect itself closely with specific occasions and circumstances, hence admits (apart from its typical bearing on the experiences of Israel, outward and spiritual) of manifold applications to all states, churches, families; and with justice, for it is really designed for all that could be named figuratively shepherd and flock, like a mathematical formula which expresses a law that may be applied to innumerable cases" (SCHMIEDER).

4. From the second verse of this chapter the Lord Jesus appears to have quoted the repeated "woe" against the Scribes and Pharisees (Matt. xxiii.). The application to these throws light specially on the days of Christ, but generally on the period subsequent to the exile. The hierarchy, as it appears in its antagonism to Christ, is the final degradation of the theocratic officialism of Israel. Prophecy ceased with Haggai, Zechariah, and Malachi. In its place, as the characteristic appearance of Ezra shows, and as fabled also by the Jewish traditions of the "Great Sanhedrim" and the "Great Synagogue," came the learning of the Scribes. As it was already with the three last prophets in relation to the earlier prophetic office, so also did the princely dignity of Zerubbabel stand related to the Davidic kingdom of former times. Zerubbabel was leader to the returning captives, and was appointed royal governor over the new colony, in which his character as a born prince of Judah was lost sight of. Although he stood as governor directly under the Persian kings, still the Persian governors in Samaria were instructed to keep their eye upon his administration. What, however, in his appointment by Cyrus, carried, according to the Jewish mode of contemplation, a specially royal, that is, Davidic aspect, presently again fell into abeyance with the person of Zerubbabel. On this account alone the application by some of ver. 23 to Zerubbabel is shown to be untenable. None of Zerubbabel's sons succeeded him as governor. If from the time of Nehemiah's death the post of provincial governor gradually disappeared, as is with much probability supposed, then, for the purpose of taking the oversight of civic affairs (and of any other kind of oversight we know nothing), only the office of the high-priesthood remained, the history of which henceforth became a very worldly one, full of ambition and crime. The Maccabees united with it the dignity of military general; afterwards, as conferred upon them by the people, a hereditary princedom, over against which the Sanhedrim, which had meanwhile been constituted, and was under pharisaical-priestly influence, strove to maintain its position; and then at last the title of king. That the dignity of high priest as combined with princely rank, especially when the prince was a Sadducee, formed a kind of caricature of Ps. cx. 4, does not hinder on the other side the noting of an important feature therein with regard to Christ; just as in the resolutions of the people and their counsellors there is apprehended, with a clear consciousness, the future

appearance of a faithful prophet (1 Macc. xiv. 41). The dissolution-process now indicated of the theocratic offices in Israel after the exile suffices for the chapter of Ezekiel before us.

5. Israel, as remarked by Beck, "should, amid the tumult of desolation and the luxurious forms of development of the God-forgetting worldly nationalities, have stood forth as a strictly separate sanctuary of God, to which not the present, indeed, but so much the more certainly the future belonged; and even the falling away from this simple isolation of the whole state-economy justified its real wisdom by means of the desolating results that ensued." "A many-membered organism of law, like a comprehensive ring, encompassed the whole individual and commercial life, woven into the elements of the world's fellowship, while the more determinative arrangements of the outward natural life, of the reckoning of time, of the physical and social human life, were consecrated as serviceable organs for the establishment of a pious fellowship with God, of a righteous ordering and wholesome direction of the life." It was "an externality," but "no hollow-surface existence ending in itself; rather a vessel and framework of a spiritual inwardness of being, destined to future development, and bearing this in itself in a manner pregnant with promise." The proof of this is specially furnished by prophecy, whose foundation was already laid among the fathers of the Israelitish people, which came forth into peculiar external activity under the constitution of the Mosaic economy, and at last assumed formally the place of an order in the State. Hence its cessation was pre-eminently a mark of the time, as being that of the approaching advent of Him whose Spirit was in the prophets! Were but the whole people of Jehovah prophets! was the wish of Moses (Num. xi. 29); expressing as regards Israel the design of prophecy, and at the same time with an eye toward the Pentecostal future. Still more, however, was this import involved in the priesthood, which was no caste foreign to the people, but rooted in a brotherly stem of the same, giving promise of a priestly position to the whole of Israel, with corresponding fulness of obligation to duties of service. So close and inward, because a service rendered to the whole, and springing out of its innermost idea, was the relation of these offices in Israel to Israel itself, that their unfolding and Israel's unfolding overlap each other, are congenial. The destination of Israel to the kingdom lies enfolded in Ex. xix. 6 (Rev. i. 6), although in what is merely the outward governing power of one, the civic subordination of the others may come more prominently out. The full prospect for the future looks toward those who are without, to the heathen nations, the world.

6. What "the servant" Moses (Heb. iii. 5) represented individually for the whole theocracy, this found its representation as regards Jehovah's supreme authority in the entire community in David, who, as "servant of Jehovah," takes up into himself "the servant Moses," as prince in Israel represents the divine supremacy.

7. So much has the being "without a shepherd," ver. 5, become the case with Israel, that by the extirpation of the Good Shepherd through the bad shepherds of Israel, the scattering of the people has become complete; and certainly also the gathering of the true Israel has been fulfilled. Comp. on this Zech. xiii. 7; Isa. liii. 6; 1 Pet. ii. 25.

8. Maintaining their position over against the world was "the one thing needful" for Israel as the people of God; so that the gathering through Christ, as on the one side it was restitution in conformity to the ideal of Israel, so on the other generally it was for them the condition of life, life's deliverance. Thus Israel lives on still, not merely as to its character as a people, while the other peoples of antiquity have historically vanished, but the idea of Israel as a people is in Christ the idea of humanity.

9. "God's will has from the first been directed to the object of gathering a new humanity out of the world, of a people of God out of all peoples; and the choosing of Israel as the people of God was only a first provisional step toward the accomplishment of this will: God gathers Israel to Himself as His people only for the purpose of gathering through their instrumentality a people from among all nations. But now it seemed, in the days of Ezekiel, as if through the scattering of Israel, as those in whom for the time being the people of God appeared, the collecting of a people of God had been abandoned and become impossible. To that, however, it could not be allowed to come; and in the text, which is quite general in its terms, there is embraced alike the bringing back of Israel from exile, the gathering of the Church of Christ by means of His word, and the final gathering of the children of God out of the world generally, as certainly as the matter itself belongs to the formation of a new humanity (KLIEFOTH). The fourteenth verse is by the same expositor similarly explained in a quite general way, though he has a spiritual and external addition of this sort, that "the future return of the converted Jews to their land" should be taken into account.

10. The ceasing of the offices in Israel is not simply, therefore, a historical fact, a ceasing of life-forms that once existed, but it is the emptying of those forms in the spirit, and consequently in respect to truth. Office-bearing of the kind that belonged to Israel can no more be found in Christ; so that all churchism which would turn back to lay hold of that, or even look aslant toward it, merely (as statecraft also with respect to the kingdom) surrenders its Christianity, or places it in question. What the official constitution of things in Israel signified, has its correspondence in the anointing with the Spirit for all Christians, 1 John ii. 20, 27; Rev. i. 6. What is called "office" in Christianity can only be ordinances as to service, or χαρίσματα, Rom. xii. 6, or the powers that be, which are ordained by God (Rom. xiii.).

11. (Religion falls radically into the three distinctive actings of the three offices, beginning with a prophetic function as the knowledge of God and manifestation of God, maintaining always a high-priestly relation toward God in the spirit of consecration and surrender to Him, and perpetually unfolding its kingly character by the renewal and enlargement of soul in God, and a walk in God's freedom and power. After P. Lange.)

12. Upon the judging between sheep and sheep Hengstenberg remarks that "the main fulfilment here also is to be sought in Christ, whose govern

ment and secret yet powerful guidance permits no tyranny and injustice to endure." "A principal phase was the decision between the synagogue and the Christian church." "But that this judging goes through the whole history, that we have to do in it with a true prophecy and not with a patriotic phantasy, appears from a comparison of the existing Christian-world with that of the heathen and Mahometan, and also with the Old Testament judicial relationships. Since the appearance of Christ, there has been at work a reforming agency among the people of God."

13. "A rich man in Scripture is not one who has many goods, but whose heart clings to what he possesses, so that it ceases to be for him something accidental; while a poor man is he only who knows and feels himself to be poor, who is so not merely in an outward respect, but in spirit also—in his consciousness" (HENGST.).

14. The introduction of David, as already remarked in the exposition, without anything farther or particular, confirms what is stated by Hengst., that "the Messiah, the glorious offspring of David, had in the time of the prophet been for long a lesson of the Catechism." David, however, according to his personality in sacred history, not only appears as the readiest thought when a shepherd is the subject of discourse—though certainly the shepherd-state with him is so entirely his style and manner, that from being the shepherd of a flock he became the shepherd of Israel (Ps. lxxviii 70; 2 Sam. vii. 8)—but also, in an especial manner for the promised gathering of the flock, he suggests more than any one else who might be brought into consideration, since through him the tribal supremacy of Judah, toward which even in Egypt the hope of Israel was directed (Gen. xlix.), effected that the tribes of Israel, which had been in a state of division, should unite, and remain together for the glorious kingdom of Solomon under its ascendency. Much more, however, does the personality of David bring into view and represent in relation to the Messianic idea—viz. that he, the anointed of Jehovah, and the king who had been raised up from a low estate, was after God's own heart, himself possessed of the prophetic Spirit (Acts ii. 30; Matt. xxii. 43),—one who manifested earnest desire and love for the worship of Jehovah, by invigorating and supporting both it and the priesthood, as well as in his psalms, and by the building of the temple, which originated with him. There was then provided, as Beck says, "the substratum for a new aspect of salvation, and there was opened up by the promise a new mental horizon in the seed of David, who was chosen for an abiding reign of peace, and for the building of God's house, and upheld with perpetual experiences of Fatherly grace, and that even amid chastisements for sin, and in the everlasting continuance of David's house, kingdom, and throne (2 Sam. vii. 8 sq., xxiii. 1 sq.; Ps. lxxxix. 30, 37 sq., lxxii.)." To the idea of a ruling power, which was contemplated by Moses, there was added the dynastic in the case of David, who became the founder not only of a kingly dynasty, but of one through which the kingdom of Israel was to reach its highest culmination. The entire image of the people's shepherd, which expresses the divine title of this dynasty, stretches so manifestly beyond all the individual rulers belonging to the Davidic line, that "for the receiver of the promise, David, said promise does not at all stand or fall with Solomon, the first member in the chosen line, whose conditional rejection rather appears not to be excluded by the divine favour promised inalienably to the seed, 1 Chron. xxviii. 9" (BECK). The individual members of the Davidic dynasty served in their working and suffering as offerings and harvests to future times; "their blossom-seasons were far from reaching the height of the ideal of their house—formed merely the foil for the more definite limning of the glory which glimmered through it (Ps. lxxii.); but, on the other hand, their periods of depression did not bring that ideal to destruction, only imprinted it more deeply in the heart, taking the divine grace and truth as a pledge for its realization (Ps. lxxxix.), and so left it over to the Son of David, in whom the image of the divine government and kingdom was concentrated, Luke i. 32 sq." (BECK).

15. In the Messiah the whole existence of Israel as a people is comprised, its organization as plastically working itself out through the theocratic offices; while, on the other side, salvation and blessing, which these offices had instrumentally to administer to the people, attained to perfection in His consecrated personality with an elevation, which is also indicated in the expression of ver. 24: "a prince among them." The parallel expressions in this verse: "Jehovah a God to them," and: "David a prince in their midst," serve for the form of the salvation and the blessing to be made good, if the one statement is taken as the theme, and the other as its exposition. A moral signification like Keil's: "pasturing in full unison with Jehovah, carrying out the will of Jehovah only," imports too little into this text, and the filling of it up by pointing to "unity of being with God," again, imports too much. To the theological judgment the relation will, perhaps, represent itself much as Ps. ii. does in respect to the sonship in its connection with the kingdom. In the psalm the theocratic temporal sonship is indicated, according to which mention is made in Rom. i. 4 of his being "determined to be the Son of God;" and in like manner, here in Ezekiel, it is only the realization of the promised salvation and blessing, as it is suggested by the covenant-relation of Jehovah to Israel, which can immediately come into consideration. The verses that follow bring into notice the grace of the covenant; the covenant graciousness manifests itself, according to ver. 24, in the David-Messiah, as the one who generally was to prove the covenant of Jehovah to be an abiding one with His people, and in particular the eternity of the kingdom of David. If the: "I have begotten thee," in Ps. ii. 7, seems to import more than: "I appoint (or raise up)," here, the expression in Ps. ii. 6: "I have anointed" (נָסַכְתִּי), does not indicate more (comp. at ch. xxii. 30); and both expressions in the psalm, like the one here (הֲקִימֹתִי), refer to 2 Sam. vii., where the decree (חֹק) in Ps. ii 7 is obvious: "I will be to him a father, and he will be to me a son" (ver. 14). While He is so called there on account of the unceasing filial relation to the divine favour, of course in connection with the promise of an eternal sovereignty, with Ezekiel, vers. 23, 24, it is the latter only which

has a place, an everlasting princedom of David, the divine ideal of His sole governmental personality. In another light, however, will the parallel-membered passage of ver. 24 appear to us, if we add in thought the: "Behold I" (הִנְנִי־אָנִי), which is so expressively repeated (vers. 11, 20). In that case Jehovah Himself will have to be thought of as present in this David. If in the term "shepherd" a reference is made to the circumstance that David was literally such before he became king, so by the designation "servant" David, which likewise is twice used with emphasis, a relation is expressed, which Nitzsch characterizes as an Old Testament mode of describing "the religion of human life" (*System*, p. 187); since "the servant of God generally is the subject of the honour that comes from God, and as such is the chosen one, the one who is specially privileged, set up for the maintenance of the true religion in behalf of others, and actively engaged in doing so—nor merely a true and proved, but also an atoning, and finally a glorified human personality." Farther, there is now on both occasions used the epithet "My" servant, with all the more emphasis in ver. 24 as it is preceded by the expression: "I Jehovah"; and there is to be compared the: "My shepherd," in Zech. xiii. 7, coupled with the words of explanation: "against the man that is My fellow." Indeed, as the whole passage from ver. 9 onwards is the self-manifestation of Jehovah, a divine background must form the gold-ground of the Messianic picture.

16. There is no need for placing any constraint on the אֶחָד of ver. 23; so much it quite naturally implies, that although the basis of the "one" shepherd is the house of David destined to an everlasting continuance, and one can, with Hengstenberg, "understand by David the stem of David culminating in Christ, so that the fulfilment in Christ is not the sole, but only the highest, the true one," still a definite, and indeed a unique personality, an individual, is contemplated here—one who has not his like. Comp. Jer. xxiii. 5.

17. "The typical element in Israel's condition, or the prefigurative representation of the future spiritual life, of which Israel itself was more or less unconscious,—a representation which was called forth and animated by the essential principles of that life,—was, like the typical character of the Israelitish religion generally, the basis of prophecy" (P. LANGE, *Philos. Dogm.*).

18. Christ, "as the Anointed of God in the theocratic sense, the Messiah promised by the prophets," is "the true Servant of God in the law of the Spirit, whom the Old Testament Israel prefigured in the law of the letter, the richly Anointed of God, whose precursors were all officially anointed typical sons of Jehovah under the Old Covenant." "Jesus is the Christ, since His whole life was the discharge of a holy office." "Jesus has not merely in some sense the office of a Christ, of a God-anointed person devoted to the wellbeing of the world; He is the Christ Himself. Hence His office is designated as the absolute office, as the sum of all the offices inseparably connected with salvation; and it is at the same time declared, that His office first represented in full reality and completeness what the separate callings in respect to salvation in the world could represent only figuratively, partly in a typical, partly in a symbolical manner." "As guiding organs of the Old Testament life, the theocratic offices were such also for the future divine-human life." "With the organic separation of these offices was connected the feature of their transitory character, their incompleteness. Hence the fulfilment of the religion in the person of Jesus was at the same time the fulfilment and completion of these offices. His life is, as the individualizing of the completed religion—absolute life from God, for God, and in and with God. Hence, also, must Christ comprise in His personality the three offices as a unity in their completed essence-form, and in the fundamental characteristics of His life they must shine forth in their rounded completeness" (P. LANGE, *Pos. Dogm.*).

19. "The dark caricature and counterpart of the prophetic activity of Christ or of the revelation in Him is the Jewish Talmud; the reverse image of His high-priestly function is the penal wandering of Israel throughout the world; and over against His royal administration and kingdom stands the demoniacal worldly-mindedness of the Jews, with its important results" (P. LANGE).

20. Upon the prophecy as a whole with respect to its fulfilment it may be said, that in its trichotomy the servant David, as the third piece, is the simultaneous discharge of the two parts that had preceded. Through Him has it come to an end with the offices of Israel (vers. 1–10); with Him comes the manifestation of Jehovah Himself as the shepherd (vers. 11–22). Now, if He who perfects Himself after this manner is the Messiah, then also everything that is essentially connected therewith must plainly be found in Jesus Christ. The appearance of the Son of God in the flesh, especially in the insight afforded into His mighty working by His resurrection from the dead, is so much the more the fulfilment of our prophecy, as this has in manifold ways been testified by Himself and His apostles. As in the exile and during the time that followed, till Christ, the dissolution of the theocratic offices in Israel as such (comp. ver. 4) took effect, so did the gathering of the people, in contrast to the scattering (ver. 5), by means of the return from Babylon, become a reality (ver. 13, and comp. Isa. xliv. 28, where Cyrus is called "My shepherd"). But the so strongly marked scattering of ver. 5 is only one thing; another is the wandering upon the mountains and hills (ver. 6), to which not the gathering effected by the return to their home corresponds, but feeding upon the mountains, etc. (ver. 13 sq., comp. also Isa. liii. 6), which had locally its fulfilment in Christ (Matt. ix. 36; Luke xv.), especially the distinctive characteristics described in ver. 16. In like manner, also, the judgment of separation exercised through the person of Christ within Israel (Luke ii. 34; Matt. xxi. 44) stands connected with what is written in ver. 17 sq.; and immediately thereafter the Messiah-David (ver. 23 sq.) is made distinctly to shine forth out of the prophetic representation. What is said, *e.g.*, by Keil of "the twofold judgment of scattering along with the twofold gathering of Israel," as being in this prophecy "not distinguished, but thrown complexly together," has

been imported into it from another quarter. "That only a small part of Israel," as he says, "received the Messiah when appearing in Jesus as their shepherd," gave occasion not so properly for a new judgment of dispersion among all nations, as rather, we may say, that the Babylonish judgment was in consequence thereof confirmed for unbelieving Israel as such, and also completed. For Israel was still, at the time of Christ's appearing, in a state of dispersion among all nations, because scattered throughout the Roman world, so that even the gathering from Babylon must be referred to the advent of Jesus Christ, since thereby His birth in the City of David, as well as His resurrection in the place where He was crucified, after being loosed from the pains of death, and hence the turning of the promised land into a blessing after the manner indicated in ver. 26, were rendered possible. One must not say that the fulfilment of this prophecy had begun "with the redemption of Israel from the Babylonish exile," and still less that it began with the appearing of Jesus Christ as the Good Shepherd of the seed of David; but this latter appearing is the fulfilment, so that we have no other to expect, and the bringing back from Babylon to Canaan was merely its preparation; and the true understanding of this preparatory gathering as a gathering is to be sought in the Church of Jesus Christ, in the gathering of the Israel after the Spirit out of the whole world (John x. 16). If it "admits of no doubt" (KLIEFOTH), that what is said of the establishing of a new covenant in ver. 25 "has been already fulfilled by the appearance of the Lord in the flesh, and by His work," it should have given this intelligent expositor no further concern, as if the fulfilment of our prophecy could have "belonged entirely to what still is future." This prophecy, also, has not been fulfilled by successive stages, but the fulfilment through Christ only presents itself separately in Christ, while the Church of Christ lives the Messianic life of the Son of God in the world as His body. The "judging between sheep and sheep, the separating of the he-goats, the purifying of the people of God into a sinless community," wherein Kliefoth finds essential parts of the prophecy, which "belong even to the very close of time,"—all this comes into realization through the efficacious working of the Holy Spirit sent by Christ (comp. John xvi. 8; Rom. viii. 9)—does so onwards till the day of Christ, since as the Lord is the Spirit, so the Son of man has been appointed the Judge of the world. The delineation of blessing in ver. 25 sq. is in form taken from the land and the people, but so as to be emblematical of the kingdom of the Anointed. Yes, even "the formation of a new paradise, and the restoration of humanity to its condition of original innocence," does not lie in the text of Ezekiel, but in the exegesis of Kliefoth, who, with such a view of the meaning, cannot get the better of that Chiliasm which he opposes.

21. The characteristic manifestation of the Good Shepherd takes place when He calls His own sheep each by its name, while the sheep on their part hear His voice (John x.). Thus are they led out of the fold, the economy of the Old Covenant, after their state of wandering upon all mountains and on every high hill; and if Jehovah (Isa. liii. 6) lays upon Him the iniquity of all, so He who in John x. 10 testifies that He came in order that they might have life, and have it more abundantly, says also in vers. 11 and 15 there, that He was going to give His life for the sheep.

22. "Christ had to come to them, first, as the teaching Shepherd; secondly, as the Shepherd that should give His life for the sheep, in order that He might set them free from the bondage of the law, and at the same time from their rulers; thirdly, He should Himself become manifest among them as Prince. Thus should the promise to Abraham, that God would be a God to his seed, become yea and amen.—The Sadducees and Pharisees troubled and corrupted to the sheep of the flock, who were obliged to hear them, the pure doctrine; whereupon Christ appeared, and healed the sicknesses of Israel, and gave Himself up to death for His sheep. This is the one period in the prophecy; the other period is, when Christ is given as a prince, quickened from the dead, raised to heaven, and before all Jerusalem anointed through the outpouring of the Holy Spirit on the apostles, when, by the preaching of the apostles, sheep was distinguished from sheep" (COCCEIUS).

23. After the import of the similitude upon Israel has been given in ver. 30, a still deeper thought is subjoined to this import, namely, the bearing of Israel on mankind generally. What of Israel attains to salvation does so not under the national title ("house of Israel"), which has been rendered obsolete through the new covenant, but simply as connected with "Adam," whose antitype Christ is (Rom. v.). Consequently, we have here the exposition of the people of the old covenant in relation to humanity at large.

HOMILETIC HINTS.

Vers. 1, 2. Corruption in the upper, the governing classes, those who give the tone and measure to society, carries along with it corruption among the whole people, and that not merely for a time, but for ever.—"It is a very honourable title to be called a shepherd, but to be so is a heavy burden, with much trouble, care, and labour" (STCK.).—"An entire tribe also of Israel, that guides the other tribes, and stands at their head, feeds the tribes of Israel, like a shepherd, 2 Sam. vii. 7. And there are many degrees of upper and lower shepherds, down even to single householders. So also in Christendom are all authorities, whether in the State, the Church, or the family, to be regarded as shepherds of their respective flocks, smaller or greater. Every pastor is really a shepherd in the biblical sense. The same person can, however, be at once shepherd and sheep, according as he has to discharge the office of ruling, or the duty of letting himself be ruled. It is also a matter of indifference through what instrument the shepherd governs his flock, whether by means of the staff or the dog, whether by the rod, or the sword, or the word. The schoolmaster, too, in so far as he commands, and exercises discipline, and governs the school, is a shepherd" (SCHMIEDER).—"Whoever would be a proper teacher must possess and manifest the true shepherd-faithfulness, must seek simply and alone what is Christ's, Phil. ii. 21" (STARKE).—"They are hirelings who seek after spiritual work, that they may thereby enrich themselves, or gain their bread, Acts xx. 18 sq.; Rom. xvi. 18" (TÜB. BIBLE).—"I ask you on your conscience, Are ye not obliged to feed the souls of your hearers with the living word of God, if ye would be shepherds?" (BERL. BIB.)—"As shepherds, rulers also must not suck the blood of their subjects" (STARKE).—Justice and injustice, blessing and cursing of feeding one's self. The shepherd must also go upon the right pasture for his own poor soul.—The shepherd-office as at the same time duty to one's self.

Ver. 3. "The shepherd receives from the flock his necessary support, his recompense from the Lord" (AUGUSTINE).—Ver. 4. "Pastors should confirm those who are not strong in the faith, cherish the weak and such as cannot go forward, that they may be strengthened, and step firmly on the way of God; should bind up those who have a wounded conscience, so that they may not be consumed by mourning; should bring back those who have been misled and seduced by other teachers; but should seek out such as are perishing for want of guidance and have lost the right way, guiding them to wholesome pasture," etc. (COCC.).—"Preachers should especially commend themselves to the corporeally and spiritually sick among their hearers" (STARKE).—The shepherd-office is sheer service (and those whose it is to serve have προβατων ἦθος); it is not lordship, nor must be, either over the goods or the consciences of men.—The obligations of the shepherd-office a mirror of human wretchedness.—The fivefold nature of a shepherd's work. "Paul became all things to all men, that he might save some."—Ver. 5. "Scattering, isolation, so that people know not rightly to whom they belong and what they should do, is the consequence of an inactive, tyrannical, luxurious government" (SCHMIEDER).—What is the consequence of bad shepherds, that is also unmistakably the curse for great communities.—The shepherd on an earthly domain knows well how many the sheep of his flock number; but how many spiritual shepherds, if they know it externally, and have the number of their church members in their head, bear them upon their hearts according to their internal states?—"Not merely in the bodily, but pre-eminently in the spiritual enemies of the people of God, inheres the wolf-spirit, the devil" (SCHMIEDER).—The many shepherds (the hierarchy) may possibly disguise the *one* Good Shepherd to the sheep, as though He were not there.—Ver. 6. Scattering can become evil, wandering may be still worse; as in life, so in doctrine.—In front of the spiritual heights, as well as before flatness in spiritual things, a shepherd has to keep his flock together.

Vers. 7–14. To have not done according to the word of the Lord must lead to great trouble from the Lord's word, namely, to hear its judgments.—God's judgment on bad shepherds, a righteous and severe one.—The frightful judgment, which is contained even in the beautiful name of the shepherd.—"Corruption in the shepherds, princes, priests, is mentioned among the signs of the Lord's advent" (BERL. BIB.).—Ver. 10. "In this, that those shepherds should no more be, it is not indicated that the shepherds then existing should perish, and others come into their place, who should bear the same office and have the same power, for this would not have been a full deliverance. Nor is this declared by the prophet, that, after the abolition of the shepherds of that time, no wolves should arise and false prophets, who would not care for the flock of God—comp. Acts xx. 29; Zech. xi. 16. But this is what is meant, that even if such should arise, they were by no means to be accounted shepherds, but their commands and instructions might safely be repudiated, etc.; whereas under the Old Covenant the people were so placed under their shepherds as to be constrained to adhere to them, since the temple must be frequented by those who drew near to God" (COCCEIUS).—"The right shepherd is also the judge of the false shepherds" (BERL. BIB.).—A reward will be given to shepherds in righteousness, but also with a gracious recompense.—Ver. 11. "Christ the Chief Shepherd of our souls. Oh, with what love does He seek them! How does He bring them into the right condition, convert them through His Spirit, and guide them to the right pasture!" (TÜB. BIB.)—Ver. 12. Redemption out of all places the great prospect of faith, the blessed hope also of the resurrection.—"There comes a day of the Lord; a morning-star must appear after a dreary night" (A. KRUMMACHER).—Ver. 13. "So again at last, when God poured out His Spirit upon the apostles, there was a gathering together from all places of the flock of God, Acts ii. 9 sq." (COCC.).—"The genuine land of Israel is the new earth with the new heavens" (SCHMIEDER).—Godliness has the promise not only of the life that now is, but also of that which is to come, 1 Tim. iv.—The divine refreshments of the Lord, images of the spiritual here, of the eternal hereafter.—Death a shepherd, Ps. xlix. 15 [14]. But while he does his work, there is also for believers the shepherd-staff of the Good Shepherd.—"This world is only an inn; not our home, rather a prison, since we have been made and redeemed for heaven" (STCK.).—"Hence we should not despair when we see that in troublous times only a few are left. The flock may continue small, but it can never happen that there shall be no flock. If the woman has fled with her children into the wilderness, Rev. xii., she must again return to be among men" (HEIM-HOFF.).—Union of the faithful the work of the Lord; and the more that the churches, through the general falling away of the members, come to be composed of believers, will the union of the churches also come to be regarded as a matter of the Lord, and no merely political maxim.—Ver. 14. "The secret of the pasture of Christ" (SCHMIEDER).—"How few consider the blessedness of the righteous, and how well it goes with them!" (STCK.)—Good pasture and bad pasture.—The high mountains of Israel, his promises in respect to their fulfilment, his worship in spirit and truth.

Ver. 15. Food and rest, the two great necessities of human life.—"Their rest will nourish them, and their nourishment will bring them new rest" (BERL. BIB.).—"Nothing can be more frequently repeated to believing souls, nothing more deeply impressed upon them, than what has been promised to them in Christ Jesus their Lord" (STCK.).—Rest, true, eternal repose, is only to be had under the shepherd-staff of Christ.—What can the whole world offer instead with all its enjoyments?—The everlasting promises of God in Christ, and the delusive shows of the devil in the lust of this passing world.—Ver. 16 sq. The Lord's inspection of the flock at the same time a call to self-examination. (Preparation-sermon before the holy communion.)—"The lost, those who are cut off from grace, excommunicated, these, in our Lord's time, were the publicans and sinners; now, those who are excluded and condemned by the alone blessed-making Church (or confession). The wandering are those who no longer hold to the Church,—the sects, separatists. The wounded are such as have taken some offence, like a sheep that has been bitten by a dog. The sick are those who, through false teaching and bad example, have become weak in the faith. The case of all these the Good Shepherd promises to take in hand" (SCHMIEDER).—"But the Lord feeds with judgment, that is, with befitting difference, since He dispenses to each what is proper to him,—to one this, to another something else. He performs to the weak no more than is good for them. The children He feeds with milk, and defends them. He acts mildly or severely, consoles, frightens, blames, caresses, as at any time is good for us; for the fearful He relaxes the reins, and those who place their confidence in Him He draws to Himself. If some are fat, and corrupt the weak, He takes from them their strength. Some are proud of the gifts lent to them, and despise the simplicity of others; for these it is good when they are humbled, and are deprived of their gifts, so that they may obtain the salvation of Christ. Thus He accomplishes the judgment, and the separation between sheep and sheep; and so each one should be concerned about himself, and not trouble himself respecting others. The separation is already going on here in secret, but at last it will become manifest, and be seen to issue in a wide gulf" (HEIM-HOFF.).—"The kingdom of God belongs to those who are weary and heavy laden (Matt. xi. 28); by and by their turn shall be to rejoice in the Lord's goodness, Luke xvi. 25" (HITZIG).—"Why should the he-goats be in the flock of God? on the same pastures, beside the same brooks as the sheep? They are at present tolerated, afterwards separated from it" (AUGUSTINE).—"A stern judge is the Good Shepherd; not merely the unscrupulous leaders of the flock, but even the sheep themselves, will be brought to account by Him" (UMBREIT).—"Believers are thereby admonished to consider on what side they should place themselves, so that they may escape the future day of slaughter; and at the same time are comforted, so as to be able to hold out with patience during this life. Religious strifes and controversies also will be brought to an end by the judgment of the Lord" (LUTHER).—Ver. 18. Compare what is set forth here with what the King says in Matt. xxv. 34 sq. Would our so-called "men of culture" also but consider it, who only tread under foot the pure doctrine, or trouble it by their goat-like gambols!—"And keep thee from the judgments of men, whereby the noble treasure is corrupted: this I leave thee at the close" (LUTHER).—Ver. 19. "This, alas! represents so many church services in which unbelieving men preach, just as ver. 21 points reprovingly to the empty churches" (RICHT.).—Ver. 21 sq. The mischievous polemic in the Church.—A theology that is quarrelsome and combative scatters the churches in the world.—Spiritual dogmatism.—A more correct estimate of separation from the Bible point of view, than from that of a corrupt church with its anathemas.—"The righteous may certainly be oppressed, yet not wholly suppressed" (STCK.).—Redemption a judgment, and the judgment of the Lord a redemption.—The help of the flock is its Shepherd alone; therefore must we withdraw our confidence from all creatures, and expect nothing from new laws and constitutions.—"This is the manner of the divine compassion, that it takes our misery as an invitation" (HEIM-HOFF.).

Ver. 23 sq. "Christ has not come without a call, but with the good-will and mission of His heavenly Father, John v. 43" (CR.).—One, because all pointed to Him, in word and in deed, and because no one, except in Him, is anything.—"God names Him His servant, since Christ, made under the law, has fulfilled it, that He might extirpate sin, and bring in righteousness, and so might be complete *goel* and propitiation, Ps. xl. 9, 10 [8, 9]" (COCC.).—"David: 1, as to the name, His beloved, Matt. iii. 17; 2, as to His birth, in Bethlehem; 3, as to His humble state and littleness, Isa. liii. 3; 4, as to His shepherd-service; 5, as to His anointing; 6, as to His devotedness, David for the law, Christ for the flock; 7, as to His victories" (STCK.).—"He will not only feed them, but also discharge in their behalf all shepherd-duty besides needful for their preservation and support, their refreshment and invigoration, and will remain their Shepherd for ever. Thus will He teach and heal, and take away sicknesses—not do and act merely, but suffer also, purchase the sheep with His precious blood, whereby He will prove Himself to be the True Shepherd," etc. (COCC.).—"He is the Prince among believers, because He is the Mediator between God and men; because as Head He communicates grace to the members and the living Spirit; and because, moreover, we see in His countenance the fatherly heart of God. Through Him is the Lord our God, that is, He is reconciled to us, and unites Himself to us" (HEIM-HOFF.).—Where Christ reigns, there God is with us, Matt. xxviii. 20.—Vers. 23, 24. The One Shepherd according to the promise in its fulfilment: 1, His official position through all times; 2, His shepherd-service in the flesh and in the spirit; 3, His personality in respect to God and as regards the flock.

Ver. 25. "1. Justified by faith, we have peace with God through Christ. God is for us, who can be against us? 2. He blesses us with all spiritual blessings. The apostles teach and sow, but the Lord gives the showers of blessing, that the seed of the word may spring forth, and the trees yield their fruit; that is, that the great and the small may believe in Christ Jesus, and confess Him with the mouth. 3. He breaks the yoke of slavery to sin, and gives freedom from all enemies. Whence, naturally, there arises a strong confidence, Rom. viii. 35-39" (HEIM-HOFF.).—The covenant of peace in Christ—its divine ground, its invincible strength, its blessed peace. The secure land even now in the midst of the world.—The evil beasts in the land,—spiritual false guides, worldly persecutors, plausible hypocrites.—"False teachers and tyrants God causes either to die or to change their mind; but the Son of God has conquered the roaring lion, who is the devil" (LUTHER).—In the world ye may be of good cheer, is the saying of the Good Shepherd to His own (John xvi. 33), as it certainly was their experience (John xiv. 27).—Security and security, carnal and spiritual, how different!—He gives sleep to His own, even in the wilderness (Ps. cxxvii. 3 [2]).—Ver. 26. Salvation is of the Jews, John iv.—What the father of the faithful was to be to the world (Gen. xii.), namely, a blessing, that should believers be in this world.—Zion, as after the flesh in Christ, so after the Spirit in the spiritual Zion, in its destination to bless, its task of blessing, and its duty of service for the earth.—There the Church is a blessing where there is the rain of the Holy Spirit. Without this rain nothing grows in the kingdom of God; one cannot even say, Jesus is Lord (1 Cor. xii. 3).—Ver. 27. The blessed earth, and the land of Israel, when smitten with the curse.—"Where faith is, there is a good tree, and there also is produced good fruit" (STCK.).—Not only shall the axe be laid to the root of the trees, but for the trees also there is a promise of fruit.—Fruit and increase in spiritual things: the former, glory to the man himself, example and enjoyment for others; the latter, the thankfulness we owe to God.—The knowledge derived as well from the misery of servitude as from redemption out of all sin and misery.—The sinner a tool of the devil; the redeemed a servant of God.—The rest in Christ from the bondage in sin.—Ver. 28. Blessedness, to be no longer compelled to belong to the world; to be chosen out of it, although one must still be in it!—Spiritual boldness, over against the powers of the world, over against the wickedness of sin, over against the transitoriness and uncertainty of our earthly life, over against the solicitude of our own heart.

Ver. 29. The planting of the Heavenly Father, Matt. xv. 13.—The kingdom of the Anointed a planting, inasmuch as the members of the kingdom are—1, sown by the word; 2, reared, fostered by the Holy Spirit; 3, grown in time for eternity, to the honour of God the Father.—The kingdom of God is righteousness, and peace, and joy in the Holy Ghost; how, then, can there ever be want? (Luke xxii. 35.)—The good, the glorious name, which the people of God should have in the world.—We should, however, not merely have the name to live (Rev. iii. 1), and still be dead.—Hungering after righteousness as the means and preservative against the eternal hunger and distress on account of sin; hunger against hunger. Hunger in order not to hunger, as the way to everlasting satisfaction.—Eternal glory and temporal reproach in the world and from the world.—The rod of wickedness shall not rest for ever or the lot of the righteous (Ps. cxxv. 3).—Ver. 30. "God at times conceals from His own His countenance, that He may thereafter embrace them with everlasting favour" (STCK.).—The last knowledge is the experience that God is our God, and we are His people.—The survey from the end back upon the beginning of the way leads us to recognise the eternal election of God above all else.—Only by the way do the pilgrims of God doubt; not at the beginning, and at the end not at all. At first they proceed in faith, at last they shall see face to face.—Ver. 31. "Under the more immediate interpretation of the similitude, that men are meant, there is at the same time indicated the universality of grace,—that not Israel alone, but Adam, humanity, are named as the flock; and the greatness also of the grace is perceptible in this, that Israel is not designated by its honourable name, that which expresses its election of grace (yet ver. 30?), but 'man,' which calls to remembrance dust of the ground, sin, and death. Such significant addresses, containing much in little, in simple language both fulness and greatness of thought, we fitly call profound (rich in spirit, *geistreich*). And God, the Spirit of all spirits, should not His speech be with spiritual richness?" (SCHMIEDER.)—The kindness and love of God toward man in Christ Jesus our Lord, Tit. iii. 4.—Israel in his significance for humanity.—That the true Israel is the Son of man, itself shows the wide horizon of the grace of God in Christ.—The Christian application of "My fatherland must be greater."—Neither the shepherds nor the sheep of the flock are saints, but simply men.—God manifests in flesh a divine *nil humani a me alienum*.—The tabernacle of God with men, Rev. xxi., the end and aim of Jehovah's action as shepherd.

2. AGAINST EDOM, WITH RESPECT TO THE MOUNTAINS OF ISRAEL, IN CONSEQUENCE OF JEHOVAH'S SANCTIFICATION OF HIS OWN NAME (CH. XXXV.–XXXVI.).

1, 2 CH. XXXV. And the word of Jehovah came to me, saying, Son of man, set
thy face towards [against] the Mount [the mountain range of] Seir, and prophesy con-
3 cerning [against] it; And say to it, Thus saith the Lord Jehovah, Behold, I
am against thee, Mount Seir, and I stretch out My hand over thee, and I
4 make thee a waste and a desolation. Thy cities will I make ruins, and thou
5 shalt be a waste, and dost know that I am Jehovah. Because thou hast
enmity for ever, and deliveredst the children of Israel into the hands of the
sword, in the time of their calamity, in the time of the guilt of the end;
6 Therefore, as I live,—sentence of the Lord Jehovah,—blood will I make thee,
and blood shall pursue thee; where thou hatedst not blood, there shall blood
7 pursue thee. And I make Mount Seir a desolation and a waste, and I cut off
8 from it him that passes over, and him that returns. And I fill his mountains
with his slain; thy hills, and thy valleys, and all thy ravines, the slain with
9 the sword shall fall in them. I will give thee up to perpetual desolations,
and thy cities shall not be inhabited, and ye know that I am Jehovah.
10 Because thou saidst, The two nations (*haggoïim*) and the two lands, mine
11 shall they be, and we possess it (Jerusalem?), and Jehovah was there: There-

fore, as I live,—sentence of the Lord Jehovah,—so do I according to thy
anger and according to thy envy, which thou out of thy hatred hast shown
towards them; and I make Myself known among them as Him who shall
12 judge thee. And thou knowest that I Jehovah have heard all thy scornful
speeches which thou utteredst against the mountains of Israel, saying, Lay
13 waste, to us they are given for food. And ye magnified yourselves against
Me with your mouth, and heaped up your words against Me; I have heard.
14 Thus saith the Lord Jehovah, as [when] the whole land [the whole earth] rejoices,
15 I will make thee a desolation. According to thy rejoicing for the inheritance
of the house of Israel because it was made desolate, so will I do to thee; a
desolation shalt thou be, Mount Seir, and all Edom, the whole of it, and they
know that I am Jehovah.

Ver. 3. Sept.: . . . δωσω σε ἐρημον κ. ἐρημωθησῃ. Vulg.: . . . *desolatum atque desertum.*

Ver. 5. . . . γενεσθαι σε ἐχθραν αἰωνιον κ. ἐνεκαθισας τω οἰκω 'Ισρ. δολω ἐν καιρω ἐχθρων ἐν χειρί μαχαιρας ἐν καιρω ἀδικιας ἐπ' ἐσχατων,

Ver. 6. . . . εἰ μην εἰς αἱμα ἡμαρτες κ. αἱμα σε διωξεται. Vulg.: *et cum sanguinem oderis—*

Ver. 7. . . . ἀνθρωπους κ. κτηνη. (Anoth. read.: ומשמה, *et stuporem.*)

Ver. 9. Anoth. read.: תשובנה, *revertentur.*

Ver. 11. Sept.: . . . γνωσθησομαι σοι— (Anoth. read.: באפך, as also יבקנאתך.)

Ver. 15. . . . κ. πασα ἡ 'Ιδουμαια ἐξολεθρευθήσεται— (Anoth. read.: כלה, *totus ipse.*)

EXEGETICAL REMARKS.

In looking forward to the restoration of Israel, ch. xxxiv., the false shepherds chiefly furnished the connection; in what follows regarding Israel as a nation, Edom and its hatred form the connecting link. Comp. also what is said in p. 245, and Doct. Reflection 5, p. 246. Hävernick aptly points out the "glaring contrast" to the preceding. "The light of Israel is set in relief by the shadow of Edom" (HENGST.). After the "marvellous blessings of the theocracy," comes "the curse which overtakes Edom." Now since, as regards the blessings, the true Israel in Christ, that is, redeemed humanity, has ultimately to be looked to, so the curse here is attached not so much to the heathen world (HÄV.) as to the heathenish, that is, the Antichristian world. Hengstenberg thinks that the reference is not to the heathen world "at large," but "only to the small neighbouring nations, which stand in a similar relation as Edom, and resemble it in intensity of hatred"! Yet, as he says, Edom appears here "as a radically corrupt people, that is to have no share in the Messianic salvation." Our prophecy has nothing to do with ch. xxxiv. 29 (against Keil). Cocceius maintains that, as the dismissal of the shepherds formed the subject in ch. xxxiv., so the subject here is the dissolution, by the coming of Christ, as foretold in Num. xxiv. 18, 19, of the Jewish nation, represented here by Edom and Seir. The Jewish nation is called Seir *per synecdochen partis*, "because Edom was included in the Jewish community; the Idumæans formed a part of the nation, and the kings were of Edomite descent; just as the land of Palestine is called Idumæa, whence Christ comes, Isa. lxiii." The signification of Edom is here, however, mainly symbolical and not literal, as in ch. xxv. 12 sq. Hengstenberg makes the prophecy there against Edom to be resumed here on the "report given by the fugitive of the injustice committed at the destruction of Jerusalem," etc. (??).

["Superficial readers will be disposed to ask, what has Edom to do here? The Lord's judgment has already been pronounced against Edom (ch. xxv. 12–14), among the enemies of the covenant-people; and this fresh denunciation against it is inserted among predictions which, both before and after, have immediate respect to the covenant-people themselves. It is, however, in its proper place; and brings out another element in the prosperity which the Lord promises to His Church and people. It gives body and prominence to the thought expressed in ver. 28 of the preceding chapter, that 'they should no more be a prey to the heathen.' So far from it, the prophet now declares that the worst and bitterest of all the heathen shall be utterly destroyed and made desolate; and that those who were then rejoicing over Israel's calamities must themselves become a spoil, without any prospect of recovery."—FAIRBAIRN'S *Ezekiel*, p. 381.—W. F.]

Vers. 2–9. *Against Edom, i.e. his Bloodthirsty Enmity to Israel.*

Ver. 2. Ch. vi. 2 (ch. xxv. 2, xxviii. 21, xix. 2).—Gen. xxxvi. 9.—הַר שֵׂעִיר, the woody mountain region in the south of that part of Palestine which lies to the east of Jordan, from the Dead Sea to the Ælanitic Gulf; the land for the people, corresponding antithetically to the prominence given to the land in the foregoing (ch. xxxiv. 25 sq.).—Ver. 3. Ch. xxxiv. 10, xiii. 8, 20, xxvi. 3, *et passim.*—Ch. xxv. 7, 13, vi. 14.—Ch. xxxiii. 28, 29.—Ver. 4. Exemplification. **Thy cities** and חָרְבָּה ranked together; the latter not exactly: "destruction," but rather: "destroyed," heaps of ruins.—Ch. xii. 20, xiv. 15, 16.—Ver. 5. **Enmity for ever**, as in ch. xxv. 15, but more expressive here on account of the kinship between Edom and Israel (comp. Ps. cxxxvii. 7). Infinitive construction passing over to the verb fin. The enmity is an abiding one; the next word, נָגַר (Hiphil, imperf. ap.), is an expression of that enmity. Besides, in this as well as in the expression בְּנֵי־יִשׂ', the people already come distinctly out from the land. אֵיד is

oppression; hence: burden, calamity, misfortune, farther and sufficiently defined by what immediately follows (comp. ch. xxi. 30, 34 [25, 29]). Oppression of brethren calls at once for the exercise of compassion, which is best manifested where no one is innocent; when guilt makes the end, ancient enmity should not be let loose (Obad. 13).—Ver. 6. לָדָם, is there an allusion here to אֱדֹם? a suggesting, although not an express naming of Edom? In this case could there be also an antithetic allusion to "Adam" (men) in ch. xxxiv. 31, and at the same time an allusion to Gen. xxv. 30!? At all events, the fourfold repetition of דָּם has some significance. Edom shall, as it were, become entirely blood (ch. xvi. 38), and still farther, blood shall follow him, which might mean that he will leave behind him a track of blood, or, the effusion of blood will follow him; so that by this phrase, which is again repeated at the end of the verse, the words: **blood will I make thee**, are explained to mean: *the effusion of blood, namely, of thy own blood, shall cleave fast to thy footsteps* (comp. ver. 8). [HÄVERN.: I will make the event authenticate thy name, and blood-guiltiness shall pursue thee everywhere as a murderer, to cry for vengeance and to give thee up to punishment. EWALD, who reads מַעֲשְׂךָ instead of אֶעֱשְׂךָ: "because thy inclination is after blood, blood shall," etc.] אִם־לֹא דָם ׳ scarcely implies an oath; affirmative, as HENGST.: "forsooth thou hast hated blood," inasmuch as the murderer hates the blood which he sheds, in which is the hated life of the murdered man; and although the significant play upon the word דָּם might include a reference to the blood-relationship of Edom and Israel (THEODORET), had not the Hebrew word for that been בָּשָׂר, it is simpler to adhere to the negation that Edom thus hated not bloodshed. ["The most peculiar part of the verse is the clause אִם־לֹא דָם שָׂנֵאתָ, which not only our version, but also nearly all commentators, render: 'since thou hast not hated blood.' But no examples can be produced to justify such a rendering, and the remark of Hitzig, that as the words stand, they must be regarded as an affirmative protestation, is quite correct. Taking blood in the usual sense, I do not see why, in a passage so strongly epigrammatic and alliteral as this, the hatred of it might not be affirmed of Edom; for the grand point on which the desires of the Edomites were centred was life, life in themselves, as opposed to the bloody extermination they sought for Israel; the shedding of their blood was what they would on no account think of. I take the meaning to be, therefore: The preservation of thy life is what thou art intent on securing; the thought of blood being shed among thee is what thou art putting far from thee as an object of aversion; but God's purposes are contrary to thine, and what thou hatest He will send—blood shall pursue thee."—FAIRBAIRN's *Ezekiel*.—W. F.]—Ver. 7. שִׁמְמָה instead of שְׁמָמָה; the same as שְׁמָמָה. The land is made so because the people fill it only as slain (ver. 8). There is no going to and fro, no traffic, ch. xxxiii. 28. [Sept. according to ch. xxv. 13.]—Ver. 8. Ch. xxxii. 5 sq., xxxi. 12. Hence the desolation of death.—Ver. 9. שִׁמְ׳ עוֹלָם, a rejoinder to אֵיבַת עוֹלָם, ver 5. Instead of תִּישַׁבְנָה, from יָשַׁב (KEIL), to be read with י quiescent, the Qeri has תָּשֹׁבְנָה, from שׁוּב, "not to return" to its original condition. HENGST.: "thy cities shall not sit," but lie prostrate (ch. xxvi. 20).

Vers. 10–15. *Against Edom, his Covetousness towards Israel.*

Ver. 10. יַעַן, parallel to ver. 5. The other side of Edom's guilt in respect to Israel. With significant allusion to their separation, Israel and Judah are called שְׁנֵי הַגּוֹיִם. In speaking thus, Edom considered them as heathen nations, and not the people of Jehovah; or this is the prophet's representation. Hence שְׁתֵּי הָאֲרָצוֹת can mean nothing else than the land of Israel and the land of Judah, not Idumæa and the land of Judah (JEROME). Grotius sees here a reference to the Assyrian and also the Babylonian captivity. וִירֵשְׁנוּהָ, neuter (KEIL): the one land as well as the other (ROSENM.); HITZIG: referring to the plur. fem. If we understand the clause וַיהוָה שָׁם ׳ of Jehovah's presence in the temple, then for believers ideally, as it also in reality was in the kingdom of Israel, it comes into consideration for both kingdoms, and we may, with other expositors, make the suffix refer to Jerusalem. On this comp. ch. ix. 3, xi. 23. But certainly the divine presence in the temple was only the sensible symbol of Jehovah's governing agency among His people generally; hence, finally, the disregarding of Israel's divine election, the ignoring of this, was the mistake in the reckoning which Edom made. Better thus than to say that Edom insulted Jehovah by coveting His possession (HITZIG); or (as Keil): "as if Jehovah were a feeble and unreal God, unable to protect His people;" but that which had been said in Israel, ch. viii. 12 (ch. ix. 9), in excuse for heathen superstition, the heathen unbelief of Edom repeats here with respect to Israel's eternal destiny, which rests on the ground of Jehovah's covenant revelation. It was practical atheism in both cases,—childish neglect of God in Israel, but active hostility to Him in Edom. Edom's reckoning took sin into account, calling to remembrance the injury done by Jacob, the father of Israel, to Esau, their ancestor; but took no account of grace, and never thought that "Jehovah" should come into consideration. [From ver. 12 שָׁם has been also interpreted as referring to Idumæa.]

Ver. 11. לָכֵן ׳, as in ver. 6. From the **hating** (infinitive) come **anger** and **envy**, expressing themselves not only in word (ver. 10), but also in deed (עֲשִׂיתָה). Jehovah acts according to Edom's doings.—The making known בָּם, not, as Hengst., among "the children of Israel," which is too remote (ver. 5), but among the two גּוֹיִם (ver.

10), just as תִּהְיֶינָה there refers to the two lands coveted by Edom. The making known among Israel shall happen as well as the judgment on Edom—comp. ch. xxviii. 25 (ch. xxvi. 20); not, however, as if both had like proportion (HENGST.), but because the making known is effected by the judgment. כַּאֲשֶׁר, as Him who, etc.—Ver. 12. Thus Edom shall know by experience that Jehovah does not leave unpunished such a saying as Edom has said. After speaking of doings in ver. 11, there is now a return to the sayings (ver. 10). He has heard all. The **mountains of Israel**, preparing for ch. xxxvi. 1, come forth in antithesis to the mountain range of Seir. Qeri שָׁמֵמוּ, simplifying, but needlessly, for the abrupt and significant שְׁמָמָה (ver. 15), 3 perf. fem. sing., may refer to the land or be understood of what is meant; or we may with Rosenm. read: שְׁמָמָה, "a waste," ch. xxxiii. 28. The following plural brings in the people.—Ch. xxxiv. 5, 8, 10.—Ver. 13. Thus their sayings were not only insults to Israel (עַל־הָרֵי יִשׂ'), land and people, but at the same time boastings with their mouth heaped up against Jehovah (עָלַי), who was there (ver. 10), wherewith they already, as it were, took joyful possession of the land. They exulted over Jehovah with haughty words and much speaking. But now—Ver. 14—He who hitherto has heard all these boastings speaks and acts (אֶעֱשֶׂה'). According as the one happens, so shall the other happen to thee. [EWALD: "I will make thee a sport (a comedy) to the whole earth," etc. HITZIG: While all the world rejoices even over thy desolation (?).] However natural it is at כָּל־הָאָרֶץ to think of the "whole earth," such a thought is very foreign to the connection. Hävernick, on the other hand, insists on the necessary harmony with the following verse, according to which the interpretation must be: as all Edom exulted, so also should all Edom be subjected to punishment. The curious explanation, to take כְּ here as an adverb of time (so also Hitzig), and in ver. 15 as a word of comparison, readily suggests itself. But better (KIMCHI), the one כְּ illustrates the other; hence כֵּן expressly in ver. 15, as also the infinitive שְׂמֹחַ here points to שִׂמְחָתְךָ in ver. 15. **To rejoice** and **desolation** must correspond to one another, while the latter, however, must be the punishment. For and instead of joy of the **whole land, desolation** now. The לָּךְ at the end of the verse already intimates what land is meant. There is not a word said in the whole chapter of the "earth"; it is always land as opposed to land, the mountain range of Seir to the mountains of Israel (ver. 12). Hengst. best shows what the "whole earth" introduces into the clear text: "The glorious salvation which comes to Zion is a subject of rejoicing for the whole earth, because it gives testimony to the glory of God, who can only bless His people, so that in them all the nations of the earth shall be blessed, Deut. xxxii. 43 sq.; Isa. xlii. 10 sq.; Ps. xcvii. 1, xlviii. 3; Lam. ii. 15." [KLIEF.: "But when all that bears the name of Edom shall, through the judgment of God, be subjected to devastation, then the whole earth shall rejoice, as Edom rejoiced when Jerusalem fell." Where is such an extravagant idea even hinted at in the text? Ch. xxxvi. 2, 5 speaks only of Edom's exultation. Hence Keil thus applies כִּשְׂמֹחַ: "When joy shall be prepared for all the world (all mankind!), then shall," etc.]—Ver. 15. That the rejoicing of Edom, which is to be requited to him, had respect to the **inheritance**, etc., that is, the land given to the family of Israel as distinguished from Esau-Edom (Gen. xxvii., xxviii. 4), is now brought in at the close; and as thereby כִּשְׂמֹחַ in ver. 14 is explained, so the motive for שְׁמָמָה is given by עַל אֲשֶׁר־שָׁמֵמָה. In accordance with this, כֵּן אֶעֱשֶׂה־לָּךְ' repeats שְׁמָמָה אֶעֱשֶׂה־לָּךְ (ver. 14), and consequently is not to be interpreted, with Hitzig: so will I make others rejoice over thy desolation. שְׁמָמָה תִהְיֶה, which forms the complement to כֵּן אֶעֱ', is the second, not the third person. The following feminine suffix indicates the land, so that with כָּל־הָאָרֶץ the meaning also of כָּל־אֱדוֹם כֻּלָּהּ (ver. 14) is quite clear. **Mount Seir, and all Edom, the whole of it**, is set in contrast to **the inheritance of the house of Israel.**

DOCTRINAL REFLECTIONS.

1. As the ideas by which the national life of Israel was upheld express themselves in a great variety and fulness of forms of worship, as to places, times, materials, and persons, so also in the course of the divine history of Israel, individuals and whole tribes and nations became symbolized into spiritual, and also unspiritual, very expressive types of character, which may serve as studies for the minister of the gospel.

2. The symbolical or typical signification of Esau-Edom, while treated more historically in ch. xxv. (p. 246), comes out with perfect clearness when we take also Heb. xii. into consideration. Whether he is called (Heb. xii. 16) πόρνος in the literal sense, with reference to Gen. xxvi. 34 sq., or in a figurative and spiritual sense, so that the expression is synonymous with βέβηλος, at all events the picture given of Edom in Ezekiel corresponds to the latter sense of the word. To Edom, Judah and Israel (*divide et impera* in his thoughts) are merely nations and lands. Anything higher, as that Jehovah was there, enters not into his thoughts. It is the ordinary profane kind of a materialism, which takes its stand on natural rights, and does not want to know of grace and election, and so repays Jacob's sin with abiding enmity, and actually carries out as Edom (Ezek. xxxv. 5) what Esau only threatened (Gen. xxvii. 41); as, on the other hand, the carnal appetite (βρώσεως μιᾶς) is still exhibited in ver. 12 of our chapter (לְאָכְלָה).

3. In this sense the elder son Esau forms the

Sadducean parallel to the Pharisaic elder son, Luke xv. 25 sq.

4. There is also in Ezekiel an ἀπεδοκιμάσθη, namely, rejection which is complete desolation. As Esau receives not the blessing which he wished to inherit, so the inheritance of the house of Israel does not fall to Edom to devour, however often and widely he opened his mouth to snatch it (ver. 13). The anger and jealousy of Edom are as vain (ver. 11) as the tears of Esau (Heb. xii. 17). Instead of μετανοια, Edom exhibits perpetual enmity and his hatred.

5. Israel has now, on the contrary, eaten up Edom, incorporated it into itself by circumcision. Thus the two who were separated, finally come together. But the contest, which began even in their mother's womb, continues to the end. Jacob-Israel subdued the elder brother, but in this way the family of the Idumæan Herod obtained the Jewish sovereignty, and the persecution of the true Israel (Matt. ii. 13 sq.) was carried out to the full by the Edomite spirit of murder which took possession of the people (Matt. xxvii. 25). Because the Herodians favoured and imported Roman heathenism, the circus, wild-beast fights, etc., the conceptions of Edom and Rome run into each other in the later Jewish writers.

HOMILETIC HINTS.

Ver. 1 sq. After the blessing upon His people, and their revival and prosperity, comes now the contrast, namely, the curse upon the ungodly, and their desolation and miserable end.—"For who else are the Idumæans but Esau, who always persecutes Israel (Gal. iv. 20)? That raises up our hope when we are tried in the present. For if Christ is our Redeemer, He has redeemed us completely, and we have not to fear the ungodly. If suffering is a means to conduct us to the height of salvation, then the temporal prosperity of the wicked only increases the cause of their destruction; and one day there comes a change of affairs, when we experience the goodness of God, and they His deserved wrath" (HEIM-HOFFMANN).—"He who has God against him has also God's word against him" (RICHT.).—"The word of the Lord is a veritable treasury, out of which continually come forth things new and old. It leads into the past and the future, and would gladly have all applied to the present" (BERL. BIB.).

Ver. 3 sq. The hand of God is the solemn mark of interrogation over every earthly height to which we look up, whether things or persons.—"When punishments break in and are already taking their course, in this God as it were stretches out His hand. Now, since His hand is not shortened to help His children, so also it is not too weak to punish His enemies, Isa. lix. 1" (STARKE).—Desolateness is the lot of the wicked, for the world passes away with all its pleasure for man; but this comes in all its force only to him who was at home there, and set his confidence thereon.

Ver. 4. "When godliness goes out of cities, confusion and devastation enter in" (STARCK).—We can never sufficiently recognise that God alone is the Eternal.

Ver. 5. Where enmity leads to: it perpetuates itself by degrees in the heart, it is not afraid even to use the sword; first the malice of the tongue, and then the violence of malice.—Therefore always become reconciled at once and completely, that no roots may remain in the heart which may shoot up afterwards.—The prayer of an implacable man is certain not to be heard.—Forgive us our debts, as we also forgive our debtors.—"Woe unto you who are glad at evil to your neighbour and rejoice over his misfortune, Matt. v. 25" (TÜB. BIB.). "God makes finally an end of sin even when the sinner will not cease, and thus many a one has been hurried away by death in the midst of a course of sin. Hence all are not godly who cease to sin. When one has no longer the power, then he must cease, when otherwise he would be still very willing. In old age, in sickness, in imprisonment, in poverty, much must be dispensed with because hands and feet are bound, when in other circumstances there would be no want of will; in the will, however, above all consists the sin" (BERL. BIB.).

Ver. 6. God's judgment for blood over Edom an instructive example, a disclosure for warning.—Blood a peculiar sap.—The Lord an avenger of blood.—The track of blood behind so many celebrated figures in history, behind so many so-called great exploits.—The shedding of blood a characteristic symptom of the world, a mark of the spirit that rules in the world, and of the wickedness in which it lies.—Ver. 7 sq. Trade and intercourse cease where God sends His judgments.—"The Lord destroys nations that delight in war" (TÜB. BIB.).—Ver. 9. "Sin is not to become eternalized, therefore eternal punishment" (STARCK).—"God's aim is the acknowledgment in all things of His sole and supreme dominion" (STARKE).—Where sinners have dwelt, there punishment finally bears sway; not only Edom, but also Judæa serves as a visible example of this.—Ver. 10. Bear always in mind that God still is there!—Every sin against man is always at the same time sinning against God; unbelief, practical blasphemy.—Bloodthirstiness and covetousness two satanic sisters.—Disdain of others a non-recognition of God, who has bestowed something on every one.—The world's delight in blood, and also its contempt of believers, a proof how little the world knows what still holds together the earth under their feet.—The meek, however, shall, according to Matt. v., inherit the land.—"Most men speak and act as if God could neither hear nor see" (STARCK).—Ver. 11 sq. Wrath and jealousy, when proceeding from hatred, do not escape the divine judgment.—God beholds Himself in His people.—The revelation of God to His own is also at last the judgment over the world.—The omniscient and omnipresent, the incorruptible eye- and ear-witness.—Thirst for fresh territory an Edomitish characteristic.—The hatred against the sacred things of humanity now become the fashion.—Ver. 14 sq. Only the children of God shall inherit, although it doth not yet appear what we shall be, etc.—"The acceptable year of Jehovah is inseparably and necessarily connected with a day of vengeance of our God, Isa. lxi. 2. No true grace without justice. The theocracy must, accordingly, pass through the fire of affliction and become purified (ch. xxxiv.); for the same reason the heathenism whose iniquity is full must show that it has fallen under the divine justice. For grace is not toleration of the bad" (HÄVERNICK).

CHAPTER XXXVI.

1 And thou, son of man, prophesy to the mountains of Israel, and say,
2 Mountains of Israel, hear the word of Jehovah. Thus saith the Lord
Jehovah, Because the enemy says over you, Aha! and the everlasting
3 heights have become a possession for us; Therefore prophesy and say, Thus
saith the Lord Jehovah, Because, because "make desolate" [is said to you], and
they snap after you round about, that ye may be [become] a possession to the
remnant of the heathen, and ye are lifted up on the lip of the tongue and
4 are become a people's talk [a calumny]; Therefore, mountains of Israel, hear
the word of the Lord Jehovah. Thus saith the Lord Jehovah to the mountains and to the hills, to the ravines and to the valleys, to the desolate ruins
and to the forsaken cities, which have become a prey [booty] and a derision to
5 the remnant of the heathen who are round about; Therefore, thus saith the
Lord Jehovah, Surely in the fire of My jealousy I have spoken regarding the
remnant of the heathen and regarding the whole of Edom, who gave themselves My land for a possession, in joy of the whole heart, in contempt of
6 soul, on account of its pasturage, for a prey. Therefore prophesy concerning
the land of Israel, and say to the mountains and to the hills, to the ravines
and to the valleys, Thus saith the Lord Jehovah, Behold, I, I have spoken in
My jealousy and in My fury, because ye have borne the reproach of the
7 heathen; Therefore thus saith the Lord Jehovah, I, I have lifted up My
hand; surely the heathen that are round about you, they shall bear their
8 shame. And ye mountains of Israel shall give your foliage and bear your
9 fruit to My people Israel; for they draw near to come. For, behold, I come
10 to you, and turn Myself to you, and ye are tilled and down. And I multiply upon you men, the whole house of Israel, all of it; and the cities are
11 inhabited and the ruins built. And I multiply upon you man and beast,
and they multiply themselves and are fruitful, and I settle you [make you inhabited] as at your origin, yea, I do you good more than in your beginnings,
12 and ye know that I am Jehovah. And I make men walk over you, My
people Israel, and they shall possess thee, and thou art to them for an in-
13 heritance, and thou shalt no more make them childless. Thus saith the Lord
Jehovah, Because they say to you, A devourer of men art thou, and hast made
14 thy people childless; Therefore shalt thou no more devour men, and no more
15 make thy people stumble,—sentence of the Lord Jehovah. And I will no
more let be heard against [over] thee the reproach of the heathen, and thou
shalt no more bear the contumely [mockery, scorn] of the nations, and shalt no
16 more make thy people stumble,—sentence of the Lord Jehovah. And the
17 word of Jehovah came to me, saying, Son of man, the house of Israel were
dwelling on their land, and they defiled it by their way and by their works,
as the uncleanness of the monthly separation was their way before Me.
18 And I poured out My fury upon them on account of the blood which they
19 shed upon the land, and by their foul idols defiled they it. And I dispersed
them among the heathen, and they were scattered in the lands; according to
20 their way and according to their works have I judged them. And it came to
the heathen whither they came, and they profaned the name of My holiness,
since it was said of them, Jehovah's people are these, and out of His land
21 have they gone forth. And I felt pity for the name of My holiness, which
they, the house of Israel, profaned among the heathen whither they came.
22 Therefore say to the house of Israel, Thus saith the Lord Jehovah, Not for
your sakes act I, O house of Israel, but on account of the name of My
23 holiness, which ye profaned among the heathen whither ye came. And I
sanctify My name, the great, the profaned among the heathen, which ye profaned in their midst, and the heathen know that I am Jehovah,—sentence of
the Lord Jehovah,—when I sanctify Myself on [in] you before their [your] eyes.
24 And I take you out of the heathen, and gather you out of all lands, and

25 bring you into your land. And I sprinkle upon you clean water, and ye
become clean from all your defilements [uncleannesses, ver. 17 sq.], and from all your
26 foul idols will I cleanse you. And I give you a new heart, and a new
spirit will I put within you, and I take away the heart of stone out of your
27 flesh and give you a heart of flesh. And My Spirit will I put within you,
and cause that ye shall walk in My statutes, and keep and do My judgments.
28 And ye dwell in the land which I have given to your fathers, and are to Me
29 a people, and I will be to you a God. And [yea] I help you from all your
defilements, and I call to the corn and multiply it, and will not send upon
30 you hunger. And I multiply the fruit of the tree, and the produce of the
field, that ye may no longer have to bear the reproach of hunger among the
31 heathen. And ye remember your evil ways, and your doings that were not
good, and loathe your own faces for your iniquities and for your abomina-
32 tions. Not for your sakes act I,—sentence of the Lord Jehovah,—be it known
to you; be ashamed, yea, shame yourselves away from your ways, O house
33 of Israel. Thus saith the Lord Jehovah, In the day of My cleansing you
from all your iniquities, I make the cities inhabited, and the ruins shall be
34 built. And the desolated [devastated] land shall be cultivated, instead of being
35 a waste in the eyes of every passer-by. And they say, This land, the deso-
lated, is become as the garden of Eden, and the ruined and desolated and
36 demolished cities are securely inhabited. And the heathen that are left
round about you know that I, Jehovah, built the demolished [cities], and
37 planted the desolated [land]; I, Jehovah, spoke and did. Thus saith the
Lord Jehovah, I will still in regard to this let Myself be inquired of by the
house of Israel to do it for them; I will multiply them in men as a flock.
38 As a flock of sacred rites, as the flock of Jerusalem in her festal seasons, so
shall the ruined cities be full of flocks of men, and they know that I am
Jehovah.

Ver. 2. Sept.: . . . εἰπεν . . . ἐρημα αἰωνια—

Ver. 3. . . . 'Αντι του ἀτιμασθηναι ὑμας κ. μισηθηναι ὑμας ὑπο τ. ἐθνων— Vulg.: *quod desolati estis et conculcati per circuitum*— (Another reading: בהיותכם.)

Ver. 4. . . . κ. τ. ναπαις τ. ἐρημωμεναις κ. ἠφανισμεναις, κ. τ. πολεσιν τ. καταλελειμμεναις . . . κ. εἰς καταπατημα—

Ver. 5. Another reading: כלה c. ה and בנפש. Sept.: . . . ἀτιμασαντες ψυχας του ἀφανισαι ἐν προνομῃ. Vulg.: . . . *et ex animo, et ejecerunt eam ut vastarent.*

Ver. 8. Sept.: . . . την σταφυλην κ. τον καρπον ὑμων φαγεται ὁ λαος μου, ὁτι ἐλπιζουσιν του ἐλθειν.

Ver. 10. . . . παν οἰκον 'Ισρ. εἰς τελος·

Ver. 12. . . . ἐτι ἀτεκνωθηναι ἀπ' αὐτων. Vulg.: *et non addes ultra, ut absque eis sis.*

Ver. 13. . . . κ. ἠτεκνωμενη ὑπο του ἐθνους σου ἐγενου, Vulg.: . . . *et suffocans gentem tuam.*

Ver. 14. Vulg.: . . . *Gentem tuam non necabis ultra*—

Ver. 17. Sept.: . . . ὁδω . . κ. ἐν τ. εἰδωλοις . . . κ. ἐν τ. ἀκαθαρσιαις αὐτοων·

Ver. 19. . . . κ. ἐλικμησα αὐτους—

Ver. 20. Another reading: ויבאו, so the old translations.

Ver. 21. K. ἐφεισαμην αὐτων— *Et peperci nomini*—

Ver. 23. Another reading: בהם and לעיניהם (so also the Masora).

Ver. 31. Sept.: . . . κ. προσοχθιειτε κατα προσωπον αὐτων ἐν ταις—

Ver. 32. Sept.: . . . κ. ἐντραπητε ἐκ τ. ὁδων—

Ver. 35. . . . ὡς κηπος τρυφης . . . ὀχυραι ἐκαθισαν.

Ver. 37. . . . ζητηθησομαι τω— Vulg.: . . . *invenient me*— Another reading: אדרש, active (Syr. Arabs.)

Ver. 38. . . . ὡς προβατα ἁγια—

["In this chapter we have a continuation of the present great theme of the prophet—Israel's prospective revival and prosperity as the Lord's covenant-people. But it treats of this under different aspects. In the first section (vers. 1–15) the prophet unfolds the essential distinction between Israel and Edom with the other nations of heathendom, in that the former had, what the others had not, an interest in the power and faithfulness of God, in consequence of which Israel's heritage must revive and flourish, and the hopes of the heathen concerning it must be disappointed. In the next section (vers. 16–21) the reason is given why the Lord had for a time acted toward His land and people as if their connection with Him was an evil rather than a blessing; it is traced up to the incorrigible wickedness of the people, and the necessity of God's vindicating the cause of His holiness by exercising upon them the severity of His displeasure. Then in another section (vers. 22–33) the purpose of the Lord for their future good is unfolded—His purpose for His own name's sake to revive His cause among His people, and that in the most effectual manner, by first renewing their hearts to holiness, and then by restoring them to a flourishing condition outwardly. And in a short concluding section (vers. 34–38) the general result is summed up, and the impressions noticed which the whole was fitted to produce upon the minds of others."—FAIRBAIRN'S *Ezekiel*, p. 386. —W. F.]

EXEGETICAL REMARKS.

Vers. 1–15. *The Mountains of Israel.*

After that ch. xxxv., which is connected with the one that follows as antithesis and thesis, has already (ver. 12) introduced the **mountains of Israel**, parallel to Mount Seir (again ch. xxxv. 15 for the last time), and reminding us of ch. vi. (comp. also ch. xxxiii. 28), as that to which the prophecy before us is directly addressed, they now form the immediate theme of the divine sayings.

Ver. 1. אֶל, see on ch. vi. 2. Here, too, by the **mountains of Israel** it is not the land that is characterized after its most prominent part, but, as ver. 2 will immediately show, the mountains come into consideration according to their religious signification for Israel.—Ver. 2. The phrase: **thus saith the Lord Jehovah,** which, when one cannot put one's self in the position of those concerned, is repeated to weariness in our chapter, belongs to its peculiarities. It is intended not only to contradict the saying of the adversary, but still more to contravene what the poor doubting heart itself says, when looking at that which the eyes see; at the same time the divine comfort appears in presence of this visibility as a comfort solely in word, as correspondingly in the closing part of the chapter the name of the Lord will come forth above all.—The **enemy** is, as the word implies, he who turns himself against any one, in the connection here Edom (ch. xxxv. 10), but in the signification developed ch. xxxv.; hence, as we go on farther, illustrated **also** by **the heathen round about** (ver. 5; ch. xxv. 3, 8, 12).—Comp. on ch. xxv. 3. That the **everlasting heights** refer primarily to the temple is clear; at the same time, however, Zion will have to be viewed as the seat of the everlasting royal dominion. "An allusion to the inmost and most tender feelings of Israel" (SCHMIEDER). [Hävernick refers to Gen. xlix. 26 (Deut. xxxiii. 15), according to which the mountains are held to stand in relation to the promises of Israel as imperishable memorials of the patriarch's blessing. HENGST.: The natural mountains as a figure of the unchangeable grandeur of which Israel boasted, because it had in the Eternal its protector and the guarantee of its own perpetuity (Ps. cxxv. 2).]—Ch. xxxv. 10.—Ver. 3. Ewald directs attention to the first five repetitions of **therefore,** because the grounds against these enemies always press on anew before the discourse becomes calmer, and will have it observed that, as in ch. v. 12 sq., sacred numbers (ch. iii. 5) fit into one another, and that in various ways, as for most certain assurance; there is a threefold address to the mountains; and the assignment of reasons has five steps in its process.—Ch. xxi. 14, xxxiii.—יַעַן בְּיַעַן, see ch. xiii. 10.—שַׁמּוֹת (EWALD, *Ausf.-Lehrb.* 8th ed. p. 611), according to Gesenius, properly *nom. verbale,* but here only for the inf. Kal of שָׁמֵם transitive: "to devastate." [EWALD: "they snap and puff at you round about." HITZIG: "they puff and snap after you," under a mistaken comparison of Isa. xlii. 14 from נָשַׁם.] Now if it cannot be rendered: "they devastate you" (KEIL), and will scarcely be rendered, with Hengst.: "ye are devastated," then perhaps the most obvious thing is, in accordance with ch. xxxv. 12, 14 sq., to think of the standing: "make desolate," "desolation"! They appear to the enemy round about as a morsel ready for swallowing, that they are already a possession for **the remnant of the heathen,** as מִסָּבִיב is more definitely explained to be. The presupposition in שְׁאֵרִית (what remains after defeat) is the judgment inflicted by the Chaldeans. As with a little brotherly love the injury received would have kept them back, so with their enmity against Israel it goaded them on to commit still farther injury to indemnify themselves on Israel.—וַתֵּעָלוּ, according to Rosenm., imperf. Niph. from עָלָה (to be lifted or taken up); according to Ewald, intransitive imperf. Kal from עָלַל (Aramaic, "to press in," "to go in"); according to Hitzig, 2d plur. Kal from עָלָה, for וַתַּעֲלוּ ("ye are gone up"). The **lip** as instrument, the **tongue** as originator; the former having as its parallel **calumny,** and the latter, **people**; so that שָׂפָה is not = talk, and לָשׁוֹן not a personification for talkers, as Klief. thinks, yet it need not be tautology (GESEN.), or לָשׁוֹן = speech, people (HÄVERN.).—Ver. 4. Ch. vi. 3. ("The mountains are for the land what the heads of the tribes are for the people; as it were the elders, the venerable fathers of the land, to whom the word of the Lord which is applicable to the whole land is announced," SCHMIEDER.) The mention of particulars is meant to point to the eye which observes all, the divine care which beholds each and all, over which only a human eye weeps, or on the contrary rejoices. As **a prey** points back to the beginning of ver. 3, so **a derision** points to its close.—Ver. 5. The **fire of my jealousy** reminds of ch. xxxv. 11.—Ch. xxxv. 15.—Ch. xxv. and xxxv. also testify that Jehovah has **spoken** in this manner.—Comp. ch. xxv. 6, 5, although the application here is somewhat different. EWALD: "in mortal contempt." HITZIG: "contempt from the soul" (?).—מִגְרָשָׁהּ, according to Gesenius, an Aramaic infinitive from גָּרַשׁ, "in order to empty it (the uninhabited land) for a prey." But what would be still there to empty? Ewald's translation: "in order to drive it out for pillage," is quite as unsuitable. Hitzig does better, taking it as a substantive, but wrongly in the sense of "produce," and according to a peculiar construction translating: "in order to plunder (לָבֹז) its produce." HENGST. (COCC.): "that its environs should be a prey to them." But which environs?

of the land? Hence he is obliged to substitute the capital as the centre! The signification **pasturage** would at least be simpler; and the emptied land is in keeping with this, and is consequently a desirable prey. [Many interpret also: "on account of the expulsion of the land" (land for people), ch. xxxi. 11; whereby it (now again the land) has become a prey.]—Ver. 6. עַל־אַדְמַת, hence as the native home of Israel, with precursory reference to the return of the people, ver. 8 sq., 28 sq.—Partly a repetition of ver. 4.—Ver. 5. The **reproach** is to be understood of words (invectives, vers. 3, 4) as well as of deeds.—Ver. 7. Ch. xx. 5. The attitude of swearing, yet not that alone, but also a sign of the intended action.—The roles shall change. Ver. 6, ch. xvi. 52. Upon the heathen the reproach shall abide, but not upon the land which they have thus reproached to its inhabitants!—Ver. 8. The honour to be restored to the land is represented as the causing of it to yield leaves and fruit; Hengst. thinks: leaves and branches as food for cattle, while the fruit is for man.—קֵרְבוּ לָבוֹא can only be the individuals concerned of the people. "Of the seventy years of Jeremiah, twenty had already elapsed (ch. xxxiii. 21)" (HENGST.).—Ver. 9. Because hitherto (as late as ch. xxxiv. 10) employed in a hostile sense, an explanation follows the הִנְנִי אֲלֵ' (Deut. xi. 12). The **sowing** shows that the work of cultivation is the subject spoken of, hence already with reference to men.—Ver. 10. Then farther in correspondence with the cultivation of the land is the peopling of it.—כָּל־בֵּית' כֻּלֹּה, antithesis to ch. xxxv. 15.—Ver. 4.—Ver. 11. To the men also cattle.—Gen. i. 28. "A new creation-blessing, as it were" (HÄVERN.). The **more than** indicates the figurative in the manner of expression (Deut. xxx. 5), as does also the fact that the mountains are addressed.—Ver. 12 rounds off as commerce (וְהוֹלַכְתִּי) what has been said of the peopling, after there has previously been a rural population with tilling of fields and rearing of cattle, and a town population with building of ruins; and the mention is made of the abiding, enduring possession of the land (לְנַחֲלָה, as inheritance).—־ךְ, what must be meant is the land, mountains and all; masc., which אֶרֶץ (ver. 5) may be also, as afterwards *fem. gen.*—The **make childless**, said of the land, may also be referred to the wild beasts introduced in consequence of its desolation (ch. v. 17, xiv. 15).—Ver. 13. What is here said has in reality as little to do with Num. xiii. 32 (observe, however, the statement of motive there) as with 2 Kings ii. 24 (a mere particular case). The promised land was neither in itself of such a kind (Deut. viii. 7 sq., xi. 10 sq.), nor, without giving a forced meaning, can we, with Hengst., understand a reference to its position between Asiatic and African powers; but what is here said to the mountains of Israel (as previously, ver. 12, of the land) is directed against the reproach, the scorn of the heathen (ver. 15), who would draw an inference from the desolation of the capital against its holy character as this land of divine promise. The reference here made to Num. xiii. can only be this, that what the adversaries say appears as a repetition of the unbelieving speech of those spies (אֶרֶץ אֹכֶלֶת יוֹשְׁבֶיהָ), with which they brought out דִּבַּת הָאָרֶץ (comp. here ver. 3); hence here somewhat in the sense of: Israel should have stayed away from it, not have come into the land, not have trod on the trap (bird-lime) of the promise. [EWALD: "an exterminator of men art thou, and an unnatural mother of thy people wast thou." HÄVERN.: "a swallower of men," and "making nations (Israel and Judah) childless." Hitzig observes: שִׁכֵּל is said of a mother—to bring children dead into the world, or to kill them afterwards. But is it, then, the children of the land, and not rather of the inhabitants, that are here spoken of?] The land is desolation, fit now only for pasture (ver. 5), thinks and says the surrounding heathen world. In opposition to this there was forcibly set forth the cultivation of the land already and the peopling of it with men, to whom the cattle (ver. 11) were only an adjunct; also the rebuilding of the ruins, in view, however, of the cities being again inhabited (ver. 10). But the sight of the desolation of the land took this general form in the mind and the mouth of the heathen, that this promised land consumes those who receive it, and especially that it can be no possession for their children, and consequently no inheritance. Comp. on this what was said in reference to the wilderness, Num. xiv. 16; Deut. ix. 28; Exod. xxxii. 12 sq. (Ezek. xx.). To this repeated reproaching, which is at the same time a reproaching of the name of Jehovah as the promiser of the land,—especially, however, to the second part of it (vers. 12, 13), the **making childless**, a statement immediately, ver. 12, explained perfectly by: **and thou art to them for an inheritance,**—ver. 14 forms a parallel, with repetition only of the phrase: **to devour men.** The alliterative (כִּשֵּׁל, Piel instead of שִׁכֵּל), "making to stumble (to fall)," of the Kethib is significant, for thus is brought to view what the heathen standpoint of reproach so entirely overlooked, what, when the promised land had to be spoken of, should have been said of its abundance and beauty, namely, that thereby, by the misuse of its resources, *it had been the occasion of Israel's sin and downfall;* and thus also a preparation is already made for speaking of, first, the profaning, and then the sanctifying of the name of Jehovah treated of in the course of the chapter. (KEIL: "if the consuming of the population stands connected with the stumbling, then the people are devoured by the consequences of their sins, that is, by judicial punishments, sterility, pestilence, and war," etc.) And inasmuch as Israel is now to possess the land abidingly, hence in his descendants, שִׁכֵּל, "to make childless," is accordingly not repeated. This decides as completely as possible against the Qeri תְּשַׁכְּלִי (also against Hitzig); while, moreover, כשל is repeated in ver. 15 without Qeri in the Hiphil. [Hengst.

understands the **stumbling** in the sense of the Qeri, and evidently under the influence of Hitzig's absurd objection, as signifying "to make unfortunate"!]—Ver. 15. According to another translation: "and I will no longer make thee hear" (Keil).—Vers. 6, 3, 4.

Vers. 16–38. *Profanation of the Name of Jehovah by Israel* (vers. 16–21), *and Sanctification of it by Jehovah Himself* (vers. 22–38).

Ver. 16. A new word of God, but, as we have seen, prepared for by what has preceded (vers. 14, 15).—Ver. 17 begins with a retrospect into the moral history of the house of Israel, for which comp. Lev. xviii. 28; Num. xxxv. 34; Jer. ii. 7.—Their **way**, their walk, as the expression **their works** explains (ch. xiv. 22, 23), and כְּטֻמְאַת' renders still more clear. נִדָּה (from נָדַד) is: "rejection"=abhorrence, abomination, ch. vii. 19 sq.; then: **separation** = purification, especially the monthly purification of a woman by separation, issue of blood (Lev. xv.). Gesen., on the other hand, explains the word by "uncleanness," *i.e.* an unclean issue of blood. Comp. besides Isa. lxiv. 5 [6]. Yet not, however, as the "most loathsome uncleanness" (Keil)—it is in reality the natural peculiarity of woman—but the comparison appears to be used on account of the blood, as ver. 18 makes obvious. Concerning the tenses comp. Hitzig. In ver. 17 a habitual state in the past, on which the action in ver. 18 breaks in. Ch. vii. 8.—Ch. xxii. 3, 6, xxxiii. 25.—Comp. on ch. vi. 4 (ch. viii. 10). "Murder and idolatry, with reference to the first commandment of the first table and the first of the second" (Hengst.).—Ver. 19. Ch. xxii. 15.—Ch. vii. 3, 8.—Ver. 20. The singular is interpreted by Hengst. of the fate spoken of in ver. 19, namely, the news (!) of it, although he goes on giving the following turn: the news came at the same time with themselves; they were the embodied intelligence. Keil understands it more simply as meaning the house of Israel. Hitzig, like the ancient versions, reads the plural, which, however, should be doubly avoided. That they themselves came to the heathen is repeatedly expressed in what follows, and that for the very purpose of explaining the fact therewith connected, the actual profanation of the name of the Lord by Israel's presence there. As in their own land, so also outside of it. The **name of My holiness** is not simply: the holy name of Jehovah, but the name in which His holiness is manifest, so that by it man names His holiness, and hence the Holy God Himself. The profanation is traced home to the Jews as originators, as occasion of the saying which follows; and hence it is said indefinitely בֶּאֱמֹר לָהֶם, so that the heathen, who certainly also desecrated the name of Jehovah in their mouth, are yet not looked upon as the desecrators of the name of His **holiness**, but the Jews [Hengst.: "not by their doing, Rom. ii. 24, but by their suffering, because they had brought on the fate by their active desecration"], who, moreover, unrepentingly remained silent concerning their sin and guilt. They just **came** where they came; and with their impenitence gave there the impression merely of wretched, unfortunate, deceived, betrayed beings, in whom the blame was not to be sought, but in their God, who was powerless in comparison with the gods of the heathen, or unfaithful to His chosen people.—עַם' has also been interpreted interrogatively by various expositors.—יָצָאוּ is as much as to say: and they have run away out of Jehovah's land which He had promised to them, where He dwelt among them; so that their having gone might be ironically held as a voluntary departure.—Ver. 21. חָמַל is: to draw one's self together, to bend over (עַל) any one, to incline one's self to him; hence: to compassionate him. [Hävern. wrongly: "and I spared for My holy name's sake" (Sept.). The Vulgate is confused. Rosenm.: "I will take care for it, so that it shall not come to harm." In this striking expression also lies something more active than: "to have compassion" (Klief.), or as Hengst.: "I had pity for My," sq.] What follows shows what is contained in this prophetic preterite.

Ver. 22. There is first the announcement, which is at the same time an explanation of the divine pity, as His pitying of Himself in harmony with His holiness, in short, as a holy love,—an explanation which cuts off everything possible with men. The self-existent majesty of the Holy One of Israel, who stands in need of no one, says: לֹא לְמַעַנְכֶם (Deut. ix. 6). Neither in Israel's virtue, nor yet in his misery, is there now any ground for Jehovah to act. Israel has no qualification whatever.—אֲנִי עֹשֶׂה, namely, what I do,—thus spoken absolutely, denoting the pure action, just as is specially suitable here. He does it, however, for glory and honour to (לְ, *dat. comm.*) His name.—Ver. 23. The "acting" of Jehovah is expressed and here announced as a sanctifying, *i.e.* of My holiness as expressed in My name, securing due weight to it, so that it shall not simply be named as name, but evidently experienced as fact. In its being the name of His holiness lies the necessity, when the people who can thus name God do not sanctify it, but on the contrary only contribute everywhere to its profanation, that then Jehovah should take in hand the sanctification of His name and thereby of Himself (בְּהִקָּדְשִׁי).—הַגָּדוֹל, together with the following הַמְחֻלָּל, makes observable the infinite grandeur as well as the omnipotence which are able to secure due regard for themselves (Josh. vii. 9; Mal. i. 11). That we might well expect: "before their (instead of: before your) eyes," which reading is almost universally preferred, Hengst. also acknowledges, but finds, however, the thought of the manifest salvation better expressed in those immediately concerned. These, however, are not the Jews, because they have beheld the misery (Job xix. 27), but the heathen as spectators of the profanation of the divine name by the Jews (ch. xx. 41, xxviii. 25). The Jews' part in the matter is sufficiently expressed by בָּכֶם (in your persons).

["The expression: 'when I sanctify Myself in you before your eyes,' for which many critical authorities, both ancient and modern, would substitute 'before their eyes,' namely, those of the heathen—this expression creates no difficulty to a person who enters thoroughly into the import of the passage. For it points to the fact that Israel, as well as the heathen, needed the manifestation in question of Jehovah's righteousness. It must be done first before the eyes of the people, who by their depravity had lost sight of God's real character; and then what was seen by them experimentally would also be seen reflectively by the heathen who dwelt around. This twofold perception of God's character is also brought out in other passages of our prophet; as in ch. xx. 41, 42: 'And I will be sanctified in you before the eyes of the heathen, and ye shall know that I am Jehovah.'"—FAIRBAIRN'S *Ezekiel.*—W. F.]

Ver. 24. The first thing in this self-sanctification of Jehovah is an act of power, which puts an end to the outward occasion for the saying in ver. 20, and to the actual profanation of the name of His holiness among the heathen (ch. xi. 17, xx. 34, 41).—Ver. 25. The next thing, to which the first only subserves, is the raising up of Israel inwardly to a holy nation, so that בָּכֶם (ver. 23) signifies: **in them**, as well as: **on them**; this, too, is a forthputting, yea, the most mighty forthputting of power, because wrought in the core of the national life. In ver. 24, *Israel's justification before the heathen;* in ver. 25, *Israel's sanctification in himself as also among the heathen.*—The "sprinkling," as it will be in respect to a nation the only imaginable method of lustration, so, moreover, from the **clean water** (מַיִם טְהוֹרִים cannot be = מֵי נִדָּה) it cannot in the least point to the rite with the ashes, Num. xix. (HENGST.); it would be preferable, with Hävern., to think of Num. viii. 7 sq., but מֵי חַטָּאת there also is something different from what **clean water** expresses here. The latter is meant expressly to symbolize the idea of purification, and specially **from all** etc., the טֻמְאוֹתֵיכֶם of the people, which, if not directly explained, is yet illustrated by גִּלּוּלֵיכֶם; the "sprinkling," again (comp. Exod. xxiv.), is doubtless meant to signify an act of consecration. Because sacrificial blood is not mentioned here, but such emphasis is laid on clean water, the best known means of purification, and also the most suitable for stains which show outwardly, we are as little at liberty to import without farther mediation—as Hengst. attempts under citation of Isa. liii. 11, lii. 15—New Testament ideas into our chapter as into ch. xi. 19 sq. (see Comm. there). Neither does Ps. li. coincide with our passage. The immediate sense of our verse is: *That Jehovah leads back Israel from exile into their own land, and consecrates them there to be a people, since the punishment, so characteristic for the sin that occasioned it, is shown to be removed by the bringing of them again into their own land; the forgiveness of sin thereby already proclaimed at once evinces and manifests itself as purification of the people, and the people* (as in point of fact took place after the exile) *put from them their old life, especially their idolatry* (ch. xi. 18, xviii. 31). Certainly not without some ground has Abarbanel referred back to the comparison of the issue of blood used in ver. 17.—As to how ver. 26 is to be understood, comp. on ch. xi. 19. Instead of the **new heart** here, לֵב אֶחָד is mentioned there, and only the "new spirit" is spoken of; while here both heart and spirit (as ch. xviii. 31) appear as **new**, whereby the religious moral regeneration of the nation, a national restoration, is placed in prospect. "It is very consonant to the priestly character to portray the new community as a truly spiritually purified band of Levites or priests, Isa. lxi. 6" (HÄVERN. ?).—Ver. 27. Since Jehovah's Spirit is put בְּקִרְבְּכֶם, and thus is brought to pass that Israel's conformity to law in walk and honesty of dealing return again, therefore the "new spirit" of ver. 26 is primarily to be understood as a divine spiritual impulse back to the law of Jehovah (ch. xi. 20).—Ver. 28. By the dwelling in the land, etc. (the "renewal of old gifts"), we are reminded of the close of ch. xxxiv. [Kliefoth here looks forward as far as the "last times," since God will gather out of the whole world His people, who are still scattered in a quite different manner and far wider in the world, and will place them in the heavenly Canaan, free them absolutely from sin (ver. 25), and as absolutely renew them inwardly (ver. 26), and by both acts as absolutely sanctify them (ver. 27).] Comp. Lev. xxv. 18, xxvi. 12.

Ver. 29. וְהוֹשַׁעְתִּי is by anticipation understood Messianically (Matt. i. 21) by those resolved to find the New Testament *ordo salutis* in Ezekiel, interpreted of the divine protection (ch. xxxiv. 22), or, by way of distinction from ver. 25, referred to the consequences of the defilements of Israel. The expression rather sums up the foregoing, which regarded the people, while now, subjoined to ver. 28, a transition is made to the land. *Idolatry disappears, and the promises concerning the land are fulfilled,* ch. xxxiv. 29. (The opposite, although in the same figure, we find in 2 Kings viii. 1.)—Ver. 30. Ch. xxxiv. 27, 29.—Ver. 31. Ch. xx. 43; comp. on ch. vi. 9. The anti-heathen abhorrence and loathing became national, and still speaks out of its distorted pietism in Pharisaism. If the gospel order of salvation were to be sought in ver. 25 sq., then we would rather expect to find here joy in the Holy Ghost (Lev. xxvi. 40).—Ver. 32. Comp. on ver. 22.—That this acting of Jehovah, irrespective of them, is still so particularly placed before and inculcated on them, is, however, by no means designed to leave the Jews undisturbed, as if they might simply wait for the things which would come upon them and happen to them; but as the love of God, without worthiness deserving it, certainly excludes any merit on the part of man, yet should so much the more awaken to reception and love in return, so there is attached to the promise here the imperative, repeated with additional emphasis, in relation to the family, the household of Israel.

Ver. 33. Ver. 25.—Hitzig translates וְהוֹשַׁבְתִּי: "then I again erect the cities," make them to sit instead of lying, since he denies that it ever (Isa. liv. 3) signifies: "to make inhabited." So also Hengstenberg always: "sit," in contrast to: lie prostrate, and here: "cause to sit." Gesenius, Ewald, etc., on the other hand, support the causative signification, as: to cause that one sit, dwell therein, to make inhabited. KEIL: make stocked with inhabitants.—Ver. 34. Ver. 9.—Ch.

xxxv. 3, vi. 14.—Ch. v. 14.—Ver. 35. וְאָמְרוּ are those individualized from כָּל־עוֹבֵר, ver. 34. (הַלָּזוּ only here, = הַלָּזֶה, but probably fem.) Observe the antithesis to ch. xxxv. 12, 9, and the probable allusion in **Eden** to Edom (ch. xxxi. 8, 9; Gen. xiii. 10; Isa. li. 3; Joel ii. 3). From this allegorical way of speaking, Hengstenberg justly rejects the idea of "the restoration of Canaan to a really paradisaic glory."—EWALD: "flourish, well fortified." HENGST.: "sit fortified;" whereas a city whose wall is broken lies on the ground. According to another translation, said of the inhabitants, who feel themselves secure, protected therein as in fortresses. (Comp. on ch. xxxviii. 11.)—Ver. 36. The heathen brought in as **left** ("the remnant of the heathen," ver. 3) are, on the contrary, made known only by the judgments that have passed over them, but by no restitution. Comp. ch. xvii. 24.—Ver. 37. Ch. xiv. 3 (1 Sam. xxviii. 6, 7). On לַעֲשׂ' לָהֶם, comp. on the opposite, the לֹא' אֲנִי־עֹשֶׂה (vers. 32, 22).—The land—well, we are again in it, but where are the people? This question Jehovah will answer by actual (לַעֲשׂוֹת) increase (ver. 10 sq.), in that He will show them as a **flock** (ch. xxxiv.; Micah ii. 12). [While Hitzig takes אָדָם as in apposition to אֹתָם (them, the men, as a flock), Kliefoth translates incorrectly: "that they became the flock of mankind."] Hävernick cites Bochart for the particularly great increase of flocks of sheep. (Comp. also ch. xxxiv. 31.) But what Ver. 38 says on this is more significant. According to Hengstenberg, formal mention is made of the festivals in general, but the connection (as Mark xv. 6) points to the great accumulation of sheep at the passover (2 Chron. xxxv. 7), with which the abundance in men of restored Israel is compared. (Thus the Chaldee.) Hengstenberg translates: "as consecrated flocks of sheep" (the people of the saints of the Lord), and seeks the fulfilment in the Church of Christ rather than in the times between the exile and Christ.—קֳדָשִׁים, that is, of hallowed ones, in this sense: of sacrificial beasts (Rom. xii. 1); whereby the reference to the consecration of the people (ver. 25) gains confirmation. The people is embraced in its chief points of worship, Deut. xvi. 16.

DOCTRINAL REFLECTIONS.

1. The comparison of our chapter with ch. vi. indicates that, in considering the "mountains of Israel," especially when they are by the best interpreter, the "enemy," sneeringly termed the "everlasting heights," we are not to direct our attention to the mountainous character of the Holy Land. Palestine is a hilly country, which leans upon the towering heights of Lebanon and Hermon; but this conformation did not so much qualify it for its significance in the Old World, so that we might at once recur to that, as its position on the boundaries of Asia, Africa, and Europe, and again its peculiar isolation, while occupying such a position in the centre of the Old World. In considering this position of the land, its littleness, ridiculed as is well known by Cicero, and from which the Roman statesman would infer the little god of the Jews, has as little, or rather as much, to say as the grain of mustard seed in the parable, Matt. xiii. The focus of the concave mirror is, in like manner, merely a point. The outward littleness of the Holy Land only compels us to one thing, and that is, to keep always in view its spiritual significance. As, then, for such a view, its separation from the other countries, and again, at the same time, its position in the midst of them (ch. v. 5) (the former, that amid the universal blowing of the world and the nations there might be a protecting hand before the light; the latter, that when the light burst forth, its brilliancy might easily shine in all directions), claim our attention much more than its mountainous character,—so under the "everlasting heights," the "mountains of Israel," Zion, as seat of the Davidic-Messianic kingdom (Ps. ii.), and the temple-mountain, in so far as Israel worshipped what it knew (John iv.), and the σωτηρια ἐκ των Ἰουδαιων ἐστιν, must come into consideration (ch. xxxiv. 26; Isa. ii. 2; Micah iv. 1); however beautifully that reads which has been said by Schmieder, accordant, no doubt, with "natural human feeling," while citing Ps. xc. 2 and Job xv. 7, and referring to the "ways and manners of mountaineers," and the thread of "remembrances," especially Israel's (Gen. xxii.; 1 Kings xviii.).

2. The antithesis of Seir places before our eyes the rugged mountain height and the rude mountain strength, that is, exactly the things which have no value for enduring victory, for abiding blessing in the higher order of things.

3. The combating of the allegorizing method of explanation—for example, by J. A. Crusius, from whom Rosenmüller quotes when commenting on our chapter—is unquestionably in the right against the arbitrary extravagances and exaggerations of Cocceius and his followers; but where the Bible language in general is symbolical, with the prophets, above all, a symbolical way of speaking will be conceded. A natural or historical substratum on which the symbolical is based is supposed with the symbolical itself. Consequently, all that is here said in Ezekiel has a fulfilment in the time after the exile. On the other hand, modern apocalypticism, by its converting the letter of prophecy into future revelations of any and every kind, sets itself against the apocalyptic mode of expression, the characteristic of which is certainly not literality. The national physiognomy of Israel, as Genesis traces it back to Adam, the father of all men, indicates a reference to humanity as a whole. This reference prevails in Noah's prophetic discourse, Gen. ix., when Japhet is destined to dwell in the tents of Shem, and Canaan, the son of Ham, to be a servant in the house. The Holy Land fits in with Abraham to this symbolism of the nation, and Abraham is to be a blessing (as is said in Gen. xii.: "to all the families of the earth, *Adamah*"), through his seed, which is Christ, as the apostle says in Gal. iii. Hence humanity in Christ will also be the theological point of view in the case of the land of Israel. So long as He who is τέλος νόμου (Rom. x. 4) was not born in the land of promise, the land remained, in respect to the realization of the blessing of Abraham to the race of Adam, a prophetic symbol of the earth, just as the nation was symbolico-prophetic for the nations of mankind

The land of Israel is also νομός (from νέμω), and, like the legal nationality of Israel, has its final fulfilment in Christ. As His beatitudes (Matt. v.) assign to His people the kingdom of heaven, so also do they the inheritance of the land. Hitherto out of Israel shines humanity, and representatively for it the Son of man, the true Israel. The Christian interpretation of the people of Israel as the Church, the kingdom of God, the kingdom of heaven, embraces now also the Holy Land in the signification of the land of glory, paradise, and Eden. From the standpoint of the fulfilling of Israel as to its universal human signification by Christ, the Old Testament outward expression of the letter, that is, what is said propædeutically and pædagogically in accordance with the economy of the Old Covenant, in the style of the people and the land, may remain in its full force; but what is given with the idea of Israel, namely, that the promises in question are to be fulfilled in a very different sense from the outward literal sense, that they are to be fulfilled "in spirit and in truth,"—this even the literal expression itself demands from its unmistakable depth of meaning, which often makes plainly ridiculous a merely literal interpretation, whether looking to the time after the exile, or to the very last time. All the prophets and the law prophesied until John, the baptizer of Christ (Matt. xi. 13; Luke xvi. 16). And what Christ said (John iv.) of worshipping at Jerusalem: "the hour cometh, and now is," bears witness to the Messianic (Christological) and in general the spiritual sense of the Old Testament letter; as the setting of it free from every temporary limitation as to place or nation bears witness to its sense for eternity, and to the spiritual interpretation as that which is at the same time interpretation "in truth," the true understanding, so that the Christian truth of the prophecies is also to be regarded as their true and full reality. The Jewish Christianity of individual expositors (*e.g.* of Baumgarten) is not the Old Testament Christianity of the prophets.

4. On ch. iii. 17 the characteristic individualization was noted as a mark of the time; but that which is peculiar to the Christological utterances of our prophet (Introd. § 9), his putting of the Christological thought, as ch. xl. sq., in the form of Palestinian worship, and so generally in the manner of the people and land of Israel, is always to be adhered to. Fundamentally, the latter form was only that of the law as early as Ex. xx. 12. But when the Son of man, of the seed of David according to the flesh, realized the kingdom of Israel as eternal—when, by the outpouring of the Holy Ghost, His gift of prophecy became the common property of mankind, then, as with the worshipping in spirit and in truth, the peculiar localization of the sanctuary and the priestly service, always accomplished for the time, ceased; Israel also could, in whatever part of the earth, consider themselves as in their own land, and so much the more as their true King had (John xviii.) witnessed the good confession of the supramundane nature of His kingdom before the representative of the Roman earthly world-power. For the Israel of fulfilment Canaan lay, in the first instance, in the world above with Christ, as the apostle Paul says in Phil. i. 23, where also paradise is (Luke xxiii. 43; 2 Cor. xii. 4); and in this world only, in the renewal of heaven and earth according to the Christian hope. So, likewise, the true, the fulfilled nationality of Israel is to be sought for in the Christian world, in humanity, according to the Spirit of Christ; now in measure, in fulness only hereafter, Rev. xxi. 3.

5. Schmieder sums up the moral guilt of Edom as threefold: (1) taking possession at his own hand; (2) doing this in a bad frame of mind, with malignant joy and scornful laughter; (3) doing this not to keep and cultivate the land (for which man was ordained of God in paradise), but to devastate and plunder it.

6. It belongs to the local colour of the land, that, when it is spoken of distinctively, its fruitfulness also is spoken of. Comp. for climate and nature of the soil, the well-known passages of Scripture. Writers in the first century still bear witness to what heathens and Jews of former times celebrated with one accord, the immense population of the land, corresponding to its great fertility. At present, indeed, Jerusalem, the largest city of Palestine, has scarcely more inhabitants than the smaller towns of Galilee had in the time of Josephus.

7. On the parallel minatory prophecy in ch. vi. it was observed (p. 94) how Israel's idolatrous self-righteousness is broken in pieces in every way by God's judgment. A parallel observation will correspond to the kernel and inmost contents of our chapter, namely, that divine grace alone will restore Israel, land and people—the latter especially, in the way of Jehovah's sanctifying His own name. In this, Israel's misery is as little the motive as any righteousness on the side of Israel. What befalls the heathen, indeed, with respect to Israel, happens to them because they have insulted in His people the name of Jehovah revealed in Israel. Hence the fundamental reference which Jehovah takes is finally Himself. Israel, as has been repeatedly said, four times in succession (in the cosmic number, vers. 20-23), gave by their exile, and hence by their misery, occasion for the profanation of the name of Jehovah. Their misery made the heathen sin against Jehovah; thus it was viewed, but by no means as cause of the divine pity. What is said of pity is Jehovah's pity for His own name, ver. 21. The divine love appears not as compassion in relation to misery, but the misery itself appears as sin, so that the reference is taken simply to sin; the divine love appears purely as grace.

8. Hävernick emphasizes this, that "the holiness of God forms the centre of the discourse before us;" but he makes too little account of the holiness of Jehovah, when he makes no more of it than "the relation therein established of God to the evil." So also it is not acutely thought, when, in explanation of vers. 1-15, that "the punitive judgment threatened against the heathen must have its ultimate explanation" from the holiness of God, Hävernick places the essence of heathenism in assailing the holiness of God. It must be observed, however, that heathenism knows nothing of God's holiness. The name of Jehovah's holiness, as the expression, chosen three times in succession (according to the number of the godhead, vers. 20, 21, 22), and which is not to be resolved into the "holy name of Jehovah," significantly runs, is even as "name" (as Beck justly observes) "the expression with living power of the divine presence in revelation," so that by the name of Jehovah's holiness this revelation of God as adapted exclusively to

Israel is set forth; hence, as to the "transgressions of the heathen," no direct relation of them to the holiness of God is expressed, but a misapprehension of the revelation of the holy in Israel, consequently a relation to Israel as the people of Jehovah. The holiness of God has, however, so much the more significance in our chapter, as the setting of it forth in Israel is thoroughly in accordance with what is thus emphasized, that what Jehovah does (vers. 22, 32) He does for His own sake. For God's holiness is "the real intrinsic ideality of God, His harmoniousness of essence, as it manifests itself also in this, that He makes Himself known in a church of His pure divine consciousness, and preserves and perfects this church in the ideality of its pure essence, until by it the world is restored to perfection in the real ideality, the personal harmoniousness of essence" (P. LANGE, *Pos. Dogm.* p. 95). By setting forth the holiness of God, as is done in our chapter, Ezekiel puts himself in harmony with Isaiah (p. 41).

9. Lange observes on the holiness of God, that the concept of it is "mediated to us through the Old Testament almost more than any other concept;" "the leading thought of the Hebrew view of the world is holiness; the קָדוֹשׁ, or קְדוֹשׁ יִשְׂרָאֵל, is He who is pure in essence, true to Himself, corresponding to His name." Lange finds the "mythologico-typical reflection" of holiness in ideality, the "leading thought of the Hellenic view of the world," just as he calls "the Greek culture the mythologico-typical counterpart of the theocracy."

10. Because love, which is God, is holy, breaking of the law, and still more the dishonouring of divine benefits, as in ver. 16 sq., can expect no support or indulgence in Him, the righteous God, the "Founder and Guardian of right" (LANGE). Since He as the "Holy One," who is the absolute opposite of the evil, can originate nothing evil, so contrariety to Him as such, and especially misuse of His gifts, here of the land, can find no encouragement with the "Holy One of Israel," the Giver of righteous recompense. Since the native land of a people, especially like Israel, may be misused as the δος μοι που στω in relation to heaven or higher interests than the earth, the corresponding righteous opposition and reaction of the holiness of God will be either deterioration of such a land (failure of crops and the like), or expulsion of the people from it, or both. So, too, the earth must finally pass away for mankind, although for the people of God there is hope of a "new earth." The latter gives proof of God's truth and faithfulness, which, keeping promise, provides for the need of finite spirits not only a corporeity, but also a locality in harmony therewith, according to the purpose of His wise and holy will; and perhaps this is typified also in Israel's possession of the land in the signification of their native land. But with God not only is goodness accompanied by justice, as that according to which God gave Israel scope and opportunity to expel (exile) themselves from their land among the heathen—just as man can procure hell for himself—and thus left as well as gave their right to Israel, but divine justice as revelation of God's holiness is more than mere retribution; it becomes on and in the sinner self-sanctification of God.

11. As the Holy One, Jehovah is the God of Israel (Lev. xi. 44 sq.); and it is only in keeping with this relation that Israel, His people, have to appear before Him, not merely in symbolical but still more in legal moral purity of life, above all in that they keep themselves religiously pure from idols. It is not only this mutual relation that results to Israel from the fact that their God is the Holy One, but also that, so long as the relation of the Holy One to Israel has not ceased, in like manner the holiness of this people is not to be surrendered; hence that, as *on* them by exile and by restoration, so *in* them Jehovah will sanctify His name or Himself. "The command: Be ye holy, for I am holy, contains (says Hävernick) at the same time the promise of the realization of a holy kingdom of God as surely as God Himself is holy. But God reveals Himself as the Holy One not merely in condemning evil and destroying the offender, but also in the extirpation of evil and the transformation and renewal of the sinner by virtue of a new divine breath of life, the spiritual creation of God in man."

12. Sanctification implies in general that something is removed from its common worldly relations. Since this does not usually take place without reference to sinful concomitants, the symbolical act of washing readily connects itself with sanctification; but it is by no means to have a merely negative interpretation, as "annulling of the false profane world-relation of the object" (LANGE), especially when, as here in Ezekiel, no mention is made of the positive symbol of anointing; which, moreover, does not symbolize induction into the service of the Lord, the "restoration of the true religious world-relation," but the divine equipment for the service of the Lord. Even in itself, and still more from its thus standing alone, washing will represent purification, which is consecration.

13. Jehovah sanctifies Himself *on* Israel before the eyes of the rest of the world (ver. 23), in that by taking and gathering Israel out of all nations and countries He actually places them again as His people in the land of promise (ver. 24). Jehovah sanctifies Himself *in* Israel, hence in Israel's own consciousness, by making them experience, as a fresh national dedication, a moral and religious purification. The expressions employed are to be interpreted as referring to the nation as such, and not to single individuals; we have not so much to understand spiritual states of mind as to think of national regeneration. But if what has been already remarked on ch. xi. suffices as to the letter for our chapter also and ch. xviii., the sprinkling of the clean water in ver. 25 symbolizes the national moral and religious cleansing of Israel, and the "new heart" in ver. 26 is nothing else than a "heart of flesh" instead of a "heart of stone" in the flesh; yet in ver. 27 the Spirit of Jehovah (רוּחִי), which the "new spirit" within Israel is interpreted to mean, points beyond ch. xi. 19 (ch. xviii. 31); the Holy One of Israel appears as the spirit of Israel, just as "God as Spirit of the Church and indweller in the human heart is preeminently the Holy One" (NITZSCH). And although ver. 25 sq. in relation to ver. 8 sq. may be taken as complement of the promise given there, or even as the condition for the promised inheritance continuing to the children, and hence

parallel thereto (ver. 24 carrying out the declaration: "for they draw near to come," ver. 8), yet we are not hindered from making the Messianic salvation of the people, as the true and full sanctification of Jehovah *in* as well as *on* them, shine forth behind all this (p. 24), and the "clean water" of ver. 25 approximates to the Holy Ghost (Joel ii. 28 sq.). Comp. Umbreit.

14. "The true essence of the Messianic time," says Hävernick, "its very kernel, from which all its other blessings flow, and its entire glory unfolds itself, is the purification of the people. At the time of Christ this idea was deeply rooted in the national consciousness, and John the Baptist unquestionably adapted to it his rite of lustration, the βαπτισμα της μετανοιας."

15. Jesus could (John iii. 5) refer to ver. 25 sq. of our chapter, namely, that water and spirit are requisite for regeneration for the kingdom of God, which truth the master in Israel (ver. 10) should have known. "For Ezekiel teaches here in clear words that Israel had to receive another and new heart and spirit—that it had to be sprinkled with clean water by the Spirit of God. Thus should a master in Israel have known regarding water and spirit in this relation" (COCCEIUS).

16. "Striking is the word of the prophet, and pointing exactly to the times of Christian fulfilment,—the people of the new planting shall never again experience the reproach of hunger among the heathen. A deep saying, when we divest it of its allegorical covering, and understand by it the eternal appeasing of hunger of spirit. It was indeed a reproach to Israel, that, nourished as they were by the divine food of life in the words of Moses and the prophets, they went after the imaginary gods of the heathen, and, being carried away into the countries of strangers, were obliged to suffer hunger in a dry land," etc. (UMBREIT).

HOMILETIC HINTS.

Ver. 1 sq. The mountains of Israel not only figures, but also places of the promises to Israel. —Word and name of the Lord; the former the revelation of His will, the latter the revelation of His nature.—Ver. 2. "Thus they mocked at the promises of God, as if their eternity were now come to an end" (BERL. BIB.).—The scorn of the world an old experience.—"Thus were the prophets and Christ reproached, and the Lord said that men would speak all manner of evil against His disciples, Matt. v. 11, and Paul, that we should be a spectacle to the world, 1 Cor. iv. 9" (HEIM-HOFFMANN).—"All things may and shall work for good to Christians, Rom. viii. 28" (CR.).—The wicked also shall have an eternity, but of what kind? Just the eternity into the possession of which they have put themselves, according as their works deserve, as death is the wages of sin.—Ver. 3 sq. God knows, sees, and hears the misery of His children; that must comfort them, therefore they cannot despair.—"How ready men often are not only to count up the sufferings of others, but also in their talk to exaggerate them still more!" (STARCK.)—Ver. 5 sq. What God calls His cannot be lost for ever. He is jealous *with* but also *for* His possession.—God lets His people be stricken only by whom He will; one cannot simply open the mouth and devour them at pleasure.—Ver. 8 sq. "Thus shall the ruined churches bring fruit, wine, and bread, that is, the mysteries of doctrine, to the profit of the people, that they may no longer be rude and ignorant, but a people taught of God. Therefore the spiritual husbandmen, vine-dressers, till and sow diligently. With the plough of fear they turn up the soil of the heart, in which they sow the new word of the gospel, whereby the forsaken churches become planted anew; and these are the mountains which the Lord addresses" (HEIM-HOFFMANN).—"When He appeared in the holy land who could say of Himself, 'Come unto Me, ye who labour and are heavy laden,' He far outshone Solomon in all his glory" (HENGST.).—"The wicked have no cause to rejoice over the chastisement of God's children, Jer. xlviii. 27" (STARKE).—"The affairs of the people of God are never in so bad a state that God should be unable to set them right again; nay, experience has taught that the Church after persecution only increases so much the more" (O.).—"They are far wrong who consider a great increase of men as a curse, because it gives rise to want and distress. God can nourish many as well as few, and we should live moderately, avoid endeavouring to surpass others in expenditure, and seek for concord in families, etc." (LUTHER).—Ver. 12 sq. "The promised good is always to be understood with the condition that men repent, Mal. iii. 7" (STARKE).—"The self-evident condition is, that they do not fill up the measure of their sins anew. There is no charter of immunity against Ye would not" (HENGST.).—"How often is the country or a district made to bear the blame when there comes a pestilence among men or cattle, when, however, it should be known that sin gaining the upper hand provoked God's wrath thereto" (O.).—"As already observed by Jerome, the Jews refer this to a kingdom of a thousand years, when Jerusalem shall be built and the temple of the latter chapters of our prophet erected; while in the opinion of others, the fulfilment took place under Zerubbabel, which cannot possibly be the case, as also Jerome grants, and then compares the Christian Chiliasts with the Jewish dreamers of their millennium. Hence we must abide by the spiritual interpretation regarding these blessings promised to the people, to which we are directed besides by Christ and the apostles" (LUTHER).

Ver. 16 sq. "Man's previous course of action is the cause of God's subsequent course of action, Jer. ii. 19" (STARKE).—"The goodness of God invites us to repentance, but not to evil-doing and pride" (STARCK).—We shall have to give account not only because of the evil which we have done, but also for the good things which we have had.—The earth should not be full of wickedness and folly, but full of the knowledge of the Lord and of love unfeigned.—"The world is perfect throughout where man does not come in to disturb it."—In our impure acting our impure nature also always comes forth. Storms clear the air, an observation which bears application in regard to the judgments of God.—Ver. 19. The scattering power of sin; in truth, it scatters the souls of men into the whole world, and that is already their judgment which sinners have to experience.—Ver. 20. With the sinner goes also his curse, his other shadow.—Our misfortunes and mistakes are very often God's sentence on our transgressions, which, indeed, are best known to Him and ourselves.—How much blasphemy against God and offence against the truth do not those very persons occasion who are called to make God's word and name honoured, acknowledged, and exalted above the world!—To have regard to the enemy,—a point to be well attended to for the walk of the friends of God in this world.—"Thus this chapter teaches us how the first petition of the Lord's prayer should be understood. The name of the Lord, to wit, is hallowed as well by the prosperity of the elect, which may obtain even under the cross, as by their purification from sin" (RICHTER).—A bad life ought not to put good doctrine in question. —Ver. 21 sq. God His own justification in this world (Theodicy).—"God sanctifies His name among men by benefits as well as by judgments and punishments" (STARCK).—"So saints are accustomed to pray who put no trust in their own merit, but humbly entreat God to look to His own name, that it may be praised and sanctified. But Christ is the holy name of God, for whose sake God is gracious to us; whoever calls upon the name of the Lord shall be saved" (HEIM-HOFFMANN).

Ver. 24. We shall come home out of this world.—Gathering even in the midst of the scattering of this world is of the grace of God.—Ver. 25 sq. "It is God alone who can truly convert us to Himself, and purify our hearts by His almighty Spirit, Jer. xxxi. 18" (TÜB. BIB.).—"Without true purification from sin no one can come into real union and communion with God, Isa. i. 16 sq." (STARKE).—"No unclean person shall enter into the New Jerusalem, Rev. xxii., hence our cleansing has to take place in this life" (STARCK).—"Purification must precede the filling of men with the new spirit. David in the first place supplicates God to wash him quite clean from his guilt, and then prays for the creation in him of a clean heart and of a new stedfast spirit, Ps. li." (UMBREIT).—"The prophets frequently reproach the Jews, as a stiff-necked people, that they will not hearken to the word of the Lord. Here, on the contrary, a heart and spirit which shall be new is promised to them, that they may not henceforth live after their former custom, but begin a new manner of life, so that the old and disobedient heart of stone may become the new but pliant and submissive heart" (LUTHER).—"The heart of stone does not bear bending according to God's will, whereas the heart of flesh is soft, and of such a texture that God can impress into its understanding a living knowledge, into its will a voluntary obedience, and into the inclinations a holy order" (STARKE).—"Our heart and inward parts are designed to be occupied as an abode by God Himself, John xiv. 23" (STARCK).—For the furniture with which God is accustomed to furnish His abode in man, see Gal. v. 22.—"Of flesh and fleshly (carnal) are two different things; the former may be dealt with, the latter becomes always harder" (STARCK).—"The new birth does not consist in annihilating the man, nor in the entire removal of sinful corruption and of the old Adamic disposition, but in the creation of an entirely new disposition and nature, 2 Cor. v. 17; Gal. vi. 15; Ephes. iv. 24" (STARKE).—"God gives the Holy Ghost and all the riches of grace not for gold, but He gives all things without price to all who ask Him for them, Isa. lv." (CR.).—Ver. 27. "The Holy Ghost is not inactive in the regenerate, but active and powerful, Rom. viii. 15 sq." (STARKE).—First the inward and then the outward change is God's order, while we men always proceed in the reverse order.—"What good, however, a man does is not his, but God's work in him, Phil. ii. 13" (STARKE).

Ver. 28 sq. To the heavenly among men there is no lack even on earth; to him who has what alone is worth having nothing shall be wanting. —So long as Christ was not born in the land of promise, the land of promise had to be also the home of Israel. Since the time that Christ is in heaven, only heaven can be the true home of the true Israel.—"The regenerate man stands in the covenant of grace with God" (STARKE).—Ver. 30. God will not only finally redeem us from all distress of body and soul, but will also free us from all reproach; so, then, we do not in vain believe in a resurrection of the body and an eternal life.—Ver. 31. In conversion man regains his memory. —A man can be of good courage when he loathes himself.—Loathing is not a sign of sickness only, but in matters spiritual it is a sign of convalescence.—The loathing of oneself, the requital of self-complacency.—Our life must become sorrow to us, otherwise sorrow will not become life to us. —Ver. 32 sq. Grace works shame, and so much the more as it makes the wilderness a paradise, the beggar a king, and the sinner a priest.—"Blessed shame" (SCHMIEDER).—We boast of nothing in Christ, and we boast of all things.—Ver. 35 sq. The last sentence of the world on the people of God will be its own self-condemnation, just as it will be our justification. It will not be in vain that we have comforted ourselves with God in this world.—Our help stands in the name of the Lord.—The comfort of the Church, that God is Builder and Planter.—"Yea, this is the honour of the holy name of God. He, the Creator, who created what was not, is also the Restorer, who creates anew that which was ruined and laid waste by the guilt of disobedient creatures" (SCHMIEDER).—Ver. 37 sq. "But the men of this flock shall also be as the sheep, that is, no wild beasts shall be among them; hence it follows that God will purify His Church from these noxious animals" (COCC.).

3. THE VISION OF THE RESURRECTION AND RE-QUICKENING OF THE DEAD BONES, AND THE SYMBOLICAL ACTION WITH THE ONE STICK OUT OF THE TWO STICKS, ALONG WITH THE INTERPRETATION (CH. XXXVII.).

1 The hand of Jehovah was upon me, and [as] Jehovah took me out
in the Spirit and made me rest [brought me, set me down] in the midst of the
2 valley, and it was full of bones. And He led me over by them round about,
and behold, [there were] very many on the surface of the valley, and behold,

3 [they were] very dry. And He said to me, Son of man, will these bones
4 live [become alive]? And I said, Lord Jehovah, Thou knowest. And He said
to me, Prophesy over these bones, and say to them, Ye dry bones, hear the
5 word of Jehovah, Thus saith the Lord Jehovah to these bones, Behold, I
6 bring spirit into you, and ye live. And I give sinews on you, and make
flesh to come up over you, and cover you with skin, and give breath in you, and
7 ye live, and know that I am Jehovah. And I prophesied as I was com-
manded; and there came a voice as I prophesied, and behold, a rustling, and
8 the bones drew near, bone to his bone. And I looked, and behold, sinews
and flesh came up on them, and skin covered them from above, yet breath
9 [was] not in them. And He said to me, Prophesy to the Spirit; prophesy,
son of man, and say to the Spirit, Thus saith the Lord Jehovah, Come from
the four winds, thou Spirit, and breathe into these slain, that they may live
10 [become alive]. And I prophesied as He commanded me, and the Spirit came
into them, and they lived [became alive], and stood upon their feet a very great
11 army. And He said to me, Son of man, these bones [are] the whole house of
Israel; Behold, they say, our bones were dried and our hope perished, for us,
12 we are undone. Therefore prophesy, and say to them, Thus saith the Lord
Jehovah, Behold, I open your graves, and lead you up out of your graves,
13 My people, and bring you to the land of Israel. And ye know that I am
Jehovah, when I open your graves and lead you up out of your graves, My
14 people; And I give My Spirit in you, and ye live, and I bring you to rest
upon your land, and ye know that I, Jehovah, spoke and did—sentence of
15, 16 Jehovah. And the word of Jehovah came to me, saying, And thou, son of
man, take to thee a stick, and write on it, For Judah and for the sons of
Israel, his associates; and take another stick, and write on it, For Joseph, the
17 stick of Ephraim, and of the whole house of Israel, his associates. And bring
them near the one to the other for thee into one stick, that they may be
18 [become] one in thy hand. And when the sons of thy people shall speak to
19 thee, saying, Wilt thou not show us what these [sticks] are to thee? Then say
to them, Thus saith the Lord Jehovah, Behold, I take the stick of Joseph,
which is in the hand of Ephraim, and the tribes of Israel his associates, and
put them on it, that is, the stick of Judah, and make them one stick, that
20 they may be one in My hand. And the sticks on which thou shalt write are
21 in thy hand before their eyes. And say to them, Thus saith the Lord
Jehovah, Behold, I take the sons of Israel out from among the heathen,
whither they went, and gather them from round about, and bring them to
22 their land. And I make them one people in the land, on the mountains of
Israel, and one king shall be king to them all; and they [there] shall no more
be two peoples, and they shall never again be divided into two kingdoms.
23 And they shall no more defile themselves with their foul idols, and with their
detestable things, and with all their transgressions; and I help them from all
their dwelling-places where they have sinned, and cleanse them; and they
24 shall be My people, and I will be their God. And My servant David shall
be king over them, and one shepherd shall be to them all; and they shall
25 walk in My judgments, and shall keep My statutes, and do them. And they
dwell upon the land which I gave to My servant Jacob, in which your fathers
dwelt, and they dwell on it, they and their sons, and their sons' sons, for ever,
26 and David My servant [is] prince to them for ever. And I make for them a
covenant of peace, an everlasting covenant [covenant of eternity] shall be with
them; and I give them and multiply them, and give My sanctuary in their
27 midst for ever. And My dwelling is over them, and I am their God and
28 they shall be My people. And the heathen know that I, Jehovah, sanctify
Israel, in that My sanctuary is in their midst for ever.

Ver. 1. Vulg.: . . . *in spiritu domini*—
Ver. 5. Sept.: . . . *εἰς ὑμας πνευμα ζωης*.
Ver. 6. . . . *νευρα* . . . . *πνευμα μου ἐφ' ὑμας*—
Ver. 7. *καθως ἐνετειλατο μοι κυριος*— (Another reading: כאשר צוני, Syr., Vulg., Arabs.)

Ver. 9. . . . κ. ἐμφυσησον εἰς τ. νεκρους τουτους κ. ζησατωσαν.
Ver. 10. . . . συναγωγη μεγαλη σφοδρα.
Ver. 11. . . διαπεφωνηκαμεν.
Ver. 14. . . . κ. θησομαι ὑμας ἐπι τ. γην ὑμων—
Ver. 16. . . ῥαβδον . . . τους προσκειμενους προς αὐτον.
Ver. 17. . . . εἰς ῥ. μιαν του δησαι αὐτας, κ. ἐσονται ἐν τ. χειρι σου. (Another reading: plur. בידיך.)
Ver. 19. Sept.: . . . την φυλην Ἰωσηφ την δια χειρος Ἐφραιμ . . . ἐπι τ. φυλην του Ἰουδα . . . ἐν τ. χειρι Ἰουδα. Vulg.: *et dabo eas pariter cum ligno J. . . . in manu ejus.* (Anoth. reading: בידו.)
Ver. 21. Sept.: . . . λαμβανω παντα οἰκον Ἰ. . . . γην Ἰ.
Ver. 22. . . . αὐτους εἰς ἐθνος ἐν τ. γη μου—
Ver. 23. . . . ἱνα μη . . . εν οἱς ἡμαρτοσαν ἐν αὐτοις, κ. ἐν τ. προσοχθισμασιν αὐτων κ. . . . ἀπο πασων τ. ἀνομιων ων ἡμαρτοσαν ἐν αὐταις— (Another reading: פשעיהם *et* Arabs.)
Ver. 24. . . . ἀρχων ἐν μεσω αὐτων . . . ὁτι ἐν—.
Ver. 25. . . . οἱ πατερες αὐτων—
Ver. 28. Sept.: . . . ὁ ἁγιαζων αὐτους—

EXEGETICAL REMARKS.

The two sections of the chapter, vers. 1–14 and vers. 15–28, are already distinguished by the introductory formula (vers. 1, 15); still more decidedly by their difference of form,—first a vision, and then a symbolic action; as also by their contents, which, however, with all their diversity, show the most intimate connection—what in the first section is prophesied of the whole of Israel is in the second ratified by promise in relation to the parts. [Hengst.: "the restoration of Israel as a covenant-people, and the restoration of Israel as a brotherhood."] The requickening and reunion of Israel. The interpretation is connected with both prophetic sections of our chapter, appended (vers. 11–14) to the first, while in the second it is given along with the prophecy. The connection with ch. xxx. is apparent from the close of that chapter, ver. 24 sq.

Vers. 1–10. *The Quickening of the Bones in the Valley.*

Ver. 1. הָיְתָה, comp. ch. i. 3 (וַתְּהִי עָלָיו) and ch. xxxiii. 22 (הָיְתָה אֵלַי). Although not the stronger introductory formula (as in ch. viii. 1), yet the description given of Ezekiel's condition is sufficient simply to set aside a mere "product of poetical intuition" (Hitzig). "The abrupt commencement without *and*" is, according to Hengstenberg, meant to point out that "the fact here related is extraordinary, and out of connection with the usual prophetic activity." ["As the subject itself is a quite unusual one, so also the description is such as Ezekiel never elsewhere draws. Such a never-seen sight is seen by itself in a moment of higher inspiration, or never," Ewald.] As the Vulgate, so also Hitzig, against the accent: "in the Spirit of Jehovah;" but יְהוָה is subject, and בְּרוּחַ simply: ἐν πνευματι (Matt. xxii. 43), in contrast to ἐν σωματι (2 Cor. xii. 2), to which it is easy to supply אֱלֹהִים (ch. xi. 24), which (as Keil justly observes) was omitted because of the יְהוָה (comp. ch. viii. 3). Ecstatic state in which he was inwardly transported from the things around him.—The **valley** can only be the one mentioned in ch. iii. 22, when we consider that those who speak in ver. 11 were settled there in the neighbourhood, and consequently could be represented as the **bones** in the valley. At all events, it is not a valley in general, but a certain valley; and if nothing else, that (וְהִיא) which was full of bones. Hengstenberg points out the contrast to the mountain (ch. xvii. 22), the "lowness of condition"! Hitzig: "The valley is fitted to represent a huge grave; but the thought is less of graves than of their opposite (עַל־פְּנֵי, ver. 2), namely, that the slain (ver. 9) have remained unburied, their bones bleach and dry there.—The **bones** are men's bones (Isa. lxvi. 14); in the connection here: *the remains of the slain*, abundance of which might be in the disturbed districts of Judah; according to the Talmudists: slain Ephraimites, 1 Chron. vii. 20 sq. Looking from the **midst** of the valley, he could warrant that it was **full** of bones.—Ver. 2. עֲלֵיהֶם, **over by them**, or "over past them;" hence not: "over," to tread them with the feet, or to hover over them, but: **round about**, so that he might be able to view them exactly, as the repeated וְהִנֵּה, as the result of such inspection, brings to view the **very many** and their being **very dry**, neither sap nor strength in them. Comp. moreover, ch. vi. [Ewald refers for "the rapid narration, with its constant fall into the present," to his *Grammar*, § 342 b.]

The question in Ver. 3 is fitted to bring the prophet, and, through him, his hearers and readers, to the consciousness of the impossibility presented to human eyes (**son of man**); and considering the words uttered by Israel (ver. 11), its intention doubtless is to bring out the despair of the people, in order to make room in their hearts for the prophecy of salvation (ver. 12). Ezekiel's answer refers the matter to God (Rev. vii. 14), for with God there is no impossibility, unless He wills it, and that God alone can know. Comp. on this point Isa. xxvi. 19.—Ver. 4. When Ezekiel is summoned to prophesy **over** the bones, their future, asked (ver. 3) by Jehovah in relation to them, comes to view as an affair of Jehovah's, or His counsel, will, and purpose; they may therefore be addressed (וְאָמ' אֲלֵיהֶם), however **dry** they are. Grotius observes: so much the more as the prisoners in the exile are to be understood. —The **word of Jehovah** (ch. xxxvi. 1, 4) mediates the salvation, the life to be prophesied. Hence not *see*, for then death, and nothing but death, will come to view. In Ezekiel's vision all depends on "**hearing**;" recognise God's word, and trust to it (John iv. 48, xx. 19). This, at the same time, legitimates as divine the word of Ezekiel's prophetic announcement. The tenor, however, of the divine word—Jehovah announces what will take place, what He purposes to do (Amos iii. 7)—follows in Ver. 5. What is said *to* them is, from the certainty of its being accomplished, in reality said *of* them, as הִנֵּה already formally points to the accomplishment.—רוּחַ, although followed by וִחְיִיתֶם of the effect generally on the whole, is yet not exactly ר׳ חַיִּים of Gen. vi. 17, or נִשְׁמַת־ר׳ ח׳ of Gen. vii. 22, "breath"; for it is just that which is in a living being that is here left out of view, and, in contrast to that which is dried up, above all, simply the creative divine power, hence **spirit** quite objectively and generally is contemplated. ("The Spirit of God is the principle of all real life in the creaturely existence," HÄV.) That we have here another order (HENGST.) than in the execution (ver. 7 sq.) is not the case, for the more detailed description which follows immediately in ver. 6 presents the same order as the execution follows. The **Spirit** also does not press forward at the beginning as the (HITZIG) chief thing, without which the rest, the merely bodily resurrection, is of no importance (HENGST.), but as וִחְיִיתֶם implies: "to live" in general, without separation for the present into political and spiritual, so אֲנִי מֵבִיא בָכֶם ר׳ introduces the divine causality simply as first, as *conditio sine qua non*. The more special is expressed—Ver. 6—by a parallel וְנָתַתִּי; and afterwards by גִּידִים, the "binding matter," the **sinews**, and by the making of "flesh to come up," and by the קרם (a word only found in Ezekiel), with **skin**, the outward form of life is completed, from which the spirit which enlivens the flesh is distinguished, but is as yet to be considered as natural, now as **breath**, the individual life, in consequence of which it certainly can be said: וִידַעְתֶּם׳. But the spiritual element, although intimated in this, is first expressly stated in the interpretation (ver. 14), with reference back to ch. xxxvi. 27.

The prophecy, in accordance with the command given to Ezekiel (ver. 4), is not limited (as HENGST.) in Ver. 7 to the summons to the bones to "hear," sq., but comprehends also what Jehovah says to these bones in vers. 5, 6; for that He is the speaker makes the saying a prophecy, although to prophesy in general may be said to mean the same as: "to speak in the Spirit."—The **voice** which **came** was audible; its simplest interpretation is in accordance with ch. i. 25. The prophet was to prophesy; what Jehovah purposed to say to the bones (vers. 4–6), the prophet now prophesies; and since he prophesies according to the command, Thus saith Jehovah, that which was prophesied to the bones is from God, and the voice is to be understood as *Jehovah's*, from which the New Testament representation is perhaps coloured (John v. 28), and neither a "noise" nor "sound" in general—anything like a thunder-clap would be out of place in this sublime and orderly connection—nor in particular: "the sound of a trumpet." Keil's position, that it cannot be supposed that God should bind His voice of power to the prophecy of the prophet, has in reality no significance. On the other hand, he is right in referring רַעַשׁ (ch. iii. 12, xii. 18) to the noise by which the effect of the word of Jehovah announced itself to the bones, now coming together in consequence thereof. [Hävernick makes the "sound" pass into a "mighty peal." Hitzig, in order to have the "fitting impulse" from the ground, translates: "earthquake" (Matt. xxvii. 51), under reference to ch. xxxviii. 19.] God's voice of power is followed by a rustling, caused by the bones coming rustling up from the surface of the valley. Thereafter (וְ consecutive) "the bones come together," which may be thus distinguished from what follows, that it refers to whatever belongs to one body, while עֶצֶם אֶל־עַצ׳ specializes a single bone in relation to another, *e.g.* the upper to the lower part of the arm (on the form תִּקְרְבוּ, see EWALD, *Gr.* p. 505).

["This may also be interpreted of the first movements of the scattered Israelites in the various settlements in Chaldea, and their assembling for quiet consultation, where the members of the people met again in secret," SCHMIEDER.]—Ver. 8, as was promised in ver. 6. ["May be interpreted of Israel's first growth in hope, conscious strength, and vigour," SCHMIEDER.] The remark that yet **breath was not in them** may serve formally for the dramatic colouring of the event in the representation; as to actual fact, it sets forth the creative power of God in the action, which is in this way twofold. That thereby is shown that "the restoration is first pre-eminently an external, political one" (HENGST.), is not of necessity contained in the text, but the original creation of man, as related in Gen. ii. 7, forms a pattern for the text. (John vii. 39 makes the deepest application of the וְרוּחַ׳.)—Correspondingly, therefore, Ezekiel has in Ver. 9 to prophesy once more,—this time to the **Spirit** (ver. 5), that is, not to the "breath," for that is רוּחַ only in a living person, as we have already said, and still less to the "wind," which is the sensuous natural symbol of the Spirit. And from what follows it is still clearer that the "outpouring of the Spirit" cannot be spoken of here, but what is spoken of is *the universal spirituality which pervades all creation*. Hence the Spirit is to come **from the four winds**; not without reference, moreover, to ch. v. 10, 12, xii. 14, xvii. 21 (Matt. xxiv. 31; Rev. vii. 1). מֵאַרְבַּע׳ makes clear the distinction between רוחות and הָרוּחַ. Our passage has nothing to do with the "breathing on" in John xx. 22, and just as little is "the fulness and force of the Spirit's operations, Acts ii. 2" (HENGST.), indicated by the "wind from the four winds." וּפְחִי makes a very plain allusion to Gen. ii. 7. ["The quickening Spirit of God awakens the resolution to return to God's covenant and to the land of their fathers," SCHMIEDER.]—**Slain**: killed, not deceased (Doct. Reflect. 5). The colouring is taken from those condemned and executed by the Chaldeans (ver. 11). Regarding וִיחִיוּ, comp. on ver. 5.—Ver. 10. Exchanging Hithp. וְהִנַּבֵּאתִי (EWALD, *Gr.* p. 331) for Niphal of ver. 7, and צִוָּנִי Piel in place of Pual in ver. 7.—Ver. 9, 5. The **Spirit**, in order to become the breath of life in them (comp. ch. ii. 2, iii. 24).—2 Kings xiii. 21 ; Rev. xi. 11.

Vers. 11–14. *The Divine Interpretation of the Vision.*

The process in the vision vers. 1–10 is symbolical, as shown by the phrase in ver. 11: **these bones are**, etc., which refers to the whole vision as it treated of the bones. Hence the bones, which lay there **very dry**, but at Jehovah's word became alive, which were **very many** (ver. 2), a **very great army** (ver. 10), bear the sense of and signify **the whole house of Israel** ; and this already prepares for the second section of our chapter. According to Hitzig, Judah and Israel combined denote the State broken up by the war, and also the generation cut off by it ; against which view we observe that the dead cannot be "saying" here any more than the bones, but, as in ch. xi. 15 sq., the Israel in exile must be contemplated, who now indeed compared themselves to the dead, but to whom, on the contrary, life is immediately (ver. 12) to be proclaimed and promised. In what they say (comp. ch. xxxiii. 10) is contained the so frequently overlooked *tertium comparationis*, and the cause for the vision in vers. 1–10. Hence the divine interpretation does not primarily start from the outward condition of the people in general, and still less from that of a part of them, the dead of Israel, but from what the despair of those in exile says, hence from the frame of mind which thus found voice: **our bones are dried**, etc. The relation of יָבְשׁוּ and יְבֵשׁוֹת (ver. 2) to each other is evident.—נִגְזַרְנוּ, properly: "cut off," separated, shut out from God's help (Ps. lxxxviii. 6 [5], xxxi. 23 [22] ; Isa. liii. 8).—לָנוּ, according to Gesenius, a superfluous pronominal dative, as much as to say: We are undone. HITZIG : Reduced to ourselves. [DELITZSCH : It is over with us. HENGST.: We are cut off for us, referring the "for us" to the sadness of the fact for those concerned.] The language which they employ corresponds thoroughly to the question in ver. 3. That which, believing themselves abandoned, without any **hope** (ch. xix. 5) of again rising up to be a nation, they say of themselves, Ezekiel beheld in the valley,—merely **very dry bones**. So much the more, and the more literally, can what was done with these bones, a procedure which the prophet had to prophesy, and was afterwards permitted to behold, avail as a promise to them.—Ver. 12 therefore parallel to ver. 4 sq., but still keeping primarily in view the despairing speech of the exiles : הִנָּבֵא וְאָמַרְתָּ, not yet, however, הִנֵּה אֲנִי מֵבִיא בָכֶם רוּחַ' (ver. 5), as ver. 14 hereafter, but first: **behold, I open your graves**, meaning thereby the *abodes of the exile*, since the Jews who were in exile considered themselves like dead men. The accommodating interpretation changes the valley with the many bones on its surface into many **graves**, which have "to be opened," etc. **My people**, here and in the following a very comforting title. Israel, however, ought always to be so, and therefore also to have constantly been so. Consequently we have at the same time prominence given to the contrast between Israel's destiny and its deadly despair, and hence a notification of its unbelief and offences in general.—What in the vision the clothing with sinews, flesh, and skin was in relation to the bones (ver. 6 sq.), could in the interpretation applying to the living be regarded as political restoration, as this has to begin with leading out of Babylon and bringing back to Canaan.—Ver. 13. וִידַעְתֶּם reminds of וִידַעְתֶּם in ver. 6.—Ver. 14 takes up וְנָתַתִּי בָכֶם רוּחַ of ver. 6 and the rest of the vision, pointing, however, by רוּחִי to ch. xxxvi. 27, as by וְהִנַּחְתִּי to לְעוֹלָם in the following, for which comp. ch. xxviii. 26, xxxiv. The inspiriting and quickening for a home system which is to have permanence, and especially in the case of a people like Israel, will of necessity be spiritual and religious. —Isa. xiv. 1.—Ch. xvii. 24, xxii. 14, xxxvi. 36

Vers. 15–18. *The Reunion of Israel and Judah.*

After the vision thus interpreted, there follows in Ver. 16—accompanied by an interpretation—a *symbolic action*, the outward reality of which there is no difficulty in admitting. Both the contents (comp. ver. 11) and the transition with וְ connect what follows with the first section of the chapter, of which it forms the continuation and completion. Israel again become a nation, must, overcoming the separation which had taken place, also again become *one* nation. What follows draws the consequence from what has preceded.—עֵץ, "board" (tablet), or "staff," or simply "wood," **stick**.—For the "writing," comp. Num. xvii.—The **sons of Israel, his associates** (while the text reads the singular for "association"), are, according to Hengstenberg, a "small" part of Benjamin, Simeon, and Levi, and the members of the kingdom of the ten tribes who had attached themselves to Judah ; according to Keil: the "greater" part of Benjamin and Simeon, the tribe of Levi, and the pious Israelites who had at various times immigrated into Judah from the kingdom of the ten tribes, 2 Chron. xi. 13 sq., xv. 9, xxx. 11, 18, xxxi. 1. —Joseph is placed first, as Hengstenberg says, because Ephraim's equality with Judah rests upon him in consequence of the blessing of Jacob; more simply, because it is the *genealogical title of the patriarch*. That **the stick of Ephraim** (comp. ver. 19), which has been looked on as a later interpolation, is subjoined, is an addition taken from historical reality, for Ephraim was the head of the kingdom of the ten tribes.—Ver. 17. וְקָרַב אֹתָם אֶחָד אֶל־אֶחָד reminds of וַתִּקְרְבוּ עֲצָמוֹת עֶצֶם אֶל־עַצְמוֹ in ver. 7.—בְּיָדֶךָ illustrates לְךָ, corresponding to the symbolic action—here in the hand of Ezekiel, as hereafter in his word. In order to make them appear as one **stick,** they must have been adapted for that, and could scarcely have been "staves."

Ver. 18. Comp. ch. xxiv. 19. The purpose of the symbolic action, what it was meant to incite, on which account it is to be conceived of as externally real (ver. 20).—**What** (are) **these sticks to thee?** that is: what is their signification?—Ver. 19, the interpretation. Where ver. 16 has **the stick of Ephraim,** we have now **the stick of Joseph,** which first of all implies exactly the same as the stick described "for Joseph." In what respect it is designated the **stick of Ephraim** is then made plain by the words: **which is in the hand of Ephraim** (the expression בְּיַד doubtless suggested by בְּיָדֶךָ, ver. 17); and thereby, at the same time, the transition is made from the sign to the thing signified, for to be **in the hand** = to be in the possession, in the power, hence it denotes the supremacy of this tribe. Hence, too, instead of וְכָל־בֵּית יִשְׂרָאֵל, more expressly יִשְׁבְטֵי יִשְׂרָאֵל ("staves," "sticks," as "tribes").—If the noun is anticipated by עָלָיו, it would certainly be better to read, with Hitzig, אֶל, than אֶת: "to it, to the stick of Judah." It lies away, however, from לָקַח, as Keil connects, to combine אוֹתָם, namely, the tribes, after they have been put on the stick of Joseph (עָלָיו), by אֶת with the stick of Judah; besides, one does not see why the tribes already joined to Joseph should still have to be united with him. The "taking" is ended with the **tribes of Israel, his associates**; the "giving" relates to those (אוֹתָם) taken together (וְ), that is, Joseph-Ephraim and his tribes, for the purpose of union (וַעֲשִׂיתִם לְעֵץ אֶחָד) with Judah, and it is only to this that עָלָיו can refer. Hengstenberg explains אֶת: "the stick of Judah, I mean," "to indicate that Judah is the proper stem of the people of God." The interpretation still keeps a firm hold of the symbolic action (לְעֵץ אֶחָד), and אֶחָד בְּיָדִי evidently expresses an antithesis to Ephraim's hand,—*the union by and in God*, as opposed to *the separation by and in Ephraim* (comp. Isa. xi. 13).

Ver. 20. The symbolic sign which the prophet is to perform (ver. 16) is expressly designed for the eyes of those concerned, and, with the repetition of the thing to be done, at the same time mediates the connection with what follows.—Ver. 21 sq. treats of the effecting of the reunion of the nation, after first glancing back to ver. 12 sq. Comp. ch. xxxvi. 24, xi. 17, xx. 34, 41, xxxiv. 13.—Ver. 22. וְעָשִׂיתִי אוֹתָם לְגוֹי אֶחָד is the וַעֲשִׂיתִם לְעֵץ אֶחָד of ver. 19. The now plainly expressed signification of the stick.—Ch. xxxiv. 13, 14.—The one nation will be one kingdom. Comp. vers. 24, 25; comp. Hos. iii. 5. [According to Hävernick, the unity of the kingdom testifies to its truth, that it represents Jehovah.] Qeri יִהְיוּ, but גּוֹי might also serve as subject to יִהְיֶה. Strong and effective negation of the old, *that* has passed away for ever.—Since sin, and especially idolatry, had contributed to the separation spoken of, the discourse turns to that, ver. 23. Comp. ch. xiv. 11, xxxvi. 25, v. 11.—מוֹשְׁבֹתֵיהֶם ought not, after ch. vi. 6, 14, to cause so much difficulty to expositors. The worship of idols, which is the subject of discourse, is just localized "transgression." The relief consists in this, that idolatry disappears, ch. xxxvi. 29. To think with Hengstenberg of the places of abode in the exile, so that the earlier sins in Canaan did not come into account—that they, as it were, left their sins behind them in the foreign land, etc., neither suits the present connection,—is a thought here postponed, as Hitzig justly observes,—nor harmonizes with ver. 12 sq., according to which the exile, on the contrary, localizes the wages of sin, *i.e.* death. Alteration of the text is equally unnecessary, just as Keil's "preserving from," and Kliefoth's idea of leading out into the glorified Canaan, are imported into the text. Comp. besides, ch. xxxiv. 13.—Ch. xxxvi. 25, xxxiii. 28, xxxiv. 24. The closing statement, recurring in ver. 27, only in reverse order, seems to interrupt the consecution of the verses, so that the prophecy forms itself into two sections—vers. 21–23 and vers. 24–27—with one conclusion. What the first section contains more as to the thing done and generally, is given in the second Messianically and as to the individual, for the full completion of the thought.

Ver. 24. See on ch. xxxiv. 23.—Ver. 22.—Ch xi. 20, xxxvi. 27.—Ver. 25. Ch. xxxvi. 28, xxviii. 25, xxxiv. 24.—עַד־עוֹלָם, so that the *terminus ad quem* is "concealed," cannot be seen; hence for an interminable future, is to be understood Messianically, that is, in Christ, as shown by the immediately following לְעוֹלָם, and all that comes after. As we find expressed here without interruption (this is the peculiarity of the whole prophecy here, in distinction to that repeated from ch. xxxiv. and xxxvi.) the unity of the nation, its continued possession of Canaan, and that very plainly of the earthly Canaan, so just as plainly is all conceived of *under the dominion of the King Messiah.* Israel's nationality in Canaan is bound up (ver. 22) with this one kingdom. As to the moral and spiritual condition of the people, their position towards God (ver. 23), ver. 24 connects likewise with the one shepherd, the King David = Messiah, the "walking in, sq.," "keeping," and "doing." And in the same connection occurs Ver. 26 (likewise לְעוֹלָם, and also בְּרִית עוֹלָם), for which comp. ch. xxxiv. 25 (Isa. lv. 3; Jer. xxxii. 40). As shown by comparing ch. xxxiv. 25, and confirmed by the connection with vers. 21–23, especially ver. 23, as that is the peculiar, the leading idea of the divine covenant, to which the לָהֶם corresponds, and by the whole mode of expression here, including the repeated "giving," the making of the covenant proceeds from God in the most manifest exhibition of grace. The fact that בְּרִית שָׁלוֹם is alike explained and completed by בְּרִית עוֹלָם, expresses the Messianic character of this covenant; for the *terminus ad quem* (עוֹלָם) of Israel, still hid to appearance, is just the Messiah. In the "salvation" (שָׁלוֹם), when it embraces time and eternity, eternity in time, alongside of the ideal reference in the whole, the real side in the particular cannot be wanting; hence what is the daily bread for a nation, namely, putting them in the position of increase, cannot be wanting; therefore: **And I give them** [KEIL: to be a nation] **and multiply them**, ch. xxxvi. 10, 11, 37. But with the giving of the **sanctuary** of Jehovah **in their midst for ever,** *another Messianic type*, now in close preparation for ch. xl. sq., is presented to us in the text, in addition to the one king and shepherd for all, the servant of Jehovah, David. Comp. on ch. xi. 16. The reference to Lev. xxvi. 9, 11 is shown by the harmony of the prophecy with the promise given by Moses. And although the מִשְׁכָּן there in ver. 11 (as שָׁכַן is said of the symbol of Jehovah's presence in the wilderness) does not so much signify the outward building, and in Ezekiel too (ver. 27) it is regarded as עֲלֵיהֶם, yet בְּתוֹכָם, which stands beside מִקְדָּשׁ, points to the midst of the people; comp. Ex. xxv. 8. Hitzig is right in this, and also as to what distinguishes this passage from ch. xi. 16. But he overlooks the express reference to each other of מִקְדָּשִׁי בְּתוֹכָם לְעוֹלָם and מְקַדֵּשׁ אֶת־יִשְׂרָאֵל, ver. 28. There is, at all events, expressed a visible national unity in Canaan as formerly, one political government, which, however, as mediated by the one King Messiah, exhibits itself as a national life purified from idolatry and conformed to law, hence moral, so also an outward serving of God by Israel is here prophesied, the sanctuary of Jehovah in the midst of Israel—that this cannot be Zerubbabel's temple is triumphantly proved to the Jews by Keil, from the fact conceded by themselves, that the Shechinah was wanting to it;—but the heathen see therein (בִּהְיוֹת, ver. 28) something yet different, namely, the continuing (particip.) sanctification of Israel by God, hence religious-moral conditions. [Not merely *gratiosa Dei habitatio in cordibus eorum*, as PISCATOR.] We remember here, where what is prophesied of the **sanctuary** is so evidently connected with the promised **servant David** as **king** and **prince,** that the kingship is specially prominent in Ezekiel's figure of the Messiah (Introd. § 9); and besides this, the passage here shows that, as likewise observed in the Introduction, § 9, with Ezekiel the main point of view continues to be the Messianic nation, the Messianic salvation of the nation. And so the phrase: **My sanctuary in their midst for ever,** לְעוֹלָם explaining itself in מְקַדֵּשׁ (ver. 28), appears essentially as prophesied of the future church of salvation, the realized kingdom of priests (Introd. § 9). (Comp. Zech. ii. 14 [10]; John i. 14; Rev. xxi. 3, vii. 15; 1 Cor. iii. 16, vi. 19; 2 Cor. vi. 16.) ["This promise has, at all events, come to be gloriously fulfilled in the election which forms the stem of the Christian Church. It is again taken up in the saying of Christ: 'Lo, I am with you alway, even unto the end of the world,'" HENGST.]

At this point of the understanding of our prophecy—and herein its most important advance, in distinction to ch. xi. 16, is perhaps announced—the certainly not unintentional exchange of: **My sanctuary in their midst**, of ver. 26, for: **My dwelling over them**, in ver. 27, must decidedly be taken more spiritually than is done when Hengstenberg refers it to the "protecting power" which is afforded in the house of God (Ps. lxviii. 29 [30]), or Keil, to the "position of the temple towering up over the city." Hitzig comes nearer the truth when he directs attention to God's dwelling in heaven, directly (?) over the temple of Jerusalem (Isa. xxxiii. 5; Ps. xxix. 9, civ. 3; 1 Kings viii. 33, 34; Gen. xxviii. 17; Ps. vii. 7 [8]). The sanctification of Israel before the world, as connected with the Kingship of the Messiah, and the establishing of the eternal sanctuary of God in Israel's midst, as effected by the founding of the Church of Christ, serve for illustration and fulfilment of the עֲלֵיהֶם in Ezekiel here, as is very clear from Acts ch. ii., to which is prefixed a repeated (comp. Luke xxiv. 50 sq.) and circumstantial account of the exaltation of the Son of man, ch. i.—Ver. 23. Ch. xi. 20; Gen. xvii. 7.—Ch. xxxiv. 30.—Ver. 28 (ch. xxxvi. 23, 36). Although the mention of the heathen is still confined to the "knowing" of the sanctification of Israel, yet such knowledge cannot remain without result, without fruit; comp. Isa. xliv. 5.—"Indication of the participation of the heathen in the promised salvation" (HENGST.).—Ch. xx. 12. "To sanctify" is to purge from sin as well as to consecrate, hence embracing forgiveness of sin, and quickening. The former must become clear to the heathen from the latter, and so much the clearer as they have seen the judgment of God executed on His people—have even executed it themselves. Comp. for the harmony with the promises in the Pentateuch, Ex. xxxi. 13; Lev. xxii. 32.

ADDITIONAL NOTE ON CH. XXXVII.

["In closing this section, we present a brief outline of the view that has been taken of the prophecies contained in the three closely related chapters, xxxiv., xxxvi., xxxvii., and which in substance applies equally to many other portions of the prophetical Scriptures. 1. They were originally given to revive and animate the hearts of God's covenant-people, by holding out to them the assured prospect of a reversion from the present evil, and their still certain destination in God's purpose to the highest and most honourable place on the earth. 2. It was the duty of those to whom such prophecies were delivered at once to believe the word spoken to them, and apply themselves in earnest to do what was needed to secure its accomplishment; and had they only done this, a far larger measure of the promised good would have been reaped than they actually experienced; this later prospect of blessing, like the earlier, given before entering Canaan, greatly failed through their own sinful unbelief. 3. But there being manifestly ideal features introduced into the delineation, especially the good spoken of being so peculiarly connected with the rule and presidency of David, clearly betokens a kind and degree of blessing which could not have been completely fulfilled under the Old Covenant, nor intended to be altogether fulfilled any time according to the letter. It shows the prophecies in question to be, like several of an earlier kind in Ezekiel, descriptions of the future under the form and image of the past—not as if the past were actually to return again, but that its general spirit and character were to revive. 4. The new things thus to be looked for in the future could only meet with their full and adequate accomplishment in Christ, who is certainly the David of the promise. They are consequently of a higher and more comprehensive nature than any that could be enjoyed under the Old Covenant, when the kingdom of God was so straitened in its dimensions, and so outward and earthly in its visible constitution. But still they were of necessity described under the hue and aspect of the things belonging to the Old Covenant—as if it were these only returning again, or these with certain alterations and improvements, such as might give the future a pre-eminence in glory over the past. For only by means of what belonged to existing or previous dispensations of God could the prophet have given any detailed exhibition of what might be expected under another and higher dispensation. The details of the future *must* have been cast into the mould of things already perceived or known. 5. Therefore, in forming one's conceptions now of the real import of such prophecies—now that the transition has been made into the new and higher dispensation—we must throw ourselves back upon the narrower and more imperfect relations amid which they were written, and thence judge of what is still to come. Thus, as the David of the promise is Christ, so the covenant-people are no longer the Jews distinctively, but the faithful in Christ; and the territory of blessing no longer Canaan, but the region of which Christ is king and lord. What was spoken immediately of the one class of personages and relations, may most fully be applied to the other; and by such a method of interpretation alone do we get a uniform and consistent principle to carry us through the whole. While those, on the other hand, who would find a literal Israel, and a non-literal David, or a literal restoration in Christian times, and a non-literal tabernacle and ritual of worship, arbitrarily confound together things dissimilar and incongruous, and render certainty of interpretation absolutely impossible. 6. Sixthly, the view thus given is confirmed by the reproduction of some of these prophecies in the field of the New Testament Church, set free, as was to be expected, from the outward distinctions and limits of the Old. Thus, in particular, the resurrection-scene of this 37th chapter substantially recurs in the 20th chapter of Revelation, and is followed precisely as here by the attack from the embattled forces of Gog and Magog; while not a word is said which would confine the things spoken to the land of Canaan, or the literal Israel; it is the Church and people of Christ at large that are discoursed of. We say nothing respecting the probable time and nature of the events there referred to, but simply point to the identity in character of what is written with the prophecies before us. In those visions of the Apocalypse, the inspired evangelist stretches out the hand to Ezekiel, and shows how the word spoken so long before by that servant of God, freed from the peculiarities of its Jewish form, is to find its application to the Christian Church. The shell has gone, but the substance remains. 7. We may add, lastly, that the common interpretation, which understands Christ by David, and takes all the rest literally, must inevitably tend to justify the Jew in his unbelief. For he naturally says, Your Messiah has not done the thing you yourselves hold must be done—to fulfil the prophecy; He has not set up His throne in Canaan, and gathered Israel there, and re-established the old worship in its purity; this was the very purpose for which He was to appear, and we must wait till He comes to do it. On the basis of the literal interpretation, there seems no satisfactory answer to this; and it is well known that since it has become prevalent, many Jews believe that Christians are coming over to their view of the matter. We are not surprised to hear, as we have heard, of converted Jews declaring that such a mode of interpretation would carry them back to Judaism."—FAIRBAIRN'S *Ezekiel*, pp. 412-414.—W. F.]

DOCTRINAL REFLECTIONS.

1. What has Jehovah caused, vers. 1–10, to be prophesied for comfort to His people (vers. 12, 13)? The resurrection of the dead in the literal sense Kliefoth still maintains, a view which is the older ecclesiastical one, shared by Jews and Christians, so that Jerome, when expressing a different opinion regarding *famosam hanc visionen, omnium ecclesiarum Christi lectione celebratam*, thought it necessary to state that he did not therefore by any means wish to deny the doctrine of the resurrection. How little the connection in Ezekiel says in favour of the dogma of the general resurrection of the dead is best seen from the artificial way in which ver. 11 sq. is disposed of. Kliefoth interprets the prophesied bringing of Israel into their own land (as already, ch. xxxvi. 28) of the "final introduction of the people of God into the eternal Canaan," and the quickening in ver. 14, of "inward renewal by the Spirit of God;" an interpretation which he has also put upon ch. xxxvi. 25 sq. From similar perplexity, ver. 11 has been combined with the "first resurrection" of Rev. xx., and the bringing of Israel into their own land understood in accordance with Matt. v. 5. Hengstenberg, holding that "all the other comforting words of the prophet relate to things of this world," insists upon this connection in general, and singles out in particular ch. xxxvi. 8, "which was soon to take its beginning," and the connection of ver. 15 sq. and the vision. If the relation is this, that the house of Israel of the vision, reanimated by the Spirit of God, is "the whole" (ver. 11), and hence is to experience the reunion symbolized (ver. 15 sq.), then this union, which cannot be sought for among "the last things," will also not suppose the re-quickening of Israel past. But in addition to the contradiction between the wider and the narrower connection, comes also the contrariety of the picture drawn here to the

doctrine laid down in 1 Cor. xv.; those who rise again in Ezekiel's vision simply return into earthly existence, with skin and flesh and bones. If the doctrine of the general resurrection is maintained in ver. 1 sq., then ver. 11 sq. must more or less, as also Kliefoth gives to understand, be denied to be "in the proper sense an interpretation and explanation of the significant occurence:" we must content ourselves with an application for an express purpose, namely, in order to comfort and raise up the hope of Israel with the prospect in question (see above, ver. 1). Against this Hengstenberg, appealing at the same time to analogies in Daniel, Zechariah, and Ezekiel himself, justly observes: "Whosoever feels himself constrained to take vers. 11–14 not as an interpretation, even thereby expresses judgment concerning his view of vers. 1–10." Ver. 11 begins expressly with an explanation of the signification of "these bones," which formed the subject of discourse, vers. 1–10.

2. A question which, unless one dismisses entirely the doctrine of the *resurrectio mortuorum* from the text before us, comes into consideration is, whether this dogma already existed in the time of Ezekiel? Hengstenberg, for example, denies indeed the express application of the doctrine to our passage, but makes the dogma serve as "figure." Hence he must answer the question put in the affirmative. It is a necessary supposition, not only—as already Tertullian, *de resurr. carnis*, points out to the Gnostics, and Jerome expresses himself—that the typical application of the resurrection of the dead by Ezekiel implies the actual taking place of that resurrection, and consequently its truth must be beyond doubt, but also that the doctrine of the resurrection was already at that time a common property of religious popular knowledge in Israel, if it could thus be figuratively applied in Ezekiel. Hengstenberg (*Christology*, vol. iii. p. 51, Clark's trans.) cites Pareau's *Comment. de Immortal.* p. 109, and refers to Isa. xxv. 8, xxvi. 19; Dan. xii. 2. The raising of the dead (1 Kings xvii. 22; 2 Kings iv. 35, xiii. 21) can, as isolated cases, prove nothing in its behalf; and passages like Deut. xxxii. 39, 1 Sam. ii. 6, attest only the omnipotence of the living God. Comp. HÄVERN. *Vorles. über die Theol. des A. T.* p. 109, and his *Comment.* p. 581; OEHLER, *V. T. sententia de rebus p. mort. fut.* p. 37 sq., 42 sq. Furthermore, ver. 3 of our vision, where the prophet leaves to the Lord the answering of the question put to him, says nothing in favour of the consciousness of the doctrine of the resurrection of the dead. If there was such a consciousness, we should certainly expect a corresponding answer from the prophet. Comp. John xi. 23, 24. (Hävernick: "If the prophet could have supposed such a general belief, he would necessarily (?) have appealed to it in order to establish thereon the restoration of the people, etc. But in such a hopeless case as ver. 11 the prophet cannot make suppositions, nor will he; he will just build anew—establish firmly a new hope in the heart.")

3. Hengstenberg says: "The prophet, however, does not merely set out from this doctrine and use it as a means of representation; his primarily figurative representation, and the historical confirmation which it received, must also have served to awaken powerfully the belief in the resurrection. If God proves Himself the master of death in the figurative sense, if He redeems His people from outward and the spiritual misery into which they had fallen during the exile, how should the death of the body set a limit to His grace?" And again: "The salvation announced here under the figure of the resurrection is completed in the resurrection; comp. 1 Cor. xv. 19."

4. But the text protests also against this merely typical acceptation of the doctrine of the resurrection. There are indeed (ver. 2) "very many," according to ver. 10 "a very great army," sufficient to suggest all the dead, at any rate sufficient for the interpretation in ver. 11 of the "whole" house of Israel. They are, however, not the bones of deceased men, but of slain men, as expressly stated in ver. 9. The open surface of the valley, moreover, hardly corresponds to the situation of the resurrection of the dead; the graves in the interpretation, still closed and yet to be opened, would be more suitable. Finally, the twofold transaction in regard to the re-quickening in the vision (ver. 7 sq., ver. 9 sq.) can hardly set before the eye the representation of the awakening of the dead; but as the direct design of the vision is to make prominent the creative in what is prophesied, the thing that is possible with God alone (ver. 3), so the first and the second act, especially the observation after the first in ver. 8, that "yet breath was not in them," serves from the outset to make prominent the point of the interpretation, namely, God's putting His Spirit in them, ver. 14.

5. Hitzig's view of the vision takes more account of the noteworthy circumstance that it treats of slain men. But how? He makes (as already in ch. xxxiv., King David) the Israelites slain in the destruction of the two kingdoms be called upon by the prophet to rise again. Thus the vision is a vision of a partial resurrection. There was already a similar opinion among the Talmudists (Sanhedr. xcii. 2)—comp. on ver. 1; and it is also maintained that such a resurrection did actually take place, and even that those who rose again begot offspring in Canaan; thus one Talmudist expressly declares his descent from one of them.[1] To say nothing of the strangeness of such a view,—for which certainly the "supernatural character of the Hebrew system" offers, as Hitzig must grant, no sufficient support,—"the idea itself of the resurrection" proves nothing, but it must be maintained in ch. xxxiv. 23, 24, xxxvii. 24, 25, in order that it may be referred to for the vision before us; moreover, as to the context, such a resurrection prophecy does not fit in excellently before and after, as Hitzig supposes. For the multiplication of the people promised in ch. xxxvi. 37, 38 (comp. ch. xxxvi. 10) surely points to something else than specially a multiplication by resurrection of the slain; and the combination of the vision in the chapter here with ch. xxxviii., however ingenious and plausible, is by no means the necessary combination imperatively required by the text. Comp. the exegesis *in loc.*

[1] It may be remarked in passing, that Hävernick misapprehends the dealings between Pharisees and Sadducees in the Talmud regarding the resurrection, for the Sadducees there do not, when appealing to Ezek. xxxvii., claim the figurative as the received explanation of our passage, but only suppose in the passage not the *resurrectio futuri sæculi*, but on the contrary a merely particular, and not the general resurrection.

6. Thus the dogma of the resurrection of the dead, as well as the announcement of a "first resurrection" of Israel, or of his slain, literally understood, must be dismissed from our chapter. So also the parabolical application of that dogma is not the sense of the text. If the view is put forward that the whole is figurative, then a mere poetical figure excogitated by Ezekiel cannot certainly be harmonized with the express character of vers. 1–10; comp. on ver. 1. We have before us a divine vision, which the Lord in express revelation gave His prophet to behold. Hence there must be more to find in this vision than the clothing of an idea, "well conceived and carried out with dramatic effect" (PHILIPPS.). The objection raised by Hävernick against the view of only outward liberation of the people and the flourishing of the State anew already under Zerubbabel (GROTIUS, VATABLUS, AMMON'S *Bibl. Theol.*), and also against Ewald's deeper penetration into the matter, the objection, namely, that it is not permissible to repeat this idea from ch. xxxvi., cannot be maintained. But we have first to deal with the form, and then we will have to remember that the conformation of the thought as contained in the vision cannot be suggested by what is known and suitable for restoration of any kind, as is coming to life again out of a state of death, but on the contrary will have to be accounted for on other grounds. The vision—and this is the reason why it proceeds in the form before us—is intended to afford to Israel a strong ground for what is already prophesied to him, a specially strong encouragement against his hopelessness. The ground on which what is promised to the people is based is the creative power of God (comp. on vers. 5 and 8). "God Himself appears to the prophet as the quickener of the bones," as Hävernick justly observes. "A thoroughly real relation is treated of, namely, the relation of God to death." Then, as regards the encouragement to Israel on this ground, it must speak so much the more powerfully to their hearts, when, taking them at their word, it borrows from their despairing words the answer against all doubts. The vision (vers. 1–10) is such a thorough answer in a matter-of-fact form, because He who answers, the Promiser, is the Almighty God of Israel, who "speaks and does," ver. 14. Comp. how very near Calvin (*Inst.* ii. 10) came to this understanding. Only because Kliefoth is so confused in the exposition of our chapter does it appear that he could gather nothing from Hävernick's remarks, which so often hit the sense, and who refers with far better right than the expositors of the literal resurrection of the dead to Deut. xxxii. 39; 1 Sam. ii. 6; Hos. xiii. 14, etc.

7. The vision of Ezekiel in our chapter takes, as has been said, the discouraged of the Israelites at their word. Already in ver. 3, where the question put to the prophet tends in this direction, the way is opened up for the after interpretation. At the very outset in ver. 2, where the bones filling the valley (ver. 1), which are very many, are described as "very dry," the whole house of Israel lies before us, namely, those who say, "Our bones were dried," as the interpretation (ver. 11) puts beyond all doubt. By their speaking thus—since their "perished hope" was Jerusalem and the people in the land of Judah—the exiles in their despondency compare themselves to those who had perished in their native land; and this explains the designation "slain" given in the vision, which takes them for what they give themselves out to be, as, on the other hand, from the close interweaving of vers. 1–10 and vers. 11–14, the interpretation speaks of their places of residence in exile as their "graves." At the same time, by the bones which He places before the prophet in the valley, the judgment formerly (comp. ch. vi.) threatened by Jehovah is conceded to have taken place. Since this judgment was executed as killing,[1] to which death what of Israel still exists has given itself up (ver. 11) with full sympathy, if there is still prospect of salvation after the judgment and arising out of the judgment, this salvation can only be life, God's act of salvation, and consequently nothing but re-quickening.[2] And because the slain, to whom Israel in exile compare themselves, are to be supposed in Canaan, the bringing back of Israel to their own land is connected repeatedly (ver. 12 sq.) with the re-quickening of the nation. Thus the salvation to be prophesied is externally restoration of the nation—Israel is again in his own land. There is one element which the vision could not set forth (unless, perhaps, it is hinted at by the expression: "and stood upon their feet," ver. 10), but which the interpretation brings in felicitously through the dead bones of the vision, by the bringing of them "out of the graves." The vision has chiefly in view the inward side, namely, the quickening by the Spirit, in general the national life as such, although, as is clear from the interpretation (ver. 14), not without spiritual reference back to ch. xxxvi.; comp. the exposition.

8. "The faith of Israel in his redemption was to rest not so much on the belief in a resurrection of the dead, as on belief in God the Creator, who brings being out of nothing, who awakens life out of death, even in its most fearful form, the annihilation of all existence" (HÄVERN.). It may be said more generally regarding the significance of hope for faith, that hope demonstrates the blessedness of faith, yet is not the ground of its knowledge or certainty, but as certainly as I believe, so certainly shall I also behold—the future, which hope expectantly anticipates.

9. As has been above remarked, Rev. xx. was early introduced into the discussion. Kliefoth recently, while making "the resurrection of the dead generally, limited, however, to a single definitely bounded field of dead" (בִּקְעָה), be

[1] "It is from the beginning a fundamental law for all human development, that death is decreed for the transgression of the divine commandment; holding good in the first instance for the individual life, but also for the national domain, where the law lays hold of Jehovah's Israel as an individual personality, and sets in view before it life and death, particularly the latter, for the decision of the nation from the beginning onward takes always more plainly the similitude of Adam's decision. Captivity, or the separation of Israel from their land, announced as the last and worst punishment, is, according to the law, to be conceived of as the death of the nation. This the Old Testament consciousness looks upon as death, for the individual is related to his body as the nation to its land, and the land separated from the nation is subjected to the most fearful desolation and devastation (ch. xxxvi.), like the human body bereft of the soul. Or, as death dissolves into dust, so the captivity of Israel is its dissolution into the primal elements out of which it was at first formed, etc."—BAUMGARTEN.

[2] Hofmann rightly observes, that what is illustrated i Ezekiel is "not so much the newness of the life *into which*, as rather the completeness of the state of death *out of which* Israel is to be restored."

shown to the prophet (vers. 1–10), "because it is afterwards to be referred to the appointed resurrection of the people of God," borrows from Rev. xx. a very peculiar confirmation of this exposition of his. The ἀναστασις ἡ πρωτη in ver. 5 there, namely, is based on our passage, and the proof of this he makes to be that the souls of the πεπελεκισμενων there (who are the הֲרוּגִים here) are seen, and that both here and there Gog and Magog follow on the resurrection. He who is constrained to recognise in the first section of our chapter the re-quickening of Israel as a nation, will not be thereby hindered from conceding that it will be followed by the re-quickening of all Israel, that is, as Paul expresses it in 1 Cor. xv. 23, of οἱ χριστου ἐν τῃ παρουσια αὐτου. If this ζωοποιησις is likewise meant in Rev. xx. 4 (ἐζησαν), then the reference of our passage to it can as little be denied as that the βασιλευειν μετα χριστου may be prefigured in ver. 23 sq., the repeated לְעוֹלָם here can be interpreted by χιλια ἐτη there, the ἱνα μη πλανηση τα ἐθνη ἐτι in Rev. xx. 3 compared with ver. 28 here, and that the κριμα, Rev. xx. 4, refers to ch. xxxviii. But the beheaded witnesses of the Apocalypse of John by no means harmonize with the slain of Ezekiel; and although Gog and Magog make their appearance in Rev. xx. 8 sq., as here in ch. xxxviii., yet already Rev. xix. 17 sq. makes reference to ch. xxxix. and xxxviii. in Ezekiel. Moreover, Rev. xx. 6 also can be compared to the so often used לְעוֹלָם of our chapter.

10. "Since God as the self-existent life in itself is Spirit, all life in its various grades and forms originates and subsists only through the Spirit, which proceeds from God; the possession of spirit forms the universal ground of life, connecting the whole creation with God" (BECK.).

11. We have here ἐγειρειν and ζωοποιειν together, the full and entire conception of the sovereignty of the Father and of the working of the Son in the Holy Ghost; comp. John v. 21 sq.

12. In regard to the religious spirit which animated the returned exiles, reference has been rightly made to the prophecies of Haggai and Zechariah, and also to the psalms belonging to this period.

13. The truth of the section vers. 1–14 is not so well expressed by saying with Ewald, "that the individual or the nation that does not despair of the Divine Spirit is never in any situation forsaken by that Spirit, but is always borne onward to new life," as by saying that it has its expression in the eternity of the Church of God. "We need not," says Hengstenberg, "extend our prophecy to the unbelieving Jewish people and their future conversion. As expressly stated in vers. 12, 13, it applies only to Israel as the people of God, and the dispensation of grace grows out of this relation."

14. "It is doubtless the power of his people which the prophet sees in this vision rising up to new life; it is the sons of Israel, held in captivity and scattered, who are destined to return to the soil of their beloved heritage. But on the ground of the deep word of typical representation we read the joyous announcement: I live, and ye shall live also" (UMBREIT).

15. The reunion of Israel and Judah has, in consequence of the pronounced heathenizing character (still continuing in the Samaritans) of the former (Doct. Reflec. 4 on ch. xx.), a co-reference to the heathen; and this is more to be thought of than "the separation between believers and unbelievers," which Hengstenberg makes ensue "after the coming of Christ," as "a still worse" separation. Yea, the less Israel-Judah has become one in the Messiah, who is Christ, the more has the heathen world come into consideration for the fulfilling of the prophesied union, Rom. xi. 26: κ. οὑτω πας Ἰσραηλ.

16. As the exile of the Jews ceases in Christ, so the alienship of the heathen ends in Christ, Eph. ii.

17. "A continued separate existence of the ten tribes in some unknown region is a fable" (HENGST.).

18. Why could not the Jews, like other nations of the sinking world-dominion of Rome, preserve their nationality in a distinct state? Think of the Maccabees. Not only their exclusive national habits, but still more the Messianic hope in the heart of the nation, fitted the Jews for this above other nations. From within and from without everything was here conjoined for building up a strong and important nationality among the fluctuating nations and gods of the Old World. In both respects there was given with the return from exile a new tone to their history. (On the characteristic peculiarities of Israel, their particular national disposition, comp. the Doct. Reflec. on ch. xxxiv.) Their greater zeal for the law of Jehovah, the more decided antithesis of the national life to the heathen world-form after the exile, has been often remarked on; and also that a more definite expectation of the Messiah is clear consciousness of the pious of the land, and not of the prophetic circle alone. The Jewish people have, in the great part of them scattered through all nations, served to prepare the heathen for Christianity. Consider the importance of Jewish Hellenism; think of the net of the proselytism "of the gate" drawn through the heathen world; and do not overlook the Septuagint. How much might their gathering together in Christ into a Christian people and state have contributed to the ingathering of the heathen! When the kingdom of priests which Israel should have been became contracted to the number twelve of the apostles (Matt. xix. 28), still the effect of this mission into the world is the fulness of the Gentiles. What the emphasizing of Judah (ver. 19) already signifies, is expressly uttered in a Messianic sense by the repeated naming of the "one king" (ver. 22) as David the servant of Jehovah (vers. 24, 25). Our promise can relate only to Christian Israel, for the Jewish nation either completed itself in the Messiah by receiving Christ, or deprived itself of Him, as may be read in John xix. 15. Then with the perishing of its spirit, its flesh also perished; what still remained in form of Israel was therefore broken up by the false Messiahs, the Romans, etc. It is a fundamental mistake still to seek at the present day to see in the Jews a nation, especially when the remains of nationality—the offspring of pride—which still manifested themselves in the Middle Ages in the individual members of the race, are being ever more and more spiritualized, or even materialized, by the spirit of indifference, into cosmopolitanism.

Because they are "My people" (vers. 12, 13), Jehovah makes the leading out of exile and the return to Canaan to be prophesied to them. In view of the Messiah, He promises them a united nationality (ver. 21 sq.), and the inhabiting of Canaan for ever, the peaceable possession of the land. The promise here has nothing to do with "individuals," and what Hengstenberg says of its conditionality in this respect is superfluous. After the people of Israel relinquished their claim to nationality in presence of the manifested Messiah, there can be no further talk of their conversion as a nation to Christ (KEIL); and so much the less as the kingdom of God over Israel as a nation has passed over for fulfilment to the idea of humanity given in Israel. In this last and at the same time highest respect, the unity and eternity, kingly and priestly, under the one shepherd, here prophesied, have in Christianity—alike as regards the kingship and as regards the sanctuary (ver. 26 sq.)—their universal and also their progressive realization (John x. 16; Rev. i. 6, xxi. 3, 22 sq., xxii. 3 sq.).

19. The literally verbal interpretation of our prophet has been repeatedly spoken against. For in whatever way the prophets may prophesy the glorious future of Israel, the popular form of their discourse, expressed in accordance with the times, must not keep out of view the eternal hope of Israel, the Spirit-anointed One. Since the beginning and the end of God's march in history through the world is man, is humanity, it must seem childish to believe that the "millennial kingdom" will be centralized at Jerusalem, that this will be its capital under the Jews brought back to Palestine, that the Lord will at His coming again dwell in a real temple, and that the law of Moses, and even the ceremonial and the civil law of Moses, will be the law of the kingdom, etc. This is "realistic" exposition indeed; and while people cross and bless themselves with it against "spiritualism," the thought never troubles them that they are borne along by the materialistic current of the age. The New Testament has not thus understood, not thus expounded the Old. Comp. moreover, the penetrating and partially conclusive arguments of Keil *in loc.* against the Chiliasm of the modern Apocalyptic. From God's covenant with Abraham onward, the development of Israel moves in the direction of the formation of a nation and the possession of a land, the land of Canaan. The prophets would have been unintelligible to Israel had they prophesied to it a future without regard to these two particulars. How far that which after the judgment of the exile was prophesied, as restitution of people, land, and cultus, had to serve the purpose of affording the historical nexus and point of departure for the Messiah—to what extent what was prophesied on these points would have political earthly reality, could be discerned from the very character of the coming Messianic kingdom. A kingdom which, according to the confession before Pilate, is not of this world, could not fail to show that the apparent sensuousness of the prophecies portraying the future of the people and land of Israel is in reality spiritual allegory. In the history of the nation, in its institutions, etc., the vessels were sufficiently well placed for types and symbols, in order in due time to change the water in them into the wine of Christ.

[See additional note above, at the close of the Exegetical Remarks.—W. F.]

20. "The New Testament," says Hengstenberg, "knows nothing of a future possession of the land of Canaan." "If the fulfilment is sought in this, then the interruption of two thousand years is inconceivable, since a constant possession is here placed in prospect. With respect to the perpetual possession, we must rather look to Matt. xxiii. 37," etc. "For supplementing Ezekiel we have Zechariah, one of his immediate successors, who soon after the return from the exile predicts (ch. xi.) a desolation of the land in consequence of the rejection of the Good Shepherd."

21. The two powers which in the second section of our chapter (ver. 15 sq.) are destined to realize the idea of the symbolized unity of the nation, are the royal power (ver. 22) and the sanctuary (ver. 26). As these express that which from the commencement Israel was appointed to be (Ex. xix. 6), Israel's destiny as a nation, they are the two pillars of its unity. When the kingdom was divided, and the sanctuary was no longer the one sanctuary for all, then there came an end, first to Israel, and then to Judah. As without the raising up again of the kingdom of David, and without the restoration of the sanctuary of Jehovah, there can be no re-quickening, so there can be no reunion of Israel. That which the last destruction of the temple, on the one hand, gives to the Jews to ponder to this very hour, Pilate on the other, by his question (John xix. 15), laid on the consciences of their national representatives of that time, and in such a manner that we feel reminded of verses like ver. 22 and others here.

22. In relation to ch. xi. 16 it has to be observed, 1st, that where מְעַט occurs there we find here לְעוֹלָם—in contrast to the temporary the completion appears in a permanent form; 2d, that where we have there וָאֱהִי לָהֶם לְמִקְדָּשׁ, we have here וְנָתַתִּי מִקְדָּשִׁי בְּתוֹכָם; hence, instead of the "I, the temple" of the exile, which also appeared in Christ (John ii.), the perfect and also the final will be (Rev. xxi. 22)—as Paul says—"the temple of God are ye." As the latter will be an enduring, an eternal one, inasmuch as it forms the other side of the final tabernacle (Rev. xxi. 3), so it is explained in ver. 27 by this, that the presence of the Eternal, formerly represented by the angel of the covenant in the cloud, will now as our flesh be exalted to heaven, in consequence of which Christ "by His Holy Spirit pours out the heavenly gifts into us, His members, as He also protects and preserves us by His power against all enemies" (HEIDELB CAT. Question 51).

HOMILETIC HINTS.

Ver. 1 sq. "The hope of the Israelites lay quite prostrate; but the hope of the people of God shall never cease, because God will assuredly reveal and glorify His grace on us. Therefore God by His word always furnishes fresh courage in every affliction," etc. (DIEDRICH.)—"This valley is found indeed everywhere. In other words, is there not plenty of dead bones? The best thing is, that God still cares even for such"

(BERL. BIB.).—Ver. 2. "When our state seems to us so extremely miserable that none of God's promises will apply to it, then we should remember these bones" (STARCK).—The Church of Christ, too, may at times look like such a field of the dead.—"What else are we, too, through our corrupt nature, than dry bones, empty and alienated from the life of God and from the righteousness of Jesus Christ, until the Lord gives us His Spirit of life?" (BERL. BIB.)—"It is the Lord who makes the dead to live, who visits His people in grace and raises them again from the dust, who redeems us by His Spirit from spiritual bondage, yea, who will also in the last days awaken the dead," etc. (TÜB. BIB.)—Ver. 3. "God asks counsel of us, that we may learn to acknowledge our ignorance, John vi. 6, 7" (CR.).—"Would that all theologians had thus confessed their ignorance, and not sought to cover it with a semblance of knowledge!" (SCHMIEDER.)—"It is God Himself who gives in us the first presentiments of regeneration and resurrection" (DIEDRICH).—Not only, however, in that which is impossible with men, but in all things should we look to God.—The recourse of faith when assailed to the divine omnipotence.—"Since God is omniscient and omnipotent, the resurrection of the dead is possible; but since He has also promised it, and cannot break His word, it is also certain, John v. 25" (STARKE).—Vers. 1–3. Faith in the field of the dead world and of the dead church; what it sees (death, and with men the impossibility of life); on what it trusts (on the Lord alone).

Ver. 4 sq. "As God here addresses the bones by the prophet, so He also by the gospel speaks to the dead in sin. He says, namely, that He can quicken from death in sin; and commands the dead to hear, and to arise from the dead, or to repent, that is, to believe that they are dead in sins, and in want of divine illumination and sanctification, and to lift up their eyes to the truth which is in Christ," etc.; Rom. iv. 17; John v. 28, 29; Eph. v. 14 (COCC.).—"Even the dead must hear the word of God from the lips of men; the man of God speaks to them" (DIEDRICH).—We are in our whole life and in death directed above all to the word of the Lord—entirely to the Lord who is the Word, John i.—"The wretched state of sin dominant in a man cannot be more forcibly typified than by the state of the dead, 1 Tim. v. 6" (LANGE).—"From this we may draw an important lesson both for ourselves and others, namely, that however worn out, however unconscious and dead to our condition we may be, yet God is able to redeem us from it, and to impart a life so much the greater the less hope of life there is apparent. This makes the soul still hope against all hope, Rom. iv. 18. The worse and the more hopeless the prospect around the soul, the more is it aware that it is well with it, and that God is able of stones to raise up children to Abraham, Matt. iii. 9. Although the soul esteems all as lost, yet it troubles not itself about that, and does not say, I am lost and shall never come back, which is the language of self-love," etc. (BERL. BIB.)—"Without God there is only death, whether natural or spiritual, whereas God's Spirit is able to quicken all and everything" (STARCK).—"We have, however, chiefly to see to it that we ourselves are alive, and so, above all, may have part in the first resurrection. For blessed and holy," etc. (BERL. BIB.)—Vers. 4, 5. The word of God over the dead bones, how it *is* spirit, and *promises* life.—Ver. 6. In the resurrection of the dead it will not, however, be as the hymn says: "Then shall this very skin, as I believe, surround me."—"As this spiritual resurrection here is a gradual process, so also in conversion and renewal, the man proceeds from glory to glory, until he stands fast in the Lord, and in the power of His might, in order to walk henceforth in the ways of the Lord" (STARCK).—Ver. 7 sq.: When it is prophesied according to God's word, there are still always voices, noise, movement, and things that belong to one another come together.—"If the voice of the Holy Ghost is heard in the heart, then there is a movement of the heart, and blessed is he who obeys the impulse" (STARCK).—The wonderful experiences on the field of the dead in the churches.—But what do bones, sinews, flesh, and skin, all brought together and fitted to one another, avail without the spirit? This remark applies not so much to the confessions of the churches, as to the attempts at revival through constitutions and liturgies. Certainly the coming together of members of each body—if the passage is made to apply to "reunion" (as by Richter)—is God's work; but not when the bodies, taken from different bodies, are as a matter of compulsion bound together promiscuously. The spirit, and not the uniform, is that which truly unifies; and the consciences of men are not to be dealt with as the regimental tailor deals with soldiers. The fact that an "army" is spoken of, ver. 10, cannot certainly give the tone to our view of the Church of Christ.—Pure doctrine is not skin and bones, flesh and sinews, but spirit, which has and brings life. But those who teach their own wisdom and holiness still seek life where it cannot be found.—Ver. 9. Thou mayest prophesy to the wind, provided thou prophesiest only God's word: "Thus saith the Lord," and not: Thus must ye do.—Ver. 10. Richter suggests of this "very great army," that, consisting of those drawn "from restored Israel," it "will serve for the spiritual conquest of all the Gentile nations, and especially for the gaining over of the Mohammedans to the kingdom of Christ."—"All (?) Scripture announces that the children of Israel, once converted, will be full of zeal to subject to the gentle rule of Jesus Christ and His grace those nations which will not be extirpated as anti-Christian (!) by divine justice. These dry bones, still scattered at present upon the earth, shall be changed into preachers and apostles," etc. (Where is it said that the "army" has to conquer the world?)—"One needs no power or army when there is nothing to fight with and conquer, and no enemy to overcome. But this conversion of the world will first take place in the kingdom of the Lord when, Rev. xx., the devil shall be bound in the bottomless pit, etc. The spirit of grace and of supplication will, however, make them invincible; and the blood of the New Covenant, which their fathers shed with blind fury, will so inspire them, that they would, if necessary, drink even the cup which their Saviour drank (Matt. xx. 22). By the confession of their sin, above all, will they work to procure entrance for His name and His mysteries into the remotest lands, etc. In this the natural ability, warmth, and activity of this people will be exceedingly useful, especially, however, through the Spirit of God, Zech. ix. 15, 13, 14."—The Berleburg Bible subjoins to ver. 9 sq. the prayer: "Would that it might also please our great prophet Jesus Christ to prophesy with power, and by His intercession and mission compel the Spirit to come! Oh, what a great army will then come forth to do battle against the beast and the whore!"

Ver. 11 sq. These bones are, that is, *signify*, *sq.*, and yet: "this bread is my body," etc., is held *not* to signify!—"We see the foolishness of our flesh when we are pressed by afflictions which go quite contrary to our expectations; we then either forget the divine promises, or accord to them scarcely a half faith" (LUTHER).—The language of unbelief makes the calamity great, and God's power to help little.—Ver. 12 sq. "But He opens the graves of despair, and makes the light of a better state arise to the house of Israel, to which all the elect belong. As the spirit of life is given to the bones from all the four corners of the world, so must the true Israelites be brought together by the same spirit out of the four corners of the world, from all places, to the unity of the faith, and these obtain the inheritance that passeth not away" (HEIM-HOFFMANN).—Ver. 14. Only let us not forget that heaven is our fatherland, and that we should delight to be with Christ.—"The Lord has always shown Himself such a God in His people. His people remain for ever, and have already often experienced resurrection" (DIEDRICH).

Ver. 15 sq. "How often does God repeat His promises! how many seals does He append to them! Is it not wonderful that men doubt not withstanding? Isa. xi. 12; Hos. i. 11" (STARKE).—(We may mention here the wooden alphabets of the ancient Britons, *e.g.* the runes written or engraved upon wood.)—Ver. 19 sq. "That was a type of the union of all believers in the whole world, Jews and Gentiles, through one spirit and faith, under one Head, King, and Saviour, the promised Messiah" (TOSSANUS).—"Thus the kingdom of Israel was to cease entirely, and not to rise up again" (STARKE).—"Unity is a mark of the Spirit" (HEIM-HOFFMANN).—Vers. 22, 23. The union which is not merely two sticks in one hand (above all in a secular hand): (1) That which is preceded by separation from the State, it is a purely ecclesiastical, and *e.g.* not a military one; (2) Where the unifying Head in everything is seen ever more and more to be Christ, and not the king, as bishop of the country; (3) Where the essential thing is: to be God's people, and not so much a German Established Church.—"The separation arose from the worship of idols, and the earthly-minded never ask after unity and purity of doctrine" (DIEDRICH).—Ver. 24. Comp. on ch. xxxiv.—The royal dominion of the Anointed One as the fulfilment of God's promises, as the pledge rich in promise of eternity.—"Of the kingdom of Christ there shall be no end" (STARCK).—Ver. 26 sq. "Jesus is the temple of the Godhead, through which we obtain what we ask" (HEIM-HOFFMANN).—The covenant of peace, an everlasting covenant and a holy covenant.—The everlasting priestly kingdom of the Messiah (Ps. cx. 4), the revelation for the heathen.

4. AGAINST GOG AND MAGOG FOR THE GLORIFICATION OF JEHOVAH IN THE WORLD (CH. XXXVIII. AND XXXIX.).

CHAP. XXXVIII. 1, 2. And the word of Jehovah came to me, saying, Son of man,
set thy face towards [against] Gog, of the land of Magog, the prince of Rosh, Me-
3 shech, and Tubal, and prophesy concerning him. And say, Thus saith the Lord
Jehovah, Behold, I am against thee, Gog, prince of Rosh, Meshech, and Tubal.
4 And I lead thee back, and give rings in thy jaws, and bring thee forth, and thy
whole army, horses and riders, all of them perfectly clothed, a numerous assem-
5 blage, with long shield and short shield, all handling swords: Persia, Cush, and
6 Phut with them, all of them with shield and helmet: Gomer and all his squad-
rons; the house of Togarmah, the farthest north, and all his squadrons; many
7 nations with thee. Be prepared and hold prepared for thyself, thou and all thy
8 assemblages which assemble around thee, and be a guard unto them. After
many days thou art visited; at the end of the years thou shalt come to a land
recovered from the sword, gathered from many nations, upon the mountains of
Israel, which were perpetually for devastation; and it was brought forth out
9 of the nations, and all of them dwell securely. And thou ascendest, as a tem-
pest shalt thou come, like a cloud to cover the land shalt thou be, thou and all
10 thy squadrons, and many nations with thee. Thus saith the Lord Jehovah:
And it comes to pass on that day, words shall ascend upon thy heart, and
11 thou devisest an evil device; And sayest, I will go up to a plain country, I will
come upon those who are at rest [quiet], who dwell securely, all of them dwell-
12 ing where there is no wall, and they have no bars and gates, To take spoil
and to seize prey, to draw back thy hand over (re-) inhabited ruins, and to a
people gathered from the heathen, who acquire cattle and goods, dwelling upon
13 the navel of the earth. Sheba and Dedan, and the merchants of Tarshish, and
all his [her] young lions, will say to thee, Comest thou to take spoil? hast thou

assembled thy assemblages to seize prey? to lift silver and gold? to take cattle
14 and goods? to take great spoil?—Therefore prophesy, son of man, and say to
Gog: Thus saith the Lord Jehovah, In that day when My people Israel dwell
15 securely, shalt thou not know [experience] it? And [yet] thou comest out of thy
place, from the farthest north, thou and many nations with thee, all of them
16 riding upon horses, a great assemblage [community], and a numerous army; And
goest up upon My people Israel, like a cloud to cover the land; in the end
of the days it shall be, and [yet] I make thee come upon My land, that the
heathen may know Me when I sanctify Myself on thee before their eyes, O Gog.
17 Thus saith the Lord Jehovah: Art thou he of whom I spoke in former
days by the hand of My servants, the prophets of Israel, who in those days
18 prophesied for years that I would bring thee upon them? And it comes to
pass on that day on the day of the coming of Gog upon the land of Israel—
19 sentence of the Lord Jehovah—My fury shall come up in My nose. And in
My jealousy, in the fire of My wrath, do I speak, if there shall not be on that
20 day a great shaking over the land of Israel! And the fishes of the sea, and
the fowl of heaven, and the beast of the field, and every creeping thing that
creepeth upon the ground, and every man that is on the face of the earth shall
tremble before My face; and the mountains are thrown down, and the cliffs
21 fall, and every wall shall fall to the earth. And I call the sword upon him at
all My mountains—sentence of the Lord Jehovah—the sword of every one
22 shall be against his brother. And I carry on My plea with him in pestilence
and in blood; and overflowing [gushing] rain and hailstones, fire and brimstone,
will I rain upon him and upon his squadrons, and upon the many nations that
23 are with him. And I show Myself great, and sanctify Myself, and make My-
self known before the eyes of many heathen nations, and they know that I am
Jehovah.

Ver. 2. Sept.: . . . κ. την γην τ. M. Vulg.: *terram M., principem capitis . . . de eo.* (Another read.: על ג׳.)
Ver. 3. . . . Γωγ και ἀρχοντα.
Ver. 4. K. περιστρεψω σε . . . κ. συναξω σε . . . ἐνδεδυμενους θωρακας παντας πελται κ. περικεφαλαιαι κ. μαχαιραι. Vulg.: *Et circumagam te*—
Ver. 6. Another read.: תורגמה.
Ver. 7. Sept.: . . . κ. ἐση μοι εἰς προφυλακην. Vulg.: . . . *eis in præceptum.*
Ver. 8. ἑτοιμασθησεται . . . ἐπι τ. γην τ. Ἰσρ.
Ver. 11. Sept.: . . . ἐπι γην ἀπεριμμενην,—
Ver. 12. . . . του ἐπιστρεψαι την χειραν μου . . . πεποιηκοτας κτησεις,—
Ver. 13. . . . κ. οἱ ἐμποροι Καρχηδονιοι κ. πασαι αἱ κωμαι αὐτων—
Ver. 14. . . . ἐξεγερθηση—
Ver. 16. . . . παντα τ. ἐθνη— גוג is omitted, or they transfer it to following verse.
Ver. 19. . . . σεισμος— Vulg.: . . . *commotio*—
Ver. 20. . . . κ. ῥαγησονται τ. ὀρη κ. πεσουνται αἱ φαραγγες— Vulg.: . . . *et cadent sepes et.*
Ver. 21. . . . ἐπ' αὐτο παν φοβον μαχαιρας—
Ver. 22. K. κρινω αὐτον—
Ver. 24. Sept. . . . κ. ἐνδοξασθησομαι—

EXEGETICAL REMARKS.

Ver. 2. See ch. vi. 2 **Magog** is known from Gen. x. 2 (1 Chron. i. 5); he is one of the Japhetites. The article pointing to what is known, הַמָּגוֹג, shows that he, or rather the people denoted by him, is meant. Already Josephus, and doubtless in accordance with generally received tradition, recognises in them the Scythians. Comp. Häv. p. 599 sq., and also Gesen. *Lex.* When אֶרֶץ is expressly added, it is not necessary, with Hitzig, to seek in the syllable *Ma* from the Coptic and the Sanscrit the idea of land. Even if the translation is not to be "Gog, prince of the land of Magog," yet it does not need to be translated, with Hävernick and Ewald, as dependent on שִׂים פָּנֶיךָ: "against Gog, towards the land of Magog;" but אֶרֶץ הַמָּגוֹג is a brief expression for: *in* or *of* the land of Magog. As he is immediately entitled נְשִׂיא, it lies on the surface to see in גּוֹג the king of the land of the people of Magog. A Reubenite "Gog" is named in 1 Chron. v. 4.—It appears that we have before us rather an official than a personal name. A comparison of the word (in full יָגוֹג, like the Arab. "yagug") with גַּג, "roof," the "top" of the altar, would countenance this, if the latter is to be derived from גָּאָה, גָּא, "to be high;" hence: the high, sublime, supreme. The Tartaric and Turkish "kak," "chakan," "khan," has been thought of (a traveller calls a Tartaric chief of the 13th century "Gog Khan"). [Cocc.: "Gog denotes him who sets himself like the roof in the midst between heaven and earth, between God and men" (ch. xxviii. 14, 16).] The very probable formation of the name from "Magog" would confirm the interpretation and derivation which it implies, since the national character (for this people is to be conceived of as on the Caucasus, which Herodotus calls the greatest mountain range of the earth), and thus their nature and residence in the high north, might be very suitably outlined in the official name of their leader and representative. In form it would be as if we said, instead of the Chinese Emperor: the Chin of China. Rev. xx. 8 takes "Gog and Magog" from Ezekiel as title for "the nations which are in the four corners of the earth." That Gog represents Magog is the less surprising, because Magog on its side represents a whole complex of nations: **Rosh, Meshech, and Tubal.** For the two latter see on ch. xxvii. 13, xxxii. 26; the former between the sources of the Phasis and Cyrus, below Colchis, the latter on the coast of the Euxine, west of Trapezus. It is not exactly said that "they dwelt in the neighbourhood of Magog" (Keil), but that they are in a state of subjection, as vassals, to Gog; and this Hengstenberg, like Ewald, and ancient translators and expositors before them, find expressed by נְשִׂיא רֹאשׁ, which they render: "chief prince" (king of kings)—a combination which would be allowable (מלך ראש on coins) if it were meant to be the translation of נגד, whence also it might be repeated unabbreviated in ver. 3; ch. xxxix. 1. (It cannot be translated appositionally: "the prince, the head of Meshech and Tubal.") But some who are of this opinion appeal more to the non-occurrence elsewhere (in Scripture or in Josephus) of a people **Rosh**; while on the other side, reference has been made to the Byzantines of the tenth century, who mention *οἱ Ῥῶς*, a barbarous people about the north of Taurus. An Arabian writer of the same age knew of the heathen nation "Rus," on the Wolga itself. (Whether the inhabitants of "Rass," Koran xxv. 50, are to be cited, is very questionable.) Gesenius observes that it can scarcely be doubtful that the first trace of the Russians is here given. Comp. Hävernick, p. 604. It is curious that Hengstenberg cannot bear to see the "poor Russians" ranged among the enemies of the kingdom of God. Hitzig points out that also in Gen. x. there is subjoined to Meshech and Tubal a third nation, Tiras, which von Hammer brings into connection with Rosh, conjecturing their original abode to have been on the Araxes. The name (*Ross*, horse) seems to indicate an equestrian people, like the Scythians, under which name the Greeks very early comprehended all the nations of the north; especially, as living from mare's milk, they are described (*Iliad*, xiii. 5, 6) as "mare-milkers." In the name Roxolani (Rhoxalani), whom Bochart combines, "ala" means the same as horse (Hitzig).—Ver. 3. Comp. xxvi. 3, xxviii. 22, xxix. 3, 10.

Ver. 4. Hitzig translates the Pilel שׁוֹבֵב, "allure," just as the Targ.: "decoy." [Keil: in the sense of: to a dangerous undertaking. Hävern.: with force, as a will-less beast out of his land, away from his former path, and on to the way of destruction.] Hitzig: "The Scythian is in the outset thought of as a wild beast, which rushes aside from the path, and must first be brought back." But שׁוֹבֵב means properly: to cause one to return (a repeating and strengthening form), a meaning which Hengstenberg justly retains as the simplest and most natural. He interprets thus: in Gog, the earlier enemies of God's people, namely, the Chaldeans, reappear. For the signification of the word adopted by him he appeals to ver. 8 and ch. xxxix. 27, and compares also ver. 12, remarking at the same time, that in the appearance of Gog, ver. 17 and ch. xxxix. 8, the fulfilment of earlier prophecies is recognised in which Gog is not expressly contemplated. The giving of special prominence to the Chaldeans is not in accordance with Ezekiel's manner (see Introd. to ch. xxv.–xxxii., and on ch. xxi. 28 sq.). It is at all events more obvious, and permits us to retain exactly the proper signification of שׁוֹבֵב, to assume a reference to the inroad of the Scythians (B.C. 633) related by Herodotus (I. 103–6), the news of which induced Cyaxares to raise the siege of Nineveh. This effect, and still more the fact that the Scythians were a powerful army (as Herodotus says), which under the command of their king Madyas defeated the Medes, who thereby lost the dominion over Asia, of which the Scythians took entire possession, fitted these latter to be a serviceable form for our prophecy. It was a kind of collision of nations, like the later barbarian migrations. The polemic of Delitzsch (comp. Strauss on Zephaniah) against the "Scythian hypothesis," which Winer also calls most uncertain, is well founded as regards Zephaniah, Jeremiah, and Habakkuk. But if the Scythians, whose equestrian hordes, marching south through Syria in B.C. 626, overran Judea, neither plundered nor laid waste Palestine, etc. (Delitzsch, *Habakkuk*, p. xviii.), but "quietly went up again along the coast of the Mediterranean as they had come down as far as Philistia" (?), at any rate left behind them pre-eminently the impression of a quite sudden (that is the Apocalyptic feature, comp. Luke xvii. 24) and unexpected irruption, and not that of a definite judgment of God on Israel, like the Assyrians and Babylonians,—then the silence of the sacred record regarding this inroad of the Scythians, who (according to Herodotus) let themselves be turned away from Egypt by Psammetichus through means of presents and entreaties, is comprehensible, the question of ver. 17 made intelligible, and the compulsory bringing back in our verse explained. As they disappeared after they had shown themselves, to people's great surprise, so would they also have remained out of sight; but Jehovah will bring them back, according to His purpose and by His power, otherwise than they came the first time, and in a still different manner of appearing. For Kliefoth's observation regarding nations hitherto unhistoric, more properly nations not yet come into consideration for the kingdom of God, is applicable to the matter in hand. The prophecy points, as we shall see, far beyond the immediate historic present and its nations; and a complex of nations coming thus from the far north, such as the generic name "Scythians" (for: uncultivated barbarians) suggested, after the above-men tioned inroad into Media, etc., was excellently adapted for that purpose. Moreover, what is here said in order to give due prominence to the divine direction, and above all to the higher intention and guidance: **And give, etc., and bring thee forth,** is accounted for in ver. 10 sq. from the natural will of the people in these respects. Their wild ungovernableness is evident from the figurative expression: **give rings in thy jaws** (for which comp. ch. xxix. 4), coming between .שׁוֹבַבְתִּיךָ and הוֹצֵאתִי, and explaining both; even to the shambles (EWALD). The force which makes Gog return takes him from his own land.—סוּסִים וּפָרָשִׁים, comp. ch. xxvii. 14. Here, at all events, **horses and riders** is a decidedly Scythian trait, for the richness in horses of these hordes, mostly equestrian tribes, was already known to Herodotus; while with the expression: **all of them perfectly clothed** (see ch. xxiii. 12), an Assyrian element is introduced, thus the figure of Gog is enlarged.—קָהָל רָב (ch. xvii. 17) resumes כָּל־חֵילֶךָ, in order by the description of the armour (comp. ch. xxiii. 24) to suggest doubtless the Chaldeans. Hitzig rightly considers the large shield as respecting only an army of cavalry. We may suppose infantry, but it is better to suppose a description embracing all and sundry kinds (**handling swords,** etc.), for the Scythians are only the nucleus (צִנָּה וּמָגֵן, loosely combined). To such a description correspond also—Ver. 5—**Persia** (ch. xxvii. 10), representing the far East, **Cush** (ch. xxx. 4 sq.), the remote south, and **Phut** (ch. xxx. 5, xxvii. 10), the south-west; thus, especially as the **farthest north** is expressely added in ver. 6, altogether (like Rev. xx. 8) τα ἐθνη τα ἐν ταις τεσσαρσι γωνιαις της γης.—(**Shield and helmet,** as in ch. xxvii. 10.)—**Gomer,** Gen. x. 2 (1 Chron. i. 5), the Cimmerians, already mentioned by Homer (*Odyss.* xi. 14 sq.), dwelling at the end of the earth and Okeanos, where the entrance to the lower world is,—wretched men, enveloped in cloud, darkness, and night, and never shone upon by Helios; afterwards placed on the west coast of Lower Italy, near Cumæ, and still later supposed to be on the northern shores of the Euxine, so that the entrance into the Palus Mæotis was called the Cimmerian Bosporus; after this they were removed to the Rhipæan Mountains, into the neighbourhood of the Hyperboreans, and finally became identified with the German Cimbri and the Celtic Cymry. "The old sound of their name is still retained in the mouth of the inhabitants of Wales, who call themselves Cumri or Cymry, and their land Cymru" (DELITZSCH). May **not** the name be derived from χειμεριοι, corresponding to the cloudy, wintry nature of their territory? (Hesychius interprets κεμμερος ἀχλυς ὀμιχλη.) See DUNCKER, *Gesch. d. Alterth.* i. p. 739 sq.—On וְכָל־אֲגַפֶּיהָ, comp. on ch. xii. 14.—**The house of Togarmah** (ch. xxvii. 14), as Knobel thinks, including the Phrygians; just as the Armenians still to this day call themselves "house of Torgom" (Torkomatsi)—on Assyrian monuments "Tarkheler," from "Tagoma."—A pictorial and manifestly symbolical grouping of nations.

Ver. 7 announces from the decree concerning Gog the demand made upon him. הִכֹּן, *inf. abs. Niph. pro imperativo,* very energetic, and the more so as *imperat. Hiph.* וְהָכֵן (ch. vii. 14) follows: he himself is to be ready, and to make everything ready for leading out; or, the former referring to אַתָּה and the latter to וְכָל־קְהָלֶיךָ', recapitulated and combined by וְהָיִיתָ לָהֶם לְמִשְׁמָר, abstract for concrete, that is, he who takes care of them. [HENGST.: Thou art authority to them = they are obedient to thee. HÄVERN.: And thou art a law to them, as leader and commander-in-chief. EWALD: And thou servest as ensign to them. HITZIG (SEPT.): And thou shalt be to Me a reserve, which I hold in readiness for the coming day (ver. 8), etc., or: and stand thou at My order.] Half ironical, for it will be seen immediately how the matter turns out.—Ver. 8. The time when and the direction in which this preparation and equipment shall take place. מִיָּמִים רַבִּים', comp. Isa. xxiv. 22, according to which parallel, תִּפָּקֵד seems to signify: to "visit," and that in wrath, as the word (according to Delitzsch) does not occur in the sense of gracious visitation. Hitzig replies that it is not yet time to speak in the connection here of the infliction of punishment, and denies that פָּקַד with *accus.* of the person signifies to visit in a bad sense. But the ambiguous expression only says even here that the judgment upon Gog will begin to be prepared, hence it is not immediate infliction of punishment; the sallying forth from his land, to which he will be moved, is his visitation referred to in the connection—תִּפָּקֵד equivalent to שׁוֹבַבְתִּיךָ', ver. 4. The radical signification of the word in the Hebrew is: to seek = to examine, to inspect, to survey, from which "to visit" easily follows; hardly, however, as HITZIG: "thou shalt receive command," or as HÄVERN.: "thou art missed," that is, considered as a nation that has disappeared and perished; "then, however, thou burstest forth unexpectedly with so much the more formidable forces into the land of promise." Hävern. according to this takes בְּאַחֲרִית הַשָּׁנִים as antithetical to מִיָּמִים רַבִּים, whereas the expiration of a long time is expressly supposed to be in the last time, which is the consummation not only of the kingdom of God, but of the world generally. **Days** and **years** interchange harmoniously; that which appears in the single event as **many days** is, for the Apocalyptic eye, which ranges over the whole, the summation for that which is still outstanding, that is, still in arrears, in **years** or time generally. Of the future in general, and hence of an indefinite time, nothing is accordingly said. HENGST.: the catastrophe belongs to a quite new order of things; both phrases denote the Messianic epoch. (But as to its final terminus), Rev. xx. 7 sq.—That now the **land** comes to view is for the purpose of joining on to ch. xxxvii., as **the mountains of Israel** point to ch. xxxvi. What is said of the land, מְשׁוֹבֶבֶת' (*part. p. Pil.,* comp. שׁוֹבַבְתִּיךָ, ver. 4), "made to return from the sword," that is, after war had raged over it (ch. vi. 5), applies in substance to the people of the land, as also מְקֻבֶּצֶת' (*Pu. pass.*)—comp. ch. xi. 17, xx. 34, 41, xxxvi. 24, xxxvii. 21—shows, and still more clearly וְיָשְׁבוּ', as conclusion. [HITZIG: the turned away from the sword, not in the sense of: which has desisted from war, but: which expects no war, in careless security.] Keil connects עַל הָרֵי' with תָּבוֹא. Comp. ch. xxxvii. 22. The closer designation of them as **perpetually**, that is, continuing a long time **for devastation** (ch. v. 14), rather connects the mountains of Israel with the people assembled upon them, who possess and inhabit them. The time referred to during which they were laid waste is to be considered as previous to what was prophesied in ch. xxxvi. xxxvii.; moreover, the phrase: **from many nations**, does not necessarily point beyond the Babylonian exile, although the spiritual sense: that "the Son of God gathers, protects, and upholds for Himself an elect church, etc., out of the whole human race," readily results from it. Comp. on לָבֶטַח, ch. xxviii. 26, xxxiv. 25, 27.—Ver. 9. וְעָלִיתָ, not a mere *vox militaris* (Isa. vii. 1; comp. Rev. xx. 9), but coloured by כַּשֹּׁאָה, which signifies "subversion," destruction, as well the state (waste, desolation), as the cause which produces it; storm, as it may also denote the moment of devastation, the crash (שׁוֹא, שָׁאָה, "to come smashing down"). The continuation of the comparison by כֶּעָנָן (ch. xxx. 18) makes the translation given too obvious for its needing to be interpreted, with Hengstenberg, "like ruin." ("Gog is, as it were, desolation incarnate.") ["The cavalry of the Tanjou frequently consisted of two or three hundred thousand men, formidable by the matchless dexterity with which they managed their bows and their horses, by their hardy patience in supporting the inclemency of the weather: unchecked by torrents or by precipices, by the deepest rivers or by the most lofty mountains, they spread themselves over the face of the country, and overthrew all who opposed them."—GIBBON.]—But that, notwithstanding this, only the "covering" is held up to view, limits essentially the evil significance of this expedition; it is in the first instance merely threatening.

Ver. 10 completes, through means of subjective morality, the representation given theocratically in principle from the divine purpose in ver. 4. For although a host not only so numerous, but also so tumultuous, wild, and disorderly, is a temptation, yet Gog too is put in the position with respect to the people and land of peace on the mountains of Israel, to settle down in this peace with his nations and participate in it, as the salvation from the Jews is announced to all the world, even to its remotest corners and ends. If, therefore, Gog's impetuosity and urgency to depart from his abodes is not thence explained, then behind the thoughts of his heart we will have to assume in addition (Rev. xx. 7 sq.) ὁ σατανᾶς and his πλανῆσαι τὰ ἔθνη, and to conceive of the relation to ver. 4 as of that of 1 Chron. xxi. 1 to 2 Sam. xxiv. 1, and generally to direct our view to the world of nations, which has remained unreceptive, notwithstanding that the gospel has been preached in the whole world πάσῃ τῇ κτίσει. On the expression: **on that day**, comp. ch. xxix. 21.—יַעֲלוּ illustrates וְעָלִיתָ in ver. 9.—דְּבָרִים are not: "things," but (as **and sayest**, ver. 11, immediately proves) in the first instance: **words**, which ascend upon the heart, after they were thoughts in the heart (and so proceed out of the heart, Mark vii. 21). חָשַׁב, to settle something inwardly, to conceive in thought, to devise, especially in a bad sense, denotes the inward process which precedes and accompanies.—Ver. 11. The evil purpose is well characterized by the contrast to אֶרֶץ פְּרָזוֹת, **a plain country**, which has no mountain fortresses, no walled cities; whereby is intended, not so much: which lies open on all sides (HITZIG), as: which offers no incentive for conquest; comp. Esth. ix. 19; Zech. ii. 4. In accordance with this, בְּצוּרוֹת, in ch. xxxvi. 35, is to be understood of a high secure position. The whole description, and particularly what follows, is an idyl, which, rather than matter for dogmatism, has a symbolic character, and is especially designed to bring out the guilt of Gog through his device against such peace of God. Comp. in addition, Judg. xviii. 7; Jer. xlix. 31; Micah v. 10 sq.

Ver. 12. As such an attack is an **evil device**, so also is the intention of plundering. [Hengst. makes "the community of God to be depicted in its want of earthly defence or help, in this its disadvantage against the world, while God has reserved to Himself to be its defence." It is not, however, "the perception of this defenceless state which presents the occasion for the undertaking of the enemy;" this proceeds rather from the wanton self-sufficiency of carnal power and might.] לְהָשִׁיב יָדְךָ, a fresh instance of what the heathen had done before, connects itself with the "and sayest" in ver. 11. In מִקְנֶה (see GES. *Lex.*) here, while in other passages the sense of the word is otherwise defined (Gen. xxxi. 18, xxxvi. 6, xxxiv. 23), the possession of flocks by the patriarchs is referred to, and the synonym קִנְיָן is to be defined in accordance therewith; comp. on ver. 13. "Very beautifully does the Archaic expression delineate the revival of the patriarchal state, the resemblance which the future bears to the past" (HÄVERN.). [HITZIG: "attending to productive labour and commerce." EWALD: "who possess land and goods." Both translations obliterate the idyllic character of the description.] As טַבּוּר can be said of any height, curved elevation (Mount Tabor!), so it here signifies the same as τὸ πλάτος τῆς γῆς (Rev. xx. 9), the symbolical elevated plateau of the earth, in contradistinction to the four corners of the earth,—a position thus of prominent centrality (see Hitzig)—"the highlands of the Spirit," as Lange expresses it. Comp. on ch. v. 5. "The designation applies so much the more closely, because the land itself lies high, and, sloping both to the east and the west, exposes a navel to view" (HITZIG). Israel's peacefulness and significance—the Israel of the fulfilment in Christ—are meant to be counter-types to the restless and the essentially mean, to the rapacious, materialistic disposition of the Christless heathen world. שָׁלָל and בַּז show what alone Gog wants with the Lord's people. Hävernick rightly remarks that "the inward significance" of the conflict is meant to be portrayed. "The heathen power has assembled its forces, as if about to fight with one of the greatest world-kingdoms. According to mere human opinion, and in view of such disparity of outward power, the evil appears here to march to certain victory." Ought we not also to be able to infer from the representation given, that the community of God has at the time ceased to appear in "dominant churches," and has also dispensed with the support of the temporal arm in the way of state churches? It looks here quite like *το μικρον ποιμνιον*, Luke xii. 32, which possesses nothing except the *εὐδοκησιν* of the Father and the *δουναι την βασιλειαν*. Hävernick mentions in this connection the "true destination of the theocracy, as it is already set before us in the law," and then adds: "Israel was not intended to stand out among other nations as a politically great people in the outward sense; its weapons and honour were, in direct contrast to the powers of this world, to belong to an incomparably higher sphere." He nevertheless makes "the theocracy be an object of allurement for covetousness and plunder," in that he makes "the new nation rich in flocks and possessions," as already the Chaldee Paraphrast does,—an idea, however, which the text does not express, and which is not contained in 'עָשָׂה. In that case one could not but choose to hear in Ver. 13 the "similar interest of avarice," the "participation in joy over such a robbing expedition;" against which Hitzig: "but why are traders named, and not rather arch-enemies, like Edom and Moab?" **Sheba**; see ch. xxvii. 22, 23. **Dedan**; ch. xxvii. 15, 20. **The merchants of Tarshish**; ch. xxvii. 21, 36, 12, 25. First of all, traffic which crosses sea and land presents a contrast to the settled system and peaceful procedure, vers. 11, 12. Then further, those named by means of the clause: וְכָל־כְּפִירֶיהָ (Hitzig: "its," the land of Tarshish's, "authorities;" Keil: "the rapacious rulers of these commercial nations;" Grotius: "sea pirates"),—comp. ch. xix. 2, 3 (ch. xxxii. 2),—are placed alongside of the greedy and rapacious Gog. ("The magnates of Tarshish are designated as fierce lions on account of the heartless cruelty which goes hand in hand with the spirit of trade," Hengst.) The meaning, however, is not: "where there is spoil the traders gather," so that "the question, in the case of affirmation, implies a prospect of joyful participation" (Hengst.), for finally they figure as *connoisseurs*, as men skilled in robbery and plunder; and this not merely "for bringing out the evident desire of Gog's hordes" (Keil)—for if it is "evident," what need is there of the "bringing out"?—but rather to place an almost ironical point of interrogation after the greed and rapacity of Gog in respect to the patriarchal possessions and goods mentioned in ver. 12; somewhat thus: what wilt thou get then? as if even for them who delight to rob and plunder for their living, the greatness of the attack bore no proportion to the smallness of the object! Moreover, what is put into their mouth is in keeping with this. In the first place, they simply take up Gog's intention (ver. 12), asking in his own words, Comest thou with this intention? are thine assemblages for this? Then, however, very characteristically, the merchants, the *connoisseurs*, immediately speak of "silver and gold" as that above all which should reward such an expedition as Gog's. This, however, is not mentioned in the description in ver. 12, so that the naming again of the מִקְנֶה וְקִנְיָן looks antithetical, and this the more as the questioners conclude: **to take great spoil. To take cattle and goods** of that kind must recommend itself poorly to hordes which have come from such a distance.

After those skilled in pillage have given their dictum by their question, Jehovah now says, Ver. 14, that Gog will find it just as those of kindred spirit to him have already said.—**Therefore**, because in fact it is as those say, the prophet also shall, on God's part, confirm it (הִנָּבֵא). The interrogatory: And say to Gog, Thus saith the Lord Jehovah, In that day . . . **shalt thou not know it**? is parallel to the interrogating speakers in ver. 13 (יֹאמְרוּ לְךָ). It is so, and therefore will also be so when Gog shall be in a position to know it. [תֵּדָע has been most commonly, as already by the Chaldee Paraphrast, understood of knowing through punishment. Hävernick regards at least "the whole foregoing leading forth" as that "of the truth" of which "Gog shall have living experience." Ewald and Hitzig read תֵּעֹר (Sept.): "wilt thou set thyself in motion?"]—On that day, ver. 10.—Ver. 11.—Ver. 15. Although thou comest to this knowledge, nevertheless thou comest, etc., because (ver. 16) I make thee come according to My intention.—Comp. vers. 8, 6, 9.—**Riding horses**, etc., comp. ch. xxiii. 6. It is related of the Scythians that they eat, drink, and sleep in the saddle. Duncker remarks on Herodotus' expedition of the Scythians: "Only on the west shore of the Caspian Sea, only through the pass of Denbend was it possible that the numerous bands of cavalry (he supposes the Sarmatian tribes, which pressed forward towards the Caucasus, and that neighbouring hordes of the Scolots, from the Tanais (Don) to the Tyras (Dniester), joined in this movement) could take and open up for themselves the way to the south. It led into the heart of the Median territory."—Ch. xxvi. 7.—Ver. 16. Comp. ver. 9.—בְּאַחֲרִית הַיָּמִים combining the two designations of ver. 8.—'לְמַעַן, the divine purpose at ver. 4, in distinction to Gog's purposes, ver. 12. That which was meant to end in a plundering expedition issues in the knowledge of Jehovah; while by the expression: **when I sanctify Myself on thee**, Gog is exhibited as a parallel and at the same time an antithesis to Israel,—a parallel as Jehovah has sanctified Himself in judgment, an antithesis as He has sanctified Himself in mercy in His people. ["Known as the Holy One, whose honour and estate no one is permitted to touch, even in His weak *protegées*," SCHMIEDER.] Comp. ch. xx. 41, xxviii. 22, xxxvi. 23.

The vocative גּוֹג, ver. 16, prepares for הַאַתָּה־הוּא, Ver. 17. The interrogative form is not so much intended to make a stronger affirmation, as to call special attention to the former prophetic announcement. The affirmation to the question also does not lie in the last clause of the verse (KEIL), for this clause rather expresses the immediate contents of the earlier prophecy referred to,—what will come upon the community of God as end and consummation. That the prophets of Israel had already named Gog is directly excluded by the interrogation. If they mentioned names, these were rather other national forms, but behind all these there remained a point of interrogation; and for this reason, that especially accompanying all the prospects of grace for Israel, there remained in prospect a final judgment over his and God's enemies, over the world that withstands the kingdom of God (over the heathen world). This interrogative realizes itself here in Ezekiel by this Gog. Hence it is not only difficult to point out distinct sayings of the older prophets (EWALD: Isa. x. 6, xvii. 14; HENGST.: Joel iii. 3 [ii. 30] sq.; Isa. xxiv.–xxvii., xxxiv.; Deut. xxxii.; KEIL: Joel iii. 2, 11 sq.; Isa. xxv. 5, 10 sq., xxvi. 21; Jer. xxx. 23, 25), but also superfluous to do so, and above all to imagine "lost" passages (EWALD). The judgment of the world shall, according to the word of the prophets of Israel, be the transforming of the Church militant into the Church triumphant. ["The predictions of the earlier prophets are in so far alluded to as the victory of the kingdom of God over the heathen world, and the judgment of the Lord on it, are announced in them. It is only thus that the reference to the prophecies accords with the other contents of the section. The special announcements regarding the invasion and overthrow of Assyria and Babylon may also be included," HENGST.]—קַדְמֹנִים, קַדְמֹנִי, what in relation to the speaker, or some one else referred to, belongs to ancient times.—בְּיַד׳, Dan. ix. 10.—בַּיָּמִים הָהֵם reproduces בְּיָמִים קַדְמוֹנִים, in order to designate by the accusative of duration, שָׁנִים, "during years," the prophecy as one "going through the whole course of the times" (HENGST.). [Others, *e.g.* Hävernick, take it as an asyndeton. EWALD: "who prophesied in those days of years."]

Ver. 18 is, according to Hitzig, a quotation from the former prophecy, of which we do not see the necessity. Our verse brings to actual fulfilment what was prophesied by: **that I would bring thee upon them** (ver. 17).—**On that day,** more definitely: **on the day of the coming of Gog, etc., upon the land of Israel,** explains **upon them** (ver. 17).—Comp. moreover, Ps. xviii. 9, 16 (8, 15). בְּאַפִּי, not: "in my wrath," but the short breathing of the nose, anthropopathically as the gesture indicative of an angry man, or poetically, as in general also of the horse, lion, crocodile, etc. (אַף, from אָנַף, *i.e.* to breathe through the nose, to puff, *correl.* נָשַׁף, נָפַשׁ, through the mouth). Comp. ch. xxiv. 8.—Ver. 19. (Ch. v. 13, xxxvi. 6.) Comp. ch. xxi. 31, xxii. 21.—דִּבַּרְתִּי, prophetic perfect, not, as Hitzig, = דִּבַּרְתִּי in ver. 17, as repetition before introducing the expression left out in ver. 18, so that ver. 18 continues itself with ver. 19*b*. Forced and artificial.—By אִם־לֹא, דִּבַּרְתִּי becomes an oath: surely. The "shaking" is not merely a shaking of the earth, because the land of Israel is immediately mentioned. For this reference is made obvious by the locality of the judgment, and besides, רַעַשׁ takes place over (עַל) the ground and soil of Israel, just as Hupf. on Ps. xviii. directs attention to the shaking of the earth by thunder, and the violence of Eastern tempests. What is meant by רַעַשׁ is explained in Ver. 20; and at the same time the "greatness" of the shaking: וְרָעֲשׁוּ מִפָּנַי׳. That the mountains, etc., **are thrown down** (ch. xxx. 4), is only one element in the whole, which, as a whole, is described as a cosmic catastrophe, sympathized in by every κτισις (comp. Zeph. i. 3; Jer. iv. 25; Gen. vii. 21), like a world's overthrow. הַמַּדְרֵגוֹת, according to Gesenius, particularly: "stair-like rocks" (like κλιμαξ), from דָּרַג, from which Meier deduces the signification: rift, fissure. Proceeding from the Arabic, מַדְרֵגָה might denote something to be ascended, a height.—Every **wall** that is to fall includes natural walls, as well as those made by man.

Ver. 21. עָלָיו, because the judgment of the fury and jealousy of Jehovah is aimed at Gog and his bands.—The **sword,** thus his own weapon (ver. 4).—לְכָל, etc., HITZIG distributive: on all, sq.; KEIL: towards all, sq., indicating the direction. This, which is certainly not "forced into the connection" (HITZIG), is explained from ver. 9 (16) from the cloud covering the land. Gog's bands are in all directions, therefore also the sword is in all directions (ch. xxxix. 4).—**My mountains,** the Lord says, casting a glance at His people there (ver. 8). [Hitzig grounds it on Zech. xiv. 4 sq. (?).] For what purpose the **sword** is called for is indeed self-evident; but here one assails the other therewith in discord (contrast to the assembling at first, ver. 7), probably as usual at the dividing of the booty made. Comp. Zech. xiv. 13. Previous types, Judg. vii. 22; 2 Chron. xx. 23. In the first instance Jehovah merely "calls."—Ver. 22. He grasps it still more personally as a judge: נִשְׁפַּטְתִּי, ch. xvii. 20. The colouring for the farther description reminds us of the plagues of Egypt, whence Hengstenberg makes them be "partly taken, and from the destruction of Sodom and Gomorrah," Gen. xix. 24. Comp. also ch. xxviii. 23, and on ch. xiii. 11, 13 (Josh. x. 11). Ver. 23 proves that it is an intervention of Jehovah Himself, His fighting for His people, who are small compared with the greatness of Gog (ver. 15). — הִתְגַּדִּלְתִּי is to be understood from the contrast to the greatness of Gog. Comp. on ch. xxxvi. 23. On הִתְקַדִּשְׁתִּי, comp. on ver. 16.—נוֹדַעְתִּי, comp. ch. xxxv. 11 (ch. xxxix. 7, xx. 5, 9).—The **many heathen nations**, corresponding antithetically to the repeatedly-mentioned "many nations" (according to ver. 22).—Comp. ver. 16.

CHAPTER XXXIX.

1 And thou, Son of man, prophesy against Gog, and say, Thus saith the
Lord Jehovah, Behold, I am against thee, Gog, prince of Rosh, Meshech, and
2 Tubal; And I lead thee back, and drive thee on, and make thee come up from
3 the farthest north, and make thee come to the mountains of Israel. And I dash
thy bow out of thy left hand, and will make thy arrows fall out of thy right hand.
4 On the mountains of Israel shalt thou fall, thou and all thy squadrons, and the
nations that are with thee; to birds of prey of every kind, and to the beasts
5 of the field I give thee for food. Upon the face [flat] of the field shalt thou
6 fall, for I have spoken it: sentence of the Lord Jehovah.—And I send fire
into Magog and into [among] those that dwell securely in the isles, and they
7 know that I am Jehovah. And the name of My holiness will I make known
in the midst of My people Israel, and I will not let the name of My holiness
be profaned any more; and the heathen nations know that I am Jehovah,
8 holy in Israel. Behold it came and was done,—sentence of the Lord Jehovah,
9 —this is the day of which I spoke. And the inhabitants of the cities of
Israel go out and set on fire and burn the armour, short shield and long
shield, the bow and the arrows, and the hand-cane and the spear, and they
10 keep a fire burning with them seven years. And they shall not carry [fetch]
wood from the field, nor cut it out of the forests, for they shall keep a fire
burning with the armour; and they spoil their spoilers and plunder their
11 plunderers: sentence of the Lord Jehovah. And it comes to pass on that
day, that I will give to Gog a place of burial in Israel, the valley of the
passers-through east of the sea, and it stops the passers-through; and there
they bury Gog and all his tumult, and they call it the valley of the tumult of
12 Gog. And the house of Israel are seven months burying them, in order to
13 cleanse the land. And the whole people of the land bury them, and it is to
them for a name, on the day of My glorifying Myself: sentence of the Lord
14 Jehovah.—And they shall sever out [appoint] set men, who pass through in the
land, who bury with the passers-through those that remain on the face of the
land, to cleanse it; after the end of seven months they shall hold a search.
15 And the passers-through in the land pass through, and he [one of them] sees a
human skeleton, and sets up by it a mark, until the buriers bury it [the
16 skeleton] in the valley of the tumult of Gog. And also the name of a city
17 [is, shall be] "Hamonah" [tumult]. And they cleanse the land. And thou, Son
of man, thus saith the Lord Jehovah, Say to birds of every kind, and to
every beast of the field, Assemble and come, gather around over My sacri-
fice which I kill for you, a great sacrifice on the mountains of Israel, and ye
18 eat flesh and drink blood! Flesh of mighty men [heroes] shall ye eat, and
blood of princes of the earth shall ye drink; rams, lambs, and he-goats, bul-
19 locks, fatlings of Bashan all of them. And ye eat fat to the full, and drink
20 blood to drunkenness from My sacrifice which I have killed for you. And
ye become full at My table, with horse and chariot, mighty man and every
21 kind of soldier: sentence of the Lord Jehovah. And I give My glory
[honour] among the heathen, and all the heathen see My judgment [justice] which
22 I have executed, and My hand which I have laid upon them. And the house
of Israel know that I am Jehovah, their God, from this day and henceforth.
23 And the heathen know that the house of Israel wandered out [were carried away
captive] for their iniquity, because they were unfaithful to Me; and I hid My
face from them, and gave them into the hand of their oppressors, and they
24 all fell by the sword. According to their uncleanness and according to their

25 transgressions have I done unto them, and I hid My face from them. There-
fore thus saith the Lord Jehovah, Now will I turn the calamity of Jacob,
and I have mercy on the whole house of Israel, and I am jealous for the name
26 of My holiness. And they bear their reproach, and all their unfaithfulness
which they have unfaithfully done towards Me, when they dwell securely
27 upon their land, and there is none that makes them afraid; When I bring
them back from the nations, and gather them out of the lands of their
enemies, and sanctify Myself on them before the eyes of many heathen.
28 And they know that I, Jehovah, am their God, in that I led them captive tc
the heathen, and have gathered [gather] them to their own land, and I will
29 leave no more of them there; And I will no more hide My face from them,
because I poured out My Spirit upon the house of Israel: sentence of the
Lord Jehovah.

Ver. 2. Sept.: K. *συναξω σε κ. καθοδηγησω κ. αναβιβασω σε . . . κ. συναξω σε ἐπι*— Vulg.: *Et circumagam te et educam*— (Another reading: אל הרי.)

Ver. 3. K. *ἀπολω . . . κ. . . . της δεξιας κ. καταβαλω σε* (4) *ἐπι τα ὀρη* . . . K. *πεσῃ . . . εἰς πληθη ὀρνεων. Παντι πετεινω κ. πασιν τ. θηριοις*— Vulg.: *Feris avibus omnique volatili.* (Another reading: ועמים הבים, ולכל חית.)

Ver. 6. Sept.: . . . *κ. κατοικισθησονται αἱ νησοι ἐπ' εἰρηνης.*

Ver. 7. . . . *παντα τ. ἐθνη*—

Ver. 8. . . . *κ. γνωσῃ ὁτι ἐσται*—

Ver. 11. . . . *τοπον ὀνομαστον, μνημειον . . . το πολυανδριον των ἐπελθοντων προς τ. θαλασσαν: κ. περιοικοδομησουσιν το περιστομιον της φαραγγος κ. κατορυξουσιν ἐκει . . . κ. κληθησεται το Γαΐ το πολυανδριον του Γωγ.* Vulg.: . . . *vallem viatorum . . . quæ obstupescere faciet prætereuntes,*—

Ver. 13. Sept.: . . . *εἰς ὀνομαστον.*

Ver. 14. . . . *πασαν τ. γην, θαψαι τ. καταλελειμμενους ἐπι . . . καθαρισαι . . . μετα την ἑπταμηνον*— Vulg.: *qui sepeliant et requirant*—

Ver. 15. . . . K. *ἐσται, πας ὁ διαπορευομενος πασαν τ. γην κ. ἰδων*—

Ver. 16. . . . *της πολεως* Πολυανδριον. Vulg.: *Amona.*

Ver. 18. . . . *κριους κ. μοσχους κ. τραγους: οἱ μοσχοι ἐστεατωμενοι παντες.* Vulg.: . . . *et altilium et pinguium omnium.*

Ver. 21. . . . *ἐν ὑμιν*—

Ver. 23. Sept.: . . . *παντα τ. ἐθνη.*

Ver. 25. . . . *κ. ἐλεησω τ. οἰκον* I.

Ver. 26. Vulg.: . . . *neminem formidantes.* (Another reading: ונשאו.)

Ver. 27. Sept.: . . . *ἐκ τ. χωρων τ. ἐθνων*—

Ver. 28. . . . *ἐν τω ἐπιφανηναι με αὐτοις ἐν τ. ἐθνεσιν.* (Another reading: על אד, etc.)

Ver. 29. . . . *ἐξεχεα τον θυμον μου.*

EXEGETICAL REMARKS.

The further execution of the divine judgment, already announced at the close of ch. xxxviii., begins in ver. 1 with a repetition from ch. xxxviii. 2, 3, of the most formal address to Gog.—Ver. 2, comp. on ch. xxxviii. 4. If וְהַעֲלִיתִיךָ, etc., did not immediately follow,—and it could not follow after the execution of the judgment on Gog,—and if וְשִׁשֵּׁאתִיךָ did not stand between וְשֹׁבַבְתִּיךָ and וְהַעֲלִיתִיךָ, whereby a signification not so very far removed from this connection is suggested, then we might listen to Hengstenberg's translation (J. Kimchi): "and I six thee,"—by which he understands the infliction on Gog of the six plagues of ch. xxxviii. 22. Others, too, appealing to ch. xlv. 13 (שִׁשִּׁיתֶם), have interpreted from שֵׁשׁ: I leave a sixth part of thee. But the position of the word (which is Ezekiel's own) here assigns to it most fittingly an intensifying sense, such as: drive, or the like (see Hävern. *in loc.*). Meier holds the Piel שִׁשֵּׁא to be an abbreviated form = שִׁאשֵׁא. Gesenius (שָׁשָׁא) translates: "and lead thee forth." It is said that the signification: "to walk along," "to march," is admissible from the Ethiopic, hence here conjugated only transitively. Following the Chaldee ("I lead thee astray"), Ewald renders it: "and entice thee away and keep thee in leading-strings," which Hitzig finds good (!). Rashi: "deceive thee."—Ch. xxxviii. 9, 16.—Ch. xxxviii. 6, 15.—Ch. xxxviii. 16, 8.—Ver. 3. The left hand holds the bow, the right bends it and fits on the arrow. It does not even come to an attack, because, ch. xxxviii. 21 sq., a **sword**, etc. consumes Gog.—Ver. 4. אַפִּיל of ver. 3 leads to תִּפּוֹל here.—On עַל הָרֵי׳, comp. ch. xxxviii. 6, 9, 22.—עַיִט is: "animal of prey," therefore more exactly described here by צִפּוֹר, "bird generally."—Comp. ch. xvii. 23. Hengst.: "as many as have wings."—Ch. xxix. 5.—Ver. 5. On account of the previous "beast of the field," the "mountains of Israel" are changed for **the face of the field.**—Ch. xxiii. 34, xxvi. 5.

Ver. 6. If we are not to extend the judgment "also over the land of Gog and all (?) the heathen who dwell securely" (Keil), which, however, **is** plainly expressed both by בְּמָגוֹג and by וּבְיֹשְׁבֵי

לָבֶטַח הָאִיִּים, then we must, with Hengst., take הָאִיִּים for "states and countries in general," "islands in the sea of the world," and understand the "security" to be such as "induces them to the expedition against the people of God" (!!); or we must, with Rosenm. at וּבְיֹשְׁבֵי, etc., think of ch. xxxviii. 13. But the **fire** does not necessarily compel us to agree with either of these, for it does not stand here as in ch. xxxviii. 22, but apart by itself, so that we have to compare here, *e.g.* ch. v. 4, and the many similar passages in which it occurs as a symbol of the divine vengeance. Our chapter, while it carries into further detail, also supplements the picture given in ch. xxxviii. Thus the judgment extends from the mountains of Israel, as also שִׁלַּחְתִּי expresses, "to Magog," the people concerned, in among them at home; while their collective character (comp. ch. xxxviii. 2) is then again depicted by the expression: **those that dwell securely in the isles.** Gog's expedition is made by land, but has its sympathisers in islands and coast lands as well as at home—in fact, over sea and land (לָבֶטַח appears to be retaliation, with a reference to ch. xxxviii. 8, 11, 14). The return to the point of departure of this extension of judgment, as indicated in ver. 7, by the expression: **in the midst of my people Israel,** forms no argument against the so plain contents of ver. 6; for not only has the purposed knowledge of Jehovah (ver. 6) to be more closely defined, but preparation has also to be made for the execution, ver. 9 sq.—Comp. on ch. xxxvi. 20 sq. (ch. xxxviii. 23). Hengst. translates thus: "and I will not any more profane," etc. אַחֵל is Hiphil. The revelation of holiness in Israel precludes further profanation of Jehovah in reference to Israel among the heathen; comp. in addition, ch. xxxvii. 28.

Ver. 8. The fulfilment is assured to the prophet with as much certainty as if it were already an accomplished fact. That which **came and was done** is made abundantly plain by the **day, etc.,** for which comp. ch. xxxviii. 18, 19 (not ver. 17). —Ver. 9. Israel, for whom the Lord has put an end to the fearful assault in a manner still more fearful, now takes a walk, as it were, out to the place of judgment. Everything by which the enemy could terrify,—in general: **armour,** properly: what is joined together (נֶשֶׁק), as distinguished from specialties which follow—wooden helmet and breastplate, probably covered with leather; then (comp. ch. xxxviii. 4) **short shield,** etc., and מַקֵּל, of uncertain derivation, "twig," "cane," "staff"—with יָד certainly not: "handstaff," or "cudgel" (Num. xxii. 27), or "baton of the commander," but the riding-switch so suitable for bands of riders as here,—all these have so lost their terrors, that they now come into consideration only as firewood—for useful appliance, in direct contrast to the terror and injury they were meant to produce. For the weapons of the enemy are not here, as often elsewhere, burnt at once after the battle; and with this Hävernick connects Isa. ix. 4, and recognises in the destruction of the most diverse kinds of weapons, and the cleansing of the land in this (?) respect, the character of the Messianic times; while Hitzig brings out simply the thought that Israel under his protecting God, who has just now fought for His people, needs no weapons, but the inhabitants of the cities of Israel (יֹשְׁבֵי עָרֵי, etc., antithetic to יֹשְׁבֵי הָאִיִּים, ver. 6) make fires of and burn the wood in question **seven years** long. Hitzig makes בִּעֲרוּ inchoative ("to set on fire"), and הִשִּׂיקוּ "to make a fire." The undoubtedly symbolic character of the number seven (symbol of the divine covenant) illustrates at the same time the very dramatic character of the whole of the rest of the account. HENGST.: "the word on which faith has to live puts on, as it were, flesh and blood, to gain an influence over the fancy, in which frightful forms so readily take their seat. It would be against the evidence to attribute a real import to the specialties, which are so obviously only means of representation." "He who has seen the battle of nations at Leipzig," observes Schmieder, "has a weak copy of Ezekiel's sublime description of the days after the battle."—Ver. 10 strengthens what has been said positively by a corresponding negative description, and subjoins שָׁלְלוּ and בָּזְזוּ—not, however, in order to make the riches now, as the heaps of wood formerly, to fall into the hands of Israel, but simply to make manifest the retaliation (comp. ch. xxxviii. 12), and perhaps also to bring to remembrance the question (ch. xxxviii. 13), but how differently now over the dead bodies. For what the weapons as firewood for Israel, as well as the spoiling and robbing, declare is this, which consequently is meant as preparation for ver. 11, namely, that Gog and his bands are all dead corpses (Isa. xxxvii. 36); comp. besides, Jer. xxx. 16.

Ver. 11. What Jehovah gives to Gog in Israel, how different from that which he intended to take to himself in Israel! מְקוֹם־שָׁם קֶבֶר, not so much: "a spot where he may be buried in Israel" (HITZIG), as: "a place where there is a grave in Israel," to wit, nothing else is for him in Israel; HÄVERNICK: "namely, a quite special one, like no other in Israel." Thus will God settle accounts with the predatory and rapacious Gog. [The Sept. doubtless read שֵׁם.]—גֵּי הָעֹבְרִים Hitzig translates: "the valley of the opposite heights," formed by mountains standing over against one another (1 Sam. xvii. 3); he reads גֵּי־הָעֲבָרִים, and makes a very far-fetched reference to Zech. xiv. 4, 5! According to Hävernick, the passage reminds of Joel iii. (the valley of Jehoshaphat), but the name belongs purely to the idea, to which it entirely corresponds, for a "valley of the passers-through" is not found elsewhere in the Old Testament; but the prophet himself gives a threefold explanation of the name—in ver. 11, as an annoyance, an object of horror for the passers-by; in ver. 14 reminding of the men that pass through the land to cleanse it; and thirdly, of the hostile bands that formerly passed through here. Only the latter reference can come into consideration if the traditional punctuation is to be retained, and the appellation: "valley of the passers-through," is, like the "valley of the multitude of Gog," to be considered as given as a memorial of what had taken place. The text, however, seems rather to suppose a valley which can be designated as that "of the passers-through," and, because it can be a valley for the passers-through, is fitted to be a burial-place for Gog and his followers; moreover, גֵּי, "low ground," may remind us of יַעֲלוּ, etc. in ch. xxxviii. 10, אֶעֱלֶה in ver. 11, etc., as a contrast thereto. Gog and his bands can be beheld in their Scythian prototypes (as described by Herodotus), as well as with reference to "passing through" (passing by), because their whole appearance was to be merely that of a passing thunder-cloud (ch. xxxviii. 9, 16); nothing was abiding except their grave. That which Jehovah will give to Gog as מְקוֹם־שָׁם קֶבֶר, is more exactly described by גֵּי הָעֹבְרִים; and "the valley of the passers-through," again, is the one fitted to be "the valley of the tumult of Gog." The situation of this is more exactly fixed, and consequently conceived of as an actual locality, by קִדְמַת הַיָּם, which (קִדְמַת, *stat. constr.* prefixed as a preposition) can yield no other meaning than: **east of the sea.** But the context tells nothing about what sea is spoken of, although in other instances it always fixes the particular sea, and indicates when it does not expressly mention the nearest. Hence, and so also with גֵּי הָעֹבְרִים, we are referred to the idea which upholds and animates the whole with its symbolic character. בְּיִשְׂרָאֵל excludes only the Red Sea. Ewald translates thus: "as a place where a grave in Israel is possible (!), the valley of the devourers opposite the sea, and which confines the breath of travellers;" and he understands thereby "the frightful, unhealthy valley opposite the Dead Sea (ch. xlvii. 8), which covers the proud of old, the Sodomites, and still has its name from them, and the smell of which, even far off, stops up the nose of travellers (Rev. xx. 10; comp. with ch. xiv. 10)." There can be no doubt that when expositors understand here the Dead Sea, its designation as הַיָּם הַקַּדְמֹנִי is floating in their mind. Hitzig's objection, that the valley did not as yet, and never did, generally bear the name, is of no weight, when the only thing that comes into consideration is, whether Jehovah in the prophet can say of it עֹבְרִים. The introduction of "proud" is far-fetched, unfounded. Keil, who makes the valley to be "without a doubt the valley of the Jordan above the Dead Sea" [so also SCHMIEDER: "the valley of salt, on the extreme border of the land of Israel, near Mount Seir (comp. ch. xxxv. 2), reminds us of a defeat of the Edomites (comp. Ps. lx., David's psalm of victory), and of Chedorlaomer, Lot, and Abraham (Gen. xiv.); and the adjacent Dead Sea is the abiding type of all divine judgments"], denies, under appeal to Gen. ii. 14, that קִדְמַת הַיָּם can (?) mean "east of the sea," and translates thus: "facing the sea." But the Mediterranean Sea is by no means excluded by the fact that "the whole land of Israel lay east of the Mediterranean," for קִדְמַת הַיָּם can very well be made parallel with בְּיִשְׂרָאֵל, just to qualify the description, especially if we would reflect on the apocalyptic signification of the sea as the fluctuating life of nations! Keil's exposition of the הָעֹבְרִים, as referring to the "travellers (?) who pass through the land, or more particularly those who pass over from Peræa to Canaan," has no significance for the explanation from the type of the Scythians, or from Ezekiel's description of Gog's expedition (see above), and also very little significance in itself, as it is supported by no other passage of the Old Testament. What is affirmed by the expression regarding the valley: וְחֹסֶמֶת, etc., is made quite clear by the following phrase: וְקָבְרוּ שָׁם, etc., whether we assume a reference to ver. 14 sq., or infer from ver. 12 sq. who are the buriers as also the callers (וְקָרְאוּ), or simply render it: they bury and they call it. The עֹבְרִים are of course the same as those alluded to in גֵּי הָעֹבְרִים. By the valley in question they (Gog and his bands) are hemmed, shut up, enclosed, bridled in, which is the meaning of חָסַם (Deut. xxv. 4); it is, as it were, their muzzle (מַחְסוֹם, Ps. xxxix. 2 [1]), after all their "words" which rose up, ch. xxxviii. 10. It cannot be a "blocking up of the way" that is spoken of, when it is plainly said: "the passers-through." Their grave in the valley is the stopping and finishing of them and their going up. A blocking up of the way for travellers can hardly be thought of, since—and perhaps not without significance, as we shall see—the following representation in ver. 14 sq. supposes an unhindered passing through in the land. [The Sept. dreamt of a walling round of the unclean place. Hitzig, indeed, does the same.] Hengstenberg, too, removes the valley, on account of its name, to "the great commercial and military road,"—the one, namely, "between Egypt and the Euphrates,"—and seeks to show from HERGT (*Palæstina*, p. 77) that it is the valley of Megiddo, famed as a battlefield; the expression: "east of the sea," implies that "a well-known and celebrated valley pretty near the sea" must be meant, such as Megiddo, a narrow pass or region abounding in ravines, which hinder the passers-through. Such passes, he observes, are found there. In this "dangerous locality the prophet makes Gog be overtaken by the divine judgment." But where is that said in the text which simply makes Gog be buried there? In all probability, says Hengstenberg, Lejun (Legio), the later name of Megiddo, is derived from our passage, corresponding to the multitude here (**tumult**); and this is the more probable, as in ver. 16 the adjacent city also will receive the name "great multitude." Since the prophecy regarding Gog (he goes on to say) was during the Roman rule certainly applied pre-eminently to it, men eagerly anticipated the time when the great heathen grave at Megiddo should receive the Roman legions. Hengstenberg further observes: "From גֵּיא הֲמוֹן (ver. 11) is formed the Κυαμων of Judith vii. 3, to which the camp of Holofernes extends; and so also Καμμώνα is, according to the *Onom.* of Eusebius, six Roman miles from Legio." Rashi, following the Chaldee paraphrase, places the valley to the east of the Sea of Tiberias (Lake of Gennesaret), and Βαιθσὰν (בֵּית שְׁאָן, "house of rest"), as named by the Greeks Σκυθόπολις, has been said to favour this. This latter name is certainly inconceivable from "Succothpolis" (as Grimm on 1 Macc. v. 52 still maintains), yet it requires no settlement of Scythians in the seventh century B.C.; but from the population, in great part heathen, which settled there during the Babylonian exile, the name may have become current in the post-Maccabæan age, while the exposition or application of our prophecy, particularly ver. 16, may also have had some influence in the matter (see Häv. p. 599 sq.). Comp. besides, ch. xxxi. 18, xxxii. 31; on הֲמוֹן, ch. xxiii. 42. A kind of pendant to this, ch. xxvi. 13!

Ver. 12. Since קֶבֶר בְּיִשְׂרָאֵל (ver. 11) is the main element in the description, this קֶבֶר is repeated immediately, and again in Ver. 13. First, **the house of Israel** is mentioned, and then **the whole people of the land;** neither of these have needed to fight. Their enemies fell by Jehovah, who has left nothing for them to do but to bury. —According to this parallelism of the two verses, the clause: **in order to cleanse the land** (the number seven, as in ver. 9), will have to be illustrated by the statement: **and it is to them for a name;** hence, that the cleansing of the land from the dead bodies, and the zeal displayed therein (ver. 14 sq.), will cause the people of the land to be named, to wit, a holy people, or will thereby make them a name. [HÄV.: "As the people thoroughly separated from heathenism." HENGST.: "That the house of Israel should bury the foe, not the reverse, serves them for fame; which, however, has its root not in themselves, but in their God, who can deliver from death, and send destruction on their enemies."] Comp. moreover, ch. xxxiv. 29. As there: blessing instead of reproach, so here: holiness instead of the former uncleannesses of Israel. Those now cleanse the land with all diligence who formerly defiled it with all manner of abominations, etc. Perhaps there is also an allusion to the name Israel (בֵּית יִשְׂרָאֵל, ver. 12), intimating that this people wrestles with God, and therefore prevails! יוֹם, **on the day**, accusative of the time of Jehovah's glorification of Himself by the overthrow of Gog, and, finally, by his grave in Israel.

Ver. 14. To be understood in the sacred interest of the cleansing of the land.—"Men of constant continuance" (תָּמִיד) are appointed to the office permanently, or at least for a lengthened period. There are two kinds of them: "the passers-through in the land" (antithetical to Gog's "passing through"), and those who bury with the "passers-through," *i.e.* as ver. 15 explains, with their help, and following the marks they set up.—הַנּוֹתָרִים (Niphal particip. from יָתַר) are those who, notwithstanding the seven months' burying, still remain on the face of the land, forgotten, neglected corpses or skeletons. Therefore, after the expiration of the seven months, the appointed men that have been spoken of enter on their office.—Ver. 15. It can hardly be without intention that the עֹבֵר is thus repeated, and so strongly emphasized: וְעָבְרוּ הָעֹבְרִים. These "passers-through" for the purpose of burying are set in characteristic contrast to the "passers-through" who passed through the land.—וְרָאָה, etc. explains, by way of example, the task of the "passers-through." After seven months it must indeed be עֶצֶם.—צִיּוּן is a guide-post of stone—here as a mark for the buriers proper. But all comes finally into the one great grave of Gog.—Ver. 16. The great burying still perpetuates itself in the name of a city: הֲמוֹנָה, an echo of הֲמוֹן. Thus what has taken place lives on with posterity. Comp. besides on ver. 11. [SCHMIEDER: "There could not be an inhabited city in this valley of the dead; it must be a city which consists not of houses but of graves."] The cleansing of the land, however, remains the chief thing; hence it is again added by way of conclusion.

Ver. 17, linking on to ver. 4, does not bring forward a parallel to the burying of Gog and his bands. We have rather to think of something that came in immediately after Gog's fall on the mountains of Israel. A further carrying out of the statement: "to birds of prey," etc. in ver. 4. But Gog's grave in Israel is the divine monument, the actual token, that Jehovah is the Holy One in Israel (ver. 7); and this result, this old truth, Israel at the same time proves on his part with all zeal; through the repeated and finally emphasized burying in order to cleanse the land. Now, as the skeletons are buried in that valley, so, on the other hand, the flesh of them is immediately devoured on the mountains of Israel by the birds and beasts of prey. Not only is Israel to prove itself a holy nation, a nation of priests, but Jehovah will forthwith, on the fall of Gog, make known His holiness in the land, in the midst of Israel (ch. xxxvii. 26 sq.); and זִבְחִי, etc., the likewise repeatedly-mentioned "sacrifice," will have to be taken in connection with this. It has been commonly observed that Ezekiel had in view only Jer. xlvi. 10; Isa. xxxiv. 6; but comp. also Zeph. i. 7. Jehovah as Sacrificer. That "the Lord takes for Himself the sacrifice refused to Him," whereby the idea of the *cherem*, the contrast of the sacrifice, is introduced, has been dragged into the text by Hengstenberg. The **sacrifice** (זֶבַח) is, however, expressly declared to be the "sacrifice which I have killed for you" (ver. 19). In this way the idea of sacrifice is essentially resolved into that of the sacrificial feast connected with the זֶבַח (ch. xxix. 5, xxxi. 13, xxxii. 4 sq.; Rev. xix. 17). Jehovah as Host, who sends forth the invitation by the prophets. There is no want of food or of drink. Ver. 18 makes prominent, in this respect, גִּבּוֹרִים (ch. xxxii. 12, 27), captains, and נְשִׂיאֵי הָאָרֶץ (**princes of the earth**); comp. Rev. xix. 18; and also in the following figurative expression: פָּרִים (**bullocks**), strengthened by מְרִיאֵי בָשָׁן כֻּלָּם, **fatlings of Bashan all of them** (since Bashan, renowned for its fat meadows, is often applied in the prophets to proud, despotic, wanton enemies of God and His people; comp. also Ps. xxii. 13 [12]), enlarges upon those set forth at the beginning. There is, besides, a comparison with the small cattle fit for sacrifice, on which Schmieder observes: "for food to the beasts, as the flesh of the sacrificial animals for the priests."—Ver. 19 (ch. xvi. 28, xxiii. 33) describes a lavish sacrificial banquet. לְשָׂבְעָה, continued still more definitely by וּשְׂבַעְתֶּם, etc., in Ver. 20.—Jehovah's table is the battlefield.—If רֶכֶב alongside of סוּס is "chariot," then, of course, the fighters in chariots are meant. Hitzig will not admit the supposition of chariots of war in respect to the Scythians. Hence others think of "cavalry" (GESEN.) or "cart-horses."—גִּבּוֹר, from ver. 18, whoever has proved himself brave, like the captains, as distinguished from whom אִישׁ מִלְחָמָה, the equipped and practised men of war individually.

Ver. 21. On כְּבוֹדִי (**My glory**), comp. pp. 40, 52. Even until the final judgment over the world—yea, how significantly here!—does the leading thought of Ezekiel's prophecy sound forth perceptibly; in respect to the heathen, explained by the clause: **and all the heathen see,** etc., it lies before their eyes (ch. xxxviii. 23); comp. Rev. xvi. 7. יָדִי is inferred from עָשִׂיתִי.—Ver. 22. The converse relation, to wit, to Israel. In this relation the text notes the knowledge of Jehovah as Israel's God, the God of them who belong to Israel (אֱלֹהֵיהֶם, וְיָדְעוּ), and that by His having manifested Himself as such in the final judgment and thenceforth; hence an abiding relation that can no more be disturbed. The יָדְעוּ (ver. 22) now leads over in Ver. 23 to a corresponding knowledge, in addition to the וְרָאוּ, ver. 21, on the part of the heathen also. From the end Jehovah directs their regard back to their oppression of Israel, by carrying them away captive. The heathen now know that their power over Israel was Israel's guilt, defined more particularly as מָעֲלוּ, etc. (comp. on ch. xiv. 13), their unfaithfulness to Jehovah, in consequence of which Jehovah hid His face from them (Deut. xxxi. 17), and abandoned them (comp. ch. xvi. 27). כֻּלָּם, in general, *exceptis excipiendis.*—Ver. 24 (ch. xxxvi. 17 sq., xiv. 11). Comp. ch. vii. 27.

Hengstenberg sees in vers. 25-29 a "close of the whole system of prophecies of a predominantly comforting character, from ch. xxxiii. 21 (?) onward, as the prophet had already closed complete sections with a like finale." After the heathen are pointed back to the past, the application is made with לָכֵן, **therefore** (because Jehovah has dealt with them as in ver. 24), to the present (עַתָּה) of Israel.—Comp. on ch. xvi. 53.—**Jacob** corresponding as much to "misery" as **Israel to** "pity;" a significant alternation. Comp. ch. xxxvi. 5, 6, 21 sq.; comp. first on ver. 7.—Ver. 26. וְנָשׂוּ, etc. [HENGST.: "they take upon them, sq."] is to be read: נָשְׂאוּ. Comp. ch. xvi. 54. Jehovah's jealousy for His holy name (ver. 25) shows itself among Israel subjectively *in*, as well as objectively *on* them. Because their guilt against Jehovah (ver. 23 sq.) shall be known, as by the heathen so by themselves, and fully only by themselves, they bear their misery as their reproach (כְּלִמָּתָם); hence to **reproach** is added **unfaithfulness**, etc. (ver. 23). Only they appear miserable (ver. 21); only Jehovah appears glorious. Where deserved punishment comes over *them*, righteousness appears before Jehovah: they exhibit themselves as worthy of reproach, obliged to reproach themselves because of their faithlessness; Jehovah manifests Himself as holy, but, at the same time, as their God (ver. 22), faithful in pity as in judgment, who will turn aside their misery (ver. 25). Their reproach and all their unfaithfulness must burden them so much the more from the very fact that they dwell securely, etc. Comp. on ch. xxviii. 25, 26, xxxiv. 28. This humbling grace is the objective practical proof of Jehovah's jealousy over them, which Ver. 27, stretching back beyond ver. 26*b*, and casting a glance at their desire during the present state of exile, follows out farther. [Hitzig, who reads וְנָשׁוּ, translates: "and they shall forget their reproach," which they have hitherto borne. It has also been proposed to translate: they shall "take away," *i.e.* expiate, etc. Ewald would admit the rendering: "they bear," if we were to read מִכֹּל for וְאֵת כָּל; and so he too translates: "that they may forget their shame," etc., and assumes a play of words, because "in fact the whole is a play of words upon the Chaldeans."—בְּשִׁבְתָּם has been understood by others, *e.g.* Grotius: "when they dwelt."] For the rest, comp. as to ver. 27, ch. xxxviii. 8, xxxvii. 21, xxxvi. 23 sq., xx. 41.—Ver. 28 (ver. 22).—Ewald wrests בְּהַגְלוֹתִי, etc. into its direct opposite, for, reading מִן instead of אֶל, he now finds the sense to be: "in that I caused them to return from among the heathen." The context certainly does not compel him to this. On the contrary, it suggests the significant parallel: אֶל, אֶל.—Ch. xxii. 21.—אוֹתִיר, comp. ch. vi. 8, xii. 16. Hengstenberg observes on this: "after the fall of the Chaldean monarchy, access to their native land was free to all Israel, and those who voluntarily remained yet had in Canaan their home, and in the temple at Jerusalem their spiritual dwelling-place."—Ver. 29. Comp. vers. 23, 24. A promise of never-failing grace on account of (אֲשֶׁר, "because") God's having poured **out His Spirit,** where formerly His "**fury,**" ***e.g.***

ch. xiv. 19, xxii. 22; comp. on ch. xxxvi. 27; but here more significant, as perhaps שָׁפַךְ indicates. Ewald remarks on the "ebullient language," although he expounds the outpouring of the Spirit to this effect: that Israel, "just because including in it from of old the Divine Spirit, is the indefeasible foundation of the true Church." Comp. Isa. xxxii. 15, 16, xliv. 3; Joel ii. 28 (ch. iii. 1 sq.). SCHMIEDER: "Spoken in anticipation of the time which the Lord promises. And the Lord, through Jesus after His glorification, actually poured out the Spirit in Jerusalem, according to His promise. But the house of Israel would not; and is the spiritual Israel of Christendom more thankful to God?"

ADDITIONAL NOTE ON CH. XXXVIII., XXXIX.

[Ezekiel's object in the chapters before us was, "through the Spirit, to present a picture of what might be expected in the last scenes of the world's history; and according to the native bent and constitution of his mind, the picture must be lifelike. Not only must it be formed of the materials of existing relations, but it must be formed into a perspective with manifold and intricate details; yet so constructed and arranged, that while nothing but the most superficial eye could look for a literal realization, the great truths and prospects embodied in it should be patent to the view of all. What, then, are these? Let it be remembered at what point it is in Ezekiel's prospective exhibitions that this prophecy is brought in. He has already represented the covenant-people as recovered from all their existing troubles, and made victorious over all their surrounding enemies. The best in the past has again revived in their experience, freed even from its former imperfections, and secured against its ever-recurring evils. For the new David, the all-perfect and continually-abiding Shepherd, presides over them, and at once prevents the outbreaking of internal disorders, and shields them from the attacks of hostile neighbours. All around, therefore, is peace and quietness; the old enemies vanish from the field; Israel dwells securely in his habitation. But let it not be supposed that the conflict is over, and that the victory is finally won. It is a world-wide dominion which this David is destined to wield, and the kingdom of righteousness and peace established at the centre must expand and grow till it embrace the entire circumference of the globe. But will Satan yield his empire without a struggle? Will he not rather, when he sees the kingdom of God taking firmer root and rising to a higher elevation, seek to effect its dismemberment or its downfall, by stirring up in hostile array against it the multitudinous and gigantic forces that lie scattered in the extremities of the earth? Assuredly he will do so; and God also will direct events into this channel, in order to break effectually the power of the adversary, and secure the diffusion of Jehovah's truth and the glory of His name to the remotest regions. A conflict, therefore, must ensue between the embattled forces of heathenism, gathered out of their far-distant territories, and the nation that holds the truth of God. But the issue is certain. For God's people being now holiness to Him, He cannot but fight with them and give success to their endeavours. So that the arm of heathenism shall be completely broken. Its mightiest efforts only end in the more signal display of its own weakness, as compared with the truth and cause of God; and the name of God as the Holy One of Israel is magnified and feared to the utmost bounds of the earth.

"Such is the general course and issue of things as marked out in this prophecy, under the form and aspect of what belonged to the Old Covenant, and its relation to the world as then existing. But stripping the vision of this merely temporary and imperfect exterior, since now the higher objects and relations of the New Covenant have come, we find in the prophecy the following series of important and salutary truths. 1. In the first place, while the appearance of the new David to take the rule and presidency over God's heritage would have the effect of setting His people free from the old troubles and dangers which had hitherto assailed them, and laying sure and broad the foundations of their peace, it should be very far from securing them against all future conflicts with evil. It would rather tend to call up other adversaries, and enlarge the field of conflict, so as to make it embrace the most distant and barbarous regions of the earth. For the whole earth is Christ's heritage, and sooner or later it must come to an issue between the adherents of His cause and the children of error and corruption. Though the latter might have no thought of interfering with the affairs of Christ's kingdom, and would rather wish to pursue their own courses undisturbed (see on xxxviii. 4), yet the Lord will not permit them to do so. He must bring the light of heaven into contact with their darkness; so as to necessitate a trial of strength between the powers of evil working in them, and the truth and grace of God as displayed in the kingdom of Christ. 2. From the very nature of the case, this trial would fall to be made on a very large scale, and with most gigantic resources; for the battlefield now is the world to its farthest extremities, and the question to be practically determined is, whether God's truth or man's sin is to have possession of the field. So that all preceding contests should appear small, and vanish out of sight, in comparison of this last great struggle, in which the world's destiny was to be decided for good or evil. Hence it seemed, in the distance, as if not thousands, as formerly, but myriads upon myriads, numbers without number, were to stand here in battle array. 3. Though the odds in this conflict could not but appear beforehand very great against the people and cause of Christ, yet the result should be entirely on their side; and simply because with them is the truth and the might of Jehovah. Had it been only carnal resources that were to be brought into play on either side, victory must inevitably have been with those whose numbers were so overwhelmingly great. But these being only flesh, and not spirit, they must fall before the omnipotent energy of the living God, who can make His people more than conquerors over all that is against them. And so in this mighty conflict, in which all that the powers of darkness could muster from the world was to stand, as it were, front to front with the people of God, there were to be found remaining only, on the part of the adversaries, the signs of defeat and ruin. 4.

Lastly, as all originated in the claim of Messiah and His truth to the entire possession of the world, so the whole is represented as ending in the complete establishment of the claim. The kingdom through every region of the earth becomes the Lord's. He is now universally known and sanctified as the God of truth and holiness. It is understood at last, that it was His zeal for the interests of righteousness which led Him to chastise in former times His own professing people; and that the same now has induced Him to render them triumphant over every form and agency of evil. And now, all counter rule and authority being put down, all disturbing elements finally hushed to rest, the prospect stretches out before the Church of eternal peace and blessedness, in what have at length become the new heavens and the new earth, wherein dwelleth righteousness.

"It may still, perhaps, seem strange to some, if this be the real meaning and import of the vision, that the prophet should have presented it under the aspect of a single individual gathering immense forces from particular regions, and at the head of these fighting in single conflict, and falling on the land of Israel. They may feel it difficult to believe that a form so concrete and fully developed should have been adopted, if nothing more local and specific had been intended. But let such persons look back to other portions of this book, especially to what is written of the king of Tyre in ch. xxviii. (which in form, perhaps, most nearly resembles the prophecy before us), and judge from the shape and aspect there given to the past, whether it is not in perfect accordance with the ascertained characteristics of Ezekiel's style to find him giving here such a detailed and fleshly appearance to the future. There Tyre is not only viewed as personified in her political head, but that head is represented as passing through all the experiences of the best and highest of humanity. It is, as we showed, a *historical* parable, in which every feature is admirably chosen, and pregnant with meaning, but all of an ideal and not a literal or prosaic kind. And what is the present vision, as now explained, but a *prophetical* parable, in which, again, every trait in the delineation is full of important meaning, only couched in the language of a symbolical representation? Surely we must concede to the prophet, what we would never think of withholding from a mere literary author, that he has a right to employ his own method; and that the surest way of ascertaining this is to compare one part of his writings with another, so as to make the better known reflect light upon the less known—the delineations of the past upon the visions of the future.

"At the same time, let us not be understood as declaring for certain that the delineation in this prophecy must have nothing to do with any particular crisis or decisive moment in the Church's history. It is perfectly possible that in this case, as in most others, there may be a culminating point, at which the spiritual controversy is to rise to a gigantic magnitude, and virtually range on either side all that is good and all that is evil in the world. It may be so; I see nothing against such a supposition in the nature of the prophecy; but I must add, I see nothing conclusively for it. For when we look back to the other prophecy just referred to, we find the work of judgment represented as taking effect upon Tyre, precisely as if it were one individual that was concerned, and one brief period of his history; while still we know blow after blow was required, and even age after age, to carry forward and consummate the process. Perfectly similar, too, was the case of Babylon, as described in the thirteenth and fourteenth chapters of Isaiah; it seems as if almost one act were to do the whole, yet how many instruments had a hand in it, and over how many centuries was the work of destruction spread! We see no necessity in the form of the representation, or in the nature of things, why it should be otherwise here; none, at least, why a different mode of reaching the result should be expected as certain. We believe that as the judgment of Tyre began when the first breach was made in the walls by Nebuchadnezzar, and as the judgment of Babylon began when the Medes and Persians entered her two-leaved gates, so the controversy with Gog and his heathenish forces has been proceeding since Christ, the new David, came to lay the everlasting foundations of His kingdom, and asserted His claim to the dominion of the earth as His purchased possession. Every stroke that has been dealt since against the idolatry and corruption of the world is a part of that great conflict which the prophet in vision saw collected as into a single locality, and accomplished in a moment of time. He would thus more clearly assure us of the certainty of the result. And though, from the vast extent of the field, and the many imperfections that still cleave to the Church, there may be much delay and many partial reverses experienced in the process; though there may, too, at particular times, be more desperate struggles than usual between the powers of evil in the world and the confessors of the truth, when the controversy assumes a gigantic aspect, yet the prophecy is at all times proceeding onwards in its accomplishment. Let the Church therefore do her part, and be faithful to her calling. Let her grasp with a firm hand the banner of truth, and in all lands display it in the name of her risen Lord. And whichever way He may choose to finish and consummate the process,—whether by giving fresh impulses to the hearts of His people, and more signally blessing the work of their hands, or by shining forth in visible manifestations of His power and glory, such as may at once and for ever shame into confusion the adversaries of His cause and kingdom,—leaving this to Himself, to whom it properly belongs, let the blessed hope of a triumphant issue animate every Christian bosom, and nerve every Christian arm to maintain the conflict, and do all that zeal and love can accomplish to hasten forward the final result."—FAIRBAIRN'S *Ezekiel*, pp. 425-430.—W. F.]

DOCTRINAL REFLECTIONS.

1. With our two chapters the prophecy of Ezekiel passes over to the apocalyptic (comp. Introd. pp. 19, 20. Comp. in general what is said by Lange in the introduction to the Revelation of St. John, p. 2 sq.). Characteristic apocalyptic features as to form and contents are perceptible, just as the very circumstance that the New Testament Apocalypse begins with the transition of ch. xxxvii. to ch. xxxviii., to borrow important (eschatological) elements for its closing

visions, must suggest something apocalyptic. The prophetic element, the element of doctrine and of application, still pervades ch. xxxviii., xxxix., but this element will subside, ch. xl. sq.; and our chapters, too, present to us and delineate a tableau of unity,—the impressive picture of a national expedition, a migration of nations, a battle of nations, and still more of God. Although contained in the word of prophecy ("Thus saith the Lord"), yet the description of the march of the army (ch. xxxviii.), and of its fearful overthrow in Israel (ch. xxxix.), assumes, as elsewhere, the appearance of a vision. Scene succeeds scene. The style is typical to such a degree, that what of historical from the past or present may here form the basis, assumes at once the form of pure symbols, whose idea stretches far beyond the Old Testament theocracy, and on to the end of time. The consummation of Israel shows itself as the consummation of the world. The contrast of the world to Israel is in our chapters not so much the traditional one of the heathen as opposed to the people of God, as coarse callousness, resembling insensibility, in relation to the peace in which the royal priesthood, the people of the possession of an eternal covenant of Jehovah (ch. xxxvii. 26), delight themselves. Compare the impressions and utterances of Balaam in Num. xxiii. 9, 10, so very different from ch. xxxviii. 11 sq.! On the other hand, the impelling force to the savage irruption into the quietness of such a people in the land is appropriately conceived, viz. on the one part, as divine compulsion of the Judge overruling to the end in view, it is high as heaven (but comp. ch. xxxviii. 4 with xxxviii. 10 sq.); on the other part, as demoniac selfishness and worldly-mindedness, it is deep as hell. Considering the apocalyptic character of our two chapters, with which the remainder of the book of Ezekiel announces itself, the suddenness of Gog's appearance on the scene and also of his overthrow is worthy of observation, reminding us of the ἐν ταχει (Luke xviii. 8), and of the oft-repeated ταχυ of the Revelation of St. John, and also of the final completeness of the judgment and its execution.

2. Hengstenberg has very justly observed: "We have here a good preparation for the exposition of the vision of the new temple." But what he pronounces a specialty of Ezekiel,—how "wide a space" is given by him to "painting," how "attentive" he is "to fill the imagination with holy figures,"—depends rather on the apocalyptic character of the prophecy regarding Gog. Moreover, to confront the imagination of timidity with the imagination of faith, to pour forth light and comfort in opposition to thoughts despairing of the future, is precisely a mark of all apocalypse proper. Lange says beautifully and strikingly of apocalypses in this respect: "As they have proceeded from the divine quieting and comforting of a longing of the hearts of elect prophets, which flamed aloft in times of great oppression of the kingdom of God, so they are also designed to direct and guide, to comfort and calm, in the first place, the servants of God, and through them the Church, in times of similar and fresh oppression in the future—nay, even to change for them all tokens of terror into tokens of hope and promise."

3. In Hengstenberg's interpretation, at all events, not only does the "so-called biblical realism" entirely disappear, to which, as he says, it so often happens to take the garb for the man, but, as the exposition has already incidentally indicated, the nations named in ch. xxxviii., although in themselves historical, appear in the connection here as elements of an idea which is summed up in the symbolic Gog of the land of Magog, namely, as the last outbreak of enmity against the kingdom of God. This symbolized idea is at all events also historical—nay, even world-historical in the highest sense, or pertaining to the universal judgment. The world's history is theocratically determined by it, determined by the kingdom of God finally developing itself into the consummation of humanity and the world. But Magog, Gomer, Meshech, Tubal, Sheba, Dedan, and Phut are as such no longer historically to be found. Of Cush Hengstenberg asserts: that it is "a Christian people, and such a one as, according to recent experience, will scarcely again attain to world-wide influence."

4. As Grotius and others, *e.g.* Jahn (Introd. ii.), interpret of the days of the Maccabees and Antiochus Epiphanes, so Luther found in our chapters the Turk, who, even in the hymns and prayers of the Church, was for a long time firmly held to be, together with the Pope, the chief enemy of German Christianity. While individual Jewish expositors apply what is said sometimes to Rome, and sometimes interpret it of the Crusades, yet we find also in Shabb. cxviii. 1; Berach. vii. 2; the Jerusalem Targum on Num. xi. 25; Deut. xxxiv. 2, Gog shifted into the times previous to the Messiah, and the battle, in which the Messiah annihilates Gog, discoursed of. Likewise, in reference to the Messianic kingdom, the Sibylline books speak of Gog and Magog, placing him in the farthest south of Egypt (see Hävernick, p. 602). In the notices which the Koran makes of *Dzu-Ikarnayn, i.e.* Alexander the Great and his adventurous warlike expeditions (*Sur.* 18 and 21), Yagug and Magug are designated as mischief-makers on earth, and enclosed by an iron wall; which, however, will be at last turned to dust, whereupon Gog and Magog break forth, and the universal judgment ensues. (SPRENGER: *Das Leben und die Lehre des Mohammad*, ii. p. 474 sq.) "The fear of these northern nations," says W. Menzel, "is very ancient, and has been justified by the Scythian, and afterwards by the Hunnish-Mongolian warlike expeditions, which have already often overrun both Europe and Asia; and this Oriental popular tradition coincides (?) with the widespread German tradition of the armies of Charlemagne or Barbarossa sleeping in the mountain, which will burst forth at the end of the world, and conquer a new golden age."

5. Hävernick adduces the following reasons for the interpretation of the time as the time of the completion of the kingdom of God. (1.) The names, which do not so much indicate single nations then existing, as that we have to do with a "view of future new relations only starting from the present." "Whatever far remote, more or less known, national names can be named, the prophet collects here; and specially important is the free formation of the name Gog." (2.) The connection with ch. xxxvi., xxxvii. represents the way prepared for the glorification and completion of the theocracy; the judgment over Edom (ch. xxxv.) is regarded as having taken place, in which old hereditary enemy, the enemies hitherto

of the covenant-people appear judged in their immediate neighbourhood. It still remains, however, "to marshal the entire (?) world-power in its sinful insurrection against God (?), and thus to perfect the salvation," just as this idea lies at the foundation of the fourth, the Roman empire, prophesied by Daniel, the contemporary of Ezekiel (EUSEB. *Demonstr. Ev.* ix. 3). (3.) The prophetic denunciation of heathen nations always regards them as representatives and supporters of definite ideas,—in Edom the hitherto antitheocratic tendency, in our prophecy the idea of future enmity as experienced by Israel in the completion of its salvation. (4.) The fulfilment is, in ch. xxxviii. 8, 16, expressly placed in the latter days. (5.) The announcements of former prophets, referred to in ch. xxxviii. 17, point to the judgment of the last day, just as also the prophet's picture is made to conform with those models. (6.) Lastly, the resumption of the subject in Rev. xx.—It tells particularly for the apocalyptic character of the representation given by Gog, that it is pervaded not only by reminiscences of Assyrians and Chaldeans—of Edom only locally, indeed ("on the mountains of Israel," comp. on this point ch. xxxv. with ch. xxxvi.)—but also by presentiments of much later heathen powers. For it is quite in the apocalyptic way and manner always to present to us types stamped anew from history as it gravitates towards the end of the world.

6. In the Introduction, p. 19, the importance of Ezekiel's position in the midst of the Babylonian world, and with that his acquaintance with foreign nations and their relations, have been adverted to. In Babylon, if anywhere, there was a standing-place for surveying the rolling waves of the sea of nations. The prediction regarding Gog, peculiar to our prophet, will have to be conceived of as to its human side from his peculiar abode on such a watch-tower in the midst of the heathen. Philippson justly observes: "We must remember that Ezekiel was placed in the midst of the inner-Asiatic world, and hence had opportunity of observing the great movements therein. Here, in the bosom of the national movements of Asia, it must have been clear to the prophet that these movements were far from having reached their end, that the dynasties would still change often, and that these concussions could not fail to affect also the countries on the Mediterranean." At all events, although our prophecy is not the result of the incidental observations, the far-sighted political reflections, etc., of a gifted man, yet, as the magnificent architecture of Nebuchadnezzar might furnish Ezekiel with views for ch. xl. sq., so the fluctuating sea of nations, which he saw and heard of in Babylonia, may perhaps have furnished him with the colours in which he paints the figure of Gog and his bands.

7. Our prophecy has been explained from the very natural question after ch. xxxvii. — will this peace of Israel continue always undisturbed? will the relations of the rest of the world take such a shape that Israel can remain in peace? So Philippson. "The dogmatic idea of the prophecy," says Hengstenberg, "is very simple: the community of God, renewed by His grace, will victoriously resist all the assaults of the world. This idea the prophet has here clothed with flesh and blood," etc. The prophecy, then, is more or less a parable. We come back to this. "The starting-point," continues Hengstenberg, "is the fear which penetrates the sick heart. What avails it, is the question that met the prophet, even if we recover, according to thy announcement, from the present catastrophe? The predominance of the heathen still remains. Soon shall we sink under another attack into permanent ruin. Against such desponding thoughts the prophet here offers comfort. He unites all the battles which the restored community has in future still to endure into one great battle, and makes this be decided by *one* glorious victory of the Lord and His people." The latter is as arbitrary as what has been said regarding the idea of the prophecy is general and superficial. Hävernick, connecting with ch. xxxvii., says: "How powerful that protection is which the Lord accords to the new glorified theocracy, is shown by its new relation to the heathen world and its power. The holy people are truly an unassailable, inviolable possession of their God. As such, Israel in its glory is the grandest, the most thorough victory over the heathen world. Hence the future of Israel stands in the most striking contrast to its present. While heathendom is now an instrument in the hand of Jehovah for the chastisement and purification of Israel, then comes the time when Israel's destiny is fulfilled, namely, to execute the final judgment on heathendom. In it is then revealed the completion of the victory of the kingdom of God over the heathen world-power." However much of what has been said is right and proper, yet the reason assigned by Hävernick for "this fundamental idea" is not quite satisfactory as he puts it, namely, that "God Himself occasions the battle (the last rallying of the power of heathendom to annihilate the king- of God), that His judgment may in it be revealed." God, however, will judge only that which, whether in self-righteousness (Pharisaism), or in worldliness (Sadducism), has, by the rejection of His counsel of salvation in Christ, shown itself ripe for judgment. In connection with this subjective ripeness for judgment, we are reminded of the deceiving by Satan, Rev. xx. World, or heathendom without further qualification, is not the idea of this so individual prophecy regarding Gog. Lange is entirely in the right when he doubts (*Pos. Dogm.* p. 1280) whether Gog and Magog represent generally all the future enemies of the kingdom of God; and he gives the hint to the understanding of the chapters before us when he declares: "We must, however, think chiefly of the obscure residue of nations which has not come under the full operation of the kingdom of Christ, of barbarous and haughty tribes."

[On the whole of this 7th section, compare the above Additional Note at the close of the Exegetical Remarks.—W. F.]

8. For the explanation of the prophecy before us we have not to search after questions of this or that kind put by Israel, which the prophet was bound to answer, as, indeed, nothing like this is intimated in the text (comp. in opposition on ch. xxxvii.); but Jehovah, in ch. xxxviii. and xxxix., simply sets the end clearly and truly before His people, at that time in Israel, and in this sense we have here ἀποκαλυψις before us. If we want an inscription on the double picture in Ezekiel, ch. xxxviii. and xxxix., there is no more appropriate one than the saying of Christ in Matt. xvi. 18: και πυλαι ἁδου οὐ κατισχυσουσιν αὐτης—a

saying not understood in its apocalyptic significance. If we have to understand ch. xxxvii. in Christ, how much more free from doubt will the proper understanding be when the subject is again referred to in such a manner at the end of ch. xxxix. And so Gog, etc. cannot mean heathenism, or heathenism in the last effects which it may produce, but must mean the obdurate world as opposed to Christianity, the world which has remained farthest away from the spirit and frame of Christianity as we find it described in Ezekiel; the most remote north as opposed to the central in this world (ch. xxxviii. 6, 15; comp. on ver. 12). That which has been maintained regarding the final stiffening down of our planet into ice, has its apocalyptic truth rather in respect of the definitive position of the human heart to Christianity, as possibly our Lord also intimates when He says, Matt. xxiv. 12: δια το πληθυνθηναι την ἀνομιαν ψυγησεται ἡ ἀγαπη των πολλων. To a finally developed egoism and worldliness, to a materialism ripe for judgment which can no longer think of anything except plunder and robbery, the μαμωνας της ἀδικιας, as opposed to the ideal powers which go to make up Christianity (righteousness, peace, and joy in the Holy Ghost, Rom. xiv. 17), the community of God, the Lord's people, appear—and this Ezekiel plainly pictures out (comp. ch. xxxviii. 12 with ver. 11)—in its meaning and essence a high-flown ideal, which men, after having at least ceased to persecute it, partly because they purely ignore it, and partly because they expect with scientific certitude its collapse, its death, after the manner of the old heathen religions (the πυλαι ἀδου), will have to take down from its height and simply crush with force. This, according to ch. xxxviii., is the position of the world in the time of Gog. If the "millennial kingdom" is to approximate to the picture with which ch. xxxvii. closes, the conception of it will necessarily be very different from what the imagination of many apocalypticists, still adhering to the old Jewish sensuous tradition, dreams it to be. But even in the *locus classicus* of the millennium, Rev. xx., the putting of Satan in chains is mentioned as the main point for the symbolical thousand years. The binding of him is the necessary preliminary of the millennial kingdom. If he is not to deceive the nations during this time, but after this does so again, then it is clear, even from that to which he afterwards deceives them, that his confinement is above all the cessation of war with violence, of violent combating of the community of God, just as also the immediately following vision of the witnesses unto blood (Rev. xx. 4) seems particularly to point in the same direction. Regarding the "fair reality of the kingdom in its glorious manifestation," the ἐζησαν, certainly distinct from the ἀνεζησαν (ver. 5), only tells us forcibly thus much in relation to a certain number, that they, given over, indeed, to death by the world, are in reality alive (comp. also John xi. 25 sq. with Rev. xx. 6); the "thrones," however, and the "judgment," already express virtually the "reigning as kings," which is only more exactly defined by the expression: "with Christ," and that as a reigning in heaven without any express reference to earth, to which the only reference mentioned is the binding of Satan. But this heavenly vision (ver. 4 sq.) is assuredly meant for comfort, as is the certainty of final victory (comp. moreover, μικρον χρονον, ver. 3), when Gog and Magog (Rev. xx. 8) march to battle upon the centre of the earth (ver. 9).

9. The misconceptions of the traditional exegesis in respect of the chapters before us, and the corresponding passages in the Revelation of John, thus relate on the one hand to the appearance of Gog, and on the other to the position and state of the true Israel, the Church of Christ, in the last days. With respect to the latter, we have remarked on the idyllic picture in ch. xxxviii.; comp. also the exposition. Rev. xx. 9, by means of το πλατος της γης (ch. xxxviii. 12) belonging here, points with παρεμβολη των ἁγιων and πολις ἡ ἠγαπημενη rather to ch. xl.–xlviii. (at least more to them than to Zech. xii. 7, 8), if these two Old Testament theocratic designations of Israel are not meant simply to denote the Church, the people of God, without any special reference. Yet, considering the reciprocal action between the unseen world and the seen, especially in the last days, when the transformation of the world is at hand and everything is prepared for it, any reflex whatever of the Church triumphant in heaven will unquestionably affect its earthly compeer, the Church on earth, during the thousand years. If it holds true for this time also that ἡμων γαρ το πολιτευμα ἐν οὐρανοις ὑπαρχει, ἐξ οὑ sq., according to Phil. iii. 20 sq., then something corresponding in the Church on earth of the last days must run parallel to the life, the enthronement, the reigning with Christ of them who have overcome,—a "time of great peace and festivity," as Lange expresses it, an ideality of life, shining so much the more brightly as the rest of mankind are under the sway of materialism, have become the slaves of enjoyment, and serve Mammon; and if the judgment on the world will be realized in presence of the latter-day community, yet on the other hand a time of final, and perhaps "most successful activity" previous to that may be reckoned upon; comp. in our prophet ch. xxxvii. 28, xxxvi. 36. As the Chaldean world-power of Ezekiel's time, with its "many nations" (עַמִּים), out of which, in the first place, Israel is gathered, ch. xxxviii. 38 (ver. 12, גּוֹיִם) is reproduced as Βαβυλων (Rev. xiv. 8, xvii. 5, xviii. 2), so also, as in Ezekiel from the passages cited, not only will "many nations" (Ezek. xxxviii. 16, 23) besides Gog and Magog have to be supposed in the Revelation of John, but the binding also of Satan, "that he should deceive the nations no more" (Rev. xx. 3), suggests the operation of the community of God upon them to bring them to the knowledge of Him. Nay, since Gog, brought up by Jehovah, like Balaam formerly, is in a position to view the people of peace assembled and encamped upon their hills—this view, which can scarcely entice a nation supposed to be rude and barbarous but still simple, may symbolize to us a virtual mission, the latest missionary activity which the community of God on earth, as such, puts forth; so that, alongside of the temptation which leads to being deceived by Satan through the besetting sin of Gog (ch. xxxviii. 10 sq.), who is perfectly conscious of what his heart purposes and expresses in vers. 11, 12, we not only hear the ironical incitements of ver. 13, but above all the aspect of the community of God, virtually giving testimony everywhere of salvation and peace upon this earth, as it lives securely solely by faith in its King, without worldly protection or power, is to be looked upon as a last

dispensation and expression of God's long-suffering and grace in relation to Gog, which he in his ripeness for judgment despises (comp. the exposition). That Gog's purpose and expedition are to be aimed directly against God is a feature at least foreign to Gog as drawn by Ezekiel, and has to be inferred even in Rev. xx. 9; for the final attack is rather directly against the people of the Lord, and only indirectly against Himself, who, however, manifests Himself from heaven in behalf of His people.

10. Although the Reformation regained the knowledge of the truth, both as respects the supreme authority, the word of God, and the foundation laid, namely, Christ, yet church life as church life was not reformed, but only the Cæsar Pope succeeded to the Pope Pope. The episcopal power was given over to the hands of the State, and thereby the Church only sank into a new servitude, which was a purely secular one. This may well be called the "Babylonish captivity" of the community of God. Pietism, however much it emphasized life in opposition to creed, furnished the theory for this, since its method is solely to influence and form the individual. Thus the Reformation made no breach with Byzantinism—it may be said that that was not the antithesis of the Reformers; but they left it possible for the State also to become evangelical. As since the Reformation—*i.e.* the attempt of ecclesiastical reconstruction upon the foundation of the apostles and prophets, in which Christ is the corner-stone—the modern sovereign-powers have come forward politically, as Ranke says, so since then, under the title of the gospel, a State-churchism has been more and more developed, which, when compared with the fundamental declaration of Christ regarding His kingdom (John xviii. 36), is no less a caricature of the holy than is the Church-state. If the whore become wife (Rev. xvii.), who formerly rode upon the beast, is finally to be destroyed by the beast, perhaps we are near to this point of time. The complete apocalyptic history of Antichristianism, however (Rev. xiii.), sets also in prospect the case that the spirit of a fallen Christianity, the false prophet, can be active, in the service of the political world-power, to bring about something of the form of a universal world-church, with legally social exclusiveness. The judgment of Antichristianism, as of pseudo-Christianity (Rev. xix. 17 sq.), appears in relation to their adherents as a spiritual, moral destruction, namely, by the sword of Him who sits upon the white horse, and which goes out from His mouth; so that the Antichristian world, slain as with a sword by the word of Christ, which should have rescued them to life, now affords room for the enjoyment of peace and dominion to the quiet community of the latter days. If the description of the closing battle against Christ in the Apocalypse of John, borrowed from Ezek. xxxix. sq., consciously conforms itself to the description given there, that will intimate that it has an affinity with Gog's final war against the Christian Church, that what begins with the Head has to be completed with the members, but that the victory of the King with His army contains in it the assurance of victory for His people to the end. But does not the very fact that rude force like that of Gog and his bands will bring about the conclusion of the development of Christian salvation for this world, also imply the corresponding recompense for the being sunk in materialism, in the common mock-reality of earthly things? And how, then, accordingly do the first heavens and the first earth pass away? It may farther be worth observing, for the social form of the world during the time previous to Gog's making his appearance, that after the judgment in Rev. xix. 17 sq. no "kings of the earth" figure any more, that the Revelation of John significantly renews "Gog and Magog" solely as national titles. The "social democracy" threatened for the future discuss only materialistic themes, just as the science destitute of philosophy labours in a similar sphere. But the victory of Christianity, the absolutely religious truth, will always be on this earth only a spiritual victory. The victory that overcame the world is our faith, 1 John v. 4. Comp. besides, John xviii. 36, which is called, in 1 Tim. vi. 13, the καλη ὁμολογια της πιστεως (ver. 12). The idea of a preliminary transformation of the world, even when put into a more real shape, as a mediating transition-period, conformable to the laws of life and to the development of life, remains, however, affected with a certain show, a mere display, the necessity of which is so much the more difficult to see, as Gog, notwithstanding, again comes up over it; and it would be much more in accordance with the moralo-theocratic law of the ripening of mankind for final judgment, that this ripening for judgment should fill up its measure on the quiet community of God, which presents in opposition to the materialistic world and its spirit of the times nothing but its unique ideality in Christ and with Christ—this indeed in a purity and sanctity unsullied by any secularity and worldliness. Comp. ch. xxxvi. 38, xxxvii. 28, and the burying of Gog's dead recorded afterwards, ch. xxxix., in a way that tells for such a character. The church-idyl of Ezekiel in the chapters before us may be compared with the apostolic church of primitive Christianity. The first period and the last, when thus laid together, form a circle.

11. "Neither as to letter or spirit was this prophecy fulfilled under the Old Covenant, and, moreover, many single passages of it are incapable of being understood in the literal sense. For example, when at the end of ch. xxxix. the Israelites are to be brought back from the lands of their enemies without a single one of them remaining behind, and that God poured out His Spirit on the house of Israel. As the kingdom promised in ch. xxxvi. is in this world, indeed, but not of this world, so the resurrection of the dead in ch. xxxvii. places itself under the saying of Christ, John v. 25," etc. (COCCEIUS).

12. "The enemies of the Old Covenant were curbed; and those of the New, who will once more rise up against the kingdom of the Messiah, are, to the terror of the world, overthrown on the day of judgment, and the New Covenant solemnizes its final victory" (UMBREIT).

13. The appearance of Gog shall be liable to no contingency, and its necessity for the consummation of things is apparent, ch. xxxviii. 4, 8, 16, etc. That even evil intent only serves the cause of God's kingdom is a fundamental view of Holy Scripture.

14. From the symbolical style and character which pervades the chapters before us, a geographical inquiry respecting the burial-place of Gog (ch. **xxxix.**) will be of little use. All the more,

however, may such thoughts suggest themselves as the contrast generally of the low ground, where Gog's lofty purpose makes a grave for himself, with his going up on the mountains of Israel, and then also the contrast of these heights with their security and his grave, which secures against him, confines him. Gog's grave in Israel, lying east of the sea, makes significant allusion to the sea, the apocalyptic term for the birthplace and cradle of the heathen nations; who, moreover, ought not to have found downfall and destruction in Israel, but, on the contrary, sunrise, to which they are described as coming virtually out of darkness and the shadow of death, from the farthest north. That Gog finds his grave in Israel is so much the more striking as Israel himself comes out of his grave in ch. xxxvii.

15. But still more significant is the closing verse of ch. xxxix., which refers back to ch. xxxvii. and xxxvi. What Israel is to be or to signify according to his idea, he becomes only through divine sanctification in the Spirit, whose final and full impartation, in contradistinction to all occasional and partial givings, is made plain, as pouring out upon the house of Israel. "As the outpouring of the Spirit, according to the earlier announcements of the prophet himself and his predecessors, bears an essentially Messianic character, and is connected with the coming of the Good Shepherd of David's line, on whom (Isa. xi. 1) the whole fulness of the Spirit rests" (HENGST.), so the predictions of the chapters before us point to the course in the world of the Christian Church, which was founded by the outpouring of the Divine Spirit, and may live in the certainty that not one soul destined to be gathered into it shall remain behind in the world, as its faith, its confession, is to rely with confidence on a grace which is eternal.

HOMILETIC HINTS

On Ch. xxxviii.

Ver. 1 sq. "The prophet evidently speaks of the last times. A good part of his sayings are riddles, which the fulfilment alone must solve and explain" (BERL. BIB.).—"The enemies of the Church are great, strong, and many; but however great their strength may be, it can effect nothing against the community of the Lord, for the Lord is its protection, 2 Chron. xxxii. 7, 8" (TÜB. BIB.).—"The Christian Church never remains unmolested, but is always persecuted by internal and external enemies, or otherwise plagued with crosses, tribulations, and adversities of all kinds, 2 Tim. iii. 12; 1 Cor. xi. 19" (W.).—"The adversity which befalls the Church of God does not befall her accidentally, but according to the divine counsel and will, Rev. ii. 9, 10" (STARKE).—"Gog is so briefly mentioned in Rev. xx. according to the economy of Holy Scripture, because here so fully" (RICHTER).—Gog is not the Antichrist (the beast), nor yet the pseudo-Christ (the false prophet), but the anti-Israel of the latter days. The last attack on the community of God, in contempt of its mission of peace and salvation, from self-confidence and worldliness.—Ver. 3. "He will, however, be of kindred disposition with Antichrist, a circumstance which is to be observed, and which at the same time explains why the Lord is so angry at him" (BERL. BIB.).—Ver. 4. "He means to march against Jehovah, but in reality Jehovah has him in tow: he must march whither He wills to his own destruction, as Pharaoh of old did not set aside the purposes of the God of Israel when he refused to let His people go, but acted so because Jehovah Himself had hardened his heart in order to hurl him to destruction" (HENGST.).—Ver. 5 sq. "It is, however, of little moment to know whether the present nations and which of them are to be understood under those designations; for those ancient nations no longer exist separately, and the Holy Spirit intended to designate under this name generally only such peoples and nations as in the latter days lie outside of the sphere of the civilisation of the Church of Christ" (HEIM-HOFFMANN).—Ver. 7. The equipment even of His enemies is subject to God's word.—"The ungodly are bound with and to one another by the cord of malice" (STARCK).—Ver 8. A glance into the latter days of the Church of God and of the world.—"Gog meant to visit the people of God, but in reality he is himself visited. It is very consolatory to the Church, that God not merely conquers her enemies, but that even their hostile undertaking is under His guidance, that they move neither hand nor foot except at His command" (HENGST.).—"Thus God visits in grace and also in wrath" (STARCK).—"The Church is thus described: from her persecutions, according to her calling, as the fulfilment of Israel, from her devastation by Antichrist, because of her separation from the world, according to her rest in God" (COCC.).—Ver 9. In the world we have anguish to the end; before we expect it, a tempest arises, and heaven and earth appear to be hid from our eyes. Our security is peace with God: Christians wish, indeed, peace with all men, but the world keeps no peace with them. Such is its turbulence that it has no rest, such its darkness that it would like to shut out all light; even God is not to be our lamp.—"If great armies resemble clouds, how soon can a wind disperse them! 2 Kings xix. 35" (STARKE).

Ver. 10. "Thus God is a heart-searcher, He knows the evil purpose in the man himself"—(STARCK).—Ver. 11. What a confession from the mouth of an enemy! for the Church and against himself.—Ver. 12. How good it is to possess the goods which cannot be stolen,—the joy, for example, which no one shall take from us!—To the end the world seeks only the temporal, the earthly.—Ver. 14. It is bad when we observe only when it is too late.—Ver. 15 sq. That is already the victory when God says, It is My people that ye seek to injure.—"Yea, all things revolve around the community of God on earth; hell must assail it, and yet suffer shipwreck on the faith of the true confessors. Therefore we ought simply to keep God's word pure, and not to care about the great multitude" (DIEDRICH).—Ver. 17. Everything has been told before; they who hold to the word have to fear no surprises.—Ver. 18 sq. "Fury is the glow which bursts forth in the breathing of wrath. The wrath of God is the holy jealousy with which He, for the protection of His kingdom, the kingdom of peace, dashes down the wicked; and this wrath of eternal protecting love is fearful" (SCHMIEDER).

Quantus tremor est futurus,
Quando Judex est venturus,
Cuncta stricte discussurus.

"Even the saints will tremble, but with adoration and hope. Comp. Ps. xlvi." (SCHMIEDER).—Ver. 21. Even the sword is the Lord's servant, which He needs only to call for and it comes at His word.—How one may become the sword of another!—"When God determines to inflict His judgments, the best friends must become the worst enemies, that one may receive from the other the merited reward, Judg. vii. 22" (STARKE).—Ver. 23. The conclusion is, that the result of everything is to magnify and sanctify God. We ought, therefore, to begin all our affairs with God.

On Ch. xxxix.

Ver. 1 sq. God does not mislay the address of His enemies. As Jerusalem, so also Gog and his company stand always before Him.—Him whom God makes to go up, He is also able in due time to make come down.—Ver. 4 sq. "By the mountains of Israel, where Gog is to be slain, we must not understand the mountains near Jerusalem, but the Christian churches in various lands; he shall fall under the Christians" (HEIM-HOFF.).—Ver. 6. The fire of God upon sympathies with evil.—The far-reaching effect of divine judgment.—Ver. 9 sq. "We see from this that outward force, whether rude or refined, does not furnish the measure for great and little with regard to religion" (LUTHER).—God prepares a way of escape for His own people from even the most terrible terrors.—All things must serve the God of love.—The fire of Christianity at last comes over all the weapons of this world. They then warn instead of injuring.—"These weapons are an appropriate figure of earthly things, of which the enemies of the kingdom of God boast as of their weapons" (STARCK).—If God is our shield, then it is seen what becomes of all the shields of men, long and short. Let not yourself be covered and screened by the world! Happy is he who enjoys and confides in the protection of God.—See there what is the value of human armour, what trust is to be put in it, what fear we are to have or rather not to have for it.—The world with its pomp and power after all exists only to furnish fuel for the children of God.—Thus the godly man finally gains the upper hand, however long and strongly the ungodly have behaved proudly.—Ver. 11. Like Gog, many a one finds his grave where he least expected it.—Gog thought of obtaining prey, but by no means a grave.—The grave, a quiet answer to so many loud questions, the echo to so many and various forms of: I will!—Here the proudest and most foaming waves will subside.—Masters cease at the brink of the grave; the continuation follows—that is to say, rottenness, horror, judgment of survivors on the dead, to say nothing of the judgment of God, who has from the beginning had the same decision regarding them.

Ver. 12 sq. The burial of the world, daily to carry out denial of self and the world.—"Men often take great pains to put away bodily uncleanness: would that they were equally careful to purge themselves from all pollution of spirit! 2 Cor. v. 17, 18" (STARKE).—"Teacher and preacher are for this purpose, that they may point out what sin and uncleanness is to be found in a church and in every individual member of it. Oh that so many would not so much forget their office! Isa. lviii. 1" (STARKE).—Ver. 16 sq. The world, the city of the dead, Hamonah.—What a stillness of death after the bustle of so many departing things and departed men!—"The enemies of the Church leave after their death a shameful name behind them, Acts xii." (O.)

Ver. 17 sq. "A communion; the communicants are here the wild beasts and birds" (HENGST.).—The fearful irony of the service of the sanctuary on every worldly interest, even the highest.—What an end, after such a beginning! The beginning was, Israel should fall a prey to Gog; now the end is, that Gog lies there a prey to the very beasts of the field.—Ver. 21. "Let us not be blind and stupid spectators of the acts of God, but let us lift up our hearts, and celebrate the goodness and power of God" (STARCK).—The punishing hand of God on others is, in a certain sense, laid on us also; He takes hold of us when He crushes others.—Ver. 22. God for us and with us, God our God! the blessed knowledge in Israel henceforth and for ever, Ps. cxliv. 15.—The doxology of the Lord's Prayer.—Ver. 23 sq. Our transgressions, the key to our frequently so dark experience on earth.—Our acts of unfaithfulness bring us into manifold miseries, but God is faithful.—By the punishment of God's people the world shall know the misery of sin as well as the righteousness—so much the more threatening for it—of the Holy One of Israel.—"The beginning is made with the house of God, the end with the world" (HÄV.).—The apostasy in Christendom makes the world apparently so powerful.—Ver. 25 sq. "After chastisement, believers again find grace—not, however, because of their goodness, but for the sake of Christ, Ps. cvi. 47" (W.).—The jealousy of God in His compassion.—"When sin is rightly acknowledged, it brings men to shame and repentance, Luke xviii. 13" (STARKE).—The knowledge of sin makes heavy-laden sinners; but grace experienced humbles still more than punishment can do.—The security of the humbled; the security of those who think that they stand; the security of the children of this world.—We men are well able to bring ourselves into distress and sorrow of heart, but only God's love is able to bring us out again.—"There is, however, no sorrow which God could not prevent" (STARCK).—The salvation of Israel, a sermon to the heathen of God's compassion and holiness alike. Hallowed be Thy name, and Thy kingdom come, stand side by side in the Lord's Prayer.—Ver. 28. Not one of the elect shall remain behind in the world.—Ver. 29. Grace as eternal grace and grace for me is the seal of the Holy Spirit.—Thus believers are kept by the power of God to a salvation which is ready to be revealed in the last time, 1 Pet. i. 5.—Israel, the true, the people of the Spirit.—The outpouring of the Spirit of Jehovah is the end of all the ways which He has gone with Israel in anger and compassion, and the consummation of Israel in the Christian Church.

5. The Closing Vision: of the Glory of Jehovah's Kingdom (Ch. xl.-xlviii.).

(1.) *The Temple and its Service* (Ch. xl.-xlvi.).

Chap. xl. 1. In the five and twentieth year of our captivity, in the beginning of the
year, on the tenth of the month, in the fourteenth year after the city was
smitten, in the selfsame day, the hand of Jehovah was upon me [came over me],
2 and He brought me thither: In visions of God brought He me to the land
of Israel, and made me rest [set me down] beside [on] a very high mountain, and
3 on [over] it [was, rose up] a city-like building to the south. And He brought me
thither, and, behold, a man whose appearance was as the appearance of brass,
and a line of flax in his hand, and a measuring rod; and he stood in the gate.
4 And the man said to me, Son of man, behold with thine eyes, and hear with
thine ears, and apply thine heart to all that I show thee, for in order to let
thee see it wert [art] thou brought hither; declare all that thou seest to the
5 house of Israel. And behold a wall outside the house round about, and in the
man's hand the measuring rod of six cubits by [measured by] the cubit and an
handbreadth; and he measured the breadth of the building one rod, and the
6 height one rod. And he came to the gate which looketh towards the east,
and went up on its steps, and measured the threshold of the gate—one rod
7 broad, even one threshold one rod broad: And the chamber [the guardroom]
one rod long and one rod broad; and between the chambers five cubits; and
8 the threshold of the gate beside the porch of the gate within, one rod. And
9 he measured the porch of the gate within, one rod. And he measured the
porch of the gate, eight cubits; and its pillars [literally, its pillar, *i.e.* one by one], two
10 cubits; and the porch of the gate [was, or, thus was the porch of the gate] within. And
the chambers of the gate towards the east [literally, the way of the east] were three
on this side, and three on that; the three of them of one measure; and the
11 pillars on this side and on that were of one measure. And he measured the
breadth of the opening of the gate, ten cubits; the length [height] of the gate,
12 thirteen cubits. And a barrier was before the chambers [guardrooms], one cubit
[on this side], and one cubit the barrier on that side; and the chamber six cubits
13 on this side, and six cubits on that. And he measured the gate from the roof
of the chamber to its roof, the breadth five and twenty cubits, opening against
14 opening [door against door]. And he made the pillars (ver. 9) sixty cubits, and at
15 the pillars [literally, at the pillar] was the court round and round the gate. And
from the front of the entrance-gate to the front of the porch of the inner gate,
16 fifty cubits. And closed windows were in the chambers [guardrooms] and in their
pillars within the gate round and round, and likewise in the wall-projections, and
there were windows round and round inward; and on the pillars [literally, the pillar],
17 palms. And he brought me to the outer court, and behold apartments [cells]
and a stone pavement [Mosaic], made for the court round about; thirty apart-
18 ments by the pavement. And the pavement was by the side of the gates,
19 exactly the length of the gates, [namely] the lower pavement. And he mea-
sured the breadth from the front of the gate of the lower [pavement] to the front
of the inner court from without, a hundred cubits; the east and the north.
20 And the gate which was towards the north on the outer court he measured
21 in its length and its breadth. And its chambers [guardrooms], three on this
side and three on that, and its pillars and its wall-projections; it was after the
measure of the first [former] gate, fifty cubits its length, and the breadth five
22 and twenty cubits. And its windows and its wall-projections and its palms
were after the measure of the gate that is towards the east, and they shall
ascend [one goes up on them] by seven steps, and its wall-projections are before them.
23 And [there was] a gate to the inner court opposite that to the north and to the
24 east; and he measured from gate to gate a hundred cubits. And he brought
me towards the south, and behold a gate towards the south, and he measured
25 its pillars and its wall-projections by those measures. And there were win-

dows to it and to its wall-projections round about, like those windows; fifty
26 cubits the length, and the breadth five and twenty cubits. And its ascent
had seven steps, and its wall-projections before them; and there were palms
27 to it, one on this side and one on that at its pillars. And there was a gate to
the inner court towards the south, and he measured from that gate to the gate
28 towards the south, a hundred cubits. And he brought me to the inner court
into the south gate [through the south gate], and he measured the south gate after
29 those measures; And its chambers and its pillars and its wall-projections
after those measures. And its windows [were] to it and to its wall-projections
round about; fifty cubits the length, and the breadth five and twenty cubits.
30 And wall-projections round about, the length five and twenty cubits, and the
31 breadth five cubits. And its wall-projections were towards the outer court;
32 and palms on its pillars, and eight steps [were] its steps. And he brought me
to the inner court towards the east, and measured the gate after those mea-
33 sures; And its chambers and its pillars and its wall-projections after those
measures. And [there were] windows to it and to its wall-projections round
34 about; fifty cubits the length, and the breadth five and twenty cubits. And
its wall-projections [were] towards the outer court, and palms on its pillars on
35 this side and on that, and its steps eight steps. And he brought me to the
36 north gate, and measured after those measures; Its chambers, its pillars,
and its wall-projections and windows [were] round about, fifty cubits the length,
37 and the breadth five and twenty cubits. And its pillars were towards the
outer court, and palms on its pillars on this side and on that, and its steps
38 eight steps. And a cell and its opening was by the pillars at the gates; there
39 shall they wash the burnt-offering. And in the porch of the gate were two
tables on this side and two tables on that side, to slay in relation to them
[or, on them] the burnt-offering and the sin-offering and the trespass-offering.
40 And at the side without for him that goeth up, at the extreme of the gate
towards the north, were two tables; and at the other side, which [belongeth] to
41 the porch of the gate, two tables. Four tables on this side and four tables
on that, by the side of the gate; eight tables, on them will they slaughter.
42 And four tables at the ascent [for the burnt-offering] of hewn stone, the length a
cubit and a half, and the breadth a cubit and a half, and the height one cubit;
on them will they lay the instruments with which they will slay the burnt-
43 offering and the slain-offering. And the double staples of a handbreadth were
fastened on the house round and round [on the walls around the temple]; and on the
44 tables is the flesh of the offering. And outside at the inner gate were cells for
the singers in the inner court which was at the side of the north gate, and their
45 front towards the south; a part at the side of the east gate, fronting towards
the north. And he said to me, This cell, whose front is towards the south, is
46 for the priests that wait upon the charge [service] of the house; And the cell
whose front is towards the north, for the priests that wait upon the charge of
the altars; these are the sons of Zadok, who of the sons of Levi draw near to
47 Jehovah to minister to Him. And he measured the court; the length a hun-
dred cubits and the breadth a hundred cubits, forming a square; and the altar
48 was before the house. And he brought me to the porch of the house, and
measured the pillar of the porch, five cubits on this side and five cubits on
that; and the breadth of the gate, three cubits on this side and three cubits
49 on that. The length of the porch was twenty cubits, and the breadth eleven
cubits, and [that] at the steps by which they will go up to it; and there were
posts by the pillars, one on this side and one on that.

Ver. 1. Sept.: Κ. ἐγενετο . . . ἐν τ. πρωτω μηνι *omittunt* שָׁמָּה *et* v. 2 הֵבִיאַנִי.

Ver. 2. ἐν ὁρασει θ. . . . ἀπεναντι.

Ver. 3. . . . χαλκου στιλβοντος . . . σπαρτιον οἰκοδομων κ.— Sept., Vulg.: *leg. bis* ἐν τη χειρι αὐτου.

Ver. 4. Sept.: *interrogativè* ἑωρακας συ; ἰδε . . . κ. ταξον εἰς τ. καρδιαν σ. παντα . . . και δειξεις παντα—

Ver. 5. . . . περιβολος . . . διεμετρησεν το προτειχισμα— Vulg.: . . . *sex cubitorum et palmo*—

Ver. 6. . . . εἰσηλθεν εἰς . . . ἐν ἑπτα ἀναβαθμοις . . διεμετρησεν θεε ἐξ ἐνθεν κ. ἐξ ἐνθεν κ. το αἰλαμ τ. πυλης ἰσον τω καλαμω

Ver. 7. . . . κ. το αἰλαμ ἀνα μεσον του θεηλαθ πηχων ἑξ κ. το θεε το δευτερον ἰσον τ. καλαμω το πλατος κ. ἰσον τ. καλαμω μηκος; κ. το αἰλαμ πηχεων πεντε κ. τ. θεε τ. τριτον ἰσον τ. καλαμω τ. μηκος κ. ἰσον τ. καλ. τ. πλατος, κ. τ. αἰλαμ τ. πυλωνος (8) πλησιον του αἰλαμ τ. πυλης ἐσωθεν ἰσον τ. καλαμω. Vulg.: . . . *portæ juxta vestibulum.*

Ver. 8. Vulg.: *portæ intrinsecus calamo uno.* (The verse is wanting in the Sept., in the Vulg., in the Syriac version, and in many manuscripts.)

Ver. 9. . . . K. το αἰλευ . . . κ. τ. αἰλαμ τ. πυλης ἐσωθεν, Vulg.: . . . *et frontem ejus duobus cubitis, vestibulum autem portæ erat intrinsecus.*

Ver. 10. . . . θεε κατεναντι . . . κ. μετρον ἐν ἐν τ. αἰλαμ ἐνθεν κ. ἐνθεν. Vulg.: . . . *mensura una frontium ex utraque parte.*

Ver. 12. K. πηχυς ἐπισυναγομενος κατα προσωπον τ. θεειμ πηχεος ἑνος κ. πηχ. ἑνος, ὁριον ἐνθεν κ. ἐνθεν,— Vulg.: . . . *et marginem ante . . . cubiti unius, et cubitus unus finis utrimque—*

Ver. 14. κ. το αἰθριον του αἰλαμ τ. πυλης ἐξωθεν πηχεις εἰκοσι πεντε κ. το θεεμ τ. πυλης κυκλω. Vulg.: . . . *fecit frontes . . . et ad frontem atrium portæ undique per circuitum.*

Ver. 15. K. το αἰθριον τ. πυλης ἐξωθεν εἰς τ. αἰθριον του αἰλαμ τ. πυλης ἐσωθεν— Vulg.: *et ante faciem portæ quæ pertingebat usque ad faciem vestibuli portæ interioris—*

Ver. 16. Sept.: K. θυριδες κρυπται ἐπι τα θεειμ κ. ἐπι τα αἰλαμ ἐσωθεν της αὐλης . . . κ. ὡσαυτως τοις αἰλαμ θυριδες— *fenestras obliquas in thalamis et in frontibus eorum, quæ erant intra portam undique per circuitum . . . et in vestibulis—*

Ver. 17. . . . εἰσηγαγεν . . . εἰς . . . παστοφορια κ. περιστυλα— Vulg.: . . . *gazophylacia . . . in circuitu pavimenti.*

Ver. 18. K. αἱ στοαι— *in fronte portarum secundum—*

Ver. 19. . . . ἐσωθεν ἐπι τ. αἰθριον τ. πυλης βλεπουσης ἐξω, πηχ. ἑκατον τ. βλεπουσης κατ' ἀνατολας. K. εἰσηγαγεν με ἐπ βορραν (20) κ. ἰδου πυλη βλεπουσα προς βορραν—

Ver. 22. . . . κ. τα αἰλαμμων ἐσωθεν.

Ver. 24. . . . κ. τα θεε κ. τα αἰλευ κ. τα αἰλαμμωθ—

Ver. 25. . . . καθως αἱ θυριδες του αἰλαμ—

Ver. 26. . . . αἰλαμμωθ ἐσωθεν—

Ver. 27. . . . κ. το εὐρος προς νοτον πηχεις εἰκοσι πεντε.

Ver. 32. . . . με εἰς τ. πυλην . . . αὐτην—

Ver. 33. Vulg.: *thalamum ejus et frontem ej. et vestibulum ejus—*

Ver. 36. . . . θυριδες αὐτω κυκλω, κ. τα αἰλαμμωθ αὐτης κυκλω, πηχεις—

Ver. 37. Vulg.: *Et vestibulum ejus respiciebat . . . et cælatura palmarum in fronte—*

Ver. 38. Τα παστοφορια αὐτης κ. τα θυρωματα αὐτης κ. τα αἰλαμμωθ αὐτης ἐπι τ. πυλης τ. δευτερας ἐκρυσις· ἐκει πλυνουσιν— Vulg.: *Et per singula gazophylacia ostium in frontibus portarum; ibi—*

Ver. 40. Sept.: K. κατα νωτου του ῥυακος τ. ὁλοκαυτωματων τ. θυρας βλεπουσης προς . . . προς ἀνατολας κατα νωτου τ δευτερας κ. του αἰλαμ . . . κ. ὀκτω τραπεζαι κατ' ἀνατολας. Vulg.: . . . *latus . . . quod ascendit . . . portæ, quæ . . . ante vestibulum portæ.*

Ver. 41. . . . ἐπ' αὐτας . . . τα θυματα, κατεναντι των ὀκτω τραπεζων των θυματων. Vulg.: . . . *per latera portæ octo mensæ erant—*

Ver. 42. . . . των ὁλοκαυτωματων λιθιναι, λελαξευμεναι—

Ver. 43. . . . K. παλαιστην ἑξουσιν γεισος λελαξευμενον ἐσωθεν κυκλω, κ. ἐπι . . . ἐπανωθεν στεγας του καλυπτεσθαι ἀπο του ὑετου κ. ἀπο της ξηρασιας. Vulg.: *Et labia earum . . . reflexa intrinsecus per circuitum—*

Ver. 44. K. εἰσηγαγεν με εἰς τ. αὐλην τ. ἐσωτεραν, κ. ἰδου δυο ἐξεδραι ἐν τ. αὐλη τ. ἐσωτερα, μια κατα νωτου τ. πυλης τ. βλεπουσης προς βορραν φερουσα προς νοτον, κ. μια κατα νωτου τ. πυλης της προς νοτον, βλεπουσης δε προς βορραν. Vulg.: . . . *una ex latere portæ orientalis—*

Ver. 48. . . . πεντε το πλατος ἐνθε κ. . . . πεντε ἐνθεν, κ. το εὐρος . . . πηχεων δεκατεσσαρων, κ. ἐπωμιδες τ. θυρας του αἰλαμ πηχεων τριων ἐνθεν— Vulg.: . . . *mensus est vestibulum quinque—*

Ver. 49. . . . το εὐρος πηχεις δωδεκα, κ. ἐπι δεκα ἀναβαθμων— Vulg.: . . . *et octo gradibus ascendebatur . . . erant in frontibus, una hinc—*

EXEGETICAL REMARKS.

LITERATURE.—In addition to Böttcher's treatise, already mentioned in the Introduction, p. 30, we have to mention: THENIUS, *Proben altt. Schrifterkl. nach wissensch. Sprachforschung*, Leipzig 1833; BALMER-RINCK, *Des Propheten Ezechiel Ansicht vom Tempel*, Ludwigsburg 1858. Of the older authors: VITRINGA, *Aanleydinge tot het rechte Verstant*, etc., and his defence against Cocceius, the son (*Naeder Ondersoeck van het rechte Verstant van den Tempel Ezechiels*); STURM, *Sciagraphia Templi*, etc., Leipzig 1694; and a little earlier: VILLALPANDUS (p. 29); and, in a ponderous monograph, MATTH. HAFENREFFER, *Templ. Ez.*, Tübing. 1613.—Great diligence and acute combination distinguish KLIEFOTH, whose second part treats entirely of the following chapters in 390 pages.—OEDER, in his *Freye Untersuch. über einige BB. des Alten Testaments*, Halle 1771, and L. VOGEL, the editor of this treatise, and CORRODI also in the anonymous treatise, *Beleuchtung d. jüd. und chr. Bibelkanons*, have criticised away the following nine chapters from our prophet, and capriciously attributed them to a Samaritan or a very late returned Jew; for what they have adduced upon "grounds" has been already refuted by J. D. MICHAELIS, EICHHORN, BERTHOLDT, and JAHN.

Vers. 1–4. Exordium—Introductory.

As in ch. i., with which the divine mission of our prophet opens, so also in ch. xl. here, an exordium, stating the point of time, the condition of Ezekiel, the locality, as well as the first and immediate view which he got, introduces us to what follows.

Ver. 1. By the first date given: **in the five and twentieth year of our** (Introd. § 3) **captivity,** the reference back to ch. i. (comp. ver. 2) is still more express. According to Bunsen and Duncker, 573 B.C. According to Schmieder, 574. According to Hitzig, 575. As to sense and meaning, this reference back to ch. i. implies on the one hand, that *the glory of Jehovah solemnizes its consummation in the glory of His kingdom* (Introd. § 5), and on the other, *that the divine mission of Ezekiel has now come to the close which befits its commencement.* Ezekiel's prophecy, ch. xxix. 17 sq., is chronologically his last (comp. on it). "The prophet has introduced it as an appendix to an earlier prophecy, in order to conclude with this great vision of restoration, in contrast to the great opening vision of destruction" (HENGST.). According to J. H. Michaelis, we have to remember in regard to the twenty-fifth year in Ezekiel here, that the Babylonish captivity of the Jews began in the fourth year of Jehoiakim, when Daniel and his companions were carried away, so that there were in all thirty-two years of exile to take into account. — Hitzig interprets בְּרֹאשׁ הַשָּׁנָה in the sense of "new year," and regards the phrase: **on the tenth of the month**, as explanatory, since he (as also Jewish tradition) takes it to be a year of jubilee (Lev. xxv. 9). The previous year must have been a sabbatic year; such a year ended in the autumn of 575, and may have been a 49th year. The significant element in this coincidence (on a day of atonement commencing a year of jubilee) would, moreover, still continue even if we should not be able, like Kliefoth, to speak of an "absolutely eschatological vision." Rdak observes: "God let the prophet see the temple and the future freedom of Israel on the day of jubilee, because then servants become free, and on the day of atonement, because then the sins of Israel are forgiven." If what is intended is the beginning of the civil year and the month Tisri, then, in order to that, this much later alteration of the beginning of the Hebrew year—the old Mosaic reckoning constantly prevails still in the post-exile Old Testament writings — must be proved to have been already in practice in Ezekiel's time; to say nothing of the fact that such a departure from the law in our prophet, with his specially priestly and other peculiarities of mind and spirit, is scarcely suitable, at least without more definite indication, even to the character of our chapter. For this reason Hävernick, with the majority of expositors, holds to the commencement of the ecclesiastical year, and thus to the month Nisan, making the phrase: רֹאשׁ הַשָּׁנָה, not found elsewhere in the Old Testament, look back to Ex. xii. 2 as a brief mode of expression for the full form there, and connecting the mention of the tenth day directly with Ex. xii. 3 (on which day the lambs for the passover were set apart, SCHMIEDER). "It is the period when the preparation begins for the solemnization of the feast of the passover. To the prophet, inspired by the Spirit of God, the future shapes itself as the consummated glorification of the past, of the first history of development of the people of God" (HÄV.). "The month did not need to be stated more exactly; from the words: **In the beginning of the year**, it was self-evident that the first month only could be intended. That the day is significant for the thing is confirmed by the emphatic form: **On the selfsame day.** On the day when of old the passover was instituted in Egypt, and the people were brought as it were into the sacred precincts of the approaching redemption, the day on which the coming sealing afresh of God's redeeming grace had thus for centuries been solemnly announced, along with the increased pain just on account of the cessation of these festivals, hope also must have arisen more strongly than at any other time, since God had given in the redemption of the olden time a pledge to His people. The day occurs elsewhere also as significant, *e.g.* the leading across Jordan, **Josh. iv. 19, etc.** On the same day was the entrance of Christ into Jerusalem, the inauguration of His kingdom. The day was thus as significant here as the day of His resurrection in Rev. i. 10. How even in later times the popular hope of deliverance was connected with the passover appears from the release at the feast of a prisoner, who, in the eyes of the Jews, represented the people enslaved by the Romans" (HENGST.). Next to the **captivity,** the circumstance that **the city was smitten,** which points back to ch. xxxiii. 21, forms the second element in fixing the date. It is a verbal reference to prepare us for understanding how the renewed divine mission of the prophet, in view of that accomplished act of judgment, would now, for the first time, fully open his mouth for the prophecy of God's compassions on His people. At all events, *the capture of Jerusalem was the consummation of the misery of the Old Testament covenant-people, but with it was presented also the exactly corresponding background for the consummation of Jehovah's glory in His kingdom in the world.* And so, in this respect also, Ezekiel cannot, in conformity with his continuous mission as prophet of Jehovah's glory in the exile, withdraw more fully from the theatre of his activity. What the prophet had been obliged to announce regarding the wrath and judgment of God on Israel throughout ch. ii.–xxiv., has been all fulfilled,—God has made a *tabula rasa;* but the strictly fulfilled threatening presents itself also as guarantee for the realization of the promise already wrapt up in it, which, in the transition portion of our book (ch. xxv.–xxxii., see Introd. § 5), prepared for itself a background in the kingdoms of this world, in order with ch. xxxiii. to set forth in prospect with increasing clearness and energy the purification, sanctification, restoration, and final victory of the new Israel, the Israel after the Spirit, over the world. What had been there prophesied in isolated instances of the future salvation becomes now collected into a united whole, so that to all appearance, as if a separate book by itself began with ch. xl., our opening verses only confirm more expressly that which already results from a reconsideration of the previous chapters. "Even in the first prophecy, in the rainbow which surrounds the appearance of the offended Deity," says Hengstenberg, "lies the germ of this last prophecy;" and Hitzig says: "Not only ch. xxxiii.–xxxix., the previous section" (to which specially our prophecy forms the conclusion), "but Ezekiel's prophecy in general, advances here also to internal completion."—**In the selfsame day;** comp. ch. xxiv. 2.—Comp. ch. i. 3, xxxiii. 22, xxxvii. 1. "Not merely a divine word, but he shall experience something" (KLIEF.).—Not directly, but certainly indirectly, there is also a reference to ch. viii. sq.; for although **thither** is explained from what precedes as the site of the smitten city, yet Jerusalem comes immediately—just as in ch. viii. sq.—into consideration principally as regards the temple. [Hävernick finds in the **thither** the direction of the longing expressed.] —Ver. 2. **In visions of God;** comp. on ch. i. 1. The state of Ezekiel.—Ch. xxxvii. 1.—Now comes the *locality* of the vision,—in general: **the land of Israel,** and then, in what follows, the first and immediate view in particular. Against Kliefoth's observation, correct in itself, that אֶל and עַל stand for each other in Ezekiel, we remark that here, however, occurring as they do close together, they can hardly be otherwise than distinct. Ezekiel is, in the Spirit, set down at all events at the foot or the side of a mountain, which to him, looking up in vision, appears **very high.** Had Ezekiel been "upon" it, he could have spoken more fitly of its size or breadth than of its height. First of all, the **mountain,** since it has to be taken in contrast with the smitten city, refers neither to Moriah nor Zion in particular, but symbolizes generally the loftily situated Jerusalem (comp. ch. xvii. 22, 23); but that it appears **very high** points, above all, to a glorious restoration, and indicates spiritual elevation, for which comp. Isa. ii. 2 (where the exaltation is immediately explained from the consciousness, the religious movement of the nations, and as no merely outward one); Zech. xiv. 9, 10, 16; Mic. iv. 1 (Rev. xxi. 10). This establishes in the outset the ideality of the further views vouchsafed to Ezekiel. Where the first vision (ch. i.) "exhibits in prospect anger and judgment," the last exhibits in prospect "the healing of the wounds." There the prophet went against the dream of a God gracious to (self-righteous) sinners, and an immediately approaching future of salvation; here at the end, after that announcement has been made, he deals a last powerful blow against the second dangerous enemy of God's people, that has now come into the foreground,—the despair, which as effectually as the former false security leads away from treading the God-ordained path of repentance" (HENGST.). That, however, which is made prominent for Jerusalem in general, and described as **a city-like building,** is, according to what follows, the temple. [Hävernick makes the prophet see from the mount of the temple, as the building in the south, the New Jerusalem (Heb. xii. 22), situated south of the mountain where the prophet stood, and consequently makes sanctuary and city to be at once announced as the two (?) main parts of the vision. According to Abarbanel, Ezekiel saw even the builders in the south building the city. Hengstenberg finds in עִיר the substitute for the smitten city (ver. 1), and the temple here, as also in Heb. xii., included in the city in the wider sense. The reverse is the correct view, as even Hengstenberg himself goes on to call the temple "the proper essence of the city," "the spiritual dwelling-place of the whole people." His reference to ch. viii. concerning the central position of the temple is good.] Apart from the fact, observed also by Keil against Kliefoth, that the city is not thus described in ch. xlv. 6, xlviii. 15 sq., 30 sq., everything is made clear by the distinction between אֶל and עַל; to the prophet set down at the mountain, from Babylon, and hence coming from the north, the building on the mountain appears מִנֶּגֶב, that is, looking from the south (as in ch. xxi. 2 sq., Judea in general), which the ἀπέναντι of the Sept. (מִנֶּגֶד) renders quite correctly.

Ver. 3. **And He brought,** etc. Resumption from ver. 1, after that the parenthesis ver. 2 has treated of the locality in general, and the first immediate view in particular. Now comes the vision proper: **And behold.** The description: **a man,** the less excludes the angel of the Lord, the known mediator of divine revelations, whom even Hitzig accepts here, "since He is called 'Jehovah' in ch. xliv. 2, 5," as the comparison of his appearance: **as the appearance of brass** (see on ch. i. 5), seems to point to ch. i. (ver. 7), and the line **of flax** to ch. ix. 2. Comp. generally what has been said on ch. ix. 2; also Zech. ii. 1 sq. (Matt. xvi. 18; Heb. xi. 16). The brass suggests to Hengstenberg: "solidity, durability, power of resistance," which is so comforting to the Church of God, because its earthly representatives rather resemble soft wax. Hitzig, like the Sept., makes it denote a "brilliant appearance;" Kliefoth: "an ordinary *angelus interpres*" (Rev. xxi. 9). The **brass** not only removes the appearance from the human sphere, but also gives in the outset an idea of firmness, hence certainty, for everything which it will determine. For that the man has to measure is shown by his equipment, as that in its completeness denotes, according to Hengstenberg: "building activity in general, in contrast to the instruments of destruction (ch. ix. 1);" according to Hävernick (BÖTTCHER), that it is: "for the greater and the lesser measurements,—**the line of flax** more for the site; the **measuring rod** more for the masonry;" according to KLIEF.: "that he has much to measure of various descriptions." HENGST., referring to Rev. xxi. 15, calls attention to *the* **measuring rod** as distinguished from *a* **line of flax.**—He **stood in the** (at the) **gate.** HITZIG, correctly: "waiting for the new-comer." Which gate, namely, of that which looked as **a city-like building** (ver. 2), therefore which temple-gate it was, is not particularized here. But as Ezekiel comes from the north, the first that met him was probably the north gate, from which the man escorts him to the east gate (ver. 6).—Ver. 4. The supposition is (ver. 2), that the building is already erected; hence: **behold with thine eyes.** That he should "hear with his ears" gives promise of oral explanation also, as, for example, ver. 45 sq. But because the expression of the building as to its proportions will be made known to the prophet specially by measuring, Ezekiel has "to apply his heart to all" that he will in this way obtain a sight of (all that I show thee), for through him Israel is to obtain knowledge of it (comp. Ex. xxv. 9).

Ver. 5. *The Enclosing Wall.*

As חוֹמָה ("checking," "keeping off"), the wall is a barrier against what might come from without (מִחוּץ). It runs right round the house, and will thus in relation to it, that is, to the temple generally, symbolize the warding off of the profane, the unclean, the false; and not so much protection. Comp. ch. xlii. 20, and Ps. xv. The height, at least, to be mentioned immediately, is nothing particular in the way of protection. [HÄV.: "In the former sanctuary such an enclosing wall appeared more arbitrary, a construction called forth by external circumstances. Here the wall is an essential constituent part. The Babylonian temples, too, had their surrounding walls, but here is certainly a contrast to the colossal structures of the Babylonians. The wall on the east side in the later temple, begun by Solomon, was 300 cubits high at the lowest parts."] [The wall "bears the square form, as broad as it is high; but this being only twelve feet at the utmost, it was manifestly not designed to present, by its altitude, an imposing aspect, or by its strength to constitute a bulwark of safety. In these respects it could not for a moment be compared with many of the moral erections which existed in antiquity. But as the boundary-line between the sacred and the profane, which, being drawn by the hand of God, must therefore remain free from all interference on the part of man, it is precisely such as might have been expected."—FAIRBAIRN'S *Ezekiel.*—W. F.] But the measuring begins with it, and so the measuring rod is here fixed at 6 cubits—the cubit, however, with the addition of a handbreadth (ch. xliii. 13), hence 6 cubits and 6 handbreadths = 1 rod. The measure is accordingly greater than that of the usual rod of 6 cubits. Comp. 2 Chron. iii. 3, and Deut. iii. 11. A cubit measure found in the ruins of Memphis shows both measures, one of 6 and one of 7 handbreadths. See a lengthened disquisition on Jewish measurement by J. D. Michaelis on our passage, p. 112 sq. [HENGST.: In the case of Solomon's temple the former cubit, because then current, was the measure, hence it was the more needful to give the relation of the one to the other here. The greater cubit, which meets us first in Ezekiel, was probably borrowed in the exile from the Chaldeans. Keil assumes a shortening of the common cubit from the old Mosaic sacred cubit, which, he says, still formed the measure for Solomon's temple, and will do so for the new temple likewise.] From this statement of a greater measure, we may presume that what is to be measured is uncommon, magnificent, surpassing that which actually exists.—Inasmuch as by measuring the dimension is made known as distinguished from the mere mass, we may say with Bähr that law and proportion, hence order, consequently the spiritual, the divine ideality, are displayed. This is what is expressed generally in the numbers occurring here. But the very preponderance of the number six, in itself non-significant, forbids us to attach to them special significance. In this respect, also, Hengstenberg's observation, that in order to get the significant number seven, it is necessary to revert to the cubit, which after the prophet's explanation no longer comes into consideration, tells against Kliefoth. Moreover, מִדַּד comes from "extending," and serves here rather to elucidate in detail to the prophet that which he beholds as already completed work.—הַבִּנְיָן is the mason-work of the wall, the equality of which in breadth and height corresponds strikingly to the purpose assigned to it—to separate.

Vers. 6–16. *The East Gate.*

After the wall now follows in Ver. 6 the most noteworthy part of it, the gates, of which, as being "the chief," as Hengstenberg supposes ("because of the rising sun"), the east gate is described. It lay opposite the entrance into the sanctuary, and hence was the one among the gates which could first come into consideration with reference to the **house** in the narrower sense, in respect to which it is also several times expressly defined in what follows. On the significance of the gates of Ezekiel's temple, comp. the Doctrinal Reflections on ch. xl.–xlvi. The steps, seven in number, according to vers. 22, 26 (SEPT.), are the first thing observed about the gate. Since the man arrives at it by them, they can hardly be conceived of otherwise than as before, and not running into the gate; they show, moreover, that the court to which the east gate leads lies higher by these seven steps. Thus the ascent, an exaltation (Col. iii.), is conjoined with the separating character of the wall.—סַף is a border or panel on the ground at the entrance, thus **threshold**; nothing can be made of "projecting lower cornice" (HITZIG). As the threshold enters into the gate a rod-breadth, which is the breadth of the wall, it fills up exactly the opening made by the gate in the wall.—וְאֵת סַף אֶחָד explains the threshold measured as "one" (HÄV.: only one, because so broad), that is, for the present, for a second follows in addition, ver. 7; hence אֶחָד, in the sense of "first."

Ver. 7. וְהַתָּא placed here, at the entrance into the gate, so simply as to explain itself, is the chamber which is wont to be in this place, the guardroom for the gate-watch (ch. xliv. 11). "An arrangement dating from David and Solomon; a sacred temple-guard was appointed to surround it" (HÄV.). [FAIRBAIRN: "Furnished, as the gates were, so amply with guard-chambers for those who should be charged with maintaining the sanctity of the house (ch. xliv. 11, 14), they were formed more especially with a view to the holiness, which must be the all-pervading characteristic of the place. It was imprinting on the architecture of this portion of the buildings the solemn truth, 'that there shall in no wise enter into it anything that defileth, neither worketh abomination, or maketh a lie' (Rev. xxi. 27),—a truth which, in past times, partly from defective arrangements, partly from the wilful disregard of such as existed, had been most grievously suffered to fall into abeyance. But henceforth it must be made known to all that holiness becometh God's house, and that they only who possess this shall be allowed to come and minister before Him."—W. F.] Since the gate extends from the wall into the court, and Ezekiel has first to pass through to the end, the first thing determined is as to the guardroom, of which, moreover, there were several (הַתָּאִים),—the "length" (from east to west), and with that also the breadth, and in this way the form, that of a square.—It is to be understood that the intervening spaces also (the distances from chamber to chamber) were measured as they went onward, and thus made clear to the prophet.—The conclusion is formed by the **threshold of the gate**, which, in distinction from the entrance one (ver. 6) of the same dimension, is named from the porch (אוּלָם or אֵלָם is vestibule or portico, often with pillars), into which the whole gate-building runs out, as the porch and thereby this threshold is fixed with respect to the temple, that is, westward. אֵצֶל indicates that this threshold lay close to the porch, adjoined it.—Ver. 8. The porch, because it opens the way to the court, is a principal part of the gate, hence its lengthened description. The Sept. and Hitzig erase this verse on account of the dimension being different from that given in Ver. 9. Kliefoth finds given in ver. 8 the size of the porch in the light, the width of its inner space from east to west, namely, 6 cubits of Ezekiel's measure (ver. 5). The width was naturally the same as that of the gate. Consequently the measurement given in ver. 9 would be that of the porch in the wider sense, including the projecting side-walls upon it (2 cubits) and the אֵילִים fronting each other (ver. 10), and each 2 cubits thick. אַיִל, mostly plural, signifies that which is "firm," "strong," which can be a prop, can afford support. The signification of the verb אוּל, "to be in front," accepted by Kliefoth, is the derived one. The "Elim" (אֵילִים) undoubtedly project, as observed, but in reality they are pillar-like props attached to the walls, to form sides and supports for doors and windows. **And the porch,** etc., forming a conclusion; in connection with which Kliefoth directs attention to the מֵהַבַּיִת, repeated for the third time, as marking the difference from the gates of the inner court (vers. 31, 34, 37).

Ver. 10. A return to the "guardrooms of the east gate" (ver. 7). They are six in number, three on one side fronting three on the other, and all of the same size. [Kliefoth: 2 × 3 watches at each of the three outer gates, and the same at the three inner gates, in all 3 × 12; "for God Himself will be the proper Guardian and Protector of this sanctuary of His people."] —The one measure spoken of the אֵילִים on this occasion seems to refer to those mentioned in ver. 9. Klief.: "the gate-pillars of the porch." [Hengstenberg supposes "pillars" one cubit thick, as in ver. 9 (?), standing in front of the walls at both sides of the guardrooms; others otherwise.]—Ver. 11. The **opening of the gate** is its entire width, and along with the statement of its **breadth** there is given at the same time the still undetermined length of the two thresholds and the steps.—In distinction from the width, הַשַּׁעַר (from שָׁעַר, to make fast, to close, and so meaning literally: "closed place" [*Schloss*] —cognate to סָהַר) as such signifies the ward, wherefore the gate too is very suitably treated of here in the midst of the more exact description of the guardrooms (vers. 10, 12). (Comp. ch. xliv. 1 sq.) Viewed with respect to its **opening,** it opens the way to the court; as a **gate** it is a silent but stedfast guardian (comp. on ver. 48). —As every other interpretation hitherto attempted leads only to quite uncertain suppositions not contained in the text (roofed and open spaces, courtyards, and the like), the **length** of 13 cubits here must mean the height. In itself, אֹרֶךְ signifies: what is extended in time and space, hence: what is long. When the breadth has been given already, the extension of the gate-barricade proper (the door) can scarcely be conceived of otherwise than in height (comp. on ver. 15), and the guardrooms supply all that is requisite to fix the length here. Length, therefore, does not in general stand for height; neither does the special application need to be explained from the circumstance that the door was lying when measured. ["To the last number of perfection, ten (δέκα, implying that it takes into it the other numbers), is added the first number of perfection, three," Hengst.]—Ver. 12. In unison with the shutting character of the gate, the idea of the guardrooms is completed by the barrier (גְּבוּל) of one cubit in breadth before each of them. As is evident from what follows, a מִפֹּה has to be supplied between אַמָּה אֶחָת and וְאַמָּה־אַחַת. [Klief.: "And the barrier on this side was a cubit, but the guardroom was 6 cubits on this side and 6 cubits on that," that is to say: the guardroom formed a square of 6 cubits each side; but the barrier-space formed an oblong of 6 cubits in length before the guardroom, and 1 cubit in breadth; and the barrier-space was not taken from the space of the guardroom, which on the contrary remained a square of 6 cubits, but joined on before the guardroom.] The statement that that which was guardroom (הַתָּא, collective, generic) occupied 6 cubits on either side, is here understood of the length, and hence is neither formally nor virtually (as Keil) a repetition of ver. 7, but is made expressly for giving a clear notion of the barriers, namely, how they ran along the entire length of each guardroom. From this it follows that these guardrooms are niche-like cells, opening into the gate, and hence closed in by the barriers, and that when one cubit on each side is taken from the 10 cubits (ver. 11), the passage leading through is limited to 8 cubits. The barrier is hardly constructed in order that the watchman "stepping out may look around right and left, and while doing so be protected against the too near approach of the people, and hindrance by them" (Hitzig); it lessens the available space in the thoroughfare, and thereby facilitates the control on both sides, and it protects the guardroom, which without it would stand entirely open, from those who wished to press into the court in this way through the doors to be mentioned immediately. [Hengst.: "The arrangement supposes that there are impudent people among the entrants who wished to force an entrance not allowed to them; comp. Luke xiii. 24."]

Ver. 13. The entire breadth of the gate-buildings: 25 cubits, measured from the guardroom (הַתָּא, as ver. 12), as this is what has just been spoken of, and the guardrooms represent the greatest breadth. Thus guardroom opposite guardroom, from roof to roof, from north to south, or *vice versâ*, so that the whole breadth comes out. The explanation: פֶּתַח נֶגֶד פָּתַח, indicates an opening of the guardrooms out towards the court, for the barriers close them up towards the interior of the gate. This at the same time explains to us the measuring; for since there is only a barrier closing up on either side, there is a free view on both sides into the respective guardrooms to their openings (under the end of each roof) into the court, so the man needs not go out (as KLIEF.) to determine the measure; moreover, **And he measured** will immediately (Ver. 14) pass over into: **And he made!** Accordingly, ver. 7 gave only the dimensions of the interior of the guardrooms in the light, whereas now the space of the outside walls ($1\frac{1}{2}$ cubits each, according to ver. 42) is included. [HITZIG: גָּג is not the cover of a chamber, but its ridge = גַּב.] The barriers may be imagined as situated in the gateway, but also as in the guardrooms, of course without lessening their space. The object of the barriers recommends the first view.—In order to give the entire extension of the gate-buildings in this direction, we have in ver. 14 the statement of the height of the אֵילִים, the two wall-pillars (ver. 9) adjoining the porch. From their height as stated, Kliefoth explains the change of expression. [HENGST.: "The usual height of the gate-building might be gathered from th height of the gate-door, ver. 11."] That it is the length (height) of the gate-structure which is meant to be determined is shown by the description of these pillars. "They are as it were the head of the whole, that which the steeples are in our churches, towering up towards and pointing to heaven" (HENGST.). Kliefoth excellently observes: "They are 60 cubits high. If one had reflected that our church towers also have grown out of gate-pillars, that one can see not only by Egyptian obelisks and Turkish minarets, but also by our factory chimneys, which, moreover, are hollow, how pillars 60 cubits high can be erected on a base of 4 cubits square, and that finally the thing spoken of is a colossal building seen in vision, one would have felt no critical anxieties at this statement of height." On: **he made,** Hengstenberg says: "The prophet goes back to the time when he who here explains the building to him prepared it. In reality the meaning is: he had made."—וְאֶל־אַיִל collectively, and this the rather because the pillars are the highest parts of the gate-structure. It is quite clear from the description in ver. 9 that the court (הֶחָצֵר) was immediately adjoining; an inner court is out of the question. Accordingly, הַשַּׁעַר must be accusative; in relation to the gate, as to the gate,—אֶל with אַיִל, in which the gate terminates in the court, precedes,—hence: the outer court of the temple surrounded the gate-structure round about, this structure was built in the court. When the relation to the court into which the gate extended has been thus considered, the entire length of the gate-structure can now—Ver. 15—be noted. For this purpose the gate on the side from which the measuring begins, that is, from the ascending steps of ver. 6, is designated as הָאִיתוֹן, which word is only here in the Qeri (Kethibh: הַיְאתוֹן). Either adjective or substantive, it is derived from אָתָה, "to come," and designates, as the point of departure, the entrance-gate to which one comes when one wishes to go to the temple. As the opposite standpoint, towards the court, פֶּתַח־הַשַּׁעַר, has been mentioned in ver. 11, the special designation of the gate was so much the more in place.—Although for fixing the *terminus ad quem*, עַל־ will have to be taken as *versus*, "towards," yet when, as here, it stands in conjunction with לִפְנֵי, it has not its full force. There lies in it something like: "upon," "above," which seeks to assert itself; for in ver. 11 the height of the gate, and in ver. 13 the roofing of the gate-chambers, and in ver. 14 the summit of the entire gate-structure, came into consideration. ["From" and "to" are omitted, says Hengstenberg, because the relation is clear in itself.] The **porch** is known from ver. 7 sq., and thereby, as from the contrast to הַיְאתוֹן, the "inner" gate, the gate leading into the court, and hence to the interior of the temple; especially when the east gate is *vis à vis* the sanctuary proper.—For this the man needs only step forward on the seventh step, look up, and, passing through the gate-buildings, calculate his starting-point: first threshold, 6 cubits; three guardrooms with two intervening spaces, 28 cubits; second threshold, 6 cubits; porch, 6 cubits; projection of the side and gate-pillars, 4 cubits = 50 cubits. This length is the double of the breadth. ["When the Psalmist calls upon the gates of the temple or of the holy city to lift themselves up, to widen themselves, at the entering in of the ark of the covenant (Ps. xxiv.), the idea which underlies this song is here symbolically embodied and expressed."]

Ver. 16 appropriately closes the description with an explanation of the way in which the gate-structure was lighted; for it needs light for the inspection of the watchmen especially. Hence there were **windows;** first of all, **in the guardrooms,** namely, **in their wall-pillars,** by which they are distinguished from the אֵילִים in ver. 10 (אֵלִים, written defectively). Pillars projecting from the wall enclosed the windows of the guardrooms. That these windows were **closed** (1 Kings vi. 4) certainly does not mean that they were not to let the light pass through, but that they were only for light, and not to be opened for any other purpose; that they were windows meant "for a sacred purpose" (HÄV.), and "not so much for looking through" (HITZIG). The being **closed** explains itself fully when we once consider that they, as also the doors of these chambers, led into the court, into which, therefore, no one was to press forward, either through the doors or by means of these windows, and then consider that their relation to the gateway given as **within** must put them on the same line with the other windows to be mentioned immediately, which came directly into the gateway, and had to be made "so" (כֵּן). Although the windows of the guardrooms are for the use of **the gate,** yet the word **within** shows that the gate gets the light first of all from the guardrooms, which indeed are also open inward up to the barrier. But since the guardrooms on both sides of the gate come forward to the court, it can be said of their windows that they were **round and round** the gate, as was said of the court (ver. 14) in relation to the gate. [KLIEF.: "In the inside of the gate-structure round about" (?).] For the purpose, however, of giving more light to the gate-structure, there were such windows לְאֵלַמּוֹת. Since nothing is nearer to the guardrooms than their partition-walls (ver. 7), we will have to think, in the first place, of them. אֵילָם is etymologically connected with אֵילִים and with אוּלָם, but is, however, as Klief. has satisfactorily shown, distinct from both. The signification: "projecting part," which Keil gives to the word, that is, what is on a solid wall for architectural ornament or necessity,—as for the windows in question, moulding, frieze, frame, and such like,—suits perfectly to the partition-walls with their windows, for these walls are, according to ver. 30, to be taken here too as 5 cubits broad, and thus were a projection on the gate-structure. [Klief. translates: "porch walls."] If, then, they projected likewise into the court on both sides, the "round and round" is as apposite and illustrative in respect to them as in respect to the guardrooms formerly. The carrying out of the parallel thus, the **windows round and round,** and the concluding expressly (**inwards**) with the lighting of the gateway, shows that that has been sufficiently cared for. [What Hengst. quotes from BALMER-RINCK about the **pillars,** by which "the windows are as it were latticed," would have been more suitable had it been said that the Elim were on the windows, and not the reverse, as here.] —Kliefoth, however, understands by the "Elammoth" or "Elammim" not only "the parapets and walls filling up the spaces between the guardrooms, but also the sides of the porch and the sides adjoining the second threshold" as pierced through with windows. The observation also is perhaps correct, as the measuring (ver. 13) from roof to roof of the guardrooms possibly shows already, that when the gate-structure thus has windows all over, it was roofed and covered. Since אַיִל in a collective sense may possibly include the just now mentioned "Elim" of the guardrooms, while in vers. 9 and 14, on the other hand, mention is specially made of the two high pillars at the porch, it will be a question whether we have, with Kliefoth, to imagine the whole of the "Elim" decorated with palm-leaf work. Hengst. (who insists on its "inseparable connection with the cherubim," of which we may remark there is here no mention) makes the palms "indicate that the gate leads to a building consecrated to the Lord of creation; it corresponds to the merely introductory character of the gate that the creation is here represented not by the animal kingdom, but by the lower region of the vegetable kingdom, of which the palm is king." HÄV.: "By this symbol nothing else is meant to be impressed upon the temple than the stamp of the noblest and grandest prosperity." More fully BÄHR (see *der Salom. Tempel*, p. 120 sq.): "Since all fulness, riches, and glory of vegetable life is comprehended in the palm, it above all is adapted for the habitation of Jehovah, which is called a habitation of glory; it stands, therefore, parallel to the cherub, nothing vegetable can so announce the glory of the Creator. By it the habitation of Jehovah is indicated as a perpetually flourishing habitation, abiding in vigorous strength, concealing in itself the fulness of life; it becomes the place of salvation, life, peace, and joy, a paradise of God. But since the sanctification of Israel is the end and aim of Jehovah's dwelling among them, these ideas are of an ethical character (Ps. i. 3, lii. 10 [8]; Jer. xvii. 8; Prov. xi. 28, 30; Ezek. xlvii. 12; Rev. xxii. 2; particularly Ps. xcii. 13 [12] sq.). The fact that the temple was adorned with these figures, while the tabernacle was destitute of them, has its ground in the Promised Land. Palestine is the native land of the palm, hence these armorial bearings and badges of the land and people of Israel on the coins of the age of the Maccabees, and on Phœnician coins, while on those of Titus we have a palm tree with *Judœa capta.* In Solomon's temple, on the other hand, *Judœa victrix* had been represented, for the temple was at once the monument of Israel's victory over its enemies and of Jehovah's covenant faithfulness, and a pledge of the firm possession of the land (comp. ch. xxxvii.). The palm, already pointing in this way to salvation, peace, joy, and rest, was very specially a symbol of that which had dawned for Israel with the period of the 'house' and its builder, the Prince of Peace. Thus there is a relation of Jehovah's habitation to the land, and of the land to the sanctuary; both relations are bound up with each other in the palm. The place of Jehovah's residence and revelation is a place of palms, thus the land of palms is a land of Jehovah's residence and revelation, a heavenly land." [KLIEF.: "The palm branches stand in close relation to the feast of tabernacles, and it is the eschatological signification of that feast which is designed to be stamped by this adorning with palms upon the edifice of the sanctuary" (?).] Comp. however, here, for the entrance into the temple of the New Jerusalem, the entry of the Messiah through the midst of palms, Matt. xxi. 8; Mark xi. 8.

[FAIRBAIRN: "Here also nothing was left to men's caprice or corrupt fancies, as had been the case of old" in the outer court of Solomon's temple. "A more perfect state of things was to be brought in; and even all in the outer court was to be regulated by God's hand, and bear the impress of His holiness. This, too, must be hallowed ground, fashioned and ruled in all its parts after the perfect measure of the divine mind and the just requirements of His service; therefore such was evidently the practical result aimed at,—let not the ungodly and profane any longer presume to tread such courts (Isa. i. 12), or desecrate them by the introduction of their own unwarranted inventions. Let all feel that in coming here they have to do with a God of purer eyes than to behold iniquity."—W. F.]

Vers. 17–19. *The Outer Court.*

It is necessary to pass over it to come to the other gates. Comp. ch. x. 5.—לִשְׁכָּה is properly: "appendage," and so: annexed building or side-room; specially used for small chambers at the sides, which served for keeping utensils and provisions, for the residence of the priests, and also for sacrificial feasts (1 Sam. ix. 22). Comp. **Jer. xxxv.**

2. Hengst. describes well the use of the "*Leshachoth:*" a refuge from storm and rain, as the pavement preserved the feet from mud, but principally for rejoicing before the Lord, for the eating and drinking before Him (Deut. xii.; Luke xiii. 26), in which the necessitous also participated, the *agapæ* of the Old Covenant. — רִצְפָה, a stone-covered floor, literally: what is "made firm," pavement, stone-cover, like *pavimentum*, from *pavire* (παιω), to ram tight.—עָשׂוּי is particip. masc. sing., referring, according to Hengst., to the chambers and the stone pavement as a whole in a neuter sense; according to Kliefoth, only to the stone pavement, which is feminine; but, as Keil justly observes, his grounds for this are not cogent. That both the chambers and the pavement were **made for the court round about**, brings them near to the wall, and makes them run along it round about the court, except its west side. Thirty such chambers are easily divided into ten in each of the three possible directions, although in ver. 18 only the stone pavement is expressly placed in relation to the three gates; for the "Leshachoth" are described as "beside" (not "upon") the stone pavement; according to Hengst.: opening on it, meaning probably that they bounded the pavement. Since these chambers may be supposed spacious, each like an annexe by itself,—whence also it may be seen how they presented themselves singly to the eye for numbering,—they might, reaching, as they did, nearly from gate to gate, have been like a connection between these.—Ver. 18. As the chambers were אֶל־הָרִצְפָה, so the stone pavement was אֶל־כֶּתֶף, by the "shoulder," that is, side **of the gates**, for the gates of the outer court are already looked on collectively; and this אֶל־כֶּתֶף is more exactly explained by לְעֻמַּת אֹרֶךְ הַשְּׁעָרִים, meaning that the length of the gates fixed the breadth of the stone pavement. As the **lower**, it is to be distinguished from that situated higher, that is, the upper, inner court. — Ver. 19 measures the breadth of the outer court, starting from the east gate, the gate hitherto spoken of, and that, doubtless, from the front of its porch.—הַתַּחְתּוֹנָה refers neither to שַׁעַר nor to an omitted הֶחָצֵר, but simply to the stone pavement of the outer court, called in ver. 18 הַתַּחְתּוֹנָה.—**To the front**, etc., this *terminus ad quem* is indicated by מִחוּץ in respect to the gates of the inner court, as they advance 50 cubits into the outer court; and here, in respect to the east gate of the inner court, *to the front of the porch of this gate*, where, accordingly, one stepped **from without** on to the inner court (vers. 23, 27). The man neither measured into the inner court nor yet up to its wall. The מִחוּץ also, doubtless, belongs to the starting-point of the measuring,—100 cubits + 2 gate lengths of 50 = 200 cubits. The breviloquent expression: "the east and the north," which latter points to what follows, would, when resolved, run as follows: Thus with respect to the east side, and the same with respect to the north side.

Vers. 20–23. *The North Gate.*

The length and breadth, only mentioned as measured in Ver. 20, are in Ver. 21 determined **after the measure** of the gate. הָיָה refers, according to Keil, to the north gate (ver. 20), but may be referred more exactly to the collectives תָאָו, אֵילָו, and אֵלַמָּו: all that was, etc. In citing particulars, the porch and thresholds are omitted. The number of the guardrooms is again given with more exactitude. — בָּאַמָּה, strictly: measured "by the cubit."—While brevity thus characterizes the repetition, with which the use of collectives harmonizes, Ver. 22 subjoins the number of the steps, applicable to the east gate also. In addition to the windows, the "Elammim" and the palms are again expressly mentioned, and what the אֵילַמִּים are is made plainer by their being indicated as **before** those who go up. לִפְנֵיהֶם refers, not to מַעֲלוֹת, but to יַעֲלוּ. The mention of the "Elammim" here, for the third time, is in order to supplement the description of the east gate, in which only those between the guardrooms had been thought of. Thus the entrance threshold, too, had "Elammim"; these, of course, being without windows, because filling the breadth of the wall (ver. 6), but furnished with projecting cornices. It lay *vis à vis* level with the last step.—Ver. 23. Now that the parts **opposite** have been spoken of, the not hitherto observed relation of the gate (of the inner court) to the gate (of the outer court) is given with reference to the two gates described northward and eastward.

Vers. 24–27. *The South Gate.*

Ver. 24. כַּמִּדּוֹת הָאֵלֶּה, **by those measures** which were observed on the east and north gates; and also of which the dimension had not been stated in definite numbers, but yet had its measured definite magnitude. — The guardrooms are not mentioned here.—Ver. 25. That the windows here are described as: **like those windows**, shows how the כַּמִּדָּה regarding them in ver. 22 is to be understood.—לוֹ, referring to the gate-structure, is prefixed in order to be able to give as briefly as is done the length and breadth of the gate.—Ver. 26. לִפְנֵיהֶם, to be understood from ver. 22.—אֶל־אֵילָו refers to the two pillars at the porch. Comp. on ver. 16. Hengst. supposes that by every pillar stood two artificial palms, which put it between them (?).—Ver. 27 to be understood from ver. 23.—Kliefoth calculates the entire extent of the temple building as a square of 500 cubits.

Vers. 28–37. *The Gates of the Inner Court.*

We already know that the inner court **has**, opposite the three gates of the outer court, likewise three gates. The measuring reached in **ver.** 27 to the south gate, which is therefore **spoken of** first in Ver. 28. בַּשַּׁעַר: so that I found myself in the south gate; others translate: through, etc. The general statement retains the same dimensions as in the outer gates.—Ver. 29, befitting the brevity, almost entirely collectives.—Ver. 30 tells how many cubits the "Elammoth" claimed from the gates in length and, because **round about**, in breadth, thus advancing into the court. Twenty-five cubits' length makes the half of the whole length of the gate. Keil accordingly includes in this latter: 10 cubits of the two partition-walls of the guardrooms, 12 for two threshold walls, and 2 cubits for the porch walls; the missing cubit forms mouldings. Hengst. does not allow the side walls of the porch to extend to the space before the terminating pillars, and deducts from the 10+12+6=28 cubits, the special side walls of the guardrooms, 3 cubits thick on the whole, which, however, are to be reckoned into the 5 cubits of the space between the guardrooms, and into the 6 cubits of the threshold. So Kliefoth previously. — The 5 cubits' breadth, which is likewise included in the entire breadth of 25 cubits, gives Hengst. occasion to remark that, since a bulwark of 5 cubits would have been useless, we may suppose two walls with a dark space within, the breadth of the guardrooms projecting 1½ or 2½ cubits before the side parapets. The statement in Ver. 31 that the side walls in the length and breadth mentioned, collectively וְאֵילָמוֹ, were directed towards the outer court, makes this inner gate, like the outer gates, seem built in the outer court, and, as its אֵיל (ver. 9) is spoken of immediately, with the two gate pillars (ver. 37), hence towards the side of the porch, and thus in reverse relation to the outer gates, and consequently so that the one porch faced the other. So Kliefoth, who then places the steps here before the porch. But how can he (and Keil after him) say of the inner gates, that the "second threshold lay between the surrounding walls of the inner court, and the gate-structure extended thence into the outer court," and yet maintain that the gate of the inner court lay "with its whole length" within the outer court? Reckoned from the "second threshold" that cannot be said; the porch only with the gate pillars was there. Hengst., on the other hand, makes the terminating point towards the inner court be the pillars with their palms, between which one went forth into the inner court; and the commencement of the gateway which reached farthest into the outer court he makes to be the stair.—מַעֲלוֹ (HITZIG: singular; KEIL: plural of מַעֲלָה, "ascent") instead of עֹלוֹת in ver. 26, the "ascending steps which form the stair" (HITZIG). On the steps being eight, a number elsewhere without import, Hengst. says: "It is here to be regarded merely as an advance on the number at the outer court, a hint at the superior dignity of the inner court, which, with its altar of burnt-offering, rises still higher above the outer court than this does above the profane exterior." [KLIEF.: "Eight is the number of the new beginning, and so the signature of the New Covenant, and of the *res novissimæ* in general; those who ascend to this priests' court will be a new priestly race, when God has established a new beginning. The number eight does not occur in John's vision of the New Jerusalem, because the new beginning is already given."]

Ver. 32. The inner east gate.—Ver. 33 as ver. 29. — Ver. 34. Comp. ver. 31. — Ver. 35. The inner north gate.—Ver. 36. More abbreviated than ver. 33.—Ver. 37. וְאֵילָו instead of וְאֵלַמּוֹ in ver. 34. "To this" (the north gate), says Hengst., "the prophet is brought last, because to it alone (?) belonged the noteworthy things of the inner court, to be described in the following section,—the arrangements for the slaughter of the victims, and the preparation of their flesh."

Vers. 38–47. *The Inner Court in respect of certain Arrangements for the Temple Service.*

The temple and its service is the theme of these closing chapters of our prophet. Hence it is easy to understand that what follows of the description of the inner court, which has hitherto been occupied with the consideration of the three gates, merely can be given in orderly connection. [FAIRBAIRN: "Everything connected even with the killing and preparing of victims must now be regulated by the word of God. Even *there*, all is to have an impress of sacredness, such as has not hitherto been found, in consequence of the higher elevation to which the divine kingdom was to attain." — W. F.] —The **opening** of the annexe, the side-chamber (ver. 17), is בָּאֵילִים, that is, beside the two pillars of the court. Hengstenberg limits the plural הַשְּׁעָרִים (="at the gates"), as a generic designation in distinction from the pillars in the interior, to the north gate. Böttcher likewise supposes two of such cells at the entrance to and two at the exit from this gate-structure, all of them on the side walls close by the thresholds. Keil finds with reason that הַשְּׁעָרִים indicates a cell with a door to each of the three interior gates, a view supported by the intended use: **there shall they wash the burnt-offering** (a thing belonging to the priests' court). יָדִיחוּ, Hiphil from דּוּחַ, to "thrust out," to "cast away," the filth, hence: to **wash**. "The Old Testament and the Talmud recognise only the washing of the entrails and the legs of the victims for the burnt-offering (Lev. i. 9; 2 Chron. iv. 6)" (KEIL). This, however, does not hinder us from taking הָעֹלָה here in its character of fulness, which makes it the first in the list of offerings in ver. 39, not so much *per synecdoche* for the bloody offerings in general, as (like ver. 43, הַקָּרְבָּן more externally) bringing to view the idea of offering from its inmost and most fundamental conception. One cell at each gate is sufficient for the purpose (it is the last stage for the victim's flesh before it is laid on the altar); but that there is such a cell at each gate is evident from the idea itself, which KLIEF. (who places the washing-cells in pairs, one on each side of each gate porch) thus expresses: "The slaying took place at the gate beside the porch, and no longer at the side of the altar of burnt-offering, as laid down in the law (Lev. i. 11); in the new temple the service will be so much more regular, zealous, and frequent; thither shall prince and people flow to bring their offerings; they will slay and (as there shall then be clean offerings) still more wash before all the gates." Hengstenberg, on the other hand, insists upon the direction in Lev. i. 11: "northward."—Passing over to the slaying, Ver. 39 speaks, according to HENGST., of the north gate (vers. 35, 40, 44) alone; but הַשַּׁעַר may comprehend collectively הַשְּׁעָרִים of the former verse, or (comp. on ver. 40) may mean a definite gate at which what holds good of all the gates is to be exemplified.—The four **tables,** two and two opposite on opposite sides, are **in the porch,** as the cells for washing beside the gate pillars are there also. שָׁחַט, "to slay," is either to be taken in a wider sense, comprehending the whole preparation of the flesh for the sacrifice, particularly the laying (comp. ver. 43) of the pieces of flesh on the tables, which, however, would be strangely expressed by לִשְׁחֹט, or אֲלֵיהֶם only simply indicates that the slaying of the victim took place without, in the direction towards these tables, in relation to them.—In the enumeration of the offerings the expiatory sacrifices are fully represented, namely, by the sin-offering and the trespass-offering,—a hint for the understanding of Ezekiel's temple, for the idea of the expiatory sacrifice has in view the restoration of the state of grace, or reception into that state. Although the burnt-offering stands first, as hitherto it has been treated of as *instar omnium*, and hence the relation in the state of grace must come principally into consideration, yet we are not to imagine an absolute purity of the people from sin in the time of this temple.—Ver. 40 adds two pairs of tables to these inner tables. The first pair, as they are said to be placed **at the side,** in contrast to the porch, so in contrast to the interior of the gate-structure they are described as **without**; and this is so much the more expressive, as reference is to be made **immediately to him that goeth up** (לָעוֹלֶה, particip.). The figurative expression: אֶל־הַכָּתֵף, which Kliefoth here and in ver. 18 presses far too much and unnecessarily, demands even as such a closer and proper definition, as here מִחוּצָה (KEIL: "outside"). But the phrase: "him that goeth up," clearly shows that the steps (מַעֲלוֹת), and, since they lie before, with them לְפֶתַח הַשַּׁעַר (comp. ver. 11), are to be understood as belonging to the porch; and הַצָּפוֹנָה (thus correctly Keil) clearly explains the כָּתֵף to be the north side of the gate; whence Kliefoth infers that הַשַּׁעַר in question is, just as in the case of the outer gates, the east gate. [Kliefoth, as others also, translates: "for him that goeth up to the gate-opening towards the north." HENGST.: "to the door of the north gate." HITZIG: northward, that is, to the right hand. Böttcher takes לָעוֹלָה to mean: "at the stair."]—The two other tables (in confirmation of the exposition given) were at the "following" ("other") side, הָאַחֶרֶת, which designation forms a brief contrast to the הַצָּפוֹנָה, as in like manner אֲשֶׁר לָאוּלָם comprises in brief the rest that has been said.—Ver. 41. A summing up to the number eight of the tables designated as within and without in vers. 39 and 40: because the latter four are tables set apart for slaying, אֲלֵיהֶם may be rendered: "on," or: "at them." Ver. 42 shows that the summing up with such indication of what is distinctive in the two latter pairs is made because there is still a third set of four tables to be mentioned. In accordance with the foregoing, one would expect here too a fixing of where they stood; hence עֹלָה can hardly mean: "burnt-offering," which is spoken of at the close, and much more completely.—They are stone tables (גָּזִית, the "cutting" of the stones), formed of square blocks, as are also the stair steps. Hence those previously mentioned were doubtless of wood, particularly the second set, named as specially appointed for slaying, while this third set had to support heavy instruments. Finally, in addition and parallel to the **burnt-offering,** comes the **slain-offering,** which includes the sin-offering, trespass-offering, and thank-offering. [HENGST.: "There are twelve tables in all, according to the number of the tribes of Israel, Ezra vi. 17, viii. 35."]—Ver. 43. הַשְׁפַתַּיִם must be something definite, something well known, and at the same time (from the dual) double or biform. Gesen. has given up the meaning: *stabula*, "cattle-stalls," held by Hupf. on Ps. lxviii. 14 [13], for that of "stakes" or "staples" standing out on the wall and bifurcated, to which they bound the beasts about to be slain. Meier, again, who rejects the idea of a fundamental signification: "to place," accepts the meaning: "to draw together," to separate, to make fast as such, and imagines: "enclosures of wicker-work for the cattle, of two rows, between which the herdsman used to rest." But what purpose do these serve here? KEIL therefore: "double staples," on which the slaughtered animals were hung for skinning. The article may denote the kind (of staple). (Others: "drinking troughs," or: conduits for conveying away the fluids.) But how does בַּבַּיִת harmonize? It only remains to make it a slip of the pen for בִּנְיָן, as the wall is called in ver. 5, or an abbreviation, or, like Keil, to think of בִּנְיָה ("house" = building). מוּכָנִים is particip. Hoph. from כּוּן. The description: **round and round,** would, moreover, answer well for the wall of the inner court, which surrounded the temple edifice on three sides; and the sacrificial victims may well be conceived of as bound to this wall. [KEIL: "On the three outsides of the porch building."] Kliefoth (and so Hengstenberg) understands raised ledges (border enclosures), with which the tables for laying the sacrificial flesh on were surrounded at the edge round about, so that the flesh lay securely between the ledges as between hurdles, and did not fall off; the ledges were opposite one another in pairs, hence the dual, a handbreadth high. But even with such an interpretation, בַּבַּיִת still causes a difficulty, for according to this, "in the house" must be taken as = in the interior of the porch (בָּאֻלָם, ver. 39), and that in distinction from the tables in vers. 40 and 42, or, as already סָבִיב סָבִיב of the tables ("round about the table-tops," KLIEF.), be taken as a figurative expression for "within" the tables (how does **round and round** harmonize with this?), and thus either the porch or a table must be taken as a house! Only the transition to the last clause would be easy, and this doubtless has given occasion to this interpretation; but, on the other hand, the new element would be wanting which the **double staples** give in this so exact representation. The ellipsis: **And on the tables,** etc., states the purpose for which the tables in ver. 39 was intended, in distinction from that of the tables in vers. 40 and 42. Keil makes the statement refer to all the tables in vers. 39–42.—הַקָּרְבָּן ("approaching," "presenting"), like "offering," from *offerre*, is the most general and comprehensive name for offerings. Mark vii. 11: Κορβαν ὁ ἐστι δωρον. Hengstenberg observes in addition: "The very going into details apparently so minute showed how clearly and sharply the prophet in faith beheld the non-existent as existent, and was well fitted to draw away the minds of the people from the fixed look at the smitten city. We must indeed always keep in view the object of the prophet, to set up an interim temple for the imagination (!), in which it might expatiate as long as the real temple, and with it the kingdom of God, actually lay in ruins."

Hitherto we have had arrangements for slaying and preparing the sacrificial victims (vers. 38–43) in reference to the inner court. With Ver. 44 we come to the *personelle* of the service.—Since we have been in the foregoing at the side of the porch of the inner gate, hence properly in the outer court, and only in relation to the inner court, the more exact description of: **outside at the inner gate,** by: **in the inner court,** is only correct. On the other hand, the cells for the singers at once present an insuperable difficulty for those who, like Keil, still draw sharply, and apply here, the Old Testament distinction "between the Levitical singers and the Aaronites who administer the priesthood" (against this sharp distinction comp. ver. 46). That Ezekiel selected certain descendants of Aaron —who, by the way, is not named in ver. 46, although Levi is—for the service of this sanctuary, is no reason why these should not come into consideration here primarily as **singers,** especially when we consider the idea thereby expressed, and so made impressive. Hengstenberg says excellently: "That the singers are here so prominent is explained by this, that in the state of exaltation of the community of God, more ample material will be given to them for new songs, so that in the worship of the new temple the singing must play a chief part, as, indeed, the multiplication of the singers and musicians under David stood in connection with the advance which, under him, the people of God had made. According to Ps. lxxxvii., when the future of salvation has come, the singers with the dancers say: All my springs are in Thee. The second part of Isaiah, and its lyric echo, Ps. xci.–c., are full of the thought, that in the time of salvation all things shall sing and play. Even in the times soon after the return from the exile, singing revived in a degree that had not been since David. In a long series of psalms, from Ps. cvii. onward, the people thank God for the blessing of restoration. Hallelujah was the watchword." The difficulties connected with the locality of these cells for the singer-priests, which have induced even Keil to enter on the slippery path of text-revision, guided by the Septuagint,—of which, however, we must first have some authentic text, if, on its authority, anything is to be altered in the Masoretic text,—are sufficiently solved by Kliefoth. He observes on 'מִחוּצָה, that, consequently, they "were not constructed in or on the gate building itself, like the cells in ver. 38." He rightly makes 'אֲשֶׁר refer to that part and space of the inner court which is contiguous to the side of the north gate, and hence not contiguous to the east gate. The description of the locality of the cells becomes perfect by this, that their front is stated to be towards the south, that is, nearer to the temple edifice than to the altar of burnt-offering, while the definition: "toward the north," approaches nearer to the altar of burnt-offering. KLIEFOTH: "The entrance of the temple lay to the southwest from the north gate; from it the priests had the temple in their view." HENGST.: "The chambers of the singers generally faced the south, where they (1 Chron. xvi. 37) chiefly had to perform."—As the number is indefinite at the beginning, and it is simply said in the plural, just as the priests, afterwards distinguished, are here comprehended in **the singers,** so the limitation in the second part of the verse, before the pendant in question fronting the north, is applicable also to that fronting the south, so that we really have to suppose likewise, in the first part of the verse, if not only one cell, yet only one range of cells (with several chambers). The masculine אֶחָד can be understood of **a part** of the cells, and so the better corresponds to the previous plural, and especially to the ופְּנֵיהֶם.—That it cannot mean "another" range of cells is self-evident, against Kliefoth. Situated **at the side of the east gate** signifies: if one steps out of the east gate into the inner court, as the following shows, with *the front towards the north.* HENGST.: "There, in the court, stood the altar of burnt-offering, where the singers had to perform at the offering of the great national sacrifices, 1 Chron. xvi. 41." [KLIEF: On account of the "superintendence over the altar" (ver. 46), and the "overseeing of the east gate."] Keil translates ver. 44: "And outside of the inner gate were two cells in the inner court, one at the shoulder of the north gate, with its front to the south, and one at the shoulder of the south gate, with the front to the north."

Vers. 45, 46. Explanation of the purpose for which the two ranges of cells were intended with respect to the persons performing service.—Ver.

45. Therefore וַיְדַבֵּר אֵלָי.—שָׁמַר מִשְׁמֶרֶת means: **the** waiting upon a business, to take care of an office, to attend to it. To make prominent the significance of temple and altar, the priestly service in respect to the **house** is kept separate from that with respect to the **altar** in ver. 46, yet so that the significant general character of those ministering according to ver. 44 is not thereby abolished.—The **sons of Zadok** are selected not as Aaronites in particular, but from among the **sons of Levi** (see the fuller treatment of this point on ch. xliv. 15).—הַקְּרֵבִים' is the general expression for the priestly function in general, as is also שָׁרֵת (Heb. vii. 19; James iv. 8).

Ver. 47. A finishing off with the inner court by stating its length and breadth as 100 cubits each, forming a square, at the same time already making mention of its proper furniture, namely, the **altar before the house**, the altar of burnt-offering. On this comp. on ch. xliii. 13 sq.

Vers. 48, 49. *The Porch of the Temple.*

The description is surprisingly short in comparison with that of the parts previously delineated, and likewise when we compare it with the description of Solomon's temple, in which reversely the courts are briefly treated of. Hengst. explains this latter circumstance from the familiarity of the people with the courts, while this had to be compensated for by a copious description of the part of the sanctuary inaccessible to them; and makes Ezekiel refer back to this description, and only in the case of the courts to enter more into detail in consideration of the people, and especially those of them to whom the courts might be wholly unknown.—Ver. 48 describes the porch before the holy place (1 Kings vi. 3), by giving the measurement of its two pillars, and the breadth of the gate. The expressions: **on this side**, and: **on that**, easily explain themselves as regards the corner pillar on each side, but not sufficiently in respect to the breadth of the gate. What is meant there by מִפּוֹ מִפּוֹ? This statement cannot be occasioned merely by the pillar on this side and on that, but must have its cause in the construction of the gate, which then (comp. on ch. xl. 11) would be represented as a barricade with two halves, which had their hinges on the respectively contiguous corner pillars, so that from this construction the measure of each half of the gate is given by itself; so here and so there. The measurement of the gate given in the text comes out still more plainly if each half of the gate (probably lattice-work) shut up only a part, its own part, of the breadth of the porch; and since this made up only three cubits on either side, a breadth of five cubits remained open in the middle for looking in and walking in. This view of Kliefoth's (also Hengstenberg's) harmonizes exactly with the measurements which immediately follow; whereas Keil, with an entire breadth of sixteen cubits, has only six cubits left for the breadth of the gate. For Ver. 49, which measures twenty cubits for the length of the porch of the temple, that is, from east to west (comp. 1 Kings vi. 3), gives its breadth, hence from north to south, or *vice versâ*, at eleven cubits, both measurements being taken in the light, and hence excluding the thickness of the walls. This interior breadth of the porch is shown to belong also to the outside by the statement: **and that** (also) **at the steps**, sq.; namely, the breadth was eleven cubits. The stair extended in equal breadth before the porch. In this way, as Kliefoth observes, the porch was wider by half a cubit on either side than the door leading from the porch into the holy place (ch. xli. 2), which door was thereby rendered as visible as its character of fixing the length of the porch demanded. [Hengst., referring to the ten cubits' breadth of the porch in Solomon's temple, supposes the eleventh cubit here to be occupied by the posts of the door on both sides.] From the height (six cubits), ch. xli. 8, Hengst. estimates the number of the steps, which is not given, to be "probably fourteen." Kliefoth and Hengstenberg compute the entire breadth of the portal, inclusive of the two corner pillars (5 + 5), to be twenty-one cubits. For enclosing the porch from the pillars to the east wall of the temple, we have to suppose, as with the gates of the court, side-walls ("Elammoth"), which Keil puts down at two and a half cubits each, so that the five cubits broad pillars would have only half their breadth on the inside of the porch. [Hengst., in opposition to most expositions of Solomon's temple, holds that the length of the porch of the temple given here "corresponds to that of the porch in Solomon's temple in 1 Kings vi. 3."] The height of the two corner pillars of the porch, which also is wanting in Ezekiel's vision, is supplied by Hengst., from 2 Chron. iii. 4 (JOSEPHUS, *Arch.* viii. 3. 2), as 5 cubits thick and 120 cubits high. The עַמֻּדִים, two in number, are set down as "at" or "beside" the corner pillars (the "Elim"), which remind us of "Jachin" and "Boaz" in Solomon's temple (1 Kings vii. 15 sq.), and, doubtless, for that very reason their position is not given more exactly. Kliefoth and Hitzig place them one at each side of the steps; and the same is done by Hengst., who says, regarding their import: taken away by the Chaldeans, Jer. lii. 20 sq., they were "as it were the programme of the temple and of the kingdom of God represented by it; they represented what the people of God have in their God: Jachin ('He establishes me') and Boaz ('in Him strong'); made of brass, very thick, uniform to the top, they are a figure of the unchangeable stability and strength which was only in appearance practically disproved by the Chaldeans," etc. —The Septuagint is all confused in these verses; for example, its statement that the steps were ten rests on this, that it has transformed אֲשֶׁר into the similar עֶשֶׂר. Böttcher, Hitzig, and Maurer ground thereon their treatment of the text, and Hävernick is simply at a loss what to make of it.

CHAPTER XLI.

1 And he brought me to the temple, and measured the wall-pillars, six cubits
broad on this side, and six cubits broad on that, the breadth of the tent [was
2 that]. And the breadth of the entrance [the door] was ten cubits, and the sides
of the entrance five cubits on this side and five cubits on that; and he mea-
3 sured its [the temple's] length, forty cubits, and the breadth, twenty cubits. And
he went inward, and measured the wall-pillar of the entrance, two cubits;
and the entrance, six cubits; and the breadth of the entrance, seven cubits.
4 And he measured its [the interior's] length, twenty cubits; and the breadth, twenty
cubits, before the temple: and he said unto me, This is the most holy place.
5 And he measured the wall of the house, six cubits; and the breadth of the
6 side building, four cubits round and round about the house [all around]. And
of the side chambers [there were], chamber on chamber, three, and that thirty
times; and they came into [on] the wall, which was to the house at the side
chambers round and round, so that they are held fast, and [yet] they are not
7 held fast in the wall of the house. And it became broader, and changed
[and in so far it changed] still upwards in the case of the side chambers; for all the
changing in the house [went on] still upwards round and round on the house;
therefore was the breadth to the house upwards, and so the lower [story] will
8 ascend to the upper by the middle. And I saw on the house a height round
and round; the foundations of the side chambers were the full rod, six cubits
9 according to that to the wrist. The breadth of the wall, which was for the
side building without, was five cubits, and [five cubits] the place that was left
free [with respect to] the house of the side chambers, which was annexed to the
10 house. And between the chambers was a breadth of twenty cubits round
11 about the house. And the opening of the side building was towards the free
place, one opening towards the north, and one opening towards the south;
and the breadth of the place [the space] left free was five cubits round and round.
12 And the building which was before the gizrah [off place] on the side towards
the west [literally: towards the sea] had a breadth of seventy cubits; and the wall of
the building was five cubits broad round and round, and its length was ninety
13 cubits. And he measured the house, a hundred cubits long; and the gizrah,
14 and the building, and its walls, a hundred cubits long. And the breadth of
the front of the house, and of the gizrah towards the east, a hundred cubits.
15 And he measured [so measured he] the length of the building which was in front
of the gizrah [namely] on its back part, and [that was] its galleries on this side
and on that, a hundred cubits, and the inner temple and the porches of the
16 court; The thresholds, and the closed windows, and the galleries round
about on all three,—over against the threshold [was] a boarding of wood
round and round,—and the ground up to the windows [measured he, or: had measures],
17 and the windows [were] covered; Up above the opening and [that] to the
inner house and outside, and on the whole wall round and round within and
18 without [were] measures. And [there were] made cherubim and palms, [so that] a
19 palm was between a cherub and a cherub, and on the cherub two faces. And
the face of a man was towards the palm on this side, and the face of a lion
towards the palm on that side; it was made on the whole house round and
20 round. From the ground to above the opening were the cherubim and the
palms made, and [this on the; or: so much of the, etc.; or: this is] the wall of the temple.
21 The post of the temple was square, and the front of the sanctuary; the view
22 [was] as the view [had the same view]. The altar of wood was three cubits high,
and its length two cubits; and it had its corners; and its length and its walls
were of wood: and he said unto me, This is the table that is before Jehovah.
23, 24 And two doors were to the temple and to the sanctuary. And there were
two leaves to the doors, two turning leaves, two to the one door, and two
25 leaves to the other. And on them, on the doors of the temple, were made

cherubim and palms, as they were made on the walls; and a wooden pedi-
26 ment was on the front of the porch without. And closed windows and palms
were on this side and on that, on the sides of the porch; thus [as respects] the
side chambers of the house, thus [as regards] the pediments.

Ver. 1. Sept.: . . . *εἰσηγαγεν με εἰς . . . το αἰλαμ . . . το πλατος ἐνθεν κ. . . . το εὐρος του αἰλαμ ἐνθεν.* Vulg.: . . *et sex cubitos inde, latitudinem—*

Ver. 2. . . . *του πυλωνος . . . κ. ἐπωμιδες τ. πυλωνος—*

Ver. 3. . . . *εἰς τ. αὐλην την ἐσωτεραν . . . κ. τας ἐπωμιδας του θυρωματος πηχεις ἑπτα ἐνθεν κ. πηχ. ἑπτα ἐνθεν.*

Ver. 4. . . . *το μηκος των θυρωματων πηχ. τεσσαρακοντα κ. εὐρος—*

Ver. 6. . . . K. *τα πλευρα . . . τριακοντα κ. τρις δις· κ. διαστημα ἐν τ. τοιχω του οἰκου ἐν τ. πλευροις τ. οἰκου κυκλω του εἰναι τοις ἐπιλαμβανομενοις ὁραν, ὁπως το παραπαν μη ἁπτωνται των τοιχων—* Vulg.: . . . *bis triginta tria, et erant eminentia, quæ ingrederentur per parietem domus in lateribus per circuitum, ut continerent et non attingerent parietem templi.*

Ver. 7. K. *το εὐρος της ἀνωτερας των πλευρων κατα το προσθεμα ἐκ του οἰκου, προς την ἀνωτεραν κυκλω του οἰκου, ὁπως διαπλατυνηται ἀνωθεν, κ. ἐκ των κατωθεν ἀναβαινωσι ἐπι τα ὑπερωα κ. ἐκ των μεσων ἐπι τα τριωροφα.* Vulg.: *Et platea erat in rotundum. ascendens sursum per cochleam, et in cœnaculum templi deferebat per gyrum, idcirco latius erat templum in superioribus. Et sic de inferioribus ascendebatur ad superiora in medium.*

Ver. 8. Sept.: K. *το θραελ τ. οἰκου ὑψος κυκλω διαστημα των πλευρων ἰσον τω καλαμω πηχεων ἑξ. Διαστηματα* (9.) *κ. εὐρος τ. τοιχου . . . κ. τα ἀπολοιπα ἀνα μεσον τ. πλευρων τ. οἰκου* (10.) *κ. ἀνα μεσον των ἐξεδρων.* Vulg.: . . . *fundata latera*—(9.) *et latitudinem per parietem lateris. . . . Et erat interior domus in lateribus domus.*

Ver. 11. . . . *ἐπι το ἀπολοιπον της θυρας τ. μιας της προς βορραν, κ. ἡ θυρα . . . κ. το εὐρος του φωτος . . . πλατος κυκλωθεν.* Vulg.: *ad orationem.*

Ver. 12. . . . *το διοριζον κατα προσωπον του ἀπολοιπου ὡς προς . . . πλατος . . . του διοριζοντος . . . εὐρος κυκλωθεν κ μηκος αὐτου—* Vulg.: *ædificium quod erat separatum—*

Ver. 13. . . . *κατεναντι του οἰκου . . . κ. τα ἀπολοιπα κ. τα διοριζοντα—*

Ver. 14. . . . *κατεναντι—*

Ver. 15. . . . *κ. τα ἀπολοιπα ἐνθεν* . . . K. *ὁ ναος κ. αἱ γωνιαι κ. το αἰλαμ το ἐξωτερον πεφατνωμενα.* Vulg.: . . . *contra faciem . . . ethecas ex utraque—*

Ver. 16. K. *αἱ θυριδες δικτυωται, ὑποφαυσεις κυκλω . . ὡστε διακυπτειν.* K. *ὁ οἰκος κ. τα πλησιον ἐξυλωμενα κυκλω, κ. το ἐδαφος κ. ἐκ του ἐδαφους ἑως τ. θυριδων, κ. αἱ θυριδες ἀναπτυσσομεναι τρισσως εἰς το διακυπτειν.*

Ver. 17. K. *ἑως πλησιον της ἐσωτερας κ. ἑως της ἐξωτερας—* Vulg.: *et usque ad domum—*

Ver. 18. . . . *γεγλυμμενα.*

Ver. 19. . . . *ἐνθεν κ. ἐνθεν . . . ἐνθεν κ. ἐνθεν. Διαγεγλυμμενος ὁλος ὁ οἰκος . . .* (20.) *ἐκ του ἐδαφους ἑως του φατνωματος . . . διαγεγλυμμενοι.* Vulg.: . . . *in pariete templi.*

K. *το ἁγιον* (21.) *κ. ὁ ναος ἀναπτυσσομενα τετραγωνα, . . . ὁρασις ὡς ὀψις* (22.) *θυσιαστηριου . . . κ. το εὐρος πηχεων δυο κ. κερατα εἰχεν, κ. ἡ βασις αὐτου—* Vulg.: . . . *aspectus contra aspectum.*

Ver. 25. Sept.: K. *γλυφη . . . κ. ἐπι . . . κατα τ. γλυφην των ἁγιων, κ. σπουδαια ξυλα κατα προσωπον—* Vulg.: . . . *quam ob rem et grossiora erant ligna in vestibuli fronte—*

Ver. 26. *κ. θυριδες κρυπται.* K. *διεμετρησεν ἐνθεν κ. ἐνθεν, εἰς τα ὀροφωματα του αἰλαμ, κ. τα πλευρα τ. οἰκου ἐζυγωμενα.* Vulg.: *Super quæ fenestræ . . . secundum latera domus latitudinemque parietum.*

EXEGETICAL REMARKS.

Vers. 1–4. *The Temple.*

The edifice of the temple proper is now described in continuation of ch. xl. 48, 49. We proceed from the temple porch to the "house," as it is called there; to הַהֵיכָל, as it is named in Ver. 1. The idea of greatness, height, like יָכֹל, "to be able," "to have the power of" (HUPF.: "to seize," be capable), lying at the root of this word, suggests a large and spacious edifice, in short, a palace, such as, doubtless, David had in his mind (2 Sam. vii. 2), and in agreement also with the character of Solomon's temple, as a palace of Jehovah (*e.g.* 1 Kings vii. 12). הַהֵיכָל does not need to be understood in the narrower sense of the holy place, any more than does הָאֹהֶל, which designation, embracing both the holy and the most holy place (without the porch), simply subjoins the Mosaic element to the Solomonic.—The "Elim" (see ch. xl. 9) are two wall-pillars, one on each side, six cubits broad, so that by this statement of the breadth of the pillars, the breadth of the whole sanctuary is given as to its bounding points, extending from the extremity of the one to the extremity of the other. For—Ver. 2—there was still between them a door ten cubits broad, and on each side, literally: "shoulders," five cubits broad, making thus the inside breadth twenty cubits, the half of the length.—In Ver. 3 it is said that he **went**; not: he brought me, etc. For, as ver. 4 shows, the place in question was the most holy place, which the mere priest was not permitted to enter. Of the collective door-pillars, one is on the right and one on the left, on the wall between the two divisions of the sanctuary. On account of the following breadth of seven cubits, the six cubits have been taken to be the height of the door, or an additional cubit has been understood as the breadth of the door-posts.—Ver. 4. The measuring of the **length** leads into the interior, to its extreme point; hence the **breadth** is again in front, where the temple appears as a whole, as the palace of holiness.

Vers. 5–11. *The Side Building.*

In Ver. 5 the measuring turns to the outside. As the wall and the side building are spoken of, it is now said the **house**. The **wall** is the wall that begins with the pillars (ver. 1).—The thrice-repeated סָבִיב undoubtedly refers to the three sides, which come into consideration, the two lengthwise and the one at the back.—According to Ver. 6, the **side building** was a complex of ninety chambers or rooms in three stories, sacristies for the priests, and for the custody of the manifold sacred objects, clothes, utensils, etc. (הַצֵּלָע, in ver. 5 collective, like יָצוּעַ in 1 Kings vi. From צָלַע, "to turn," "to bend," it signifies: turning, bending, and thence: side, rib, etc. The הַצְּלָעוֹת in ver. 6 are single chambers which compose the צֵלָע as a whole.) **Chamber** "on" **chamber**; אֶל here = עַל, as is evident from what follows, and still more so from Solomon's temple, through which that becomes clear which otherwise might remain dark. The eye first looks upward, and in this direction there was chamber rising **on** chamber. (KEIL: on the north and south walls, twelve each; on the shorter west wall, six.)—As to the fastening of their floor-beams, these side chambers came "**into the wall** (the proper temple wall which ran around them inside);" the immediately following explanation shows that the בְּ implies such a connection with the wall in question that "into" rather implies: "on," or: "upon"; they were indeed caught and held fast (אָחַז) there, but not in the temple wall itself, for ledges ran round about the temple, *upon* but not *into* which the ends of the beams were put. (Comp. 1 Kings vi. 6, 10.)—Ver. 7 speaks impersonally (it), although, according to what precedes and what immediately follows, it is the **house** that will be thought of under reference to the side building. The widening as it went upwards (לְמַעְלָה לְמַעְלָה) related to the side chambers (לַצְּלָעוֹת). Its explanation is already given in ver. 6, namely, where the ledges let us suppose a gradual narrowing of the temple wall adapted to the three stories. As now said in ver. 7, it was **still upwards** and **round about the house**, thus not on the outer wall of the side building, so that this wall rose perpendicular without any ledges. Accordingly, the width of the side building and relatively of the side chambers necessarily increased as the temple wall grew narrower from story to story. This is the מוּסַב־הַבַּיִת' (from סָבַב, Niph.: וְנָסַבָּה); this widening was the **changing**, which could be said of the temple house (HENGST.: "and altered itself," "the alteration of the house"), כִּי expressing the וְנָסַבָּה with so much the better reason as the מוּסַב was **round and round on the house**, and **therefore** (עַל־כֵּן) רֹחַב־לַבַּיִת, that is, this "width" increasing "with the ascent," this "changing" pertained in fact only to the house, with which the side building of three stories was connected on every possible side. [Keil translates: "and was surrounded," "the surrounding of the house," and understands by that very simply the side building; while Kliefoth understands a gallery-like "corridor" running round the house, by which one could get to the chambers of the upper story, and derives the widening above not from the temple wall, but from the corridors of the second and third stories; comp. the convincing refutation in Keil.]—If the most generally accepted translation: "and so one ascends from the lower story to the upper by the middle," is held to say something not quite clear in itself, one must with Hengstenberg supply from 1 Kings vi. 8 the winding stair, for which room was got by the breadth increasing upwards; we do not need with Keil to suppose the stair on the outside, and to contend against its leading from the lower into the upper, and thence (!) into the middle story; it was self-evidently in the interior of the side building;—or by this translation of the close of the verse one can find the thought expressed that the priests did not step from the temple into the side chambers, but within the widening upwards which the house had through the side buildings. KEIL: "proportionately to the middle story"; the difference of gender decides nothing against הַתַּחְתּוֹנָה as subject to יַעֲלֶה, and וְכֵן indicates that the ascent took place in the way stated of the widening.

What Ezekiel sees—Ver. 8—was **on the house**, and hence still relates to the side building, without its being taken as = "house." [HENGST.: "the height round about," namely, of the side building, may be given.] What we may take as meant by the **height** (KEIL: = elevation) is probably told by מיסדות (Qeri: מוּסְדוֹת). According to Keil, particip. dual of יָסַד; according to Gesenius, a substantive, signifying: the foundations of the side chambers, the basement of which, accordingly, a full rod high, reached to the house; and this harmonizes with the steps leading to the porch of the temple (ch. xl. 49); and so מְלוֹ הַקָּנֶה (only here, elsewhere מְלוֹא, מְלֹא) will hardly be added, "because the elevation above the ground might easily be supposed less" (HENGST.). On the contrary, the six cubits אַצִּילָה has quite the appearance of a closer definition of that which Ezekiel calls **the full rod**, although whether from the elbow to the wrist, where hand and arm meet, or how, cannot be determined. J. D. Michaelis supposes short cubits. Such a more exact definition of the measure would be the more in place were it different from that of ch. xl. 5. [Hengstenberg and Kliefoth understand אַצִּיל of each of the three stories: "the foundations one full rod, six cubits its story." Irrespective of whether אַצִּיל can mean that, וְ is wanting.]—In Ver. 9, besides the five cubits' breadth of the outer wall of the side building, the same extent (וַאֲשֶׁר) is set apart for מֻנָּח (particip. Hoph. of נוּחַ, left "over," "free," "empty"), that is, for the space not built upon (ver. 11). KLIEF.: *par terre* round about the first story of the side building, still to be distinguished from the wider unbuilt-on space which surrounded the temple in a width of twenty cubits.—בַּיִת' regards the side building connected with the temple in this relation separately as a "house," while the clause: אֲשֶׁר לַבַּיִת, still retains the fact that the **house** after all is the temple.—Ver. 10. "The cells" are described in ch. xlii. The breadth of twenty cubits bounds the three sides of the temple, north, south, and west. The breviloquent expression: **between**, etc., Hengstenberg takes to mean: between the outer wall of the side building and the cells. KEIL: between the free space and the cells.—Ver. 11 shows that the side building opened with two doors towards the free space (HENGST.: "between the wall of the side building and the surrounding wall"). The five cubits **round and round** (in distinction from the two door-sides) are those already indicated in ver. 9.

Vers. 12–14. *The Off-place.*

Ver. 12. Now the side building which stands in connection with the house has been treated of, and its relation to the outside too shown, a **building** (as the wall was called in ch. xl. 5) comes to be spoken of which is said to be **before the gizrah**, from which appellation accordingly we have to find its situation and explanation. Since it is not spoken of so incidentally and epenthetically, as Kliefoth supposes, but next to the side building which belongs to the house its measurements also being given, it must be supposed to stand in some relation or another to the temple. And so it is called הַגִּזְרָה, by which is indicated something known, self-intelligible. גָּזַר means: "to separate," "to cut," and is here said of a space; and thus **the gizrah** is an off-place. The goat bears (Lev. xvi. 22) "upon him all their iniquities," אֶל־אֶרֶץ גְּזֵרָה. HENGST.: "The place and the building thereon serve negatively the same purpose which the temple serves positively. If this is to retain its dignity and sanctity, a place must be assigned to which all uncleanness is removed. Already in Deut. xxiii. 13 sq. we find the order for setting apart such a place outside the camp, which corresponded to the temple (?) with its courts; and also the injunction that this place is to be kept clean, which is laid down as a religious duty." With this has been compared in Solomon's temple 2 Kings xxiii. 11; 1 Chron. xxvi. 16, 18 (the "refuse-gate"). See Lange on Kings, p. 262 sq. Nothing whatever is told us expressly regarding the purpose for which this place, situated behind the temple at the west, was intended, perhaps just because the name itself was quite enough. Where bloody sacrifices were brought, sacrificial feasts held, places for preparing them stood, and a numerous body of persons kept moving about, an off-place for the great quantity of all kinds of refuse was a self-evident necessity.—פְּאַת' means the same thing, whether it be taken as defining more closely 'אֲשֶׁר or הַגִּזְרָה, for since the building stood with its east front towards the temple, the side towards the west can only denote its position in some other respect; that is, the position of the place generally. Keil's translation is not clear: "And the building in front of the separate place was on the side towards the west seventy cubits broad."—By the **wall . . . round and round**, the breadth of which is particularly noticed, is to be understood with Kliefoth the wall of the building. Thus "it extended westward to the outer enclosing wall of the court, and had (HENGST.) by a gate built in this its egress into the city." In Ver. 13 the length of the gizrah (inclusive of all) is placed parallel to the length of the temple, as in Ver. 14 the breadth by which the relation, although antithetical, of the gizrah to the temple becomes very clear. Deducting accordingly the $70+2\times5=80$ cubits (ver. 12), there remains of the 100 cubits a free space 20 cubits broad, doubtless 10 on the north and 10 on the south, for approaches to the gizrah building, whose length ran along the whole extent.

Vers. 15–26. *Supplementary.*

Ver. 15, summing up in accordance with ver. 12: $90 + 2 \times 5 = 100$, just like ver. 13, thus being a recapitulation, intimates by this the character of the notices that still follow, as supplementary additions to the preceding.—The measuring of this length proceeds in such a way that the measurer measured the building situated before the gizrah (according to ver. 12) in the direction towards the back part of the place. This is the meaning of the definition: אֲשֶׁר עַל־אַחֲרֶיהָ, the feminine suffix referring to הַגִּזְרָה, the **back part** being the natural antithesis to אֶל־פְּנֵי; so that אֲשֶׁר may either signify "which," or it may also be referred to the length, which extended in front over the back part of the gizrah, if it is not with Keil to be referred to הַבִּנְיָן. This definition is intended, namely, to form the transition to supplementary statements as to the not yet mentioned אַתּוּקֶיהָא (Qeri: אַתִּיקֶיהָא). MEIER: אַתַּק, from אַת, allied to אָתָה, "to go through" = עָדָה, whence אַתִּיק, "walk," as gallery is properly derived from the German *wallen* = *quellen* (to issue forth). GESEN.: properly: "landing place," then a short piazza, from נָתַק, "to break off." The signification: walks, galleries, for the word—occurring only here and in ch. xlii.—is certainly demanded by the latter passage. The analogy to the temple retained throughout speaks in favour of this, as does also the fact that the free space of ten cubits on each side (ver. 14, see exposition) is in this way satisfactorily disposed of. Keil makes the suffix look back to הַבִּנְיָה in ver. 13. The repeated statement of the hundred cubits' length is intended to show that the galleries were as long as the building.—Since now the **inner temple**, *i.e.* that which stood in the inner court (KEIL), or because it is so called in distinction from the gizrah building and the courts (HENGST.), and finally the **porches of the court**, that is, the projections of the gates into the court generally or into the court in question, are mentioned, all that was hitherto measured is summarily repeated; in which manner Ver. 16 continues, to which Hengst. supplies: "and he measured" (ver. 15), while Keil takes them as nominatives absolute, and finds the predicate in מִדּוֹת, ver. 17.—הַסִּפִּים, mentioned in ch. xl. 6, 7, according to Kliefoth: window sills (?).—The **closed windows**, see ch. xl. 16.—The **galleries**, see ver. 15. The definition: **round about on all three** (the gizrah, the temple, and the porches of the court, ver. 15), is either to be understood with respect to the description given in the foregoing of the parts designated by the article as known, and hence to be understood under limitation, or we must, for example, suppose galleries to the temple also, and likewise to the porches of the court; for which Hengst. cites John x. 23, and Josephus, *Arch.* xx. 9. 7. The recapitulatory character of these verses—meant, as they are, for a supplement—speaks in favour of the first view, that of Keil. But that which is to be supplied is in respect of the thresholds or sills (הַסַּף collectively) over against them; and, taken strictly, it denotes the upper moulding of the door, or the door-case generally, on both sides (סָבִיב סָבִיב). [HENGST.: the ground floor when one looked over the threshold; KEIL: the wooden case of the window openings.] שְׁחַף is: "to make thin," whence שְׂחִיף, "thin, fine" wood. Hengst. discovers such wooden boarding also in the words: "and also from the ground to the windows," and places the windows up in the roof, as in the ark (Gen. vi. 16), for one reason, because of the adjoining house, which was probably as high as the temple. Kliefoth, on the other hand, places the windows immediately on the ground floor, and makes the earth of the foundation rise up to the windows (!). As what has been just said had respect to the thresholds, so what follows with וְהָאָרֶץ' is supplementary to the second thing mentioned, the windows; beginning with this, that even the ground up to them, this distance, was a measured distance (ver. 17), which had not yet been said, after which the more intelligible expression: מְכֻסּוֹת (particip. Pual of כָּסָה), illustrates the above-mentioned הָאֲטֻמוֹת. Finally, with respect to the walks which ran along the doors, and the wall rounding off the whole, Ver. 17 accordingly adds, that each and all was according to measure; the space above the door (collective), even into the inner **house**,—the temple in its entirety is spoken of as to its principal parts,—and outside, and the whole wall round about within and without were so. [HENGST.: "a house worthy of the God who has wisely arranged all things in His creation (Ps. civ. 24), and left nothing to caprice and chance."]

The expression: **made**, in Ver. 18, which is resumed in ver. 19, refers to sculpture or carved work; but comp. Lange on Kings, p. 67. On the cherubim, see the same work, p. 66, and in this Commentary on ch. i. 4–14, and Doct. Reflec. 10 on ch. ix.; on the palms, see on ch. xl. 16. HENGST.: "There are the carved works in the temple, the destruction of which by the Chaldeans is lamented in Ps. lxxiv. 6; and now they are there again." Comp. as to the significance of the grouping, Lange on Kings, p. 74 sq. Hengst. brings out the reference that the house is dedicated to the Lord of the whole terrestrial creation.—The arrangement was that a cherub and a palm, and again a cherub, always followed in order.—It is further observed, in distinction from chap. i., that the cherub had **two faces**, as expositors generally say, because only two could be visible, inasmuch as figures were treated of which could present only one side. On this Bähr observes: "But certainly the wings of the eagle and the feet of the bullock were not wanting." Two, however, is specially the number of creation (heaven and earth), of the creaturely contrast, which therefore everything **made** will have in itself, harmonized here by the palm as the third between cherub and cherub into the number of the divine life.—Ver. 19. The two faces were that of man and of the lion, which most aptly represents the wild animal named by way of eminence חַיָּה (ζῶον). The cherub turned the one face to the palm on this side, and the other to the palm on that, whereby the union of the two with the palm to form three was made very manifest.—Ver. 20 illustrates what ver. 19 intends by: **on the whole house round and round**; that it was from the ground or floor to the wall-work above the door, that is, to the roof, and this on the temple within to which the door led, of which, therefore, mention is made.—וְקִיר', local accusative or concluding formula.

But with Ver. 21 comes an additional supplement in relation to the door-post work on the temple, namely, that each pair of door-posts had the significant square form already met with in Solomon's temple, and first fully carried out in Ezekiel (see Lange on Kings, p. 73). In this way the revelation of Jehovah, the God of the world, in the world, in its cosmic relations, comes into prominence; KLIEF.: the number four is "the signature of the coming universality;" it will extend itself into all the world, and to it they shall enter in from all the world. (According to Klief. מְזוּזַת is not *stat. constr.*, but an unusual form for מְזוּזָה. רְבֻעָה, an adjective, literally: "post of the square." Keil remarks on the breviloquence.)—The **sanctuary** (הַקֹּדֶשׁ) is the most holy place (ver. 23). The **front**, which it presented to the priest-prophet treading the holy place, had the view as the view just described, that is, the quadriform view of the door-posts. [HENGST.: "at the front was," etc., since the new view is compared with a former one which the prophet himself had had (ch. xliii. 3). KLIEF.: "And the superficies of the whole sanctuary was likewise square." The Targum and Rashi suppose a reference to the vision by the Chebar.]

Ver. 22 describes with similar brevity of diction the wooden altar of incense, in distinction from the brazen altar of burnt-offerings. The abrupt עֵץ forms also a contrast to the coating of gold in Solomon's temple ("just as there is a deep silence throughout in Ezekiel concerning gold, which plays so great a part in Solomon's temple," HENGST.). While observing that, "in the case of the floor also and the walls mention is made only of the wooden boarding," Hengst. refers to the "troublous times in which temple and city should be built again," and compares Dan. ix. 25; Zech. iv. 10 (comp. Doct. Reflec. 8).—The height and

length (which, considering its square form, gives **at** the same time its breadth)—not given in the case of Solomon's altar,—may, however, be here borrowed from it (HENGST.). Keil includes in **its corners** the four horns found on Solomon's altar. But in what follows: **and its length**, etc., he sees in וארכו a mistake for אדנו, "its pedestal;" while Hengst. can find in it only the top of the altar. But why should we not suppose it to say plainly, because it came in the way here, that the altar in **all** its length and round and round was wood? Ezekiel says nothing of the candlestick, and the table for the shew-bread, and indeed nothing of a furnishing of the most holy place. Keil therefore interprets the explanation: **this is the table**, etc., from the Pentateuch designation of the offerings "as the bread of God." HENGST.: "because that which is set upon this altar—the incense denoting the prayers of the saints (Ps. cxli. 2; Rev. v. 8, viii. 3)—is regarded as a spiritual food which the people present to their Heavenly King. The altar appears as the table of the Lord also in ch. xliv. 16; the offering as food of God in Mal. i. 7. The loaves laid on the table of shew-bread denoted good works;" to which Hengst. compares Matt. xxi. 18 sq., the fruit of the fig-tree, that is, of the Jewish people, after which Jesus hungered. Compare also Bähr's (*der Salom. Tempel*, p. 185 sq.) objections to the view of Hengstenberg and Keil. After all, the express declaration: **This is the table that**, etc., has in it something surprising, which is rather strengthened than explained by ch. xliv. 16. Böttcher thinks that "the altar-table was meant to combine in one the old table of shew-bread and the altar of incense" (see Doct. Reflec. 8). For the rest, the expression: **before Jehovah**, is explained from the place where the altar of incense stood, immediately before the ark of the covenant, which was separated from it by the veil of the most holy place.

In Ver. 23 supplementary mention is made of two doors (1 Kings vi. 32, 33), to be explained, without doubt, by the altar of incense standing at the separating point of the two divisions of the temple, that is, one door belonging to the holy place, and one to the most holy place, both which —Ver. 24—had two leaves each. These two-leaved doors are, however, still more closely described by the following phrase: **two turning leaves**, so that each leaf had two parts which could be opened and shut,—a very suitable arrangement, considering the breadth of these doors. According to Ver. 25, the ornaments on these temple doors are the same as those mentioned in ver. 18 sq.—On the front of the porch (of the temple) without there was a wooden עב. GESEN.: probably a threshold which formed a kind of pediment as stepping-place to a colonnade or temple. How is that to be conceived of? It was evidently made of wood. A threshold-like approach, a perron?—As the beholder's look returns again and again to the ample materials presented to it, something additional is always to be observed. Thus Ver. 26: **closed windows** and simple **palms** on the two shoulders, that is, side-walls, right and left. Either not mentioned hitherto, or at least now more exactly.—The brief concluding clause: וצלעות הבית והעבים, probably simply intimates, that as there were closed windows and palms on the two sides of the porch, so there were windows of the kind on the side chambers, and palms on the wooden pediments. KLIEF.: On the side buildings (?) of the porch and of the side stories were windows and palms, and so also the עבים. Hengst. thinks that the words: "and the steps" [pediments] (= "and besides, the steps also are to be noticed in the porch," ver. 25), "place the extreme end to the east over against the extreme end to the west of the gizrah, with which the section began in ver. 15."

CHAPTER XLII.

1 And he led me forth to the outer court, the way northwards, and brought
me to the chamber [that is, what there was of chambers] which is over against the
gizrah, and [in fact] which is over against the building, toward the north.
2 Before the length [in front of the length] of a hundred cubits, the opening toward
3 the north, and the breadth fifty cubits. Over against the twenty of the inner
court, and over against the pavement of the outer court; gallery [was] before
4 gallery in the third (that is, galleries). And before the chambers was a walk
ten cubits broad, to the inner [court] way of one cubit, and their openings to
5 the north. And the upper chambers were shortened, for the galleries consume [take away] from them, from the [the space of the] lower and also from the
6 [the space of the] middle as respects the building. For they were three-storied
and had no pillars as the pillars of the courts: therefore [space was] taken
7 away from the lowest and the middle, from the ground. And a dividing-wall which is outside, close by the chambers, toward the outer court, in front
8 of the chambers, its length was fifty cubits. For the length of the chambers
which are to the outer court was fifty cubits; and [yet] lo, before the temple
9 a hundred cubits. And from under it [the dividing-wal] were these chambers:
10 the entrance was on the east in coming to them from the outer court. In the
breadth of the dividing-wall of the court, toward the east, fronting the gizrah,
11 and fronting the building, were chambers. And a way before them; as the look

of the chambers which were towards the north, as their length so their breadth
12 and all their outgoings, and as their arrangements, and as their openings, So
also the openings of the chambers which were toward the south, an opening
was at the head of the way, the way in face of the dividing-wall turned to it,
toward the east in coming [thence] to them [or: eastwards when one came to them (the
13 chambers)]. And he said to me, The chambers of the north, the chambers of
the south, which are in front of the gizrah, these are chambers of holi-
ness, where the priests who approach Jehovah shall eat the most holy things;
there shall they set down the most holy things, and [that] the meat-offer-
14 ing, and the sin-offering, and the guilt-offering, for the place is holy. The
priests when entering shall not go out of the holy place to the outer court,
and [but] there they shall lay down their garments wherein they shall minister;
for they are holiness; they shall put on other garments, and [so] approach to
15 that which [belongs] to the people. And he finished the measures of the inner
house, and led me out the way of the gate whose face is toward the east, and
16 measured it [the house] round and round. He measured the east side on [with]
the measuring-rod five hundred [cubits?] rods [measured by rods] on the measuring-
17 rod around. He measured the north side, "five hundred" in rods with the
18 measuring-rod. He measured the south side, "five hundred" in rods with the
19 measuring-rod. He turned to the west side; he measured "five hundred" in
20 rods with the measuring-rod. Toward the four winds measured he it; a wall
was to it round and round, the length "five hundred," and the breadth "five
hundred," to separate between the holy and the profane.

Ver. 1. Sept.: . . . *κατα ἀνατολας κατεναντι τ. πυλης τ. προς βορραν κ. εἰσηγαγεν με· κ. ἰδου ἐξεδραι δεκαπεντε, ἐχομεναι του ἀπολοιπου κ. ἐχομεναι του διοριζοντος προς βορραν.* Vulg.: . . . *et contra ædem vergentem ad aquilonem.*

Ver. 2. . . . *ἑκατον μηκος προς βορραν*— Vulg.: . . . *in facie . . . ostii aquilonis et latitudinis.*

Ver. 3. *διαγεγραμμεναι ὁν τροπον αἱ πυλαι τ. αὐλης τ. ἐσωτερας, κ. ὁν τροπον τα περιστυλα τ. αὐλης τ. ἐξωτερας ἐστιχισμεναι, ἀντιπροσωποι στοαι τρισσαι.* Vulg.: . . . *ubi erat porticus juncta porticui triplici.*

Ver. 4. . . . *ἐπι πηχεις ἑκατον το μηκος, κ. τα*— Vulg.: . . . *ad interiora respiciens viæ cubiti unius. Et . . .* (5.) *ubi erant . . . humiliora, quia supportabant porticus, quæ ex illis eminebant de inferioribus et de mediis ædificii.* (Another reading: ופתחיהן, fem.)

Ver. 5. *κ. οἱ περιπατοι οἱ ὑπερωοι ὡσαυτως· ὁτι ἐξειχετο το περιστυλον ἐξ αὐτου, ἐκ του ὑποκατωθεν περιστυλου, κ. το διαστημα· οὑτως περιστυλον κ. διαστημα, κ. οὑτως στοαι.*

Ver. 6. *Διοτι . . . στυλοι των ἐξωτερων· δια τουτο ἐξειχοντο των . . . ἀπο τ. γης.* Vulg.: . . . *Tristega . . . propterea eminebant de . . . a terra cubitis quinquaginta.*

Ver. 7. K. *φως ἐξωθεν, ὁν τροπον κ. αἱ ἐξεδραι . . . της ἐξωτερας αἱ βλεπουσαι ἀπεναντι τ. ἐξεδρων των προς βορραν*— Vulg. *Et peribolus exterior secundum*—

Ver. 8. . . . *των βλεπουσων εἰς τ. αὐλην . . . κ. αὑται εἰσιν ἀντιπροσωποι ταυταις, το παν*—

Ver. 9. Sept.: *κ. αἱ θυραι τ. ἐξεδρων τουτων της εἰσοδου τ. προς ἀνατολας . . . δι' αὐτων*— Vulg.: *Et erat subter gazophylacia hæc introitus ab oriente ingredientium in ea*— (Qeri: וּמִתַּחַת הַלְּשָׁכוֹת and הַמֵּבִיא).

Ver. 10. *κατα το φως του ἐν ἀρχῃ του περιπατου· κ. τα προς νοτον κατα προσωπον του διοριζοντος· κ. αἱ ἐξεδραι*—

Ver. 11. *κ. ὁ περιπατος κατα προσωπον αὐτων, κατα τα μετρα τ. ἐξεδρων . . . κ. κατα πασας τας ἐπιστροφας αὐτων κ. κατα τα φωτα αὐτων κ. κατα τα θυρωματα αὐτων.* Vulg.: . . . *et omnis introitus eorum et similitudines et ostia eorum.*

Ver. 12. *των ἐξεδρων . . . κ. κατα τα θυρωματα ἀπ' ἀρχης του περιπατου ὡς ἐπι φως διαστηματος καλαμου, κ. κατ' ἀνατολας του εἰσπορευεσθαι δι' αὐτων.* Vulg.: *Secundum . . . quæ via erat ante vestibulum separatum per viam orientalem ingredientibus.*

Ver. 13. . . . *κατα προσωπον των διαστηματων, . . . αἱ ἐξεδραι του ἁγιου . . . οἱ υἱοι Σαδδουκ*— Vulg.: . . . *ante ædificium separatum . . . gazophylacia sancta . . . ad dominum in sancta sanctorum.*

Ver. 14. *Οὐκ εἰσελευσονται ἐκει παρεξ των ἱερεων, κ. οὐκ ἐξελευσονται . . . ὁπως διαπαντος ἁγιοι ὡσιν οἱ προσαγοντες· κ. μη ἁπτωνται του στολισμου αὐτων . . . ἐν αὐτοις, διοτι ἁγια ἐστιν· . . . ὁταν ἁπτωνται του λαου.* (Another reading: בהם, masc. Qeri: וְלָבְשׁוּ).

Ver. 15. . . . *συνετελεσθη ἡ διαμετρησις . . . ἐσωθεν . . . διεμετρησεν το ὑποδειγμα τ. οἰκου . . . ἐν διαταξει.*

Ver. 16. K. *ἐστη κατα νωτου τ. πυλης τ. βλεπουσης κατ' ἀνατολας κ. διεμετρησεν πεντακοσιους ἐν τ. καλαμῳ τ. μετρου.* Vulg.: . . . *contra ventum . . . calamos in calamo mensuræ*—(many codd. and all translations read מאות instead of אמות.)

Ver. 17. K. *ἐπεστρεψεν προς . . . κ. διεμετρησεν το κατα προσωπον του βορρα πηχεις πεντακοσιους ἐν τ. καλαμῳ*—

Ver. 18. K. *ἐπεστρεψεν προς θαλασσαν κ. διεμετρ. το κατ. προσωπ. τ. θαλασσης, πεντακοσιους.* Vulg.: . . . *quingentos calamos . . . per circuitum.*

Ver. 19. K. *ἐπεστρ. πρ. νοτον κ. διεμ. κατα προσωπ. τ. νοτου, πεντακοσ. ἐν*— Vulg.: *Et ad ventum occidentalem.*

Ver. 20. *εἰς τα τεσσαρα μερη του αὐτου μετρου.* K. *διεταξεν αὐτον κ. περιβολον αὐτῳ κυκλῳ, πεντακοσιων προς ἀνατολας κ. πεντακοσιων πηχεων εὐρος, του διαστελλειν ἀνα μεσον των ἁγιων κ. ἀνα μεσον του προτειχισματος του ἐν διαταξει του οἰκου.*— Vulg.: . . . *mensus est murum ejus undique . . . cubitorum . . . cubitorum, dividentem inter*—

EXEGETICAL REMARKS.

Vers. 1–14. *The Chambers of Holiness.*

The leading forth of Ver. 1 is easy to be understood, both from ch. xli. and from the outer court, where the structure of cells for the priests about to be described is situated, for הַלִּשְׁכָּה suggests to us such a structure. Comp. moreover, ch. xl. 17 sq. and xl. 44 sq. The outer court here harmonizes with the first passage, while its purpose does not; the one there was designed for the people. It would harmonize with the second passage that there too the purpose was for the priests; on the other hand, the inner court does not harmonize.—That it is added: **and brought me,** etc., is quite in the copious style of Ezekiel, as the immediately following will likewise show. The general statement: **the way northwards,** is made more precise by the closer fixing of the locality, in which the expression: **over against the gizrah,** repeats itself in: **over against the building** (situated there, ch. xli. 12 sq.), just as the northern direction mentioned in the outset does by: **towards the north.** Hengst. expresses the opinion that, considering the object of the gizrah-building, an adjacent building on either side withdrawing it from view was very appropriate, and that the description is designed to point to that.—In Ver. 2, אֶל־פְּנֵי can hardly (as HENGST.) mean: "before the length" (determined for the gizrah from east to west), for the repeated אֶל is merely a continuation. It was the front-length of the cell building to which Ezekiel sees himself brought, as also the **opening toward the north** shows that the doors of the building opened northwards. — The hundred cubits of length agree with ch. xli. 13, so that both buildings simply cover each other as to length; whereas the sacrificial kitchens (ch. xlvi. 19) embarrass Keil, who needs for them still forty cubits of length westwards behind the cell building; while Hengstenberg claims for them no separate building, but, as is usually the case with kitchens, places them below in the cell building. According to Keil, the cell building would stretch along still before the temple.—By the description in Ver. 3: **over against the twenty,** etc., the breadth of fifty cubits is put in relation to the twenty cubits' breadth of free space belonging to the inner court (ch. xli. 10), and at the same time more closely stated to be in a southern direction towards the temple (HENGST.: eastward), as the following: **over against the pavement** (ch. xl. 17), on its part points out clearly the northern direction; or a reference to what is farthest out, the outer court, is added to the reference made by the first נֶגֶד to what is inmost.—By the statement that **gallery ran before gallery in the third,** Hengst. understands: that one looked down from the walk before the chambers of the third story to another walk that was before the chambers of the second story (?). KEIL: one gallery in front of the other or towards it (?). Kliefoth takes אֶל = עַל ("on," "over"), but what would עַל־פְּנֵי mean? Also, בַּשְּׁלִשִׁים does not mean, as he supposes with Böttcher: "into the threefold." As ch. xli. 10 can refer only to our verse, we shall in the case of אֶל־פְּנֵי־אַתִּיק have to think of the first-mentioned galleries of the gizrah house, ch. xli. 15 sq.; and this so much the more as the description of the cell structure was determined immediately (ver. 1) after this building. Thus the galleries of the two buildings ran front to front; and this is said only of the **third,** namely, the two third galleries, for the first mention of the middle ones is in ver. 5; the highest also caught the eye first, and with them at the same time the height of the building could be given as of three stories.

The **walk**—Ver. 4—**before the chambers,** which was **ten cubits broad,** can only be supposed as extending from west to east before the northern long side of the building. **To the inner court** (ch. viii. 3, 16, x. 3) was **a way of one cubit** in breadth; this denotes the narrow approach to the inner court, on which the wider passage round the east wall of the building abutted; and according to this account, returning to the walk, it is said of the doors of the chambers or of the galleries, that they opened on the passage to the north. Hengstenberg makes the **walk** to be the "approach to the chambers," from which one had access to the interior of the chambers, and this interior to be "one cubit from the street, which was the thickness of the walls" (!). Keil, who can extract no suitable sense from the text, reads with the Sept.: מֵאָה אַמּוֹת, thus making a way of a hundred cubits long lead through the north gate into the inner court (!).—Ver. 5 harmonizes the galleries with the chambers, speaking first of the **upper** as ver. 3 had spoken of the **third** galleries. These chambers are said to be **shortened,** and indeed they were the narrowest; and therefore it is remarked of them alone in the first place, for (the details will become clear in ver. 6) the galleries took away from their breadth (יוּכְלוּ only here, instead of יֹאכְלוּ). They were shorter, it is said, than the **lower** above all, but also than the **middle.** So Keil understands the second and third מִן in a comparative sense. If it is to be taken as the first, that in מֵהֵנָּה, then that one must be understood of the chambers in general, and the more exact definition must be given with the two following מִ, as Hengstenberg says: "in the case of the middle ones, the half of the space which in relation to the lower was cut off by the galleries from the upper." He makes בִּנְיָן to be "building space—space which otherwise might have been built upon." The mode of expression indicates that the prophet means to say: the structure, which had lower, middle, and upper chambers (**for they were three-storied,** ver. 6), was shortened in the upper chambers, since the galleries there in particular occupied part of the breadth which the under chambers had entire, and which even the middle chambers had; the reason is, they had no **pillars** to support the upper galleries to the three stories of chambers, and so the upper chambers were necessarily contracted, and consequently had to lose in breadth, since **the galleries which ran along the outer walls had** to seek support in rests which were taken from the chambers. The explanatory expression: **from the ground**, throws light upon the בִּנְיָן of the previous verse; hence the building there comes into consideration as to the ground-space which it could afford on its lower floor for the under and the middle chambers, which thus, especially the first, were broader than the upper, although self-evidently the middle chambers too must have been shortened by their gallery in comparison with the under. As the building became higher, the chambers became shorter.—We have to notice the reference to the **pillars of the courts**, of which nothing has been said hitherto, and we shall have to suppose them where they are wanting here, namely, in ch. xl. 17 sq. and 44 sq. The chambers there, too, may have had stories.—The whole description of the galleries, and the way in which this description is kept in connection with the building on the gizrah, is hardly intended merely to make plain the possibility of access to the chambers of the second and third stories, but is designed to give us the impression, that from the galleries, so easily accessible from the chambers, an equally prompt supervision over this hinder and interior part of the environs of the sanctuary was made possible, as by the guardrooms in the case of the gates; if the chambers here correspond to these guardrooms, then the galleries here correspond to the barriers there.

Ver. 7. גָּדֵר, that which "fences off," is a dividing-wall, a boundary-fence, which is measured fifty cubits long, and consequently is to be sought for opposite the breadth of the building and on the east side, where the narrow way (ver. 4) led to the inner court, in distinction from which the further description will have respect to the outer court. In the first place however, it is said to be **outside**, for if this wall ran along the chambers, its position is made plainer by the phrase: **towards the outer court** (where דֶּרֶךְ may remind us of דֶּרֶךְ, ver. 4); as also: **in front of the chambers**, illustrates still better the phrase: **close by** (running equally with) **the chambers**. If this wall concealed the narrow access to the inner court, still more so did it the under chambers on the east towards the outer court, and what had to be performed in these chambers, for—Ver. 8—the length of the wall corresponded to the **length of the chambers which are to the outer court**, that is, which here come into consideration for this court, as the eye fell on them in looking from the east. The proper length of a hundred cubits on the north side—**before the temple**, because the temple rose behind in its length as point of view and boundary—is very perceptibly distinguished by וְהִנֵּה from the above-mentioned so-called **length** (the breadth of fifty cubits). The reason why there is no mention of a dividing-wall in the case of the chambers of this northern long side perhaps is, that their windows and galleries (comp. on ver. 3) lay towards the gizrah, and only the doors opened towards the north (ver. 4). Ver. 9. So the east side chambers rose up **from under** the dividing-wall, which concealed them only below, but did not cover them so as to cut off the light from them.—The observation regarding **the entrance**, that it was **on the east**, which is still further described by: **in coming to them from the outer court**, may indeed be understood in distinction from the narrow way which led along there to the inner court (vers. 7, 4), but is rather to be taken as a corroboration, that whereas people for the most part got at these chambers from the east, a fence was requisite on this side also of the outer court. Hengstenberg converts the הַמְּבוֹא, sufficiently intelligible by the clause: **in coming**, etc., into a door which the "fence-wall" must have had.

Ver. 10 makes the transition to a parallel building on the other side, by first repeating the last described, in such a manner, however, that no misunderstanding is possible; hence **breadth** is said, and not "length," as in ver. 7. The chambers were **in the breadth of the dividing-wall**, for they were situated in this breadth. The **court** to this wall is the just now mentioned (ver. 9) outer court, and the expression: **toward the east**, likewise borrowed from ver. 9, is a closer description of the position of the dividing-wall and consequently of the chambers, so that הַקָּדִים is not to be changed into הַדָּרוֹם, which definition comes afterward in ver. 12. The description: **fronting the gizrah**, and (as ver. 1): **fronting the building** (upon it), which occupied the whole length, signifies exactly the same as: "in front of the length of a hundred cubits," in ver. 2; hence the chambers were concealed on this side also by the gizrah building. That which in ver. 4 is called מַהֲלָךְ, is in ver. 11 by way of variety called דֶּרֶךְ, but any misunderstanding is guarded against by the observation: **as the look**, etc. (that the chambers had the same look as those **toward the north**). The comprehensive: **as the look**, etc., said on the occasion of mentioning the **way**, is specialized by what follows. We would express it thus: As in relation to their length, so in relation to their breadth and in relation to all their, etc. The **arrangements** are what concerns the way and manner of the whole, and the particulars. Finally, the **openings**, although already comprehended in the **outgoings**, are, on account of an appendage to be immediately given to the north chambers, once more specially mentioned. —Ver. 12, in the first place, shows that the chambers spoken of are to be conceived of **as toward the south**, in the same way as their patterns were "toward the north" (ver. 11); it then proceeds to mention "a door-opening," which, while only supposed in vers. 4, 7, is now described in detail. Leading into the inner court, it was situated where the way began, or had its head at the wall of the court; hence it was constructed in this wall, wherefore it is added that the way proceeded בִּפְנֵי, **in face of the dividing-wall**, that is, so that this wall had it as it were before its eyes. דֶּרֶךְ is perhaps so often repeated because the narrower walk in question (ver. 4) is distinguished as דֶּרֶךְ from the longer and broader "walks." הַגְּדֶרֶת is collective, because said at the same time for the north side. הֲגִינָה occurs only here; it is derived from הָגָן, which Meier interprets by: "to bend off," "to bend," "to incline," translating the adjective here: "bending," "turning," or "stretching" towards, which would be quite suitable to 'בִּפְנֵי, but would still more vividly express the thought: the dividing-wall inclined itself to the way passing before its eyes. Gesenius, taking for guide the rabbinical הָגוּן, which means: "noble," "graceful," but also: "insignificant," renders הָגִין by: "convenient," "suitable," which Keil transforms into this, that it denotes the wall corresponding to the cells, and running the same distance with them before the east narrow side of the building. In the remainder, similar to ver. 9.—The interpretation given of ver. 10 sq., almost the same as that of Keil, supposes only two cell buildings, whereas Kliefoth and Hengstenberg reckon three, adding an eastern "priests' court." Keil places the building here "at or on the broad-side (?) of the court-wall over against the separate place."

In Ver. 13 (as ch. xl. 45 sq.) his guide tells the prophet the purpose for which the north and south chambers were intended (only these two kinds of chambers are mentioned, completely refuting the idea of more than two buildings of the kind).—**Which are in front**, etc., since they ran along in front of the long side (hence also simply **gizrah**) of the off-place.—הַקֹּדֶשׁ, not *abstr. pro concr.*, but as throughout, **holiness**, corresponding to the holiness of Jehovah, which is no single divine attribute (comp. ch. xx. 39 sq., and on ch. xxxvi. p. 343, etc.), but the expression of the entire relation of God to Israel (BÄHR, *der Salom. Tempel*, p. 56 sq.). This relation is once more strongly pronounced in קָדְשֵׁי הַקֳּדָשִׁים, by which are designated the priests' portions of the offerings, that is, of the offerings named (**meat-offering, sin-offering**, and **guilt-offering**), which had to be eaten by the priests alone, to the exclusion of their families (Lev. ii. 3, 10, vi. 9 sq., 19 sq., vii. 6, x. 12); hence the detailed account of their status (HENGST.: "who are near the Lord") and official character. In the case of the heave-offering or wave-offering, the priests' portion was partaken of even by the female members of the priests' families (Lev. x. 14). Comp. BÄHR, *Symb. des Mos. Kultus*; KURTZ, *Der Alttestamentliche Opferkultus*. On the distinction between "eating" and "setting down" Keil says: "Because neither the meal mingled with oil of the meat-offering, nor the flesh of the sin and guilt-offerings, could be eaten by the priests immediately after the presentation of the offering, but first the one had to be baked and the other cooked, they were, until this preparation, allowed to be set aside, but not in any place one pleased." —The different designation: כִּי הַמָּקוֹם קָדֹשׁ, shows the distinction from the previous הַקֹּדֶשׁ.—Ver. 14 still adds, with similar emphasizing of the **priests**, that after performing their functions (בְּבֹאָם, as the context shows, is not: when they come to the service) in the **holy place**, that is, the inner room, they are not to repair without ceremony **to the outer court** (as Keil supposes, had they "been obliged to pass out through the inner gate in order to get to the sacred cells"), but—and for this the door, ver. 12, is excellently adapted—the official garments in which they (שָׁרַת, "to order well," "to administer," in the Piel of respectful services before kings and princes, especially of service before Jehovah) performed the sacred service are to be put aside, laid down in the chambers mentioned, and exchanged for common garments.—הֵנָּה, namely: the priestly garments.—In וְקָרְבוּ we are instinctively reminded of קְרוֹבִים in ver. 13.—אֶל־אֲשֶׁר לָעָם explains more closely the אֶל־הֶחָצֵר הַחִיצוֹנָה, that the people come into consideration there. Not until the service of God is completed are the priests allowed to come into converse with them.

Vers. 15–20.—*The Circumference of the whole.*

Ver. 15. What was begun in ch. xl. 3 sq. was now **finished**. The antithesis of the **measures of the inner house** is: **and he measured it round and round.** The prophet therefore is led out,—דֶּרֶךְ הַשַּׁעַר, which may mean the way to the gate, but also the way through it. The return to the east gate (comp. ch. xl. 6) depicts to us Ezekiel's re-entrance into the outer court; and thus the expression: **round and round**, will the more readily point to the wall (ch. xl. 5) from which he then (hence now from the opposite direction) came to the east gate. The **inner house** comprehends the whole interior up to the wall, of which it is said, ch. xl. 5, that it was מִחוּץ לַבַּיִת סָבִיב סָבִיב. Keil disputes, without due grounds, the reference of the suffix in וּמְדָדוֹ to 'הַבַּיִת, although we must concede to him that some indefiniteness may adhere to the suffix; at all events, **round and round** is not the wall as wall, which would have also its inner side, but as that which surrounded the house from without, and denoted the outside in reference to the house, so that we are pointed to the outside of the wall-girt sanctuary. Meanwhile, however, if nothing more definite follows, this only says that, after finishing all the measurings in the interior, a total measurement of the whole was taken outside on the circumference of the sanctuary.

Ver. 16. The measuring begins with the east gate; and hence on the east, רוּחַ, in the signification it has in the common expression: to the four winds, meaning the four directions whence the wind principally comes, is here said of the east side, as in the following of the north, south, and west sides.—Hengst. takes אֲמוֹת as a blending of אַמּוֹת and מֵאוֹת, and translates: "five hundred cubits, measured in rods with the measuring-rod." That חֲמֵשׁ־אֲמוֹת cannot mean "five hundred" is clear, but what is the meaning of "five cubits"? Hence the Qeri: מֵאוֹת. Then, however, we get by what follows: "five hundred rods," or we must say with Hengst. that by **rods on the measuring-rod around**, is intended to be observed that the measure would be obtained by measuring not in cubits, but in rods, with the measuring-rod described at the commencement. At all events, ch. xl. 5 favours this view, as also the square of five hundred cubits for the whole of the sanctuary, already, on ch. xl. 27, observed to be correct, has to be harmonized with the detailed statements. The blending, too, of "a hundred" and "cubits" would agree well with the brevity of similar statements; only, such brevity and obscurity in the case of a summing up, a general survey of the spatial relations of the sanctuary, as Hengst. supposes, is difficult to conceive and hard to accept. On the other hand, the abbreviation: **five hundred** (thus read with the Qeri), measured by rods, is easy of acceptation, when it is so very clear, not only from the definition of the "rod" given in ch. xl. 5, but from a presupposed after-reckoning of all the statements of measuring hitherto coming into consideration, that only cubits can be meant; even in ver. 20, where otherwise it might be expected, all mention of rods is omitted. Ewald, too, and Böttcher and Hitzig have decided in favour of cubits. That Ezekiel "gives elsewhere all the greater measures in cubits and not in rods," as Hengst. insists on, has, however, no significance when the prophet had to refer to a wider space, a space separating the sanctuary from the rest of the land, a space independent of all that had gone before, and which therefore might have been measured by rods, as Klief. and Keil hold. Comp. however, ch. xlv. 2.—Ver. 17. **Five hundred,** and the same in Ver. 18 and Ver. 19, merely the number; and this Hengst. explains by saying that, in the case of the other sides, the mere number suffices, so that the number given is self-evidently of cubits, according to ver. 16.—Is the question decided in Ver. 20? But **toward the four winds,** that is, in the direction of the four cardinal points (it is said סָבַב in ver. 19, by which, however, at the same time, may be indicated the going round and round), is a mere *résumé* of what has been described singly in vers. 16–19. Accordingly, the suffix also in מִדָּדוֹ is to be understood exactly as in ver. 15, that is, as referring to the house.—What now is to be understood by the wall which was to the house (לוֹ)? It is called חוֹמָה, as in ch. xl. 5, and, exactly as there, it is said that it was סָבִיב סָבִיב. It is not, indeed, said, as Hengst. expresses himself: "he measured it, namely, the wall, round about;" but the observation here, that the house had a wall, gives no further information than that the measuring will have had respect to this compass of the house! Keil, indeed, refuses to understand the סָבִיב in vers. 16 and 17 of a square five hundred rods in length and breadth on these two sides, yet he gets in ver. 20 a space which measured five hundred rods towards each of the cardinal points, that is, a surrounding wall five hundred rods in length on each side; in whole, an area of two hundred and fifty thousand square rods, while the temple, with its courts, claims only two hundred and fifty thousand square cubits. Hengstenberg, at the mention of this in fact so much more considerable space than that of the sanctuary, but neither further defined nor filled up, is reminded of the Hungarian who, looking at a bare expanse, said: "Nothing but space," and finds a mere vacuum on each of the four sides "intolerable." But when he finds nothing corresponding in Solomon's temple, the form of which, however, is perpetually before the prophet's eyes, and in reply to what he otherwise expresses regarding the "enormous extent" of "useless space," Kliefoth, in giving the purpose intended: **to separate,** etc., says: "In the case of the tabernacle and Solomon's temple the outer court served for this purpose, whereas, in the case of Ezekiel's temple, the outer court also still belongs to the sanctuary, and is itself holy; and the purpose of separating the sanctuary from the common ground must be effected by this surrounding space, which, in this respect, takes the place in regard to Ezekiel's temple which the outer court took in the case of that of Solomon." Keil disputes the latter statement, and says that "the tabernacle had no outer court, and in Solomon's temple the outer court already formed a part of the sanctuary." He continues: "Only in the case of the latter temple, the outer court bordered immediately on the common soil of the city and of the land, so that the pollution of the land produced by the sin of the people could press without obstacle even into the sacred space of the courts. To this a limit shall be set in the sanctuary of the future, by this environing space set apart for separating the holy from the profane." That the extent of the temple, with its courts, is not rendered insignificant by the twenty-five times' greater size of the space in question, Keil proves from the circumstance that it "is not covered with buildings," and hence comes into consideration merely as so significant a separation from the profane, by which "strongly marked separation peculiar to Ezekiel's temple," the "inviolable holiness of this sanctuary" is, on the contrary, illustrated in an enhanced measure. That the surface of Mount Moriah affords no room for this is certainly no proof against the above-mentioned view of Keil and Kliefoth, for ch. xl. 2 speaks only of a very high mountain.

[Throughout vers. 16–20 Dr. Fairbairn abides by the rendering of the English version: "reeds" or "rods," not "cubits," and adds: "We regard the immense extent of the sacred area as a symbol of the vast enlargement that was to be given to the kingdom of God in the times of Messiah. It was immeasurably to surpass the old in the extent of its territory, and in the number of its adherents, as well as in the purity of its worship. The wall that surrounded the sacred buildings is expressly said, in ver. 20, to have been for separating between the holy and profane; not, therefore, as in Rev. xxi. 12, and very common elsewhere, for defence and safety; as, indeed, its comparative want of elevation might seem to render it unfit for such a purpose. But its square form, and the square appearance of the entire buildings (as in John's city, Rev. xxi. 16), betokened the strength and solidity of the whole, along with a vast increase in extent and number. A perfect cube, it was the emblem of a kingdom that could not be shaken or removed. And thus every way it exhibited, to the eye of faith, the true ideal of that pure and glorious temple, which, resting on the foundation of the Eternal Son, and girt round by all the perfections of Godhead, shall shine forth the best and noblest workmanship of Heaven."—FAIRBAIRN'S *Ezekiel*, p. 470.—W. F.]

CHAPTER XLIII.

1, 2 And he led me to the gate, the gate that looks toward the east: And,
behold, the glory of the God of Israel came from the east, and its [His] voice
3 was as the voice of many waters, and the earth shone with His glory. And
as the appearance [was] the appearance which I saw, as the appearance which
I saw when I came to destroy the city, and [there were] sights like the appear-
4 ance which I saw by the river Chebar; and I fell upon my face. And the
glory of Jehovah came to the house by the way of the gate whose face [front]
5 is toward the east. And the Spirit lifted me up, and brought me to the
6 inner court, and, behold, the glory of Jehovah filled the house. And I heard
one speaking to me from the house, and a man was standing beside me.
7 And He said to me: Son of man, [behold] the place of My throne and the place
of the soles of My feet, where I will dwell in the midst of the sons [children]
of Israel for ever, and the house of Israel shall no more defile the name of
My holiness, they and their kings, by their whoredom and by the corpses of
8 their kings, their high places; When they gave their threshold beside My
threshold and their post beside My post, and [only] the wall [was] between Me
and them, and they defiled [so defiled they] the name of My holiness by their
abominations which they did, and I consumed them in My anger [breath of
9 anger]. Now shall they put away their whoredom, and the corpses of their
10 kings from Me, and I dwell in their midst for ever. Thou, son of man, show
to the house of Israel the [this] house, that they may be ashamed because of
their iniquities, and they measure [so they measure] the harmony of proportion.
11 And if they be ashamed because of all that they did, make them know the
conformation of the house, and its arrangement, and its out-goings, and its in-
comings, and all its forms, and what relates to all its ordinances, and all its
forms, and all its precepts [laws]; and write before their eyes, that they may
12 keep its whole conformation and all its ordinances, and they do them. This is
the law [the Thorah] of the house; on the head [top] of the mountain all its
border round and round is most holy! Behold, this is the law of the house.
13 And these are the measures of the altar [altar of burnt-offering] in cubits; the cubit
a cubit and a hand-breadth, and [indeed] the [a] bosom (the girth) had the
cubit, and [i.e.] one cubit broad [thick], and its border at its lip [its edge] round
14 about was a span, and this is the elevation of the altar; And [namely] from
the bosom [at] the ground to the lower rest were two cubits, and a breadth
of one cubit; and from the lesser rest to the greater rest, four cubits and a
15 breadth of one cubit. And the mountain of God four cubits; and from the
16 hearth of God and upwards were the four horns. And the hearth of God
17 twelve in length by twelve in breadth, square in all its four sides. And the
rest fourteen in length by fourteen in breadth in its four sides, and the border
round about it was half a cubit, and its bosom [girth was] a cubit round about,
18 and its [the altar's] steps toward the east. And He said unto me, Son of man,
thus saith the Lord Jehovah: These are the ordinances of the altar on the
day when it is made, to cause burnt-offerings to ascend upon it, and to sprinkle
19 blood upon it. And thou givest to the priests, the Levites, those who are of
the seed of Zadok, who draw near to Me,—sentence of the Lord Jehovah,—
20 to minister to Me, a bullock, a young steer, for a sin-offering. And thou
takest of its blood, and givest it upon its [the altar's] four horns, and on the four
corners of the rest, and on the border round about, and thou dost cleanse and
21 expiate it. And thou takest the bullock of the sin-offering, and one burns it
22 in the assigned [appointed] place of the house, without the sanctuary. And on
the second day thou shalt offer a kid of the goats without blemish for a sin-
23 offering, and they cleanse the altar as they cleansed with the bullock. When
thou hast completed the cleansing, thou shalt offer a bullock, a young steer
24 without blemish, and a ram of the flock without blemish. And thou offerest

them before Jehovah, and the priests cast salt upon them, and make
25 them ascend as a burnt-offering [olah] to Jehovah. Seven days shalt thou
prepare a kid for a sin-offering daily, and they shall prepare a bullock, a
26 young steer, and a ram of the flock without blemish. Seven days do they
27 expiate the altar, and purify it, and fill its hand. And they shall have
completed the [these] days; thus it comes to pass on the eighth day and
onwards, that the priests shall make upon the altar your burnt-offerings,
and your peace-offerings; and I receive you graciously,—sentence of the
Lord Jehovah.

Ver. 2. Sept.: . . . *κατα τ. ὁδον της πυλης τ. βλεπουσης προς . . . φωνη της παρεμβολης ὡς φωνη διπλασιαζοντων πολλων . . . ὡς φεγγος ἀπο τ. δοξης κυριου κυκλοθεν.*

Ver. 3. K. *ἡ ορασις ἡν ἰδον κατα τ. ὁρασιν ἡν ἰδον ὁτε εἰσεπορευομην του χρισαι τ. πολιν· κ. ἡ ὁρασις του ἁρματος οὑ εἰδον,*— Vulg.: *Et vidi visionem secundum speciem, quam videram quando venit ut disperderet . . . et speciem secundum aspectum quem videram*— (Another reading: בבאו, *i.e. cum venit dominus.*)

Ver. 4. . . . *ingressa est templum*—

Ver. 6. K. *ἐστην κ. ἰδου φωνη ἐκ . . . εἱστηκει ἐχομενος μου,*

Ver. 7. . . . *Ἑωρακας, υἱε . . . του ἰχνους των ποδων . . . ἐν οἱς . . . το ὀνομα μου ἐν μεσω του οἰκου Ἰσρ. . . . ; κ. ἐν τοις φονοις των ἡγουμενων ἐν μεσω αὐτων; (8.) ἐν τω τιθεναι αὐτους το προθυρον μου ἐν τ. προθυροις αὐτων κ. τας φλιας μου ἐχομενας των φλιων αὐτων, κ. ἐδωκαν τ. τοιχον μου ὡς συνεχομενον ἐμου κ. αὐτων, κ. . . . κ. ἐξετριψα αὐτους ἐν θυμω μου κ. ἐν φονω.* Vulg.: . . . *vestigiorum pedum meorum, ubi habito . . . et in ruinis regum suorum et in excelsis,* (8.) *qui fabricati sunt . . . propter quod consumpsi eos*— (Another reading: בְּמוֹתָם, *in morte eorum.*)

Ver. 9. . . . *κ. τ. φονους*— Vulg.: . . . *ruinas regum . . . semper.*

Ver. 10. Another reading: ואתה—תבנית *pro* תכנית.

Ver. 10. . . . *δειξον τω . . . κ. κοπασουσιν ἀπο των ἁμαρτιων . . . κ. την ὁρασιν αὐτου κ. την διαταξιν αὐτων* (11.) *κ. αὐτοι λημψονται την κολασιν αὐτων περι παντων . . .* K. *διαγραψεις τ. οἰκον . . . κ. την ὑποστασιν αὐτου κ. παντα τ. προσταγματα αὐτου κ. παντα τα νομιμα αὐτου γνωριεις αὐτοις . . . κ. φυλαξονται παντα τα δικαιωματα μου κ. παντα τ. προσταγματα μου*— Vulg.: . . . *ostende . . . templum . . . et metiantur fabricam* (11.) *et erubescant . . . Figuram domus et fabricæ . . . et omnem descriptionem . . . præcepta . . . cunctumque ordinem . . . ostende eis . . . omnes descriptiones*— (*Desunt in nonnullis codd.*: ואת כל חקתיו וכל צורתו, or only וכל צורתו. *In fine versus legitur plur.*: כל צורותיו.)

Ver. 12. K. *την διαγραφην τ. οἰκου ἐπι της κορυφης του ὀρους.* Παντα τα ὁρια— Vulg.: . . . *domus in summitate montis.*

Ver. 13. . . . *Το κολπωμα βαθος πηχυς ἐπι πηχυν, κ. πηχυς το εὐρος· κ. γεισος ἐπι του χειλους αὐτου κυκλοθεν, σπιθαμης.* K. *τουτο το ὑψος*— Vulg.: . . . *In sinu ejus erat cubitus . . . hæc quoque erat fossa altaris.*

Ver. 14. Sept.: *ἐκ βαθους τ. ἀρχης του κοιλωματος . . . προς το ἱλαστηριον το μεγα το ὑποκατωθεν . . . κ. ἀπο του ἱλαστηριου τ. μικρου ἐπι τ. ἱλαστηριον το μεγα*— Vulg.: . . . *usque ad crepidinem novissimam . . . a crepidine minore*—

Ver. 15. K. *το ἀριηλ . . . ἀπο του ἀριηλ . . . των κερατων πηχυς.* (Another reading: וההריאל, *montes dei.* Syr.: Adiel.—ומהאריאל, *litteris transpositis.*)

Ver. 16. K. *το ἀριηλ* (*eadem codicum varietas*).

Ver. 17. K. *το ἱλαστηριον . . . το εὐρος τετραγωνον ἐπι τα τεσσαρα . . . κ. το γεισος αὐτου κυκλοθεν κυκλομενον αὐτω.*— Vulg.: *Et crepido . . . et corona in circuitu ejus*—

Ver. 19. . . . *ὁ θεος του Λευι, . . . μοσχον ἐκ βοων περι ἁμαρτιας*— Vulg.: . . . *vitulum de armento pro peccato.*

Ver. 20. K. *λημψονται . . . κ. ἐπιθησουσιν . . . του ἱλαστηριου κ. ἐπι τ. βασιν κυκλω, κ. περιραντιεις αὐτο κ. ἐξιλασονται αὐτο.* Vulg.: . . . *angulos crepidinis et super coronam . . . et mundabis illud et expiabis.*

Ver. 21. K. *λημψονται . . . κ. κατακαυθησεται ἐν τ. ἀποκεχωρισμενω του*—

Ver. 22. . . . *λημψονται ἐριφους δυο ἀπο αἰγων ἀμωμους*—

Ver. 23. . . . *προσοισουσιν*— Vulg.: . . . *de armento et . . . de grege*—

Ver. 24. *κ. προσοισετε*—

Ver. 25. . . . *ποιησουσιν* (26.) *ἑπτα ἡμερας, κ.*—

Ver. 26. Qeri: יְכַפְּרוּ. *Idem legunt quam plurimi codices.*

Ver. 27. . . . *κ. προσδεξομαι ὑμας*— Vulg.: . . . *et placatus ero vobis*—

EXEGETICAL REMARKS.

Vers. 1–12. *The Entrance of the Glory of Jehovah.*

The measuring is over, the house is in this respect finished as an actual house (ch. xlii. 15), that is, its measurements are completed. But heaven and earth are said to be finished (Gen. ii.) only when the Eternal rested. And so the prophet's guide leads him back—Ver. 1—**to the gate** (הַשַּׁעַר), to the one that principally comes into consideration (comp. what has been remarked in the foregoing chapters regarding the significance of this gate, and also the Doctrinal Reflections), to the east gate,—we will have to imagine Ezekiel standing before this gate,—that after all the measuring he—Ver. 2—may see the **glory**, sq. (see pp. 38 sq., 52), coming to its rest. HENGST.: a parallel to Ex. xl. 34 sq., and 1 Kings viii. 10 sq., and the counterpart to ch. xi. of our prophet (comp. ch. x. 19, xi. 1, 23). The gate of exit then is the gate of re-entrance now.—וְקוֹלוֹ; comp. on ch. i. 24. The **voice** might refer more to the manifestation of the glory; comp. however, Rev. i. 15: **His glory** is at all events the glory of the God of Israel (Luke ii. 9; Rev. xviii. 1). The significant addition **and the earth**, etc., is not sufficiently explained by a brilliant light cast upon the ground; but as the land of Canaan is hardly meant here, by this burst of light extending far beyond Israel is meant to be symbolized an enlightenment also of the face of the whole earth, that is, of the entire region of humanity, thus shown to have been in itself and hitherto dark, Isa. vi. 3, lx. 1 sq. It is like sunrise (אוֹר in the Hiphil, to "make" or "give" "light," Gen. i. 15, 17) for the world through Israel's temple-gate, and in so far is certainly something additional which was not in the tabernacle or Solomon's temple; just as in general the temple of Ezekiel is a symbol of the future. — Ver. 3 in no way contradicts this. 'וּכְמַרְאֵה הַמַּרְאֶה אֲשֶׁר may be translated: "and as the appearance of the appearance which, etc., as the appearance (closer definition) which I saw when," etc., that is, quite as conspicuous as that was, was the appearance of glory this time also. KEIL: "And the appearance which I saw was to look upon just like the appearance which I saw when I," etc. כְּ is evidently a resumption of וּכְ. The former appearance (וּכְמַרְאֵה) comes first before the prophet's mind when he wishes to describe what he saw, and seeks therefore for an appearance with which he can compare it; and then he characterizes more closely this appearance (כַּמַּרְאֶה), with which he compares that now seen. Keil's observation against Hitzig does not meet the point, but neither is Hitzig's alteration of the text necessary. In the first place, by means of this comparison the re-entrance of the divine glory is attested in the strongest way, and therefore so circumstantially. It was the same glory then as now. For all this, the prophet does not intend to deny the anger in the execution of judgment then, for he expressly defines more closely בְּבֹאִי לְשַׁחֵת, which alone is the correct text, since the Lord did not come, but rather went, giving over the city to destruction, and in reality Ezekiel was the person coming—of course in the vision of God, the subject to be spoken of immediately. The prophet did not come in order to see the destruction of the city, but his coming was a seeing which had for its aim and issue his announcement of the overthrow; and then this ideal destruction on the part of the prophet was also realized by the judgment of God fulfilling it. Ezekiel first, Nebuchadnezzar afterwards (ch. xxx. 11), but by both certainly Jehovah. In the second place, the prophet, as he had already done in ch. x. 15, 20, compares the last visions (comp. ch. xl. 2), hence the coming of the glory with its individual manifestations, with the appearance which the manifestation had had on the Chebar (ch. i.).—On his falling down Hengstenberg observes: "In ch. i. 28 it was before the majesty of the angry God; here before the majesty of God appearing in His grace (Rev. i. 17)." Comp. also on ch. iii. 23.—Ver. 4. A continuation of ver. 2; there: whence **the glory of the God of Israel** came; here: whither **the glory of Jehovah** came; there: **from the east**; here: **to the house** through the east gate, to its dwelling, to its rest.

Ver. 5. Comp. on ch. iii. 12. There is still less need of the "wind" here; to arrive at the inner court, the prophet needed only to go, as hitherto, in vision. But Ezekiel needs taking up by the **Spirit**, not only because the impression of ver. 2 has cast him to the ground (HENGST.), but also in order to be able to follow, so far as was permitted to him as priest, the fresh revelation of the glory of Jehovah filling the temple. For the form of manifestation, 1 Kings viii. 10 sq. might be compared, and so much the more as that becomes quite plain there, which indeed is already indicated in Ex. xl. 35 sq., that the cloud is as significant in the manner of manifestation as the glory is in the actual fact, according as the cloud is one of fire or of light (Matt. xvii. 5).—Ver. 6. Evidently, however, the מְדַבֵּר אֵלַי [Häv. understands the Hithpael of a conversation in the interior of the sanctuary (?), of a command to the angel to communicate to the seer the revelation of God], that is, the one speaking to him **from the house** whom Ezekiel hears first, is meant to be represented as visible by 'וְאִישׁ הָיָה, so that the **man** is the medium between Jehovah and the prophet, and so must certainly be conceived of in analogy with ch. xl. 3 (which comp.), as Keil: ὁ λογος, John i. Hengst. supposes: "the man has entered the door to speak to him." וַיֹּאמֶר in Ver. 7 is certainly the אִישׁ of ver. 6.—אֶת־ מְקוֹם denotes an accusative, and requires a "behold" to be supplied. What the man says identifies him entirely with Jehovah, wherefore the reference by the article back to the man in ch. xl. 3 is intentionally omitted. We no longer walk with the prophet through the courts of the sanctuary to the measurings of his guide, but the vision is interpreted to Ezekiel, and through him to us, from the most holy place. The man's speech, legitimating itself as word of Jehovah, shows him to be essentially the glory of the God of Israel, so that we now know why nothing farther was said regarding the way and manner in which the glory of Jehovah filled the house (ver. 5), and the form of its manifestation. "Between the statement," rightly remarks Hengst., "that one spake, and the speech that was spoken, stands the account of the person of the speaker, to which the prophet has his attention first directed by the speech; the seeing was first occasioned by the hearing." We have before us in the man the essential revelation of Jehovah's glory. Comp. on ch. i. 26, pp. 55, 56; Rev. i. 10 sq. The Messianic-christological interpretation is the only explanation corresponding to the connection, so much the more significantly, as there is no mention in Ezekiel of the ark of the covenant, with which elsewhere the dwelling of Jehovah in the midst of Israel is wont to be connected; and hence also the לְעוֹלָם here, and in ver. 9, is to be taken as unconditionally literal (ch. xxxvii. 26, 28). Neither in the tabernacle nor in the temple of Solomon had Jehovah dwelt **for ever**, although these might be called the "place of His throne," that is, of the ark of the covenant (1 Sam. iv. 4; Ex. xxv. 22); see Bähr, *Symb. der Mos. Kult.* i. p. 387 sq., and parallel therewith מְקוֹם כַּפּוֹת

רַגְלַי, by which the lower part of the throne, more exactly the ground whereon it stands, is particularized. Comp. for the latter mode of expression, Isa. lx. 13. According to ch. lxvi. 1: **place of the soles of My feet,** hence the same footstool (the earth) as here, perhaps alludes to the most holy place of the temple, where the ark stood, while the ark which was set up upon the floor of the most holy place is to be compared to heaven, Isa. lxvi. 1; Ps. xcix. 5, cxxxii. 7. Reference is also made hereby to the ark of the covenant (1 Chron. xxviii. 2). Both modes of expression symbolize the temple in the traditional legal manner as the dwelling-place of Jehovah (אֲשֶׁר אֶשְׁכָּן־שָׁם),—the first referring chiefly to the ark, and the second chiefly to the most holy place (for which see ver. 12). Bähr says: "What the dwelling is in a larger sense and generally, the ark of the covenant is in a narrower sense and in particular; in it the dwelling of Jehovah is concentrated in a single point," etc.—In conformity with his theory of the conditionality of certain promises, Hengst. finds in the statement: **shall no more,** etc., reference to a condition, whereas it simply repeats negatively what the dwelling of Jehovah for ever has already said positively (ch. xxxvii. 23 sq., xxxix. 24, 29; comp. John x. 28).—On: **the name of My holiness,** comp. on ch. xxxvi. 20 sq. Ch. xvi., xx.—פֶּגֶר is something "fallen down," "flaccid," a corpse. It cannot be proved that the burial-places of kings were in the neighbourhood of the temple. It will not do to take the **corpses** for dead idols, even although it should be a quotation from Lev. xxvi. 30, for that passage speaks of demolished idols, whereas flourishing idols are treated of here. Moreover, a closer definition could hardly be omitted (Jer. xvi. 18), which Keil, indeed, finds here in the context. Häv. insists on finding the idols in the **kings** (Amos v. 26; Zeph. i. 5), holding it to be a contemptuous expression for: the lifeless idols. On the other hand, Keil and Hengstenberg remind us of kings like Manasseh and Amon, who took to do with dead bodies, which according to the law were to be avoided as unclean and polluting, had built for them altars or high places in the courts of the temple (2 Kings xxi. 4, 5, 7), and patronized the worship of idols. As **whoredom** designates idolatry in general, so what is meant to be said by the **corpses of their kings** applies to the worship of kings, the forgotten subjection to Jehovah under them, who, if kings, yet are perpetuated only as corpses; one might be allowed to call to mind Schubert's poem: "The Princes' Vault." To this the appositional, loosely strung בָּמוֹתָם the more fittingly attaches itself, as in בָּמוֹת the thought of the kings as also high points, points of worship in social life, easily connects itself with the worship on the high places, which was specially popular in the time of the kings, and tolerated even by the better kings; the worship of the king, and the worship favoured by the kings, would border on one another. As idolatry in general constitutes the defilement of the name of Jehovah, the doings on the part alike of the house of Israel in general, and of their kings in particular, so the figurative and literal worshipping on high places forms, with special reference to the kings, a contrast to the enthronement of the King Jehovah, and to His dwelling in the literal sense in the midst of Israel. [In the interest of the different explanation of בְּפִגְרֵי מַלְכֵיהֶם, it has been proposed to read בְּמוֹתָם, "in their death," as the Chaldee paraphrase already interprets. Zunz makes בְּמוֹתָם dependent on יְטַמְּאוּ, but the בְּ wanting before בְּמוֹתָם can be easily supplied from the preceding בִּזְנוּתָם and בְּפִגְרֵי.]—Ver. 8. The subject in בְּתִתָּם is not the kings (Hengst.), but what was subject in ver. 7, the house of Israel and their kings. The suffix in סִפָּם means, if any particular persons, the kings, but better, Israel in general. What is then said refers neither to the temples of the high places, which had been placed so close beside the temple of God (Keil), for **their** threshold cannot refer to **their high places,** nor to idol-chambers there (comp. for this ch. viii.), and idol-altars in the courts of the temple, which the kings of Judah built (such things would require to be expressed more plainly); nor is this disparaging expression meant to condemn the building of royal palaces like that of Solomon (1 Kings vii.); but if kings are specially aimed at, then the figurative mode of expression, as given by the temple of Jehovah, will pronounce sentence on the conduct of the kings who assumed an equality with Jehovah (1 Kings xii. 28, 32), by their idolatrous appointments and arrangements with respect to religion and worship. It is better, however, to hold that the defilement of the name of the holiness of Jehovah by the people and the kings consisted in this, that the consciousness of the distance between Jehovah and Israel had entirely disappeared from the life of the latter, the dwelling of Jehovah was as if it were not present in Israel, Israel performed his domestic and secret worship of idols as his worship of Jehovah, so that only the temple wall (הַקִּיר) still protested, and preserved, or at least marked to Israel the boundary between the Holy One and His people. [Keil understands הַקִּיר of the temple wall, which was "the only thing between Jehovah and the corpse-gods."]—וָאֲכַל, from כָּלָה imperf. apoc. Piel (Ex. xxxii. 10, xxx. 3!), signifies: to make the measure full, to finish sin by death (Jas. i. 15).—בְּאַפִּי, comp. on ch. xxxviii. 18.—Ver. 9 resumes, in conclusion, the subject of ver. 7, as also to the same purpose; "the eternal duration of the new and perfect revelation of God as distinguished from the Old Testament merely temporary one, which is at this time passing over into complete fulfilment and glorification" (Häv.), is repeatedly set forth.—יְרַחֲקוּ (Piel: "to put far away") מִמֶּנִּי corroborates with respect to the corpses of kings the interpretation proposed (ver. 7) of idolatrous adulation and adoration of them and their edicts regarding worship.

Ver. 10. הַגֵּד, ch. xl. 4.—*The Aim of the Announcement of the Temple-vision, and consequently of the Vision itself as regards Israel.*

It is not said that Israel is again to build a temple of the kind; but neither is it said that he is to build up his phantasy on this architectonic interim phantasy. But with the perception that Jehovah still, and now first in the proper sense, desires to dwell in the midst of Israel,—a perception which will be brought about by the announcement of this **house** to the **house of Israel,**—shame shall come over them through the knowledge of their **iniquities,** from a comparison of these iniquities with the mercy and grace of God (ch. xxxvi. 31, 32), so that the goodness of God leads them to repentance (Rom. ii. 4). This moral-prophetic tendency is thoroughly in accordance with the Messianic acceptation of the temple-vision.—תָּכְנִית (comp. ch. xxviii. 12), not so much: "plan," model (HENGST.), but ("proportionality," says Fürst): the harmony of the proportions, the regular character of the edifice. KEIL: "the well-apportioned edifice." Hengst. observes on this measuring: "not as architects, but as Abraham went through the length and breadth of the Promised Land (Gen. xiii. 17) with the interest of the family belonging to the house, in a meditating and loving and thankful spirit, following the measures shown," etc.

Ver. 11. And the announcement for this purpose is not, if they are ashamed of themselves, to be confined to the harmony of the whole, but will enter into particulars, which, being enumerated at the beginning, and in a profusion of words, are well fitted to produce from the outset the impression of something important. צוּרָה, from צוּר, "to form" (Ps. xlix. 15 [14]), is the shape, the form, hence primarily the outside, with which is joined תְּכוּנָה, which Gesenius would derive from תָּכַן, and compares with תָּכְנִית. The word is derived from כּוּן, and signifies the inside plenishing of a dwelling-place, as also the dwelling-place itself (Job xxiii. 3), for which its **out-goings and its in-comings,** taking into account both the exterior and the interior, come above all into consideration. כָּל־צוּרֹתָו is everything that צוּרָה is in the particular, the individual forms; כָּל־חֻקֹּתָיו the regulations in regard to the particulars of the arrangement; according to KEIL: "regarding what Israel has to observe, the ordinances of worship." [HENGST.: All here has a practical import (2 Tim. iii. 16). The high mountain, for example, on which the house is situated proclaims: "Hearts upward." The wall which surrounded the whole (ch. xlii. 20) proclaims: "Ye shall be holy, for I am holy." The guardrooms of the gates embody the word: "Without are dogs, whoremongers, murderers, idolaters." The chambers for the people in the outer court preached: "Rejoice before the Lord always," and: "Be ye thankful." The arrangements for the priests reminded of sin, and demanded that one should consecrate himself to God in the burnt-offering, present to Him always the thank-offering and the meat-offering of good works. The altar of incense proclaimed to all: "Pray without ceasing."] That the dwelling of the Holy One among His people has as its aim their sanctification in repentance and faith as to every part of them, is clear from the accompanying כָּל־חֻקֹּתָיו, which is, moreover, repeated by a parallel expression, and so strengthened (**and all its forms and** כָּל־תּוֹרֹתָו), that is, all instructions and directions, what has thereby been given in doctrine according to which a man should live. And thus the symbolical view of the section (see Doct. Reflec.) has no need to seek elsewhere for farther justification. By the command: **write,** etc., the: **make them know,** passes over from oral annunciation into a more abiding form, into the written outline we have before us of the new temple, into the description given of the vision.—The: **do,** corresponding to the preceding: **all that they did,** certainly does not mean that they are to build such a temple, and just as little that they were to console themselves therewith. They are to repent, for the kingdom of heaven is at hand. The "doing" intended is a spiritual, ethical doing.

Ver. 12. The mention of the תּוֹרֹתָו leads to the summary of all doctrine and precepts in respect to this temple, which is significantly—in contrast with the law of Moses which Israel has not kept—one might indeed say: as the law of Christ—laid down repeatedly (ver. 13) as *the Thorah of the house.* For all is summed up in this, that what has been represented on the (going back to ch. xl. 2) top of the mountain ("head" of the mountain and head article of the doctrine!), the whole boundary marked out for the house round and round, is **most holy** (ch. xlv. 3). The summary thought which underlies the whole, the holiness of Jehovah, the sanctification of Israel, is in a way set forth by this, that even the courts appear in the light of the most peculiar abode of Jehovah, so that the perfection of a new temple as the completion of the old is here proclaimed as a close to the temple-vision proper. Hengst. quite uselessly takes pains to tone down the קֹדֶשׁ קָדָשִׁים into "eminently holy." For if it is conceded to him that "ideally" (as he says) such (a holy place) was already extant in the tabernacle and the temple of Solomon, and all behoved in view of it to strive to be holy in their whole conversation (for which he appeals to 1 Pet. i. 15), then he will have to concede that this "ideal" is set down here as a real, as the fulfilled law, since its ideality was nothing else than the idea of the future, the promised fulfilment in Christ. Num. xviii. 10 rather proves this advance than furnishes ground for contending against it, with Hengstenberg; for what is said in that passage of the court of the tabernacle is expressly limited to the priestly families representing the people, and, moreover, to the male portion of them. The Old Testament form, indeed, still obtains on the top of the mountain here, but yet the *novum quod in vetere latet* is distinctly apparent. The question is not concerning the "world surrounding" the sanctuary, but when the vision here finishes with the temple, the mutual relation of its parts must be viewed—a view rendered possible just by this, that the most holy place still remains, as the prophet has shown. Certainly the point of view is a "practical" one; but when Hengst. says: "the passage serves as the foundation for the confident expectation expressed in vers. 7 and 9, that the people will in future lay aside all unholy dispositions," then this looks forward to a future which points far beyond the immediatly post-exile period, namely, that God (to speak with Hengstenberg) "holds in prospect to the children of Israel a help against themselves, whereby they may succeed in conquering the enemy that makes the dwelling of God among them impossible," this help being, of course, the Spirit of the Anointed One, of the fulfilling of the law, somewhat as in the passage cited by Hengst., 1 Pet. i. 3 sq. Comp. 1 Cor. i. 30: ὃς ἐγενήθη ἡμῖν καὶ ἁγιασμός (2 Thess. ii. 13 sq.; Eph. iv. 20 sq., and similar passages). COCCEIUS: "And the least on this mountain, within this wall of God, is greater than the high priest in the temple of Solomon, Matt. xi. 11; Rev. i. 6, v. 10; 1 Pet. ii. 9; comp. also Zech. xiv. 20, 21."

ADDITIONAL NOTE ON VERS. 1–12.

["In this striking passage we are first of all to note the character in which the Lord now appears to dwell and manifest Himself among His people. It is as their divine King, occupying that house as the throne of His kingdom. God had always claimed this position, and had at first resisted their desires to have an earthly sovereign, because this virtually implied a rejection of Him as the proper head of the State. Even when He consented to their request, it was with a solemn and earnest protest against the person chosen ruling in his own name, and for selfish purposes, or in any other way than as the Lord's vicegerent. The protest, however, was soon forgotten. The king looked upon himself, and the people also looked upon him, as possessing an absolute title to the throne, and the earthly head came very much to occupy, in men's eyes, the place of the true and proper King. But in the new and more perfect order of things now unfolded in vision to the prophet, this flagrant perversion of the past must be rectified; God must be known and honoured as alone properly 'King in Jeshurun.' And hence, not only here does He declare that He had come to occupy His throne in the house, but, as mentioned in the note on ver. 7, the earthly head, when spoken of in a subsequent chapter, is simply called 'the prince.' The supremacy and glory of Jehovah were henceforth to appear in their full splendour. We have farther to notice in the preceding passage the essentially moral character of all that was here displayed in vision respecting the future things of God's kingdom. It was not a pattern which God was going to carry out anyhow, and accomplish as by a simple fiat of Omnipotence. It depended upon the condition of the people, and only if they agreed to put away sin from among them, and give God the supreme place in their hearts, could He manifest Himself toward them in the manner described. And finally, while the whole scheme was fraught with lessons of instruction, and inlaid with principles of holiness, the grand and distinguishing peculiarity of this pattern of the future, as compared with the past, we are expressly informed, was to be a general and all-pervading sanctity. The law of the house—what was pre-eminently entitled to be called *the* law—consisted in the whole region of the temple-mount being most holy. Not, as hitherto, was this characteristic to be confined to a single apartment of the temple; it was to embrace the entire circumference occupied by the symbolical institutions of the kingdom,—the chambers allotted to the priest, and even the courts trodden by the people, as well as the immediate dwelling-place of Jehovah. All were to have one character of sacredness, because all connected with them were to occupy a like position of felt nearness to God, and equally to enjoy the privilege of access to Him. So that the pattern delineated is that of a true theocracy, having God himself for king, with the community in all its members for true denizens of the kingdom, and acceptable ministers of righteousness before the Lord."—FAIRBAIRN'S *Ezekiel*, pp. 473, 474.—W. F.]

Vers. 13–27. *The Altar of Burnt-offering* (vers. 13–17), *and its Consecration* (vers. 18–27).

["The remaining verses of this chapter (vers. 13–27), which contain a description of the altar of burnt-offering, and of the necessary rites of consecration connected with it, seem at first view somewhat out of place. But there is an historical reason for such a description being given here. Now that the Lord has taken possession of the house, the prophet goes on to show how the work of fellowship and communion with Him is to proceed on the part of the people. It must, as it were, commence anew, and of course be conducted after the old manner; for no other could here come into contemplation. But in ancient times the grand medium of divine intercourse was the altar, at which all gifts and sacrifices were to be presented for the divine favour and blessing. And therefore, the prophet here, to show that the way was open, and that the people might have free access to the fellowship of God, after having briefly sketched the dimensions of the altar, gives instructions for its consecration, and the consecration of the priesthood, which was all that was needed to complete the arrangements. . . . The seven days' purification services for the altar have respect to the original directions of Moses for the same purpose, in Ex. xxix. 37, and are simply a preparation for the great end aimed at—that God might accept the sacrifices of the people, and be gracious to them (ver. 27). This indispensably required that there should first be a consecrated way of access—a holy altar, and a holy priesthood to minister at it."—FAIRBAIRN'S *Ezekiel*, pp. 474, 475.—W. F.]

Ver. 13, with which the vision already turns more expressly to the second particular, the service in the temple of Jehovah, has been prepared for by occasional references, such as ch. xl. 38 sq., xlii. 13 sq., but is introduced in particular by the "ordinances" and "precepts" commanded to be made known in ver. 11 of our chapter. We remark, as regards the predominating evangelical tone of the vision, that the statement that Jehovah's sanctuary, as well as Jehovah Himself, will dwell among His people, precedes any commandment or ordinance in regard to it. So the time of the wandering patriarchs was likewise before the time of the law, which simply came in between promise and fulfilment.—**And these are the measures**, the idea is symbolized in the "measure."—הַמִּזְבֵּחַ is the altar of burnt-offering (ch. xl. 47, ix. 2; Ex. xxx. 28 sq.). Both on account of its significance in regard to the people in their relation to Jehovah,—since it is for the court what the ark which is wanting in Ezekiel is for the most holy place, and the altar of incense for the holy place (comp. Ezra iii.),—and also because a fresh section of the vision announces itself here, the more exact statement of the measures is repeated in accordance with ch. xl. 5.—חֵיק, from חוּק, "to surround," is the so-called **bosom**,—GESENIUS: the hallowed part of the altar, where the fire burnt; KEIL: its base; HENGST.: the same as its back (?), namely, the enclosure, which was of brass,—as being on the outside; "back," because it formed the periphery of the altar; "bosom," because it embraces and grasps the heart, since חֵיק properly means something that grasps. Evidently the whole circumference of the altar will be first given. Keil translates: "a bottom-frame one cubit high and one cubit broad" (?). In the case of that which encloses the earth and stone, the kernel of the altar, the breadth is the thickness.—גְּבוּלָהּ (the feminine suffix here and in שְׂפָתָהּ, referring to חֵיק, has been explained from the transferred relation), more closely defined by אֶל־שְׂפָתָהּ סָבִיב, is, since anything else can scarcely be understood from the foregoing, the one span, that is, half cubit broad edging projecting over the circumference. הָאֶחָד, as noun: a span of unity, of the one = one span. Keil, who interprets from below upwards, places here a moulding a half cubit high.—וְזֶה גַּב הַמִּזְבֵּחַ is commonly translated: the "back," which גַּב must as little signify as it can denote the "socle" of the altar, the bottom-frame with its moulding. According to the fundamental idea of the root-word, to be "drawn together," "heaped up," גַּב may at least quite as well denote something elevated or high, which is so easily expressed by this object (*altare*), as what is bowed or bent, especially when circumference and edging have preceded, and when in this way the configuration in height was not yet touched on.—Ver. 14 would describe this from the bottom upwards; hence מֵחֵיק הָאָרֶץ = from the circumference (starting from that with which the description began in ver. 13), where it rose above the earth, apparently as belonging to it and raising itself out of it. [And for this reason Hävernick already in ver. 13 makes the bosom mean: the lowest part of the altar, the part immediately on the earth, the support of the whole. Keil understands הָאָרֶץ of the filling up of the חֵיק with earth (?).]—הָעֲזָרָה, HENGST.: "closing;" KEIL: "walling round." The Aramaicized word, which is derived as a softened form from עָצַר, denotes in 2 Chron. iv. 9, vi. 13, the court (חָצֵר, the "enclosure"). If derived from עָזַר, "to hold off" (hence, "to protect," "to help"), **the word would indicate a rest or landing-place,** as the courts formed such ascending landing-places or terraces. It can hardly be a third designation for the wall of the altar (HENGST.: "especially the external wall of the two cubits thick enclosure"). When, as here, the height of the altar is treated of, two rests are to be understood, one above the other,—first a **lower** one, because only two cubits high, and therefore called the **lesser**, in relation to the **greater** of four cubits high, the next and higher one. The repeatedly stated breadth of one cubit makes the detailed description of the more general description in ver. 13 more intelligible. We make by addition the height six cubits; Keil, seven cubits, but where is his half cubit גְּבוּל?

Ver. 15. הַהַרְאֵל, "the mountain of God," four cubits high, denotes after the two court-like rests, in the priestly mode of expression, the altar proper, as it were the sanctuary upon the very high mountain (ch. xl. 2). The height of the altar which is being described suggested the expression; and accordingly the entire temple edifice, as it has been designated after the temple proper, "house" or "palace," concentrates itself in the altar with its rests, designated as it is after its upper part: **mountain of God.** From this, however, the genuine priestly term: הָאֲרִאֵיל, is still to be distinguished. The Qeri reads: אֲרִיאֵל, adopting which Keil interprets, in conformity with Isa. xxix. 1, not: "lion of God," but, from אָרָה, "to burn" (*ara Dei*): "hearth of God." Hengst. holds for the reading in the text: אֲרִי, "lion," and takes אַיִל, the י being elided by the Masoretes, as "ram," while he thinks it possible that the original form was אֲרַיְאֵל, instead of אֲרִאֵיל, so that a double sense had been intended. Lion of God and ram-lion, the lion that consumes the rams for God! At all events, what is meant is the upper surface, that is, in reality the fire-hearth of the altar from the four corners of which the four horns extended, and these, according to Jewish tradition, belonged to the essential requisites of the altar, and indicate the insignia of kingly dominion, hence the revelation of divine power and glory, etc. (BÄHR, *Symb.* i. p. 473); with these our description is completed as regards extent upwards. The altar has, like that of Solomon, a height of ten cubits.—Ver. 16. The account of the height is followed by that of the length and breadth, measured at the highest point of the altar, and given for the whole four sides from the ground up.—Ver. 17. Setting out now from that which is not a part of the altar proper (וְהָעֲזָרָה, collective, comp. ver. 14), the lower ledge, in contrast and as complement to וְהָאֲרִאֵיל (ver. 16), the top surface, ver. 17, measures fourteen instead of twelve cubits square, since it adds from vers. 13, 14 the thickness of the "bosom," a cubit on each side, to the length and the breadth; this is referred to in what follows: **and the border round about it,** etc. = "and its border at its lip round about" (ver. 13), although for the sake of variety we have **half a**

cubit here, instead of a span there.—**And its bosom,** etc. (ver. 13); this explains the difference in the measurement here from that of ver. 16. The mention of the **bosom** and the **border** reverts to the beginning of the description of the altar (ver. 13), so that only גַּב there still needs to be mentioned, and this is now done by naming the **steps,** in distinction from Ex. xx. 26, indicating the elevation of the altar of burnt-offering. [Bähr carries an inclined plane round the altar for a similar purpose as the two rests here.]—פְּנוֹת, infinitive = when one turns, equivalent to: **toward;** according to others, a noun, read by Hitzig as participle פֹּנוֹת.

Ver. 18 leads to the consecration of the altar of burnt-offering, forming an introduction to its ritual for the purpose stated, and to its service. In other words, as the entire temple-edifice was referred to the underlying idea by means of the measuring, that is, was set forth as to its symbolical signification, so, in accordance with its intention as respects the people, in whom the idea is to be realized, the altar of burnt-offering has been purposely described at such length; but this intention will be effected only by this means, that, strictly parallel with the entrance of the glory into the sanctuary, a formal act of sacrificial consecration in respect of the altar of burnt-offering is provided for beforehand. The clothing of the idea is a kind of dramatic transaction between Ezekiel and the priests of the new temple, an act of the future with which we can compare from the past Lev. viii. (Ex. xxix. 10 sq.); 1 Kings viii. 62 sq.; 2 Chron. viii. 4 sq.—By the words: **on the day when it is made,** the **ordinances of the altar** are more closely defined as ordinances which are fulfilled (as to their idea) as soon as the whole temple, including this altar, will be in actual existence. A "being made" is also spoken of in the sense of the reference throughout to the people, just as the whole consecration points to men, who as such can do nothing pure or holy. Comp. Ex. xx. 22; Lev. xvi. 16. But the consecration of the altar, the ritual of which is told to the prophet in the Old Testament mode of expression, particularly by the solemn: "thus saith the Lord," etc., holds out the prospect of a *consecration of the people by Jehovah.*—By the avowed purpose of the altar, "to cause ascendings" (as the burnt-offerings meant to be wholly burnt, specially fulfilling the view, are called) "to ascend upon it" (with reference to the altar, the raising up of the gift), **and to sprinkle blood upon it** (which precisely in these offerings was done merely on the altar round about), is therefore signified in the first instance, and corresponding at the same time to the act of consecration here, the *consecration of the people to Jehovah,* their entire surrender and presentation of themselves to Him. The burnt-offerings usher in the class of offerings which obtains in the state of grace. The justified man lives henceforth not to himself; the service of the Lord which is ministered in the Church is symbolized by this purpose of the altar of burnt-offering; hence there is no act of worship without burnt-offering. Its expiatory significance comes out only in a secondary way in referring to the altar, just as the sprinkling with blood in the case of the burnt-offering takes place in the most general form. But since, in the time before the law, the burnt-offerings were at the same time the sin-offerings,—just as their atoning nature reminds of the sin which continually adheres to us, although the awakened conscience is again hushed,—so likewise the history of sacrifice is represented to us by this oldest of all sacrifices; thus the self-surrendering reliance on grace continues to be taken into account, as in the past, so for the future, and so the burnt-offering may be called the perpetual offering of the Church of God.

Ver. 19 passes over from the altar as to its purpose to the priests and the appropriate victims. The former are simply presupposed as a body of priests descended from Levi, belonging through the tribe to the whole people as their natural and official representatives, and that without consecration, which took place at the tabernacle; nevertheless, instead of consecration the elective appointment is repeated (comp. ch. xl. 46), so that only the race of Zadok who draw near to Jehovah (ch. xlii. 13) are qualified for the service (comp. on ch. xliv. 15 sq.). As to the second element, the victim, פַּר בֶּן־בָּקָר, a young bullock was fixed on. The male was the fitting victim for the burnt-offering, and the bullock was the most distinguished among the animals coming into consideration for a **sin-offering**; and so the high priest, as priestly head and representative of the community, offered for his cleansing a bullock still in the full flower of his strength (Lev. iv. 3 sq., comp. 13 sq.).—Ver. 20. Comp. ver. 15; vers. 14, 17; ver. 13. The sprinkling of the blood is the sprinkling in detail of the particular parts characteristic of the sin-offering. The cleansing and expiation of the altar have a reflex influence on the people that made it, and that, at the word of God (in Lev. xvii. 11 the altar is a place of God), raise themselves up there to God. That which the two words employed express (**cleanse,** and **expiate**), that which the procedure above and below and around the extremities symbolizes, will be a complete sanctification of the people. With such a strong representation of the cleansing, an anointing of the altar, etc. (Lev. viii. 11) was not necessary in order to give expression to the idea.—Ver. 21. הַפָּר הַחַטָּאת, the article before the *stat. constr.* It is quite as unwarranted simply to suppose everything omitted, as from what is not said to make the prophet be in contradiction with the Mosaic ceremonial. The statements in this vision are mainly determined by the idea to be set forth, and which shows itself everywhere. Thus there was no need of saying anything about the blood which was not consumed, and which elsewhere was poured out at the foot of the altar of burnt-offering to prevent its being profaned, since the sanctification is so strongly expressed in that no mention is once made of the fat upon the inwards which came upon the altar, but it is so spoken as if the fire consumed the whole animal (comp. besides in Lev. iv. 12, viii. 17, the manner of expression) **without the sanctuary**; comp. Lev. iv. 21, vi. 23. Thus not within the **house,** and if in a place that may be supposed related to it, certainly (comp. what was remarked in speaking of the gizrah, ch. xli.) in the **"off-place,"** hardly ch. xlvi. 19 sq.

Ver. 22. The goat is the atonement for a prince (Lev. iv. 23), but also the characteristic offering for the people on the great day of atonement (Lev. xvi.). Thus the people might be looked upon as perfectly represented at the altar of the court, ver. 19 sq. ecclesiastically, and here civilly, by their two heads the high priest and the prince (comp. ch. xliv. 3 sq.), with reference at the same time to the great yearly atonement. At any rate, only the **second day** is marked at the beginning which is made with the bullock as sin-offering; the following days up to the seventh are, as respects sin-offering, introduced and indicated by the second.—תָּמִים, *integer*, which had to be the quality of every victim, but clearly more noteworthy here when the civil side is treated of.—וְחִטְּאוּ, the priests, or: one, etc., while at the same time ver. 21 sq. is illustrated in this respect by כַּאֲשֶׁר'. The prophet does it by instructing the priests to do it.—After what has been stated regarding these two days, that the bullock cleanses the altar, etc. (ver. 20), to which reference is expressly made in speaking of the goat of the second day (ver. 22), then בְּכַלּוֹתְךָ מֵחַטֵּא in ver. 23 can be understood only of the completion of the two sin-offerings, to which the subordinate purpose of the altar, the mention of the sprinkling of blood (ver. 18), had led the prophet, so that he now comes to what is spoken of as the principal purpose, to the burnt-offering, which, in the indefiniteness as regards time with which the bullock and ram of which it consists are spoken of, can be quite as easily assigned to the first day as it is expressly assigned in ver. 25 to seven days.—Ver. 24. What remained still indefinite in ver. 22 now becomes quite clear by the mention of **the priests.**—Very significant, however, and exceedingly telling for the setting forth of the idea of sanctification already remarked in Ezekiel, is the casting of salt by the priests, which in the law is expressly demanded for the meat-offering, and appears here connected in a similar manner (שָׁלַךְ) with the burnt-offering, although salt (Lev. ii. 13) was to be put on every oblation. Salt (especially in contrast with leaven and honey), by its seasoning and antiseptic power, with its hidden cleansing fire which consumes everything unclean, is meant to bring out the signification of the powerful truth which keeps off impurity and hypocritical legal sanctity, viz. the surrender to the service of the Lord symbolized in the burnt-offering. Perhaps its character as salt of the covenant of God, with reference to the eternity thereof (Num. xviii. 19; 2 Chron. xiii. 5), comes additionally into consideration for the act of consecration. The quality of human nature, observes Hengst., is unsalted, and may not enter into relation with God.

Ver. 25. The **seven days** can be neither nine nor eight days, *i.e.* excluding the first two days, or at least the first day, for they are expressly seven; as also it is said again in ver. 26, וְכִפְּרוּ (Qeri: יְכַפְּרוּ), with evident allusion to וְכִפַּרְתָּהוּ in ver. 20. Moreover, apart from the significance of the number seven as the number of the covenant, consecration, sanctification, etc., it is the basis of all solemnities in Israel, as Keil observes: prescribed in the law without exception for every act of consecration continuing over one day. Comp. particularly Ex. xxix. 37; 2 Chron. vii. 9. The one **kid for a sin-offering daily** cannot possibly be held to run counter to this, for it expresses what relates to the majority of these days, six days; and in respect of the first day, the bullock (ver. 19 sq.) stood clearly defined from the outset. The two victims appointed for burnt-offering (ver. 23 sq.) are also distinguished from the kid by the change from תַּעֲשֶׂה to יַעֲשׂוּ. And not without significance could the cleansing sin-offering, in distinction from the burnt-offering, be ascribed—although only formally—to the prophet; in this keeping separate he represents the sanctifying grace of God, and the priests the community sanctifying themselves to God.—As ver. 23 sq. is supplemented by the שִׁבְעַת יָמִים placed at the beginning of ver. 25, and qualifying the whole verse, the burnt-offering in question is to be offered daily during the seven days after the daily completion of the cleansing.—Ver. 26, concluding the act of consecration,—hence couched in general terms,—confirms both the merely seven days' duration of the consecration of the altar (for nothing else is meant by טִהֲרוּ), and also, in virtue of the entire consecration above mentioned, its perfect purification, on the ground and in consequence of the expiation (וכפרו) of the altar, which according to ver. 20 is its cleansing. We might translate: a pronouncing clean for the present use, treated of in ver. 27. It is certainly also in harmony with this when, in making over to the altar thereby represented as entering personally on its functions, the peculiar phrase: **fill its hand**, is used. After the use previously in the description of the altar of the words "bosom" and "lip" in reference to it, **its hand** (יָדָיו, plur., is a needless gloss) can cause no surprise, especially in Ezekiel, who delights in bold symbols. The altar representing the people in the priests, even of itself, easily becomes a person, and still more readily if the idea of it is to be made prominent. But to "fill the hand" is the expression used in Lev. viii. on occasion of the offering for consecrating the priests, inasmuch as those parts of the offering, which otherwise were heaved and waved in the thank-offering, were laid, along with the loaves and cakes, into the hands of the priests. With exception of the breast and shoulder, all this was laid on the altar as a sacrifice of consecration (מִלֻּאִים). The expression: מִלֵּא יָד, occurs similarly in Ex. xxxii. 29; 1 Chron. xxix. 5; 2 Chron. xxix. 31 (יֶדְכֶם), in reference to Jehovah, so that the application to the priests in general denotes the giving of a present to them, which, although by the people, is yet as from Jehovah. It indicates in particular, however, their official right to their ministry, and the obligation of this ministry to offer to Jehovah in the fire of the altar. Since the expression, different from the consecration proper of priests, implies the conferring of the priestly office, the formal installation into it, —the making of it over to the altar here, corresponding to its purification, is designed to represent the making over of the altar of burnt-offering for the service assigned to it, as ver. 27 farther describes. The use for which this altar will have to be employed henceforth, after the completion of what has to be completed in regard to it in the seven days, as, moreover, it is expressly said: **on the eighth day and onwards**, is intimated by the burnt-offering and the *Shelamim*, which, however, appear not exactly as the principal and most frequent offerings, *instar omnium* (KEIL, HENGST.), but to make prominent the idea of a people of God in the state of grace, as the kinds of offering befitting such a relation to Jehovah. Hence also the *Shelamim* are not called here זְבָחִים, "slain offerings," in order to give a general designation for offerings, or to mark the distinction from the burnt-offering, which falls entirely to Jehovah, but שְׁלָמִים, that is, salvation-offerings (**peace-offerings**), a designation well fitted to place them on a level with the "whole offering" (כָּלִיל), as the burnt-offering is also called: full surrender is met by full grace, salvation perfect in respect to the past and for the future, and the individual's enjoyment of peace resting on and flowing from it (in which perhaps the more private character of this species of offering compared with the more official character of the burnt-offering should be noticed). The burnt-offerings mentioned first give the key-note, just as they are also strengthened through the bullock in the seven days' consecration. As supplicatory offerings, the *Shelamim*, therefore, are also rather thank-offerings, because the praying Church knows on whom she believes (as John xi. 41). Finally, the *Shelamim* were in the Old Covenant the oldest flesh-offerings after the burnt-offerings. Comp. also Ex. x. 25, xviii. 12 (in reference to the delivering of Israel out of Egypt), and Gen. xlvi. 1.—רָצָא, thus only here, elsewhere רָצָה (ch. xx. 40, 41), refers to: "restraining," so that the guilt presupposed in having recourse to the sacrifice is confessed; hence Niphal in Isa. xl. 2 (Lev. xxvi. 41, 43: ר' עון) of guilt being recompensed, here: to receive as unrestrained by guilt (the idea of justification is perceptible in the word), equivalent to: to receive graciously.

CHAPTER XLIV.

1 And he led me back the way of the outer gate of the sanctuary that
2 looks to the east; and it was shut. And Jehovah said to me: This gate
shall be shut, it shall not be opened, and no man shall go in through it;
3 because Jehovah, the God of Israel, went in through it; thus it is shut. As
to the prince, he [is] prince, he shall sit in it, to eat bread [food] before
Jehovah; from the way of the [to the] porch of the gate shall he go in, and
4 from its way shall he go out. And he brought me the way of the north
gate before the house, and I looked, and behold, the glory of Jehovah filled
5 the house of Jehovah; and I fell upon my face. And Jehovah said to me:
Son of man, set thy heart, and behold with thine eyes, and hear with thine
ears all that I say unto thee concerning all the ordinances of the house of
Jehovah, and all its laws [or: its whole law]; and thou settest [shalt set] thy heart
to the approach of the house in [conjunction with] all the out-goings of the
6 sanctuary. And thou sayest to the contumacy, to the house of Israel, Thus
saith the Lord Jehovah: Cease at last from all your abominations, O house
7 of Israel, When ye brought sons of the outland, uncircumcised in heart and
uncircumcised in flesh, to be in My sanctuary, to desecrate it, even My house;
when ye offered My bread [My food] (through them), fat and blood, and they
8 broke My covenant in addition to all your abominations. And [yea] ye have
not kept the charge of My holy things, and [but] ye set [such, those] to keep My
9 charge for you in My sanctuary. Thus saith the Lord Jehovah: A son of
the outland, uncircumcised in heart and uncircumcised in flesh, shall not come
to My sanctuary; in respect of every son of the outland [shall it be said] that is
10 in the midst of the children of Israel. Nay, but the Levites who went far
from Me when Israel went astray, who went astray from Me after their
11 detestable idols, they bear their guilt; And they are servants in My sanctuary, sentinels at the gates of the house and servants of the house; they
shall slay the burnt-offering and the slain-offering for the people, and they
12 shall stand before them to serve them. Because they used to serve them
before their detestable idols, and were to the house of Israel a stumbling-
block of guilt, therefore have I lifted My hand over them,—sentence of the
13 Lord Jehovah,—and they bear their guilt. And they shall not draw near to
Me, to minister as priests to Me, and to draw near over all My holy things

to the most holy place, and [but] they bear their reproach and their abomina-
14 tions which they did. And I have given them to be keepers of the charge
15 of the house, for all its service and for all that is to be done in it. And [but]
the priests the [these] Levites, the sons of Zadok, who kept the charge of My
sanctuary when the children of Israel went astray from Me, they shall come
near to Me to minister unto Me, and stand before Me to offer unto Me fat
16 and blood,—sentence of the Lord Jehovah. They shall come to My sanc-
tuary, and they shall draw near to My table to minister unto Me, and to
17 keep My charge. And it comes to pass, when they go to the gates of the
inner court, they shall put on linen garments, and wool shall not come upon
them when they minister in the gates of the inner court and at the house.
18 Linen turbans shall be upon their heads, and linen breeches upon their loins;
19 they shall not gird themselves in sweat. And on their going out to the outer
court, to the outer court to the people, they shall put off their garments in
which they minister [ministered], and lay them away [down] in the cells of holi-
ness, and put on other garments; and they shall not sanctify the people in
20 [with] their garments. And their head they shall not shave, nor suffer their
21 locks to grow long; polling they shall poll their heads. And no priest shall
22 drink wine when they go to the inner court. And a widow and a divorced
woman shall they not take to themselves for wives; but maidens of the seed
of the house of Israel, and the widow who was widow of a priest they may take.
23 And they shall teach My people; what [the difference is] between the holy and
the common, and between the unclean and the clean, they shall make them
24 know. And over [matters of] strife shall they stand to judge in My judgments,
and judge them [so]; and My laws and Mine ordinances on all My festivals
25 shall they keep; and My Sabbaths shall they hallow. And to a dead body
of a man shall he not go to be defiled; but for father, and for mother, and
for son, and for daughter, for brother, and for sister who had no husband,
26 they may defile themselves. And after his cleansing they shall count to him
27 seven days. And on the day of his coming to the sanctuary to the inner
court, to minister in the sanctuary, he shall offer his sin-offering,—sentence of
28 the Lord Jehovah. And it is to them for an inheritance [namely], I am their
inheritance; and a possession shall ye not give them in Israel, I am their
29 possession. The meat-offering, and the sin-offering, and the guilt-offering,
30 they shall eat it; and every devoted thing in Israel shall be theirs. And the
first of all the firstlings of everything, and every oblation of all, out of all
your oblations, shall be to the priests, and the first of your [ground] corn shall
31 ye give to the priest, to bring down a blessing upon thy house. Whatever is
carrion, or torn, whether of fowl or of beast, the priests shall not eat.

Ver. 2. Sept.: . . . ὁτι κυριος . . . εἰσελευσεται . . . κ. ἐσται κεκλεισμενη. Vulg.: . . . *eritque clausa* (3.) *principi. Princeps ipse . . . per viam portæ vestibuli ingredietur et per viam ejus*—

Ver. 3. Διοτι ὁ ἡγουμενος οὑτος . . . κατα τ. ὁδον αἰλαμ—

Ver. 4. K. εἰσηγαγεν με . . . πληρης δοξης ὁ οἰκος— (Another reading: ואפל על־פני.)

Ver. 5. . . . ταξον εἰς τ. καρδιαν . . . κατα παντα . . . ἐν πασιν τοις ἁγιοις. Vulg.: . . . *de universis ceremoniis in viis templi per omnes exitus*—

Ver. 7. . . . κ. παρεβαινετε τ. διαθηκην μου ἐν πασαις— (Another reading: את כל and תועבתיהם.)

Ver. 8. . . . κ. διεταξατε του φυλασσειν φυλακας— Vulg.: *et non servastis præcepta . . . et posuistis custodes observationum mearum in . . . vobismet ipsis.*

Ver. 10. ἀλλ' ἡ οἱ— Vulg.: *Sed et . . . qui longe recesserunt*—

Ver. 11. Vulg.: . . . *æditui et janitores portarum*—

Ver. 12. . . . και ἐγενετο τω οἰκω—

Ver. 13. . . . οὐδε του προσαγαγειν προς τα ἁγια υἱων Ἰσρ· οὐδε προς τ. ἁγια τ. ἁγιων μου . . . τ. ἀτιμιαν αὐτων ἐν τη πλανησει ἡ ἐπλανηθησαν. Vulg.: . . . *juxta sancta sanctorum* (Another reading: אל כל.)

Ver. 14. K. ταξουσιν αὐτους . . . ὁσα ἀν ποιησωσιν. (Another reading: לו.)

Ver. 15. . . . του προσφερειν μοι θυσιαν, στεαρ—

Ver. 17. Sept.: . . . ἀπο της πυλης . . . κ. ἐσω.

Ver. 18. βια.

Ver. 19. The words repeated are wanting in several manuscripts, and in the Sept., Syr., Vulg., Arab., and Chaldee.

Ver. 20. . . . κ. τας κομας αὐτων οὐ μη ψιλωσουσιν, καλυπτοντες καλυψωσιν τας κεφαλας αὐτων. Vulg.: . . . *neque comam nutrient, sed tondentes attondent capita sua.*

Ver. 23. . . . κ. ἀνα μεσον καθαρου κ. ἀνα μεσον ἀκαθαρτου—

Ver. 24. K. ἐπι κρισιν αἱματος . . . τα δικαιωματα μου δικαιωσουσιν, κ. τα κριματα μου κρινουσιν, κ. τα νομιμα— Vulg.: . . . *controversia, stabunt in judiciis meis et judicabunt;*— (Another reading: למשפט.)

Ver. 25. K. ἐπι ψυχην ἀνθρωπου οὐκ εἰσελευσονται— Vulg.: . . . *ad mortuum hominem . . . quæ alterum virum non habuerit,*—

Ver. 26. Another reading: יספר.

Ver. 27. . . . εἰσπορευωνται εἰς τ. αὐλην . . . προσοισουσιν ἱλασμον— Vulg.: . . . *ut ministret mihi*—

Ver. 28. κ. ἐσται αὐτοις . . . 'Εγω . . . και— Vulg.: *Non erit autem eis*—

Ver. 29. K. τας θυσιας—

Ver. 30. K. ἀπαρχαι παντων κ. τα πρωτοτοκα παντων κ. τα ἀφαιρεματα παντα ὑμων ἐκ παντων τ. ἀπαρχων . . . κ. τα πρωτογεννηματα ὑμων— Vulg.: *Et primitiva omnium primogenitorum et omnia libamenta ex omnibus quæ offeruntur . . . et primitiva ciborum vestrorum . . . ut reponat*—

Ver. 31. . . . θνησιμαιον κ. θηριαλωτον—

EXEGETICAL REMARKS.

Vers. 1–3. *The Prince in the East Gate.*

[As the preceding chapter had disclosed the purpose of God to re-occupy, and that for ever, this new temple, and had described the necessary means and rites of consecration in order to its being a source of blessing to His people, so the present chapter lays down regulations for preventing any new desecration of the house, such as might again compel God to withdraw His gracious presence. These regulations refer successively to the prince and the priesthood—the two classes through whom directly the former pollutions had been introduced into the house of God.—FAIRBAIRN.—W. F.]

The prophet observed in the priests' court (ch. xliii. 5) all that relates to the altar of burnt-offering. He is thence brought back, as we shall have to suppose, through the inner north or south gate the way to the outer east gate. It is not without significance that the east gate of the outer court (comp. ch. xliii. 12) is designated as "gate of the sanctuary, the outer one which," etc. Looking into it from the court (not as Hitzig and Hengstenberg: from before the outer east gate, as ch. xliii. 1), Ezekiel perceived that it was **shut** (comp. ch. xl. 11); and this must the more astonish him, as this entrance to the sanctuary had been described to him in ch. xl. as forming the rule for all the other gates of the temple. The fact, then, of its being closed demands an explanation, which also **Jehovah** (comp. on ch. xliii. 6, 7) gives him in Ver. 2. Since the whole vision points to the future, it is said first of all in reference thereto: **This gate shall be shut** (יִהְיֶה). Hence the closing shall continue for all futurity, as is again expressly confirmed by the statement: **It shall not be opened**, and strengthened by this other declaration: **And no man** (whoever he may be) **shall go in through it,**—in other words, by the exclusion of every one. When it is thereafter said: **Because Jehovah,** etc., the כִּי explains certainly the immediate present (וְהָיָה), the present closing of the gate, which, as we see in ver. 1, is the first thing treated of; but we shall have to draw upon it for the explanation for the future likewise, for this future has been announced as the continuance of the closing in the present. The way which the glory of Jehovah went (ch. xliii. 4) is thus a unique **way,** and will remain such, no man shall tread it **henceforth;** and this, when we look upon the fulfilment in Christ of all that had been written aforetime, reads like a Messianic prophecy, without its being necessary for us to suppose with the Church Fathers a direct reference to the virginity of Mary (*fit porta Christi pervia, referta, plena gratia, transitque rex et permanet clausa ut fuit per sæcula*). [The Rabbins have interpreted the closing of the gate to this effect: that the Shechinah shall no longer be able to come out, an idea which Lightfoot has transformed into the ever-during dwelling of the glory of God in the Christian Church; while Hengst. expresses it thus: that the glory of the impending revelation of the Lord "embodies" itself in the door's remaining shut.]—When, after this quite universal explanation in respect to future and present of the shut east gate, Ver. 3, by its very commencing with the absolute construction אֶת־הַנָּשִׂיא, directs attention to the prince, and, besides, gives as reason for what is to be said of him in reference to the east gate, נָשִׂיא הוּא, that is as much as to say: *qua* prince it belongs to him; then an exception from the rule just laid down, that is, an exceptional entering of the prince through this gate at certain times and for certain contingencies, is not to be supposed, especially as what is announced regarding him is not: יָבֹא בוֹ, but simply: יֵשֶׁב־בּוֹ, that he shall sit in this gate, namely (comp. for the expression: to eat bread before God, Ex. xviii. 12; Luke xiii. 26), to enjoy the sacrificial banquets. Of this place of the prince in the east gate, Hengst. exclaims: "How glorious must the entering Lord be, when the prince cannot be more highly honoured than by a place in the gate by which He entered!" Now, since according to vers. 1, 2 the entrance through the east gate was closed to him, the way by which the prince arrived at his place of honour will necessarily have to be given, as is accordingly done; and this account is not to be interpreted, with Keil, of the outside stair over the threshold at the guardroom, and onward to the gate-porch at the inner end of the gate-structure. For such a way surely מִדֶּרֶךְ אוּלָם' would be a strange mode of expression! On the contrary, this mode of expression is quite conceivable when we consider the way of the prophet (ver. 1), who had been brought from the north or south to the east gate, and finds himself there on the side of the court west of the gate, and hence has the porch right before him, so that he will the more readily define from it the way of the prince into the gate (**from its way** he shall also **go out**), as the entering **from the way of the porch of the gate** forms self-evidently the contrast to an entering from the way of the gate without. Consequently, the prince has (as Hitzig rightly understands) to come through the outer north or south gate into the outer court, and to cross the same, in order to arrive at the place where he will sit, etc. Whether the gate-porch which thus lay on this side (toward the court) of the gate-barrier is meant to be given as the place for the banquets of the prince may be questioned; Hengstenberg recommends, as "specially" adapted for them, "the inner threshold immediately adjacent to the porch." According to all this, the exception of the prince symbolizes merely, in its own way, the holiness of the sanctuary, the solemnity of drawing near to Jehovah and appearing before Him. It will no longer be as in the former temple, that any one (אִישׁ) will march straight to the sanctuary through the east gate; but the saints of God, His people sanctified for ever, will know how to honour the holiness of Him who sanctified them. ("In the case of the tabernacle and its court there was only one entrance, from the east, through which all had to go," KLIEF.) But it is significant that the civil head of the people (comp. on ch. xliii. 22), the prince, sits and eats in the east gate closed for every one, on the way which the glory of Jehovah went to fill the **house** (ver. 4), and there enjoys the fruit of that which has been provided. For the significance of the banquets has regard to the communion and friendly relation in which the participants stand to one another, and with the provider of the feast, who in the last resort is Jehovah—at least He participates therein in the sense of Rev. iii. 20; just as also the gladness and joy before the Lord, and even the joys of the kingdom of heaven, appear under the figure of a feast (Ps. xxiii. 5, xxxvi. 9 [8]; Matt. viii. 11; Luke xiv. 15; Rev. xix. 9). We have in this the genuine gospel feature, which excels in glory the face of the law. So much the more, however, as regards the prince—who, as has been said, is rather a reflex of the people (comp. ch. xlvi. 10), just as to them also the entrance to the temple has been opened by the setting in operation of the altar of burnt-offering (ch. xliii. 26)—must we avoid the interpretation which accentuates in him the David of Messianic times (ch. xxxiv. 23 sq., xxxvii. 24). On this comp. also ch. xlv. 22, xlvi. 2, 16. It would be better to insist with Hengst. on his "cheering" form, as opposed to the ceasing of the magisterial office in the exile, especially when his presence is so incidentally "presupposed." But this princeship, which makes orderly civil relations again obtain in Israel, had its post-exile appearance in Zerubbabel, for instance (Zech. iv.), and has at all events been perfected in the Messianic kingdom, even as to the side applicable here, which Isa. liii. 10 expresses thus: "The pleasure of Jehovah shall prosper through his hand;" while in ver. 11 he is said: "to see," "to be refreshed;" and similarly ver. 12.

["In regard to the *prince*, it is impossible for us to think of any one but the royal head, as he is throughout spoken of as an individual, and in the next chapter is directed 'to prepare for himself, and for all the people of the land,' a sin-offering (ch. xlv. 22). So that the idea of Hävernick, that the word is used collectively for the rulers and presidents generally of the people, is quite untenable. And not less so is the opinion, that by the expression is simply to be understood the Messiah; for this is utterly irreconcilable with all the prescriptions given, and in particular with those requiring the presentation of sacrifices and sin-offerings for the prince. It is to be explained precisely as the whole delineation here, and in the preceding visions (ch. xxxiv.–xxxix.), by viewing it as part of an ideal description of coming realities under the form and aspect of the old relations. And no more than we expect other parts of the vision to find their accomplishment under the gospel by a restoration of the carnal sacrifices and institutions of Judaism, should we look here for an actual prince to follow the regulations prescribed. Standing on the position he did, the prophet *must* speak of the future under the image of the past; and as it was by means of the earthly head of the Jewish state that many of the former corruptions had been introduced, he now shows how a repetition of such evils is to be guarded against in the future. Whether the kingly power should ever again be concentrated in one person, or should be shared by many, is of no moment as regards the substance of the truth here unfolded." As for the connection between the prince and the east gate (vers. 1–3), "what could this import, but that the prince should feel he now occupied a place of peculiar nearness to God? As God's vicegerent and deputy among the people, it became him to be the most distinguished representative in public life of God's holiness, to tread the higher walks of spiritual communion and fellowship with Heaven, and stand pre-eminent in his zeal for the interests of truth and righteousness. Far now from usurping the authority that belonged to God, and abusing to selfish ends and purposes the power which was given by Him for higher ends, all authority and power in Israel should be exercised—if this divine ideal were reduced to practice—in a solemn feeling of subordination to God's majesty, and with an unfeigned desire for His glory."—FAIRBAIRN'S *Ezekiel*, pp. 477, 478.—W. F.]

Vers. 4–16. *The Priests.*

Ver. 4. The outer north gate cannot be the one spoken of, for the prophet stands in the outer court before the porch of the east gate. He is brought אֶל־פְּנֵי הַבַּיִת, and so דֶּרֶךְ־שַׁעַר־הַצָּפוֹן must be the way to the inner north gate, as this was also the way by which to get near to the temple-house.—Comp. for the rest on ch. xliii. 5 and 3. As there the filling of the house with the glory of Jehovah introduced the Thorah of the temple, especially the consecration of the altar of burnt-offering, which certainly forms also the transition to the temple-service, so here by a similar introduction, in which Ver. 5 refers so far back as to ch. xl. 4, the service before Jehovah is now introduced, and that with attentive regard to the *personelle*. Thus the two parts of the section, ch. xl.–xlvi., are even formally separated.—**Jehovah**, as in ver. 2.—The threefold demand upon the prophet, of which the first, which as the most inward strikes the key for the seeing and hearing, has its ground not exactly in the glory just now seen (HENGST.), but rather in what Jehovah will say to him, and in the abominations committed by Israel, to which it has reference.—What concerns the **ordinances** and **laws** of the **house** (comp. ch. xliii. 11, 12) is certainly limited here by הַמִּקְדָּשׁ to the temple building proper, as is also indicated by the designation: **house of Jehovah**, repeated from ver. 4, so that **the approach of the house with all the out-goings** is to be understood in reference to the priests.—Ver. 6. That the **house of Israel** is to be addressed (ch. ii. 7) shows the more plainly how it had been represented by the priesthood of the past.—רַב־לָכֶם מִכָּל', literally: there is much to you from all your abominations, sufficient, enough for you, so that you may at last abstain (1 Pet. iv. 3). Like priest, like people; but also, like people, like priest (Hos. iv. 9).

Ver. 7, in this connection, in which the temple-house accessible to the priests alone is treated of, and priestly ministration is had regard to, can hardly refer to heathens or foreigners living amongst Israel (comp. for this Lev. xvii. 10, 12; Num. xv. 13 sq.; Ex. xii. 43, 44; 1 Kings viii. 41 sq.), foreign merchants as sellers of sacrificial victims, etc., nor heathenized Israelites in general, but must be understood as referring to the introduction of priests, who, as the children of Israel were called "heathens" (גּוֹיִם) in ch. ii. 3, were בְּנֵי־נֵכָר, instead of being sons of Jehovah's house. In what sense the term employed is to be taken is shown by the next clause: **uncircumcised in heart**, which, if said of genuine born heathens, would be nonsense; whereas, said of Israelites, of the priests here, and conjoined with the following clause: **and uncircumcised in flesh**, it expresses exactly the same as Rom. ii. 25, when the περιτομη ἀκροβυστια γεγονεν,—when the direct opposite of the idea of the symbol realizes itself (comp. besides, Deut. xxx. 6), the distinction also which the symbol denotes will disappear, the Jew has become heathen. Comp. also ch. xvi. 3; Zech. xiv. 21 (Phil. iii. 3). The expression: **to be in My sanctuary**, which more closely defines the בַּהֲבִיאֲכֶם as the bringing in to the priestly ministration, is still farther illustrated by the clause: **to desecrate it, My house.** When it is farther said: **when ye offered** לַחְמִי (in a manner, the daily bread of Jehovah, which is immediately explained to mean the sacrificial food as to its elements: **fat and blood**, for which comp. Num. xxviii. 2; Lev. iii. 11, xxi. 6, 8, etc.), this parallel phrase to: **when ye brought to be in My sanctuary**, etc., confirms the view that priests are meant who formed the pure contrast to the Israelitish priesthood according to its idea, and this the more plainly as וַיָּפֵרוּ (ch. xvi. 59, xvii. 18, 19) can scarcely be said of heathens as such, who were outside of the covenant; but when understood of such priests, it looks straight into the inmost relation, from which are derived the sanctuary, the service in it, and the sanctification of Israel. The interchange of **ye** and **they** is farther shown to be intentional by the next clause: in addition to **all your abominations**, inasmuch as not even the priests were correct, with whose holiness the people so frequently think they may venture to dispense with their own. Ver. 8 accordingly goes on to reprimand such shameful priestly representation of the people in respect to the **holy things** (ch. xxii. 8) of Jehovah (comp. ch. xl. 45, 46). Of this Keil gives a superficial view, when he says that "the people, by unlawfully admitting ungodly heathen into the temple, had not only forgotten the reverence due to the holy things of God (!), but had also made for themselves these heathen, so to say (?), ministers of God in His sanctuary." How can "permission to tread the temple" be "put on the same level," even only "spiritually," with "placing in the temple for superintending the worship"? What is meant flows, moreover, from the general statement, impossible to be understood except in its constant sense: **And ye set** (namely, such parties) . . . **for you in My sanctuary.** לָכֶם implies also the representation of the people by such keepers of the charge, which the sanctuary and the covenant of Jehovah with them bound Israel to keep. (Comp. 1 Kings xii. 31.) Häv.: "Not to serve God, but to serve your own sinful inclination."

[Fairbairn: "The children of Israel are spoken of as doing all this, because the corrupt priesthood was inseparably connected with the sins of the people—the one continually acting and re-acting on the other. And the corruption in the priesthood, it will be observed, is expressed as if persons had been put into the office who were not of the tribe of Levi, or even of the seed of Israel, but uncircumcised heathen. Not that literally persons of this description had been admitted into the priestly office; that did not take place, not even in the kingdom of Israel, where still the Israelites were employed, though not of the family of Aaron. But the prophet is viewing all in a spiritual light; he is reading forth the import of the outward transactions, as they appeared to the eye of God; and as in that respect the officiating priesthood had been no better than uncircumcised strangers, so he speaks of them as having actually been such."—W. F.]

Ver. 9. We have now, in condemnation of such profanation, Jehovah's solemn declaration regarding the *personelle* of His service in future. In the first place, a simple negativing of what has been, that shall no longer be; hence כָּל־בֶּן־נֵכָר, to be understood in the same sense as in ver. 7; also the phrase: **shall not come to**, etc., corresponding to what has been previously said, is to be understood of priests, as: **My sanctuary**, proves beyond a doubt. But the summary winding up (לְכָל', Ewald, *Gram.* § 310a): **that is in the midst of**, etc., precludes, by the explanation it gives, every thought of genuine foreigners, or even of the גֵּרִים, strangers, ch. xlvii. 22 sq. "Jewish heathen," as Hengstenberg designates them, are most expressly excluded by this canon of church discipline, which begins at the house of God. To be a "son of Israel" is the first qualification which Jehovah demands for His priesthood, and this taken strictly explains likewise as antithesis thereto the **son of the outland.** Ver. 10. כִּי אִם' (a strong "but," Ewald, *Gram.* p. 856), after the ample negativing (**ver. 9**), introduces the position which makes everything perfectly clear that the discourse is to be concerning the tribe of Levi. This designation is given in the outset, because there will still take place a *choix sur choix*, a narrower election in respect of the Aaronites, the peculiarly priestly family, and a degradation of priests to be servants and assistants, like the Levites given as such to Aaron and his lineage (Num. iii.).—רחק (ch. xi. 6, viii. 15), "to be away," to depart from, Jer. ii. 5, 8.—תָּעָה is: "to stagger" (Isa. xxviii. 7), in the wider signification: to go astray (Isa. liii. 6).—אֲשֶׁר' can explain "Israel's going astray" (ch. vi. 4), and then it is still people and priest taken together as formerly; and this is especially clear when אֲשֶׁר תָּעוּ', corresponding to the אֲשֶׁר רָחֲקוּ, makes it conformable to "Israel's going astray."—וְנָשְׂאוּ', ch. xiv. 10, xvi. 52, 58 (HENGST.: "they shall take their iniquity upon them"), the guilt to be borne will be made clear by the immediately following punishment. This idolatrous staggering had at different times seized hold of priest and people, sometimes more, sometimes less. Instead of allowing themselves to be dragged along by the people to active or even passive participation in the service of idols, they ought, from their office, to have restrained the people, Jer. ii. 8. Comp. moreover, Ps. xvi. 4. [Hävernick thinks here of "even the old misdeeds of Levi, which will make themselves observable."]—Ver. 11. They shall not be excluded from all service in the sanctuary, but degraded from the functions of priests to those of simple Levites; as Rashi expresses it: "to do what strangers and servants and women can perform." שֵׁרֵת is used also of priestly service; it is only פְּקֻדָּה (the function for those discharging it) that with the words expressly added points to the gates of the house, although the word in itself is equivalent to מִשְׁמֶרֶת, מִשְׁמָר. It is still in respectful terms that these degraded priests are spoken of (it is not said: לַעֲבֹד אֶת־עֲבֹדַת, as is said of the Levites specifically, Num. xvi. 9). They are porters and house-servants, yet in this at least they still represent the people, that they relieve them of the slaying of the victims; it is only with their "standing before them to serve them" that their being degraded to Levites becomes more marked (comp. Num. xvi. 9), because now the punishment corresponding to the guilt is —Ver. 12—to be mentioned; the guilt which they shall bear is characterized by the punishment for it in this way; what they were accustomed to do in the apostasy at the will of the people—and thus as **a stumbling-block** which caused to fall into guilt—is now officially imposed upon them.—Comp. on ch. xx. 5, 6, 15, 23, xxxvi. 7.—Ver. 13 hereupon expressly cuts them off from being priests as hitherto. כֹּהֵן, the fuller stem of כּוּן, signifies: those who establish anything as it should be according to the divine ordinance, the people continuing always in their functions; according to others: those bending themselves, namely, doing homage to the Eternal; Num. xvi. 10 of the priesthood, as distinguished from mere Levite service. לְ is therefore antithesis to לְשָׁרְתָם, ver. 11. Further details are given in what follows. By the appositional אֶל־קָדָשַׁי הַקֳּדָשִׁים, the expression: **to draw near over all My holy things**, is—as itself suggests, and the plural קָדָשַׁי' (comp. Num. iv. 19) confirms—interpreted as referring to the eating of the most holy things (comp. on ch. xlii. 13), appertaining to the priests alone. For the rest, comp. ch. xvi. 52.—Ver. 14 recapitulates and sums up the reproach and guilt to be borne, with respectful reference to their former priestly calling; hence שֹׁמְרֵי מִשׁ', which mode of expression, however, receives its levitical limitation through לְכֹל עֲבֹדָתוֹ (comp. Num. xvi. 9, ch. iii.).

Ver. 15. Those likewise are called **Levites** who in contrast to the punishment of the former priests are all the more exalted as priests.—צָדוֹק, the son of Ahitub (1 Chron. v. 34 [vi. 8]), of the line of Eleazar (1 Chron. xxiv. 1 sq.), was co-high priest with Abiathar of the line of Ithamar, in consequence of the twofold service of worship in David's time, that at Jerusalem and that at Gibeon (1 Chron. xvi. [xvii.] 39). After Abiathar had like Joab repeatedly attached himself to Adonijah, the pretender to the crown, and had brought about his own fall and banishment to Anathoth (1 Kings ii.), Zadok was appointed by Solomon sole high priest, and with him the line of Eleazar again became the alone high-priestly one. We are not to go along with Hengstenberg when he, in order to interpret **the sons** of Zadok, goes back even to the relation of fatherhood in the Decalogue, and drags in the pope too as a holy father, simply to get a father-priest, after whom all priests (since 1 Kings ii.) are to be designated as his sons, "even the unfaithful," says Hengstenberg, "who were excluded in the foregoing passage" (!!). He hazards this contradiction to the connection in order to get the faithful priests first in ch. xlviii. 11, and because he finds in ch. xliii. 19, instead of "sons of Zadok" (as in ch. xl. 46), "that are of the seed of Zadok," "the heads (!) of the high-priesthood, those who are of the high priest's kindred (Acts iv. 6), officiating at the consecration of the altar of burnt-offering" (that is, it is incorrect to say that in the whole vision the high priest never meets us!). In Zadok we might indeed be reminded of Melchizedek, had not the very name Zadok ("righteous"), and still more what is historically known of him, symbolized him as a type of the true priestly character. The faithful position which he had taken towards David he did not forsake towards Solomon, as Abiathar did (1 Kings i. 7, 8, 25, 26, ii. 22); he even anointed Solomon king over Israel. Consequently, in the theocratic (Messianic) signification of the kingdom of David and Solomon, Zadok kept himself precisely in the relation which is so significant for our vision (see Doct. Reflec.). Comp. also 1 Sam. ii. 35.—[FAIRBAIRN: "The promise of a priesthood of the house of Zadok entirely corresponded to the promise of a shepherd with the name of David. It simply indicated a race of faithful and devoted servants, in whom the outward and the inward, the name and the idea, should properly coincide,—a priesthood serving God in newness of spirit, not in the oldness of the letter, as the people whom they represented should also have become true Israelites, themselves a royal priesthood offering up spiritual sacrifices to the Lord. In truth, it is the raising up of a people who should be such a priesthood that is meant by the description, and the sons of Zadok came into notice only because in connection with them there was an historical ground for taking them as representatives of a right-hearted spiritual community."—W. F.]—But as not all the children of Abraham are of his faith, so here the **sons of Zadok** are only those **who kept**, etc., who have kept and will keep themselves faithful to Me. Not until after this essential personal qualification for priest, is the formal and official service described: in general, the "drawing near," etc. (ch. xl. 46, xliii. 19), in particular, the "standing before Me (in contrast to 'before them,' ver. 11) **to offer unto Me** (comp. ver. 7) **fat**," etc., part of the service at the altar of burnt-offering.—Then in Ver. 16 comes the treading of the dwelling in the holy place, especially the drawing near to the altar of incense (ch. xli. 22), for which the name **table** is significantly retained. Finally, וְשָׁמְרוּ אֶת־מִשְׁמַרְתִּי reverts to the starting-point in ver. 15, אֲשֶׁר שָׁמְרוּ'.

Vers. 17–31. *Priestly Duties and Privileges.*

Ver. 17 begins with the most external, the clothing; the duty in this respect will make the symbolized inward obligation the more apparent. The coming to the inner gates implies the intention of service at or in the sanctuary, and thereby involves the duty of putting on (פִּשְׁתָּה, "flax") linen garments, and this makes שֵׁשׁ, as already ordained by Moses, perfectly clear (comp. Ex. xxxix. 28, xxviii. 39 sq.; Lev. vi. 3 [10], xvi. 4, 23). The express prohibition of wool (צֶמֶר, what is "drawn together," hanging together like *vellus*, ἔρος, εἶρος) gives additional emphasis to the linen, and makes the ministering **in the gates of the inner court**, that is, within them, **and at the house**, said of functions discharged within the house, the former in relation to the altar of burnt-offering, and the latter in relation to the altar of incense, still more distinctly prominent.—Ver. 18, like ver. 17, refers to the priest's garments; פְּאֵר is properly: "adornment," diadem, which might suggest the special high-priestly מִצְנֶפֶת; the word, however, occurs rather in connection with מִגְבָּעֹת, Ex. xxxix. 28 ("goodly bonnets"), and we have no warrant for supposing it is a special head-covering for priests in general. It is rather meant to be remarked that they are adorned (פְּאֵר is suggestive of floral ornaments), **although with linen**.—The covering for the loins (מִכְנְסֵי, plural or dual), reaching from high above the loins down to about the thigh (comp. Ex. xxviii. 42), forms the third of the four articles, as Bähr says, designed for the official dress of the priests (in accordance with "the symbolical place of Jehovah's testimony and revelation"); while the injunction about "girding," which, moreover, explains the sense and spirit of the whole linen dress, subjoins the אַבְנֵט, that is, girdle of the priests, as the fourth article. This was worn higher up toward the breast, as would then be confirmed by the added defining clause: **not in sweat**; which certainly will not bear the meaning: while they sweat, but according to Bähr is meant to imply: where they sweat. But בַּיָּזַע (יֶזַע, found only here, elsewhere זֵעָה, from זוּעַ: what is forced out by pressure or anguish) certainly means nothing but what has been said already: that no wool shall come upon them; for as the white linen makes the cleanness apparent, so sweat, so readily produced by woollen stuff, especially when forming a girdle and thus confining the body, is meant to be guarded against as uncleanness, and on the whole accordingly the holiness of the priests for the sanctification of the people to be signified. [Did the Septuagint mean too tight girding, or girding in violent haste?]

Ver. 19. The repetition: **to the outer court**, is meant to strengthen the prohibition, which is particularly strong in our verse; to call attention to the distinction between the outer court and the inner, while both, however, are still only courts; and to the altar in the inner court, where the sanctification of the people willed by Jehovah has to take place. After this (comp. ch. xlii. 14) comes the laying aside of the priest's official dress, and the laying of it down at the place suitable to the "holiness of Jehovah" (ch. xlii. 13), and the putting on of other garments, for the purpose of guarding against the thought of another sanctification than the God-ordained one by the way of sacrifice. Not **in their garments**, that is, it is not they, although they are priests, who are to **sanctify the people** (comp. John xvii. 19!). Consequently, the going out **to the people** is to be understood in reference to sanctification, and shows moreover that this outer court was for the people. Expositors generally refer here to Lev. vi. 11, 20 (יִקְדָּשׁ); Ex. xxix. 37, xxx. 29; comp. besides, Ex. xxviii. 43; Lev. vi. 4 [11], xvi. 23. [That contact with the people defiles the priests when in their official dress, as Keil referring to Lev. xxi. supposes, is not said here.]

Ver. 20 forbids, as already Lev. xix. 27, xxi. 5, the shaving of the head smooth, as heathenish; censuring the Creator (!?), says Hengst.; according to Bähr, as mourning, a sign of fellowship with the dead, inasmuch as the hair is a proof of life and vigour of body. The Egyptian priests kept the head always close shaved. On the contrary, the priests of Israel are to bear their head high, as the mediators of an eternal life in holiness through grace. — פֶּרַע implies: "breaking forth," "being on the top;" hence, the hair on the head. The covering for the head is treated of next to the garments for the body. Keil cites for שַׁלַּח ("to let loose"), as "to let grow freely," Lev. x. 6 and Num. vi. 5. But the first passage must not be so understood, and we need not suppose here, in accordance with the second, a prohibition of Nazaritism, but, as the markedly positive clause shows, the hair is simply to be kept short, to be polled. Comp. 1 Cor. xi. 14 sq. (Rev. ix. 8). (כָּסַם is found only here.) On this Hengstenberg observes: "That which is the sign of a wild, disorderly man, who lets nature take its free course, might indeed be permitted to the Nazarite, in consequence of a vow undertaken for a time, in order thereby to typify his separation from the world; but not to the priest, whose duty it was to hold converse with the world, and adapt himself to society, to enter which with shorn hair was the custom even in Joseph's time. The priest should be no separated person." If flowing locks and the growth of hair generally is the sign of vigorous natural life, as the forbidden shaving also on its part symbolizes, then by forbidding the priest as representative of a holy people to let his locks grow long, the false positive, in addition to the false negative, is forbidden; the maxim that: every one is his own law (as every one his own devil), unbounded naturalism is forbidden. Neither annihilation nor yet glorification of nature, neither askesis unto death nor honouring of the flesh, but simply law, divine order, is the watchword for the servant of Jehovah. The sanctification treated of is neither heathenishly self-chosen, one's own fabrication, self-sanctification, nor is it a natural holiness of one's own, which needs not a sanctification in Jehovah's way. —Ver. 21. Although abstinence from wine is demanded, yet our passage has nothing to do with the Nazarite proper. His was a vow regulated by law; but always a free-will dedication *pro tempore*, where the man thus devoted himself to God with all his naturalism, just as he had grown up. That the priests are not to drink wine (Lev. x. 9) is grounded on no temporary, formal separation from the world, is no drastic consecration, as in the case of the Nazarite, but is simply an emblem of what is seemly, of sobriety of soul, of the true spirit of a servant of God, who goes into the **inner court**,—the reason assigned for the prohibition.

Ver. 22. From their manner of life in respect to drinking, and no doubt generally (Rom. xiii. 14), the obligation of the priests turns to their married life. The injunction not to marry a widow (Lev. xxi. 14, 13) is extended here from the high priest to the whole body of priests, who in this respect then appear high-priestly, just as in ch. xliii. 12 everything upon the mountain round about was most holy. The ordinary priest also is not allowed to marry (Lev. xxi. 7) אִשָּׁה גְּרוּשָׁה, a woman put away by her husband, of course with reason, because of guilt; one of this kind is classified as a factitious widow with those who are really widows. The permission to take a priest's widow forms a pendant to the judgment pronounced on the daughter of a priest in Lev. xxi. 9. For the rest, the verse relates to the priests' being holy with reference to the holiness of Jehovah. [The Jewish Talmudic view limits the first part to the high priest, understanding מִכֹּהֵן of **the other priests: "Yet the widow who is (really)** a widow, those who occupy the position of ordinary priests may take."]

Ver. 23 defines the official duties of the priests. יָרָה (Hiph.), "to spread out," the hand, for example, to point to something, to teach, here the people, of whom Jehovah says: **My** people (Deut. xvii. 10 sq., xxxiii. 10; Lev. x. 10); and above all to teach them the difference **between**, etc., for which comp. ch. xxii. 26. The priestly service, then, is to comprehend worship and doctrine, representation of the people before God, and representation of God before the people. (Comp. Mal. ii. 7.) But above all, everything with an eye to sanctification.—Ver. 24 gives in addition to this the court of judicature which they form in disputed cases (Deut. xvii. 8 sq., xix. 17): עַל־רִיב, they are to stand over the confused and complicated points raised by the parties, and because they have the power to stand over them as judges, since they have to judge **in My judgments**, they will always find in the law of Jehovah what is right in every case. Qeri: לְמִשְׁפָּט, and Qeri: יִשְׁפְּטֻהוּ, are both equally unnecessary. What this administration of justice is in civil life—it too being a sanctification of the people through the judgment of God—has its counterpart in church life, in the observance of all the laws and ordinances, on all the **festivals** of Jehovah, the key-note for which is given with the hallowing of the **Sabbaths** (comp. for the reverse, ch. xxii. 26), while at the same time we are told what is always the main matter in priestly ministration.

Ver. 25 therefore shows how the priests have to keep themselves from defilement.—לֹא יָבוֹא individualizes, to speak exactly.—The exception (כִּי אִם) affects the same blood-relations as Lev. xxi. The exception of the high priest (Lev. xxi. 10 sq.) is not noticed, just as there is no notice of the high priest in the whole book. Ver. 26 is, according to Keil, the command to purify from uncleanness by the dead sharpened, inasmuch as he believes the seven days are appointed over and above the space of seven days prescribed by the law (Num. xix. 11 sq.), and finds this indicated in טָהֳרָתוֹ, in which he thinks he sees a compensation for the previously permitted coming of the priests to the dead, which in the law had been forbidden to the high priest even in the case of father or mother. Rather perhaps the number seven simply points the more strongly to holiness and sanctification. Hengstenberg, on the other hand, insists on the distinction between: having been cleansed, and: "cleansing," which, he says, began with the beginning of the seven days (Num. xix.), seven days being the longest period which any uncleanness lasts. At all events it cannot be denied that Ver. 27 still demands the offering of a sin-offering when the priest enters again on his ministry.

After the duties come now the privileges of the priests, what is to accrue to them for their service.—In Ver. 28 we have, first of all, the fundamental condition known from the law (comp. Num. xviii. 20; Deut. x. 9, xviii. 1), expressed first positively, then negatively, and finally once more positively; which the Israelite priestly consciousness received **and retained in living and in** dying. For, since the priests of Israel are no foreigners, no dominant race, but of Israel, like all their brethren, it would be natural, when Canaan was promised by God as נַחֲלָה to the people to whom they belonged, that to them also there should be a definite tribal territory for inheritance and possession (אֲחֻזָּה, something which one grasps and retains). But they represent Israel not as to the flesh but as to the spirit, as to the idea which from the outset makes of this people God's peculiar possession, and thereby God their peculiar possession: "My" people, and I am Jehovah, "thy God." Now, as the Lord already (Gen. xv. 1) says to Abraham, the father of all believers: I am thy very great reward, so this is to the priests **for an inheritance, that I am their inheritance** (נַחֲלָה), as Jehovah says. They are thereby in such a position that nothing more is to be given to them (לֹא־תִתְּנוּ לָהֶם), at least by their fellow-countrymen, to whom on the contrary they give an earnest of the ideality of their nationality, of the eternal inheritance, of the possession of Canaan in truth, in that they as matter of fact teach Israel its better self, its true aspiration, its eternal future. [Ver. 28 does not, as Keil supposes, treat of cities to dwell in, with the houses and pasture-grounds belonging thereto, which in the Mosaic economy Jehovah assigns to the Levites and priests from His own peculiar possession in land; comp. ch. xlv.]

Ver. 29. On the contrary, they have their livelihood from the offerings, and in so far live from Jehovah's hand. On the meat, sin, and guilt-offerings here mentioned, comp. in the law Lev. ii. 1-10; 1 Cor. ix. 13.—חֵרֶם ("separating") is what is devoted to Jehovah without possibility of redemption; for this comp. Lev. xxvii. 21, 28.—Ver. 30. בִּכּוּרִים are the first-fruits of tree-fruit and of corn (from בָּכַר, "to break forth"). Comp. Ex. xxiii. 19, xxxiv. 26; Num. xviii. 13; Deut. xviii. 4.—תְּרוּמָה is said of parts of the offerings with reference to the ceremonial of heaving and waving, which likewise signified consecration to Jehovah. The Rabbins explain the word of the gift "separated" for the Lord; for thus it took place with all the first-fruits, sheaves as well as loaves. At all events, **the heave-offering** is in general whatever is according to precept or of free will lifted up for Jehovah as a consecrated gift to the sanctuary, indirectly to its ministers (Ex. xxv. 2 sq., xxx. 13 sq.; Num. xv. 19 sq., xviii. 27 sq.). Comp. ch. xx. 40.—עֲרִיסָה, used only in the plural, is supposed to be "groats," or "peeled grain" (GESENIUS), with which רֵאשִׁית does not well harmonize; hence Meier supposes grain-corn. Comp. Num. xv. 20 sq.—Everything mentioned in ver. 29 tends to sanctification; the heaving and waving in particular involved the thought, that in consequence of such gifts to the priest the blessing of God is brought down on the individual house. Hengstenberg translates: "and that thou mayest make blessing rest in thy house," and cites Matt. xv. 4, 5. Comp. Mal. iii. 10.—Ver. 31 brings to a close what refers to the sustenance of the priests, mentioning the things to be excluded therefrom. נְבֵלָה, a dead body, what lies stretched out of men and beasts, *cadaver*. טְרֵפָה, "something torn off," torn by wild beasts. Comp. ch. iv. 14; Ex. xxii. 30 [31]; Lev. xxii. 8. Lev. xvii. 15 marks this as defiling for any man, how much more so for the priests of Jehovah; so that by this the idea of holiness is exemplified. "Only what Jehovah gives to them and His sanctuary in offerings and dues, which, however, must never be unclean, shall accrue to them; and this at the same time forms the best transition to the awards which follow" (EWALD).

CHAPTER XLV.

1 And when ye allot [divide] the land as inheritance, ye shall make an obla-
tion to Jehovah, a holiness from the land; the length five and twenty thou-
sand and the breadth ten thousand; holiness [is] it in all its border round
2 about. Of this shall be [come, belong] to the sanctuary five hundred by five
hundred, a square round about; and fifty cubits of environs for it round
3 about. And from [according to] this measure shalt thou measure a length of
five and twenty thousand and a breadth of ten thousand, and in it shall be
4 the sanctuary, the most holy place. Holiness from the land is this; for the
priests, the ministers of the sanctuary shall it be, who draw near to minister
to Jehovah; and it is to them a place for houses, and a holy place for the
5 sanctuary. And five and twenty thousand in length and ten thousand in
breadth shall be [belong] to the Levites, the ministers of the house, to them
6 for a possession, twenty chambers. And as a possession of the city ye shall
give five thousand in breadth, and in length five and twenty thousand, beside
[running along] the oblation of holiness; it shall be for the whole house of Israel.
7 And for the prince: adjoining the oblation of holiness on both sides and the
possession of the city, before the oblation of holiness and before the possession
of the city, on the west side westward, and on the east side eastward, and

the length, beside [running along] one of the [tribal] portions from the west border
8 to the east border. It shall be land to him for a possession in Israel; and
My princes shall no more oppress My people; and [but] the land shall they
9 give to the house of Israel according to their tribes. Thus saith the Lord
Jehovah: Enough for you, O princes of Israel; remove [put away] violence and
rapine, and do judgment and justice, take away your expulsions from My
10 people,—sentence of the Lord Jehovah. Ye shall have just balances, and a
11 just ephah, and a just bath. The ephah and the bath shall be of one mea-
sure; that the bath may contain [amount to] the tenth of the homer, and the
12 ephah a tenth of the homer; its measure shall be after the homer. And the
shekel [shall be] twenty gerahs; twenty shekels, five and twenty shekels, fifteen
13 shekels, shall be your maneh. This is the oblation which ye shall make:
the sixth of the ephah from the homer of wheat, and ye shall six the ephah
14 from the homer of barley. And the ordinance of the oil: the bath of oil
[what is to be offered as bath from the oil shall be] the tenth of the bath out of the cor,
15 [which is] ten baths, a homer; for ten baths are a homer. And one sheep
[or goat] out of the flock, from two hundred from the watered [land] of Israel,
for the meat-offering, and for the burnt-offering, and for peace-offerings, to
16 atone for [to cover] them,—sentence of the Lord Jehovah. All the people of
17 the land, they shall be [held] to this oblation for the prince in Israel. And
upon the prince shall be the burnt-offerings, and the meat-offering, and the
drink-offering, on the feasts, and on the new moons, and on the Sabbaths, in
all the festal seasons of the house of Israel; he shall prepare the sin-offering,
and the meat-offering, and the burnt-offering, and the peace-offerings, to atone
18 for [to cover] the house of Israel. Thus saith the Lord Jehovah: In the first
[month], on the first of the month, thou shalt take a bullock, a young steer,
19 without blemish, and cleanse the sanctuary: And the priest takes of the
blood of the sin-offering, and puts it upon the posts of the house, and
upon the four corners of the ledge of the altar, and upon the posts of
20 the gate of the inner court. And so shalt thou do on the seventh of
the month for the erring man and for the fool, and ye atone for the house.
21 In the first [month], on the fourteenth day of the month, shall the passover
be to you, a feast of seven days; unleavened bread shall be eaten [one shall eat
22 *mazzoth*]. And the prince brings on this day for himself and for the whole
23 people of the land a bullock as a sin-offering. And the seven days of the
feast he shall bring as a burnt-offering to Jehovah seven bullocks and seven
rams without blemish, daily the seven days; and as a sin-offering a kid of the
24 goats for the day [daily]. And as a meat-offering he shall offer an ephah for a
25 bullock, and an ephah for a ram, and of oil an hin for the ephah. In the
seventh [month], on the fifteenth day of the month, in the feast he shall bring
just such [offerings] seven days, as the sin-offering, as the burnt-offering, and as
the meat-offering, and as the oil.

Ver. 1. Sept.: . . . *ἀπαρχην . . . κ. εὐρος εἰκοσι χιλιαδας*— (The second or the first ארך is omitted in the various manuscripts.)

Ver. 2. . . . *εἰς ἁγιασμα . . . διαστημα αὐτων*— Vulg.: *Et erit ex omni parte sanctificatum . . . in suburbano ejus*—

Ver. 3. . . . *διαμετρησεως . . . το ἁγιασμα των ἁγιων.* Vulg.: . . . *templum sanctumque sanctorum.*

Ver. 4. . . . *εἰς οἰκους ἀφωρισμενους τω ἁγιασμω αὐτων.*

Ver. 5. . . . *αὐτοις εἰς κατασχεσιν πολεις του κατοικειν.*

Ver. 6. . . . *ὁν τροπον και ἡ ἀπαρχη των ἁγιων παντι οἰκω 'Ισρ. ἐσονται.*

Ver. 7. . . . *εἰς τας ἀπαρχας τ. ἁγιων, εἰς κατασχεσιν τ. πολεως, κατα προσωπον των ἀπαρχων . . . τα προς θαλασσαν κ. ἀπο των προς θαλασσαν τα προς ἀνατολας· κ. το μηκος ὡς μια των μεριδων ἀπο των ὁριων των προς θαλασσαν, κ. το μηκος ἐπι τα ὁρια τα προς ἀνατολας* (8.) *της γης.* K. *ἐστω αὐτω . . . οὐκετι οἱ ἀφηγουμενοι του 'Ισρ. . . . κ. την γην κατακληρονομησουσιν οἰκος 'Ισρ.*—Vulg.: . . . *et non depopulabuntur*— (Another reading: לְעַמִּת.)

Ver. 9. *'Ικανουσθω ὑμιν . . . κ. ταλαιπωριαν . . . κ. ἐξαρατε καταδυναστειαν*— Vulg.: . . . *Iniquitatem et rapinas . . . separate confinia vestra a populo meo*—

Ver 10. . . . *κ. μετρον δικαιον κ. χοινιξ δικαια ἐσται ὑμιν του μετρου.*

Ver. 11. . . . K. *ἡ χοινιξ ὁμοιως μια ἐσται του λαμβανειν, το δεκατον του γομορ ἡ χοινιξ, κ. το δεκατον του γομορ το μετρον προς το γομορ ἐσται ἰσον.* Vulg.: . . . *æqualia et unius mensuræ . . . partem cori . . . juxta mensuram cori erit æqua libratio eorum.*

Ver. 12. K. τα σταθμια εἰκοσι ὀβολοι, οἱ πεντε σικλοι πεντε κ. οἱ δεκα σικλοι δεκα κ. πεντηκοντα σικλοι ἡ μνια ἐσται ὑμιν. Vulg.: . . . *obolos . . . Porro viginti sicli et . . . et . . . mnam faciunt.* (Another reading: שקלים.)

Ver. 13. . . . ἑκτον του μετρου . . . κ. το ἑκτον του οἰφι— Vulg.: . . . *primitiæ.*

Ver. 14. Sept: . . . κοτυλην ἐλαιου ἀπο των δεκα κοτυλων, ὁτι οἱ δεκα κοτυλοι εἰσιν γομορ. Vulg.: . . . *batus olei, decima pars cori est; et decem bati corum faciunt, quia decem bati implent corum.*

Ver. 15. K. προβατον ἐν ἀπο τ. δεκα προβατων ἀφαιρεμα ἐκ πασων των πατριων τ. Ἰσρ.— Vulg.: *Et arietem unum de grege ducentorum, de his quæ nutriunt Israel—*

Ver. 17. K. δια του ἀφηγουμενου ἐσται— (Other readings: העולה and ובכל מועדי.)

Ver. 18. . . . ληψεσθε—

Ver. 19. Another reading: מזוזות.

Ver. 20. . . . ἐν τ. μηνι τω ἑβδομω μια του μηνος ληψη παρ' ἑκαστου ἀγνοουντος κ. ἀπο νηπιου, Vulg.: . . . *qui ignoravit et errore deceptus est—*

Ver. 22. . . . ὑπερ αὐτου κ. ὑπερ τ. οἰκου κ. ὑπερ παντος τ. λαου τ. γης—

Ver. 23. . . . κ. θυσιαν. (24.) K. πεμμα τω μοσχω—

Ver. 24. Vulg.: *Et sacrificium ephi per vitulum—*

Ver. 25. . . . ποιησεις κατα τα αὐτα . . . κ. καθως το μαναα— Vulg.: . . . *sicut supra dicta sunt—*

EXEGETICAL REMARKS.

Vers. 1–9. *The Oblation of Holiness, the Land of the Levites, the Possession of the City, and the Portion of the Prince.*

That Jehovah is the inheritance and possession of His priests (ch. xliv. 28) is a reality even for this world, as godliness in like manner has the promise "of the life that now is." In order to give form to this truth, Ver. 1 connects what follows with the preceding.—הִפִּיל, from נָפַל, signifies: "to make to fall," and is used peculiarly of the lot (ch. xxiv. 6); but when nothing suggests this, and when לְ is not prefixed to the word, it is to be taken in its general sense, and בְּנַחֲלָה, *cum* בְּ *essentiæ*, is to be understood as meaning: to divide in general. Comp. Ps. xvi. 6. (The reference to the time immediately after the Babylonian servitude, hitherto maintained by Hengstenberg, must now, as we may well conceive, be abandoned; and so then he makes the prophet travel to Utopia, etc.)—תָּרִימוּ תְרוּמָה (Hiphil of רוּם, referring to what was done in the case of the peace or thank-offerings with the shoulder of the victim—the waving with the breast) has here the more general signification, although not that of: "to present a present," nor that of: "to offer an offering," but that of: to consecrate, to hallow to the Lord (לַיהוָה), which, moreover, was the meaning of the ceremony of heaving on high as well as of the heaving up upon the altar. Comp. also on ch. xliv. 30. For details see on ch. xlviii.—**Holiness** (corresponding to Jehovah) **from the land**, and thus separated, "partly for sacred and partly at least for higher, more general purposes" (Bunsen); but see the intended use in what follows.—The word **length** is repeated, perhaps on account of the significant number mentioned for the first time, or because the natural length of the land is not to be regarded, but by **length** reference is meant to be made to that which is forthwith so called in the vision, the extension from east to west, and so the repetition is not exactly pleonastic. Whether rods (Jerome, Rashi, Häv.) or cubits (Ewald, Hitzig, Hengst.) are meant, is not said. The supporters of both interpretations appeal to ch. **xlii. 16 sq.**; hence compare what is said there.—The express mention, too, of cubits in ver. 2 is pressed into the service of both parties. Those who hold for rods say: Thus rods are always meant in what goes before, because here cubits are excepted; those who contend for cubits reply: Thus in what goes before, too, as everywhere in the case of all the large measurements, cubits are to be understood, otherwise rods would need to be expressly named. That cubits are mentioned first in ver. 2, Hengstenberg explains from "the unexpectedly small measure there, so that one might easily think of a larger scale." Böttcher, moreover, adduces against the measurement by rod which he calculates would give 40 German [about 900 English] square miles (?), *i.e.* almost the tenth of the whole land, the colossal disproportion to the statements elsewhere, especially as to the temple, which measures only 500 cubits square. Keil, on the other hand, maintains that ch. xlviii. with its proportions corresponds throughout to the τεμενος of 25,000 rods in length and 10,000 rods in breadth. Comp. therefore ch. xlviii.—The **breadth** trends from north to south (ch. xlviii. 10).—Keil finds עֲשָׂרָה אֶלֶף for 10,000 surprising, for which, he observes, עֲשֶׂרֶת אֲלָפִים is constantly used in vers. 3, 5, and in ch. xlviii. He therefore prefers the 20,000 of the Sept., giving as additional reasons for this, that the part mentioned in ver. 3 is to be measured off from what was measured in ver. 1; also that the Levites of ver. 5 are to be considered, whose possession is likewise "Terumah of holiness" (ch. xlviii. 14 sq.), as is plain from other passages of our chapter; ver. 1 comprehends the land of the priests and of the Levites [25,000 and 20,000], which vers. 2 and 3 divide into two districts.—Finally, the character of the **oblation**, because **to Jehovah**, is again insisted on, and that in respect of **all its border round about**.

Ver. 2, after this general statement, marks off from the above-mentioned (מִזֶּה) the **sanctuary** described and measured in ch. xl., that is, the 500 cubits square forming the temple edifice, or, as Keil, in accordance with his view of ch. xlii 15 sq.: the 500 square rods pertaining to the sacred enclosures of the temple. But as he adds: "there is still to be around this enclosure, which separates between the sacred and the common, a free space of fifty cubits on each side to keep the priests' dwellings from being built too near to the sacred square of the temple buildings," how, we ask, does he leave this latter entirely out of account!?—מִגְרָשׁ, comp. on ch. xxvii. 28. "A free space of 50 cubits to a sanctuary of 500 rods would be much too small. It was evidently intended to be an interspace between the house of God and the houses of the priests" (HENGST.).—Ver. 3. מִן־הַמִּדָּה הַזֹּאת is not the same as מִזֶּה in ver. 2; for if so, this distinct and different mode of expression would not have been chosen, which, as it refers to the measuring of the **sanctuary**, so it designates as the sanctuary the temple building, and not the "sacred enclosure of the temple." Keil needs 10,000 rods more in ver. 1, because he makes הַמִּדָּה הַזֹּאת here = "this measured piece of land." מִן־, as modified by הַמִּדָּה, which has had always hitherto to be translated "measure," denotes that from which the prophet has to take the measure, and is therefore entrusted with the "measuring" (תָּמוֹד, as it is expressly said); it had, indeed, been measured before him in ch. xl. The temple building, just referred to in ver. 2 as the principal part, is normal for the whole **oblation**, which as such is again referred to in Ver. 3, where also the centrality of the temple, already indicated by the phrase: **and in it shall be the sanctuary,** is distinctly denoted by the epithet: **most holy**, pointing to ch. xliii. 12. After that the **holiness**, the separation **from the land** for the holy purpose (for Jehovah, for His sanctuary) of the land of which the **oblation** consists (הוּא), with (ver. 3) the sanctuary in it (inclusive of the courts), has been again insisted on. Ver. 4 treats now of the area in question in its relation to the priests, who, as hitherto (ch. xl. 46, xlii. 13, xliv. 15)—here, however, with a view to the sanctuary and its central position—are described, both as respects their official functions and their dwelling-places. Since they are such, since this is their official calling, it is befitting to assign to them the **holiness from the land** as a **place for houses**, explained in the clause following to be: **a holy place for the sanctuary,** so that this latter defines the priests' houses to be a dependency of the sanctuary, just as similarly in ch. xliii. 12 the whole was even called most holy (ver. 3 here). The last clause of the verse is commonly taken as indicating a second use for the area of the **oblation**, namely, for the temple, a superfluous repetition. The mention of houses is in harmony with the law, in which the thirteen cities for the priests (Josh. xxi.) likewise come into consideration simply as regards the houses in them. From that which is His own through the **oblation** Jehovah gives to the priests as His ministers, and as ministers of the sanctuary in the neighbourhood, the space necessary for dwellings (just as in ch. xliv. the necessaries of life). This is an arrangement which doubtless is to be taken in connection with the entire division of the land, but differs from that laid down in Num. xxxv., so that it will have to be understood from the idea meant to be illustrated (Doct. Reflec. 19).

Still more surprising is the new arrangement in Ver. 5, where an area equal to that occupied by the sanctuary and priests' houses is assigned to the Levites as ministers **of the house** (ch. xliv. 11 sq.), without any farther description, while **the priests** were described (ver. 4) as ministers of the sanctuary, making thus a marked difference between them; and this distinction of the Levites is also marked by the phrase: **to them for a possession;** for the next verse goes on to speak likewise of **a possession of the city,** although this latter is "given" (comp. on the other hand ch. xliv. 28, לֹא־תִתְּנוּ), and does not simply belong (יִהְיֶה), and לָהֶם לַאֲחֻזָּה stands evidently opposed to the וּמִקְדָּשׁ לַמִּקְדָּשׁ of ver. 4. But this area will be different from the one demanded in general in ver. 1, although the Levites too belong to the ministers of the Lord, and the twenty chambers correspond very little to a special landed possession of the extent mentioned. Keil includes **the** land of the Levites in ver. 1; but indeed with his 20,000 rods in breadth there, of which 10,000 fall to the priests and the sanctuary, he has still a breadth of 10,000 rods left for the Levites. Hengst. on the other hand says: "Along with the priests the Levites receive a portion of land of like extent; then follows the district of the holy city with the same length, and a breadth of 5000 cubits; so that the whole portion marked off in advance for priests, Levites, and city is in breadth as in length 25,000 cubits."—Instead of יִהְיֶה, the Qeri reads: יִהְיֶה.—The words עֶשְׂרִים לְשָׁכֹת formed a difficulty to the LXX., who perhaps imagined the text to be עָרִים לָשֶׁבֶת. The **chambers,** instead of the thirty-five Levitical cities of Moses with pasturage, form, as regards the expression, no difficulty; they are very suitable diminutives of the "houses" of the priests. The priests have houses, the Levites as inferiors only **chambers**, which possibly may mean ranges of cells (ROSENM.) or courts, with one-twentieth of the pasturage for each. Keil, who cannot understand the Masoretic text, and holds עֶשְׂרִים to be a corruption of שְׁעָרִים, reads: לָשָׁבֶת, by which, however, he obtains only "gates (!!) as dwellings" for the Levites, understanding indeed the "gates" as equivalent in meaning to cities. Hengst. calls them the barracks of the Levites; the departure from the ordinance of Moses, according to which the Levites dwelt scattered through the whole land, is so much the more surprising.

Ver. 6. The land of the Levites could be properly **oblation** only if it were the same portion of land as that of the priests and the sanctuary, or if the reading in ver. 1 be 20,000 rods in breadth. Hence Hengst. limits the **oblation** to the sanctuary and the priests' portion. Only "in the wider sense" does he make it include also the portion of the Levites and the circuit of the city; it may include even the portion of the prince (he says), "since the prince acts as the minister of God." The structure of the clause in ver. 5 speaks in favour of a special area of 10,000 in breadth as Levites' land; and so does the consideration that by such a possession in land the so much greater number of cities than of priests' cities, which according to the ordinance of Moses belonged to them, is perhaps given expression to. Comp. besides on ch. xlviii. 20. But however much the definition in ver. 5: **to them for a possession,** indicates a special portion of Levites' land outside of the *Terumah* ("oblation") demanded in ver. 1, yet the **possession of the city** lies still farther outside, as likewise תִּתְּנוּ seems to separate it even from the land of the Levites. The **city** is the capital of the land. Its area has the same length as that hitherto given (25,000), but differs in breadth, which therefore is mentioned first; we have in this respect 10,000 + 10,000 + 5000 = 25,000. The possession of the city "is to be distinguished from the city itself, which (ch. xlviii. 16) is square, the length being equal to the breadth" (HENGST.). The length of this possession runs along the **oblation of holiness**, by which designation is meant specially the land of the priests and the sanctuary. Its destined purpose, **for the whole house of Israel**, shows that it is to belong to no single tribe merely. Comp. ch. xlviii.

The transition to לַנָּשִׂיא in Ver. 7 is mediated by **the whole house of Israel** in ver. 6, of which the prince is the civil head and representative.—Either a kind of protasis to which Ver. 8 forms the apodosis, or we may supply: "ye shall give," from ver. 6.—מִזֶּה וּמִזֶּה = on both sides, so that the **oblation of holiness**, which certainly may here include the land of the Levites, and the possession of the city lie between, running before these from north to south, so that seen from the west side what is westward as far as the Mediterranean Sea, seen from the east side what lies east as far as the Jordan is to belong to the prince; just as וְאֹרֶךְ explains that as to the length, that is from west to east, the territory shall run the same length with **one**, *i.e.* any one of the portions of the tribes, shall neither go beyond nor fall short of any single tribal portion. Jerome remarks that the prince received for himself a whole tribal portion, with the exclusion, however, of the land of the sanctuary, the priests, the Levites, and the city; but in return he has not only the duty of protecting the square in question, but also the honour of possessing on his territory whatever is holy pertaining to the nation.—Ver. 8. לָאָרֶץ, more exactly defined by לַאֲחֻזָּה: the land described in ver. 7 shall be the land assigned **to him for a possession in Israel**. The reason for this arrangement follows: 'וְלֹא. The former state of things, in which no landed possession, no crown estate, was allotted to them *qua* princes, had tempted them to misuse of their power, to acquire for themselves possessions.—**My princes** corresponds to **My people**; hence those who will in future have princely power over the people. This **My** applied to both parties contains at the same time the divine sentence on the former princes, who may be considered persons as little conscious of their high and responsible position as of the significance of Israel. Instead of taking to themselves, they are rather to **give** to the house of Israel, that is, to leave in possession, and also, if need be, to restore. The phrase: **according to their tribes**, shows what land is meant. [FAIRBAIRN: "That the whole ground for the priesthood, the prince, and the people of the city was to form together a square, betokened the perfect harmony and agreement which should subsist between these different classes, as well as the settled order and stability which should distinguish the sacred commonwealth, in which they held the highest place. That the priesthood were to occupy what was emphatically holy ground, was a symbol of the singular degree of holiness which should characterize those who stood in their official position the nearest to the Lord. And that the prince was to have a separate possession assigned him was to cut off all occasion for his lawlessly interfering with the possessions of the people, and to exhibit the friendly bearing and upright administration which was to be expected of him (ver. 8). And not only must he personally abstain from all oppressive behaviour, but as the divinely constituted head of a righteous commonwealth, he must take effective measures for establishing justice and judgment throughout the whole. Particular examples are given of this in regard to the using of just weights and measures in the transactions of business (vers. 9–12)."—W. F.]—Ver. 9 concludes what specially regards the princes, by whose conduct in good and in bad a mirror and example was held up to the people, while at the same time it solemnly introduces the more general regulations which follow in regard to judgment and justice in trade and commerce.—The subject in ch. xliv. 6 was the people with reference to the priesthood, here it is the prince in reference to the people; as there holiness and sanctification, so here **judgment and justice**. (Jerome interprets 'רַב: let this tribe-like possession suffice you!) What has already taken place far too often is now so much the more enough, as all natural temptation has been taken away by the assigning of domains (ver. 7 sq.).—שֹׁד (שָׁדַד) is virtually the same as חָמָס, a violent mode of acting, misuse of power, only stronger, because the consequence thereof: "devastation," is implied in the word, as in the corresponding **justice** the exercise of **judgment** is manifested. Hengstenberg thinks: the direct address shows that representatives or descendants of the princes who had formerly committed injustice were also in exile.—גְּרֻשָׁה is expulsion of the lawful possessor from his property, as in 1 Kings xxi.—The burden which this was to the community, the pressure which thereby was inflicted on Israel, is depicted in the words: 'הָרִימוּ מֵעַל "The political parties especially," observes Hengstenberg, "gave occasion for the confiscations." Comp. besides, 1 Sam. viii. 14.

Vers. 10–12. *Justice in Common Life.*

The transition which is made by Ver. 10 shows what an example for the community the conduct of the prince *may be* in evil and *ought to be* in good.—("Princes have in all times attempted to take advantage of their subjects by alteration of coinage and weights," PHILIPPSON.)—מֹאזְנַיִם, dual, denotes the two scales of the balance, from אָזַן, "to make ready," "to fix;" in reference to the way this can be done, "to weigh," to determine the weight.—אֵיפָה (אֵפָה), according to Josephus' statement in Greek, a measure about the same as a Berlin bushel [about $1\frac{1}{12}$ bushels English]; see GESEN. *Lexicon.* In the same way as the ephah for dry goods, the בַּת was used for liquids, as Delitzsch observes on Isa. v. 10. This measure occurs first in the days of the kings, and from Josephus' calculation it might contain somewhat more than 33 Berlin quarts [about 7 gallons English].—Ver. 11 now begins to discuss what is right as to measure (תֹּכֶן, *pensum*, Ex. v. 18), that which the ephah and bath are to represent, in order clearly to set forth exactness in trade and commerce as the divine characteristic of the people, as their holiness in ordinary life. Ver. 10 is expounded and illustrated by examples.—לָשֵׂאת Rashi explains by לָקַחַת, "to bear" = to hold, to contain. The חֹמֶר (a heap collected together) shall be the measure, the norm, for ephah and bath, as the greatest dry goods measure, commonly called "cor" from the time of the kings, and (from Josephus) estimated at a little more than 15 Berlin pecks [about 600 English pints].—Ver. 12 proceeds to speak of the standard for money, the shekel. An exactly weighed and hence definite (small) pound of silver, called by the Rabbins "rock" in distinction from the gerah, which they called "little stone," is the oldest biblical standard of value, originally, in barter a weight, afterwards a coin, like the *drachma* among the Greeks and the *as* among the Romans. The value doubtless affixed by common agreement of the dealers to the ordinary shekel before the time of Moses cannot now be determined; but originating probably in Babylon, and coming through the Phœnicians, the word meets us also in Greek (σικλος, σιγλος).—גֵּרָה is what is "made small," hence grain as a small piece, like "grain" (a weight), from *granum;* Gesenius supposes it to be the carob bean (κερατιον), which the Greeks, Romans, and Arabians used as the smallest weight, in the same way as barley and pepper-corns have been so used,—the smallest biblical silver coin.—After the value of the shekel has been thus defined from the parts it contains (comp. Ex. xxx. 13; Lev. xxvii. 25; Num. iii. 47), there may perhaps, as Cocceius and J. D. Michaelis think, be three different kinds of shekel given, a larger, an intermediate, and a smaller. Hengstenberg better: "the maneh, probably of foreign origin, which explains its rare and late occurrence, is stated at a threefold value," according to its different worth in the several countries from which it came. The normal maneh = 20 shekels, corresponding to the 20 gerahs, stands first.—מָנֶה (1 Kings x. 17; Ezra ii. 69; Neh. vii. 71, 72), from a comparison of the first passage—in which Hengstenberg, indeed, prefers to read מֵאוֹת instead of מָנִים—with 2 Chron. ix. 16, it appears that a maneh is equal to 100 shekels, a result usually reconciled with our passage by saying that civil shekels, that is, Mosaic half-shekels, are intended to be meant in 2 Chron. ix., since the בֶּקַע in the course of time became as shekel the widest spread large silver piece. But still 100 such shekels, or 50 Mosaic ones, by which Ezekiel reckons, would not be 20 + 25 + 15, the numbers given here, added together = 60 shekels; and besides, the three divisions and the putting of the 20 first remain unexplained! Hence Keil infers a very ancient corruption of the text. Hitzig, accepting like Hengstenberg three manehs, the only reasonable interpretation of the present text, supposes computation in gold, silver, and copper; that is, a gold, a silver, and a copper maneh. The Chaldee paraphrast, on the other hand, took the 60 shekels as the extraordinary value of the happy Messianic age (ומני רבא קודשא יהי לכון). The interpretation of the LXX., accepted by Boeckh (*Metrol. Unters.*) and Bertheau (*Gesch. der Isr.*), gives the following very insignificant proposition: The 5-shekel weight shall be to you 5 shekels, and the 10-shekel weight 10, and 50 shekels shall be a maneh.

Vers. 13–17. *The Oblation of the People.*

As formerly it was from the prince to the people, so now it is what the people have to render to the prince. The foregoing fixing of measures forms the transition, and the designation הַתְּרוּמָה in Ver. 13, taken from ver. 1 sq., is also an intermediate link. The **oblation** is offered to Jehovah as being set apart for purposes of worship. It is to be the sixtieth part of wheat and barley. שִׁשָּׁה, to divide into six parts, hence here: to take off the sixth part.—Ver. 14. חֹק הַשֶּׁמֶן is the ordinance of the oil, what the law of the **oblation** is to be in respect to the oil; namely, as explained by the apposition: הַבַּת הַשֶּׁמֶן, which Hengstenberg makes a parenthesis, and paraphrases thus: "the bath is the measure for the oil,"—the quantity taken from the bath of oil shall be the tenth part of it. The **cor** (1 Kings v. 2 [iv. 22]; 2 Chron. ii. 9 [10], xxvii. 5), for dry goods and liquids, a post-Mosaic name of a measure; and hence it is not only added that the cor is ten baths, but also that it is the same as the homer, for ten baths (ver. 11) make a homer. [HENGST.: homer without doubt the native name; cor introduced from the Aramaic during or after the exile.] Thus the tenth of the bath is as regards the oil the hundredth part of the harvest.—Wine (specifically for the drink-offering) is not mentioned; small cattle however are—Ver. 15—(the "oblation" in their case is to be one out of two hundred, and that one to come from fat pastures, to be well fed), but not oxen. The enumeration, says Keil, is not complete, but contains only the norm for levying the contributions; as Hengstenberg expresses himself: to serve as proof that the regulations here "do not bear the character of an actual tax," but are only by way of example and outline. Philippson remarks: "This impost appears intended to serve as substitute for the tithes prescribed by Moses, which are not mentioned here."—מַשְׁקֶה is "a watered district," like Gen. xiii. 10; a significant allusion: Israel after their return to their own land will be as richly blessed as ever the valley of Jordan was before its devastation.

Ver. 16 consigns **this oblation** to the **princes.**—

יהיו אל, they are to see to it that they render it. The prince is hereby on the one hand enabled to provide for the service of worship, as on the other his representation of the people is made manifest. Hengstenberg holds the amount of this oblation to be too great, and barley moreover was not used in worship, unless we understand that "the other expenses for the general good" were to be included.—Ver. 17. Instead of היה אל, which applies to all the people, we have now היה על, that which concerns the prince only ; on him it shall be incumbent. First, the things incumbent upon him are enumerated, and then is added what he has to do (הוא־יעשה), namely, as is obvious from his very position, that he shall defray the material expenses of worship, and in so far perform it. He is indeed "governor of the feast," but not "officiator in presenting the atoning sacrifice on the feast days," with a priestly dignity, such as Umbreit attributes to him. יעשה may simply be : cause to be done (ch. xlvi. 2). Hävernick again well observes: "Thus there arises a beautiful contrast to the former state of matters. Instead of violent exactions, harsh oppression, infamous tyranny, and mutual injustice and disloyalty, comes a settled order of things, conscientious gifts of the people which are holy gifts. The prince appears as the theocratic head, who truly cares for the weal and safety of Israel, who supports in the liveliest and demands in the strongest manner the close communion of the people with their God ; not only administering justice, but also caring for the most sacred interests of the people," etc.

Vers. 18-20. *The Sin-offering in the First Month.*

A solemn introduction : **Thus saith,** etc.—("Taking occasion from the thought in ver. 17, the prophet now portrays, as a new, solemn cycle of feasts begins in Israel, what also the prophets elsewhere announce regarding the sacred festivals in the Messianic period, *e.g.* Isa. lxvi. 23 ; Zech. xiv. 16," Häv.) The whole mode of expression in Ver. 18, as well as the comparison of ch. xliii. 18 sq. (of the difference between that and this), and the connection with what follows,—all this compels us to reject the view given by Hengstenberg, that corresponding to the consecration of the altar of burnt-offerings, we have to regard the consecration of the sanctuary as a solemnity occurring only once. Hengstenberg compares the seven days' solemnity in the case of Solomon's temple (2 Chron. vii. 8), and the fresh consecration of the temple under Hezekiah (2 Chron. xxix. 18 sq.), but especially the consecration of the tabernacle on the first day of the first month in Ex. xl. Besides what we have said already, the following consideration tells against this view. Surely we may suppose a difference between these sanctuaries built by men, like the altar of burnt-offerings (ביום העשותו), and the divine temple beheld by Ezekiel, when its consecration in this sense had already taken place by the coming in of the divine glory (ch. xliii. 2 sq.). The solemnity here ordained on the first and seventh days of the month (Nisan, ver. 21) is a yearly returning one, as is shown also by the reference in ver. 20 to continual recurrence. Num. xxviii. 11 sq. shows that the beginning of every month is to be solemnized, and Num. xxix. that there is to be additionally a special solemnity on the first day of the seventh month. On this comp. Ezek. xlvi.—The cleansing of the sanctuary is effected here through a young bullock, instead of the goat prescribed by Moses for the new moon,—an augmentation of the sin-offering as to the victim, just as in Ver. 19 through the process which accomplishes the cleansing. The **posts of the house** (ch. xli. 21) refer to the **sanctuary** (ver. 18), without distinction in respect to its two divisions, the altar of burnt-offerings and the gate (doubtless collective for all the three gates, for if only the east gate were meant, specific mention of it would hardly be omitted) of the inner court.—Ver. 20, however, explains in direct terms that this cleansing of the **sanctuary** on the first and seventh days of the first month takes place from the ground (מן), the cause which, in view of the holiness of the house, may be found in איש שגה, that is : the erring, frail man, and פתי, either : folly, or, *abstr. pro concreto :* the fool (properly, the man open to every impression, easily led astray). The two designations are distinguished as *actus* and *potentia*, the occasional act and the natural disposition ; but it has been rightly remarked that both denote sins of weakness. [Keil wrongly interprets מן: "from, away from," setting him free from his sin ; for this neither agrees with the immediately following וכפרתם את־הבית, nor can it be found in the וכן תעשה, which refers back to ver. 19.] "Thus shall the year, newly consecrated by such a beginning, most truly present the appearance of a holy year. At the same time this is the preparation for the feast of the passover in ver. 21" (Häv.). Since the great day of atonement (Lev. xvi. 16 sq.) had the same end in view as the very expressive and augmented solemnity ordained here on the first day of the month, the single yearly day of atonement is otherwise quite passed over, and thus there is ground for the opinion that the solemnity here is meant to express the idea of the day of atonement for the worship of the future.

Vers. 21–25. *The Passover and the Feast of Tabernacles.*

Ver. 21. The chief fundamental feast of Israel, the beginning of the feast-cycle, as afterwards its close, so that with the passover and the feast of tabernacles the whole circle of feasts in the narrower sense is either embraced (Häv.), or decreed as the annual feasts of the future (Keil). Comp. the original institution of the feast of the passover in Ex. xii.—חג שבעות, to which is here added ימים, is: **feast of seven days,** because it always lasted seven days (comp. Num. xxviii. 17), so that the "continuous" feast is denoted, but not, as Hengst.: "in contrast to the feast of consecration," but rather implying that in this con nection recurring feasts are spoken of. The old translations render the designation simply: "a feast of seven days"; the addition: יָמִים, will at least distinguish it as seven-dayed from the "feast of weeks" (חַג שָׁבֻעוֹת), celebrated later at the close of harvest. Kliefoth, on the other hand, supposes that in future the passover will be held as a feast of seven weeks, which lasts seven weeks; and so not merely the seven days of unleavened bread, but the whole seven weeks will be passover—the feast of weeks shall be one with the passover. The ordinance regarding the מַצּוֹת relates (he holds) to the whole seven weeks up to the feast of first-fruits. See the refutation of this in Keil on the passage. The seven days of the feast in ver. 23 also tell very plainly what is meant. Comp. on Deut. xvi.—Ver. 22 exhibits the prince in the charge imposed upon him (הוא־יַעֲשֶׂה, here וְעָשָׂה). — בַּיּוֹם הַהוּא is the above-mentioned fourteenth day of the first month, the feast-day proper (הַפֶּסַח), on the evening of which the paschal lamb was slain and eaten. — The sin-offering precedes, whereas in Num. xxviii. it follows after. In this way the idea of the day of atonement pervades also the passover of the future (**for himself and for the whole people of the land**). The victim, too, of the sin-offering on the first feast-day proper is not a goat, but a bullock! For the seven following days of the mazzoth there are ordained—Ver. 23—as a **burnt-offering**, instead of the two bullocks of Moses, seven bullocks, and instead of the one ram in the law, here seven rams, all without blemish, לַיּוֹם, "for the day," each of the seven days; and only the one goat as daily **sin-offering** is retained from the law of Moses. This enhancement of the feast-offerings, 49 bullocks and 49 rams as burnt-offering, is additional proof of an element which has already repeatedly shown itself, to wit, Israel's state of grace for the future. In reference to the passover Hengstenberg observes: "That precisely the grace of redemption sealed by this festival was to receive so rich an accession by the events of the future." The seven lambs of the first year ordained in the law are omitted by Ezekiel; we might say, because the Lamb of God, who is the fulfilment of this feast, will be sufficient in the Messianic times.' But, as only befits the symbolized idea meant to be made prominent, the **meat-offering**—Ver. 24—accompanying the burnt-offering surpasses even the measure of the latter. In the law there are to each bullock only three-tenths of an ephah of flour mingled with oil, two-tenths to the ram, and only one-tenth to each of the seven lambs; here a whole ephah, namely of flour, is appointed for each bullock and each ram, finally of oil one הִין (ch. iv. 11).

Ver. 25 describes the feast of tabernacles, the feast (בֶּחָג) falling on the 15th day of the 7th month, so designated because not expressed by name. Keil and Kliefoth assign as the reason for its not being named: "without doubt because the dwelling in tabernacles will for the future be discontinued." What the prince has to perform **in this feast is, as to time (seven days) and kinds** of offering, the same as in the passover. Hengstenberg excepts from this similarity the number of victims. Comp. Num. xxix. 13 sq. But the definition: **as meat-offering**, leaves us to suppose for the rest also nothing but a matter relative to number and measure, and Hengstenberg's solicitude about the passover as "the root of all feasts," seems in the case of such a comparison as is made here to overlook the fact that the number of victims, which indeed daily decreased, was far more signal and greater in the Mosaic feast of tabernacles; moreover, the eighth day, as concluding feast with its special offerings, is, as Keil observes, wanting here. Hävernick farther observes: "The sacred number seven dominates here both in the passover and in the offerings of the feast of tabernacles. The gradual decrease of the number of victims in the latter, explained by Bähr as a gradual decrease of the festal character of the seven feast-days, receives a fresh confirmation. Here, namely, an equal number of victims is appointed for every day. The distinction between the feasts themselves thereby almost disappears. Each day comes forth in its proper and symmetrical holiness. The sacred number seven pervades the whole cycle of feasts. The defective and imperfect character of the ancient mode gives place to a higher and more perfect form."

ADDITIONAL NOTE ON VERS. 18-25.

["As it was more especially in connection with the stated and yearly festivals that the prince had to represent the people in the public service of God, so the prophet takes a rapid glance of these, and refers particularly to the first and the last. But he first mentions a consecration service with which the year was always to begin, and of which no mention whatever was made in the law (vers. 18-20). On the first and again on the seventh day of the first month, the sanctuary was always to be cleansed, that the year might be commenced in sacredness, and that all might be in preparation for the feast of the passover on the fourteenth day of the month. As the prophet has introduced a new solemnity before the passover, so for the passover itself he appoints quite different sacrifices from those named by Moses; instead of one ram and seven lambs for the daily burnt-offering, he has seven bullocks and seven rams; and the meat-offerings also vary. And while there were quite peculiar offerings prescribed in the law for the feast of tabernacles, constantly diminishing as the days of the feast proceeded; here, on the other hand, the prophet appoints the same as in the case of the passover. This shows how free a use was made by the prophet of the Old Testament ritual, and how he only employed it as a cover for the great spiritual truths he sought to unfold. They were not permanently fixed and immutable things, he virtually said, those external services of Judaism, as if they had an absolute and independent value of their own, so that precisely those and no other should be thought of; they were all symbolical of the spiritual and eternal truths of God's kingdom, and may be variously adjusted, as is now done, in order to make them more distinctly expressive of the greater degree of holiness and purity that is in future times to distinguish the people and service of God over all that has been in the past."—FAIRBAIRN'S *Ezekiel*, pp. 485, 486.—W. F.]

CHAPTER XLVI.

1 Thus saith the Lord Jehovah: The gate of the inner court that looketh
toward the east shall be shut the six working days; and on the Sabbath day
2 it shall be opened, and on the day of the new moon it shall be opened. And
the prince cometh the way of [to] the porch of the gate from without, and
will stand at the post of the gate; and the priests offer up his burnt-offering
and his peace-offerings; and he worships at the threshold of the gate, and
3 will go out; and the gate shall not be shut until the evening. And the
people of the land worship at the door of this gate in the Sabbaths and in
4 the new moons before Jehovah. And the burnt-offering which the prince
shall offer to Jehovah on the Sabbath day is six lambs without blemish, and
5 a ram without blemish. And the meat-offering [shall be] an ephah for the
ram, and for the lambs the meat-offering [shall be] what his hand gives, and
6 oil a hin to the ephah. And on the day of the new moon without blemish
a bullock—a young steer, and six lambs and a ram; without blemish shall
7 they be. And an ephah for the bullock and an ephah for the ram shall he
make the meat-offering, and for the lambs so much as his hand will attain
8 to, and oil a hin to the ephah. And when the prince cometh he shall come
the way of the porch of the gate, and by the same way shall he go out.
9 And when the people of the land come before Jehovah in the set times, he
that cometh the way of the north gate to worship shall go out the way of
the south gate, and he that cometh the way of the south gate shall go out
the way of the north gate; he shall not return the way of the gate by which
10 he came, but they shall go out each straight before him. And the prince
shall come in their midst; when they come and when they go out, they shall
11 go out [together]. And in the feasts and in the set times the meat-offering
shall be an ephah for the bullock and an ephah for the ram, and for the
12 lambs what his hand gives, and oil a hin to the ephah. And when the
prince shall offer a free-will offering, burnt-offering, or peace-offering, as a
free-will offering to Jehovah, then one opens to him the gate that looketh
toward the east, and he offers his burnt-offering and his peace-offering, as he
will do on the Sabbath day; and he goeth out, and one shuts the door after
13 his going out. And a lamb a year old without blemish shalt thou daily
14 offer as a burnt-offering to Jehovah; every morning shalt thou offer it. And
a meat-offering shalt thou offer with it every morning, the sixth of an ephah,
and oil the third of a hin, to moisten the fine flour,—a meat-offering to
15 Jehovah, ordinances perpetual, continual. And they offer the lamb and the
meat-offering and the oil every morning, as a continual burnt-offering.
16 Thus saith the Lord Jehovah: When the prince shall give a gift to one of
his sons, it [is] his inheritance, to his sons shall it be [become], their possession
17 as an inheritance. And when he shall give a gift from his inheritance to one
of his servants, then it is his until the year of freedom, when it returns to
18 the prince; only his inheritance of his sons shall belong to them. And the
prince shall not take of the people's inheritance to thrust them out of their
possession; from his own possession he may endow his sons, that My people
19 be not scattered every man from his possession. And he brought me, in the
entry which was at the side of the gate, to the chambers of holiness, to the
priests, that look toward the north; and, behold, there was a place on the
20 hinder side westward. And he said to me, This is the place where the
priests shall boil the guilt-offering and the sin-offering, where they shall bake
the meat-offering, so as not to bring it forth to the outer court, to sanctify
21 the people. And he brought me forth to the outer court, and made me pass
on to the four corners of the court, and, behold, in each corner of the court
22 was a court. In the four corners of the court were smoking courts, forty
[cubits] long and thirty [cubits] broad; one measure was to them to the four

23 corner-rooms. And a range was round about in them, round about the four
24 of them, and cooking-places were made under the ranges round about. And
he said to me: These are the house of the cooks, where the ministers of the
house shall boil the slain-offering of the people

Ver. 2. Sept.: . . . της πυλης της ἐξωθεν . . . ἐπι τα προθυρα— Vulg.: . . . *stabit in limine*—
Ver. 3. . . . κατα τα προθυρα—
Ver. 4. K. το ὁλοκαυτωμα προσοισει—
Ver. 6. Another reading: תקח פר and תמים; all the old translations read singular as the latter.
Ver. 9. . . . ἀλλ' ἡ κατ' εὐθυ αὐτης ἐξελευσεται. Vulg.: . . . *sed e regione illius egredietur*. (Another reading: יצא, also ver. 10.)
Ver. 10. . . . εἰσελευσεται μετ' αὐτων, κ. ἐν τω . . . ἐξελευσεται μετ' αὐτων.
Ver. 11. . . . και ἐν ταις πανηγυρεσιν—
Ver. 12. . . . ὁμολογιαν ὁλοκαυτωμα σωτηριου τω κυριω κ. ἀνοιξει—
Ver. 13. . . . ποιησει . . . ποιησει— (Another reading: יעשה, also ver. 14.)
Ver. 14. Sept.: . . . προσταγμα αἰωνιον διαπαντος (15.) ποιησετε τον ἀμνον κ. . . . ποιησετε— Vulg.: . . . *cata mane sacrificium domino legitimum, juge atque perpetuum.*
Ver. 15. *Faciet . . . cata mane mane*— (Qeri: יַעֲשׂוּ.)
Ver. 16. . . . υἱων αὐτου του ἐκ τ. κληρονομιας αὐτου, τουτο—
Ver. 17. . . . κ. ἀποδωσει . . . πλην τ. κληρονομιας τ. υἱων αὐτου— Vulg.: . . *hæreditas autem ejus filiis ejus erit.*
Ver. 18. Vulg.: . . . *per violentiam et de possessione eorum,*
Ver. 19. . . . ἐκει τοπος κεχωρισμενος.
Ver. 20. . . . ἐπι τα τεσσαρα μερη τ. αὐλης· . . . αὐλη κατα τα κλιτη τ. αὐλης, αὐλη κατα το κλιτος, αὐλη (22.) ἐπι τα τεσσ. κλιτη τ. αὐλης, αὐλη μικρα μηκους— Vulg.: . . . *in angulo atrii, atriola singula per angulos atrii.*
Ver. 22. Vulg.: . . . *atriola disposita*—
Ver. 23. K. ἐξεδραι . . . ἐν αὐταις, . . . κ. μαγειρεια γεγονοτα ὑποκατω των ἐξεδρων— Vulg.: *Et paries per circuitum ambiens quatuor atriola . . . subter porticus*—
Ver. 24. . . . οἱ οἰκοι των μαγειρειων— Vulg.: . . . *domus culinarum*—

EXEGETICAL REMARKS.

Vers. 1–12. *The Prince and People at Sacrifice.*

Ch. xliv. 1 sq. treated of the outer east gate, while here the inner east gate comes into consideration. There the prince appears as sitting feasting upon the offerings; here he is viewed as standing, in accordance with his duty of offering. Both passages accord to him precedence of the people. In Keil's view the two passages supplement each other in this way, that we have here the exceptions to the rule there. But ch. xliv. permits no exception in regard to the shutting of the gate (comp. on ch. xliii. 5, also xlvii. 2); and besides, it is the outer gate that is spoken of there, whereas here it is the inner. If one is to call it a case of supplementing, he can say: whereas ch. xliv. shuts the outer east gate always, the inner east gate also, according to our passage, should as a rule be shut; the Sabbath day and the day of the new moon are to form the exceptions. —Ver. 2. We are told in ch. xliv. how the prince arrives at the outer gate, namely, by the way of the porch of the gate (מִדֶּרֶךְ'); that same way, only in respect to the inner east gate,—which, however, as we have seen on ch. xl. 31, has its porch likewise turned to the outer court,—the prince comes here also, so that מחוץ means just the same as מִן in מִדֶּרֶךְ (ch. xliv. 3): from the outer court, into which he entered by the north or south gate. מחוץ only makes the gate intended, but not expressly named in ver. 2, more plain as the inner gate, the gate that leads into the inner court. [Hengst. takes it as: "without," "beyond"; he makes the prince proceed through the opened door of the inner east gate as far as its threshold and post; not pass through the porch, but remain standing on this side of it, beyond the gate-opening, but close by it, on the threshold between the gate-opening and the porch. Keil, again, understands מחוץ as meaning from outside of the temple through the outer east gate. Ewald makes as correction in ver. 1 the gate of the "outer" court.] The mention again of the east gate repeats, in reference to the prince, the distinction conferred upon him in ch. xliv. It is, however, rather a distinction from the people, or a distinction of the people in his person, than a distinguishing approximation of the prince to the priests. Compare with what is here said Solomon's probably pulpit-like brazen scaffold, on which he knelt, and which thus was situated before the altar of burnt-offering in the inner court (2 Chron. vi. 13); likewise 2 Kings xi. 14, xxiii. 3; 2 Chron. xxiii. 13, xxxiv. 31. According to the passage before us, the position even of the prince inside of the environs of the temple suffers a noteworthy modification. A definite, fixed, elevated standing place, a *suggestus* for the bearer of princely power at the entrance into the inner court, as occupied since Solomon by the pre-exile kings, is no longer spoken of. The king of the future is the Messiah; the princedom shines in His light (Doct. Reflec. 14), in the brightness of the glory that entered through the east gate, which in view thereof is shut for ever toward the outside, and it (namely, the east gate) is temporarily opened only toward the interior, to be shut again at even. The Messianic idea dominates the modification of the prerogative of the possession derived from the pre-exile kingdom within the architectonic symbolism of the theocracy. Hengst. says: "What is treated of here is not merely a subordination of the prince to God; there is also as regards worship a sharp line drawn between prince and priest." Hävernick observes: "As on the one hand the prince is unreservedly acknowledged in his special exaltation, so on the other his rights appear in due limitation, in reference to encroachment of any kind on the priestly prerogatives. With regard to this, a position is assigned to him at the post of the gate leading to the inner court, on the threshold of the gate, hence at the head of the people, yet not in the priests' court proper." While he stands, the priests "do" what the prince cannot do, but must cause to be done by them. הִשְׁתַּחֲוָה (שָׁחָה, "to bow"), Hithp. with וה as reduplication of the third radical, reflexive.--**And will go out** by the way that he came (ch. xliv. 3). As what has been said invests the prince with privileges only above the people, Ver. 3 fixes the people's place at worship. פֶּתַח׳ [HENGST.: "opposite the opened door, through which they catch a glimpse of the altar of burnt-offering, which the prince—this is the only difference (? he enters the inner east gate, however)—sees from a nearer point"] is, according to Klief., equivalent to: through the opening of the gate, inasmuch as the people before the outer east gate have to look at the temple through it, and also through the inner gate (comp. ver. 9). The arrangement intimates that the people shall worship outside of the threshold of the inner east gate, the gate spoken of (הַהוּא). Ps. xcv. 6.

Ver. 4. The Sabbath-offerings to be brought and offered by the prince are instead of: two lambs of the first year without blemish for a burnt-offering, and two-tenth deals of flour and oil for a meat-offering and drink-offering (Num. xxviii. 9); in future: three times as many lambs and a ram besides.—Ver. 5. This increase of offerings extends also to the meat-offering: an ephah for the ram (ch. xlv. 24). This may, and doubtless does, imply a proportionate increase with respect to the lambs likewise; מַתַּת יָדוֹ, however, which does not necessarily mean the same as the formula in ver. 7, expresses free-willingness as the other element in the ordinance. A range of freedom along with the obligation, as HENGST., is not, however, so much the thought here, as, on the one hand, greater richness and splendour, which on the other presupposes a liberal and munificent disposition in the individual. "The disposition has become changed; with the greater blessings, demands higher than hitherto present themselves. But the more the amount to be spent is left to the free will of the individual, the more of zeal and faithfulness is presupposed" (HÄV.).—Ver. 6. The new-moon offerings, on the contrary, show a decrease; namely, instead of: two bullocks, one ram, seven lambs (Num. xxviii. 11 sq.), we have here only: one bullock, one ram, six lambs. Hengst., indeed, disputes this; the number of bullocks, he says, "is left to the free judgment, only it may not fall short of the two required by the law." In support of this view he takes פַּר as collective (an "ideal unity"), and appeals to the plural תְּמִימִים, which certainly cannot be interpreted as referring to the frequent recurrence of the feast. (According to Keil, it is a "blunder of the transcriber" for תְּמִים.) Not only one bullock and one ram, however, but also the goat for the **sin-offering** (Num. xxviii. 15) is wanting here.—Ver. 7. The increase appears to be retained only through the meat-offering (comp. ch. xlv. 24), and to be expressed by the formula: כַּאֲשֶׁר תַּשִּׂיג יָדוֹ, which takes as measure, not the free will, like ver. 5, but ability (Lev. xiv. 30).

In order to pass over from Sabbaths and new moons to other seasons of worship, Ver. 8 first repeats what has been said in ver. 2. בְּדַרְכּוֹ = by the same way.—Ver. 9. Keil notices as a distinction from ver. 3, that there the people were spoken of "only incidentally" ("provided some of them came"), since they were "not bound to come on Sabbaths and new moons." Such a distinction, however, would require to be more definitely noted. In reality, Ezekiel as much supposes the people coming in ver. 3 as here, where the coming and going of individuals (הַבָּא) is expressly mentioned. Something similar to Deut. xvi. 16 is not exactly expressed here. The most that can be said is, that בְּמוֹעֲדִים (this is what makes the distinction from ver. 3)—מוֹעֵד (יָעַד) the set time and assembling of the community—the coming and going of the people, might make more of a throng, so that here the relative rank of people and prince, expressed in ver. 3, is not so much regarded, but care is taken for due order in the temple; and while in vers. 2, 3 the prince was distinguished from the people, here he and they are taken together. [FAIRBAIRN: "At the great festivals the prince was to depart from the state of isolation which it was proper for him to observe at other times, and at the head of the people join in the great throng of worshippers that were to pass through the temple courts from one side to another. It reminds us of David, who in this was doubtless the exemplar in the eye of the prophet: 'I had gone with the multitude, I went with them to the house of God, with the voice of joy and praise, with a multitude that kept holyday.' A beautiful picture of a religious people: the highest in rank freely mingling with the mass of worshippers, and inspiriting their devotions by the elevating influence of his presence and example."—W. F.] ("The reason of the regulation in ver. 9 can only be a theological one, that each should go out of the sanctuary another man than he came in (Phil. iii. 13); to avoid a throng, all must have been obliged to go in by the same gate, and out by the opposite one."—HENGST.) Hengst. renders בְּמוֹעֲדִים here: "in the feast seasons;" in ver. 11: "on the feast days;" in order to assure himself of the continuance of the great day of atonement; and hence he renders בַּחַגִּים: "on the joyous feasts." Keil makes מוֹעֲדִים comprehend "Sabbaths, new moons, and the day of atonement, all the seasons and days sanctified to the Lord." This in itself cannot be disputed, but in the connection here in Ezekiel may be very questionable. Keil at all events overthrows by this his own distinction of vers. 9 and 10 from ver. 3, which rests on the ground that vers. 9 and 10 speak of the high feasts, at which every one has to appear. בְּמוֹעֲדִים in ver. 9 points rather to the two days appointed for the first month, ch. xlv. 18, 20.—**Since mention is made of two ways of coming** the singular Qeri (יֵצֵא) must be rejected.—Ver. 10, very suitably for the two days of the first month, views the prince and people together. Here, too, the Qeri is to be rejected; יֵצֵאוּ are prince and people. Hengstenberg rightly compares Ps. xlii. 5 [4].—Ver. 11 introduces the "feasts" strictly so called (see ch. xlv. 21 and 25) in addition to the "set seasons" (ch. xlv. 18, 20); but, as the statement of the meat-offering shows, the מוֹעֲדִים are chiefly meant, for as to the **feasts** comp. the meat-offering ordained in ch. xlv. 24 sq., while the **lambs** are explained from ver. 6 of our chapter, which tells of those for the new moon. Hence what is there mentioned for burnt-offering must hold good also in ch. xlv. 18–20, and likewise the meat-offering here, for which comp. ver. 7 of our chapter. While the formula there measures according to ability, the one here expresses also that which corresponds to free-will, and this the more appropriately as free-will offerings are treated of in what follows.—Ver. 12. נְדָבָה (Ps. cx. 3), from נָדַב, "to impel," is the peculiar inward impulse, the joyful readiness for good and for all sacrifices which comes from the Spirit of God (Ps. li. 14 [12]). The expression is used, as of the impulse originally, so of that to which one feels himself impelled, of the gift, and especially of the sacrifice to which a man was bound by no vow (Lev. xxii. 23). The repetition in our verse of this element makes it specially prominent. [FAIRBAIRN: "To show that his worship was not merely of a public and official nature, that it should spring from a heart truly alive to divine things, and itself delighting in fellowship with God, the prophet passes from those holiday services to the voluntary offerings and the daily morning sacrifice, which the prince was also to present to the Lord. In a word, the proper head of a religious people, he was to surpass them all, and be an example to them all, in the multitude and variety of his acts of homage and adoration."—W. F.] Keil observes on the modified regulation in regard to opening and shutting the gate, as compared with ver. 2, that the free-will offering could be brought on any day of the week; Hengst. points to the distinction that "in the free-will offering the prince appears as an individual, in the Sabbath-offering as the representative of the people."

Vers. 13–15. *The Daily Sacrifice.*

Ver. 13. The address to the people (תַּעֲשֶׂה), where hitherto we have had to do with the prince, and the comparison of what was imposed on him in ch. xlv. 17, make it probable that the daily sacrifice is to be "an affair of the community," which "the priests have to provide" (KEIL). "Yet," observes Hengstenberg, "the conclusion is not certain; the transition from the prince to the people is an easy one, since in the foregoing passage also the prince represents the people. Ch. xlv. 18–20 likewise began with the address to the people, and undoubtedly the close here corresponds to the beginning there; the prince is encompassed on both sides by the people." According to Num. xxviii. 3 sq., two such lambs were to be offered daily for a burnt-offering, namely, one in the morning and the other in the evening. The more exact statement here: בַּבֹּקֶר בַּבֹּקֶר, that it shall be done **every morning**, either abolishes the evening burnt-offering (KEIL), or silently supposes it (HENGST.). The aim is, corresponding to ch. xlv. 18 sq., a similar sanctification of the commencement of the day as of that of the month and year; hence the sanctification of the whole of time in all its divisions, in distinction, perhaps, from the significance of the evening for Israel (Ex. xii. 6). If the evening sacrifice is to be discontinued, the increase of the meat-offering **every morning** in Ver. 14 (compared with Num. xxviii. 5, one-tenth of an ephah and one-fourth of a hin) perhaps comes into consideration for the deficit.—לָרֹס, from רָסַס, "to rend," to scatter, to sprinkle. HENGST. and KEIL: to moisten.—סֹלֶת, probably from סָלַל (but of doubtful signification; MEIER: to split, to widen; GESEN.: to lift up, to oscillate), is the finest wheat meal. The plural חֻקּוֹת refers both to the burnt-offering in ver. 13, and the meat-offering here. The significance of such a solemnity every morning is emphasized by the תָּמִיד strengthening the עוֹלָם, for which, with Hitzig, Lev. xxiii. 14, 21, 31 is to be compared.—Ver. 15. Keil takes וְעָשׂוּ as imperative; it is preterite with *vav.* The Qeri reads the imperfect.—Again the emphatic תָּמִיד. ("That which is to be done daily forms a contrast to the festivities; it is to be acknowledged and honoured in due dignity and significance as a perpetual burnt-offering," HÄV.) HENGST.: "We move here entirely on the realm of Old Testament worship, and there is not the slightest (?) indication that, by the sacrifice of bulls, lambs, and goats, other forms of worship are here denoted. Even if the details were only colouring and means of representation, yet an intimation in regard to the whole should not be wanting" (neither is it wanting, it is manifest throughout the whole and in every part!) "if the announcement were to extend to a time when, by the offered sacrifice of Christ, a total revolution in the worship was produced. This is certainly correct; although the prophecy refers primarily to the restoration of the Old Testament worship, and in this respect has long ago found its fulfilment, and indeed a fulfilment that has long disappeared again,—the disappearance was proclaimed by the word of Christ: Behold, your house is left unto you desolate;—yet at the same time it conceals in the details the kernel of a general truth,—the imperishability of the worship in the community of God on earth, which is demonstrated among other things also by this, that as the worship here predicted had to perish by the Roman destruction, the worship in the Christian Church rose again gloriously." Any misunderstanding, as if Ezekiel should have predicted the Roman or Greek-Catholic worship, or a new evangelical worship of kindred form, might have been obviated by the consideration, that in everything here relative to the *service* of the temple of the future, the object aimed at is to give to the idea an expression as distinct as possible, although in terms of the Old Testament, and so in a symbolizing prophetic form, here specially to the idea, that whereas the Church Militant is a teaching church, the Church Triumphant of eternity (עוֹלָם תָּמִיד) will on the contrary be a liturgic one; as also the so much debated question of constitution will be overcome, because solved.

Vers. 16-24. *Appendices*:—Vers. 16-18. *The Right of the Prince as regards the Disposal of his Property.*—Vers. 19-24. *The Sacrificial Kitchens.*

Just as supplementary matter to the temple building is appended in ch. xli. 15 sq. in the transition to the service of the temple, so we have here a supplementary statement in reference to the prince and the priests,—the former as the procurer and defrayer of the material of worship, the latter as the persons formally celebrating it, after the order of worship was finished in the foregoing.

Vers. 16-18. *The Prince and his Possession.*

Ver. 16. 'כֹּה־אָמַר expressly introduces what follows as a divine ordinance, and not the fancy of the prophet; and this connects itself with that which was assigned to the prince in ch. xlv. 8 as his "possession in Israel." As we know from that passage, reference is made here too to the former despotic regime. When Hengstenberg says that "the prophet does not set himself up as a lawgiver, but only seeks to give a representation of the thought that the princes of the future are to be no despots, are to beware of the unjust absolutism of the princes of the past," it is clear, and Hengstenberg cannot deny it, that an ideal future is kept in view. But the ideality of the whole Old Testament is the future of the Messiah. Hengstenberg, indeed, observes quite correctly: "The prince cannot be Christ. He is one who may have several sons of his own body; who in the prospect of his death disposes of his property; who does not stand beyond the region of sin, else he should not need to be warned against it." The concession in respect of one of his **sons** preserves the character of the princely possession; **it becomes an inheritance**, but it remains in the princely family. Hengstenberg connects נַחֲלָתוֹ הִיא with the principal clause, and makes the suffix refer to the prince: "this shall become his inheritance (surely: his possession, which in this case he bequeaths) to his sons." It is more natural to connect it with לְאִישׁ מִבָּנָיו, and to make the suffix refer to the prince's son in question: the inheritance shall be his, bequeathed to him by his father (comp. on ver. 18); and this is confirmed by the immediately following clause, which does not generalize, so that, with Keil, the suffix in לְבָנָיו should now revert to the prince; but **his sons** are the sons of the just-mentioned **prince's** son, and the idea of the נַחֲלָתוֹ is only farther carried out: **it shall be their possession**, so that it can be bequeathed (בְּנַחֲלָה) to their sons also.—Ver. 17. The idea of "inheritance" remains the key-note as formerly, so that the farther concession in respect of a meritorious or favourite servant of the prince does not indeed forbid a present to the servant in land from that which the prince possesses as hereditary property, but yet alienation and so lessening of the crown estates is guarded against by the limitation: **until the year of freedom.** דְּרוֹר (from דָּרַר), which denotes free outflowing (Ex. xxx. 23), is free motion in general, freedom, as the year of jubilee is consequently named in Lev. xxv. 10, 13. The reversion is the same as in the case of an Israelitish heritable landed possession, when it passes by sale to another.—The meaning of the phrase: **only his inheritance of his sons,** is clear from the foregoing: only what the prince has presented to his sons from his inheritance shall remain to them. [KEIL: "only his inheritance is it (?); as regards his sons, to them it shall belong."]—Ver. 18. That which is to be preserved in the case of the prince, is also to be preserved for the people: **inheritance** in their case as in his. יָנָה, "to oppress," in general, hence: to exercise violence, to treat one with violence (ch. xviii. 7 sq., xlv. 8), here with מִן.—On פּוּץ, comp. ch. xxxiv. (1 Sam. viii. 14, xxii. 7).

Vers. 19-24. *The Sacrificial Kitchens for Priests and People.*

Ewald inserts this section after ch. xlii. 13, 14, as he does the preceding ch. xlv. between vers. 8 and 9. The prophet, who has not changed his standing-place since ch. xliv. 4 sq., is brought to the הַלְּשָׁכוֹת described in ch. xlii. 1 sq. (which comp.).—On בַּמָּבוֹא, comp. on ch. xlii. 9.—As the chambers in question are the priests', Hengst. explains the appositional phrase: **to the priests,** as in Roman Catholic countries one may say, for example: "to the Carmelites," etc.—The description: **that look toward the north,** refers of course to **chambers.** The **gate,** accordingly, is the north inner gate; according to Hengst., the entry leads "from the inner court gate on the west to the east entrance gate of the fence-wall of the priests' cells."—שָׁם, KEIL: "At the cells on the extreme hinder side toward the west;" HENGST.: "Thus the kitchens are in the cell building, not by and outside of it."—The Qeri has בְּיַרְכָתַיִם (HENGST.: יַרְכָתָם, "on their west side;" "singular, as in Gen. xlix. 13; the suffix refers in fact to the chambers, in form to the priests, including under them the chambers"). Gesenius derives the dual from the original signification: limb.—Ver. 20. Here the guilt-offering comes first, whereas in ch. xl. 39, xlii. 13, xliv. 29, it always comes after the sin-offering, as it did in the law also, and hence appeared as a subordinate kind of sin-offering, ordained merely for certain cases; in accordance with the leading thought that the sinner should not only desire atonement of his sin before God by a sin-offering, but likewise endeavour as far as possible to pay what was owing, make good the damage, make restitution for the crime com mitted.—בָּשַׁל, "to swell;" hence, naturally: "to ripen;" artificially: "to cook" (Piel).—אָפָה, properly: to draw together, is: "to bake." Comp. moreover, ch. xlii. 13.—לְבִלְתִּי, to be understood as in ch. xliv. 19, which comp.; הוֹצִיא, namely: out of the kitchens, which were situated in the corners of the outer court, like those which follow, where the priests had to pass through the crowd in order to get to their cells. **To the outer court**, mentioned to prepare for what follows, forms the transition to ver. 21.—The repetition: חָצֵר בְּמִקְצֹעַ, repeats in words what was repeatedly seen: "a court in the corner of the court, and again a court in the corner of the court" (as HENGST.), so that ver. 22 first gives the exact number of four.—The being brought forth **to the outer court** is explained by its distinction from the inner, the priests' court, against whose wall the cells and kitchens rested, as belonging to the sanctuary. Comp. ver. 19.—Ver. 22. These kitchens for the people are distinguished by the detailed description given from those formerly mentioned for the priests. Hengst. considers them: "as off-rooms of the chambers of the people in the sides of the court," and translates חֲצֵרוֹת קְטֻרוֹת: "smoking courts," saying that the ascending smoke is the characteristic mark of these "buildings," and asserting that the verb קָטַר, with all its derivatives, signifies in Hebrew only: to exhale, to smoke, etc. Gesenius assumes another root, קָטַר, "to bind," "to close," and understands: closed (*partic. pass.*) with walls and doors. This latter description would express as little as the other meanings, which Keil rightly rejects, and which the expression cannot have, such as "uncovered" (KLIEF.), "firm" (HÄV.), "pressed over" (HITZIG.), and the like. The description from the smoke has, on the other hand, something pictorial and emblematic, in so far as it might point to this, that in these kitchens meat to cook will never be wanting.—מִקְצוֹעַ, plur. ים— and וֹת—, is: corner, from קָצַע, to "cut off."—The Sept. and Vulgate omit מְהֻקְצָעוֹת, the last word of the verse, and the Masoretes, by points placed over it, mark it as suspicious. Hengst. holds it to be "a kind of priestly proper name for those rooms (HÄV.: a peculiar technical term for: placed in the corner), which Ezekiel here brings forward as a fond reminiscence." It is part. Hophal, and signifies: "cornered," "a corner room," as Hengstenberg says; according to Keil: "cornered off," "cut off in corners" (apposition to the suffix in לְאַרְבַּעְתָּם). Hävernick observes that the word still depends upon חֲצֵרוֹת.—Ver. 23. טוּר is something on which one walks round. Keil translates: "a row of standing places was in it round about." [KLIEF.: "a framework was in it round about."] Evidently the range of cooking-places (מְבַשְּׁלוֹת, **literally: "which cause to cook," partic. Piel),** running below the court-walls (טִירָה) and along them, is meant to be described. [KEIL: a tier of wall-work had several single tiers, under which the cooking-hearths were constructed. HÄV.: "the surrounding boundary-wall rises so high above the kitchens, that these are constructed below the wall."]—Ver. 24. בֵּית הַמְבַשְּׁלִים is in fact: the "kitchen-house," but formally: the house where the cooks cook.—**The ministers of the house**, as formerly, are the mere Levites, in contradistinction from the priests.—"Not without reason is only the slain-offering mentioned (the name bearing reference to the form; earlier the name denoted the essence: *Shelamim*), in distinction from the sin and guilt-offerings to be prepared in the kitchens of the priests. Only with the slain-offerings, such offerings as are akin to common slaughtering, was a communion connected. The greater part fell to the offerers, and was consumed in the sacrificial meals. But the slain-offering was not allowed to be prepared by the people themselves" (HENGST.).

DOCTRINAL REFLECTIONS ON CH. XL.-XLVI.

1. Hävernick rightly finds "the nervous and lofty unity" in the prophecies of Ezekiel "manifested in this section also." "The visions of the prophet find here their fairest completion and perfect rounding off." Already in the exposition (on ver. 1 sq.) the harmony with the former part of Ezekiel's prophecy has been remarked. Ch. xliii. 3 expressly refers back to ch. i. and viii. The free conformity in expression between our chapters and the whole closing portion generally, and the earlier chapters, has been often proved (comp. Philippson, p. 1294). The proof is the more striking when we consider the complete difference of the subject. That we have a vision here too harmonizes not only with ch. i. and viii., but in general with the prophetic character of Ezekiel, ch. viii., xv., xvii. The prophet has repeatedly hinted at this close of his book. Thus ch. xi. 16, xx. 40, xxxvi. 38, xxxvii. 26 sq. The last passage in particular might be regarded as the text for ch. xl. sq. The eighth and following chapters required by the necessity of the idea our conclusion of the book.

2. In regard to analogies in the other prophets, Ezekiel's contemporaries, as we may well conceive, will chiefly come into consideration. Hence, above all, Ezekiel's fellow-labourer Jeremiah. Jeremiah represents the restoration and renewal of Israel as a rebuilding of Jerusalem, ch. xxxi. 38 sq. (with this comp. in our prophet, ch. xlvii. 13 sq., ch. xlviii.). Jer. xxxiii. 18 is similar to Ezek. xliv. 9 sq. Hag. ii. 7 sq. follows entirely the thought here of a new temple, insisting on its glory in view of a meagre present. But still more analogous are the night-visions of Zechariah (ch. ii. 5 [1] sq., ch. iv., ch. vi. 13 sq., ch. xiv.).

3. The parallel between Isaiah and Ezekiel, as it stands in relation to the vision in ch. i. (p. 41), is not completed by citing Isa. lx. as corresponding to the close of our book; but we shall have to seek the culminating point of Isaiah's prophecy for the culmination of Ezekiel's, in accordance with the office of this prophet to be the **prophet of Jehovah's holiness to obdurate Israel,**

—just as for the commencement Isa. vi. is covered by Ezek. i.—not so much in the close as in ch. liii. The corresponding pendant to our closing chapters is the life-like description given there of the Messiah and His sacrifice of Himself. It is this self-sanctification of Jehovah through His servant Israel which in Isaiah corresponds to the self-glorification of Jehovah in Ezekiel (ch. xl. sq.) by means of the new sanctuary and the new nationality; and this, again, accords with Ezekiel's office, to behold the glory of Jehovah in the misery of the exile. In this respect Ezekiel stands to Isaiah somewhat as Easter and Pentecost do to Good Friday.

4. The different views, especially regarding the vision of the temple, may be distinguished generally as subjective and objective. I. The views which derive the explanation of ch. xl. sq. solely or chiefly from Ezekiel's subjectivity: (1) Already Villalpandus saw everywhere here only reminiscences of Solomon's temple and of Solomon's era, and consequently a similar line of thought to that in Ezra iii. 12. Similarly Grotius, only that he reconciled the differences between Ezekiel's temple and that of Solomon by ascribing them to the temple at the time of its destruction, just as Bunsen refers in this connection to 2 Kings xvi. According to both these expositors, Ezekiel traced out from reminiscences a pattern for the future restoration. Thus, according to Ewald, Ezekiel becomes "a prophetic lawgiver." "Such an undertaking, quite unusual in the case of earlier prophets," is explained from the "predominating thoughts and aspirations of the better class of those days for the restoration of the subverted kingdom." "Ezekiel probably meditated long, with passionate longing and lively remembrance, on the institutions of the demolished temple, etc.; what appeared to him great and glorious became impressed upon his mind as a pattern, with which he compared the Messianic expectations and demands, etc., until at length the outline of the whole arrangement which he here writes down pressed itself upon him!" "Above all, he sketches the holy objects, temple and altar, with the utmost exactness and vividness, as if a spirit (!) impelled him, now, when they were destroyed, at least to catch up their image in a faithful and worthy form for the redemption that will one day certainly come; so that he must have diligently instructed himself in these matters from the best written and oral sources" (!). "Thus it is quite in keeping with Ezekiel's way of prophesying, that he introduces everything as if he had been borne in spirit into the restored and completed temple, accompanied throughout by a heavenly guide, and had learned exactly from him all the single parts of this unique building as to their nature and use." The paragraph ch. xlvii. 1–12 is, in Ewald's opinion, "from its great, all-embracing sense, quite adapted to bring to a close briefly and pithily all these presentiments!" "Yet when precepts more moral are to be given, or the perfected kingdom has to be described in its extent, reaching even beyond the temple, this assumed form (!) easily passes over into the simple prophetic discourse." (2) While the foregoing view looks to realization, Hitzig, for example, entirely rejects the idea that Ezekiel "considered such things (as our chapters contain) possible, feasible, or probable, and relatively commanded and prescribed them." "One does not or did not reflect that the prophet's calling was to express the demands of the idea, indifferent in the first instance about their realization." All is pure fancy, a mere castle-in-the-air, a kind of "Platonic sketch," as Herder expresses himself. The self-criticism of this view of our chapters can hardly be more suitably given than when Hitzig continues: "Inasmuch as this or that could be set in order otherwise than he imagines, he would not in regard to plans and proposals have resisted obstinately, but would have known how to distinguish the unessential of the execution from the essential of the thing itself. He sketches the future in the form he must wish it to take, in which it really would have the fairest appearance. If the reality falls short of the image, then the idea is defectively realized; but the fault lies in the reality, not in the idea, and Ezekiel is not responsible for it." This, moreover, is merely what already Doederlein and others have held with respect to the closing portion of our book. Similarly Herder: "Ezekiel's manner is to paint an image entire and at length; his mode of conception appears to demand great visions, figures written over on all sides, even tiresome, difficult, symbolical acts, of which his whole book is full. Israel in his wandering upon the mountains of his dispersal, among other tongues and peoples, had need of a prophet such as this one was, etc. So also as regards this temple. Another would have sketched it with soaring figures in lofty utterances; he does so in definite measurements. And not only the temple, but also appurtenances, tribes, administration, land, etc. How far has Israel always, so far as depended on his own efforts, remained below the commands, counsels, and promises of God!" (3) Böttcher has attempted to combine both views, and after him Philippson, who expresses himself to the following effect: "Ezekiel the prophet, sunk in himself, brooding over matters in the distance and in solitude, had not, like Jeremiah, upon whom the immediate reality pressed, viewed the occurrences simply as punishment of defection and degeneracy, but was conscious also of their inward signification, which came to him in the appearance of a vision. Hence he represented the destruction of the temple as a suspension of the relation of revelation between God and Israel; and so much the more necessary was it to represent the restoration of that same relation as the return of God into the restored sanctuary. Now, from the peculiar character of Ezekiel, this necessarily had to assume a form at once ideal and real,—ideal in its entirety as something future, real as individual and special, matter of fact in its appearance." As the "indubitable motive of the prophet," the following is given: "to keep alive in the exiles in the midst of Babylonian idolatry the idea of the one temple, and the priestly institute consecrated to it, as the centre of the religion of the one God; and at the return into Palestine to confirm the life of the people in their calling, by the removal of all elements of strife, and by approximation to the Mosaic state of things." Hengstenberg's view is surprisingly near the above one; he says: "With the exception of the Messianic section in ch. xlvii. 1–12, the fulfilment of all (!) the rest of the prophecy belongs to the times immediately after the return from the Chaldean exile. So must every one of its first hearers and readers have under-

stood it. Jeremiah, whom Ezekiel follows throughout, had prophesied the restoration of the city and temple 70 years after the beginning of the Chaldean servitude, falling in the fourth year of Jehoiakim. Thirty-two years had already elapsed. Forty years after the devastation of Egypt (ch. xxix. 13), the nations visited by the Chaldeans shall get back to their former state. According to ch. xi. 16, the restoration is to follow in a brief space after the destruction of the temple. We have before us a prophecy for which it is essential (!) to give truth and poetry (! !), which contains a kernel of real thoughts, yet does not present them naked, but clothed with flesh and blood, that they may be a counterpoise to the sad reality, because they fill the fancy, that fruitful workshop of despair, with bright (!) images, and thus make it an easier task to live in the word at a time when all that is visible cries aloud, Where is now thy God? The incongruity between the prophecy of Ezekiel and the state of things after the exile, vanishes at once by distinguishing between the thoughts and their clothing, and if we can rightly figure to ourselves the wounds for which the healing plaster is here presented, and at the same time the mental world of the priest (Ezekiel), and the materials given in the circumstances surrounding him, for clothing the higher verities which he had to announce to the people." II. The views which above all look to and keep hold of the objectivity of the divine inspiration of Ezekiel. The very regard which must, in one way or other, be paid to the circumstances under which the people for whom, and the Babylonian exile in which, Ezekiel prophesied, objectivizes in some measure his subjectivity, so that not all the views hitherto cited of our chapters and the ones that follow are to be designated as purely subjective; the properly objective, however, will be, that "the hand of Jehovah was upon him," that he was brought "in visions of God" to the land of Israel. Here the distinction is drawn by his own hand between the prophet of Israel and the fanciful Jewish priest; and not only this, but the unavoidable and irreconcilable alternative presents itself: either Ezekiel was a man of God, or a deceiver, for whom the fact that he had deceived himself also with assumed divine objectivity were no excuse, but would only be his self-condemnation. The case of Ezekiel, for the sake of truth, is too solemn for thinking of "poetic clothing" in the case before us. The subjective for the form before us, is to keep in mind when considering it what that form is. It has pleased God to speak to us through men. If we take full account of the national peculiarity of Israel in general during the whole old covenant, and of the peculiar personality in the case of our vision here, that is, that Ezekiel is the priest-prophet, that he above all other prophets is, as Umbreit says, a "born symbolist" ("in the temple which he erects he makes known his greatness as a symbolist, as well by what he says as by what he passes over in silence"),—if we concede to Umbreit the "surprising skill in popularizing instruction" which he observes in Ezekiel, we shall have to accept as the ultimate ground why Israel was the mediator of the world's salvation, and Ezekiel was chosen to behold the temple of the future, divine wisdom and its purpose for the world, that is, the objective κατ' ἐξοχήν above everything subjective. In accordance with this principle, we have to judge of (1) the view objectivized in this sense of a model for the rebuilding of the temple after the return from the exile, the supporters of which assume a building-plan "issued under divine authority," given by Jehovah through the prophet. Although there is a resemblance between Ex. xxv. 9, 40 and Ezek. xl. 4, yet it is not said to Ezekiel regarding Israel: "according to all that I show thee, the pattern of the dwelling, etc., even so shall ye make it;" the prophet is only to "convey," announce (נָגַד) all that he sees to the house of Israel. From this circumstance, and not because the reality fell short of the idea (HITZIG, HERDER), or, as Philippson adduces here, "the similar fate of so many Mosaic precepts," the fact is explained that the post-exile temple was built without any regard to our vision. Only the fundamental reference to Solomon's temple, which in general obtains in Ezekiel also, meets us in Ezra iii. 12. This fact, the more remarkable considering the nearness of time, shows that ch. xl. 4, soon after it was written, and when fully known, was not regarded as a divine building-specification. We do not need, therefore, to express, as Hengst., "the obvious impossibility of erecting a building according to the specifications here given." The circumstance that the building materials are not given has at least not prevented the temple of Ezekiel from being, with more or less success, constructed and fashioned after his statements. Bunsen says that "the temple here forms a very easily realized, congruous whole, of which an exact outline may be made, as the prophet also has evidently done." Umbreit, too, holds this latter view. And although we have to do not with an architect but with a prophet, yet nothing stands in the way of our believing that the subjectivity of Ezekiel was pre-eminently qualified for this vision, from the fact that he possessed architectural capacity" (Introd. § 7). (2) The symbolical view. It corresponds generally to the character of Holy Writ. (Comp. Lange, Rev. Introd. p. 11.) In particular it pays due regard to the law of Moses, to the part of it relating to worship, the subject here. Especially when the whole worship of Israel is concentrated in the temple, a symbolical view respecting a vision thereof will be quite in place. Thereby only its due right is given to this objective, to the divine idea, in the shape which it has above all assumed in Israelitish worship. The symbolical character, moreover, is specially appropriate for the prophetic writings. As has already been often said and pointed out, the symbolical predominates in Ezekiel; and as to these concluding chapters, Hävernick adduces, as indicating their general character, the description of the circuit of the new temple (ch. xlii. 15 sq.), the representation of the entrance, etc. of the divine glory (ch. xliii. 1 sq.), the river (ch. xlvii. 1 sq. etc.), and observes that "it is just such passages that form the conclusion to the previous description, and hence cast a light on it." Comp. on ch. xliii. 10 sq. But everything architectonic is not a symbol, although everything of that nature will indeed primarily relate to the building to be erected, and will thereby at the same time in some way serve the idea of the whole. This character comes out clearly even in individual statements of number, yet all such measurements are not therefore to be interpreted symbolically. Nay, as the exposition shows, there are here bare numbers, resisting every attempt to trace them back to the idea. It is sufficient in respect to the numbers, that (comp. Umbreit, p. 259 sq.) 4, as "signature not only of regularity but also of the revelation of God in space," *e.g.* in the quadrangle of the temple; 3, "the signature of the divine," *e.g.* in the sets of three gates; 10, "perfection complete in itself," occurring often; likewise the "sacred number" 7; and the number 12 in the tables for preparing the offerings (ch. xl.), represent symbolism. (On the symbolism of numbers, comp. Lange on Rev. Introd. p. 14.) Umbreit rightly maintains: "It is a symbolical temple, notwithstanding the arid and dry description, in which only exact specifications of the number of cubits and the apparently most insignificant calculations and measurings occur;" as he says, "quite in keeping with the poverty of the immediately succeeding age and the dignity of the most significant inwardness." (3) The Messianic view (for which comp. Lange on Kings, p. 60 sq.) is only the taking full advantage of and applying the symbolic view in general. Symbol and type, emblem and pattern, must mutually interpenetrate one another in a law like that of Israel. What separates Israel from the heathen is its law; what qualifies Israel for the whole world is its promise. But now, because of sin, the law has come in between the promise and the fulfilment; that sin becoming the more powerful as transgression may make manifest for faith the grace which alone is still more powerful, and that consequently the necessity of the promise should be the more apparent; that is, the pedagogy of the law (and especially of its ethical part) to Christ. Thus the law of Israel is the theocratic expression of Israel, the servant of God, as be ought to be, and hence prefigures the servant of Jehovah who is the fulfilling of the law, as He is the personal fulfilling of Israel, inasmuch as in Him who was delivered for our transgressions, and raised again for our δικαιωσις, Israel after the Spirit is represented; so that here out of the law relating to worship rise up, as on the one hand sacrifice and the priesthood, so on the other the concentration of the whole of worship in the temple, this parable of the future, with reference to which Christ, John ii., gives the σημειον: Destroy (λυσατε) this temple, and in three days I will raise it up (εγειρω), saying this of the temple of His body; as also the disciples remembered when He had risen from the dead, and as the accusation against Him ran (Matt. xxvi. 61). Accordingly the law, and especially the temple and its service, is σκιαν εχων των μελλοντων; the future σωμα is given in the σωμα του Χριστου (σωμα δε κατηρτισω μου, Heb. x.). "This reference to the future," says Ziegler (in his thoughtful little work on the "historical development of divine revelation"), "is the most dynamical among all the references of the law; its significance for its own time is so weak and unimportant, that it seems to exist solely for the sake of the future, although its office is the opposite of the office of the New Testament, which is formed and abiding in the hearts of men (διακονια της δικαιοσυνης, του πνευματος); still it was a sensible type, a strongly marked and distinctly stamped shadow of the coming substances, and yet, moreover, a veil which concealed it." What has been said shows the typical signification of the vision of Ezekiel, in which the symbolical view of it is completed, and the pedagogic and providential necessity of that form borrowed from the legal worship in which it is enshrined. Here is more than what (as Hengstenberg can say) "suffices to employ the fancy." For the anointed one is τελος του νομου. But as the Messianic view of our chapters is thus justified by the symbolic view, when we have taken into account the law, particularly the law of worship in Israel, so likewise the already (Doct. Reflec. 1) noted connection of ch. xl. sq. with the previous chapters, especially with ch. xxxvii. 26 sq. (p. 351), yields the same result, as also the position after ch. xxxviii. and xxxix. and the relation to this prophecy will have to be taken into consideration. What holds good of ch. xxxvii. 26 sq. will also be a hint for our chapters. But even the Talmudists saw themselves compelled (principally because of the treatment of the law of Moses, to be spoken of presently) to acknowledge "that the exposition of this portion would be first given in Messianic times," as the "best" (according to Philippson) Jewish expositors recognised here "the type of a third temple." The saying of Jesus in John ii. possibly alluded to the exegetical tradition of the Jews. Hävernick accommodates as follows: "The shattered old theocratic forms rather than new ones were above all cognate to the priestly mind of Ezekiel;" so "he sees nothing perish of that which Jehovah has founded for eternity; those forms beam before him revivified, animated with fresh breath, and lit up in the splendour of true glory; he recognises their full realization as coming in first in Messianic times." As errors are still committed, *e.g.* by Schmieder, in the symbolizing of particulars, so the Messianic typology of a Cocceius has deserved, although only in part, the anathema on "mystical allegories," which above all modern criticism utters; for our defect in understanding in respect of many particulars will always have to be conceded. The Christian idea, however, the Old Testament typical symbolizing of which we have here to expound, is not only the idea of Christ, but also the idea of the Christian Church, the kingdom of God in Christ. If the resurrection of the Anointed One comes into consideration in the first respect, so in the latter does the consummation of the kingdom of grace, after its last affliction, into the kingdom of glory; comp. Rev. xxi. 22. The one is as eschatological in the wider, that is, christological in the narrower sense, as the other is eschatological in the narrower, or christological in the wider sense. By the translating of our passage into the higher key of John's Apocalypse, the relation of ch. xl. sq. to ch. xxxviii. xxxix. must be so much the more evident. Comp. Doct. Reflec. on xxxviii. and xxxix. We refer, finally, to what has been said in the Introduction, § 7, that Jehovah's building in Ezekiel here (still more in its already actual reality for the seer, so that what already existed had only to be measured to him) forms the architectonic antithesis to the buildings of Nebuchadnezzar. As the figure of Gog with his people may have presented itself to our prophet through means of Babylon (comp. Doct. Reflec. on ch. xxxviii. xxxix., p. 375), so from that same quarter may have been derived the representation given of the kingdom of God in its victorious opposition to the world. Hitzig, too (as we now first see when treating of the closing chapters), supposes that there probably "flitted before the eyes of the author living in Chaldea, when describing his quadrangle, the capital of the country and the temple of Belus,—the former, like the latter, forming a square, with streets intersecting one another at right angles." Umbreit says of the vision of Ezekiel as a whole: "It is a great thought, which presents itself unadorned to our view in the prophetico-symbolic temple: God henceforth dwells in perfect peace, revealing Himself in the unbounded fulness of His glory, which is returning to Jerusalem, in the purest and most blissful unison with His sanctified people, making Himself known in the living word of progressive, saving, and sanctifying redemption. Everything is placed upon the ample circuit of the temple, whose extended courts receive all people, and through whose high and open gates the King of Glory is to enter in (Ps. xxiv. 7, 9), and then upon the order and harmony of the divine habitation, the well-proportioned building (ch. xlii. 10); and the revelations of the holiest are stored up in the pure, deep water of His word, which in life-giving streams issues from the temple. The stone tables of the law are consumed (?), and the fresh and free fountain of eternal truth streams forth from the temple of the Spirit, quickening and vivifying in land and sea, awakening by its creative and fructifying power a new and mighty race on earth. And thus hast thou, much misjudged yet lofty seer, in the unconscious depth of thy mysteriously flowing language, set up upon the great, undistinguishing (comp. Jer. xxxi. 34), well-proportioned, and beautifully compacted building, a type of the simple yet lofty temple of Christ, from which flows the spiritual fountain of life!" From this Messianic view of the section we have to reject (4) the chiliastic-literal view, according to which Ezekiel describes what may be called either the Jewish temple of the future, or the Jewish future of the Christian Church. It is interesting to observe what kind of spirits meet together here in the flesh; *e.g.* Baumgarten and Auberlen, Hofmann and Volck (who acts as champion for him, and that partly with striking power of demonstration against Kliefoth), are combined here only in general because they make the community of God at our Lord's *Parousia* to be an Israelite one. Comp. moreover, p. 357 and § 10 of the Introduction. Auberlen (*Daniel and the Revelation of John*, p. 348 sq., Clark's tr.) expresses the apocalyptic phantasm as follows: "Israel brought back to his own land becomes the people of God in a far higher and more inward sense than before, etc.; a new period of revelation begins, the Spirit of God is richly poured forth, and a fulness of gracious gifts is conferred, such as the apostolic Church possessed typically" (!). (One can hardly go farther in the delusion of "deeper" knowledge of Scripture than to make primitive and original Christianity a type of Judaism!) "But this rich spirit-imparted life finds its completed representation in a priestly as well as in a kingly manner. That which in the ages of the Old Covenant obtained only outwardly in the letter, and that which conversely in the age of the Church withdrew itself into inward, hidden spirituality, will then in a pneumatic (!) manner assume also an outward appearance and form. In the Old Covenant the whole national life of Israel in its various manifestations — household and state, labour and art, literature and culture—was determined by religion, but only in an external legal manner; the Church, again, has to insist above all on a renewal of the heart, and must leave those outward forms of life free, enjoining it on the conscience of each individual to glorify Christ in these relations also; but in the millennial kingdom all these spheres of life will be truly Christianized from within outwardly. Thus looked at, it will no longer be offensive (?) to say that the Mosaic ceremonial law corresponds to the priesthood of Israel, and the civil law to its kingship. The Gentile Church could adopt only the moral law; so certainly the sole means of influence assigned to her is that which works inwardly,—the preaching of the word, the exercise of the prophetic office."

(The Romish Church, however, has known how to serve itself heir *satis superque* to the Jewish ceremonial law!) "But when once the priesthood and the kingship arise again, then also—without prejudice to the principles laid down in the Epistle to the Hebrews (?)—the ceremonial and civil law of Moses will unfold its spiritual depths in the cultus and the constitution of the millennial kingdom (Matt. v. 17–19). The present is still the time of preaching, but then the time of the liturgy shall have come, which presupposes a congregation consisting solely of converted people," etc. etc. When Hengstenberg calls such interpretation "altogether unhappy," that is the least that one can say about it; but even that could not have been said if Ezekiel's descriptions really had the "Utopian character" which Hengstenberg attributes to them. He, however, justly animadverts upon the incongruity of expecting the restoration of the temple, the Old Testament festivals, the bloody sacrifices (!!), and the priesthood of the sons of Zadok, within the bounds of the New Covenant. Comp. Keil, p. 500 sq., who, both from the prophetic parts of the Old Testament and from the New, refutes at length the notion of a transformation of Canaan before the last judgment, and a kingdom of glory at Jerusalem before the end of the world. (Auberlen, who looks on the "first resurrection" as a "bodily coming forth of the whole community of believers from their hitherto invisibility with Christ in heaven," makes the now "transformed Church again return thither with Christ, and the saints rule from heaven over the earth;" and from this he concludes that "the intercourse between the world above and the world below will then be more active and free," etc. Hofmann's transference of the glorified Church to earth, and his further connecting therewith the national regeneration of Israel, Auberlen declares to be "incompatible with the whole of Old Testament prophecy, to say nothing of its internal improbability.")

ADDITIONAL NOTE ON CH. XL.–XLVI.

[Dr. Fairbairn's classification of the views which have been held of Ezekiel's closing vision generally, and in particular of the description contained in it respecting the temple, is as follows: 1. The *historico-literal* view, "which takes all as a prosaic description of what had existed in the times immediately before the captivity, in connection with the temple which is usually called Solomon's." 2. The *historico-ideal* view, that "the pattern exhibited to Ezekiel differed materially from anything that previously existed, and presented for the first time what *should have been* after the return from the captivity, though, from the remissness and corruption of the people, it never was properly realized." 3. The *Jewish-carnal* view, held by certain Jewish writers, who maintain that Ezekiel's description was actually followed, although in a necessarily imperfect manner, by the children of the captivity, and afterwards by Herod; but that "it waits to be properly accomplished by the Messiah, who, when He appears, shall cause the temple to be reared precisely as here described, and carry out all the other subordinate arrangements,"—a view which, strangely enough, is in substance held also by certain parties in the Christian Church, who "expect the vision to receive a complete and literal fulfilment at the period of Christ's second coming." 4. The *Christian-spiritual* or typical view, "according to which the whole representation was not intended to find either in Jewish or Christian times an express and formal realization, but was a grand, complicated symbol of the good God had in reserve for His Church, especially under the coming dispensation of the gospel. From the Fathers downwards this has been the prevailing view in the Christian Church. The greater part have held it, to the exclusion of every other; in particular, among the Reformers and their successors, Luther, Calvin, Capellus, Cocceius, Pfeiffer, followed by the majority of evangelical divines of our own country."

To this fourth and last view Dr. Fairbairn himself strenuously adheres, expounding, illustrating, and defending it at considerable length, and with marked ability and success. We give his remarks in a somewhat condensed form.

"1. First of all, it is to be borne in mind that the description purports to be a vision,—a scheme of things exhibited to the mental eye of the prophet 'in the visions of God.' This alone marks it to be of an ideal character, as contradistinguished from anything that ever had been, or ever was to be found in actual existence after the precise form given to it in the description. Such we have uniformly seen to be the character of the earlier visions imparted to the prophet. The things described in chap. i.–iii. and viii.–xi., which were seen by him 'in the visions of God,' were all of this nature. They presented a vivid picture of what either then actually existed or was soon to take place, but in a form quite different from the external reality. Not the very image or the formal appearance of things was given, but rather a compressed delineation of their inward being and substance. And such, too, was found to be the case with other portions, which are of an entirely similar nature, though not expressly designated visions; such, for example, as ch. iv., xii., xxi., all containing delineations and precepts, as if speaking of what was to be done and transacted in real life, and yet it is necessary to understand them as ideal representations, exhibiting the character, but not the precise form and lineaments, of the coming transactions. . . . Never at any period of His Church has God given laws and ordinances to it simply by vision; and when Moses was commissioned to give such in the wilderness, his authority to do so was formally based on the ground of his office being different from the ordinarily prophetical, and of his instructions being communicated otherwise than by vision (Num. xii. 6). So that to speak by way of vision, and at the same time in the form of precept, as if enjoining laws and ordinances materially differing from those of Moses, was itself a palpable and incontrovertible proof of the ideal character of the revelation. It was a distinct testimony that Ezekiel was no new lawgiver coming to modify or supplant what had been written by him with whom God spake face to face upon the mount.

"2. What has been said respecting the *form* of the prophet's communication, is confirmed by the *substance* of it—as there is much in this that seems obviously designed to force on us the conviction of its ideal character. There are things in the description which, taken literally, are in the highest degree improbable, and even involve natural impossibilities." Thus, for example, "according to the most exact modes of computation, the prophet's measurements give for the outer wall of the temple a square of an English mile and about a seventh on each side, and for the whole city [*i.e.* including the oblation of holy ground for the prince, the priests, and the Levites] a space of between three and four thousand square miles. Now there is no reason to suppose that the boundaries of the ancient city exceeded two miles and a half in circumference (see Robinson's *Researches*, vol. i.), while here the circumference of the wall of the temple is nearly twice as much." And then, taking the land of Canaan at the largest, as including all that Israel ever possessed on both sides of the Jordan, it amounted only to somewhere between ten and eleven thousand square miles. Surely "the allotment of a portion nearly equal to one-half of the whole for the prince, the priests, and Levites is a manifest proof of the ideal character of the representation; the more especially, when we consider that that sacred portion is laid off in a regular square, with the temple on Mount Zion in the centre. . . . The measurements of the prophet were made to involve a literal incongruity, as did also the literal extravagances of the vision in chap. xxxviii. xxxix., that men might be forced to look for something else than a literal accomplishment. . . .

"3. Some, perhaps, may be disposed to imagine that, as they expect certain physical changes to be effected upon the land before the prophecy can be carried into fulfilment, these may be adjusted in such a manner as to admit of the prophet's measurements being literally applied. It is impossible, however, to admit such a supposition. For the boundaries of the land itself are given, not new boundaries of the prophet's own, but those originally laid down by Moses. And as the measurements of the temple and city are out of all proportion to these, no alterations can be made on the physical condition of the country that could bring the one into proper agreement with the other. Then there are other things in the description, which, if they could not of themselves so conclusively prove the impossibility of a literal sense as the consideration arising from the measurements, lend great force to this consideration, and, on any other supposition than their being parts of an ideal representation, must wear an improbable and fanciful aspect. Of this kind is the distribution of the remainder of the land in equal portions among the twelve tribes, in parallel sections, running straight across from east to west, without any respect to the particular circumstances of each, or their relative numbers. More especially, the assignment of five of these parallel sections to the south of the city, which, after making allowance for the sacred portion, would leave at the farthest a breadth of only three or four miles a-piece! Of the same kind also is the supposed separate existence of the twelve tribes, which *now*, at least, can scarcely be regarded otherwise than a natural impossibility, since it is an ascertained fact that such separate tribeships no longer exist; the course of Providence has been ordered so as to destroy them; and once destroyed, they cannot possibly be reproduced. . . . Of the same kind, farther, is 'the very high mountain' on which the vision of the temple was presented to the eye of the prophet; for as this unquestionably refers to the old site of the temple, the little eminence on which it stood could only be designated thus in a moral or ideal, and not in a literal sense. Finally, of the same kind is the account given of the stream issuing from the eastern threshold of the temple, and flowing into the Dead Sea, which, both for the rapidity of its increase and for the quality of its waters, is unlike anything that ever was known in Judea, or in any other region of the world. Putting all together, it seems as if the prophet had taken every possible precaution, by the general character of the delineation, to debar the expectation of a literal fulfilment; and I should despair of being able in any case to draw the line of demarcation between the ideal and the literal, if the circumstances now mentioned did not warrant us in looking for something else than a fulfilment according to the letter of the vision.

"4. Yet there is the farther consideration to be mentioned, viz. that the vision of the prophet, as it must, if understood literally, imply the ultimate restoration of the ceremonials of Judaism, so it inevitably places the prophet in direct contradiction to the writers of the New Testament. The entire and total cessation of the peculiarities of Jewish worship is as plainly taught by our Lord and His apostles as language could do it, and on grounds which are not of temporary, but of permanent validity and force. The word of Christ to the woman of Samaria: 'Woman, believe me, the hour cometh when ye shall neither in this mountain, nor yet at Jerusalem, worship the Father,' is alone conclusive of the matter; for if it means anything worthy of so solemn an asseveration, it indicates that Jerusalem was presently to lose its distinctive character, and a mode of worship to be introduced capable of being celebrated in any other place as well as there. But when we find the apostles afterwards contending for the cessation of the Jewish ritual, because suited only to a church 'in bondage to the elements of the world,' and consisting of what were comparatively but 'weak and beggarly elements;' and when, in the Epistle to the Hebrews, we also find the disannulling of the Old Covenant, with its Aaronic priesthood and carnal ordinances, argued at length, and especially 'because of the weakness and unprofitableness thereof,' that is, its own inherent imperfections, we must certainly hold, either that the shadowy services of Judaism are finally and for ever gone, or that these sacred writers very much misrepresented their Master's mind regarding them. No intelligent and sincere Christian can adopt the latter alternative; he ought, therefore, to rest in the former. And he *will* do so, in the rational persuasion, that as in the wise administration of God there must ever be a conformity in the condition of men to the laws and ordinances under which they are placed, so the carnal institutions, which were adapted to the Church's pupilage, can never, in the nature of things, be in proper correspondence with her state of manhood, perfection, and millennial glory. To regard the prophet here as exhibiting a prospect founded on such an unnatural conjunction, is to ascribe to him the foolish part of seeking to have the new wine of the kingdom put back into the old bottles again, and while occupying himself with the highest hopes of the Church, treating her only to a showy spectacle of carnal superficialities. We have far too high ideas of the spiritual insight and calling of an Old Testament prophet, to believe that it was possible for him to act so unseemly a part, or contemplate a state of things so utterly anomalous. And we are perfectly justified by the explicit statement of Scripture in saying, that 'a temple with sacrifices now would be the most daring denial of the all-sufficiency of the sacrifice of Christ, and of the efficacy of the blood of His atonement. He who sacrificed before, confessed the Messiah; he who should sacrifice now, would most solemnly and sacrilegiously deny Him.'[1]

"5. Holding the description, then, in this last vision to be conclusively of an ideal character, we advance a step farther, and affirm that the idealism here is precisely of the same kind as that which appeared in some of the earlier visions,—visions that must necessarily have already passed into fulfilment, and which therefore may justly be regarded as furnishing a key to the right understanding of the one before us. The leading characteristic of those earlier visions, which coincide in nature with this, we have found to be the historical cast of their idealism. The representation of things to come is thrown into the mould of something similar in the past, and presented as simply a reproduction of the old, or a returning back again of what is past, only with such diversities as might be necessary to adapt it to the altered circumstances contemplated; while still the thing meant was, not that the outward form, but that the essential nature of the past should revive." In this connection, Dr. Fairbairn refers to the vision of the iniquity-bearing in ch. iv.; to the sojourn in the wilderness spoken of in ch. xx.; to the ideal representation given of the king of Tyre in ch. xxviii. 11–19; and to the prediction of Egypt's humiliation in ch. xxix. 1–16. "Now in all these cases," he goes on to remark, "of an apparent, we should entirely err if we looked for an actual repetition of the past. It is the *nature* of the transactions and events, not their precise form or external conditions, that is unfolded to our view. The representation is of an ideal kind, and the history of the past merely supplies the mould into which it is cast. The spiritual eye of the prophet discerned the old, as to its real character, becoming alive again in the new. He saw substantially the same procedure followed again, and the unchangeable Jehovah must display the uniformity of His character and dealings by visiting it with substantially

[1] Douglas' *Structure of Prophecy*, p. 71.

the same treatment. If, now, we bring the light furnished by those earlier revelations of the prophet, in respect to which we can compare the prediction with the fulfilment, so as to read by its help, and according to its instruction, the vision before us, we shall only be giving the prophet the benefit of the common rule, of interpreting a writer by a special respect to his own peculiar method, and explaining the more obscure by the more intelligible parts of his writings. In all the other cases referred to, where his representation takes the form of a revival of the past, we see it is the spirit and not the letter of the representation that is mainly to be regarded; and why should we expect it to be otherwise here? In this remarkable vision we have the old produced again, in respect to what was most excellent and glorious in Israel's past condition,—its temple, with every necessary accompaniment of sacredness and attraction — the symbol of the divine presence within — the ministrations and ordinances proceeding in due order without—the prince and the priesthood—everything, in short, required to constitute the beau-ideal of a sacred commonwealth according to the ancient patterns of things. But, at the same time, there are such changes and alterations superinduced upon the old as sufficiently indicate that something far greater and better than the past was concealed under this antiquated form. Not the coming realities, in their exact nature and glorious fulness—not even the very image of these things, could the prophet as yet distinctly unfold. While the old dispensation lasted, they must be thrown into the narrow and imperfect shell of its earthly relations. But those who lived under that dispensation might get the liveliest idea they were able to obtain of the brighter future, by simply letting their minds rest on the past, as here modified and shaped anew by the prophet; just as now, the highest notions *we* can form to ourselves of the state of glory is by conceiving the best of the Church's present condition refined and elevated to heavenly perfection. Exhibited at the time the vision was, and constructed as it is, one should no more expect to see a visible temple realizing the conditions, and a reoccupied Canaan, after the regular squares and parallelograms of the prophet, than in the case of Tyre to find her monarch literally dwelling in Eden, and, as a cherub, occupying the immediate presence of God, or to behold Israel sent back again to make trial of Egyptian bondage and the troubles of the desert. Whatever might be granted in providence of an outward conformity to the plan of the vision, it should only be regarded as a pledge of the far greater good really contemplated, and a help to faith in waiting for its proper accomplishment.

"6. But still, looking to the manifold and minute particulars given in the description, some may be disposed to think it highly improbable that anything short of an exact and literal fulfilment should have been intended. Had it been only a general sketch of a city and temple, as in the 60th chapter of Isaiah, and other portions of prophecy, they could more easily enter into the ideal character of the description, and understand how it might chiefly point to the better things of the gospel dispensation. But with so many exact measurements before them, and such an infinite variety of particulars of all sorts, they cannot conceive how there can be a proper fulfilment without corresponding objective realities. It is precisely here, however, that we are met by another very marked characteristic of our prophet. Above all the prophetical writers, he is distinguished, as we have seen, for his numberless particularisms. What Isaiah depicts in a few bold and graphic strokes, as in the case of Tyre, for example, Ezekiel spreads over a series of chapters, filling up the picture with all manner of details,—not only telling us of her singular greatness, but also of every element, far and near, that contributed to produce it, and not only predicting her downfall, but coupling it with every conceivable circumstance that might add to its mortification and completeness. We have seen the same features strikingly exhibited in the prophecy on Egypt, in the description of Jerusalem's condition and punishment under the images of the boiling caldron (ch. xxiv.) and the exposed infant (ch. xvi.), in the vision of the iniquity-bearing (ch. iv.), in the typical representation of going into exile (ch. xiii.), and indeed in all the more important delineations of the prophet, which, even when descriptive of ideal scenes, are characterized by such minute and varied details as to give them the appearance of a most definitely shaped and lifelike reality.

". . . Considering his peculiar manner, it was no more than might have been expected, that when going to present a grand outline of the good in store for God's Church and people, the picture should be drawn with the fullest detail. If he has done so on similar but less important occasions, he could not fail to do it here, when rising to the very top and climax of all his revelations. For it is pre-eminently by means of the minuteness and completeness of his descriptions that he seeks to impress our minds with a feeling of the divine certainty of the truth disclosed in them, and to give, as it were, weight and body to our apprehensions.

"7. In farther support of the view we have given, it may also be asked, whether the feeling against a spiritual understanding of the vision, and a demand for outward scenes and objects literally corresponding to it, does not spring, to a large extent, from false notions regarding the ancient temple and its ministrations and ordinances of worship, as if these possessed an independent value apart from the spiritual truths they symbolically expressed? On the contrary the temple, with all that belonged to it, was an embodied representation of divine realities. It presented to the eye of the worshippers a manifold and varied instruction respecting the things of God's kingdom. And it was by what they saw embodied in those visible forms and external transactions that the people were to learn how they should think of God, and act toward Him in the different relations and scenes of life—when they were absent from the temple, as well as when they were near and around it. It was an image and emblem of the kingdom of God itself, whether viewed in respect to the temporary dispensation then present, or to the grander development everything was to receive at the advent of Christ. And it was one of the capital errors of the Jews, in all periods of their history, to pay too exclusive a regard to the mere externals of the temple and its worship, without discerning the spiritual truths and principles that lay concealed under them. But such being the case, the necessity for an outward an literal realization of Ezekiel's plan obviously falls to the ground. For if all connected with it was ordered and arranged chiefly for its symbolical value at any rate, why might not the description itself be given forth for the edification and comfort of the Church, on account of what it contained of symbolical instruction? Even if the plan had been fitted and designed for being actually reduced to practice, it would still have been principally with a view to its being a mirror in which to see reflected the mind and purposes of God. But if so, why might not the delineation itself be made to serve for such a mirror? In other words, why might not God have spoken to His Church of good things to come by the wise adjustment of a symbolical plan? . . . Let the same rules be applied to the interpretation of Ezekiel's visionary temple which, on the express warrant of Scripture, we apply to Solomon's literal one, and it will be impossible to show why, so far as the ends of instruction are concerned, the same great purposes might not be served by the simple delineation of the one, as by the actual construction of the other.[1]

"It is also not to be overlooked, in support of this line of reflection, that in other and earlier communications Ezekiel makes much account of the symbolical character of the temple and the things belonging to it. It is as a priest he gives us to understand at the outset, and for the purpose of doing priest-like service for the covenant-people, that he received his prophetical calling, and had visions of God displayed to him (see on ch. i. 1–3). In the series of visions contained in ch. viii.–xi., the guilt of the people was represented as concentrating itself there, and determining God's procedure in regard to it. By the divine glory being seen to leave the temple was symbolized the withdrawing of God's gracious presence from Jerusalem; and by His promising to become for a little a sanctuary to the pious remnant in Chaldea, it was virtually said that the temple, as to its spiritual reality, was going to be transferred thither. This closing vision comes now as the happy counterpart of those earlier ones, giving promise of a complete rectification of preceding evils and disorders. It assured the Church that all should yet be set right again; nay, that greater and better things should be found in the future than had ever been known in the past,—things too great and good to be presented merely under the old symbolical forms; these must be modelled and adjusted anew to adapt them to the higher objects in prospect. Nor is Ezekiel at all singular in this. The other prophets represent the coming future with a reference to the symbolical places and ordinances of the past, adjusting and modifying these to suit their immediate design. Thus Jeremiah says, in ch. xxxi. 38–40: 'Behold, the days come, saith the Lord, that the city shall be built to the Lord from the gate of Hananeel to the corner gate. And the measuring line shall go forth opposite to it still farther over the hill Gareb (the hill of the leprous), and shall compass about to Goath (the place of execution). And the whole valley of the dead bodies, and of the ashes, and all the fields to the brook Kedron, unto the corner of the horse-gate toward the east, shall be holy to the Lord.' That is, there shall be a rebuilt Jerusalem in token of the revival of God's cause, in consequence of which even the places formerly unclean shall become holiness to the Lord: not only shall the loss be recovered, but also the evil inherent in the past purged out, and the cause of righteousness made completely triumphant. The sublime passage in Isa. lx. is entirely parallel as to its general import. And in the two last chapters of Revelation we have a quite similar vision to the one before us, employed to set forth the ultimate condition of the redeemed Church. There are differences in the one as compared with the other, precisely as in the vision of Ezekiel there are differences as compared with anything that existed under the Old Covenant. In particular, while the temple forms the very heart and centre of Ezekiel's plan, in John's no temple whatever was to be seen. But in the two descriptions the same truth is symbolized, though in the last it appears in a state of more perfect development than in the other. The temple in Ezekiel, with God's glory returned to it, bespoke God's presence among His people to sanctify and bless them; the no-temple in John indicated that such a select spot was no longer needed, that the gracious presence of God was everywhere seen and felt. It is the same truth in both, only in the latter represented, in accordance with the genius of the new dispensation, as less connected with the circumstantials of place and form.

"8. It only remains to be stated, that in the interpretation of the vision we must keep carefully in mind the circumstances in which it was given, and look at it, not as from a New, but as from an Old Testament point of view. We must throw ourselves back as far as possible into the position of the prophet himself. We must think of him as having just seen the divine fabric which had been reared in the sacred and civil constitution of Israel dashed in pieces, and apparently become a hopeless wreck. But in strong faith in Jehovah's word, and with divine insight into His future purposes, he sees that that never can perish which carries in its bosom the element of God's unchangeableness; that the hand of the Spirit will assuredly be applied to raise up the old anew; and not only that, but also that it shall be inspired with fresh life and vigour, enabling it to burst the former limits, and rise into a greatness and perfection and majesty never known or conceived of in the past. He speaks, therefore, chiefly of gospel times, but as one still dwelling under the veil, and uttering the language of legal times. And of the substance of his communication, both as to its general correspondence with the past and its difference in particular parts, we submit the following summary, as given by Hävernick:—'1. In the gospel times there is to be on the part of Jehovah a solemn occupation anew of His sanctuary, in which the entire fulness of the divine glory shall dwell and manifest itself. At the last there is to rise a new temple, diverse from the old, to be made every way suitable to that grand and lofty intention, and worthy of it; in particular, of vast compass for the new community, and with a holiness stretching over the entire extent of the temple, so that in this respect there should no longer be any distinction between the different parts. Throughout, every-

[1] See the *Typology of Scripture*, vol. i. ch. i. and ii., for the establishment of the principles referred to regarding the tabernacle; and vol. ii. part iii., for the application of them to particular parts.

thing is subjected to the most exact and particular appointments; individual parts, and especially such as had formerly remained indeterminate, obtain now an immediate divine sanction; so that every idea of any kind of arbitrariness must be altogether excluded from this temple. Accordingly, this sanctuary is the thoroughly sufficient, perfect manifestation of God for the salvation of His people (ch. xl.–xliii. 12). 2. From this sanctuary, as from the new centre of all religious life, there gushes forth an unbounded fulness of blessings upon the people, who in consequence attain to a new condition. There come also into being a new glorious worship, a truly acceptable priesthood and theocratical ruler, and equity and righteousness reign among the entire community, who, being purified from all stains, rise indeed to possess the life that is in God (ch. xliii. 13–xlvii. 12). 3. To the people who have become renewed by such blessings, the Lord gives the land of promise; Canaan is a second time divided among them, where, in perfect harmony and blessed fellowship, they serve the living God, who abides and manifests Himself among them'[1] (ch. xlvii. 13–xlviii.)."—FAIRBAIRN'S *Ezekiel*, pp. 436–450.—W. F.]

5. In connection with the wall with which the description begins, mention is forthwith made (ch. xl. 5) of the "house." This makes clear in the outset what is the principal building, to which all else is subordinate, although the wall is called a "building." However large, then, that which the wall comprehends may appear to be,—and it is said in ver. 2 to be "a city-like building,"—the "house" is still the kernel. Comp. the measuring from it in ver. 7 sq. Hence the symbolized idea is the dwelling of Jehovah as a permanent one, especially when we compare ch. xxxvii. 26 sq. As type, the realization of the idea is to be found in the Word become flesh (John i. 14), as also the καὶ νῦν ἐστιν (John iv. 23) farther shows that the worship in spirit and in truth, and thereby the fulfilling of the worship at Jerusalem, has come with Christ. Salvation (ἡ σωτηρία) is of the Jews, as our vision also sets forth in an architectonic form; they worship what they know. But as the law was given by Moses, so grace and truth came by Jesus Christ. The original influence of the sanctuary on the first constituting of Israel as a people through the making of a divine covenant is still held by in ch. xxxvii. 26 sq. (Yes, Israel is Jehovah's family, His house, εἰς τὰ ἴδια ἦλθε, John i. 11; Jehovah's covenant with Israel is a marriage-covenant, Ezek. xvi.) The visibility of Jehovah's dwelling, even in the vision here, although spiritual, must be looked on as a pledge of the entire relation of Jehovah to Israel, and especially of the promise of the Messiah. This is the sacramental character of Ezekiel's vision of the temple specially insisted on by Hengstenberg. But the temple as the abode of Jehovah is a place of farther revelation, for Jehovah is the Self-revealing One. The very name Jehovah contains a pledge for the whole future of the kingdom of God, the Church of the future. Now this name, as is well known, coincides most essentially and intimately with the destination of this "house;" Ezekiel repeatedly emphasizes the fact that it is the name of His holiness, just as in connection therewith the sanctification of Israel is again and again expressed. Now, as this expresses also the ultimate aim of all Jehovah's revelation in Israel, we must have got before us in the sanctuary the perspective to the end of God's way with Israel and mankind in general, the vision of Israel fulfilling its destiny of being God's tabernacle with men, and the consummation of the world in glory, Rev. xxi. xxii. But the holiness of Jehovah, the sanctification of Israel, is signified forthwith by the wall "round about the house."

6. The significance of the wall, however, comes first into consideration in respect to the court of the people, so that in special the sanctification of Israel as the end and object of Jehovah's dwelling in their midst is before all thus symbolically expressed. If the "house" is the central point of the whole, still the court completes the idea of the house; as we have the temple in its entirety, as it was meant to be, only when it has the two courts conjoined with it. The reference to the city, and farther to the whole land, which undoubtedly was always contained in the idea of the court, is moreover expressly given shape to in Ezekiel (comp. ch. xlviii.). The court here represents the Israel in the widest extent that appears before Jehovah, as it lives in the light of His countenance and of intercourse with Him; that is to say, it refers to the idea proper of a holy people. When, accordingly, the visionary-prophetic description in Ezekiel exhibits a striking difference from the brevity, incompleteness, and indefiniteness of the historical account in the books of Kings and Chronicles, this indicates, as respects the idea, another Israel than the people had hitherto been. Hävernick remarks on "the wide compass, in order to contain the new community," and "the sanctuary extending itself on all sides of the temple indiscriminately," "that which was formerly undefined is now," as he says, "to receive a higher, a divine sanction." Bähr, speaking of Solomon's temple, says that the "almost total indefiniteness" of its court is owing to its "human character" in contrast to the idea and purpose of the house, and that even the court of the tabernacle, although measured and defined more exactly than that of the temple, shows numbers and measurements which indicate "imperfection and incompleteness." This latter statement might possibly give a hint as to Ezekiel's description of the courts of the temple, which is, on the contrary, so exact and detailed, and would at least be plainer than what Bähr says of the human as "not divine," etc., while yet he must concede to the court a mediate divineness. Israel in the wilderness might, as Jehovah's host, as the people under His most special guidance, still in some measure stamp this relation on the court of the tabernacle. In Solomon's temple, on the contrary, the self-development, left more to the freedom of the people, especially as they now had kings like other nations, and when their position under Solomon was so influential, would be expressed in the characteristic indefiniteness of the people's part in the sanctuary. But the Israel of the future, Ezekiel in fine would say, will be exactly and distinctly Jehovah's possession. Hävernick (and Bähr too) cites for the conformation of the court, "shaping itself according to the need of the people and the times," its well-known division by Solomon into two courts. After referring to 2 Chron. xx. 5, and the various *annexes*, the cells, and the frequent defilement of this locality (2 Kings xxiii. 11, 12), he concludes

[1] Hävernick, *Comm.* p. 623.

thus: "The treading of the courts (Isa. i. 12) has now come to an end; the repentant people are ashamed of their sins, and draw near to their God in a new spirit, Ezek. xliii. 10. The new condition of the courts is a figure, an expression of the new condition of the community. (Comp. Zech. iii. 7; Rev. xi. 2.) Thus in Ezekiel's symbolism the new garnishing of the courts comes to view as the quickening anew, the glorious restoration of the community of Israel." [Comp. additional note on p. 388.—W. F.]

7. But the description in our vision begins with the gates, dwelling specially on the east gate. For the copiousness with which the gates are described, comp. ch. xliii. 11, xlviii. 31 sq. Hävernick, against Böttcher, dwells on their significance (p. 641 sq.); makes them since Solomon have acquired under his successors the "disturbing character of the incidental;" remarks that the law says nothing definitely regarding them; points out the profane use to which they were put (Jer. xx. 2); and maintains that, on the contrary, "the prophet assigns to them a definite relation to the whole of the building, so that they are thoroughly in conformity with the idea of the building." But the contrast to ch. viii. and those that follow is to be very specially observed. "Brought to the gates of the temple, the prophet had been witness of the idol-worship prevalent there. And he had seen the Shechinah departing out of the east gate. To this we have now a beautiful and complete contrast. Henceforth Jehovah will no longer see the holy passages in and out so contemptuously desecrated and defiled (ch. xliii. 7 sq.); on the contrary, the holy bands that keep the feast and offer sacrifice shall go in and out with the prince of the people in their midst (ch. xlvi. 8 sq.; comp. Rev. xxi. 25 sq.). But above all, the glory of Jehovah shall enter in by the east gate (ch. xliii. 1 sq.). Hence this gate is the pattern for all the others," etc.

8. From the relation on the whole to the temple of Solomon, Bunsen thinks that "in general the old temple was the model;" only, on the one hand, the disposition of the parts was "simpler and less showy," and on the other, "an effort was exhibited to attain to symmetry in the proportions and regularity in general." While Tholuck and others remark on "the colossal size" in different respects, as indicating the pre-eminence of the future community, Hengstenberg finds throughout "always very moderate dimensions." Unmistakeably there is a reference throughout to the temple which Ezekiel had seen with his own eyes; this explains the brevity and incompleteness partially attaching to the description, although in respect to the sanctuary proper this peculiarity of Ezekiel, who is otherwise so pictorial, demands some farther explanation. That the knowledge of the temple, whenever it could be supposed, is supposed in our vision (comp. on ch. xli.), especially when what was seen presented itself, as it were, in short-hand to the prophet, is only what we should naturally expect. But it corresponded also to the typology of Solomon and the glorious age of Solomon, which had entered so deeply into the consciousness of Israel, and was so popular, when Solomon's temple forms the foil for the still future revelation of glory and the form it assumes. Ezekiel's vision presupposes, indeed, that which it passes over in silence, but certainly not always that which it suppresses, as having to be supplied from the days of Solomon. A supposition of this kind is least of all permissible for the metallic ornaments, of which nothing whatever is said in passages in which, on the contrary, *e.g.* ch. xli. 22, what is made "of wood" is particularly mentioned, or when explanations are made, such, for example, as: "This is the table which is before Jehovah.". The old is presupposed, and also something new and different is inserted in the old when not put in its place. What Hävernick observes generally regarding the use made of the sacred symbols of the Old Testament and the allusions to the law by our prophet, may be applied to the way in which reference is made to Solomon's temple and the knowledge of it supposed: "He lives therein with his whole soul, but by the Spirit of God he is led beyond the merely legal consciousness, he rises superior to the legal symbolism," etc. In the prophetic description in the chapters before us, we can perceive a struggle as of a dawning day with the clouds of morning; and if something testifies to the derivation of our vision from a higher source than a fancy, however pious, would be, we may take that something to be the sudden advent of peculiar and quite unexpected lights, which have in them at least something strange and surprising in the case of Ezekiel, who was not only familiar with ancestral tenets and priestly tradition, but strongly attached to both. One might sometimes say a less than Solomon is here (Matt. xii. 42), and yet not be satisfied with Hengstenberg's reference to the troublous times in which temple and city were to be rebuilt, but (as Umbreit beautifully says) will feel constrained to take still more into consideration the "worth of the most significant inwardness" for "the poverty of the immediately succeeding times," in view of "the new temple for the new covenant," so that whatever of "apparently meagre simplicity" attaches to our temple-vision may have to be read according to the rule given in Matt. vi. 29. Umbreit aptly says: "In the interior of the abode of the Holy One of Israel, quite a different appearance indeed is presented from that in Solomon's temple, and the splendour of gold and brilliant hues is in vain sought for therein; no special mention is made of the sacred vessels, and only the altar of incense is changed into a table of the Lord, which, instead of all other symbols, simply suggests the purely spiritual impartation of the divine life. The ark of the covenant was destroyed by the fire of God, and our prophet no more than Jeremiah cared to know about a new one being made, as also, indeed, it was actually wanting in the so-called second temple. It is enough that the cherubim resume their place in the sanctuary, and, entering through the open doors, now fill the whole empty house, in which the distinctions of the old temple are very significantly left out; for we no longer see the veils, and the whole temple has become a holy of holies." In the same strain Hävernick says: "If Jehovah wills to dwell among a new people, He must do so in a new manner, although in one analogous to the former. It is the same temple, but its precincts have become different, in order to contain a much more numerous people; and all the arrangements and adjustments here testify to the faithfulness and zeal with which the Lord is sought and served. The whole sacred temple area has become a holy of holies; in this temple there is no place for the ark of the cove-

nant (Jer. iii. 16), instead of which comes the full revelation of the Shechinah." On the one hand, the legal form of worship is retained in every iota, or tacitly supposed; on the other, a new element, as with ch. xli. 22, almost exactly what Christendom calls "the Lord's table," sheds its light over everything previously existing. On the one hand, the numbers and proportions express a magnitude and beauty, a majestic harmony, surpassing both the "tent" and the "temple" (ch. xli. 1); on the other, there are unmistakeable indications, as respects the μορφη θεου, in the simplicity and plainness of the whole and the parts, of an ἐν ὁμοιωματι ἀνθρωπων γενομενος, a κενωσις, and ταπεινωσις, and here and there even a hint is perceptible of the outward poverty of the Church in the last times. Moreover, as the temple of Ezekiel consolingly presented to those who returned from the exile, approaching the more closely to them as respects its human character, its divinity and spirituality in their temple building, so again it contained a sacred criticism on the splendid edifice erected by Herod 500 years later (of the *immensa opulentia* of which the Roman Tacitus speaks),—a criticism which He who walked in this last temple of Israel, and who was Himself the fulfilling of the temple, completed κατα πνευμα, and as κρισις, κριμα.

9. The treatment of the side-building (ch. xli. 5 sq.), especially in its connection with the temple-house, and the detailed description, kept now first in due correspondence with the sanctuary, of the building on the gizrah (ch. xli. 12 sq.), are worthy of observation, although not so important as Hävernick makes them. With a touch of human nature, Hengstenberg connects the side-chambers with Ezekiel's dearest youthful reminiscences, reminding us at the same time of Samuel, who, as well as Eli, had even his bedroom in such a side-chamber of the tabernacle. According to Hävernick, Ezekiel's description is meant to keep the *annexe* in fairest proportion to the sanctuary itself, etc.; it is the perfect building, instead of the still defective and imperfect one described in 1 Kings vi. The side-building and the gizrah are evidently distinguished in relation to the temple as addition and contrast. The description, too, given of both, suggests a still farther realization of the temple-idea, as regards priestly service and other modes of showing reverence to God, and also of the "in spirit and in truth" for this future worship.

10. As to the temple of Ezekiel's vision considered æsthetically, Bähr's thoughtful analysis (*Der sal. Tempel*, pp. 7 sq., 269 sq.) is so much the more applicable, as this visionary temple is still more animated and dominated by the religious idea of Israel, which in its futurity is the Messianic idea. The temple before us is in the highest sense of the word music of the future, although only a variation of an old theme. The import of this old theme, Solomon's temple and the original tabernacle, will first find full expression in Ezekiel's temple, whether its measures and numbers are the old ones or different. We must not employ here the classical criterion of the beautiful; sensuous beauty of form is not to be found here. The adornment of the edifice is limited to cherubim and palms, either together or separate; and of the cherubim it must be granted that, æsthetically considered, they are figures the reverse of beautiful. We meet, however, with nothing tasteless or repulsive, like the dog or bird-headed human forms, the green and blue faces of the Egyptian gods, or the many-armed idols of the Indian cultus. But what a difference is there between the temple of Ezekiel's vision and the fancy edifice, for example, the description of which is to be found in the younger Titurel (strophe 311–415, edited by Hahn; comp. Sulp. Boisseree on the description of the temple of the Holy Grail, Munich 1834),—the wondrous sanctuary on Mont Salvage, in which the ideal German architecture consecrates its poetic expression under the influence of reminiscences of Rev. xxi. 11 sq.! (The chapel of the Holy Cross at Castle Karlstein, near Prague, presents to this day a partial imitation, and on a reduced scale, of the temple of the Grail.) A large fortress with walls and innumerable towers surrounds the temple of the Grail, like an extensive and dense forest of ebony trees, cypresses, and cedars. Instead of the guard-rooms (ch. xl.) and the express charge of the house (ch. xliv.) of Ezekiel, are the guardians and protectors of the Grail,—the templars, a band of spiritual knights of the noblest kind, humble, pure, faithful, chaste men. And whatever of precious stones, imagery, gold, and pearls the poetic fancy was able to imagine, is collected around the shrine of the Holy Grail. In the heathen temple, with its attempts to represent the divine, and especially in the Greek temple, conformably to the innate artistic taste of the Greeks, with such beautiful natural scenery cherishing and demanding this taste, where sky, earth, and sea on every side suggest the divine as also the beautiful, the execution, form, and shape, distribution and arrangement of the parts, as well as all its decorations, correspond to the demands of æsthetics; but already in Solomon's temple the ethical-religious principle of the covenant, and consequently of the theocratic presence of Jehovah among His people, penetrates and pervades everything else. Thus the tabernacle, and also the whole temple building, culminates in the holy of holies, which contains the ark of the covenant with the tables of the law, and in which the atonement *par excellence* is completed. A relation like this, then, is served by any form which rather fulfils its office than strives after artistic configuration, and the form has answered its purpose, provided it only is a religiously significant form. "Solomon's temple," says Bähr, "cannot stand as a great work of art before the forum of the æsthetic." Human art in general goes along with nature, hence its mainly heathenish, its cosmic (κοσμος, "decoration") character. Jehovah, on the contrary, is holiness, and no necessity of nature of any kind, no nationality as such, no deification of nature, no magic consecration binds Him to Israel, but the freest covenant grace, which has as its aim the sanctification of Israel as His people, with a view to all mankind. That Phœnician artists executed the building of Solomon's temple (comp. for this the exhaustive critique of Bähr in the work quoted above, p. 250 sq.)—although (KRAUSE, *die drei ältesten Kunsturkunden der Freimaurer-brüderschaft*, Dresden 1819) freemasonry makes grand masters after Solomon, who is held to represent the Father (omnipotence), King Hiram as Son (wisdom), and Hiram Abif as Spirit (harmony, beauty)—concerns chiefly the technical working in wood and metal. If the artistic execution, thus

limited, of the temple decoration bore on it a Phœnician character, and the employment of table work coated with silver showed signs of Hither Asia in general, yet the Phœnician element, this mundane configuration, would not amount to much more than what the Greek language was, in which the gospel of the New Covenant, as well as that of the Old, came before the world. But a specifically Christian element, the really fundamental element in the first and oldest Christian church architecture, namely, that what is also called (it is true) "God's house" is simply an enclosure of the congregation (οἶκος ἐκκλησίας, τῶν ἐκκλησιῶν οἶκος, *domus ecclesiæ*), is an approximation to the extension of the outer court in Ezekiel, which extension is quite in unison with the Christological method of our prophet, with the peculiar regard he pays to the people of the Messiah (Introd. § 9). Comp. 2 Cor. vi. 16; Eph. ii. 20 sq.; 1 Pet. ii. 4. The Christian community forms in future the house of God, the temple; as also its development, externally and internally, is in the New Testament called edification, building. Voltaire has declared that he could remember in all antiquity no public building, no national temple, so small as Solomon's; and J. D. Michaelis held that his house in Göttingen was larger; whereas Hengstenberg ascribes to Solomon's temple, "inclusive of the courts, an imposing size." The prominence given in Ezekiel to the east gate of the new temple, although the holy of holies still lies towards the west, may remind us of the projecting eastward of Christian church buildings from the earliest age, and especially of the Concha closing them on the east. As the glory of the God of Israel comes from the east (ch. xliii.), so in the east is the Dayspring from on high (Luke i. 78; the Sun of Righteousness, Mal. iii. 20 [iv. 2]), the Light of the world (John viii. 12; Isa. ix.), which has brought a new day, the precursor and pledge of the future new morning and day of eternal glory (Rom. xiii. 12; 2 Tim. iv. 8). If the light-concealing stained windows of the Middle Ages are not to be traced back to the parts shut up and covered in Ezekiel's temple, still the powerful tendency to elevation upwards, so appropriate to the Gothic style, has at least some support in the pillars (ch. xl. 14), and even suggests an ἄνω τὸν νοῦν (Phil. iii. 20; Col. iii. 1 sq.).

11. The designation of the temple in ch. xliii. as the place of Jehovah's throne, etc., might make us suppose the existence of the ark of the covenant, unless its significance as (to borrow Bähr's words) "centre, heart, root, and soul of the whole edifice" necessarily demanded an express mention, when, for example, we have in Ezekiel most exact accounts of the altars; comp on ch. xli. 22. Solomon's temple (1 Kings viii.) first became what it was meant to be from the fact that the ark of the covenant came into it. But the post-exile temple had an empty holy of holies, as Tacitus (*Hist.* v. 9) relates of Pompey, that "he by his right as conqueror entered the temple, from which time it became known that no divine image was in it, but only an empty abode, and that there was nothing in the mystery of the Jews." (Comp. Josephus, *Bell. Jud.* v. 5. 5.) The most probable supposition is, that the ark of the covenant disappeared at the destruction of Solomon's temple, that it was consumed by fire. For the traditions of what became of it are mere myths; *e.g.* in 2 Macc. ii., that Jeremiah, among other things, by divine command hid the ark in a cave in Mount Nebo, but when they who had gone with him could not again find the place, he rebuked them, and pointed to the future, when the Lord would again be gracious to His people and reveal i to them, and the glory of the Lord and the cloud would appear as formerly. [The Mishna makes it be hid in a cave under the temple, a statement which the Rabbins endeavour to confirm from 2 Chron. xxxv. 3. Carpzov supposes the ark included in 2 Chron. xxxvi. 10, and holds that it was restored by Cyrus, Ezra i. 7; a statement which Winer rightly cannot find in that passage, but rather the reverse; while at the same time he is unable to agree with Hitzig, who concludes from Jer. iii. 16 that the ark of the covenant was no longer in existence even in the days of this prophet. According to the Mishna (Joma v. 2), there had been put in its place an altar-stone rising three fingers above the ground, on which the high priest on the great day of atonement set the censer.] That the symbolical designation of the temple expressed in Ezekiel with reference to the ark of the covenant is simply a legal technical term may be the more readily believed, as in certain respects in contrast thereto, at least in distinction therefrom (although this is strangely denied by Hengst.), the whole precincts of the temple, in consequence of the re-entrance of the glory of Jehovah, became a holy of holies in accordance with the law of this house; comp. on ch. xliii. 12. W. Neumann expounds Jer. iii. 16 of the new birth of Israel, when Jehovah will be glorified in the midst of His saints, that these shall no longer celebrate the ark of the covenant. He rejects the opinion of Abendana, who, from ver. 17 of the same chapter, inferred that the whole of Jerusalem is to be a holy dwelling-place, and holds to Rashi's view, that the entire community will be holy, and that Jehovah will dwell in its midst as if it were the ark of the covenant. "For the ark of the covenant as such is a symbolical vessel. As it contains within it the law, which testifies to the covenant (Deut. iv. 13, xxvi. 17 sq.), so the covenant-people are represented in it, the bearers of the law through worldly life, until the days when it shall be written on the hearts of the saints (Jer. xxxi. 31 sq.). The Capporeth represents the transformation of the creature transformed by Israel's perfection in the Lord (?), the new heavens and the new earth wherein dwelleth righteousness, Isa. lxvi. 22, 23. If this is the thought which lies at the root of the symbolism, then when the ark of the covenant is no longer kept in commemoration, the shadows of the Old Covenant have passed away, all has become new, and the redeemed are the holy seed (Isa. vi. 13), to whom Jehovah's law has become the law of their life." The eloquent silence in our prophet regarding the ark of the covenant will, moreover, be understood in respect to the man who speaks as Jehovah (comp. on ch. xliii. 7), that is, in a Messianic-christological sense, notwithstanding that Ezekiel's Christology (Introd. § 9) has the Messianic people principally in view.

12. Ezekiel's vision rests throughout on the law of Moses. Were it otherwise in our chapters, Ezekiel could have been no prophet of Israel, nor the Mosaic law the law of God. This legal character was, moreover, well adapted to put an arrest

on a mere fancy portraiture, if not to make it altogether impossible. As to the departure from the law of Moses, which, however, he must concede, Philippson maintains that it is "not great," and "is limited to the number of victims" (? ?). Hengstenberg denies any difference, calling it merely "alleged." On the other hand, Hävernick, with whom many agree, speaks of Ezekiel's "many differences and definitions going beyond the law of the Old Covenant," while at the same time he rejects the idea that the prophet forms the transition to the farther improved system of the Pentateuch (VATKE), and affirms against J. D. Michaelis the unchangeable character of the law of Moses. Hävernick says: "These discrepancies rather show with so much the more stringent necessity, that a new condition of things is spoken of in the prophet, in which the old law will continue in glorious transformation, not abrogated, but fulfilled and to be fulfilled, coming into full truth and reality." Bunsen speaks to this effect: "Ezekiel's design was to make the ritual more spiritual, and to break the tyranny of the high-priesthood. For mention is nowhere made of a high priest, whereas a high-priestly obligation, although slightly relaxed, is laid upon the priests (ch. xliv. 22). The daily evening sacrifice falls away, and among the yearly feasts we miss Pentecost and the Great Day of Atonement, all which accords with the absence of the high priest and the ark of the covenant; instead of these comes an additional feast of atonement at the beginning of the year (ch. xlv. 18 sq.), and the amount of the morning sacrifice and the festal sacrifices is enhanced. There is, indeed, much reference to the original law throughout, and it is anew set forth with respect to transgressions and abuses that had crept in, special weight being laid on the precepts concerning clean and unclean (ch. xliv. 17 sq.; comp. ch. xxii. 26); but still more does Ezekiel go beyond the law, and gives additional force to its precepts." We must call to mind the position generally of prophecy to the law of Moses. As prophecy is provided for in the law in the proper place (comp. our Comment on Deut. p. 134), namely, when Moses' departure demanded it, so its foundation is traced back in Deut. xviii. 16 sq. to Sinai, and thus it is thenceforth comprehended historically in the legislation. But although it thus stands and falls with the law, having by its own account, like all the institutions of Israel, its norm in the law, yet it rejoices in its extraordinary fellowship with God, its divine endowment and inspiration. And this not in order, like the priesthood, to teach after the letter, and to serve in the ceremonial; but the provision made and charge given already on Mount Sinai, as they make the official duty of prophecy to be the representation of God's holy will against every other will, so they give to it the character of a legitimate as well as legitimatized officiality, which, like Moses, has to serve as the chosen means of intermediation in relation to the will of the Most High Lawgiver revealing itself; the calling is ordained in Israel for the continuity of the divine legislation. This latter qualification of the prophets of Jehovah in Israel afforded a foundation for their deepening of the legal worship, as opposed to hypocrisy and torpid formality, for their spiritual interpretation of the ceremonial; as, in view of their position towards the future, a consideration of the ecclesiastical and civil law in their bearing on the future followed as a matter of course. The idea which for this end dominates Ezekiel's closing vision is the holiness of Jehovah, and the corresponding sanctification of Israel, their separation to Jehovah as a possession. It is the root idea which the law expresses and symbolizes in all its forms, whether of morality, worship, or polity. And as it is said already in Ex. xix.: "Ye shall be unto me a kingdom of priests," so it is also said in 1 Pet. ii. of the Christian community, that they who are lively stones are built up a spiritual house, a holy priesthood, to offer up spiritual sacrifices, acceptable to God through Jesus Christ (comp. ver. 9). Peter thus makes a New Testament use of the same mode of expression regarding worship, which, carried out in Old Testament form, is Ezekiel's representation of Jehovah's service of the future, when Jehovah shall dwell for ever in His people. Comp. ch. xx. 40. Ezekiel's position, therefore, to the law of Moses is not that of freedom from legal restraints,—a position which might be subjective and arbitrary,—but what he applies from the law for the illustration of the future, and the way in which he does so, passing by some things, more strongly emphasizing others, or putting them into new shapes, derives its legal justification from the idea of the law as it shall be realized in a true Israel, that is, the Messianic Israel. That the Messiah, who says in John xvii.: "And for them I sanctify myself, that they also may be sanctified in truth," remains as a person in the background, is quite in correspondence with Ezekiel's Christology (Introd. § 9), which, as already said, characterizes the times and the salvation of the Messiah through the Messianic people.

13. "The proper significance of the new temple lies in the full revelation of Jehovah in His sanctuary, in the new and living fellowship into which God enters with His people by this His dwelling among them" (HÄV.). As being a return, which it is in relation to ch. xi., the entrance of the glory of the Eternal has, although with a New Testament application, corresponding to the: ἐγω μεθ' ὑμων πασας τας ἡμερας ἑως της συντελειας του αἰωνος (Matt. xxviii. 20), also its Apocalyptic significance, as John says before the close of his Revelation (ch. xxii.): ναι ἐρχου, Κυριε Ἰησου.

14. If the idea of the court is unquestionably that of the people, whose Messianic perfection as Israel Ezekiel is to behold, then, since everything on the mountain of the vision here is "most holy" (ch. xliii. 12), the immediately following detailed description of the altar of burnt-offering and its consecration can only point to the future manifestation of Jehovah's holiness and the sanctification of His peculiar people (1 Pet. ii. 9). "What holds good of the altar refers also to the whole court; the blessing of the altar includes in it that of the community. By means of the expiation of the altar, the purpose of the divine love, to see a holy people assembled, is effected. The first act, consequently, in which the significance of the new sanctuary is expressed, is the complete expiation of the people, and its efficacy in this respect far surpasses in extent and glory that of the old sanctuary" (HÄV.). Accordingly, if they who are sanctified are perfected εἰς το διηνεκες by the προσφορα μια (Heb. x. 14), the full and complete offering on Golgotha, then the idea also of this altar of burnt-offering upon the very high

mountain must be fulfilled. But as the offering which fulfils is the most personal priestly offering, so the sanctification of the people in Ezekiel's typical temple takes place on the altar of burnt-offering in the priests' court, which therefore still remains separated from the court of the people, as in Solomon's temple, whereas in the tabernacle there was only one court. The symbolical representation of the dominant idea of the sanctification of the people was, from their being represented by the priests, rightly localized in a priests' court, which gives it due prominence here, where everything hinges on locality and arrangement. Thus also, as Bähr observes, in the camp of Israel the priestly family in its four main branches encamped close around the sanctuary on its four sides. [Comp. with this section the Additional Note on ch. xliii. 13–27, p. 410.—W. F.]

15. As the shutting of the east gate (ch. xliv.) for the future puts the key of Ezekiel's temple into the hand of Him who, according to the typology of the law and the prediction of the prophets, is the Coming One of Israel, so the prince's sitting and eating in the east gate must be taken as throwing light on the Messianic future of the people of the promise. It is very evident that by the "prince" is not to be understood the high priest of Israel. This interpretation, which was a Maccabean prolepsis, has now been abandoned. Kliefoth, Keil, and Hitzig justly dispute the indefinite sense which Hävernick gives to the נָשִׂיא, yet they do not sufficiently attend to what may be said in defence of Hävernick's indefiniteness, and which certainly tells against those who make the future theocratic ruler to be one with the King David of ch. xxxiv. and xxxvii., because he too is called נָשִׂיא, as indeed he is also called רֹעֶה. They must own, however, that there is a difference between: "My servant David shall be king over them," between the "one shepherd" who is "prince for ever," and the הַנָּשִׂיא here, who comes into consideration *quâ* נָשִׂיא. Now if this must be granted, then it is only with justice that Hävernick observes that the designation נָשִׂיא sets before us the original, or, as he calls it, "the purely natural constitution of the Israelites" (Ex. xxii. 27 [28]), although not so much because "the time of the exile had again limited the people to this original constitution, or left them only a poor remainder of it," as because, looking, as in our vision we always should do, at the Messiah and His times, the discrepancy between theocracy and kingly power, which showed itself at the rise of the latter under Samuel, is to be adjusted on the original ground of the peculiarity of Israel. The נָשִׂיא is the prince of the tribe, as the tribal constitution of Israel put the juridical power and the executive into the hands of the natural superiors, the heads of families and tribes. And even when in time of need, as in the days of the judges, a dictatorship, the power of one over all others, is had recourse to, it is *potestas delegata*, and is on both sides considered as nothing else. With a tribal constitution such as the natural constitution of Israel was, the want of an outward *centrum unitatis* might in itself be painfully felt, and the instituting of one be looked on as a political necessity; but that for Israel the necessity of the time as such should have demanded a permanent institution of the kind, is strikingly refuted by the days of the judges, for the present aid of Jehovah answered to the momentary distress, and raised up the competent helper from out of the tribes of Israel,—"then when they entreated and wept, the faithfulness of God helped them, and sooner than they supposed all distress was over,"—just as the former examples of Moses and Joshua showed that in the Israelitish theocracy the right men were not wanting at the right time. Jehovah alone, as on another side the fundamental canon of the priesthood still held up before the people, claimed as His due to be Israel's king in political respects also. Originally there could be beside Him no other political sovereign, but merely the institution, in subordination to Him, of the princes of the tribes, and a sort of hegemony of a single tribe. The unity of the religious sentiment, which made the twelve externally separate tribes internally one community, had in earlier times made up for the want of an external *centrum unitatis*, and the free authority of certain individual representatives of this sentiment was quite in harmony therewith. Hence Jehovah says in 1 Sam. viii.: "They have not rejected thee, but they have rejected Me, that I should not reign over them." Thus the demand of the people requesting a king must, having regard to Samuel, who occupied in Israel a position similar to that of Moses, be looked on as a symptom of disease, although the disease was one of development. We may concede to the elders of Israel who come before Samuel, Samuel's age, which they urge; and still more, as the occasion of their demand, the evil walk of his sons. We can point to the picture exhibited in the later period of the judges, when everything, even the temporary alliance of individual tribes, appears to be in a state of dissolution; we can along therewith take into account the pride of Ephraim, in whose midst the sanctuary stood, and to whose claims of superiority, even over Judah, all the tribes were more or less compelled to bow. Nay, even in the law (Deut. xvii. 14 sq.), where it refers to the future taking possession of Canaan, the future development of an Israelitish kingdom is taken into view by Jehovah Himself, and the very form foreseen in which the demand came to Samuel: "I will set a king over me, like all the nations that are about me." But although this possible desire of the people, because tolerated, is not expressly blamed, yet neither the self-derived resolution there: "when thou sayest: I will," etc., nor the pattern: "like all the nations that are about me," is spoken of approvingly; nor can there be behind the emphatic command: "thou shalt in any wise set him to be king over thee whom Jehovah thy God shall choose," anything but a presupposed conflict with the kingly authority of Jehovah, against which provision must be made in the very outset. Accordingly, when Jehovah Himself takes into view the earthly kingship for Israel, He does so in a way not very different from what Christ says in Matt. xix. regarding the Mosaic permission of divorce because of Israel's hard-heartedness: ἀπ' ἀρχῆς δὲ οὐ γέγονεν οὕτω. But Jehovah is the Physician of Israel, who (Num. xxi.) made Moses set the brazen serpent on a pole, as a remedy against the bite of the fiery serpents. That which expresses to the full the sentiment of the people under Samuel is

also the undisguised: "like all the nations;" with this their request before Samuel closes emphatically as its culminating point. Although to Samuel the thing that personally concerned him: "that he may judge us," which they gave as their object in the case of the king to be appointed, was displeasing, was in his eyes the bad element in the request, Jehovah first set the matter before him in the light that in His eyes the request for the "king" (מֶלֶךְ) was rather a rejection of His reigning over them, and explained to him the: "like all the nations," in the mouth of the elders of the people, by their hereditary disposition: "they forsook Me, and served other gods." Kingly power, such as the heathen nations have from early times, is a necessary self-defence of polytheism against its own divisive and centrifugal elements in the realm of politics; it is a socialistic attempt to arrange a life in community, and that is to unite, both to make the internal unity and order strong and powerful externally, and to keep them so. For מֶלֶךְ, from מָלַךְ, is derived from: "judging," as still attested by the Syrian signification: "to advise," and also by the fact that the kingly power in Israel arose from that of the judges: the ruler is he who stands over the opposing parties, over the strife, he who unites; very different from whom is מוֹשֵׁל, the tyrant, עָרִיץ, the coming to power by the right of the strongest. Thus kingly power is from the first peculiar to heathenism; and because the boundary between the human and the divine is to the heathen consciousness a fluctuating one, kingship, especially in connection with the idolatrous worship thereof which grew up among the heathen nations, comes to be regarded as the contrast to the theocratic relations of the monotheistic people of Israel. Accordingly, when the people of Jehovah ask a king such as all the nations have (comp. 1 Sam. viii. 20), this indicates that the theocratic consciousness is darkened and weakened in them; and thus a visible king appears necessary to them, because the invisible Ruler has, as it were, disappeared from their view. In times of religious and moral insensibility, inquiries are always directed to the political constitution; not to the state of society, but to the civil arrangements. And when Israel, forgetting the divine national prerogative they had enjoyed since leaving Egypt, placed themselves on a level with the heathen, then they must have looked on themselves with eyes like those of the heathen; it could not but occur to them, that in comparison with heathen monarchy they were, as Ziegler says, "a people poorly and weakly organized, visibly only republican, and therefore easy to be overcome by the heathen, whose power was concentrated in monarchy." Thus Israel's disease in desiring a monarchy "like the nations" was, that they had become infected by the political miasma of the polytheistic spirit of the age. For while the first king of Israel, Saul, very soon entered on the path of the heathen, the monarchy which is in accordance with the law of Israel first assumes shape with David, and then chiefly internally, and with Solomon, and then almost entirely externally. This, too, explains the significance of these two types of kings for the Messianic idea. Ziegler calls David: "the king among kings." "He comprehended thoroughly the office of a king in a theocracy; he was the best mediator between the people and Jehovah. Because he was the servant of Jehovah, he was also the lawful king. Through him the kingdom became the very best means for attaining to the divine purposes." Comp. Doct. Reflec. 14, etc. on ch. xxxiv., and Doct. Reflec. 21 on ch. xxxvii. But already with David—so that Solomon's sinking down from the greatest external kingly glory into the surrounding polytheism, and the after-division of the royal power through its being broken into two kingdoms, only furnish the foil to it—the wider and higher future of Israel was founded in spirit, namely, as this future should be realized in the Messiah. According to the flesh, the Coming One of Israel is the son of David; according to the spirit of Messianic prophecy, David is the historico-personal basis, its personal foundation, a thoroughly prophetic personality; as Ziegler says: "Partly inasmuch as he is manifestly a τυπος του μελλοντος in many phases of his character and life, even in the minute particulars,—that, like Christ, he began his official career in his thirtieth year, and that he went weeping over the Kedron, and ascended the Mount of Olives with covered head; but also partly because in his psalms he manifests himself a prophet in the narrower sense of the word, a prophet who by his psalms really adds new elements of revelation to the old, his prophecies entering into the most minute details, his Son is the Spirit of his poetry. If the people were comprehended in Moses as the κεφαλη as to the law, we may say of David that they are gathered together in him as to the theocratic kingdom." Hence these are far-seeing divine thoughts, and bearing special reference to the Messianic salvation which in 1 Sam. viii. Jehovah repeatedly urged upon Samuel, viz. to listen to the voice of the people, although the people will not at all listen to Samuel's voice. Not that Israel had, as Ziegler supposes, to be set by the monarchy on a level with he world in order to be preserved in the world,—for it was just the monarchy that destroyed its national existence, by drawing it into the politics of the great world,—but (and this is the sole object in view in the law regarding the king in Deut. xvii.) the possible conflict with Jehovah's royal dominion over Israel was guarded against by this, that in the Israelitish monarchy, especially as represented by David personally and by Solomon regally, Jehovah made His "Anointed" for eternity assume a preparatory shape, that is, filled the heathen-political form of government, which might be and still more might become such a contrast to the true, the theocratic Israel, with that which is the final purpose of God's dominion over Israel (just as already to the patriarchs kings were promised as their descendants). Accordingly in Deuteronomy also, as the Israelitish kingship rises up as on the foundation of the judgeship, so, parallel therewith, and in connection with the priestly office, the prophetic office rises up as a continuation of the revelation by Moses (כָּמֹנִי or כָּמוֹךָ, Deut. xviii.), in whom, according to Peter, was the πνευμα Χριστου. And not less significantly does "the prince" in Ezekiel sit and eat in the gate, through which the glory of Jehovah had entered, and which it has Messianically sanctified. With him Israel appears again as what it was, just as the elders of Israel asked from Samuel a king like the nations, to be chief representative of Israel according to its tribal constitution; he who can be styled directly הַנָּשִׂיא,[1] will be so in Messianic consecration and sanctification, so that Christian kingship might be symbolized. Umbreit observes: "Whereas at first every particular tribe had its *Nasi*, they now are all reunited under a single one. Thus an old name, and yet again new in its signification." From this Umbreit infers a prince "clothed with great splendour (?), like another Melchizedek, who may combine well the rights of the state and of the Church in one spirit," etc. etc. Yet surely Hävernick is right in finding indicated here the "true and complete harmony of civil and ecclesiastical order in the days of the Messiah." "Christ has no vicar; to no one but Himself shall the kingdoms of the world belong; but to pious princes (to princes as they ought to be), to lawful magistrates and lords, pertains a prerogative over the faithful, which again is a duty and a service" (Cocc.). Comp. what is said on this point in the exposition of ch. xlvi. 2. [See also Additional Note on p. 417.]

16. In regard to the priests of Ezekiel's temple, Hengstenberg thinks the prophet "wishes to draw away the view from the dreary present,—the priests without prospect of office, the ruins of the priesthood,—and, on the contrary, presents to the eye priests in office and honour, in whom the Mosaic ordinances are again in full exercise and authority; and next he wishes to labour for the regeneration of the priesthood." It is only surprising, when in accordance with Hengstenberg's general view of our chapters the fancy is worked on here too by ideas of Mosaic priests, that the idea of the high priest is wanting, that this most powerful impression is disregarded. But as regards the removal of the degradation of the pre-exile priesthood, the mention of Zadok sets forth too prominently for this end just the age of David and Solomon. Ezekiel's priests certainly are Mosaic priests, but the Mosaic priests had a people to represent of whom it is said in Ex. xix. 6: "Ye shall be unto Me a kingdom of priests, and an holy nation" (at the passover the whole people acted as priests); so that it is certainly Mosaic, although according to the inmost idea of the Mosaic law, when the people of the future are in Ezekiel specially represented by the priests. But it is quite peculiar to Ezekiel, that, in order duly to set forth the sanctification of the people by the lofty holiness of their priests, the high priest appears in certain respects absorbed into the priests, and these are represented in a high-priestly aspect. As the people are dealt with in ch. xliv. 6 sq. for the bad priests set to keep the charge of Jehovah's holy things (ver. 8), so the exemplification of priestly instruction of the people given in ver. 23 is that of the true priests' teaching to discern the difference between the holy and the profane, the unclean and the clean: the high-priestly sanctity of the priests is to serve for a high-priestly sanctification of the people; the high-priestly idea is to become a national reality, just as the aggregate of these Old Testament letters (for which comp. Zech. vi.) is the fulfilling word of the "body of Christ" as the Church. For the figure of Zadok, the typical high priest, taken from the very specially Messianically-typical age of David and Solomon, corresponds to only such a Messianic prospect. Zadok's sons are called the true priests of the people, just as the true Shepherd of the people (ch. xxxiv. and xxxvii.) is a descendant of David. And here we have a parallel exactly similar to that of Jer. xxxiii., where the continuance of the Levitical priesthood is guaranteed in like manner as the continuance of the race of David, and similarly as to the increase of both,—in which respect there shall, according to Isa. lxvi., be taken of the Gentiles for priests and for Levites; and so in this way the position of priests among the Gentiles, promised to Israel in Isa. lxi., fulfils itself as a universal priestly position. Hävernick makes a "special" blessing for the priesthood be connected with the "general blessing of the theocracy," inasmuch as "not its hitherto meagre (?) form," but the priestly office, "as a faithful expression of the idea inherent in it, will be established in perpetuity;" and he compares Mal. iii. 3: "A new priesthood, made anew by the power of the Lord, arises on the soil of the Old Testament priesthood in the new theocracy;" just as Ezekiel's main concern is "the priestly office in general," so also the idea "of a really spiritual priesthood" comes to light in his writings, etc. When Hengstenberg compares Ps. xxiv. for the reformation of the priesthood, we observe that the "demands on His people," spoken of there "from the coming of the Lord of glory," are no specially priestly demands, but are addressed to the whole house of Israel; and the same is really the case with Isa. xl., which he also cites. The Messianic references of the priesthood of the sons of Zadok, whereby (neither by Zadok personally, nor by Samuel) the prophetic word spoken to Eli (1 Sam. ii. 27 sq.) is fulfilled, is not only maintained by the Fathers, but also by Keil;[1] comp. on 1 Sam. ii. 35 sq. The Berleburg Bible observes: "As in the person of Solomon the Spirit of prophecy pointed to the true and anointed Solomon, so also in this priest it points to the great High Priest, Jesus Christ.' Hengst. remains "quite on the ordinary priestly ground; the prospect into the New Testament relations remains completely closed." According to him, the prophet has to do only with what is "to be accomplished after brief delay," etc. On the other hand, Umbreit says: "The priesthood is quite in accordance with the transformation of the house of God. The old class of mediators between Jehovah and His people, consecrated by descent, has disappeared, and we no more find the high priest than we find the ark of the covenant. Instead of the Levites, who, together with the people, have to bear the guilt of the profanation of the covenant, there have come now only the inwardly worthy, the sons of Zadok, who should fulfil their significant name by main-

[1] It will each time be a more definite person, but that does not determine who it will be: only this perhaps is implied, that each nation may retain what is natural to it, what accords with its special character and historic development. The Bible dictates neither a church constitution nor a state constitution; but in Ezekiel there is symbolized what in every constitution, in itself human, ought to be the abiding, the higher: the humanly highest one (הַנָּשִׂיא) sits and eats in the east gate of the Highest, of Jehovah.

[1] "The final fulfilment comes with Christ and His kingdom; accordingly, the Lord's Anointed, before whom the approved priest shall alway walk, is not Solomon, but David and David's Son, whose kingdom shall endure for ever" (KEIL).

taining fidelity in this ideal sense; and the supreme enhanced law of the new priesthood is the maintaining of inward purity from every outward stain, etc. Their outward support is the holy gift of Jehovah, so that they can say with the godly man in Ps. xvi.: 'Jehovah is my portion and my cup; my lot has fallen to me in pleasant places' (ver. 5 sq.)." [Comp. Additional Note at pp. 419, 420.]

17. The temple building, with its sacred architecture on the basis of the first tabernacle, as Solomon's temple most richly displays it, symbolizes essentially the same as that which in the priesthood of the temple of Ezekiel's vision is illustrated liturgically by the ministrations in this temple. For the accomplished dwelling of the Holy One in Israel proclaims His people to be a sanctified, and therefore a holy people. These are the worshippers that the Father desires (John iv.), a kingdom of priests, or a royal priesthood (1 Pet. ii.); just as the "prince," representing the people civilly and politically, fulfils his idea in King-Messiah; while the priests, the "sons of Zadok," represent them ecclesiastically and spiritually. This is the purpose and constitution of Israel, the people of God. What the temple is "in spirit," the representation by the priesthood of the new temple gives "in truth," that is, in faithfulness and trueness of life. In the former, everything is most holy; in the latter, all are high-priestly. But in Christ the idea to be represented is realized in so much the more priestly a manner, because we have here the community of the Lord, the κυριακον, where, in the case of Israel, was the congregation of the people, the עֵדָה, the קָהָל. We might, moreover, find some difficulty in reconciling the omissions, and also the occasional so pregnant additions and stricter definitions taken from the idea of the law, in the ordinances regarding the priesthood, with what Hengst. maintains, namely, that the aim is, "by a few well-chosen strokes, to bring out the thought of the restoration of the Mosaic priesthood in its customs and its rights," while it has been so easy for the exposition (which comp.) to show the prominence given throughout to the priestliness and sanctity of the priests' office and the priestly order with reference to the people to be represented. As, moreover, the prince is, in ch. xliv., advanced to a privileged relation to the sanctuary (comp. ch. xlv. 13 sq.), so along with teaching, instruction, especially in holiness (בֵּין קֹדֶשׁ לְחֹל) and sanctification (וּבֵין־טָמֵא לְטָהוֹר, ch. xliv. 23), the settlement of disputes by the judgment of God, the establishing of righteousness (as is perhaps indicated in the name "Zadok"), is specified in ver. 24 among the official duties of the priests. The prince eats in the east gate in the enjoyment of peace; the priests have always to restore peace.

18. As, on the one hand, the burnt-offering is the predominant note in this temple-system of the future, so, on the other, in ch. xlv. "oblation" is said in reference to the whole land. It is the same idea of devotion to Jehovah which is expressed by both,—the national life consecrated to the Lord in fellowship with Him (comp. the sacrificial feasts, in the east gate, of the prince of this people), Israel's state of grace. The disquisition on the oblation of holiness, etc., preliminary to ch. xlvii. and xlviii., and for which ch. xliv. 28 sq. furnishes the occasion, is significant from the very fact of being thus occasioned. For where priests and Levites are taken account of expressly according to their ministry in relation to Jehovah (ch. xlv.), there the whole house of Israel (ver. 6), and the prince in particular, with their portions of land, appear in the light of sacred property belonging to Jehovah, and also as His servants, who, while His more peculiar servants, the priests, are to see to holiness and sanctification, have to endeavour after judgment and righteousness. In this way the new nationality dedicated to the Lord (chiefly by the burnt-offering, and symbolized by the "oblation") has to exhibit itself in civil, social, and secular life. It is actually a new nationality in relation to land and people; but, considered by itself, and apart from ch. xliv. 28 sq., it appears to mean the division of the land, and especially the "oblation." Spring has come, yea, the fields are now already white for the harvest (John iv.). The "oblation of holiness" announces itself as the commencement of the future harvest. EWALD: "The holy portion, which is previously taken from the rest of the land (like the tithes from the fruits of the field), and set apart for its own special purpose, is here very expressively mentioned in the outset, and with manifest reference to the now completed description of the temple (ver. 2; comp. ch. xlii. 20); while the prophet evidently hastens more quickly over the portions connected therewith of the common Levites and the city of Jerusalem, in order to come to the portion and duties of the prince," etc.

19. Hävernick says on ch. xlv.: "After the description of a so newly reviving order of things in church matters, it appears as a matter of course that the land itself must be treated as a new land, and stand in need of a new special division. This division stands in a converse relation to that under Joshua. While at that time the people before all, each particular tribe, receive their portion, and not until afterwards was a fixed seat in the land assigned to Jehovah, here Jehovah first of all receives a holy gift, which is presented to Him. A portion of land is separated for the sanctuary and the priests, and one of equal size for the Levites. The new temple is moreover kept separate by a kind of suburb, in order to point out its special holiness."

20. The design of the Mosaic regulation, according to which priests and Levites, especially the latter, were to dwell dispersed among all the tribes, whereby the curse formerly uttered with respect to Levi by Jacob in his blessing of the patriarchs (Gen. xlix.) became fulfilled as a blessing for Levi and for all Israel, was to settle the tribe among Israel in accordance with its calling. Bähr says: "If the Levites were to preserve the law and word of God, and thereby spread religious knowledge, promote religious life, pronounce judicial decisions in accordance therewith, etc., then it was not only suitable, but necessary, that they should not all dwell in one place, in one district. Their dwelling dispersed reminded them to spread the light of the fear of God and piety among the whole people, to give preference to no tribe, and to neglect none." On this we observe, that it is certainly not to be looked on as an abolition of

the Mosaic ordinance that in Ezekiel priests and Levites are all concentrated in one place,—the negation of the former would necessarily have to be formally announced,—but the fulfilment simply comes in place of the former arrangement, inasmuch as the end proposed by that arrangement and regulation is present with and in the future Church. Hengst. thinks the relation of the priests and Levites to the sanctuary is meant to be made clear by their concentration in its neighbourhood. But already before this the cities of the priests at least were to be found in those tribal districts which lay nearest to the place of worship. The idea from which the grouping of the priests and Levites around the sanctuary has to be understood is rather what Jeremiah predicts: that they shall no more teach every man his brother, etc., that from the least to the greatest they all shall know Jehovah (ch. xxxi. 34). The aim of dividing Levi among all the tribes, viz. to care for, preserve, and spread abroad everywhere the law and the testimony, is thus attained. The people of the future will be such that their liturgical representation and the dwelling of their priests and Levites in the neighbourhood of the temple suffice; and besides, this significantly brings out the thought that Levi, this election from the elect people, is a "people of God in the people of God" (Bähr). For, what was designed by the appointed cities, in which we already see them collected while they were dispersed among all the tribes, is fully accomplished in the land of the priests and the Levites (ch. xlv.); and if Bähr's interpretation of the number of the 48 cities of the priests and Levites as referring to the sanctuary (*Symb. d. mos. Kult.* ii. p. 51) needed confirmation, it might have it here, where what this interpretation makes of Levi's dwelling in the midst of Israel is expressly stated of the dwelling-place of the priestly Levites: "a holy place for the sanctuary" (ver. 4). Accordingly it is with this diversity as respects the Mosaic law, which Philippson calls "the real" diversity, exactly as Christ says in Matt. v.: "I am come not to destroy (καταλυσαι), but to fulfil," and that: "not one jot or one tittle shall pass from the law till all be fulfilled."

21. The sanctuary, the land of the priests and Levites, and the prince's portion, form almost the centre of the land. The city does not include the sanctuary, but is situated beside it, also in the midst of the land. "No jealousy about the possession of them can any longer separate the tribes" (Häv.). "This whole district," says Bunsen, "is not to lie in the territory of a single tribe, which might thereby appear privileged, but, as accords with its sanctity, is separated from the tribal territories. In other words, the union-authority of the confederacy is to have a special seat for manifesting its activity. No wiser political idea could be devised. Hence Jerusalem still remains Jerusalem, but it no longer belongs to Benjamin." The central sanctuary is that which unifies also the tribes of Israel, just as the priesthood, royalty, and public property grouped around it give local expression to the unity and oneness of the whole. Instead of the "violence-inflicting and heaven-assailing tower of Babel" (Neteler), "the tabernacle of Shem" has become "a divine sanctuary," which then no longer symbolizes solely Jehovah's dwelling in Israel, but is at the same time a type for mankind in general of His tabernacle with men (Rev. xxi. 3), and of their being united to and under Him. Comp. the Doct. Reflec. on ch. xlvii., xlviii.

22. Chiliasm—and this is conceivable of the Jewish Chiliasm, whereas such a final Judaism cannot but prove injurious to modern Christian Chiliasm (Gal. iii. 3)—forgets, while studying these closing chapters of our prophet, the beginning of his prophecy, the cosmic character of ch. i., which relates to creation generally, and on which the whole book is based. But indeed if πας Ἰσραηλ in Rom. xi. is the people, *i.e.* Israel after the flesh, then it is only logically consistent to interpret the requickening in ch. xxxvii. as a bodily resurrection of all dead Jews. Those who are raised become by this fact, or as at one stroke, converted to Christ; those who are alive are Christians already, or will become so in consequence of this; and this whole Israel returns to Palestine, and forms in a transformed state, as it is already marked out for being by this awakening, the focus of the "millennial kingdom" for fresh salvation to all nations. It is illogical to wish to pick out one piece here, and to understand another merely spiritually; but he who here says A must also say B. Whether the converted Jews are to live in their own land, "under kings of the house of David, as a people who are to be preserved and finally also converted," as Kliefoth allows to be the doctrine of Scripture, or whether King David will then return and rule over Israel in glory, is rather an antiquarian than a theological question. Scripture teaches none of these fancies; nor does it speak of a kingdom of glory in the earthly Jerusalem, in which the Gentile Church is to be joined to Israel under the dominion of the then reappeared Christ-Messiah (as Baumgarten). According to the Scriptures of the Old and New Testaments, it has been the destination of Israel, as the people separated from all nations from the time of their first fathers, to be a blessing to mankind. And the more its national theocracy expanded itself to universal Christocracy, which comprehended also the Gentiles under the blessing of the Messiah, the more evidently there becomes exhibited in Israel, with its ecclesiastical and political forms, the preformation of an Israel which wholly is what Israel exhibits only in type,—a people of God that comprehends the redeemed, the saints of all mankind; in which accordingly, as to its worship, and as to its nationality in general, traced back to its original idea, and also viewed with respect to its future realization, the whole and (what is specially emphasized) every part always exhibits holiness and sanctification, the service of the holy God in spirit and in truth (Ps. xxii. 28 [27] sq., xlvii. 10 [9], cii. 16 [15] sq.; Isa. xxvi. 2, li., lx.; Luke i. 17; Rom. ix. 24 sq.; 2 Cor. vi. 16; Tit. ii. 14; 1 Pet. ii. 5 sq., 9, 10, etc.). Nation and nationality are historical and hence perishable colourings of the idea of mankind, which have entirely faded since the eternal idea of Israel has been fulfilled in Christ, in whom there is neither Jew nor Greek (Gal. iii.), but man, the new man (Eph. ii.) ἐν δικαιοσυνῃ και ὁσιοτητι της ἀληθειας. What could be fulfilled according to the letter—which, however, is the expression borne by the spirit of fulfilment—has been fulfilled in the people of Israel by their rising and revival from the graves of the exile, by their return thence-forth to Canaan under Judah as "Jews," by the period of the Maccabees, certainly in historical

prelude only to the ideal, the entire, true fulfilment of the spirit-letter in the kingdom of God through Christ; according to which fulfilment the elect people are the people of the elect from all mankind, and the Jewish people now neither exist as a people, nor have a future such as Kliefoth would assign to them, namely, to be "holy in the same way that every Christianized nation (!) now is," for ἔφθασε ἐπ' αὐτους ἡ ὀργη εἰς τελος (1 Thess. ii. 16). For the Church of God in Christ, so far as it belongs to this world, the representation of its spiritual life in a service of atoning sacrifices and cleansings, as here in Ezekiel, can be no antithesis; for still, according to Heb. xii., the εὐπεριστατος ἁμαρτια has to be laid aside, and (James iii. 2) πολλα πταιομεν ἁπαντες (comp. Ezek. xlv. 20). But to Ezekiel no other representation of the future could be given than in types of the sacred past of Israel—as of its law, so of the Davidic royalty and of Canaan as the land of promise. "But however prominent," observes Keil, "is the Old Testament clothing of the Messianic prophecy in Ezekiel, yet even in this guise lineaments are found by which we recognise that the Israelitish-theocratic guise is only the drapery in which is concealed the New Testament form of the kingdom of God;" and he very justly refers to 1 Pet. i. 10 sq., while he farther says: "Even although the prophets, in their uninspired meditations on what they had prophesied as moved by the Holy Ghost, may not have known the typical signification of their own utterances, yet we who live in the times of fulfilment, and know not only the beginning in the appearing of our Lord, etc., but a considerable course of the fulfilment too in the eighteen hundred years' spread of the kingdom of heaven on earth, have not so much to inquire after what the Old Testament prophets thought in their searching into the prophecies with which they were inspired by the Holy Ghost,—if these thoughts of theirs could be in any way ascertained,—but we have to inquire, in the light of the present measure of fulfilment (comp. 2 Pet. i. 19), what the Spirit of Christ, which enabled the prophets to behold and prophesy the future of His kingdom in figures of the Old Testament kingdom of God, has announced and revealed to us by these figures." Apart from the occasional references of Ezekiel's representation to paradise, to the first creation (comp. on ch. xxxvi. 35, xvi. 53), to which there is a return in Christ through God's new creation, the whole handling of the Mosaic law in Ezekiel, of its forms of worship as hieroglyphs of the future to be prophesied of the true Israel, can be understood only from the point of view of a transmutation of the law into its fulfilment.

HOMILETIC HINTS

On Ch. xl.

Ver. 1 sq. Jerome, despairing of the possibility, and especially of his own ability, to expound these chapters of Ezekiel, wished to break off and finish his commentary here. Only the urgency and importunity of friends urged him to continue; but every instant he acknowledges his inability, etc.—"The commencement and close, the cherubim and the new temple, are what every one first thinks of when Ezekiel's name is mentioned" (HENGST.).—The vision of the temple, as regards the date given, a trilogy of thoughts: from judgment to mercy, from prison to freedom, from the world to Christ and into the community of God.—"Under the material promises of God are concealed spiritual ones; take that to heart in these chapters too, therefore, *sursum corda*" (STARCK).—"God raises up His own in their misery by His comfort, and keeps them through the hope of things to come in faith and patience. When there is no prospect of deliverance, when no help, no refuge appears, then the Lord is present with His comfort" (HAFENREFFER).—"When it seems that all will be over with the Church of God, then God thinks of its maintenance and amelioration" (STARKE).—"To human eyes Canaan was lost for Israel, to human eyes Jerusalem lay in the dust; but the prophet sees it again far more glorious. Such seeing again is, however, truly given by God in the Spirit. Land and city and temple had been lost through the sins of the people; yet Israel must remain and fulfil its eternal purpose for the glory of God. God makes it even already in this prophet and in all like-minded bloom forth only the more gloriously, so that neither the sins of the people nor the power of its enemies can put an end to Israel. A fairer and loftier Jerusalem and temple must be still in store for Israel, which the prophet represents entirely by figures taken from the old land, the old royal seat, and the old temple. Yet he does not merely make the old be renewed; everything becomes quite different, in order to indicate that the kingdom of God will, in its completion, present a quite different figure" (DIEDRICH).—"The word of God, too, counts the years and months and days of our distress, to make us understand that it is not unknown to God how long we have borne the yoke of the cross and the oppression of tyrants" (STARCK).—"Ezekiel was already five and twenty years in a foreign land. We must be prepared and purified in many ways by God's Spirit before we can rightly understand the consolations of God; and one grows in God when one learns, under present sufferings, to see more and more of the eternal comfort" (DIEDRICH).—"It is manifest that this vision ought to have comforted the Israelites,—that they who neither had nor saw a temple were meanwhile to busy themselves with considering this temple, and to study what such a vision might denote" (COCC.).—"In the selfsame day the hand of Jehovah was upon me: in this is verified anew the name of the prophet. God is strong; for in Him as in all others flesh and blood cry out: Gone is gone, lost is lost" (HENGST.).

Ver. 2. "Give me eyes to see the glorious grace of Thy kingdom; give me strength to go even into the sanctuary!" (LAMPE.)—"The prophet's visions are not deceptive dreams, but true, divine inspirations, Jer. xxvi. 12" (CR.).—"The land of Israel is the hieroglyph of the inheritance which God will give to His people from the whole world, which in contrast thereto is called the sea or the wilderness" (COCC.).—"The Church of God is the city set upon a hill, Matt. v. 14" (TÜB. BIB.).—How different was it in Matt. iv., when the tempter took Jesus to an exceeding high mountain, and showed Him all the kingdoms of the world and the glory of them!—"Through Christ we come even here in the kingdom of grace to the mount of God, to the heavenly Jerusalem, but the true e trance still awaits us in the kingdom of glory, Heb. xii. 22" (STARKE).—In the world, and yet high above the world; yea, the kingdom of the Anointed One is not of this world, and our citizenship is in heaven (Phil. iii. 20); and they who live by faith of the Son of God seek the things that are above (Col. iii.). The very high mountain points to the highest height.—On Mount Zion stands (Rev. xiv.) the Lamb, with His hundred and forty and four thousand.—"The high mountain is Christ, on whom the Church is founded" (GREGORY).—"The very high mountain is Mount Zion; not, however, in its present form, the state of humiliation, but in glorious exaltation. The high place already existed in the days before the destruction of the temple, Ps. xlviii. 3 [2], lxviii. 17 [16]. It now returns. The new exaltation took its beginning in the return from the exile, and found its completion in the coming of Christ (ch. xvii. 22, 23)" (HENGST.).—This is indeed a place to sit down in and meditate. Jerusalem in the Old Covenant, the Jerusalem which is the Christian Church, and the Jerusalem above,—what a theme for contemplation throughout time and eternity!—The repose in the contemplation of human and divine things.—Jerusalem a Sabbatic place in the working days of the world's history.—Ver. 3. "Christ is indeed the foundation and corner-stone of His Church; but He is also the Builder, who has laid the foundation and brings the building erected thereon always more and more to perfection, Matt. xvi. 18" (STARKE).—"The brass signifies holiness and purity, also life and permanent strength" (COCC.).—"He gives the holy and eternal temple, in which will be unchangeable repose" (ŒCOLAMPADIUS).—"He is the strong and invincible Hero" (STARCK).—"The serpent in the wilderness, too, was brazen; and Christ is the same yesterday, to-day, and for ever" (LUTHER).—"In the Church everything must be ordered and judged by the rule of the divine word, Acts xvii. 11" (STARKE).—The harmony of the kingdom of God.—"In the Church everything should be done decently and in order (1 Cor. xiv. 40); in it there is to be no confused teaching or dissolute life" (STARCK).—"Let every man examine himself by this measuring-rod, how far he has advanced" (GREGORY).—"Here applies what Plato wrote on his school: Let no one enter who is ignorant of geometry" (HAFENREFFER).—"Every believer ought to measure the temple of God and its magnitude, towers and palaces, and distinguish it from that which is not God's house, Ps. xlviii. 13, 14 [12, 13]" (COCC.).—"Elsewhere also Christ stands at the door and calls, invites in, shows the way, and opens the entrance to the temple and into the inner sanctuary" (BERL. BIB.).

Ver. 4. "Christ by His Spirit speaks with us as man with man" (COCC.).—"There has been a difference of opinion among teachers regarding the signification of this temple, altar, city, and territory. But the opinion to be rejected above all is that of the Jews and men like them, who think that it is to be the third temple, which must be built by their coming Messiah, and in their vain and foolish hope boast much of its great glory, and do not see, blinded and dull people that they are, that the text will not bear such dreams as theirs. Therefore this building of Ezekiel's is not to be understood of a new material building, but, like the chariot at the beginning, and also the building at the end, is nothing else than the kingdom of Christ, the holy Church of Christendom here on earth even to the last day. But how all the parts are to be properly interpreted and placed, that we will defer until that life in which we shall see the whole building prepared and ready. Now, while it is still in process of building, and much stone and wood belonging thereto are not yet born, not to speak of their being squared, we cannot see it all; it is enough for us to know that it is God's house and His own building wherein we all are" (LUTHER).—The thing is to see and hear exactly and lay to heart what serves for our peace; and this Israel has not done (Luke xix. 42).—"But all Israel must know its eternal calling; and if God gives special revelation to particular prophets, that revelation must accrue to the good of all" (DIEDRICH).—Although it *is* a mystery, it ought not to *remain* a mystery.—But what Israel was contemplated in this? Certainly not that which is called Israel after the flesh, but the spiritual, true Israel. The former built not after the pattern; the latter still continues to build itself in this temple.

Ver. 5. "To learn to understand the arrangement, the holy building, begin with the most distant things. We must not despise even those who stand employed at the threshold. The will, not the ability, is pleasing to God. Beware, therefore, of despising those who are still engaged in laying the foundations, and give only distant hope of life," etc. (ŒCOL.)—"The boundary of the wall had a twofold signification. To the community it was a warning not to approach the sanctuary with unrenewed hearts (Ps. xv.). With respect to God, it was a pledge that He would eventually separate His Church from the world. Because the people of God had neglected the admonition contained in the boundary, the boundary was as a righteous punishment destroyed also in the latter respect. Desecration as punishment followed desecration as guilt. In the broken-down wall of the smitten city was typified the abandoning of the people of God to the world. That this relation will in the future take another shape, that God will again raise up His reformed people to be an independent power, is typified by the erection of the new wall, which is in this respect an embodiment of God's protection and grace, that are to be imparted to the covenant-people renewed in spirit" (HENGST.).—"The Church has a triple wall: God as protection, the angels as guardians, and believers, in other words their prayers" (λ LAPIDE).—"God has indeed broken down by the death of Christ the wall of separation which was in the Old Testament between Jew and Gentile, yet He makes in the New Testament an invariable distinction between believers and unbelievers, Eph. ii. 14" (STARKE).—"If even among men the king's measure is larger than the ordinary one, not so much because kings require a more abundant measure, as because kings should replenish their subjects with all munificence, why should not God's measure overflow with grace, truth, and power?" (COCC.)—The larger measure of the sanctuary: (1) from the love wherewith God loves us; (2) according to the love wherewith we ought in return to love God in the brethren.—"One should be more liberal for the advancement of God's service than for other and worldly things, Gal. vi. 9" (O.).—"The breadth of the Church points to love, for nothing is broader; the height embraces the contemplation and knowledge, which alway ascend higher" (GREGORY).

Ver. 6. "How beautifully is everything measured and arranged in the community of the Lord by the eternal counsel of God! This is done by the wisdom of the great Founder and Master-builder (Eph. iii. 10, 11, iv. 12); which prepares by the measuring-rod of the gospel (Gal. vi. 16; Phil. iii. 16) living stones for the building of the Church, that it may become a habitation of God in the Spirit (1 Pet. ii. 5)" (TÜB. BIB.).—"When believers enter, they have (1) a Guide with them into all truth; (2) without Him they can do nothing; (3) progress is made toward full knowledge of God and Christ," etc. (COCC.)—"We ought to increase and grow, as in age, so in wisdom and grace, Luke ii. 52" (STARCK).—"Christ is the dayspring from on high, who for us has opened the way for the rising of the light" (GREGORY).—The east gate as model and pattern gate in its homiletic significance; every sermon ought to lead to the Father through Christ.—"In order to educate us by His Spirit, Christ undertook freely in our name this labour here, in that He became man for us, and ascended to the Father through suffering. Those also ascend these steps who will not, staying outside, give themselves up to lusts, but, wiser than the foolish multitude, attach themselves to God's people" (ŒCOL.).—"One must not so thoughtlessly imagine that only a single leap is required to come into heaven, but constant ascent is requisite and necessary in order to seek after the things that are above, Col. iii." (BERL. BIB.)—Ver. 7. "In the Lord's house are many mansions, according to the distinction of offices and gifts; each mansion, however, serves to ornament the house, John xiv. 2" (TÜB. BIB.).—"Since there are many mansions in the Lord's temple, there is certainly still room there. Let no one wantonly exclude himself therefrom, Acts xiii. 46" (STARKE).—The manifold positions and ministrations, and hence the manifold occupations in the kingdom of God.—"The thresholds show that entrance and exit are alike; as the beginning, so the end: he who begins well shall and will end well" (STARCK).—Ver. 8 sq. Behold, a wall round about; thou shalt not dream of overleaping it, or esteem it as non-existent; those whom God chose for Himself went out from the world, and are not of the world. There are also gates through which we have to enter in; but the way for mankind to God is through the one door, which is and continues to be Christ. Finally, the charge of the house for goings in and out is committed to the Spirit of Truth. No one shall enter in through the gate by lying and hypocrisy, and without the seal of the Spirit no one shall go out of the sanctuary into the world or pass over to eternity.—We first ascend the mountain on which the sanctuary is situated; next we must go up through the gate; and then we have before us the most holy place, namely, the manifestly revealed heart of the Father, with its blessed thoughts of peace.—"As he who no longer remains without is sheltered from the storms which rage there, so the Christian is not driven about by any wind. The porch reminds us of the peace and repose connected with the consciousness of the grace of God" (ŒCOL.).—"Truly, they who are preparing for the holy office of the ministry are measured in many ways, and they should still farther test themselves by the measure of the sanctuary" (STARCK).—"O soul, when so many depths, breadths, and heights of knowledge come before thee in the commencement of thy Christian course, let not that discourage thee! Christ gives thee the Holy Spirit, who will by degrees teach thee all things, John xiv. 26" (STARKE).—Ver. 12. Ministers of the Church should be protected against being too much pressed upon, for they are still but men. There is, however, a professedly pious impertinence, which addresses them as if their bones were iron and brass; *e.g.*, "The Lord is able to strengthen you," and the like. The Lord has in Ezekiel set a fence around the chambers of the keepers of the gate.—"We ought to avoid a brother who walks disorderly" (STARCK).—Ver. 13 sq. "Thus those who are in this way are walled around, covered, and protected on all sides; so that nothing can befall them in Him who is the Door and the Way, but everything leads forward to the sanctuary when we walk in Christ Jesus" (COCC.).—Ver. 16. "In the Church of God darkness has no place, but the light of truth and faith shines everywhere; yea, believers themselves are a light in the Lord, whose works shine before men, Matt. v." (STARCK.)—"Teachers and preachers ought to have a fuller knowledge of the divine mysteries than others, 1 Tim. iii. 9" (O.).—"They who walk in the ways of the Lord have the true, cheerful, and clear light; while the natural soul is a gateway without windows" (STARCK).—"What is signified by the palms is already fulfilled in the essential nature of believers, and will be so in particular in Christ's glorious kingdom (Ps. xcii. 13 [12] sq.), when they shall sing of victory in the tabernacles of the righteous (Ps. cxviii.), with palms in their hands, Rev. vii. 9" (BERL. BIB.).

Ver. 17 sq. "In the Church of God provision is also made for satisfying the need of spiritual fellowship on the part of those who are like-minded, and no one requires for this reason to wander about outside the wall in this or that sect, hole-and-corner conventicle, or society for any object whatever. Notice the 'apartments' here, and how Christ hallows them (Matt. xviii. 20), and comp. Zech. iii. 10" (COCC.).—"Those who are employed in God's house ought to keep even their feet clean, for holiness is the ornament of His house" (STARCK).—Ver. 20 sq. "By the diversity of the gates you may recognise the diversity of those who enter" (ŒCOL.).—"The way to the sanctuary has been opened to the nations of the north also" (STARKE).—"As in our cathedrals every part tells something to the deeper-seeing connoisseur, so this is still more the case in Ezekiel's temple" (RICHTER).—"Everything here is in harmony and mutual correspondence, like the Old and the New Testaments, Moses and Christ, the prophets and the apostles" (STARCK).—Ver. 28 sq. "The courts are separated, for the covenant of Abraham is one thing, the covenant of Moses another, and the covenant of Christ still another. Yet they only mutually confirm one another. For are not the contents of the covenant the promises of God, who graciously forgives sin? One court, however, is nearer than another to the sanctuary. Walkest thou unhindered in the court of the priests, busied with spiritual sacrifices; then thank the Lord and extend meanwhile the hand to others, that by thy support they may overcome difficulties" (ŒCOL.).—"The inward and the outward measure must correspond perfectly in Christians" (STARKE).—Ver. 31. "So 2 Pet. i. 5-7 enumerates eight virtues" (BERL. BIB.).—Ver. 38 sq. "This signifies that our heart may remain unclean, even when we give our bodies to be burned for the glory of God. The constant mortification of the flesh must ground itself on Christ, otherwise we will lose courage," etc. (ŒCOL.)—"The believing soul presents its heart, as one sets a table, on which Christ as sacrifice is beheld, for faith lays hold of this alone" (STARCK).—Ver. 44 sq. "A place in the house of God is justly due to them who sing the praise of God in spiritual and heavenly songs, which contribute so powerfully to spiritual edification" (TÜB. BIB.).—"The spiritual songs of them who rejoice in the Lord, because they have been enabled to come to the altar and stand before God, form part of the spiritual sacrifice" (ŒCOL.).—"In these corrupt days music is used more for sin and vanity than for the praise of God. When will it be free from this service to vanity? Ps. cxvii. 1; Isa. xii. 1" (STARKE).—"He who draws near to God sings to Him also in his heart; they, however, sing best who in the midst of troubles are full of joy. They incite others to sing," etc. (COCC.)—Ver. 46. "Since 'sons of Zadok' is in our language equivalent to: sons of righteousness, this implies that only those duly keep the charge who are justified by faith and born of God, whom Jesus Christ has begotten and upholds by the word of His power" (ŒCOL.).—Ver. 47 sq. "The true temple is the body of Christ as He took it out of the grave on the third day, for it surpasses all figures and is pure life. The prophet here prophesies of it; but he does so in lisping words, and for the sake of his contemporaries his understanding of Christ in these chapters, where he speaks of Christ's kingdom and sanctuary, is still, as it were, in swaddling clothes" (DIEDRICH).

On Ch. xli.

Ver. 1 sq. "We ought to go forward under God's guidance in the ways of the Lord from glory to glory, but not to go backward or stand still except in meditation" (STARCK).—"The temple a figure of the Church of Christ; as the former was gloriously built, so also the spiritual form of the Church of Christ is glorious, Ps. xlv. 14 [13]" (TÜB. BIB.).—"The Good Spirit leads men to the Church, there to listen devoutly to the word of God; the evil spirit keeps them back from it, 1 John iv. 6" (STARKE).—That that can be entitled a palace which is at the same time called a tabernacle, shows how the King had resolved to become a pilgrim, just as He who is enthroned in the sanctuary on high walks with pilgrims, and is at home in the tabernacles of those who are humble and contrite in heart.—Ver. 4 sq. "The most holy place is set before us as the goal, and we understand thereby a heavenly state on earth, namely, the Church of the New Testament. Accordingly, in ch. xliii. the entire circuit of the mountain is called most holy, from which it is evident that no one is truly inside of this temple, or even in its courts, who is devoid of the New Testament perfection," etc. (COCC.)—Heavenly glory or eternal bliss is no doubt the only complete holy of holies; yet he who has entered the kingdom of grace has come to a glory which eye hath not seen, nor ear heard, neither hath entered into the heart of any man, to praise and glorify God for ever.—"When we meet together, God is present in the temple (Matt. xviii.); for our heart is the dwelling-place of the Father and the Son in the Holy Ghost" (STARCK).—Ver. 5 sq. That the chambers are connected denotes the brotherly relation in the sanctuary, Ps. cxxxiii.; 1 John iii. 1 sq.—God provides for His servants covert and shelter in this world.—The chambers are not all of the same size, but they are all connected with the sanctuary; the same is the case with the progress and growth of the members of the body of which Christ is the Head.—The saints of God are also measured round and round; no heavier task is laid upon them, no greater temptation befalls them, than what is their Father's will.—Indefiniteness in spiritual endeavours is a token of disease, a want of sobriety and obedience of faith.—Ver. 6. Leaning upon God, upheld by Him, but not mixed up with Him in our affairs.—Of ourselves we cannot stand a single moment.—Ver. 7. "In God's house we must go upward by growth in grace, that the mind may be always the more firmly directed heavenward" (BERL. BIB.).—The breadth in the top part.—"Christians ought not to contract, but to expand as they grow older" (STARCK).—Higher grace gives expansion in width and breadth. The narrower points of view with which we ascend gradually disappear.—The broader heart on the height of the Christian life in theory and practice.—Prayer an ascending stair.—But let us not forget that which lies in the middle! In the middle is the means, the way of mediation.—Ver. 8. The secret of the height depends on the foundation.—Ver. 12 sq. The history of dogmas is in many respects the off-place in Ezekiel's temple.—Ver. 15 sq. God knows and determines the magnitude of the Church on earth.—Ver. 17. "Enlightenment is from above; only thus do we obtain a conception of heavenly things" (STARKE).—Faith is a window, and, as compared with vision, a narrow one.—"Through His wounds we see into the heart of Christ as through a window" (A LAPIDE).—Ver. 18 sq. "The ever-flourishing palm is the righteous one who has overcome sin and is in the eternal habitations. And so also we are genuine men, in God's strength, with the heart of a lion" (HEIM-HOFF.).—The palm a sign of victory, of life, of eternal glory.—The view of the palm which is promised to the victor.—"Teachers ought to be men, especially to humbled consciences, but also to be lions against enemies" (O.).—Ver. 21. The New Testament presents no other view than the Old.—Ver. 22. "This altar is at the same time a table, as Christ is to our souls in the Holy Supper" (STARCK).—Wood: the humanity, too, of Jesus was like us in all things except sin.—Ver. 23 sq. Doors let in and shut out; so also does the Church.—Ornament is here combined with solemnness. We have not here the joyous worldly beauty of Greece, but neither have we the solemnness dark as death, as in Egypt. The world opens its doors half to frivolity and half to despondency.—"The sanctuary of the heart also must be shut, and not with one door only. Our treasure is incomparable, and ought to be preserved with much watchfulness and strong exhortation" (HEIM-HOFF.).—"There is no mention of a veil before the holy of holies, because it was rent at the death of Christ, and must not reappear. This the Lord knew, who showed Ezekiel everything, and Himself rent the veil. Christ is the fulfilment and substitute for everything in the former temple that is wanting in the latter" (RICHTER).—Here on earth, however, are only windows; face to face will be first in heaven.

On Ch. xlii.

Ver. 1 sq.: "As this temple was provided with many chambers, but each had its own purpose, so believing Christians must be sanctified chambers for the glory of God,—one for this use and another for that, 2 Tim. ii. 21" (STARKE).—Ver. 5 sq. While in the previous chapter the breadth increased with the elevation, it here becomes narrower. The progressive growth in grace is a wider consciousness of Christ, but a constantly narrowing self-consciousness (1 Cor. xv. 9).—So is the service in the gospel, when with increasing years our view into eternity expands, and similarly contracts in temporal matters; the nearer the day of reckoning is, our responsibility becomes the clearer to us, and the more clearly do we see our many mistakes and disloyalties.—"There are three stages of life: youth, manhood, and old age, and the last is the narrowest of all" (STARCK).—Ver. 7 sq. God is able to set walls around those who desire to keep themselves pure from the stains of the flesh, and to protect them in the hour of trial and temptation.—"True believers are protected, no one can injure them, John x. 27 sq." (STARKE.)—The protection which is in an evangelically-understood official and priestly dignity.—"If God's servants have no place under heaven, yet they have one in heaven" (STARCK).—"By these buildings connected with the temple, and pertaining to its outward economy, we should be reminded that the Lord bestows upon the pious the other necessaries of life also. In Him they find their entire satisfaction; but they use food, drink, intercourse with men, and this whole world, as if they did not use all this. Thus, to the pure all things are pure that they do with pure and upright heart. The word of God makes us strong when it is with us, and blesses also outward things. David never saw a righteous man forsaken (Ps. xxxvii.). So also has the Lord ordained that they who preach the gospel should live of the gospel, 1 Cor. ix. 13, 14" (ŒCOL.).—"Oh, how sweet it is to cling to the temple like Anna! Luke ii. 37" (STARCK).—Ver. 13 sq. "If we have to understand by the priests the early Christians, or those brought up from childhood in the faith of Christ and walking in this way, then in these verses is figured their fellowship with one another in particular, their united inquiry into the word and meditation thereon and on the mystery of Christ for growth of knowledge and increase of joy, so that they are prepared and adorned in one and the same faith, alway to return to and worship at the altar, which is Christ" (COCC.).—"In word, in work, in everything, be Jesus read, and He alone" (TERSTEEGEN).—Glory and holiness in their connection; how this connection is stamped on this temple and its arrangements and purposes, even to the most minute particulars.—His office secures enjoyment, too, to the minister of the gospel, but enjoyment from the holy; the Lord wills to be enjoyment to His own.—Profane ministers profane the sanctuary.—These two verses form a fitting text for introduction and ordination sermons.—That which is seemly for every Christian is, however, special duty for the priests. One should be able to discover in a preacher of the gospel, above all else, above all science, knowledge, culture, etc., that he is in the enjoyment of the sacrifice of Jesus Christ for the sins of the world.—"So also we ought not to approach the holy table of the Lord with worldly, impenitent hearts" (CALOV.).—From ver. 14 much pastoral wisdom may be learned.—"But the lesson is not that a pastor may for a time lay aside his clerical robes or hang them on a nail to make merry with the world" (BERL. BIB.).—A true minister of the gospel does not want to be called a clergyman in distinction from the laity,—a Pharisaic title, which the church regulations of our fathers do not know, and which modern State bureaucracy ought to abolish,—but as he is so in the spirit of the gospel in contrast to the world, even to the so-called world of culture.—The wrong and dangerous sociability of a minister of the word. The clerical coat does not make the clergyman, yet it is a defence and an admonition. The best clerical garment, and one which we may always put on and wear everywhere, is our sanctification in Christ.—It is as great a mistake to carry about the clerical coat everywhere, like a monk, as to leave it at home from unclerical frivolity or worldly-mindedness.—Paul became all things to all men (1 Cor. ix. 19, 22), but not at the expense of his ministerial office.—"When we sinners come in contact with Christ by faith, we are made clean, and become a holy, reasonable sacrifice, acceptable to God. But when once we are consecrated to God, we have to be on our guard that we on no occasion defile ourselves" (ŒCOL.).—Ver. 15 sq. "God gathers His Church from all the four quarters of the world, Isa. xlix. 12" (STARKE).—"So wide and spacious will the New Testament Church be, in distinction from the Old Testament Church. A greater than Solomon in all his pomp and glory is here; for Jesus is the Light of all nations, Isa. xlii. 6, xlix. 6; Luke ii. 32" (STARCK).—"All believers in the whole world belong to this temple. The true Church is the collection of the scattered believers that are in the world" (STARCK).—"Observe, only after he had learned exactly the internal magnitude did the prophet learn the external. It is labour in vain to labour in investigating nature until we have first laid a good foundation in godliness. Without this we continue too much devoted to the contemplation of visible things, and make them our idols, so that they become a stumbling-block and a snare to ourselves and other inexperienced persons. But when thou hast come to know the inner meaning of spiritual things, and hast tasted the length, height, and depth of the love of God, then thou mayest busy thyself with all visible things. Thou wilt everywhere pause, and, contemplating things with the spiritual eye, say: O Lord our God, how excellent is Thy name in all the earth!

Thou who hast made the heavens, declare Thy glory, etc. For by the contemplation of outward things thou wilt be borne along to the praise of the divine glory and the overflowing love of the heavenly Father toward His people, for whose sake He has made also this whole artistically-compacted framework of visible things" (HEIM-HOFF.).—"The prophet has now depicted everything so fully and clearly, in order to preach to his contemporaries, as babes in understanding, in a way intelligible to them, the consoling truth that God's Church is eternal through His grace, and that He will always rebuild His house among us, provided we only desire to be His. Whatever is lost must truly be restored more glorious than ever to them who love God; and where God's word finds lovers, His kingdom, too, increasingly assumes shape. But in Christ all has assumed such a shape, that through Him the sanctuary now always continues present in humanity; and the true altar of burnt-offering, Golgotha, is always before the eyes of the Most Holy Father, in order, for the sake of the sacrifice thereon offered, to love, sanctify, and protect us all. We thank thee, O most gracious eternal God and Father, who hast set up an eternal sanctuary for us sinners, never to depart from us, and hast sanctified us by the blood of Thy Son, and now givest unto us the four ends of the earth to embrace by Thy gospel; grant unto us to remain faithful in contemplation of Thee, and, ever fuller and fuller of Thy Spirit, to praise Thee through Jesus Christ. Amen" (DIEDRICH).

On Ch. xliii.

Ver. 1. "Jerusalem, how gladly would our foot stand in thy gates!" (Ps. cxxii.)—"Open to me the pearl gates, Thou who art the Ornament of heaven's city, Light from Light, chosen as the Light before the world began," etc. (DESSLER).—To come to Christ is really to find out the bearings of this world.—"The entrance took place after the measuring of the temple and consideration of its adornment. So did Christ show His disciples, represented in the person of the prophet, the whole heavenly edifice by word and work (John xvii. 6); and everything pertaining to the building of this spiritual temple was finished on the cross. The entrance of the glory from the east for lighting the temple took place when the apostles, on the day of Pentecost, were endued with power from on high," etc. (ŒCOL.)—"When Jesus comes there is light; darkness must disappear, and all is pure joy and comfort, Ps. xcvii. 11" (CR.).—Ver. 2 sq. "The gracious advent of Jehovah indicates the visitation of grace in the forgiveness of all sins, in light, salvation, and blessedness" (STARCK).—"The voice is that of Ps. xix., the voice of the gospel, which resounds through the whole world" (STARCK).—Where the gospel is preached, the waters of life make a noise not only of themselves, but also from the stones which men cast in, and from the rocky banks of worldly hearts which make resistance; but the glory of eternity shines upon earth.—"The loud noise of the glory is the voice of them who praise the Lord with one heart and one voice, here on earth as there in heaven, Rev. xiv. 1" (HEIM-HOFF.).—"We have here the hymn of praise and the triumphant joy of the saints as they cheer and encourage one another; the contradiction, confutation, and blasphemy of the wicked at the confessions of believers; the cries of the spectators expressing their various opinions, and the songs of the witnesses unto blood at the stake; just as in a triumphal procession the victors shout with joy, the vanquished howl. There is no more glorious victory than that of faith" (COCC.).—"The creature has its voice only from the Creator; and therefore His voice must sound louder than its, however loud it is, Ps. xciii. 3, 4 (Dan. x. 6; Rev. i. 15). He who said: 'Let there be light,' Himself shines forth at His appearing in the clearest light, as He who dwelleth in light that is inaccessible, 1 Tim. vi. 16; James i. 17 [Ps. l. 2; Deut. xxxiii. 2; Rev. xviii. 1]" (HENGST.).—"The justice and wisdom of God, kept secret since the world began, are set before the eyes of all. There was no corner in which the truth was not heard, whether it met with approval or contradiction. Thus no one perishes unless he is an enemy to the light. Christ is altar, priest, and sacrifice; hence they who are near the altar cannot but have a sight of His glory" (COCC.).—"Let us pray God to enlighten the dark earth of our heart with that holy light of His glory!" (ŒCOL.)—Ver. 3. The terror of the prophet on account of the past and in the present; what will be the future terrors of the wicked!—"The thought of the perdition of the lost always causes pain and alarm to the true prophets" (STARCK).—"The knowledge of God never causes pride, but humility, because it at the same time discovers the corruption of the heart. The more modest a man is, and the less he trusts to himself, the more is he endowed with the knowledge of God. The bowed down are, however, revived by the Lord and led by the Spirit to the place where the majesty of the God of glory shines" (HEIM-HOFF.).—Ver. 4 sq. Whom the Spirit has cast down, the Spirit raises up again.—This is life in dying, rising up in falling.—"Yea, thus shall God's temple be, full of divine spirit and life; but then it must consist of other materials than brick or stone" (DIEDRICH).—"What hinders this glory from filling also thy heart, provided it is not full of other things, and needs first to become empty, that thy hunger and desire may by the breath of the Spirit seek and find satisfaction in its fulness?" (BERL. BIB.)

Ver. 6 sq. "God does not relinquish mankind; He continually creates anew His Israel for Himself" (DIEDRICH).—"That Jesus aimed at the preservation of the temple is shown by His cleansing of the temple at the commencement of His ministry, whereby He intimated His intention to effect a wholesome reformation. Not until after this reformation was decisively rejected did He, at the close of His ministry, effect the second cleansing of the temple, which is the symbolical announcement of its destruction: Ye would not have reformation, therefore ye must have revolution. The sentence: 'Behold, your house is left unto you desolate' (Matt. xxiii.), immediately follows the saying: 'How often would I have gathered thy children,' etc. Had they let themselves be gathered, their house would not have been destroyed; it would have become 'a house of prayer for all people' (Isa. lvi. 7). Jesus speaks first in view of His passion in Matt. xxiv. 2, when the stiff-necked obduracy of the people had been completely revealed. Had the Jews listened to Him, had they not imposed silence on His disciples, the stones of the temple would not have cried out (Luke xix. 40; comp. Hab. ii. 11). Not until they had stopped up the mouths of the true witnesses did the preaching of the stones sound forth. But while the abolition of the form was brought on by the mass of the people, who once more, and in the most culpable manner, thrust away from them their Creator, and lightly esteemed the Rock of their salvation (Deut. xxxii. 15), the election, far from being deprived of the blessing pertaining to them, found a glorious compensation for the loss of the temple in the Church of Christ, the legitimate continuation of the temple, John ii. 19" (HENGST.).—"It is man in whom, as in a temple chosen for Himself, He sets the throne of His glory. This is a New Testament word of promise; for what else does it imply than that sins are forgiven, our heart renewed, confirmed, and made obedient to the truth?" (HEIM-HOFF.)—"(1) This temple shall be the true temple; (2) this temple is different from the former temple. Into it nations and kings bring indeed their glory, but the kings and people of Israel no longer their abominations" (COCC.).—False doctrine brings the threshold of God and the threshold of men close to each other.—"Where the government of the Church is conducted by and according to the spirit of the State" (BERL. BIB.).—In this way the divine becomes human, and the human looks as if divine; and this is the devil's union-work.—Therefore the sanctuary of the king is still not Jehovah's sanctuary.—"A table at once the Lord's and the devil's, Paul has expelled from the Church" (STARCK).—Ver. 9. "God now first returns to the apostates; but His grace is designed to work repentance, and then He will never more depart from them" (DIEDRICH).—Ver. 10 sq. "Solomon's temple left the people in their disobedience and worship of idols; but this house belongs to a higher order. He who lays it to heart will cease sinning, and duly examine the temple and its measurements. For the measuring of the temple, which is not visibly present, must be done in the Spirit, 'which temple, however, are ye' (1 Cor. iii.). And therefore each one should examine with abasement his heart and conscience, and be displeased with himself because he has lived so long in ingratitude toward God," etc. (ŒCOL.)—The shame of the poor sinner finds in the temple, which is Christ, exactly the right measure.—The understanding of Ezekiel's temple-vision from the self-knowledge of the heart.—The turning to repentance through the promises of the gospel.—"The contemplation of the goodness and the works of God ought to bring shame into our hearts" (STARCK).—"The form of the divine economy of grace is, in outline, here described" (BERL. BIB.).—Ver. 11 sq. "They who repent of their sins are capable of knowing the temple and its arrangements, while those who wantonly pursue fleshly desires receive not the Spirit of wisdom, and are incapable of knowing the law of the Lord (2 Tim. ii. 19; 1 John iii. 3). For the law of the house is God's law, that everything be most holy" (HEIM-HOFF.).—"That the temple stood on the top of the mountain lets the whole land have it continually before its eyes in its midst, and not now and then only on occasional visits" (DIEDRICH).

Ver. 13 sq. "Christ is the true altar (Heb. xiii. 10); for He is the propitiation for our sins (1 John ii. 2; Rom. iii. 25), and He has sanctified Himself for us, John xvii. 19" (CR.).—"No one could go into the temple without passing by the altar, and so no one can go into heaven without the sacrifice of the death of Christ, Acts iv. 12" (STARCK).—Golgotha the true altar of burnt-offering: "here hangs the antitype of all the sacrifices" (LAMPE).—Ver. 18 sq. "Thus God comes, first and gives grace; His grace makes ashamed, chastises, sanctifies, reconciles, and produces intimate eternal fellowship. This is always God's way with us men, provided only we recognise it aright in these days of ours, when now it is set in the most glorious light; Christ and the apostles have given additional clearness to Ezekiel" (DIEDRICH).—"In the New Testament we no longer offer material, but spiritual sacrifices through Jesus Christ, etc., 1 Pet. ii. 5" (TÜB. BIB.).—"He who would bring an offering pleasing to God must be of the race of Zadok, Isa. i. 15 sq." (STARKE).—The prayer of a righteous man availeth much, because it is effectual, Jas. v. 16.—"All true believers are priests who can draw near to God, for access to the throne of grace has been opened to us through Christ" (STARCK).—The ministers of a king are glorious; how much more so are they who minister before the King of all kings!—Ver. 21. Comp. Heb. xiii. 11 sq.—"All this only illustrates more clearly the sacrifice of Christ" (RICHTER).—Ver. 22. Golgotha the place of purification of all altars.—Ver. 23 sq. "A man can offer himself as a burn-sacrifice to the Lord, when he fully, entirely, and unreservedly devotes himself to Him in faith and love. The end of our creation, redemption, and sanctification, involves this" (BERL. BIB.).—Ver. 25 sq. Christ finishes His work in His people too.—"It is not enough to begin well in what is good; we must also stand fast in the Lord, and continue stedfast unto the end, 2 Thess. iii. 13; Heb. iii. 14; Rev. ii. 10, iii. 11" (CR.).—"But those who are sanctified to the Lord by the sacrifice of Christ ought to praise God's benefits, and especially to remember them at the Holy Supper, according to the saying: This do in remembrance of Me, and: Show the Lord's death till He come" (HEIM-HOFF.).—Ver. 27. "They who were in Christ before others ought in this to serve as priests to the younger believers" (BERL. BIB.).

On Ch. xliv.

Ver. 1 sq. "Blessed are they who walk under God's guidance, whom He brings back as here to the principal gate toward the east" (STARCK).—"God's connection with mankind remains a secret" (DIEDRICH).—"The shut gate is the book sealed with seven seals, which only the victorious Lion of the tribe of Judah opens, and no one shuts (Rev. v. 5). When we draw near to Him who is the Door of the sheepfold, He, because He is the only-begotten of the Father, will open unto us and show us the Father" (ŒCOL.).—"Christ needs no successor to figure as His vicar in the Church" (BERL. BIB.).—"But certainly in what follows a prerogative is indicated which pious princes, magistrates, and lords may have" (COCC.).—"Our heart, too, should be shut to the world and the devil, when once the Holy God has entered into it, and His glory has swallowed up sin and misery in us" (STARKE).—"Alas, if the door of heaven should be shut!" (STARCK.)—Ver. 3. The position of the prince in the sanctuary of the Lord.—Even the highest civil power has nothing to complete here, but only enjoys the fruits of the completed, perfect sacrifice of Christ.—Princedom and power in the light of the glory of Christ.—The Christian ruler and the rule of Christ.—Privileges and the corresponding responsibility.—"The nearer we are to the sanctuary, the more holy and godly ought we to be" (STARCK).—The Christian ruler ought to be the Christian pattern to his people.—He is not to preach, just as it is not his office to offer sacrifice; but he is to nourish and protect the Church and avow its faith.—"Christ is the gate, the only gate; through Him the glory of God has entered into the Church. It also belongs to Him alone to speak the word of God. Hence even the prince is not allowed to enter the Church for the purpose of making his own discourses be heard there. For in the Church is the throne of Christ alone, and of no one else. What is said of the prince is rather this, that he ought to have a good conscience and joy before the Lord because of his princely office, which does not merely consist in this, that we live in peace and quiet under his sceptre, but also that the people may hear the word of God, and without fear offer to Him the sacrifices of their worship" (COCC.). (Interpreting the prince as the Messiah: "No one knoweth the Father but the Son, who is from God, because He says: My meat is to do the will of Him that sent me" (John iv. 34), ŒCOL.)—Ver. 4. "If the prophet here again falls to the ground before the glory of the Lord, have we not humbly to acknowledge and confess our frailty and weakness in presence of the divine mysteries? No plummet of the understanding sounds the abyss of the mysteries of God. Let us be content with what revelation presents to us" (after JEROME).—"God reveals His glory to His servants, especially when He calls on them to make known His will to the people, Acts xviii. 9, xxiii. 11" (TÜB. BIB.).—"Consider, O Christian, whether thou art what thou art called; whether thou hast God or some one else dwelling in thy heart; whether thou art full of glory or of worldliness, sensuality, and carnality!" (STARKE.)—Ver. 5 sq. Divine things are not to be drowsily listened to, or drowsily engaged in.—In everything there must be heart—in seeing, in hearing, in doing.—*Pectus theologum facit,* not pathos.—The goings in and out of the sanctuary, a solemn consideration for every one, but especially for those who keep the charge of the sanctuary, whatever their rank in the service.—"The sin which still adheres to believers makes them often inattentive in the most necessary things; hence they need many a stirring up and putting in remembrance, 2 Pet. i. 13" (STARKE).—Ver. 6. Sinners make light of their doings; but God suddenly says: Enough.—"He who seeks to be saved out of this lost world must once for all have enough of it" (STARCK).—The feeling of final surfeit of the world must, however, include aversion; for repentance is conversion, not so weariness of the world, disgust with the world, or such like.—There is a difference between the Israel after the flesh and the Israel after the Spirit.—Ver. 7. "The false Israel gives the sacraments to the heathen, and elects heretics to office" (DIEDRICH).—I know thy works, saith the Lord, but of thy faithfulness I know nothing. Quite enough to remove the candlestick, although baptizing, marrying, and dispensing the Lord's Supper still go on.—The so-called liberal clergy.—The voice of the people, the choice of the people, is not God's voice, God's choice, but frequently God's judgment to the full.—Strange doctrine indicates an uncircumcised heart; and where that is, in spite of ordination and consistorial confirmation, and whatever else pertains to circumcision, there is nothing but the foreskin of a hireling, a thief, and a murderer of the sheep.—"Self-chosen divine service is an abomination to the Lord" (STARKE).—The responsibility in the election of a pastor.—The outward discharge of the ministerial office, however exact, does not make a minister such as he should be according to God's word.—A person baptized in due form may yet be no Christian after the Spirit.—Ver. 8. The false teachers, who please the spirit of the age and have the applause of the world.—What general can employ a soldier who is everything else, but no soldier? And the general superintendents [bishops, presbyteries] ordain year by year men who have got through their examinations and are of canonical age, but who are fitter for anything else than for being pastors.—Ver. 9. "It is accordingly a token of the greatest decline of the Church when the wicked and manifest hypocrites are not only not expelled, but go freely in and out, and even have the ruling power" (BERL. BIB.).—The Church of the future of Jesus Christ, a pure church.—Ver. 10 sq. The judgment on the priests of the sanctuary, already begun inwardly, is their evil conscience, that cripples all energy in presence of the world, and degrades them to the position of paid domestics; and outwardly too, for even men of the world have no respect for them, although they do not revile them as fanatics.—The false righteousness, which is not God's righteousness, is also a detestable idol, behind which so many preachers commit adultery.—"Where there are ungodly teachers there is no want of ungodly hearers, Jer. v. 31" (STARKE).—The lower service in the sanctuary a question of conscience reaching into many a pastor's life.—Degraded priests a mirror for pastors.—Ver. 11. But even in the performance of subordinate service, where one originally stood higher, the grace of God may be with us, provided we let God's humbling of us issue in conversion of heart, and look upon the punishment as a righteous recompense. It is not at all necessary that we should, as the world calls it, make a successful career in the clerical profession.—It is not natural gifts, but heartfelt piety, which decides as to the testimonials which the Lord grants, and as to capacity for office in His eyes.—Ver. 12. Least of all should a preacher be a stumbling-block and cause of destruction to others. Yet the grace of God will still raise up from their fall even those who caused others to fall. Grace and always grace. Let us not despise the offer, let us not neglect the day of grace.—But there is no grace without self-judgment and self-condemnation.—The sins of the preacher in their consequences as regards the life of the community.—"A minister of the Church ought to be a pattern to the flock in doctrine and life, 1 Tim. iv. 12; 2 Tim. i. 13; Tit. ii. 7" (STARCK).—The servant who knows his lord's will and does it not shall receive a double amount of stripes.—

Vers. 13, 14. The ignominy of failure in ministerial life: personal access to God is hindered, and the office becomes a torment.—"Wherein can they who have cause to be ashamed before others of their former doings, and have given much offence to others, complain of God that the first have become last, when God still finally receives and takes hold of them, although they do not attain to such a high position as otherwise they might have attained to, and which others have attained to? Should they not rather extol God's exceeding great and undeserved mercy to them?" (BERL. BIB.)

Vers. 15, 16. The sons of Zadok are those who have neither received the mark of the beast in their hand nor in their forehead (Rev. xiii.).—"Faithful servants of God are highly esteemed in His sight, Ps. cv. 15" (CR.).—Ver. 16 sq. Blessed are the pure in heart, for they shall see God (Matt. v.).—"Sheep they ought to be, but neither to keep the sheep for the sake of the fleece, nor to enter in in sheep's clothing" (BERL. BIB.).—"Let him who desires to be found at last among them that are clothed in white robes, be diligent to have a conscience void of offence, Acts xxiv. 15 sq." (STARKE).—The precepts according to the law should remind us that preachers particularly run within lists, as Paul writes of the Christians. What is fitting for any one else may yet be far from seemly in a preacher. —But it is just those who take things easy that speak most of their severe toil and the heavy labour they have to undergo.—Ver. 19 sq. "Let them manifest their intimate fellowship with God and the glorious privileges over which their soul rejoices in a becoming walk and conversation. They are not to conform to the world, but to shine as lights among men (Phil. ii. 15); while at the same time they are not to make a show of their inward life, lest the people from hypocrisy should imitate that to which their mind is a stranger" (HEIM-HOFF.).—"They certainly should go among the people, but not seek to exalt themselves over the people because of their prerogatives, but to hold converse with them as brethren with brethren" (COCC.). (Comp. on ch. xlii. 14.)—He who ministers at the sanctuary must never seem profane, nor a fop in his attire, nor comic in his speech, nor a man of the world in his transactions. He may seem ridiculous to the world, only never conformed to the world.—But the pretended sanctification through holy priests is also of the devil, for of God Christ is made to us sanctification, etc., and there is no other mediator than He, the only Mediator between God and men.—Ver. 20 sq. Seemly, but not remarkable either in defect or excess.—Men of extremes are unfit for the holy ministry.—"The spirit of believers is a spirit of power, and of love, and of a sound mind, 2 Tim. i. 7" (BERL. BIB.).—Ver. 22. Ministers' widows an exception among widows.—But this neither bids ministers marry, nor forbids their remaining unmarried, only the marriage ought to be a priestly one.—The spiritual side of the married state.—Ver. 23. As their life, so above all their teaching ought to preserve the people from defilement, and train them to purity. —Ver. 24. God's word is God's judgment, the righteous Judge, right law and upright judgment. —The servant of God as umpire in disputes. He must not be a party man, but stands over the parties.—The Sabbath in the pastor's house also a subject for reflection.—Ver. 25 sq. They who are the messengers, heralds, and representatives of an eternal life shall neither have their serenity disturbed by the death of believers, which is no death, nor their pure walk defiled by the life of the spiritually dead, which is no life.—"Have no fellowship with those who love dead works but hate the life of God" (BERL. BIB.).—We too are allowed to wipe our eyes, as God wipes away every tear from the eyes of His saints.—At Jehovah's altar is peace and joy in the Holy Ghost (Ps. cxxxii. 9, 16).—Ver. 28. "Why dost thou, O teacher, strive for a larger stipend and greater income? Knowest thou not that the Lord Himself will be thine inheritance and thy exceeding great reward, or wishest thou not that He should be so?" (TÜB. BIB.)—"All who have first the kingdom of God for their possession, are also truly priests. God feeds them wholly on what is hallowed, and he who will have a blessing in his house must evince love to them" (DIEDRICH).—What greater inheritance can there be than God, the Lord of all; and what greater possession than He who made, who sustains, and rules heaven and earth?—"So Christians ought not to endeavour after filthy lucre; they are not to have their portion in this world, but to have their home in heaven" (ŒCOL.).—Ver. 31. "In God's service there is no filthy lucre. The Lord purifies everything for them who eat with Him" (DIEDRICH).

On Ch. xlv.

Ver. 1 sq. "Here in particular I acknowledge the weakness of my knowledge. I silently revere the mysteries of this passage. Neither will any mortal explain them completely, because that which God has prepared for them that love Him does not come into the heart of man. This indeed I see, that he speaks of the possession of the land of the living, as also the Revelation of John has borrowed much from this passage." Thus Œcolampadius expresses himself. —"God promises believers an inheritance, and will also give it them in due time, but that is in heaven" (STARCK).—"God the Lord needs indeed no land for Himself, yet it is for His honour when real estates are bequeathed to churches and schools, that those who labour in them may receive their support from them, Gen. xlvii. 22" (STARKE).—"They who live from God's hand are content with His measure, even when it turns out small and modest" (STARCK).—"It ought to be our joy to be near God, to be associated with Him" (STARCK).—Ver. 2. "There is nothing twisted and crooked with God; with Him everything is straight" (STARCK).—"The paths are often crooked and yet straight on which Thou makest Thy children come to Thee," etc. (ARNOLD.)—Ver. 3. The sanctuary was situated in the centre of all; so ought religion to be the central point of all life, and Christ the centre of true religion. — Religion, faith, Christianity ought not, either in the life of nations or of individuals, to be placed in a corner merely as a tolerated piece of antiquity.—Ver. 4. "If those who labour in the church and the school have no official houses, still they must have houses to dwell in. Therefore it is fitting that the community should build such, and keep them in a habitable condition" (STARKE).—"When ministers' houses are near the church, they can the-better attend to their office, 1 Chron. ix. 27" (O.).—"The Lord's faithful priests shall dwell beside Him, and be with Christ, for refreshment and revival from the strife and disquiet of men among whom they are scattered" (Cocc.).—Ver. 5 sq. "Although a lesser service in the Church appears to be incumbent on church officers and schoolmasters, yet care must be taken to provide them with food and lodging," etc. (Starck.)—"Hence offices and ranks which are not mutually destructive ought to continue; only let each in his place belong to the Lord" (Tossani).—"The sanctuary is not included in the city or state as formerly, for God will not permit His kingdom to be confounded with the temporal power; this, however, does not mean that God cannot rule in the state, bu only that God's kingdom and human kingdoms are different. For human authority is not to interfere in the kingdom of God, but the divine authority does interfere in the kingdoms of men, and God makes subjects obey their princes, servants their masters, and children their parents; and all obedience, if of the right kind, is paid to Him as the Lord, and to men as brethren and fellow-servants whom the common Lord has placed in authority for the Lord's sake. But we do not obey God for the sake of a man, nor can any man by his power make us obedient to God," etc. (Cocc.)—"Hence when this prophecy places the sanctuary outside of the city, and yet annexes the sanctuary to the city, that indicates that in the kingdom of Christ states and governments will belong to the people of God; in which, however, the kingdom of God will not be absorbed nor confined" (Cocc.).—"The magisterial office is holy, and has also part in the holy, Num. vii. 1 sq." (Cr.)—"For princes to have their domains is not unjust, but they should not seek to draw everything into these domains," etc. (Starke.)—Ver. 8 sq. "To protect, but not to fleece.—"Governments ought to give good heed to weights, measures, and coinage, and allow no inequalities to creep in" (Tüb. Bib.).—"Christians ought to be upright in their dealings, 1 Thess. iv. 6" (O.).—"Knowingly to pass spurious coin is intentional deceit, and so is the clipping of coins in order to lessen their weight" (Starke).—"Unjust gain does not profit the third generation. Lightly come, lightly gone" (Hafenreffer).—Ver. 13 sq. "Even the small gifts of the poor, when given in true love, are an acceptable offering, Heb. xiii. 16" (Cocc.).—"It is reasonable that a man set apart a considerable portion of his income for the glory of God and the support of the true worship, Rom. xv. 16" (Tüb. Bib.).—"The revenue for spiritual objects is most defrauded" (Starke).—There are liberals and liberals; the liberals of former days built churches, the liberals of to-day would like to tear them down; to the former, church endowment was an aim, to the latter an eyesore.—"Almsgiving in private is a fruit of faith; but not less so is liberality in endowments for churches and schools" (Cocc.).—The Christian munificence of our fathers was a very different thing from the duty of subscribing to associations imposed on their children, and from the whole ordinary system of collecting as it is carried on to raise supplies for the kingdom of God.—Ver. 15. "The antitype of the lambs, the Lamb that bore the sin of the world" (Starck).—The sacrifices considered in Christ.—Christian sacrifices are spiritual sacrifices.—The fulfilling of the sacrifices in the Spirit of Christ.—Ver. 17. "When Christ on the cross consecrated the new temple, He cancelled our sins" (Heim-Hoff.).—Ver. 18 sq. The new year of grace.—"At the beginning of the new year of grace, and with the newly rising light, the temple was again raised up or opened, and the true justification and sanctification through the sacrifice of Christ recognised and proclaimed" (Berl. Bib.).—Without cleansing there is no sanctuary for man, nor sanctification of him: "Let him who desires to be clean cleanse himself in the blood of Christ, 1 John i. 7" (Starck).—Ver. 20. Sin as error and seduction, and error and seduction as sin.—"We ought to attend divine service from beginning to end" (Cr.).—Ver. 21 sq. The ever-renewed remembrance of redemption in every participation of the Lord's Supper, and also in the experience of believers.—Every solemnization of the Lord's Supper a fulfilled paschal solemnity.—But our passover is Christ, 1 Cor. v.—How wearisome are church festivals to the men of our time!—"This prophetic representation contains a beautiful pattern for many a land; yet the main matter is this, that the Holy Ghost teaches us here how firmly and fixedly God with His grace has settled down among us men, and how priesthood and royalty are upheld in Christendom from His fulness. But they must keep close to the sanctuary, and the magistracy must protect the confessors of the truth on the right and on the left. The deepest ground, however, is this: Christ's disciples are all of them priests, and they themselves are also the royalty; they themselves offer sacrifice and also protect themselves, for God Himself is their strength through Christ. He who has the Spirit of Christ will easily understand the whole of this figure," etc. (Diedrich).—"It behoves us to celebrate the feast of tabernacles in spirit and in truth so much more than the Jews the nearer we approach eternity. For the nearer we come thereto, the less ought we to hold by this world, but on the contrary ought to withdraw our thoughts from the earth, from houses, cities, and lands, and allow scarcely a thought to arise in us that we still have a portion on earth and in the world; but, since we only dwell in tabernacles, let us have our loins girded, as those who are ready to depart, that they may be with the Lord" (Berl. Bib.).—"Our home is above, to which we draw nearer every moment" (Heim-Hoff.).—Tabernacles ought to be as passover; that is, we ought to pursue our pilgrimage on the ground of eternal redemption.

On Ch. xlvi.

Ver. 1. "There is a time for prayer and a time for work. On work-days we are not to rest, as on the Sabbath. He who does not work ought not to eat, whatever his pretences are. The door to the Father, the Source of all grace, opens itself to us when the gracious light of the love of God again shines forth, as it often does after great darkness. The way to the Father, on which Christ preceded us when He prayed for us, now stands always open to us, for the Sabbath is eternal, and we see the door to the inner sanctuary of the temple: only in a figure through a glass do we see the glory of the Lord" (Heim-Hoff.).—At the door, but not at the altar.—

The temporal power, moreover, ought, in reverence for what is sacred,—which is and ought to remain sacred to its subjects,—not to overstep the privileged position assigned to it, not to command or forbid when it has no authority for the one or the other.—"Princes and lords should abide in their calling" (CR.).—"But the temporal power and teachers and preachers ought also to live in harmony with one another, and to assist one another in furthering the glory of God, 2 Chron. xix. 11" (W.).—Ver. 3 sq. Prayer and diligent attendance on divine service are becoming alike for people and prince.—In the Old Covenant it is said: before the Lord; in the New Covenant: in the Lord.—Ver. 8 sq. Every one has his assigned path under God's guidance, and on it he should abide.—"God's guidance demands quiet; where the foot itself makes a noise, the will of the eternal Father is exchanged for our own choice" (ZINZENDORF).—"But many shall come from the north and from the south to worship in the Lord's house, Matt. viii. 11" (STARKE).—"The influence of love shall extend into the whole world from the south to the north, so that they from the north and they from the south shall go to meet one another, in order to receive and embrace one another as brethren" (BERL. BIB.).—"He that will serve God must never go backward, but always forward, growing in grace, 2 Pet. iii. 18" (STARCK).—"No one should go out of the church as he came into it; he should always take home with him something for his edification, Eccles. iv. 17 [v. 1]; Acts xvi. 14" (STARKE).—The prince has to go in the midst of his people, that his prerogative be not perverted into injustice; for the people do not exist for the sake of the prince, but the prince for the sake of the people.—"When magistrates and authorities give a good example to subjects and subordinates, that is a stronger motive than much teaching and exhortation, 2 Sam. vi. 15" (STARKE).—Ver. 11 sq. Grace makes the heart free, and so also willing. Voluntariness is a measure of grace, as mercifulness is a sign that we ourselves shall obtain mercy.—"He who confines his prayers and devotions to Sundays and festivals does not yet know what it is to serve God, what it is always to pray (Luke xviii. 1) and to worship God in spirit and in truth. Daily ought we to exhort and arouse ourselves, that we fall not again into sin; daily ought the praise of God to be heard from our mouth, Heb. iii. 13" (STARKE).—In every gift God looks on the giver's heart: My son, give me thine heart.—A people that shall be pure willingness, the prospect held out in Ps. cx.—As God's grace is new every morning, so also ought our devotion to Him to be renewed every morning.—The whole life of man ought to be a life consecrated to God.—"Our whole life should be a sacrifice, from morning to night, and next morning again" (BERL. BIB.).—The consecration of time.—Since Christ's appearance the night has disappeared, and the day has come; there are now only morning sacrifices.—Watchman, what of the night? was a question of pre-Christian longing. Is there not yet light towards Hebron? was the daily question of the priest in the old temple.—"The whole section is of the deepest importance for us, inasmuch as it instructs us to live in the word, when God's grace does not make itself known to us in the visible" (HENGST.).—Ver. 16 sq. If the prince is understood to be the Messiah, then according to that view Christ's gifts here to the children are different from those to servants, which are only temporary, and taken from them again!—"The year of freedom shall be 'the day of revelation of righteous judgment,' which is already exercised in secret. The hypocrites, who are condemned by the silent judgment of their heart, shall one day be manifest also to the world" (HEIM-HOFF.).—"Rulers ought not to invade the rights of their subjects, 1 Kings xxi. 2 sq." (TÜB. BIB.)—"He who is profuse in giving is (easily) compelled to take from others what belongs to them" (HENGST.).—"The kingdom of Christ is very different from an earthly one, for He supports His subjects, not His subjects Him, John x. 11" (STARCK).—In Christ's kingdom injustice has no formula, either socially or judicially.—"Spiritual things ought to be left in the spiritual order, and temporal in the temporal; confusion in this particular confuses the position of the people in other particulars also" (HEIM-HOFF.).—Ver. 19 sq. In the kingdom of God, as in the kingdom of nature, and in the full sense of the expression, everything has its own place. Only the things of men are in disorder, because they are sinners, and sin is disorder in every respect.—Servants of the Church should have the gift of distinguishing times and places, and above all, of discerning the spirits.—Consideration for the people, an important part of pastoral prudence.—To cook is to bring to a proper condition, so that the food tastes well and is agreeable; so ought also the truth to be prepared:—Is not homiletics a kind of sacred cookery?—"When teachers have rightly experienced wholesome truths in their heart, then they understand also how to set them rightly before others, Matt xiii. 52" (STARKE).—"The same kind of food does not do for the simple and children and for grown men" (BERL. BIB.).

(2.) *The Holy Land and the Holy City* (ch. xlvii., xlviii.).

CH. XLVII. 1. And he brought me back to the opening of the house, and, behold,
waters issued from below the threshold of the house eastward: for the
front [the face] of the house is toward the east, and the waters came down
2 from under, from the right side of the house, south of the altar. And he
brought me forth the way of the north gate, and made me go round the way
without to the outer gate, the way of the eastward-looking [gate]; and, behold,
3 waters came purling out from the right side. When the man went forth to
the east, there was a measuring-line in his hand. And he measured a thousand cubits, and made me pass through in the water—waters to the ankles.

4 And he measured a thousand, and made me pass through in the water—waters
to the knees [they reached]. And he measured a thousand, and made me pass
5 through—waters to the loins. And he measured a thousand—a river [was it
then] which I could not pass through, because the waters rose up, waters of
6 swimming, a river that could not be waded. And he said unto me, Hast
thou seen, son of man? And he led me, and brought me back to the bank
7 of the river. When I returned, behold, on the bank of the river very many
8 trees, on this side and on that. And he said unto me, These waters, going
out as they do to the east boundary, then flow down over the steppe, and
come to the sea, brought forth [they come] to the sea, and the waters are healed.
9 And it cometh to pass that every living thing which shall creep, whithersoever
ever the double stream shall come, shall live; and very many fish are there,
for these waters come thither, and they shall be healed; and everything
10 liveth to which the river cometh. And it cometh to pass that fishers shall
stand on it [shall place themselves over it], from En-gedi even unto En-eglaim there
shall be a spreading-place for nets; as to their kind, their fishes shall be as
11 the fishes of the great sea, very many. Its mire [its swamps] and its pools [holes],
12 these shall not be healed; they are given to salt. And [yet] on the river there
shall rise up, on its bank, on this side and on that, every kind of tree for
food; its leaf [foliage] shall not fade, nor its fruit cease; according to its months
it bears first-fruits, for its waters flow forth from the sanctuary; and its fruit
13 is for food and its leaf [foliage] for healing. Thus saith the Lord Jehovah:
The territory itself, the land which ye shall take to you for an inheritance,
14 [shall be] for the twelve tribes of Israel; for Joseph [two] portions. And ye
inherit it, every one as his brother, which I lifted up My hand to give to
15 your fathers; and [so] this land falleth to you for inheritance. And this is
the border of the land on the north side, from the great sea on the way to
16 Hethlon, to come to Zedad; Hamath, Berothah, Sibraim, which is between
the border of Damascus and the border of Hamath; Hazar the middle, which
17 is on the border of Hauran. And the border from the sea is from Hazar-
Enon, the border of Damascus, and [in the] north northward there is the bor-
18 der of Hamath; and [this] as the north side. And as to the east side, from
between Hauran, and Damascus, and Gilead, and the land of Israel, is
the Jordan; from the border ye shall measure to the east sea; and [this] as
19 the east side. And as to the south side, to the right; from Tamar to the
waters of Meriboth-Kadesh is the inheritance [to the river] to the great sea; and
20 [this] as the side to the right southward. And with respect to the west side,
the great sea from the border to over against the way to Hamath; this is the
21 west side. And ye divide this land for you according to the tribes of Israel.
22 And it cometh to pass that ye shall allot [divide] it as an inheritance to you
and to the strangers sojourning in your midst, who have begotten children in
your midst; and they are to you as the native among the children of Israel;
23 with you shall they share in the inheritance among the tribes of Israel. And
it cometh to pass, that in the tribe with which the stranger sojourns, there
shall ye give him his inheritance. Sentence of the Lord Jehovah.

Ver. 1. Sept.: K. εἰσηγαγεν με ἐπι τα προθυρα . . . ἀπο του κλιτους του δεξιου ἀπο νοτου ἐπι το θυσιαστηριον.

Ver. 2. . . . το ὑδωρ κατεφερετο— Vulg.: . . . *aquæ redundantes*—

Ver. 3. καθως ἐξοδος ἀνδρος ἐξεναντιας. K. μητρον . . . κ. διηλθεν ἐν . . . ὑδωρ ἀφεσεως. Vulg.: . . . *et traduxit me per aquam*—

Ver. 4. . . . κ. διηλθεν . . . ὑδωρ ἑως των μηρων . . . ἑως ὀσφυος—

Ver. 5. . . . χειμαρρους, κ. οὐκ ἠδυνατο . . . ἐξυβριζεν . . . ὑδωρ ὡς ῥοιζος χειμαρρου ὁ οὐ διαβησονται. Another reading: לא יוכל, Syr., Arabs.)

Ver. 6. Sept.: . . . ἐπι το χειλος του ποταμου (7.) ἐν τ. ἐπιστροφη μου.

Ver. 8. . . . εἰς την Γαλιλαιαν την προς ἀνατολας . . . ἐπι την Ἀραβιαν . . . θαλασσαν ἐπι το ὑδωρ της ἐκβολης— Vulg.: . . . *quæ egrediuntur ad tumulos sabuli orientalis . . . ad plana deserti, intrabunt mare et exibunt*— (Another reading: הגלילה, Syr., Chald., Arabs., *in hexaplis Origenes*.)

Ver. 9. . . . πασα ψυχη των ζωων των ἐκζεοντων . . . ὁ ποταμος . . . ὑγιασει κ. ζησεται παν . . . ἐκει ζησεται.

Ver. 10. . . . ψυγμος σαγηνων ἐσται, κατ' αὐτην ἐσται κ. ὡς οἱ— Vulg.: . . . *plurimæ species erunt piscium ejus, sicut*— (Another reading: דיגים.)

Ver. 11. . . . ἐν τη διεκβολη αὐτου κ. ἐν τ. ἐπιστροφη αὐτου κ. ἐν τ. ὑπεραρσει αὐτου— Vulg.: *In littoribus autem . . . in salinas dabuntur.* (Another reading: ובבאיו, *et in redditibus suis.* Sept., Syr.)

Ver. 12. . . . παν ξυλον βρωσιμον οὐ μη παλαιωθη ἐπ' αὐτου, οὐδε μη ἐκλειπη ὁ καρπος αὐτου· της καινοτητος αὐτου πρωτοβολησει . . . κ. ἡ ἀναβασις αὐτων εἰς ὑγειαν. Vulg.: . . . *afferet primitiva—*

Ver. 13. . . . Ταυτα τα ὁρια κατακληρονομησετε της γης, ταις δωδεκα . . . προσθεσις σχοινισματος. Vulg.: *Hic est terminus in quo possidebitis terram in . . . quia Joseph duplicem funiculum habet.* (Another reading: זה, גיא.)

Ver. 15. . . . της μεγαλης τ. καταβαινουσης κ. περισχιζουσης, της εἰσοδου Ἡμαθελδαμ.

Ver. 16. Μαωσθηρας, Ἐφραμηλειαμ, ἀνα μεσον τ. ὁριων Ἡμαθ . . . Δαμασκου, Εὐναν κ. του Εὐναν, αἱ εἰσιν ἐπανω— Vulg.: . . . *et confinium Emath, domus Tichon quæ est—*

Ver. 17. . . . ἀπο τ. αὐλης του Αἰναν. (Another reading: זאת פאת.)

Ver. 18. . . . ἀνα μεσον της Ὡρανιτιδος . . . ὁ Ἰορδανης διοριζει ἐπι τ. θαλασσαν τ. προς ἀνατολας Φοινικωνος·— Vulg. . . . *de medio Auran . . . Jordanis disterminans ad mare orientale; metiemini etiam plagam—* (Another reading: זאת פאת; עד הים, *etiam*, Ver. 19.)

Ver. 19. . . . προς νοτον κ. λιβα ἀπο Θαιμαν κ. Φοινικωνος ἑως ὑδατος Μαριμωθ Καδης, παρεκτεινον ἐπι— Vulg.: *Plaga autem australis meridiana . . . aquas contradictionis Cades, et torrens usque—* (Another reading: מְרִיבַת, Vulg., Syr., Chald.)

Ver. 20. Τουτο το μερος νοτος κ. λιψ, τουτο το μερος της θαλασσης τ. μεγαλης διοριζει, ἑως κατεναντι της εἰσοδου Ἡμαθ, ἑως εἰσοδου αὐτου·— Vulg.: . . . *a confinio per directum, donec venias—* (Another reading: זאת פאת־ים.)

Ver. 22. Sept: Βαλειτε αὐτην ἐν κληρω . . . προσηλυτοις . . . μεθ' ὑμων φαγονται ἐν κληρονομια— Vulg.: . . . *vobiscum divident possessionem—*

Ver. 23. . . . ἐν φυλη προσηλυτων ἐν τοις προσηλυτοις μετ' αὐτων. Ἐκει δωσετε . . . αὐτοις—

EXEGETICAL REMARKS.

As the entrance of the glory of the God of Israel (ch. xliii. and xliv.) forms the centre for the first section of this closing vision of the glory of Jehovah's kingdom, namely, for the temple and its service, so the waters of life from the temple give the key-note for the second section,—the holy land and the holy city,—and at the same time furnish the interpretation of the second and thereby of the first section.

Vers. 1–12. *The Waters of Life.*[1]

ADDITIONAL NOTE.

["It is necessary to take the first part of this chapter apart from the second, which relates to a different subject, the new division of the land, and which ought to have formed part of ch. xlviii. The vision contained in the first twelve verses of this chapter is a thing by itself, although it stands in close connection with what precedes, and springs naturally out of it. The prophet has been exhibiting, by means of a variety of detailed representations, the blessed results to the Lord's people of His re-occupying His temple. The way now stands open to them for a free and elevating communion with the Lord; and the work proceeds, on their part, by the regular employment of all spiritual privileges and the faithful discharge of holy ministrations. God is duly glorified in His people, and His people are blessed in the enjoyment of His gracious presence and the benefit of His fatherly administration. But what is to be the nature of the kingdom in this new form, in respect to the world without? Is it to be of a restrictive or expansive character? Is the good it discloses and provides for a regenerated people to be confined, as of old, to a select spot, or is it to spread forth and communicate itself abroad for the salvation of the world at large? In an earlier prophecy (ch. xvii.), when speaking of the future Head of the divine kingdom under the image of a little twig, plucked from the top of a cedar in Lebanon, and planted upon a lofty mountain in Israel, the prophet had represented this not only as growing and taking root there, but as winning the regard of all the trees of the field, and gathering under its ample foliage beasts of every kind and birds of every wing. The kingdom of God, as thus exhibited, seemed to carry a benign and diffusive aspect toward the entire world. And should it be otherwise now, when presented under the different but more detailed and variegated form of a spiritual house, with the living God Himself for the glorious Inhabitant, and a royal priesthood for its ministering servants? No; it is for humanity, mankind as a whole, that God was thus seen dwelling with men; and though everything presents itself, according to the relations then existing, as connected with a local habitation and circumscribed bounds, yet the good in store was to be confined within no such narrow limits; it was to flow forth with healthful and restorative energy, even upon the waste and dead places of the earth, and invest them with the freshness of life and beauty.

"This fine idea is presented by the prophet under a pleasing natural image. He is brought back by the angel from the outer court, where he was standing, to the door of the temple on the east; and there he sees a stream of water gushing from beneath the threshold, and running in the direction of south-east, so as to pass the altar on the south. He is then brought outside by the north gate, and carried round to where the waters appeared beyond the temple-grounds, that he might witness the measurements that were to be made of them, and the genial effects they produced."—FAIRBAIRN'S *Ezekiel*, pp. 489–491.—W. F.]

The bringing back of the prophet in Ver. 1 is explained from the circumstance that he had tarried (ch. xlvi. 21) in the outer court; latterly, at the sacrificial kitchens for the people. The **opening of the house** is the temple gate, where the entrance into the holy place of the temple opens.—מִתַּחַת stands first by itself, both times parallel to each other, to describe the very first impression, namely, that the waters (HÄV.: "in particular, living spring water is often in Scripture a symbol of the divine blessings, Isa. xli. 17 sq., xliv. 3") came forth **from below**, and so

[1] W. NEUMANN: *The Waters of Life.* An Exegetical Disquisition on Ezekiel xlvii. 1–12. Berlin, 1848. Somewhat hyperbolical, but written with intelligent and hearty appreciation, in the spirit of the language and faith of the prophets of Israel.

did not pour down from the heavens, but issued from the depth of the sacred foundation upon the mountain; and this is without doubt to be thought of in connection with the filling of the house with the glory of Johovah (ch. xliii., xliv.). What Tacitus observes (*Hist.* v. 12) about "a never-drying fountain, whole mountains hollowed out below the surface, and ponds and cisterns for keeping the rain water;" or when Robinson does not doubt that there is in the rock "an artificial well at a depth of some 80 feet below the Haram,"—all this serves for understanding the prophet only by way of contrast;—he means and intends to describe nothing of the kind. [W. Kraft (*Topographie von Jerusalem*) thinks that the prophetic contrast refers to the spring known only to the priests as hidden, and whose water served only for the outward cleansing of the people.]—The מִפְתַּן הַבַּיִת that follows subjoins the more exact definition of the first מִתַּחַת, as: below the threshold of the door of the temple, מִתַּחַת without a לְ, so that we have to seek the fountain-head not at this threshold, but farther in in the house.—The reason for saying **eastward** is the "eastern" position of the temple front; the waters which issued from below the house flowed toward the place where the glory of the Eternal had entered the house. Even Hitzig's dictum, which makes קָדִימָה to mean: "in the east," does not destroy the very expressive causal nexus of the two sections of these concluding chapters of Ezekiel; but W. Neumann acutely observes: "The circumstance that the water flows east appears significant to the seer, and yet again, on the other hand, natural; for, says he, the front of the house is toward the east. According to ver. 12, the spring is the bearer of the mysteries of the sanctuary, and consequently the means of bearing along its ideal substance; and to this the פָּנִים [properly: 'the constantly changing multiform aspects or manifestations of the soul through the exterior, the complex unity of which we call the countenance,' STIER] corresponds; because the soul of the temple looks to the east, the gushing stream flows in the same direction."—This already indicates the farther course of the water as to its direction immediately after its gushing forth under the threshold of the door of the temple. But before treating of this direction, mention is again made of this so characteristic gushing forth. While, however, after the first מִתַּחַת, to avoid repeating the מ before מִפְתַּן, it is merely said: מִתַּחַת מִפְתַּן הַבַּיִת, there now follows after the second מִתַּחַת the more exact statement: מִכֶּתֶף הַבַּיִת, from the "shoulder" of the house, *i.e.* the right one. מִתַּחַת means here neither: in the south = beneath (Judg. vii. 8 which is sufficiently expressed by מִנֶּגֶב, nor downwards (HITZIG), which is sufficiently expressed by יֹרְדִים. What is meant to be described is a stream of water flowing from the temple, not one conducted into the temple; hence the brook Etham cannot be supposed, from which Lightfoot brings the water by means of subterranean channels for washing the victims and cleansing the house. (Comp. also the combination of Judah Leo in Lundius, *die alten jüd. Heiligth.*) Dereser infers from יֹרְדִים, that the fountain "fell into the earth on the south side of the altar of burnt-offering in the court of the priests, and flowed on under it until it reappeared outside of the courts of the temple." יָרַד is employed to accord both with ver. 8, and also in general with the view current in Israel, according to which that which tends towards the abode of the Highest ascends, and hence that which comes out from it will descend. KEIL: "because the temple lay higher than the inner court."—הַיְמָנִית. After the repeatedly marked eastern direction, there can be no doubt which right side is meant; a person looking to the east has the south on his right, as also מִנֶּגֶב plainly indicates. This מִנֶּגֶב has its signification in reference to the altar of burnt-offering, which stood before the porch of the temple (ch. xl. 47): לַמִּזְבֵּחַ, the right (south) side of the house, the south part of the east side. The fact that the water issued "from the south end of the threshold," Hengst. explains from the circumstance that "the altar of burnt-offering lay immediately before the east door of the sanctuary; the water must therefore issue not from the middle of the threshold, if it was not to meet with an immediate hindrance; it must first come forth where the altar no longer stood in the way." This is quite natural. Neumann speaks of "the prominence given to the right side as the side of good fortune and power." He says: "If even in the feasts of the Bedouins the cup-bearer must hand the cup to the drinker from the right, to prevent complaint of want of respect, how could that which was here commanded by a heavenly hand for healing (ver. 8) come from another quarter?" [KLIEF.: "But the temple had two thresholds, one before the flight of steps at the door of the fore-porch, and one at the west end of the porch, before the temple gate. If, then, ver. 1 speaks in the outset of the door of the temple, that shows us that we have to understand the latter threshold. If the temple is the body, and its fore-porch the head, then its right shoulder is in the angle which the south wall of the temple porch forms with the east wall of the temple. The threshold of the door of the temple abutted with its south end on this corner, and thence under the threshold the fountain gushed out and ran down into the inner court."] "The water," says Häv., "comes from the sanctuary;" that is to say, "it is the fulness of blessing which is poured out over the community from the new manifestation of God. Without this going before, the people cannot serve the Lord in the new manner; and the service of God, again, is itself a grace and a gift from Him. If the fountain proceeding from God is simply a testimony to His revelation of Himself, then it cannot be a mere material fountain."

Ver. 2. In the court, surrounded with buildings and walls, Ezekiel cannot descry the farther course of the waters. For this he is **brought forth through the north gate, for the outer east gate is** always shut, and to go out through the south gate the prophet would be obliged to cross over the waters. [Neumann infers, from comparing ch. xl. 35, xliv. 4, that the guide had a preference for the north gate (but see ch. xlvi. 9), and seeks the reason in the significance of the north in the prophecies.] He proceeds on the outside along the wall of the outer court, the way to the east gate, as the **outer gate** is more exactly designated. [Neumann erroneously, because against the prophet's uniform mode of expression, refers the epithet **eastward-looking** to the **way**.] The thrice repeated דֶּרֶךְ thus emphasizes and depicts the circuit which Ezekiel had to take, because the aim of the prophet's going—the regaining a view of the waters—is the main matter. Whether the waters flowed forth *over* or *under* the courts is not expressly stated; at all events they ran under the surrounding walls, and doubtless under the stone pavement of the outer court.—וְהִנֵּה־מַיִם resumes verbally, when the waters were seen again, the וְהִנֵּה־מַיִם of ver. 1, so that the מַיִם without the article occasions no difficulty whatever; no other waters can be imagined than those which the prophet had seen before.—מְפַכִּים (Piel particip. of פָּכָה) only in this passage, thus a unique and not less pictorial expression. GES.: "to trickle;" and Umbreit adduces its affinity with בָּכָה, so that he gets "weeping" waters, which would portray such an "insignificant commencement of the issue" as does not harmonize with ver. 1. How can that be thought of as trickling here which has already flowed through the courts? The affinity of the expression with בָּקַק, "to pour out," likewise observed by Gesenius, would lead to a signification such as: to gush out. Hitzig goes back to פָּכַךְ, a word which does not exist; and Meier to בָּכַךְ, "to burst forth" (?). Hengst. thinks of פַּךְ, "a bottle," and supposes a "gurgling," like the "sound which the emptying bottle makes," which, however, does not correspond to the "character of fulness and livingness" which, according to him, the waters in themselves must have; he translates, indeed: "gushed out." Neumann assumes a radical signification: "to break up," "to set free;" hence: פָּכָה, "to break forth." To translate it with Keil: "to purl," very probably comes nearest the figure.—מִן־הַכָּתֵף הַיְמָנִית; HITZIG: "not the south side of the whole temple-circuit, but: the southern half of the east front;" NEUM.: "on the beholder's right hand, when he has come out here from the north;" HENGST.: "the right side is here also the south-east, the south side of the east gate, where the water comes forth only because it has taken its rise on the south-east side of the temple;" KLIEF.: "the angle which the eastern outer gate formed with the wall of the outer court is meant." At all events this is meant to be expressed, that the waters which Ezekiel here saw again were the waters which came from the sanctuary.

Ver. 3. Hengstenberg translates: "When the man went forth to the east with the measuring-line in his hand, he measured a thousand cubits," etc. Ezekiel's guide is, in distinction from ver. 2 (וַיּוֹצִיאֵנִי), now considered by himself (בְּצֵאת־הָאִישׁ). He had קָו (ch. xl. 3: פְּתִיל)—from קָוָה, according to Gesenius: "to twist;" according to Meier: "to bring together"—in his hand, which is remarked because of what follows, where not merely the farther course of the waters, but still more their peculiarities during the course, are set forth. Following the waters in an eastern direction, the man measured a thousand cubits.—מֵי אָפְסָיִם gives the experience of the prophet, whom the man makes to wade in the water from one bank to the other; hence it is not appositional to בַּמַּיִם, but an independent clause, the meaning of which many attempts have been made to distort, when yet it must contain a statement corresponding to the following increments. Kimchi, making use of Gen. xlvii. 15, interprets it: "water of vanishing" = little water. The dual form: אָפְסַיִם, certainly does not refer to an abstraction, but, as uniformly, denotes things paired naturally or artificially; in the connection here, without doubt, a corporeal duality, but not, as Genesius: "foot-soles" ("shallow water which only wets the soles"); against which Hitzig justly observes that the water reached to the foot-soles in the very beginning. אֶפֶס is not exactly the same as פַּס, that is, "extension," flat of the hand, and hence also flat of the foot, foot-sole, but אָפְסַיִם rather suggests כְּתֹנֶת פַּסִּים, a garment extended so as to reach to the ankles. [Neumann thinks that "waters of the foot-soles" probably were waters of only the depth of the sandals, which the prophet had put off (!) in the court of the priests, and again put on; and that, in conformity with the phrase: אַפְסֵי אֶרֶץ, we have to think of the two ends, the two lower extremities of the body, that is, the feet: waters of the extremities were waters which scarcely covered the feet.]—בָּאַמָּה, measured by the measure, which was a cubit-measure.

Ver. 4. After the second measuring of a thousand cubits, *i.e.* of distance along the course of the waters, the result of the waters becoming always deeper is מַיִם בִּרְכַּיִם; an ungrammatical form, so much the more striking, as we have the *stat. constr.* מֵי before and after. See Hitzig's explanation, which, however, is a mere conjecture, while the supposition of a separate clause (**waters, to the knee they reach**) is easier, and at the same time more emphatic. After a third measuring, we have **waters to the loins**. But after the fourth measuring of another thousand cubits, *i.e.* in all, at a distance of four thousand cubits, it is —Ver. 5—a river! נַחַל looks like an exclamation of Ezekiel's surprise on seeing what reminds him of the impetuous rush of a mountain torrent. The going through, hitherto possible, is no longer so, for the waters נָאוּ, "swelled," "grew in height" (Job viii. 11, x. 16; comp. also Ex. xv. 1) to מֵי־שָׂחוּ, in which swimming was possible, yea, necessary, if one were to cross from bank to bank—to a river which cannot be waded. The prophet describes the increasing volume of water by the two parallel clauses: "waters of swimming," "a river that could not be waded."

The question in Ver. 6 indicates the halting-place in the vision, whereby what had been already seen, that is, the *out*-flow and *on*-flow of the waters in gradually increasing strength, is, in passing over to what follows, marked off as a thing apart by itself. Yet it is specially the continuous increase of the waters to which the prophet's attention is called. KEIL: "A natural brook cannot in so short distances have increased so mightily, unless brooks fell into it on all sides, which was not the case here." HENGST.: "The Messianic salvation *crescit eundo*, while the streams of worldly enterprise dry up after a brief course—are streams whose waters lie (Isa. lviii. 11; Job vi. 15 sq.). Comp. the supplement through the person of the Mediator of salvation in Ezek. xvii. 22, 23; and in the New Testament, the parables of the mustard seed and the leaven. The same progress which is exhibited in its efficacy among the nations shows itself also in the life of individuals, making them become great out of small, fathers in God out of children." Neum. calls attention to the Messianic element in the designation: **son of man**, and observes that "the seer was thereby reminded that his vision was for mankind, that this swelling stream flowed on to the days of the completion of the human race." The וַיּוֹלִכֵנִי taken by itself may be a mere recording here of what had taken place before,—"a wading in to the neck" (Isa. viii. 8), as Hengst. expresses it,—in order to get the knowledge indicated in ver. 5; or, according to others, it is to be taken in conjunction with וַיְשִׁבֵנִי, as defining it more exactly: he brought me back to come up again out of the water.—עַל־שְׂפַת, **to the bank** (up to the bank), etc. Neumann, Kliefoth, and Keil understand it thus: And he made me go, namely, away from the last-mentioned place, and brought me back to the bank of the river (Ewald, too, in his last edition: "and made me go and return on the bank of the stream"). According to this, the prophet was led on the bank, in order to learn the depth of the waters,—but he was rather led through three times, and hence the fourth time probably just in and out again!—and brought back to the bank, to see that it was covered with trees. It seems, however, to agree better with the end intended, to understand עַל as stating the purpose; for, as Hengst. says, the attention is now to be turned to the bank, to observe it, and not as hitherto the waters in their bed. [Hitzig makes the guide measure at a distance from the water, and the prophet, after his last vain attempt, come to the guide; whereupon the latter put his question to the prophet, and returned with him to the bank of the river, and during the time that Ezekiel's back was turned to the river, its bank became adorned with trees. HÄV.: "from the end, from the point where the river flows into the Dead Sea (!), the prophet returned once more to its bank."]—Ver. 7. בְּשׁוּבֵנִי, literally: "when I turned myself back." Hitzig disputes the transitive signification of the verb, but indisputably the objective suffix נִי is attached to the infinitive; whereas Hitzig takes the suffix as genitive of possession: "when he came back with me." On the return of the prophet (בְּשׁוּבֵנִי seems to comprehend the וַיּוֹלִכֵנִי וַיְשִׁבֵנִי of ver. 6)—who would probably have followed the course of the water still farther had it depended on him, but is obliged to return to the edge of the bank, just because he has to notice the bank of the river, and that (as ver. 8 shows) as far back as the sanctuary—that is realized which was intended with a וְהִנֵּה, as in vers. 1 and 2; it is the third stage in the vision. How much the matter treated of refers to the **brink of the river**, the repeated mention of it shows. But the fact that "so long as the beholder followed the measurer, he saw nothing of the trees on the bank," arises from the nature of the process in the vision. The looking forward gave Ezekiel the knowledge of the progressive fulness and depth of the waters; not until he looks back does he come to know—with a view to what follows—the fertilizing, enlivening effect of these waters. עֵץ, as the words: **very many**, show, is collective (Gen. i. 11 sq., ii. 9), and in accordance with ver. 12 is to be understood of fruit-bearing trees. (The phrase: **on the brink of the river**, indicates the cause. It has been said that Ezekiel interchanges עַל and אֶל; but when the bringing of the prophet out of the water and on to the bank was referred to, עַל was employed in ver. 6; here, where the reference is to the trees growing on and overshadowing the bank, we have simply אֶל.) But it confuses the meaning of the waters when Hengst. finds here "the need of salvation denoted by hungering as well as by thirsting." Nothing has been said of this in connection with the waters. It is not the case that "life or salvation is here represented in the shape of the fruit-tree, as before by the water" (for which Hengst. compares Isa. lv. 1 sq.).—It cannot with strictness be said that "the trees have here no independent import, but come into account only for their fruit," for there is not the slightest mention here of their fruit. It would be better, with Hitzig, to call to mind ch. xxxvi. 35, and to think of the restoration, cultivation, and fertilization of the land in general, as a blessed dwelling-place for Israel. The trees are not very "great," but very "many,"—not one tree, as in ch. xvii. 22 sq.; Dan. iv. 7 [10] sq. "That this stream here depends on the four streams watering the garden of Eden (Gen. ii.), and this forest on the tree of life, is a gratuitous assertion. Nothing is said of the immortality-giving power of the trees, and the waters no more bear fish of paradise on their waves than do the rivers in Ps. i. 3." (NEUM.).

Ver. 8. Corresponding to the twofold direction of the prophet's observation, the interpretation, which now begins, tells us regarding the course of the waters and the effects they shall produce. Had the prophet desired to follow the water farther, this desire would have been met by the saying: "these waters go out;" in other words, as they come out from the sanctuary, vers. 1, 2 (יֹצְאִים, ver. 1), *i.e.* take their departure thence, so their progress is directed out "toward," "to" (אֶל), etc.—The statement: הַגְּלִילָה הַקַּדְמוֹנָה, is no such "general" determination of the region in which the waters are to prove themselves effectual as Hengstenberg supposes. At any rate, what is thereby designated is not—as the exegesis of the Fathers, following the Sept., delighted to maintain, in view of Jesus' residence there—הַגָּלִיל of Josh. xx. 7; the גְּלִיל הַגּוֹיִם of Isa. viii. 23 [ix. 1]; the northern district in the tribe of Naphtali, called הַגָּלִילָה in 2 Kings xv. 29—the later Galilee. On the contrary, הַקַּדְמוֹנָה expressly distinguishes it from that Galilee. The very word גְּלִילָה, the feminine formation from גָּלִיל, evidently denotes with the article a definite district; there were several גְּלִילוֹת, Josh. xiii. 2 (Joel iv. 4 [iii. 9]), xxii. 10 sq. Derived as it is from גָּלַל, "to break off," "to roll off," a "section," something "bounded off," is to be understood; and because it is here in the east, the border-land there, lying opposite the centre of the land, would be meant, as distinguished from every other border district.—After the statement of the direction (יָצָא אֶל), there follows the account of the course of the waters, as also it is said in the outset in ver. 1 (יֹרְדִים) that the waters, namely, came down (וַיֵּרְדוּ), "flowed down," עַל, that is, over.—הָעֲרָבָה, defined by the article, is to be interpreted by the context. From the intransitive עָרַב, to be "contracted," hence to be "arid," "dry," heath, wilderness, steppe is meant.—Geographically, the Arabah is the whole valley of the Jordan, extending even beyond the Dead Sea; comp. our Comment. on Deut. i.; but in accordance with the previous definition, we find ourselves in that part of the Ghor which lies above the Dead Sea.—After יָצָא and יָרַד, we have now בּוֹא, the coming to the goal. How much stress is laid upon this goal, as that which is to be defined in respect to the course of the waters, is shown by the repetition of אֶל־הַיָּמָּה after הַיָּמָּה. As the Dead Sea is called in Deut. iii. 17, iv. 49, יָם הָעֲרָבָה, so in ver. 18 of our chapter it is designated the "east sea;" and thus we cannot with other expositors understand here the western, the Mediterranean Sea, which, moreover, is distinguished in ver. 10 as "the great sea." If the Arabah, the μεγα πεδιον of Josephus, which he names ἐρημιαν, is an unhealthy plain "full of salt clay," then this is only the fitting introduction to the Dead Sea, with its well-known peculiarity.—הַמּוּצָאִים (particip. Hoph.) אֶל־הַיָּמָּה has, following the Sept., been translated: "into the sea of the mouths," inasmuch as the Jordan falls into it, and, according to Gadow (in the *Journal of the German Oriental Society*, 1848, i. p. 61), forms "a slimy delta." [EWALD: "into the sea, into the sea of the muddy waters;" מוֹצָא, "muddy," "foul"!] The comparison of Zech. xiv. 8 and the dual form in ver. 9 have led others to suppose a dividing of the waters, so that יָמָּה refers one time to the east, but afterwards also to the west. "The prophet," says Umbreit, "sets out first and specially from the Dead Sea; he does not, however, confine himself to it, but makes the waters flow also into the great west and world sea. For the sea of the wilderness appears, indeed, as the most fitting symbol of the death of sin ('the Lord hath no pleasure in the death of the sinner, but that he should turn and live'); but until now there is no water altogether healthy, and for this very reason there is a flowing forth of the fountain of life still farther into the world of sin and of death." [According to the Midrashim, the river divides itself into twelve waters, which flow to the twelve tribes; it is even said to flow on so far as to Calabria and into Barbary.] It only remains that, in accordance with the stress laid upon the issuing forth of the waters in question in vers. 1 and 2, and again in ver. 12, we understand the expression: **brought forth**, used of the waters on their way **to the sea**, as an emphasizing again of the fact that they proceeded from the temple, and that this is done just here in order to pass on to the purpose effected by them when they have reached their goal. (HENGST.: reference "to the higher hand, which executes, according to deliberate counsel, the plan of salvation." NEUM.: "waters that well forth from the threshold of the temple, that come to the Dead Sea. Not only that, but, moreover, having arrived at the Dead Sea, they are **brought forth**; thus the sanctuary of the blessing expressly connects itself with the doomed domain of the curse.")—The waters of which it is said that they **are healed** are self-evidently (2 Kings ii. 22) the waters of the Dead Sea, as is shown also by what follows. The spiritual signification of the waters is now told to the prophet: healing of the dead, which accordingly means only sick unto death, is the aim of their being brought forth from the sanctuary to the Dead Sea, to the east boundary; that is, we might say, from Israel into the world, which is thereby auspiciously symbolized as in the east, consequently with a reference to the rising of the Sun of Righteousness (Mal. iii. 20 [iv. 2]). [Grotius explains וְנִרְפְּאוּ in this way, that the waters flowing in continue wholesome, notwithstanding their flowing through.] The character of the water of the Dead Sea has already been correspondingly described by Diodorus: ἐχει διαπικρον και καθ' ὑπερβολην δυσωδες. Comp. Tacitus, *Hist.* v. 6. Jerome calls it *mare amarissimum, quod Græce λιμνη ἀσφαλτου, id est, stagnum bituminis vocatur.* Comp. von Schubert (*Reise in d. Morgenl.* iii

p. 85), who remarks on the deceptive appearance for thirsty persons of the "clear and pure" water. Comp. moreover, von Raumer's *Palästina*, p. 61 sq.; Robinson's *Physical Geography of the Holy Land*, p. 209 sq. [HENGST.: "The wilderness is in Scripture a figure of ungodliness (?), and so a fitting emblem of the world estranged from God and excluded from His kingdom, Ps. cvii. 5. In Joel, the valley of the acacias, the tree of the wilderness, corresponds to the Arabah here. Comp. also Isa. xxxv. 6. As a symbol of the corrupt world lying in wickedness (1 John v. 19), the Dead Sea is the more appropriate, as it owes its origin to a judgment on the corrupt world, and the spiritual eye discerns under its waves the figure of Sodom and Gomorrah (ch. xvi.)."]

The transition is now made to the effects of the waters flowing to the Dead Sea. Very impressively Ver. 9 begins first of all with the prophetic וְהָיָה (NEUM.: "it has *then* come to pass, then the fact lies open to observation"): what manifests itself in consequence of the healing of the water, in reference to the water itself, as an effect of the healing waters of the sanctuary.—But what of כָּל־נֶפֶשׁ חַיָּה? Is there, then, any **living thing** in the Dead Sea? There is not, although Prince Pückler asserts that he ate there fishes taken living from the Dead Sea. The Jordan carries in some, or "they voluntarily accompany its waves" (VON SCHUBERT), but "they must soon pay with their life for their love of travel, because they die in the salt brine, or because this brine thrusts out their light bodies to the shore." A fish seen by Robinson, and said to have been caught in the Dead Sea, was found near the mouth of the Jordan, and dying in a state of exhaustion. "Neither fishes nor snails live in this very salt lake" (VON SCHUBERT). "Some herons," Gadow relates, "sought the little fishes washed into the sea, that died instantly in the sharp lye; I myself observed some wrestling with death. Sea fishes which Marshal Marmont at Alexandria cast into water taken from the Dead Sea, died in two or three minutes." Thus "living things" can only be spoken of in respect to the Dead Sea as things that were alive and then died there, or that live but must die when they come thither. But the mode of expression employed is rather a prophetic anticipation, picturing as it does in the healed water, in contrast to the death dominating it, life already preserved,—life, too, which, through אֲשֶׁר יִשְׁרֹץ, significantly alludes to Gen. vii. 21, viii. 17 (death and preservation), and Gen. i. 21 (creation). Quite as readily could a contrast to the Jordan carrying the living to death in the Dead Sea be found in the following words: **everything whithersoever the double stream shall come shall live.** HITZIG: "which creeps in every place to which rivers (נְחָלִים, pointed as plural) come." (EWALD: נַחְלָם.) KEIL: "which swarms wherever the brook comes."—נַחֲלַיִם. What is the meaning of the dual, where hitherto we have always had נַחַל? Keil thinks the best solution is that of Hengstenberg, who, referring to Jer. l. 21, explains "two rivers" as equivalent to strong river, remarking that the doubled often stands for the distinguished (Job xi. 6; Isa. lxi. 7). He might have known that already Umbreit translates it: "two rivers," and in doing so refers to "the fulness of the water." The *dualis emphaticus*, too, of Stier (*Lehrgeb.* p. 218) comes to the same thing, as he also cites for it Jer. l. The original "waters" (מַיִם) have grown in ver. 5 to a נַחַל; may they not now, when they have mixed with the waters of the Dead Sea, when הַמַּיִם הָאֵלֶּה and the healed הַמַּיִם have been expressly named side by side in ver. 8, be very appropriately (not indeed as Maurer: because of the similarity with מַיִם) expressed succinctly by the dual form נַחֲלַיִם, and by נְחָלִים indefinitely, because of their rushing streams sweeping away death and opening up the way to life? Thus, as Neum.: "We see it at once, the result of the flowing in is manifest in the sea itself; the river is not lost in it, but neither does the river swallow up the sea; it impenetrates it with its living power, and wherever the eye follows these united streams, it beholds the swarming newly produced life," etc. KLIEF.: "When the waters of the river shall come into the waters of the sea, they will divide themselves," etc.—יְחִיֶה, to retain life and to enjoy life, in pregnant contrast to the dying of which this sea is suggestive. KEIL: "to revive, to come to life." [Hitzig, too, remarks on the masculine construction of נֶפֶשׁ (יְחִיֶה and יִשְׁרֹץ), so that חַיָּה appears as a substantive in the genitive dependent on נֶפֶשׁ. NEUM.: "Thus everything, that in the power of life bears in itself the germ of life, shall unfold this germ; the view which underlies is not that of the feminine, of what is upheld by the Spirit, but of what breathes independently."]—The description of this life accords with the nature of the water, the healthy vital power of which finds expression in its fulness and the multitude of its fishes. But we have first "everything that creeps and moves quickly, שָׁרַץ, said of every kind of animal mobility" (NEUM.), in order primarily to give pictorial expression to life in general in the all-sided manifold swarm. The following clause adds the more special: and there are **very many** הַדָּגָה (a collective, expressing at the same time the most different kinds), a feminine form of דָּג, which, from דָּגָה, "to become thick," denotes first of all, as here too in accordance with the context, the strong large sea-fish, and then fish in general. (UMBR.: "to live and multiply most abundantly.")—The cause of this, which was formerly incorporated in the general description, is now taken by itself, in order to explain the special case of the fishes: **for these waters come thither and they shall be healed,** *i.e.*, as this repetition from ver. 8 clearly shows, the waters of the Dead Sea, to which שָׁמָּה also points.—But the description reaches its full height of expression of life with the clause: **and everything liveth,** etc. First, **everything,** etc.; then, the many fishes of various kinds in particular—in other words, the Dead Sea in its piscine life; finally, the whole Dead Sea as such. Hence formerly שָׁם, whereas the two following times שָׁמָּה; as also the preceding וְיֵרָפְאוּ (imperf. Niphal) is illustrated by וָחַי כֹּל, and therefore also we have הַנַּחַל, from ver. 5 sq., in antithesis to the waters of the Dead Sea. "The Dead Sea has become a sea of life" (NEUM.). [EWALD: every one that draws water out of it. CALMET: every land, however unfruitful, provided only the river waters it, shall be at once made most fruitful. DERESER: "all the regions of the Dead Sea, to which the water penetrates, shall swarm with fish."]

Ver. 10. וְהָיָה again. ["Out of death there arises, by the omnipotence and grace of God, a rich life. The new community is numerous, innumerable as the fishes of the sea," HÄV.] Because not only the life of the sea, but the (Dead) Sea itself as alive is exemplified in the abundance of fish, this abundance is described partly as to the employment it occasions, and partly as to the numerous kinds of fish. In the former respect, יעמדו עליו (Qeri: עָמְדוּ, "they have placed themselves," one sees them standing), "fishers place themselves over it" (the river, not the Dead Sea, but also not the whole length of the river on its banks, but where the Dead Sea touches it, because the filling of it with fish-life is the subject in hand). With this agrees also the statement as to locality given: מֵעֵין גֶּדִי וְעַד־עֵין עֶנְלַיִם, which has given occasion to so many disquisitions. These must be two points lying near each other, as the same expression: עֵין and עֵין, and not less the difference, which is simply that between a "kid" and "two calves," seems designed to show. Hengst. thinks that perhaps עֶנְלַיִם is a dual, such as that in ver. 9: "the double calf in parallelism with the kid." He supposes "the fountains are named after the finders," "the calf had distinguished itself by the discovery" (!). Seriously, however, En-gedi ("kid's fountain," which reminds Sepp of the ibex, seldom pursued here by a hunter) is "Ain-Didi," on the west bank of the Dead Sea, the southmost point inhabited by the Israelites, with an Egyptian climate and Egyptian products; and regarding En-eglaim ("two-calves' fountain"), Jerome says that it is situated at the beginning of the Dead Sea, where the Jordan flows in, that is, northward. Since the death of living things occurs at the entrance into the Dead Sea, we feel certain that this is the right place. Hengst. finds "En-gedi obliquely over against the Eglaim mentioned in Isa. xv. 8;" for, "as obviously the whole compass of the sea is intended, En-eglaim is to be looked for on the east side." EWALD: "the whole present stretch along the Dead Sea." Neum. disregards any geographical basis: "Two fountains (עין) flow now into the Dead Sea, both of them living and full of fish, into the dark depths of death; but in those days of salvation, a river of life shall flow from the one to the other. No longer shall there be only small and quickly-dying fishes moving here and there before the mouths of the fountains; the whole intervening water, now waste and dead, shall then become alive, and swarm with the fishes of the great sea."—מִשְׁטוֹחַ [EWALD: "a casting-place for nets"] is distinguished by Neumann from מִשְׁטַח in ch. xxvi. 5, 14. Gesenius holds both forms to have the same signification: place of spreading out. In order, however, to suppose the act of spreading out, we must with Neumann take the fishers as a spreading out of the nets; they will be quite absorbed in that occupation, will be nothing else; and this is not so inadmissible as Kliefoth supposes; while Rosenmüller's interpretation of the יִהְיוּ, as referring to the places, that they shall be places for spreading out the nets, can quite well be extracted out of the phrase: **from En-gedi even unto**, etc., although it is not so obvious.—לַחֲרָמִים, whether for the take, or, after the take, for drying, which, however, is done as fresh preparation for new labour, for a new take. [HENGST.: "The question is not of fishers who will arrange after their kind the fish caught, but only of those who catch fish of different kinds."] By the nets is characterized not only the fulness, but also the manifoldness, the various kinds of fishes that may be or are caught.—לְמִינָה, "as to the kind" (collective), intentionally (as Raphe shows) **without** Mappiq, means at bottom the same as with ה: "in respect to their kind;" care is always taken to express the variety of kinds corresponding to the דָּגָה here and in ver. 9. "Life is depicted with far more significance not by multitudes alone, but by the variegated mixture of the most different kinds, which are commingled together" (NEUM.).—"Allusion to the account of creation (comp. also ver. 9): the new community, a similar creation of God's" (HÄV.).—דְּגָתָם, not: of the healed מַיִם of the sea, nor of the נְחָלִים of ver. 9, nor of the banks between En-gedi and En-eglaim, but of the fishers, or the nets.—The comparison with **the fishes of the great sea**, said to be **very many**, is connected, as Hitzig observes, with the לְמִינָה: there shall live in it the many kinds of fish of the great sea, and many of each kind,—**as the fishes**, sq., is proverbial for this—and not merely the few kinds of small fresh-water fish. The fish of the Mediterranean thus compared are, moreover, conceived of as living, so that this too shows that the Mediterranean cannot have been spoken of previously. [HENGST.: "The sea is a symbol of the world; accordingly men appear as the living creatures in the sea, as the fishes (Rev. viii. 9). Hitherto there were only dead fishes, only unspiritual, unsaved men. Thus the meaning of the fishers cannot be doubtful: the fishes are the men who have attained to life through the Messianic salvation; the fishers are the messengers of this salvation, who gather those who are quickened into the kingdom of God, introduce them into the fellowship of the Church," Luke v. 11; Matt. xiii. 47, etc.]

Ver. 11. בִּצָּאת (Qeri: בצאתיו) is singular; the plural of the Qeri appears to be put because of the following plural, וּגְבָאָיו. Gesenius: בִּצֹּאתָיו, incorrectly written for בִּצּוֹתָיו. בִּצָּה is a moist place. RASHI: *marais* (marsh). One might perhaps make the distinction to be what is turned into swamp by the natural recession of the sea from the bank, and the artificially constructed salt-pits (Zeph. ii. 9). These form the exception from the rule of healing and quickening; they are the places in which the healing waters produce no effect. "We have just observed the fishers placing themselves from one fountain to the other, that the life of the sea may become conspicuous through them; but here in the pools is death" (NEUM.). "The waters even which the river brought to them," thinks Hitzig, "would become corrupt, if left standing along with the whole mass of water without any fresh inflow." J. D. MICHAELIS: "Palestine would lose much were it to lose this salt, got without labour, and were the Dead Sea to become quite fresh; hence this gift of nature is to remain." Hitzig's view and reasons, even if satisfactory for the וְלֹא יֵרָפְאוּ, are certainly not so for the לְמֶלַח נִתָּנוּ; which clause, moreover, is not to be explained on the ground of utility (as is done by Michaelis), it is the expression of a judgment. "Those districts," says Hävernick, "in which the salt-deposits proper were formerly found, shall also henceforth be such waste places. The thought is this: only those who bar themselves against the gracious stream of divine love, and are unwilling to regain health, are henceforth to be given over to the curse, continuing to exist as monuments thereof (Zech. xiv. 17)." Around the sea of death there lingers on a death which abides: this is the second death, the death unto death. What is **given to salt** is entirely forfeited to death. KLIEF.: "They shall be made into salt." HENGST.: "The salt comes into consideration here not as seasoning, as frequently, but as the foe of fertility, life, and prosperity (Job xxxix. 6). A contrast to deliverance from the corrosive power of the salt, which would be effected by the waters from the sanctuary were access afforded to them; they remain given over to salt: he that believeth not the Son of God shall not see life, etc., John iii. 36."—In Ver. 12, that of which the seer obtained merely a general view in ver. 7 is now more exactly particularized to him, as the conclusion of the entire section. After the contrast (ver. 11) to the healing effect of the waters of the sanctuary (ver. 8), there comes in what follows something antithetical, and therefore parallel to ver. 9 sq.: the quickening effects as regards the banks of the river, and so back to the source of the waters, form a parallel to the quickening effects as regards the goal, in relation to the Dead Sea. In fine, viewed forward or backward, they are the waters of life; as on the one hand they sustain life, so on the other they produce fruit.—הַנַּחַל, as the waters since ver. 5, on their way to the Dead Sea, and considered in contrast thereto (ver. 9), have been designated, so that the reference is to their course from their coming out of the temple walls.—The description: **on the river,** is amplified thus: "on its bank on both sides." The "rising up" forms also, no doubt, an antithetical pendant to the former deepening and deepening and descending of the waters.—מַאֲכָל, "what is edible" (HENGST.: "all fruit-bearing trees;" HITZIG: "every tree of edible fruit"). KLIEF.: "they shall bear edible fruits of all sorts." Their described quality, however, is not this alone, that they are trees of food, and hence yield food—not wild, acid, hard fruit; but an abiding freshness of life and vigour distinguishes this growth of trees (which is elsewhere expressed by ever-flowing, never-failing waters), both as to the **leaf** (נָבֵל, Ps. i. 3, "to fade," "to fall off," cognate with נָפַל) and the **fruit** (תָּמֹם). In respect to the latter it is said: **according to its months,** that is, as these change (HITZIG: distributively), יְבַכֵּר, said of the "first commencement," of the "first of a thing;" hence בִּכּוּרִים, the first-fruits, signify, according to Hitzig, that the trees produce fresh fruit every month; and this, according to Hengst., "indicates the uninterrupted enjoyment of salvation;" or the fruit is as eagerly desired and hailed with as much joy as early first-fruits, or generally as superior fruit, which can claim, as it were, the right of the first-born (Deut. xxi. 16). Comp. Rev. xxii. 2. NEUM.: "The thought in fact is: what used to delight the heart every year, will henceforth be furnished every month. According to Horapollo, the palm puts forth a new branch with every new moon. The month is looked on as the property of the trees, because the change of the moon always enables them to put forth in similar change the life welling up in them." We are not to compare here the enchanted gardens of Alcinous (*Odyss.* vii. 114 sq.). The reason assigned, too, which makes the leading thought the active principle of the effects, accords with the closing character of the verse: **its** (not: the stream's, as Neumann, but: the trees', this forest's) **waters,** namely, the waters "proceeding from the sanctuary." HITZIG: "from the dwelling-place of Him who is the Author of all life and fertility." NEUM.: "a deep disclosure regarding what the temple of his God was to the prophet. With Him is the fountain of life, and in His light we see light, Ps. xxxvi. 10 [9]. But this is just the sanctuary; because its source is holy, therefore the flood of the river produces fruitful germs. And קָדוֹשׁ is not moral purity, but sublime, transcendent purity, which sheds its enlightening beams over all the dark places of the earth. Hence the lofty praise of the seraphim in Isa. vi. 3."—As formerly the fishes were for the nets of the fishers, so now the fruit of the trees is **for food,** etc. וְהָיוּ (Qeri: וְהָיָה, which is unnecessary), for פִּרְיוֹ is not necessarily the fruit of each and every tree, but can be taken collectively with the plural. As we have here a reference to paradise and the first creation (Gen. ii. 9), so we have also to redemption, the future salvation, in the phrase: **and its** (the forest's) **leaf,** לִתְרוּפָה—HITZIG: "for medicine;" on which he remarks: "doubtless for external application, since the leaf is laid upon wounds as soft and cooling, apart from its special healing virtue; תְּרוּפָה is derived from רָפָא." In this, too, the thought of mending and of healing is united and conjoined in this closing clause, so that in this sense "medicine" is by no means "a very unsuitable disharmony in these figures of perfection," as Neumann says, whose thoughts run on "the blessed salvation enlivened by a sweet life of rapture," and on "adorning life with fragrant chaplets." This last would as mere ornament be altogether out of place here. HENGST.: "Salvation must present itself for the terribly sick heathen world, above all, in the form of saving grace. Besides the nourishing fruits, therefore, are named also the healing leaves." HÄV.: "The trees are trees of life, with allusion at the same time to Ps. i.; the figure of the fishes refers to the extent, the greatness of the community; and this figure of the trees to its nature, in so far as the divine grace transforms it into truly living members, who themselves bear rich fruit, and thereby become a means of life and recovery to others also." [Philippson says of the entire section: "This description answers to no fountain actually existing in Jerusalem, and contains suppositions which no actually existing fountain could fulfil. Hence it belongs to the realm of those prophetic intuitions of the future land, in which this land appeared, altered in its nature, endowed with the most glorious fertility and wonderful virtues. We have to consider this section as a poetical resting-point of the prophet, in which, between dry narration and representation, the prophet's enraptured soul expatiated on the prospects of his people." According to this, the hope of the Jews of the present should finally be æsthetics.]

Vers. 13–23. *The Fixing of the Boundaries in the Holy Land.*

Hengstenberg, in accordance with his view of the concluding portion of Ezekiel, makes the prophet return from the distant Messianic future, the prospect into which, according to him, suddenly opened in vers. 1–12, to the lower salvation, the temple and city of the future, which formed the presupposition of the higher salvation. According to Hitzig, "the previous section forms the transition to this, inasmuch as in that section Ezekiel first of all, following the course of the river, turns himself away from the temple and the idea of the Terumah; in other words, it still remains to treat of the land itself from which that Terumah was selected." It would be an entire break in these closing chapters, which hang so closely together, were vers. 1–12 an insertion of essentially different character, meaning, and signification from that which precedes them, and that which follows them. But if vers. 1–12 are decidedly symbolical, and their contents specially Messianic, then we have in them the key for everything in these chapters, both what precedes and what follows, not merely "the transition" to what follows. Then the temple is a symbol of the new revelation of God among Israel in their own land; then the partly indicated, partly instituted worship as to acts, persons, and times, symbolizes the future worshipping in spirit and in truth; then the blessing, which abolishes even the Dead Sea in its character of curse, cannot leave the Holy Land untouched, but only with the fixing of its boundaries and the division of the enclosed territory among the tribes (ch. xlviii.) will the theocracy of the future be complete. We cannot say, with Ewald, that "the whole book might have been perfectly well concluded with the last great figure in ch. xlvii. 1–12." Ewald himself is compelled to admit that "the position of the sanctuary and its immediate environs in ch. xlvii. 1–8 is not yet explained with sufficient clearness;" but what still follows finds its explanation less by reference to this, than by the fact that in ch. xlv. 1 the division of the land by inheritance is presupposed, without our having up to this point heard anything regarding it, except the prophecy of the return of Israel into their again reviving land (ch. xxxiv. 25 sq., xxxvi. 8 sq., xxxvii. 21 sq.). Only by what follows from ver. 13 to the end of the book do the people of God attain to rest, as the glory of God came to its rest by its re-entrance into the sanctuary (ch. xliii.). In the sense of such a connection, comp. Rev. xxi. 3: καὶ σκηνώσει μετ' αὐτῶν, καὶ αὐτοὶ λαοὶ αὐτοῦ ἔσονται; the sanctuary with its environs still continues in ch. xlviii. the main point of view. Not merely, as Häv. says, "does the whole representation take its departure from the sanctuary, and so naturally also returns thither," but the close of Ezekiel's book is intended to depict the glory of God by the glory of His kingdom (Introd. § 5). Thus neither the incidental presupposition of the division of the land by inheritance, nor the oblation to be set apart as defined in ch. xlv., nor, in particular, the city—which, it is true, is to belong to Israel as a whole (ch. xlv. 6)—can suffice; but all Israel must in their tribes colonize the land, in order, after everything has been bounded off externally and internally, to see the glory of Jehovah in the sanctuary, as the foundation of the glory of Israel in their own land, brought to full expression. "Hence," as Hävernick observes, "this impresses also upon the whole land a new aspect, a more glorified conformation."

Ver. 13. A solemn introduction marks off the following section (comp. ch. xlvi. 1, 16). גֵּה, GESENIUS: "unquestionably a false reading for זֶה (as ver. 15). So read also the Sept., Vulg., Chald., and fourteen manuscripts." This is easy to say, also easy to imagine, but the analogy of בֵּג for בַּז, after ch. xxv. 7 (which see), cannot be applied here. Although we can hardly say, with Hengstenberg, that it "would almost seem as if Ezekiel wished to tease scribes and critics, and to put them to the test" (!!), still, the propagation of such a clerical error as גֵּה for זֶה in ver. 13 is so much the more difficult to imagine, as the matter is really different in ver. 15, where we have זֶה, from what it is here. Hengst. makes גֵּה to be of similar import with גֵּהָה in Prov. xvii. 22, which word, occurring only there, signifies, according to him, "the inwards"! He translates thus: "(this is) the inside of the border," and observes on it: "The stem is גָּהָה or גָּוָה; cognate is גַּו, middle (in Chald. גּוֹ), גַּיְא, valley, as the interior enclosed by mountains." All this might be allowed; but that גּוֹי, "people," is "the interior, the centre, in antithesis to individuals as the periphery," is so far from correct, that the direct opposite would be nearer the mark. The stem signifies: to draw together; and hence גּוֹי (people) and גֵּו (body) refer to "connection." A signification such as: body, suits the גֵּהָה of Prov. xvii. 22 in its parallelism there with גָּרֶם, and a similar signification would be the suitable one here in Ezekiel. For the question in ver. 13 is not concerning גְּבוּל in the sense of "border," as in ver. 15, but concerning the territory itself, whose borders are first defined in ver. 15 sq. Vers. 13 and 14, introductory to the fixing of the boundaries, and vers. 22 and 23, which conclude it, give us to understand that the division of the land among the twelve tribes of Israel is the dominating design; only with reference to this, that is to say, preparatively, are the boundaries of the land to be treated of.—אֶת־הָאָרֶץ explains גֵּה גְבוּל sufficiently; אֲשֶׁר is accusative.—לִשְׁנֵי׳ is, according to Hitzig, distributive, and denotes the point of view which is to obtain in the division of the land, since all Israel, the re-united people of God, shall return to their land (ch. xxxvii.); from which point of view, also, the curt יוֹסֵף חֲבָלִים = Joseph shall receive of it (plural) "inheritances" (measured off portions of land), is directly explained, without our needing, with Ewald, to punctuate dual חֲבָלַיִם, although two portions are meant, in accordance with the ancient prophetic injunction of Jacob, the patriarch of the tribes (Gen. xlviii. 5). The more exact determination is so much the more presupposed as understood; "as Levi is to have no other portion of land except that in the sacred Terumah, the tribes can only be made twelve in number when (as always) the tribe of Joseph is counted and treated as two, Ephraim and Manasseh" (KLIEF.). Comp. Josh. xvii. 14 sq. [The Sept. translate the *nom. pr.* יוֹסֵף.] Already Eusebius has observed in the *Præp. ev.*, that Plato, too, divides his ideal state into twelve parts, and the capital likewise.

After the determination concerning the point of view of the number twelve for the division of the land, as it has been in ver. 13 first stated generally, and then specialized in Joseph, Ver. 14 lays down the second principle for the division of the land: into equal parts. What was said regarding Joseph is not in contradiction with this principle, as Hitzig maintains, for, as Keil justly replies, the words: **ye inherit it,** אִישׁ כְּאָחִיו, only affirm that of the twelve tribes which Israel numbers in relation to נַחֲלָה, the one shall receive as much as the other. Comp. the opposite principle in Num. xxvi. 54, xxxiii. 54; and comp. Ezek. xlviii. 1 sq. There is no reason for supposing that אֲשֶׁר signifies: "inasmuch as," or: "because." Comp. ch. xx. 28, 42.—The symbolical character of these introductory regulations, which the very norm of the symbolical number twelve leaves scarcely questionable, must be beyond all question, unless the principle of equality in division here laid down should go on the strange supposition that each tribe would comprehend the same number of individual members, or, in contrast to the first division of the land, the new division, with all its appearance of justice, should yet in fact and reality be practically unjust, namely, because treating the more populous tribe exactly as the weaker. This Philippson also admits, when he remarks "that this would be more contradictory to the Mosaic law than all the other deviations of the prophet taken together;" but he gets over the difficulty by saying that only the same direction from east to west is given for the tribal portions, and that the equal division among the individual Israelites is spoken of. Bunsen, on the contrary, maintains "the ideal nature of the plan." *The number twelve of the tribes of Israel expresses the whole of the people, but it does so according to their idea, and thus in a spiritual manner; but still more does the equal share of each tribe in the common inheritance make the land of promise become a symbol of something else than the earthly Canaan.* (Comp. 2 Pet. i. 1; Ps. xxxvii. 11, 29.) The seed now has come to whom the land was promised by Jehovah (Gen. xii. 7, xvii. 8; Gal. iii. 7, 16).

Ver. 15. We have here the fixing of the boundaries, which (as in Num. xxxiv., Josh. xv.) is done with reference to the four cardinal points; but here, instead of south, west, north, and east, the order is north, east, south, west, just as also in ch. xlviii. the several tribes follow from north to south. Hengst. explains the difference "from this circumstance, that in ancient times Israel came from the south into the land; here, on the contrary, the return is from the land of the north." KLIEF.: "We must so understand this deviation that the Holy Land will in that future be indeed the same as the old Holy Land, but yet in a certain sense opposed to the old, the counterpart of the old Canaan."—After that גֵּה has preceded with vers. 13 and 14, it can now be said with וְ of the boundaries proper: וְזֶה גְבוּל׳.—The north boundary begins from the Mediterranean Sea (as in Num. xxxiv. 7 sq.), hence in the west, and proceeds **on the way to Hethlon, to come to Zedad** (לְבוֹא, of the direction whither). Since צְדָד or צְדָדָה with ה *locale* helps also to determine the boundary in Num. xxxiv. 8, doubtless on the north-east, as the antithesis to the point of departure on the west naturally suggests, so certainly no other **Zedad** is to be thought of. Robinson holds it to be Sudud, four hours from Hasia, on the west entrance of the wilderness, east of the road which leads from Damascus to Emesa; Keil declares himself against this. **Hethlon** is unknown. Gesenius places it in Syria of Damascus.—Ver. 16. A more detailed account, by means of several other places, of the north boundary as compared with the other boundaries.—**Hamath,** of which Keil says: not the city on the Orontes, but the kingdom whose south border forms the north border of Canaan; while Gesenius takes it for this important Syrian city (Epiphania), and compares Num. xiii. 21, xxxiv. 8. Hitzig denies that here at the beginning the land of the city could be meant, and therefore, appealing to the Sept., he takes it as a gloss (from ch. xlviii. 1) to Zedad, the word before it.—בֵּרוֹתָה is, according to Gesenius = בֵּרוֹתַי (2 Sam. viii. 8), a city in the kingdom of Aram-Zobah; is it perhaps the seaport of Berytus in Phœnicia?—סִבְרַיִם (identical with זִפְרֹן in Num. xxxiv. 9?) is further defined by the clause: **which is between**, etc., without thereby becoming clearer.—The closer definition: **which is on**, or: "toward" **the border of Hauran** (חַוְרָן), brings the middle Hazer (חָצֵר הַתִּיכוֹן, "middle court") into relation with the transjordanic Auranitis, without, however, defining the latter more exactly.—Ver. 17 "states the north border for the third time," says Klief. (without, however, being able to solve the difficulty of the double Hamath in ver. 16), "but so that it, after ver. 16 has named the series of Israelitish border places, defines the boundary by border places outside of Israel." His view is, that "Damascus and Hamath are the boundaries on the north, in this way, that the north-east Damascene border place opposite the north-east Israelitish border place, Zedad, is Hazar-Enon, while on the north side the land of Hamath extends itself."—The point of departure from the Mediterranean Sea is once more repeated; hence this must be the most western point of the north border.—חֲצַר עֵינוֹן (עֵינָן), "fountain court" (Num. xxxiv. 9), Keil sets down as "the fountain of Lebweh in the Beca, on the watershed between the Orontes and Leontes. The calling of Hazar-Enon **the border from the sea**, indicates that it forms the most eastern boundary-point for the north border drawn from the sea, as it is added: **the border of Damascus**, that is: the border place from Damascus, or: "on the border," etc. (HENGST.), or: toward the border, etc.—וְצָפוֹן צָפוֹנָה, according to Hengst., "denotes first the north border, to which all the places named belong," and then "northward" gives the "special in the general;" for "the north border was no straight line, but had its more northern and less northern points; the most northern was Hamath." HÄV.: "The repetition strengthens the conception: northward and northward."—וְאֵת פְּאַת', doubtless as accusative, with: looks to, or: measures off, understood. Hävernick finds "the boundary-line drawn here with still greater exactness than in Num. xxxiv., partly to indicate the still sharper and more definite fixing of the limits of the new Canaan than of the old, and partly to express here too the thought that the new community shall obtain the fullest possible possession of the promised land." However unknown the various places named may be, thus much seems certain, that the only design of the many names is to draw the boundary with full sufficiency.

Ver. 18 defines as the east border briefly the Jordan, agreeing in this with Num. xxxiv. 10 sq., only with different local colouring. Hauran, Damascus, and Gilead are put on the east, and the land of Israel on the west side. Keil makes the remarkable sequence: Hauran, Damascus, Gilead, to have arisen through regard to the Jordan, which does not reach so far as Damascus; if it had, the sequence must have been Damascus, Hauran, Gilead. While Klief. insists on this, that Num. xxxiv. gives in addition the district east of the Jordan conceded to the transjordanic tribes, whereas, according to the statement here, the Holy Land of the future shall no longer have any portion not fully incorporated; Hengst., on the contrary, maintains the continuance of the frontier land, referring for this to Ps. lx.; Mic. vii. 14; Jer. l. 19; Zech. x. 10: also in Num. xxxii. 30, xxxiii. 51; Josh. xxii. 9, the land of Canaan lying west of Jordan is in the same way set over against, *e.g.*, Gilead.—The **border** from which they are to measure is the above-defined north border. The **east sea** is the Dead Sea, in distinction from the west, the Mediterranean Sea.

Ver. 19. The south border. The nearer definition of the direction by תֵּימָנָה marks only the transition to the place where the determination of the southern boundary begins. Tamar, says Hengst., "does not occur elsewhere in the Old Testament;" it is, according to him, to be sought for "in the extreme south-east, at the end of the Dead Sea." Robinson's conjecture in favour of Thamara, that is, Kurnub, lies open to many objections. On the other hand, **the waters of Meriboth-Kadesh**, that is, the waters of strife, are those known of old. Hengst. observes: "Only instead of the singular in Num. xxvii. 14, the plural Meriboth is put, to point to this, that the strife there involves in it a whole fulness of rebelliousness,—a solemn *nota bene* for those who, like their fathers, were still to the present day a house of rebelliousness." These waters of Kadesh (Num. xx.) in the wilderness of Zin were near Kadesh Barnea (Num. xxxiv. 4).—נַחֲלָה, accented as "inheritance," is retained by Hengstenberg: "the inheritance (reaches) to the great sea," who cites for this the oldest translators, Sept., Jonathan, and the Syriac. The possession here (according to him) corresponds to the border of the land in the case of the first two sides. On the other hand, already Hävernick (Vulg.) thinks of the "river of Egypt," the Wady el Arish, which appears throughout in the Old Testament as the extreme south-western boundary of Palestine; also Num. xxxiv. 5 is (in his view) decisive for this acceptation, and consequently for a change of the punctuation into נַחְלָה. Comp. Josh. xv. 4. HITZIG: "in the direction of the river to the great sea;" and for this he urges in addition that 'Ρινὰ κορούρα is also called simply Νεελ, that is, נַחַל, with the omission of the genitive.—The Mediterranean Sea is given as boundary-point on the south-west.

Ver. 20. The west border, with which the fixing of the boundaries concludes. As it is formed by the Mediterranean Sea, only the terminating points south and north have to be noticed. In the former respect stands מִגְּבוּל, that is, from the south border defined in ver. 19; in the latter, עַד־נֹכַח לְבוֹא חֲמָת, that is, to over against the place where one comes into the territory of Hamath, which was set down in ver. 17 as the north boundary; comp. Num. xxxiv. 6. Klief. further observes: "The Philistine coast district is here, as with Moses, included in the Holy Land; the fact that it was not conquered by the Israelites happened against the will of God: the Holy Land of the future shall be the real, entire, full Holy Land."—Ver. 21. A concluding clause referring back to ver. 13, as well as preparing for ver. 22 sq.

Ver. 22. Like a codicil to a will; EWALD: "and with the genuine prophetic innovation, that the protected should have quite as many rights as the ancient sons of the soil." וְהָיָה, comp. vers. 9, 10.—HÄV.: "The prophet's perspective extends itself beyond the borders of Israel to those of the Gentile nations. Israel arrived at the goal of its development forms at the same time a fresh point of connection for the Gentiles. He who connects himself with the true, perfect Church, enjoys the same privileges and blessings as Israel itself. That which the Old Testament contains in the weak type in relation to strangers passes here into complete fulfilment." HITZIG: The prophet draws here the inference from Lev. xix. 34; the limitation and exception in Deut. xxiii. 3, 4 is here omitted. For this he gives as reasons: inasmuch as "residence in a strange land could even weaken an exclusive disposition," and "the lessening of the population of Israel made them wish for and favour the accession of strangers." Hengst., on the contrary, holds that what is here said does not primarily refer to "strangers in general," but to those **who have begotten children in your midst**, hence to those "who have been naturalized in Israel in the times of affliction," as similarly Abarbanel. Hengst. urges against "the hosts of the heathen," "the boundaries of the land confined between the Jordan and the Mediterranean." (Might we not imagine we perceived here the *rationalismus vulgaris?*) The question, too, "concerns only the strangers already naturalized in Israel." He says: the exception which the Ammonites and Moabites make (Deut. xxiii.) in regard to the reception of born heathen into the community of God serves only to confirm the rule. "Already, in the state in which Moses found the people, there was a considerable foreign element, the whole posterity of the servants who went down to Egypt with Jacob. A fresh accession took place in Egypt at the time of the exodus (Ex. xii. 38; Num. xi. 4). In 1 Chron. ii. 34, 35 we have an example that these Egyptian strangers were considered in the partition of the land, and, indeed, in the territory of the tribe to which they had attached themselves. Further, Moses gives in Num. x. 29 sq. the friendly invitation to his Midianitish brother-in-law to share with his tribe the lot of Israel. Hobab, says Knobel, shall accordingly have a share in the land. Hobab consented, and we find his race afterward in the Hebrew land. Comp. Judg. i. 16, iv. 11; Jer. xxxv. Only apparently at variance with Ezekiel is the conduct of Ezra toward the heathen wives (Ezra ix. 10), and that of Nehemiah (ch. xiii.) toward the heathen men who had settled among the Israelites. Ezekiel speaks of those who had attached themselves to Israel by inward inclination at a time when it had no form nor comeliness, and when there was nothing in it to desire but the true God; Ezra and Nehemiah are zealous against the attempt to give heathendom equal rights in the midst of Israel, and to break down the partition-wall so necessary in the pre-Christian times. Both the attraction which Ezekiel commends, and the repulsion for which Ezra and Nehemiah are zealous, arise rather from the same principle; it is the true God who here binds and there severs."—Hitzig remarks on the clause: **who have begotten children**, etc., that for their sake the fathers received a landed possession, but the childless proselyte did not. Keil understands it of permanent settlement in Israel, in contrast to temporary or transitory residence there. "Here too there is, analogous to Isa. lvi. 3 sq., attached to the promise a condition, the idea of which is already involved in Deut. xxiii. 7, 8 (that Edomites and Egyptians shall only in the third generation enter into the congregation of the Lord). This involves the close, firm, and faithful attaching of oneself to the congregation, whereby one has to the utmost removed and excluded himself from the national communion of heathens. Comp. also Lev. xxv. 45." Certainly not testifying to an already very prevalent custom, but in a prophetic mode of expression, Ver. 23 adds again a וְהָיָה. The more general sense of this specializing Hävernick expresses to the following effect: "Heathendom forms no new church alongside of Israel, no proper tribe alongside of the twelve families of Israel. It is absorbed into Israel as God's holy ordinance, which continues unalterable, as an ensign for the Gentiles, into the one true Church, which has existed from the beginning and shall exist for ever." Very rightly does Kliefoth point out the connection of our prophetic passage with the prediction in ch. xxxvi. 36, xxxvii. 9, 28; only he wrongly adduces ch. xliv. 9, which compare. "There shall henceforth be no distinction between the members of God's people born of the seed of Abraham and those born of the Gentiles."

CHAP. XLVIII.

1 And these are the names of the tribes: from the north end by the way of
[toward] Hethlon, as one cometh to Hamath, Hazar-Enon, the border of
Damascus northward to the border of Hamath, and they are to him the east
2 side, the sea: Dan one. And on the border of Dan, from the east side to
3 the westward side: Asher one. And on the border of Asher, from the east-
4 ward side to the westward side: Naphtali one. And on the border of
Naphtali, from the eastward side to the westward side: Manasseh one.
5 And on the border of Manasseh, from the eastward side to the westward
6 side: Ephraim one. And on the border of Ephraim, from the east side and

7 to the westward side: Reuben one. And on the border of Reuben, from the
8 east side to the westward side: Judah one. And on the border of Judah,
from the east side to the westward side, shall be the oblation which ye shall
offer, five and twenty thousand in breadth, and the length as one of the tribe-
portions from the eastward side to the westward side; and the sanctuary is
9 in the midst of it. The oblation which ye shall offer to Jehovah is in length
10 five and twenty thousand, and in breadth ten thousand. And to these, to
the priests, shall the oblation of holiness be; northward five and twenty
thousand, and seaward in breadth ten thousand, and southward in length five
and twenty thousand; and the sanctuary of Jehovah is in the midst of it.
11 To the priests is the hallowed portion, [to those descending] from the sons of
Zadok, who kept My charge, who went not astray when the sons of Israel
12 went astray, as the Levites went astray. And there is to them a heave-por-
tion from the oblation of the land most holy, by the border [border district] of
13 the Levites. And the Levites [receive], over against the border of the priests,
five and twenty thousand in length, and in breadth ten thousand; the whole
14 length five and twenty thousand, and the breadth ten thousand. And they
shall not sell of it, nor exchange, nor shall the first-fruits of the land pass
15 over [into another hand]; for [it is] holiness to Jehovah. And five thousand that
are left in breadth before the five and twenty thousand that is profane, for
16 the city, for dwelling, and for open space; and the city is in its midst. And
these are its measures: the north side four thousand and five hundred,
and the south side four thousand and five hundred, and on the east side four
thousand and five hundred, and the westward side four thousand and five
17 hundred. And there is an open space for the city, northward two hundred
and fifty, and southward two hundred and fifty, and eastward two hundred
18 and fifty, and westward two hundred and fifty. And the residue in length,
over against the oblation of holiness, ten thousand eastward and ten thousand
westward; and it is over against the oblation of holiness, and the produce
19 thereof is for food for the labourers of the city. And as to the labourers of
20 the city, they shall labour it out of all the tribes of Israel. The whole obla-
tion is five and twenty thousand by five and twenty thousand: a fourth-part
21 shall ye offer the oblation of holiness, for a possession of the city. And the
residue [belongs] to the prince, on this side and on that of the oblation of
holiness, and of the possession of the city, before the five and twenty thousand
of the oblation unto the border eastward, and westward before the five and
twenty thousand toward the westward border, over against the tribe-portions,
[it belongs] to the prince; and the oblation of holiness and the sanctuary of the
22 house are in its midst. And [namely] from the possession of the Levites, from
the possession of the city [from that] in the midst, shall be the prince's, between
the border of Judah and between the border of Benjamin—the prince's it
23 shall be. And the rest of the tribes: from the eastward side to the westward
24 side: Benjamin one. And on the border of Benjamin, from the eastward
25 side to the westward side: Simeon one. And on the border of Simeon, from
26 the eastward side to the westward side: Issachar one. And on the border
27 of Issachar, from the eastward side to the westward side: Zebulon one. And
on the border of Zebulon, from the eastward side to the westward side: Gad
28 one. And on the border of Gad, toward the south side, to the right is the
border: from Tamar to the strife-waters of Kadesh is the inheritance [along
29 the brook] to the great sea. This is the land which ye shall divide of the
inheritance to the tribes of Israel, and these are their portions: sentence of
30 the Lord Jehovah. And these are the out-goings of the city: on the north
31 side, four thousand and five hundred by measure. And the gates of the city
after the names of the tribes of Israel: three gates northward; the gate of
32 Reuben one, the gate of Judah one, the gate of Levi one. And on the east-
ward side four thousand and five hundred: and three gates; the gate of
33 Joseph one, the gate of Benjamin one, the gate of Dan one. And as to the
southward side, four thousand and five hundred by measure: and three gates;

the gate of Simeon one, the gate of Issachar one, the gate of Zebulon: one.
34 As to the westward side, four thousand and five hundred: its gates three;
35 the gate of Gad one, the gate of Asher one, the gate of Naphtali one. Round
about eighteen thousand; and the name of the city from that day: "Jehovah
thither" (Jehovah Shammah).

Ver. 1. Sept.: . . . *ἀπο τ. ἀρχης . . . κατα το μερος της καταβασεως του περισχιζοντος ἐπι την εἰσοδον της* Ἡμαθ *αὐλης* *του* Αἰναν, . . . Ἡμαθ *αὐλης· κ. ἐσται αὐτοις τα προς ἀνατολας ἑως προς θαλασσαν*— Vulg.: . . . *juxta viam . . . pergentibus Emath atrium Enan*—

Ver. 8. . . . *ἡ ἀπαρχη του ἀφορισμου*— Vulg.: . . . *primitiæ, quas separabitis*—

Ver. 9. . . . *ἡν ἀφοριουσιν*—

Ver. 10. Τουτων *ἐσται . . . τοις ἱερευσιν* . . . Κ. *το ὁρος των ἁγιων*— Vulg.: *Hæ autem erunt primitiæ sanctuarii sacerdotum*—

Ver. 11. . . . *τοις ἡγιασμενοις υἱοις*— Vulg.: *Sacerdotibus sanctuarium erit de filiis*— (Another reading: בני המקדש, Sept. Arabs.)

Ver. 12. . . . *ἡ ἀπαρχη δεδομενη ἐκ τ. ἀπαρχων τ. γης*— (Another reading: מתרמות; הקדש *pro* הארץ.)

Ver. 14. Οὐ *πραθησεται ἐξ αὐτου οὐδε καταμετρηθησεται, οὐδε ἀφαιρεθησεται τα πρωτογεννηματα τ. γης*—

Ver. 15. . . . *προτειχισμα ἐσται τη πολει*—

Ver. 17. Another reading: ופאת' instead of ומפאת קדים, and ומפאת' instead of ופאת־ימה.

Ver. 18. . . . *κ. ἐσονται αἱ ἀπαρχαι τ. ἁγιου, κ. ἐσται . . . τοις ἐργαζομενοις την πολιν.* Vulg.: . . . *erunt sicut primitiæ sanctuarii . . . fruges in panes his qui serviunt civitati.*

Ver. 20. Sept.: . . . *ἀφοριειτε αὐτου την ἀπαρχην . . . ἀπο της κατασχεσεως τ. πολεως.* Vulg.: *Omnes primitiæ . . . in quadrum, separabuntur in primitias sanctuarii et in possessionem civitatis.*

Ver. 21. . . . *ἐκ τουτου, κ. ἐκ τουτου ἀπο τ. ἀπαρχων . . . κ. εἰς τ. κατασχεσιν . . . κατα προσωπον . . . χιλιαδας μηκος, ἑως των ὁριων τ. προς θαλασσαν, κ. ἐχομενα των μεριδων τ. ἀφηγουμενου·* (Another reading: על גבול instead of עד'.)

Ver. 22. . . . *ἐν μεσω των ἀφηγουμενων . . . των ἀφηγουμενων ἐσται.*

Ver. 28. . . . *κ. ἑως των προς λιβα, κ. ἐσται ὁρια αὐτου ἀπο Θαιμαν κ. ὑδατος* Βαριμωθ Καδης, *κληρονομια, ἑως θαλασσης*— (Another reading: מפאת *pro* אל פאת; עד מי'; עד הים.)

Ver. 29. Another reading: בנחלה.

Ver. 34. Another reading: שערים.

Ver. 35. Κυκλωμα . . . Κ. *τ. ὀνομα τ. πολεως, ἀφ' ἡς ἀν ἡμερας γενηται· Κυριος ἐκει ἐσται τ. ὀνομα αὐτης.*

EXEGETICAL REMARKS.

Vers. 1–29.—*The Division of the Land among the Tribes, with the Separation of the Part to be separated.*

Vers. 1–7.—*The Seven Upper Tribe-portions.*

The division of the land, like the fixing of the boundaries (ch. xlvii. 15 sq.), begins in the north, inclining thence to the south. Hitzig denies the significance of the number seven here: "As the section itself regarding the Terumah is put in the middle, so his object is to move the central sanctuary, which must lie between Judah and Benjamin, but historically lay far nearer the south border than the north, as near indeed as possible to the centre, yet also toward the south." Hengst., on the contrary, argues from the division of the number twelve into seven and five,—a division which often occurs also in the grouping of the Psalms, where "the sacred number seven is always the chief number, and five appears only as its supplement." "Even upon the land," says Häv., "is the character of pleasing to God to be stamped throughout."

["The territory to be divided being thus obviously viewed in an ideal light, the division itself is conducted in the same manner,—not as it ever could have taken place in the reality, but after rule and measure, in exact and regular portions, running alongside of each other the whole breadth from west to east, and standing in a common relation to the temple in the centre. Seven of the tribes have their portions on the north, on account of the greater stretch of the land in that direction with respect to the actual Jerusalem, and in the following order:—Dan, Asher, Naphtali, Manasseh, Ephraim, Reuben, Judah; the latter having its place close by the central portion on the north, as Benjamin had on its south. This honour appears to have been given to these two tribes in consideration of their relative historical superiority, having so long adhered to the temple and ordinances of God, when the others deserted them. Dan, on the contrary, was placed at the extreme north, on account of the low religious character of the tribe, precisely as John, in representing the whole elect Church by twelve thousand from the several tribes of Israel, leaves Dan out altogether (Rev. vii.). As there were actually thirteen tribes, he finds his twelve times twelve by omitting Dan, whose idolatrous and semi-heathen character made it border morally, as it did locally, on the Gentiles. Here the two tribes of Joseph are thrown into one, to admit of Dan's having a place, but it is still the lowest place in the ideal territory of a blessed world. With these exceptions, we can discern no specific grounds for the particular places assigned to the tribes respectively. The order on the south side was, Benjamin, Simeon, Issachar, Zebulon, Gad. But the city, the temple, the prince, and priesthood, with their respective portions, being situated precisely in the middle, and not within the boundaries of any of the tribes, was intended to intimate that all were now to be regarded as having a common interest in them; and that the miserable and mischievous jealousies which had of old exercised so disastrous an influence, especially between

Judah and Ephraim, should finally and for ever cease. All now should stand related as a united and compact brotherhood to the sanctuary of the Lord, from which, as a central fountainhead of life and blessing, there should continually stream forth manifestations of grace to all the people."—FAIRBAIRN'S *Ezekiel*, pp. 498, 499.—W. F.]

Ver. 1. The starting-point: **the north end**, ch. xlvii. 15.—The course goes from west to east; hence "Hethlon" and "Hamath," and "Hazar-Enon" as the eastmost point. HENGST.: "from Hazar, etc., to the border," etc., so that the northmost point is Hamath, ch. xlvii. 17.—The words: **and they are** (pertain) **to him**, refer to the tribe immediately named, **Dan.**—פְּאַת־קָדִים הַיָּם, KEIL: asyndeton = the east side and the west, the tract toward both sides. HITZIG: "the east side of the sea," that is, what lies east from the sea, namely, from the north end of this east side, from Hazar-Enon. HENGST.: "the east side, the west sea." But he takes "him" as the ideal unity of the tribes as a whole, although Dan (he says) was specially in the prophet's mind. At the division of the land under Joshua, Dan had, west of Benjamin, taken possession of only a part of the land's breadth; but in the days of the Judges, Danites had pressed northward, and had named the conquered Laish Dan, so that Dan denoted the north border. Hengst. makes one of the prophet's points of view to be to show the equality of all the tribes as "members of equal rank in the body of the people of God." Thus in the case of the tribe allotments, and afterwards in the case of the gates, "the sons of the handmaids and of the wives, and those of the latter again among one another, were intentionally and skilfully intermixed (Rev. vii. 5–8), and Dan the son of the handmaid stands at the head, because there is with God no respect of persons: Israel is a brotherly people, in which no member may raise itself above another."—דָּן אֶחָד means: that Dan shall receive an inheritance, as Keil supplies חֵלֶק, from ch. xlvii. 13. KLIEF.: "the single equal heritage for each tribe being considered as a monad." Similarly in what follows; and always, in distinction from the former order of things, taking in the whole breadth of Canaan, "from the east side to the seaward side."—Ver. 2. **Asher.**—Ver. 3. **Naphtali.**—Ver. 4. **Manasseh.**—Ver. 5. **Ephraim.**—Ver. 6. **Reuben.**—Ver. 7. **Judah**, who is thus preceded by three pair of tribes, the list of the seven upper tribes closing with him, just as from him the whole people received even their name. Keil observes: "Asher and Naphtali, who formerly occupied the most northern district, are ranged beside Dan; then follows Manasseh, since half-Manasseh formerly dwelt to the east of Naphtali; and Ephraim is ranged beside Manasseh, as formerly beside the western half-Manasseh. The reason for bringing in Reuben between Ephraim and Judah seems to be that Reuben was the first-born of Jacob's sons."

Vera. 8–22. *The Special Portion cut off from the Land.*

Ver. 8 places, moreover, the Terumah on the border of Judah. "The normal condition of Israel is reached, according to which all the life of the whole land streams forth from its truly spiritual centre, and the unity of the whole community rests entirely upon the Lord Himself and His self-revelation in the midst of the people. In this way the fact also is explained that Judah dwells nearest the sanctuary, while Benjamin occupies a corresponding position on the south side of the temple. The reason of this is not so much the warlike character of these two tribes, as their attachment to the temple when the ten tribes revolted from it. Both tribes represent such a disposition, and the prophet's higher spiritual point of view manifests itself in this division of the tribes, as differing essentially from the old division, inasmuch as this latter was determined principally by outward need and external relations" (HÄV.). According to Bunsen, Judah lay sufficiently near the centre in order, with Ephraim, "to form the fulcrum of defence." The Terumah, which refers us back to ch. xlv. 1 sq., is employed, according to Hengst., *sensu latiori*, including also the portion of the prince; it rather appears, however, to be denominated *a parte potiori*, as it is expressly said: **and the sanctuary is in the midst of it**, although the **five and twenty thousand in breadth** will comprehend all, if the clause: **and the length as one** (any one) **of the tribe portions from the eastward side to the westward** (seaward) **side**, is to be understood in accordance with ch. xlv. 7. Then, however, Ver. 9, the **oblation**, as it is distinctively called, **which ye shall offer to Jehovah**, will not, like that: **which ye shall offer**, in ver. 8, be the Terumah in the special sense. The "sanctuary" in ver. 8 forms the transition to this specializing.—Thus also it cannot be misunderstood when in Ver. 10 **the oblation of holiness** (comp. on ch. xlv.) is adjudged to the **priests**, for the sanctuary lies in their portion.—The clause: **northward**, etc., makes the upper boundary of this main division of the whole the same (25,000) **in length**, that is, from east to west, as the last-measured boundary **southward**. Westward and eastward, whereby the **breadth** is given, that is, in the direction from north to south, the measurement yields the same result in each case, 10,000.—וְהָיָה בְּתוֹכוֹ fixes in some measure more exactly the בְּתוֹכוֹ of ver. 8, whose suffix Keil makes refer *ad sensum* to חֵלֶק, instead of to תְּרוּמָה. At all events, בְּתוֹכוֹ there is not = "therein" (HITZIG). The expression: "in the midst," refers, however, neither to one of the tribe-portions nor to the "oblation," but to the priests' portion, which the oblation bounds off on all sides. In our verse the suffix refers more definitely to the **oblation of holiness** in its length and breadth, which are given as to the four sides.—Ver. 11. Kliefoth renders הַמְקֻדָּשׁ, "the hallowed portion," to the priests it shall belong. So also Rashi. Pual pass., as it is, can here denote nothing more suitably, especially as the suffix in the previous בְּתוֹכוֹ is thereby most easily explained. Most expositors, following the old translations, and influenced by Isa. xiii. 3, render it in a plural sense; and similarly Kimchi takes it distributively: "he who is hallowed of the sons of Zadok." The participle certainly lies inconveniently between לַכֹּהֲנִים and מִבְּנֵי, but the plural in 2 Chron. xxvi. 18 cannot decide in favour of the singular here, for the singular here would, as Hengst grants, denote "the hallowed part as distinct from the unconsecrated part,"— a restriction which can no longer be introduced in the case of the sons of Zadok (comp. xliv. 15 sq.), after they have been repeatedly represented as the hallowed priestly *personelle.* What does this saying of Hengstenberg's mean: that they are sanctified "by their fidelity, by which they made their election sure"? It ought rather to be said that the part of the Terumah which is specially the Terumah—the "oblation of holiness" (as in ver. 10), or הַמִּקְדָּשׁ, as is said here—belongs to those who are the priests of the future, namely, to the priests who are taken **from the sons of Zadok, who kept,** etc. (referring to the "sons of Zadok"); comp. ch. xliv. 15. The מִ denotes no selection or restriction among the sons of Zadok, but simply their descent, whence these priests are, with a reference back to what is contained on that subject in the previous chapters. [Keil's objection in respect to הַמִּקְדָּשׁ tells, moreover, against such a view as this: "to the priests it is consecrated,"—a view which indeed would correspond neither to the form of the text nor the facts of the case.] The mention of the going astray of the **Levites,** like whom the children of Israel went astray, shows, what hitherto is manifest throughout, namely, that the tribe of Levi, not the priestly family of Aaron, was intended; whereas Hengst., in order to have the necessary distinction and contrast, thinks of those who were "as a punishment desecrated (?), degraded, and reduced to mere Levites." The meaning, on the contrary, is simply this: the sons of Zadok stood firm when the rest of Levi stumbled, and along with Levi, Israel. That some of the sons of Zadok also had gone astray, and in contrast to them the description here is given, is not the case.—Ver. 12. וְהָיְתָה לָהֶם, although no formal apodosis to ver. 11, most expressly confirms the view taken of ver. 11.—תְּרוּמִיָּה, as the following מִן likewise shows, is less a part (KLIEF.) of the **oblation,** than an abstraction therefrom; hence in a spiritual respect somehow in relation to the oblation, what is **most holy** in relation to the sanctuary; KEIL correctly: "the offering from the oblation." But this "Terumiah" from the "Terumah" is designated **most holy** because it is this in relation to the part which belongs to the Levites. Observe how the old ordinances as regards places are converted into ordinances in reference to persons, and thereby Jehovah's relation comes out as a relation appearing in men. [HENGST.: "the heave-portion which fell to the priests is designated most holy, because it has God's sanctuary in the midst of it, and belongs to His most eminent ministers, in distinction from the part of the Levites, which has only the second degree of holiness, and from that of the city, which has only the third" (?).] The closing definition: אֶל־גְּבוּל, not merely forms the transition to what follows, but also indicates that we have to imagine the priests' portion as adjoining the south or the north side of the Levites' portion.—In Ver. 13, accordingly, this latter is expressed, as it had to be expressed in respect of the Levites, namely: that they are to have their appointed portion **close to the border of the priests** (לְעֻמַּת). HENGST.: "In the description of the oblation, the prophet, for theological reasons, began with the middle portion, the priests' part; it was then necessary to guard against the thought that the Levites' part was separated by the city, or the city by the Levites' part, from the sanctuary. The servants of the house, and likewise the inhabitants of the city, as constituting the holy assembly at the divine services, behoved to have the sanctuary as near as possible." Comp. for the determination of the circumference, ch. xlv. 5. As to the repeated closing clause: **the whole length,** it will lose its appearance of tautology if we assume with Kliefoth that it is meant to express briefly the two lengths (north and south) and the two breadths (east and west), instead of going through the cardinal points one by one, as in ver. 10.—Ver. 14. Comp. Lev. xxv. 34. "It is regarded as the gift of first-fruits to Jehovah, to which the Lord has the sole right, and which thus may never come into the hands of another" (HÄV.). "The ordinance applies naturally also to the priests' land, although it is expressly given only for the Levites' part, because its holiness is less, so that the thought of its being saleable might more readily arise" (HENGST.).—יַעֲבוֹר (Qeri: יַעֲבִיר); the Kal is quite sufficient, there is no need of a Hiphil form.—That which is acknowledged as **first-fruits of the land** is holy to Jehovah. "Traffic is excluded where God is the landowner and the Levites only usufructuaries" (HENGST.). "This land is an offering; the heaving is one form for it, and the gift of first-fruits the other" (KLIEF.).

As in ch. xlv. 6, so now in Ver. 15, the possession of the city comes after the land of the priests and Levites. Kliefoth observes, referring to ch. xl. 2 (?), that the prophet beheld the city to the south; hence it lay south of the priests' portion and the sanctuary, and so the Levites' portion lay north of that of the priests. Ezekiel, he goes on to say, setting out as he does from the middle of the Terumah, does not, as in the division of the land among the tribes, follow the direction from north to south, but takes first the more central priests' portion (vers. 9-12); but the fact that he then (vers. 13, 14) describes the Levites' portion, lying north of it, and thereafter takes up the city-possession, lying south of the priests' portion, has its ground in this, that the portion of the Levites is also holy, whereas the portion of the city is profane. It is still simpler to take as motive for the order observed, besides the reference to ch. xlv., the connection of priests and Levites with the central sanctuary. In this way the Levites necessarily preceded the city. The five thousand are left when we subtract twice ten thousand in breadth (vers. 9 and 13) from five and twenty thousand in breadth, that is, from north to south (ver. 8).—הַנּוֹתָר is neuter, according to Hitzig; it is the particip. Niph. of יָתַר.—עַל פְּנֵי, before the side in question, namely, from east to west; this gives a third oblong, which, however, is only half the breadth of the two former.—חוֹל is profane, in contrast to the former "most holy" and "holy" of the portion of the priests and Levites. PHILIPPSON: "they are common land for the city, for dwellings, and for environs." These five thousand are set apart generally for the city (לָעִיר), and specially for dwellings and as precincts for free use, pasture, arable land, etc. As the city is the title for this portion of land, so the verse concludes by stating that the city is בתוכה: Hengst. makes the feminine suffix refer to the city in the wider sense (לָעִיר), within which the city in the narrower sense lies. Kliefoth translates: "in the middle in it." Since the city lies in the midst of the city-district, this makes it, as Klief. observes, lie right opposite the sanctuary in the south.

Ver. 16 first subjoins the more exact statement in regard to the length from east to west, previously only indicated by עַל פְּנֵי. The oblation affords it a front of five and twenty thousand; its measure, however, is such as to make a square of four thousand five hundred on each side, to which is added in Ver. 17 an open space of two hundred and fifty on each of the four sides. The חמשׁ found in the text, and left by the Masorites unpunctuated, is almost universally considered an error of transcription; Hengst., on the contrary, says: "It points to this, that the south side *equally* with the north side has 4500 cubits; five stands for: on the five, or: to the five," etc. The length of the city-district (namely, city and free space), from east to west, amounts to 4500 + 250 + 250 = 5000, and to the same in breadth from north to south, so that the square in this respect occupies the entire breadth of the city-district, while it only comes to a fifth of the 25,000 in length from east to west. ["The small compass of the city district" (cubits!), observes Hengst., "wholly excludes the inhabitants from agriculture."]—Ver. 18 disposes of what remains of the length (Klief.: "in the length") along the holy oblation, the section eastward and the section seaward, 10,000 each. "This is to remain over against the holy Terumah, that is, as a part of it, although it is assigned neither to the priests, nor the Levites, nor the city" (Klief.). Hengst. explains the phrase: "over against the holy oblation," as indicating "that we are not to imagine that the Levitical part is shoved in between, whereby the holy oblation would be separated from its guardians." The *proventus*, the תְּבוּאָה of the הַנּוֹתָר, what of fruit the soil of these two districts yields, is destined for support (לְלֶחֶם) for the **labourers of the city**. They are further described in Ver. 19, where it is said of them: יַעַבְדוּהוּ. (1) Häv.: "By these are not meant slaves, nor (as Kimchi) such as cultivate gardens and fields (against which there is the הָעִיר), but, as Gesenius puts it: those who perform service in building the city, which the prophet represents as an honourable office. The holy city as well as the temple belongs now to no single tribe, but to all Israel, so all the tribes take part in building and maintaining it, by workmen chosen for the purpose, who receive their support from land assigned to them situated in the immediate vicinity of the holy temple-district." Hävernick makes יַעַבְדוּהוּ refer to הַנּוֹתָר, and the last thought of ver. 18 to be: "the residue of the city-district shall serve for support to the workmen, and they shall cultivate it, for which they shall be bound to the service of the city." (2) Hengst. translates thus: "who serve the city;" and "can only understand by this a militia (!) that take the city in the midst,—military service is the only possible service on a large scale to a city,—and, as is so emphatically stated, are encamped as a guard beside the holy oblation with the temple." "On the north side of the holy oblation are the Levites as the *militia sacra* (Num. iv. 23, viii. 24); on the south side the ministers of the secular arm, which has to protect the Church." "Adjoining the provision made for these servants on both sides is the domain of the prince (?!), who is to be considered the commander of these guards." For עָבַד, in the sense of "military service," Hengst. refers to ch. xxix. 20. But if ever an exposition has missed the mark, it is here. We hear the mounting of guard on the Berlin University Platz, and Hengst. must also mention Egypt as an example "of such military colonies endowed with land;" he comforts himself with the thought that this militia "is not to be gathered out of the lands of other lords, as formerly the Cherethites and Pelethites, but is to consist of such as are willing also to serve their Lord in this lower (!) sphere." (3) Klief.: "The workmen of the city are the labouring class dwelling in it; in this city they are not to be destitute of possession, as is usual in the cities of men, therefore considerable portions of land are assigned to them for support; and to explain this ver. 19 subjoins, that from all the tribes of Israel (עָבַד, transitively with the accus.) they are to employ these in labour; namely, when they come from all parts of the land to the holy city to the feasts, and because the land in the capital gives employment to labourers," etc. (4) Hitzig takes עָבַד as *colere locum*, of cultivating through residence = to inhabit: hence, "for the inhabitants of the city;" ver. 19: "And as to the inhabitants of the city, people from all the tribes of Israel shall inhabit it."—הָעֹבֵד, singular, stands as collective, "but the suffix in יַעַבְדוּהוּ does not refer to it, and to make it refer to הַנּוֹתָר would yield no suitable sense; hence we are to read: יַעַבְדוּהָ, and the reference to עִיר, which is certainly not of the common gender, is to be accepted." As in ver. 18 the masculine suffix in תְּבוּאָתֹה refers to הַנּוֹתָר, so also does the suffix in יַעַבְדוּהוּ. Ewald translates thus: "And every labourer of the city will cultivate it." Neteler: "and as to the workman of the city, one will take him for workman out of," etc.—Ver. 20 sums up the **whole**, namely, of the previously described oblation, as a square of 25,000, *i.e.* inclusive of the possession of the city; and then describes the possession of the city as a fourth-part of the "oblation of holiness," as the portions of the priests and Levites in the narrower sense are called, which have a breadth of 20,000, of which the 5000 of the possession of the city are a fourth. Philippson, on the other hand, translates thus: "In square form shall ye offer the holy oblation, together with the property of the city;" as similarly Ewald. And already Hävernick took אֶל־ as: "in addition to the possession of the city."

Ver. 21; comp. ch. xlv. 7. The portion of the prince on both sides, east and west, of the "oblation" described in ver. 8 (25,000 from east to west). אֶל־פְּנֵי, translated by Ewald: "close to;" by Hengst.: "over against;" by others: "along," with reference to the east and west skirt of the Terumah, which was only 25,000 long. The position is described first eastward, and then, with some variations (instead of אֶל, now עַל, with omission of the "oblation;" instead of עַד־גְּבוּל, now עַל־גְּ'), westward likewise; while in conclusion there is added: **close to the tribe-portions.** It is scarcely necessary to remark in explanation, that the prince's portion abuts on the north (like the Levites' portion) on the portion of Judah, on the south (like the possession of the city) on the portion of Benjamin. That which lies eastward and westward between Judah and Benjamin belongs to the prince, to whose domain the suffix in בְּתוֹכָהּ refers, namely, to הַנּוֹתָר.—Ver. 22 describes the same object, only instead of eastward and westward, it is now from north to south; hence, setting out **from the possession of the Levites,** namely, in the north, and **from the possession of the city.**—The designation בְּתוֹךְ does not belong to הָעִיר (KEIL), but stands as an asyndeton, like: **possession of the Levites,** and: **possession of the city;** and counts as the third the central part, namely, the portion of the priests, with the lately-mentioned temple-sanctuary, after mention has been made of the two outer parts. Thus, what is to be the prince's domain extends from north to south, namely, on both sides (ver. 21); and when it is described as in the direction of north to south, it is represented as lying **between the border of Judah and between the border of Benjamin.** The question, moreover, of ch. xlv. is renewed here: rods? or cubits? Keil and Kliefoth reckon by rods, because, reckoned by cubits, "the prince's land would be more than six times as large as the whole Terumah;" whereas, measuring by rods, the actual size of the land is in correspondence. Hengst. adduces the fifty stadia of Hecatæus in proof of the 18,000 cubits of Jerusalem.

Vers. 23–29.—*The Five Lower Tribe-portions.*

Ver. 23.—**The rest of the tribes** follow southward: first, Benjamin, which tribe opens the series on this side, as Judah closed it on the other. Three pairs precede Judah, and two pairs follow Benjamin: first, Ver. 24, **Simeon**; thereafter, Ver. 25, **Issachar**; then, Ver. 26, **Zebulon**; and, finally, Ver. 27, **Gad.**—For Ver. 28 comp. on ch. xlvii. 19.—Ver. 29, a closing formula. HENGST.: "It is said of the inheritance, because a part of the whole was not to be distributed, but to be previously set apart as holy ground."

["The desire of giving due prominence to the sacred portions in the centre, leads the prophet again to enter into some statements regarding the Terumah, or oblation, and its subdivisions. Nothing of importance is added to what was said before, except that the 5000 rods apportioned out of the 25,000 square to the city is here laid off in a square of 4500, with the 250 all round for suburbs. This space for the city was not strictly holy ground, in the sense that the sacerdotal portions were, and hence it is called profane or common. But being thus immediately connected with the sacred portions, and standing apart from the individual tribes, the city built on it formed a fit and proper centre to the whole land—in its position and its structure the beau-ideal of a theocratic capital, encompassed by the most hallowed influences, and fitted to exert a uniting and healthful effect upon the entire community. Hence the prophet closes the description by the mention of some things regarding the city which might serve more deeply to impress the feeling of its being the suitable representative and common centre of the community. Itself occupying a central position, and immediately in front of the house of God, it was also to have twelve gates, bearing the names of the twelve tribes of the children of Israel; in token that all the family of faith had their representation in it, and, as if they were actually resident in it, stood before the Lord for the enjoyment of His favour and blessing. He specifies, again, the entire circumference of the city, 18,000 rods (between twenty and thirty miles), as a symbol of the immense numbers of the covenant-people under the new and better dispensation of the future, immeasurably transcending what had existed under the old. And to exhibit the character of the city itself as representative of the community at large, and indicative of its own relative position, it was to bear from that day, namely, from the period of the beginning of this new and better order of things, the honourable name of 'Jehovah-Shammah'—not, as has been already stated, Jehovah-there, but Jehovah-thither, or thereupon. For it was in the temple, rather than in the city, that the Lord was represented as having His peculiar dwelling-place. But His eyes were to be ever from the temple toward the city, and again from the city toward the whole land. The manifestations of His love and goodness were to radiate from the chosen seat of the kingdom through all its borders; He in all, and all united and blessed in Him. So that the consummation of this vision substantially corresponds with the object prayed for by our Lord, when He sought respecting His people that they might be where He was, and that they might be all one, as He and the Father are one; He in them, and they in Him, that they might be made perfect in one."—FAIRBAIRN'S *Ezekiel*, pp. 499, 500.—W. F.]

Vers. 30–35.—*The City as to Extent, Gates, and Name.*

In continuation of Ver. 15 sq., we have now in Ver. 30 **the out-goings of the city,** that is, the outlets, with evident reference to the gates; for "the boundary-lines marked out by walls" (HENGST.), "the extremities into which a city runs out" (KEIL), are only such in virtue of the gates. The measure here on each of the four sides is 4500; comp. ver. 16.—The detailed account begins, as in the dividing of the land, and so with evident reference thereto, from the north.—Ver. 31. The gates are designated after the names of the tribes of Israel. There are three gates to each side, hence twelve in all; comp. Rev. xxi. 12. The naming does not follow the position of the tribe-district, and thus the omitted tribe of Levi appears here in the north, honoured by a gate named after it. The three sons of Leah (as Deut. xxxiii.) are first mentioned; as Keil observes: "the first-born by age, the first-born in virtue of the patriarchal blessing, and the one chosen of Jehovah for His service instead of the first-born of Israel." In Ver. 32 the three east gates, where Joseph is named next after Levi, and comprehends in his name his two sons, Ephraim and Manasseh ("Rachel's sons and the son of her handmaid," KEIL). In Ver. 33 the three south gates bear the names of the other three sons of Leah; and, lastly, in Ver. 34 the west gates are given, after the names of the other three sons of the handmaids, as Keil observes.

Ver. 35. Then follows the close of the book; it closes with a name, with the symbolical name of the city, whose whole compass—doubtless calculated likewise in a symbolical point of view—is given as: $4 \times 4500 = 18{,}000$. Kliefoth remarks on this number, that it is $= 12 \times 1500$; hence, a product of 12 by a multiple of 10. "The city of the people of God," says he, "has now become the capital of the new world." Neteler connects with it the millennial kingdom, saying: "A thousand years are with God as one day, and one day as a thousand years; hence the city is called the millennial kingdom" (!).—The name of the city is annexed to its whole circumference, just as before the gates named follow the statement of the extent. Thus it appears that the name of the city itself now expresses the same relation to Jehovah which the names of the gates did to the people of the covenant. Hitzig translates: "The name of the city is from that day: Jehovah there," and understands this to mean: from the day of its being built. Hävernick makes the following excellent remarks on the whole connection: "Already in the foregoing the thought was made prominent, that Jerusalem should be the common property of all the tribes. Over against the temple, the place of the divine revelation is Jerusalem, the Church of God, living before and in Him. As such, it forms a closely knit together, indissoluble whole, a stately unity rooting itself in God. In order duly to set forth this thought, there is annexed to the division of the land among the individual tribes a consideration of the city itself. For that division is nothing less than an isolating or dissevering of the individual tribes; but forthwith the higher unity of the prophetic intuition, again embracing and knitting all firmly together, presents itself. The community is one accepted of God and hallowed to Him; standing itself in the presence of God, it forms the one true stem of the new Church, and has thereby reached its full destination. In the first place, the greatness of the community expresses itself to the prophet in the compass of the city; and then in its name, its quality, its holiness. 'From that day,' that is: henceforth for ever, Isa. xliii. 13. The name itself is: 'Jehovah thither,' not: Jehovah shall dwell there. For Ezekiel distinguishes between temple and city: Jehovah does not properly dwell in Jerusalem, but, in the proper and highest sense, only in His sanctuary. Thence He looks toward Jerusalem, is turned thither with the fulness of His love and grace. What now makes Jerusalem a true city of God is the love entirely turned toward it, the good pleasure of God resting upon it," etc. HENGST.: מִיּוֹם means: from the day when what is described will be so; it does not and cannot mean: "always," and just as little can it mean: "from to-day." שָׁמָּה is not: "there," but, as always: "thither." But query ch. xxiii. 3 in Ezekiel himself, if not ch. xxxii. 29 sq. He explains the name from Deut. xi. 12. "This 'Jehovah thither' manifested itself in the most glorious manner in the appearing of Christ, in the many attempts He made to gather the children of Jerusalem, in His tears over Jerusalem. When, however, His own would not receive Him, then the 'Jehovah thither,' which had availed for the restored city five hundred years, passed over to the new people of God, the legitimate continuation of Israel and Jerusalem (Matt. xxi. 43), to which Jesus had promised to be with them unto the end of the world."—Kliefoth with right expresses himself against an alteration of the punctuation (שָׁמָּה into שְׁמָהּ, "and the name of the city is henceforth: Jehovah is its name"), and also against the idea that שָׁמָּה can mean anything else than: "thither." "But then the name purports that Jehovah will raise Himself up thither, toward the city, and will do so from the day, that is, from to-day, that this city and what depends upon it may come into being."

In view of the total ruin of the people of God, the whole comfort of the prophet's predictions, the full significance of his labours, is yet once more completely summed up in the last words of his ministry. Schmieder says: "Notwithstanding the irregularity of the natural boundaries, Ezekiel views the Holy Land as a rectangular, oblong quadrilateral, etc. The centre falls exactly at Sychar, where Jesus speaks to the woman of Samaria (John iv.). Mount Gerizim is the site of the new temple, but the Holy City is at a distance of about five miles off; the place in which it is situated is 'the place of Bethel.' The revelation of John contains in its closing chapters cognate views, which presuppose and surpass, but do not exactly interpret Ezekiel."

ADDITIONAL NOTE.

["Thus ends the marvellous vision of the prophet—alike marvellous whether we look to the lofty pattern (true in the spirit, though unavoidably wearing the garb of imperfect forms and shadowy relations) which it embodied of better things to come in God's kingdom, or to the time chosen for presenting this to the Church of God. The cause of Heaven was then at its lowest ebb. The temple that had been, together with the kingdom it symbolized and represented, were laid in ruins; they were to be seen only in broken fragments and mournful dilapidations, as if smitten with the powerful curse of an irrecoverable perdition. Yet from the midst of these howling desolations, as from the very 'suburbs of hell,' the prophet ascends, with assured step, the mount of vision, and has there exhibited to his view, not, indeed, the very image of better things to come, but the ideal pattern after which the blessed and glorious future was to be fashioned. He even sees it as already present; and, with such imperfect materials of thought and utterance as then stood at his command, he gives it forth to the Church and the world as a thing which his own eyes had beheld, showing how God would certainly dwell with His people in a manner He had never done before—how He would at once immeasurably extend the sphere of His kingdom, and greatly elevate the condition of those who belonged to it—and how, through the copious effusions of His life-giving Spirit, the former imperfections should be done away, the most remote regions of the divine territory hallowed and blessed, and even the peculiar haunts of cursing and desolation made to rejoice and blossom like the rose.

> 'O scenes surpassing fable, and yet true!
> Scenes of accomplished bliss! which, who can see,
> Though but in distant prospect, and not feel
> His soul refreshed with foretaste of the joy?'

"That such scenes should have been described with such assured confidence, and at a time so deeply overspread with gloom, was indeed an ennobling triumph of faith over sight. It gave a most illustrious proof of the height in spiritual discernment, and far-reaching insight into the purposes of Heaven, which is sometimes imparted in the hour of greatest need, especially to the more select instruments of the Spirit's working. And surely the children of the kingdom now must be chargeable with neglecting an important privilege, if they fail to profit by so inspiriting an example. Here the heart of faith is taught never to despair—not even in the darkest seasons. And when it is seen how much of the scheme delineated in the prophetic vision has already been accomplished, should not believers feel encouraged to look and strive for its complete realization, assured that God is ready to hear their cry, and to second with the aid of His Spirit the efforts that are made to dispossess and drive out the hostile powers that continue to linger in His kingdom? It is theirs, if they feel thus, not only to contend in the best of causes, but also with the surest prospect of success; for the Lord Himself is upon their side, and His word of promise must be established.

> 'Thus heavenward all things tend. For all were once
> Perfect, and all must be at length restored.
> So God has greatly purposed; who would else
> In His dishonoured works Himself endure
> Dishonour, and be wronged without redress!
> —Come, then, and added to Thy many crowns,
> Receive yet one as radiant as the rest,
> Due to Thy last and most effectual work,
> Thy word fulfilled, the conquest of a world.'"

—FAIRBAIRN'S *Ezekiel*, pp. 501, 502.—W. F.]

DOCTRINAL REFLECTIONS.

1. Ch. xl.-xlvi. show the temple and its service; ch. xlvii. and xlviii., the land and the city. It may be said that in these two parallels temple and service stand related to each other, as do land and city. The temple comes to expression in its service, as the land finds its most expressive name in the city, ch. xlviii. 35. But the land gets sanctification, healing, and quickening from the temple; so that the waters which stream forth from the temple in connection with the entrance of the glory of Jehovah into the sanctuary, and transmit the blessing of the temple to the land, are the kernel, as they are the connecting link between the two closing sections of our prophetic book.

2. Hävernick sums up what has preceded in the expression (Rev. xxii. 3): "And the throne of God, etc., shall be in it, and His servants shall serve Him." Ch. xl.-xliii. treat of "the new and glorious indwelling of the Lord in Israel;" ch. xliv.-xlvi. "of the new service of the Lord which shall follow on the ground of that completion of all the divine manifestations of grace;" now, however, according to him, "the rich blessing of God which comes upon the new community from the new indwelling of God" is described. This latter assertion cannot be upheld in the face of ch. xlvii.; at least, vers. 1-12 of that chapter, keeping, as they do, within Canaan, appear to exhibit in a very characteristic manner the perfection of Israel, rather than to contain an account of what accrues to the new community of the Lord in the way of a rich blessing of God. The community of the future, with the service which obtains in this temple, is described as being what it should be. For as Jehovah (ch. xxxvi. 27) puts His Spirit within Israel, so He makes them walk in His statutes, and keep and do His judgments. But this sanctification of Israel comes (ch. xxxvii. 28) with the sanctuary in the midst of them. Hence not only the specially priestly temple-service (ch. xliv.), but likewise the representation therein of the people by the prince, yea, the people themselves (ch. xlvi. 3, 9), and that, as ch. xlv. shows, as to judgment and justice (comp. ch. xliv. 24) in all their affairs (ch. xlv. 9 sq.), appear in connection with the sanctuary. When Ezekiel portrays the new community as conformed to the law in their worship, this specially manifests the connection of the sanctification of Israel with the sanctuary of Jehovah (in accordance with ch. xxxvii. 28); in general, however, the prophet comes in this way only to that which he has always throughout his book prophesied as the form of the sanctification and holiness of Israel. Only the deviations here and there from the Mosaic law in the service of the future defined by the temple, and in general, the freedom which prevails in this respect in the ordinances (while Ezra's scrupulously exact adherence to the law shows the direct opposite), presuppose so very significantly for this future of which Ezekiel prophesies the fulfilling of the law in the popular life. The letter of the law is, as to its spirit, learned in the Spirit which Jehovah put within Israel (comp. also ch. xxxix. 29), in that it is lived, in that the idea of the law has become the life of the people. Thus there is an end to the pædagogy of the law. The fulfilled idea of the law, as exemplified by our prophet, realizes itself in a newness of life. But that this newness has still its expression in a legal form, in the forms of the Mosaic worship, as little disparages the new reality of the future, as when in the New Testament the sacrificial service furnishes clothing for the thoughts of the Christian life. It is, however, a proof not only of the priestly, but of the historical standpoint generally of Ezekiel's prophecy; it is the necessary shell which adheres thereto. Comp. besides the Doct. Reflec. on ch. xl.-xlvi.

3. The waters from the sanctuary—to which they are finally traced back again in ver. 12, and consequently are represented as belonging thereto —no doubt raise up fruit-bearing trees on their banks; but the significance of this is not the amplification, *e.g.* of ch. xxxiv. 26 sq., that is, the fruitfulness of the land (ch. xxxvi. 8 sq., 29 sq.); for as the aim of this water is the healing of the Dead Sea (ch. xlvii. 8 sq.), so likewise the foliage of these fruit-trees serves for healing (ch. xlvii. 12). We may say: As the aim of the temple-sanctuary is sanctification, so that of the waters from the sanctuary is healing, so that sanctification and healing are the two leading theological thoughts dominating the whole closing part of Ezekiel. But with the thought of healing the completion of Israel is already alluded to.

4. Ch. xvi. 53 prophesied the ethical restoration of Sodom, and the same thought returns here with the healing of the waters of the Dead Sea. Since the Dead Sea, like Sodom and Gomorrah, stands throughout the whole of Scripture as a type of judgment, the judgment is, in the character of threatening, by its healing symbolically removed from the sight of Israel. Israel by its sanctification is exempted from judgment, has no further judgment to fear (ch. xxxix. 29). The healing of the Dead Sea in its land, which immediately precedes the settling of the boundaries and the division of the land (ch. xlvii. 13 sq.), is the characteristic symbol of the completion of Israel, the community of God. Only the salt pools and pits of ch. xlvii. 11 still remain, but in the same way as when in the closing verse of Isaiah (ch. lxvi. 24) they go out and look upon the carcases of the apostates, whose worm dieth not, etc., and who are an abhorring unto all flesh.

5. From Genesis onward, which also relates the genesis of Israel as the people of God, there runs through Holy Scripture a twofold reference, namely, to the people of the promise, and to the Promised Land. This twofold reference meets us here also in these closing chapters. But as we have repeatedly seen, the people of Israel are to be taken in their prophetical character of the future as referring to mankind, and the land of Israel is to be taken as referring to the earth. Now in Ezekiel, people and land become united in the symbol of the sanctuary, of the temple in the midst of the twelve tribes and their portions of land, as indeed the prophet accentuates this centre, which thus unites all the parts into a whole. By this the idea is symbolized which has realized itself in the Son of man, who unites mankind in Himself; who as the second Adam is the centre for the whole earth; who can say: To Me is given all power in heaven and on earth, go ye therefore and make disciples of all nations, and preach the gospel to the whole creation! We have there the sanctuary for sanctification, and here the Saviour for healing; preparation and fulfilment, beginning and end.

6. Stier on John vii. 38 rightly interprets the word of Scripture to which our Lord appeals there as referring to Christ Himself (*Words of the Lord Jesus*, vol. v. p. 282 sq.; Clark's Tr.). When here in Ezekiel the healing, life-giving waters flow from the temple, then, at least according to what Scripture here says (but comp. also Joel iv. [iii.] 18; and afterwards Zech. xiv. 8), the fulfilment cannot possibly be sought for in him who believes in Christ. (ὁ πιστευων εἰς ἐμε corresponds to the ἐρχεσθω προς ἐμε (ver. 37), just as in John vi. 35 ὁ ἐρχομενος προς με and ὁ πιστευων εἰς ἐμε mutually correspond.) The αὐτος, out of whose κοιλια ποταμοι ῥευσουσιν ὑδατος ζωντος, can also according to John only be He ἐφ' ὁν the Baptist (John i. 33) saw το πνευμα καταβαινον και μενον ἐπ' αὐτον, and with allusion to whom he says in general (John iii. 34): οὐ γαρ ἐκ μετρου διδωσιν ὁ θεος το πνευμα. This One who is the Anointed κατ' ἐξοχην explains to the Jews (John ii.) the temple of His body. Consequently He not only could, but must have understood of Himself what the Scripture says of the "rivers of living water flowing out," as He also began by saying: If any man thirst, let him come unto Me; and this quite apart from the circumstance that, as the feast suggested ever since the march through the wilderness, "the spiritual rock that followed" was, as Paul expressly says in 1 Cor. x. 4, the Anointed One. Zech. xii. 10 also was very clearly uttered with this reference, as Jesus, too, in John vii. 39 spoke of the Spirit, not that should flow out from him that believes on Him, but "that they should receive (λαμβανειν) who believe on Him; for πνευμα ἁγιον (in the sense of the outpouring of Zech. xii. 10) was not yet, because Jesus was not yet glorified." Comp. John xx. 22. Thus Christ has interpreted Ezekiel xlvii. 1–12 as referring to the Spirit of Pentecost. When Stier, in accordance with his apocalyptic mysticism, makes the thought be included here of "the community of the Lord, particularly in its glorious final perfection, but only the community as a whole, in so far as the Lord Himself flows through and fills it, sends forth from it His streams of blessing,"—that goes beyond the letter, upon which Stier insists so much, and beyond the sense and spirit of the letter in John; and, moreover, the word of prophecy in Ezekiel does not point to such a perfection. We may at all events say with Roffhack (*Ev. Johannis*, i. p. 302 sq.): "In the derived sense the saying may hold good of believers; for twelve Galilean fishermen and publicans produced that spiritual movement in the world, the swell of whose waves still at the present time presses onward to the remotest ends of the earth." "Interpreted as referring to believers generally," observes Roffhack, "it could not but wholly mislead thousands regarding their own faith and that of their brethren."

7. Hengstenberg says in his commentary on our prophet: "We shall have to regard as the Mediator of this salvation for the whole world the exalted Descendant of David, who, according to ch. xvii. 23, grows up from a feeble sapling to a glorious cedar, under which all fowls dwell; to the fowls of every wing there, correspond here the fish of every kind in ver. 10. In harmony with our prophecy, the salvation here announced took its beginning in the time of the second temple, and poured itself forth from the place where Jesus had the chief seat of His activity over the nations of the earth" (comp. on John vii. 3, 4). In the *Christology*, 2d ed., he observes in particular: "In Ezekiel the water issues forth under the threshold of the house toward the east; according to the Apocalypse, the stream of water proceeds from the throne of God and of the Lamb. John has completed Ezek. xlvii. 1 from ch. xliii. 7. The reason why the streams of salvation now proceed from the sanctuary, is that the Lord has entered into it with His glory. From the temple, now lying in ruins, they could not issue, because the

temple was not yet truly the place of God's throne. This the sanctuary, that is, the Church, first became through Him in whom dwells the fulness of the Godhead bodily. Henceforth it is called 'Jehovah there,' ch. xlviii. 35. As the announcement of the indwelling of the glory of the Lord in ch. xliii. found its fulfilment in Christ, so John points to this when he speaks of the throne of God *and of the Lamb.*" In his commentary he says: "The relations of the New Testament to our section (ch. xlvii. 1–12) are very rich and manifold. In reference to it the Lord, in Matt. iv. 18, 19, speaks to Peter and Andrew. On it rests the miraculous draught of fishes by Peter at the beginning of the ministry of Jesus (Luke v.), and likewise the draught after the resurrection (John xxi.). Jesus with evident design embodies, at the commencement and the close, the contents of our prophecy in a symbolic act. Not less allusive to our prophecy is the parable of the net which gathered of every kind (Matt. xiii. 47). Finally, in Rev. xxii. 1, 2, the last and most glorious fulfilment is announced."

8. "Other prophets, too, have the symbol of a temple fountain (comp. Joel iv. [iii.] 18, and Zech. xiv. 8), but nowhere is it seen so beautifully carried out as here" (UMBREIT). The fundamental passage, or at least the older passage, is Joel's. It is not necessary, however, to consider Ezekiel as borrowing from Joel; the thought is applied as originally in him as in Joel or Zechariah; the only thing common to the three is the water. But unmistakeably there is a connection between the three prophetic passages. That which the healing of the Dead Sea, this removal of a spectacle of judgment as old as the days of Abraham, signifies in Ezekiel as to the fulfilment of Israel, is in Joel, likewise as to Israel, expressed in the watering of the valley of Shittim, which symbolizes as fulfilled the wilderness-journey of Israel, their period of probation generally. With the east sea Zechariah takes up Ezekiel's thought of judgment of the Dead Sea, but with the west sea he subjoins thereto reference to the salvation coming from the Jews unto the Gentiles. The Israel completed in the Messiah, in Christ, the temple, draws water with joy from the wells of salvation (Isa. xii. 3). When Jehovah counts and writes up His people among the nations (Ps. lxxxvii.), all His springs are in Zion. "Ho, every one that thirsteth, come ye to the waters," it is said in Isa. lv., for there is a river whose streams make glad the city of God, the dwelling-place of the Most High (Ps. xlvi.), whereas judgment passes over the world in the morning of the day of the Lord. Peace to him that is far off, and to him that is near, saith the Lord; I healed it, Isa. lvii. 19.

9. Before we take up for comparison the representation given in the Revelation of John, let us first consider the order in our prophet. That which was prophesied to Israel specially in ch. xxxvii. 26 is carried into effect in ch. xl.–xlviii., in which the Messianic salvation as to land and city is symbolically set forth in the temple, its service, and the waters. These chapters are eschatological in the sense that Christ and the Christian Church are the end, the fulfilment of Israel. Ch. xxxviii. and xxxix., again, contain eschatology in another sense, that is, the Christian sense; see p. 374 sq. These chapters are a specifically apocalyptic *enclave* in Ezekiel, whose close (ch. xxxix. 21 sq.) then points back to ch. xxxvii., by way of preparation for the following chapters, and to form connection with them. Thus Gog and Magog stretch beyond ch. xl.–xlviii. Since, then, the *schema* of the fulfilment of Israel, as sanctification to be God's people in the spirit that is to be poured forth—this fulfilment set down just as it took place through the Messiah, by means of the Christian Church—is summarily expressed in ch. xxxvii. 26 sq. and xxxix. 29, the last conflict of this fulfilled Israel, that is, of the Christian Church, is foreseen in the apocalyptic chapters xxxviii. and xxxix., so that the world-progress of the gospel, and the development of the nationalities for and against Christ and His community, will lie between ch. xxxvii. 26 sq., or, we may say, between ch. xxxix. 21 sq., and ch. xxxviii.–xxxix. 1–20. After the legal γραμμα, with which, although according to the freedom of the spirit of fulfilment, the completion of the Old Testament Church is described in ch. xl. sq., there comes, as early as ch. xlv., but much more in ch. xlvii. 13 sq., the historical γραμμα of the taking possession of and dividing the Promised Land. As, in order to understand the temple, we must go back to its idea, especially after the entrance of the glory of the Lord (ch. xliii.), and as in connection therewith (ch. xliv.) the service of the community of this sanctuary is understood of the worship of the Father through the Son in the Holy Ghost, so in like manner the only significance which the undeniably symbolical temple-water assigns to the land and the twelve tribes, and to the city with its gates, is that which the people of Israel has, through the Christian Church, obtained for the earth, "the *territorium* of the kingdom of God" (KEIL); for, in the Church of Christ, Israel has become complete as to the members, just as in Christ, the Messiah of Israel, as to the head. The Chiliastic interpretation of our chapters, even if correct in assuming that the letter of Ezekiel's prophecy—which, however, is symbolical—relates to Israel and Canaan, that is, that what is meant is an earthly, historical fulfilment, must still be regarded as advocating a restoration to the pristine condition, irrespective of the fulfilment of the Old Covenant in the New.

10. It harmonizes with the chronological order given in Ezekiel that John's Apocalypse takes up in ch. xx. 8 sq. the prophecy of Ezekiel through Gog and Magog (ch. xxxviii.), that is, in its specifically apocalyptic passage (p. 373), and this after previously introducing in Rev. xix. 17 sq. the final conflict against Christ of antichristianism and pseudo-Christianity, and the judgment and overthrow of the latter as the beginning of the end; we have seen (p. 377) why the colouring of the description in the Apocalypse is borrowed from Ezek. xxxix. 17 sq. That this and the other final conflict (Gog's) both belong to the history of the Christian Church of Israel, is perhaps indicated by the mention of the χαραγμα του θηριου, both as to those who have it (Rev. xix. 20) and those who have it not (Rev. xx. 4), which reads as parallel to ch. xliv. 15, although the Old Testament framework of the description of the sons of Zadok has something essentially different of its own (not yet overthrow, but degradation is inflicted upon those who stumbled, in contrast to the sons of Zadok). But if Ezekiel in ch. xl.–xlviii. beholds Israel perfected on earth

in the temple and its service, and placed in its twelve tribes within the bounds of Canaan, and if this symbolical representation is a prophecy of Christ and the Christian Church, the kingdom of God in this guise on earth, then the Apocalypse of John interprets the certainly apocalyptic hint that these closing chapters of our prophet come after the attack, etc. of Gog, and, beginning by making Rev. xx. 11 sq. the end of the world, the last resurrection and the final judgment precede Gog's attack; hence it interprets our ch. xl.–xlviii. as referring to the perfection of the Christian Church, the kingdom of glory (Rev. xxi. 1–xxii. 4); and here, corresponding to Ezekiel's earthly description (Canaan), the Apocalypse describes a new earth, and also retains throughout the Old Testament colouring of our prophet. The justification of interpreting John's Apocalypse with this application is to be found in the principle that the perfection of the Christian kingdom of God at the end of the world is just the full final perfection of Israel in Christ, just as Israel after the Spirit and the Church of Christ are only one continuous thing. That which the general judgment in John carries out in its reference is indicated by the giving over to salt in Ezek. xlvii. 11, with respect to the completion of Israel; and as the (Dead) Sea, in ver. 8 there, is healed to life, so in Rev. xx. 13 the sea gives up its dead, and there is no more sea (ch. xxi. 1), and there shall be no more death (ch. xxi. 4). That Keil says too much when he says: "The prophetic picture in Ezek. xl.–xlviii. gives a clear idea of the kingdom of God erected by Christ in its full configuration," is already evident from his own limitation of this assertion, for he supposes merely a "partial Old Testament outline to this New Testament image of the heavenly Jerusalem, Rev. xxi. and xxii." But still more markedly does the comparison of the Apocalypse present essential differences. While Ezekiel's temple is situated in Canaan, as repeatedly stated in ch. xlv. and xlviii., the New Jerusalem (Rev. xxi. 2, 10) comes down out of heaven from God. The distinction is not this, that in Ezekiel city and temple are separated, but that the New Jerusalem of the Apocalypse has no temple whatever, God and the Lamb are its temple (ch. xxi. 22); and this furnishes the most express confirmation of the explanation given of Ezekiel's temple, as referring to the dwelling of God in Christ. While in Ezekiel the entire circuit of the temple is most holy (ch. xliii. 12, xlv. 3), in John this now holds of the city. The glory of God entering into and filling the temple in Ezekiel (ch. xliii., xliv.) lightens the city, etc., in Rev. xxi. 23; its gates, too, are not shut; compare, on the contrary, Ezek. xliv. 2, xlvi. 1 sq. So also it can be said that the holy city of the Apocalypse is called the "bride" (ch. xxi. 2, 9) of the Lamb, just as He is alike her Temple and her Bridegroom. The closing representation of John's Revelation is occupied with this city of twelve gates, and is accordingly borrowed from the close of Ezekiel, from the city "Jehovah Shammah" (ch. xlviii. 35). Apart from particulars, the ample magnificence of precious stones and gold, etc. in Rev. xxi. 18 sq. forms a noteworthy contrast to the meagre simplicity of Ezekiel's temple (p. 445). Moreover, the cube form (Rev. xxi. 16), like the most holy place, comes very specially into consideration for the New Jerusalem. But in respect of the river of the water of life (Rev. xxii. 1 sq.), it has to be noticed that in the Apocalypse it flows in the midst of the street of the city, and that the leaves of the tree of life on either side are designated as εἰς θεραπείαν τῶν ἐθνῶν, a still clearer reference to Ezekiel (ch. xlvii.), and, in accordance with the original promise that in Abraham's seed all the nations of the earth should be blessed, removing for the Gentile world (as already in Rev. xxi. 24) the apparent limitation to Israel of Ezekiel's prophetic description; as Neumann expresses it: "The transformation of Israel to a blessed eternity is the consecration of the nations, Isa. lx. 3 sq." Hengst., who in the 2d edition of his *Christology* makes the symbolical view of our closing chapters be confirmed beyond question by the Apocalypse, just as he attributes "to the entire description of the new temple, in its main points, a Messianic character" ("and of such a kind that under the New Testament the fulfilment is always going on, while the completion belongs to the future"), in his commentary on Ezekiel cannot keep the Apocalypse and the prophet far enough apart, simply, indeed, on the ground that "in Ezekiel everything is mundane, there everything is supramundane;" neither of which is the case, not even in the form of expression, and also not so in the sense expressed. At all events, Hengstenberg finally concedes in his commentary that "the fact cannot be mistaken, that in a certain (?) sense the entire description of the new temple bears a Messianic character," etc.

11. The Mosaic law may, in respect to worship, be said to culminate in the temple, just as its goal and that of the temple is the Anointed One, as the fulfilling of the law in general; and so the spirit of the law, as well as the Spirit of Christ, may be considered as the water flowing from the temple. Both met together at the first Pentecost of the Christian Church, and moreover, those of Israel on whom the Spirit was poured forth were assembled in the temple; and the preaching of Peter was like a first bursting forth of these waters from the temple.

12. "The Dead Sea has its place in worship also. The Talmud *Menachoth* prescribes that the salt used in sacrifice should be salt of Sodom. Every sacrifice receives in the salt the death-consecration, and consequently it is just this use which explains why the waters of life flow into the sea of death. As all the health and blessedness of a glorified future well forth in the former, so in the latter surges the torment of the curse, all the woe of the divine judgments which culminate in death" (NEUM.).

13. The fishers in the vision (ch. xlvii. 1–12) are not mere figures in the landscape, however true it is not for the East alone that fishing is part of the picturesque in a well-watered region. For what Ezekiel treats of is not so much the abundance of water as the abundance of life, of living fishes. And so, too, Neumann has no right to bring in the fishes as palatable food (Num. xi. 5; Neh. xiii. 16), as the third kind of Sabbath food among the Jews, in order to get "an inviting attraction," which is altogether foreign to our vision. True it is, however, and needing no reference to the fishponds beside the temples of Paphos and Hierapolis, and the fish idols Derceto, Oannes, and Dagon, that "in the multitude of fish is mirrored the most exuberant (!) and richest fulness of life." Neumann observes, moreover

"the lively movement in the element of all purity, in order to contemplate in this figure the most blessed existence of the sinless." In the Talmud the Messiah, too, is called "fish," and according to Abarbanel the constellation Pisces announces His birth. The swarming life of the fishes in ver. 9 sq. is dramatized by means of the fishes. Neumann says on this occasion: "To man was given the dominion also over the fish of the sea, Gen. i. 28; Ps. viii. 9 [8]. He has now grasped the sceptre. Comp. Isa. xix. 5, 8. The greatness of the affliction there testifies to the greatness of the blessing here. In Jer. xvi. 16 the fishers are the executors of the judgment; in Ezek. xxvi. 3 they are sureties for the fulfilled judgment. Yet where a Dead Sea became alive, there the fishers in their ceaseless movement, in the ardour of their activity, testify that here the curse is changed into a blessing."

14. The palms of Engedi continued to be known to a late period, and although the vineyards of Cant. i. 14 have disappeared, still there was here a place of life not far from the seat of death. May not (asks Neumann) the other fountain (Eneglaim) have been in equally beautiful natural scenery? like two oases on the border of the Dead Sea? "And the names fountain for oxen and fountain for goats surely indicate pasture grounds. Thus the fountains would encompass like a silver frame the steppe that was to be transformed, and from their brilliancy the figure itself would become light."

15. It is only in accordance with the specifically Israelitish tenor of Ezekiel's prophecy, particularly in this closing section, that in ch. xlvii. 22 the reference to the Gentiles keeps itself within Israel; enough has been said in the earlier chapters for supplementing and explaining. Hofmann compares Isa. xiv. 1 sq.; on which Delitzsch observes that "the letter of the promise at all events is not in a New Testament form, because the community (*ecclesia*) has no other mode of manifestation for Old Testament days and Old Testament perception than the national form. This national form of the community is broken up in the New Testament, and will never be restored."

16. "When the new earth is designated as Canaan, and the new humanity as the nation of Israel with its twelve tribes, this is because that has appeared in the new humanity and the new earth which was aimed at, begun, and prefigured in Israel and Canaan. In proportion, however, as the kingdom of God extends itself on earth, and the salvation of Christ finds faith in men, the people of God become œcumenical, gain over the earth, and obtain the mastery of the world, until God gifts it to them as a new world. The Revelation of John omits all features which refer back to the previous development, because it has to do with the absolute consummation. God will one day make the new altar; life will give health to the sea of nations; at last we have the consummation before our eyes. Our temple-vision may be compared to paintings" (Kaulbach's frescoes), "which attempt to represent historical developments upon one sheet, and must be interpreted and understood like these" (KLIEF.).

17. The city Jehovah Shammah forms the antithesis not to Babylon alone, but also to the city of Gog (ch. xxxix. 16). Perhaps, too, the permanent grave of Gog (ch. xxxix. 11 sq.) and the healed Dead Sea stand to each other in significant contrast.

18. Hofmann thinks "the hope which was ever and anon whispered to the national community of God under all circumstances is not lost either to the community of God which then existed in the form of a nation, or to the nation which was called as such to be the community of God; and the fulfilment will correspond in both respects to the prophecy."

HOMILETIC HINTS

On Ch. xlvii.

Ver. 1 sq. "Before his view stands a paradise of the nation returned to God, from whom the fountain of life flows forth in richest effusion, filling the land and all waters with healing virtues,—behold in this the word of God in its vigour of heavenly life, destroying disease and death!" (UMBREIT.)—"From the restored temple issues finally salvation for the whole world" (HENGST.).—"For this is the most intrinsic characteristic of these waters, that they spread through the world the consecration of the most holy place" (NEUM.).—The waters of life in their significance, whence they come, and whither they flow.—"Water, which makes the unfruitful land fruitful, and affords refreshing drink to the thirsty, is in Scripture a figure of the blessing and salvation which already in paradise are represented as a watering of the ground (Gen. xiii. 10). Comp. in Isa. xii. 3 the wells of salvation, and in Isa. xliv. 3 the Spirit as the blessing, for the root of disease is sin" (HENGST.).—"In the Church of the New Covenant there is a river of living water, the rich gifts of the Holy Ghost, which flow out into it. Only we must come and taste this water, that we may be made whole, John vii. 37 sq." (TÜB. BIB.)—"The watering of Canaan implies a great spiritual fruitfulness" (LAMPE).—"The gospel is no invention of man, but an outflow from God in Christ" (STARCK).—The Eastern and the Western Church.—"The water is the fatherly kindness and compassion of God, out of whose treasury innumerable benefits flow to us. The water turns at once to the altar of Christ, because we behold in Christ the love of God, and from Him flow upon mankind the spiritual streams of blessing which are to quicken and give health to the world, John xiii. 10, iv. 10" (HEIM-HOFF.).—"By this water is signified the preaching of the gospel, which offers to us grace and the forgiveness of sins in Christ. Water cleanses, so do God's word and grace (John xiii.), of which baptism is the symbol. Also the course of the gospel, as the course of these waters, no one can stop" (LAVATER).—"It is the water of life, which Oriental mysticism in vain seeks for in other places" (UMBREIT).—Ver. 2. "The kingdom of God cometh not with outward show (Luke xvii. 20); at first it has even an insignificant appearance, but soon it grows and increases mightily (Matt. xiii. 31, 32)" (W.).—"That the waters at first flow out so gently is meant to intimate how entirely different is the process in the kingdom of grace from that in the course of worldly things. For whatever glorious or great thing takes place in the kingdoms of the world creates great wonder and surprise in its very beginning; but the kingdom of God cometh not so (Luke xvii. 20). In the kingdom of God, things proceed from little to great; in the kingdoms of the world, often from great to little; Satan, as Luther says, begins his things with lofty impetuosity, but finally they end in nothing, and everything comes to disgrace" (HAFENREFFER).—"At first it appeared an insignificant work, with a few disciples in Judea; then it was preached in Samaria, and soon after in the whole world" (LAVATER).—Ver. 3 sq. "Faith has always to do with the water here, namely, because it is constantly occupied with consideration of the word of God" (STARCK).—"No one has learned so much, that there is not more to learn still. Christianity is prefigured in the water through which Ezekiel was brought. Experience teaches that the longer Christians exercise themselves in godliness, the less value they set on themselves; they confess finally that they cannot reach the bottom; they can depend upon nothing that is theirs, but must submit themselves simply and solely to the grace and mercy of God" (SCRIVER).—To him that hath shall be given, that he may have abundance.—"The mysteries of the gospel are like a deep river, which finally becomes so deep that one cannot sound it, Eph. iii. 18" (TÜB. BIB.).—"When reason cannot fathom the divine mysteries because of their depth, the faith which trusts to the truth and wisdom of God, as it were, swims across, Luke i. 34 sq." (STARCK).—"We find here a twofold figure; the one is the four measurements of a thousand cubits each, the other is the four depths of the waters. The one refers to the exceeding great extension of the kingdom of Christ toward all the four quarters of the globe; the other to the different degrees in the measure of the Spirit to which the nations called to the kingdom of Christ shall gradually attain," etc. (MEYER.)—"The four world-kingdoms in Daniel are like a shadow of the four great epochs in space and time, through which the waters of life diffuse their fulness over the world, gradually transforming it until its peace shall become as a river, and its righteousness as the waves of the sea (Isa. xlviii. 18); until the earth shall be full of the knowledge of Jehovah as the waters cover the sea," Isa. xi. 9 (NEUM.).—"So the books, too, of the Holy Scriptures are, as to their contents, like these waters, of dissimilar depth. Some come only to the ankles, others to the knees, or even to the loins, and some are altogether unfathomable, like these last nine chapters of our prophet" (PFEIFFER).—"At first the word of God seems to us like water which reaches only to the ankles; one thinks it is not so deep, one will easily wade through. But when a man reflects diligently with heartfelt prayer, then his understanding is more and more opened in the divine illumination; then it already reaches his knees—he acquires a far higher esteem for it (Ps. cxix. 129). When he advances farther, he gets always deeper into the hidden wisdom, and Holy Writ is to him a water which comes to his loins; he is so captivated therewith, that he finds in it his highest satisfaction, and forgets over it everything else in the world. Finally, it becomes a water over which he must swim; he cannot fathom the mysteries" (GLASSIUS).—"The river of life, which is at first small, always grows in volume, because the grace and knowledge of Christ should always increase in us; and the divine love and mercy should appear to us always greater, more glorious, and more worthy of admiration, the more attentively we consider them. For who can comprehend their height and depth! Who is so void of understanding as not to be astonished, when he considers that the God of immortality interests Himself in poor mortal man, yea, in the sinner, who so often rises up against Him and breaks His word, imparts to him heavenly treasures, makes him immortal and a partaker of the divine nature? Of this spiritual blessing more and more is always imparted to believers. Here we have sprinkling, cleansing, the taking away of the heart of stone, and the impartation of the new heart, and the anointing with the Holy Ghost. In such measure does the water of life increase" (HEIM-HOFF.).—"Friends of missions behold here a glorious emblem of missions, particularly of the most blessed missionary activity proceeding from Israel" (RICHTER).—Ver. 6. "In this life we see darkly and through means of the word, hereafter face to face, 1 Cor. xiii. 12" (STARCK).—Ver. 7. The gospel makes fruitful trees on all sides.—"How wholesome, how fruitful is the living water of the gospel, and of the gifts of the Spirit which it gives us! They restore health, they bring forth fruits of blessedness which endure unto eternity, John iv. 14" (TÜB. BIB.).—Blessed is the man that trusteth in the Lord (Jer. xvii. 7 sq.).—"Believers are trees planted by the rivers of water (Ps. i.); they flourish to the glory of God (Isa. lxi.), and produce rich and ripe fruit (Ps. xcii. 13 sq.)" (STARKE).—Ver. 8. First *urbi*, and then *orbi*, holds good of the Messiah.—Salvation is of the Jews, but it is a salvation for the world.—"Covered with loose pebbles and wild rifted rocks, furrowed by dry torrent-beds, enclosed and obscured at the sides by lofty chains of mountains, the Arabah exhibits only here and there traces of fertility in the growth of herbs and plants, where fountains and streams flow down from the mountains; it is the evening gloom of the wilderness-night, the land in which is the darkness of evening (Isa. xxiv. 11; Jer. ii. 6). The steppe a world in the bonds of death, where the mystery moulders below in silence, and shoots up in roses of the grave" (NEUM.).—God's sanctuary a well-spring of life for the Dead Sea of the world (Ps. lxxxvii. 7).—The Dead Sea in the darkness of nature, in the light of the promise.—God's thoughts of peace over the abysses of the world's wretchedness.—Judgment and grace.—The world is a desert and a Dead Sea.—"Oh the greatness of the grace of God, which desires not the death of the sinner, but his healing!" (STARCK.)—By conversion we lose our former salt.—"In other cases a clear and wholesome stream, which flows into a muddy and putrid lake like this, becomes corrupt; it is otherwise with the gospel, which brings recovery and health to the earthly-minded heart" (STARKE).—"The gospel is a word of life to them who believe in it (John vi. 68); and its spiritual rivers are living waters to them who drink thereof (John iv. 10)" (TÜB. BIB.).—"It is a power of God, but man will not let the power work, Heb. iv. 2" (STARKE).—Ver. 9. "The sea, the restlessly swelling depth, an emblem of disquiet (Isa. lvii. 20), unfruitful (Isa. xxiii. 3), boiling up with violent impetuosity (Job vii. 12; Ps. xlvi. 4 [3]), even in its most glorious aspect only darkling night, like phosphorescent gleams around a corrupt tree, awakening a painful desire and longing for launching forth on distant voyages (Deut.

xxx. 13), and down even to the shady abyss (Lam. ii. 13), unfathomable and dark, the most natural expression of the dark and destructive power of death (Jer. li. 42; Mic. vii. 19), its harshness increased by the flood supersaturated with salt," etc. (NEUM.).—"In the Dead Sea of the world there arises just such a gladsome swarm of those who have become partakers of life from God, as formerly of ordinary fishes in the natural sea at the creation. The salvation is for all, without distinction of nation, rank, or age" (HENGST.).—"From death into life, from the service of sin into the glorious liberty of the children of God, come rich and poor, young and old, bond and free, Jews and Greeks, who receive into them the law of the spirit of life. For whosoever calls upon the name of the Lord shall be saved" (HEIM-HOFF.).—"The fishes in the water and the drops in a river are innumerable; so also the multitude of believers shall be amazing, Isa. lx. 7" (STARKE).—"The two rivers are the two Testaments, the two sacraments" (STARCK).—Ver. 10. "The ministers of the Church are compared to fishers, because of the contempt with which they are regarded by the rich and powerful of this world; because of their labour by day and by night, in heat and in cold; because of the fruitlessness of their labour at times, when they say with Peter, We have caught nothing; because, too, of the dangers they incur in stormy weather; because of their confidence, which, as in the case of the husbandman, must rest on God; because of the various kinds of implements which they use, nets, hooks, etc., preaching, inviting, admonishing, etc. And they rescue souls from the abyss" (STARCK).—Nets and fishers everywhere, this is the appearance which the world in Christ presents.—"The world is the sea, the fishes are the men; so long as the fishes swim freely hither and thither at their own will, they profit no one, but when caught they are profitable. In the same way, so long as men walk according to their own lusts and pleasures, they are of no real use either to God or their neighbour; but when they are caught or converted by the gospel net, then they are profitable to God and their neighbour, Philem. 11" (STARKE).—Ver. 11. "In the Dead Sea of the world the marshes and swamps are originally of the same nature as the main sea; the only difference is, that they shut themselves off from the healing waters, which flow from the sanctuary. Comp. the saying: Ye would not, and the drawing of the Father (John vi. 44), which comes to meet the longing of the soul. It is, however, sufficient punishment for the world that lieth in wickedness that it continues as it is" (HENGST.).—"The mud-puddles probably indicate separatist, self-contained parties, which do not receive those streams of salvation, and consequently cannot be healed. To these belong Gog's adherents, ch. xxxviii." (RICHTER.)—"Such, too, are those who entrench themselves against the truth and craftily wrest the Scriptures throughout; people of this kind are not easily brought to the knowledge of the truth" (BERL. BIB.).—"Over the figures of light there comes once more a dark shadow. Yea, nothing can rescue from death that which is his own (Isa. xxvi. 14). All transformation is only the fruit of a ripening, during which there is constant need of being put in mind of the day of wrath, which comes on the earth, as here on Israel" (NEUM.).—He who will not have Christ wills to have eternal death.—No salvation out of Christ.—"The eyes of God regard him who opposes Christ as a morass, because he prefers the wilderness of sin to eternal salvation, John iii. 19" (STARCK).—"He who, in case of conversion, still seeks to retain bypaths and bosom sins, is not upright before God. Divided allegiance is of no avail here, Matt. vi. 24" (STARKE).—"The ungodly, who despise God's word, or do not persevere in the path of life, remain dry and unfruitful. Blessed, on the contrary, is the godly man who meditates on the law of the Lord day and night (Ps. i.). He is always flourishing, always alike; he walks in the ways of the Lord, and edifies and elevates others" (HEIM-HOFF.).—Ver. 12. The blessed growth close by the river of life.—Evergreen leaves, yet not leaves merely, but also fruit! Thus it is with life from God's sanctuary.—Hypocrisy and true piety.—"The never-fading of the leaves implies the perseverance of believers in temptations, in persecutions, in death" (STARCK).—"The works of believers, which in other respects are done even by unbelievers, are fragrant of faith and love, and are therefore fitted for converting the heathen" (BERL. BIB.).—"Would that all men knew how well it is with him who is included in the number of Christians, of true members of Jesus! Then one always goes onward (and never backward) in his happiness; he is in the path of life, and always receives grace for grace" (ROTHE).—Healing and sanctification.—"A pleasant figure of the blessing imparted to mankind from the dwelling among us of the God-man. His word flows forth from Him, swelling through all lands with ever-increasing power, and always more and more disclosing its fulness. He who holds to it and is rooted in it brings forth fruit continually, and it has power to quicken even what has long been lifeless, and to turn the curse into a blessing. In Christ we have this as a matter of daily experience; Ezekiel in vision saw it in the future; his prophecies have respect to us" (DIEDRICH).—Ver. 13 sq. "In the community of God every one has his place and his share according to his gifts, 1 Cor. xii. 28" (TÜB. BIB.).—"Who can define the boundaries of the Church, especially in the last days? But as here the boundaries of Canaan are defined, so the boundaries of the Church are faith and life in the Scriptures of the apostles and prophets, which accordingly no one is to overpass, Gal. vi. 16" (STARKE).—The Church of God has her boundaries within and without. The inheritance of the saints in light (1 John iii. 1 sq.).—"God gives to His children very differently; from him to whom a double portion has been given, a corresponding return is required" (STARCK).—"In the New Covenant the same grace is offered to all men. God is not a respecter of persons. It is one and the same Christ, one Spirit for all, Gal. iii. 26" (STARCK).—Ver. 22 sq. "Oh what comfort it is that the Gentiles are no longer to be strangers and foreigners from the promise, but citizens, and of the household of God! Eph. ii. 19" (STARKE).—"It is not birth, but the new birth, that makes men children of God" (STARCK).—"Here, under earthly figures, the Jerusalem that is above, with her children, is typified, and the calling of the Gentiles from east and west and the utmost bounds of the earth is described; for many shall come from the east and from the west, and sit down to eat with Abraham, Isaac, and Jacob in the kingdom of God, Ps. xlvii. 10 [9]" (HEIM-HOFF.).—"God here opens to all the holy gates of His Church, and prescribes to the Church herself the commandment of meekness, love, and brotherly kindness" (HAFENREFFER).—"Those who were formerly strangers shall then be heirs of the whole world. In Christ, in faith, in the New Covenant, the alien disappears. Those who were aliens from the commonwealth of Israel, and far off, and they who are nigh, are made one; the two are made one new man, Eph. ii. 12. For he who is in Christ is through faith Abraham's seed, and an heir and possessor of his promise, Gal. iii. 28, 29. The incorporation of believers into Christ makes a complete unity, and a new spiritual body, consisting of all true members without distinction, for in the new creation all members prosper alike before God, etc." (BERL. BIB.)—Right and title in the faith.

On Ch. xlviii.

Ver. 1 sq. "As the tribe of Dan stands at the beginning, so in the kingdom of God the last are first, Matt. xix. 30" (STARCK).—Believers are all Israel, and are so in truth, because according to the Spirit of sanctification.—Ver. 8 sq. "Thy heart is in thy midst; take heed to whom it belongs: is it a temple of God in which His Spirit dwells, 1 Cor. iii. ? or is it a habitation of unclean spirits, Luke xi. 26?" (STARKE.)—God has an eternal right to the centre of man; hence He says to man: Give Me thine heart; God is the centre of the spirit world, and in Him everything lives and moves.—"We ourselves ought to be God's oblation" (STARCK).—Ver. 11 sq. "Teachers, above all men, ought to keep God's commands and do that which they teach others. They ought to attach themselves chiefly to the sanctuary of the Lord, around which they dwell" (STARKE).—God is near to them who show themselves to be His priests and ministers in this world.—"To err with the erring excuses no one; the way is broad, not for us to walk on it, but to call attention to the narrow path of life" (STARCK).—Ver. 14. "Simon Magus wanted to buy the power of imparting the Spirit; but that is not permitted, because it comes solely from the Lord's portion, which may not be bought or sold" (HEIM-HOFF.).—"In the administration of church-estates nothing ought to be applied to one's own use" (STARKE).—Ver. 15 sq. Wherever believers dwell, their city is always one and the same.—"The city pertains to the holy, as respects the eternal destination of its inhabitants, for the members of the Church are called with a holy calling; it is in very truth the fellowship of the saints, of the truly anointed, for Christ, the glorious Head, is its Temple and Sanctuary. But in the actual state in which the Church appears in this world, the righteous and the hypocrites are intermixed, and there are many nominal Christians who count as dead, that is, in the death-list of the Church, in which list, indeed, those who have died in the Lord are not inserted; but from the appearance which she presents here, the Church universal on earth must also be regarded as a profane Church" (after STARCK).—On all the four sides which bound the world, and always by thousands. Thus the Church has spread from the fulness of the Godhead. This her false friends forget when they believe they must enrich her; but not less so her enemies and persecutors, when they imagine they needed only to rush upon her at full speed, thinking her small and contemptible, and that she and God and conscience, etc., are nothing but vain imaginations inherited from our ancestors.—Ver. 18 sq. "Behold here the great goodness of God, who thinks of even the labourers in the city and cares for them, Jas. v. 4" (STARCK).—But every Christian ought to be an upright labourer, as every stone, wherever it is placed, belongs to the building and contributes to its erection.—Ver. 21 sq. The prince protects the holy portion, the centre of the whole land, "on the east and on the west;" by which may be signified, that a state which has comprehended the nature and signification of the Church, both in her eastern and western course, shall stand alongside of her.—Ver. 23 sq. "Let every man be content with the portion of temporal goods which he possesses, for the Lord has apportioned it, Matt. xx. 14" (TÜB. BIB.).—Ver. 29. "Thou rejoicest when thou obtainest an earthly inheritance, which thou often canst possess only a very short time: strive rather for the heavenly inheritance, for the inheritance that fadeth not away, which is reserved in heaven for the children of God, 1 Pet. i. 4" (STARKE).—Ver. 30 sq. The goings-out of the city of God are toward the four quarters of the world; its power, like its mission, extends to all places; yea, our faith is the victory which overcometh the world.—The names of the gates are the names of the tribes, the names of the tribes are the names of the sons of Israel; thus the gates taken together are the whole of Israel—that is, however, Israel in spirit and in truth.—"In this holy city, which represents the Church of Christ, the Lord is always graciously present, who says: Where two or three, etc. (Matt. xviii. 20), and: I am with you alway, etc. (Matt. xxviii. 20). Comp. also John xiv. 23. Happy are we when we receive such a name that it can be said of us, The Lord is there! When the Lord dwells in us, then our hope ascends to the New Jerusalem, which cometh down from heaven, etc., Rev. xxi." (HEIM-HOFF.)—"The dream of the patriarch Jacob has been fulfilled: God has a city upon earth, in which all nations are to share. The Word was made flesh, and dwelt among us, and we beheld His glory, etc. Bethel has by this obtained its fulfilment even to the name. Thus, then, God Himself has set the prophet free from Jerusalem, and the old temple, and the old ordinances, and shown him a higher form of the kingdom of God. Ezekiel proves that he was a true prophet of God by the fact that he withdrew his nation from the service of the flesh, and with plain words, and also in figures, prepared them for Christ," etc. (DIEDRICH.)—"The name of the prophet denotes one in relation to whom God is strong, who speaks not from his own heart, but is impelled and guided by a supra-mundane power. We have the verification of this name in the prophecies before us. That holds good of them throughout which the Lord said to Peter: Flesh and blood hath not revealed it unto thee, but My Father which is in heaven. Not one of His words has fallen to the ground. The whole course of history has verified His saying in ch. xxxiii. 33: They shall know that a prophet hath been among them" (HENGST.).